A Matter of Taste

Opera noua chiamata Epulario
Quale tracta il modo de cucinare ogni carne jacelli/
pesci/de ogni sorte. Et fare sapori/torte/pastel/
li/al modo de tutte le prouincie: z molte
altre gétilezze. Cópofta p Maeftro
Giouáne de roffelli. Fráceíe.

Rosselli's Opera nova chiamata Epulario, (Venice 1517)
The earlies known printed illustration of a kitchen.

A Matter of Taste

*A Bibliographical Catalogue of International
Books on Food and Drink in
The Lilly Library, Indiana University*

William R. Cagle

Oak Knoll Press
New Castle, Delaware
1999

Second edition, revised and expanded. First edition was printed by
Garland Publishing, New York, N.Y. in 1990.

Published in 1999 by Oak Knoll Press
310 Delaware Street, New Castle, DE 19720
All rights reserved.

Title: A Matter of Taste
Author : William R. Cagle
Publication Director: J. Lewis von Hoelle
Editor: L.K. Stafford
Cover Design: J. von Hoelle & Michael Hohne

Copyright 1999 by William R. Cagle

ISBN: 1-884718-86-8

Library of Congress Cataloging- in-Publication Data

Cagle, William R. (William Rea)
    A Matter of Taste: a bibliographical catalogue of the Gernon collection of books on   food and
drink / William R. Cagle   -- 2nd ed.,rev. and   expanded.
        p.   cm.
    Includes bibliographical references and indexes.
    ISBN: 1-884718-86-8
    1. Cookery--Europe--Bibliography--Catalogs. 2. Cookery-Bibliography--Catalogs.
    3. Gernon, John Talbot--Library--Catalogs. 4. Gernon, John Talbot, Mrs.--Library
    --Catalogs. 5. Lilly Library (Indiana University, Bloomington) -- Catalogs.
II. Title.
    Z5776.G2C177   1999
    [TX651]
    016.641594--dc21   99-19304
                                                            CIP

This edition was printed in the United States of America at Quinn-Woodbine, Woodbine,
N.J. on 60# natural acid-free archival paper.

TABLE OF CONTENTS

A Note on the Second Edition

The original edition of *A Matter of Taste* was issued by Garland Publishing in 1990 in a small press run of 150 copies that sold out in eighteen months. Although reviews published after the book was out of print brought more orders, changes in Garland's management at that time took the firm in new directions and it was decided not to reprint the book, the rights to which were returned to the author. When a companion volume, *American Books on Food and Drink*, describing the American books in the Gernon collection, was offered to Oak Knoll Books, they inquired about the possibility of issuing a new edition of *A Matter of Taste* at the same time. In the eight years since the earlier volume had been published the Lilly Library has added eighty significant British and European gastronomic books to the collection, most notably the extremely rare parts issue of Mrs. Beeton's *Book of Household Management*, so an enlarged edition adding these works was proposed. This also gave us a chance to revise and correct some of the earlier descriptions based on new information.

It was decided to place the new entries in their proper location within the volume rather than to add them as a supplement. This presented a question of how to number them. Renumbering the entire work would cause confusion between citations to the original and the revised editions so it was decided to number the new entries by adding an "a" or occasionally an "a" and a "b" to the number of the previous item. While this has the disadvantage of seeming to link unrelated books it at least makes the location clear when going from the index to locate a work in the main body of text.

Several new bibliographical works published since 1990 have been added to the list of bibliographies consulted. Citations in these have been recorded in the entries in this edition of *A Matter of Taste*.

This second edition was edited and revised with the generous assistance of Lisa Killion Stafford.

William R. Cagle

This second edition would not have been completed without the assistance and guidance of Mr. John Lewis von Hoelle and Mr. Joel Silver. It should be noted that the reacquiring of the Frankfort type, used throughout this work, would not have been available without the aid of Sandy Vincent. Special thanks go to my husband, Rick, and my parents for their constant love, support and understanding while editing and revising this second edition. Without the aforementioned people this book would not have been completed.

Lisa Killion Stafford

Preface

I first became interested in cookbooks in rather an unusual way. On Saturday afternoons, I used to visit the office of Mr. Walter Hill, a famous book dealer whose place of business was in the same building in Chicago as my medical office.

Mr. Hill and I became quite friendly and when he asked me what type of books I was interested in I told him that I would like to collect original editions of English literature. This remark was much to Mr. Hill's liking and he supplied me with a choice collection of material to peruse.

One afternoon Mr. Hill said to me, "You know I have a very rare and famous English book here that you should buy but it is not literature." I said in a very indifferent fashion, "OK, let me see it." Hill produced a beautifully bound (full blue morocco) book which I casually examined and here was the original edition (subscribers' copy) of the *Art of Cookery* by Hannah Glasse. I was not particularly impressed at the time and handed it back to Mr. Hill with the remark, "I have no interest in cooking or books of cookery. Please show me some more literature." Mr. Hill regarded me with a jaundiced eye and repeated, "You should buy this book."

The next day was Sunday and somehow I couldn't get that cookbook out of my mind. I decided to call Hill on Monday and purchase the book. When Monday came around, Hill told me that he was very sorry but the book had been sold Saturday afternoon after I left his shop. This upset me. I told Mr. Hill that whenever he obtained a desirable cookbook to let me know. He agreed and that's how it all started.

Dr. John T. Gernon

Introduction

The literature on food and drink is vast; every culture, every corner of the world, and every era since man began to record history has contributed something. Further, as a subject that tends to shade gradually into other fields--medicine, agriculture, social history--its boundaries are difficult to define. The sheer mass of the material it includes has made compiling a comprehensive record of all the books and pamphlets comprising the literature of gastronomy a task too intimidating to be contemplated. Even Georges Vicaire, in his monumental *Bibliographie gastronomique* (Paris, 1890), did not attempt a complete listing. Instead, bibliographers in the field, as Lord Westbury in his *Handlist of Italian Cookery Books* (Florence, 1963) and Virginia Maclean in her excellent *A Short-title Catalogue of Household and Cookery Books Published in the English Tongue 1701-1800* (London, 1981) have, of necessity, confined their efforts to limited and clearly defined areas within the larger body of the literature. Cookery book collectors, on the other hand, have largely resisted such limitations and have taken the whole world as their oyster. The greatest of them, including Baron Jérôme Pichon, Georges Vicaire, Katherine Bitting, Harry Schraemli, André Simon, and Erna Horn and Dr. Julius Arndt, have ranged widely in their collecting interests, covering a broad spectrum of centuries, nations, languages, and categories within the field. It is in the catalogues of their libraries that we find the best overview of gastronomic literature and it is in the tradition of these catalogues that we present this description of the collection of books on food and drink formed by Dr. and Mrs. John Talbot Gernon of Evanston, Illinois, now housed in the Lilly Library at Indiana University.

At the heart of the Gernon collection, as in any gastronomic library, are the cookery books themselves with their recipes and instructions for preparing food. These include approximately half of the 1,350 books and manuscripts described in this catalogue and range from specialized works devoted entirely to such items as pastries, desserts, ices, oysters, mushrooms, truffles, and even a book dedicated entirely to cooking with onions, to general cookery books, some written for young housewives and others for professional chefs. A number of household management books with information on everything from training the parlor maid to curing a lame horse also have sections on cookery and, hence, have a place in the collection.

Drink is the inevitable companion of food and, until early in the twentieth century when brewing, distilling and wine-making had largely left the home, information on all these subjects found its way into most cookery and household management books. There also grew up a separate beverage literature that has become nearly as extensive as that on food. While this is well represented in the Gernon collection with something over one hundred books, it appears in a supporting rather than a main role. Among the key books present are Brunschwig on distilling (Strassburg, 1519)[*], Dufour's *Traitez nouveaux et curieux du*

---

[*]Dates cited in this introduction refer to copies described in this catalogue, not necessarily to the date of original publication.

café, du thé et du chocolate (Lyon, 1685), Pasteur's studies on wine and beer (Paris, 1866 and 1876), and Viala's great *Ampélographie* (Paris, 1901-1910). But these are representative titles. The emphasis in the Gernon collection is much more the literature of food than the literature of drink.

From the medieval banquet where pheasants were presented dressed in their own feathers, through the pièce-montées of Carême, to the kiwi decorated oversized plates of nouvelle cuisine, chefs have known that the presentation of a dish can be almost as important as its preparation. Writers on food have devoted many volumes to the subject. From the sixteenth century there is Christoforo di Messibugo's *Banchetti compositioni di vivande, et apparecchio generale* (Ferrara, 1549) with its detailed accounts of banquets held in the household of Hippolito da Este, cardinal of Ferrara, describing the procession of courses and the ceremony that accompanied them. In the seventeenth century carving was done with great ceremony and generated an extensive literature of its own represented in the Gernon collection by twenty-five books, sixteen of which were printed before the end of the seventeenth century. In the eighteenth century, before the *service à la russe* replaced *service à la française,* great tables with vast arrays of dishes were the order of the day and the cookery books of the time include engraved plates illustrating various table arrangements. One of the more elaborate volumes, Charles Carter's *The Complete Practical Cook* (London, 1730) contains sixty engraved plates showing table settings for anything from a modest dinner to a coronation banquet. Finally, with the nineteenth century decorative cuisine reaches its apex in the works of Carême and Urbain Dubois. The famous gastronomic books treating ceremony and display form a substantial part of this collection.

The relationship between diet and health has been a concern of writers on food from earliest times and is a subject well documented in the Gernon collection. The emphasis here is on early writers beginning with Galen's *De alimentorum facultatibus* (Paris, 1530, but written in the second century AD) and including works by Paulus Aegineta, Michael Scott, Antonio Gazio, Jean-Baptiste Bruyerin, Lobera d'Avila, Sir Thomas Elyot, and Platina whose *De honesta voluptate et valitudine* (Venice, 1475) is the earliest printed book described in this catalogue. A few more recent books, such as volumes of recipes for the sick, are also present but strictly medical books on diet and nutrition fall outside the scope of the collection.

Agriculture, like medicine, occasionally crosses into the realm of gastronomic literature. The Gernon collection contains a small number of books on viticulture, farming and gardening and to these we have added descriptions of a few like books that were already in the Lilly Library. Here our additions have been fairly arbitrary and relate principally to kitchen gardening and raising fruit trees but not venturing into the broader areas of agriculture such as farm management or raising livestock or grain, though even these are touched on in some of the more general works such as the *Maison rustique* (London, 1616).

In addition to practical guides and theoretical treatises by cooks, physicians, and gardeners there appeared in the nineteenth century a new genre in the literature of food: the gastronomic essay. Its co-creators were Alexandre-Balthazar-Laurent Grimod de la Reynière who began writing about the aesthetics of dining in his *Almanach des gourmands*

(Paris, 1803-1808, 1810, 1812) and Jean-Anthelme Brillat-Savarin whose *Physiologie du goût* (Paris, 1826) stands as the unsurpassed classic in the field. These arbiters of taste and their successors (Alexandre Dumas, Charles Monselet, William Kitchiner, Abraham Hayward, and others) were the forerunners of the present-day restaurant critic and food commentator. They are well represented in the collection.

While the Gernons placed no strict limits on time or place of publication for the books they acquired – the dates range from 1475 to 1962 and there are a few Canadian, Mexican, Indian, and Japanese imprints as well as those from Britain and European countries – the bulk of the collection is composed of books published between the seventeenth and nineteenth centuries in Britain, France, Germany and Italy. For those interested, there is a chronological index at the end of this catalogue that shows the distribution of works in the collection by date and country of origin. The Gernons also showed flexibility in not limiting themselves to first editions. This was wise for two reasons. First, cookery books frequently were revised from edition to edition, making their later versions as interesting as the original. Second, the survival rate of cookery books, as of children's books, is much lower than with other works; books that went into the kitchen or the nursery fared less well than those that found a home on the library shelf. Several of the later editions described in this catalogue represent the only form, and sometimes the only copy, in which the book has survived.

It remains to stress that this is a bibliographic catalogue of a particular collection of books and that the copies described are the copies in hand. In contrast with earlier catalogues in this tradition, notably those of Georges Vicaire, Katherine Bitting, André Simon, and Erna Horn and Dr. Julius Arndt, which are on the order of short-title lists, a full bibliographical description, including a complete quasi-facsimile transcription of the title-page or title-pages, a collation of the book by signature, a pagination statement, and a record of the illustrations, whether in the text or on inserted plates, is given for each of the books in the collection. It is hoped that this more precise and more detailed information will allow other collectors, both private and in libraries, to compare their copies with these descriptions and to discover as yet unrecorded bibliographical variants. As these variants are noted by booksellers and in library catalogues, the record of gastronomic literature will be made more complete and the evidence needed by the specialists who will fully map the many compartments of this field will be more readily available.

Certainly, without the dedicated efforts and the strong commitment of private collectors who, like the Gernons, have not only assembled great collections of gastronomic literature, but have seen that their collections are kept intact and made available to scholars, the study of these books, whether for bibliography or the wealth of social history they preserve, would have been far more difficult. Indiana University, and especially the Lilly Library, acknowledge their debt of gratitude to the Gernons with the publication of this catalogue.

William R. Cagle
Lilly Librarian Emeritus

Explanation of the Descriptions

Title-page transcriptions.

Each title-page is given in quasi-facsimile transcription following the precepts laid down by Fredson Bowers in his *Principles of Bibliographical Description* (Princeton, 1948) with minor modifications. Transcriptions indicate upper and lower case letters, line endings, and roman, italic and gothic typefaces. Decorative typefaces are transcribed as roman or italic depending on the verticality or slant of the letters; script is transcribed as italic; full and small upper case letters are not distinguished one from the other as this proved beyond the capabilities of our laser printer. The long "s", common until the end of the eighteenth century, and the two forms of "r" found in gothic type are recorded as the standard modern "s" and "r." Symbols used in the fifteenth and sixteenth centuries for abbreviations, and not available in modern fonts, are represented by giving the abbreviated portion of the word in brackets, as q[bue]. We did not have the German double s or the s-zed available on our printer and, therefore, have transcribed these as ss and sz. The latter produced some abnormal spellings, such as Hausz, but provides an accurate record of the German ligature used in the original. The statement [rule] indicates a rule the full width of the type page; shorter rules are indicated as [short rule]. Tapered, wavy, or other decorative rules appear as [fancy rule] or [short fancy rule]. Colored inks are designated before the words, rule, or ornament for which they have been used. Unless the color notation is repeated, the ink reverts to black after the end of the line.

In works of more than one volume in which the title-pages are the same except for the volume number statement, one transcription is given with the change indicated in brackets: VOLUME ONE [TWO] [THREE]. If differences are more substantial, the title-pages are separately transcribed. Sectional titles within a volume are transcribed if they are a full title-page complete with imprint. In early works where the imprint appears in a colophon rather than on the title-page, the colophon is transcribed immediately after the title-page transcription.

Edition statement.

A book known to be a first edition is so described. Statements assigning a book to a later edition derive either from the title-page or from other bibliographical information. If these conflict, a statement as "third edition, styled second on the title-page," indicates that, while the title-page describes the work as the second edition, other evidence has shown it to be the third. If no earlier edition of the book has been found and it contains no internal evidence of prior publication, it may be described as presumed, or probable, first edition. Later editions for which a numerical position cannot be determined are recorded as "new edition."

When the book described is not the first edition, the place and date of the first edition, or the earliest recorded edition, is provided. Changes in title between the edition described and the original edition are recorded as, in the case of translations, are the title and the place and date of publication of the first edition in the original language.

Collation.

The collation statement includes the format for books printed through the eighteenth century and the page size in millimeters for nineteenth and twentieth century books, the collation of the book by signature, and a statement of the pagination or foliation of the book. Collations signed with letters are based on the twenty-three letter Roman alphabet (omitting j, u and w) generally used for this purpose by printers. In those few instances in which the printer has used the full twenty-six letter alphabet in the collation this is indicated as, for example, A-I^4 J^4 K-U^4 V^4 W^4 X-Z^4.

The pagination statement follows the rules as given in Bowers' *Principles of Bibliographical Description*. Unnumbered pages for which no numbering sequence has been inferred are given by their total in italics enclosed in brackets; unnumbered pages for which numbering may be inferred are given in brackets. If the recto of a leaf is numbered and the verso is not, the page number of the verso is inferred and if the same section of text continues on subsequent unnumbered pages, numbers for those pages also are inferred. Numbering is not inferred for unnumbered separate sections of text (as an index or appendix) but the total number of pages for the section is stated in italics in brackets. Unnumbered or misnumbered pages within a numbered sequence are not indicated unless they effect the total.

Publisher's bindings are noted briefly at the end of the collation statement. Other bindings are not described.

Illustrations.

Illustrations are distinguished as (1) those that are separately printed and inserted in the volumes and, therefore, not recorded in the collation, or (2) those that are printed on the text pages. The latter are always noted as "in the text" or by designation of the leaf on which it appears (e.g. "numerous woodcuts in the text" or "engraved frontispiece on A1^v"). While a full count is not always given for illustrations in the text, it is for separately printed illustrations, with a count of folding illustrations also noted (e.g. "five etched illustrations, two folding"). The type of illustration (etching, engraving, woodcut, etc.) is reported but the subject matter is noted only when it can be stated in a few words.

Bibliographies.

All of the books described in this catalogue have been checked against other bibliographies and catalogues covering similar works and citations to these are provided in this paragraph in each description. Citations are to the specific edition described. If no reference to this edition has been found it is noted that "this edition is unrecorded in the bibliographies consulted." If no reference to any edition of the book described has been found it is noted as "unrecorded in the bibliographies consulted." A list of these bibliographies appears at the end of this preface.

Copies.

Each book described in the catalogue has been checked against the *British Museum General Catalogue of Printed Books, Photolithographic edition to 1955,* London, 1959-1966, 263 volumes, cited as *BMC,* the *Catalogue général des livres imprimés de la Bibliothèque Nationale,* Paris, 1898-1981, 231 volumes, cited as *BNC,* and *The National Union Catalog, Pre-1956 Imprints,* Chicago, 1968-1980, 685 volumes, cited as *NUC.* Where applicable, the books also have been checked in those bibliographies that cite locations of copies.

Our original intention had been to list all copies cited but on writing to a number of libraries with questions about bibliographical variants in the books the *NUC* reported they owned, we found that in about one case in four the *NUC* was in error. Some libraries reported owning other editions, some had photocopies, and others had no record of the book at all. Rather than perpetuate a list of ghost copies, it was decided to give *NUC* locations only when three or fewer copies were listed on the theory that in these cases the record was more likely to be accurate. When four or more copies are listed in the *NUC* the citation records only the number of copies as an indication of the relative scarcity of the book. Citations are to the specific edition of the book described in the catalogue. In a few instances, and particularly in cases of extreme rarity, the location of copies of one or more other editions may be noted.

Bibliographies Consulted

Arents	Brooks, Jerome E. *Tobacco, Its History Illustrated by the Books, Manuscripts and Engravings in the Library of George Arents, Jr.* New York, 1937-1942. 5 vols.
Attar	Attar, Dena. *A Bibliography of Household Books Published in Britain 1800-1914.* London, 1987.
Axford	Axford, Lavonne. *English Language Cookbooks, 1600-1973.* Detroit, 1976.
Beaupré	Beaupré, Jean Nicolas. *Recherches historiques et bibliographiques sur les commencement de l'imprimerie en Lorraine et sur ses progrès jusqu'à la fin du XVIIe siècle.* Saint-Nicolas-de-Port, 1845.
Benzing	Benzing, Josef. *Walther H. Ryff und sein literarisches Werk, eine Bibliographie.* Hamburg, 1959.
B. In. G.	Fondation Bibliothèque Internationale de Gastronomie. *Catalogo del Fondo Italiano e Latino delle Opera di Gastronomia Sec. XIV-XIX.* Sorengo, 1994. 3 vols.
Bitting	Bitting, Katherine. *Gastronomic Bibliography.* San Francisco, 1939.
Blake	Blake, D. *A Short Title Catalogue of the Eighteenth Century Printed Books in the National Library of Medicine.* Bethesda, 1979.
Brunet	Brunet, Jacques. *Manuel du libraire et de l'amateur de livres.* Paris, 1860-1865. 6 vols and Supplement 2 vols.
Cohn	Cohn, Albert M. *George Cruikshank, a Catalogue raisonné of the Work Executed during the Years 1806- 1877 . . .* London, 1924.
Crahan	*The Marcus and Elizabeth Crahan Collection of Books on Food, Drink and Related Subjects.* Sotheby's 9-10 October 1984. New York, 1984.
Craig	*Four Hundred Years of English Diet & Cookery. A Selection of books printed between 1541 & 1939 from the collection of Dr. and Mrs. John C. Craig.* Berkeley, 1987.

Drexel   Drexel, Theodor. *Catalog der Kochbücher-Sammlung von Theodor Drexel.* Frankfurt a.M., 1887-1895. Catalog and five supplements.

Driver   Driver, Elizabeth. *A Bibliography of Cookery Books Published in Britain, 1875-1914.* London and New York, 1989.

Durling   Durling, Richard. *A Catalogue of Sixteenth Century Printed Books in the National Library of Medicine.* Bethesda, 1967.

Favier   Favier, Justin. *Trésor du bibliophile Lorrain.* Nancy, 1889.

Foxon   Foxon, David F. *English Verse 1701-1750: a Catalogue of Separately Printed Poems.* London, 1975. 2 vols.

Fussell (1)   Fussell, George Edwin. *Old English Farming Books 1523-1730.* London, 1947.

Fussell (2)   Fussell, George Edwin. *More Old English Farming Books, 1731-1793.* London, 1950.

Fussell (3)   Fussell, George Edwin. *Old English Farming Books. Vol. III 1793-1839.* London, 1983.

GW   *Gesamtkatalog der Wiegendrucke.* Leipzig, 1925-1940. 8 vols.

Gabler   Gabler, James M. *Wine into Words: A History and Bibliography of Wine Books in the English Language.* Baltimore, 1985.

Gambacorta/   Gambacorta, Gorgias, and Alberto Giordano. *Regimen Sanitatis* Giordano *Salernitanum: Bibliografia.* Milano, 1983.

Garrison/   Garrison, Fielding, and Leslie Morton. *Garrison and Morton's*
Morton   *Medical Bibliography.* Second edition. New York, 1961.

Goff   Goff, Frederick R. *Incunabula in American Libraries, a third census . .* New York, 1973.

Graesse   Graesse, Johann. *Trésor de livres rares et précieux.* Milan and New York, 1951. 8 vols.

Gumuchian   Gumuchian & Cie. *Les Livres de l'enfance du XVe au XIXe siècle.* Paris, 1931. 2 vols.

Henrey	Henrey, Blanche. *British Botanical and Horticultural Literature before 1800*. Oxford, 1975. 3 vols.
Holzmann/ Bohatta	Holzmann, Michael, and Hanns Bohatta. *Deutsches Anonymen-Lexikon, 1501-[1926]*. Hildesheim, 1961. 7 vols.
Horn-Arndt	Horn, Erna, and Julius Arndt. *Schöne alte Kochbuchsammlung Erna Horn und Dr. Julius Arndt*. Munich, 1982.
Hunt	*Hunt Botanical Catalogue*. Pittsburgh, 1961. 3 vols.
Keynes	Keynes, Geoffrey. *John Evelyn, a Study in Bibliophily and a Bibliography of his writings*. New York, 1937.
Kress	*The Kress Library of Business and Economics Catalogue*, Cambridge, Mass., 1940-1967. 4 vols.
Lisbon	*Livros Portugueses de cozinha*. Lisboa, Biblioteca Nacional, 1988.
Maclean	Maclean, Virginia. *A Short-title Catalogue of Household and Cookery Books Published in the English Tongue 1701-1800*. London, 1981.
Maggs	Maggs Bros. Ltd. Catalogue 645. *Food and Drink Through the Ages*. London, 1937.
Malortie	Malortie, Ernst von. *Das Menu*. Third edition. Hannover, 1888. 2 vols. All references are to the item numbers in the bibliography in vol. I.
Muther	Muther, Richard. *Die deutsche Bücherillustration der Gothik und Frührenaissance (1460-1530)*. München und Leipzig, 1884. 2 vols.
Noling	Noling, A. W. *Beverage Literature, a Bibliography*. Metuchen, 1971.
Oberlé (1)	Oberlé, Gérard. *Les Fastes de Bacchus et de Comus; ou, Histoire de boire et du manger en Europe, d'antiquité a nos jours, à traverse les livres*. Paris, 1989.
Oberlé (2)	Oberlé, Gérard. *Une Bibliothèque Bachique*. Paris, 1992.
Oxford	Oxford, Arnold Whitaker. *English Cookery Books to the Year 1850*. London, 1979.

Palau Palau y Dulcet, Antonio. *Manual del Librero Hispano-Americano, Bibliografia general Española e Hispano-Americana* . . . Barcelona, 1948-1977. 28 vols.

Pearl Pearl, Morris Leonard. *William Cobbett, a Bibliographical Account of His Life and Times.* London, 1953.

Pellechet Pellechet, Marie. *Catalogue général des incunables des bibliothèques publiques de France.* Nendeln, Liechtenstein, 1970. 26 vols.

Pennell Pennell, Elizabeth Robins. *My Cookery Books.* Boston, 1903.

Poynter Poynter, Frederick. *A Bibliography of Gervase Markham, 1568?-1637.* Oxford, 1962.

Renouard Renouard, Antoine Augustin. *Annales de l'Imprimerie des Estienne.* Paris, 1837-1838. 2 vols.

Renzi Renzi, Salvatore de. *Collectio salernitana* . . . Napoli, 1859. Vol. V.

Roscoe Roscoe, Sydney. *J. Newbery and his Successors, 1740-1814, a Bibliography.* Wormley, 1973.

STC *A Short-Title Catalogue of Books Printed in England, Scotland, & Ireland and of English Books Printed Abroad 1475-1640,* compiled by A.W. Pollard & G.R. Redgrave. Second edition. London, 1976. 2 vols.

Sander Sander, Max. *Le Livre à figures italien, dupuis 1467 jusqu'à 1530.* Milan, 1942. 6 vols.

Schraemli (1) Schraemli, Harry. *Catalogue of a Collection of Books and Manuscripts of the 15th to 20th century on food and wine from the well known library of Harry Schraemli.* Sotheby 22-23 February 1971. London, 1971.

Schraemli (2) Schraemli, Harry. *Schloss Jegenstorf 1952. Bibliophile Köstlichkeiten der Gastronomie Sammlung Harry Schraemli.* Zurich and Bern, 1952.

Schraemli (3) *Zweitausend Jahre gastronomische Literatur.* Zürich, 1942.

Simon BB Simon, André. *Bibliotheca Bacchica.* London, 1927-1932. 2 vols.

Simon BG Simon, André. *Bibliotheca Gastronomica.* London, 1953.

Simon BV   Simon, André. *Bibliotheca Vinaria*. Enlarged edition. London, 1979.

ULS   *Union List of Serials in Libraries of the United States and Canada*. Third edition. New York, 1965. 5 vols.

Vicaire   Vicaire, Georges. *Bibliographie gastronomique*. Paris, 1890.

Vicaire ML   Vicaire, Georges. *Manuel de l'amateur de livres du XIXe siècle, 1801-1893*. Paris, 1894-1920. 8 vols.

Watt   Watt, Robert. *Bibliotheca Britannica*. Edinburgh, 1824. 4 vols.

Westbury   Westbury, Lord. *Handlist of Italian Cookery Books*. Florence, 1963.

Wheaton and Kelly   Wheaton, Barbara Ketcham and Patricia Kelly. *Bibliography of Culinary History*. Boston, 1987.

Wing   *A Short-Title Catalogue of Books Printed in England, Scotland, Ireland, Wales and British America and of English Books Printed in Other Countries 1641-1700*, compiled by Donald Wing. Second edition. New York, 1972-1988. 3 vols.

AUSTRIA

1.   Allerneuestes Brünner Kochbuch

Allerneuestes | Brünner | Kochbuch | für | herrschaftliche und andere Tafeln. | [short fancy rule] | Herausgegeben | von einem erfahrnen fürstlichen Koch. | Nebst einer | Deutschen Erklärung der im Buche vorkommenden | Französischen Kunst- und andern Wörtern, | dann einigen | beiläufigen Anmerkungen zu Jedermanns Verständigung, | und einem | Anhange, | alle Arten von Gefrornen, und eingemachte | Früchte zu verfertigen. | [thick-thin rule] | Grätz 1791. | Im Verlag bei Christian Friedrich Trötscher, und in | Brünn in Kommission zu haben bei Johann Georg | Gastl in der Sattlergasse.

First edition, first issue under this title, Grätz and Brünn, 1791. Four issues of this book are known. It was published under the title *Allerneustes oesterreichisches Kochbuch*, Grätz, 1791, and reissued under the same title with a cancel title-page stating "2te Auflage" with the date changed to 1792. It also was published under the title *Allerneuestes Brünner Kochbuch*, Grätz and Brünn, 1791, and reissued under this title, but spelling Brüner with one n, with a cancel title-page stating "2te Auflage" with the Grätz imprint only and the date changed to 1792 (item 1a). All four issues are from the first and only printing of the book.

8vo. A-Cc⁸; 208 leaves, pp. [8] [1] 2-381 [382-406] [2]. Last leaf blank. Signature A is signed A2-A5 on leaves A3-A6.

Illustrations: Copperplate engraved frontispiece on A1ᵛ depicting a kitchen scene.

Bibliographies: The issue with this title unrecorded in the bibliographies consulted or in RLIN. Horn-Arndt 211 and Schraemli (1) 8 record the second issue with the title *Allerneuestes oesterreichisches Kochbuch*, Grätz, 1792.

Copies: No other copy of this issue located. *NUC* records the two issues under the *Allerneuestes oesterreichisches Kochbuch* title, Grätz, 1791 (Cornell only) and Grätz, 1792 (New York Academy of Medicine only).

1a. Allerneuestes Brüner Kochbuch.

Allerneuestes | Brüner | Kochbuch | für | herrschaftliche und andere Tafeln. | [fancy rule] | Herausgegeben | von einem erfahrnen fürstlichen Koch. | Nebst einer | Deutschen Erklärung der im Buche vorkommenden | Französischen Kunst- und anderen Wörtern, | dann einigen | beiläufigen Anmerkungen zu jedermanns Verständigung, | und einem | Anhange, | alle Arten von Gefrornen, und eingemachte | Früchte zu verfertigen. | 2te Auflage. | [rule] | Grätz 1792. | Bei Christian Friedrich Trötscher.

First edition, second issued under this title, Grätz, 1792, styled second edition on the title-page. See note under item 1, above.

8vo. A^8 ($\pm$A2) B-Cc^8; 208 leaves, pp. [8] [1] 2-381 [382-406] [2]. Last leaf blank. Signature A signed A2-A5 on leaves A3-A6.

Illustrations. Copperplate engraved frontispiece on A1^v depicting kitchen scene.

Bibliographies: The issue with this title unrecorded in the bibliographies consulted or in RLIN. Horn-Arndt 211 and Schraemli (1) 8 record the second issue with the title *Allerneuestes oesterreichisches Kochbuch*, Grätz, 1792.

Copies: No other copy of this issue located. *NUC* records the two issues under the *Allerneuestes oesterreichisches Kochbuch*, title Grätz, 1791 (Cornell only) and Grätz, 1792, (New York Academy of Medicine only).

2. Bewehrtes Koch-Buch.

Bewehrtes | Koch=Buch | In sechs Absätze vertheilet; | In welchem zu finden: | Wie man verschiedene Speisen | von allerhand Wild=Prät, Fleisch, Geflü= | gelwerk, Fisch und Garten=Gewächsen, | Wie auch | Torten, Pasteten, und anderes, Geba= | ckenes, niedlich zurichten könne. | Wegen guter, und sicher=gestell= | ten Eintheilung dienet jedermann, | besonders der in der Kocherey sich | übenden Jugend. | Verbesserte Sechste Auflage. | Mit Röm. Kais. auch Kais. Kön. Apost. Majestät | Allergnädigsten Freyheit. | [fancy rule] | Wien in Oesterreich, | Gedruckt und zu finden, bey Leopold Kaliwoda, | auf dem Dominicaner=Platz, N. 724.

Sixth edition, Vienna, ca. 1760. The date of the first edition is not known; the second was published, Vienna, 1748, and the third, Vienna, 1750.

8vo. A-X^8; 168 leaves, pp. [1-2] 3-317 [318-336]. Last leaf (blank?) wanting in this copy.

Note: Some of the recipes in this collection are almost identical to those in the *Wienerisches bewährtes Kochbuch* by Ignaz Gartler (items 3 and 4).

Bibliographies: This edition unrecorded in the bibliographies consulted. Schraemli (1) 248 records the third edition, Vienna, 1750.

Copies: No other copy of this edition located. *NUC* records a second edition, Vienna, 1748 (New York Academy of Medicine only).

3. Gartler, Ignaz.

Wienerisches bewahrtes | Kochbuch | in | sechs Absätzen. | Enthält | Tausend fünfhundert achtzig Kochregeln | für | Fleisch = und Fasttäge | alle auf das deutlichste und gründlichste beschrieben, | nebst einen | Anhang in fünf Abschnitten, | worinnen | ein allgemeiner Unterricht, was man in der | Küche, beym Einkaufen, Anrichten der Speisen und | Anordnung der Tafeln zu beobachten habe, | als auch bequeme | Speis = und Suppeezettel. | [short fancy rule] | Anfangs herausgegeben | von | Ignaz Gartler | nunmehro aber verbessert und vermehrt von der | Barbara Hikmann. | Zwey und zwanzigste mit einem alphabetischen | Register versehene Auflage. | [fancy rule] | Wien, | verlegt bey Joseph Gerold, K. K. Hofbuchdrucker und | Universitäts Buchhändler am Dominikanerplatz Nro. 711. | [short fancy rule] | 1799.

Twenty-second edition, Vienna, 1799. Originally published under the title *Nutzliches Kochbuch*. The date of the original edition has not been determined; the earliest edition recorded is the second, Steyr, 1740, and the earliest edition located is Bamberg, 1768 (Cornell).

8vo.)(^{6} A-Qq^8 Rr^2 a-d^8 e^6; 358 leaves, pp. [*12*] 1-628, ^{2}[1-2] 3-59 [60-76].

Illustration: Engraved frontispiece titled "Die Wienerische Köchin."

Bibliographies: This edition unrecorded in the bibliographies consulted. Horn-Arndt records editions of 1804, 1812, and 1831; Schraemli (3) 37 records the Steyr, 1740, edition.

Copies: *NUC* (Indiana University only). *NUC* also records editions of 1768 and 1812 (both Cornell only).

4. Gartler, Ignaz.

𝔚ienerisches bewährtes │ 𝔎ochbuch │ in │ sechs Absätzen. │ Enthält: │ 𝔗ausend sechshundert 20 𝔎ochregeln │ für │ 𝔉leisch- und 𝔉asttage, │ alle auf das deutlichste und gründlichste beschreiben, │ nebst einem │ Anhange in fünf Abschnitten, │ worinnen │ ein allgemeiner Unterricht, was man in der │ 𝔎üche, beym Einkaufen, Anrichten der Speisen und │ Anordnung der 𝔗afeln zu beobachten habe, │ als auch bequeme │ Speis- und Suppeezettel. │ [short fancy rule] │ Anfangs herausgegeben │ von │ 𝔍gnaz 𝔊artler, │ nunmehro aber verbessert und vermehrt von der │ 𝔅arbara 𝔥ikmann. │ 𝔑eun und zwanzigste mit einem alphabetischen 𝔑e- │ gister versehene Auflage. │ [two rules] │ 𝔚ien, 1810. │ 𝔍m 𝔙erlage der 𝔊eroldschen 𝔅uchhandlung.

Twenty-ninth edition, Vienna, 1810. Originally published under the title *Nutzliches Kochbuch*. The date of the original edition has not been determined; the earliest edition recorded is the second, Steyr, 1740, and the earliest edition located is Bamberg, 1768 (Cornell).

187 x 115 mm. π^2)(^{2} A-Rr^8 Ss^2 [Tt-Vv]^2; 330 leaves, pp. [8] 1-528, 527-642 [8], page numbers 527 and 528 repeated.

Illustrations: Engraved frontispiece depicting kitchen scene and two engravings of kitchen utensils and table settings.

Bibliographies: This edition unrecorded in the bibliographies consulted. Horn-Arndt records editions of 1804, 1812, and 1831; Schraemli (3) 37 records the Steyr, 1740, edition.

Copies: No other copy of this edition located. *NUC* records editions of 1768 (Cornell), 1799 (Indiana University), and 1812 (Cornell).

5. M., J.

𝔊rätzerisches │ durch Erfahrung geprüftes │ 𝔎ochbuch. │ Eingerichtet │ für alle Stände. │ 𝔃um │ 𝔊ebrauch für 𝔉leisch- und 𝔉asttage. │ [short rule] │ Enthaltend: │ deutlich und gründlich beschriebene 𝔙orschriften │ von der 𝔃ubereitung verschiedener für jeden Stand taug- │ licher 𝔊erichte, 𝔊ebackenen, 𝔗orten, 𝔃uckergebäcke, 𝔊e- │ frornen, Sulzen und Eingesottenen, 𝔊elleen,

Galler- | ten, &c. Getränken, von Fleischeinpökeln: &c. nebst | andern häuslichen Erfahrungen, und einer Anwei- | sung zum Trenschiren und Vorlegen. | Herausgegeben von J. M. | Zehnte | mit einer grossen Menge bewährter Speise-Vorschriften neuer- | dings vermehrte und veränderte Auflage. | [short rule] | [two rules] | Grätz, | gedruckt und verlegt bey Johann Andreas Kienreich | 1811.

Tenth edition, Grätz, 1811. The date of the original edition has not been determined; the earliest edition located is the fifth, Grätz, 1799 (Library of Congress).

176 x 107 mm. π1 ❊² A-Gg⁸ Hh⁴ χ1; 248 leaves, pp. [6] [1] 2-464 [26].

176 x 107 mm. $\pi 1$ ❊^{2} A-Gg^8 Hh^4 $\chi 1$; 248 leaves, pp. [6] [1] 2-464 [26].

Illustration: Etched frontispiece on $\pi 1^v$ of kitchen scene.

Bibliographies: This edition unrecorded in the bibliographies consulted; Horn-Arndt records an edition of Grätz, 1818.

Copies: No other copy of this edition located. *NUC* locates the Grätz, 1799, edition (Library of Congress).

6. Neubauer, Jean.

Neues | Kochbuch, | bestehend | in ganz Ordinairen oder | auf burgerliche Art zubereiteten | Fleisch- und Fastenspeisen, | es lehrnet: | wie man solche ohne viele Kösten, jedoch | von guten Geschmack zubereiten kann. | Herausgegeben von | Mr. JEAN NEUBAUER, | welcher die zwey herrschaftlichen Kochbücher an | Tag gegeben hat. | [ornament] | [two rules] | Wien, | im Verlage bey Joh. Georg Weingand, | Buchhändlern. | [short rule] | 1777.

New edition, Vienna, 1777. Originally published, Munich, 1776. Neubauer published another book similarly titled in Munich, 1741, treating "Herrschaftliche Küche" as opposed to "Bürgerliche Küche" covered in this work.

8vo. A-I⁸ K⁴; 76 leaves, pp. [1-3] 4-147 [148-152].

8vo. A-I^8 K^4; 76 leaves, pp. [1-3] 4-147 [148-152].

Bibliographies: Unrecorded in the bibliographies consulted.

Copies: No other copy located.

7. Niederederin, Maria Elisabetha.

𝕯𝖆𝖘 │ neue, grosse, geprüfte und bewährte │ 𝕷𝖎𝖓𝖟𝖊𝖗 𝕶𝖔𝖈𝖍𝖇𝖚𝖈𝖍 │ in zehn 𝕬𝖇𝖘𝖈𝖍𝖓𝖎𝖙𝖙𝖊𝖓. │ [short fancy rule] │ 𝕰𝖓𝖙𝖍ä𝖑𝖙: │ ein tausend fünf hundert und zwey und dreyzig │ 𝕶𝖔𝖈𝖍𝖗𝖊𝖌𝖊𝖑𝖓 │ für │ 𝕱𝖑𝖊𝖎𝖘𝖈𝖍- und 𝕱𝖆𝖘𝖙𝖙ä𝖌𝖊 │ sehr deutlich und fasslich beschrieben │ [short fancy rule] │ 𝕹𝖊𝖇𝖘𝖙 einem │ 𝕬𝖓𝖍𝖆𝖓𝖌 in zwey 𝕬𝖇𝖘𝖈𝖍𝖓𝖎𝖙𝖙𝖊𝖓 │ worinnen ein allgemeiner 𝖀𝖓𝖙𝖊𝖗𝖗𝖎𝖈𝖍𝖙 vom 𝕶𝖔𝖈𝖍𝖊𝖓 überhaupt │ — von der 𝕺𝖗𝖉𝖓𝖚𝖓𝖌 — von der 𝕽𝖊𝖎𝖓𝖑𝖎𝖈𝖍𝖐𝖊𝖎𝖙 — von der │ 𝖅𝖎𝖊𝖗𝖑𝖎𝖈𝖍𝖐𝖊𝖎𝖙 im 𝕬𝖓𝖗𝖎𝖈𝖍𝖙𝖊𝖓 — von dem 𝕱𝖑𝖊𝖎𝖘𝖘 — von der │ 𝕾𝖕𝖆𝖗𝖘𝖆𝖒𝖐𝖊𝖎𝖙 — vom 𝕿𝖗𝖆𝖓𝖘𝖈𝖍𝖎𝖗𝖊𝖓 und 𝖁𝖔𝖗𝖑𝖊𝖌𝖊𝖓, gründ- │ lich und ausführlich abgehandelt wird. │ [short fancy rule] │ 𝕭𝖊𝖞𝖌𝖊𝖋ü𝖌𝖙 sind noch: │ mehrere bequem eingerichtete 𝕾𝖕𝖊𝖎𝖘𝖟𝖊𝖙𝖙𝖊𝖑𝖓 mit einem voll- │ ständigen 𝕽𝖊𝖌𝖎𝖘𝖙𝖊𝖗. │ 𝖁𝖊𝖗𝖋𝖆𝖘𝖘𝖙 von │ 𝕸𝖆𝖗𝖎𝖆 𝕰𝖑𝖎𝖘𝖆𝖇𝖊𝖙𝖍𝖆 𝕹𝖎𝖊𝖉𝖊𝖗𝖊𝖉𝖊𝖗𝖎𝖓. │ [fancy rule] │ 𝕯𝖗𝖎𝖙𝖙𝖊, verbesserte und mit 146 𝕾𝖕𝖊𝖎𝖘𝖊𝖓 vermehrte 𝕬𝖚𝖘𝖌𝖆𝖇𝖊. │ [fancy rule] │ 𝕷𝖎𝖓𝖟, 1815. │ Im 𝖁𝖊𝖗𝖑𝖆𝖌𝖊 der k.k. priv. akademischen 𝕶𝖚𝖓𝖘𝖙= 𝕸𝖚𝖘𝖎𝖐= │ und 𝕭𝖚𝖈𝖍𝖍𝖆𝖓𝖉𝖑𝖚𝖓𝖌.

Third edition, Linz, 1815. Originally published, Linz, 1804.

170 x 108 mm.)(^{8} A-Vv^8; 360 leaves, pp. [i-iii] iv-xvi [1] 2-688.

Illustration: Etched frontispiece of kitchen scene.

Bibliographies: Malortie I.434.

Copies: No other copy located.

8. Plenck, Josef Jacob von, 1738-1807.

𝕵𝖔𝖘𝖊𝖕𝖍 𝕵𝖆𝖐𝖔𝖇 𝕻𝖑𝖊𝖓𝖐'𝖘, │ der 𝖂𝖚𝖓𝖉𝖆𝖗𝖟𝖓𝖊𝖎𝖐𝖚𝖓𝖘𝖙 𝕯𝖔𝖐𝖙𝖔𝖗, der 𝕮𝖍𝖊𝖒𝖎𝖊 und 𝕭𝖔𝖙𝖆𝖓𝖎𝖐 │ ordentlicher öffentlicher 𝕷𝖊𝖍𝖗𝖊𝖗 an der chirurgischen 𝕸𝖎𝖑𝖎= │ tairakademie, 𝕯𝖎𝖗𝖊𝖐𝖙𝖔𝖗 der 𝕱𝖊𝖑𝖉𝖆𝖕𝖔𝖙𝖍𝖊𝖐𝖊𝖓 und │ 𝕾𝖙𝖆𝖇𝖘𝖈𝖍𝖎𝖗𝖚𝖗𝖌𝖚𝖘, │ 𝕭𝖗𝖔𝖒𝖆𝖙𝖔𝖑𝖔𝖌𝖎𝖊 │ oder │ 𝕷𝖊𝖍𝖗𝖊 │ von │ den 𝕾𝖕𝖊𝖎𝖘𝖊𝖓 und 𝕲𝖊𝖙𝖗ä𝖓𝖐𝖊𝖓. │ [short rule] │ [vignette] │ 𝕬𝖚𝖘 bem 𝕷𝖆𝖙𝖊𝖎𝖓𝖎𝖘𝖈𝖍𝖊𝖓 übersezt. │ [fancy rule] │ 𝖂𝖎𝖊𝖓, │ bey 𝕽𝖚𝖉𝖔𝖑𝖕𝖍 𝕲𝖗ä𝖋𝖋𝖊𝖗. 1785.

Second edition in German, Vienna, 1785. Originally published in Latin under the title *Bromatologia seu Doctrina de esculentis et potulentis*, Vienna, 1783, and then in German, with the Latin title-page, Vienna, 1784.

8vo. A-Dd^8; 216 leaves, pp. [1-3] 4-432.

Bibliographies: Horn-Arndt 323.

Copies: *NUC* (John Crerar Library and National Library of Medicine).

Allerneuestes Brünner Kochbuch

für

herrschaftliche und andere Tafeln.

Herausgegeben

von einem erfahrnen fürstlichen Koch.

Nebst einer

Deutschen Erklärung der im Buche vorkommenden
Französischen Kunst= und anderen Wörtern,

dann einigen

beiläufigen Anmerkungen zu jedermanns Verständigung,

und einem

Anhange,

alle Arten von Gefrornen, und eingemachte
Früchte zu verfertigen.

2te Auflage.

Grätz 1792.

Bei Christian Friedrich Trassler.

Grätzerisches
durch Erfahrung geprüftes
KOCHBUCH
Eingerichtet
für alle Stände.

Zum
Gebrauch für Fleisch- und Fasttage.

Enthaltend:

deutlich und gründlich beschriebene Vorschriften von der Zubereitung verschiedener für jeden Stand tauglicher Gerichte, Gebacknen, Torten, Zuckergebäcke, Gefrornen, Sulzen und Eingesottenen, Gelleen, Gallerten, rc. Getränken, von Fleischeinpöcein: rc. nebst andern häuslichen Erfahrungen, und einer Anweisung zum Trenschiren und Vorlegen.

Herausgegeben von J. M.

Zehnte
mit einer großen Menge bewährter Speise-Vorschriften neuerdings vermehrte und verbesserte Auflage.

Grätz,
1811.

gedruckt und verlegt bey Johann Andreas Kienreich

BELGIUM

9. Annulaire agathopédique et saugial.

[Engraved title-page] ANNULAIRE | AGATHOPÉDIQUE ET SAUGIAL |
[illustration of pig with knife and fork and three figures] | [below, in letterpress]
IMPRIM·E PAR LES PRESSES ICONOGRAPHIQUES A LA CONGRÈVE | DE
L'ORDRE DES AGATH ∷, | CHEZ A. LABROUE ET COMPAGNIE, | RUE DE
LA FOURCHE, 36, A BRUXELLES. | [short rule] | CYCLE IV.

First edition, Brussels, 1849.

226 x 143 mm. π^2 1-2^4 [3]^4 4-16^4 17^2 18$_1$; 69 leaves, pp. [*4*] [1] 2-134. Page 134
misnumbered "130."

Illustrations: Wood-engraved title-page and frequent wood engravings in the text.
Four pages of engraved music, not reckoned in the signatures or pagination, follow
page 134.

Bibliographies: Maggs 477; Vicaire 26.

Copies: *BMC*, *NUC* (New York Public Library and Newberry Library).

10. Audot, Louis-Eustache, 1783-1870.

LA CUISINIÈRE | DE LA VILLE | ET DE LA CAMPAGNE, | OU | LA
NOUVELLE CUISINE | ÉCONOMIQUE; | Précédée d'instructions sur la Dissection
des viandes à table, et suivie de Recettes | précieuses pour l'économie domestique, et
d'un Traité sur les soins à donner aux | caves et aux vins. | DÉDIÉE AUX BONNES
MÉNAGÈRES. | [short rule] | HUITIÈME ÉDITION, | REVUE, CORRIGEÉ ET
AUGMENTEÉ, | PAR M. SULPICE BARUÉ, | CHEF DE CUISINE. | AVEC
NEUF PLANCHES GRAVÉES, DONT UNE COLORIÉE. | [short fancy rule] |
𝕭𝖗𝖚𝖝𝖊𝖑𝖑𝖊𝖘, | AUGUSTE WAHLEN, LIBR.-IMPR. DE LA COUR. | LEIPZIG ET
LIVOURNE, MÊME MAISON. | [short rule] | 1829.

Eighth edition, Brussels, 1829. Originally published under the title *La Cuisinière de la
campagne et de la ville*, Paris, 1818 (item 52).

195 x 120 mm. 1-10^{12}; 120 leaves, pp. [1-5] 6-240. Publisher's printed wrappers.

Illustrations: Engraved frontispiece "Le Mardi Gras" and eight engraved plates, one of
which is hand colored.

Bibliographies: This edition unrecorded in the bibliographies consulted.

Copies: OCLC (February 1995): Cornell and Library of Congress.

11. Bernardi.

L'ART DE DONNER | DES | BALS ET SOIRÉES, | OU | le 𝕲lacier 𝕽oyal, | PAR
BERNARDI, | OFFICIER DE BOUCHE. | Contenant les meilleures recettes pour
faire les *Glaces, Sorbets, Café, Punch, Cho-* | *colats, Thé, Marmelades, Confitures,*
Pâtes, Fruits à l'eau-de-vie, Sirops, etc; | suivi de la construction d'une glacière, d'une
distribution indiquant la quantité et | l'ordre du service à faire pour recevoir depuis 25
jusqu'à 200 personnes; de menus | de desserts de Déjeuners, Diners et Soupers pour les
quatre saisons; orné de *six* | *planches* gravées pour le service des desserts, et indiquant
les ustensiles néces- | saires à la confection des glaces. | Ouvrage entièrement neuf, |
Utile aux gens du monde, et indispensable aux limonadires, restaurateurs, | confiseurs,
maîtres d'hôtel, épiciers, etc. | [short fancy rule] | 𝕭ruxelles. | SOCIÉTÉ
TYPOGRAPHIQUE BELGE, | ADOLPHE WAHLEN ET Cie. | [short rule] | 1844

First Brussels edition, 1844. Originally published under the title *Le Glacier royal*,
Paris, 1844.

182 x 119 mm. π^2 1^4 2-24^6; 144 leaves, pp. [i-v] vi-x [11] 12-285 [286] [2]. Last leaf
blank. Publisher's printed wrappers.

Illustrations: Five full page wood engravings in signature 22, one of utensils and four
of table settings.

Bibliographies: Maggs 463; Vicaire 87; Wheaton and Kelly 613.

Copies: *NUC* (Boston Atheneum and University of California, Berkeley).

Bonnefons, Nicholas de: see items 16 and 17.

12. Brillat-Savarin, Jean-Anthelme, 1755-1826.

PHYSIOLOGIE | DU GOÛT, | OU | MÉDITATIONS DE GASTRONOMIE |
TRANSCENDANTE; | OUVRAGE THÉORIQUE, HISTORIQUE ET A L'ORDRE
DU JOUR, | 𝕯édié aux 𝕲astronomes parisiens. | PAR UN PROFESSEUR, |
MEMBRE DE PLUSIEURS SOCIÉTÉS SAVANTES. | Dis-moi ce que tu manges, je

te dirai qui tu es. | APHOR. DU PROF. | TOME PREMIER. [TOME SECOND.] | [short fancy rule] | BRUXELLES, | P. J. VOGLET, IMPRIMEUR-LIBRAIRE, | PRÈS LE PALAIS DE JUSTICE. | [short rule] | 1828.

First Brussels edition, 1828. The half titles state "Troisième édition" because this followed the second Paris edition. Originally published, Paris, 1826 (item 98).

142 x 92 mm. 2 vols. Vol. I π^2 1-27^6 28^8; 172 leaves, pp. [*4*] [1] 2-340. Vol. II π^2 *✱*^{2} 1-31^6 32$_1$; 191 leaves, pp. [2] [i-iii] iv-vi [1] 2-374. Publisher's printed wrappers.

Bibliographies: Unrecorded in the bibliographies consulted.

Copies: No other copy of this edition located.

13. Casteele, Pieter van de, 1585-1632.

ΚΡΕΩΦΑΓΙΑ | SIVE | DE ESV CARNIVM | LIBRI IV. | Authore | PETRO CASTELLANO, | *In Academiâ Louaniensi Graecarum litera-* | *rum & Medicinae Professore Regio.* | [printer's device] | ANTVERPIAE, | Ex Officina HIERONYMI VERDVSSII. | [rule] | *ANNO M. DC. XXVI.*

First edition, Antwerp, 1626.

8vo. *✱*^{4} A-S^8 T^4; 152 leaves, pp. [8] 1-296.

Bibliographies: Vicaire 152.

Copies: *BMC, BNC,* and *NUC* (National Library of Medicine only).

14. Le Cuisinier familier.

LE | CUISINIER | FAMILIER | Tant pour les Grandes Maisons & Familles | Bourgeoises que pour les Gens de la Cam- | pagne & autres de toutes sortes de Con- | ditions. | *Enseignant outre quantité d'Aprêts & de nou-* | *veaux Ragoûts, plusieurs Curiositez de Cuisine* | *& les manieres de faire la Patisserie & les* | *Confitures; comme aussi les preparations neces-* | *saires pour les Festins.* | [ornament] | A BRUXELLES,

| Chez JEAN-BAPTISTE DE LEENEER, Im- | primeur & Libraire sur le Marché au Bois. | M. D C C. V. | [rule] | *Avec Acte de Privilege.*

First edition, Brussels, 1705.

8vo. π^4 A-R^4; 72 leaves, pp. [8] 1-133 [134-136].

Bibliographies: Unrecorded in bibliographies consulted.

Copies: *BMC.*

15. Dubrunfaut, Auguste-Pierre, 1797-1881.

TRAITÉ COMPLET | DE L'ART | DE LA DISTILLATION, | CONTENANT, | DANS UN ORDRE MÉTHODIQUE, | Les instructions théoriques et pratiques les plus exactes et les | plus nouvelles sur la préparation des liqueurs alcoholiques | avec les raisins, les grains, les pommes de terre, les fé- | cules et tous les végétaux sucrés ou farineux; | *Par M. Dubrunfaut,* | Membre de la Société d'Encouragement pour l'industrie nationale, et | Auteur d'un Mémoire sur la Saccharification des fécules, couronné, | en 1823, par la Société royale et centrale d'Agriculture de Paris. | SECONDE ÉDITION, | Ornée de huit planches. | [short fancy rule] | BRUXELLES, | Chez la Ve. AD. STAPLEAUX, Imprimeur-Libraire du ROI, et de | S.A.R. le PRINCE D'ORANGE, Marché aux Herbes, No. 323. | [short rule] | 1825.

Second edition, Brussels, 1825. Originally published Paris, 1824.

196 x 120 mm. π^2 1-28^8 29^2; 228 leaves, pp. [4] [1] 2-451 [452].

Illustrations: Eight etched folding plates of distilling apparatus.

Bibliographies: Unrecorded in bibliographies consulted.

Copies: No other copy located.

15a. Lessius, Leonardus, 1554-1623.

[fancy] L' ART | *DE JOUIR* | D'UNE SANTÉ PARFAITE, | *ET* | DE VIVRE HEUREUX JUSQU'A | UNE GRANDE VIEILLESSE. | *Traduction nouvelle des*

Traités de LESSIUS | *& de CORNARO, sur la vie sobre & sur* | *les moyens de vivre cent ans.* | [short rule] Abstinentia adjicit vitam. [short rule] | [ornament] | A SALERNE, | *Et se trouve à LIÉGE* | Chez F. J. DESOER, Imprimeur-Libraire, sur | le Pont-d' Isle. | [short fancy rule] | M. DCC. LXXXV.

New edition, Liége, 1785. Leonardus Lessius's *Hygiasticon* was originally published, Antwerp, 1613, and Luigi Cornaro's *Trattato de la vita sobria*, Padua, 1558. The translation by J.-R. Allaneau de la Bonnodière was first published Paris, 1701.

12mo. a^6 A-I^{12} K^6; 120 leaves, pp. [i-v] vi-xii [1] 2-228.

Bibliographies: Unrecorded in the bibliographies consulted.

Copies: *BNC*.

16. Liger, Louis, sieur d'Auxerre, 1658-1717.

LE MENAGE | DE LA VILLE | ET DES CHAMPS, | ET | LE JARDINIER | FRANÇOIS | ACCOMMODEZ AU GOUT DU TEMS; | Ou la maniere facile d'aprêter tout ce qui | est necessaire pour l'usage de la vie, & de | cultiver parfaitement les Jardins fruitiers, | potagers & à fleurs. | *Avec un Traité de la Chasse & de la Pêche.* | Ouvrage utile à toutes sortes de Personnes. | *Par le Sieur LIGER.* | [ornament] | A BRUXELLES, | Chez JEAN LEONARD Libraire-Impri- | meur, ruë de la Cour. 1712. | [rule] | *AVEC APPROBATION ET PRIVILEGE.*

Second edition, Brussels, 1712. This is, in fact, a compilation from Nicolas de Bonnefons' *Jardinier françois* and his *Délices de la campagne*. It was first published in this form, with the privilège assigned to Liger, in Paris, 1711 (Vicaire mentions a 1710 edition which, however, is not recorded in any other bibliography or collection and appears an error). It was reprinted frequently in both Paris and Brussels.

12mo. ✱^{12} A-S^{12}; 228 leaves, pp. [*24*] 1-428 [429-430] [2]. Last leaf blank.

Bibliographies: Vicaire 523.

Copies: *BMC* and *NUC* (New York Public Library and University of California, Davis).

17. Liger, Louis, sieur d'Auxerre, 1658-1717.

LE MENAGE | UNIVERSEL | DE LA VILLE | ET DES CHAMPS, | ET | LE
JARDINIER | ACOMODEZ AU GOUT DU TEMS; | *CONTENANT* | [in two
columns separated by four type figures arranged vertically, column one] LA
PATISSERIE, | CONFITURES, | LIQUEURS, | LA CUISINE, | [column two] LE
JARDINAGE, | LA CHASSE ET | LA PESCHE, | SECRETS DU MENAGE. [end of
columns] | Ouvrage utile à toutes sortes de Personnes. | NOUVELLE EDITION
AUGMENTÉE D'UN | TRAITÉ DES ABEILLES, | Où l'on voit la véritable maniére
de les gouver- | ner & d'en tirer du profit. | *Par Mr.* DE LA FERRIERE. | [ornament]
| A BRUXELLES, | Chez JEAN LEONARD, Libraire-Imprimeur, | ruë de la Cour.
1725. | [rule] | *AVEC APROBATION ET PRIVILEGE.*

New edition, Brussels, 1725. Originally published in this form, Paris, 1711. See the
edition note in item 16.

8vo. ✳⁸ ✳✳⁸ A-Ii⁸; 272 leaves, pp. [*32*] 1-507 [508-512].

Illustration: Engraved frontispiece depicting garden, kitchen and bakery, on ✳1ᵛ.

Bibliographies: This edition unrecorded in bibliographies consulted.

Copies: No other copy of this edition located.

18. Nonnius, Ludovicus, ca. 1555-1645?

LVDOVICI NONNI | DIAETETICON | SIVE | DE RE CIBARIA | LIBRI IV: |
[ornament] | ANTVERPIAE, | Apud PETRVM & IOANNEM | Belleros. M. DC.
XXVII.

First edition, Antwerp, 1627.

8vo. ✳⁸ ✳✳⁸ A-Rr⁸; 336 leaves, pp. [*32*] 1-638 [639-640].

Bibliographies: Horn-Arndt 176; Schraemli (1) 369; Vicaire 626.

Copies: *BMC, BNC,* and *NUC* (4 copies).

19. Nonnius, Ludovicus, ca. 1555-1645?

[Engraved pictorial title-page lettered] LVDOVICI | NONNI | MEDICI ANTVERPIENSIS | DIAETETICON | SIVE | DE RE CIBARIA | LIBRI IV. | NVNC PRIMVM | LVCEM VIDIT. | ANTVERPIAE, EX OFFICINIA PETRI BELLERI. M.DC.XLVI.

Third edition, Antwerp, 1646. Originally published, Antwerp, 1627 (item 18).

4to. a⁴ e⁴ i⁴ A-Vvv⁴; 312 leaves, pp. [24] [1] 2-526 [527-528].

Illustration: Engraved title-page on a1ʳ.

Bibliographies: Crahan 181A; Oberlé (1) 33; Oberlé (2) 33.

Copies: *BMC.*

20. Nouvel Almanach de cuisine.

[within an ornamental border] NOUVEL ALMANACH | DE CUISINE, | *OU* | LA CUISINIERE | MODERNE, | *Contenans les XII. Articles suivans:* | I. Instruction sur les Richesses que la | Nature produit pour notre subsistance | pendant toute l'année. II. La façon de | faire toutes sortes de Potages & Soupes. | III. De la Dessection des Viandes. IV. La | maniere de préparer & déguiser toutes | sortes de Viandes de Boucherie. V. L'art | de bien apprêter la Volaille. VI. La ma- | niere d'apprêter toutes sortes de menu | & gros Gibier. VII. Des divers apprêts | convenables au Poisson d'eau douce & de | mer. VIII. La maniere d'apprêter toutes | sortes de Racines, Légumes, Herbages | & Fruits de Jardin, & comment il faut | les assaisonnier. IX. Du Laitage, des Oeufs | & Bignets. X. Des Gateaux, Tartes, | Pâtes & Tourtes. XI. Des Confitures | liquides & séches, Gélées, Conserves, | Massepains & Compotes de plusieurs sor- | tes. XII. Instruction pour ordonner des | Repas réglés, tant en gras qu'en maigre. | [ornament] | A GAND, chez les FRERES GIMBLET.

First edition, Gand, ca. 1781.

12mo. π⁶ A-G¹² H⁴; pp. [12] [1] 2-176. This copy lacks π1.

Bibliographies: Unrecorded in bibliographies consulted.

Copies: No other copy located.

21. Oettinger, Edouard-Marie, 1808-1872.

UN | AGATHOPÈDE | DE L'EMPIRE, | OU | ESSAI SUR LA VIE ET LES
TRAVAUX GASTRONOMICO-LITTÉRAIRES | DE FEU GRIMOD DE LA
REYNIÈRE. | PAR | Edouard-Marie Oettinger. | [short rule] | TIRÉ A 300
EXEMPLAIRES. | [short rule] BRUXELLES ET LEIPZIG, | KIESSLING, SCHNÉE
ET Cie, ÉDITEURS, | RUE VILLA-HERMOSA, 1. | [short rule] | 1854

First edition, Brussels, 1854.

130 x 86 mm. π^2 1-3^8 4^4; 30 leaves, pp. [1-5] 6-57 [58] [2].   Last leaf (blank?) wanting
in this copy.

Bibliographies: Oberlé (1) 139-140; Vicaire 638.

Copies: Only the Oberlé copy located.

22. De Verstandighe Kock.

DE | VERSTANDIGHE KOCK, | OFT SORGHVULDIGHE HUYS-HOUDSTER: |
BESCHRYVENDE, | Hoe-men op de beste en beguaemste manier alderhande
Spijsen sal koken/ stoven/ bra- | den/ backen en bereyden ; met de Saussen daer
toe dienende/ seer dienstigh | en profijtelijck in alle Huys-houdinghen; | Oock om
veelderleye slagh van TAERTEN en PASTEYEN toe te stellen. | Vermeerdert met de
| NEDERLANDTSCHE SLACHT-TYDT. | Hier is noch achter by-ghevoeght de |
VERSTANDIGHE CONFITUER-MAKER, | Onderwijsende, hoe-men van
veelderhande Vruchten, Wortelen, Bloemen en Bladeren, &c. | goede en nutte
Confituren sal konnen toe-maken en bewaren. | [illustration of kitchen with two cooks,
fireplace with roasting fowl, and a cat] | TOT BRUSSEL, | By Philips Vleugaert,
ghezworen Boeck-Drucker/ achter't Stadt-huys/ in | den Enghel- bewaerder.
1672. | [short rule] | Met Gratie en Privilegie.

New Edition. Brussels, 1672. Originally published in Amsterdam, 1669. *De
Verstandige Kock* is the third section in part three of *Het Vermakelijck Landt-leven.*
See item 1096a.

4to. H-L^4; 16 leaves, pp. [4] 61-88.

Illustration: Woodcut of kitchen scene on title-page.

Bibliographies: Maggs 172.

Copies: *BNC.*

23. De Verstandige Kock.

De | VERSTANDIGE KOCK, | Oft Sorghvuldighe Huyshoudster: | Beschrijbende/ hoemen op de Beste en bequaemste manier/ alderhande Spijsen sal koocken/ | stooven/ braden/ backen en bereyden: met de Saussen daer toe dienende. | Seer dienstigh en profijtelijck in alle Huyshoudinghen. | Oock om veelderleye slagh van TAERTEN en PASTEYEN toc te stellen. | Vermeerdert met de Winter-probiste/ ende | SLACHT-TYDT. | Als de kennis van de Fongi oft Cam pernoillien, ende des selfs regeringhe. | Hier is achter by-ghevoeght / de | VERSTANDIGE CONFITUURMAKER | Onderwijsende/ hoemen van veelderhande Vruchten/ Wortelen/ Bloemen | en Bladen &c. goede en nutte Confituren sal konnen | toemaken en bewaren. | [illustration of kitchen scene] | T' ANTWERPEN. By de Weduwe van Regnier Sleghers; Boeck-brucker ende | Boeck- verkooper in de Cammer-straet/ Inden Schilt van Urtops. 1682.

New Edition. Originally published, Amsterdam, 1669, as the third section in part three of *Het Vermakelijck Landt-leven*. See item 1096a.

4to. A-D⁴, ²A⁴, ³A⁴ B²; 26 leaves; pp. [1-4] 5-32; ²[1] 2-8; ³[1] 2-11 [12]. Part two has head title "De Verstandighe Confitur-Maker" and part three head title "Tractaet van de Campernoillien, ghenant Duyvels-broot."

Illustration: Engraved illustration of kitchen on title-page. This is a mirror image of the woodcut on the title-page of the Brussels, 1672, edition (item 22).

Bibliographies: This edition unrecorded in bibliographies consulted.

Copies: No other copy of this edition located.

24. Den Verstandigen Kok.

DEN VERSTANDIGEN | KOK, | OF DE ZORGVULDIGE | KEUKEMEYD, | BESCHRYVENDE | Hoe men op de beste en bekwaemste manier alder- | hande Spyzen zal beryden, Gezoden, Gestoven, | Gebraden en Gebakken met de saussen daer toe | dienende. -- Alsook om veelderlye slag van Taer- | ten, Pastyen, Pottingen,

Bingeéts en Champions | te beryden welke delicieus zyn. | BENEVENS DEN
ERVAREN | CONFITUERMAKER, | Onderwyzende hoe men vele vruchten van
Confitueren, | Conserven, Geleyen en Siropen maken, die men | kan bewaren. | *Alles*
zeer nut en dienstig voor Huyshoudende Per- | *soonen en Dienstboden.* |
VERMEERDERD MET | Onderwys wegens het Tafeldienen en vouwen der |
Serveeten op eene nette wys. | [ornament] | GENT, | DRUKKERY VAN I.-C. VAN
PAEMEL, | Lange Violettestraet, 3.

New edition, Gent, ca. 1820.

147 x 91 mm. 1-6⁶; 36 leaves, pp. [1-3] 4-70 [71-72].

Bibliographies: Bitting, p. 615; Maggs 383.

Copies: *NUC* (Library of Congress only).

LVDOVICI
NONNI
MEDICI ANTVERPII
DIÆTETICON
SIVE
DE RE CIBAR.
LIBRI IV.
NVNC PRIMVM
LVCEM VIDIT.

Item no. 19

ANTVERPIÆ, EX OFFICINA PETRI BELLERI. M.DC.XLVI.

De
VERSTANDIGE KOCK,

Oft Sorghvuldighe Huyshoudster:

Beschrijvende / hoemen op de Beste en bequaemste manier / alderhande Spijsen sal koocken/
stooven / braden / backen en bereyden; met de Saussen daer toe dienende.
Seer dienstigh en profijtelijck in alle Huyshoudinghen.
Oock om veelderleye slagh van **TAERTEN** en **PASTEYEN** toe te stellen.
Vermeerdert met de Winter-provisie/ en de

SLACHT-TYDT.

Als de kennis van de Fongi oft Cam pernoillien, ende des selfs regeringhe.
Hier is achter by-ghevoeght / de

VERSTANDIGE CONFITUURMAKER.

Onderwijsende / hoemen van beelderhande Vruchten / Wortelen / Bloemen
en Bladen &c. goede en nutte Confituren sal konnen
toemaken en bewaren.

T'ANTWERPEN, By de Wedúwe van Reynier Sleghers; Boeck-drucker ende
Boeck-verkooper in de Cammer-straet / Inden Schilt van Artoys. 1682.

Item no.

CANADA

25. Nouvelle cuisinière canadienne.

NOUVELLE | CUISINIÈRE | CANADIENNE | CONTENANT: | Tout ce qui est nécessaire de savoir dans un ménage, tel que l'achat | des diverses sortes de denrées; les recettes les plus nouvelles | et les plus simples de préparer les potages, les rotis de | toutes espèces, la pâtisserie, les gelées, glaces, sirops, | confitures, fruits, sauces, puddings, crêmes et | charlottes; poissons, volailles, gibiers, oeufs, | légumes, salades, marinades; différentes | recettes pour faire diverses sortes de | breuvages, liqueurs, etc., etc. | [short fancy rule] | QUATRIEME EDITION, | Revue, corrigée et considérablement augmentée. | [short fancy rule] | Montréal: | C. O. BEAUCHEMIN & VALOIS, | LIBRAIRES-ÉDITEURS, | *Rue St. Paul, Nos. 237 et 239.* | 1865.

Fourth edition, Montréal, 1865. No earlier edition located.

140 x 87 mm. 1-16⁸; 128 leaves, pp. [i-iii] iv-viii [9] 10-256.

Bibliographies: Vicaire 238; Wheaton and Kelly 4486.

Copies: *NUC* (New York Public Library only). Wheaton and Kelly (American Antiquarian Society).

26. Traill, Catherine Parr (Strickland) 1802-1899.

THE | CANADIAN | EMIGRANT HOUSEKEEPER'S | GUIDE. | [short rule] | BY MRS. C. P. TRAILL. | [short rule] | PUBLISHED BY AUTHORITY. | [short rule] | [ornament] | FIFTH THOUSAND. | [short rule] | PRICE TWO SHILLINGS, POST PAID. | [short rule] | PUBLISHED BY JAMES LOVELL, | MONTREAL, QUEBEC AND TORONTO. | [short rule] | 1861.

Fifth edition, Montréal, 1861. This work reprints material from the author's *The Female Emigrant's Guide*, Toronto, 1854, which was retitled *The Canadian Settler's Guide* after 1855.

166 x 114 mm. π^2 A⁴ B-I⁸; 70 leaves, pp. [2] [1-3] 4-133 [134-138].

Illustrations: Wood-engraved frontispiece "Emigrant's First Home in the Back Woods" and two wood-engravings "Design for a church and School" and "Maple sugar-making in the bush" on A4ᵛ and F5ᵛ.

Bibliographies: Unrecorded in bibliographies consulted.

Copies: No other copy of this edition located. *NUC* locates two copies of the 1862 edition (University of Toronto and University of British Columbia).

THE

CANADIAN

EMIGRANT HOUSEKEEPER'S

GUIDE.

BY MRS. C. P. TRAILL.

PUBLISHED BY AUTHORITY.

FIFTH THOUSAND.

PRICE TWO SHILLINGS, POST PAID.

PUBLISHED BY JAMES LOVELL,

MONTREAL, QUEBEC AND TORONTO.

1861.

EMIGRANT'S FIRST HOME IN THE BACK WOODS.

CZECHOSLOVAKIA

26a. Neues Lexikon.

𝔑eues | 𝔏exikon | der | französischen, sächischen, österreichischen und | böhmischen | 𝔎ochkunst. | [vignette of a kitchen scene] | [rule] |𝔓rag und 𝔚ien, | in der von 𝔖chönfeldischen 𝔥andlung, | 1785.

First edition, Prague and Vienna, 1785.

8vo. π^8 A-Ff^8 Gg^4; 244 leaves, pp. [*16*] [1] 2-472.

Bibliographies: Drexel 43.

Copies: *NUC* (New York Academy of Medicine only).

FRANCE

Abraham, Nicolas, sieur de La Framboisière. See La Framboisière.

27. Agrippa von Nettesheim, Henricus Cornelius, 1486?-1535.

DECLAMATION │ SVR │ L'INCERTITV- │ DE, VANITÉ, │ ET ABVS DES │ SCIENCES, │ * │ *Traduite en François du Latin de Henry* │ *Corneille Agr.* │ Oeuure qui peut proffiter, & qui apporte mer- │ ueilleux contentement à ceux qui frequen- │ tent les Cours des grands Seigneurs, & qui │ veulent apprendre à discourir d'une infinité │ de choses contre la commune opinion. │ [ornament] │ PER IEAN DVRAND. │ [short rule] │ M. D. LXXXII.

First edition of the translation into French by Louis Turquet de Meyerne, Paris, 1582. Originally published in Latin under the title *De incertitudine et vanitate scientiorum et artium atque excellentia verbi Dei declamatio*, Antwerp, 1530.

8vo. *⁸ a-z⁸ A-L⁸ M⁴; 284 leaves, pp. [*16*] 1-551 [552].

Bibliographies: Brunet I, 114, in a note; Graesse I, p. 45.

Copies: *BMC*, *BNC*, and *NUC* (New York Public Library, Princeton, and University of Wisconsin).

28. Albert, B.

LE │ CUISINIER PARISIEN, │ OU │ MANUEL COMPLET │ D'ÉCONOMIE DOMESTIQUE, │ CONTENANT: │ LA CUISINE, LA CHARCUTERIE, LA GROSSE PATISSERIE ET LA PATIS- │ SERIE FINE, L'OFFICE DANS TOUTES SES BRANCHES; │ LA CUISINE DES MALADES; │ Les remèdes urgens qu'on doit administrer en attendant le médecin, │ dans les cas d'empoisonnemens par les champignons, le vert- │ de-gris, les moules, etc.; contre l'asphyxie, les brûlures, les │ indigestions, etc.; │ Les propriétés diététiques des substances alimentaires; │ LES PROCÉDÉS LES PLUS SURS POUR LA CONSERVATION DES VIANDES, │ DES FRUITS, DES LÉGUMES, DES OEUFS, ETC.; │ LA CONDUITE DE LA CAVE; │ Un recueil de recettes choisies sur toutes les branches de l'économie │ domestique; │ ENFIN LA DESCRIPTION ET L'USAGE DES FOURNEAUX ET USTENSILES ÉCONOMIQUES │ RÉCEMMENT INTRODUITS DANS LES CUISINES. │ AVEC QUATRE PLANCHES. │ PAR B. ALBERT, │ EX-CHEF DE CUISINE DE SON EXC. LE CARINAL FESCH. │ CINQUIÉME ÉDITION. │ [short fancy rule] │ PARIS, │ LOUIS TENRÉ, LIBRAIRE, │ RUE DU PAON, No 1. │ [short rule] │ 1833.

Fifth edition, Paris, 1833. Originally published, Paris, 1812, under the title *Manuel complet d'économie domestique*. The title changed with the third edition, 1825.

207 x 124 mm. [1]^8 2-28^8 29^8 (-29$_8$); 231 leaves, pp. [i-v] vi-viii [1] 2-454.

Illustrations: Engraved frontispiece titled "intérieur d'une cuisine bien ordonnée" and three engraved plates depicting ovens and cooking utensils.

Bookplate: De la bibliothèque du comte de Chambord (Henry V de France, duc de Bordeaux) Né en 1820. Aquise par Maggs Bros. Ltd. de Londres.

Bibliographies: Vicaire 9, in a note; Wheaton and Kelly 51.

Copies: *BNC*. Wheaton and Kelly (Radcliffe only).

28a. Alletz, Pons-Augustin, 1703-1785.

L'AGRONOME. │ DICTIONNAIRE PORTATIF │ DU CULTIVATEUR, │ CONTENANT │ Toutes les Connoissances nécessaires pour gouver- │ ner les Biens de Campagne, & les faire valoir │ utilement, pour soutenir ses droits, conserver sa │ santé, & rendre gracieuse la vie champêtre. │ *CE QUI A POUR OBJET,* │ 1^0. Les Terres à Grains, la Vigne, les Prés, les Bois, │ la Chasse, la Pêche, les Jardins, tant de propreté que │ d'utilité; les Fleurs recherchées, les Plantes usuelles, │ les Bestiaux, Chevaux & autres animaux. │ 2^0. Les principales notions qui peuvent donner l'intelli- │ gence des affaires, jusqu'au degré suffisant pour défen- │ dre son bien, tant dans les matieres Rurales que Civiles. │ 3^0. Les Remedes dans les maladies ordinaries, & autres │ accidens qui arrivent aux Hommes & aux Animaux. │ 4^0. Les divers apprêts des Alimens; & tout ce qui peut │ procurer une nourriture saine & agréable. │ *Avec un nombre considérable d'autres instructions utiles &.* │ *curieuses à tout Homme quis passe sa vie à la Campagne.* │ TOME PREMEIER. [TOME SECOND.] │ [ornament] │ *A PARIS*; │ Chez [next five lines bracketed to left] La Veuve DIDOT, Quai des Aug. à la Bible d'Or. │ NYON, Quai des Augustins, à l'Óccafion. │ La Veuve DAMONNEVILLE, Quai des Augustins. │ SAVOYE, rue S. Jacques, à l'Espérance. │ DURAND, rue du Foin, près de la rue S. Jacques. │ [rule] │ M. DCC. LXIII. │ *Avec Approbation, & Privilege du Roi.*

Fourth edition, Paris, 1763. Originally published, Paris, 1760, followed by Liège, 1761, and Paris, 1762. There were numerous later editions.

8vo. 2 vols. Vol. I. a^8 A-Ss^8 Tt^4 Vv1; 341 leaves, pp. [i-iii] iv-xvi [1] 2-666. Vol. II. A-Rr^8 Ss^4 (-Ss 3 = Vol. I Vv1); 323 leaves, pp. [2] [1] 2-302, 323-664.

Bibliographies: Oberlé (1) 629.

Copies: Oberlé copy only.

28b. Alletz, Pons-Augustin, 1703-1785.

L'AGRONOME, │ *OU* │ DICTIONNAIRE PORTATIF │ DU CULTIVATEUR, │ *CONTENANT* │ Toutes les connoissances nécessaires pour gouverner les │ Biens de Campagne, & les faire valoir utilement; │ pour soutenir ses droits, conserver sa santé, & rendre │ gracieuse la vie champêtre. │ *CE QUI A POUR OBJET;* │ 1⁰. Les Terres à Grains, la Vigne, les Prés, les Bois, │ la Chasse, la Pêche, les Jardins, tant de propreté que │ d'utilité, les Fleurs recherchées, les Plantes usuel- │ les, les Bestiaux, Chevaux & autres Animaux. │ 2⁰. Les principales notions qui peuvent donner l'intelli- │ gence des affaires, jusqu'au dégré suffisant pour défen- │ dre son bien, tant dans les Matieres rurales que civiles. │ 3⁰. Les Remedes dans les Maladies ordinaires, & autres │ accidents qui arrivent aux Hommes & aux Animaux. │ 4⁰. Les divers Apprêts des Aliments, & tout ce qui │ peut procurer une nourriture saine & agréable; │ *Avec un nombre considérable d'autres Instructions utiles &* │ *curieuses à tout homme qui passe sa vie à la Campagne.* │ DERNIERE ÉDITION, │ Revue, corrigée & augmentée, dans laquelle on a remis dans │ leur ordre alphabétique le Supplément & les Observations. │ TOME PREMIER. [TOME SECOND.] │ [ornament] │ *Des fonds de M. Pierre Machuel.* │ *A ROUEN,* │ Chez JEAN RACINE, Libraire, rue Ganterie. │ [rule] │ M. DCC. LXXXIV. │ *AVEC PERMISSION.*

Note: In addition to "TOME SECOND." for "TOME PREMIER." the title-page of Vol. II differs from that of Vol. I in the following: line 13, "usuelles," for "usuel- │ les," and line 23 "*Homme*" for "*homme.*"

New edition, Rouen, 1784. Originally published, Paris, 1760.

8vo. 2 vols. Vol. I. π² a⁸ A-Ff⁸ Gg⁴; 246 leaves, pp. [4] [i] ii-xiv [xv-xvi] [1] 2-472 (p. 472 misnumbered 462). Vol. II π² A-Ff⁸; 234 leaves, pp. [4] [1] 2-464.

Bibliographies: This edition unrecorded in the bibliographies consulted.

Copies: *NUC* (Yale only).

28c. Alletz, Pons-Augustin, 1705?-1785.

L'ALBERT MODERNE, | *OU* | NOUVEAUX SECRETS ÉPROUVÉS, | ET LICITES, | *RECUEILLIS D'APRÈS LES DÉCOUVERTES* | *LES PLUS RÉCENTES.* | Les uns ayant pour objet de remédier à un | grand nombre d'accidens qui intéressent | la santé: | *Les autres, quantité de choses utiles à sçavoir* | *pour les différens besoins* *de la vie*: | D'autres, enfin tout ce qui concerne le pur | agrément, tantaux Champs qu'à la Ville. | *Le tout divisé en trois parties, & rangé par* | *ordre alphabétique.* | [ornament] | A PARIS, | Chez la Veuve DUCHESNE, Libraire, rue | St. Jacques, au Temple du Goût. | [two short rules] | M. DCC. LXVIII. | *Avec Approbation &* *Privilége du Roi.*

First edition, Paris, 1768.

12mo. a^{12} A-S^{12}; 228 leaves, pp. [i-ii] iii-xxiv [1] 2-430 [431-432].

Bibliographies: Vicaire 9.

Copies: *BNC* and *NUC* (4 copies).

29. Alletz, Pons-Augustin, 1705?-1785.

L'ALBERT MODERNE, | *OU* | NOUVEAUX SECRETS | ÉPROUVÉS ET LICITES, | *RECUEILLIS D'APRÈS LES DÉCOUVERTES* | *LES PLUS RÉCENTES.* | Les uns ayant pour objet de remédier | à un grand nombre d'accidens qui | intéressent | la sante·: | *Les autres, quantité de choses utiles à savoir* | *pour les différens besoins de* *la vie*: | D'autres enfin, tout ce qui concerne le pur | agrément, tant aux Champs qu'à la Ville. | *Le tout divisé en trois parties, & rangé par* | *ordre alphabétique.* | SECONDE ÉDITION, | *AUGMENTÉE DE PLUSIEURS SECRETS NOUVEAUX.* | [ornament] | *A PARIS,* | Chez la Veuve DUCHESNE, Libraire, rue Saint | Jacques, au-dessous de la Fontaine S. Benoît, | au Temple du Goût. | [short fancy rule] | M. DCC. LXIX. | *Avec Approbation & Privilége du Roi.*

Second edition, Paris, 1769. Originally published, Paris, 1768 (item 28c).

12mo. π^4 A-S^{12} T^8; 228 leaves, pp. [i-iv] v-viii [1] 2-429 [430] [*18*].

Bibliographies: This edition unrecorded in the bibliographies consulted. Vicaire 9 records the first edition, 1768, *BMC* lists a "second edition" dated 1770, Horn-Arndt 212 and Simon BG 78 record a third edition, 1772.

Copies: *BNC* and *NUC* (Columbia, Folger and Harvard).

30. Andry de Bois-Reynard, Nicolas, 1658-1742.

LE REGIME │ DU CARESME, │ CONSIDERÉ │ PAR RAPPORT A LA NATURE │ du corps, & des alimens. │ *EN TROIS PARTIES,* │ OU L'ON EXAMINE LE SENTIMENT │ de ceux qui prétendent que les alimens mai- │ gres sont plus convenables à l'homme que la │ viande: où l'on traite, à ce sujet, de la qua- │ lité & de l'usage des legumes, des herbages, │ des racines, des fruits, du poisson, &c. │ Et òu l'on éclaircit plusieurs questions, touchant │ l'abstinence, & le jeûne, suivant les princi- │ pes de la Physique & de la Medecine, entre │ autres, si l'on doit défendre en Caresme, l'usa- │ ge de la Macreuse & du Tabac. │ *Par Me.* NICOLAS ANDRY, *Docteur,* │ *Regent de la Faculté de Medecine de Paris,* │ *Lecteur & Professeur Royal.* │ [ornament] │ A PARIS, │ Chez JEAN BAPTISTE COIGNARD, Imprimeur │ ordinaire du Roy, rüe S. Jacques, à la Bible d'or. │ [short rule] │ M D C C X. │ *AVEC PRIVILEGE DE SA MAJESTÉ.*

First edition, Paris, 1710.

12mo. a^{12} A-V^{12} X^{12} (-X12) Y-Dd^{12}; 335 leaves, pp. [*24*] 1-631 [*632-646*].

Written in response to Philippe Hecquet's *Traité des dispenses de caresme*, Paris, 1709.

Bibliographies: Maggs 206; Schraemli (1) 18; Simon BG 114; Vicaire 24.

Copies: *BMC, BNC,* and *NUC* (Cornell and New York Academy of Medicine).

31. Andry de Bois-Regnard, Nicolas, 1658-1742.

TRAITÉ │ DES ALIMENS │ DE CARESME, │ OÚ L'ON EXPLIQUE LES │ differentes qualitez des légumes, es herba- │ ges, des racines, des fruits, des poissons, │ des amphibies, des assaisonnemens: des │ boissons même les plus en usage, comme de │ l'eau, du vin, de la bierre, du cidre, du │ thé, du caffé, du chocolat. │ Et où l'on éclaircit plusieurs questions impor- │ tantes sur l'abstinence & sur le jeûne, tant │ par rapport au Carême, que par rapport à │ la sante·. │ *Par Me* NICOLAS ANDRY, *Conseiller, Lecteur &* │ *Professeu Roïal, Docteur Regent de la Faculté de* │ *Medecine de Paris, Professeur des Ecoles de la même* │ *Faculté, & Censeur Roïal des Livres.* │ TOME I. [TOME II.] │ [ornament] │ A PARIS, │ Chez JEAN-BAPTISTE

COIGNARD, Imprimeur | ordinaire du Roi, ruë S. Jacques, à la Bible d'or. | [short rule] | M D C C X I I I. | *Avec Approbation, & Privilege de Sa Majesté.*

First edition, Paris, 1713.

12mo. 2 vols. Vol. I. a^6 A-Tt$^{8.4}$ Vv^6 Xx^8 Yy-Zz^4; 280 leaves, pp. [*12*] [1] 2-519 [520] [*28*]. Vol. II. a^4 A-Ll$^{8.4}$ Mm^8 (±Mm8) cancellans of Mm8 signed Nn; 216 leaves, pp. [*8*] [1] 2-402 [*22*].

Bibliographies: Horn-Arndt 217; Maggs 207; Vicaire 24.

Copies: *BNC* and *NUC* (Kansas State University and the National Library of Medicine).

31a. Annuaire de la Boulangerie de Paris.

ANNUAIRE | DE LA | BOULANGERIE | [fancy] DE PARIS | POUR | L'EXERCICE DE L'AN 1860 | COMPRENANT | Les Arrêtés et Décrets, Ordonnances, Décisions, Délibérations | et Instructions | CONCERNANT LE COMMERCE DE LA BOULANGERIE DE PARIS. | [short fancy rule] | PARIS | AU BUREAU DU SYNDICAT | QUAI D'ANJOU, 7. | [short rule] | 1860

First edition, Paris, 1860.

208 x 130 mm. [1]^8 2-12^8 [13-14]^8 15-40^8 41^4; 324 leaves, pp. [1-6] 7-648.

Bibliographies: Unrecorded in the bibliographies consulted or in RLIN. Oberlé (1) 825 and 826 records issues for 1835 and 1861.

Copies: No other copy of this issue located. *BMC* locates issues for 1850 and 1856 "etc." with a note "not published in 1864-72."

32. Apicius.

CAELII | APITII, SVM | MI ADVLATRICIS | MEDICINAE ARTIFICIS, | De re Culinaria libri | Decem. | [ornament] | B. PLATINAE CREMONEN- | *sis De Tuenda ualetudine, Natura rerum, & Popinae* | *scientia Libri X.* | PAVLI AEGINETAE DE FA- | *cultatibus alimentorum Tractatus,* | *Albano Torino Inter-* | *prete.* | ✳ | [printer's device] | APVD SEB. GRYPHIVM | LVGVDVNI, | 1541.

New edition, Lyon, 1541. Originally published under the title *De re coquinaria*, Milan, 1498.

8vo. a-u⁸ x⁴; 164 leaves, pp. [1-2] 3-314 [315-328].

Bibliographies: Bitting, p. 11; Malortie 12; Oberlé (1) 6; Schraemli (1) 22; Simon BG 123; Vicaire 31.

Copies. *BMC*, *BNC*, and *NUC* (12 copies).

33. Apicius.

LES DIX LIVRES | DE CUISINE | [in green] D'APICIUS | Traduits du latin | pour la première fois et commentés | par | BERTRAND GUÉGAN | [in green: ornament] | PARIS | RENÉ BONNEL ÉDITEUR | RUE BLANCHE, No 8

First edition in French, Paris, 1933. No. 471 of 650 copies on vélin de Vidalon after 4 copies on vélin de Montval and 25 on Hollande Pannekoek.

225 x 140 mm. [a]⁸ b-e⁸ 1-20⁸ 21⁴; 204 leaves, pp. [2] [i-ix] x-lxxviii [1-3] 4-322 [323-324] [*4*], first four and last four pages blank. Publisher's printed wrappers.

Bibliographies: Bitting, p. 13; Oberlé (1) 7; Schraemli (3) 5.

Copies: *BMC* and *NUC* (5 copies).

34. Appert, Nicolas, 1750?-1841.

L'ART DE CONSERVER, |PENDANT PLUSIEURS ANNÉES, | TOUTES LES SUBSTANCES ANIMALES ET VÉGÉTALES; | OUVRAGE soumis au Bureau consultatif des Arts et | Manufactures, revêtu de son approbation, et publié | sur l'invitation de S. Exc. le Ministre de l'Intérieur. | PAR APPERT, | *Propriétaire à Massy, département de Seine et Oise,* | *ancien Confiseur et Distillanteur, Élève de la bouche de* | *la Maison ducale de Christian IV.* | [short rule] | "J'ai pensé que votre découverte méritait | "un témoignage particulier de la bienveillance | "du Gouvernement." | *Lettre de S. Exc. le Ministre de l'Intérieur.* | [short rule] | A PARIS, | CHEZ PATRIS ET Cie, IMPRIMEURS-LIBRAIRES, QUAI | NAPOLÉON, AU COIN DE LA RUE DE LA COLOMBE, No 4. | [short fancy rule] | 1810.

First edition, Paris, 1810. Vicarie 34 records a Paris, 1810, edition with the imprint of Barrois who published the third and later editions under an altered title (see items 35 and 36). However, as all recorded copies of the first edition have the Patris imprint, Vicaire may be in error.

The verso of the half-title contains a printed warning against pirated editions and is signed in holograph by Appert.

215 x 135 mm. pp. [*a*]^8 b^8 1-7^8 8^2; 74 leaves, pp. [i-v] vi-xxxii [1] 2-116. Uncut in original wrappers.

Illustration: Engraved folding plate depicting a machine for corking bottles.

Bibliographies: Bitting, p. 13 (Patris imprint); Oberlé (1) 184 and 185 (Patris imprint); Oberlé (2) 125 (Patris imprint); Schraemli (1) 27 (imprint not noted); Vicaire 34 (Barrois imprint); Wheaton and Kelly 193 (Patris imprint).

Copies: *NUC* (8 copies).

Note: Appert's first name is variously recorded as Nicolas (*NUC*); Charles (*BMC*, *BNC* and Horn-Arndt); and Françoise (Vicaire). The *Dictionnaire de Biographie française* has elected Appert, Nicolas (Charles? Françoise?)

35. Appert, Nicolas, 1750?-1841.

LE LIVRE | DE TOUS LES MÉNAGES, | OU | L'ART DE CONSERVER, | PENDANT PLUSIEURS ANNÉES, | TOUTES LES SUBSTANCES | ANIMALES ET VÉGÉTALES; | OUVRAGE soumis au Bureau consultatif des Arts et | Manufactures, revêtu de son approbation, et publié | sur l'invitation de S. Exc. le Ministre de l'Intérieur; | PAR M. APPERT, | Propriétaire à Massy (Seine-et-Oise), ancien Confiseur et Distillateur, | Elève de la bouche de la maison ducale de Christian IV. | TROISIÈME ÉDITION, | REVUE ET AUGMENTÉE DE PROCÉDÉS NOUVEAUX, | D'EXPÉRIENCES ET D'OBSERVATIONS NOUVELLES. | [short rule] | "J'ai pensé que votre découverte méritoit un témoignage | "particulier de la bienveillance du Gouvernement." | *Lettre de S. Exc. le* MINISTRE DE L'INTÉRIEUR. | [short rule] | A PARIS. | Chez BARROIS l'aîné, libraire, rue de | Savoie, no. 13. | [short rule] | 1813. | DE L'IMPRIMERIE DE DOUBLET.

Third edition, Paris, 1813. Originally published in Paris, 1810, under the title *L'Art de Conserver, pendant plusieurs années, toutes les substances animales et végétales* (item 34).

214 x 136 mm. a-c⁸ A-L⁸; 112 leaves, pp. [i-iii] iv-xlviii [1] 2-176. Uncut in original wrappers.

Illustration: Engraved folding plate depicting the machine for corking bottles, as in the 1810 edition, but adding a top and side view of a still.

Bibliographies: Bitting, p. 14; Simon BG 136; Vicaire 35; Wheaton and Kelly 201.

Copies: *BMC*, *BNC* and *NUC* (5 copies).

36. Appert, Nicholas, 1750?-1841.

LE LIVRE | DE TOUS LES MÉNAGES, | OU | L'ART DE CONSERVER, | PENDANT PLUSIEURS ANNÉES, | TOUTES LES SUBSTANCES | ANIMALES ET VÉGÉTALÉS; | OUVRAGE soumis au Bureau consultatif des Arts et Manufactures, | revêtu de son approbation, et publié sur l'invitation de S. Exc. | le Ministre de l'Intérieur; | PAR M. APPERT, | Propriétaire à Massy (Seine-et-Oise), ancien Confiseur et Distillateur, Élève de la | bouche de la maison ducale de Christian IV. | TROISIÈME ÉDITION, | REVUE ET AUGMENTÉE DE PROCÉDÉS NOUVEAUX, D'EXPÉRIENCES | ET D'OBSERVATIONS NOUVELLES. | [short rule] | "J'ai pensé que votre découverte méritoit un témoignage | "particulier de la bienveillance du Gouvernement." | *Lettre de S. Exc. le* MINISTRE DE L'INTÉRIEUR. | [short rule] | A PARIS, | CHEZ BARROIS L'AÎNÉ, LIBRAIRE, | RUE DE SAVOIE, No. 15. | 1821.

Fourth edition, styled "troisième édition" on the title-page, Paris, 1821. Originally published, Paris, 1810, under the title *L'Art de Conserver* . . . (item 34).

214 x 131 mm. π² 1-11⁸ 12⁴; 94 leaves, pp. [i-v] vi-xli [xlii] [1] 2-146.

Illustration: Engraved folding plate crudely redrawn after that in the third edition (item 35).

Bibliographies: This edition unrecorded in the bibliographies consulted.

Copies: *BMC* and *BNC*.

37. Arbuthnot, John, 1667-1735.

ESSAI | SUR | LA NATURE, | ET LE CHOIX | DES ALIMENS, | SUIVANT LES | DIFFÉRENTES | CONSTITUTIONS; | *OU* | On explique les différens effets, les | avantages & les désavantages de | la nourriture animale & végétale. | *Par* JEAN ARBUTHNOT, *Docteur en* | *Médecine, Membre des Collges des* | *Médecins de Londres & d'Edimbourg,* | *& de la Société Royale.* | Traduite de l'Anglois | PREMIERE PARTIE. | [ornament] | A PARIS, | Chez la Veuve CAVELIER & Fils, | rue | S. Jacques, au Lys d'Or. | [short rule] | M. DCC. LV. | *Avec Approbation & Privilége du Roi.*

Title-page of second part:

REGLES PRATIQUES | SUR | LA DIÉTE. | DANS LES DIFFERENTES | CONSTITUTIONS | ET MALADIES | DU CORPS HUMAIN. | *Par* JEAN ARBUTHNOT, *Docteur en* | *Médecine, Membre du Collège des Méde-* | *cins de Londres, & de la Société Royale.* | SECONDE PARTIE. | [ornament] | A PARIS, | Chez la Veuve CAVELIER & Fils, rue | S. Jacques, au Lys d'Or. | [short rule] | M. DCC. LV. | *Avec Approbation & Privilége du Roi.*

Second edition of the translation into French by M. Boyer de Prebandier, Paris, 1755. Originally published in English under the title *An Essay Concerning the Nature of Ailments*, London, 1731, and in French, Paris, 1741.

12mo. a^{12} A-O^{12}; 180 leaves, pp. [i-ii] iii-xxiv [1] 2-330 [331-336].

Bibliographies: This edition unrecorded in the bibliographies consulted.

Copies: *BNC* and *NUC* (John Crerar Library and the National Library of Medicine).

38. Arcet, Jean-Pierre-Joseph d', 1777-1844.

Wrapper title:

[Within a border of two rules] COLLECTION | DES | MÉMOIRES ET NOTICES | (AVEC DES PLANCHES), | Publiés depuis 1829 jusqu'en 1843, | RELATIVEMENT A L'EMPLOI ALIMENTAIRE | DE LA | GÉLATINE DES OS, | PAR M. D'ARCET, | Membre de l'Institut (Académie des Sciences), du Conseil de | Salubrité, de la Société Centrale et Royale d'Agriculture, etc. | [short fancy rule] | A PARIS, | Au Bureau de l'Administration de la Société Polytechnique, | RUE DE LA PAIX, No 20; | [short fancy rule] 1843.

A collection of the pamphlets, originally published between 1829 and 1843 with an "avis" at the beginning and a "table" at the end and a printed wrapper to provide a title.

Contents:

1. "Avis" signed V. de Moléon. π^2; 2 leaves, pp. [2] [1] 2.

2. "Mémoire sur les os provenant de la viande de boucherie, dans lequel on traite de la conservation de ces os, de l'extraction de leur gélatine, par le moyen de la vapeur, et des usages alimentaires de la dissolution gélantineuse qu'on en obtient. Par M. d'Arcet." $1\text{-}4^8\ 5_1$; 33 leaves pp. [1] 2-66. With two engraved folding plates.

3. "Note relative a l'emploi de l'appareil servant a préparer, a l'hospice de la charité, mille rations de dissolution gélatineuse par jour; par M. Darcet." Paris, Gaultier Laguionie, 1830. π^4; 4 leaves, pp. [1-3] 4-7 [8]. With an engraved folding plate.

4. "Recueil de diverses notes relatives à la extraite des os provenant de la viande de boucherie." By d'Arcet. $[1]^8\ 2^4\ \chi1$; 13 leaves, pp. [1-3] 4-25 [26].

5. "Instruction sur les précautions à prendre pour bien conduire l'appareil servant à extraire la gélatine des os de la viande de boucherie, par M. d'Arcet." π^8; 8 leaves, pp. [1] 2-15 [16]. With an engraved folding plate.

6. "Rapport fait en 1814, sur un travail de M. d'Arcet, ayant pour objet l'extraction de la gélatine des os et son application aux différens usages économiques, par MM. Leroux, Dubois, Pelletan, Duméril et Vauquelin." $[10]^8\ (\text{-}10_{1,2})\ 11^2$; 8 leaves, pp. [149] 150-164.

7. "Rapport fait le 20 janvier 1830 au Conseil général des hospices, sur l'emploi de la gélatine, à l'Hotel-Dieu de Paris, par M. B. Desportes, membre de la commission administrative." $\pi^4\ \chi1$; 5 leaves, pp. [3] 4-11 [12].

8. "Note relative à l'extraction de la gélatine des os de la viande de boucherie, et à son emploi, en grand et pendant toute une année, dans le régime alimentaire de l'hôpital Saint-Louis, Par. M. d'Arcet." $\pi^8\ \chi1$; 9 leaves, pp. [1] 2-15 [16-18].

9. "Notice sur la fabrication des biscuits animalisés au moyen de la viande de boucherie, par M. d'Arcet." $\pi^2\chi1$; 3 leaves, pp. [1] 2-6.

10. "Résumé concernant l'emploi alimentaire de la gélatine des os de la viande de boucherie, par M. d'Arcet." 1^4; 4 leaves, pp. [1] 2-7 [8].

11. "Extrait de deux lettres adressées à M. d'Arcet, par M. Commesny, pharmacien à Reims, et administrateur du bureau de bienfaisance de cette ville, relativement à l'appareil extracteur de la gélatine des os, établi pour le soulagement des pauvres et des ouvriers sans travail." π^4; 4 leaves, pp. [1] 2-7 [8].

12. "Résumé de ce qui a été fait depuis deux ans pour améliorer le régime alimentaire des pauvres, en y introduisant l'usage de la gélatine des os, par M. d'Arcet, lu le 28 avril, à la séance générale de la Société des Établissemens charitables." $\pi^8(-\pi1)$; 7 leaves, pp. [1] 2-14.

13. "Note sur l'emploi alimentaire de la gélatine des os, en réponse au mémoire et à la lettre que M. Donné a lus à l'Académie sur le même sujet. Par. M d'Arcet." π^8; 8 leaves, pp. [1] 2-16.

14. "Note relative au bouillon que l'on fait en aromatisant la dissolution gélatineuse au moyen de la viande de boucherie, par M. d'Arcet." π^6; 6 leaves. pp. [1] 2-12.

15. "Résultats de l'emploi alimentaire de la gélatine des os, continué, sans interruption, à l'hôpital Saint-Louis, pendant trois ans et trois mois, par M. d'Arcet . . ." $\pi^4(-\pi4)$; 3 leaves, pp. [1-3] 4-6.

16. "Recette de potages et de ragouts à la gélatine." 1^4; 4 leaves, pp. [1] 2-8.

17. "Note sur l'emploi arimentaire [sic] de la gélatine, pendant sept ans, dans le régime alimentaire de l'hôpital Saint-Louis. Par M. d'Arcet . . ." $3\text{-}4^8$ 5^6; 22 leaves, pp. [1] 2-44.

18. "Note sur l'emploi continu et régulier de la gélatine, pendant neuf années, dans la régime alimentaire de l'hôpital Saint-Louis, par M. d'Arcet." 1^6; 6 leaves, pp. [1] 2-11 [12].

19. "Note sur l'emploi continu et régulier de la gélatine pendant dix années, dans le régime alimentaire de l'hôpital Saint-Louis, suivie de quelques autres documents relatifs à la même question, par M. d'Arcet." $*^2$ 6^8 7^4; 14 leaves, pp. [1] 2-28. With a folding chart.

20. "Extrait du Recueil de la Société polytechnique, ou du receueil industriel et des beaux-arts (Février 1840.) . . . Documens sur l'emploi de la gélatine. Rapport fait à l'administration du Dépôt de Mendicité de la ville de Lyon sur l'emploi alimentaire de la gélatine dans cet établissement en 1838 et 1839." 1^4; 4 leaves, pp. [1] 2-8.

21. "Emploi alimentaire de la gélatine. (Recueil industriel, no. 32, août 1840.)" 1^4; 4 leaves, pp. [1] 2-8.

22. "Nouveaux documens relatifs à l'emploi alimentaire de la gélatine en 1840." [1-2]^8 3^4; 20 leaves, pp. [1-3] 4-37 [38-40] with folding chart facing p. 4. pp. 38-40 blank.

23. "Extrait du Recueil de la Société polytechnique, Septembre 1842. Emploi de la gélatine. Documens envoyés par les Departemens et l'Etranger." [1]^8; 8 leaves, pp. [1] 2-15 [16].

24. "Table des documens composant le collection des mémoires, notices et rapports publiés depuis 1829 jusqu'à 1843, relativement à l'emploi de la gélatine des os; par M. d'Arcet." π^4; 4 leaves, pp. [1] 2-7 [8].

Bibliographies: This collection unrecorded in the bibliographies consulted.

Copies: No other copy of this collection located. Some of the individual pieces are listed in *BMC*, *BNC*, and *NUC*.

Note: The author's name appears as Darcet in *NUC* and Vicaire and as d'Arcet in *BMC*, *BNC* and the pieces themselves.

39. Arcet, Jean-Pierre-Joseph d', 1777-1844.

RECHERCHES | SUR | LES SUBSTANCES NUTRITIVES QUE RENFERMENT | LES OS, | OU | MÉMOIRE SUR LES OS PROVENANT DE LA VIANDE DE BOUCHE- | RIE, SUR LES MOYENS DE LES CONSERVER, D'EN EXTRAIRE DE LA | GÉLATINE PAR LA VAPEUR, ETC., | PAR M. D'ARCET, | Membre de l'Académie royale des sciences et du Conseil de salubrité, etc; | ET | MÉMOIRE SUR L'APPLICATION SPÉCIALE DE CE PROCÉDÉ A LA NOUR- | RITURE DES OUVRIERS DE LA MONNAIE ROYALE DES MÉDAILLES ET | SUR LES APPLICATIONS GÉNÉRALES QU'IL PEUT RECEVOIR, | PAR M. A. DE PUYMAURIN, | Directeur de la Monnaie royale des médailles, Membre de la Société | d'Encouragement, etc. | [short fancy rule] | *Avec 5 Planches.* | [short fancy rule] | A PARIS, | A LA MONNAIE DES MÉDAILLES, rue Guénégaud, no. 8; | MADAME HUZARD (NEÉ VALLAT LA CHAPELLE), Imprimeur- | Libraire, rue de l'Éperon, no. 7; | BÉCHET jeune, Libraire, place de l'École de Médecine, no. 4. | [short fancy rule] | 1829.

First edition, Paris, 1829.

217 x 135 mm. π^4 a^2 1-10^8 11^2; 88 leaves, pp. [i-v] vi-xi [xii] [1] 2-164. Uncut in contemporary plain wrappers; bound with Arcet's *Recueil de diverses notes* (item 40).

Bibliographies: Crahan 538.

Copies: *BMC* and *BNC*.

40. Arcet, Jean-Pierre-Joseph d', 1777-1844.

RECUEIL | DE DIVERSES NOTES | RELATIVES A LA GÉLATINE EXTRAITE DES OS PROVENANT DE LA | VIANDE DE BOUCHERIE.

First edition, Paris, ca. 1829.

217 x 135 mm. [1]^8 2^4 χ1; 13 leaves, pp. [1-3] 4-25 [26]. Uncut in contemporary plain wrappers; bound with Arcet's *Recherches sur les substances* (item 39).

Illustrations: Five engraved folding plates of apparatus for extracting gelatine from bones.

Bibliographies: Unrecorded in the bibliographies consulted.

Copies: No other copy located.

41. Archambault.

LE | CUISINIER ÉCONOME, | OU | ÉLÉMENS NOUVEAUX | DE CUISINE, DE PATISSERIE ET D'OFFICE, | RENFERMANT: | 1°. Des notices sur les diverses espèces d'alimens; des moyens de reconnaître les | meilleures qualités des denrées; et des procédés de cuisine beaucoup plus simples | et moins dispendieux; | 2°. Des méthodes pour préparer et conserver les fruits et les légumes. | 3°. Une Notice sur les Vins, et l'ordre du service, avec cinq planches. | Ouvrage indispensable aux maisons les plus somptueuses comme | aux tables les plus simples, à la ville et à la campagne; | PAR FEU ARCHAMBAULT, | ANCIEN RESTAURATEUR. | [short rule] | Bonne chère, économie. | [short rule] | PARIS, | ANT. BAILLEUL, Imprimeur du Commerce et du Constitutionnel, | rue Thibautodé, no. 8; | RENARD, à la Librairie du Commerce, rue Sainte-Anne, no. 71; | BAUDOUIN frères, Libraires, rue de Vaugirard, no. 36. | [short fancy rule] | 1821.

First edition, Paris, 1821.

204 x 121 mm. π^4 1-27^8 28^6; 226 leaves, pp. [i-v] vi-viii [1] 2-444.

Illustrations: Four lithographed folding plates illustrating table settings. Note: The title-page calls for five plates, but the first is double, containing two services.

Bibliographies: Vicaire 37.

Copies: *BNC*.

42. Archambault.

LE | CUISINIER ÉCONOME, | OU | ÉLÉMENS NOUVEAUX | DE CUISINE, DE PATISSERIE ET D'OFFICE; | RENFERMANT | 1° Des notices sur les diverses espèces d'alimens, et des moyens de recon- | naître les meilleures qualités de denrées; 2° Des procédés de cuisine | beaucoup plus simples et moins dispendieux; 3° Des méthodes pour | préparer et conserver les fruits et les légumes: | Ouvrage indispensable aux maisons somptueuses comme | aux tables les plus simples, à la ville et à la campagne; | PAR ARCHAMBAULT. | TROISÈME ÉDITION, | Revue, corrigée et ornée de cinq planches pour l'ordre du service des tables; | SUIVIE | D'une Notice sur les Vins, par M. JULLIEN, auteur de la | *Topographie des Vignobles* et du *Manuel du Sommelier.* | Bonne chère, économie. | [short fancy rule] | PARIS, | A LA LIBRAIRIE DU COMMERCE, | CHEZ RENARD, LIBRAIRE, RUE SAINTE-ANNE, No 71. | [short fancy rule] | 1825.

Third edition, Paris, 1825. Originally published, Paris, 1821 (item 41).

199 x 122 mm. π^4 1-24^8 25-28^4 29^2; 214 leaves, pp. [i-v] vi-viii [1] 2-420.

Illustrations: Three engraved folding plates depicting table settings.

Bibliographies: Bitting, p. 15; Oberlé (1) 199; Vicaire 37.

Copies: *NUC* (Library of Congress and New York Public Library).

43. Arnauld d'Andilly, Robert, 1588-1674.

LA MANIERE | DE CVLTIVER | LES ARBRES | FRVITIERS | *Par le Sieur LE GENDRE* | *Curé d'Henonuille.* | OÙ IL EST TRAITTÉ | des Pepinieres. Des Espaliers. | Des Contr'espaliers. Des Arbres | en buisson, & à haute tige. |

TROISIESME EDITION. | [ornament] | A PARIS, | Chcz Antoine Vitré, Imprimeur | ordinaire du Roy, & du Clergé | de France. | [short rule] | M. DC. LV. | *Auec Priuilege du Roy.*

Third edition, Paris, 1655. Originally published, Paris, 1652.

12mo. a⁸ e⁴ i⁸ o⁴ u² A-S⁸·⁴ T⁸ V²; 144 leaves, pp. [*52*] 1-235 [236].

Bibliographies: Unrecorded in the bibliographies consulted.

Copies: *BNC.*

44. Arnauld d'Andilly, Robert, 1588-1674.

LA | MANIERE DE CVLTIVER | LES | ARBRES | FRVITIERS. | *Par le Sieur LE GENDRE,* | *Curé d'Henonville.* | OV IL EST TRAITÉ DES | Pepinieres, des Espaliers, des contre- | Espaliers, des arbres en buisson & à | haute tige. | *NOVVELLE EDITION.* | [vignette] | A PARIS, | Par la Compagnie des Libraires | du Palais. | [short rule] | M. DC. LXV.

Fifth edition, Paris, 1665. Originally published, Paris, 1652.

12mo. A-E¹² F⁶; 66 leaves, pp. [1-2] 3-132.

Bound with *Le Jardinier françois*, Paris, 1665, by Nicolas de Bonnefons (item 91).

Bibliographies: Unrecorded in the bibliographies consulted.

Copies: *BNC* and *NUC* (William Andrews Clark Library only).

45. L'Art d'employer les fruits.

L'ART | D'EMPLOYER | LES FRUITS, | ET DE COMPOSER A PEU DE FRAIS TOUTES SORTES | DE CONFITURES ET DE LIQUEURS | POUR FAIRE SUITE A LA *CUISINIÈRE DE LA CAMPAGNE* | [short fancy rule] | A PARIS, | CHEZ AUDOT, LIBRAIRE, | rue des Mathurins-St.-Jacques, no 18. | 1818.

First edition, Paris, 1818.

168 x 96 mm. [1]^8 2^4 3-12$^{8.4}$ 13^4 14^2; 78 leaves, pp. [i-v] vi-viii [9] 10-155 [156]. Bound with *La Cuisinière de la campagne et de la ville*, Paris, 1818, by Louis-Eustache Audot (item 52).

Illustration: Engraved plate titled "Coupe d'une Glacière en Pierre et en Charpente" facing p. 117.

Bibliographies: Vicaire 47.

Copies: No other copy located.

46. L'Art de conserver et d'employer les fruits.

L'ART | DE | CONSERVER ET D'EMPLOYER | LES FRUITS, | CONTENANT TOUS LES PROCÉDÉS LES PLUS ÉCONOMIQUES | POUR LES CONFIRE ET POUR COMPOSER LES LIQUEURS | SIROPS, GLACES, BOISSONS DE MÉNAGE, etc.; | Pour faire suite à la Cuisinière de la campagne | et de la ville. | SECONDE ÉDITION, | Entièrement refondue, et augmentée de beaucoup de recettes | nouvelles. | PARIS, | AUDOT, LIBRAIRE-ÉDITEUR, | RUE DES MAÇONS-SORBONNE, No. 11. | 1823.

Second edition, Paris, 1823. Originally published, Paris, 1818, under the title *L'Art d'employer les fruits et de composer à peu de frais toutes sortes de confitures et de liqueurs* (item 45).

177 x 116 mm. ✱^{6} 1-7^{12} 8^2 ✱8^4; 96 leaves, pp. [i-v] vi-xii [1] 2-171 [2] 172-178. Contemporary wrappers, uncut. 24 page publisher's catalogue, dated décembre 1825 at end.

Illustration: Engraved plate titled "Coupe d'un Glacière en Pierre et en Charpente" intended to face p. 112 here used as a frontispiece.

Bibliographies: Vicaire 48.

Copies: *NUC* (Library of Congress only).

47. L'Art de conserver et d'employer les fruits.

L'ART | DE | CONSERVER ET D'EMPLOYER | LES FRUITS, | CONTENANT TOUS LES PROCÉDÉS LES PLUS ÉCONOMIQUES POUR | LES CONFIRE ET POUR COMPOSER LES LIQUEURS, SIROPS, | GLACES, BOISSONS DE MÉNAGE, etc.; | Pour faire suite à la Cuisinière de la campagne | et de la ville. | TROISIÈME ÉDITION, | Augmentée de descriptions de plusieurs glacières domestiques et | économiques, et d'une fontaine à conserver la glace. | AVEC FIGURES. | PARIS. | AUDOT, LIBRAIRE-ÉDITEUR, | RUE DES MAÇONS-SORBONNE, No. 11. | [short rule] | 1829.

Third edition, Paris, 1829. Originally published, Paris, 1818, under the title *L'Art d'employer les fruits* . . . (item 45).

172 x 97 mm. π^6 1-7^{12} 8^6; 96 leaves, pp. [i-v] vi-xii [1] 2-180.

Illustration: Engraved frontispiece of a "Glacière" with three figures and not the same as the illustration used in the 1818 and 1823 editions, above.

Bibliographies: Vicarie 48.

Copies: *NUC* (Longwood Gardens, Kennet Square, Pa., only).

48. L'Art du limonadier.

L'ART | DU LIMONADIER, | CONTENANT la manière de préparer les Bavaroises, le | Cachou, le Café, le Chocolat; de former les Conserves | de Roses, les Crêmes et Fromages glacés; de distiller | les Eaux odoriférantes; de procéder à la confection des | Elixirs, des Essences, des émulsions, des Huiles, des | Extraits, de confire les Fruits à l'eau-de-vie et au sucre, | de composer l'Hydromel, les Liqueurs aqueuses, spé- | cialement la Limonade, les rafraîchissantes, les spiri- | tueuses, les Ratafias; de faire des Loochs, des Pas- | tilles, des Pâtes, des Sorbets; la Teinture, principale- | ment de Thé; et les Vins artificiels. | Ouvrage utile, non-seulement aux Limonadiers, | aux Distillateurs, mais à tous les Économes | et Pères de famille. | EXTRAIT DE DUBUISSON. | [short fancy rule] | A PARIS, | CHEZ CAUSETTE, LIBRAIRE, | Quai des Augustins, n.o 35 *bis*.

New edition, Paris, ca. 1810. This is a compilation from several earlier works, especially Dubuisson's *L'Art du distillateur et marchand de liqueurs considérées comme alimens médicamenteux*, 2 vols., Paris, 1779. The earliest edition of this compilation located is Paris, 1804.

210 x 120 mm. [1]^8 2-18^8 19^4; 148 leaves, pp. [1-5] 6-294 [2]. Last leaf (blank?) wanting in this copy.

Bookplate: Westbury.

Bibliographies: This edition unrecorded in the bibliographies consulted. Bitting records a Paris, 1804, edition and Maggs and Vicaire a Paris, 1807, edition.

Copies: No other copy of this edition located. *NUC* locates the 1804 edition (Library of Congress only).

49. Audiger.

LA │ MAISON │ REGLÉE │ ET │ L'ART DE DIRIGER LA MAISON │ d'un grand Seigneur & autres, tant à │ la Ville qu'à la Campagne, & le devoir │ de tous les Officiers, & autres Dome- │ stiques en general. │ AVEC │ *LA VERITABLE METHODE* │ *de faire toutes sortes d'Essences d'Eaux &* │ *de Liqueurs, fortes & rafraîchissantes* │ *à la mode d'Italie.* │ OUVRAGE UTILE ET NECESSAIRE A TOUTES │ sortes de personnes de qualité, Gentils hommes de │ Provinces, Etrangers, Bourgeois, Officiers de grandes │ Maisons, Limonadiers & autres Marchands de Liqueurs. │ *Dedié à* *Monseigneur* PHELYPEAUX. │ A PARIS, │ *au Palais.* │ Chez NICOLAS LE GRAS, dans la grande Salle au troi- │ siéme Pillier à L. Couronnée. │ AUGUSTIN BESONGNE, devant la Cour des Aydes │ aux Rozes Vermeilles. │ Et HILAIRE FOUCAULT, rue" S. Jacques, vis à vis │ la rue" du Plâtre aux Armes du Roy & de la Ville. │ [rule] │ M. DC. XCII. │ *AVEC PRIVILEGE DU ROY.*

First edition, Paris, 1692. Three issues of the first edition are known: with the imprint of Nicolas Le Gras; with the imprint of Nicolas Le Gras, Augustin Besonge and Hilaire Foucault; and with the imprint of Michel Brunet.

12mo. a^{12} A-L^{12} M^{12} (-M10-12); 153 leaves, pp. [*24*] 1-267 [*268*] [*14*].

Illustrations: Six engraved folding plates showing table settings.

Bibliographies: Simon BG 148 (Le Gras imprint); Vicaire 53 (Le Gras imprint).

Copies: *BNC* (Le Gras imprint and Le Gras, Besonge, Foucault imprint) and *NUC* (Michel Brunet imprint; 6 copies).

50. Audiger.

LA | MAISON | REGLÉE | ET | L'ART DE DIRIGER LA MAISON | d'un grand
Seigneur, & autres, tant à | la Ville qu'à la Campagne, & le devoir | de tous les
Officiers, & autres Dome- | stiques en general. | AVEC | *LA VERITABLE METHODE*
| *de faire toutes sortes d'Essences d'Eaux &* | *de Liqueurs, fortes & rafraîchissantes à
la* | *mode d'Italie.* | OUVRAGE UTILE ET NECESSAIRE | à toutes sortes de
personnes de qualité, Gentils- | hommes de Provinces, Etrangers, Bourgeois, |
Officiers de grandes Maisons, Limonadiers & | autres Marchands de Liqueurs. | *Dedié
à Monseigneur* PHELYPEAUX. | [ornament] | A PARIS, | Chez NICOLAS LE
GRAS, au Palais, | dans la grand' Salle, au autroisiéme Pillier, | à l'L couronnée. |
[rule] | M. DCC. | *AVEC PRIVILEGE DU ROY.*

Second French edition, Paris, 1700. Originally published in Paris in 1692 (item 49),
and reprinted in Amsterdam in 1697. Vicaire records an edition published in Paris in
1700 with the imprint of Michel Brunet and mentions another in a note with the imprint
of Paul Marret.

12mo. ✱^{8} ✱✱^{4} A-Cc$^{8.4}$ Dd^6; 174 leaves, pp. [*24*] 1-305 [306-324].

Illustrations: Six engraved folding plates showing table settings.

Bibliographies: This issue, with the Le Gras imprint, unrecorded in the bibliographies
consulted. Bitting, p. 19, Schraemli (1) 40, and Vicaire 53 record the issue with the
Michel Brunet imprint.

Copies: *NUC* (Michel Brunet imprint; Folger Library, Library of Congress, and
Northwestern University).

51. Audot, Louis-Eustache, 1783-1870.

ALMANACH | DES MÉNAGÈRES | ET DES | GASTRONOMES | POUR 1854, |
PRODUITS DE CHAQUE MOIS, PROVISIONS, | SERVICES ACTUELS A LA
FRANÇAISE ET A LA RUSSE | AVEC FIGURES, | RECETTES NOUVELLES OU
PEU CONNUES, ANECDOTES, ETC.; | PAR L'AUTEUR | de la Cuisiniére de la
Campagne et de la Ville. | [short fancy rule] | PARIS | AUDOT,
LIBRAIRE-ÉDITEUR, | Rue Larrey, ci-devant du Paon, 8, École-de-Mécine.

First edition, Paris, 1854. First year of this almanac which continued with issues for
1855 and 1856.

185 x 116 mm. [1]^{12} 2^6 3-6$^{12.6}$ 7^6; 60 leaves, pp. [1-17] 18-119 [120]. Publisher's printed wrappers. Eight pages of publisher's ads at the end.

Illustrations: Eleven wood engravings in the text.

Bibliographies: Bitting, p. 20; Vicaire 17.

Copies: *NUC* (Library of Congress only).

52. Audot, Louis-Eustache, 1783-1870.

LA CUISINIÈRE | DE LA CAMPAGNE | ET DE LA VILLE, | OU | LA NOUVELLE CUISINE | ÉCONOMIQUE; | Précédée d'OBSERVATIONS très-importantes sur les soins qu'exige | une Cave et d'une INSTRUCTION sur la manière de servir à | table, et sur la Dissection des viandes. | AVEC FIGURES. | [short fancy rule] | A PARIS, | CHEZ AUDOT, LIBRAIRE, | rue des Mathurins-St.-Jacques, no 18. | 1818.

First edition, Paris, 1818.

167 x 97 mm. [a]^8 b^4 c-f$^{8.4}$ 1-20$^{8.4}$ 21^4; 124 leaves, pp. [i-v] vi-lxxii [1] 2-248. Bound with *L'Art d'employer les fruits*, Paris, 1818 (item 45).

Illustrations: Eight engraved plates, printed in brown, illustrating carving.

Bibliographies: Maggs 375; Oberlé (1) 179; Vicaire 54.

Copies: *BNC*.

53. Audot, Louis-Eustache, 1783-1870.

LA CUISINIÈRE | DE LA CAMPAGNE | ET DE LA VILLE, | OU | LA NOUVELLE CUISINE | ECONOMIQUE; | Précédée d'un TRAITÉ sur les soins qu'exige une cave, et sur | la Dissection des viandes à table. | DÉDIÉE AUX BONNES MÉNAGÈRES; | PAR M. L.-E. A. | AVEC DIX PLANCHES GRAVÉES. | TROISIÈME ÉDITION, | REVUE, CORRIGÉE ET AUGMENTÉE. | PARIS, | AUDOT, LIBRAIRE- ÉDITEUR, | RUE DES MAÇONS-SORBONNE, No. 11. | 1823.

Third edition, Paris, 1823. Originally published, Paris, 1818 (item 52).

170 x 100 mm. π^4 1-12^{12} 13$_1$; 149 leaves, pp. [i-v] vi-viii [1] 2-289 [290].

Illustrations: Engraved frontispiece titled "Le Mardi Gras" and nine engraved plates, one folding, on carving.

Bibliographies: Maggs 376; Vicaire 54.

Copies: *BNC*.

54. Audot, Louis-Eustache, 1783-1870.

LA CUISINIÈRE │ DE LA CAMPAGNE │ ET DE LA VILLE │ OU │ NOUVELLE CUISINE ÉCONOMIQUE; │ CONTENANT: │ Table des mets selon l'ordre du service. │ Ustensiles, instrumens et procédés nouveaux, avec figures. │ Service de la table par les domestiques, avec figures. │ Manière de servir et de découper à table, avec figures. │ Cuisines française, anglaise et italienne, au nombre de plus de mille │ recettes; d'un exécution simple et facile. │ Divers moyens et recettes d'économie domestique, de conservation des │ viandes, poissons, légumes, fruits, oeufs, etc. etc. │ Des vins et des soins qu'ils exigent. │ Table des mets par ordre alphabétique. │ PAR M. L.-E. A. │ VINGTIÈME ÉDITION, │ CORRIGÉ ET AUGMENTÉE, │ AVEC 65 FIGURES, DONT 2 COLORIÉES │ PARIS. │ AUDOT, LIBRAIRE-ÉDITEUR, │ RUE DU PAON, 8, ÉCOLE DE MÉDECINE. │ 1836.

Twentieth edition, Paris, 1836. Originally published, Paris, 1818 (item 52).

177 x 104 mm. π^2 1^{12} 2^4 3-20^{12} 21^6; 240 leaves, pp. [1-5] 6-480.

Illustrations: Sixty-five wood engraved illustrations in the text. Two, on p. 35, are hand colored.

Bibliographies: This edition unrecorded in the bibliographies consulted.

Copies: No other copy of this edition located.

55. Audot, Louis-Eustache, 1783-1870.

LA CUISINIÈRE │ DE LA CAMPAGNE │ ET DE LA VILLE, │ OU │ NOUVELLE CUISINE ÉCONOMIQUE, │ CONTENANT │ Indication des Jours maigres │ Table des mets selon l'ordre du service. | Ustensiles, instruments et procédés nouveaux, avec figures. | Service de la table par les domestiques, avec figures. | Manière de servir et de découper à table, avec figures. | Cuisines Française, Anglaise, Allemande, Flamande, Polonaise, Russe, | Espagnole, Provençale, Languedocienne, Italienne et Gothique, | au nombre de 1,500 recettes, d'une exécution simple et facile. | Divers moyens et recettes d'économie domestique, de conservation des | viandes, poisson, légumes, fruits, oeufs, etc., etc. | Article détaillé sur la Pâtisserie, avec figures. Moyen facile de faire les glaces. | Des caves, des vins et des soins qu'ils exigent. | Propriétés sanitaires et digestives des aliments. | Table des mets par ordre alphabétique. | *Cinquante-quatrième édition* | MISE AU COURANT DU PROGRÈS ANNUEL. | 300 FIGURES. | PARIS, 1876. | LIBRAIRIE AUDOT | NICLAUS ET Cie, SUCCESSEURS, LIBRAIRES-ÉDITEURS | RUE GARANCIÈRE SAINT-SULPICE, No 8 | [short rule] | Ouvrage admis spécialement à l'Exposition | universelle de 1867, classe 90, galerie II.

Fifty-fourth edition, Paris, 1876. Originally published, Paris, 1818 (item 52).

187 x 117 mm. π^4 1-38$^{12.6}$ 39^4; pp. [1-5] 6-84, 84A-84D, 85-242, 242A-242D, 243-688 [689-690] ^{2}1-2. Publisher's printed boards dated 1878. 24 page publisher's catalogue dated 1878 bound in at end.

Illustrations: 300 wood engraved illustrations in the text, including the hand colored frontispiece on $\pi1^v$.

Bibliographies: Bitting, p. 20.

Copies: *BNC* and *NUC* (Library of Congress only).

56. Audot, Louis-Eustache, 1783-1870.

SUPPLÉMENT | A | LA CUISINIÈRE | DE LA CAMPAGNE ET DE LA VILLE | [short rule] | SERVICE DE TABLE | *A la Française et à la Russe* | ART DE PLIER LES SERVIETTES | [illustration with two women; one taste sampling, the other reading a copy of *La Cuisinière*] | PAR MM. AUDOT, GRANDI ET MOTTON | La Cuisinière Entrées, Pose du couvert, Arrangement des fruits, | Service des Vins, Vermoutn, Entremets, Dessert, Café, Thé, | Bals, Soirées, Ambigu, Observations générales sur le service des mets, Relevés, | Hors-d'oeuvre, Rôts, Salades, Instructions sur les huitres, Menus pour saisons, Déjeuners, | Diners, Dessert, Calendrier des ménagères. | Jardin d'utilité, Surveillance, Produits, Provisions. | Notes gastronomiques de chaque mois sur les fromages, avec calendrier. | Potages, Gâteaux,

Recettes diverses, Économie domestique. | [short rule] | SIXIÈME ÉDITION | [short fancy rule] | PARIS | LIBRAIRIE AUDOT, Vve LEBROC ET Cie, ÉDITEURS | 62, RUE DES ÉCOLES

Sixth edition, Paris, ca. 1860. Originally published, Paris, 1852.

187 x 118 mm. π^2 1-12$^{12.6}$ 13^{12} 14^4; 126 leaves, pp. [*4*] [1] 2-228, ^{2}[1] 2-20. Publisher's printed wrappers.

Illustrations: Numerous wood engravings in the text.

Bibliographies: This edition unrecorded in the bibliographies consulted.

Copies: *NUC* (University of Utah only).

57. Aulagnier, Alexis-François, 1767-1839.

DICTIONNAIRE | DES ALIMENS | ET DES BOISSONS | EN USAGE | DANS LES DIVERS CLIMATS | ET | CHEZ LES DIFFÉRENS PEUPLES. | CET OUVRAGE CONTIENT | L'HISTOIRE NATURELLE DE CHAQUE SUBSTANCE ALIMENTAIRE, SON | ORIGINE, SES PRINCIPES CONSTITUANS, SES PROPRIÉTÉS, SES | ALTÉRATIONS ET LES MOYENS DE LES RECONNAÎTRE, ET FINA- | LEMENT LES RÈGLES LES PLUS IMPORTANTES A SUIVRE POUR | CONSERVER LA SANTÉ. | PAR A.-F. AULAGNIER, | MEMBRE DE L'ACADÉMIE ROYALE DE MÉDECINE. | [short fancy rule] | *Précédé* | DE CONSIDÉRATIONS GÉNÉRALES | *SUR LA NOURRITURE DE L'HOMME;* | (Extrait du Dictionnaire pittoresque d'Histoire naturelle). | PARIS, | [in two columns, column one] COSSON, IMPRIMEUR, | rue St. Germain- des-Prés, 9. | [two vertical rules between columns] | [column two] COUSIN, ÉDITEUR, | rue Jacob, 25. [end columns] | 𝔅𝔯𝔲𝔵𝔢𝔩𝔩𝔢𝔰, | Mertens, libraire, rue de Flandre, 155. | 1839.

Second edition, Paris, 1839. Originally published under the title *Dictionnaire des substances alimentaires indigènes et exotiques et de leurs proprietes*, Paris, 1830.

205 x 128 mm. π^2 χ^2 a-d^8 1-45^8 46^6; 402 leaves, pp. [*8*] 1-63 [64], ^{2}1-731 [732].

Bibliographies: Maggs 456; Oberlé (1) 466; Vicaire 56.

Copies: *BMC*, *BNC*, and *NUC* (4 copies).

57a. Babinski, Henri, b. 1855.

Gastronomie | *pratique* | [fancy] ÉTUDES CULINAIRES | SUIVIES | DU |
Traitement de l'Obésité des Gourmands | PAR | ALI-BAB | [ornament] | PARIS |
ERNEST FLAMMARION, EDITEUR | 26, RUE RACINE, 26 | [short rule] | 1907 |
Droits de traduction et de reproduction réservés pour tous les pays, | y compris la
Suède et la Norvège.

First edition, Paris, 1907.

204 x 143 mm. π^2 1-19^8 20^6; 160 leaves, pp. [*4*] [1] 2-314 [*2*]. Last leaf blank.

Note: This copy inscribed "A mon vieil ami G. Stiegler souvenir affectueux H.
Babinski."

Bibliographies: The first edition unrecorded in the bibliographies consulted or in
RLIN. Bitting, p. 23, and Oberlé (1) record the second edition, Paris, 1912.

Copies: No other copy of the first edition located.

58. Bailleux, Louis.

LE | PATISSIER MODERNE | OU | TRAITÉ | ÉLÉMENTAIRE ET PRATIQUE |
DE LA PATISSERIE FRANÇAISE | AU DIX-NEUVIÈME SIÈCLE | PAR | LOUIS
BAILLEUX. | [short fancy rule] | PARIS | CHEZ L'AUTEUR, BOULEVARD
MONTMARTRE, 3 | ET CHEZ TOUS LES LIBRAIRES. | [short rule] | 1856

First edition, Paris, 1856.

275 x 175 mm. 1^8 (1$_2$+1) 2-16^8 17^6; 135 leaves, pp. [*6*] [5] 6-267 [*268*]. Publisher's
printed wrappers.

Illustrations: 34 lithographed plates of which five are double and five folding showing
a plan for an oven and designs for pastry.

Bibliographies: Bitting, p. 25; Vicaire 61.

Copies: *BMC*, *BNC*, and *NUC* (Library of Congress and Peabody Institute).

59. Balinghem, Antoine de, 1571-1630.

APRESDINEES | ET PROPOS DE TABLE | CONTRE L'EXCEZ AV | *BOIRE, ET AV MANGER* | POVR VIVRE LONGVEMENT | SAINEMENT ET SAINCTEMENT. | *DIALOGISEZ ENTRE VN PRINCE* | *& sept scauants personnages:* | VN THEOLOGIEN, CANONISTE, IVRISCON- | SVLTE, POLITIQVE, MEDECIN, PHILO- | SOPHE MORAL, ET HISTORIEN. | Par le P. ANTHOINE DE BALINGHEM de la | Compagnie de IESVS. | [printer's device] | A LILLE, | De l'Imprimerie de Pierre de Rache, à la | Bible d'or, l'an 1615. | [short rule] | *Avec Permission des Superieurs.*

First edition, Lille, 1615.

8vo. a^8 e^4 χ1 A-Nn^8 Oo^4 Pp^2; 307 leaves, pp. [*26*] 1-588.

Bibliographies: Horn-Arndt 105; Oberlé (2) 71; Vicaire 62.

Copies: *BMC* and *NUC* (Yale only).

60. Barbier-Duval.

L'ART | DU | CONFISEUR MODERNE | CONTENANT | LES PROCÉDÉS LES PLUS NOUVEAUX ET LES MEILLEURS | A L'USAGE DES CONFISEURS | ET DES MÉNAGÈRES | FABRICATION EN GROS ET EN DÉTAIL | PAR | BARBIER-DUVAL | Confiseur à Nancy. | MÉDAILLE DE 1re CLASSE | [short rule] | OUVRAGE ORNÉ DE 100 FIGURES | [within single rule border] FOURNEAUX ET OFFICES. – DRAGÉES, FOURS, DESSERTS, PASTILLAGE. | – DISTILLATION DES SUBSTANCES AROMATIQUES. – ALCOOLATS, | ESSENCES. – CHOIX DES MATIÈRES, LEURS PROPRIÉTÉS, LEUR | NATURE. – SUBSTANCES VÉGÉTALES, RACINES, PLANTES, FRUITS, | GRAINES, ETC., ETC. – SUBSTANCES ANIMALES, MINÉRALES. – SELS, | ACIDES, COULEURS. – MOYENS DE RECONNAITRE LES FALSIFICATIONS | DE TOUS LES PRODUITS. – APPAREILS MÉCANIQUES, MACHINES, | MOULES ET USTENSILES DIVERS. | [below the border] PARIS | LIBRAIRIE AUDOT | LEBROC ET Cie, SUCCESSEURS | 8, RUE GARANCIÈRE | [short rule] | 1879 | *Tous droits réservés*

First edition, Paris, 1879.

176 x 110 mm. π^2 a^2 1-46$^{12.6}$ 47^2; 420 leaves, pp. [i-v] vi-vii [viii] [1] 2-828 [*4*].

Illustrations: 108 illustrations in the text.

Bibliographies: Bitting, p. 27; Vicaire 65.

Copies: *BMC*.

61. Barra, Pierre.

L'VSAGE | DE LA | GLACE, | DE LA NEIGE | ET DV FROID. | *Par* M. P.
BARRA' *D. Medecin,* | *Aggregé au College de Lyon.* | [ornament] | A LYON, | Chez
ANTOINE CELLIER fils, ruë | Merciere, à l'Enseigne de la Constance. | [rule] |
AVEC PERMISSION. | M. DC. LXXV.

First edition, Lyon, 1675.

12mo. a^8 A-L^{12} M^4; 144 leaves, pp. [*16*] 1-249 [250-270] [2]. Last two pages blank.

Bibliographies: Oberlé (1) 431; Simon BG 167.

Copies: *BMC, BNC,* and *NUC* (4 copies).

62. Barra, Pierre.

L'VSAGE | DE LA | GLACE, | DE LA NEIGE | ET DV FROID. | *Par* M. P.
BARRA' *D. Medecin,* | *Aggregé au College de Lyon.* | [ornament] | A LYON, | Chez
ANTOINE CELLIER fils, ruë | Merciere, à l'Enseigne de la Constance. | [rule] |
AVEC PERMISSION. | M. DC. LXXVI.

Second edition, Lyon, 1676. Originally published, Lyon, 1675 (item 61).

12mo. a^8 A-L^{12} M^4; 144 leaves, pp. [*16*] 1-249 [250-270] [2]. Last two pages blank.

Bibliographies: Vicaire 66.

Copies: *BNC*.

63. Barthélemy, Nicolas.

APOLOGIE | DV BANQVET | SANCTIFIÉ | DE LA VEILLE | DES ROIS. | *Par Maistre* NICOLAS BAR- | THELEMY, *Aduocat en* | *Parlement, & au Bailliage* | *& Siege Presidial de Senlis.* | [ornament] | A PARIS, | Chez GILLES TOMPERE, ruë Char- | tiere, prés le Puits Certain, | au Treilly-vert. | [rule] | M. DC. LXV. | *Auec Priuilege & Approbation.*

Second edition, Paris, 1665. Originally published, Paris, 1664.

12mo. a^{12} e^{8} A-F^{12} G^{6}; 98 leaves, pp. [*40*] 1-156.

Bibliographies: This edition unrecorded in the bibliographies consulted. Vicaire described the 1664 edition.

Copies: No other copy of this edition located.

64. Bayle-Mouillard, Élizabeth-Félicie (Canard), 1796-1865.

MANUEL COMPLET | DES | DOMESTIQUES, | OU | L'ART DE FORMER DE BONS SERVITEURS; | SAVOIR: | Maitres-d'hôtel, – Cuisiniers, – Cuisinières, | – Femmes et Valets de chambre, – Frot- | teurs, – Portiers. – Concierges, – Bonnes | d'enfants, – Cochers, – Valets d'écurie, | – etc.; | contenant | D'IMPORTANTS DÉTAILS SUR LE SERVICE DES MALADES, | ET BEAUCOUP D'UTILES RECETTES | D'ÉCONOMIE DOMESTIQUE. | PAR Mme CELNART. | [short fancy rule] | PARIS, | A LA LIBRAIRIE ENCYCLOPÉDIQUE DE RORET, | RUE HAUTEFEUILLE, No 10 BIS. | 1836.

Second edition, Paris, 1836. Originally published, Paris, 1835.

150 x 90 mm. 1-19^{6} [20]^{2}; 116 leaves, pp. [i-v] vi-viii [1] 2-224. Publisher's printed wrappers.

Bibliographies: Unrecorded in the bibliographies consulted.

Copies: *BMC*, *BNC*, and *NUC* (4 copies).

65. Beauvillers.

LE BON | ET | PARFAIT CUISINIER | UNIVERSEL, | CONTENANT | LES
RECETTES DE LA CUISINE PROPREMENT DITE, | DE LA CHARCUTERIE, DE
LA PATISSERIE, DE L'OFFICE, ETC., | SUIVI | D'UNE INSTRUCTION SUR LE
CHOIX DES VINS, | RÉDIGÉ ET MIS EN ORDRE | D'APRÈS NOS PLUS
CÉLÈBRES CUISINIERS. | PAR M. BEAUVILLERS, | Ancien maître d'hôtel. |
ORNÉ DE PLANCHES. | [short fancy rule] | PARIS, | LEBIGRE FRÈRES,
LIBRAIRES, | RUE DE LA HARPE, No 26. | [short rule] | 1837.

First edition, Paris, 1837. Simon BG 182 describes this as a later edition of the
Manuel de la cuisine ou l'art d'irriter la gueule par une Sociéte de gens de bouche,
Metz, 1811, which Vicaire notes as the original edition of *Le Nouveau cuisinier royal*,
Paris, 1835, and 1836 (see Vicaire 75-76). However, Vicaire describes this work as
made up of articles arranged in alphabetical order, which *Le Bon et parfait cuisinier
universel* is not. It appears, therefore, Simon is incorrect to associate *Le Bon et parfait
cuisinier universel* with the earlier works mentioned by Vicaire. Vicaire, in his entry
under Bauvillers, discusses the names Bauvillers and Beauvillers as possible
pseudonyms of authors hoping to capitalize on the fame of Antoine Beauvilliers.

203 x 125 mm. π^2 1-27^8; 218 leaves, pp. [4] [1] 2-432.

Illustrations: Lithograph frontispiece of kitchen utensils and three lithographs of table
settings.

Bibliographies: Simon BG 182.

Copies: No other copy located.

66. Beauvilliers, Antoine, 1754-1817.

L'ART | DU CUISINIER, | PAR A. BEAUVILLIERS, | Ancien Officier de
MONSIEUR, comte de Provence, attaché | aux Extraordinaires des Maisons royales, et
actuellement | Restaurateur, rue de Richelieu, no 26, à la grande Taverne | de
Londres. | [short rule] | TOME PREMIER. [TOME SECOND.] | [engraved
illustration] | A PARIS, | CHEZ PILET, IMPRIMEUR-LIBRAIRE, RUE
CHRISTINE, No 5. | IL SE VEND AUSSI | CHEZ { COLNET, LIBRAIRE, QUAI
DES PETITS-AUGUSTINS, | ET LENOIR, LIBRAIRE, RUE DE RICHELIEU, No
35. | [short fancy rule] | 1814.

First edition, second issue, Paris, 1816 (for 1817). Signed "Ve Beauvilliers" by the author's widow on the title-page of Vol. I and with the date altered in the same hand from 1814 to 1816 on both title-pages. This issue adds a "Supplément à *L'Art du Cuisinier*" to Vol. II and an eight-page preface to Vol. I in which it is stated: "La première édition de *l'Art du Cuisinier*, que j'ai publiée à la fin de 1814, fut bientôt épuisée; il ne m'appartient pas d'en rien dire: le public, à ce qu'il paraît, l'a jugée avantageusement sou le report de l'économie domestique: et je lui présente aujourd'hui cette seconde édition, à laquelle j'ai donné l'attention dont je suis capable." In spite of this statement, the sheets of this issue are from the same printing as those of the first issue, with the addition of the preface and supplement. It might be noted here that while the title-page of Vol. I of the 1814 issue is signed by A. Beauvilliers, the later issues of the sheets are signed Ve Beauvilliers, Ve short for veuve (widow) and therefore, while dated 1816, the reissue did not occur until after Antoine Beauvilliers' death on 31 January 1817.

210 x 135 mm. 2 vols. Vol. I. π^2 a-b^4 1^6 2-23^8 24-25^6; 204 leaves, pp. [i-v] vi-xx [1] 2-388. Vol. II. π^2 1-23^8 24^4; ^{2}[1]^8 2^8 3^4; 210 leaves, pp. [4] [1] 2-376; ^{2}[1-3] 4-38 [2]. Last leaf blank. Uncut, in plain publisher's wrappers with printed labels on spines.

Illustrations: Vol. I. Engraved illustration of a kitchen by Jubin on the title-page and three engraved folding plates showing table settings. Vol. II. Engraved illustration of a kitchen by Jubin after Démarais on title-page and six engraved folding plates showing table settings.

Bibliographies: Bitting, p. 31 (second issue); Horn-Arndt 370 (first issue); Maggs 363 (first issue); Simon BG 183 (first issue); Vicaire 78, in note.

Copies: *BMC*, *BNC*, and *NUC* (Library of Congress and University of Oregon).

66a. Beauvilliers, Antoine, 1754-1817.

L'ART | DU CUISINIER, | PAR A. BEAUVILLIERS, | Ancien Officier de MONSIEUR, comte de Provence, attaché | aux Extraordinaires des Maisons royales, et actuellement | Restaurateur, rue de Richelieu, n° 26, à la grande Taverne | de Londres. | [short rule] | TOME PREMIER. [TOME DEUXIÈME.] | [illustration of kitchen scene] | A PARIS, | CHEZ PILLET, IMPRIMEUR-LIBRAIRE, RUE CHRISTINE, N° 5. | IL SE VEND AUSSI | CHES [next two lines bracketed to left] COLNET, LIBRAIRE, QUAI DES PETITS-AUGUSTINS, | ET LENOIR, LIBRAIRE, RUE DE RICHELIEU, N° 35. | [short wavy rule] | 1816.

First edition, third issue, Paris, 1816. Originally published, Paris, 1814.

210 x 140 mm. 2 vols. Vol. I. π^2 ($\pm\pi^2$) a-b^4 1^6 2-23^8 24-25^6; 204 leaves, pp. [i-v] vi-xx [1] 2-388. Vol. II. π^2 ($\pm\pi^2$) 1-23^8 24^4; ^{2}[1]^8 2^8 3^4; 210 leaves, pp. [4] [1] 2-376; ^{2}[1-3] 4-38 [2]. Last leaf blank. Uncut.

Illustrations: Vol. I. Engraved illustration of a kitchen by Jubin on the title-page and three engraved folding plates showing table settings. Vol. II. Engraved illustration of a kitchen by Jubin after Démarais on the title-page and six engraved folding plates showing table settings.

Bibliographies: Vicaire 78.

Copies: No other copy of this issue located.

67. Beauvilliers, Antoine, 1754-1817.

L'ART | DU CUISINIER, | PAR A. BEAUVILLIERS, | Ancien Officier de MONSIEUR, comte de Provence, attaché | aux Extraordinaires des Maisons royales, et actuellement | Restaurateur, rue de Richelieu, no 26, à la grande Taverne | de Londres. | [short rule] | TOME PREMIER. [TOME DEUXIÈME.] | [engraved illustration] | A PARIS, | CHEZ PILLET AÎNÉ, IMPRIMEUR-LIBRAIRE, | ÉDITEUR DE LA COLLECTION DES MOEURS FRANÇAISES, | RUE CHRISTINE, No 5; | CHEZ COLNET, LIBRAIRE, QUAI MALAQUAIS, No 9. | [short fancy rule] | 1824.

Second edition, Paris, 1824. The preface to this edition carries the same statement as that quoted in the edition statement in item 66, only changing "seconde édition" to "troisième édition." Although referred to as the third edition in the preface, it is in fact only the second, the copies dated 1814 and 1816 being different issues of the first edition sheets.

205 x 125 mm. 2 vols. Vol. I. π^2 a^8 1^6 2-23^8 24-25^6; 204 leaves, pp. [i-v] vi-xx [1] 2-388. Vol. II. π^2 1-25^8 26^6(-26$_6$); 207 leaves, pp. [4] [1] 2-408 [2].

Illustrations: Vol. I. Engraved illustration of a kitchen by Jubin on the title-page and three engraved folding plates showing table settings. Vol. II. Engraved illustration of a kitchen by Jubin after Démarais on the title-page and six engraved folding plates showing table settings.

Bookplate: De la bibliothèque du comte de Chambord (Henri V de France, duc de Bordeaux). Né en 1829. Aquise par Maggs Bros. Ltd. Londres.

Bibliographies: Maggs 364; Malortie, 1086; Vicaire 77.

Copies: *BNC* and *NUC* (New York Public Library and University of Oregon).

68. Bégin, M.-E.

DU VIN | DANS LES DIVERSES FORMES DE L'ANÉMIE | ET | DANS LA GOUTTE ATONIQUE | PAR | M. M.-E. BÉGIN | [short fancy rule] | Prix: 50 centimes | [ornament] | PARIS | J.-B. BAILLIÈRE ET FILS | LIBRAIRES DE L'ACADÉMIE DE MÉDECINE | Rue Hautefeuille, 19, près le boulevard Saint-Germain | [in two columns, column one] LONDRES | Hipp. BAILLIÈRE, 219, Regent street | [vertical rule between columns] | [column two] NEW-YORK | Ch. BAILLIÈRE, 440, Broadway [end columns] | Madrid, C. BAILLY-BAILLIÈRE, plaza del Principe Alfonso, 8.

First edition, Paris, 1877. Note: The National Library of Medicine (U.S.) cataloging for this work in the *NUC* assigns the date 1878. There is, however, an English translation of it published by Ch. Baillière in New York dated 1877.

239 x 149 mm. [1]^{12}; 12 leaves, pp. [1-3] 4-24. Publisher's printed wrappers. Presentation copy inscribed from Bégin to doctor Deshayes.

Bibliographies: Simon BV, p. 193.

Copies: *NUC* (National Library of Medicine only).

68a. Béguillet, Edmé, d. 1786.

DISCOURS | SUR | LA MOUTURE | ÉCONOMIQUE, | *PRÉSENTÉ pour concourir au prix proposé | par l'Académie des Belles-Lettres, Arts & | Sciences de Lyon, sur les moyens les plus | convenables de moudre les Bleds nécessaires à | la subsistance de la Ville de Lyon.* | Par M. BEGUILLET, Avocat en Parlement, premier | Notaire des Etats de Bourgogne, Correspondant de | l'Académie Royale des Inscriptions & Belles-Lettres | de Paris, Honoraire de l'Institut de Bologne, des | Arcades de Rome, de la Société économique de | Berne, des Georgofili de Florence, des Académies | de Marseille, Montpellier, Beziers, Caen, Metz, | &c. &c. | [short rule] | E culmo fpicam conjicere. | [short rule] | [ornament] | *A PARIS,* | Chez PANKOUCHKE, Libraire, rue des Poitevins. | [short fancy rule] | M. DCC. LXXV. | *AVEC APPROBATION ET PRIVILEGE DU ROI.*

First edition, Paris, 1775.

8vo. a^8 A-R^8 S^6; 150 leaves, pp. [i-iii] iv-xiv [xv-xvi] [1] 2-283 [284].

Bibliographies: Unrecorded in the bibliographies consulted.

Copies: *BNC* and *NUC* (Eleutherian Mills Historical Library, Greenville, Delaware, and Union Library Catalog of Pennsylvania).

68b. Béguillet, Edmé, d. 1786.

MANUEL | DU MEUNIER | ET | DU CHARPENTIER | DE MOULINS; | OU | ABREGÉ CLASSIQUE | DU TRAITÉ | DE LA MOUTURE PAR ÉCONOMIE, | *Orné de Gravures en taille douce,* | Et rédigé sur les Mémoires du Sieur CÉSAR BUQUET, | *PAR M. BÉGUILLET,* | *Avocat & premier Notaire des Etats de* | *Bourgogne,* | *Correspondant des Académies Royales des Sciences* | *& des Belles-* | *Lettres, Honoraire de l'Institut de* | *Bologne, des Arcades de Rome, &c. &c.* | [ornament] | A PARIS, | Chez [next two lines bracketed on left] PANCKOUCHKE, Libraire, rue des Poitevins. | DELALAIN, Libraire, rue & près de la Comédie | Françoise. | [short thick-thin rule] | M. DCC. LXXV. | *Avec Approbation, &* | *Privilege du Roi.*

First edition, Paris, 1775.

8vo. [a]^4 b^8 A-L^8; 100 leaves, pp. [i-v] vi-xxiv [1] 2-171 [172-176].

Illustrations: Engraved frontispiece captioned Elévation d'un Moulin, and four folding engraved plates illustrating a mill and milling machinery.

Bibliographies: Unrecorded in the bibliographies consulted.

Copies: *BNC* and *NUC* (Harvard and New York Public Library).

69. Beguillet, Edmé, d. 1786.

OENOLOGIE | *OU* | DISCOURS | *SUR la meilleure Méthode de cultiver* | *la Vigne.* | Avec un Précis sur la maniere de faire le | Vin, pour le rendre, dans tous cantons, | aussi agréable que le fin Vin de Bour- | gogne, qui peut servir de suite aux | Ouvrages de M. M. BIDET & MAUPIN. | *Par l'Auteur du Traité de la Mouture écono-* | *mique,* | *Aggrégé à la Société d' Agriculture* | *de Lyon, & de la Société royale des Sciences* | *&* | *Arts de la Ville de Metz.* | [rule] | *Vitis ament alii succum, cultura docentem* | *me* | *juvat.* | [rule] | [ornament] | *A DIJON,* | Chez EDME BIDAULT, Libraire au Palais. | [two short rules] | M. DCC. LXX. | *AVEC APPROBATION ET PERMISSION.*

First edition, issue with Bidault imprint, Dijon, 1770. Copies also are recorded with the imprint Dijon, Capel, 1770 and the double imprint, Dijon, Capel et Bidault. The verso of the half-title lists booksellers in Paris, Lyon, Besançon, Lausanne, Genève, and Metz where the book was sold raising the possibility of yet further imprints.

12mo. $\pi^2 \chi^2$ a^8 b^4 c^8 A-Y$^{8.4}$ Z^8; 164 leaves, pp. [*8*] i-xxxv [xxxvi-xl] 1-280. Bound with Chambray's *L'Art de faire le bon cidre* (item 129).

Bibliographies: Crahan 249 (Capel imprint); Oberlé (2) 108 (Capel and Bidault imprint); Simon BG 187 (Bidault imprint); Simon BV, p. 16; Vicaire 79 (Capel imprint).

Copies: *BNC*.

70. Benoit, Philippe-Martin-Narcisse, 1791-1867.

MANUEL COMPLET | DU | BOULANGER, | DU | NÉGOCIANT EN GRAINS, | *DU MEUNIER* | ET DU | CONSTRUCTEUR DE MOULINS. | TROISIÈME ÉDITION | ENTIÈREMENT REFONDUE, ET ENRICHIE DE TOUTES LES DÉ- | COUVERTES ET PERFECTIONNEMENS QUI SE RATTACHENT A | LA FABRICATION DU PAIN, A LA CONSTRUCTION DES MOULINS | ET A LA CONNAISSANCE DES CÉRÉALES ET DES LÉGUMINEUSES. | PAR M. BENOIT, | Ingénieur pour les Usines, Manufactures, Machines, etc.; l'un des | Fondateurs de l'Ecole centrale des Arts; | ET M. JULIA DE FONTENELLE. | *Ouvrage orné de planches.* | [two short rules] | *Première Partie. [Deuxième Partie.]* | [two short rules] | *PARIS,* | A LA LIBRAIRIE ENCYCLOPÉDIQUE DE RORET, | rue Hautefeuille, N.o 10, bis. | [short rule] | 1836.

Third edition, enlarged to two volumes, Paris, 1836. The date of the original edition has not been determined, but the second was published, Paris, 1829.

137 x 83 mm. 2 vols. Vol. I. π^4 1-21^6; 130 leaves, pp. [*4*] [i] ii-iv [1] 2-252. Two folding letterpress charts not included in the signatures or pagination. Vol. II. π^2 22-45^6 46^6(-46$_6$); 151 leaves, pp. [*4*] [253] 254-550. One folding letterpress chart not included in the signatures or pagination. Contemporary quarter morocco, with publisher's printed front wrappers preserved.

Illustrations: Vol. II. Five engraved folding plates, one illustrating apparatus for baking, and four milling machinery.

Bibliographies: This edition unrecorded in the bibliographies consulted. Wheaton and Kelly 604 record the second edition, Paris, 1829.

Copies: *BNC*.

71. Berchoux, Joseph de, 1762-1838.

LA GASTRONOMIE, | OU | L'HOMME DES CHAMPS | A TABLE, | Pour servir de suite à *l'Homme des Champs* | PAR J. DELILLE. | Seconde édition, revue et augmentée, | AVEC FIGURE. | A PARIS, | CHEZ GIGUET ET MICHAUD, IMP.-LIBRAIRES, | RUE DES BONS-ENFANS, No. 6. | [short rule] | 1803. – (AN XI.)

Second edition, Paris, 1803. Originally published, Paris, 1801.

143 x 90 mm. $1\text{-}14^6$ 15^6 $(-15_{5,6})$; 88 leaves, pp. [1-7] 8-176.

Illustration: Engraved frontispiece with the caption, "Le Senat mis aux voix cette affaire importante, / Et le Turbot fut mis à la sauce piquante."

L'Homme des champs is by Jacques Montanier, called Delille, 1738-1813.

Bibliographies: Bitting, p. 37; Oberlé (1) 385; Vicaire 83; Wheaton and Kelly 608.

Copies: *BMC*, *BNC*, and *NUC* (4 copies).

72. Berchoux, Joseph de, 1762-1838.

LA GASTRONOMIE, | OU | L'HOMME DES CHAMPS | A TABLE, | POËME DIDACTIQUE EN IV CHANTS; | PAR J. B..., DU DÉP. DE LA LOIRE. | TROISIÈME ÉDITION revue, corrigée et augmen- | tée d'un grand nombre de Pièces fugitives du même | auteur. | AVEC FIGURE. | A PARIS, | CHEZ GIGUET ET MICHAUD, IMP.-LIBRAIRES, | RUE DES BONS-ENFANS, No. 6. | [short rule] | 1804. – AN XII.

Third edition, Paris, 1804. Originally published, Paris, 1801.

141 x 90 mm. $1\text{-}18^6$ 19^4 20^6 $(-20_{5,6})$; 118 leaves, pp. [1-7] 8-228 [*4*]. Last two leaves blank and the final one pasted to the free portion of the marbled endpapers.

Illustration: Engraved frontispiece by Bovinet after Monsiau with the caption
" . . . et je prétends, dans ma reconnoissance, / Dérobant les Lauriers d'un Jambon de
Mayence, / D'une couronne un jour décorer ton bonnet."

Bibliographies: Simon BG 195; Vicaire 83.

Copies: *BMC*, *BNC*, and *NUC* (Brown University only).

73. Berchoux, Joseph de, 1762-1838.

LA GASTRONOMIE, | POËME, | PAR J. BERCHOUX, | SUIVI DES POÉSIES
FUGITIVES DE L'AUTEUR. | QUATRIÈME ÉDITION, CORRIGÉE ET
AUGMENTÉE. | [publisher's monogram] | A PARIS, | CHEZ GIGUET ET
MICHAUD, IMP.-LIBRAIRES, | RUE DES BONS ENFANS, No. 6. | [short rule] |
1805. − AN XIII.

Fourth edition, Paris, 1805. Originally published, Paris, 1801.

142 x 92 mm. 1-22^6 [23]^2 (-23$_2$); 133 leaves, pp. [1-7] 8-266.

Illustrations: Engraved frontispiece by Delignon after Myris captioned "Viens, aimable
Lysbé, que les heureuses mains / Nous versent à longs traits ce nector des humains"
and three engraved plates by Baquoy and R. Delvaux after Myris and by Bovinet after
Monsiau.

Bibliographies: Crahan 479; Horn-Arndt 373; Maggs 327; Oberlé (1) 386 and 387;
Schraemli (1) 49; Schraemli (3) 52; Simon BG 196; Vicaire 84; Wheaton and Kelly
609.

Copies: *BMC*, *BNC*, and *NUC* (9 copies).

74. Berchoux, Joseph de, 1762-1838.

LA GASTRONOMIE, | Poëme, | Par J. BERCHOUX, | *Suivi* | des Poésies Fugitives
de l'Auteur. | *Cinquième Edition* | *Corrigée et augmentée.* | [publisher's monogram] |
à Paris, | *Chez* L. G. MICHAUD, *Libraire,* | Rue de Cléry, No. 13. | [short fancy
rule] *1819* [short fancy rule]

Fifth edition, Paris, 1819. Originally published, Paris, 1801.

143 x 91 mm. [1]⁶ 2-21⁶ [22]²; 128 leaves, pp. [2] [v] vi-xvii [xviii] [19] 20-258.

Illustrations: Engraved frontispiece and three engraved plates as in the fourth edition (item 73).

Bibliographies: Bitting, p. 37; Vicaire 84.

Copies: *NUC* (Library of Congress only).

75. Berchoux, Joseph de, 1762-1838.

J. DE BERCHOUX | [short rule] | [in red] LA GASTRONOMIE | POËME EN QUATRE CHANTS | *Publiée avec une Notice et des Notes* | PAR | [in red] FÉLIX DESVERNAY | [publisher's device] | PARIS | [in red] LIBRAIRIE DES BIBLIOPHILES | Rue Saint-Honoré, 338 | [short rule] | M DCCC LXXVI

First printing of this edition, Paris, 1876. No. 53 of 30 copies on papier Whatman after 30 copies on papier de Chine. Berchoux's poem was originally published, Paris, 1801.

170 x 109 to 150 mm. π² a-d⁴ 1-11⁴; 62 leaves, [4] [i] ii-xxix [xxx] [2] [1] 2-87 [88]. Three quarter brown morocco with marbled boards; publisher's printed wrappers preserved.

Bibliographies: Maggs 530; Vicaire 84.

Copies: *BMC*, *BNC*, and *NUC* (Franklin and Marshall College, Lancaster, Pa., only).

76. Bernardi.

L'ÉCUYER | TRANCHANT | OU L'ART DE DÉCOUPER ET SERVIR A TABLE. | COMPLÉMENT INDISPENSABLE DU CUISINIER ROYAL, | PAR BERNARDI, | AUTEUR DU GLACIER ROYAL. | Ouvrage entièrement neuf, | Contenant l'art de découper et de servir à table; la manière de disposer le couvert; des | Menus en gras et en maigre pour tous les jours de l'année, depuis deux con- | verts jusqu'à cent cinquante; la composition de diners avec la desserte, | des repas de corps, des ambigus, des buffets; la manière de com- | mander un déjeuner ou un diner au restaurant, avec | l'indication du temps qu'il faut pour préparer les | mets; une nomenclature culinaire pour chaque | mois de l'année; un traité des hors- | d'oeuvre d'office; des remarques |

sur les sauces, etc., etc. | ORNÉ DE 24 PLANCHES EXPLICATIVES | GRAVÉES
SUR ACIER. | [publisher's device] | PARIS, | GUSTAVE BARBA, ÉDITEUR, |
RUE MAZARINE, 34. | 1845

First edition, Paris, 1845.

223 x 137 mm. π^2 1-22^8 23^6 24^4 pp. [*4*] [1] 2-371 [372]. Publisher's printed wrappers.

Illustrations: 24 lithographs, 15 on carving and 9 of table settings.

Bibliographies: Bitting, p. 38; Simon BG 203; Vicaire 86.

Copies: *BMC*, *BNC*, and *NUC* (Kansas State University and the Library of Congress).

77. Bertall, Charles-Albert, vicomte d'Arnould, called, 1820-1882.

[in red] LA VIGNE | VOYAGE | AUTOUR DES VINS DE FRANCE | ÉTUDE
PHYSIOLOGIQUE, ANECDOTIQUE | HISTORIQUE, HUMORISTIQUE ET
MÊME SCIENTIFIQUE | PAR | [in red] BERTRALL | [illustration] | [in red] PARIS
| E. PLON ET Cie, IMPRIMEURS-ÉDITEURS | RUE GARANCIÈRE, 10 | [short
rule] | 1878 | *Tous droits réservés*

First edition, Paris, 1878.

276 x 188 mm. π^4 1-82^4 83^2; 334 leaves, pp. [*8*] [1] 2-659 [660].

Illustrations: Numerous wood engravings in the text. Vicaire calls for 64 plates hors
texte but, in fact, these engravings are on text paper and are part of the normal
signatures.

Bibliographies: Bitting, p. 38; Crahan 482; Oberlé (2) 138; Schraemli (1) 50;
Schraemli (2) 122; Vicaire 87.

Copies: *BMC*, *BNC*, and *NUC* (6 copies).

78. Berthe, Th.

TRAITÉ | DE | L'OFFICE | PAR | T. BERTHE | EX-OFFICEIR DE BOUCHE DE
FEU SON EXC. M. LE COMTE POZZO DI BORGO | OUVRAGE

INDISPENSABLE | AUX MAITRES D'HOTEL, VALETS DE CHAMBRE | CUISINIERS ET CUISINIÈRES | ET UTILES AUX GENS DU MONDE | [short rule] | PARIS | GARNIER FRÈRES, LIBRAIRES-ÉDITEURS | 6, RUE DES SAINTS-PÈRES, 6 | [short rule] | 1876

New edition, Paris, 1876. Originally published, Paris, 1844.

179 x 109 mm. π^4 1-20$^{12.6}$ 21^{10}; 194 leaves, pp. [i-v] vi-viii [1] 2-380.

Bibliographies: Bitting, p. 38; Vicaire 88.

Copies: *BMC*, *BNC*, and *NUC* (Library of Congress only).

79. Bibliotheque physico-économique, instructive et amusante.

BIBLIOTHEQUE | PHYSICO-ÉCONOMIQUE, | *INSTRUCTIVE ET AMUSANTE,* | ANNÉE 1786, OU 5e ANNÉE; | *CONTENANT des Mémoires, Observations-Pratiques* | *sur l'Economie rurale; -- les nouvelles Découvertes* | *les plus intéressantes dans les* | *Arts utiles & agréables; -- la Description & la Figure des nouvelles Ma-* | *chines, des* | *Instrumens qu'on doit y employer, d'après* | *les Expériences des Auteurs qui les ont* | *imaginées; -- des Recettes, Pratiques, Procédés, Médicamens* | *nouveaux, externes ou* | *internes, qui peuvent inté-* | *resser les Hommes & les Animaux; -- les Moyens* | *d'arrêter les Incendies & autres Evénemens, provenans* | *des vices & de l'altération de* | *l'Air; -- de mouvelles* | *Vues sur plusieurs points d'Economie domestique, &* | *en* | *général sur tous les objets d'Utilité & d'Agrément* | *dans la Vie civile & privée,* &c &c. On y a joint | des Notes que l'on a cru nécessaires à plusieurs | Articles. | AVEC DES PLANCHES EN TAILLE-DOUCE. | TOME I. [TOME II.] | [rule] | Prix 3 livres chaque Volume relié. | Et franc de port par le Poste, 2 livres 12 sols, broché. | [rule] | [ornament] | *A PARIS,* | Chez BUISSON, Libraire, Hôtel de Mesgrigny, | rue des Poitevins, No. 13. | [short fancy rule] | M. DCC. LXXXVI. | *Avec Approbation & Privilège du Roi.*

First edition, Paris, 1786. The series began in 1782.

12mo. 2 vols. Vol. I. a^6 A-S^{12}; 222 leaves, pp. [i-ii] iii-xii [1] 2-432. Vol. II. π^6 A-S^{12} T^6; 228 leaves, pp. [i-ii] iii-xii [1] 2-444.

Illustrations: Vol. I. Three engraved folding plates. Vol. II. Three engraved folding plates.

Bibliographies: Unrecorded in the bibliographies consulted.

Copies: *BMC* and *NUC* (eight copies).

80. Biscuits Pernot.

[lithographed art nouveau title-page printed in blue] MANUFACTURE |
DIJONNAISE | des | BISCUITS PERNOT | USINES | A | DIJON & GENÈVE |
ADMINISTRATION: | 14. Rue Courtepée | DIJON | TÉLÉPHONE No. 150 | IMP.
M. J. STAERCK & Cie, PARIS

Probable first edition, Paris, ca. 1898.

234 x 162 mm. 64 page trade catalogue; 4 pages of text, 30 pages of colored
illustrations and 30 pages of text describing the products of Biscuits Pernot of Dijon.
Publisher's paper covered boards.

Bibliographies: Unrecorded in the bibliographies consulted.

Copies: No other copy located.

81. Blanquet, Rosalie.

LA | CUISINIÈRE | DES MÉNAGES | OU | MANUEL PRATIQUE | DE CUISINE
ET D'ÉCONOMIE DOMESTIQUE | POUR LA VILLE ET LA CAMPAGNE |
CONTENANT | L'ART DE DÉCOUPER, LE SERVICE DE TABLE | LES
DEVOIRS D'UNE MAITRESSE DE MAISON, DES MENUS GRAS ET MAIGRES |
POUR TOUTES LES SAISONS | UN TRAITÉ DE LA CAVE ET DES MALADIES
DES VINS | ET UN GRAND NOMBRE DE RECETTES D'ÉCONOMIE
DOMESTIQUE | PAR | MME ROSALIE BLANQUET | Ouvrage illustré de 217
figures. | [short rule] | PARIS | LIBRAIRIE DU LOUVRE | 2, RUE MARENGO

New edition, Paris, ca. 1865. Originally published, Paris, Lefèvre [1863].

183 x 117 mm. π^2 1-28$^{12.6}$ 29^{12} 30^4; 270 leaves, pp. [4] [1] 2-536. First leaf wanting in
this copy. Publisher's printed boards.

Illustrations: 217 wood engravings in the text.

Bibliographies: This edition unrecorded in the bibliographies consulted. Vicaire 95
records the first edition; Wheaton and Kelly 658, the 29th edition, n.d.

Copies: No other copy with the Librairie du Louvre imprint located.

82. Blegny, Nicolas de, 1642?-1722.

ABREGE' | DES TRAITEZ | DV CAFFE', | DV THE' | ET DU | CHOCOLAT, | POUR LA PRESERVATION. | & pour la guerison des | maladies. | *Ante languorem adhibe medicinam* | Eccl. cap. 18. v.20. | [ornament] | A LYON, | Chez ESPRIT VITALIS, ruë | Merciere. | [short rule] | M. DC. LXXXVII. | *AVEC APPROBATION ET PERMISSION.*

First edition, Lyon, 1687. This is an abridgement of Blegny's *Le Bon Usage du thé, du caffé et du chocolat . . .* (item 83).

12mo. A-F^6; 36 leaves, pp. [1-2] 3-70 [71-72].

Bibliographies: Pennell, p. 122; Vicaire 2.

Copies: *BNC.*

83. Blegny, Nicolas de, 1642?-1722.

LE BON USAGE | DU THE' | DU CAFFE' | ET | DU CHOCOLAT | POUR LA PRESERVATION | & pour la guerison des | Maladies. | *Par Mr DE BLEGNY, Conseiller, Medecin* | *Artiste ordinaire du Roy & de Monsieur,* | *& préposé par ordre de Sa Majesté, à la* | *Recherche & Verification des nouvelles* | *découvertes de Medecine.* | [ornament] | A LYON, | Chez THOMAS AMAULRY ruë | Merciere, au Mercure Galant. | [short rule] | *M. DC. LXXXVII.* | AVEC PRIVILEGE DU ROY.

Cancel label over imprint: *A Lyon, & se vend* | A PARIS, | Chez JACQUES COLLOMBAT, ruë | S. Jacques, au Pelican. |

First edition, Lyon, 1687. Vicaire 97 reports that copies of this work are known with three imprints: Paris, chez l'Auteur; Paris, Etienne Michallet; Lyon, Thomas Amaulry. This copy has the Amaulry imprint covered by a cancel label for Jacques Collombat in Paris. London bookseller Stephanie Hoppen's catalogue, *Four Centuries of Food and Drink*, vol. II, item 24, records yet another imprint: Paris, Veuve d'Houry et la Veuve Nion, 1687.

12mo. a^{12} A-P^{12}; 192 leaves, pp. [24] 1-120, 131-226, 219-357 [358-362] = 384.

Illustrations: Thirteen integral engraved illustrations by Johann Hainzelmann in the text.

Bibliographies: Bitting, p. 44 (Amaulry imprint); Crahan 96 (Amaulry imprint); Horn-Arndt 109 (Michallet imprint); Hunt 376 (Amaulry imprint); Oberlé (1) 734 (Amaulry imprint); Vicaire 97 (all three imprints). The Collombat cancel label is unrecorded in the bibliographies consulted.

Copies: *BMC* (Amaulry and Michallet imprints); *BNC* (all three imprints); *NUC* (5 copies with chez l'Auteur imprint, 7 with Amaulry imprint and 3 with Michallet imprint). No other copy located with the Collombat cancel label.

84. Blocquel, Simon, 1780-1863.

GUIDE | DES FEMMES DE MÉNAGE, | DES CUISINIÈRES, | ET DES BONNES D'ENFANTS, | *Contenant* | L'indication des qualités que doivent posséder les | femmes attachées au service d'une maison; des con- | seils sur la conduite qu'elles | doivent tenir dans tou- | tes les circonstances ; des instructions sur les tra- | vaux journaliers dont elles sont chargées; des conseils | particuliers aux bonnes d'enfants; des recettes et des | procédés avantageux pour le nettoiement des meubles | et des ustensiles de toutes espèces, pour le blanchissage | du linge et de plusieurs effets d'habillement, etc.; la | manière de servir les personnes malades, de préparer | les aliments et les boissons dont elles ont besoin, et | d'appliquer ou d'administrer certains médicaments | ordonnés pour leur rétablissement; une série de remè- | des contre plusieurs maladies ou accidents qui peuvent | être traités sans l'intervention d'un médecin; et enfin | quantité de renseignements d'une utilité incontestable; | PAR BLISMON. | [short fancy rule] | A PARIS, | Chez DELARUE, Libraire, quai des Augustins, 11; | Et à LILLE, chez BLOCQUEL-CASTIAUX, Libraire.

First edition, Paris, 1841.

149 x 92 mm. 1-10^6 11^2; 62 leaves, pp. [i-v] vi [7] 8-118 [*6*]. Publisher's printed wrappers.

Illustrations: Lithographed folding frontispiece of three femmes de ménage.

Bibliographies: Vicaire 97.

Copies: *BNC*.

85. Bock, Hieronimus, 1498-1554.

Teütsche Speiszkam= | mer. | Inn welcher du findest/ | Was gesunden unnd krancken men- | schen zur Leibs narung und desselben gepresten von | nöten/ Auch wie alle speis und dranck Gesun= | den und Krancken jeder zeit zur | Kost und artznei gerei= | chet werden | sollen. | Zü dienst und wolfart allen frommen Teutschen | durch HIERONYM'VM BOCK mit fleisziger | trewer arbeit/ vormalns nie gese= | hen/ beschriben und ans | liecht gegeben. | Den jnnhalt dises Büchs findestu auff | der andern seitten verzeichnet. | Sampt einem nutzlichen Register. | Dit Röm Kais. Baie. Freiheit | auff vij jar. | Gedruckt zü Strassburg bei Wendel Rihel. | Im jar M. D. L.

First edition, Strassburg, 1550.

4to. $^\pi A^6$ π^4 χ^4 A-Z^4 a-g^4 ; 134 leaves, ff. [*14*] i-xcv, xcv-cxix.

Bibliographies: Bitting, p. 46.

Copies: *BMC* and *NUC* (Library of Congress only).

86. Bonnefons, Nicholas de.

LES | DELICES | DE LA CAMPAGNE. | Suitte du | IARDINIER | FRANÇOIS. | OV EST ENSEIGNE' A | preparer pour l'vsage de la vie tout | ce qui croist sur la Terre, & dans | les Eaux. | *DEDIE' AVX DAMES* | *Mesnageres.* | [ornament] | A PARIS, | Chez PIERRE DES-HAYES, ruë | de la Harpe, aux Gands Couronnez, | prés la Roze Rouge. | [rule] | M. DC. LIV. | *Avec Privilege du Roy.*

First edition, Paris, 1654.

12mo. a^8 e^4 A-Ii$^{8.4}$; 204 leaves, pp. [*24*] 1-384.

Illustrations: Engraved title-page and three engraved plates by F. Chauveau.

From the library of the baron Pichon.

Bibliographies: Vicaire 261 (this copy).

Copies: No other copy of the first edition located.

87. Bonnefons, Nicolas de.

LES | DELICES | DE LA CAMPAGNE. | Suitte du | IARDINIER | FRANÇOIS, | OV EST ENSEIGNE' A | preparer pour l'usage de la vie tout | ce qui croist sur la Terre, & dans | les Eaux. | *DEDIE' AVX DAMES MESNAGERES.* | SECONDE EDITION, | Augmentée par l'Autheur. | [ornament] | A PARIS, | Chez PIERRE DES-HAYES, ruë | de la Harpe, aux Gands Couron- | nez, prés la Roze Rouge. | [rule] | M. DC. LVI. | *Avec Privilege du Roy.*

Second Paris edition, Paris, 1656. Originally published, Paris, 1654, (item 86) and reprinted, Amsterdam, 1655.

12mo. a⁸ e⁴ A-Ii⁸·⁴; 204 leaves, pp. [*24*] 1-384. Bound with the author's *Le Jardinier françois*, Paris, 1659 (item 90).

Illustrations: Engraved title-page and three engraved plates by F. Chauveau.

Bibliographies: Vicaire 262; Wheaton and Kelly 729.

Copies: *NUC* (Harvard, John Crerar Library and Peabody Institute).

88. Bonnefons, Nicholas de.

LES | DELICES | DE LA CAMPAGNE. | Suitte du | IARDINIER | FRANÇOIS, | OV EST ENSEIGNE' A | preparer pour l'usage de la vie tout | ce qui croist sur la Terre, & dans | les Eaux. | *DEDIE' AVX DAMES MESNAGERES.* | TROISIESME EDITION, | Augmentée par l'Autheur. | [ornament] | A PARIS, | Chez ANTHOINE CELLIER, ruë de la | Harpe, aux Gands Couronnez, & à | l'Imprimerie des Roziers. | [rule] | M. DC. LXII. | *Avec Privilege du Roy.*

Third edition, Paris, 1662. Originally published, Paris, 1654 (item 86).

12mo. a⁸ e⁴ A-Ii⁸·⁴; 204 leaves, pp. [*24*] 1-384.

Illustrations: Engraved title-page and three engraved plates by F. Chauveau.

Bibliographies: Vicaire 262; Wheaton and Kelly 730.

Copies: *BMC*, *BNC*, and *NUC* (National Agricultural Library only). Wheaton and Kelly (Harvard only).

89. Bonnefons, Nicolas de.

LE | IARDINIER | FRANÇOIS, | QVI ENSEIGNE A | Cultiver les Arbres, & Herbes | Potageres; Avec la maniere de | conserver les Fruicts, & faire | toutes sortes de Confitures, | Conserves, & Massepans. | *DEDIE' AVX DAMES.* | SIXIESME EDITION | Augmentée par l'Autheur de plusieurs | experiences qu'il a faites. | [ornament] | A PARIS, | Chez PIERRE DES-HAYES, ruë | de la Harpe, aux Gands Couronnez, | prés la Roze Rouge. | [rule] | M. DC. LVI. | *Avec Privilege du Roy.*

Sixth edition, Paris, 1656. Originally published, Paris, 1651.

12mo. a^8 e^8 A-Ii$^{8.4}$; 204 leaves, pp. [*24*] 1-382 [383-384].

Illustrations: Engraved title-page and three engraved plates by F. Chauveau.

Bibliographies: Wheaton and Kelly 745.

Copies: *NUC* (Brooklyn Public Library only). Wheaton and Kelly (Harvard only).

90. Bonnefons, Nicolas de.

LE | IARDINIER | FRANÇOIS, | QVI ENSEIGNE A CVLTIVER | les Arbres, & Herbes Potageres; Avec | la maniere de conseruer les Fruicts, | & faire toutes sortes de Confitures, | Conserues, & Massepans. | *DEDIE' AVX DAMES.* | SEPTIEME EDITION, | Augmentée par l'Autheur de plusieurs | experiences qui'il a faites. | [ornament] | A PARIS, | Chez ANTHOINE CELLIER, ruë | de la Harpe, aux Gands Couronnez, | & à l'Imprimerie des Roziers. | [short rule] | M. DC. LIX. | *AVEC PRIVILEGE DV ROY.*

Seventh edition, Paris, 1659. Originally published, Paris, 1651.

12mo. a^8 e^8 A-Ii$^{8.4}$; 204 leaves, pp. [*24*] 1-382 [383-384]. Bound with the author's *Les Delices de la campagne*, Paris, 1656 (item 87).

Illustrations: Engraved title-page and three engraved plates by F. Chauveau.

Bibliographies: Vicaire 462 in note.

Copies: *NUC* (Brooklyn Public Library only).

91. Bonnefons, Nicolas de.

LE | IARDINIER | FRANÇOIS, | QVI ENSEIGNE A CVLTIVER | les Arbres, & Herbes Potageres; | Auec la maniere de conseruer les | Fruits, & faire toutes sortes de Con- | fitures, Conserues, & Massepains. | *DEDIE' AVX DAMES.* | HVITIESME EDITION, | Augmentée par l'Autheur de plusieurs | experiences qu'il a faites. | [engraved vignette] | A PARIS, | Par la Compagnie des Marchands | Libraires du Palais. | [rule] | M. DC. LXV.

Eighth edition, Paris, 1665. Originally published, Paris, 1651.

12mo. A-V$^{8.4}$ X^6 e^2; 128 leaves, pp. [*14*] 1-238 [*4*]. Bound with *La Manire de cultiver les arbres fruitiers*, Paris, 1665, by Robert Arnauld d'Andilly (item 44).

Illustrations: Engraved title-page and three engraved illustrations after those by F. Chauveau executed for the original edition, Paris, 1651. The three illustrations are mirror images of the originals. The engraved title-page is separately printed and not reckoned in the signatures or pagination; the three engraved illustrations are on leaves A7^v, H1^v and P3^v.

Bibliographies: This edition unrecorded in the bibliographies consulted.

Copies: *NUC* (William Andrews Clark Library only).

92. Bonnefons, Nicolas de.

LE | *JARDINIER* | FRANÇOIS, | QUI ENSEIGNE A CULTIVER | les Arbres & Herbes Potageres. | *Avec la maniere de conserver les Fruits, &* | *faire toutes sortes de* *Confitures,* | *Conserves & Massepains.* | DEDIE' AUX DAMES. | *Derniere Edition.* | [ornament] | A PARIS, | Chez SAUGRAIN Fils, au Palais, au sixiéeme | Pilier de la Grand' Salle, vis-à-vis l'Escalier de la | Cour des Aydes, à la Bonne-Foi couronnée | [two short rules] | M DCC. LV. | *Avec Privilege du Roi.*

New edition, Paris, 1755. Originally published, Paris, 1651.

12mo. a^8 A-Ii$^{8.4}$ Kk^4; 204 leaves, pp. [*16*] [1] 2-387 [388-392].

Illustrations: Woodcut title-page and three woodcuts after the engraved plates by F. Chauveau for the original edition, Paris, 1651, on a1^r, a8^v, P6^v and Aa^r.

Bibliographies: This edition unrecorded in the bibliographies consulted.

Copies: *NUC* (Rutgers University only).

93. Boulenger, Jules-César, 1558-1628.

DE | CONVIVIIS | *LIBRI QVATVOR.* | Ad Illustriss. & Integerrimum Dominum, | D. NICOLAVM DE VERDVN, Senatus | Parisiensis Principem, Equitem Tor- | quatum, & sanctioris Consistorij | Consiliarium. | *Auctore* | IVLIO CAESARE BVLENGERO, | Societatis IESV Presbytero. | [vertically at left] IN VIRTVTE, | [ornament; vertically at right] ET FORTVNA. | *LVGDVNI,* | Sumptibus LVDOVICI PROST, | Haeredis ROVILLE. | [short rule] | *M. DC. XXVII.* | CVM PRIVILEGIO.

First edition, Lyon, 1627.

8vo. ✷✷✷✷⁸ Aaaa-Bbbbb⁸ Ccccc⁴; 212 leaves, pp. [*16*] 1-394 [*14*].

Bibliographies: Crahan 101; Malortie 76; Simon BG 231; Vicaire 131; Wheaton and Kelly 953.

Copies: *BMC*, *BNC* (3 copies), and *NUC* (7 copies).

94. Bourdon, Arthur-Charles, b. 1842.

LA PATISSERIE | POUR TOUS | MANIÈRE DE LA FAIRE, DÉMONTRÉE ET EXPLIQUÉE | A L'USAGE DES CUISINIERS & CUISINIÈRES DE MAISON BOURGEOISE | ILLUSTRÉE DE 25 PLANCHES | [illustration of three medals] | SE TROUVE CHEZ L'AUTEUR: PATISSERIE DES TUILERIES | BOURDON | 167, – RUE SAINT-HONORÉ, – 167 | Innovateur et Fondateur de la Société de Secours mutuels | des Pâtissiers-Glaciers de Paris, 1868. | [short fancy rule] | MÉDAILLE D'ARGENT A L'EXPOSITON GASTRONOMIQUE, PARIS 1873 | [short fancy rule] | MÉDAILLE ET DIPLOME D'HONNEUR, PALAIS DE L'INDUSTRIE 1874 | [short fancy rule] | PRIX: 5 FR. | [short fancy rule] | PARIS | ASSOCIATION GÉNÉRALE TYPOGRAPHIQUE | RODIÈRE ET Ce | 19, Rue du Faubourg-Saint-Denis, 19 | [short rule] | 1874

First edition, Paris, 1874.

208 x 131 mm. [1]⁸ 2-8⁸; 64 leaves, pp. [i-iii] iv [5] 6-117 [118] [*10*]. Last leaf blank.

Illustrations: Wood engraved illustrations in the text depicting pastries.

Bibliographies: Bitting, p. 52; Vicaire 109; Wheaton and Kelly 788.

Copies: *BNC* and *NUC* (Library of Congress only). Wheaton and Kelly (Essex Institute only).

95. Breteuil, Jules.

LE | CUISINIER | EUROPÉEN | Ouvrage contenant | LES MEILLEURES RECETTES DES CUISINES FRANÇAISES | ET ÉTRANGÈRES | Pour la préparation des Potages, Sauces, Ragoûts, Entrées, Rôtis | Fritures, Entremets, Dessert et Pâtisseries | COMPLÉTÉ PAR | UN APPENDICE | Comprenant la desserte ou l'art d'utiliser les restes d'un bon repas, le service | de table, la manière de faire les honneurs d'un repas | et de servir les vins, les confitures, les sirops, les bonbons de ménage, les liqueurs, | les soins à donner à une cave bien montée. | PAR JULES BRETEUIL | ANCIEN CHEF DE CUISINE | NOUVELLE ÉDITION | REVUE ET CORRIGÉE | [short fancy rule] | PARIS | GARNIER FRÈRES, LIBRAIRES-ÉDITEURS | 6, RUE DES SAINTS- PÈRES, 6

New edition, Paris, ca. 1868. Originally published, Paris, 1860.

174 x 111 mm. $\pi^2 \chi^2$ 1-40$^{12.6}$ 41^{12} 42^2; 380 leaves, pp. [i-v] vi-viii [1] 2-748. Publisher's red cloth stamped in black and gold.

Illustrations: Numerous wood engravings in the text.

Bibliographies: Bitting, p. 58; Oberlé (1) 234; Vicaire cites editions of 1860, 1863, and 1872.

Copies: *BNC* and *NUC* (Library of Congress and Yale).

96. Briand.

DICTIONNAIRE | DES | ALIMENS, | *VINS ET LIQUEURS,* | LEURS QUALITE'S, LEURS EFFETS, | relativement aux différens âges, & aux | différens tempéramens; | *AVEC* | LA MANIERE DE LES APPRÊTER, | ANCIENNE ET MODERNE, | *Suivant la méthode des plus habiles Chefs-* | *d'Office & Chefs de Cuisine, de la Cour,* | *& de la Ville.* | Ouvrage très-utile dans toutes les familles. | *Opinor.* | *Haec res & jungit, junctos & servat amicos.* | Horat. 5. L. I. V. 54. | Par M. C. D. Chef de Cuisine de M. le | Prince de ✱✱✱. | TOME PREMIER. [TOME

SECOND.] [TOME TROISIÉME.] | [ornament] | A PARIS, | Chez { GISSEY, rue de la vieille Bouclerie. | BORDELET, rue Saint Jacques. | [two short rules] | M. DCC. L. | *Avec Approbation & Privilege du Roi.*

First edition, Paris, 1750.

12mo. 3 vols. Vol. I. $^{\pi}a^8$ a^8 b^4 c^2 A-X$^{8.4}$; 292 leaves, pp. [i-v] vi-xvi; ^{2}[i] ii-xxviii [1] 2-538 [2]. Vol. II. π^2 A-Bbb$^{8.4}$; 290 leaves. pp. [4] [1] 2-576. Vol. III. π^2 A-Zz$^{8.4}$ Aaa^4; 282 leaves. pp. [4] [1] 2-559 [560].

Bibliographies: Bitting, p. 59; Horn-Arndt 231; Oberlé (1) 113; Pennell, p. 125; Oberlé (1) 113; Simon BG 250; Vicaire 276.

Copies: *BMC, BNC,* and *NUC* (4 copies).

97. Briffault, Eugène-Victor, 1799-1854.

PARIS | A TABLE | PAR | EUGÈNE BRIFFAULT. | Illustré par Bertall. | [vignette] | PARIS | PUBLIÉ PAR J. HETZEL, | RUE DE RICHELIEU, 76. – RUE DE MÉNARS, 10. | [short fancy rule] | 1846

First edition, Paris, 1846.

188 x 125 mm. π^2 χ1 1-46^2 [47]^2; pp. [6] [1] 2-184 [i] ii-iv. Publisher's gold and blind stamped green cloth.

Illustrations: Wood engraved frontispiece, vignette on title-page and numerous wood engravings by "Bertall" (pseud. of Charles Albert, vicomte d'Arnoux) in the text. Frontispiece tipped in and not counted in the signatures or pagination.

Bibliographies: Bitting, p. 60; Horn-Arndt 385; Simon BG 252; Vicarie 115; Wheaton and Kelly 841.

Copies: *BNC* and *NUC* (6 copies).

98. Brillat-Savarin, Jean-Anthelme, 1755-1826.

PHYSIOLOGIE | DU GOUT, | OU | MÉDITATIONS DE GASTRONOMIE | TRANSCENDANTE; | OUVRAGE THÉORIQUE, HISTORIQUE ET A L'ORDRE

DU JOUR, | *Dedié aux Gastronomes parisiens,* | PAR UN PROFESSEUR, |
MEMBRE DE PLUSIEURS SOCIÉTÉS LITTÉRAIRES ET SAVANTES. | Dis-moi
ce que tu mangqes, je te dirai qui tu es. | APHOR. DU PROF. | TOME PREMIER.
[TOME SECOND.] | [ornament] | PARIS, | CHEZ A. SAUTELET ET Cie
LIBRAIRES, | PLACE DE LA BOURSE, PRÈS LA RUE FEYDEAU. | [short rule] |
1826.

First edition, Paris, 1826.

206 x 127 mm. 2 vols. Vol. I. π^2 $*^6$ 1-9^8 [10]^8 11-24^8 25$_1$; 201 leaves, pp. [2] [i-vii]
viii-xiv [5] 6-390. Vol. II. π^2 1-27^8 28^4(-28$_4$); 221 leaves, pp. [1-5] 6-442.
Publisher's printed boards.

Bibliographies: Crahan 491; Horn-Arndt 386; Oberlé (1) 144; Schraemli (1) 68;
Vicaire 116; Wheaton and Kelly 860.

Copies: *BNC* and *NUC* (6 copies).

99. Brillat-Savarin, Jean-Anthelme, 1755-1826.

BRILLAT SAVARIN | [short rule] | PHYSIOLOGIE | DU GOUT | PRÉCÉDÉE |
D'UNE NOTICE PAR ALP. KARR | DESSINS DE BERTALL | [illustration] |
PARIS | FURNE ET CIE, LIBRAIRES-ÉDITEURS | 45, RUE
SAINT-ANDRÉ-DES-ARTS | MDCCCLXIV

Second printing of this edition, Paris, 1864, which was originally published, Paris
1848.

258 x 168 mm. π^4 1-57^4 58^2; 234 leaves, pp. [*8*] [1] 2-459 [460].

Illustrations: Engraved frontispiece and six engraved plates as well as numerous wood
engravings in the text all by "Bertall" (pseud. of Charles Albert, vicomte d'Arnoux).

Bibliographies: Schraemli (1) 75; Vicaire 119.

Copies: *BNC* and *NUC* (4 copies).

100. Brillat-Savarin, Jean-Anthelme, 1755-1826.

PHYSIOLOGIE | DU GOUT | OU | MÉDITATIONS DE GASTRONOMIE
TRANSCENDANTE | Ouvrage théorique, historique, et à l'ordre du jour | *DÉDIÉ*
AUX GASTRONOMES PARISIENS | PAR BRILLAT-SAVARIN | AVEC UNE
NOTICE SUR L'AUTEUR | ÉDITION ACCOMPAGNÉE DES OUVRAGES
SUIVANTS | TRAITÉ DES EXCITANTS MODERNES | PAR H. DE BALZAC |
ANECDOTES ET FRAGMENTS D'HISTOIRE CULINAIRE | PAR DES
AMATEURS | PENSÉES ET PRÉCEPTES | RECUEILLIS | PAR UN
PHILOSOPHE | RECETTES ET FORMULES | PAR UN CORDON-BLEU | LA
GASTRONOMIE | POÈME, PAR BERCHOUX | L'ART DE DINER EN VILLE |
POÈME, PAR COLNET | PARIS | CHARPENTIER ET Cie,
LIBRAIRES-ÉDITEURS | 28, QUAI DU LOUVRE, 28 | [short rule] | 1874

Later printing of this edition, Paris, 1874, which was originally published, Paris, 1853.

174 x 110 mm. π^2 a^4 1-44^6; 270 leaves, pp. [i-v] vi-xi [xii] [1] 2-525 [526-528].

Bibliographies: This printing unrecorded in the bibliographies consulted. Vicaire 119
records the original printing, Paris, 1853, and reprints of 1858 and 1862.

Copies: *BNC* and *NUC* (Vassar College only).

101. Brillat-Savarin, Jean-Anthelme, 1755-1826.

PHYSIOLOGIE | [in red] DU GOUT | DE BRILLAT-SAVARIN | AVEC UNE | [in
red] PRÉFACE PAR CH. MONSELET | *Eaux-fortes par Ad. Lalauze* | [short rule] |
TOME PREMIER [TOME SECOND] | [printers device] | PARIS | [in red]
LIBRAIRIE DES BIBLIOPHILES | Rue Saint-Honoré, 338 | [short rule] | M DCCC
LXXIX

First printing of this edition, Paris, 1879. No. 171 of 170 copies on Holland paper
after 20 on China paper and 20 on Whatman paper.

218 x 136 mm. 2 vols. Vol. I. π^2 a-b^4 1-37^4; 158 leaves, pp. [*4*] [i] ii-xvi [1] 2-296.
Vol. II. π^2 1-40^4; 162 leaves, pp. [*4*] [1] 2-320. Publisher's printed wrappers.

Illustrations: Vol. I. Etched portrait of the author as frontispiece and 27 etched head
and tailpieces in the text. Vol. II. 24 etched head and tailpieces in the text.

Bibliographies: Schraemli (1) 77; Vicaire 120.

Copies: *BMC*, *BNC*, and *NUC* (Boston Anthenaeum, Detroit Institute of Arts, New York Public Library).

102. Brillat-Savarin, Jean-Anthelme, 1755-1826.

PHYSIOLOGIE | DU GOUT | DE BRILLAT-SAVARIN | AVEC UNE | PRÉFACE PAR CH. MONSELET | TOME PREMIER [TOME SECOND] | [printers device] | PARIS | LIBRAIRIE DES BIBLIOPHILES | E. FLAMMARION, SUCCESSEUR | 26, Rue Racine, 26 | [short rule] | Tous droits réservés.

Later printing, Paris, ca. 1880, of this edition which was originally published, Paris, 1879 (item 101).

121 x 108 mm. 2 vols. Vol. I. π^2 1-20^8 21^2; 204 leaves, pp. [*4*] [i] ii-xlviii [1] 2-276. Vol. II. π^2 1-20^8 21^4; 166 leaves, pp. [*4*] [1] 2-327 [328].

Bibliographies: This edition unrecorded in the bibliographies consulted.

Copies: *NUC* (University of Iowa only).

103. Brunschwig, Hieronymus, ca. 1450-1512.

Das buch zu distillieren | die zusamen gethonen ding Composi= | ta genant/ durch die eintzige ding/ vnd das büch Thesaurus pau | perü/ für die armen/ durch experiment von mix Jheronymo | Brunschwick vff geklubt vnd geoffenbart/ zü trost vn | heil dē menschen vn nutzlich ir leben vnd leib daruss | .°. zü erlengeren vnd in gesuntheit zü behalten. .°. | [woodcut]

Colophon: Hie endet sich diss buoch | seligklich getruckt vnd bolēdet in der Kei= | serlichen stat Strassburg durch Johā | nem Grüninger vff Sāt Adolffs | abent In dem Jar so mā zalt | nach Christi geburt, M.cccc | vnd.xix.

Second edition, Strassburg, 1519, of the so-called Grosses Destillierbuch, originally published under the title *Liber de arte distillandi de compositis*, Strassburg, 1512.

Folio: A-Zz^6 a-i^6; 330 leaves, ff. [i] ii-cccxxx.

Illustrations: Numerous woodcuts in the text.

Bibliographies: This edition unrecorded in the bibliographies consulted. Durling lists other editions.

Copies: *BMC* and *NUC* (University of Michigan only).

104. Brunschwig, Hieronymus, ca. 1450-1512.

ᴅAs Büch zü Distilieren die züsa | men gethonen ding: Composita genant: durch die einzigen | ding/ vñ das büch Thesaurus pauperum genant/ für die armen getz von neüwem wider ge= | truckt vnd von vnzalbarn urthumen geregnigt vnnd gebessert/ für alle voraussgangen truck/ | etwan von Hieronimo Brunsschwick auff geklaubt vnd geoffenbart zü trost vnd | beyl den menschen/ nützlich yr leben darauss züerlengern vnd yre | leib in gesuntheyt zübehalten. | [ornament] | [woodcut]

Colophon: Hie endet sich diss buoch seligklich getruckt | vnnd volendet in der loblichen stat Strassburg durch | Bartholomeü Grüniger vff Sant Adolffs | tag In déJar so man zalt nach | Christi geburt. M. | cccce.xxxij.

New edition, Strassburg, 1532, of the so-called Grosses Destillierbuch, originally published under the title *Liber de arte distillandi de compositis*, Strassburg, 1512.

Folio: a^8 A-Zz^6 aa^4; 288 leaves, ff. [8] i-cclxxx.

Illustrations: Numerous woodcuts in the text.

Note: Bound with Brunschwig's *Das New Distilier Büch der rechten Kunst*, Strassburg, 1537 (item 105).

Bibliographies: Durling 749.

Copies: *BMC* and *NUC* (four copies).

105. Brunschwig, Hieronymus, ca. 1450-1512.

ᴅAs New Distilier Büch der | rechten kunst/ von meister Hieronimo Brunschwig col | ligiert/ zü distilieren auss allen Kreütern die wasser/ mit einem leichtern sinn an= | gezeigt/ vnnd vorab das Register gerechtuertiget. Auch das Büch | des hoch berümbten Herren Marsilij Ficini/ das lang leben | betreffend/ vnnd sunst vil nützlicher stück. Deren | so vil/ das sie von manchem veracht/ | doch probiert/ vñ ye lenger | ye meer recht erfun= | den seind. | [woodcut] | Vnd zü merer besserung diss büchs/ so ist auss Galieno vnd der alt berümpten | Artzren hie durch den gantzen Herbarium ersücht/ durch alle Capitel ausserle= | sen die besten stuck/ vff dz du den Herbarium darbey magst | haben/ so doch alle figuren im disti= | lier büch stond. | M. D. xxxvij.

Second title-page:

Das Büch des lebens | MArsilij Ficini des hothge | lerten vnd wol erfarnen Florentiners/ zü behal= | ten gesundes vnd langwiriges leben/ Artzney büch. Vom La= | tin erst neüw züteütsch gemacht/ anderst emendiert | vnd gebessert/ mit vil neüwen vnd nützlichen | zü satzen der Nuinta essentia/ auch | anderer stuck/ so in den vo= | rigen nit gesehen | seind wor= | den. | [woodcut]

Colophon: Getruckt vnd volendet in der löblichen freyen Statt Strass= | burg/ durch Bartholomeum Grüninger/ Jm jar als | man zalt von vnsers Herren geburt. | M. D. xxxvij.

New edition, Strassburg, 1537, of the so-called Kleines Destillierbuch, originally published under the title *Liber de arte distillandi, de Simplicibus*, Strassburg, 1500.

Folio: A-B⁶ C⁴ D⁶ E⁴ F-V⁶ AA-HH⁶; 164 leaves, ff. [1] viii-xxviii, xxxi-cxxiiii, ²[i-ii] iii-xlviii.

Illustrations: Numerous woodcuts in the text.

Note: Bound with Brunschwig's *Das Büch zü Distilieren* . . . Strassburg, 1532 (item 104).

Bibliographies: Durling 762.

Copies: *NUC* (New York Public Library only).

106. Bruyerin, Jean-Baptiste, fl. 1560.

DE | RE CIBARIA | LIBRI XXII | OMNIVM CIBORVM | genera, omnium gentium mo- | ribus, & vsu probata | complectentes, | *Io. Bruyerino Campegio Lugdun authore.* | PRIMA EDITIO. | [vignette] | LVGDVNI, | APVD SEBAST. HONORATVM, | [short rule] | M. D. LX. | Cum Priuilegio Regio.

First edition, Lyon, 1560.

8vo. πa^8 a^4 b-z^8 A-Zz^8 AA-BB^8 CC^6; 578 leaves, pp. [*24*] 1-957, 956-1129 [1130].

The author was physician-in-ordinary to Henri II.

Bibliographies: Crahan 22; Horn-Arndt 23; Oberlé (1) 66; Pennell, p. 112; Schraemli (1) 93; Vicaire 124.

Copies: *BMC*, *BNC*, and *NUC* (5 copies).

107. Buc'hoz, Pierre-Joseph, 1731-1807.

L'ART | *ALIMENTAIRE,* | OU | *METHODE* | Pour préparer les Aliments les plus | sains pour l'Homme. | *Par M. BUC'HOZ, Auteur de différents* | *Ouvrages économiques.* | [ornament] | A PARIS, | Chez l'Auteur, rue de la Harpe. | [two short rules] | M. DCC. LXXXIII.

First edition, Paris, 1783.

12mo. π^4 (-π1) A-O^{12} P^8; 175 leaves, pp. [*6*] [1] 2-352.

Bibliographies: Bitting, p. 66; Malortie 175; Vicaire 128.

Copies: *BMC* and *NUC* (Library of Congress only).

108. Buc'hoz, Pierre-Joseph, 1731-1807.

MANUEL | *ALIMENTAIRE* | DES PLANTES, | TANT indigênes qu'exotiques, qui peuvent servir de | nourriture & de boisson aux différens Peuples de | la terre; | *CONTENANT leurs noms triviaux & botaniques*; | *suivant les Auteurs les plus célebres,* | *l'utilité qu'on* | *en peut tirer dans la vie animale, & les différentes* | *manieres de les* | *préparer pour la cuisine, l'office, la* | *distillation, &c.* | Par M. BUC'HOZ, Médecin du feu Roi de Pologne, &c. | [ornament] | A PARIS. | Chez J. P. COSTARD, Libraire, rue | Saint-Jean-de-Beauvais. | [two short rules] | M. DCC. LXXI. | *Avec Approbation & Privilége du Roi.*

First edition, Paris, 1771.

8vo. π^4 A-Ss^8 Tt^4; 336 leaves, pp. [i-iv] v-viii [1] 2-663 [664].

Bibliographies: Simon BG 266; Oberlé (2) 486; Vicaire 128.

Copies: *BMC*, *BNC*, and *NUC* (John Carter Brown Library and New York Academy of Medicine).

109. Bullett, Jean-Baptiste, 1699-1775.

[within a border of type ornaments] DU FESTIN | DU | *ROI-BOIT.* | [group of type ornaments] | *A BESANÇON,* | De l'Imprimerie de JEAN-FELIX | CHARMET. | [two short rules] | M. DCC. LXII.

First edition, Besançon, 1762.

4to. A^{10}; 10 leaves, pp. [2] [1] 2-16 [2]. Last leaf blank.

Bibliographies: Bitting, p. 68; Oberlé (2) 486; Vicaire 131.

Copies: *BNC* and *NUC* (Boston Public Library, Library of Congress and Yale University).

110. Burnet.

DICTIONNAIRE | DE | CUISINE | ET D'ÉCONOMIE MÉNAGÈRE. | A l'usage des Maîtres et Maîtresses de maison, Fermiers, Maître-d'hôtel, Chefs de cuisine, | Chefs d'office, Restaurateurs, Pâtissiers, Marchands de comestibles, Confiseurs, | Distillateurs, &c. | CONTENANT | L'EXPLICATION DE TOUS LES TERMES TECHNIQUES. | – LES DIVERS PROCÉDÉS EMPLOYÉS DANS LA | HAUTE, MOYENNE ET PETITE CUISINE. – LES | MENUS DE REPAS. – LA MANIÈRE DE DRESSER | LES PLATS ET DE DISPOSER LES DIFFÉRENS | SERVICES. – L'ART DE DÉCOUPER. – L'ART | DU PATISSIER, CONFISEUR ET DU DISTIL- | LATEUR. – LES MEILLEURS MOYENS A | EMPLOYER POUR LA CONSERVATION DES | ALIMENS DE TOUTE NATURE, LA | MANIÈRE DE

RECONNAITRE LA BONNE │ OU MAUVAISE QUALITÉ DES ALI- │ MENS, SOIT SOLIDES, SOIT LI- │ QUIDES, ET DE TOUTES LES │ SUBSTANCES QUI SERVENT A │ L'ALIMENTATION. – DES OB- │ SERVATIONS HYGIÉNIQUES │ SUR LA NATURE DES ALI- │ MENS ET SUR CE QUI │ REGARDE LEUR PRÉ- │ PARATION. – LES │ PARTIES LES PLUS │ INTÉRESSANTES DE │ L'HISTOIRE DE LA │ CUISINE. – LES │ SOINS A DON- │ NER A LA │ CAVE. – │ LA MA- │ NIÈRE │ DE │ FAIRE │ TOUS │ LES │ VINAI │ GRES │ CON- │ NUS. │ – │ ENFIN TOUTES LES NOTIONS RELATIVES A │ L'ART CULINAIRE ET L'ÉCONOMIE MÉNAGÈRE. │ *Par M. Burnet, Ex-Officier de bouche.* │ [short fancy rule] │ PARIS. │ A LA LIBRAIRIE USUELLE, 6, RUE NEUVE-SAINT-MARC. │ [short rule] │ 1836.

First edition, Paris, 1836.

8vo. π^2 χ^2 1-8^8 [9]^8 10-49^8 50^2; 398 leaves, pp. [*4*] [i] ii-iii [iv] [1] 2-788.

Illustrations: Wood engravings in the text and eleven etched plates (a dessert table; a group of serving dishes; and nine plates showing table settings). Note: Vicaire calls for eight plates rather than eleven as here.

Bibliographies: Bitting, p. 69; Horn-Arndt 401; Simon BG 270; Vicaire 132; Wheaton and Kelly 970.

Copies: *BNC* and *NUC* (National Agricultural Library and Northwestern University).

111. Les Cabarets de Rouen.

LES CABARETS │ *DE ROUEN* │ en 1556 │ [short rule] │ 3e ÉDITION │ Réimprimée sur les deux premières │ et accompagnée d'un avant-propos │ PAR UN BIBLIOPHILE │ DU QUARTIER MARTAINVILLE │ [ornament] │ *A ROUEN* │ chez tous les débitants │ [short rule] │ 1870

Third edition, Rouen, 1870. No. 62 of 96 copies on vélin anglais in a total edition of 100.

157 x 99 mm. [1]^4 [2]^6; 10 leaves, pp. [i-v] vi-viii [9-11] 12-19 [20].

Illustrations: Vignette on p. 9 and ornamental head and tail pieces.

Bibliographies: Bitting, p. 526.

Copies: *NUC* (Library of Congress only).

112. Cadet de Gassicourt, Charles-Louis, 1769-1821.

COURS | GASTRONOMIQUE, | OU | LES DINERS DE MANANT-VILLE, |
Ouvrage Anecdotique, Philosophique et Littéraire; | SECONDE ÉDITION | *dédiée* | *à*
la Société Epicurienne du Caveau moderne, | *séaute au Rochev de Chancalle*; | Par feu
M. C✱✱✱, ancien avocat au Parlement de Paris. | [short rule] | Trahit sua quemque
Voluptas. | [short rule] | IMPRIMERIE DE BRASSEUR AINÉ. | PARIS, |
CAPELLE ET RENAND, Libraires-Commissionnaires, | rue Jean-Jacques-Rousseau,
no. 6. | *1809.*

First edition, Paris, 1809. The publishers styled this the second edition on the title-
page because several chapters of the work had appeared in the journal *L'Epicurien*
français.

203 x 127 mm. π^2 [1]^8 2-22^8 23^6; 184 leaves, pp. [i-v] vi-xx [17] 18-364 = 368.

Illustration: Frontispiece engraved gastronomic map of France by Tourcaty.

Bibliographies: Bitting, p. 71; Crahan 500; Maggs 343; Oberlé (1) 171 and 172;
Schraemli (3) 66; Vicaire 137.

Copies: *BNC* and *NUC* (4 copies).

113. Cadet-de-Vaux, Antoine-Alexis, 1743-1828.

DE LA | GÉLATINE DES OS | ET DE SON BOUILLON, | PRÉCÉDÉE | De
considérations sur le vice du régime alimen- | taire des classes populeuses, et la
nécessité ainsi | que les moyens de leur assurer la subsistance | la plus salutaire et la
plus économique. | PAR. A.-A. CADET DE VAUX, | Ancien Président de la Société
philanthropique, et Admi- | nistrateur d'hôpitaux civils et militaires; de diverses |
Académies impériales, royales, étrangères et natio- | nales de la Société royale
d'agriculture; honoraire de | la Société helvétique des sciences naturelles, etc., etc. |
[short rule] | *Infelix cujus in potestate est tantorum animas* | *à morte defendere, et non*
est voluntas! | ST.-AMBR. | [short rule] | A PARIS, | CHEZ L. COLAS FILS,
IMPRIMEUR-LIBRAIRE, | Rue du Petit-Bourbon Saint-Sulpice, No. 14. | [two short
rules] | 1818.

First edition, Paris, 1818.

180 x 116 mm. π^4 χ^2 1^8 $^\pi$2^4 2^8 2✱^{4} 3^8 3✱^{4} 4^8 4✱^{4} 5^4 (-5$_1$); 57 leaves, pp. [i-v] vi-xii [1]
2-102.

Bibliographies: Vicaire 138 in a note.

Copies: *BNC* and *NUC* (National Library of Medicine and University of Wisconsin).

114. Cadet-de-Vaux, Antoine-Alexis, 1743-1828.

DISSERTATION | SUR LE CAFÉ; | SON HISTORIQUE, SES PROPRIÉTÉS, et le Procédé | pour en obtenir la boisson la plus agréable, la | plus salutaire et la plus économique; | PAR ANT.-ALEXIS CADET-DE-VAUX, | MEMBRE des Sociétés d'Agriculture de la Seine, de Seine et | Oise, etc.; Académiques des Sciences, etc. du Haut-Rhin; | des Sciences et Arts des Deux-Sèvres; des Sciences, Arts et | Belles-Lettres de Dijon; des Sciences, Lettres et Arts de | Nancy, etc.; du Lycée du Gard; d'Académies et Sociétés | savantes étrangères. | SUIVIE | DE SON ANALYSE; | PAR CHARLES-LOUIS CADET, *Pharmacien ordinaire* | *de* S. M. L'EMPEREUR, *Membre de la Société de Médecine* | *de Paris, Professeur de Chimie.* | [short rule] | Et je crois, du Génie éprouvant le réveil, | Boire, dans chaque goutte, un rayon du Soleil. | DELILLE. | [short rule] | A PARIS. | [two short rules] | 1806.

First edition, Paris, 1806.

163 x 98 mm. π^2 1-10$^{8.4}$; 62 leaves, pp. [*4*] [1] 2-120.

Bibliographies: Wheaton and Kelly 1011.

Copies: *NUC* (4 copies).

115. Cadet-de-Vaux, Antoine-Alexis, 1743-1828.

DISSERTATION | SUR LE CAFÉ; | SON HISTORIQUE, SES PROPRIÉTIÉS, et le Procédé | pour en obtenir la boisson la plus agréable, la | plus salutaire et la plus 1économique; | PAR ANT.-ALEXIS CADET-DE-VAUX, | MEMBRE des Sociétés d'Agriculture de la Seine, de Seine et | Oise, etc.; Académiques des Sciences, etc. du Haut-Rhin; | des Sciences et Arts des Deux-Sèvres; des Sciences, Arts et |Belles-Lettres de Dijon; des Sciences, Lettres et Arts de | Nancy, etc.; du Lycée du Gard; d'Académies et Sociétés | savantes étrangères. | SUIVIE | DE SON ANALYSE; | PAR CHARLES-LOUIS CADET, *Parmacien ordinaire* | *de* S. M. L'EMPEREUR, *Membre de la Société de Médecine* | *de Paris, Professeur de Chimie.* | [short rule] | Et je crois, du Génie éprouvant le réveil, | Boire, à chaque goutte, un rayon du Soleil. | DELILLE. | [short rule] | A PARIS. | [two short rules] | 1807.

Second edition, Paris, 1807. Originally published, Paris, 1806 (item 114).

185 x 110 mm. π^2 1-10$^{8.4}$; 62 leaves, pp. [*4*] [1] 2-119 [120].

Bibliographies: Bitting, p. 72; Vicaire 138; Wheaton and Kelly 1012.

Copies: *NUC* (Harvard and Library of Congress).

116. Cadet-de-Vaux, Antoine-Alexis, 1743-1828.

MÉMOIRE | SUR | LA MATIÈRE SUCRÉE | DE LA POMME, | *Et sur ses* *appropriations aux divers* | *besoins de l'Economie.* | PAR A.-ALEXIS CADET-DE-VAUX, | De l'Académie Impériale des Curieux de la Nature, de | l'Académie Royale des Sciences de Madrid, Corres- | pondant de celle de Munich, membre de diverses Aca- | démies et Sociétés savantes et agricoles de France. | [short rule] | Combien de choses que nous voyons | et que nous n'apercevons point! | MONTAIGNE. | [short rule] | [publisher's monogram] | A PARIS, | CHEZ D. COLAS, IMPRIMEUR-LIBRAIRE, | Rue du Vieux-Colombier, No 26, faub. St.-Germain. | [two short rules] | 1808.

First edition, Paris, 1808.

175 x 110 mm. [1]^8 2-5^8; 40 leaves, pp. [1-5] 6-80.

Bibliographies: Vicaire 138 in a note.

Copies: *BNC* and *NUC* (Franklin Institute, Philadelphia, and Yale).

117. Cadet-de-Vaux, Antoine-Alexis, 1743-1828.

LE MÉNAGE | OU | L'EMPLOI | DES FRUITS, | DANS | L'ÉCONOMIE DOMESTIQUE; | PROCÉDÉS A L'USAGE | DE LA MÈRE DE FAMILLE. | *Ouvrage destiné* | A rendre usuelles les différentes préparations des Fruits, | à mettre à profit leur propre matière sucrée, et à en | obtenir à peu de frais tout ce qu'ils peuvent donner à | l'Économie domestique, tels que Sirops, Compotes, | Confitures, Gelées, Vins, Vins de liqueurs, Rata- | fias, etc. | PAR A.-A. CADET-DE-VAUX. | [short fancy rule] | A PARIS, | CHEZ D. COLAS, IMPRIMEUR-LIBRAIRE, | rue du Vieux-Colombier, No 26, faubourg S. G. | [short fancy rule] | 1810.

First edition, Paris, 1810.

170 x 106 mm. π^2 a^8 b^4 1-24$^{8.4}$; 158 leaves, pp. [*4*] [i] ii-xxiv [1] 2-288.

Illustration: Engraved folding plate illustrating an ice cream maker.

Bibliographies: Maggs 347; Oberlé (1) 704; Vicaire 138.

Copies: *BMC*, *BNC*, and *NUC* (University of California, Berkeley, and Kansas State University).

Cardelli, P. see Duval, Henri-Louis-Nicolas.

118. Carême, Antonin, 1784-1833.

Ire Livraison

L'ART | DE | LA CUISINE FRANÇAISE | *Au dix-neuvième siècle.* | TRAITÉ | ÉLÉMENTAIRE ET PRATIQUE | DES BOUILLONS EN GRAS ET EN MAIGRE, DES ESSENCES, FUMETS, DES | POTAGES FRANÇAIS ET ÉTRANGERS; DES GROSSES PIÈCES DE POISSON; | DES GRANDES ET PETITES SAUCES; DES RAGOUTS ET DES GARNITURES; | DES GROSSES PIÈCES DE BOUCHEIRE, DE JAMBON, DE VOLAILLE, ET | DE GIBIER; SUIVI DE DISSERTATIONS CULINAIRES ET GASTRONOMIQUES | UTILES AUX PROGRÈS DE CET ART. | PAR | M. A. CARÊME, DE PARIS, | *Auteur du Pâtissier Royal, du Pâtissier pittoresque, du Maître d'Hôtel | français, du Cuisinier Parisien, et de deux recueils de Projets d'archi- | tecture, destinés aux embellissements de Paris et de Saint-Pétersbourg* | Ire LIVRAISON. | TOME PREMIER. [TOME SECOND.] | [short fancy rule] | PARIS, | CHEZ L'AUTEUR, RUE NEUVE-SAINT-ROCH, No 37. | [short rule] | 1833.

IIe Livraison

L'ART | DE | LA CUISINE FRANÇAISE | *Au dix-neuvième siècle,* | OU | TRAITÉ ÉLÉMENTAIRE ET PRATIQUE | DU TRAVAIL EN GRAS ET EN MAIGRE | DES BOUILLONS, CONSOMMÉS, FUMETS ET BOUILLONS MÉDICINAUX; | DES POTAGES FRANÇAIS, ANGLAIS, NAPOLITAINS, SICILIENS, | ITALIENS, ESPAGNOLS, ALLEMANDS, RUSSES, POLONAIS, HOLLANDAIS, | AMÉRICAINS ET INDIENS; DES GRANDES ET PETITES SAUCES; DES | ESSENCES, DES RAGOUTS ET DES GARNITURES EN GÉNÉRAL; DES | GROSSES PIÈCES DE POISSON, DE BOUCHERIE, DE PORC FRAIS, | DE

JAMBON, DE VOLAILLE ET DE GIBEIR; | SUIVIE D'OBSERVATIONS SUR LA CONNAISSANCE ET LES PROPRIÉTÉS DES ALIMENTS, | ET DE DISSERTATIONS CULINAIRES UTILES AUX PROGRÈS DE CET ART; | ORNE DE 12 PLANCHES, | DESSINÉES PAR L'AUTEUR, ET GRAVÉES AU TRAIT. | PAR | M. A. CARÊME, DE PARIS, | *Auteur du Pâtissier Royal, du Pâtissier pittoresque, du Maître d'Hôtel* | *français, du Cuisinier Parisien, et de deux recueils de Projets d'archi-* | *tecture, destinés aux embellissements de Paris et de Saint-Pétersbourg* | Lacuisine est le plus ancien des arts. | BRILLAT-SAVARIN. | [short fancy rule] | PARIS, | CHEZ L'ÉDITEUR, RUE NEUVE-PETITS-CHAMPS, No 71. | [short rule] | 1835.

First edition, Paris, 1833-1835.

204 x 129 mm. 3 vols. Vol. I. [a]^8 b-h^8 1-19^8 20^8(-20$_{4,5,6}$); 231 leaves, pp. [i-iv] v-cxxvii [cxxviii] [1] 2-313 [314]. Vol. II. [1]^8 2-21^8 22^8(-22$_{1,8,2,7,3}$) a-b^8; 187 leaves, pp. [1-6] 7-342, i-xxxi [xxxii]. Vol. III. π^4 1-32^8 33^4 ^{2}33^8 34^4; 276 leaves, pp. [8] [1] 2-544.

Illustrations: Vol. I. Lithographed title-page and etched frontispiece portrait of the author, two lithographed plates and wood engraved ornaments in the text. Vol. II. Lithographed title-page, nine lithographed folding plates of elaborate dishes, and wood engraved ornaments in the text. Vol. III. Lithographed title-page, twelve lithographed folding plates of elaborate dishes, and wood engraved ornaments in the text.

Two further volumes, written by Armand Plumerey, were published in 1844 (item 394).

Bibliographies: Bitting, p. 75; Maggs 441; Schraemli (1) 107; Schraemli (2) 45; Schraemli (3) 70; Simon BG 283; Vicaire 146.

Copies: *BNC* (vols. I and II only) and *NUC* (Boston Public Library, Library of Congress, and National Library of Medicine).

119. Carême, Antonin, 1784-1832.

LA | CUISINE | ORDINAIRE | PAR | BEAUVILLIERS, et Antonin CARÊME, | [in two columns, column one] Ancien Officier du Comte de Provence (depuis | Louis XVIII), attaché aux extraordinaires | des maisons royales, ancien Restaurateur, | rue Richelieu, 26. | [two vertical rules] | [column two] Chef des cuisines du prince régent d'Angleterre | (Georges IV), de l'empereur Alexandre, du | marquis de Londonderry, de la princesse de | Bagration, de M. le baron J. de Rothschild, etc. [end column two]

| 4° ÉDITION TRÉS-AUGMENTÉE, | CONTENANT: | 1° l'*Art du Cuisinier*, de BEAUVILLIERS. — Une série de *Bouillons* et de *Po-* | *tages*, par ANTONIN, CARÊME; — Une série de Mets froids, Gelées, d'Entre- | mets de Sucre, par le même; | 2° Un Travail spécial, intitulé: le *Premier Déjeuner*: Lait, Café, Thé, Cho- | colat, par BRILLAT-SAVARIN, CADET GASSICOURT; les docteurs GAS- | TALDI, JOSEPH ROQUES, PAUL GAUBERT, DONNÉ, QUEVENNE, etc. | [short fancy rule] | TOME PREMIER. [TOME DEUXIÈME.] | [short fancy rule] | A PARIS, | A LA LIBRAIRIE DE E. BRIÈRE | Editeur de la Collection d'Antonin CARÊME et de la Collection de CHASSE d'ELZÉAR BLAZE, | RUE SAINTE-ANNE, 55, | 1848.

First edition, Paris, 1848, of this compilation, styled the fourth edition as it followed the third edition of Carême's *Le Cuisinier parisien*, Paris, 1842. Second issue, with the cancel label over the imprint: AU BUREAU DE LA COLLECTION CULINAIRE D'ANTONIN CARÊME, | DE LA COLLECTION DE TOUTES LES CHASSES, AVEC ALBUMS DE CHASSE, | DU COURS COMPLET D'AGRICULTURE, | EN 20 VOLUMES IN-8, | AVEC ENVIRON 4000 SUJETS GRAVÉS SUR ACIER; 110 FR. | Paris, rue des Moulins, 8. | [short rule]

198 x 124 mm. 2 vols. Vol. I. π^2 $2\pi^4$ 1-23^8 24-25^6; 202 leaves, pp. [i-v] vi-xi [xii] 1-2; ^{2}[1] 2-12, 1-2 [13] 14-388. Vol. II. π^2 1-25^8 26^6(-26$_6$); $^2\pi^2$ 1-2^8; ^{3}1^6 2^8 3^4; ^{4}a-d^8; $^5\pi^6$; 281 leaves, pp. [4] [1] 2-408 [2]; ^{2}[4] [1] 2-32; ^{3}[1] 2-35 [36]; ^{4}[i] ii-lxiii [lxiv]; ^{5}[1] 2-12.

Illustrations: Vol. I. Wood engraved vignette on p. xi and six lithographed folding plates of table settings. Vol II. Three lithographed folding plates of table settings and a wood engraving of a kitchen on the sectional title following signature 26.

Bibliographies: Vicaire 148 with the date 1847 which is probably an error as the preface in Vol. I is dated ler Janvier 1848.

Copies: *BNC*.

120. Carême, Antonin, 1784-1832.

LE CUISINIER | PARISIEN, | OU | L'ART DE LA CUISINE FRANÇAISE | AU DIX-NEUVIÈME SIÈCLE, | TRAITÉ ÉLÉMENTAIRE ET PRATIQUE | DES ENTRÉES FROIDES, DES SOCLES ET DE L'ENTREMETS | DE SUCRE, | SUIVI D'OBSERVATIONS UTILES AUX PROGRÈS DE CES DEUX PARTIES | DE LA CUISINE MODERNE. | Par M. A. Carême, de Paris, | Auteur du *Pâtissier royal parisien*, du *Pâtissier pittoresque*, du *Maître-* | *d'hôtel français*, et de deux *Recueils de projets d'architecture destinés* | *aux embellissements de Paris et de Saint-Pétersbourg.* | [short fancy rule] | 𝕯𝖊𝖚𝖝𝖎𝖊̀𝖒𝖊 𝕰̀𝖉𝖎𝖙𝖎𝖔𝖓, 𝖗𝖊𝖛𝖚𝖊, 𝖈𝖔𝖗𝖗𝖎𝖌𝖊́𝖊 𝖊𝖙 𝖆𝖚𝖌𝖒𝖊𝖓𝖙𝖊́𝖊. | OUVRAGE ORNÉ DE 25 PLANCHES DESSINÉES PAR L'AUTEUR, ET GRAVÉES AU | TRAIT PAR MM. NORMAND FILS, HIBON ET THIERRY. | [short fancy rule] | PARIS, | DE L'IMPRIMERIE DE FIRMIN DIDOT, | IMPRIMEUR DU ROI, RUE JACOB, No 24. | [short fancy rule] | 1828.

Second edition, Paris, 1828. Original edition, also Paris, 1828.

205 x 127 mm. [1]⁸ 2-26⁸ 27⁴(-27₄); 211 leaves, pp. [1-7] 8-422.

Illustrations: Lithographed title-page and 24 lithographed folding plates of elaborate pastry dishes, numbered 2-25.

Bibliographies: Drexel 149; Horn-Arndt 404; Maggs 419; Oberlé (1) 188; Schraemli (1) 103; Vicaire 146; Wheaton and Kelly 1061.

Copies: *BMC* and *NUC* (Library of Congress only). Wheaton and Kelly (Radcliffe only).

121. Carême, Antonin, 1784-1832.

LE | CUISINIER PARISIEN, | OU | L'ART DE LA CUISINE FRANÇAISE AU DIX-NEUVIÈME SIÈCLE, | TRAITÉ | ELÉMENTAIRE ET PRATIQUE | DES ENTRÉES FROIDES, DES SOCLES, | ET DE L'ENTREMETS DE SUCRE; | SUIVI | D'OBSERVATIONS UTILES AUX PROGRÈS DE CES DEUX PARTIES | DE LA CUISINE MODERNE; | PAR ANTONIN CARÊME, | Auteur du PATISSIER ROYAL PARISIEN, – du PATISSIER PITTORESQUE, – du MAITRE-D'HÔTEL | FRANÇAIS, et de l'ART DE LA CUISINE FRANÇAISE AU XIXe SIÈCLE. | [short rule] | TROISIÈME ÉDITION, | REVUE, CORRIGÉE ET AUGMENTÉE. | OUVRAGE ORNÉ DE 25 PLANCHES DESSINÉES PAR L'AUTEUR ET GRAVÉES AU TRAIT | PAR MM. NORMAND FILS, HIBON ET THIERRY. | [short fancy rule] | PARIS. | Au dépôt principal, rue Thérèse, 11; | ET CHEZ MM. | [in two columns, column one] J. RENOUARD et Cie, libraires, 6, rue de Tournon. | MANSUT, libraire, 30, place St-André-des-Arts. | TRESSE, libraire, 3, galerie de Chartres. | [vertical rule] | [column two] MAISON, libraire, 29, quai des Augustins. | DAUVIN et FONTAINE, libr., pass. des Panoramas. | DENTU, libraire, Palais-Royal. [end columns] | A LONDRES, CHEZ W. JEFFS, 15, BURLINGTON-ARCADE. | [short rule] | 1842.

Third edition, Paris, 1842. Originally published, Paris, 1828, and reprinted the same year.

226 x 135 mm. [a]^4 b^4 1-25^8 26^4; 212 leaves, pp. [i-vii] viii-xvi [1] 2-408.

Illustrations: Engraved title-page (styled "Deuxieme Edition") and twenty-four engraved folding plates illustrating elaborate pastry dishes numbered 2-25.

Bibliographies: Bitting, pp. 74-75; Horn-Arndt 405; Vicaire 146 in a note.

Copies: *NUC* (Library of Congress and University of California, Berkeley).

122. Carême, Antonin, 1784-1832.

LE | MAITRE D'HOTEL | FRANÇAIS, | OU | PARALLÈLE DE LA CUISINE ANCIENNE ET MODERNE, CONSIDÉRÉE | SOUS LE RAPPORT DE L'ORDONNANCE DES MENUS SELON | LES QUATRE SAISONS. | OUVRAGE CONTENANT UN TRAITÉ DES MENUS SERVIS A PARIS, | A SAINT-PÉTERSBOURG, A LONDRES ET A VIENNE. | PAR M. A. CARÊME, DE PARIS. | [short rule] | TOME PREMIER. [TOME DEUXIÈME.] | [printers monogram] | A PARIS, | DE L'IMPRIMERIE DE FIRMIN DIDOT, | IMPRIMEUR DU ROI ET DE L'INSTITUT, RUE JACOB, No 24. | [short fancy rule] | M DCCC XXII.

First edition, Paris, 1822.

218 x 130 mm. 2 vols. Vol. I. π^2 ($\pm\pi$2) 2π^4 1-21^8 22^6; 180 leaves, pp. [8] [i] ii-iv [1] 2-348. Vol. II. π^2 1-17^8 18^6; 144 leaves, pp. [4] [1] 2-282 [2]. Vol. I contains 12 and Vol. II 13 folding printed menus not reckoned in the signatures or paginations.

Illustrations: Vol. I. Engraved title-page and two folding plates of table settings numbered 2 and 3. Vol. II. Engraved frontispiece of two chefs and six engraved folding plates, three of table settings, two illustrating "grands buffets de la cuisine moderne" and one of a plan for a grand buffet.

Bibliographies: Maggs 388; Oberlé (1) 187; Vicaire 145; Wheaton and Kelly 1063.

Copies: *BNC* and *NUC* (Iowa State University, Library of Congress and New York Public Library).

123. Carême, Antonin, 1784-1832.

LE | MAITRE-D'HOTEL | FRANÇAIS, | TRAITÉ DES MENUS | A SERVIR A PARIS, A ST-PÉTERSBOURG, A LONDRES ET A VIENNE; | PAR ANTONIN CARÊME, | Auteur du PATISSIER ROYAL PARISIEN, – du PATISSIER PITTORESQUE, du CUISINEIR ROYAL PARISIEN | et de l'ART DE LA CUISINE FRANÇAISE AU XIXe SIÈCLE. | [short rule] | NOUVELLE ÉDITION, | REVUE, CORRIGÉE ET AUGEMENTÉE | [short fancy rule] | TOME PREMIER. [TOME SECOND.] | [short fancy rule] | PARIS. | Au dépôt principal, rue Thérèse, 11; | ET CHEZ MM. | [in two columns, column one] J. RENOUARD et Cie, libraires, 8, rue de Tournon. | MANSUT, libraire, 30, place St-André-des-Arts. | TRESSE, libraire, galerie de Chartres. | [vertical rule] | [column two] MAISON, libraire, 29, quai des Augustins. | DAUVIN et FONTAINE, libr., pass. des Panoramas, | DENTU, Libraire, Palais-Royal. [end columns] | A LONDRES, CHEZ W. JEFFS, 15, BURLINGTON-ARCADE. | [short rule] | 1842.

Second edition, Paris, 1842. Originally published, Paris, 1822 (item 122).

227 x 139 mm. 2 vols. Vol. I π^4 $*^2$ 1-22^8; 182 leaves, pp. [i-ix] x-xi [xii] [1] 2-352. Vol. II. π^2 1-17^8 18^6(-18$_6$); 143 leaves, pp. [4] [1-2] 3-282. Vol. I contains 12 and Vol. II 13 folding printed menus not reckoned in the pagination.

Illustrations: As in the first edition (item 122).

Bibliographies: Bitting, p. 75; Drexel 160; Schraemli (1) 105; Simon BG 288; Vicaire 146.

Copies: *BMC*, *BNC*, and *NUC* (Cornell and University of Pennsylvania).

124. Carême, Antonin, 1784-1832.

LE PATISSIER | PITTORESQUE, | COMPOSÉ ET DESSINÉ | PAR M. A. CARÊME, | CONTENANT | Cent vingt-cinq Planches gravées au trait, dont cent dix repré- | sentent une variété de Modèles, de Pavillons, de Rotondes, de | Temples, de Ruines, de Tours, de Belvéders, de Forts, de | Cascades, de Fontaines, de Maisons de Plaisance, de Chau- | mières, de Moulins, et d'Hermitages; | PRÉCÉDÉ | D'un traité des cinq Ordres d'Architecture, selon VIGNOLE; auquel | on a joint des détails des Ordres Cariatide, Poestum, Égyptien, | Chinois et Gothiques; tirés de l'Ouvrage de M. DURAND, Parallèle | des Monuments antiques et modernes. | [publisher's monogram] | A PARIS, | DE L'IMPRIMERIE DE FIRMIN DIDOT, LIBRAIRE, | IMPRIMEUR DU ROI, ET DE L'INSTITUT, | RUE JACOB, No 24. | [two short rules] | 1815.

First edition, Paris, 1815.

258 x 166 mm. [1]^4 2-3^4 4^2; 14 leaves, pp. [1-7] 8-27 [28].

Illustrations: 125 engraved plates consisting of an engraved title-page, plates 1-123 of architectural designs to be made of pastry and one folding plate of a "Colonne royale" numbered 125.

Bibliographies: Schraemli (2) 41; Schraemli (3) 69; Vicarie 145 in a note.

Copies: *BNC* and *NUC* (John Crerar Library only).

125. Carême, Antonin, 1784-1832.

LE | PATISSIER | PITTORESQUE, | COMPOSÉ ET DESSINÉ | Par M. Antonin Carême, | *De Paris* | CONTENANT | CENT VINGT-CINQ PLANCHES GRAVÉES AU TRAIT, DONT CENT DIX REPRÉ- | SENTENT UNE VARIÉTÉ DE MODÈLES DE PAVILLONS, DE ROTONDES, DE | TEMPLES, DE RUINES, DE TOURS, DE BELVÉDÈRES, DE FORTS, DE CAS- | CADES, DE FONTAINES, DE MAISONS DE PLAISANCE, DE CHAUMIÈRES, | DE MOULINS ET D'ERMITAGES; | PRÉCÉDÉ, | D'un Traité des cinq ordres d'Architecture, selon VIGNOLE; auquel on a joint | des détails des ordres Cariatide, Poestum, Égyptien, Chinois et Gothiques; | tirés de l'Ouvrage de M. DURAND, Parallèle des Monuments antiques et | modernes. | 3e Edition, revue et augmentée. | [short fancy rule] | PARIS. | IMPRIMERIE DE FIRMIN DIDOT, | IMPRIMEUR DU ROI, RUE JACOB, No 24. | [short fancy rule] | 1828.

Third edition, Paris, 1828. Originally published, Paris, 1815 (item 124).

238 x 154 mm. π^2 [1]^8 2-4^8 χ1; 35 leaves, pp. [*4*] [i-iii] iv-v [vi] [7] 8-66.

Illustrations: 126 engraved plates consisting of an engraved title-page, two unnumbered plates showing bases for sixteen of the designs that follow, and plates 1-123 of architectural designs to be made of pastry.

Bookplate: Ex libris Georges Vicaire.

Bibliographies: Maggs 420; Oberlé (1) 186; Wheaton and Kelly 1064.

Copies: *BNC* and *NUC* (Kansas State University and Peabody Institute). Wheaton and Kelly (Radcliffe only).

126. Carême, Antonin, 1784-1832.

LE | PATISSIER ROYAL | PARISIEN, | OU | TRAITÉ ÉLÉMENTAIRE | ET PRATIQUE | *de la Pâtisserie* | ANCIENNE ET MODERNE, | DE L'ENTREMETS DE SUCRE, | DES ENTRÉES FROIDES ET DES SOCLES; | SUIVI D'OBSERVATIONS UTILES AUX PROGRÈS DE CET ART, | D'UNE SÉRIE DE PLUS DE SOIXANTE MENUS, | ET D'UNE REVUE CRITIQUE DES GRANDS BALS DE 1810 ET 1811. | *Composé par* M. A. CARÊME, *de Paris,* | CHEF-PATISSIER DES GRANDS EXTRAORDINAIRES. | OUVRAGE ORNÉ DE 70 PLANCHES DESSINÉES PAR L'AUTEUR, | COMPRENANT PLUS DE 250 SUJETS. | TOME PREMIER. [TOME DEUXIÈME.] | [ornament] | PARIS, | J. G. DENTU, IMPRIMEUR-LIBRAIRE, | RUE DU PONT DE LODI, No 3, PRÈS LE PONT-NEUF. | 1815.

First edition, Paris, 1815.

203 x 126 mm. 2 vols. Vol. I. π^2 [a]^8 b^6 1-30^8 31^2(-31$_2$); 257 leaves, pp. [8] [i] ii-xxi [xxii-xxiv] [1] 2-482. Vol. II. π^2 1-28^8; 226 leaves, pp. [4] [1] 2-447 [448].

Illustrations: Vol. I. Engraved title-page on $\pi2^r$ with an explanation on the facing page signed by the author, and 31 engraved folding plates, illustrating pastries and pastry designs, numbered 2-32. Vol. II. 38 engraved plates, 23 of which are folding, illustrating pastries and pastry designs, numbered 33-70.

Bibliographies: Crahan 509; Maggs 422; Schraemli (1) 101; Schraemli (2) 43; Vicaire 144; Wheaton and Kelly 1065.

Copies: *BMC* and *NUC* (Library of Congress only). Wheaton and Kelly (Vol. II. Radcliffe only).

127. Carême, Antonin, 1784-1832.

LE | PATISSIER ROYAL | PARISIEN, | OU | TRAITÉ ÉLÉMENTAIRE | ET PRATIQUE | DE LA | PATISSERIE ANCIENNE ET MODERNE; | SUIVI D'OBSERVATIONS UTILES AUX PROGRÈS DE CET ART, | ET D'UNE REVUE CRITIQUE DES GRANDS BALS DE 1810 ET 1811. | Par M. A. Carême, de Paris, | Auteur du *Pâtissier pittoresque,* du *Maître-d'hôtel français,* du *Cuisinier* | *parisien* ou *l'Art de la Cuisine française au* 19e *siècle,* et de deux *Re-* | *cueils de projets d'architecture destinés aux embelissements de Paris et* | *de Saint-Pétersbourg.* | [short fancy rule] | 𝔇𝔢𝔲𝔵𝔦è𝔪𝔢 𝔈𝔡𝔦𝔱𝔦𝔬𝔫, 𝔯𝔢𝔟𝔲𝔢 𝔢𝔱 𝔠𝔬𝔯𝔯𝔦𝔤é𝔢. | OUVRAGE ORNÉ DE 41 PLANCHES DESSINÉES PAR L'AUTEUR, COMPRENANT 182 | SUJETS, GRAVÉS AU TRAIT PAR MM. NORMAND FILS, HIBON ET THIERRY. | [short fancy rule] | TOME PREMIER. [TOME SECOND.] | [short fancy rule] | PARIS, | DE L'IMPRIMERIE DE FIRMIN DIDOT, | IMPRIMEUR DU ROI, RUE JACOB, No 24. | [short fancy rule] | 1828.

Second edition, Paris, 1828. Originally published, Paris, 1815 (item 126).

208 x 131 mm. 2 vols. Vol. I. [a]^8 b-e^8 f^2 1-24^8 25^6(-25$_6$); 239 leaves, pp. [i-vii] viii-lxxxiii [lxxxiv] [1] 2-394. Vol. II. π^2 1-27^8 28^2; 220 leaves, pp. [4] [1] 2-435 [436].

Illustrations: Vol. I. Lithographed title-page and 12 lithographed folding plates of pastries and pastry designs, numbered 2-13. Vol. II. 24 lithographed folding plates of pastries and pastry designs, numbered 14-41.

Bibliographies: Schraemli (1) 102; Schraemli (2) 44; Vicaire 144 in a note.

Copies: *BNC* and *NUC* (University of California, Berkeley, and Northwestern University).

128. Carême, Antonin, 1784-1832.

LE | PATISSIER ROYAL | PARISIEN, | OU | TRAITÉ ÉLÉMENTAIRE | ET PRATIQUE | DE LA PATISSERIE ANCIENNE ET MODERNE; | Suivi | D'OBSERVATIONS UTILES AUX PROGRÈS DE CET ART, | ET D'UNE REVUE CRITIQUE DES GRANDS BALS DE 1810 ET 1811; | PAR ANTONIN CARÊME, | Auteur du PATISSIER PITTORESQUE, du MAITRE-D'HOTEL FRANÇAIS, | du CUISINIER ROYAL PARISIEN, de l'ART DE LA CUISINE FRANÇAISE AU XIXe SIÈCLE, et de DEUX RECUEILS | de projets d'architecture destinés aux embellissements de Paris et de St-Pétersbourg. | [short rule] | TROISIÈME ÉDITION, | REVUE, CORRIGÉE ET AUGMENTÉE. | OUVRAGE ORNÉ DE 41 PLANCHES DESSINÉES PAR L'AUTEUR, COMPRENANT 182 SUJETS | GRAVÉS AU TRAIT PAR MM. NORMAND FILS, HIBON ET THIERRY. | [short fancy rule] | TOME PREMIER. [TOME SECOND.] | [short fancy rule] | A PARIS, CHEZ MM. | [in two columns, column one] J. RENOUARD et Cie, libraires, 6, rue de Tournon. | TRESSE, libraire 3, galerie de Chartres. | A. ROYER, libraire, 241, rue Saint-Honoré. | [vertical rule] | [column two] MANSUT, libraire, 30, place St-André-des-Arts. | MAISON, libraire, 29, quai des Augustins. | DAUVIN et

FONTAINE, libr., pass. des Panoramas. | [end columns] | *Et à la Librairie des Étrangers, rue Neuve-Saint-Augustin*, 55. | A LONDRES, CHEZ W. JEFFS, 15, BURLINGTON-ARCADE. | [short rule] | 1841.

Third edition, Paris, 1841. Originally published, Paris, 1815 (item 126).

212 x 129 mm. 2 vols. Vol. I. π^2 a-e^8 f^4 1-25^8; 246 leaves, pp. [i-vii] viii-xcii [1] 2-399 [400]. Vol. II. π^2 1-27^8 28^6; 224 leaves, pp. [*4*] [1] 2-443 [444].

Illustrations: Vol. I. 12 lithographed folding plates of pastries and pastry designs, numbered 2-13. Vol. II. 24 lithographed folding plates of pastries and pastry designs, numbered 14-41.

Bibliographies: Bitting, p. 74; Drexel 159; Horn-Arndt 407; Oberlé (1) 189 and 190; Schraemli (1) 104; Simon BG 287; Vicaire 144 in a note; Wheaton and Kelly 1066.

Copies: *NUC* (Buffalo and Erie County Public Library and Library of Congress). Wheaton and Kelly (Radcliffe only).

128a. Chambray, Louis, marquis de, 1713-1783.

L'ART | DE CULTIVER | *LES POMMIERS,* | *LES POIRIERS,* | ET DE FAIRE DES CIDRES | *Selon l'usage de la Normandie.* | Par M. le Marquis de Chambray. | [ornament] | *A PARIS,* | Chez GANEAU rue Saint- Séverin, près- | Église, | aux armes de Dombes & à Saint-Louis | [two short rules] | M. DCC. LXV. | *AVEC PERMISSION.*

First edition, Paris, 1765.

12 mo. π^2 A-D$^{8.4}$ E^8 F^2; 36 leaves, pp. [*4*] [1] 2-66 [2].

Bibliographies: Vicaire 160.

Copies: *BMC*, *BNC* and *NUC* (National Agricultural Library and University of California Davis).

129. Chambray, Louis, marquis de, 1713-1783.

L'ART DE FAIRE | LE | BON CIDRE, | Avec la manière de cultiver les | Pommiers et Poiriers selon l'usage | de la Normandie; | Par le Marquis DE CHAMBRAY. |

Précédé | DE L'ESSAI | SUR LES PRINCIPES DE LA GREFFE, | Par CABANIS; | On y a joint | La Composition pur guérir les maladies | des arbres, par M. FORSITH. | [short fancy rule] | A PARIS, | Chez MARCHANT, rue des Grands-Augustins, no. 12. | AN XI (1803).

Fourth edition, Paris, 1803. Originally published as *L'Art de cultiver les pommiers, les poiries, et de faire des cidres selon l'usage de la Normandie*, Paris, 1765 (item 128a). Other editions were published in 1781, 1782, and 1803.

164 x 90 mm. π^4 1-6^{12} 7^2; 78 leaves, pp. [i-iii] iv-vii [viii] [1] 2-148. Bound with Edmé Beguillet's *OEnologie* (item 69).

Illustration: Engraved folding plate on grafting with explanation on pp. 106-108.

Bibliographies: Bitting, p. 82; Vicaire 160 in a note.

Copies: *NUC* (Library of Congress only).

130. Champier, Symphorien.

Rosa Gallica aggrega | toris Lugdunēsis domini Symphoriani Chāperij omnibus | sanitatē affectātibus vtilis & necessaria. Que in se cōtinet pre | cepta, auctoritates, atq[ue] sentētias memoratu dignas, ex Hip | pocratis, Galeni, Erasistrati, Asclepiadis, Diascoridis, Ra= | sis, Haliabatis, Isaac, Auicēnae, multorūq[ue] aliorū clarorum | virorum libris in vnum collectas: quae ad medicam artem re | ctāq[ue] viuendi formā plurimū conducūt. Vna cū sua pretio= | sa Margarita: De Medici atq[ue] egri officio. | [woodcut] | Venundatur ab Iodoco Badio.

Colophon: Emissum hoc opus interum ex officina Ascē | siana. Anno Domini. M.DXVIII. ad Calen- | das Nouembres.

Second edition, Paris, 1518. Brunet claims the work was originally published in Nancy in 1512 but P. Allut, in his *Etude biographique et bibliographique sur Symphorica Champier* (Lyon, 1859) doubts the existence of this edition, crediting the Paris, 1514, edition, as the first.

8vo. A^8 a-r^8; 144 leaves; ff. [*8*] 1-136.

Illustration: Woodcut on title-page.

Bibliographies: Durling 944; Maggs 54; Oberlé (1) 59 and 60; Simon BB II, 135; Vicaire, 160.

Copies: *BMC, BNC,* and *NUC* (Countway Library, National Library of Medicine and New York Academy of Medicine). Note: *NUC* records a Nancy, 1512, edition at the Countway Library but Richard J. Wolfe, Curator of Rare Books and Manuscripts there, reports that they have no edition earlier than that of 1514.

131. Chanvalon, d. 1765.

MANUEL │ *DES* │ CHAMPS, │ OU │ *RECUEIL CHOISI,* │ INSTRUCTIF ET AMUSANT, │ de tout ce qui est le plus nécessaire │ & le plus utile pour vivre avec ai- │ sance & agrément à la Campagne. │ *Par M. DE CHANVALON, Prêtre* │ *de l'Ordre de Malthe.* │ DEUXIEME ÉDITION. │ [ornament] │ A PARIS, │ Chez LOTTIN, le jeune, Libraire. │ [two short rules] │ M. DCC. LXV. │ *Avec Privilege du Roi.*

Second edition, Paris, 1765. Originally published, Paris, 1764.

8vo. a⁸ A-Dd⁸; 224 leaves, pp. [i-iv] v-xvi [1] 2-429 [430-432].

Bibliographies: Oberlé (2) 103; Wheaton and Kelly 1142.

Copies: *NUC* (Harvard and Rutgers).

131a. Chaptal, Jean-Antoine-Claude, comte de Chanteloup, 1756-1832.

L'ART │ DE │ FAIRE, GOUVERNER, │ ET │ PERFECTIONNER LES VINS. │ PAR le citoyen CHAPTAL, Ministre de │ l'Intérieur, Membre de l'Institut national, et │ des Sociétés d'Agriculture des départemens de │ la Seine, Morbihan, Hérault, etc. │ ÉDITION ORIGINALE, seule avouée par l'Auteur. │ [short wavy rule] │ A PARIS, │ DELALAIN fils, Libraire, quai des Augustins, nº. 29. │ [short double rule] │ DE L'IMPRIMERIE DE MARCHANT. │ AN X.–1801.

First edition, separate issue, first printing, Paris, 1801. Gérard Oberlé was the first bibliographer to record the two printings of this piece. In the first the publisher's address is given as quai des Augustins, no. 29 and in the later as quai des Augustins, no. 38. This work was published both separately and as the first part of volume two of the *Traité théorique et pratique sur la culture de la vigne, avec l'art de faire le vin...* (Paris, 1801, 2 vols.) (item 132). The designation "*TOME II.*" appears at the foot of the page for leaves A1^r-M1^r in both the separate issue and in the *Traité théorique*; Signature N was separately printed for each issue because in the *Traité théorique* N2 begins a new section of text. In the separate issue N2 contains a *table des chapitres*.

216 x 135 mm. π^2 A-M^8 N^2; 100 leaves, pp. [*4*] [1] 2-194 [*2*].

Bibliographies: Oberlé (1) 949; Simon BV, p. 18.

Copies: Separate issue, *NUC* (Library Company of Philadelphia, Library of Congress, University of Chicago). The *NUC* does not distinguish between the two printings of the separate issue.

132. Chaptal, Jean-Antoine-Claude, comte de Chanteloup, 1756-1832.

TRAITÉ | THÉORIQUE ET PRATIQUE | SUR LA CULTURE DE LA VIGNE, | AVEC | L'ART DE FAIRE LE VIN, | LES EAUX-DE-VIE, ESPRIT-DE-VIN, | VINAIGRES SIMPLES ET COMPOSÉS; | PAR le Cen. CHAPTAL, Ministre de l'Intérieur, Conseiller d'Etat, | membre de l'Institut national de France; des Sociétés d'Agriculture des | Départemens de la Seine, de l'Hérault, du Morbihan; etc. M. l'Abbé | ROZIER, membre de plusieurs Académies, auteur du *Cours* | *Complet d'Agriculture;* les Cens. PARMENTIER, de l'Institut | national; et DUSSIEUX, de la Société d'Agriculture de Paris. | OUVRAGE dans lequel se trouvent les meilleures méthodes pour faire, gouverner et | perfectionner les VINS et EAUX-DE-VIE; avec XXI Planches représentant les | diverses espèces de Vignes; les Machines et Instrumens servant à la fabrication des | Vins et Eaux-de-Vie. | TOME PREMIER. [TOME SECOND.] | [short fancy rule] | A PARIS, | Chez DELALAIN, fils, libraire, quai des Augustins, no. 29. | [two short rules] | DE L'IMPRIMERIE DE MARCHANT. | AN IX. – 1801.

First edition, Paris, 1801.

197 x 121 mm. 2 vols. Vol. I. a^8 A-Bb^8 Cc^4; 212 leaves, pp. [i-v] vi-xvi [1] 2-408. Vol. II. [a]^4 b^2 A-Mm^8 Nn^4; 290 leaves, pp. [i-v] vi-x [2] [1] 2-567 [568]. Folding letter press table facing page 1 in each volume, and a third folding letterpress table facing p. 508 in volume two.

Illustrations: Vol. I. Twelve engraved plates illustrating varieties of wine grapes. Vol. II. Nine engraved plates (three folding) illustrating wine making apparatus.

Bibliographies: Oberlé (2) 116-117; Simon BV 18.

Copies: *BMC*, *BNC*, and *NUC* (5 copies).

133. La Charcuterie.

LA CHARCUTERIE, | OU | L'ART | DE SALER, FUMER, APPRÊTER ET
CUIRE | TOUTES LES PARTIES DIFFÉRENTES DU | COCHON ET DU
SANGLIER. | POUR FAIRE SUITE A LA *CUISINÈRE DE CAMPAGNE.* | [short
fancy rule] | A PARIS, | CHEZ AUDOT, LIBRAIRE, | rue des
Mathurins-St.-Jacques, no 18. | 1818.

First edition, Paris, 1818.

185 x 109 mm. [1]^8 2^4 3-6$^{8.4}$ 7^6(-7$_6$); 41 leaves, pp. [i-v] vi-xii [13] 14-82. Twelve
page publisher's catalogue, dated April 1819 bound in.

Bibliographies: Vicaire 165.

Copies: No other copy of this edition located. *NUC* locates a single copy of the
second edition, 1826 (University of California, Berkeley).

134. Chareau, Paul-Benjamin.

SCIENCE | DU BIEN VIVRE | OU | MONOGRAPHIE DE LA CUISINE |
ENVISAGÉE SOUS SON ASPECT PHYSIQUE, INTELLECTUEL ET MORAL, |
GUIDE DE LA MAITRESSE DE MAISON; | SUIVIE | DE MILLE NOUVELLES
RECETTES | PAR ORDRE RÉGULIER, | DU SERVICE DE LA TABLE; | D'une
liste des provisions que l'on doit faire dans un ménage, et de l'indication des pays d'où
elles peuvent être tirées; | D'un calendrier culinaire; | D'une nomenclature des vins de
choix et de l'ordre dans lequel ils doivent être servis; | De la préparation et de
l'arrangement du dessert; | D'une nomenclautre de tous les ustensiles nécessaires dans
une cuisine; | D'un vocabulaire des termes employés à la cuisine et à l'office; | Des
travaux de l'office; | De la description des menus pour 3, 5, 7 et jusqu'à 20 convives;
| De la composition des menus de diners maigres; | Des moyens de bien faire le café,
suivis de quelques conseils sur la manière dont il doit être servi; | PAR PAUL BEN ET
A. D. | [short rule] | PARIS | CHEZ MARTINON, LIBRAIRE, 4, RUE DU
COQ-SAINT-HONORÉ; | CHEZ Mme LALLEMAND-LÉPINE, LIBRAIRE, | 52,
RUE DE RICHELIEU; | Et à la Direction du *Musée des Familles*, 4, rue Gaillon. |
[short rule] | 1844

First edition, Paris, 1844.

242 x 148 mm. π^4 1-28^4 29$_1$; 117 leaves, pp. [8] [1] 2-225 [226].

Illustrations: Numerous wood engravings in the text.

"Paul Ben" is a pseudonym of Paul-Benjamin Chareau and "A.D." are initials of A. Desrez.

Bibliographies: Vicarie 81.

Copies: *BMC* and *BNC*.

135. Chatillon-Plessis.

CHATILLON-PLESSIS | [short rule] | [in red] LA VIE A TABLE | A LA FIN DU XIXE SIÈCLE | [in red] THÉORIE PRATIQUE ET HISTORIQUE DE GASTRONOMIE MODERNE | PHYSIOLOGIE. – DISCUSSIONS. – MOEURS ET MODE | PRATIQUE. – SERVICE DE LA TABLE ET DES RÉCEPTIONS. – LE BOIRE | LA CUISINE. – GRANDES RECETTES CULINAIRES DU SIÈCLE | LA PATISSERIE. – LES RESTAURANTS. – NOUVEAUX CLASSIQUES | DE LA TABLE. – MÉLANGES ET FANTAISIES | [short rule] | Ouvrage illustré de 170 gravures hors texte ou dans le texte | sur la vie d'autrefois et la vie d'aujourd'hui | [publisher's monogram] | PARIS | [in red] LIBRAIRIE DE FIRMIN-DIDOT ET CIE | IMPRIMEURS DE L'INSTITUT, RUE JACOB, 56 | [short rule] | 1894 | Traduction et reproduction réservées

First edition, Paris 1894.

200 x 130 mm. π^4 1-25^8 26^2; 206 leaves, pp. [*8*] [1-3] 4-387 [388] [397] 398-411 [412] = 412.

Illustrations: 170 photo engraved illustrations including a two page "Galerie des Gastronomes et Patriciens français" with an attached folding leaf identifying the persons and a folding plate reproducing four pages from *Le Figaro* for 21 December 1889. The folding plates follow page 388 and account for the hiatus in the numbering.

Bibliographies: Bitting, p. 84; Maggs 568; Wheaton and Kelly 1165.

Copies: *BMC*, *BNC*, and *NUC* (4 copies).

136. Chevallier, Jean-Baptiste-Alphonse, 1793-1879.

DICTIONNAIRE | DES ALTÉRATIONS ET FALSIFICATIONS | DES
SUBSTANCES | ALIMENTAIRES | MÉDICAMENTEUSES ET COMMERCIALES
| AVEC L'INDICATION | DES MOYENS DE LES RECONNAITRE | PAR | M. A.
CHEVALLIER | Pharmacien-chimiste, Membre de la Légion-d'Honneur, Professeur
adjoint à l'École de pharmacie; | Membre de l'Académie impériale de médecine de
Paris et de l'Académie | de médecine de Belgique; des Conseils de salubrité de Paris et
de Bruxelles; du Conseil | d'administration de la Société d'encouragement pour
l'industire nationale; | Membre correspondant des Académies | de Bordeaux, de
Reims, de Rouen, de diverses Sociétés savantes de l'Allemagne, d'Anvers, de la
Bavière, | de Bruges, de Liége, de Lisbonne, de Londres, de Turin, etc. | [short rule] |
Deuxième édition | REVUE, CORRIGÉE ET CONSIDÉRABLEMENT
AUGMENTÉE. | [short fancy rule] | TOME PREMIER. [TOME SECOND.] | [short
fancy rule] | PARIS | BÉCHET JEUNE, LIBRAIRE-ÉDITEUR, | Rue
Monsieur-le-Prince, 22. | CI-DEVANT PLACE DE L'ÉCOLE-DE-MÉDECINE. |
[short rule] | 1854 [1855]

Second edition, Paris, 1854-1855. Originally published, Paris, 1850-1852.

214 x 129 mm. 2 vols. Vol. I. π^2 a^4 1-35^8 36^4; 290 leaves, pp. [6] [i] ii-v [vi] [1]
2-566 [2]. Vol. II π^2 1-42^8 43^6; 344 leaves, pp. [4] [1] 2-684.

Illustrations: Vol. I. Five engraved plates (one hand colored) of apparatus and
microscope slides. Vol. II. Six engraved plates (three partly hand colored) of
apparatus.

Bibliographies: Oberlé (1) 477. Garrison and Morton 1610 and Vicaire 169 record the
original edition.

Copies: *BNC* and *NUC* (6 copies).

137. Chevrier, A.

LE | CUISINIER | NATIONAL ET UNIVERSEL, | contenant | LES
RECETTES DE LA CUISINE PROPREMENT DITE, ET LA CHAR- |
CUTERIE, DE LA PATISSERIE, DE L'OFFICE DANS SES DIVERSES |
PARTIES; | TERMINÉ | PAR UNE NOTICE SUR TOUS LES VINS. |
RÉDIGÉ ET MIS EN ORDRE D'APRÈS LES PLUS CÉLÈBRES PRATICIENS
DANS L'ART | CULINAIRE MODERNE. | Par M. A. Chevrier, | Maitre-d'Hôtel
en chef du Cercle des Étrangers, etc. | [two short rules] | AVEC PLANCHES

GRAVÉES. | [short fancy rule] | PARIS, | CHEZ TOUS LES MARCHANDS DE NOUVEAUTÉS. | [short rule] | 1836.

First edition, Paris, 1836.

210 x 122 mm. $\pi^4(-\pi 1)$ 1^4 2^{10} χ^2 $3\text{-}27^8$ 28^6; 233 leaves, pp. [i-iii] iv [3] 4-437 [438]. Signatures 1, 2, and χ are signed as though two gatherings of eight leaves with signature 2 signed on the fifth leaf.

Illustrations: Lithographed frontispiece of a kitchen scene and two folding lithographed plates, one of kitchen utensils and one of dishes and table settings.

Bibliographies: Bitting, p. 86; Vicaire 170.

Copies: *BNC* and *NUC* (Iowa State University and Library of Congress).

138. Chevrier, A.

NOUVEAU MANUEL | DU | CUISINIER. | CONTENANT | LES RECETTES LES PLUS MODERNES | POUR FAIRE A PEU DE FRAIS UNE | CUISINE CONFORTABLE; | OUVRAGE | ENTIEREMENT NEUF, RÉDIGÉ D'APRÈS LES | OBSERVATIONS DES PLUS CÉLÈBRES HOMMES DE | BOUCHE DU DIX-NEUVIÈME SIÈCLE; | PAR M. CHEVRIER. | [short rule] | PARIS, | IMPRIMERIE DE Mme HUZARD (née VALLAT LA CHAPELLE), | Rue de l'Éperon, no 1.

First edition, Paris, 1836.

139 x 86 mm. π^2 $1\text{-}24^6$ 25^4; 150 leaves, pp. [4] [1] 2-296.

Illustration: Lithographed frontispiece of chef cooking a covered dish.

Bibliographies: Vicaire 170.

Copies: No other copy of this edition located. *BNC* lists the second edition, 1838.

139. Clerc, Louis.

MANUEL | DE | L'AMATEUR D'HUITRES, | OU | L'ART DE LES PÊCHER, | De les parquer, de les faire verdir, de les | préserver des maladies qui peuvent les at- | taquer, de les conserver fraîches pendant | un assez long espace de tems, de reconnaî- |

tre celles qui sont dans cet état et de les | ouvrir facilement; | SUIVI | DES QUALITÉS ALIMENTAIRES ET PROPRIÉTÉS | MÉDICALES DE CE MOLLUSQUE, AINSI QUE DE | L'ADRESSE DES PERSONNES QUI LE VENDENT. | PAR M. L. CLERC, F. D. M. N. | [short rule] | Ha! dans combien de déjeuners les huîtres | n'ont-elles pas fourni l'esprit d'un couplet, | le sel d'un bon mot et le trait d'un madrigal! | [short rule] | PARIS, | CHEZ L'ÉDITUER, | LIBRAIRIE FRANÇAISE ET ÉTRANGÈRE, | Palais-Royal, Galerie de Pierre, no. 185 et 186, | au coin du Passage Valois. | [two short rules] | 1828.

First edition, Paris, 1828.

131 x 81 mm. [1]^6 2-6^6 χ1 [7]^6 [8]^2; pp. [i-v] vi-viii [9] 10-79 [80]; ^{2}[i] ii-viii.

Illustration: Engraved, hand-colored, folding frontispiece.

Bibliographies: Vicaire 182.

Copies: *BNC*.

140. Cocks, Charles.

GUIDE DE L'ÉTRANGER | A BORDEAUX ET DANS LA GIRONDE. | [short rule] | BORDEAUX | SES ENVIRONS | ET | SES VINS | CLASSÉS PAR ORDRE DE MÉRITE, | PAR | CHARLES COCKS, | Agrégé de l'Université de France. | [short fancy rule] | BORDEAUX, | FERET FILS, LIBRAIRE-ÉDITEUR, | 15, Fossés de l'Intendance. | [short rule] | 1850.

First edition, Bordeaux, 1850. Cocks also wrote a work titled *Bordeaux: Its Wines and the Claret Country*, London, 1846, which evidently was a forerunner of this work. The 1850 *Guide* was the first in which Cocks classified the wines of Bordeaux in order of merit.

170 x 101 mm. π^2 1^8 1✻^{4}-7^8 7✻^{4} 8-19^6 20^4; 182 leaves, pp. [*4*] [i] ii-iii [iv] [5] 6-319 [320].

Illustrations: Four lithographed plates of Bordeaux landmarks and a folding lithographed plan of the city in 1850.

Bibliographies: Simon BV, p. 264.

Copies: *BNC*.

141. Code culinaire.

CODE | CULINAIRE, | MANUEL COMPLET | DU CUISINIER, DE LA CUISINIÈRE | ET DE LA MAITRESSE DE MAISON, | RÉCEPTION, SERVICE, OFFICE, PATISSERIE, SOIN DE LA | CAVE, CONSERVATION DES SUBSTANCES | ALIMENTAIRES, ETC. | [short fancy rule] | PARIS. | J. P. RORET, ÉDITEUR, | quai des Augustins, no 17 bis. | [two short rules] | 1830.

First edition, Paris, 1830.

152 x 96 mm. [1-3]^6 4-31^6 χ1 2χ1 3χ1 32^4(-32$_1$); 192 leaves, pp. [1-5] 6-383 [384]. Publisher's printed wrappers.

Illustrations: Lithographed frontispiece and folding "Carte gastronomique de la France."

Bibliographies: Drexel 153.

Copies: No other copy located.

142. Collet, Pierre, 1693-1770.

INSTRUCTIONS | ET PRIERES | *A L'USAGE* | DES DOMESTIQUES | ET DES PERSONNES | qui travaillent en ville, &c. | OUVRAGE | qui peut servir aux Confesseurs. | *Par M. COLLET Prêtre d.l.C. d. l.M.&c.* | [ornament] | A PARIS, | Chez les Libraires associés. | [two short rules] | M. DCC. LVIII. | *Avec Approbation & Privilege du Roi.*

First edition, Paris, 1758.

12 mo. π^2 a-f^6 A-Aa^6 Bb^6($\pm$Bb1) Cc-Ee^6; pp. [*4*] [i-ii] iii-lxxi [lxxii] [1] 2-332 [*4*]. First leaf blank. Cancellans Bb1 signed "✱Bb."

Bibliographies: Unrecorded in the bibliographies consulted.

Copies: *BNC* and *NUC* (Harvard only).

143. Colnet du Ravel, Charles-Jean-Auguste-Maximilien de, 1768-1832.

L'ART | DE DINER EN VILLE, | A L'USAGE | DES GENS DE LETTRES. | POËME EN IV CHANTS. | Savant en ce métier, si cher aux beaux-esprits, | Dont Montmaur autrefois fit leçon dans Paris. | BOILEAU, Satire I. | A PARIS, | Chez COLNET, Libraire, quai Voltaire, au coin de | la rue du Bac; | Et chez DELAUNAY, Palais-Royal, galerie de bois. | [short fancy rule] | 1810.

First edition, Paris, 1810.

152 x 99 mm. [1]^6 2-11^6 12^6 (-12$_6$); 71 leaves, pp. [1-5] 6-142.

Bibliographies: Maggs 348; Oberlé (1) 391; Vicarie 191.

Copies: *BMC* and *NUC* (Library of Congress and University of California, Berkeley).

143a. Combles, M. de, d. 1770?

L'ÉCOLE | *DU JARDIN* | *POTAGER,* | QUI COMPREND LA DESCRIPTION | exacte de toutes les Plantes Portageres; les qualités | de Terre, les situations & les climats qui leur sont | propres; la culture qu'elles demandent; leurs pro- | priétes pour la vie, & leurs vertus pour la santé; | les differens moyens de les multiplier; le tems de | récueillir les graines; leur durée, &c. La maniere | de dresser & de conduire les Couches & d'élever | des Champignons en toute saison, &c. | *Par l'Auteur du Traité de la Culture des Pêchers.* | NOUVELLE EDITION. | [short rule] | *TOME PREMIERE.* [*TOME SECONDE.*] | [illustration of people working in garden] | A PARIS, *rue S. Jacques.* | Chez [next two lines bracketed to left] ANT. BOUDET, Imprimeur du Roi. | P. A. LE PRIEUR, Imprimeur du Roi. | [thick-thin rule] | M. DCC. LII. | *AVEC APPROBATION, ET PRIVILEGE DU ROI.*

Second edition, Paris, 1752. Originally published, Paris, 1749. The fifth edition, Paris, 1802, was published as "Par M. de Combles."

12 mo. 2 vols. Vol. I. π^4 a^6 A-Y^{12} Z^4; 278 leaves, pp. [*20*] [1] 2-536. Vol. II. π^4 A-Aa^{12} Bb^8; 300 leaves, pp. [*8*] [1] 2-586 [*6*]. First leaf blank.

Illustrations: Engraved frontispiece of a garden scene on π1^v in Vol. I. Engraved vignette of two gardeners with watering can and rake looking at huge cabbage on both title-pages.

Bibliographies: Hunt 544.

Copies: *BNC*, *NUC* (National Agricultural Library only).

144. La Contre-lesine.

LA │ CONTRE-LESINE, │ Ou plustost │ DISCOVRS, CONSTITV- │ TIONS ET LOVANGES DE │ la Liberalité, remplis de moralité, de │ doctrine, & beaux traits admirables. │ *Augmentez d'vne Comedie intitulee,* │ LES NOPCES D'ANTILESINE. │ Ouurage du Pasteur Monopolitain. │ *Et traduit nouuellement de l'Italien.* │ [engraving] │ A PARIS, │ Chez ROLET BOVTONNÉ, au Palais en │ la gallerie des prisonniers, pres la │ Chancellerie. │ [short rule] │ M. DC. XVIII.

Second edition, Paris, 1618. Translation of *La Contralesina* originally published in Italian in Venice, 1603, and in this translation, Paris, 1604.

12mo. a^8 a-x^{12} y^6 z^2; 268 leaves, ff. [*8*] 1-260.

Bibliographies: Bitting, p. 535; Maggs 108; Wheaton and Kelly 1364. Vicarie 197 records the Paris, 1604, edition.

Copies: *BMC* and *NUC* (5 copies).

See also item 188.

145. Cousin, Maurice, comte de Courchamps, 1783-1849.

NÉO-PHYSIOLOGIE DU GOUT │ PAR ORDRE ALPHABÉTIQUE, │ OU │ DICTIONNAIRE GÉNÉRAL │ DE LA │ CUISINE FRANÇAISE │ ANCIENNE ET MODERNE, │ ainsi que de l'Office et de la Pharmacie domestique, │ OUVRAGE OU L'ON TROUVERA TOUTES LES PRESCRIPTIONS NÉCESSAIRES A LA CONFECTION │ DES ALIMENTS NUTRITIFS OU D'AGRÉMENT │ A L'USAGE DES PLUS GRANDES ET DES PLUS PETITES FORTUNES; │ *Publication qui doit suppléer à tous les livres de Cuisine dont le public n'a que trop expérimenté* │ *le charlatanisme, l'insuffisance et l'obscurité;* │ Enrichi de plusieurs menus, prescriptions culinaires, et autres opuscules inédits de M. de La Reynière, │ Auteur de l'ALMANACH DES GOURMANDS; │ SUIVI D'UNE COLLECTION GÉNÉRALE DES MENUS FRANÇAIS DEPUIS LE DOUZIÈME SIÈCLE, │ et terminé par une PHARMACOPÉE qui contient toutes les préparations médicinales dont l'usage est le plus utile et le plus familier, │ DÉDIÉ A L'AUTEUR DES MÉMOIRES DE LA MARQUISE DE CRÉQUY. │ Héraclite avait dit que l'homme est un animal *pleurant;*

| Démocrite avait dit que l'homme est un animal *riant*; | M. de la Reynière a dit que l'homme est un animal *cuisinier*. | [short fancy rule] | PARIS. | AU BRUEAU DU DICTIONNAIRE GÉNÉRAL DE CUISINE, | 16, BOULEVART MONTMARTRE. | [short rule] | 1839.

First edition, Paris, 1839.

246 x 158 mm. π^2 1-39^8 40^6; 320 leaves, pp. [*4*] [i] ii-iii [iv] [5] 6-635 [636].

Note: This work was published anonymously but is attributed to Cousin de Courchamps by Barbier (*Dictionnaire des ouvrages anonymes*, vol. 3, col. 409). Vicaire enters it under title, mentioning the attribution in a note. The author was baptised Pierre-Marie-Jean Cousin, but always wrote his name Cousen and used the given names Maurice or Marius. He was the author of the *Souvenirs de la Marquise de Créquy* to whom, tongue-in-cheek, the *Néophysiologie du goût* is dedicated. The second edition of this work was published under the new title *Dictionnaire général de la cuisine française ancienne et moderne*, Paris, 1853.

Bibliographies: Simon BG 1083; Vicaire 622.

Copies: *BMC*.

146. Cousin d'Avallon, Charles-Yves Cousin, *called*, 1769-1840.

LA NOUVELLE | CUISINIÈRE BOURGEOISE, | CONTENANT, | 1°. Outre les recettes générales et particulières propres | à faire une bonne cuisine à peu de frais, l'art de | découper, avec autant de dextérité que d'élégance, | toutes sortes de viande, de volaille et de gibier; | 2°. L'art de trousser la volaille et le gibier; | 3°. La manière de servir une table de huit, douze, | seize et vingt couverts; | 4°. De faire et confectionner toute espèce de confitures | au prix le plus modéré; | SUIVIE | De LA BONNE MÉNAGÈRE DE LA VILLE ET DES CHAMPS, | qui enseigne tous les moyens propres à élever la volaille, à faire | le beurre et le fromage, à conserver les légumes, les fruits; à | faire les vinaigres, les ratafias, les pâtes et toutes les boissons | économiques; ouvrage indispensable pour toutes les personnes | qui veulent, à peu de frais, faire bonne chère; terminé par un | court Appendix sur la manière de faire et d'orthographier les | divers mémoires de la comptabilité domestique. | *Par l'Auteur du Parfait Cuisinier.* | PRIX: 1 FRANC 80 CENTIMES POUR PARIS. | A PARIS, | CHEZ { DAVI et LOCARD, Libraires, rue de Seine, no. 54, | faub. St.-Germain, vis-à-vis les Deux-Magots; | PIGOREAU, Libraire, place St.-Germain-l'Auxerrois. | [short rule] | 1815.

First edition, Paris, 1815.

180 x 110 mm. π^2 1-11^{12} 12^{10}; 144 leaves, pp. [*4*] [1] 2-283 [284].

Illustration: Engraved frontispiece of a kitchen scene.

Bibliographies: Vicaire 238, in a note.

Copies: No other copy of this edition located.

147.   Cousin d'Avallon, Charles-Yves Cousin, *called*, 1769-1840.

LE | PARFAIT CUISINIER | *OU* | LE BREVIAIRE DES GOURMANDS, | *Contenant les Recettes les plus nouvelles* | *dans l'art de la Cuisine, et de nouveaux* *procédés* | *propres à porter cet art à sa dernière perfection,* | SECONDE ÉDITION, | *Entièrement refondue, augmentée du Cuisinier* | *étranger, et divers Recettes très précieuses.* | *Orné d'une Gravure désignant les trois Services,* | [fancy type] Par | A. T. RAIMBAULT, | *Homme de Bouche;* | *Revu, avec le plus grand soin,* | *Par Mr. Borel, ci-devant Chef de* | *cuisine de S. E. l'Ambassadeur de Portugal.* | A PARIS, | *Chez Delacour, Libraire, Rue J. J. Rousseau, No. 14.* | [short rule] | *Février 1811.*

Title-page of the second part:

LE | CUISINIER ÉTRANGER, | POUR FAIRE SUITE AU PARFAIT CUISINIER; | *Contenant une Notice raisonnée de tous les mêts* | *étrangers qu'on peut servir sur une* *table* | *française.* | PAR UN GASTRONOME COSMOPOLITE. | [short rule] | J'ai visité les Cuisines de tout le | globe, et j'ai écrit ces Recettes. | [short rule] | A PARIS, | Chez DELACOUR, Imprimeur-Libraire, rue J.-J. | Rousseau, no. 14, vis-à-vis la Poste aux Lettres. | [short rule] | 1811.

Second edition, Paris, 1811.   Originally published, Paris, 1809.

178 x 107 mm. π^2 1-12^{12} 13^8; ^{2}1-2^{12} 3^6; 184 leaves, pp. [*4*] [1] 2-304; ^{2}[i-v] vi [7] 8-60.

Illustrations: Engraved frontispiece titled "Le Parfait Cuisinier," engraved title-page, and engraved folding plate of table setting for three courses.

Note: A. T. Raimbault and M. Borel are both pseudonyms of Cousin d'Avallon.

Bibliographies: Vicaire 728 in a note under the third edition, 1814. Vicaire dates the first edition 1810 but the *NUC* records copies dated 1809 at the Library of Congress and the New York Public Library.

Copies: *NUC* (New York Public Library only).

148. Croisette.

LA | BONNE ET PARFAITE | CUISINIÈRE | GRANDE ET SIMPLE CUISINE | OUVRAGE NOUVEAU ET TRÈS-COMPLET | contenant | LE SERVICE, LA MANIÈRE DE DÉCOUPER LES VIANDES, L'ART | DE LA CUISINE; VIANDES, POISSONS, LÉGUMES, PATISSERIE, | SIROPS, ETC., ETC. | Par CROISETTE, | officier de bouche, cuisinier en chef. | [publisher's monogram] | PARIS. | FONTENEY ET PELTIER, ÉDITEURS, | 4, RUE HAUTEFEUILLE.

First edition, Paris, ca. 1840.

165 x 107 mm. 1-14$^{12.6}$; 126 leaves, pp. [i-v] vi [7] 8-252. Publisher's printed boards.

Illustrations: Twenty-three wood engravings in the text, three showing table settings and twenty illustrating carving.

Bibliographies: This edition unrecorded in the bibliographies consulted.

Copies: *BNC*.

149. Cussac, Jean.

PISCICEPTOLOGIE, | OU | L'ART DE LA PÊCHE | A LA LIGNE; | DISCOURS SUR LES POISSONS, | LA MANIERE | DE LES PRENDRE ET DE LES ACCOMMODER; | LA PECHE AUX FILETS | ET AUTRES INSTRUMENTS; | SUIVI | D'un TRAITÉ DES ETANGS, VIVIERS, FOSSÉS, | RÉSERVOIRS, et les moyens d'en tirer avan- | tage; avec un grand nombre de figures | en taille-douce ou *Descriptions des* | *Piéges* propres à ces différentes Pêches. | PAR J. C✳✳✳. | PARIS, | DE L'IMPRIMERIE DE CUSSAC, LIBRAIRE, | Rue Montmartre, no. 30, vis-à-vis celle du Jour. | [short rule] | 1816.

First edition, Paris, 1816.

176 x 111 mm. a^{12} A-Q^{12} R^2; 206 leaves, pp. [i-v] vi-xxiv [1] 2-388.

Illustrations: Engraved frontispiece on the recto of which is an engraving of Marcus Crassus, and twenty-eight engraved plates illustrating techniques of fishing.

Bibliographies: Unrecorded in the bibliographies consulted.

Copies: *BMC*, *BNC*, and *NUC* (American Philosophical Society, Harvard, and the University of California, Berkeley).

150. De l'usage du caphé, du thé, et du chocolate.

DE L'VSAGE | DU | CAPHE', | DV THE', | *ET DV* | CHOCOLATE. | [ornament] | *A LYON,* | Chez IEAN GIRIN, & | BARTHELEMY RIVIERE, | en ruë Merciere, à la Prudence. | [short rule] | M. DC. LXXI. | *Avec permission des Superieurs.*

First edition, Lyon, 1671.

12mo. ✻^{12} A-G^{12} H^{12}(-H11,12); 106 leaves, ; [*24*] 1-188.

Illustrations: Woodcut of coffee plant and coffee grinder on ✻12^v.

Bibliographies: Bitting, p. 612; Crahan 134; Vicaire 850; Wheaton and Kelly 1814.

Copies: *BMC*, *BNC*, and *NUC* (7 copies).

Note: The authorship of this work has been widely discussed. Vicaire, in his entry for Dufour's *Traitez nouveaux et curieux du café, du thé et du chocolate*, Lyon, 1685, notes that Dufour remarks in his preface that about twelve years before he had published a translation of a Latin manuscript on this subject. Vicaire suggests *De l'usage du caphé, du thé, et du chocolate* may be that translation. It should be noted, however, that 114 of the 188 pages of this small volume consist of a reprint of René Moreau's translation of a treatise on chocolate, itself variously attributed to Antonio Colmonero de Ledesma and Bartolomeo Marradon, which originally was published in Madrid, 1631, and in Moreau's French translation in Paris, 1643 (see Vicaire 190). The balance of the work (47 pages on coffee and 25 on tea) draws heavily on earlier published sources, both ancient and modern, and may be nothing more than a compilation by the publishers, Girin and Riviere. The *BMC* records Jacob Spon, the translator of Dufour's *Traitez* into Latin, as the compiler, but there is no evidence in the book for this attribution. See also Dufour (items 168-170).

151. Debaussaux, L. F.

L'ART | DE | FAIRE LA BIÈRE, | OUVRAGE ÉLÉMENTAIRE THÉORIQUE | ET PRATIQUE, | MIS A LA PORTÉE DE TOUT LE MONDE, | Donnant les moyens de faire la Bière en toute saison | avec nombre de végétaux et produits de végétaux, | soit racines, tiges, fruits, semences, etc.; les moyens | de la conserver plusieurs années, et de la rendre propre | aux embarcations; | CONTENANT AUSSI | La description de plusieurs Ventilateurs hydrauliques, Séchoirs | calorifères, nouveau Moulin à Drèche, nouveau Rafraîchissoir, | à l'usage des Brasseries, des Distilleries et de beaucoup d'autres | établissemens, AVEC PLANCHES ET TAILLE-DOUCE; | PAR L. F. D. | A PARIS, | CHEZ CARILIAN-GOEURY, | Libraire des Ingénieurs, de l'École royale des Ponts et Chaus- | sées et de celle des Mines, quai des Augustins, no. 41. | [short rule] | 1821.

First edition, Paris, 1821.

202 x 124 mm. $\pi^8(-\pi 1)$ 1-20^8 21^2; 169 leaves, pp. [2] [i-v] vi-xii [1] 2-323 [324].

Illustrations: Three engraved plates showing apparatus for brewing.

Bibliographies: Vicaire 47.

Copies: *BMC* and *NUC* (John Crerar Library only).

152. Decomberousse, Hyacinthe-François-Isaac, 1786-1856.

LE | MINISTÉRIEL, | OU | LA MANIE DES DINERS, | COMÉDIE EN UN ACTE ET EN VERS, | Par l'Auteur de l'*ULTRA*, Comédie en vers, | Dont la représentation u'a pas été autorisée par la Ministre de la Police. | [short rule] | ....Quel dîné! | Les Ministres m'ont donné! | DE BÉRANGER. | [short rule] | [short fancy rule] | A PARIS, | CHEZ LADVOCAT, LIBRAIRE, | ÉDITEUR DES FASTES DE LA GLOIRE, | PALAIS-ROYAL, GALERIE DE BOIS, Nos. 197 ET 198. | [short rule] | De l'Imprimerie de HOCQUET, rue de Faubourg Montmartre, no. 4. | [short fancy rule] | 1819.

First edition, Paris, 1819.

214 x 128 mm. [A]^4 B-E^4; 20 leaves, pp. [1-3] 4-39 [40]. Modern cloth, publisher's printed wrappers preserved.

Bookplate: Ex-libris Robert Viel.

Bibliographies: Unrecorded in the bibliographies consulted.

Copies: *BMC* and *BNC*.

153. Demachy, Jacques-François, 1728-1803.

ÉCONOMIE | RUSTIQUE, | *OU* | NOTIONS SIMPLES ET FACILES | Sur la Botanique, la Médecine, la Pharma- | cie, la Cuisine & l'Office : Sur la Juris- | prudence rurale : Sur le Calcul , la Géo- | métrie-Pratique, l'Arpentage, la Cons- | truction & le Toisé des Bâtimens, &c. | avec les prix des différens matériaux & | de la main-d'oeuvre, pour être à l'abri | des tromperies des Ouvriers. | *Ouvrage nécessaire sur-tout aux personnes qui | vivent à la campagne.* | [short rule] | Le prix relié est de 3 livres. | [short rule] | [ornament] | A PARIS, | Aux dépens de LOTTIN le jeune, rue S. Jacques, | vis-à-vis la rue de la Parcheminerie. | [two short rules] | M. DCC. LXIX. | *Avec Approbation, & Privilége du Roi.*

First edition, Paris, 1769.

12mo. a^{12} A-E^{12} F^{12}($\pm$F4) G^{12}($\pm$G7) H-Z^{12} Aa^4; 292 leaves, pp. [i-v] vi-xxiii [xxiv] [1] 2-560.

Bibliographies: Bitting, p. 120.

Copies: *BNC* and *NUC* (Library of Congress and National Library of Medicine).

154. Derys, Gaston, b. 1875.

MON DOCTEUR | LE VIN | [in red] *Aquarelles de Raoul Dufy* | TEXTE DE GASTON DERYS

Colophon: Achevé d'imprimer | en Janvier 1936 | sur les presses de | DRAEGER FRÈRES | à Paris | TYPOGRAPHIE DE A. M. CASSANDRE

First edition, Paris, Draeger, 1936.

316 x 258 mm. [1-6]^4; 24 leaves, pp. [48] first two leaves blank and first leaf folded under the cover. Publisher's lithographed wrappers.

Illustrations: Nineteen color reproductions of watercolors by Raoul Dufy in the text.

Bibliographies: Oberlé (1) 1006; Schraemli (1) 141; Schraemli (2) 125.

Copies: *NUC* (5 copies).

155. Deslyons, Jean, 1615-1700.

DISCOVRS | ECCLESIASTIQVES | CONTRE | LE PAGANISME | DES ROYS DE LA FEVE | ET DV ROY-BOIT, | Pratiqués par les Chrétiens | charnels en la Veille & au | Iour de l'Epiphanie de N.S. | IESVS-CHRIST. | *Par M. Iean DESLYONS,* | *Prestre Docteur de la Maison* | *& Societé de Sorbone, Doyen* | *& Theologal de l'Eglise Ca-* | *thedrale de Senlis.* | [ornament] | A PARIS, | Chez GUILLAUME DESPREZ, | ruë Saint Iacques, à S. Prosper. | [short rule] | M. DC. LXIV. | *Avec Approbation, & Privilege*

First edition, Paris, 1664.

12mo. a⁴ e¹² i¹² o⁴ A-B¹² C⁸ ²A-B¹² C⁸; 96 leaves, pp. [*64*] 1-64; ²1-60 [*4*]. Last two leaves blank.

Bibliographies: Bitting, p. 122; Oberlé (2) 483; Vicaire 272.

Copies: *BNC* and *NUC* (4 copies).

156. Deslyons, Jean, 1615-1700.

TRAITEZ | SINGULIERS ET NOUVEAUX | CONTRE LE PAGANISME | DU ROY-BOIT. | *Le I. Du Ieusne ancien de l'Eglise Catholique* | *la Veille des Roys.* | *Le II. De la Royauté des Saturnales remise* | *& contrefaite par les Chrestiens charnels* | *en cette Feste.* | *Le III. De la Superstition du Phoebé, ou de* | *la sottise du Febué.* | A MESSIEURS LES THEOLOGAUX | de toutes les Eglises de France. | *Par* JEAN DESLYONS *Docteur de Sorbonne, Doyen* | *& Theologal de l'Eglise Cathedrale de Senlis.* | Ouvrage utile aux Curez, aux Predicateurs | & au Peuple. | [ornament] | A PARIS | Chez la Veuve C. SAVREUX, Libraire-Juré, | au pied de la Tour de Nostre-Dame, | à l'Enseigne des trois Vertus. | [rule] | M. DC. LXX. | *Avec Approbation & Privilege du Roy.*

First edition, Paris, 1670, of Deslyons' second work on this subject, an answer to N. Barthelemy's *Apologies du banquet sanctifié de la veille des rois*, Paris, 1664. The catalog record in *NUC* wrongly states that this is a revised and enlarged edition of Deslyons' *Discours ecclesiastiques contre le paganisme des roys de la fève et du roy-boit*, Paris, 1664 (item 155).

12mo. ✲⁶ ✲✲1 a¹²(-a1) e⁶ i⁴ A¹² B¹²(-B4,5 + χ1) C¹² D¹² (D9 + 2χ1) E-O¹² P⁶; 202 leaves, pp. [*56*] 1-31, 34-92, 91-346 [2]. Last leaf blank.

Bibliographies: Simon BG 485; Oberlé (1) 496; Oberlé (2) 484; Vicaire 272.

Copies: *BMC*, *BNC*, and *NUC* (5 copies).

157. Destaminil.

LE | CUISINIER | FRANÇAIS | PERFECTIONNÉ, | CONTENANT | LES MEILLEURES PRESCRIPTIONS DE LA CUISINE | ANCIENNE ET MODERNE. | PRÉCÉDÉ | DE NOTIONS SUR LE SERVICE, DE MENUS DIVERS, D'UN VOCABULAIRE DES TERMES ET | DES USTENSILES EN USAGE POUR LA CUISINE, L'OFFICE ET LA CAVE, DE L'ART DE | DÉCOUPER ET DE SERVIR A TABLE, ETC.; | SUIVI | De l'Art de conserver les substances alimentaires, d'un Traité des altérations | et des falsifications des substances solides et liquides employées dans | l'économie domestique, des aliments dangereux et nuisibles, | des empoisonnements par les champignons, les mou- | les, le vert-de-gris; de l'asphyxie par la va- | peur du charbon, etc. | [vignette] | B. RENAULT, ÉDITEUR, | [short rule] | 1844.

First edition, Paris, 1844.

214 x 124 mm. [1]⁴ 2-22⁸ 23⁴; 176 leaves, pp. [i-v] vi-viii [9] 10-134, 151-368 = 352. Pp. i-ii (half-title?) lacking in this copy.

Illustrations: Wood engraved frontispiece and folding wood engraved plate showing four bills of fare.

Bibliographies: Bitting, p. 123; Vicaire 274.

Copies: *BNC* and *NUC* (Library of Congress only).

158. Deville, Albéric, 1773-1832.

RÉVOLUTIONIANA, | OU | ANECDOTES, ÉPIGRAMMES, | ET | saillies relatives à la révolution; | PAR PHILANA. | [rule] | Sur les ailes du Temps la Tristesse s'envole. | LAFONTAINE. | [short fancy rule] | A PARIS, | Chez MARADAN, Libraire, rue Pavée- | Saint-André-des-Arcs, no 16. | AN X.

First edition, Paris, 1802.

119 x 75 mm. [A]^6 B-Q^6 R^2; 98 leaves, pp. [1-7] 8-194 [2]. This copy lacks pp. 1-2 (half-title?). Bound with *Gastronomiana* (item 206) and *Poissardiana* (item 395).

Illustration: Engraved frontispiece titled "Les petites cause produisent souvent de grands effets."

Bibliographies: Unrecorded in the bibliographies consulted.

Copies: *BNC*.

159. Dictionnaire des plantes alimentaires.

DICTIONNAIRE | DES PLANTES ALIMENTAIRES, | *QUI PEUVENT SERVIR* | DE NOURRITURE ET DE BOISSON AUX | DIFFÉRENS PEUPLES DE LA TERRE. | CONTENANT les noms triviaux Latins et Français de ces | mêmes Plantes; les pays où croissent les éxotiques; la | méthode de les préparer en Pain, Pâtes, Pâtisseries, | Vermicels, Potages, Conserves, Confitures, Ratafias, | Liqueurs, et généralement de quelque manière qu'elles | puissent s'employer. | OU | Les Arts du Boulanger, du Pâtissier, du Vermicelier, du Confiseur, | du Distillateur- Liquoriste, du Cuisinier, réunis dans cet Ouvrage, | utile aux Cultivateurs et aux personnes qui habitent la campagne. | [rule] | TOME PREMIER. [TOME SECOND.] | [rule] | [short fancy rule] | A PARIS, | CHEZ SAMSON, Libraire, quai des Augustins | No. 69, près le Pont-Neuf. | [two short rules] | AN XII. − 1803.

First edition, Paris, 1803.

202 x 124 mm. 2 vols. Vol. I. π^4 A-Bb^8; 204 leaves, pp. [i-v] vi [vii-viii] [1] 2-398 [2]. Vol. II. π^2 A-Bb^8 Cc^4 Dd^2; 208 leaves, pp. [4] [1] 2-412.

Bibliographies: Oberlé (2) 122.

Copies: *NUC* (National Agricultural Library only).

160. Dictionnaire domestique portatif.

DICTIONNAIRE | *DOMESTIQUE* | PORTATIF, | *CONTENANT toutes les connoissances relatives à l'OEconomie* | *domestique & rurale; où l'on détaille les différentes branches de* | *l'Agriculture, la maniere de soigner les Chevaux, celle de* | *nourrir & de conserver toute sorte de Bestiaux, celle d'élever* | *les Abeilles, les Vers à soie; & dans lequel on trouve les* | *instructions nécessaire sur la Chasse, la Pêche, les Arts,* | *le Commerce, la Procédure, l'Office, la Cuisine, &c.* | Ouvrage également utile à ceux qui vivent de leurs rentes ou | qui ont des terres, comme aux Fermiers, aux Jardi- | niers, aux Commerçans, & aux Artistes. | *PAR UNE SOCIÉTÉ DE GENS DE LETTRES.* | TOME PREMIER. [TOME SECOND.] [TOME TROISIEME.] | [ornament] | A PARIS, | Chez VINCENT, Imprimeur-Libraire, | rue saint Severin. | [two short rules] | M DCC LXII. [Vols. II and III: M DCC LXIV.] | *AVEC APPROBATION, ET PRIVILEGE DU ROI.*

First edition, Paris, 1762-1764.

8vo. 3 vols. Vol. I. π^2 a^8 A-R^8 S^6 T-Ll^8; 280 leaves, pp. [*4*] [i-iv] v-xvi [1] 2-538 [*2*]. Vol. II. π^2 A-Oo^8; 298 leaves, pp. [*4*] [1] 2-592. Vol. III. π^2 A-Rr^8; 322 leaves, pp. [*4*] [1] 2-640.

Barbier I.972 and Quérard III.667 attribute this work to August Roux, Jean Goulin, and François Alexandre Aubert de la Chesnaye des Bois.

Bibliographies: Oberlé (1) 628; Oberlé (2) 97; Simon BG 498.

Copies: *BMC*, *BNC*, and *NUC* (4 copies).

161. Dictionnaire instructif.

DICTIONNAIRE | INSTRUCTIF, | POUR APPRENRRE FACILEMENT | TOUT CE QUI SE PRATIQUE | DANS | LA SCIENCE DE L'OFFICE; | *CONTENANT la connaissance générale de* | *tout ce qui s'emploie dans l'Office, les* | *noms, les descriptions, les usages, les* | *choix et les principes de cet Art; l'expli-* | *cation de tous le termes dont on se sert; la* | *manière de confire toutes sortes de fruits,* | *tant secs que liquides, et à l'eau-de-vie;* | *de faire tous les ouvrages de sucrerie,* | *avec la méthode de les servir; les diffé-* | *rentes cuissons du sucre; la manière de* | *faire les liqueurs rafraîchissantes et autres,* | *les pastilles, pastillages, toutes sortes* | *de neiges, mousses et fruits glacés, avec* | *la méthode de les colorer, etc.:* | Ouvrage utile non seulement à ceux qui veulent | apprendre l'Office, mais encore aux Distillateurs, | Confiseurs,

Limonadiers, Epiciers et Restaurateurs. | [short fancy rule] | A PARIS, | Chez
SERVIÈRE, Libraire, rue du Foin S.-Jacques. | [short rule] | AN XI. (1803.)

First edition, Paris, 1803.

195 x 122 mm. π^4 A-T^8; 156 leaves, pp. [i-v] vi-viii [1] 2-303 [304].

Bibliographies: Wheaton and Kelly 1707.

Copies: *NUC* (Library of Congress only). Wheaton and Kelly (Radcliffe only).

162. Dictionnaire portatif de cuisine.

DICTIONNAIRE | *PORTATIF* | DE CUISINE, | *D'OFFICE,* | ET DE
DISTILLATION; | *CONTENANT la maniere de préparer toutes sortes de* | *viandes, de*
volailles, de gibier, de poissons, de | *légumes, de fruits, &c.* | *La façon de faire toutes*
sortes de gelées, de pâtes, de | *pastilles, de gâteaux, de tourtes, de pâtés, vermichel,* |
macaronis, &c. | *Et de composer toutes sortes de liqueurs, de ratafias, de* | *syrops, de*
glaces, d'essences, &c. | OUVRAGE *également utile aux Chefs d'Office & de Cui-* |
sine les plus habiles & aux Cuisiniers qui ne sont | *employés que pour des Tables*
bourgeoises. | *ON Y A JOINT des Observations médecinales qui font* | *connoître la*
propriété de chaque Aliment, relativement | *à la Santé, & qui indiquent les mets les*
plus conve- | *nables à chaque tempérament.* | [rule] | PREMIERE PARTIE.
[SECONDE PARTIE.] | [rule] | [ornament] | *A PARIS,* | Chez VINCENT, Libraire,
rue S. Severin. | [double rule] | M. DCC. LXVII. | *AVEC APPROBATION, ET*
PRIVILEGE DU ROI.

Second edition, Paris, 1767. Originally published under the title *Dictionnaire portatif*
de la cuisine et de l'office, Paris, 1765, also in two volumes.

12mo. 2 vols. Vol. I. π^4 A-Q^{12}; 196 leaves, pp. [i-iv] v-viii [1] 2-384. Vol. II.
A-Q^{12}; 192 leaves, pp. [1-2] 3-382 [2].

Note: Vicaire describes a copy of this work in one volume paged xvi-382 [2], as in
volume two, above, but adding xvi pages of preliminaries. He states, "Cet ouvrage
anonyme est assez complet," which is curious as volume one, above, contains A-L of
the dictionary and volume two contains M-Z. He also states, "Le faux-titre indique
que la *Dictionnaire portatif de cuisine* peut servir de suite au *Dictionnaire domestique*
portatif, 1762-1763," and goes on to speculate that this may also be the work of Aubert
de la Chesnaye des Bois, Goulin and Roux (see item 160). The Gernon copy of this

work contains no such statement on the half-title. Either Vicaire had a different edition of this work in hand, or his description is in error. The copies in *BMC* and *NUC* are as the Gernon copy.

Bibliographies: Bitting, p. 543; Blake, p. 119; Maggs 277; Oberlé (2) 98; Schraemli (3) 44 in a note; Vicaire 276. Only Drexel 516 and Malortie 197 record the 1765 edition.

Copies: *BMC* and *NUC* (Library of Congress, Louisiana State University, and New York Academy of Medicine). No copy of the 1765 edition has been located.

163. Dictionnaire portatif de cuisine.

DICTIONNAIRE | *PORTATIF* | DE CUISINE, | *D'OFFICE,* | ET DE DISTILLATION; | *CONTENANT la maniere de préparer toutes sortes de* | *viandes, de volailles, de gibier, de poissons, de* | *légumes, de fruits, &c.* | *La façon de faire toutes sortes de gelées, de pâtes, de* | *pastilles, de gâteaux, de tourtes, de pâtés, vermichel,* | *macaronis, &c.* | *Et de composer toutes sortes de liqueurs, de ratafias, de* | *syrops, de glaces, d'essences, &c.* | OUVRAGE également utile aux Chefs d'Office & de Cui- | sine les plus habiles & aux Cuisiniers qui ne sont | employées que pour des Tables bourgeoises. | *ON Y A JOINT des Observations médecinales qui font* | *connoître la propriété de chaque Aliment, relativement* | *à la Santé, & qui indiquent les mets les plus conve-* | *nables à chaque Tempérament.* | NOUVELLE ÉDITION, | Revue, très-corrigée, & enrichie d'un grand nombre | d'Articles refaits en entier. | [ornament] | *A PARIS,* | Chez LOTTIN le jeune, Libraire, rue S. Jacques, | vis-à-vis la rue de la Parcheminerie. | [two short rules] | M. DCC. LXXII. | *AVEC APPROBATION, ET PRIVILEGE DU ROI.*

Fourth edition, Paris, 1772. Originally published Paris, 1765 and reprinted in 1767 (item 162), 1770 and 1772.

8vo. π^2 a^8 A-Z^8 Aa^2; ^{2}A^6 B-Z^8 Aa^2; 380 leaves, pp. [*4*] [i] ii-xiv [xv-xvi] [1] 2-372; ^{2}[1] 2-367 [368].

Bibliographies: Bitting, p. 543 in a note; Blake, p. 119; Oberlé (1) 124; Schraemli (3) 44; Simon BG 499; Vicaire 276 in a note.

Copies: *NUC* (4 copies).

164. Droyn, Gabriel.

LE ROYAL SYROP | DE POMMES, | ANTIDOTE DES | PASSIONS MELAN- | CHOLIQVES. | *PAR GABRIEL DROYN* | *Docteur en Medecine.* | [ornament] | A PARIS, | Chez Iean Moreau, ruë sainct Iacques, | à la Croix blauche.

First edition, Paris, 1615.

8vo. a⁴ A-I⁸ K⁴; 80 leaves, pp. [*8*] 1-152.

Bibliographies: Oberlé (1) 1070; Simon BG 526; Vicaire 287.

Copies: *BMC, BNC,* and *NUC* (University of Wisconsin and Yale).

164a. Dubief, L.-F.

MANUEL | THÉORIQUE ET PRATIQUE | DU | FABRICANT DE CIDRE | ET DE POIRÉ, | AVEC LES MOYES D'IMITER AVEC LE SUC DES POMMES OU DE | POIRES, LE VIN DE RAISIN, L'EAU-DE-VIE | ET LE VINAIGRE DE VIN; | suivi | De l'art de faire les vins de fruits et les vins de liqueurs artificiels; de | composer des arômes ou bouquets des vins, et de faire avec les | raisins de tous les vignobles, soit les vins de Basse-Bourgogne, du | Cher, de Tourraine, de Saint-Gilles, de Roussillon, de Bordeaux | et autres. | OUVRAGE INDISPENSABLE AUX MARCHANDS DE VINS, FABRI- | CANS DE CIDRE, CULTIVATEURS, ET AUX AMIS | DE L'ECONOMIE DOMESTIQUE. | *Avec Figures.* | PAR L.-F. DUBIEF, | Manufacturier, auteur oenologue, Membre de plusieurs Sociétés | savantes. | [short fancy rule] | PARIS, | A LA LIBRAIRIE ENCYCLOPÉDIQUE DE RORET, | RUE HAUTEFEUILLE, Nº 10 BIS. | 1834.

First edition, Paris, 1834.

145 x 93 mm. π² [1]⁶ 2-25⁶; 152 leaves, pp. [*4*] [i] ii-iv [5] 6-299 [300]. Publisher's tan printed wrappers. A 36 page publisher's catalog dated February 1836 bound in at the end.

Illustrations: Engraved folding plate illustrating various apparatus tipped in facing p. 292.

Bibliographies: Wheaton and Kelly 1783.

Copies: *BMC, BNC* and *NUC* (5 copies).

165. Dubois, Urbain, 1819-1901.

CUISINE ARTISTIQUE │ [in red] ÉTUDES DE L'ÉCOLE MODERNE. │ [short rule] │ OUVRAGE EN DEUX PARTIES │ [in red] RENFERMANT CENT ET UNE PLANCHES GRAVÉES, HORS TEXTE. │ PAR │ [in red] URBAIN-DUBOIS │ AUTEUR DE LA CUISINE DE TOUS LES PAYS, DE L'ÉCOLE DES CUISINIÈRES, DE LA CUISINE-CLASSIQUE. │ Pour longtemps encore, l'école Française restera ce │ qu'elle est: incontestée, sans rivale! │ PREMIÈRE PARTIE: 53 PLANCHES. [SECONDE PARTIE: 52 PLANCHES.] │ [in red] PARIS │ LIBRAIRIE E. DENTU, │ AU PALAIS-ROYAL │ DANS TOUTES LES GRANDES LIBRAIRIES. │ 1872. [1874.]

First edition, Paris, 1872-1874.

301 x 224 mm. 2 vols. Vol. I. π^4 1-28^4; 116 leaves, pp. [i-v] vi-viii [1-4] 5-221 [222] [2]. Vol. II. π^2 29-57^4 58^6 59-61^4 62^6; 142 leaves, pp. [4] [223] 224-415 [416] [6] 417-418 [4] 419-420 [6] 421-422 [4] 423-424 [6] 425-426 [10] 427-432 [4] 433-434 [12] 435-436 [4] 437-444 [2]. The unnumbered pages in vol. II between pp. 416 and 437 are for 26 full page illustrations, integral with the signatures in which they appear but not included in the pagination.

Illustrations: Vol. I, 53 engraved plates (one folding). Vol. II, 52 engraved plates and 26 full page illustrations in the text.

Bibliographies: Maggs 519; Schraemili (3) 90; Vicaire 290.

Copies: *BMC*, *BNC*, and *NUC* (University of Wisconsin and Yale.)

166. Dubois, Urbain, 1818-1901.

NOUVELLE │ CUISINE BOURGEOISE │ POUR LA VILLE ET POUR LA CAMPAGNE │ PAR │ URBAIN DUBOIS │ Auteur de l'ÉCOLE DES CUISINÈRES, de la CUISINE DE TOUS LES PAYS, │ de la CUISINE CLASSIQUE et de la CUISINE ARTISTIQUE. │ L'ambition d'une bonne ménagère doit │ viser à ce résultat méritoire de faire │ bien avec peu. │ VINGT-SEPTIÈME ÉDITION │ [publisher's monogram] │ PARIS │ PAUL BERNARDIN, LIBRAIRE- ÉDITEUR │ 53, QUAI DES GRANDS-AUGUSTINS, 53 │ [short rule] │ Tous droits réservés.

Twenty-seventh edition, Paris, ca. 1909. Originally published, Paris, 1878.
176 x 109 mm. π^4 1-42$^{12.6}$ 43^{12} 44^2; 396 leaves, pp. [i-v] vi-vii [viii] [1] 2-783 [784]. Publisher's printed boards with cloth spine.

Illustrations: Numerous wood engravings in the text.

Bibliographies: This edition unrecorded in the bibliographies consulted. Bitting, p. 131, cites a ninth edition, 1889; Vicaire 291 cites an eighth edition [1888]. Wheaton and Kelly cites fifth edition 1884, twenty-first edition, 1901, and twenty-fourth edition, 1905.

Copies: No other copy of this edition located.

167. Dubourg, Antony.

DICTIONNAIRE | DES MÉNAGES, | RÉPERTOIRE | DE TOUTES LES CONNAISSANCES USUELLES, | ENCYCLOPÉDIE DES VILLES ET DES CAMPAGNES, | PAR ANTONY DUBOURG, | MEMBRE DE DIVERSES SOCIÉTÉS SAVANTES, INDUSTRIELLES ET AGRICOLES. | [short rule] | TOME PREMIER. [TOME DEUXIÈME.] | [short rule] | [ornament] | PARIS, | CHEZ D'URTUBIE ET WORMS, RUE SAINT-PIERRE-MONTMARTRE, 17. | ET A HAM, | Chez M. ROUSSEAU, ancien Notaire. | [short rule] | 1839.

Second edition, Paris, 1839. Originally published, Paris, 1836.

273 x 214 mm. 2 vols. Vol. I. π^2 1-61^4 62^2; 248 leaves, pp. [4] [1] 2-491 [492]. Vol. II. π^2 1-65^4; 262 leaves, pp. [4] [1] 2-519 [520].

Antony Dubourg is a pseudonym of Paul Lacroix and Emile de la Bédollière.

Bibliographies: Bitting, p. 132; Vicaire 291.

Copies: No copy of this edition located (Bitting copy does not appear in *NUC*). *BMC* and *BNC* record first edition.

167a. Dubuisson.

L'ART | DU DISTILLATEUR | *ET* | MARCHAND DE LIQUEURS | *Considérées comme Alimens médicamenteux;* | PAR M. DUBUISSON, *ancien Maître.* | *Distillateur,* | [thick-thin rule] | PREMIÈRE PARTIE. [SECONDE PARTIE.] | [thin-thick rule] | [ornament] | *A PARIS,* | Chez l'AUTEUR, vis-à-vis l'Imprimerie du Parlement; | rue Mignon. | Chez [next four lines bracketed to left] M. DUBUISSON

Fils, au Caveau du Palais | Royal. | M. CUSIN, au Café Dubuisson, vis-a-vis | l'ancienne Comédie Françoise. | [short triple rule] | M. DCC. LXXIX. | *Avec approbation & Privilége du Roi.*

First edition, Paris, 1779. There was second edition, Paris, 1788; another "second edition," Paris, 1803; and a third edition, Paris, 1809.

8vo. 2 vols. Vol. I. a^8 A-Ee^8; 232 leaves, pp. [i-iv] v-xvi [1] 2-448. Vol. II. π^2 A-Z^8 Aa^2; 188 leaves, pp. [4] [1] 2-370 [2].

Bibliographies: The first edition is mentioned only in a note in Vicaire. The second edition, Paris, 1788, is cited in Oberlé (1) 1096, Simon BG, 527, and Vicaire 292; the third edition, Paris, 1809, is cited by Bitting, p. 133, and Vicaire 292.

Copies: *BNC*; *NUC* (University of Wisconsin and Yale).

168. Dufour, Philippe-Sylvestre, 1622-1687?

TRACTATVS | *NOVI* | DE POTV CAPHE'; | *DE* | CHINENSIVM THE'; | *ET* | DE CHOCOLATA. | [ornament] | *PARISIIS,* | Apud PETRUM MUGUET. | [rule] | *M. DC. LXXXV.*

First edition, Paris, 1685, of this Latin translation by Jacob Spon of Dufour's *Traitez nouveaux et curieux du café, du thé et du chocolate*, Lyon, 1685 (item 169).

12mo. a^4 A-H^{12} I^8; 108 leaves, pp. [8] 1-202 [6]. Last leaf blank; first leaf (blank or half-title) wanting in this copy.

Illustrations: Three engraved plates, being the frontispiece and the illustrations at the beginning of the sections on caphé and chocolata. There is no plate at the beginning of the section on Chinensium thé.

Bibliographies: Horn-Arndt 122; Maggs 191; Oberlé (1) 732; Vicaire 294; Wheaton and Kelly 1823.

Copies: *BMC*, *BNC*, and *NUC* (7 copies).

169. Dufour, Philippe-Sylvestre, 1622-1687?

[in red] TRAITEZ | Nouveaux & curieux | [in red] DV CAFE', | [in red] DV THE' |
ET DV | [in red] CHOCOLATE. | Ouvrage également necessaire aux | Medecins, & à
tous ceux qui | aiment leur santé. | [in red] PAR PHILIPPE SYLVESTRE DVFOVR
| [ornament] | [in red] A LYON, | Chez IEAN GIRIN, & B. RIVIERE, | ruë
Merciere, à la Prudence. | [in red: rule] | *M. DC. LXXXV.* | [in red] AVEC
PRIVILEGE DV ROY.

First edition, Lyon, 1685.

12mo. a^{12} A-S^{12} T^8 V^2 (-V2); 237 leaves, pp. [*24*] 1-445 [446-450].

Illustrations: Engraved frontispiece and three engraved illustrations, one at the
beginning of each section. The frontispiece and the illustrations facing the sections on
café and thé are an integral part of the signatures in which they appear; the illustration
facing the section on chocolate is a separate plate inserted after N8.

Bibliographies: Bitting, p. 134; Maggs 190; Oberlé (1) 733; Vicaire 293.

Copies: *BMC, BNC,* and *NUC* (8 copies).

170. Dufour, Philippe-Sylvestre, 1622-1687?

TRAITEZ | Nouveaux & curieux | DU CAFE', | DU THE' | ET DU |
CHOCOLATE. | *Ouvrage également necessaire aux Me-* | *decins, & à tous ceux qui*
aiment | *leur santé.* | Par PHILIPPE SYLVESTRE DUFOUR. | *SECONDE EDITION.*
| [ornament] | A LYON, | Chez JEAN BAPTISTE DEVILLE, ruë | Merciere à la
Science. | [rule] | M. DC. LXXXVIII. | *AVEC PRIVILEGE DU ROY.*

One of two Lyon, 1688, editions. The other is by the original publisher Jean Girin.
Originally published, Lyon, 1685 (item 169) and reprinted, The Hague, 1685. There
was a later edition, The Hague, 1698.

12mo. a^{12} A-S^{12} T^8 V^4; 240 leaves, pp. [*24*] [1] 2-444 [*12*]. Last leaf blank.

Illustrations: Engraved frontispiece and three engraved illustrations, one at the
beginning of each section. The frontispiece and the illustrations facing the sections on
café and thé are an integral part of the signatures in which they appear; the illustration
facing the section on chocolate is a separate plate inserted after N8.

Bibliographies: Schraemli (1) 149; Vicaire 293 in a note; Wheaton and Kelly 1827.

Copies: *BMC*, *BNC*, and *NUC* (8 copies).

171. Dumas, Alexandre, 1802-1870.

GRAND DICTIONNAIRE │ DE │ [in red] CUISINE │ PAR │ [in red] ALEXANDRE DUMAS │ [publisher's device] │ PARIS │ [in red] ALPHONSE LEMERRE, ÉDITEUR │ 27-29, PASSAGE CHOISEUL, 27-29 │ [short rule] │ M DCCC LXXIII

First edition, Paris, 1873.

266 x 170 mm. π^2 a^4 1-73^8 74^6; 596 leaves, pp. [*4*] [i-iii] iv-vi [vii-viii] [1] 2-1155 [1156]; ^{2}[1-2] 3-24. Publisher's cloth.
Illustrations: Etched portrait of Dumas facing p. iii and etched portrait of D. J. Vuillemot facing p. vii.

Bibliographies: Bitting, p. 135; Drexel 179; Horn-Arndt 424; Oberlé (1) 238; Schraemli (1) 152; Vicaire 297; Wheaton and Kelly 1832.

Copies: *BMC*, *BNC*, and *NUC* (8 copies).

172. Dumas, Alexandre, 1802-1870.

PETIT DICTIONNAIRE │ DE │ CUISINE │ PAR │ ALEXANDRE DUMAS │ [publisher's device] │ PARIS │ ALPHONSE LEMERRE, ÉDITEUR │ 27-31, PASSAGE CHOISEUL, 27-31 │ [short rule] │ M D CCC LXXXII

First edition, Paris, 1882.

184 x 115 mm. π^4 1-68^6 69^2; 414 leaves. pp. [*4*] [i] ii-iii [iv] [1] 2-819 [820]. Publisher's printed boards.

Bibliographies: Bitting pp. 135-136; Maggs 522; Oberlé (1) 240; Schraemli (3) 105; Vicaire 297; Wheaton and Kelly 1833.

Copies: *BNC* and *NUC* (6 copies).

173. Duplais, Pierre.

TRAITÉ │ DES LIQUEURS │ ET DE LA │ DISTILLATION DES ALCOOLS │ CONTENANT │ Les procédés les plus nouveaux pour la Fabrication │ des Liqueurs françaises et étrangères; │ Fruits à l'eau-de-vie et au sucre; Sirops, Conserves, │ Eaux et Esprits parfumés, Vermouts, │ Vins de Liqueur. │ EAUX ET BOISSONS GAZEUSES │ AINSI QUE │ LA DESCRIPTION COMPLÈTE │ DES OPÉRATIONS NECESSAIRES POUR LA DISTILLATION DE TOUS LES ALCOOLS │ PAR P. DUPLAIS AINÉ, │ DISTILLATEUR ET LIQUORISTE. │ [ornament] │ *DEUXIÈME ÉDITION.* │ [short rule] │ TOME PREMIER. [TOME DEUXIÈME.] │ [ornament] │ VERSAILLES │ CHEZ L'AUTEUR, PASSAGE SAINT-PIERRE, 10. │ [short rule] │ 1858

Second edition, Versailles, 1858. Originally published, Versailles, 1855.

225 x 140 mm. 2 vols. Vol. I. π^2 ^{4} 1-35^8; 286 leaves, pp. [i-vii] viii-xii [1] 2-550 [*10*]. Vol. II. π^4 1-33^8 34^4; 272 leaves, pp. [i-v] vi-viii [1] 2-534 [*2*]. Last leaf blank. Both volumes in publisher's printed wrappers.

Illustrations: Vol. I. Five lithographed folding plates of distilling apparatus. Vol. II. Nine lithographed folding plates.

Bibliographies: This edition unrecorded in the bibliographies consulted. Oberlé (2) 411 records the original edition, Paris, 1855.

Copies: *BMC*, *BNC*, and *NUC* (Yale only for this edition).

174. Duval, Henri-Louis-Nicolas, 1783-1854.

MANUEL │ DE │ LA JEUNE FEMME, │ Contenant │ TOUT CE QU'IL EST UTILE DE SAVOIR POUR │ DIRIGER AVEC AGRÉMENT, ORDRE ET │ ÉCONOMIE L'INTÉRIEUR D'UN MÉNAGE. │ Orné d'une jolie Vignette. │ PAR │ *M. Cardelli,* │ Auteur du Manuel du Limonadier, Confiseur, etc, │ et du Manuel du Cuisinier et de la Cuisinière. │ [short fancy rule] │ PARIS, │ CHARLES-BÉCHET, LIBRAIRE, │ Quai des Augustins, no 57. │ [short rule] │ 1825.

First edition, Paris, 1825.

150 x 90 mm. 1-27^6 28^{12} (-28$_{12}$); 173 leaves, pp. [i-v] vi-xi [xii] [13] 14-343 [*344*] [*2*]. Publisher's printed wrappers, dated 1826.

Illustration: Engraved frontispiece of domestic scene.

Note: Cardelli is the pseudonym of Henri-Louis-Nicolas Duval.

Bibliographies: Vicaire 144.

Copies: *BNC*.

175. Duval, Henri-Louis-Nicolas, 1783-1854.

MANUEL │ DU CUISINIER │ ET │ DE LA CUISINIÈRE, │ A L'USAGE DE LA
VILLE ET DE LA CAMPAGNE; │ Contenant toutes les Recettes les plus simples pour
faire bonne │ chère avec économie, ainsi que les meilleurs Procédés pour │ la Pâtisserie
et l'Office; │ PRÉCÉDÉ D'UN TRAITÉ SUR LA DISSECTION DES VIANDES; │
Suivi de la manière de conserver les subtances alimentaires, et d'un │ Traité sur les
vins; │ PAR P. CARDELLI, │ ANCIEN CHEF D'OFFICE. │ 4e. ÉDITION, │ Revue,
corrigée, considérablement augmentée, et ornée de │ figures. │ PARIS, │ RORET,
LIBRAIRE, RUE HAUTEFEUILLE, │ AU COIN DE CELLE DU BATTOIR. │ [two
short rules] │ 1826.

Fourth edition, Paris, 1826. Originally published, Paris, 1822.

143 x 189 mm. π^2 a^4(-a1) b^6 1-28^6 28✳✳1 (=a1); 180 leaves, pp. [*4*] [i] ii-xvii [xviii]
[1] 2-337 [338]. Modern quarter brown morocco with marbled boards, original printed
wrappers bound in.

Illustrations: Lithographed frontispiece of dining room and kitchen and three engraved
plates illustrating carving.

Note: P. Cardelli is the pseudonym of Henri-Louis-Nicolas Duval.

Bookplate: Ex-libris Robert Viel.

Bibliographies: Maggs 412 (this copy); Vicaire 142 in a note.

Copies: *BNC*.

176. Duval, Henri-Louis-Nicolas, 1783-1854.

MANUELS-RORET. | [short rule] | NOUVEAU MANUEL COMPLET | DU | CUISINIER | ET | DE LA CUISINIÈRE, | A L'USAGE DE LA VILLE ET DE LA CAMPAGNE; | CONTENANT LES RECETTES LES PLUS SIMPLES POUR FAIRE | BONNE CHÈRE AVEC ÉCONOMIE, SUIVIES DES MEILLEURS PROCÉDÉS | POUR LA PATISSERIE ET L'OFFICE | PRÉCÉDÉ | D'un Traité pour bien découper et servir | les viandes à table, | Auquel on a joint des Préceptes généraux sur le choix des substances | alimentaires, ainsi que les Méthodes à suivre pour les parer, les | attendrir et les conserver, | Terminié par un Traité sur les vins; | Par M. CARDELLI, ANCIEN CHEF-D'OFFICE. | *NOUVELLE ÉDITION,* | *Entièrement revue, considérablement augmentée, et ornée* | *d'un grand nombre de planches gravées sur acier.* | PARIS, | A LA LIBRAIRIE ENCYCLOPÉDIQUE DE RORET, | RUE HAUTEFEUILLE, 10 BIS.

New edition, Paris, 1848. Originally published under the title *Manuel complet du cuisinier et de la cuisinière*, Paris, 1822, and in this enlarged edition, Paris, 1838.

139 x 85 mm. π^4 1-39^6 40^2; 240 leaves, pp. [i-v] vi-viii [1] 2-472. This copy lacks first leaf (half-title?). Publisher's printed boards.

Illustrations: Steel engraved frontispiece of dining room and kitchen (as in item 175) and seven steel engraved folding plates illustrating carving, table settings, pastry designs (2), kitchen utensils and stoves (3).

Note: Cardelli is the pseudonym of Henri-Nicolas-Louis Duval.

Bibliographies: Vicaire 143 in a note; Wheaton and Kelly 1872.

Copies: *BNC* dated [1847] and *NUC* (Boston Public Library and New York Public Library).

177. Duval, Henri-Louis-Nicolas, 1783-1854.

MANUELS-RORET. | [short rule] | NOUVEAU MANUEL | DU | LIMONADIER, | DU | GLACIER, DU CHOCOLATIER | ET DU | CONFISEUR; | CONTENANT | Les meillieurs procédés pour préparer le café, le chocolat, le punch, les | glaces, les boissons rafraichissantes, liqueurs, fruits à l'eau-de-vie, | confitures, pâtes, vins artificiels, pâtisseries légères, bière, cidre, etc. | Ouvrage utile, non-seulement aux limonadiers, confiseurs, mais encore | aux droguistes, herboristes, chefs-d'office, économes, et indispensable | à toutes les personnes qui se font un délassement de confectionner et | d'améliorer toutes les douceurs agréables dans les usages de la vie; | Par MM. CARDELLI, chef d'office, LIONNET-CLÉMANDOT, | ancien confiseur, et JULIA DE FONTENELLE, | pour la partie chimique. | *NOUVELLE EDITION.* | *Ouvrage orné de Figures.* | [short fancy rule] | PARIS, | A LA LIBRAIRIE ENCYCLOPÉDIQUE DE RORET, | RUE HAUTEFEUILLE, NO 10 BIS. | 1838.

New edition, Paris, 1838. Originally published under the title *Manuel du limonadier, du confiseur et du distillateur*, Paris, 1822, and in this enlarged edition, Paris, 1838.

149 x 99 mm. π^4 1-38^6 39^4; 236 leaves, pp. [i-v] vi-viii [1] 2-464. 36 page publisher's catalogue, dated Mars 1842, bound in at end. Publisher's printed paper wrappers.

Illustrations: Four steel engraved folding plates with 151 figures illustrating utensils and apparatus of the limonadier.

Bibliographies: This edition unrecorded in the bibliographies consulted. Vicarie 143 records the first edition, 1822, noting various later printings, and an 1839 edition under the new title.

Copies: *BNC*.

Elimithar, Elluchasem. See Ibn Bultan (items 243 and 244).

178. L'Ecole des jardiniers.

L'ESCOLE | DES | JARDINIERS, | OV L'ON APPREND LA METHODE | de faire des Pepinieres a Pepin & à | Noyaux, avec les differentes façons | d'Enter & Planter toutes sortes | d'Arbres fruitiers : Ensemble la | maniere de les èlever en Buissons, | Espaliers, contr'Espaliers & en | haute Tige : Et en suite la saison de | les Cultiver, & le moyen de reme- | dier à leurs Maladies. | *Par le Sieur R. D. F. E.* | [ornament] | *A TOLOSE,* | Chez la Vefve d'ESTIENNE TREVENAY Marchand | Libraire, à la Potterie. | [short rule] | CIƆ IƆ C LXXII.

First edition? Toulouse, 1672.

12mo. ¶^{8} A-Q^6 R^4; 108 leaves, pp. [*16*] 1-198 [*2*]. Last leaf blank.

Bibliographies: Unrecorded in the bibliographies consulted.

Copies: No other copy located.

179. L'Ecole parfaite des officiers de bouche.

L'ESCOLE | PARFAITE | DES OFFICIERS | de Bouche; |
CONTENANT | Le vray Maistre-d'Hostel, | Le grand Escuyer-Tranchants, | Le
Sommelier Royal, | Le Confiturier Royal, | Le Cuisinier Royal, | Et le Patissier
Royal. | [ornament] | A PARIS. | Chez la Veuve PIERRE DAVID, sur le Quay des |
Augustins, au Roy Dauid. | ET | Chez IEAN RIBOV, sur le Quay des Augustins, | à
l'image sainct Louis. | [rule] | M. DC. LXII. | *AVEC PRIVILEGE DV ROY.*

First edition, Paris, 1662.

8vo. a^4 A-D^8 E^8 (-E8) F-Kk^8; 267 leaves, pp. [*8*] 1-85, 84-464, 467-494 [*32*] = 534.

Illustrations: Woodcuts in the text illustrating table settings and carving.

Bibliographies: Vicaire 338.

Copies: *NUC* (Harvard only).

180. L'Ecole parfaite des officiers de bouche.

L'ECOLE | PARFAITE | DES OFFICIERS | DE BOUCHE, | QUI ENSEIGNE LES
DEVOIRS | du Maître-d'Hôtel, & du Somme- | lier; la manier de faire les Confi- |
tures seches & liquides; les Liqueurs, | les Eaux, les Pommades & les Par- | fums; la
Cuisine, à découper les | Viandes & à faire la Patisserie. | *Septiéme Edition, corrigée
& augmentée de* | *Pâtes & Liqueurs nouvelles, & des nouveaux* | *Ragoûts qu'on sert
aujourd'huy.* | [ornament] | A PARIS, | Chez PIERRE RIBOU, sur le Quay des |
Augustins, à l'image Saint Loüis. | [rule] | M. DCCVIII. | *Avec Approbation &
Privilege du Roy.*

Seventh edition, Paris, 1708. Originally published, Paris, 1662 (item 179).

12mo. a^6 A-Tt$^{8.4}$ Vu^8 Xx^2; 268 leaves, pp. [*12*] 1-507 [508-524].

Illustrations: Woodcuts in the text illustrating carving and four engraved folding plates
at the end showing table settings.

Bibliographies: Horn-Arndt 246; Simon BG 600, Vicaire 340.

Copies: No other copy of this edition located.

181. L'Ecole parfaite des officiers de bouche.

L'ECOLE | PARFAITE | DES OFFICIERS | DE BOUCHE, | QUI
ENSEIGNE LES DEVOIRS | du Maître-d'Hôtel, & du Somme- |
lier; la manier de faire les Confi- | tures séches & liquides; les Liqueurs, | les Eaux,
les Pommades & les Par- | fums; la Cuisine, à découper les | Viandes & à faire la
Patisserie. | *Huitiéme Edition, corrigée & augmentée* | *de Pâtes & Liqueurs nouvelles,*
& | *des nouveaux Ragoûts qu'on sert* | *aujourd'huy.* | [ornament] | A PARIS, | Chez
PIERRE RIBOU, sur le Quay des | Augustins, à l'image Saint Loüis. | [rule] | M.
DCC. XVI. | *Avec Approbation & Privilege du Roy.*

Eighth edition, Paris, 1716. Originally published, Paris, 1662 (item 179).

12mo. a⁶ A-Tt⁸·⁴ Vu⁸ Xx²; 268 leaves, pp. [*12*] [1] 2-507 [508-524].

Illustrations: Woodcuts in the text illustrating carving and four engraved folding plates
showing table settings.

Bibliographies: Vicaire 340.

Copies: No other copy of this edition located.

182. Emy.

L'ART | DE BIEN FAIRE | LES GLACES D'OFFICE; | *OU* | LES VRAIS
PRINCIPES | Pour congeler tous les Rafraichissemens. | *La maniere de préparer*
toutes sortes de | *Composuions, la façon de les faire* | *prendre, d'en former des Fruits,*
Can- | *nelons, & toutes sortes de Fromages.* | Le tout expliqué avec précision selon |
l'usage actuel. | *AVEC* | UN TRAITÉ SUR LES MOUSSES. | *Ouvrage très-utile à*
ceux qui sont des Glaces | *ou Fromages glacés.* | Orné de Gravures en taille-douce. |
Par M. EMY, Officier. | [rule] | Prix, 2 liv. 10 sols *broché;* 3 liv. *relié.* | [rule] |
[ornament] | A PARIS, | Chez LE CLERC, Libraire, quai des | Augustins, à la Toison
d'or. | [two short rules] | M. DCC. LXVIII. | *Avec Approbation & Privilege du Roi.*

First edition, Paris, 1768.

12mo. π1 A-K¹² L⁶(-L1) M²; 128 leaves, pp. [2] i-viii, 1-242 [*4*].

Illustrations: Engraved frontispiece titled "L'Art de bien faire les glaces" and two
engraved plates of utensils.

Bibliographies: Bitting, pp. 144-145; Crahan 307A; Drexel 137; Maggs 279; Malortie 204; Schraemli (1) 164; Vicaire 328.

Copies: *BMC, BNC,* and *NUC* (4 copies).

183. Encyclopédie domestique.

ENCYCLOPÉDIE │ DOMESTIQUE, │ OU │ ANNALES INSTRUCTIVES, │ FORMANT RECUEIL │ *DE toutes sortes de Remedes, Recettes,* │ *Préservatifs,* *Curatifs des diverses maladies* │ *et incommodités des hommes et des animaux,* │ *de* *Secrets, d'Inventions, de Découvertes* │ *utiles et agréables, dans les Sciences et* │ *Arts,* *& généralement de tout ce qui peut* │ *intéresser la santé, la beauté, la curiosité,* │ *c'est-à-dire, les besoins & les agrémens de* │ *la vie morale & physique, à l'usage des* │ *deux Sexes de la Cour, de la Ville &* │ *de la Campagne.* │ [rule] │ Prix 4 liv. 4 s. et 5 liv. par la poste. │ [rule] │ [short fancy rule] │ A PARIS, │ Chez LAURENS jeune, Imprimeur-Libraire, │ rue Saint-Jacques No. 37. │ Et chez les Marchands de Nouveautés.

First edition? Paris, ca. 1800. The latest date found in the text is October 1790 but the absence of the long s in the book points to a date closer to 1800.

196 x 118 mm. π1 [A-B]² C-T⁴ V² X-Ll⁴ Mm⁸ Nn⁴ Pp-Xx⁸ Yy⁴ ᵖA⁴; 207 leaves, pp. [1-5] 6-406; ²[1] 2-7 [8].

Bibliographies: Unrecorded in the bibliographies consulted.

Copies: No other copy located.

183a. Eobanus, Helius *Hessus,* 1488-1540.

[Leaf] BONAE VALETVDI═ │ NIS CONSERVANDAE PRAE- │ CEPTA AD MAGNIFICVM │ D. GEORGIVM STRVTIADEN, │ AVTHORE EOBANO HESSO. │ [clover leaf] *Medicinae Laus ad Martinum Hunum.* │ [clover leaf] *Caena Baptistae &* *Fierae de Herbarum vir-* │ *tutibus, & ea medicae artis parte, quae in* │ *victus ratione* *consistit.* │ [clover leaf] *Item Polybus de salubri vistus ratione* │ *priuatorum, Ioanne* *Guinterio Andernaco* │ *Medico interprete.* │ [clover leaf] *Aristotelis problemata, quae* *ad stirpium ge-* │ *nus & oseracea pertinent.* │ PARISIIS │ Apud Simonem Colinæum. │ 1533

New edition, Paris, 1533. Originally published Erfurt, 1524.

8vo. a-h^8; 64 leaves, ff. [1] 2-64.

Bibliographies: Oberlé (1) 317, Vicaire 331.

Copies: *BMC*, *BNC* and *NUC* (National Agricultural Library, National Library of Medicine and New York Academy of Medicine).

184. Erresalde, Pierre.

NOVVEAVX | SECRETS | RARES ET CVRIEVX. | Donnés Charitablement au public | par vne personne de | Condition. | CONTENANT | *DIVERS REMEDES EPROVVEZ,* | *vtils & profitables pour toutes sortes* | *de Maladies.* | Et diuers Secrets pour la conseruation de | la Beauté des Dames: Auec vne nou- | uelle maniere pour faire toutes sortes | de confitures, tant seiches que liquides. | [ornament] | A PARIS, | Chez IEAN BAPTISTE LOYSON, | ruë Sainct Iacques prés la Poste, | à la Croix Royalle. | [rule] | M. DC. LX. | *AVEC PRIVILEGE DV ROY.*

First edition, Paris, 1660.

8vo. a^8 e^2 A-R^8 S^4; 150 leaves, pp. [*20*] [1-2] 3-280.

Bibliographies: Vicaire 333.

Copies: *BMC* and *NUC* (National Library of Medicine only).

185. Escoffier, Auguste, 1846-1935.

A. ESCOFFIER | [short fancy rule] | LES | FLEURS | EN | CIRE | [ornament] | BIBLIOTHÈQUE | DE L'ART CULINAIRE | *4, Place Saint-Michel.* – PARIS | MDCCCCX | Nouvelle Édition

Fourth edition, Paris, 1910. Originally published under the title *Traité sur l'art de travailler les fleurs en cire*, Paris, 1884. Of the fourth edition there were 50 copies on papier des Manufactures Impériales du Japon and 200 copies on papier de Hollande, de Van Gelder Zonen. These all signed by the author. This copy is on text paper, neither numbered nor signed.

188 x 141 mm. [1]^8 2-6^8; 48 leaves, pp. [1-9] 10-94 [*2*]. Publisher's printed wrappers.

Illustrations: Halftone frontispiece portrait of the author and halftone illustration titled "Fleurs de magnolia en cire" and 40 photo engraved illustrations in the text.

"La présente édition (Paris–septembre 1910), entièrement refondue et considérablement augmentée, comprend 96 pages, texte et titre, illustrées de 40 gravures dans le texte, documents de fleurs et frontispices, et 2 photogravures hors texte."

Bibliographies: Bitting, p. 145; Oberlé (1) 260. Vicaire 338 records the first edition.

Copies: *BMC*, *BNC*, and *NUC* (Kansas State University, Library of Congress and New York Public Library).

185a. Escoffier, Auguste, 1846-1935.

BIBLIOTHÈQUE PROFESSIONNELLE | [short rule] | Le Guide | Culinaire | *AIDE-MÉMOIRE DE CUISINE PRATIQUE* | Par A. ESCOFFIER | AVEC LA COLLABORATION | DE MM. PHILÉAS GILBERT - E. FÉTU | A. SUZANNE, B. REBOUL, Ch. DIETRICH, A. CAILLAT, ETC. | *Dessins de* VICTOR MORIN | *Je place ce livre sous le patronage posthume de* | *Urbain Dubois et Émile Bernard, en témoignage de* | *mon admiration pour ceux qui, depuis Carême,* | *ont porté le plus haut le gloire de l'Art Culinaire.* | A. E. | [ornament] | PARIS | 1903 | Tous droits de traduction et de reproduction péservés pour tous les pays, | y compris la Suède, la Norvège et le Danemark.

First edition, Paris, 1903.

215 x 133 mm. π^6 1-49^8 50^6; 404 leaves, pp. [i-v] vi-x [xi-xii] [1] 2-790 [*6*].

Illustrations: Steel engravings in the text.

Bibliographies: The first edition is unrecorded in the bibliographies consulted.

Copies: *BNC*, *NUC* (Cornell only).

185b. Escoffier, Auguste, 1846-1935.

A. ESCOFFIER | avec la collaboration de | MM. PHILÉAS GILBERT et ÉMILE FETU | [short rule] | Le livre | des menus | *Complément indispensable du Guide*

Culinaire | [publisher's monogram] | PARIS | ERNEST FLAMMARION, ÉDITEUR | 26, rue Racine, 26 | [short rule] | Tous droits de traduction, de reproduction et d'adaptation réservés | pour tous les pays.

First edition, Paris, 1912.

253 x 164 mm. [1]⁸ 2-10⁸ 11⁴; 84 leaves, pp. [2] [1-4] 5-164 [165-166]. First leaf, blank. Folding chart titled "Tableau de Service dans une grande Cuisine" tipped in at the end. Publisher's terra cotta colored printed wrappers.

Bibliographies: Bitting, p. 146; Wheaton and Kelly 1979.

Copies: *NUC* (4 copies). Wheaton and Kelly adds Harvard.

186. L'Esprit des usages et des coutumes des différens peuples.

L'ESPRIT | DES USAGES | *ET DES* | COUTUMES | DES DIFFÉRENS PEUPLES. | *OUVRAGE dans lequel on a réuni en corps d'H stoire* | *tout ce qu'ont imaginé les* *Hommes sur les alimens & les* | *repas, les Femmes, le mariage, la naissance & l'édu-* | *cation des Enfans, les Chefs & les Souverains, la* | *Guerre, la distribution des rangs, la* *servitude & l'es-* | *clavage, la pudeur, la parure, les modes, la société,* | *& les usages* *domestiques, les loix pénales, les* | *supplices, la Médecine, la mort, les funérailles, les* | *sepultures, &c.* | [rule] | TOME PREMIER. [TOME SECOND.] [TOME TROISIEME.] | [rule] | [ornament] | A LONDRES, | *Et se trouve à PARIS,* | Chez LAPORTE, Imprimeur-Libraire, rue des Noyers, | [two short rules] | M. DCC. LXXXV.

First edition, Paris, 1785.

8vo. 3 vols. Vol. I. a⁸ A-Cc⁸; 216 leaves, pp. [i-iv] v-xvi [1] 2-415 [416]. Vol. II. π⁴ A-Z⁸; 188 leaves, pp. [i-v] vi-viii [1] 2-365 [366] [2], last leaf (blank?) wanting in this copy. Vol. III. π⁴ A-X⁸; 172 leaves, pp. [i-v] vi-viii [1] 2-336.

Bookplate: Westbury.

Bibliographies: Vicaire 341, recording two volumes.

Copies: *BMC* (3 vols.)

187. Etienne.

TRAITÉ | DE L'OFFICE, | PAR M. ÉTIENNE, | ANCIEN OFFICIER DE L'AMBASSADE D'ANGLETERRE, | OFFICIER DE MADAME LA PRINCESSE DE BAGRATION, A PARIS. | AVEC DE BEAUX DESSINS GRAVÉS SUR ACIER. | [short fancy rule] | PARIS. | Mlle LAIGNIER, A LA LIBRAIRIE, RUE THÉRESE, 11. | PRÈS LE PALAIS-ROYAL. | [short rule] | 1845.

Title-page of second volume:

TRAITÉ | DE L'OFFICE, | PAR M. ÉTIENNE, | ANCIEN OFFICIER DE L'AMBASSADE D'ANGLETERRE, | OFFICIER DE MADAME LA PRINCESSE DE BAGRATION, A PARIS. | AVEC DE BEAUX DESSINS GRAVÉS SUR ACIER. | [short fancy rule] | TOME DEUXIÈME ET DERNIER. | [short fancy rule] | PARIS, | AU DÉPOT DE LA COLLECTION D'ANTONIN CARÊME, RUE THÉRÈSE, 11. | PRÈS LE PALAIS-ROYAL. | [short rule] | 1846.
First edition, Paris, 1845-1846.

215 x 129 mm. 2 vols. Vol. I. π^2 $*^2$ 1-2^8 3^6 4^2; $^2\pi$1 1-7^8; ^{3}1-13^8 14^6 15_1; 196 leaves, pp. [8] [1] 2-50; ^{2}[1] 2-111 [112]; ^{3}[1] 2-222 = 392. Vol. II. π^2 a^2 1-2^8 3^4; ^{2}1^6; ^{3}1^8 2^2; ^{4}1-12^8 13^6 (-13_6); ^{5}1-13^8 14^8 (-14_8); 252 leaves, pp. [4] [i] ii-iii [iv] [1] 2-40; ^{2}[1] 2-11 [12]; ^{3}[1] 2-19 [20]; ^{4}[1] 2-202; ^{5}[1] 2-220 [2] = 504. The first volume was published in three parts and the second in five. In this copy the two volumes are bound as one.

Illustrations: Vol. I. Two steel engraved plates, one of ovens and one of petits fours. Vol. II. Five steel engraved plates illustrating elaborate bonbon stands.

Bibliographies: Vicaire 347; Wheaton and Kelly 2013.

Copies: *BNC*; *NUC*, Vol. I. only (New York Public Library and University of California, Berkeley). Wheaton and Kelly, Vol. I. only (Radcliffe only).

188. La Fameuse Compagnie de la Lesine.

LA | FAMEVSE | COMPAGNIE DE LA | LESINE, | OV | ALESNE. | *C'est à dire,* | La Maniere d'espargner, acquerir | & conseruer. | *Ouurage nõ moins vtile pour le Public, que delectable | pour la varieté des rencontres, pleins de doctrine | admirable, & de moralité autãt qu'il est possible.* | Traduction nouuelle de l'Italien. | *Le contenu se pourra voir plus amplement | en la page suiuante.* | [vignette with motto OMNIA VIN | CIT SVBVLA] | A PARIS, | Chez ROLET BOVTONNÉ, au Palais, en la | gallerie des prisonniers, pres la Chancellerie. | [short rule] | M.D.C.XVIII.

Second edition, Paris, 1618, of this translation into French. Originally published in Italian under the title *La famosissima compagnia della Lesina* [Florence? 1570?] and in French, Paris, 1604.

12mo. a^{12} e^8 A-Hh^{12} Ii^4; 396 leaves, ff. [*20*] 1-374 [*2*]. Last two leaves blank.

Note: The original Italian edition of this work is recorded in *BMC* as [Florence? 1550?] but Westbury believes it may be about twenty years later. Authorship has been variously ascribed to Francesco Maria Vialardi, Tommasso Buoni, or Pietro Strozzi. See also item 144.

Bibliographies: Bitting, p. 549; Maggs 108; Oberlé (1) 367-368. Vicaire 196 for the Paris, 1604, edition.

Copies: *BMC*, *BNC*, and *NUC* (8 copies). Note: While the 1618 edition appears in several collections, there is no record of the 1604 edition outside of Vicaire.

189. Favre, Joseph, 1844-1903.

JOSEPH FAVRE | [short fancy rule] | DICTIONNAIRE UNIVERSEL | DE | CUISINE | ENCYCLOPÉDIE ILLUSTRÉE | D'HYGIENE ALIMENTAIRE | [short rule] | MODIFICATION DE L'HOMME PAR L'ALIMENTATION | [short rule] | [two columns: column one] Près de 6,000 recettes | 3 planches coloriées | 1,200 figures gravées dans le texte | [column two] L'animal se repait, l'homme mange: l'homme | d'esprit seul sait manger. | BRILLAT-SAVARIN. | Cuisine, c'est médecine : c'est la médecine | préventive, la meilleure... | J. MICHELET. [end columns] | LE DICTIONNAIRE COMPREND: | L'étymologie, | la synonymie en trois langues, | l'histoire, l'analyse chimique de tous les aliments | naturels et composés, les propriétés hygiéniques appropriées | aux äges et aux sexes, d'après le besoin réclamé par l'individu; le régime, | les prophylactiques, les eaux minérales, la climatologie, les aliments respiratoires, les | cuisines végétarienne, assyrienne, grecque, romaine, française, anglaise, | allemande; la recette des mets, entremets, charcuterie, confiserie, | pâtisserie, glacerie, distillerie et conserves alimentaires; la | biographie de tous les cuisiniers illustres et la | terminologie culinaire. | [short rule] | *PREMIÈRE ÉDITION* – DEUXIÉME *TIRAGE* | [short rule] [Vols. II and III: short fancy rule replaces two short rules and edition statement. Vol. VI: omits DEUXIÉME TIRAGE] | PARIS | LIBRAIRIE-IMPRIMERIE DES HALLES ET DE LA BOURSE DE COMMERCE | 33, rue Jean-Jacques-Rousseau, 33

Second edition, Paris, 1894. Originally published in parts, Paris, 1883-1891, and in book form, Paris, 1892. Vicaire states that this dictionary was the official organ of the Académie de Cuisine.

283 x 212 mm. 4 vols. Vol. I [a]^4 [b]^8 χ1 [1-2]^4 3-55^4; 233 leaves, pp. [6] [i-iii] iv-xiv [2] [1] 2-444. Vol. II. [56]^4 57-117^4 "118-119"^{4}; 252 leaves, pp. [i-v] vi-viii [453] 454-939 [940] [8]. Vol. III. [119]^4 120-179^4 χ^4; 248 leaves, pp. [8] [949] 950-1426 [10]. Vol. IV. [a-f]^4 [180]^4 181-244^4; 284 leaves, pp. [8] [i-iii] iv-xl, 1429-1940 [8]. First leaf blank.

Illustrations: Numerous wood engravings in the text.

Bibliographies: Bitting, p. 154; Oberlé (1) 258; Schraemli (1) 117; Vicaire 356; Wheaton and Kelly 2106.

Copies: *BNC* and *NUC* (Boston Public Library only).

190. Fayot, Charles-Fréderic-Alfred, 1797-1861, ed.

LES | CLASSIQUES | DE LA TABLE, | PETITE BIBLIOTHÈQUE DES ÉCRITS LES PLUS DISTINGUÉS | PUBLIÉS A PARIS SUR LA GASTRONOMIE ET LA VIE ÉLÉGANTE, | ORNÉS DE PORTRAITS, | VIGNETTES SUR ACIER, EAUX-FORTES, LITHOGRAPHIES, | D'APRES | MM. Paul Delaroche, Ary Scheffer, Alfred et Tony Johannot, Isabey, Gavarni, Eugène Lamy, | Roqueplan, Chenavard, Denière, | Par MM. Henriquel Dupont, Blanchard fils, Colignon, Tony Johannot, | Roqueplan, Desmadryl, etc., etc. | Dans les lettres, comme dans l'art de vivre, il n'y a | plus d'originalité que dans l'éclectisme. | Nos médecins ne font plus comme ce philosophe qui, | rencontrant un jeune homme al'ant à un grand festin, le | ramena chez lui, afin de la garantir d'un danger; loin de | là; − ils vont au festin avec le jeune homme. | 1re PARTIE. − 3e ÉDITION, AUGMENTÉE. | [short fancy rule] | PARIS. | AU DÉPOT DE LA LIBRAIRIE, RUE THÉRÈSE, 11, PRÉS LE PALAIS-ROYAL. | [in two columns, column one] DENTU, Palais-Royal; | MARTINON, rue du Coq-Saint-Honoré; | [vertical rule] | [column two] MANSUT, place Saint-André-des-Arcs, 30; | TREUTTEL ET WURTZ, rue de Lille, 19. [end columns] | 1845

Third edition, Paris, 1845. Originally published, Paris, 1843, in sixty parts.

206 x 127 mm. π^2 2π^2 a^4 χ^2 a✱^{8} 1-9^8 10^8(10$_1$ + '10(1)'^{4}, '10(2)$_1$') 11-18^8 '18(1)'^{2} '18(2)'^{2} 9-22^8 2χ1 3χ^2 23^8 (23$_4$ + '23(1)'^{2}) 24^8 25^6 (25$_2$ + '16(1)') 26-32^8 33^4(-33$_4$) 34-37^8 [38]^4 39-40^8 41^8(-41$_8$) 42^4; 353 leaves, pp. [4] [i] ii-iv [2]; ^{2}[i] ii-xxii [4] [1-3]

4-146 [xxv] xxvi-xxxiii [xxxiv] [147-149] 150-288 [xxxvii] xxxviii-xliv [289-291] 292-352 [2] [xlvii] xlviii-l, 353-360 [4] [363] 364-641 [642] [2] = 706 pp. Note: This copy is tightly bound and the collation is offered here as probable.

Illustrations: Lithographed title-page, five lithographed illustrations, two of them double page, and twenty engraved or etched portraits and illustrations all inserted as plates as well as numerous wood engraved vignettes in the text.

Bibliographies: Vicaire 179.

Copies: *NUC* (John Crerar Library and Library Company of Philadelphia).

191. Ficino, Marsilio, 1433-1499.

Ⅸ Marsilio Ficino de triplici vita: Cū | textu Salerni ad vnguem castigato. | [publisher's device: IEHAN PETIT]

Fifth edition, Paris, ca. 1495-1500. Originally published, Florence, 1489.

8vo. a-n^8; 104 leaves, unpaginated. Two index leaves, present in the Bibliothèque Mazarin copy, are not present in this or the Georgetown University copy.

Note: Colophon on n8^v reads: Xvi Septēbris M.LLLL.lxxxix. iargo caregio | Finit opus. This appears to have been copied from the original printing of the work. Inserted in this copy following the title-page is a 16 page unidentified Regimen sanitatis.

Bibliographies: Goff F162; Pellechet 4796.

Copies: *NUC* (Georgetown University only). There is also a copy in the Bibliothèque Mazarin in Paris.

192. Fleury, Claude, 1640-1723.

LES | [in red] DEVOIRS | DES | [in red] MAITRES | ET DES | [in red] DOMESTIQUES. | *Par Me.* [in red] CLAUDE FLEURY, | *prêtre, abbé du Loc-Dieu.* | [printer's monogram] | A PARIS, | [in three columns: column one] Chez { | [column two] [in red] PIERRE AUBOUIN, | [in red] PIERRE EMERY, | ET | [in red]

CHARLES CLOUZIER. | [column three] } Quay des | Augustins, | prés l'Hôtel | de Luynes, | â l'Ecu de | France. [end columns] | [rule] | [in red] M. DC. LXXXVIII. | *Avec Privilege du Roy.*

First edition, Paris, 1688.

12mo. π1 A^8 B^4 C-D^{12} E-Y$^{8.4}$ Z^8 Aa^4 (-Aa4); 156 leaves, pp. [2] 1-308 [2].

Bibliographies: Crahan 141.

Copies: *BNC* and *NUC* (4 copies). *BMC* records an Amsterdam, 1688, edition.

193. Fouquet, Marie (de Maupeou) vicomtesse de Vaux, 1590-1681.

SUITE | DU RECUEIL | DES | REMEDES | FACILES | ET DOMESTIQUES, | CHOISIS, EXPERIMENTEZ | & approuvez pour toutes sortes | de maladies internes & externes, | inveterées & difficile à guerir, | *Recueillis par les ordres charitables de l'illustre* | *& pieuse Madame* FOUQUET, *pour* | *soulager les pauvres malades.* | Avec un Regime de vie pour chaque Complexion | & pour chaque Maladie; & un Traité du | Lait: le tout par ordre alphabetique. | [ornament] | A DIJON, | Par JEAN RESSAYRE Imprimeur | & Libraire, vis-à-vis le College. | [rule] | *M DC. LXXXIX.* | Avec Approbation, & Privilege du Roy.

Second edition, Dijon, 1689. Originally published Dijon, 1687.

12mo. a^{12} e^8 A-S^{12} T^4; 240 leaves, pp. [*40*] 1-440.

Bookplate: William Charles de Meuron, Earl Fitzwilliam.

Bibliographies: Unrecorded in the bibliographies consulted.

Copies: *BMC* and *NUC* (National Library of Medicine only). *BNC* records 1687 edition.

194. Frémont d'Ablancourt, Nicolas, 1625?-1693.

DIALOGUES | DE LA | SANTÉ. | DE MR DE✳✳✳. | [ornament] | A PARIS, | Chez JACQUES VILLERY, ruë de la | Vieille Bouclerie, à l'Estoille. | [short rule] | M. DC. LXXXIII. | *AVEC PRIVILEGE DV ROY.*

First edition, Villery issue, Paris, 1683. Copies of the first edition also exist with the imprints of J. de La Caille and of J. Auboüin.

12mo. a⁴ e1 A-Aa⁸·⁴ Bb⁴ χ1; 154 leaves, pp. [*10*] 1-296 [*2*].

Bookplate: Ex libris Georges Vicaire.

Bibliographies: Vicaire 275 (this copy).

Copies: *BMC*, *BNC*, and *NUC* (5 copies).

195. Friedel, Louise-Béate-Augustine (Utrecht), d. 1818.

LE CONFISEUR | ROYAL, | OU | L'ART DU CONFISEUR | DÉVOILÉ AUX GOURMANDS; | Contenant la manière de faire les Confitures, Mar- | melades; Compotes, Dragées, Pastilles, etc.; | DES INSTRUCTIONS SUR LA DISTILLATION, | La composition des Liqueurs, Crêmes, Huiles, et la ma- | nière de faire les Ratafias et les Fruits à l'eau-de-vie; | DIVERS ARTICLES CONCERNANT L'OFFICE, | Les Crêmes d'entremets, Macarons et Biscuits; | La manière de préparer le Chocolat, le Café, le Thé, les | Sirops, la Limonade, le Punch, les Glaces et les Sorbets; | ENFIN DES RECETTES D'ÉCONOMIE DOMESTIQUE | Pour faire toutes sortes de Vinaigres et les aromatiser, les Eaux | odoriférantes, et les procédés à suivre pour conserver toute | l'année des Légumes et des Fruits comme dans leur primeur; | PAR Mme. UTRECHT-FRIEDEL. | QUATRIÈME ÉDITION. | A PARIS, | Chez TARDIEU-DENESLE, Libraire, quai des | Grands-Augustins, No. 37. | 1816.

Fourth edition, Paris, 1816. Originally published under the title *L'Art de confiseur*, Paris, 1801, and reprinted as *Le Confiseur impérial* in 1809 and 1811.

159 x 96 mm. π⁴ ✱1 1-28⁸·⁴ 29⁸; 181 leaves, pp. [i-v] vi-x [1] 2-352. Bound with Gacon-Dufour's *Recueil pratique d'économie rurale et domestique*, Paris, 1803 (item 197) and Lériguet's *La Cuisine élémentaire*, Paris, 1805 (item 280).

Illustrations: Engraved frontispiece of a confectioner's shop and two engraved folding plates of implements and patterns.

Bibliographies: Maggs 369 (this copy); Vicaire 852.

Copies: *BMC* and *BNC*.

196. Gacon-Dufour, Marie-Amande-Jeanne, 1753-1835.

MANUEL │ DU │ PATISSIER │ ET │ DE LA PATISSIÈRE, │ A L'USAGE DE LA
VILLE ET DE LA CAMPAGNE; │ CONTENANT │ Les moyens de composer toutes
sortes de Pâtisserie, soit │ fortes, soit légères; ainsi que la conservation des viandes, │
des poissons, des fruits et légumes qui doivent y entrer. │ PAR MME
GACON-DUFOUR, │ AUTEUR DE DIVERS OUVRAGES D'ÉCONOMIE, D'ARTS
│ ET DE SCIENCES. │ PARIS, │ RORET, LIBRAIRE, RUE HAUTEFEUILLE, │
AU COIN DE CELLE DU BATTOIR. │ 1825.

First edition, Paris, 1825.

133 x 84 mm. π^6 1-24^6; 150 leaves, pp. [2] [i-v] vi-x [1] 2-288. First leaf blank.

Bibliographies: Bitting, p. 174; Drexel 535; Vicaire 379.

Copies: *BNC* and *NUC* (Library of Congress only).

197. Gacon-Dufour, Marie-Armande-Jeanne, 1753-1835.

RECUEIL │ PRATIQUE │ D'ÉCONOMIE │ RURALE │ ET │ DOMESTIQUE. │ PAR
M.ME GACON-DUFOUR, │ DE PLUSIEURS SOCIÉTÉS D'AGRICULTURE │ ET
LITTÉRAIRES. │ [short rule] │ A PARIS, │ Chez FR. BUISSON, imprimeur-libraire,
rue │ Haute-Feuille, no. 20. │ [short rule] │ AN XII. (1804.)

First edition, Paris, 1804.

159 x 97 mm. π^2 A-K^{12} L^2; 124 leaves, pp. [4] [1] 2-243 [244]. Bound with Mme.
Utrecht-Friedel's *Le Confiseur royal*, Paris, 1816 (item 195) and Lériguet's *La Cuisine
élémentaire*, Paris, 1805 (item 280).

Illustration: Engraved folding plate of a fermentation tub.

Bibliographies: Maggs 369 (this copy).

Copies: *BMC* and *BNC*.

198. Galen.

[ornament] CLAVDII | GALENI DE ALIMENTO- | RVM FACVLTATIBVS | LIBRI III | IOACHINO MARTINIO GAN- | DAVO INTERPRETE. | [printer's device] | PARISIIS | APVD SIMONEM COLINAEVM | 1530.

First separate edition, Paris, 1530.

4to. A^4 a-n^8 o^6; 114 leaves, ff. [4] 1-110.

Bookplates: (1) William Charles de Meuron, Earl Fitzwilliam (2) Westbury.

Bibliographies: Bitting, p. 174; Durling 1856; Horn-Arndt 49; Simon BB2, 356; Vicaire 380.

Copies: *BMC*, *BNC*, and *NUC* (5 copies).

199. Gallais, A.

MONOGRAPHIE | DU CACAO | OU | MANUEL DE L'AMATEUR DE CHOCOLAT, | OUVRAGE CONTENANT | LA DESCRIPTION, L'HISTOIRE ET LA CULTURE DU CACAOYER, | L'ANALYSE | ET LES CARACTÈRES COMMERCIAUX DU CACAO, |LA PRÉPARATION ET LES PROPRIÉTÉS DU CHOCOLAT, | *AVEC UNE CANTATE DE MÉTASTASE*; | ORNÉ D'UNE CARTE ET DE DEUX PLANCHES; | PAR A. GALLAIS, | EX-PHARMACIEN, | ASSOCIÉ DE M. DEBAUVE, | FABRICANT DE CHOCOLATS DU ROI. | [short rule] | Utile dulci. | [short fancy rule] | A PARIS, | CHEZ DEBAUVE ET GALLAIS, | RUE DES SAINTS-PÈRES, N. 26. | 1827

First edition, Paris, 1827.

198 x 125 mm. π^4 1-13^8 14^4; 112 leaves, pp. [i-v] vi-viii [1] 2-216.

Illustrations: Lithographed folding map of the Equatorial countries of South and Central America and two lithographs (one folding) of cacao beans.

Bibliographies: Bitting, p. 175; Vicaire 382.

Copies: *BNC* and *NUC* (4 copies).

200. Gardeton, César, 1786-1831.

DICTIONNAIRE │ DES ALIMENS, │ PRÉCÉDÉ │ D'UNE HYGIÈNE DES
TEMPÉRAMENS, │ DE RÉFLEXIONS SUR LA DIGESTION │ ET LES
MALADIES DE L'ESTOMAC, etc. │ PAR M. C. G., │ DOCTEUR EN MÉDECINE.
│ Dis-moi ce que tu manges, je te dirai ce que tu es. │ BRILLAT-SAVARIN,
Physiologie du goût. │ SECONDE ÉDITION. │ [short fancy rule] │ PARIS, │
NAUDIN, LIBRAIRE, │ RUE DE MONTAIGNE, NOS 18 ET 20. │ [short fancy rule]
│ 1828

Second edition, Paris, 1828. Originally published, Paris, 1826.

203 x 125 mm. π^2 a-b^6 1-25^8 26^4; 218 leaves, pp. [i-v] vi-xxviii [1] 2-408.

Bibliographies: Maggs 423; Vicaire 384 in a note.

Copies: *NUC* (University of California at Berkeley only). *BNC* has first edition.

201. Gardeton, César, 1786-1831.

LA │ GASTRONOMIE │ POUR RIRE, │ OU │ ANECDOTES, RÉFLEXIONS, │
MAXIMES ET FOLIES GOURMANDES │ SUR LA BONNE CHÈRE, LES
INDIGESTIONS, LE VIN, LES IVROGNES, │ LES BUVEURS D'EAU, LES
GOURMANDS, LA GOURMANDISE, LES CUISINIERS, │ LES ALIMENS, LES
BOISSONS, etc.; │ Suivies de principes généraux de politesse et de bonne chère, │ de
notices gastronomiques, │ d'une topographie alimentaire de la France et de l'étranger, │
de considérations hygiéniques sur les alimens en général, │ sur les liquides qui nous
servent de boisson, etc., etc., etc. │ PAR M. CÉSAR GARDETON, │ auteur du
Directeur des estomacs, etc. │ Quand on donne à dîner, on a toujours raison. │ (*L'Art
de dîner en ville.*) │ [short fancy rule] │ A PARIS, │ CHEZ J.-G. DENTU,
IMPRIMEUR-LIBRAIRE, │ RUE DU COLOMBIER, NO 21; │ et Palais-Royal,
galeries de bois, nos 265 et 266. │ MDCCCXXVII.

First edition, Paris, 1827.

145 x 87 mm. π^2 1-23^6 24^4 (-24$_4$); 143 leaves, [*4*] [1] 2-282.

Illustration: Engraved frontispiece titled "Le cochon parlant."

Bibliographies: Vicaire 384; Wheaton and Kelly 2333.

Copies: *BMC*, *BNC*, and *NUC* (New York Public Library only). Wheaton and Kelly (Radcliffe only).

202. Gardeton, César, 1786-1831.

NOUVEAU │ DICTIONNAIRE │ DES MÉNAGES, │ DE SANTÉ, DE CUISINE ET D'ÉCONOMIE, │ CONTENANT: │ 1° Instruction sur les Alimens dont chacun, selon son âge │ et son tempérament, peut se permettre ou doit s'interdire │ l'usgage; 2°. Conservation du Linge, des Etoffes, et d'autres │ effets et meubles; 3°. Méthodes pour détuire les Insectes │ et les Animaux nuisibles; 4°. Avis importans pour se ga- │ rantir de plusieurs Maladies; 5°. Les Plantes utiles à la │ Médecine et à d'autres Arts, leurs propriétés, et les moyens │ de les employer; 6°. Enfin, toutes sortes de Remèdes, │ Recettes, Secrets, Inventions et Découvertes utiles dans │ les Sciences et dans les Arts. │ OUVRAGE UTILE │ AUX GENS DE LA VILLE ET DE LA CAMPAGNE; │ Publié, d'après les travaux des Sociétés Savantes, │ PAR C✳✳✳ G✳✳✳. │ [short fancy rule] │ PARIS, │ CHEZ CORBET AÎNÉ, LIBRAIRE, │ QUAI DES AUGUSTINS, NO. 61. │ 1825.

First edition, Paris, 1825.

178 x 115 mm. π^6 1-29^{12}; 354 leaves, pp. [i-vii] viii-xii [1] 2-696. Publisher's printed wrappers.

Bibliographies: Vicaire 383.

Copies: *BNC* and *NUC* (Rutgers University only).

202a. Garlin, Gustave, b. 1838.

LE │ CUISINIER MODERNE │ OU │ LES SECRETS DE L'ART CULINAIRE │ Menus −Haute Cuisine −Pâtisserie−Glaces−Office, etc. │ SUIVI D'UN DICTIONNAIRE COMPLET DES TERMES TECHNIQUES │ PAR │ Gustave GARLIN │ (DE TONNERRE) │ Elève des premiers Cuisiniers de Paris │ [short rule] │ OUVRAGE COMPLET ILLUSTRÉ DE 60 PLANCHES (330 DESSINS) │ COMPRENANT │ 5,000 TITRES ET 700 OBSERVATIONS │ [short wavy rule] │ TOME PREMEIER [TOME SECOND] │ [short wavy rule] │ PARIS │ GARNIER FRÈRES, LIBRAIRES-ÉDITEURS │ 6, RUE DES SAINTS-PÈRES, 6 │ [short rule] │ 1887

First edition, Paris, 1887, 2 volumes.

307 x 240 mm. 2 vols. Vol. I. [a]⁴ b-e⁴ f² 1-35⁴; 162 leaves, pp. [5] viii [4] xi-xliv [1] 2-278 [2]. Last leaf, blank. Vol. II. π⁴ 1-45⁴; 184 leaves, pp. [8] [1] 2-357 [358] [2]. Last leaf, blank.

Note: The verso of the title-page in each volume has the statement: *Tout exemplaire non revêtu ci-dessous de la signature de l'auteur propriétaire | sera considéré comme contrefaçon. |* [signed in blue ink, G. Garlin]

Illustrations: 60 engraved plates containing 330 illustrations of elaborately prepared dishes.

Bibliographies: Bitting, p. 176; Oberlé (1) 254 (mixed set, Vol. I first edition, Vol. II second edition); Vicaire 385-386.

Copies: *BNC, NUC* (Iowa State University, Kansas State University, and University of California, Berkeley).

203. Garlin, Gustave, b. 1838.

LE | PATISSIER | MODERNE | SUIVI D'UN | TRAITÉ DE CONFISERIE D'OFFICE | PAR | GUSTAVE GARLIN | (DE TONNERRE) | ÉLÈVE DES PREMIERS PATISSIERS DE PARIS | Auteur de Cuisinier moderne | [short rule] | OUVRAGE ILLUSTRÉ DE 262 DESSINS GRAVÉS PAR M. BLITZ | REPRÉSENTANT LES PRINCIPALES PIÈCES MONTÉES | DE LA CUISINE, DE LA PATISSERIE ET DES GLACES | Contenant 3,300 titres et 460 observations tirés du Cuisinier moderne | [short fancy rule] | PARIS | GARNIER FRÈRES, LIBRAIRES-ÉDITEURS | 6, RUE DES SAINTS-PÈRES, 6 | [short rule] | 1889 | Droits de traduction et de reproduction réservés.

First edition, Paris, 1889. Vicaire records the date as 1888 but all copies located are dated 1889.

261 x 173 mm. π² a⁸ 1-62⁸ 63⁴; 510 leaves, pp. [4] [i] ii-xvi [1] 2-997 [998] [2].

Illustrations: 262 photo engraved illustrations by M. Blitz in the text.

Bibliographies: Vicaire 386.

Copies: *BNC* and *NUC* (University of California, Berkeley, only).

204. Le Gastronome français.

LE | GASTRONOME | FRANÇAIS, | OU | L'ART DE BIEN VIVRE, | *Par les anciens Auteurs du Journal des Gourmands*, | MM. G. D. L. R✳✳✳, D. D✳✳✳, GASTERMANN, | G✳✳✳, CLYTOPHON, CHARLES SARTROUVILLE, C. L. C✳✳✳, C✳✳✳, | MARIE DE SAINT-URSIN, B✳✳✳, ETC.; | Ouvrage mis en ordre, accompagné de Notes, de | Dissertations et d'Observations | *Par M. C✳✳✳* | La découverte d'un mets nouveau fait plus pour le | bonheur de l'humanité que la découverte d'une étoile. | HENRION DE PANSEY. | Vaut mieux être ici bas | Gastronome. | Qu'astronome. | GENTIL. | [ornament] | PARIS. | CHARLES-BÉCHET, LIBRAIRE-COMMISSIONNAIRE, | QUAI DES AUGUSTINS, NO 57, PRÈS LE PONT-NEUF. | [ornament] | 1828.

First edition, Paris, 1828.

216 x 131 mm. π^4 1-31^8 32^4; 256 leaves, pp. [i-v] vi-viii [1] 2-503 [504].

Illustration: Engraved frontispiece.

Note: Much of this work was written by Alexandre-Balthazar-Laurent Grimod de la Reynière and Charles-Louis Cadet de Gassicourt. The preliminary discourse was written by Honoré de Balzac over the signature "l'auter de cet article." The book was printed at the Imprimerie de H. Balzac.

Bibliographies: Bitting, p. 555; Simon BG 733; Vicaire 389; Wheaton and Kelly 2556.

Copies: *NUC* (4 copies).

205. Le Gastronome français.

LE | CUISINIER DES CUISINIERS | OU LE VÉRITABLE | GASTRONOME | FRANÇAIS, | MANUEL COMPLET | DU | CUISINIER ET DE LA CUISINIÈRE, | A L'USAGE DE LA VILLE ET DE LA CAMPAGNE; | PAR VIART, | HOMME DE BOUCHE, | QUINZIÈME ÉDITION, REVUE ET AUGMENTÉE DE BEAUCOUP DE | NOUVEAUX ARTICLES, | PAR CARDELLI, ALBERT ET FOURET, | CONTENANT LES PLUS SIMPLES RECETTES POUR FAIRE BONNE CHÈRE | AVEC ÉCONOMIE, | SUIVI DES MEILLEURS PROCÉDÉS POUR LA PATISSERIE | ET L'OFFICE, ETC., ETC. | [ornament] | PARIS, | BARBA, LIBRAIRE, PALAIS ROYAL. | [short rule] | 1839.

Styled "fifteenth edition" on the title-page, but actually a reissue of the first edition sheets with a cancel title and half-title, Paris, 1839. Originally published under the title *Le Gastronome français*, Paris, 1828 (item 204).

190 x 121 mm. π^4 (-π1,2 +π1.2) 1-31^8 32^4; 256 leaves, pp. [i-v] vi-viii [1] 2-503 [504].

Bibliographies: This issue of the first edition unrecorded in the bibliographies consulted.

Copies: No other copy of this issue located.

206. Gastronomiana.

GASTRONOMIANA │ OU │ RECUEIL │ CURIEUX ET AMUSANT │ D'ANECDOTES, Bons-Mots, Plai- │ santeries, Maximes et Réflexions │ Gastronomiques, précédé d'une Dis- │ sertation historique sur la science de │ la Gueule, et entremêlé de Chan- │ sons et Propos de Table propres à │ égayer la fin d'un Repas. │ [short rule] │ Nous n'avons qu'un temps à vivre, │ Amis, passons-le à Table. │ [short rule] │ A PARIS, │ A LA LIBRAIRIE ÉCONOMIQUE, │ Ancien Collége d'Harcourt, rue de la Harpe, │ no. 94. │ [short fancy rule] │ 1809.

First edition, Paris, 1809.

Note: Attributed to Charles-Yves Cousin, called Cousin d'Avallon, 1769-1840, by Oberlé.

119 x 76 mm. π^2 1-14^6 15^4; 90 leaves, pp. [4] [1] 2-175 [176]. Bound with *Révolutioniana* (item 158) and *Poissardiana* (item 395).

Illustration: Engraved frontispiece of a military officer at a table and two others before a fire with two servants in attendance.

Bibliographies: Drexel 530; Horn-Arndt 441; Maggs 344; Malorite 521; Oberlé (1) 390; Schraemli (3) 67; Vicaire 390; Wheaton and Kelly 2340.

Copies: *NUC* (University of California, Berkeley, only). Wheaton and Kelly (Radcliffe only).

207. Gautier, Alexandre.

TRAITÉ | DES ALIMENS, | LEURS QUALITÉS, LEURS EFFETS, | ET DU
CHOIX QUE L'ON DOIT EN FAIRE, | SELON L'AGE, | LE SEXE, LE
TEMPÉRAMENT, | LA PROFESSION, LES CLIMATS, LES HABITUDES | ET
LES MALADIES, | PENDANT LA GROSSESSE, L'ALLAITEMENT, ETC.; | PAR
M. A. GAUTIER, | DOCTEUR EN MÉDECINE, | [short fancy rule] | PARIS, |
AUDOT, ÉDITEUR, | RUE DES MAÇONS-SORBONNE, NO 11. | 1828.

First edition, Paris, 1828.

133 x 82 mm. π^4 1-12$^{12.6}$ 13^{12}; 124 leaves, pp. [i-v] vi-xii [5] 6-239 [240].

Bibliographies: Vicaire 393.

Copies: *BNC*.

208. Gautier, Leopold, b. 1838.

MANUEL PRATIQUE | DE LA | FRABRICATION ET DU RAFFINAGE | DU |
SUCRE DE BETTERAVES | PAR | LE Dr L. GAUTIER | [short rule] | Ave 66
Gravures dans let texte | [short rule] | PARIS | LIBRAIRIE F. SAVY | 77,
BOULEVARD SAINT-GERMAIN, 77 | [short rule] | 1880

First edition, Paris, 1880.

244 x 153 mm. π^4(-π1) 1-13^8; 107 leaves, pp. [2] [i] ii-iv [1] 2-207 [208].

Illustrations: Sixty-six photo engraved illustrations in the text.

Bibliographies: Unrecorded in the bibliographies consulted.

Copies: *BMC*, *BNC*, and *NUC* (Franklin Institute and National Agricultural Library).

209. Gazio, Antonio, 1449-1530.

[in red] Florida Corona que ad sa= | [in red] nitatis hominum conseruationem ac | [in
red] longeuam vitam perducendam | [in red] sunt pernecessaria continens. | [in red] Ab
[in black] Anthonio Gazio [in red] Pa= | [in red] tauino medico doctissi= | [in red]
mo composita. | [in red, cross] | [woodcut of crown]

Colophon: ℂ Impressum Lugd. per Gilbertum devil | liers. Impensis honesti viri Bartholomei | trot. Anno salutis. M.ccccxiiii. Die. xvii. | mensis Octobris.

Second edition, Lyon, 1514. Originally published under the title *De conservatione sanitatis*, Venice, 1491.

4to. A^8 a-v^8; 168 leaves, ff. [*8*] 1-159 [160]. Last leaf blank.

Illustration: Woodcut of crown on title-page.

Bibliographies: Durling 2031; Oberlé (1) 424; Vicarie 397.

Copies: *BNC* and *NUC* (John Crerar Library, National Library of Medicine, and University of California, Berkeley).

210. Gazio, Antonio, 1449-1530.

[within woodcut border] [ornament] [in red] Florida Co= | [in red] rona: que ad sanitatis hominum | [in red] conseruationem [in black] ac longeuam vi= | tam perducendam sunt perne= | cessaria continens. [in red] Ab Antho= | [in red] nio Gazio Patauino medico do | [in red] ctissimo composita. [in black] Non medio= | cri vigilātia et labore [in red] recēter Im= | [in red] presta. [in black] Et mendis quibus pluri= | mum scatebat [in red] expurgata. [in black] Felici= | ter Incipit. | ℂ [in red] Venundant Lug= | [in red] duni [in black] In vico Mercuriali: apud | [in red] Scipionem de Gabiano [in black] sub Si= | gno fontis. | [in red] 1534

Fourth edition, Lyon, 1534. Originally published under the title *De conservatione sanitatis*, Venice, 1491, and reprinted, Lyon, 1514, 1516, and 1534.

8vo. A^8 a-z^8 $\&^8$ $?^8$; 208 leaves, ff. [*8*] 1-198 [*2*]. Last two leaves blank.

Bibliographies: Durling 2033; Oberlé (1) 426.

Copies: *BMC* and *NUC* (National Library of Medicine, University of California, Berkeley, and University of Minnesota).

211. Geiler von Kaisersberg, Johannes, 1445-1510.

Nauicula siue speculū fatuorū | Prestantissimi sacrarum literarum Doctoris Joan- | nis Geyler Keysersbergii Concionatoris Ar- | gentineñ. a Jacobo Othero | collecta. | Compendiosa vitae eiusdem descriptio, per | Beatum Rhenanum Selestatinum. | Ad Narragoniam. | [woodcut]

First edition, Strassburg, Matthias Schurer, 1510.

Note: While there is no separate colophon, the last paragraph on Ss8^r concludes, "Vale ex Argeñ. iii. Jdus Februarij. Anno. 1510."

4to. 1-2^8 3^4 4^6 A^4 B-C^8 D^4 E-F^8 G^4 H-I^8 K^4 L^8 M^4 N-O^8 P^4 Q^8 R^4 S-T^8 U-X^4 Y^8 Z-Aa^4 Bb^8 Cc^4 Dd^8 Ee-Ff^4 Gg-Hh^8 Ii^4 Kk^8 Ll- Mm^4 Nn-Oo^8 Pp-Qq^4 Rr-Ss^8; 278 leaves, unpaginated. Note: Some copies include a twelve page life of Geiler by Rhenanus, separately published and appended to several of Geiler's works. It is not present in this copy.

Illustrations: Woodcut of a ship on the title-page. Note: This is not the same woodcut as appears on the title-page of the 1511 edition (item 212).

Text consists of sermons on Brant's *Narrenschiff*.

Bibliographies: Unrecorded in the bibliographies consulted.

Copies: *BMC* and *NUC* (5 copies).

212. Geiler von Kaisersberg, Johannes, 1445-1510.

Nauicula siue speculū fatuo[rum] | Prestatissimi sacra[rum] literarŪ doctoris Joannis Geyler Key | sersbergij: concionatoris Argetineñ. in sermones iuxta tur | marum seriem diuisa. suis figuris iam insignita: a Jacobo | Othero diligenter collecta. | Compendiosa vite eiusdem descriptio/ per | Beatum Rhenanum Selestatinum. | Ad Narragoniam. | [woodcut]

Second edition, Strassburg, Johann Pruss, 1511. Originally published, Strassburg, 1510 (item 211).

4to. 1^8 2^6 3^8 A-X$^{4.8.4}$ Y^4 Z^8 a^4 b-k$^{4.8.4}$ l^4 m-z$^{4.8.4}$ Aa-Bb^4 Cc^6; 280 leaves, unpaginated.

Illustrations: Woodcut on the title showing the "Ship of Fools" and 105 woodcuts, five of them repeated, for a total of 110 illustrations in the text. These are the same woodcuts, printed from the same blocks, as were used in the first Basle editions of Brant's *Ship of Fools* (1494, 1497). They were for a long time attributed variously to Grünewald, Wechtlin, and Urs Graf, but now are widely believed to be the work of the young Dürer.

Bibliographies: Brunet II, 1575; Crahan 47; Maggs 52.

Copies: *BMC, BNC,* and *NUC* (12 copies).

212a. George-Grimblot, A.

EXPOSITION UNIVERSELLE DE 1878. | [short fancy rule] | MINISTÈRE DE L'AGRICULTURE ET DU COMMERCE. | [short rule] | ADMINISTRATION DES FORÊTS. | [short fancy rule] | ÉTUDES SUR LA TRUFFE | PAR | A. GEORGE-GRIMBLOT, | INSPECTEUR DES FORÊTS. | [publisher's device] | PARIS. | IMPRIMERIE NATIONALE. | [short rule] | 1878.

First edition, Paris, 1878.

269 x 211 mm. [1]⁴ 2-12⁴ 13²; 50 leaves, pp. [1-5] 6-99 [100]. Publisher's green paper printed wrappers with the text of the title-page within a three rule border on the outer front wrapper and a three rule border on the outer back wrapper.

Illustrations: Diagrams in the text.

Bibliographies: Unrecorded in the bibliographies consulted.

Copies: *BNC* and *NUC* (Harvard only).

213. Gérard de Nerval, 1808-1855.

MONSIEUR | DENTSCOURT, | OU | *LE CUISINIER D'UN GRAND HOMME,* | Tableau politique, à propos de lentilles. | PAR M. BEUGLANT, | POÈTE, AMI DE CADET ROUSSEL, | *Auteur de la fameuse Complainte sur la Mort* | *du Droit* | *d'aînesse.* | [publisher's monogram] | PARIS. | TOUQUET, GALERIE VIVIENNE. | [short rule] | M. DCCC. XXVI.

First edition, Paris, 1826.

98 x 60 mm. [1]^{16}; 16 leaves, pp. [1-7] 8-32.

A tableau in verse in seven scenes.

Bibliographies: Vicaire ML VI, 51.

Copies: *BNC*.

214. Gilliers.

LE | CANNAMELISTE | FRANÇAIS, | *OU* | NOUVELLE INSTRUCTION | POUR CEUX QUI DESIRENT D'APPRENDRE | L'OFFICE, | Rédigé en forme de Dictionnaire, | *CONTENANT* | Les noms, les descriptions, les usages, les choix & les principes de tout | ce qui se pratique dans l'Office, l'explication de tous les termes dont | on se sert; avec la maniére de dessiner, & de former toutes sortes | de contours de Tables & de Dormants. | ENRICHI DE PLANCHES EN TAILLE-DOUCE. | *Par le Sieur GILLIERS, Chef d'Office, & Distillateur de Sa Majesté le Roi | de Pologne, Duc de Lorraine & de Bar.* | [ornament] | A NANCY, | De l'Imprimerie D'ABEL-DENIS CUSSON, au Nom de JESUS. | *Et se vend à Lunéville*, Chez l'AUTEUR. | [two short rules] | *AVEC PRIVILEGE DU ROY.* | MDCCLI.

First edition, Nancy, 1751.

4to. ✱^{4} A-Hh^4 [Ii]^2; 130 leaves, pp. [*4*] i-iii [iv] [1] 2-238; ^{2}1-13 [*14*].

Illustrations: Folding engraved frontispiece and thirteen folding plates of utensils and designs for sugar constructions.

Bibliographies: Drexel 133; Horn-Arndt 260a; Maggs 259; Malorite 216; Schraemli (1) 205; Schraemli (3) 40; Vicaire 404; Wheaton and Kelly 2390.

Copies: *NUC* (Harvard and John Crerar Library).

215. Gilliers.

LE | CANNAMELISTE | FRANÇAIS, | OU | *NOUVELLE INSTRUCTION* | POUR CEUX QUI DESIRENT D'APPRENDRE | L'OFFICE, | *RÉDIGÉ EN FORME DE DICTIONNAIRE,* | CONTENANT | *LES NOMS, les descriptions, les usages, les choix & les | principes de tout ce qui se pratique dans l'Office, l'explication | de tous les termes dont on se sert; avec la maniere de dessiner,* | *& de former toutes sortes de contours de Tables & de Dor-* | *mants.* | ENRICHI DE PLANCHES EN TAILLE-DOUCE. | *Par le Sieur* GILLIERS, *Chef d'Office, & Distillateur* | *de Sa Majesté le Roi de Pologne, Duc de Lorraine* | *& de Bar.* | [ornament] | A NANCY, | Chez JEAN-BAPTISTE-HIACINTHE LECLERC, | Imprimeur-Libraire. | *Et à Paris,* | Chez MERLIN, Libraire, rue de la Harpe. | [two short rules] | M. DCC. LXVIII. | *Avec Privilege du Roi.*

Second edition, Nancy, 1768. Originally published, Nancy, 1751 (item 214).

4to. $*^4$ A-Hh^4 [Ii]^2; 130 leaves, pp. [*4*] i-iv [1] 2-238; ^{2}1-13 [14].

Illustrations: Engraved title and 13 engraved folding plates of utensils and designs for sugar construction.

Bibliographies: Bitting, p. 184-5; Maggs 260; Oberlé (1) 122; Schraemli (1) 206; Vicaire 405.

Copies: *BMC*, *BNC*, and *NUC* (6 copies).

216. Gonet, Gabriel de.

LA NOUVELLE | CUISINE SIMPLIFIÉE | DES MÉNAGES | A L'USAGE DES MAITRESSES DE MAISONS | PAR GABRIEL DE GONET | SUIVI DU | GUIDE COMPLET DU SERVICE DE TABLE | PAR MADAME LA COMTESSE DE BASSANVILLE | PRÉCÉDÉ D'UNE | INTRODUCTION SUR LES CLASSIQUES DE LA TABLE | PAR ALPHONSE KARR | [short fancy rule] | *Illustré de gravures sur acier* | Prix: 5 francs | [woodcut of kitchen scene] | Chez GENNEQUIN, Libraire, à Paris | 11, RUE GÎT-LE-COEUR, 11

First edition, Paris, ca. 1860.

211 x 130 mm. π^2 1^2 2^4 ($\pm2_2$) 3-32^8 33-35^4; 260 leaves, pp. [1-5] 6-16, ff. [17] 18-256, pp. [257] 258-276 [4]. Last three pages blank. The foliated part of the book has text on the rectos only, the versos being ruled and headed "Recettes nouvelles – Modifications." Green publisher's printed boards. This copy lacks π1 (half-title?).

Illustrations: Wood engraving of kitchen scene on the title-page; hand-colored steel engraved frontispiece and three hand-colored steel engraved plates representing personified vegetables.

Bibliographies: Bitting, p. 192; Wheaton and Kelly 2448.

Copies: Wheaton and Kelly (Radcliffe only). (Bitting copy not recorded in *NUC*).

217. Goudeau, Émile, 1849-1906.

[in red] *TABLEAUX DE PARIS* | [short rule] | ÉMILE GOUDEAU | [ornament] | [in red] PARIS | [in red] QUI CONSOMME | [ornament] | Dessins | de | PIERRE VIDAL | [publisher's monogram] | PARIS | [in red] IMPRIMÉ POUR HENRI BERALDI | [short rule] | 1893

First edition, Paris, 1893. No. 8 of 138 copies on vélin des Vosges.

270 x 189 mm. π^4 a^4 b^2 1-41^4; 174 leaves, pp. [*8*] [i] ii-ix [x-xii] [1] 2-325 [326] [*2*]. Full calf stamped in colored relief Japanese scenes, by Carayon; original wrappers preserved.

Illustrations: Colored frontispiece and fifty colored full page illustrations by Pierre Vidal integral with the signatures in which they appear.

Bibliographies: Crahan 581; Maggs 566.

Copies: *BMC*, *BNC*, and *NUC* (4 copies).

218. Gouffé, Jules, b. 1807.

LE LIVRE | [in red] DE CUISINE | PAR | JULES GOUFFÉ | COMPRENANT | [in red] LA CUISINE DE MÉNAGE ET LA GRANDE CUISINE | AVEC | 25 PLANCHES IMPRIMÉES EN CHROMO-LITHOGRAPHIE | ET 161 VIGNETTES SUR BOIS | DESSINÉES D'APRÈS NATURE PAR E. RONJAT | [wood engraving of three game hens on a skewer] | PARIS | [in red] LIBRAIRIE DE L. HACHETTE ET Cie | BOULEVARD SAINT-GERMAIN, No 77 | [short rule] | 1867 | Droits de propriété et de traduction réservés

First edition, Paris, 1867.

275 x 174 mm. π^2 a^6 1-51^8 52^6; 422 leaves, pp. [*4*] [i] ii-xi [xii] [1-3] 4-823 [824] [*4*].

Illustrations: Chromolithograph frontispiece and 24 chromolithograph plates in color and 161 wood engravings in the text.

Bibliographies: Bitting, p. 195; Drexel 172; Malortie, 1189; Oberlé (1) 226; Schraemli (2) 46; Schraemli (3) 99; Vicaire 418 in a note; Wheaton and Kelly 2469.

Copies: *BMC*, *BNC*, and *NUC* (10 copies).

219. Gouffé, Jules, b. 1807.

LE LIVRE | [in red] DE PATISSERIE | PAR | JULES GOUFFÉ | OFFICIER DE BOUCHE DU JOCKEY-CLUB DE PAIRS | OUVRAGE CONTENANT | [in red] 10 PLANCHES CHROMOLITHOGRAPHIQUES | [in red] ET 137 GRAVURES SUR BOIS | D'APRÈS LE PEINTURES A L'HUILE ET LES DESSINS | DE E. RONJAT | [wood engraving of a cake] | PARIS | [in red] LIBRAIRIE HACHETTE ET Cie | BOULEVARD SAINT-GERMAIN, 79 | [short rule] | 1873 | Droits de propriété et de traduction réservés

First edition, Paris, 1873.

266 x 169 mm. π^8 1-31^8 32^6; 262 leaves, pp. [8] [i] ii-vii [viii] [1] 2-506 [2].

Illustrations: Wood engraved frontispiece portrait of the author, ten chromolithograph plates in color and 137 wood engravings in the text.

Bibliographies: Bitting, p. 195-6; Oberlé (1) 230; Schraemli (1) 215; Schraemli (2) 48; Vicaire 418; Wheaton and Kelly 2473.

Copies: *BMC*, *BNC*, and *NUC* (John Crerar Library and National Agricultural Library). Wheaton and Kelly (Boston Anthenaeum only).

220. Gouffé, Jules, b. 1807.

LE LIVRE | DES | [in red] CONSERVES | OU | RECETTES POUR PRÉPARER ET CONSERVER | LES VIANDES ET LES POISSON SALÉS ET FUMÉS | LES TERRINES, LES GALANTINES | LES LÉGUMES, LES FRUITS, LES CONFITURES, LES LIQUEURS DE FAMILLE | LES SIROPS, LES PETITS FOURS, ETC., ETC. | PAR | JULES GOUFFÉ | Officier de bouche du Jockey-Club | AUTEUR DU LIVRE DE CUISINE | [short rule] | [in red] OUVRAGE ILLUSTRÉ

DE 34 VIGNETTES SUR BOIS | [short rule] | PARIS | [in red] LIBRAIRIE DE L. HACHETTE ET CIE | BOULEVARD SAINT-GERMAIN, No 77 | [short rule] | 1869 | Droits de traduction et de reproduction réservés

First edition, Paris, 1869.

277 x 180 mm. π^4 1-28^8 29^2; 230 leaves, pp. [2] [i-v] vi [1] 2-450 [2].

Illustrations: Steel engraved frontispiece portrait of the author and 34 wood engravings in the text.

Bibliographies: Oberlé (1) 229; Schraemli (1) 217; Vicaire 418; Wheaton and Kelly 2472.

Copies: *BMC*, *BNC*, and *NUC* (Library of Congress, Northwestern University and University of Virginia).

221. Gouriet, Jean-Baptiste, 1774-1855.

L'ANTIGASTRONOMIE, | OU | L'HOMME DE VILLE SORTANT | DE TABLE, | POÈME EN IV CHANTS. | Manuscrit trouvé dans un pâté, et aug- | menté de remarques importantes. | AVEC FIGURE. | A PARIS, | CHEZ HUBERT ET Ce. IMP.-LIB. | RUE DES GRANDS-AUGUSTINS, No. 21. | [short rule] | M. DCCC. VI.

Second edition, Paris, 1806. Originally published, Paris, 1804.

129 x 82 mm. 1-18^6 19^8; 116 leaves, pp. [1-5] 6-232.

Illustrations: Engraved frontispiece by Bovinet after Desrais of a draped figure pointing accusingly at a group at table.

Bibliographies: Bitting, p. 196; Drexel 143; Horn-Arndt 446; Maggs 334; Oberlé (1) 388; Vicaire 27.

Copies: *BMC*, *BNC*, and *NUC* (Library of Congress and New York Public Library).

222. Grandi, Ferdinando.

LES NOUVEAUTÉS | DE LA | GASTRONOMIE PRINCIÈRE | PAR | FERDINANDO GRANDI | CHEF DES CUISINES | DE SON EXCELLENCE LE PRINCE ANATOLE DE DÉMIDOFF. | Ouvrage orné de 25 figures. | [short fancy rule] | PARIS. AUDOT. | LIBRAIRIE GASTRONOMIQUE, | RUE GARANCIÈRE, 8, SAINT-SULPICE. | [short rule] | 1866 | *Tous droits de reproduction et de traduction réservés.*

First edition, Paris, 1866.

242 x 154 mm. [1]⁸ 2-13⁸ 14²; 106 leaves, pp. [1-7] 8-212. Half green morocco with marbled boards. Publisher's printed wrappers preserved.

Illustrations: Fourteen wood engraved plates illustrating elaborate dishes.

Bibliographies: Bitting, p. 197; Drexel 569; Vicaire 421.

Copies: *BMC, BNC,* and *NUC* (Library of Congress only).

223. Grapaldi, Francesco Mario, 1465?-1515.

Francisci Marij Grapaldi | De partibus aedium | Dictionari[us] lōge | lepidissimus | nec min[us] | fructuo | sus. | Beatus Arnoaldus: Selestatinus | Laudantur monumenta vel caduca. | Vt Pori domus alta: Apollinisq[ue] | Ex auro statua: Herculisq[ue] gades: | Et fanum triuiae sacrum Dianae | Nomen quo tulit impius cremator: | Aut Mēphitica Pyramis sepultae. | Quā struxisse serunt puellae amātes: | Mausoli quoq[ue] Cariae tyranni | Instructum aere pendulū sepulchrum: | Vitam quaeq[ue] dabant vel architectis: | Aedes: atria: porticus: columae: | Quae nullos meruere vt haec honores | Constructa ingenij sagacitate. | Laudata ingeniosioribusq[ue]. | Quae conspecta tibi: scio placebunt.

Colophon: Finiunt Libri. F. Grabaldi de partibus aeditū | cum regesto vocabulorum impressi in | vrbe Argentina per Industrium | Ioannem prysz In aedibus | Lustri vulgo zum thier= | garttē Anno salutis | M.ccccc.viij: | [printer's device]

New edition, Strassburg, 1508. Originally published, Parma, ca. 1494.

4to. [A]⁸ B-C⁴, ²A-B⁸ C-D⁴ E⁸ F-G⁴ H⁸ I-K⁴ L⁸ M-O⁴ P⁸ Q-S⁴ T⁸ V-X⁴ Y⁸; 136 leaves, ff. [*16*] i-cxviii, cxx [*1*].

Bibliographies: Graesse Vol. III, p. 137, in a note.

Copies: *BMC*, *BNC*, and *NUC* (four copies).

224. Grimod de la Reynière, Alexandre-Balthasar-Laurent, 1758-1838.

ALMANACH | DES GOURMANDS, | OU | CALENDRIER NUTRITIF, | SERVANT DE GUIDE DANS LES MOYENS DE | FAIRE EXCELLENTE CHÈRE; | Suivi de l'Itinéraire d'un Gourmand dans | divers quartiers de Paris, et de quel- | ques Variétés morales, apéritives et ali- | mentaires, Anecdotes gourmandes, etc. | PAR UN VIEUX AMATEUR. | [short rule] | Tanquam leo rugiens, circuit | quaerens quem devoret. | S. Petr. epist., cap. VI, vers. 8. | [short rule] | A PARIS, | Chez MARADAN, Libraire, rue Pavée- | Saint-André-des-Arcs, no. 16. | [short rule] | AN XI. − 1803.

First edition, Paris, 1803.

145 x 91 mm. π^2 $2\pi^6$ a^2 1-12$^{12.6}$ 13^{12} 14^4; 134 leaves, pp. [i-iii] iv [*12*] v-viii, ^{2}[i] ii-viii [9] 10-247 [248]. Publisher's orange wrappers with printed label on the spine.

Illustrations: Engraved frontispiece by "M." after "N." titled "Bibliothèque d'un Gourmand du XIX. Siècle."

Bibliographies: Oberlé (1) 133; Schraemli (3) 53; Simon BG 794; Vicaire 424. Bitting, p. 201-202 and Pennell, p. 131, record the second edition and Horn-Arndt 358 the fourth edition.

Copies: *BNC* and *NUC*. (Note: A check of the libraries recorded in the *NUC* as having the *Almanach des Gourmands* reveals that none owns the first edition of the first number.)

225. Grimod de la Reynière, Alexandre-Balthasar-Laurent, 1758-1838.

ALMANACH | DES GOURMANDS, | SERVANT DE GUIDE DANS LES MOYENS DE | FAIRE EXCELLENTE CHÈRE; | PAR UN VIEIL AMATEUR. | SECONDE ANNÉE, | Contenant un grand nombre de Disser- | tations philosophico-gourmandes; les | quatre Parties du jour d'un Gourmand; | des Variétés morales et nutritives; des | Anecdotes gourmandes; plusieurs | articles relatifs à la

Friandise, etc. etc. | [short rule] | Non in solo pane vivit homo. | *S. Math. cap. 4 .* |
[short rule] | A PARIS, | Chez MARADAN, Libraire, rue Pavée- |
Saint-André-des-Arcs, no. | [short rule] | AN XII. − 1804.

First edition, Paris, 1804.

142 x 90 mm. π^2 $2\pi^4$ $3\pi^6$ 1-23^6 24^4; 154 leaves, pp. [*4*] [1] 2-8 [*12*] i-xviii [19] 20-282
[*2*]. Last leaf blank. Publisher's orange wrappers with printed label on the spine.

Illustrations: Engraved frontispiece by Mariage after Dunant titled "Les audiences d'un
Gourmand."

Bibliographies: Oberlé (1) 133; Schraemli (3) 54; Vicaire 425; Wheaton and Kelly
2538. Bitting, p. 202, Horn-Arndt 358 and Simon BG 797 all list the second edition.
Pennell, p. 131, edition not stated.

Copies: *NUC* (New York Public Library only).

226. Grimod de la Reynière, Alexandre-Balthasar-Laurent, 1758-1838.

ALMANACH | DES GOURMANDS, | SERVANT DE GUIDE DANS LES
MOYENS | DE FAIRE EXCELLENTE CHÈRE. | PAR UN VIEIL AMATEUR. |
TROISIÈME ANNÉE, | Contenant plusieurs Articles de morale et | de politesse
Gourmande; une Notice rai- | sonnée des principaux Fruits qui se ser- | vent à table; la
seconde Promenade d'un | Gourmand dans Paris; les Découvertes | nouvelles de 1804;
plusieurs Recettes | alimentaires et friandes; un grand nom- | bre d'Anecdotes
Gourmandes; des prin- | cipes d'Hygiène et de savoir-vivre; un | extrait de la
Correspondance Gourmande | de l'Auteur, etc. etc. | [rule] | Jejunus rarò stomachus
vulgaria temnit. | *Horat. Sat. 2, Lib. II.* | [rule] | DE L'IMPRIMERIE DE CELLOT.
| A PARIS, | Chez MARADAN, Libraire, rue des Grands- | Augustins, no. 29. | AN
XIII. − 1805.

First edition, Paris, 1805.

143 x 91 mm. [a]^6 b^2 1-28^6 29^4; 180 leaves, pp. [2] [i-v] vi-xiv [1] 2-342 [2]. First and
last leaves blank. Publisher's orange wrappers with printed label on the spine.

Illustrations: Engraved frontispiece by Maradan after Dunant titled "Séance d'un Jury
de Gourmands dégustateurs."

Bibliographies: Bitting, p. 202; Drexel 143; Oberlé (1) 133; Schraemli (3) 55; Simon BG 798; Vicaire 425. Pennell, p. 131, edition not stated.

Copies: *BNC* and *NUC* (Kansas State University and University of Massachusetts).

227. Grimod de la Reynière, Alexandre-Balthasar-Laurent, 1758-1838.

ALMANACH | DES GOURMANDS, | SERVANT DE GUIDE DANS LES MOYENS | DE FAIRE EXCELLENTE CHÈRE. | PAR UN VIEIL AMATEUR. | QUATRIÈME ANNÉE, | Contenant un grand nombre d'Articles de | morale Gourmande et de Considérations | alimentaires; beaucoup de Recettes | Gourmandes inédites et curieuses; la | Description de plusieurs espèces de ra- | goûts, tant exotiques qu'indigènes; | la Petite Revue Gourmande, ou troi- | sième Promenade d'un Gourmand dans | Paris, les Découvertes Gourmandes et | Friandes de l'année 1805; la Nécrologie | Gourmande de 1805, etc. | [rule] | Nil actum reputans si quid superesset agendum. | *Lucan.* | [rule] | DE L'IMPRIMERIE DE CELLOT. | A PARIS, | Chez MARADAN, Libraire, rue des Grands- | Augustins, no. 9. | M. DCCC. VI.

First edition, Paris, 1806.

142 x 90 mm. a^6 b^4 1-28^6; 178 leaves, pp. [i-v] vi-xx [1] 2-336. Publisher's orange wrappers with printed label on the spine.

Illustrations: Engraved frontispiece by Maradan after Dunant titled "Les méditations d'un Gourmand."

Bibliographies: Bitting, p. 202; Drexel 143; Horn-Arndt 358; Oberlé (1) 133; Schraemli (3) 56; Simon BG 800; Vicaire 425. Pennell, p. 131, edition not stated.

Copies: *BMC*, *BNC*, and *NUC* (5 copies).

228. Grimod de la Reynière, Alexandre-Balthasar-Laurent, 1758-1838.

ALMANACH | DES GOURMANDS, | SERVANT DE GUIDE DANS LES MOYENS | DE FAIRE EXCELLENTE CHÈRE. | PAR UN VIEIL AMATEUR. | CINQUIÈME ANNÉE, | Contenant un grand nombre d'Articles de | Morale, de Politesse et d'Hygiène gour- | mandes, plusieurs Recettes gourmandes | inédites et curieuses; un petit Traité | des Diners par Coeur, du Savoir-vivre | et des Offres-réelles; les Découvertes | Gourmandes et Friandes de 1806; quel- | ques

Anecdotes gourmandes; la Corres- | pondance gourmande; la Petite Revue | de l'année 1806, formant la Quatrième | Promenade d'un Gourmand dans Paris; | Poésies gourmandes, etc. | [rule] | *Liquidum non frangit jejunium.* | [rule] | DE L'IMPRIMERIE DE CELLOT. | A PARIS, | Chez MARADAN, Libraire, rue des Grands- | Augustins, no. 9. | M. DCCC. VII.

First edition, Paris, 1807.

147 x 90 mm. a^6 b1 [c]^6 1-30^6 31$_1$; 194 leaves, pp. [i-v] vi-xiv [*12*] [1] 2-362. Publisher's orange wrappers with printed label on the spine.

Illustrations: Engraved frontispiece by Maradan after Dunant titled "Le premier devoir d'un Amphitrion."

Bibliographies: Bitting, p. 202; Drexel 143; Horn-Arndt 358; Oberlé (1) 133; Schraemli (3) 57; Simon BG 801; Vicaire 426. Pennell, p. 131, edition not stated.

Copies: *BMC*, *BNC*, and *NUC* (5 copies).

229. Grimod de la Reynière, Alexandre-Balthasar-Laurent, 1758-1838.

ALMANACH | DES GOURMANDS, | SERVANT DE GUIDE DANS LES MOYENS | DE FAIRE EXCELLENTE CHÈRE. | PAR UN VIEIL AMATEUR. | SIXIÈME ANNÉE, | Contenant plusieurs articles qu'il importe aux | Amphitryons, aux convives, et surtout aux | Gourmands, de lire et de méditer; des Décou- | vertes importantes pour les Gourments; quelques | Chapitres de Morale et de Métaphysique gour- | mandes; des Recettes inédites et curieuses; un | petit Traité des Liaison, des Braises et des | Coulis; des considérations sur les Progrès de l'art | du Four, sur plusieurs objets d'Economie domes- | tique, et sur quelques Marchés de Paris; des Poé- | sies et des Chansons gourmandes; la Petite Re- | vue de l'année 1808, formant la Sixième Prome- | nade d'un Gourmand dans Paris, etc. etc. etc. | [short rule] | *Anseris ante ipsum magni jecur, anseribus par | Altilis, et flavi dignus ferro Meleagri | Fumat aper.* | Juvénal, Sat. v. vers. 114. | [short rule] | DE L'IMPRIMERIE DE CELLOT. | A PARIS, | Chez MARADAN, Libraire, rue des Grands- | Augustins, no. 9. | M. DCCC. VIII.

First edition, Paris, 1808.

145 x 92 mm. a^6 1-27^6 28^4; 172 leaves, pp. [i-v] vi-xii, 1-331 [332]. Publisher's orange wrappers with printed label on the spine.

Illustrations: Engraved frontispiece by Maradan after Dunant titled "Les Rêves d'un Gourmand."

Bibliographies: Bitting, p. 202; Horn-Arndt 358; Oberlé (1) 133; Schraemli (3) 58; Simon BG 802; Vicaire 426. Pennell, p. 131, edition not stated.

Copies: *BMC*, *BNC*, and *NUC* (5 copies).

230. Grimod de la Reynière, Alexandre-Balthasar-Laurent, 1758-1838.

ALMANACH | DES GOURMANDS, | SERVANT DE GUIDE DANS LES MOYENS | DE FAIRE EXCELLENTE CHÈRE; | PAR UN VIEIL AMATEUR. | SEPTIÈME ANNÉE, | Contenant un grand nombre de Chapitres intéres- | sans, pour servir à l'Histoire de l'Art alimentaire; | plusieurs Recettes gourmandes inédites; un | article sur la Conserve de Café; des Considé- | rations importantes sur les Santés, le Chocolat | et les Andouilles de Vire; des Anecdotes gour- | mandes; les Découvertes nouvelles de 1808 et | de 1809; de petits Traités sur les Sardines de | Nantes, les Liqueurs de Bordeaux, le Riz de | Pommes de terre, etc.; des Aperçus nouveaux | sur les Mutations gourmandes; la Correspon- | dance gourmande; des Poésies et des Chansons | gourmandes; la Petite Revue de l'année 1809, | formant la Sixième Promenade d'un Gourmand | dans Paris, etc. etc. etc. | [rule] | *Sternitur, exanimisque tremens procumbit humi bos.* | VIRG. *AEn.* Lib. V. vers. 481. | [rule] | DE L'IMPRIMERIE DE CELLOT. | A PARIS, | Chez Joseph CHAUMEROT, Libraire, au Palais- | Royal, Galeries de bois, no. 188. | M. DCCC. X.

First edition, Paris, 1810.

140 x 89 mm. a^6 b^2 1-28^6 29^2; 178 leaves, pp. [i-v] vi-xv [xvi] [1] 2-340. Publisher's orange wrappers with printed label on the spine.

Illustrations: Engraved frontispiece by Mariage after Charles titled "Le lever d'un gourmand."

Bibliographies: Bitting, p. 203; Horn-Arndt 358; Oberlé (1) 133; Schraemli (3) 59; Simon BG 803; Vicaire 427. Pennell, p. 131, edition not stated.

Copies: *BMC*, *BNC*, and *NUC* (5 copies).

231. Grimod de la Reynière, Alexandre-Balthasar-Laurent, 1758-1838.

ALMANACH | DES GOURMANDS, | SERVANT DE GUIDE DANS LES MOYENS | DE FAIRE EXCELLENTE CHÈRE; | PAR UN VIEIL AMATEUR. | HUITIÈME ANNÉE, | Contenant, parmi un grand nombre d'Articles | intéressans sur l'Art alimentaire, une petite | Dissertation sur les Truffes; une sur les Gril- | lades, sur les Réductions, sur le Beurre, le | Vin de Madère, les Repas de Noces, les Cui- | sinières, les OEufs, les progrès de la Cuisine | dans le 18e siècle, le Kirschwasser, etc.; l'éloge | des Cure-dents; les Découvertes nouvelles de | 1810 et de 1811; des Poésies et des Anecdotes | gourmandes; la Correspondance gourmande; | la Petite Revue de l'année 1811, formant la | Septième Promenade d'un Gourmand dans la | bonne ville de Paris; quelques Articles de Gas- | tronomie étrangère, etc. etc. etc. | [short rule] | *Acceptabis.... oblationes et holocausta: tunc* | *imponent super altare* *tuum vitulos.* | Ps. 50. | [short rule] | DE L'IMPRIMERIE DE CELLOT. | A PARIS, | Chez Joseph CHAUMEROT, Libraire, au Palais- | Royal, Galeries de bois, no. 188. | M. DCCC. XI.

First edition, Paris, 1811.

142 x 89 mm. [a]^6 b1 1-30^6; 187 leaves, pp. [i-v] vi-xiv [1] 2-360. Publisher's orange wrappers with printed label on the spine.

Illustrations: Engraved frontispiece by Mariage after "Ch.F." titled "Le plus mortel ennemi du diner."

Bibliographies: Bitting, p. 203; Drexel 143; Horn-Arndt 358; Oberlé (1) 133; Schraemli (3) 60; Simon BG 804; Vicaire 427. Pennell, p. 131, edition not stated.

Copies: *BMC* and *NUC* (5 copies).

232. Grimod de la Reynière, Alexandre-Balthasar-Laurent, 1758-1838.

CHEFS-D'OEUVRE PARTICULIERS | *présentés par* | JEAN GALTIER-BOISSIÈRE | [short rule] | GRIMOD DE LA REYNIÈRE | [ornament] | [in red] CALENDRIER | [in red] GASTRONOMIQUE | suivi des | APHORISMES DU PROFESSEUR | par | *BRILLAT-SAVARIN* | et des | SONNETS GASTRONOMIQUES | par | *CHARLES* *MONSELET* | Illustrations de | LUCIEN BOUCHER | *LIBRAIRIE GRÜND* | PARIS

First edition, Paris, 1946. One of 2070 copies on vélin surglacé, not numbered.

194 x 142 mm. [1]^8 2-6^8 7^{10}; 58 leaves, pp. [1-8] 9-112 [*4*]. Last leaf blank. Folding letterpress menu tipped in facing p. 24 not reckoned in the collation or pagination. Publisher's printed wrappers.

Illustrations: Colored frontispiece and black and white vignettes in the text by Lucien Boucher.

Bibliographies: Unrecorded in the bibliographies consulted.

Copies: *NUC* (Library of Congress, New York Public Library, and Yale).

233. Grimod de la Reynière, Alexandre-Balthasar-Laurent, 1758-1838.

MANUEL │ DES │ AMPHITRYONS; │ CONTENANT │ Un Traité de la Dissection des viandes à │ table, la Nomenclature des Menus les plus │ nouveaux pour chaque saison, et des Elé- │ mens de Politesse gourmande. │ OUVRAGE indispensable à tous ceux qui sont jaloux de │ faire bonne chère, et de la faire faire aux autres; │ Orné d'un grand nombre de Planches gravées en taille-douce. │ Par l'Auteur de l'ALMANACH DES GOURMANDS. │ [short rule] │ Le véritable Amphitryon │ Est l'Amphitryon où l'on dîne. │ MOLIÈRE. │ [short rule] │ A PARIS, │ Chez CAPELLE et RENAND, Libraires-Commis- │ sionnaires, rue J. J. Rousseau. │ [two short rules] │ M. DCCC. VIII.

First edition, Paris, 1808.

208 x 129 mm. A-Y^8 [Z]^4 Aa-Cc^4; 192 leaves, pp. [1-5] 6-384.

Illustrations: Engraved frontispiece and sixteen engraved plates illustrating carving. This copy contains a second set of the plates, each hand-colored.

Bookplate: Ex Libris A.B.L. Grimod de la Reynière.

Bibliographies: Bitting, p. 203; Crahan 584; Horn-Arndt 451; Oberlé (1) 135; Pennell, p. 131; Schraemli (1) 219; Schraemli (3) 61; Simon BG 805; Vicaire 427; Wheaton and Kelly 2554.

Copies: *BMC*, *BNC*, and *NUC* (7 copies).

234. Guégan, Bertrand, b. 1892.

LA FLEUR │ DE LA CUISINE │ FRANÇAISE │ *OU` L'ON TROUVE* │ LES MEILLEURES RECETTES │ des meilleurs Cuisiniers, Pâtissiers et │ Limonadiers de France, du XIIIe au XIXe Siècle, │ *Enrichies de notices et d'un glossaire* │ PAR BERTRAND GUÉGAN, │ *Avec des images anciennes et une Préface* │ d'Ed. NIGNON, Directeur du │ Restaurant Larue. │ [ornament] │ PARIS, │ AUX ÉDITIONS DE LA SIRÈNE, │ Rue La Boétie, No 12. │ MDCCCCXX.

Title-page of the second volume:

LA FLEUR │ DE LA CUISINE │ FRANÇAISE │ TOME II │ LA CUISINE MODERNE │ (1800-1921) │ LES MEILLEURES RECETTES │ DES GRANDS CUISINIERS FRANÇAIS. │ NOTES DE BERTRAND GUÉGAN. │ INTRODUCTION DU DOCTEUR │ RAOUL BLONDEL. │ [ornament] │ PARIS. │ AUX ÉDITIONS DE LA SIRÈNE, │ BOULEVARD MALESHERBES. No 29. │ [short rule] │ 1921.

First trade edition, Paris, 1920-1921, after 30 copies of volume one and 50 copies of volume two printed on papier vélin, Paris, 1920.

225 x 143 mm. 2 vols. Vol. I π^6 [1]^8 2-23^8 24^4; 194 leaves, pp. [i-vii] viii-xi [xii] [1] 2-374 [2]. Vol. II. π^8 2π^8 [1]^8 2-35^8 36^4 37^8; 308 leaves, pp. [i-vii] viii-xxxii [1-2] 3-579 [580] [4]. Publisher's printed wrappers.

Illustrations: Reproductions of illustrations from earlier works in the text.

Bibliographies: Bitting, p. 204; Horn-Arndt 860; Schraemli (3) 123; Wheaton and Kelly 2568.

Copies: *BMC* and *NUC* (4 copies).

235. Le Guide de santé.

LE GUIDE │ *DE SANTÉ,* │ OU │ L'ART DE SE LA CONSERVER │ Par les préceptes qui donnent la vie la plus longue │ & exempte de maladies; avec différens préservatifs, │ & des moyens sûrs pour remédier promptement │ aux divers accidens qui menacent la vie, & à une │ foule d'incommodités dont on est journellement │ attaqué: │ SUIVI DES │ DONS DE LA NATURE, │ *Mis en ordre pour l'usage de la Table suivant* │ *les Saisons de l'année;* │ OU │ Recueil contenant une idée des qualités & propriétés │ des Alimens, tant animaux que végétaux, ser- │ vant à la subsistance de l'homme. │ [short

rule] | Utile dulci. *Horat.* | [short rule] | [ornament] | A PARIS, | *& se trouve à*
LIÉGE, | Chez F. J. DESOER, Imprimeur-Libraire, | sur le Pont-d'Isle. | [fancy
double rule] | *M. DCC. LXXXV.*

First edition, Paris, 1785.

12mo. A-H^{12} I^{12} (-I12); 107 leaves, pp. [1-5] 6-214.

Bibliographies: Vicaire 430.

Copies: No other copy located.

236. Guybert, Philbert, 1579?-1633.

TOVTES LES | OEVVRES | CHARITABLES | DE | PHILBERT GVYBERT, |
Escuyer, Docteur Regent en la | Faculté de Medecine à Paris. | [in two columns]
[column one] Sçavoir, | { | [column two] *Le Medecin Charitable.* | *Le prix & valeur*
des Medicamens. | *L'Apotiquaire Charitable.* | *Le Choix des Medicamens.* | *Le Traitté*
du Sené. | *La maniere de faire toutes sortes de Gelées.* | *La maniere de faire diverses*
Confitures. | *La Conservation de la Santé.* | *Le Discours de la Peste.* | *Le Traitté de la*
Saignée. | *La Methode agreable & facile de faire des* | *Vins medecinaux.* | *La maniere*
d'Embaumer les corps morts. [end columns] | Reveuës, corrigées, & augmentées en
cette | derniere Edition. | [ornament] | A PARIS, | Chez LOVIS VENDOSME, dans
la Cour du Pa- | lais, proche Monseigneur le Premier President, | au Sacrifice
d'Abraham. | [rule] | M. DC. LXIX.

New edition, Paris, 1669. Originally published, Paris, 1629.

8vo. a^4 A-Oo^8 Pp^4; 304 leaves, pp. [*8*] 1-580 [*20*].

Bibliographies: This edition unrecorded in the bibliographies consulted. Bitting, p.
206, records a 1640 edition and Vicaire 432 a 1645 edition.

Copies: *BNC* and *NUC* (University of Wisconsin only).

237. Havet, Armand-Étienne-Maurice, 1795-1820.

LE | DICTIONNAIRE | DES MÉNAGES, | OU | RECUEIL DE RECETTES ET
D'INSTRUCTIONS | POUR L'ÉCONOMIE DOMESTIQUE; | SAVOIR; Moyens de

conserver les Fruits, les Légumes, les Grains et autres | Provisions alimentaires; | De faire les Confitures, les Marmelades, les Sirops, les Liqueurs, les Ratafias, | les Fruits secs et à l'eau-de-vie; | De préparer le Café, le Chocolat, le Thé, le Punch, la Limonade, et autres | Liqueurs d'agrément; | L'art de faire le Pain, le Vin, le Cidre et les Boissons économiques; | Les Vinaigres naturels et aromatisés, les Eaux odoriférantes; | Soins à donner à la Cave, à la Basse-cour, aux Oiseaux de volière et aux | Animaux domestiques; | Destruction des Insectes nuisibles; conservation du Linge, des Etoffes, et | d'autres Effets et Meubles; | Enfin, quantité de procédés pour tirer meilleur parti de sa fortune et rendre | sa vie plux agréable. | OUVRAGE UTILE | Aux Pères et Mères de famille, et à tout Chef de maison. | PAR M. HAV.., | *Médecin et Botaniste, auteur du* MONITEUR MÉDICAL, | ET M. LANCIN, | *Propriétaire-Cultivateur.* | PARIS, | PIERRE BLANCHARD, LIBRAIRE, | GALERIE MONTESQUIEU, No. 1, AU PREMIER. | [short rule] | 1820.

First edition, Paris, 1820.

210 x 135 mm. π^4 1-31^8 32^8(-32$_8$); 259 leaves, pp. [i-v] vi-viii [9] 10-517 [518].

Bibliographies: Bitting, p. 219; Simon BG 822.

Copies: *NUC* (Library of Congress and New York Public Library).

238. Hélouis, Édouard.

LES | [in red] ROYAL-DINERS | GUIDE DU GOURMET | CONTENANT | [in red] DES MENUS POUR CHAQUE SAISON | AVEC LA MANIÈRE DE LES PRÉPARER | ET DES CONSEILS SUR LE SERVICE DE LA TABLE | PAR | [in red] ÉDOUARD HÉLOUIS | ANCIEN CHEF DE CUISINE | DES ROIS CHARLES ALBERT ET VICTOR EMMANUEL | [short rule] | [in red] Ouvrage orné de vingt-quatre planches coloriées | [vignette] | [in red] PARIS | [in two columns: column one] | CH. NOBLET, LIBRAIRE-ÉDITEUR | 13, RUE CUJAS, 13 | [fancy vertical rule] | [column two] E. DENTU, LIBRAIRE-ÉDITEUR | PALAIS-ROYAL, GALERIE D'ORELÉANS, 17-19 [end columns] | 1878

First edition, Paris, 1878.

248 x 163 mm. π^2 2π^2 1-31^8; 252 leaves, pp. [*4*] [i] ii-iii [iv] [1] 2-493 [494] [2].

Illustrations: 24 chromolithographs of utensils and elaborate dishes.

Bibliographies: Bitting, p. 223; Drexel 188; Schraemli (3) 106; Vicaire 441.

Copies: *BMC*, *BNC*, and *NUC* (Kansas State University and New York Public Library).

239. Hocquart, Édouard-Auguste-Patrice, 1787-1870.

[within a wood engraved border] Cuisine de grande Maison. | [rule] | LA CUISINIÈRE MODÈLE | OU | L'ART DE FAIRE UNE BONNE CUISINE | AVEC ÉCONOMIE; | Contenant un Vocabulaire explicatif des Termes de cuisine, | des Notes sur les Substances alimentaires, l'art de | découper à table, les Sauces, la Cuisine proprement dite, | la Pâtisserie, etc., et un nombre considérable de figures | en bois. | Par E. H. | 4e ÉDITION | revue et augmentée. | AVEC UNE TABLE ALPHABÉTIQUE. | [short rule] | PARIS. | J. LANGLUMÉ, ÉDITEUR, | Rue des Noyers, 63.

Fourth edition, Paris, 1853. Originally published, Paris, 1845.

143 x 84 mm. π^2 1-18$^{12.6}$ 19^{12} 20^4; 180 leaves, pp. [*4*] [*1*] 2-356.

Illustrations: Wood engraved frontispiece and border on title-page and wood engravings in the text.

Bibliographies: Vicaire 445 in a note.

Copies: No other copy of this edition located.

239a. Hornot, Antoine.

TRAITÉ RAISONNÉ | DE LA | DISTILLATION; | OU | LA DISTILLATION | RÉDUITE EN PRINCIPES: | Avec un Traité Odeurs. | *Par M. DÉJEAN, Distillateur.* | [ornament] | A PARIS, *Quai des Augustins.* | Chez [next three lines bracketed on right] NYON Fils, à l'Occasion. | GUILLYN, au Lys d'Or, du côté | du Pont Saint Michel. | [short thick-thin rule] | M. DCC. LIII. | *Avec Approbation & Privilége du Roi.*

First edition, Paris, 1753.

12mo. a^6 A-V^{12} X^6; 252 leaves, pp. [i-iii] iv-x [xi-xii] [*1*] 2-484 [*8*].

Bibliographies: Oberlé (1) 1085; Simon BG 457; Vicaire 258; Wheaton and Kelly 2966.

Copies: *BNC, NUC* (New York Public Library, Yale), Wheaton and Kelly (Harvard).

239b. Hornot, Antoine.

TRAITÉ RAISONNE │ DE LA │ DISTILLATION, │ OU │ LA DISTILLATION │ REDUITE EN PRINCIPES, │ Avec un Traité des Odeurs. │ *Par M. DÉJEAN,* *Distillateur.* │ SECONDE ÉDITION, │ Revue, corrigée & augmentée par l'Auteur. │ [ornament] │ A PARIS, │ Chez [next three lines bracketed to left and right] NYON, à l'Occasion. │ GUILLYN, au Lis d'Or, du │ côté du Pont Saint Michel. │ [to the right] Quai des │ Augustins. [end brackets] │ [short thick-thin rule] │ M. DCC. LIX. │ *Avec* *Approbation & Privilége du Roi.*

Second edition, Paris, 1759. Originally published, Paris, 1753 (item 239a).

12mo. a^6 A-T^{12} V^6; 240 leaves, pp. [i-iv] v-x [xi-xii] [1] 2-468.

Bibliographies: Oberlé (1) 1086; Oberlé (2) 405; Vicaire 258.

Copies: *BMC, BNC, NUC* (New York Academy of Medicine only).

240. Hornot, Antoine.

TRAITÉ RAISONNÉ │ DE LA │ DISTILLATION, │ *OU* │ LA DISTILLATION │ RÉDUITE EN PRINCIPES, │ *Par M. DÉJEAN, Distillateur.* │ QUATRIEME ÉDITION, │ Revue, corrigée & beaucoup augmentée par l'Auteur. │ [short rule] │ Prix 3 liv. │ [short rule] │ [ornament] │ *A PARIS,* │ Chez CH. G. LE CLERC, Libraire, Quai des │ Augustins, à l'Etoile. │ [two short rules] │ M. DCC. LXXVII. │ *Avec* *Approbation & Privilege du Roi.*

Fourth edition, Paris, 1777. Originally published Paris, 1753 (item 239a).

12mo. a^8 A-T^{12} V^4; 240 leaves, pp. [i-iii] iv-xvi [1] 2-461 [462-464].

Bibliographies: Blake, p. 222; Simon BG 857; Vicaire 258 in a note.

Copies: *BNC* and *NUC* (Iowa State University, John Crerar Library, and University of Wisconsin). *BMC* records a fourth edition, Paris, 1778.

241. Houssaye, J. G.

INSTRUCTIONS | SUR | LA MANIÈRE DE PRÉPARER | LA BOISSON DU THÉ, | PAR J. G. HOUSSAYE. | [short fancy rule] | A PARIS, | Chez l'Auteur, à la porte chinoise, | PLACE DE LA BOURSE. | 1832.

First edition, Paris, 1832.

205 x 123 mm. [1]^{10}; 10 leaves, pp. [1-5] 6-20. Publisher's printed wrappers. This copy lacks the back wrapper.

Bibliographies: The first edition is unrecorded in the bibliographies consulted. Vicaire 447 records a Paris, 1833, edition.

Copies: No other copy of the first edition located.

242. Houssaye, J. G.

MONOGRAPHIE | DU THÉ | DESCRIPTION BONTANIQUE, TORRÉFACTION | COMPOSITION CHIMIQUE, PROPRIÉTÉS HYGIÉNIQUES DE CETTE FEUILLE | *orné de 18 gravures* | PAR J.-G. HOUSSAYE | [engraved vignette of a Chinese tea house] | PARIS | CHEZ L'AUTEUR, 3 RUE DE LA BOURSE | [short rule] | 1843

First edition, Paris, 1843.

237 x 150 mm. π^2 1-10^8; 82 leaves, pp. [*4*] [1] 2-160. Publisher's blue cloth stamped in gold.

Illustrations: Steel engraved vignette of Chinese tea house on title-page and eighteen steel engraved plates, the last one repeating the title-page vignette with an advertisement for A La Porte Chinoise, a store specializing in oriental merchandise.

Bibliographies: Bitting, p. 235; Horn-Arndt 474; Maggs 461; Schraemli (1) 234; Simon BG 866; Vicaire 447; Wheaton and Kelly 3012.

Copies: *BMC*, *BNC*, and *NUC* (14 copies).

243. Ibn Butlan, d. ca. 1068.

[in red] TACVINI | [in red] SANITATIS | ELLVCHASEM ELI= | MITHAR | Medici de Baldath, | De sex Rebus non naturalibus, earum naturis, operationi= | bus, & rectificationibus, publico omnium usui, | conseruandae Sanitatis, recens exarati. | [in red] ALBEN= | [in red] GNEFIT | De uirtutibus Medicinarum, | & Ciborum. | [in red] IAC. ALKIN | [in red] DVS DE RERVM | GRADIBVS. | [in red: star] | ARGENTORATI | apud [in red] Ioannem Schottum [in black] Librarium. | ℂ Cum praerogatiua Caes. Maiestatis ad | sexennium. [in red] M. D. XXXI. | [in red: short rule]

First edition, Strassburg, 1531. Note: Durling lists this edition and also "a variant state, with the majority of the tables and marginalia (pp. 38-117) printed in black only, instead of red and black as in the above." Clearly, these are from two printings, not variant states. The Lilly copy is printed in red and black.

Folio: A-M⁶ N-O⁴ P⁶; 86 leaves, pp. [1-4] 5-163 [164-170] [2]. Last leaf (blank?) wanting in this copy.

Illustrations: Woodcuts along the bottoms of D2-K5 rectos.

Bibliographies: Durling 2520; Oberlé (1) 48; Schraemli (1) 162; Vicaire 323.

Copies: *BMC*, *BNC*, and *NUC* (11 copies).

244. Ibn Bultan, d. ca. 1068.

[ornament] | TACVINI | SEX RERVM | non naturalium, cum earum naturis operationi= | bus, & rectificationibus. | TACVINI | Aegritudinum, & Morborum ferme omniū corporis humani: | cum curis eorundem. Mandato christianiss. | CAROLI Imp. primi, summo | studio comportati. | ALBENGNEFIT | De uirtutibus Ciborum, & Medicinarum. | IAC. ALKINDVS | De rerum GRADIBVS. | Publico omnium usui, conseruandae Sanitatis, | recens, & denuo exarati. | [hand] ARGENTORATI | apud Ioannem Schottum Librarium. | ℂ Cum praerogatiua Caes. Maiestatis ad | [short rule] | sexeñium. M. D. XXXIII. | [ornament]

Second edition, Strassburg, 1533. Originally published, Strassburg, 1531 (item 243)

Folio: A-M⁶ N-O⁴ P⁶; 86 leaves, pp. [1-5] 6-163 [164-170] [2]. Last leaf blank.

Bound with Yahya'ibn Isa's *Tacvini aegritudinum et Morborum fere omnium Corporis humani*, Strassburg, 1532 (item 443).

Illustrations: Forty woodcuts by Hans Weiditz along the lower margins of the same number of pages, and a few historiated woodcut initials.

Bibliographies: Durling 2522; Simon BB II no. 633; Vicaire 325. Horn-Arndt 1 records the first edition in German, Strassburg, 1533.

Copies: Not in *NUC* but Durling records the copy in the National Library of Medicine.

Le Jardinier françois. See Bonnefons, Nicolas de.

245. Jobey, Charles, 1813-1877.

CHARLES JOBEY | [short fancy rule] | LA CHASSE | ET | LA TABLE | NOUVEAU TRAITÉ EN VERS ET EN PROSE | DONNANT LA MANIÈRE | DE CHASSER, DE TUER ET D'APPRÊTER | LE GIBIER | [short fancy rule] | PARIS | FURNE ET CIE, LIBRAIRES-ÉDITEURS | 45 RUE SAINT-ANDRÉ-DES-ARTS | [short rule] | Droits de traduction et de reproduction réservés.

First edition, Paris, 1864.

171 x 118 mm. π^2 1-16$^{12.6}$ 17^4 (-17$_4$); pp. [*4*] [1] 2-294.

Illustration: Lithographed title-page.

Bibliographies: Bitting, p. 246; Oberlé (1) 677; Vicaire 465.

Copies: *BMC*, *BNC*, and *NUC* (Library of Congress and New York Public Library).

246. Jourdan-Lecointe.

LA CUISINE | DE SANTÉ, | OU moyens faciles & économiques de | préparer toutes nos Productions | Alimentaires de la maniere la plus | délicate & la plus salutaire, d'après | les nouvelles découvertes de la Cuisine | Françoise & Italienne. | *PAR M.*

JOURDAN LE COINTE, Docteur en | *Médecine; revu par un Practicien de Montpellier.* | OUVRAGE destiné à l'instruction des Gens | de l'Art, à l'amusement des Amateurs & | particulierement à la conservation de la Santé. | *TOME PREMIER.* [*TOME SECOND.*] [*TOME TROISIEME.*] | [ornament] | A PARIS, | CHEZ BRIAND, Libraire, Hôtel de Villiers | rue Pavée Saint-André-des-Arts. | [two short rules] | 1789.

First edition, Paris, 1789, printing on fine paper. Note: The fine paper copies are considerably thicker than copies on ordinary paper, the three volumes measuring 30 mm., 32 mm., and 38 mm. respectively, compared with 19 mm., 21 mm., and 25 mm. for copies on ordinary paper.

12mo. 3 vols. Vol. I. A-T^{12} V^6(-V6); 233 leaves, pp. [1-5] 6-465 [466]. Vol. II. A-V^{12} X^6(-X6); 245 leaves, pp. [1-5] 6-490. Vol. III. A-Aa^{12}; 288 leaves, pp. [1-5] 6-576.

Illustrations: Vol. I. Engraved folding plate illustrating kitchen utensils and an oven.

Bibliographies: Pennell, p. 130, but not noting which paper. Bitting, p. 278, records a set with volumes I and III dated 1790 and volume II dated 1789; Vicarie 507 describes an edition dated 1790.

Copies: No other set with all three volumes dated 1789 located. *NUC* records the Bitting set (Library of Congress) with volumes I and III dated 1790 and volume II dated 1789. *BMC*, *BNC*, and *NUC* (American Philosophical Society) record sets dated 1790.

247. Jourdan-Lecointe.

LE | CUISINIER ROYAL | *OU* | *CUISINE DE SANTÉ* | Adapté aux préparations les plus | économiques et les plus salutaires | de nos Alimens. | *PAR M JOURDAN LE COINTE.* | *Docteur en Médecine.* | *TOME PREMIER.* [*TOME SECOND.*] [*TOME TROISIEME.*] | [ornament] | A PARIS. | Chez *BOSSANGE, MASSON ET BESSON* | *Libraries et Commissionres. Rue des Noyers No. 33.* | 1792

First edition of *La Cuisine de Santé*, reissued, Paris, 1792, with engraved cancel title-pages as above for all three volumes. Printing on ordinary paper (see note under item 246).

12 mo. 3 vols. Vol. I. A^{12} ($\pm$A2) B-T^{12} V^6(-V6); 223 leaves, pp. [1-5] 6-465 [466]. Vol. II. A^{12}($\pm$A2) B-V^{12} X^6(-X6); 245 leaves, pp. [1-5] 6-490. Vol. III. A^{12}($\pm$A2) B-Aa^{12}; 288 leaves, pp. [1-5] 6-576.

Illustrations: Vol. I. Engraved folding plate of a rotisserie grill. This is not the plate that appears in the 1789 issue.

Bibliographies: This issue unrecorded in the bibliographies consulted.

Copies: No other copy of this issue located.

248. Jourdan-Lecointe.

LE CUISINIER | DES | CUISINIERS, | OU | 𝕷'𝖆𝖗𝖙 𝖉𝖊 𝖑𝖆 𝕮𝖚𝖎𝖘𝖎𝖓𝖊, | ENSEIGNÉ ÉCONOMIQUEMENT | D'APRÈS LES PLUS GRANDS MAITRES ANCIENS ET MODERNES, | TELS QUE D'ALÈGRE, CHAUD, LAGUIPIERRE, MÉZELIER, | RICHAUD, SOUVENT, BALAINE, ROBERT, | SUIVI | D'UNE CHIMIE APPLIQUÉE A LA CUISINE, | PAR ACCUM; | DE L'ART DE SOIGNER LES VINS, DE CONSERVER LES | SUBSTANCES ALIMENTAIRES; | PAR A. M. V...Y, | EX-MAJORDOME DU PRINCE MARESCALCHI, EX-MAITRE-D'HÔTEL DU PRINCE | BUTERA, ETC., ETC., ETC. | [short fancy rule] | PARIS, | AUDIN, LIBRAIRE, QUAI DES AUGUSTINS, No. 25; | URBAIN CANEL, PLACE SAINT-ANDRÉ-DES-ARTS, No. 30. | [short fancy rule] | 1825.

First edition, Paris, 1825.

192 x 117 mm. π^2 a-d^4 1-29^8 30^4; 254 leaves, pp. [4] [i] ii-xxxii, 1-456.

Bibliographies: Vicaire 508.

Copies: No other copy of the first edition located.

249. Jourdan-Lecointe.

LA PATISSERIE | DE SANTÉ, | Ou moyens faciles et éonomiques | de préparer tous les genres de | Pâtisseries de la manière la plus | délicate et la plus salutaire. | PAR M. JOURDAN LE COINTRE. | *Ouvrage destiné à l'instruction des* | *Gens de l'Art, à* | *l'amusement des* | *Amateurs, et particulièrement à la* | *conservation de la santé.* | Deux volumes in-12. de 500 pages chaque | volume, orné d'une grande carte. Prix, 5

1. | broché. | TOME PREMIER. [TOME SECOND.] | [short fancy rule] | *A PARIS*, | Chez BATILLIOT, rue du Cimetière S. André, | la première porte chochère en entrant par | la rue Haute-Feuille. | [short rule] | 1793.

Third edition, Paris, 1793. Originally published, Paris, 1790.

12mo. 2 vols. Vol. I. A-Z^{12}; 276 leaves, pp. [1-5] 6-550 [2]. Last leaf blank. Vol. II. π^2 A-R^{12} S^4; 210 leaves, pp. [*4*] [1] 2-416. This copy wanting half-titles in both volumes.

Illustrations: Vicaire calls for a "grande planche" in the 1792 edition. There is an impression on the paper in volume II following p. 404 indicating that a folding plate once was present in this 1793 edition, but it is lacking in this copy.

Bibliographies: This edition unrecorded in the bibliographies consulted. Vicaire 506 records the 1792 edition.

Copies: No other copy of this edition located. *BMC* and *BNC* record the 1792 edition.

250. Joyant, Maurice.

MAURICE JOYANT | LA CUISINE | DE | MONSIEUR MOMO | CÉLIBATAIRE | ÉDITIONS PELLET | [two rules] PARIS [two rules]

First edition, Paris, 1930. One of 250 copies on papier d'Arches.

236 x 184 mm. [1-38]^4; 152 leaves, pp. [*8*] i-iv [1-4] 5-283 [*284*] [*8*].

Illustrations: Colored engraved frontispiece by Jean Édouard Vuillard and 24 colored engravings after designs by Henri Toulouse-Lautrec.

Bibliographies: Bitting, p. 251; Oberlé (1) 297; Schraemli (1) 238.

Copies: *NUC* (Library of Congress only).

250a. Julia de Fontenelle, Jean-Sébastien-Eugène, 1790-1842.

MANUEL | DE | L'HERBORISTE, | DE | L'ÉPICIER—DROGUISTE | ET DU | GRAINIER—PÉPINIÉRISTE | HORTICULTEUR; | CONTENANT | LA

DESCRIPTION DES VÉGÉTAUX, LES LIEUX DE LEUR NAISSANCE, | LEUR
ANALYSE CHIMIQUE ET LEURS PROPRIÉTÉS MÉDICALES; | PAR M. JULIA
DE FONTENELLE, | Professeur de Chimie, Président de la Société des Sciences
"physiques et chimiques, Membre de la plupart des | Sociétés savantes de France. |
TOME PREMIER. [TOME SECONDE.] | PARIS, | RORET, LIBRAIRE, RUE
HAUTEFEUILLE, | AU COIN DE CELLE DU BATTOIR. | 1828.

First edition, Paris, 1828.

144 x 92 mm. 2 vols. Vol. I. π^2 χ1 2χ1 3χ1 1-37^6 38^2; 229 leaves, pp. [6] [xiii] xiv-
xvi [1] 2-445 [445-448]. Folding tables inserted facing pp. 27, 165, 166, 168, 170 and
176. χ1, the dedication leaf, is misbound between χ2 and χ3 in this copy. Vol. II. π^2
1-45^6 46-47^4 48$_1$; 281 leaves, pp. [4] [1] 2-558. Publisher's tan printed wrappers. A
36 page publisher's catalog bound in at the end of Vol. II.

Bibliographies: Querard 4:265.

Copies: *BMC*, *BNC* and *NUC* (New York Public Library and US Patent Office).

251. Julia de Fontenelle, Jean-Sébastien-Eugène, 1790-1842.

MANUEL | THÉORIQUE ET PRATIQUE | DU VINAIGRIER | ET | DU
MOUTARDIER, | SUIVI | DE NOUVELLES RECHERCHES | SUR LA
FERMENTATION VINEUSE, | PRÉSENTÉES | A L'ACADÉMIE ROYALE DES
SCIENCES; | Par M. Julia Fontenelle, | Professeur de chimie médicale, Président
de la Société des sciences phy- | siques et chimiques de Paris, Membre honoraire de la
Société royale de | Varsovie, Membre de la Société de chimie médicale, de l'Académie
| royale de médecine, et des Académies royales des sciences de Barcelone, | Rouen,
Lyon, etc. | [short fancy rule] | PARIS, | RORET, LIBRAIRE, RUE
HAUTEFEUILLE, | AU COIN DE CELLE DU BATTOIR. | 1827
First edition, Paris, 1827.

145 x 91 mm. a^8 1.^{6} 1..^{6} 1...^{6} -7.^{6} 7..^{6} 7...^{6} 8.^{6} 8..^{4}; 144 leaves, pp. [i-vii] viii-xvi [1]
2-272. Publisher's printed wrappers.

Bibliographies: Vicarie 470.

Copies: *BMC*, *BNC*, and *NUC* (Harvard only).

252. Jullien, André, 1766-1832.

MANUEL | DU SOMMELIER, | OU | INSTRUCTION PRATIQUE | SUR LA
MANIÈRE DE SOIGNER LES VINS; | CONTENANT la Théorie de la Dégustation,
de la Clarifi- | cation, du Collage et de la Fermentation *secondaire* des | Vins; les
Moyens de prévenir leur Altération et de les | rétablir lorsqu'ils sont dégénérés ou
naturellement | défectueux, de distinguer les Vins purs des Vins | mélangés, frelatés ou
artificiels, etc.; | SUIVI | Du Tarif des Droits de mouvement, d'entrée, d'octroi, | de
vente en détail et de douanes, des Prix de loca- | tion, etc., que l'on paye à l'entrepôt
de Paris. | DÉDIÉ à M. LE COMTE CHAPTAL, | Pair de France, Membre de
l'Académie des Sciences, auteur de l'ouvrage | intitulé: l'*Art de faire le vin.* | PAR A.
JULLIEN, | Marchand de vin en gros, Auteur de la *Topographie de tous les* |
vignobles connus, inventeur des poudres pour clarifier les vins, | des cannelles aérifères
et de plusieurs autres instrumens. | AVEC TROIS PLANCHES. | Troisième Édition,
revue, corrigée et augmentée. | A PARIS, | [in two columns: column one] CHEZ { |
[column two] L'AUTEUR, rue Saint-Sauveur, no. 18. | L. COLAS,
Imprimeur-Libraire, rue Dauphine, | no. 32. | Madame HUZARD,
Imprimeur-Libraire, rue de | l'Éperon, no. 7. | [end of columns] | [two short rules] |
1822.

Third edition, Paris, 1822. Originally published, Paris, 1813.

168 x 102 mm. π^2 a^8 1-14^{12} 15^2; 180 leaves, pp. [*4*] [i] ii-xv [xvi] [1] 2-340.
Letterpress folding chart facing p. 279.

Illustrations: Three engraved folding plates depicting tools and equipment of a
sommelier.

Bibliographies: Simon BV p. 19.

Copies: *BNC.*

253. Kern, Ulrich.

Eyn new Kunstlichs wolge= | gründts Visierbuch, gar groiss vnnd behend |
auss rechter art der Geometria/ Rechnung vnd Circkelmessen/ | Darinnen
mancherley Visier rüten oder Stäb angezeygt | zemachen/ nach yeglicher landart
Eichen vnd mass/ | dergleichen noch nie getruckt oder aussgangen. | [woodcut] |
Zum Leser. | [in two columns: column one] Wöltstu visieren manches vass/ |
Vnd das mit seiner rechten mass, | So findst dess Stabes grund behend | In

disem büch/ an alle end │ Der teutschen Nation gerecht/ │ Garmanchem es bil nutzes brecht/ │ So wolt mit nasser war handtiern/ │ Auch bon im selber lern bisiern/ │ Vnd seiner sachen sein gewiss/ │ Derhalb mit fleiss diss Büch aussliss. │ Der Küten sind wol zehen gmacht │ Besonder/ grecht in jrer acht. │ [column two] Eyns gmanich dich/ dess nit bergess/ │ Die guäss an allen orten mess/ │ Hab acht der beuln (schlags nit inn windt) │ Darein dann sölche wahr berrinnt, │ Darumb besihe es eben wol/ │ Obs breyt sei truckt/ obs bodenhol/ │ Wo du es nit eben hettest bsehn, │ Wers bald bm drei/ bier/ massen gschehn. │ Gehst du dann diser kunst nit miss/ │ So triffstus bei eym gläslin gwiss/ │ Vorab so guäss wer innen glat/ │ Huldrichus Kern es gmachet hat. [end columns] │ M. D. XXXI.

Colophon: [woodcut] │ Inn der löblichen freistatt Strassburg truckts Peter Schäffer/ │ bei Nansen Schwyntzern/ bnd ward bolendet am ersten │ Aprilis/ nach der gebürt Christi bnsers Herren/ │ [short rule] │ M. D. XXXI.

First edition, Strassburg, 1531.

Folio: A⁶ B-E⁴ F⁶ G² H-O⁴; 58 leaves, ff. [1] i-lvi [1]. Last leaf blank.

Illustrations: Woodcut on title-page and colophon leaf as well as woodcuts illustrating gauging in the text.

Bibliographies: Graesse IV, 13; Muther 1402.

Copies: *BMC* and *NUC* (5 copies).

254. La Bretonnerie, M. de.

CORRESPONDANCE │ RURALE, │ *CONTENANT* │ Des Observations critiques, intérenssantes │ & utiles sur la Culture des Terres & │ des Jardins; les travaux, occupations, │ économies & amusemens de la Campagne, │ & tout ce qui peut être relatif à ces objets. │ *OUVRAGE* │ *Nécessaire aux Propriétaires de Terres, aux* │ *Régisseurs, aux Amateurs, aux Cultivateurs* │ *de tout genre, & à tous ceux qui habitent la* │ *Campagne.* │ Par M. DE LA BRETONNERIE. │ [rule] │ Intelligentia, instrumenta, vires & aurum │ Belli & Agriculturae nervi, & ars magica. │ [rule] │ TOME PREMIER. [TOME DEUXIEME.] [TOME TROISIEME.] │ [ornament] │ A PARIS, │ Chez EUGÈNE ONFROY, Libraire, │ Quai des Augustins, au Lys d'or. │ [two short rules] │ M. DCC. LXXXIII. │ *Avec Approbation, & Privilége du Roi.*

First edition, Paris, 1783.

12mo. 3 vols. Vol. I. a^{12} b^8 A-Bb^{12}; 320 leaves, pp. [i- iv] v-xxxix [xl] [1] 2-597 [598] [2]. Last leaf blank. Vol. II. π^2 a^4 A-Aa^{12} Bb^8; 202 leaves, pp. [4] i-viii [1] 2-590 [2]. Last leaf blank. Vol. III. π^2 a^4 A-R^{12} S^8; 218 leaves, pp. [4] i-viii [1-2] 3-413 [414-416], ^{2}[1] 2-8.

Bibliographies: Unrecorded in the bibliographies consulted.

Copies: *BNC* and *NUC* (National Agricultural Library, University of California, Berkeley, and Yale).

255. Lacam, Pierre, b. 1836.

LE GLACIER │ CLASSIQUE ET ARTISTIQUE │ EN FRANCE ET EN ITALIE │ PAR │ [in two columns: column one] PIERRE LACAM │ Auteur du *Mémorial de la Pâtisseire* │ Ex-chef pâtissier-glacier │ de Son Altesse S. Charles III, Prince de │ Monaco. │ [vertical rule] │ [column two] ANTOINE CHARABOT │ Ex-chef pâtissier-glacier │ du Grand Hôtel Quirinal à Rome. │ du Savoy Hôtel à Londres et des Maisons │ Quillet et Julien frères, à Paris. [end columns] │ 4 DIPLOMES D'HONNEUR 1891-92 │ MEMBRE DU JURY (EXPOSITION CULINAIRE 1893) │ [short rule] │ Ouvrage orné de gravures dans le texte et hors texte, avec les portraits de Procope │ Tortoni (Percheron), Appert, Chevet, etc. │ [short rule] │ PRIX: 8 FR. │ [short rule] │ *Première édition − Premier mille* │ [short rule] │ *EN VENTE CHEZ LES AUTEURS:* │ PIERRE LACAM, 10, rue de Paris Vincennes (Seine) │ ANTOINE CHARABOT, 194, rue Lafayette (Paris) │ [short rule] │ 1893 │ Droits de propriété et de traduction réservés

First edition, Vincennes and Paris, 1893.

218 x 130 mm. π^2 1-23^8 24^4; 190 leaves, pp. [4] [1] 2-374 [2]. Last leaf blank.

Illustrations: Numerous wood engravings in the text.

Bibliographies: Unrecorded in the bibliographies consulted.

Copies: *BNC*.

256. Lacam, Pierre, b. 1836.

LE | MÉMORIAL DES GLACES | FAISANT SUITE | AU MÉMORIAL DE LA
PATISSERIE | RENFERMANT | 3,000 Recettes de Glaces, Boissons, Entremets |
Petits-Fours, Gaufres, Confitures, Gaufrettes | Conserves de Fruits, de Jus, Purées,
Pains d'épices | Biscuiterie, Confiserie, Timbales, etc., etc. | [short rule] | PAR
PIERRE LACAM | [short rule] | PRIX: BROCHÉ 8 FR., RELIÉ 10 FR. | [short rule]
| *Avec les Portraits de* | CLAUDE GELÉE, LES TROIS FRÈRES JULIEN | CH.
MONSELET, E. BERNARD, F. GRANDI, FULBERT DUMONTEIL | 17 Portraits
et Gravures texte et hors texte | [short rule] | 2e ÉDITION – 3e MILLE | [short rule]
| *EN VENTE* | Chez l'Auteur, 81, rue Saint-Denis, Paris | 1902 | Droits de traduction
et de reproduction réservés

Second edition, second issue, Paris, 1902, with cancel label over the imprint: "Se
trouve à Paris | Chez MM. DUPONT ET MALGAT | 1, Rue Coquillière, 1."
Originally published Paris, 1899.

216 x 131 mm. π^8 [1-14]^8 15^8 [16-23]^8 24^8 [25-26]^8 27-28^8 [29-39]^8 40^8 [41]^8 42-55^8
"65"^{8} [57]^6 (-57$_6$); 461 leaves, pp. [i-vii] viii-xv [xvi] [1] 2-906.

Illustrations: Frontispiece portrait of the author and eight plates, two printed on both
sides.

Bibliographies: Bitting, p. 267.

Copies: *NUC* (John Crerar Library and Library of Congress).

257. Lacam, Pierre, b. 1836.

LE MÉMORIAL | HISTORIQUE ET GÉOGRAPHIQUE | DE LA PATISSERIE |
CONTENANT | 3000 Recettes de Pâtisserie, Glaces et Liqueurs | ORNÉ DE
GRAVURES DANS LE TEXTE | Par PIERRE LACAM | Auteur du *Pâtissier-Glacier*
publié en 1865 | Ex-pâtissier-glacier | de son Altesse Sérénissime Monseigneur
CHARLES III, prince de Monaco | 10 DIPLOMES D'HONNEUR 1891-92
93-93-94-95-96-98-1900 | Lauréat et membre de l'Académie de cuisine | Nommé 6
fois membre du Jury | [short rule] | Prix: 8 francs; Relié 10 francs. | [short rule] |
AVEC ANECDOTES ET BIOGRAPHIES | Des grands Auteurs de la Gastronomie |
Un portrait du Marquis de Cussy | un d'Antonio Carême, un de Grimod de la
Reynière, | celui de Jules Gouffé, | deux lettres autographes d'Antonin Carême
1830-1832 | un portrait de Émile Bernard, A. Ozanne, | E. Guerbois. | [short rule] |
6e ÉDITION. – 6e MILLE | [short rule] | DU MÊME AUTEUR 1899 | *LE*

MÉMORIAL DES GLACES. Même Prix. │ 3000 Rcccttcs, Glaces, Boissons, Entremets │ 2e ÉDITION. − 1902 │ [short rule] │ EN VENTE │ Chez l'auteur 81 rue Saint-Denis PARIS │ [short rule] │ 1903 │ Droits de traduction et de reproduction réservés

Sixth edition, second issue, Paris, 1903, with cancel label over imprint: "Se trouve à Paris │ Chez MM. DUPONT ET MALGAT │ 1, Rue Coquillière, 1". Originally published, Vincennes, 1890.

216 x 131 mm. π^6 a-b^8 1-26^8 27^8(27$_7$+ χ1) 28-54^8; 455 leaves, pp. [i-ix] x-xi [xii], ^{2}[i-iv] v-xxxii [1] 2-866.

Illustrations: Three folding lithographed plates with facsimiles of two letters from Antonin Carême and numerous illustrations in the text.

Bibliographies: Wheaton and Kelly 3393. Horn-Arndt records the first edition, Vincennes, 1890.

Copies: Wheaton and Kelly (Radcliffe only).

257a. La Chesnaye-Desbois, François Alexandre Aubert de, 1699-1784.

DICTIONNAIRE │ UNIVERSEL │ *D'AGRICULTURE* │ ET │ *DE JARDINAGE.* │ DE FAUCONNERIE, CHASSE, PÊCHE, │ CUISINE ET MANÉGE, │ *EN DEUX PARTIES:* │ LA PREMIERE, enseignant la maniere de faire valoir toutes sortes │ de Terres, Prés, Vignes, Bois; de cultiver les Jardins potagers, │ fruitiers, à fleurs, & d'ornement; de nourrir, élever, & gouverner │ les Bestiaux & la Volaille; avec une explication des Plantes, │ Arbrisseaux, Arbustes, & Arbres qui croissent en Europe. │ LA SECONDE, donnant des régles pur la Volerie, la Chasse & │ la Pêche, & des remedes pour les Qiseaux de Fauconnerie, les │ Chevaux, & les Chiens de chasse dans leurs maladies. │ DEUX VOLUMES, AVEC FIGURES. │ TOME PREMIER. [TOME SECOND.] │ *Dicendum, & que sint duris Agrestibus arma.* VIRG. │ [ornament] │ A PARIS, │ Chez DAVID le jeune, à l'entrée du Quai des Augustins, du côté │ du Pont Saint Michel, au Saint Esprit. │ [short thick-thin rule] │ M. DCC. LI. │ *AVEC APPROBATION ET PRIVILEGE DU ROI.*

First edition, Paris, 1751. Based on Louis Liger's *Dictionnaire pratique du bon ménager de campagne et de ville* (Paris, 1715, item 283) with augmentation by La Chesnaye-Desbois.

4to. 2 vols. Vol. I. π⁴ A-Yyyy⁴ Zzzz²; 370 leaves, pp. [8] [1] 2-730 [2]. First leaf, blank. Vol. II. π² A-Gg⁴ ²A-Mmm⁴ Nnn²; 356 leaves, pp. [4] [1] 2-238 ²[2] [1] 2-467 [468]. First leaf, blank.

Illustrations: 12 engraved folding plates bound at the end of vol. II.

Bibliographies: Vicaire 277; Wheaton & Kelly 3396.

Copies: *NUC* (9 copies).

258. La Framboisière, Nicolas-Abraham de, 1559-1634.

LE │ GOVVERNEMENT │ NECESSAIRE A CHACVN │ POVR VIVRE LONGVEMENT │ EN SANTE' │ AVEC │ *LE GOVVERNEMENT REQVIS EN* │ *l'vsage des eaux Minerales, tant pour la preser-* │ *uation, que pour la guerison des* │ *maladies rebelles.* │ PAR │ NICOLAS ABRAHAM, SIEVR DE │ LA FRAMBOISIERE, CONSEILLER │ & Medecin ordinaire du Roy. │ *Troisiesme edition reueüe, & reformée par l'Auteur.* │ [woodcut with motto: VIRTVS AD ASTRA PER ASPERA] │ A PARIS, │ Chez MARC ORRY, ruë sainct Iacques │ au Lyon rampant. │ [short rule] │ M. DC. VIII. │ *Auec Priuilege du Roy.*

Third edition, Paris, 1608. Originally published, Paris, 1600.

8vo. a⁸ A-Bb⁸; 208 leaves, pp. [16] 1-379 [380-382] 383 [384-396] [4]. Last two leaves blank.

Illustration: Engraved portrait of the author on a8ᵛ.

Note: Birth and death dates for La Framboisière are from Wellcome; *NUC* records b. 1577 and no death date.

Bibliographies: Schraemli (1) 1; Vicaire 2.

Copies: *NUC* (Kansas State University, University of Minnesota and Yale).

258a. La Quintinie, Jean de, 1626-1688.

INSTRUCTION │ POUR │ *LES JARDINS* │ FRUITIERS ET POTAGERS, │ *AVEC UN TRAITÉ DES ORANGERS,* │ ET DES RÉFLEXIONS SUR L'AGRICULTURE. │ *Par M. DE LA QUINTINYE, Directeur des Jardins* │ *Fruitiers & Potagers du ROY.* │

NOUVELLE ÉDITION REVUE, CORRIGÉE, | Et augmentée d'une Instruction pour la Culture des Fleurs. | *TOME PREMIER. [TOME SECOND.]* | [ornament] | *A PARIS,* | Par la Compagnie des Libraires Associés. | [short thick-thin rule] | M. DCC. LVI. | *AVEC PRIVILÉGE DE SA MAJESTE.*

New edition, Paris, 1756. Originally published, Paris, 1690. Translation into English by John Evelyn and published under the title *The Compleat Gardner* (London, 1693, item 814).

4to. 2 vols. Vol. I. a^4 e^4 i^4 o^4 u^4 aa^4 ee^4 ii^4 A-Eeee^4; 328 leaves, pp. [8] [1] 2-16 xvii-xlviii [8] ^{2}1-591 [592]. Vol. II. ✳^{4} ✳✳^{2} A-HHhh^4; 314 leaves, pp. [12] [1] 2-587 [588-616].

Illustrations: Vol. I. Vignettes at section heads, 4 woodcuts in the text, 10 single page engraved plates and 2 folding engraved plates. Vol. II. Vignettes at section heads, 9 woodcuts in the text and 1 single page engraved plate.

Bibliographies: This edition unrecorded in the bibliographies consulted.

Copies: *BMC, BNC, NUC,* (6 copies).

259. Laurent, Jean.

ABREGE' | POUR | LES ARBRES NAINS | ET AUTRES; | CONTENANT TOUT CE QUI LES | regarde, tiré en partie des derniers Au- | teurs qui ont écrit de cette Matiere; Joint | une experience avec application de vingt | ans & plus. Avec un Traité tres-particu- | lier pour les bons Melons, & aussi un Trai- | té general & singulier pour la culture de | toutes sortes de Fleurs, & pour les Arbu- | stes, & aussi pour faire & conduire une | grosse Vigne, & beaucoup de choses pour | les autres Vignes. | *Oeuvre qui n'a encore esté traité à fonds par | aucun, & qui provient aussi en partie de la | communication des plus entendus Curieux | en ces sortes de choses.* | Par J. L. Notaire de Laon. | [ornament] | A PARIS, | Chez CHARLES DE SERCY, au Palais, au sixiéme | Pillier de la Grand'Salle, vis-à-vis la montée de la | Cour des Aydes, à la Bonne-Foy Couronnée. | [short rule] | M. DC. LXXV. | *AVEC PRIVILEGE DV ROY.*

First edition, Paris, 1675.

12mo. a^8 e^4 A-M$^{8.4}$; 84 leaves, pp. [24] 1-142 [143-144].

Bound with Venette's *L'Art de tailler les arbres fruitiers* (item 428).

Bibliographies: Hunt 339.

Copies: *BNC* and *NUC* (4 copies).

260. Lavalle, Jean, b. 1820.

TRAITÉ PRATIQUE | DES | CHAMPIGNONS COMESTIBLES | COMPRENANT | LEUR ORGANISATION, LEURS CARACTÈRES BOTANIQUES, | LEURS PROPRIÉTÉS ALIMENTAIRES, LEUR CULTURE, LA MANIÈRE DE LES PRÉPARER, | LES MOYENS DE LES DISTINGUER DES ESPÈCES VÉNÉNEUSES | ET LES SOINS A DONNER AUX PERSONNES EMPOISONNÉES PAR CES DERNIÈRES; | PAR J. LAVALLE, | Docteur ès-sciences et Docteur en médecine, Professeur de botanique, | Professeur d'histoire naturelle médicale à l'Ecole secondaire de médecine de Dijon, | Directeur du Jardin botanique de la même ville, | Membre de la Société géologique de France, du Comité central d'Agriculture de la Côte-d'Or, | Rédacteur de la *Revue horticole de Dijon;* etc. | [short rule] | OUVRAGE ORNÉ DE GRAVURES COLORIÉES. | [ornament] | [in two columns: column one] PARIS, | J.-B. BAILLIÈRE, ÉDITEUR, | rue Hautefeuille. | [vertical rule] | [column two] DIJON, | LAMARCHE et DROUELLE, | place Saint-Etienne. [end columns] | *1852.*

Second edition? Paris, 1852. Vicaire records a Paris, 1851, edition, no copy of which is recorded in the *BMC, BNC,* or *NUC* and which may be a ghost.

246 x 165 mm. π^2 1-5^8 6-7^4 8-10^8 [11]^2; 76 leaves, pp. [4] [1] 2-146 [147-148]. Publisher's printed wrappers.

Illustrations: 12 chromolithographs (one folding).

Bibliographies: Bitting, p. 275. Vicaire 494 records a Paris, 1851, edition.

Copies: *BMC, BNC,* and *NUC* (Library of Congress and University of Michigan).

261. La Varenne, François-Pierre de.

LE | CVISINIER | FRANCOIS, | ENSEIGNANT LA MANIERE | de bien apprester, & assaisonner | toutes sortes de viandes, grasses, | & maigres, legumes, | Patisseries, &c. | Reueu, corrigé, & augmenté d'vn | Traitté de Confitures seiches & | liquides, & autres delicatesses | de bouche. | Ensemble d'vne Table Alphabetique des | matieres qui sont traittées dans tout │ le Liure. │ *Par le sieur de LA VARENNE, Escuyer de* │ *Cuisine de Monsieur le Marquis d'Vxelles,* │ SECONDE EDITION. │ A PARIS, │ Chez PIERRE DAVID, au Palais, à l'entrée │ de la Gallerie des Prisonniers. │ [short rule] │ M. DC. LII. │ *AVEC PRIVILEGE DV ROY.*

Second edition, Paris, 1652. Originally published, Paris, 1651.

8vo. a⁸ A-N⁸ OP⁸ Q-Bb⁸; 200 leaves, pp. [*16*] 1-224, 241-370 [*30*]. Note: This edition was set by two compositors, one beginning at signature A and the other at signature Q. An error in casting off brought the first compositor to the end of his text at signature O so, to avoid a hiatus in the series, he signed this OP. No attempt was made to fill the gap in page numbers between 224 and 241.

Bibliographies: Vicaire 495.

Copies: *BMC* and *NUC* (John Crerar Library and New York Academy of Medicine).

262. La Varenne, François-Pierre de.

LE │ CVISINIER │ FRANCOIS, │ ENSEIGNANT LA MANIERE │ de bien apprester & assaisonner │ toutes sortes de Viandes grasses │ & maigres, legumes, & │ Patisseries, &c. │ *Reueu, corrigé, & augmenté d'vn Traitté de* │ *Confitures seiches & liquides, &* │ *autres* │ *delicatesses de bouche.* │ Ensemble d'vne Table Alphabetique des │ Matieres qui sont traittées dans │ tout le Liure. │ *Par le Sieur DE LA VARENNE, Escuyer de* │ *Cuisine de Monsieur le Marquis d'Vxelles,* │ QVATRIESME EDITION. │ [ornament] │ A PARIS, │ Chez PIERRE DAVID, au Palais, sur le Perron │ de la Saincte Chapelle, au Roy Dauid │ [short rule] │ M. DC. LIII. │ *AVEC PRIVILEGE DV ROY.*

Fourth edition, Paris, 1653. Originally published, Paris, 1651.

8vo. a⁸ A-Aa⁸; 200 leaves, pp. [*16*] 1-354 [355-384].

Bibliographies: This edition unrecorded in the bibliographies consulted.

Copies: No other copy of this edition located.

263. La Varenne, François-Pierre de.

LE | CUISINIER | FRANÇOIS, | *OV* | EST ENSEIGNE' LA MANIERE | d'apprester toute sorte de viandes, | de faire toute sort de Patisseries, | & de Confitures. | Reveu, & augmenté d'un Traité de Confitures | seiches & liquide, & pour aprêter les festins | aux quatre Saisons de l'Année. | *Par le Sieur DE LA VARENNE* | *Ecuyer de Cuisine de Monsieur* | *le Marquis d'Vxelles*, | ONZIE'ME EDITION. | [ornament] | *A LYON*, | Chez ANTOINE MOLIN, vis-à-vis le | grand College. | [short rule] | *M. DC. LXXXV.* | AVEC PERMISSION.

Eleventh edition, Lyon, 1685. Originally published, Paris, 1651.

12mo. A-T^{12} V^6; 234 leaves, pp. [1-2] 3-384, 383-458 [*8*].

Bibliographies: Maggs 185.

Copies: No other copy of this edition located.

264. La Varenne, François-Pierre de.

LE | CUISINIER | FRANÇOIS, | *OU* | L'ECOLE | DES RAGOUTS, | OU EST ENSEIGNE' | la maniere d'apprêter toutes sortes | de viandes, de Patisseries & Con- | fitures. | *Par le Sieur* DE LA VARENNE, | *Ecuyer de Cuisine de Monsieur le Mar-* | *quis d'Uxelles.* | [ornament] | A LYON, | Par la SOCIETÉ. | [rule] | M. DC. XCIX. | *AVEC PERMISSION.*

New edition, Lyon, 1699. Originally published, Paris, 1651.

12mo. A-T^{12} V^6; 234 leaves, pp. [1-4] 5-384, 383-456 [*10*]. First leaf blank.

Bibliographies: This edition unrecorded in the bibliographies consulted.

Copies: *NUC* (John Crerar Library and University of Texas).

265. La Varenne, François-Pierre de.

LE | PARFAICT | CONFITVRIER, | *QVI ENSEIGNE A* | *bien faire toutes sortes de* | *Con-* | *fitures tant seiches que liquides,* | *de Compostes, de fruicts, de* | *Sallades, de* | *Dragées, Breu-* | *uages delicieux, & autres de-* | *licatesses de bouche.* | [group of type ornaments] | A PARIS, | Chez IEAN RIBOV, au Palais, sur le | Grand Peron, vis à vis la Porte de l'Eglise | de la Saincte Chapelle, à l'Image S. Louis. | [rule] | M. DC. LXVII. | *AVEC PRIVILEGE DV ROY.*

First edition, Paris, 1667.

12mo. A-F^{12}; 72 leaves, pp. [1-2] 3-132 [133-144].

Bibliographies: Simon BG 471; Vicaire 501.

Copies: *BNC.*

266. La Varenne, François-Pierre de?

LE | PASTISSIER | FRANÇOIS; | Où est enseigné la maniere de faire | toute sorte de Pastisserie, tres-vtile | à toutes personnes. | *ENSEMBLE* | *Le moyen d'aprester les oeufs pour les* | *iours maigres, & autres, en plus* | *de soixante façons.* | [ornament] | A PARIS, | Chez IEAN GAILLARD, ruë | Sainct Iacques à la Diligence. | [short rule] | M. DC. LIII. | *Auec Priuilege du Roy.*

First edition, Paris, 1653.

8vo. π1 A-O^8 P^8(-P8); 120 leaves, pp. [2] 1-233 [234-238].

Bibliographies: Horn-Arndt 154; Malortie 133; Vicaire 659.

Copies: No other copy of the first edition located.

Note: The attribution of this work to La Varenne is speculative. Vicaire and Malortie enter it under title; *BMC* enters it under French Pastrycook; *BNC* does not list it among La Varenne's works; *NUC* and Horn-Arndt enter it under La Varenne. Maurice des Ombiaux writes in the foreword to the 1931 edition (item 268) "cet auteur? . . . On croit que ce serait le Sieur de La Varenne . . ." In the absence of a strong consensus we have chosen to follow *NUC* and Horn-Arndt.

267. La Varenne, François-Pierre de?

LE | PASTISSIER | FRANÇOIS; | Où est enseigné la maniere de faire toute | sorte de Pastisserie, tres-vtile à toute | sorte de personnes. | ENSEMBLE | *Le moyen d'apprester toute sorte d'oeufs pour les* | *iours maigres, & autres, en plus* | *de soixante façons.* | SECONDE EDITION. | [ornament] | A PARIS, | Chez IEAN GAILLARD, ruë | S. Iacques, à la diligence. | [short rule] | M. DC. LVII. | *Auec Priuilege du Roy.*

Second Paris edition, 1657. Originally published Paris, 1653 (item 266), and reprinted, Amsterdam, 1655.

8vo. π1 A-N⁸; 105 leaves, pp. [2] 1-80, 83-146, 149-205 [206-212].

Bibliographies: Vicaire 662.

Copies: *NUC* (John Crerar Library only).

268. La Varenne, François-Pierre de?

LE | PASTISSIER | FRANÇOIS. | Où est enseigné la maniere de | faire toute sorte de Pastisse- |rie, tres-utile à toute sorte | de personnes. | *ENSEMBLE* | *Le moyen d'aprester toutes sortes d'oeufs* | *pour les jours maigres, & autres,* | *en plus de soixante façons.* | Nouvelle édition avec une introduction de | MAURICE DES OMBIAUX | [publisher's device] | *Sur l'imprimé de Louys & Daniel Elzevier, Amsterdam, 1655* | DORBON-AINÉ | 19, Boulevard Haussmann 19, | PARIS

Colophon: CETTE RÉIMPRESSION DE L'ÉDITION | DU PASTISSIER FRANÇOIS | PUBLIÉE A AMSTERDAM EN 1655 PAR | LOUYS & DANIEL ELZEVIER A ÉTÉ | EXÉCUTÉE SUR LES PRESSES DE | MAURICE DARANTIERE, A ÉPINAY | SUR SEINE, A QUATRE CENTS | EXEMPLAIRES NUMÉROTÉS DE | 1 A 400 PLUS DIX EXEMPLAIRES | HORS COMMERCE DONT CINQ | NOMINATIFS ET CINQ NUMÉROTÉS | DE I A V, TOUS SUR PAPIER | PUR CHIFFON DE VINCENT | MONTGOLFIER & TERMINÉE LE | QUINZE OCTOBRE M CM XXXI | POUR LA LIBRAIRIE DORBON | AINÉ, A PARIS. | EXEMPLAIRE NUMÉRO | 315

First printing of this edition, Paris, 1931.

270 x 200 mm. [1]⁶ [2-20]⁴ [21]⁶; 88 leaves, pp. [*12*] [1] 2-158 [*6*]. Last two leaves blank.

Bibliographies: Horn-Arndt 156; Schraemli (1) 382.

Copies: *BMC* and *NUC* (Case Western Reserve University and New York Public Library).

269. Lebas, J.

FESTIN │ JOYEUX, │ OU, │ LA CUISINE │ EN MUSIQUE, │ EN VERS LIBRES. │ *PREMIERE PARTIE.* │ *Le prix est de trois livres broché.* │ [two type ornaments] │ [single type ornament] │ A PARIS, │ Chez { LESCLAPART Pere, rue │ Saint André des arcs, vis- │ à-vis la rue Pavée, à l'Es- │ pérance couronnée. │ *ET* │ LESCLAPART Fils, Quay │ de Conti, entre la rue de Ne- │ vers & la rue Guenegaut, │ à l'Espérance couronnée. │ [rule] │ M DCC XXXVIII. │ *Avec Approbation & Privilége du Roi.*

First edition, Paris, 1738.

12mo. a^6 a-h$^{8.4}$ A-O$^{8.4}$ P^8 Q^4(-Q4); ^{2}A^8 B^4 A^8 B-C^4; 177 leaves, pp. [i-iii] iv-x [xi-xii]; ^{2}[i] ii-xciii [xciv] [2] [1] 2-189 [190]; ^{3}1-24; ^{4}[1] 2-27 [28-30] [2]. Last leaf blank. Two parts bound in one volume. Pp. ^{3}1-24 are music printed from engraved plates.

Illustrations: One engraved folding plate of table setting.

Bibliographies: Bitting, p. 277; Crahan 359; Maggs 228; Schraemli (1) 279; Schraemli (2) 35; Vicaire 360.

Copies: *NUC* (6 copies).

270. Lebault, Armand.

ARMAND LEBAULT │ [short rule] │ LA TABLE ET LE REPAS │ A TRAVERS LES SIÈCLES │ HISTOIRE DE L'ALIMENTATION, DU MOBILIER A L'USAGE DES REPAS │ DU CÉRÉMONIAL ET DES DIVERTISSEMENTS DE TABLE │ CHEZ LES PEUPLES ANCIENS ET LES FRANÇAIS │ PRÉCÉDÉE D'UNE ÉTUDE SUR LES MOEURS GASTONOMIQUES PRIMITIVES │ ET SUR LE RÔLE DU REPAS DANS LA CIVILISATION │ [short rule] │ *Ouvrage orné de 116 illustrations* │ "Les animaux se repaissent; l'homme mange; │ l'homme d'esprit, seul, sait manger." │ BRILLAT-SAVARIN. │ [publisher's monogram] │ PARIS │ LUCIEN LAVEUR, ÉDITEUR │ 13, RUE DES SAINTS-PÈRES (VIe) │ [short rule] │ Tous droits réservés

First edition, Paris, 1910.

248 x 160 mm. π^4 1-45^8; 364 leaves, pp. [i-v] vi-vii [viii] [1] 2-718 [2]. Last leaf blank. Contemporary quarter purple morocco with marbled boards, publisher's printed wrappers preserved.

Illustrations: 116 halftones and line drawings in the text.

Bibliographies: Bitting, p. 277; Maggs 524 (incorrectly assigning the date 1873); Schraemli (3) 496; Wheaton and Kelly 3512.

Copies: *BMC*, *BNC*, and *NUC* (8 copies).

271. Lebeuf, Valentin-Ferdinand, b. 1818.

L'HORTICULTEUR GASTRONOME | [short fancy rule] | BONS LÉGUMES | ET | BONS FRUITS | OU CHOIX DES MEILLEURES VARIÉTÉS DE PLANTES POTAGÈRES | ET D'ARBRES FRUITIERS, VIGNES, ETC., A CULTIVER | ET MOYEN DE CONSERVER LES FRUITS ET LÉGUMES PENDANT L'HIVER | SUIVIS | DES 365 SALADES DE L'AMI ANTOINE | DE LA MANIÈRE D'ÉTABLIR UN JARDIN POTAGER-FRUITIER DE PRODUIT | ET DU | CALENDRIER DE L'HORTICULTEUR | Indiquant les travaux à exécuter, chaque mois, dans les jardins du nord, | du centre et du midi de la France. | PAR | V.-F. LEBEUF | [short rule] | PARIS | [in two columns: column one] RORET | LIBRAIRE-ÉDITEUR | 12, RUE HAUTEFEUILLE, 12 | [vertical rule] | [column two] CHAMEROT ET LAUVEREYNS | LIBRAIRES-ÉDITEURS | 13, RUE DU JARDINET, 13 [end columns] | [short rule] | 1878

Second edition, Paris, 1878. Originally published, Paris, 1868.

165 x 108 mm. [1]^{12} 2^6 3-6$^{12.6}$ 7^{12}; 66 leaves, pp. [1-5] 6-132. Publisher's printed wrappers. 18 page horticultural catalogue bound in at the end.

Bookplate: Westbury.

Bibliographies: Vicaire 505.

Copies: *BNC* and *NUC* (Massachusetts Horticultural Society only).

272. Lebrun.

MANUELS-RORET. | [short rule] | NOUVEAU MANUEL COMPLET | DU | CHARCUTIER, | OU | L'ART DE PRÉPARER ET DE CONSERVER LES DIFFÉ- | RENTES PARTIES DU COCHON, D'APRÈS LES PLUS | NOUVEAUX PROCÉDÉS; | PRÉCÉDÉ | DE L'ART D'ÉLEVER LES PORCS, DE LES ENGRAISSER ET | DE LES GUÉRIR. | PAR UNE RÉUNION DE CHARCUTIERS, | ET RÉDIGÉ | PAR M. LEBRUN, ANCIEN CHARCUTIER A

PARIS. | *NOUVELLE ÉDITION TRÈS AUGMENTÉE.* | [short fancy rule] | PARIS, | LIBRAIRIE ENCYCLOPÉDIQUE DE RORET, | RUE HAUTEFEUILLE, N 10 BIS. | 1840.

First printing, Paris, 1840, of this substantially enlarged and revised version of the *Manuel du charcutier*, Paris, 1827, by Mme Celnart (pseud. of Elisabeth Félicie Canard Bayle-Mouillard).

139 x 86 mm. π^2 1-24^6 25^2; 148 leaves, pp. [4] [1] 2-292 (p. 292 misnumbered "192").

Illustrations: Engraved folding plate showing a meat grinder.

Bibliographies: Vicaire 506 in a note.

Copies: *BMC*, *BNC*, and *NUC* (New York Public Library only).

273. Le Cordier, Hélie, b. 1615.

LE | PONT-L'EVESQVE | POËME | DEDIE' | A | MADEMOISELLE | *Par le sieur H. LE CORDIER, M.* | [ornament] | A PARIS, | Chez CHARLES DE TVNES, ruë Chartiere | proche le Puits certain. | [short rule] | M. DC. LXII. | *AVEC PRIVILEGE DV ROY.*

First edition, Paris, 1662.

4to. a^4 e^4 π^2 χ1 A-Dd^4; pp. [22] 1-215 [216].

Illustrations: Engraved portrait of Anne Marie Louise d'Orléans (Mademoiselle), dated 1652, facing a2^r.

Bibliographies: Vicaire 509.

Copies: No other copy of this edition located.

274. Le Grand d'Aussy, Pierre-Jean-Baptiste, 1737-1800.

HISTOIRE | DE LA VIE PRIVÉE | DES FRANÇAIS, | *Depuis l'origine de la Nation jusqu' à nos jours.* | Par M. LE GRAND D'AUSSY. | *PREMIERE PARTIE.* | [short rule] | .... *Si quid novisti rectius istis,* | *Candidus imperti; si non, his utere*

mecum. HOR. | [short rule] | TOME PREMIER. [TOME SECOND.] [TOME
TROISIEME.] | [vignette] | *A PARIS*, | DE L'IMPRIMERIE DE PH.-D. PIERRES, |
Imprimeur Ordinaire du Roi, &c. rue S. Jacques. | [two short rules] | M. DCC.
LXXXII. | *AVEC APPROBATION ET PRIVILEGE DU ROI.*

First edition, Paris, 1782.

8vo. 3 vols. Vol. I. a^8 A-Z^8 Aa^4; 196 leaves, pp. [i-v] vi-xiii [xiv-xvi] [1] 2-373 [374]
[2]. Last leaf (blank?) wanting in this copy. Vol. II. π^2 A-Z^8; 186 leaves, pp. [4] [1]
2-80, 97-383 [384]. Vol. III. π^2 A-Y^8 Z^6; 186 leaves, pp. [4] [1] 2-363 [364].

Bibliographies: Bitting, p. 280; Drexel 523; Malortie 218; Simon BG 946; Vicaire
510; Wheaton and Kelly 3545.

Copies: *BMC*, *BNC*, and *NUC* (7 copies).

275. Le Grand d'Aussy, Pierre-Jean-Baptiste, 1737-1800.

HISTOIRE | DE LA VIE PRIVÉE | DES FRANÇOIS, | DEPUIS L'ORIGINE DE
LA NATION JUSQU'A NOS JOURS; | PAR LE GRAND D'AUSSY. | NOUVELLE
ÉDITION, | AVEC DES NOTES, CORRECTIONS ET ADDITIONS, | PAR J. B. B.
DE ROQUEFORT. | [short rule] | .... Si quid novisti rectius istis, |
Candidus imperti; si non, his utere mecum. | HOR. *Epist. VI, lib. I.* | [short rule] |
TOME PREMIER. [TOME DEUXIÈME.] [TOME TROISIÈME.] | PARIS, |
LAURENT-BEAUPRÉ, libraire, Palais Royal, no 218. | [short rule] | 1815.

Second edition? Paris, 1815. Originally published, Paris, 1782 (item 274). Vicaire
notes, "Quérard indique une autre édition: Paris, Onfroy, 1783, 3 vol. in-8." No other
record of a 1783 edition has been found and no copy of it appears in *BMC*, *BNC*, or
NUC.

200 x 123 mm. 3 vols. Vol. I. π^2 a^4(-a4) 1-28^8; 229 leaves, pp. [4] [i] ii-vi [1] 2-448.
Vol. II. π^2 1-27^8; 218 leaves, pp. [4] [1] 2-431 [432]. Vol. III. π^2 1-30^8 31$_1$; 243
leaves, pp. [4] [1] 2-481 [482].

Bibliographies: Bitting, p. 280; Maggs 365; Simon BG 947; Wheaton and Kelly 3546.

Copies: *BMC*, *BNC*, and *NUC* (9 copies).

276. Lémery, Louis, 1677-1743.

TRAITÉ | DES | ALIMENTS, | *OÙ L'ON TROUVE* | PAR ORDRE, ET
SEPARÉMENT | La difference & le choix qu'on doit faire de chacun d'eux | en
particulier; les bons & les mauvais effets qu'ils | peuvent produire; les principes en
quoy ils abondent; | le temps, l'âge & le temperament où ils convien- | nent. | *Avec*
des Remarques à la suite de chaque Chapitre, où | *l'on explique leur nature & leurs*
usages, suivant | *les principes Chymiques, & Méchaniques.* | Par M. LOUIS
LEMERY, Docteur Regent en la Faculté de | Medecine de Paris, de l'Academie
Royale des Sciences. | [ornament] | A PARIS, | Chez J. B. CUSSON & P. WITTE,
rue S. Jacques, | au Nom de JESUS & au Bon Pasteur, | vis à vis la rue Plâtre. |
[short rule] | M. DCCII. | *Avec Approbations & Privilege du Roy.*

First edition, Paris, 1702.

12mo. a^{12} e^{12} i^4 A-Y^{12} Z^8; 300 leaves, pp. [*56*] 1-541 [*542-544*].

Bibliographies: Blake, p. 263; Pennell, p. 122; Schraemli (1) 281; Vicaire 514 in a
note.

Copies: *BMC*, *BNC*, and *NUC* (5 copies).

277. Lémery, Louis, 1677-1743.

TRAITE' | DES | ALIMENTS, | *OÙ L'ON TROUVE*| PAR ORDRE, ET
SEPAREMENT. | La difference & le choix qu'on doit faire de chacqun d'eux | en
particulier; les bons & les mauvais effets qu'ils peu- | vent produire; les principes en
quoi ils abondent; le | temps, l'âge & le temperament où ils conviennent. | *Avec de*
Remarques à la suite de chaque Chapitre, où l'on | *explique leur nature & leurs*
usages, suivant les principes | *Chymiques, & Méchaniques.* | Par M. LOUIS
LEMERY, Docteur Regent en la | Faculté de Medecine de Paris, de l'Academie
Royale | des Sciences. | SECONDE EDITION, | *revue, corrigée & augmentée par*
l'Auteur. | [two type ornaments] | [two type ornaments] | A PARIS, | Chez PIERRE
WITTE, à l'Ange Gardien | rue saint Jacque, au-dessus de la rue | des Mathurins. |
[short rule] | MDCCV. | *AVEC APPROBATIONS ET PRIVILEGE DU ROI.*

Third edition, Paris, 1705, styled second on the title-page. Originally published, Paris,
1702 (item 276), and reprinted 1703, 1705, and 1709, the last three all styled second
edition.

12mo. a^8(-a8) ✱^{12} ✱✱^{6} A-Z^{12} Aa^4 Bb1 (=a8); 306 pp. [*14*] i-xxxv [*xxxvi*] 1-562.

Bibliographies: Bitting, p. 281; Blake, p. 263; Vicaire 514.

Copies: *BMC*, *BNC*, and *NUC* (5 copies).

278. Lémery, Louis, 1677-1743.

TRAITÉ | DES | ALIMENS, | *OU L'ON TROUVE* | La différence, & le choix, qu'on en doit faire; les | bons, & les mauvais effets, qu'ils peuvent produire; | leurs principes; les circonstances où ils convien- | nent, | *Par M. LOUIS LÉMERY, Docteur Regent en* | *la Faculté de Médecine de Paris, de l'Academie* | *Royale des Sciences.* | TROISIÈME ÉDITION, | Revue, corrigée, & augmentée sur la seconde de | l'Auteur, par M. JACQUES JEAN BRUHIER | Docteur en Médecine, Censeur Royal, des Aca- | démies d'Angers, &c. | *TOME I.* [*TOME II.*] | [ornament] | A PARIS, | Chez DURAND, rue du Foin, la premiere Porte | Cochere, en entrant par la rue S. Jacques. | [two short rules] | M. DCC. LV. | *Avec Approbations, & Privilege du Roi.*

Fifth edition, Paris, 1755, styled third on the title-page. Originally published, Paris, 1702 (item 276). Reprinted 1703, 1705 (item 277), and 1709, all styled second edition, and 1755 as the third edition.

12mo. 2 vols. Vol. I. a-c^{12} d^{4} A-Z^{12}; 316 leaves, pp. [i-iii] iv-lxxx [1] 2-552. Vol. II. π1 A-Bb^{12}; 301 leaves, pp. [2] [1] 2-595 [596-600].

Bookplates: (1) Ex libris Georges Vicaire; (2) Ex Libris Robert Viel.

Bibliographies: Blake, p. 263; Maggs 261 (this copy); Vicaire 513 (this copy).

Copies: *BNC*.

279. Lepage, Auguste, 1835-1908.

AUGUSTE LEPAGE | [short rule] | LES | DINERS | ARTISTIQUES ET LITTÉRAIRES | DE PARIS | [publisher's monogram] | PARIS | BIBLIOTHÈQUE DES DEUX MONDES | FRINZINE, KLEIN ET Cie, ÉDITEURS | I, RUE BONAPARTE, I | [short rule] | 1884 | Tous droits réservés.

First edition, Paris, 1884. Printing on ordinary paper, after 20 copies on Hollande.

178 x 110 mm. π^6 1-20$^{12.6}$; 186 leaves, pp. [i-vii] viii-xi [xii] [1-3] 4-360. First leaf (blank?) wanting in this copy.

Bibliographies: Bitting, p. 282; Vicaire 515.

Copies: *BNC* and *NUC* (Library of Congress and University of California, Berkeley). *BMC* records the second edition, also Paris, 1884.

280. Lériguet, D.

LA CUISINE | ÉLÉMENTAIRE | ET ÉCONOMIQUE, | PROPRE A TOUTES LES CONDITIONS | ET A TOUS LES PAYS; | Contenant des recettes d'un usage journalier, | la plupart inconnues jusqu'à présent, des pré- | ceptes généraux clairs et précis pour pré- | parer toutes les espèces d'alimens, de pâtis- | series, de confitures et de liqueurs de ménage; | avec une planche explicative d'un fourneau et | de différens ustensiles de cuisine, de nouvelle | invention. | PAR D. L. | SECOND ÉDITION. | [short fancy rule] | A PARIS. | Chez LEVACHER, Libraire, rue du Hurepoix, no. 12, | au bout du quai des Augustins. | [short rule] | AN XIV. – 1805.

Second edition, Paris, 1805. Originally published, Paris, also 1805.

159 x 96 mm. π^4 A-Aa$^{8.4}$ Bb^8; 156 leaves, pp. [i-iii] iv-viii [1] 2-304. Bound with Mme. Utrecht-Friedel's *Le Confiseur royal*, Paris, 1816 (item 195) and Gacon-Dufour's *Recueil pratique d'économie rurale et domestique*, Paris, 1804 (item 197).

Illustration: Engraved plate of cooking stove.

Bibliographies: Maggs 369 (this copy); Vicaire 225.

Copies: *BNC*.

281. Lessius, Leonardus, 1554-1623.

DE | LA SOBRIÉTÉ | *ET* | DE SES AVANTAGES, | OU | *Le vrai moyen de se conserver dans* | *UNE SANTÉ PARFAITE* | *jusqu'à l'âge le plus avancé.* | TRADUCTION NOUVELLE des Traités | de LESSIUS & de CORNARO | sur la vie sobre. | [rule] | *Abstinentia adjicit vitam.* | [rule] | [ornament] | A SALERNE, | *Et se trouve A PARIS*, | Chez CAILLEAU, Imprimeur-Libraire, | rue Saint-Severin. | [two short rules] | M. DCC. LXXXII.

New edition, Paris, 1782. Leonardus Lessius's *Hygiasticon* was originally published, Antwerp, 1613, and Luigi Cornaro's *Trattato de la vita sobria*, Padua, 1558. This translation by J. R. Allaneau de la Bonnodière was originally published, Paris, 1701.

139 x 78 mm. π^6 A-N^{12}; 162 leaves, pp. [i-v] vi-xii [1] 2-312.

Bibliographies: Vicaire 213.

Copies: *BNC*.

282. Leuchs, Johann Karl, b. 1797.

LA CHIMIE | APPLIQUÉE | A LA CONSERVATION | DES | SUBSTANCES ALIMENTAIRES, | OU | MANUEL COMPLET DES MÉNAGES, | DONNANT DES RECETTES INFAILLIBLES POUR CONSERVER: | [in two columns: column one] 1°. Les Fruits; | 2°. Les Viandes; | 3°. Les Légumes; | 4°. Le Lait; | 5°. Le Beurre; | [vertical double rule] | [column two] 6°. Les OEufs; | 7°. Le Pain; | 8°. Les Racines; | 9°. Les Semences; | 10°. Le Vin, etc. [end columns] | *Traduit de l'allemand, de* JEAN-CHARLES LEUCHS, | Par M. Bulos. | PARIS. | AUDIN, LIBRAIRE, quai des Augustins, no 25; | C. BÉCHET, même quai, no 57; | LECOINTE et DUREY, même quai, no. 39; | PONTHIEU, Palais-Royal. | 1827.

Second edition, Paris, 1827, of Bulos's translation. Originally published in German under the title *Haus- und Hülfsbuch für alle Stände*, Nürnberg, 1822, and in French under the title *L'Art de conserver les substances alimentaires solides ou liquides*, Paris, 1825.

168 x 98 mm. π^2 χ^6(-χ1,2) 1-20^{12}; 246 leaves, pp. [i-v] vi-xii [1] 2-480.

Bibliographies: Vicaire 132.

Copies: *BNC*.

283. Liger, Louis, sieur d'Auxerre, 1658-1717.

DICTIONAIRE | PRATIQUE | DU | BON MENAGER | DE CAMPAGNE | ET DE VILLE, | QUI APPREND GENERALEMENT LA MANIERE | de nourrir, élever & gouverner, tant en santé que malades, tou- | tes sortes de Bestiaux, Chevaux & Volailles, de sçavoir mettre à | son profit tout ce qui provient de l'Agriculture; de faire valoir tou- | tes sortes de Terres, Prez, Vignes & Bois; de cultiver les Jardins, | tant Fruitiers, Potagers, que Jardins Fleuristes; de conduire les | Eaux, & faire generalement tout ce qui convient aux Jardins d'or- | nemens. | *AVEC* | UN TRAITE' DE TOUT CE QUI CONCERNE | la Cuisine, les Confitures, la Pâtisserie, les Liqueurs de toutes sor- | tes, les Chasses differentes, la Pêche, & autres divertissemens de la | Campagne; les mots Latins de tout ce qu'on traite dans ce Livre, | & quelques Remarques curieuses sur la plûpart; le tout en faveur | des Etrangers, & de tous ceux qui se plaisent à ces sortes de lectures. | Ouvrage tres-utile dans les Familles. | *Par le Sieur L. LIGER.* | TOME PREMIER. [TOME SECOND.] | *Le prix est dix livres.* | [ornament] | A PARIS, | Chez PIERRE RIBOU, seul Libraire de l'Académie Royale de Musique, | Quai des Augustins, vis à-vis la descente du Pont-Neuf, | à l'Image S. Loüis. | [short rule] | M. DCC. XV. | *AVEC APPROBATION ET PRIVILEGE DE SA MAJESTÉ.*

First edition, Paris, 1715.

4to. 2 vols. Vol. I. $\pi^4(-\pi 4)$ A-Hhh^4 Iii^2; 221 leaves, pp. [i-ii] iii-vi [1] 2-436. Vol. II. $\pi 1$ A^2 B-Ddd^4 Eee^2; 201 leaves, pp. [2] [1] 2-400. Two volumes bound in one.

Bibliographies: Horn-Arndt 284; Vicaire 522 in a note; Wheaton and Kelly 3668.

Copies: *BMC, BNC,* and *NUC* (Cornell, Harvard, and John Crerar Library).

284. Liger, Louis, sieur d'Auxerre, 1658-1717.

LE ME'NAGE | DES CHAMPS | ET DE LA VILLE, | OU NOUVEAU | CUISINIER | FRANÇOIS | ACCOMMODE' | au goût du temps. | CONTENANT, | Tout ce qu'un parfait chef de cuisine doit sçavoir | pour servir toutes sortes de tables, depuis celles | des plus grands Seigneurs jusqu'à celles des bons | Bourgeois, avec une instruction pour faire toutes | sortes de pâtisseries, confitures seches & liqui- | des, & toutes des differentes liqueurs qui sont | aujourd'huy en usage. Premiere partie du Ménage. | A PARIS AU PALAIS, | Chëz | DAMIEN BEUGNIE', dans la grande | Salle, au pilier des Consultations, | au Lion d'or. | [short rule] | M. DCCXIV. | *AVEC PRIVILEGE DV ROY.*

Part one of a new and greatly enlarged edition, Paris, 1714, of Liger's *Le Ménage des champs, et le jardinier françois accommodez au goût du temps*, originally published, Paris, 1710. Vicarie writes, "This work which is nothing, in fact, but a compilation of the *Jardinier françois* and the *Délices de la campagne* of Nicolas de Bonnefons, is divided into four books. The first three concern cooking; the fourth treats gardens and is followed by a treatise on hunting and fishing." The above volume, published in 1714, enlarges the section on cooking and was followed in 1715 by *Le Ménage des champs et de la ville, ou nouveau jardinier françois accomodé au goût du temps . . . deuxième partie du ménage des champs* treating gardening, hunting and fishing.

12mo. a⁴ A-DDd⁸·⁴ [EEe]²; 306 leaves, pp. [8] [1] 2-384, 387-584 [22].

Illustrations: Engraved frontispiece and five engraved folding plates showing table settings.

Bibliographies: Horn-Arndt 285; Vicaire 523.

Copies: *BNC* and *NUC* (New York Academy of Medicine and University of California, Berkeley).

285. Liger, Louis, sieur d'Auxerre, 1652-1717.

LE MENAGE | DES CHAMPS | ET DE LA VILLE; | OU NOUVEAU | CUISINIER | FRANÇOIS, | *Accommodé au goût du Tems.* | Contentant tout ce qu'un parfait Chef de Cuisine doit sça- | voir pour servir toutes sortes de tables, depuis celles | des plus grands Seigneurs jusqu'à celles des bons Bour- | geois; avec une Instruction pour faire toutes sortes de | Pâtisseries, confitures séches & liquides, & toutes les | diffentes liqueurs qui sont aujourd'hui en usage. | *NOUVELLE EDITION.* | [ornament] | A PARIS, | Chez CHRIST. DAVID, Libraire-Imprimeur, rüe S. Jacq. | près la Fontaine S. Séverin, au Nom de Jesus. | [rule] | M. DCC. XXXIX. | *AVEC PRIVILEGE DU ROY*

New edition, Paris, 1739. Originally published, Paris, 1710. (See note on editions under item 284).

12mo. a⁶ A-Rr⁸·⁴; 246 leaves, pp. [*12*] 1-473 [474-480].

Bibliographies: Bitting, p. 287; Pennell, p. 124; Vicaire 523.

Copies: *NUC* (Library of Congress only).

286.   Liger, Louis, sieur d'Auxerre, 1658-1717.

LA NOUVELLE │ [in red] MAISON RUSTIQUE, │ OU │ [in red] ÉCONOMIE GENERALE │ DE TOUS LES BIENS │ [in red] DE CAMPAGNE: │ La maniere de les entretenir & de les multiplier; │ Donnée ci-devant au Public par le Sieur Liger. │ [in red] QUATRIE'ME EDITION, │ [Augmentée considérablement, & mise en meilleur ordre; │ *AVEC* │ [in red] LA VERTU DES SIMPLES, L'APOTICAIRERIE │ & les Décisions du Droit-François sur les Matieres Rurales; │ Et enrichie de Figures en Taille-douce. │ *Par M.* ✳✳✳ │ [in red] TOME PREMIER. [TOME SECOND.] │ [ornament] │ [in red] A PARIS, │ Chez la Veuve [in red] PRUDHOMME, [end red] au Palais, au sixiéme Pilier de la │ Grand'Salle, vis-à-vis l'Escalier de la Cour des Aydes, │ à la Bonne-Foy couronnée. │ [short rule] │ [in red] M. DCC. XXXVI. │ *AVEC PRIVILEGE DV ROY.*

Sixth edition, styled the fourth, Paris, 1736. Originally published under the title *OEconomie générale de la campagne, ou nouvelle maison rustique*, Paris, 1700, and reprinted Amsterdam, 1701 (2nd edition), Paris, 1708 (2nd edition), Paris, 1721 (3rd edition), Paris, 1732 (4th edition), Paris, 1736 (4th edition), etc.

4to. 2 vols. Vol. I. π^2 a^4 e^2 A-ZZzzz^4 AAAaaa^2 BBBbbb-CCCccc^4; 956 leaves. pp. [*16*] [1] 2-528, 559-970. Vol. II. π^2 a^2 A-FFFfff^4 GGGggg^2; 490 leaves, pp. [*8*] 1-971 [*972*].

Illustrations: Vol. I. Engraved frontispiece printed on $\pi2^v$, eight woodcuts in the text and eight engraved plates. Vol. II. Twenty-three engraved plates (one folding) and twenty woodcuts in the text.

Bibliographies: Vicaire 521.

Copies: *NUC* (University of Wisconsin only).

286a.   Linand, Barthelemy.

L'ABSTINENCE │ DE LA VIANDE │ RENDUE AISE'E, │ ou moins difficile à pratiquer. │ *ou* │ REGIME DE VIE │ Avec lequel on peut prévenir │ ou rendre moins grandes les │ incommoditez qui survien- │ nent à ceux qui font maigre, │ par le ménagement des tem- │ peramens, le choix & le bon │ usage des alimens maigres │ simplement aprêtez, &c. │ *Par M. BARTHELEMY LINAND, Docteur / en Medecine.* │ [ornament] │ A PARIS, │ Chez PIERRE BIENFAIT, sur le Quay des │ grands

Augustins, à l'Image S. Pierre. | *Où l'on trouve aussi le Traité des Eaux minerales* / *de Forges, du même Auteur* | [rule] | M. DCC | *Avec Approbations & Privilege du Roy.*

First edition, Paris, 1700.

12mo. a^8 e^4 A-S$^{8.4}$ T^4 χ1; 125 leaves, pp. [*24*] 1-225 [226].

Bibliographies: Bitting, p. 288; Vicaire 523; Wheaton and Kelly 3692.

Copies: *BMC, BNC, NUC* (Harvard and Library of Congress).

287. Le Livres de glace.

LE LIVRES | DE GLACE | OU | HISTOIRE CONCISE ET ABRÉGÉE | De tout ce qui regarde la Glace | Depuis son premier usage en Europe, comme article de | luxe, jusqu'au temps présent. | AVEC DES INSTRUCTIONS | Sur la manière de produire de la Glace pure et solide, au moyen de | l'Appareil frigorifque, suivies d'un recueil de recettes pour | faire les glaces et les crêmes ou fromages glacés. | [vignette] | PARIS, | AU DÉPOT DES MACHINES FRIGORIFIQUES, | *Chez* LAHOCHE, *Palais-Royal, galerie Valois, No 153.* | [short rule] | 1845.

First edition, Paris, 1845.

224 x 139 mm. π^2 2π^2 [1]^8 2-7^8 8^4; 64 leaves, pp. [*4*] i-iv [1-5] 6-120.

Illustrations: Folding lithographed plate of refrigeration machines.

Bibliographies: Drexel 164; Schraemli (1) 286; Vicaire 529.

Copies: No other copy located.

288. Lombard, Léandre-Moïse.

LE | CUISINIER | ET LE | MÉDECIN | ET LE MÉDECIN ET LE CUISINIER | OU | LE CUISINIER MÉDECIN ET LE MÉDECIN CUISINIER | OU | L'ART DE CONSERVER OU DE RÉTABLIR SA SANTÉ | PAR UNE ALIMENTATION CONVENABLE | GUIDE INDISPENSABLE | A TOUTES LES PERSONNES QUI VEULENT CONNAITRE LEUR TEMPÉRAMENT, LE GOUVERNER EN SANTÉ OU EN MALADIE, | SELON LES RÈGLES DE L'HYGIÈNE, | Suivi d'un | LIVRE

DE CUISINE │ D'ÉCONOMIE DOMESTIQUE ET D'HYGIÈNE ALIMENTAIRE APPLIQUÉE SELON LES DIVERS TEMPÉRAMENTS │ INDIQUANT PAR ORDRE ALPHABÉTIQUE │ LE MODE DE PRÉPARATION DE TOUS LES ALIMENTS FRANÇAIS ET ÉTRANGERS, │ LES QUALITÉS ET LES PRIX DE TOUS LES VINS, LIQUEURS ET BOISSONS, │ L'INDICATION DE TOUS LES VÉGÉTAUX ET ANIMAUX QUI SERVENT A L'ALIMENTATION, │ LA MANIÈRE DE DÉCOUPER TOUTES LES VIANDES ROTIES, GIBIERS, ETC.; LE SERVICE DE LA TABLE, ETC. │ LES PROPRIÉTÉS DE TOUTES LES SUBSTANCES ALIMENTAIRES, DES EAUX MINÉRALES, LEUR INFLUENCE SUR LES DIVERS │ TEMPÉRAMENTS, LES MALADIES RÉSULTANT DES ABUS ET EXCÈS, ET LE MOYEN DE S'EN PRÉSERVER, │ PAR │ UNE SOCIÉTÉ DE MÉDECINS, DE CHIMISTES, DE CUISINIERS ET D'OFFICIERS DE BOUCHE, │ SOUS LA DIRECTION DE │ MR L.-M. LOMBARD │ DOCTEUR EN MÉDECINE DE LA FACULTÉ DE PARIS. │ *L'hygiéne, c'est la santé,* │ *La santé, c'est la vie.* │ [two short rules] │ PRIX: Broché, 10 fr.   Relié en percaline, 12 fr. │ [two short rules] │ PARIS │ L. CURMER, RUE DE RICHELIEU, 47 (AU PREMIER), │ ET CHEZ TOUS LES LIBRAIRES DE FRANCE ET DE L'ÉTRANGER. │ MDCCCLV.

First edition, Paris, 1855.

240 x 152 mm. [a]⁴ b⁴ c² 1-30⁴; ²1-46⁴; 314 leaves, pp. [i-v] vi-xix [xx] [1] 2-239 [240]; ²[1] 2-368. Publisher's purple cloth stamped in gold.

Illustrations: Lithographed frontispiece of a doctor and a cook shaking hands signed in the left lower corner "Pauquet" and in the right lower corner "Brunier" and a lithographed title-page with a chef before his stove at the top and three persons and a small table at the bottom and a border of food and names of famous chefs and doctors, signed lower left "G. FATH." and lower right "PISAN." Vicaire records that there were two printings of the frontispiece and this copy bears the statement "2e TIRAGE." There are numerous wood engravings in the text.

Bibliographies: Bitting, p. 392; Drexel 169; Horn-Arndt 413; Schraemli (3) 94; Simon BG 965; Vicaire 534.

Copies: *BMC* (mis-cataloged as 1885), *BNC*, and *NUC* (7 copies).

289. Lorry, Anne-Charles, 1726-1783.

ESSAI │ *SUR* │ LES ALIMENS, │ *POUR servir de Commentaire* │ *aux Livres Diététiques* │ *d'Hippocrate.* │ TOME PREMIER. │ [ornament] │ A PARIS, │ De l'Imprimerie de VINCENT, | rue S. Severin, à l'Ange. | [two short rules] | M DCC LVII. | *Avec Approbation & Privilege du Roi.*

Title-page of Volume II:

ESSAI | *SUR USAGE* | DES | ALIMENS, | *POUR servir de Commentaire* | *aux Livres Diététiques* | *d'Hippocrate.* | TOME SECOND. | [ornament] | A PARIS, | De l'Imprimerie de VINCENT, | rue S. Severin, à l'Ange. | [two short rules] | M DCC LVII. | *Avec Approbation & Privilege du Roi.*

Second edition of volume one and the first edition of volume two, both Paris, 1757. The first edition of volume one was published, Paris, 1754.

12mo. 2 vols. Vol. I. a^{12} A-S^{12} T^6; 234 leaves, pp. [i-ix] x-xxxiv [1] 2-440 [*4*]. Vol. II. a^8 A-S^{12} T^2; 226 leaves, pp. [i-iii] iv-xv [xvi] [1] 2-436.

Bibliographies: Bitting, pp. 293-294; Blake, p. 277; Drexel 513; Maggs 267; Malortie 288; Simon BG 969; Vicaire 342.

Copies: *BNC* and *NUC* (5 copies).

290. Lune, Pierre de.

LE NOVVEAV | CVISINIER | OV IL EST TRAITTE' | DE LA VERITABLE METHODE | pour apprester toutes sortes de Viandes, | Gibbier, Volatiles, Poissons, tant | de Mer que d'eau douce: | *Suiuant les quatre saisons de l'Année.* | Ensemble la maniere de faire toutes sortes de Patis- | series, tant froides que chaudes, en perfection. | *Par le Sieur PIERRE DE LVNE, Escuyer de* | *Cuisine de feu Monsieur le Duc de Rohan.* | SECONDE EDITION. | [ornament] | A PARIS, | Chez PIERRE DAVID, sur le Quay | & proche la grande porte des Augustins, | au Roy Dauid. | [rule] | M. DC. LX. | *Auec Priuilege du Roy,*

Third edition, styled second, Paris, 1660. Originally published under the title *Le Cuisinier ou il est traitté de la véritable méthode pour apprester toutes sortes de viandes . . .*, Paris, 1656. The second edition was Paris, 1659.

8vo. a^4 A-Bb^8; 196 leaves, pp. [*8*] 1-364 [*36*].

Bibliographies: Schraemli (1) 293; Schraemli (2) 30. Vicaire 542-543 records the 1656 and 1668 editions and Malortie 121 and Simon BG 472 the 1659 edition.

Copies: *BMC* and *NUC* (New York Academy of Medicine only).

291. Machet, J. J.

LE │ CONFISEUR MODERNE, │ OU │ L'ART DU CONFISEUR ET DU DISTILLATEUR, │ CONTENANT │ Toutes les opérations du Confiseur et du Distillateur, │ et, en outre, les procédés généraux de quelques Arts │ qui s'y rapportent, particulièrement ceux du Parfu- │ meur et du Limonadier. │ OUVRAGE │ ENRICHI de plusieurs recettes nouvelles, et mis à la portée de tout │ amateur, avec les moyens de reconnaître les falsifications et les │ sophistications en tout genre; │ AUQUEL ON A JOINT: │ 1° Un Appendice ou Recueil de recettes de médicamens, rendus agréables à │ la vue et au goût, par une préparation et une forme nouvelles, avec leurs doses │ et leurs vertus; │ 2° Un petit historique de quelques substances simples les plus usuelles; │ 3° Un vocabulaire des termes techniques. │ PAR J. J. MACHET, Confiseur et Distillateur. │ Utile dulci. │ [short fancy rule] │ DE L'IMPRIMERIE DE GUILLEMINET. │ A PARIS, │ Chez MARADAN, Libraire, rue Pavée S. André-des-Arcs, no 16. │ AN XI – 1803.

First edition, Paris, 1803.

215 x 137 mm. π^8 1-28^8 29^8(-29$_8$); 239 leaves, pp. [i-v] vi-xvi [1] 2-461 [462]. Untrimmed, in contemporary wrappers with printed label on spine.

Bibliographies: Drexel 140; Schraemli (1) 297; Simon BV, p. 155.

Copies: *BNC* and *NUC* (Kansas State University and Louisiana State University).

292. Machet, J. J.

LE │ CONFISEUR MODERNE, │ OU │ L'ART DU CONFISEUR ET DU DISTILLATEUR, │ CONTENANT │ Toutes les opérations du Confiseur et du Distillateur, │ et, en outre, les procédés généraux de quelques Arts │ qui s'y rapporte, particulièrement ceux du Parfu- │ meur et du Limonadier. │ OUVRAGE │ ENRICHI de plusieurs recettes nouvelles, et mis à la portée de tout │ amateur, avec les moyens de reconnaître les falsifications et les │ sophistications en tout genre; │ AUQUEL ON A JOINT │ 1° Un Appendice ou Recueil de recettes de médicamens, rendus agréables à │ la vue et au goût, par une préparation et une forme nouvelles, avec leurs doses │ et leurs vertus. │ 2° Un petit historique de quelques substances simples les plus usuelles. │ 3° Un vocabulaire des termes techniques. │ PAR J. J. MACHET, Confiseur et Distillateur. │ Utile dulci. │ SECONDE ÉDITION. │ [short fancy rule] │ DE

L'IMPRIMERIE DE HARDY. | A PARIS, | Chez MARADAN, Libraire, rue des Grands-Augustins, no 29, | vis-à-vis celle du Pont-de-Lodi. | M. DCCC. VI.

Second edition, Paris, 1806. Originally published Paris, 1803 (item 291).

198 x 123 mm. π^8 1-29^8; 240 leaves, pp. [i-v] vi-xvi [1] 2-461 [462] [2]. Last leaf blank.

Bibliographies: Bitting, p. 299; Crahan 643; Simon BV, p. 155.

Copies: *NUC* (Library of Congress and University of Pennsylvania.)

293. Machet, J. J.

LE | CONFISEUR MODERNE, | OU | L'ART DU CONFISEUR ET DU DISTILLATEUR, | CONTENANT | Toutes les opérations du Confiseur et du Distillateur, | et, en outre, les procédés généraux de quelques | Arts qui s'y rapportent, particulièrement ceux du | Parfumeur et du Limonadier. | OUVRAGE | ENRICHI de plusieurs recettes nouvelles, et mis à la portée de tout | amateur, avec les moyens de reconnaître les falsifications et les | sophistications en tout genre; | AUQUEL ON A JOINT | 1°. Un Appendice ou Recueil de recettes de médicamens, rendus agréables | à la vue et au goût, par une préparation et une forme nouvelles, avec leurs | doses et leurs vertus. | 2°. Un petit Historique de quelques substances simples les plus usuelles. | 3°. Un Vocabulaire des termes techniques. | PAR J. J. MACHET, Confiseur et Distillateur. | Utile dulci. | QUATRIÈME ÉDITION. | [short fancy rule] | A PARIS, | CHEZ MARADAN, LIBRAIRE, RUE DES MARAIS, No 16. | 1821.

Fourth edition, Paris, 1821. Originally published Paris, 1803 (item 291).

202 x 125 mm. π^8 1-28^8 29^8(-29$_8$); 239 leaves, pp. [i-v] vi-xvi [1] 2-462.

Bibliographies: Maggs 386; Vicaire 546 in a note.

Copies: *BNC* and *NUC* (National Library of Medicine only).

294. Machet, J. J.

LE | CONFISEUR MODERNE, | OU | L'ART DU CONFISEUR, | DU DISTILLATEUR, DU RAFFINEUR DE SUCRE, | DU PARFUMEUR ET DU

LIMONADIER, | CONTENANT | TOUS LES PROCÉDÉS GÉNÉRAUX DE QUELQUES ARTS QUI S'Y RAPPOR- | TENT, AVEC LE MOYEN DE CONNAÎTRE LES FALSIFICATIONS ET LES | SOPHISTICATIONS EN TOUT GENRE; | AUQUEL ON A JOINT: | 1° Un Appendice, ou Recueil de Recettes de médicaments rendus | agréables à la vue et au goût, par une préparation et une forme | nouvelle, avec leurs doses et leurs vertus; | 2° Un petit Historique de quelques Substances simples les plus usuelles; | 3° Un Vocabulaire des Termes techniques, et enfin des Recettes d'écono- | mie domestique pour conserver toute l'année les fruits comme dans | leur primeur: | PAR J.-J. MACHET, | CONFISEUR ET DISTILLATEUR. | HUITIÈME ÉDITION, | REVUE PAR ROBINEAU, CONFISEUR. | A PARIS. | CORBET, LIBRAIRE, RUE DAUPHINE, 20; | F. BÉCHET, LIBRAIRE, 31, QUAI DES AUGUSTINS. | [short rule] | 1846.

Ninth edition, Paris, 1846. Originally published Paris, 1803 (item 291). There were two editions styled "huitième," one in 1838 and one in 1846.

206 x 125 mm. π^8 1-29^8; 240 leaves, pp. [i-v] vi-xvi [1] 2-464.

Bookplate: Ex Libris Georges Vicaire.

Bibliographies: Simon BG 979; Vicaire 545 (this copy).

Copies: No other copy of this edition located.

295. Maigne, W., 1819-1893.

MANUELS-RORET | [short rule] | NOUVEAU MANUEL COMPLET | DES | CONSERVES | ALIMENTAIRES | CONTENANT | LES PROCÉDÉS USITÉS POUR LA CONSERVATION | DES SUBSTANCES, | SOIT SOLIDES, SOIT LIQUIDES, QUI SERVENT A LA | NOURRITURE DE L'HOMME | AINSI QUE | L'HISTOIRE ET LA COMPOSITION DE CES SUBSTANCES | LES ALTÉRATIONS OU MODIFICATIONS NATURELLES | AUXQUELLES ELLES SONT EXPOSÉES, LES PROPRIÉTÉS | PARTICULIÈRES QU'ELLES POSSÈDENT, | LE RÔLE SPÉCIAL QU'ELLES JOUENT DANS L'ALIMENTATION | ET | LES FALSIFICATIONS | QUE LE COMMERCE DÉLOYAL LEUR FAIT SUBIR, AVEC LES MOYENS | DE DÉMASQUER LES

FRAUDEURS | Par M. W. MAIGNE, | Auteur de plusieurs ouvrages de Technologie, d'Hygiène | appliquée, etc. | PARIS | A LA LIBRAIRIE ENCYCLOPÉDIQUE DE RORET, | RUE HAUTEFEUILLE, 12. | 1865 | *Tous droits réservés.*

First edition, Paris, 1865.

152 x 96 mm. [a]^4 b1 1-35^6 36$_1$; 216 leaves, pp. [*4*] [i] ii-vi [1] 2-422. Publisher's printed wrappers. 72 page publisher's catalogue dated Mars 1884 bound in.

Bibliographies: Unrecorded in the bibliographies consulted.

Copies: *BMC*, *BNC*, and *NUC* (Library of Congress and Princeton).

296. Maillard, Léon.

LÉON MAILLARD | [short rule] | LES | [in red] Menus & Programmes | ILLUSTRÉS | INVITATIONS – BILLETS DE FAIRE PART – CARTES D'ADRESSE | PETITES ESTAMPES | *Du XVIIe siècle jusqu'à nos jours.* | [short rule] | OUVRAGE ORNÉ DE QUATRE CENT SOIXANTE REPRODUCTIONS | *D'après les documents originaux des meilleurs artistes* | [emblem lettered: SOCIAE LITTERIS ARTES] | PARIS | [in two columns: column one] LIBRAIRIE ARTISTIQUE | [in red] G. BOUDET, Éditeur | *197, Boulevard Saint-Germain* | [vertical rule] | [column two] VENTE EXCLUSIVE | [in red] Librairie CH. TALLANDIER | *Boulevard Saint-Germain, 197* [end columns] | [short rule] | 1898

First edition, Paris, 1898, limited to 1050 copies: 25 copies on papier des Manufactures Impériales du Japon, 25 on véritable papier de Chine; and 1000 on papier vélin. This copy is on papier de Chine.

315 x 221 mm. π^4 1-50^4 51^2; 206 leaves, pp. [i-vii] viii [1-3] 4-402 [*2*]. Half blue morocco by Ch. Septier, with original wrappers, designed by Mucha, in colored and uncolored states, preserved.

Illustrations: Nineteen lithographed plates, each present in colored and uncolored states, and 460 illustrations in the text. An original hand colored pencil sketch by François Kupka for a menu card bound in.

Bibliographies: Bitting, p. 305 (copy on Japon); Horn-Arndt 510 (copy on vélin); Oberlé (1) 873 (copy on Japon); Wheaton and Kelly 3902 (paper not specified).

Copies: *BMC*, *BNC*, and *NUC* (5 copies).

297. Le Maistre d'hostel.

LE MAISTRE │ D'HOSTEL │ QVI APPREND L'ORDRE │ DE BIEN SERVIR SVR
TABLE │ & d'y ranger les seruices. │ ENSEMBLE │ LE SOMMELIER │ QVI
ENSEIGNE LA MANIERE │ de bien plier le linge en plusieurs figures. │ *Et à faire*
toutes sortes de Confitures, tant seiches │ que liquides. │ Comme aussi toutes sortes de
Dragées, & autres │ gentillesses fort vtiles à tout le monde. │ *Auec vne Table*
Alphabetique des matieres qui │ sont traittées dans ce Liure. │ [ornament] │ A PARIS, │
Chez PIERRE DAVID, sur le Quay & proche │ la porte des Augustins du Grand
Conuent, │ au Roy Dauid. │ [short rule] │ M. DC. LIX. │ *Auec Priuilege du Roy.*
First edition, Paris, 1659.

8vo. a⁸ A-K⁸; 88 leaves, pp. [*16*] 1-145 [*146*] [*14*].

André Simon, in his *Bibliotheca Gastronomica*, assigns this work to Pierre de Lune on
the strength of the publisher's request in the dedicatory letter that de Lune give it his
protection. Vicaire enters it under title.

Bibliographies: Simon BG 472; Vicaire 553.

Copies: *BMC.*

298. Maistres boulangers de la ville et des faubourges de Paris.

[within a double rule border] STATUTS, │ *PRIVILÉGES,* │ ORDONNANCES │ ET │
REGLEMENS │ *DE LA COMMUNAUTÉ* │ DES │ MAISTRES BOULANGERS │ *de la*
ville, fauxbourgs & banlieue de Paris. │ [ornament] │ *A PARIS,* │ De l'imprimerie de
MOREAU, Libraire-Imprimeur │ de la *REINE* & de Monseigneur le *DAUPHIN.* │
[short fancy rule] │ *M. DCC. LXVI.*

First edition, Paris, 1766.

12mo. π² A-F¹² G¹⁰(-G10); 83 leaves, pp. [*4*] [1] 2-162. First leaf blank.

Note: Vicarie 800-803 records several collections of statutes and regulations governing
the master bakers of the city and suburbs of Paris published between 1721 and 1772.

Bibliographies: Vicarie 803.

Copies: No other copy located.

299. Mangin, Arthur, 1824-1887.

LE CACAO │ ET │ LE CHOCOLAT │ CONSIDÉRÉS AUX POINTS DE VUE │
BONTANIQUE, CHIMIQUE, PHYSOLOGIQUE, AGRICOLE, │ COMMERCIAL,
INDUSTRIEL ET ÉCONOMIQUE, │ PAR │ ARTHUR MANGIN │ Rédacteur de la
Revue scientifique du *Journal des Économistes*, │ un des principaux auteurs du
Dictionnaire universel du commerce et de la naviagtion, etc. │ SUIVI │ DE LA
LÉGENDE DU CACAHUATL │ PAR │ FERDINAND DENIS │ Conservateur de la
Bibliothèque Sainte-Geneviève. │ [short rule] │ Deuxième Édition. │ [short fancy rule] │
PARIS │ GUILLAUMIN ET Cie, LIBRAIRES │ Éditeurs du *Journal des Économistes*,
de la *Collection des principaux économistes*, │ du *Dictionnaire de l'Économie politique*,
│ du *Dictionnaire universel du commerce et de la navigation*, etc. │ RUE RICHELIEU,
14. │ [short rule] │ 1862

Second edition, Paris, 1862. Originally published, Paris, 1860.

185 x 119 mm. π^2 1-18$^{12.6}$ 19^4; 168 leaves, pp. [*4*] [1] 2-331 [332]. Publisher's printed
wrappers.

Illustrations: Hand colored lithographed frontispiece of a "Cacaoyer (Theobroma
Cocao)" and one hand colored lithograph of the fruit and flower of the cacaoyer.

Bibliographies: Bitting, p. 306; Vicaire 558; Wheaton and Kelly 3926.

Copies: *BNC* and *NUC* (Harvard and Library of Congress).

300. Manuel de gastronomie.

MANUEL │ DE │ GASTRONOMIE, │ CONTENANT particulièrement la manière de
dresser et de │ servir une table, et d'observer la symétrie des mets; la │ nomenclature
alphabétique de 54 potages, 27 relevés │ de potage, 40 hors-d'oeuvres, 600 plats
d'entrée, │ 100 plats de rôt, 350 plats d'entremets, et 100 ar- │ ticles de dessert, avec la
manière de les préparer et │ de les servir. │ OUVRAGE │ Mis à portée de toutes les
classes de la société, indispensable │ aux ménagères, et surtout aux personnes qui
habitent la cam- │ pagne, etc., etc. [ornament] │ PARIS, │ Chez F. G. LEVRAULT,
rue de la Harpe, n.° 81. │ Et rue des Juifs, n.° 33, à STRASBOURG. │ 1825.

First edition, Paris, 1825.

168 x 98 mm. π^2 1-28$^{8.4}$ 29^8(-29$_8$); 177 leaves, pp. [*4*] [1] 2-349 [350].

Illustrations: Lithographed folding plate showing nine table settings.

Bibliographies: Vicaire 561; Wheaton and Kelly 3950.

Copies: *NUC* (John Crerar Library only). Wheaton and Kelly (Radcliffe only).

301. Marin, François.

LES DONS | [in red] DE COMUS, | *OU* | LES DÉLICES | [in red] DE LA TABLE. | *OUVRAGE non-seulement utile aux* | *Officiers de Bouche pour ce qui concerne leur* | *art, mais principalement à l'usage des* | *personnes qui sont curieuses de sçavoir* | *donner à manger, & d'être servies délica-* | *tement, tant en gras qu'en maigre, snivant* | *les saisons, & dans le goût le plus nouveau.* | [ornament] | [in red] A PARIS, | Chez PRAULT, Fils, Quay de Conty, | vis-à-vis la descente du Pont Neuf, | à la Charité. | [three rules] | [in red] M. DCC. XXXIX. | *Avec Approbation & Privilege du Roi.*

First edition, Paris, 1739.

12mo. a-d$^{8.4}$ A-Y$^{8.4}$ Z^6; 162 leaves, pp. [i-ii] iii-xlviii [1] 2-275 [276].

Illustration: Etched frontispiece by Le Bas titled "Les attributs de la Bonne-Chere."

Bibliographies: Bitting, p. 307; Crahan 364; Oberlé (1) 108; Simon BG 1001; Vicaire 284.

Copies: *BNC* and *NUC* (Library of Congress only).

302. Marin, François.

SUITE | DES DONS | DE COMUS, | *OU* | L'ART DE LA CUISINE, | REDUIT EN PRATIQUE. | *TOME PREMIER. [TOME SECOND.] [TOME TROISIÈME.]* | [this line in first volume only] Le prix est de six livres quinze sols relié. | [ornament] | A PARIS, | Chez { | La veuve PISSOT, Quai de Conti, | à la Croix d'or, à la descente du | Pont-neuf. | DIDOT, Quai des Augustins, près | le Pont S. Michel, à la Bible d'or. | BRUNET fils, Grand'Salle du | Palais, à l'Envie. | [two short rules] | M. DCC. XLII. | *Avec Approbation & Privilege du Roi.*

First edition, Paris, 1742. Vicaire 285 describes this as an enlarged edition of *Les Dons de Comus*, Paris, 1739, (item 301) but that work, in one volume, presents lists of foods, naming the ways in which they may be prepared, recipes for a number of sauces, and menus for the different seasons of the year, while the *Suite des Dons de Comus*, Paris, 1742, in three volumes, is a collection of recipes for all manner of dishes. Even those recipes for sauces that appear in both works are completely rewritten. The matter is further confused by the fact that subsequent editions of the *Suite des Dons de Comus* take the title of the earlier work and were published as *Les Dons de Comus*. In spite of this title adoption, however, *Les Dons de Comus* of 1739 is quite a distinct work from the *Suite des Dons de Comus*, 1742, and its later editions.

12mo. 3 vols. Vol. I. π^2 a^8 e^4 i^8 o^4 u^4 A-Nn$^{8.4}$ Oo^8; 254 leaves, pp. [4] i-liii [liv-lvi] [1] 2-448. Vol. II. π^2 A-Tt$^{8.4}$ Vv^2 [Vv signed "V"]; 256 leaves, pp. [4] [1] 2-508. Vol. III. π^2 A-Fff$^{8.4}$ Ggg^4; 318 leaves, pp, [4] [1] 2-631 [632].

Illustration: Vol. I. Etched plate, after that by La Bas in *Les Dons de Comus*, Paris, 1739, facing p. 1.

Bookplate: Bibliotheca Lindesiana.

Bibliographies: Drexel 511; Malortie 200; Vicaire 285.

Copies: *BNC*.

303. Marin, François.

LES DONS | *DE COMUS,* | OU | *L'ART DE LA CUISINE,* | RÉDUIT EN PRATIQUE, | *NOUVELLE EDITION,* | Revue, corrigée & augmentée par l'Auteur. | *TOME PREMIER. [TOME SECOND.] [TOME TROISIÈME.]* | Le prix est de sept livres dix sols relié. | [ornament] | A PARIS, | Chez PISSOT, Libraire, Quai de Conti, à la | Croix d'Or, à la descente du Pont-Neuf, | au coin de la rue de Nevers. | [two short rules] | M. DCC LVIII. | *Avec Approbation & Privilége du Roi.*

New edition, Paris, 1758. Originally published, Paris, 1742 (item 302).

12mo. 3 vols. Vol. I. π1 a-b^{12} A-V^{12} X^4 *1; 270 leaves, pp. [2] i-xlviii [1] 2-490. Vol. II. π1 A-V^{12} X^4 *1; 246 leaves, pp. [2] [1] 2-490. Vol. III. π1 A-Y^{12} Z^4 $_\chi$1; 270 leaves, pp. [2] [1] 2-534 [4].

Illustration: Etched frontispiece, same as the plate in *Suite des Dons de Comus*, Paris, 1742 (item 302).

Bibliographies: Bitting, p. 309; Maggs 268; Oberlé (1) 109; Pennell, p. 126; Wheaton and Kelly 3958.

Copies: *BMC*, *BNC*, and *NUC* (Harvard, Library of Congress, and Vassar College).

304. Marin, François.

LES | DONS DE COMUS, | OU | *L'ART DE LA CUISINE,* | RÉDUIT EN PRATIQUE, | NOUVELLE ÉDITION, | Revue, corrigée & augmentée par l'Auteur. | *TOME PREMIER. [TOME SECOND.] [TOME TROISIÈME.]* | [ornament] | A PARIS, | Chez L. CELLOT, Impr.-Lib., rue & vis- | à-vis les Grands Augustins, la troisieme | porte-cochere à gauche par le Quai. | [two short rules] | M. DCC LXXV. | *Avec Approbation & Privilege du Roi.*

New edition, Paris, 1775. Originally published, Paris, 1742 (item 302).

12mo. 3 vols. Vol. I. a-b^{12} A-S^{12}; 240 leaves, pp. [i-ii] iii-xlviii [1] 2-430 [2]. Vol. II. π^2 A-R^{12} S^8; 214 leaves, pp. [4] [1] 2-424. Vol. III. π^2 A-T^{12} V^8; 238 leaves, pp. [4] [1] 2-472.

Bibliographies: Schraemli (3) 45.

Copies: *NUC* (Library of Congress, New York Academy of Medicine, and University of Wisconsin).

305. Marquis, F.

DU THÉ, | OU | NOUVEAU TRAITÉ | SUR SA CULTURE, | SA RÉCOLTE, SA PRÉPARATION ET SES USAGES; | PAR F. MARQUIS, JEUNE, | MARCHAND DE THÉS DE S. A. R. MONSIEUR, COMTE D'ARTOIS. | Orné de Gravures coloriées, faites d'après nature | et d'après des peintures originales de la Chine. | [short rule] | A PARIS, | Chez { | NEPVEU, Libraire, Passage des Panoramas, no 26. | AUDOT, Lib., rue des Mathurins S. Jacques, no 18. | F. MARQUIS, Passage des Panoramas, no 18. | MDCCCXX.

One of two editions published in Paris in 1820, one in small format containing 124 pages, as in this copy, and one in larger format containing 68 pages. Priority undetermined. A "second edition" was published, Paris, 1834.

146 x 93 mm. 1-10⁶ 11²; 62 leaves, pp. [1-5] 6-124. Publisher's printed wrappers.

Illustrations: Ten hand colored engraved plates, four single page and unnumbered, and six folding double page numbered 3-8.

Bibliographies: Vicaire 567.

Copies: *BNC* and *NUC* (Harvard, John Crerar Library, and Yale).

306. Martin, Alexandre, b. 1795.

BRÉVIAIRE │ DU GASTRONOME, │ OU │ L'ART D'ORDONNER LE DÎNER DE CHAQUE JOUR, │ SUIVANT LES DIVERSES SAISONS DE L'ANNÉE. │ POUR LA PETITE ET LA GRANDE PROPRIÉTÉ. │ PRÉCÉDÉ │ D'UNE HISTOIRE DE LA CUISINE FRANÇAISE, │ ANCIENNE ET MODERNE. │ PAR │ L'AUTEUR DU *MANUEL DE L'AMATEUR* │ *D'HUITRES.* │ PARIS. │ AUDOT, LIBRAIRE-ÉDITEUR, │ RUE DES MAÇONS-SORBONNE, No. 11. │ [short fancy rule] │ 1828.

First edition, Paris, 1828.

135 x 86 mm. π² 1-9⁶ 10²; 58 leaves, pp. [4] [1] 2-110 [111-112]. Publisher's printed wrappers.

Illustrations: Folding hand colored lithographed frontispiece by Henry Monnier and an engraved folding "Carte Gastronomique de la France" by Tourcaty.

Bibliographies: Drexel 539; Vicaire 569.

Copies: *BNC* and *NUC* (John Crerar Library only).

307. Martin, Alexandre, b. 1795.

BRÉVIAIRE │ DU GASTRONOME, │ OU │ L'ART D'ORDONNER LE DÎNER DE CHAQUE JOUR, │ SUIVANT LES DIVERSES SAISONS DE L'ANNÉE. │ POUR LA PETITE ET LA GRANDE PROPRIETE. │ PRÉCÉDÉ │ D'UNE HISTOIRE DE LA CUISINE FRANÇAISE, │ ANCIENNE ET MODERNE. │ PAR ALEXANDRE

MARTIN. | DEUXIÈME ÉDITION, | Augmentée de plusieurs menus nouveaux. | PARIS. | AUDOT, LIBRAIRE-ÉDITEUR, | RUE DES MAÇONS-SORBONNE, No. 11. | [short fancy rule] | 1828.

Second edition, Paris, 1828. Originally published, Paris, also 1828 (item 306).

148 x 90 mm. π^2 1-10^6 11^4; 66 leaves, pp. [4] [1] 2-124 [4]. Last leaf, blank, pasted to back wrapper. Publisher's printed wrappers.

Illustrations: Folding hand colored lithographed frontispiece by Henry Monnier.

Bibliographies: Bitting, p. 312; Drexel 540; Maggs 424; Oberlé (1) 201; Vicaire 569.

Copies: *BNC* and *NUC* (Library of Congress only).

308. Martin, Alexandre, b. 1795.

LE CUISINIER | DES | GOURMANDS, | OU | LA CUISINE MODERNE | ENSEIGNEE D'APRÈS LES PLUS GRANDS MAITRES; | SUIVI | DE L'ART DE DÉCOUPER LES VIANDES, | ET DE LES SERVIR A TABLE; | PAR A. MARTIN, | AUTEUR DU BRÉVIAIRE DU GASTRONOME. | [short fancy rule] | PARIS, | CHARLES FROMENT, LIBRAIRE, | QUAI DES AUGUSTINS, No 37. | 1829.

First edition, Paris, 1829.

144 x 93 mm. π^2 1-26^6 27^4; 162 leaves, pp. [4] [1] 2-320. Publisher's wrappers with printed label on spine.

Illustration: Engraved frontispiece by Pfitzer after Adam.

Bibliographies: Maggs 431; Vicaire 570.

Copies: *BNC.*

309. Martin, Alexandre, b. 1795.

MANUEL | DE | L'AMATEUR DE CAFÉ, | OU | L'ART DE PRENDRE TOUJOURS DE BON CAFÉ. | OUVRAGE | Contenant plusieurs procédés nouveaux, faciles et écono- | miques, pour préparer le café et en rendre la boisson | plus saine et plus agréable. | DÉDIÉ | AUX GOURMETS, AUX BONNES MÉNAGÈRES, ETC., ETC. | PAR M. H...., | *Doyen des habitués du café de Foi.* | PARIS. | AUDOT, ÉDITEUR DE L'ENCYCLOPÉDIE POPULAIRE, | RUE DES MAÇONS-SORBONNE, No. 11. | [short fancy rule] | 1828.

First edition, Paris, 1828.

142 x 90 mm. π^4 1^4 $2\text{-}7^6$ $\pi7^2$; 46 leaves, pp. [i-v] vi-vii [viii] [1] 2-84. Publisher's printed wrappers. Publishers twelve page catalogue bound in.

Illustrations: Folding hand colored lithographed frontispiece by Henry Monnier and one folding hand colored engraved plate titled "Coffea Arabica" by Maria Gabriel Coignet after P. Bessa.

Bibliographies: Vicaire 569.

Copies: *BNC* and *NUC* (John Crerar Library and Library of Congress).

310. Martin, Alexandre, b. 1795.

MANUEL | DE | L'AMATEUR DE MELONS, | OU | L'ART DE RECONNAITRE ET D'ACHETER | DE BONS MELONS; | PRÉCÉDÉ | D'UNE HISTOIRE DE CE FRUIT, | avec | UN TRAITÉ SUR SA CULTURE ET UNE NOMENCLATURE | DE SES DIVERSES ESPÈCES ET VARIÉTÉS, | Par Alexandre Martin. | orné de 4 planches coloriées. | [short fancy rule] | PARIS, | AUGTE UDRON, LIBRAIRE-ÉDITEUR, | RUE DU BATTOIR, No 20. | 1827.

First edition, Paris, 1827.

149 x 95 mm. π^2 $1\text{-}13^6$ $"16"^2$; 82 leaves, pp. [4] [i] ii-iv [1] 2-156. Publisher's printed wrappers.

Illustrations: Colored lithographed frontispiece and three colored lithographed plates, all of melons.

Bibliographies: Maggs 414; Vicaire 567; Wheaton and Kelly 3991.

Copies: *BNC*. Wheaton and Kelly (Harvard only).

311. Martin, Alexandre, b. 1795.

MANUEL | DE | L'AMATEUR DE TRUFFES, | OU | L'ART D'OBTENIR DES TRUFFES, | Au moyen de plants artificiels, dans les parcs, bosquets, | jardins, etc., etc.; | PRÉCÉDÉ | D'UNE HISTOIRE DE TRUFFE | et d'anecdotes gourmandes, | ET SUIVI | D'UN TRAITÉ SUR LA CULTURE DES CHAMPIGNONS. | PUBLIÉ PAR A. MARTIN, | Auteur du Manuel de l'Amateur de melons. | SECONDE ÉDITION. | A PARIS, | CHEZ LEROI, LIBRAIRE-ÉDITEUR, | RUE DU COQ, N. 4; | Et portail du Louvre, vis-à-vis la rue du Coq. | CHEZ AUDIN, LIBRAIRE, | QUAI DES AUGUSTINS, N. 25. | [short rule] | 1829.

Second edition, Paris, 1829. Originally published, Paris, 1828.

138 x 86 mm. π^2 $2\pi^6$ 1-12^6; 80 leaves, pp. [4] [i] ii-xii [1] 2-143 [144]. Recent boards, publisher's printed wrappers preserved.

Illustration: Folding hand colored lithographed frontispiece by Henry Monnier.

Bibliographies: Bitting, p. 312; Crahan 649; Vicaire 570.

Copies: *BNC* and *NUC* (Longwood Gardens, Kennett Square, Pa., only).

312. Martin, Alexandre, b. 1795.

MANUEL | DE | L'AMATEUR D'HUITRES. | CONTENANT | L'HISTOIRE NATURELLE DE L'HUITRE, | UNE NOTICE SUR LA PÈCHE, LA PARCAGE ET LE COMMERCE | DE CE MOLLUSQUE EN FRANCE, | Et des Dissertations hygiéniques et gourmandes sur l'Huître | considérée comme aliment et comme médicament. | PAR | ALEXANDRE MARTIN. | PARIS. | AUDOT, LIBRAIRE-ÉDITEUR, | RUE DES MAÇONS-SORBONNE, No 11. | [two short rules] | 1828.

First edition, Paris, 1828.

145 x 86 mm. π^4 1-7^6; 46 leaves, pp. [i-v] vi-viii [1] 2-84. Nineteenth century binder's cloth, with original publisher's printed wrappers preserved. Twelve page publisher's catalogue bound in.

Illustrations: Folding hand colored lithographed frontispiece by Henry Monnier and a folding engraved plate of an oyster knife, fork and pick.

Bibliographies: Crahan 648; Maggs 426; Vicaire 569; Wheaton and Kelly 3990.

Copies: *BNC* and *NUC* (5 copies).

313. Martin, Alexandre, b. 1795.

TRAITÉ | MEDICO-GASTRONOMIQUE | SUR LES INDIGESTIONS. | SUIVI | D'UN ESSAI SUR LES REMÈDES . . . . | A ADMINISTRER EN PAREIL CAS. | DÉDIÉ | AUX GOURMANDS DE TOUS LES PAYS. | OUVRAGE POSTHUME | DE FEU DARDANUS, |Ancien Apothicaire. | PARIS. | AUDOT, ÉDITEUR DE L'ENCYCLOPÉDIE POPULAIRE, | RUE DES MAÇONS-SORBONNE, No. 11. | [short fancy rule] | 1828.

First edition, Paris, 1828.

148 x 90 mm. π^2 1-7^6 8^6(-8$_6$); 49 leaves, pp. [*4*] [1] 2-94. Modern cloth, publisher's printed wrappers preserved.

Illustration: Hand colored lithographed frontispiece by Henry Monnier.

Bookplate: Ex-libris Robert Viel.

Bibliographies: Maggs 425 (this copy); Oberlé (1) 464; Vicaire 249.

Copies: *BNC* and *NUC* (John Crerar Library and Yale).

314. Martin, Barthélemy, 1629-1698.

TRAITE' | DU LAIT, | DU CHOIX QU'ON EN | doit faire, & de la maniere | d'en user. | *Par* BARTH. MARTIN, *Apoticaire* | *du Corps de S. A. S. Monseigneur* | *le Prince.* | *Seconde Edition, corrigée & augmentée de la* | *Pratique d'Hippocrate dans la cure des* | *maladies par l'usage de ce Médicament.* | [woodcut] | A PARIS, | Chez LAURENT D'HOURY, rue saint | Severin, au Saint-Esprit, vis à vis | la rue Zacharie. | [short rule] | M. DCC VI. | *Avec Approbations & Privilege du Roy*

Third edition, styled second, Paris, 1706. Originally published under the title *Traité de l'usage du lait*, Paris, 1684, and reprinted under the same title, Paris, 1699.

12mo. a^8 A-S$^{8.4}$ T^4; 120 leaves, pp. [*16*] 1-215 [*216*] [*8*].

Bibliographies: Vicaire 571.

Copies: *BMC*, *BNC*, and *NUC* (Kansas State University, National Library of Medicine, and Yale Medical School Library).

315. Martin, Louis.

L'ESCHOLE │ DE │ SALERNE │ En vers Burlesques. │ ET │ POEMA │ MACARONICVM, │ DE BELLO │ HVGVENOTICO. │ [ornament] │ A PARIS, │ Chez IEAN HENAVLT, au Palais, dans la Salle │ Dauphine, à l'Ange-Gardien. │ [short rule] │ M. DC. L. │ *AVEC PRIVILEGE DV ROY.*

Third edition, Paris, 1650. Originally published, Paris, 1647.

4to. [a]^2 e^2 i^2 o^2 u^2 †1 A-T^2; 49 leaves, pp. [22] 1-74 [2].

Illustration: Engraved title-page on a1^v.

Bibliographies: Horn-Arndt 164; Maggs 140; Oberlé (1) 325; Vicaire 334.

Copies: *BMC*, *BNC*, and *NUC* (National Library of Medicine and University of Chicago).

316. Massialot, François, ca. 1660-1733.

LE │ CUISINIER │ ROIAL │ ET BOURGEOIS, │ Qui apprend à ordonner toute │ sorte de Repas, & la meilleure │ maniere des Ragoûts les plus à │ la mode & les plus exquis. │ *Ouvrage tres-utile dans les Familles, & sin-* │ *gulierement necessaire à tous Maîtres* │ *d'Hôtels, & Ecuïers de Cuisine.* │ [publisher's device] │ A PARIS, │ Chez CHARLES DE SERCY, au Palais, │ au sixiéme Pilier de la Grand'Salle, vis-à- │ vis la Montée de la Cour des Aides, │ à la Bonne-Foi couronnée. │ [short rule] │ M. DC. XCI. │ *AVEC PRIVILEGE DV ROI.*

First edition, Paris, 1691.

12mo. a^8 e^2 A-Zz$^{8.4}$; 286 leaves, pp. [20] 1-505 [506-552].

Bibliographies: Malortie 83; Schraemli (2) 32; Vicaire 573.

Copies: *BNC.*

317. Massialot, François, ca. 1660-1733.

LE | CUISINIER | ROYAL | ET | BOURGEOIS, | Qui apprend à ordonner toute | sorte de Repas, & la meilleure | maniere des Ragoûts les plus à | la mode & les plus exquis. | *Ouvrage tres-utile dans les Familles, & sin-* | *gulierement necessaire à tous* | *Maîtres* | *d'Hôtels, & Ecuïers de Cuisine.* | Seconde Edition, revûë & augmentée. | [publisher's device] | A PARIS, | Chez CHARLES DE SERCY, au Palais, au sixiéme | Pilier de la Grand'Salle, vis-à-vis la Montée de | la Cour des Aydes, à la Bonne-Foy couronnée. | [rule] | M. DC. XCIII. | *AVEC PRIVILEGE DV ROI.*

Second edition, Paris, 1693. Originally published, Paris, 1691 (item 316).

12mo. a^8 e^2 A-Zz$^{8.4}$; 286 leaves, pp. [*20*] 1-505 [*506-552*].

Bibliographies: Crahan 174; Schraemli (1) 325; Vicaire 574.

Copies: *NUC* (National Agricultural Library only).

318. Massialot, François, ca. 1660-1733.

LE | CUISINIER | ROÏAL | ET | BOURGEOIS; | QUI APPREND A ORDONNER TOUTE | sorte de Repas en gras & en maigre, & | la meilleure maniere des Ragoûts les plus | delicats & les plus à la mode. | *Ouvrage tres-utile dans les Familles, &* | *singulierement necessaire à tous Maîtres* | *d'Hôtels, & Ecuïers de Cuisine.* | Nouvelle Edition, revûë, corrigée & beaucoup | augmentée, avec des Figures. | [publisher's device] | A PARIS, | Chez CLAUDE PRUDHOMME, au Palais, au sixiéme | Pilier de la Grand'Sale, vis-à-vis la Montée de la | Cour des Aides, à la Bonne-Foi couronnée. | [short rule] | M. DCC V. | *AVEC PRIVILEGE DU ROY.*

Fifth edition, Paris, 1705. Originally published, Paris, 1691 (item 316).

12mo. a^8 A-Xx$^{8.4}$ Yy^8 Zz^2; 282 leaves, pp. [*16*] 1-500 [*48*].

Illustrations: Eight folding woodcuts showing table settings.

Bibliographies: Vicaire 574.

Copies: *BNC.*

319. Massialot, François, ca. 1660-1733.

LE NOUVEAU │ CUISINIER │ ROYAL │ ET │ BOURGEOIS; │ QUI APPREND A ORDONNER TOUTE │ sorte de Repas en gras & en maigre, │ & la meilleure maniere des Ragoûts les │ plus délicats & les plus à la mode; & tou- │ tes sortes de Pâtisseries: avec des nou- │ veaux desseins de Tables. │ *Ouvrage très-utile dans les Familles, aux* │ *Maîtres d'Hôtels, & Officiers de Cuisine.* │ TOME PREMIER. [TOME SECOND.] [TOME TROISIÉME, │ *Servant de Supplément aux deux premiers Tomes.*] │ [publisher's device] │ A PARIS, │ Chez CLAUDE PRUDHOMME, au Palais, au sixiéme │ Pilier de la Grand'Salle, vis-à-vis la L'Escalier de la │ Cour des Aides, à la Bonne Foy couronnée. │ [short rule] │ M. DCCXXXIII. [DCCXXXIII.] [MDCCXXXIV.] │ *AVEC PRIVILEGE DU ROY.*

New edition, Paris, 1733-1734. Originally published, Paris, 1691 (item 316) and enlarged to two volumes, Paris, 1712. This edition of 1733-1734 is the first to add the supplementary third volume.

12mo. 3 Vols. Vol. I. a^2 e^4 A-Tt$^{8.4}$ Vu^8 Xx^2; 268 leaves, pp. [*12*] [1] 2-500 [*24*]. Vol. II. π^2 A-Xx$^{8.4}$; 266 leaves, pp. [*4*] 1-496 [*32*]. First leaf blank. Vol. III. π^2 A-Ii$^{8.4}$ Kk^4; 198 leaves, pp. [*4*] [1] 2-374 [*18*].

Illustrations: Vol. I. nine woodcuts, five of them folding, showing table settings; Vol. III. thirteen woodcuts, twelve of them folding, showing a centerpiece for the table and twelve table settings.

Bibliographies: This edition unrecorded in the bibliographies consulted. Vicaire 574-575 cites other editions.

Copies: No other copy of this edition located.

320. Massialot, François, ca. 1660-1733.

NOUVELLE │ INSTRUCTION │ POUR │ LES CONFITURES, │ LES LIQUEURS, │ ET LES FRUITS. │ AVEC LA MANIERE DE BIEN │ ordonner un Dessert, & tout le reste qui │ est du Devoir des Maîtres d'Hôtels, Som- │ meiliers Confiseurs, & autres Officiers de │ bouche. │ *Suite du Cuisinier Roïal & Bourgeois.* │ Egalement utile dans les familles, pour sçavoir │ ce qu'on sert de plus à la mode dans les │ Repas, & en d'autres occasions. │ [ornament] │ A PARIS, │ Chez CHARLES DE SERCY, au

Palais, au sixiéme | Pilier de la Grand'Salle, vis-à-vis la Montée de la | Cour des Aides, à la Bonne-Foi couronnée. | [rule] | M. DC. XCII. | *AVEC PRIVILEGE DU ROY.*

First edition, Paris, 1692.

12mo. a^8 e^4 A-Pp$^{8.4}$; 240 leaves, pp. [*24*] 1-442 [*443-456*].

Bibliographies: Horn-Arndt 169; Oberlé (1) 94; Schraemli (1) 326; Vicaire 453-454.

Copies: *BNC* and *NUC* (Cornell, John Crerar Library, and Kansas State University).

321. Massialot, François, ca. 1660-1733.

NOUVELLE | INSTRUCTION | POUR | LES CONFITURES, | LES LIQUEURS | ET LES FRUITS, | AVEC LA MANIERE DE BIEN ORDONNER | un Dessert, & tout le reste qui est du Devoir | des Maîtres d'Hôtels, Sommeliers, Confi- | seurs, & autres Officiers de bouche. | *Suite du Cuisinier Roïal & Bourgeois.* | Egalement utile dans les Familles, pour sçavoir ce | qu'on sert de plus a la mode dans les Repas, | & en d'autres occasions. | *Seconde Edition, revûë, corrigée, & beaucoup augmentée.* | [publisher's device] | A PARIS, | Chez CHARLES DE SERCY, au Palais, au sixiéme | Pilier de la Grand'Sale, vis-à-vis la Montée de la | Cour des Aides, à la Bonne-Foi couronnée. | [short rule] | M. DC. XCVIII. | *AVEC PRIVILEGE DU ROY.*

Second edition, Paris, 1698. Originally published, Paris, 1692, (item 320).

12mo. a^8 e^4 A-Rr$^{8.4}$; 252 leaves, pp. [*24*] 1-458 [*20*].

Illustrations: Folding woodcut of table of desserts and, on pp. 450 and 453, woodcuts of a "Modele de Dessert pour une Table de douze Couverts" and a "Modele de Dessert pour une table ronde."

Bibliographies: Horn-Arndt 170.

Copies: *BMC* and *NUC* (4 copies).

322. Massialot, François, ca. 1660-1733.

NOUVELLE | INSTRUCTION | POUR | LES CONFITURES, | LES LIQUEURS, | ET LES FRUITS: | Où l'on apprend à confire toutes sortes de Fruits, | tant secs que liquides; & divers Ouvrages | de Sucre qui sont du fait des Officiers & | Confiseurs; avec la maniere de bien ordon- | ner un Fruit. | *Suite du Nouveau Cuisinier Royal &* | *Bourgeois,* | *également utile aux Maitres-d'Hôtels & dans* | *les Familles, pour sçavoir* | *ce qu'on sert de plus* | *à la mode dans les Repas.* | NOUVELLE EDITION, | Revûë, | corrigée, & beaucoup augmentée, | *Avec de nouveaux Desseins de Tables.* | [ornament] | A PARIS AU PALAIS, | Chez CLAUDE PRUDHOMME, dans la Grand'Salle, | vis-à-vis l'Escalier de la Cour des Aides, | à la Bonne-Foy couronnée. | [short rule] | M. DCC XXVI. | *AVEC PRIVILEGE DU ROY.*

New edition, Paris, 1726. Originally published, Paris, 1692, (item 320).

12mo. a^6 A-Xx$^{8.4}$ Yy^4; 274 leaves, pp. [*12*] 1-508 [509-536].

Illustrations: Three folding engravings of desserts on a table.

Bibliographies: This edition unrecorded in the bibliographies consulted.

Copies: No other copy of this edition located.

323. Massialot, François, ca. 1660-1733.

NOUVELLE | INSTRUCTION | POUR | LES CONFITURES, | LES LIQUEURS, | ET LES FRUITS: | Où l'on apprend à confire toutes sortes de | Fruits, tant secs que liquides; & divers | Ouvrages de Sucre qui sont du fait des Offi- | ciers & Confiseurs; avec la maniere de bien | ordonner un Fruit. | *Suite du Nouveau Cuisinier Royal &* | *Bourgeois,* | *également utile aux Maîtres-d'Hôtels & dans* | *les Familles, pour sçavoir* | *ce qu'on sert de plus* | *à la mode dans les Repas.* | NOUVELLE EDITION, | Revûë, | corrigée, & beaucoup augmentée, | *Avec de nouveaux Desseins de Tables.* | [ornament] | A PARIS AU PALAIS, | Chez CLAUDE PRUDHOMME, dans la Grand'Salle, | vis-à-vis l'Escalier de la Cour des Aides, | à la Bonne-Foy couronnée. | [rule] | M. DCC XXXII. | *AVEC PRIVILEGE DU ROY.*

New edition, Paris, 1732. Originally published, Paris, 1692, (item 320).

12mo. a^6 A-Zz$^{8.4}$; 282 leaves, pp. [*12*] [1] 2-547 [548-554].

Illustrations: Three folding engravings of desserts on a table.

Bibliographies: This edition unrecorded in the bibliographies consulted.

Copies: No other copy of this edition located.

324. Massialot, François, ca. 1660-1733.

LE CONFITURIER │ ROYAL, │ *OU NOUVELLE* │ INSTRUCTION │ *POUR* │ LES CONFITURES, │ *LES LIQUEURS ET LES FRUITS;* │ Où l'on apprend à confire toutes sortes de │ Fruits, tant secs que liquides; la façon de │ faire différens Ratafias, & divers Ouvrages │ de Sucre qui sont du fait des Officiers & │ Confiseurs; avec la maniere de bien ordon- │ ner un Fruit & des Dessins de Table. │ *Cinquieme édition, revue &* │ *corrigée.* │ Prix, trois liv. relié. │ [ornament] │ A PARIS, │ [two short rules] │ M.DCC.LXXVI. │ *Avec Approbation & Privilége du Roi.*

New edition, styled "fifth," Paris, 1776. Originally published under the title *Nouvelle instructions pour les confitures . . .*, Paris, 1692 (item 320).

12mo. a^8(-a1) A-Z^{12} Aa1(=a1) χ^2; 286 leaves, pp. [iii-vii] viii-xvi [1] 2-554 [555-558].

Illustrations: Four folding engravings, three of desserts on a table as in the editions of 1726 and 1732, above, and a fourth of a "Surtout de table des plus leste pour les Desserts."

Bibliographies: Maggs 220; Vicaire 455.

Copies: *BMC*.

325. Masson, Pierre.

LE │ PARFAIT │ LIMONADIER │ OU │ LA MANIERE DE PREPARER │ le Thé, le Caffé, le Chocolat, & │ autres Liqueurs chaudes & froides. │ *Par P. MASSON* *Limonadier* │ [ornament] │ A PARIS, │ Ch*ez* CHARLES MOETTE ruë de la Bouclerie, │ entre le Pont S. Michel, & le bas de la │ ruë de la Harpe, à l'Etoille. │ [short rule] │ M. DCCV.

First edition, Paris, 1705.

12mo. A-H$^{8.4}$ I^8, ^{2}A^4 B^8 C^4 D^4 χ^2 (I8 signed "A"); 78 leaves, pp. [1-2] 3-96, 95-108, ^{2}1-42 [*4*].

Bibliographies: Bitting, p. 315; Vicaire 576; Wheaton and Kelly 4077.

Copies: *BNC* and *NUC* (5 copies).

326. Maupin.

[head title] [two rules] | LEÇON | *Sur la Grappe, ou Rafle des Raisins.*

First edition, Paris, ca. 1780.

8vo. A^8; 8 leaves, pp. [1] 2-15 [16]. Bound with items 327, 328, and 329.
Bibliographies: Unrecorded in the bibliographies consulted.

Copies: *BNC* (5 copies).

327. Maupin.

MOYEN | *CERTAIN ET FONDÉ* | SUR L'EXPÉRIENCE GÉNÉRALE, | *Pour assurer & prolonger, pour ainsi dire,* | *à volonté la durée des Vins, & en prévenir* | *la dépravation & toutes les maladies;* | Avec un PROCÉDÉ pour la Manipulation | & l'Amélioration de tous les Vins: | *Le tout joint à l'Art de la Vigne; contenant une* | *nouvelle méthode économique de cultiver la* | *Vigne, les expériences qui en ont été* | *faites,* | *& l'Approbation de l'Académie Royale des* | *Sciences.* | A l'usage de tous les Pays de Vignoble & même | des Marchands de Vin & des Consommateurs. | *Par M. MAUPIN, Auteur de l'Art des Vins* | *& de la seule Richesse du Peuple.* | [short rule] | Prix 3 liv. 12 s. avec le reçu signé de l'Auteur. | [short rule] | [ornament] | A PARIS, | Chez { | MUSIER, | GOBREAU, } | Libraires, Quai des | Augustins. | [two short rules] | M. DCC. LXXXI. | *Avec Approbation, & Permission.*

First edition, Paris, 1781.

8vo. A^8 B^4; 12 leaves, pp. [1-3] 4-24. Bound with items 326, 328, and 329.

Bibliographies: Unrecorded in the bibliographies consulted.

Copies: *BNC* (5 copies) and *NUC* (New York Public Library only).

328. Maupin.

[head title] [two rules] PROBLÊME | *Sur le temps juste du Décuvage des Vins;* | *avec*
l'indication la plus générale pour | *ce Décuvage.*

First edition, Paris, 1780.

8vo. A^4(-A4); 3 leaves, pp. [1] 2-6. Bound with items 326, 327, and 329.

Bibliographies: Unrecorded in the bibliographies consulted.

Copies: *BNC* (5 copies).

329. Maupin.

[head title] [vignette] | PROCÉDÉ | *POUR la Manipulation & la* | *Fermentation des*
Vins.

First edition, Paris, ca. 1780.

8vo. A-B^8; 16 leaves, pp. [1] 2-32. Bound with items 326, 327, and 328.

Bibliographies: Unrecorded in the bibliographies consulted.

Copies: *BNC* (3 copies).

330. Mazois, François, 1783-1826.

LE PALAIS | DE SCAURUS, | OU | DESCRIPTION | D'UNE MAISON
ROMAINE, | FRAGMENT D'UN VOYAGE FAIT A ROME, | VERS LA FIN DE
LA RÉPUBLIQUE, | PAR MÉROVIR, PRINCE DES SUÈVES. | [short fancy rule] |
SECONDE ÉDITION. | [publisher's monogram] | A PARIS, | DE L'IMPRIMERIE
DE FIRMIN DIDOT, | IMPRIMEUR DU ROI, RUE JACOB, No 24. | [short fancy
rule] | 1822.

Second edition, Paris, 1822. Originally published, Paris, 1819.

8vo. [1]^8 2-19^8 20^2; 154 leaves, pp. [1-7] 8-308. First leaf (half-title) wanting in this
copy.

Illustrations: Twelve lithographed plates, one folding, illustrating plans, views and details from the Palace of Scaurus in Rome.

Bibliographies: Vicaire 649.

Copies: *BNC* and *NUC* (8 copies).

331. Mémoire pour faire un festin.

MEMOIRE │ POVR FAIRE │ VN FESTIN. │ ENSEMBLE LA VIE DE │ puissante & tres-haute dame │ Madame Gueline. │ *Reueue & augmentee de nouueau par* │ *Monsieur Frippe saulce.* │ [publisher's device] │ A ROVEN, │ Chez IEAN PETIT, tenant sa boutique │ pres l'Orenger deuant S. Eloy. │ [short rule] │ M.DCVII.

First edition, Rouen, 1607.

8vo. A^4; 4 leaves, pp. [2] 1-6.

Bibliographies: Unrecorded in the bibliographies consulted.

Copies: No other copy located.

332. Mémoire sur les aliments.

[Head title] *Egalité,* [Phrygian cap] *Liberté.* │ An 2e de l'Ere Républicaine. │ [short fancy rule] │ MEMOIRE │ SUR LES ALIMENTS.

First edition, Paris(?) 1791.

8vo. [1]^6; 6 leaves, pp. [1] 2-12. Bound with Villars's *Catalogue des substances végétales,* Grenoble [1791] (item 439).

Bibliographies: Unrecorded in the bibliographies consulted.

Copies: No other copy located.

333. Le Ménagier de Paris.

LE | [in red] MÉNAGIER DE PARIS, | TRAITÉ | DE MORALE ET D'ÉCONOMIE DOMESTIQUE | COMPOSÉ VERS 1393, | [in red] PAR UN BOURGEOIS PARISIEN; | CONTENANT | Des préceptes moraux, quelques faits historiques, des instructions | sur l'art de diriger une maison, [in red] des renseignemens sur la consommation | [in red] du Roi, des Princes et de la ville de Paris, à la fin du quatorzième siècle, [in black] des conseils | sur le jardinage et sur le choix des chevaux; [in red] un traité de cuisine [in black] fort étendu, | et un autre non moins complet sur [in red] la chasse à l'épervier. | ENSEMBLE: | L'histoire de [in red] Grisélidis, Mellibée et Prudence [in black] par Albertan de Brescia (1246), | traduit par frère Renault de Louens; et [in red] le chemin de Povreté et de Richesse | poëme composé, en 1342, par Jean Bruyant, notaire au Châtelet de Paris; | PUBLIÉ POUR LA PREMIÈRE FOIS | [in red] PAR LA SOCIÉTÉ DES BIBLIOPHILES FRANÇOIS. | TOME PREMIER. [TOME SECOND] | [vignette] | [in red] A PARIS, | DE L'IMPRIMERIE DE CRAPELET, | RUE DE VAUGIRARD, 9. | [short rule] | [in red] M. D. CCC. XLVI.

First edition, Paris, 1846.

230 x 152 mm. 2 vols. Vol. I. π^4 χ1 $*^2$ $^\pi$a^4 a^4-e^4 $^\pi$e^4 f^4 $^\pi$A^4 A^4-P^4 $^\pi$P^4; 171 leaves, pp. [6] [i] ii-iii [iv] [4], ^{2}[i-iii] iv-lxxxviii [1] 2-240. Vol. II. π^2 $^\pi$A^4 A^4-C^4 $^\pi$C^4 D^4 $^\pi$D^4($\pm$$^\pi$D2.3) $^\pi$E^4 E^4-AA^4 $^\pi$AA^4; 194 leaves, pp. [4] [1] 2- 277 [278] [2] [279] 280-382. Signatures signed in eights on leaves 1-5 but gathered in fours. In this copy both cancelan and cancellandum of $^\pi$D2.3 are present.

Illustration: Etched illustration titled "Chasse à l'épervier en 1379" on S3^v.

Bibliographies: Bitting, p. 578; Oberlé (1) 50; Schraemli (1) 339; Vicaire 583; Wheaton and Kelly 4114.

Copies: *NUC* (10 copies).

334. Ménestrier, Casimir.

[Engraved title-page] Chansons | de | *Casimir-Ménestrier,* | *Convive des Soupers de Momus.* | [rule] | *Dans le plaisir et dans la peine,* | *Dans tous les tems, sur tous les tons,* | *Chantons, morguène,* | *Chantons! P. 88.* | [rule] | [vignette of browser at bookstall] | Le Flaneur. | PARIS, | *Chez SCHERFF, Libraire Editeur Place du Louvre, No. 12* | 1818.

First edition, Paris, 1818.

131 x 78 mm. π1 1⁶ [2-3]⁶ 4⁶ [5-6]⁶ 7-25⁶ χ1 (signature 11 signed "12"); 152 leaves, pp. [2] [1] 2-301 [302].

Illustrations: Engraved frontispiece titled "La Vendance" and engraved title-page.

Bibliographies: Unrecorded in bibliographies consulted.

Copies: *BNC.*

335. Menon.

CUISINE │ *ET* │ OFFICE │ *DE SANTÉ,* │ Propre à ceux qui vivent avec │ oeconomie & régime. │ [short rule] │ *Volume im-12. 50 sols relié.* │ [short rule] │ [ornament] │ A PARIS, │ Chez { LE CLERC, Quai des Augustins, à │ la Toison d'Or. │ PRAULT pere, Quai de Gêvres, au │ Paradis. │ BABUTY pere, rue S. Jacques, à │ S. Jean Chrisostome. │ [two short rules] │ M. D. CC. LVIII. │ *Avec Approbation & Privilége du Roi.*

First edition, Paris, 1758.

12mo. π⁸ A-Pp⁸·⁴ a⁴; 240 leaves, pp. [1-4] 5-12 [13-16], ²[1] 2-288, 249-416, i-viii (=480).

Bibliographies: Blake, p. 301; Oberlé (1) 119; Schraemli (1) 344; Simon BG 1037; Vicaire 591.

Copies: *BMC.*

336. Menon.

LA NOUVELLE │ CUISINIERE │ BOURGEOISE, │ SUIVIE DE L'OFFICE, │ *A L'USASE,* │ De tous ceux qui se mêlent des │ dépenses de Maison. │ [ornament] │ A PARIS, │ Chez GUILLYN, Quay des Augustins, │ entre les ruës Pavée & Gît-le-Coeur, │ au Lys d'or. │ [short rule] │ M. DCC. XLVI. │ *Avec Approbation & Privilege du Roy.*

First edition? Paris, 1746. All the standard bibliographies (Bitting, p. 320; Horn-Arndt 294; Vicaire 235) record the first edition of Menon's *La Cuisinière bourgeoise* as published in Paris by Guillyn in 1746. The title of the recorded 1746 edition and of the subsequent 18th century editions is *La Cuisinière bourgeoise*, not *La Nouvelle Cuisinière bourgeoise* as in this copy. Further, the recorded 1746 edition contains 400 pages of text and this edition 322 pages. As the "second" and "third" editions of 1748 and 1750 were enlarged and editions after those were increased to two volumes, it may be that this 322 page edition precedes the longer edition of the same year.

12mo. a⁴ A-Ee⁸·⁴ Ff²; 174 leaves, pp. [2] [i-iii] iv-v [vi] [1] 2-322 [*18*]. First leaf blank.

Bibliographies: This edition unrecorded in the bibliographies consulted.

Copies: No other copy located.

337. Menon.

LA | CUISINIERE | BOURGEOISE | SUIVIE DE L'OFFICE, | *A L'USAGE* | De tous ceux qui se mêlent de dé- | penses de Maisons. | *Contenent la maniere de disséquer, connoître &* | *servir toutes sortes de viandes.* | [first volume only] Nouvelle édition, augmentée de plusieurs Ra- | goûts des plus nouveaux, de différentes Recettes | pour des Liqueurs. | [second volume only: TOME SECOND] | [ornament] | A PARIS, | Chez GUILLYN, Quay des Augustins, | du côté du Pont S. Michel, au Lys d'Or. | [two short rules] | M. DCCLII. | *Avec Approbation & Privilége du Roi.*

Fourth edition, Paris, 1752. Originally published, Paris, 1746 (item 336).

12mo. 2 vols. Vol. I. a⁴ A-S¹² T-V⁴; 228 leaves, pp. [*8*] [1] 2-451 [452], ²[1] 2-6. Vol. II. π² A-R¹² S⁸ T²; 216 leaves, pp. [*4*] [1] 2-428. Page 1 in each volume is signed by the author.

Bibliographies: Oberlé (1) 114; Vicaire 236.

Copies: *NUC* (Cornell and University of California, Berkeley).

338. Menon.

LA | CUISINIERE | BOURGEOISE | SUIVIE DE L'OFFICE, | *A L'USAGE* | De tous ceux qui se mêlent de dé- | penses de Maisons. | *Contenent la maniere de connoître, disséquer, & ser-* | *vir toutes sortes de viandes, des avis intéressans sur* |

leurs bontés, & sur le choix qu'on en doit faire. | Nouvelle édition, augmentée de plusieurs Menus | pour les quatre Saison, & des Ragoûts des plus | nouveaux, d'une explications des termes propres, | & à l'usage de la Cuisine & de l'Office, & d'une | Liste alphabétique des ustensilles qui sont néces- | saires. | *TOME PREMIER* [*TOME SECOND*] | [ornament] | A PARIS, | Chez GUILLYN, Quay des Augustins, | du côté du Pont S. Michel, au Lys d'Or. | [two short rules] | M. DCC. LVI. | *Avec Approbation & Privilége du Roi.*

Fifth edition, Paris, 1756. Originally published, Paris, 1746 (item 336).

12mo. 2 vols. Vol. I. π^2 a^{12} A-Q^{12} R^4 S^{10}; 220 leaves, pp. [2] i-xxvi [1] 2-410 [2]. Vol. II. π^2 A^8 B-R^{12} S^4; 206 leaves, pp. [4] [1] 2-405 [406-408].

Bibliographies: Oberlé (1) 115.

Copies: Only the Oberlé copy of this edition located.

339. Menon.

LA | CUISINIERE | *BOURGEOISE,* | SUIVIE | *DE L'OFFICE.* | A l'usage de tous ceux qui se mêlent de | dépenses de Maisons. | *Contenant la maniere de disséquer, connoître* | *& servir toutes sortes de Viandes,* | NOUVELLE EDITION. | Augmentée de plusieurs ragoûts des plus nou- | veaux, & de différentes Recettes pour les | Liqueurs. | [ornament] | *A PARIS,* | Chez P. GUILLAUME CAVELIER, Libraire, | Rue S. Jacques, au Lys d'Or. | [short fancy rule] | M. DCC. LXXVII.

New edition, Paris, 1777. Originally published, Paris, 1746 (item 336).

12mo. π^2 A-R^{12} S^{10}; 216 leaves, pp. [4] [1] 2-428.

Bibliographies: Pennell, p. 127.

Copies: *NUC* (Library of Congress, New York Academy of Medicine, and Rutgers University).

340. Menon.

NOUVEAU TRAITÉ | DE | LA CUISINE, | *AVEC* | DE NOUVEAUX DESSEINS | DE TABLES | ET | VINGT-QUATRE MENUS, | Où l'on apprend ce que l'on doit servir suivant | chaque Saison, en gras, en maigre, & en | Pâtisserie; & très-utiles à toutes les personnes | qui s'en mêlent, tant pour ordonner, que | pour exécuter toutes sortes de nouveaux | ragoûts, & des plus à la mode. | TOME PREMIER. [TOME SECOND]. | [volume two only: ornament] | A PARIS, QUAY DES AUGUSTINS, | Chez MICHEL-ETIENNE DAVID, à la Providence | & au Roy David. | [short rule] | M. DCC. XXXIX. | *AVEC APPROBATION ET PRIVILEGE DU ROI.*

Title-page of the third volume:

LA NOUVELLE | CUISINE, | *AVEC* | DE NOUVEAUX MENUS | pour chaque Saison de l'année, | *Qui explique la façon de travailler* | *toutes sortes de Mets, qui se* servent | *aujourd'hui, en gras & en maigre; très-* | *utile aux personnes qui veulent* diversifier | *une Table par des Ragoûts nouveaux.* | Pour servir de continuation au nouveau | Traité de la Cuisine. | TOME TROISIÉME. | [ornament] | A PARIS, AU PALAIS, | Chez JOSEPH SAUGRAIN, au sixiéme Pilier de la | Grand'Salle, vis-à-vis l'Escalier de la Cour des | Aydes, à la Bonne Foy couronnée. | [short rule] | M. DCC. XLII. | *AVEC APPROBATION ET PRIVILEGE DU ROY.*

First edition, Paris, 1739-1742.

12mo. 3 vols. Vol. I. a^6 A-Rr$^{8.4}$; 246 leaves, pp. [i-ii] iii-viii [ix-xii] [1] 2-456 [*24*]. Vol. II. a^8 b^4 c^6 A-Ii$^{8.4}$ Kk^2; 212 leaves, pp. [*36*] [1] 2-384, 383-386. Vol. III. π^4 A-Ii$^{8.4}$ Kk^8; 204 leaves, pp. [*8*] [1] 2-400.

Illustrations: Vol. I, eight folding woodcuts showing table settings; Vol. III, four folding woodcuts showing table settings.

Bibliographies: Vicaire 588; Wheaton and Kelly 4138 (2 volumes only). Crahan 373 for volume three only (this copy).

Copies: *BNC* and *NUC* (New York Academy of Medicine only).

341. Menon.

NOUVEAU TRAITÉ | DE | LA CUISINE, | *AVEC* | DE NOUVEAUX DESSEINS | DE TABLES | ET | VINGT-QUATRE MENUS. | Où l'on apprend ce que l'on doit servir suivant | chaque Saison, en gras, en maigre, & en | Pâtisserie; & très-utiles à toutes les personnes | qui s'en mêlent, tant pour ordonner, que | pour exécuter toutes sortes de nouveaux | ragoûts, & des plus à la mode. | TOME PREMIER. | A PARIS, | Chez DAVID Pere, Quay des Augustins, | à la Providence & au Roy David. | [rule] | M. DCC. XLII. | *AVEC APPROBATION ET PRIVILEGE DU ROY.*

New edition, Paris, 1742. Originally published, Paris, 1739 (item 340).

12mo. Vol. I only. a⁴ χ² A-Rr⁸·⁴; 240 leaves, pp. [i-ii] iii-viii [ix-xii] [1] 2-456 [22]. This copy lacks leaves E3-E6 (pp. 53-60) and has χ² misbound after a2. Illustrations: Nine folding woodcuts showing table settings.

Bibliographies: This edition unrecorded in the bibliographies consulted.

Copies: No other copy of this edition located. *NUC* records a set of the three volumes with the imprint: Paris, Paulus de Mesnil, 1742.

341a. Menon.

LA NOUVELLE | CUISINE, | *AVEC* | DE NOUVEAUX DESSEINS | DE TABLES | ET | VINGT-QUATRE MENUS; | Où l'on apprend ce que l'on doit servir suivant | chaque Saison, en gras, en maigre, & en | Pâtisserie; & très-utiles à toutes les personnes | qui s'en mêlent, tant pour ordonner, que | pour executer toutes sortes de nouveaux | ragoûts, & des plus à la mode. | TOME SECOND. | [ornament] | A PARIS, | Chez DAVID Pere, Quay des Augustins, à la | Providence. | [rule] | M. DCC. LI. | *Avec Approbation & Privilége du Roy.*

New edition, Paris, 1751. Originally published, Paris, 1739 (item 340).

12mo. Vol. II only. a⁸ b⁴ c⁶ A-Gg⁸·⁴ Hh⁴; 202 leaves, pp. [*36*] [1] 2-365 [366-368].

Bibliographies: This edition unrecorded in the bibliographies consulted.

Copies: No other copy of this edition located.

342. Menon.

LA SCIENCE | DU | MAÎTRE D'HÔTEL, | CONFISEUR, | A L'USAGE DES OFFICIERS, | *AVEC* | *DES OBSERVATIONS* | *Sur la connoissance & les proprietés des* | *Fruits. Enrichie de Desseins en Décora-* | *tions & Parterres pour les Desserts.* | Suite du Maître d'Hôtel Cuisinier. | [ornament] | A PARIS, AU PALAIS, | Chez PAULUS-DU-MESNIL, Imprimeur- | Libraire, Grand'Salle au Pilier | des Consultations, au Lion d'or. | [rule] | M. DCC. L. | *Avec Approbation & Privilege du Roi.*

First edition, Paris, 1750.

12mo. π^2 a^6 b^4 A-Zz$^{8.4}$; 288 leaves, pp. [*4*] i-ix [x-xx] [1] 2-525 [526-550] [*2*]. Last leaf blank.

Illustrations: Five engraved folding plates showing table arrangements for desserts and figures to ornament the table.

Bibliographies: Bitting, pp. 320-321; Maggs 243; Schraemli (1) 340; Schraemli (3) 39; Vicaire 590.

Copies: *BMC*, *BNC*, and *NUC* (Library of Congress and New York Academy of Medicine).

343. Menon.

LA SCIENCE | DU | MAÎTRE D'HÔTEL | CUISINIER, | *AVEC* | *DES* *OBSERVATIONS* | *sur la connoissance & proprietés* | *des Alimens.* | [ornament] | A PARIS, AU PALAIS, | Chez PAULUS- DU-MESNIL, Imprimeur- | Libraire, Grand'Salle au Pilier | des Consultations, au Lion d'or. | [rule] | M. DCC. XLIX. | *Avec Approbation & Privilege du Roi.*

First edition, Paris, 1749.

12mo. π^2 a-h$^{8.4}$ A-Zz$^{8.4}$ Aaa^4; 330 leaves, pp. [*4*] [i] ii-xcvi [1] 2-552 [*8*]. Page 1 is signed by Menon.

Bibliographies: Maggs 242; Schraemli (3) 38; Vicaire 590.

Copies: *BNC* and *NUC* (University of California, Berkeley, only).

344. Menon.

LES SOUPERS | DE | LA COUR, | *OU* | L'ART DE TRAVAILLER | *TOUTES* *SORTES D'ALIMENS,* | Pour servir les meilleures Tables, suivant | les quatre Saisons. | *TOME I.* [*TOME SECOND.*] [*TOME III.*] [*TOME IV.*] | [ornament] | A PARIS, | Chez GUILLYN, Libraire, Quai des Augustins, | au Lys d'Or. | [two short rules] | M. DCC. LV. | *Avec Approbation & Privilége du Roi.*

First edition, Paris, 1755.

12mo. 4 vols. Vol. I. π^6 a^{12} A-Q^{12} R^8 S^2; 220 leaves, pp. [i-v] vi-xii, ^{2}i-xxxii [2] [1] 2-404. Vol. II. a^{12} A^2 B-V^{12}; 242 leaves, pp. [2] [i] ii-xxii [1] 2-460. Vol. III. a^{12} A-M^{12} N^6; 162 leaves, pp. [2] [i] ii-xxii [1] 2-264, 269-302 [2] (p. 302 misnumbered "300"). Last leaf blank. Vol. IV. π^2 A^6 B-P^{12} Q^{10}; 186 leaves; pp. [4] [1] 2-367 [368]. First leaf blank.

Bibliographies: Bitting, p. 321; Drexel 134; Malortie 297; Schraemli (1) 342; Vicaire 591.

Copies: *BMC*, *BNC*, and *NUC* (John Crerar Library, Library of Congress, and Newberry Library).

345. Menon.

LES SOUPERS | *DE LA COUR,* | OU | L'ART DE TRAVAILLER | *TOUTES SORTES D'ALIMENS.* | Pour servir les meilleures Tables, suivant | les quatre saisons. | NOUVELLE EDITION. | *TOME PREMIER. [TOME SECOND.] [TOME TROISIEME.]* | [ornament] | A PARIS, | Chez L. CELLOT, Imprimeur-Libraire, | rue Dauphine. | [two short rules] | M. DCC. LXXVIII. | *Avec Approbation & Permission.*

Presumed second edition, Paris, 1778. The privilege is dated 23 Novembre 1772 but no other edition between the first, Paris, 1755 (item 344) and this is known.

12mo. 3 vols. Vol. I. π1 a^4 a^{12} A-T^{12} V^2; 247 leaves, pp. [2] [i] ii-viii, ^{2}[i] ii-xxiv [1] 2-459 [460]. Vol. II. π^2 (π1 + a^{12} b^2) A-X^{12} Y^{10}; 278 leaves, pp. [2] i-xxx [1] 2-524. Vol. III. π1 a^{12} b^6 A-P^{12} Q^8; 207 leaves, pp. [2] i-xxxvi [1] 2-374 [375-376].

Bibliographies: Bitting, p. 321; Horn-Arndt 297; Vicaire 591.

Copies: *BNC* and *NUC* (Library of Congress only).

346. Menon.

TRAITÉ | HISTORIQUE ET PRATIQUE | *DE LA CUISINE.* | OU | LE CUISINIER | *INSTRUIT,* | de la connoissance des ANIMAUX, tant VOLATILES, | que TERRESTRES, AQUATIQUES & | AMPHIBIES; de la façon, de PRÉPARER les |

divers ALIMENS, & de les SERVIR. | *Suivi* | D'UN PETIT ABREGÉ. | *Sur la maniere de faire les CONFITURES liquides* | *& autres DESSERTS de toute espéce.* | Ouvrage très-utile, non-seulement pour les *Maîtres d'Hôtel &* | *Officiers de Cuisine;* mais encore pour toutes les *Communautés* | *Religieuses*, les *grandes Familles*, & tous ceux qui veulent | donner à manger honnêtement. | *Par le Sieur* ✳ ✳ ✳ | TOME PREMIER. [TOME SECOND.] | [ornament] | A PARIS, | *QUAY DES AUGUSTINS;* | Chez CL. J. B. BAUCHE, Libraire, à l'Image Sainte | Génévieve & à Saint Jean dans le Desert. | [two short rules] | M. DCC. LVIII. | *Avec Approbation & Privilége du Roi.*

First edition, Paris, 1758.

12mo. 2 vols. Vol. I. π1 a-f^{12} g^6 A-T^{12} V^6; 313 leaves, pp. [2] i-clvi [1] 2-468. Vol. II. π^2 A-Cc^{12} Dd^8; 322 leaves, pp. [*4*] [1] 2-552, ^{2}[1] 2-84 [*4*].

Illustrations: Vol. I. Woodcuts in the text. Vol. II. Woodcuts in the text and four folding woodcuts showing table settings.

Bibliographies: Schraemli (1) 343; Simon BG 1043.

Copies: *BNC* and *NUC* (Library of Congress only).

347. Menon.

Der vollständige | französische | Zuckerbecker | oder | Anweisung | allerhand Früchte einzumachen, Zuckerwerk | zuzubereiten, kühlende Getränke, gebrannte | Wasser &c. zu verfertigen. | Aus dem Französischen | des | Herrn Menon | übersetzt | [fancy rule] | Strassburg | verlegts Johann Gottfried Bauer | 1766 | [short rule] | Mit Obrigkeitlicher Erlaubniss.

First edition, Strassburg, 1766, of this translation into German of Menon's *La Science du maître d'hôtel confiseur.*

8vo.)(^{4} (-)(4) A-Ii^8 Kk^4 (-Kk4); 262 leaves, pp. [6] [1] 2-490 [*28*].

Bibliographies: Drexel 35; Malortie 298.

Copies: *BMC.*

348. Mérigot, Mme.

LA | CUISINIÈRE | RÉPUBLICAINE, | *QUI enseigne la manière* | *simple*
d'accomoder les / *Pommes de terre*; *avec* | *quelques avis sur les* | *soins nécessaires*
pour les | *conserver.* | [ornament] | *A PARIS.* | Chez MÉRIGOT jeune, Libraire, |
quai des Augustins, N.° 38. | [two short rules] | L'AN III.e DE LA RÉPUBLIQUE.

First edition, Paris, 1794.

12mo. A^{22}; 22 leaves, pp. [1-4] 5-42 [2]. Last leaf (blank?) wanting in this copy.

Bibliographies: Vicaire 240.

Copies: *BNC*.

349. Michel, Francisque-Xavier, 1809-1897.

LE LIVRE D'OR DES MÉTIERS. | [short rule] | HISTOIRE | DES |
HOTELLERIES, CABARETS, | HOTELS GARNIS, | RESTAURANTS ET CAFÉS,
| ET DES ANCIENNES COMMUNAUTÉS ET CONFRÉRIES | D'HOTELIERS, DE
MARCHANDS DE VINS, DE RESTAURATEURS, | DE LIMONADIERS, ETC.,
ETC., | PAR | FRANCISQUE MICHEL, | Docteur ès-lettres, associé correspondant
de l'Académie impériale de Vienne, | de l'Académie royale des sciences de Turin, |
des Sociétés des antiquaires de Londres et d'Ecosse. auteur de l'*Histoire des races*
maudites de la France et de l Espagne, | couronnée par l'Institut de France (*2e prix*
Gobert), des *Études de philologie comparée sur les divers Argots*, | également
couronnées par l'Institut (*prix Volney*), etc., etc., | ET PAR | ÉDOUARD
FOURNIER. | "Il y aurait à faire un travail intéressant et des recherches instructives |
sur les Corporations et leurs Statuts. C'est, on peut le dire, une législation | toute
particulière, la législation du peuple de cette époque: sous ce rap- | port, elle est digne
des investigations de érudits et de la curiosité des | lecteurs." (DE PASTORET,
membre de l'Institut, Préamb. des | *Ordonnances royales*, t. xx.) | "L'esprit de
charité, répandu sur la terre par le christianisme, donnait | aux anciennes Confréries un
caractère moral et sacreé…" | (LE ROUX DE LINCY, t. VII de la *Soc. des Antiq. de*
France.) | TOME PREMIER. [TOME SECOND.] | [short fancy rule] | PARIS –
1851, | LIBRAIRIE HISTORIQUE, ARCHÉOLOGIQUE ET SCIENTIFIQUE DE
SERÉ, | 5, RUE DU PONT-DE-LODI.

First edition, Paris, 1851.

277 x 180 mm. 2 vols. Vol. I. π^2 χ1 $2\pi^2$ [1]^4 2-43^4 44^2; 179 leaves, pp. [i-v] vi-x [1-3] 4-348 (χ1 and $2\pi^2$ misbound at end of the volume in this copy). Vol. II. π^2 [1]^4 2-51^4 52$_1$; 207 leaves, pp. [4] [1-3] 4-410. This copy bound two volumes in one.

Illustrations: Vol. I. One double and ten single wood engraved plates by A. Racinet fils after engravings by Adrien Lavieille and numerous wood engravings in the text. Vol. II. Wood engraved frontispiece birds-eye view of Paris by A. Racinet fils after an engraving by Bisson and Cottard, three double and twelve single wood engraved plates by A. Racinet fils after engravings by Adrien Lavieille and numerous wood engravings in the text. The plates were executed for Michel's *La Grande Bohême* (Paris, 1850) and, according to Vicaire, are not an integral part of this work. In some copies some plates are colored. In this one, all are black and white.

Bibliographies: Drexel 166; Vicaire 369-371; Wheaton and Kelly 4168.

Copies: *BMC*, *BNC*, and *NUC* (11 copies).

350. Mizauld, Antoine, d. 1578.

Artificiosa Methodus | COMPARANDORVM | Horensium Fructuum, olerum, | radicum, vuarum, vinorum, car- | nium & iusculorum, quae corpus | clemēter purgent, & variis mor- | bis, absque vlla noxa & nausea, | blandè succurrant. | *Autore ANT. MIZALDO* | *Monluciensi, Medico.* | [publisher's device] | LVTETIAE. | Ex Officina Federici Morelli | Typographi Regij. | 1575. | CVM PRIVILEGIO.

Second edition, revised and enlarged, Paris, 1575, of Mizauld's *Nova et mira artificia*, Paris, 1564.

8vo. A^8 b-f^8; 48 leaves, ff. [8] 1-39 [40]. Last leaf blank.

Bibliographies: Durling 3191; Oberlé (1) 686; Simon BB, II 460.

Copies: *BMC*, *BNC*, and *NUC* (7 copies).

351. Monselet, Charles, 1825-1888.

[Decorative title-page drawn by Gillot and lithographed by Jules Grass, lettered] | LE DoubLE ALMANACh | [in red] GOURMAND | PAR | CHARLES MONSELET |

POUR | [in red] 1866 | | PRIX: 1 FRANC | [in red] | PARIS | LIBRAIRIE DU PETIT JOURNAL | 21, Boulevard Montmartre.

First edition, Paris, 1865.

159 x 122 mm. π1 [1]^8 2-9^8; 73 leaves, pp. [1-31] 32-136 [*10*]. The eight unnumbered pages following p.136 contain advertisements; last leaf blank.

Illustrations: Lithographed title-page and lithographed borders and vignettes throughout the text.

Note: Monselet published an *Almanach des gourmands pour 1862* which may be why he began this series with *Le Double Almanach gourmand . . . pour 1866* and *Le Triple Almanach gourmand . . . pour 1867* after which he abandoned this system for *L'Almanach gourmand.* The series ended with the number for 1870.

Bibliographies: Bitting, p. 328; Drexel 587; Vicaire 604.

Copies: *BMC, BNC,* and *NUC* (John Crerar Library and Library of Congress).

352. Monselet, Charles, 1825-1888.

[Decorative title-page drawn by Gillot and lithographed by Jules Grass, lettered] | LE TripLE ALMANACh | [in red] GOURMAND | PAR | CHARLES MONSELET | *POUR* | [in red] 1867 | [in red] PARIS | LIBRAIRIE DU PETIT JOURNAL | 21, Boulevard Montmartre.

First edition, Paris, 1866.

159 x 122 mm. π1 [1]^{16} 2-3^{16} [4]^{16} [5]^4; 69 leaves, pp. [2] [1] 2-122 [123-124] [*12*]. The second through eleventh unnumbered pages at the end contain advertisements.

Illustrations: Lithographed title-page and lithographed borders and vignettes throughout the text.

See Note under item 351.

Bibliographies: Bitting, p. 328; Drexel 588; Vicaire 604; Wheaton and Kelly 4225.

Copies: *BMC, BNC,* and *NUC* (John Crerar Library and Library of Congress).

353. Monselet, Charles, 1825-1888.

[Decorative title-page drawn by Gillot and lithographed by Jules Grass, lettered] |
L'ALMANACh | GOURMAND | PAR | CHARLES MONSELET | *POUR* | 1868 |
PARIS | LIBRAIRIE DU PETIT JOURNAL | 21, Boulevard Montmartre.

First edition, Paris, 1867.

159 x 122 mm. [1]^8 2-7^8 [8]^4; 60 leaves, pp. [1-17] 18-112 [8]. The seven
unnumbered pages following p. 112 contain advertisements.

Illustrations: Lithographed title-page and lithographed borders and vignettes
throughout the text.

Bibliographies: Bitting, p. 328; Drexel 589; Oberlé (1) 219; Schraemli (3) 101;
Vicaire 604.

Copies: *BNC* and *NUC* (John Crerar Library and Library of Congress).

354. Monselet, Charles, 1825-1888.

[Decorative title-page drawn by Gillot and lithographed by Jules Grass, lettered] |
L'ALMANACh | GOURMAND | PAR | CHARLES MONSELET | *POUR* | 1869 |
PARIS | LIBRAIRIE DU PETIT JOURNAL | 21, Boulevard Montmartre.

First edition, Paris, 1868.

159 x 122 mm. π^4 1-6^8; 52 leaves, pp. [1-9] 10-95 [96-104]. Pp. 96-101 contain
advertisements.

Illustrations: Lithographed title-page and lithographed borders and vignettes
throughout the text.

Bibliographies: Bitting, p. 328; Drexel 590; Oberlé (1) 219; Schraemli (3) 101;
Vicaire 605.

Copies: *BNC* and *NUC* (John Crerar Library and Library of Congress).

355. Monselet, Charles, 1825-1888.

[Decorative title-page drawn by Gillot and lithographed by Jules Grass, lettered] |
L'ALMANACh | GOURMAND | PAR | CHARLES MONSELET | *POUR* | 1870 |
PARIS | LIBRAIRIE PAGNERRE | Rue de Seine, 18

First edition, Paris, 1869.

159 x 122 mm. π^4 1^8 $[2]^8$ $3\text{-}5^8$ $[6]^4$ $(6_3 + \chi^2)$; 50 leaves, pp. [2] [1-7] 8-89 [90] [8]. The
first six pages following p. 90 contain advertisements; the first and last leaves are
blank.

Illustrations: Lithographed title-page and lithographed borders and vignettes
throughout the text.

Bibliographies: Bitting, p. 328; Drexel 591; Oberlé (1) 219; Schraemli (3) 101;
Vicaire 605.

Copies: *NUC* (John Crerar Library and Library of Congress).

356. Monselet, Charles, 1825-1888.

CHARLES MONSELET | [short fancy rule] | LETTRES | GOURMANDES |
MANUEL DE L'HOMME A TABLE | [publisher's monogram] | PARIS | E. DENTU,
ÉDITEUR | *Libraire de la Société des Gens de Lettres* | PALAIS-ROYAL, 15, 17 ET
19, GALERIE D'ORLÉANS | [short rule] | 1877 | Tous droits réservés

First edition, Paris, 1877.

187 x 119 mm. π^2 $1\text{-}25^6$; 152 leaves, pp. [4] [1] 2-299 [300]. Publisher's printed
wrappers.

Bibliographies: Drexel 575; Maggs 537; Oberlé (1) 222; Schraemli (3) 103; Vicaire
606.

Copies: *BMC*, *BNC*, and *NUC* (Cornell, Kansas State University, and University of
California, Berkeley).

357. Montagné, Prosper.

[in red] LAROUSSE | [in red] GASTRONOMIQUE | PAR PROSPER MONTAGNÉ | [in red: ornament] [in black] *MAITRE CUISINIER* [in red: ornament] | AVEC LA COLLABORATION DU | DOCTEUR GOTTSCHALK | *PRÉFACE DE A. ESCOFFIER* | *ET DE PH. GILBERT* | [ornament] | *1850 gravures,* | *16 planches hors texte en couleurs.* | LIBRARIES LAROUSSE – PARIS | [in red: short rule]

First edition, Paris, 1938. The first printing is identified by the code "(612-3-38)" in the last line of the printer's imprint on p. 1088.

261 x 190 mm. π^4 1-68^8; 548 leaves, pp [*8*] [1] 2-1087 [1088]. Black morocco spine and green cloth covered boards stamped in gold and blind.

Illustrations: 16 halftone colored plates and 1850 black and white halftone illustrations in the text.

Bibliographies: Crahan 654; Schraemli (3) 472.

Copies: *BMC* and *NUC* (10 copies).

357a. Morelot, Denis.

STATISTIQUE | DE LA VIGNE | DANS LE DÉPARTEMENT | DE LA COTE-D'OR, | PAR | M. LE DR MORELOT, | MEMBRE DE LA COMMISSION D'AGRICULTURE DE L'ARRONDISSEMENT | DE BEAUNE, | ET DE PLUSIEURS SOCIÉTÉS SAVANTES. | [publisher's monogram] | DIJON. | CHEZ VICTOR LAGIER, LIBRAIRE, | PLACE SAINT-VINCENT. | PARIS. | CHEZ Mme HUZARD, LIBRAIRE, | RUE DE L'ÉPERON, N. 17. | [short rule] | 1831.

First edition, Dijon, 1831.

227 x 145 mm. π^2 1-18^8; 146 leaves, pp. [*4*] [1] 2-286 [2].

Bibliographies: Simon BV 98.

Copies: *BNC*.

358. Moseley, Benjamin, 1742-1819.

TRAITÉ | SUR | LES PROPRIÉTÉS | ET LES EFFETS | DU CAFÉ, | PAR M. B. MOSELEY, | Docteur en Médecine, Auteur des Observations | sur la Dyssenterie des Indes Occidentales; | TRADUIT DE L'ANGLOIS, | *Sur la troisieme Édition,* | PAR M. LEBRETON, | *Inspecteur-Général des Remises des Capitaineries* | *Royales, de* | *l'Académie Royale des Sciences* | *d'Upsal, & Correspondant de la Société* | *Royale* | *d'Agriculture de Paris.* | Avec les Observations sur la culture du Café, | par *M.* | *FUSÉE-AUBLET.* | [ornament] | A PARIS. | Chez PRAULT, Imprimeur du Roi, quai des | Augustins, à l'Immortalité. | [two short rules] | M. DCC. LXXXVI. | *Avec* | *Approbation & Privilége du Roi.*

First edition in French, Paris, 1786. Originally published in English, under the title *Observations on the Properties and Effects of Coffee*, London, 1785.

12mo. π^4 A-E^{12} χ^2; 66 leaves, pp. [i-v] vi-viii, ^{2}[i] ii-xxv [xxxvi] [27] 28-120 [121-124].

Bibliographies: Blake, p. 314; Oberlé (1) 747; Vicarie 610; Wheaton and Kelly 4259.

Copies: *BNC* and *NUC* (Harvard and University of Michigan).

359. Mousin, Jean.

DISCOVRS | [in red] DE L'YVRESSE, | ET YVRONGNERIE. | Auquel les causes, nature, & effects de | l'yuresse sont amplement deduictz, auec | la guerison & preseruation d'icelle. | *Ensemble la maniere de carousser, & les combats* | *Bacchiques* | *des anciens yurongnes.* | [in red] Le tout pour le contentement des | [in red] curieux. | *Par I. MOVSIN Conseiller & Medecin* | *ordinaire de son ALTESSE.* | [ornament] | [in red] A TOVL. | Par SEBASTIEN PHILIPPE Imprimeur | Iuré | [short rule] | [in red] 1612. | *Auec Priuilege du Roy.*

First edition, Toul, 1612.

8vo. †^{8} ††^{4} A-Aa^8 Bb^4; 208 leaves, pp. *[24]* 1-390 *[2]*. Last leaf blank.

Bibliographies: Beaupré, p. 279; Favier, p. 19 and plate 21; Simon BG 1071; Vicaire 611.

Copies: *BMC*, *BNC*, and *NUC* (4 copies).

360. Moynier, M.

DE LA | TRUFFE, | TRAITÉ COMPLET | DE CE TUBERCULE, | CONTENANT | SA DESCRIPTION ET SON HISTOIRE NATURELLE LA PLUS DÉTAILLÉE, | SON EXPLOITATION COMMERCIALE | ET SA POSITION DANS L'ART CULINAIRE; | SUIVI | D'UNE QUATRIÈME PARTIE | Contenant les meilleurs moyens d'employer les truffes en aprêts culinaires; | les meilleures méthodes d'en faire des conserves certaines; | les indications, recettes et moyens les plus positifs et les plus compliqués | sur tout ce qui concerne cette substance; | PAR | MM. MOYNIER. | [short fancy rule] | PARIS, | BARBA, Libraire, Palais-Royal, galeire de Chartres. | LEGRAND ET BERGOUGNIOUX, success. de Ve C. Béchet, | Quai des Grands-Augustins, n. 59. | 1836

Second edition, Paris, 1836. Originally published, Paris, 1835.

204 x 130 mm. [1]^8 2-25^8 26^2; 202 leaves, pp. [1-5] 6-404.

Bibliographies: Bitting, p. 334; Drexel 551; Maggs 451; Oberlé (1) 722; Schraemli (1) 360; Simon BG 1074; Vicaire 612; Wheaton and Kelly 4275 (misdating the work 1826).

Copies: *BNC* and *NUC* (4 copies).

360a. Munier, Jean-Baptiste.

MANUEL | DES FROMAGERIES | OU | TRAITÉ DE LA FABRICATION DES FROMAGES | de | GRUYÈRE, SEPTMONCEL, CHEVRETS, MONT-D'OR, ETC., ETC. | PAR | M. JEAN-BAPTISTE MUNIER, | DE FONCINE-LE-HAUT, | Médcein, et membre de plusieurs sociétés savantes. | [vignette] | LONS-LE-SAUNIER, | IMPRIMERIE ET LITHOGRAPHIE DE FRÉDÉRIC GAUTHIER. | [short rule] | 1858

First edition, Lons-le-Saunier, 1858.

225 x 141 mm. π^4 1-36^8; 292 leaves, pp. [i-v] vi-viii [1] 2-576.

Bibliographies: Unrecorded in the bibliographies consulted.

Copies: *BNC*.

361. Muret, Pierre, ca. 1630-ca. 1690.

TRAITE' | DES | FESTINS. | Par M. MURET. | *Atne quis modici transiliat neu-* | *nera Liberi,* | *Centaurea monet cum Lapithis rixa* | *super mero debellata.* | Horat. l. I. Od. 18. | [publisher's monogram] | A PARIS, | Chez GUILLAUME DESPREZ, ruë | S. Jacques, à S. Prosper, & aux trois | Vertus, au dessus des Mathurins. | [short rule] | M. DC. LXXXII. | *Avec Privilege du Roy.*

First edition, Paris, 1682.

12mo. a^8 e1 A-V$^{8.4}$ X^6 Y1; 136 leaves, pp. [*18*] 1-230 [*24*].

Note: In *BNC* under Jean Muret. In *BMC* under both Jean Muret and Pierre Muret (different copies). In *NUC* under Pierre Muret with a cross reference from Jean Muret. In *Nouvelle biographie générale* as Pierre Murct.

Bibliographies: Drexel 502; Malortie 127; Schraemli (1) 362; Simon BG 1078; Vicaire 614.

Copies: *BMC* (2 copies), *BNC*, and *NUC* (4 copies).

362. Nicolardot, Louis, 1822-1888.

HISTOIRE | DE | LA TABLE | CURIOSITÉS GASTRONOMIQUES | DE TOUS LES TEMPS ET DE TOUS LES PAYS | PAR | LOUIS NICOLARDOT | [publisher's monogram] | PARIS | E. DENTU, ÉDITEUR | LIBRAIRE DE LA SOCIÉTÉ DES GENS DE LETTRES | PALAIS-ROYAL, 17 ET 19, GALERIE D'ORLÉANS | [short rule] | 1868 | Tous droits réservés

First edition, Paris, 1868.

186 x 119 mm. π^2 a^{12} 1-24$^{12.6}$ [25]^2; 232 leaves, pp. [*4*] [i] ii-xxiv [1] 2-434 [435-436]. Last two pages blank. Publisher's printed wrappers.

Bibliographies: Bitting, p. 343; Drexel 570; Maggs 516; Vicaire 623; Wheaton and Kelly 4448.

Copies: *BMC*, *BNC*, and *NUC* (Library of Congress and New York Public Library).

363. Nignon, Édouard.

[Within a blue green ornamental border] E. NIGNON | ÉLOGES | DE LA | CUISINE FRANÇAISE | PRÉSENTATION DE SACHA GUITRY | [vignette in black and green] | PARIS | L'ÉDITION D'ART H. PIAZZA | 19, RUE BONAPARTE

First edition, Paris, 1933.

238 x 191 mm. [1-3]^8 4-26^8 [27]^4 28-29^8 (signature 7 signed on 7$_4$^{v}; signatures 11 and 12 mis-signed "10" and "11"); 228 leaves, pp. [4] [1-4] 5-443 [444] [8]. First two and last two leaves blank.

Illustrations: Head and tail pieces printed in green.

Bibliographies: Bitting, p. 343; Oberlé (1) 279.

Copies: *BMC* and *NUC* (Library of Congress only).

364. Nignon, Édouard.

ÉDOUARD NIGNON | [in brown] LES PLAISIRS | [in brown] DE LA TABLE | *Où,* *sous une forme nouvelle,* | *l'Auteur a dévoilé maints* | *délicieux secrets et recettes de* | *bonne Cuisine, transcrit les* | *précieux avis de Gourmets* | *fameux et de fins* *Gastronomes,* | *conseillers aimables et sûrs en* | *l'Art du Bien-Manger* | PRÉFACE | DE ROBERT DE FLERS | de l'Académie Française | [vignette in brown] | DESSINS de P. F. GRIGNON | *A PARIS CHEZ L'AUTEUR, 3, Place de la Madeleine* | *et chez* *LAPINA, ÉDITEUR, 75, rue Denfert-Rochereau* | Ouvrage Déposé

Second edition, Paris, 1930. Number 1910 of 2000 on vergé. Originally published, Paris, 1926.

237 x 190 mm. [1]^4 [2-12]^{16}; 180 leaves, pp. [4] [i] ii-viii [1-2] 3-339 [340] [4]. Last two leaves blank. Publisher's printed wrappers.

Illustrations: Designs by P. F. Grignon printed in brown in the text.

Presentation copy, inscribed, "à Monsieur Frank Hawley Respectueux hommages de l'auteur E. Nignon Paris le 3 juin 1931."

Bibliographies: Oberlé (1) 278.

Copies: *NUC* (8 copies).

365. Noulet, Jean-Baptiste, 1802-1890.

TRAITÉ | DES | CHAMPIGNONS | COMESTIBLES, | SUSPECTS ET
VÉNÉNEUX, | QUI CROISSENT DANS LE BASSIN SOUS-PYRÉNÉEN, | ORNÉ
DE FIGURES COLORIÉES DE GRANDEUR NATURELLE. | PAR J.-B. NOULET
ET A. DASSIER, | DOCTEURS EN MÉDECINE | Et membres de plusieurs Sociétés
Savantes. | [short rule] | CHEZ J.-B. PAYA, LIBRAIRE-ÉDITEUR. | [in two
columns: column one] TOULOUSE, | RUE CROIX-BARAGNON, 9, | Hôtel
Castellane. | [vertical rule] | [column two] PARIS, | AU DÉPÔT DE LA MAISON, |
17, rue des Beaux-Arts. | [short rule] | 1838.

Second edition, Paris, 1838. Originally published in two parts, Toulouse, 1835-1836.

236 x 150 mm. π^8 $2\pi^8$ 1-16^8 [17]^2 1; 167 leaves, pp. [i-v] vi-xxx [xxxi-xxxii] [1]
2-258 [259-262].

Illustrations: 42 handcolored lithographed plates of mushrooms.

Bibliographies: Unrecorded in the bibliographies consulted.

Copies: *BMC* and *NUC* (Cleveland Public Library, Cornell, and Harvard).

365a. Nouveau manuel de la cuisinière bourgeoise et économique.

NOUVEAU MANUEL | DE LA | CUISINIÈRE BOURGEOISE | ET
ÉCONOMIQUE | CONTENANT | LES MEILLEURS PROCÉDÉS POUR FAIRE
UNE EXCELLENTE CUISINE | A TRÈS-BON MARCHÉ. | L'ART DE FAIRE LES
HONNEURS D'UNE TABLE | DE DÉCOUPER TOUTE SORTE DE VIANDE,
VOLAILLE, GIBIER, POISSON | DE COMPOSER LE MENU D'UN REPAS. |
UNE NOTICE SUR LES VINS, LES SOINS DE LA CAVE, ETC. | REVU | PAR
UN ANCIEN CORDON BLEU | [short fancy rule] | PARIS | BERNARDIN-
BÉCHET, LIBRAIRE | 31, QUAI DES GRANDS-AUGUSTINS, 31 | [short rule] |
1862

First edition, Paris, 1862.

180 x 106 mm. π^2 1-13^{12} 14^{10}; 168 leaves, pp. [4] [1] 2-332.

Illustrations: Engraved folding frontispiece illustrating carving and table setting; woodcut vignettes and additional carving illustrations in the text.

Bibliographies: This edition cited only in notes in Horn-Arndt 540 and Vicaire 561-562. Wheaton and Kelly 4485 records an undated later edition.

Copies: No other copy of the first edition located.

366. Nouvel Almanach des gourmands.

NOUVEL ALMANACH | DES | GOURMANDS, | SERVANT DE GUIDE DANS LES MOYENS DE | FAIRE EXCELLENTE CHÈRE. | *Dédié au Ventre.* | PAR A. B. DE PÉRIGORD. | Première Année. | [vignette] | PARIS | BAUDOUIN FRÈRES, LIBRAIRES, | RUE DE VAUGIRARD, N. 36. | [ornament] | 1825

Second edition (so stated on half-title and printed wrappers) Paris, 1825. Originally published, Paris, also 1825.

141 x 92 mm. π^2 $2\pi^2$ a-b^6 1-19^6 20^2 21$_1$ 22^2; 136 leaves, pp. [*4*] [i] ii-iv, ^{2}[i] ii-xxiv [1] 2-238. Full green levant morocco, uncut, with publisher's printed wrappers preserved.

Illustration: Engraved frontispiece "le premier devoir du gourmond" from the 1826 issue of the almanach is present in place of "l'inspiration du gourmond" called for in the description on the verso of the title-page. The "Carte gastronomique de la France" called for by Vicaire and present in 1826 and 1827 almanachs is wanting in this copy.

A. B. Périgord is the pseudonym of Horace-Napoléon Raisson and Léon Thiessé.

Bibliographies: Vicaire 673; Wheaton and Kelly 4961. Bitting, p. 365, describes the first edition.

Copies: *BNC* and *NUC* (John Crerar Library, Library of Congress, and New York Public Library). Wheaton and Kelly (Boston Public Library).

367. Nouvel Almanach des gourmands.

NOUVEL ALMANACH | DES | GOURMANDS, | SERVANT DE GUIDE DANS LES MOYENS DE | FAIRE EXCELLENTE CHÈRE. | | PAR A. B. DE PÉRIGORD. | Deuxième Année. | [vignette] | PARIS | BAUDOUIN FRÈRES, LIBRAIRES, | RUE DE VAUGIRARD, N. 17. | [ornament] | 1826

First edition, Paris, 1826.

135 x 85 mm. [a]⁴ b⁶ 1-22⁶; 142 leaves, pp. [*20*] [1] 2-264. Full green levant morocco, uncut, with publisher's printed wrappers preserved.

Illustrations: Engraved frontispiece "le premier devoir du gourmond" and engraved folding "Carte gastronomique de la France" printed on rose paper.

Bibliographies: Horn-Arndt 541; Vicaire 673.

Copies: *NUC* (John Crerar Library, Library of Congress, and New York Public Library).

368. Nouvel Almanach des gourmands.

NOUVEL ALMANACH │ DES │ GOURMANDS, │ SERVANT DE GUIDE DANS LES MOYENS │ DE FAIRE EXCELLENTE CHÈRE. │ PAR A. B. DE PÉRIGORD. │ 𝔗𝔯𝔬𝔦𝔰𝔦è𝔪𝔢 𝔞𝔫𝔫é𝔢. │ [vignette] │ 𝔓𝔞𝔯𝔦𝔰. │ BAUDOUIN FRÈRES, LIBRAIRES, │ RUE DE VAUGIRARD, No. 17. │ [short rule] │ 1827.

First edition, Paris, 1827.

141 x 87 mm. π² 1-20⁶ 21²(21₁+1); 125 leaves, pp. [*4*] [1] 2-246. Full green levant morocco, uncut, with publisher's printed wrappers preserved.

Illustrations: Engraved frontispiece "promenade du gourmond" and engraved folding "Carte gastronomique de la France."

Bibliographies: Vicaire 673 in note.

Copies: *BNC* and *NUC* (John Crerar Library, Library of Congress, and New York Public Library).

369. Papin, Denis, 1647-1714.

LA │ MANIERE │ D'AMOLIR LES OS, │ ET │ DE FAIRE CUIRE TOUTES │ sortes de viandes en fort peu de │ temps, & à peu de frais. │ *Avec une description de la Machine* │ *dont il se faut servir pour cét effet,* │ *ses proprieteZ & ses usages, confirmez* │ *par plusieurs Experiences.* │ NOUVELLEMENT INVENTE. │ *Par Mr PAPIN,*

Docteur en | *Medecine.* | [ornament] | A PARIS, | Chez ESTIENNE MICHALLET, ruë | Saint Jacques, proche la Fontaine Saint | Severin, à l'image Saint Paul. | [short rule] | M. DC. LXXXII. | *Avec Aprobation & Permission.*

First edition in French, Paris, 1682. Originally published in English under the title *A New Digester, or Engine for Softening Bones*, London, 1681 (item 912).

12mo. a^4 e^2 A-Cc$^{4.2}$ Dd1; 85 leaves, pp. [*12*] 1-158.

Illustrations: Two engraved folding plates illustrating Papin's bone softening apparatus.

Bibliographies: Bitting, p. 355; Oberlé (1) 89; Vicaire, 651; Wheaton and Kelly 4596.

Copies: *BMC*, *BNC*, and *NUC* (5 copies).

370. Parmentier, Antoine-Augustin, 1737-1813.

APERÇU | DES RÉSULTATS OBTENUS | DE LA | FABRICATION | DES SIROPS ET DES CONSERVES | DE RAISINS | DANS LE COURS DES ANNÉES 1810 ET 1811, | *Pour servir de suite au TRAITÉ publié sur cette matière;* | AVEC | UNE NOTICE HISTORIQUE ET CHRONOLOGIQUE | DU CORPS SUCRANT; | Par A. A. PARMENTIER, Officier de la Légion d'honneur, | et Membre de l'Institut impérial de France. | *IMPRIMÉ ET PUBLIÉ PAR ORDRE DU GOUVERNEMENT.* | [short fancy rule] | A PARIS, | DE L'IMPRIMERIE IMPÉRIALE. | [short fancy rule] | 1812.

First edition, Paris, 1812.

194 x 116 mm. π^2 A-Ee^8 Ff^2; 228 leaves, pp. [*4*] [1] 2-452.

Bibliographies: Oberlé (1) 837.

Copies: *NUC* (American Philosophical Society, Library of Congress, and New York Public Library).

371. Parmentier, Antoine-Augustin, 1737-1813.

L'ART | DE FAIRE LES EAUX-DE-VIE, | D'APRÈS LA DOCTRINE DE CHAPTAL; | Ou l'on trouve les procédés de ROZIER, pour économiser | la dépense de leur distillation, et augmenter la spirituosité | des Eaus-de-vie de vin, de lie, de marcs, de cidre, | de grains, etc.; | SUIVI | DE L'ART DE FAIRE LES VINAIGRES | SIMPLES ET COMPOSÉS, | AVEC la méthode en usage à Orléans pour leur fabrication; les | recettes des Vinaigres aromatiques, et les procédés par lesquels | on obtient le Vinaigre de bière, de cidre, de lait, de malt, etc. | Par PARMENTIER de l'Institut national. | OUVRAGE orné de Cinq Planches représentans les diverses Machines et Instrumens | servant à la fabrication de EAUX-DE-VIE. | [short fancy rule] | A PARIS, | Chez DELALAIN, fils, libraire, quai des Augustins, no. 29. | [two short rules] | DE L'IMPRIMERIE DE MARCHANT. | AN X. – 1801.

First edition, Paris, 1801.

198 x 122 mm. π^2 A-N^8 O^4 (-O4); 109 leaves, pp. [4] [1] 2-210 [i] ii-iv. Letterpress folding table of tarifs facing p. 145 not included in the signatures or pagination.

Illustrations: Five engraved plates (two folding) of distilling apparatus.

Bibliographies: Oberlé (1) 410; Vicaire 657.

Copies: *BNC* and *NUC* (Yale only).

372. Parmentier, Antoine-Augustin, 1737-1813.

MANIÈRE | DE | FAIRE LE PAIN | DE | *POMMES DE TERRE,* | Sans mélange de Farine. | *Par M. PARMENTIER, Pensionnaire de l'hôtel* | *des Invalides, Censeur royal, Membre du Collége* | *de Pharmacie de Paris, de l'Académie des Sciences* | *de Rouen & de celle de Lyon, Démonstrateur* | *d'Histoire Naturelle.* | [ornament] | A PARIS, | DE L'IMPRIMERIE ROYALE. | [short rule] | M. DCCLXXIX.

First edition, Paris, 1779.

8vo. A-C^8 D^4; 28 leaves, pp. [1-3] 4-55 [56].

Bibliographies: Vicaire 656; Wheaton and Kelly 4651.

Copies: *BMC*, *BNC*, and *NUC* (Harvard and University of Wisconsin).

373. Parmentier, Antoine-Augustin, 1737-1813.

NOUVEL APERÇU | DES RÉSULTATS | OBTENUS DE LA FABRICATION | DES | SIROPS ET CONSERVES | DE RAISINS | DANS LE COURS DE L'ANNÉE

1812, | *Pour servir de suite à l'INSTRUCTION sur cette matière* | *publiée en 1809*; |
AVEC DES RÉFLEXIONS GÉNÉRALES | CONCERNANT | LES SIROPS ET LES
SUCRES | EXTRAITS DES AUTRES VÉGÉTAUX INDIGÈNES; | Par A. A.
PARMENTIER, Officier de la Légion d'honneur, | et Membre de l'Institut impérial de
France. | *IMPRIMÉ ET PUBLIÉ PAR ORDRE DU GOUVERNEMENT.* | [short fancy
rule] | A PARIS, | DE L'IMPRIMERIE IMPÉRIALE. | [short fancy rule] | 1813.

First edition, Paris, 1813.

205 x 120 mm. π^2 A-L^8 χ1 M^8 N^8(N4+1) O-Ee^8 Ff^6(-Ff6); 233 leaves, pp. [*4*] [1]
2-176 [*2*] 177-200 [*2*] 201-458.

Illustrations: Four engraved folding plates of distilling apparatus.

Bibliographies: Simon BG 1134.

Copies: *BNC* and *NUC* (University of Wisconsin and Yale).

374. Parmentier, Antoine-Augustin, 1737-1813.

LE PARFAIT | *BOULANGER,* | *OU* | TRAITÉ COMPLET | Sur la Fabrication & le
Commerce | du Pain. | *Par M. PARMENTIER, Pensionnaire de l'hôtel* | *royal des*
Invalides, Membre du Collége de | *Pharmacie de Paris, de l'Académie des Sciences* |
de Rouen & de celle de Lyon, Démonstrateur | *d'Histoire Naturelle.* | [ornament] | A
PARIS, | DE L'IMPRIMERIE ROYALE. | [short rule] | M. DCCLXXVIII.

First edition, Paris, 1778.

Bookseller's label on title-page beneath the imprint: Chez BARROIS, aîné, Libraire,
quai des | Augustins, du côté du Pont Saint-Michel.

8vo. a-c^8 d^4 A-Rr^8; 348 leaves, pp. [i-ii] iii-liii [liv-lvi] [1] 2-639 [640].

Bibliographies: Bitting, p. 357; Maggs 288; Oberlé (1) 813; Schraemli (1) 377;
Schraemli (3) 47: Vicaire 656; Wheaton and Kelly 4600.

Copies: *BMC, BNC,* and *NUC* (7 copies).

375. Parmentier, Antoine-Augustin, 1737-1813, and Nicolas Déyeux, 1745-1837.

PRÉCIX D'EXPÉRIENCES | ET OBSERVATIONS | SUR LES DIFFÉRENTES ESPÈCES | DE LAIT, | CONSIDÉRÉES DANS LEURS RAPPORTS | AVEC | LA CHIMIE, LA MÉDECINE | ET L'ÉCONOMIE RURALE; | PAR A. PARMENTIER ET N. DÉYEUX, | Membres de l'Institut national de France. | [short fancy rule] | STRASBOURG, | Chez F. G. LEVRAULT, imprimeur-libraire, rue des Juifs, N.o 33; | ET A PARIS, | Chez THÉOPH. BARROIS, libraire, rue Hautefeuille, N.o 22. | *An 7 de la République.*

First edition, Strassburg, 1799.

8vo. π^4 A-CC^8 DD^2; 214 leaves, pp. [*4*] [i] ii-iii [iv] [1] 2-420.

Bookplate: Westbury.

Bibliographies: Bitting, p. 357; Maggs 319.

Copies: *BNC* and *NUC* (4 copies).

376. Parmentier, Antoine-Augustin, 1737-1813.

RECHERCHES | SUR | LES VÉGÉTAUX | NOURRISSANS, | Qui, dans les temps de disette, peuvent | remplacer les alimens ordinaires. | Avec de nouvelles Observations sur la culture | des Pommes de terre. | *Par M. PARMENTIER, Censeur royal, Pension-* | *naire de l'Hôtel royal des Invalides, Apothicaire-major* | *des Camps & Armées du Roi, Membre du Collége* | *de Pharmacie de Paris, des Académies des Sciences* | *de Rouen, de Lyon, de Basançon & de Dijon, Hono-* | *raire de la Société économique de Berne, &c.* | [short rule] | L'abondance est trompeuse; elle endort & s'ensuit; | La disette effrayante & la faim qui la suit, | Nous arrachent trop tard à notre léthargie; | Surpris, découragé, l'homme est sans énergie; | S'il a su les prévoir, il peut les détourner. | [short rule] | [ornament] | A PARIS, | DE L'IMPRIMERIE ROYALE. | [short rule] | M. DCCLXXXI.

First edition, Paris, 1781.

8vo. π1 a^8 A-Oo^8 Pp^4; 309 leaves, pp. [2] [i] ii-xvi [1] 2-599 [600].

Illustration: Engraved folding plate by Gaitte of a Moulin-râpe (a grater), apparatus for making starch from potatoes and a table sieve.

Bibliographies: Blake, p. 339; Horn-Arndt 315; Maggs 294; Oberlé (1) 693 and 694; Vicaire 657; Wheaton and Kelly 4656.

Copies: *BMC*, *BNC*, and *NUC* (5 copies).

377. Parmentier, Antoine-Augustin, 1737-1813.

TRAITÉ | SUR | L'ART DE FABRIQUER | LES SIROPS ET LES CONSERVES | DE RAISINS, | DESTINÉS À SUPPLÉER LE SUCRE DES COLONIES | Dans les principaux Usages de l'Économie domestique; | PAR A. A. PARMENTIER, | *Membre de la Légion d'honneur et de l'Institut* | *de France, &c.* | [short rule] | TROISIÈME ÉDITION, | *Revue, corrigée et augmentée.* | [short rule] | A PARIS, | Chez MÉQUIGNON aîné, Libraire, rue de l'École | de Médecine. | [short fancy rule] | 1810.

Third edition, Paris, 1810. Originally published under the title *Instruction sur les sirops et les conserves de raisin* . . ., Paris, 1808.

210 x 133 mm. A-Aa^8 Bb^2; 194 leaves, pp. [1-5] 6-388. Publisher's boards with printed paper label on the spine.

Bibliographies: Bitting, p. 357; Oberlé (1) 835 and 836; Vicaire 658.

Copies: *BMC*, *BNC*, and *NUC* (4 copies).

378. Pasteur, Louis, 1822-1895.

ÉTUDES | SUR | LA BIÈRE, | SES MALADIES, CAUSES QUI LES PROVOQUENT, | PROCÉDÉ POUR LA RENDRE INALTÉRABLE, | AVEC UNE | THÉORIE NOUVELLE DE LA FERMENTATION, | PAR M. L. PASTEUR, | Membre de l'Institut de France et de la Société royale de Londres, | Membre de l'Académie de Médecine et de la Société centrale d'Agriculture de France, | des Sociétés royale et médicale d'Édimbourg, etc, etc. | "Le plus grand déréglement de l'esprit | est de croire les choses parce qu'on veut | qu'elles soient." | (Ce volume contient 12 planches gravées et 85 figures dans le texte.) | [short fancy rule] | PARIS, | GAUTHIER-VILLARS, IMPRIMEUR-LIBRAIRE, | DU BUREAU DES LONGITUES, DE L'ÉCOLE POLYTECHNIQUE, | SUCCESSEUR DE MALLET-BACHELIER, | Quai des Augustins, 55. | [short rule] | 1876 | (Tous droits réservés.)

First edition, Paris, 1876.

240 x 152 mm. π^4 1-24^8 25^4; 200 leaves, pp. [i-vii] viii [1] 2-387 [388], ^{2}[1] 2-4.

Illustrations: 12 engraved plates and 85 illustrations in the text, some of apparatus but largely of cells.

Bibliographies: Crahan 673; Garrison and Morton 2485; Schraemli (1) 380.

Copies: *BNC* and *NUC* (22 copies).

379. Pasteur, Louis, 1822-1895.

ÉTUDES | SUR LE VIN | SES MALADIES | CAUSES QUI LES PROVOQUENT | PROCÉDÉS NOUVEAUX | POUR LE CONSERVER ET POUR LE VIEILLIR | PAR M. L. PASTEUR | MEMBRE DE L'INSTITUT | [short rule] | ÉTUDES COURONNÉES PAR LE COMITÉ CENTRAL AGRICOLE DE SOLOGNE | [ornament] | PARIS | IMPRIMÉ PAR yAUTORISATION DE SON EXC. LE GARDE DES SCEAUX | A L'IMPRIMERIE IMPÉRIALE | [short rule] | M DCCC LXVI

First edition, Paris, 1866.

238 x 155 mm. π^4 1-16^8 17^4; 136 leaves, pp. [i-vii] viii [1] 2-264. Publisher's printed wrappers.

Illustrations: Thirty-eight colored lithographed plates.

Bibliographies: Crahan 674; Garrison-Morton 2479; Maggs 510a; Oberlé (1) 985; Simon BV, p. 22.

Copies: *BMC*, *BNC*, and *NUC* (20 copies).

380. Pasteur, Louis, 1822-1895.

ÉTUDES | SUR LE VIN | SES MALADIES | CAUSES QUI LES PROVOQUENT | PROCÉDÉS NOUVEAUX | POUR LA CONSERVER ET POUR LE VIEILLIR | PAR M. L. PASTEUR | Membre de l'Institut de France et de la Société royale de Londres | ÉTUDES COURONNÉES PAR LE COMITÉ CENTRAL AGRICOLE DE

SOLOGNE | ET PAR LE JURY DE L'EXPOSITION UNIVERSELLE DE 1867 | DEUXIÈME ÉDITION | REVUE ET AUGMENTÉE | AVEC 32 PLANCHES IMPRIMÉES EN COULEUR | ET 25 GRAVURES DANS LE TEXTE | PARIS | LIBRAIRIE F. SAVY | 24, RUE HAUTEFEUILLE | [short rule] | 1873 | Tous droits réservés.

Second edition, Paris, 1873. Originally published, Paris, 1866 (item 379).

230 x 151 mm. π^2 a^2 1-21^8 22^4; 176 leaves, pp. [4] [i] ii-iv [1] 2-344.

Illustrations: 32 chromolithographs and 25 illustrations in the text, some of apparatus but largely of cells.

Bibliographies: Bitting, p. 358; Oberlé (1) 986.

Copies: *NUC* (12 copies).

381. Pasteur, Louis, 1822-1895.

ÉTUDES | SUR LE VINAIGRE, | SA FABRICATION, | SES MALADIES, MOYENS DE LES PRÉVENIR; | NOUVELLES OBSERVATIONS | SUR LA CONSERVATION DES VINS PAR LA CHALEUR; | PAR M. L. PASTEUR, | MEMBRE DE L'INSTITUT. | [short fancy rule] | PARIS, | [in two columns: column one] GAUTHIER-VILLARS, | IMPRIMEUR-LIBRAIRE, | Quai des Grands-Augustins, 55. | [vertical rule] | [column two] VICTOR MASSON ET FILS, | LIBRAIRES, | Place de l'École de Médecine. [end columns] | 1868 | (L'Auteur et les Éditeurs de cet Ouvrage se réservent le droit de traduction.)

First edition, Paris, 1868.

236 x 156 mm. π^4 1-7^8 8^4; 56 leaves, pp. [i-v] vi-viii [1] 2-119 [120]. Publisher's printed wrappers.

Illustrations: Wood engravings in the text.

Bibliographies: Bitting, p. 358; Garrison-Morton 2480.

Copies: *BMC*, *BNC*, and *NUC* (21 copies).

382. Pasteur, Louis, 1822-1895.

EXAMEN CRITIQUE | D'UN | ÉCRIT POSTHUME DE CLAUDE BERNARD | SUR | LA FERMENTATION, | PAR M. PASTEUR, | MEMBRE DE L'INSTITUT. | [ornement] | PARIS, | GAUTHIER-VILLARS, IMPRIMEUR-LIBRAIRE | DU BUREAU DES LONGITUDES, DE L'ÉCOLE POLYTECHNIQUE, | SUCCESSEUR DE MALLET-BACHELIER, | Quai des Augustins, 55. | [short rule] | 1879 | (Tous droits réservés.)

First edition, Paris, 1879.

227 x 143 mm. [a]^8 b^4 1-9^8 10^6; 90 leaves, pp. [i-vii] viii-xxiv [1] 2-156. Publisher's printed wrappers.

Illustrations: Line cuts in the text and two engraved plates.

Bibliographies: Garrison-Morton 700.

Copies: *BNC* and *NUC* (20 copies).

383. Pasteur, Louis, 1822-1895.

MÉMOIRE | SUR LA | FERMENTATION ALCOOLIQUE, | PAR M. L. PASTEUR. | [short fancy rule] | PARIS, | IMPRIMERIE DE MALLET-BACHELIER, | Rue du Jardinet, 12. | [short rule] | 1860.

First edition, Paris, 1860.

235 x 150 mm. 1-6^8 7^6; 54 leaves, pp. [1-3] 4-106 [2]. Last leaf blank. Publisher's printed wrappers.

Inscribed: "a Monsieru Fizeau membre de l'Institut hommage de l'auteur L. Pasteur"

Bibliographies: Unrecorded in the bibliographies consulted.

Copies: *NUC* (Harvard, Jefferson Medical College, Philadelphia, and Lilly Library).

Le Pastissier françois. See La Varenne, François (items 266-268).

384. Paulus AEgineta, fl. 610-642.

℃ Pauli ęginetae praecepta salubria Guilielmo | Copo Basileiensi interprete. | [woodcut portrait of the author]

Colophon: ℃ Parisijs ex officina libraria Hen | rici stephani Anno CHRI= | STI Saluatoris | ∴ MDX ∴ | quarta A= | prilis | ∴ | [woodcut]

First edition, Paris, 1510, of this translation of book one of the author's *De re medica*. The Greek text of all seven books was published in 1528 and the complete Latin text in 1532.

4to. a⁴ b-g$^{8.4}$; 40 leaves, unpaginated.

Bibliographies: Brunet I. 60; Durling 3569.

Copies: *BMC*, *BNC*, and *NUC*, (John Crerar Library and the National Library of Medicine).

385. Payen, Anselme, 1795-1871.

PRÉCIS | THÉORIQUE ET PRATIQUE | DES | SUBSTANCES ALIMENTAIRES | ET DES MOYENS | DE LES AMÉLIORER, DE LES CONSERVER ET D'EN RECONNAITRE | LES ALTÉRATIONS | PAR A. PAYEN | Membre de l'Institut (Académie des sciences) | Secrétaire perpétuel de la Société impériale et centrale d'Agriculture de France | Professeur de chimie appliquée au Conservatoire impérial des arts et métiers | et de chimie industrielle et agricole à l'École impériale centrale des arts et manufactures | (ministère de l'agriculture, du commerce et des travaux publics) | Membre du Comité consultatif d'hygiène et du service médical des hôpitaux | au ministère de l'intérieur | du Comité des travaux historiques et des Sociétés savantes au ministère de l'instruction publique | de Conseil d'hygiène publique et de salubrité du département de la Seine | du Comité des arts chimiques, de la Société d'encouragement, etc., etc. | [short rule] | QUATRIÈME ÉDITION | AUGMENTÉE DE PLUSIEURS APPLICATIONS NOUVELLES | [short fancy rule] | PARIS | LIBRAIRIE DE L. HACHETTE ET Cie | BOULEVARD SAINT-GERMAIN, No 77 | [short rule] | 1865

Fourth edition, Paris, 1865. Original published under the title *Des substances alimentaires. . .*, Paris, 1853.

215 x 130 mm. π^6 1-35^8 36^6; 292 leaves, pp. [i-vii] viii-xii [1] 2-569 [570] [2]. First and last leaves (blanks?) wanting in this copy.

Bibliographies: Bitting, p. 360; Vicaire 668; Wheaton and Kelly 4695.

Copies: *BNC* and *NUC* (7 copies).

386. Pelletier, Eugène, b. 1827.

LE THÉ | ET | LE CHOCOLAT | DANS L'ALIMENTATION PUBLIQUE | AUX POINTS DE VUE | Historique – Botanique – Physiologique – Hygiénique – Économique | industriel et commercial | PAR | EUGÈNE ET AUGUST PELLETIER ∴ | DIRECTEURS-GÉRANTS DE LA COMPAGNIE FRANÇAISE, MEMBRES DE LA SOCIÉTÉ | D'ENCOURAGEMENT | [short fancy rule] | PARIS | CHEZ LES AUTEURS | A LA COMPAGNIE FRANÇAISE DES CHOCOLATS ET DES THÉS | Boulevard de Sébastopol, 26 | DANS TOUTES SES SUCCURSALES DE FRANCE | CHEZ TOUS LES LIBRAIRES | Et à la Librairie Dubuisson, 5, rue Coq-Héron | [short rule] | 1861 | Droits de reproduction et de traduction réservés.

First edition, Paris, 1861.

186 x 120 mm. 1-12^6; 72 leaves, [1-5] 6-142 [2]. Last leaf blank. Publisher's printed wrappers.

Bibliographies: Bitting, p. 363; Schraemli (1) 384; Vicaire 672; Wheaton and Kelly 4714.

Copies: *BMC*, *BNC*, and *NUC* (5 copies).

387. Petit, Alphonse.

LA | GASTRONOMIE | EN RUSSIE | PAR | A. PETIT, | CHEF DE CUISINE DE SON EXCELLENCE MONSIEUR LE | COMTE PANINE, MINISTRE DE LA JUSTICE. | [short fancy rule] | PARIS | CHEZ L'AUTEUR, 18, RUE MARTEL. | Dépôt, chez M. TROTTIER, fabricant de moules, | 4, RUE SAINT-HONORÉ. | ÉMILE MELLIER, LIBRAIRE-ÉDITEUR, | 17, RUE PAVÉE SAINT-ANDRÉ DES ARTS. | [short rule] | 1860

First edition, Paris, 1860.

186 x 118 mm. 1-10$^{12.6}$ 11^{12} 12^2 a^{12} b^6 c^{12} d^4; 138 leaves, pp. [i-v] vi-viii [9] 10-275 [276]. Publisher's printed wrappers.

Bibliographies: Bitting, p. 366; Drexel 566; Maggs 501; Oberlé (1) 251 and 252; Simon BG 1155; Vicaire 677.

Copies: *BMC*, *BNC*, and *NUC* (Cornell, Kansas State University, and Library of Congress).

388. Petit, Pierre.

L'ART │ De trancher la viande, │ & toutes sortes de fruits, │ nouvellement │ a la françoise. │ PAR │ PIERRE PETIT │ Écuyer tranchant.

Engraved plates with manuscript text, Paris? after 1750.

Note: This series of plates illustrating carving has its origins in Mattia Giegher's *Il Trinciante*, Padua, 1621 (item 1146). It was orginally published, probably in Paris about 1650, with an accompanying hand written text attributed to the carver Jacques Vontent (item 440). The plates were used again sometime after 1750, this time with a handwritten text by a carver named Pierre Petit. Maggs, in their catalogue *Food and Drink Through the Ages* (London, 1937) dates both the Jacques Vontet and Pierre Petit versions Lyon, ca. 1647. However, both this copy and another of the Pierre Petit version owned by Pierre Berès are printed and written on paper with the watermark of Mathieu Johannot, papermaker of Annonnay who was active during the years 1750-1780. We are indebted to Berès for correctly dating the Pierre Petit version.

Folio: 103 leaves, unsigned. Folio 1, blank; f. 2, undentified and probably made up coat of arms; f. 3, printed title-page; ff. 4-5, manuscript advise to the reader, written on rectos and versos; the remaining 98 leaves consisting of 34 engraved plates and 16 pen and ink drawings illustrating carving and 48 leaves with manuscript carving instructions.

Bookplates: (1) Arnold W. Oxford; (2) From the collection of Cookery Books formed by John Hodgkin, F.L.S.; (3) From the collection of Cookery Books formed by Fred W. Scheibe.

Bibliographies: Maggs 135. Oberlé (1) 552; Schraemli (1) 386, Schraemli (3) 24 and Vicaire 677 describe similar works.

Copies: No other copy exactly like this one located. However, see Vontet (item 440) for a similar work.

389. Pigot, Léon.

ACADÉMIE DE CUISINE │ Gastronomique │ [short rule] │ N'est pas gourmand qui veut! │ *Brillat-Savarin* │ LA │ *Chasse Gourmande* │ ou "l'Art d'accommoder tous les Gibiers" │ *ENCYCLOPÉDIE CULINAIRE DU CHASSEUR* │ par Léon PIGOT │ *Chef de Cuisine, Chevalier du Mérite Agricole* [small medal] │ Auteur du Mémorandum du Pâtissier-Entremettier │ Collaborateur à l'*Art Culinaire* et à la *Cuisine Française et Etrangère* │ *Les Gourmets me liront* │ [short rule] │ [wood engraving of boar's head]

Second edition, Paris, 1911. Originally published Mculan, 1910. The title-page of the second edition has no imprint but there is one on the front printed wrapper which reads as follows: *BIBLIOTHÈQUE DU CHASSEUR Vol. II* │ [ornament] │ La Chasse gourmande │ OU │ L'ART D'ACCOMODER TOUS LES GIBIERS │ PAR │ Léon PIGOT │ CHEF DE CUISINE │ [publisher's monogram] │ PARIS │ Librairie Générale at Internationale │ G. FICKER │ 6, Rue de Savoie, 6 │ [short rule] │ 1911

184 x 124 mm. 1-20^6; 120 leaves, [1-5] 6-239 [240]. Quarter brown morocco with marbled boards; publisher's printed wrappers preserved.

Illustrations: Numerous small cuts of animals in the text.

Bibliographies: This edition unrecorded in the bibliographies consulted. Bitting, p. 371, records the first edition.

Copies: No other copy of this edition located.

390. Pinchesne, Étienne-Martin de, sieur de, 1616-1680.

POÈTES ET GOINFRES DU XVIIe SIÈCLE │ [short rule] │ LA CHRONIQUE │ DES │ [in red] CHAPONS ET DES GÉLINOTTES │ [in red] DU MANS │ D'ETIENNE MARTIN DE PINCHESNE │ PUBLIÉE │ SUR LE MANUSCRIT ORIGINAL DE LA BIBLIOTHÈQUE NATIONALE │ PAR │ [in red] FRÉDÉRIC LACHÈVRE │ [short rule] │ Frontispice à l'eau-forte gravé par H. MANESSE │ [publisher's monogram] │ PARIS │ LIBRAIRIE HENRI LECLERC │ 219, RUE SAINT-HONORÉ, 219 │ et 16, rue d'Alger. │ [short rule] │ 1907

Colophon: CET OUVRAGE | A ETÉ TIRÉ A 301 EXEMPLAIRES | (dont un sur peau de vélin) | AUX FRAIS DE | FRÉDÉRIC LACHÈVRE | [short rule] | No. 230

First edition, Paris, 1907.

287 x 182 mm. π² 1-21⁸; 170 leaves, pp. [i-v] vi-lxxi [lxxii] [1-3] 4-259 [260] [8]. Last three pages blank.

Illustration: Etched title-page by H. Manesse.

Bibliographies: Wheaton and Kelly 3994.

Copies: *BNC* and *NUC* (7 copies).

391. Platina (Bartholomaeus Bartolomeo Sacchi de Platina) 1421-1481.

PLatine en fran/ | coys tresutile & necessaire pour le corps hu | main qui traicte de hō neste volupte et de | toutes viandes et choses que lōme men= | ge/ quelles vertus ont/ et en quoy nuysent | ou prouffitēt au corps humain, et cōment | se doyuent apprester ou appareiller/ et de faire a chascune dicelles vi= | andes soit chair ou poysson sa propre saulce/ & des proprietes & vertus | que ont lesdites viandes/ Et du lieu et place cōuenable a lōme pour | abiter/ et de plusieurs aultres gentilesses par quoy lomme se peult | maintenir en prosperite et sante sans avoir grāt indigēce davoir aul= | tre medicin sil est homme de rayson.

Colophon: ℂ Cy finist Platine leql a este trāslate de la= | tin en frācoys/ & augmēte copieusemēt de plu | sieurs docteurs, principalemēt p messire Des= | dier xpol prieur de sait Maurice pres mōtpe= | lier. Et imprime a Lyon par Frācoys fradin | pres nostre dame de cōfort. Lan mil cinq cens | & cinq. Et le dixhuitiesme jour Dauril.

Note: The title-page and colophon are set in lettre bâtarde.

First edition in French, Lyon, Francoys Fradin, 1505. Originally published in Latin under the title *De honesta voluptate*, Rome, 1474 or 1475.

Folio: ⳨⁴ a-r⁶; 106 leaves, ff. [4] i-cii.

Bibliographies: Schraemli (1) 399; Simon BB II. 528; Simon BG 1192; Vicaire 692.

Copies: *BNC* and *NUC* (College of Physicians of Philadelphia only).

392. Platina (Bartholomaeus Bartolomeo Sacchi de Platina) 1421-1481.

[ornament] BAPTISTE | PLATINE DE CREMONNE | DE LHONNESTE VOLVPTE, | liure tresnecessaire a la vie humaine | pour obseruer bonne sante. | 1559. | [woodcut] | ☞ On les vend a Paris en la rue sainct Iac= | ques au mortier dor par Viuant gauteroth.

Colophon: ☞ Cy fine Platine tresutile & necessaire pour | le corps humain, qui traicte de honneste volu= | pte & de toutes viandes profitablee a lhomme: | lequel a este translate de latin en francoys, & | augmente copieusement de plusieurs docteurs, | principallement par messire Desdier Christol | prieur de sainct Maurice pres Montpeslier. Et | imprime nouuellement a Paris. | 1539.

New edition, Paris, 1539. The date 1559 on the title-page is an error according to Vicaire. Originally published in Latin under the title *De honesta voluptate*, Rome, 1474 or 1475, and in French, Lyon, 1505 (item 391).

8vo. a-z⁸ &⁸ A-K⁸; 272 leaves, ff. [8] i-cclxiv.

Bibliographies: Oberlé (1) 55; Schraemli (1) 400; Schraemli (2) 26; Vicaire 695 cites two other issues.

Copies: Only Oberlé copy located.

393. Platina, Bartolomeo, 1421-1481.

LE | LIVRE DE | HONNESTE | VOLVPTÉ. | *Contenant la maniere d'habiller tou-* | *tes sortes de viandes, tant chair que posi-* | *son & de seruir en banquets & festes.* | Auec vn memoire pour faire escriteau | pour vn banquet: extraict de plusieurs | fort experts, & le tout reueu nouuelle- | ment, contenant cinq Chapitres. | [three fish within a border of type ornaments] | *A LYON,* | POVR PIERRE RIGAVD. | [short rule] | 1602.

New edition, Lyon, 1602. Originally published in Latin under the title *De honesta voluptate*, Rome, 1474 or 1475, and in French, Lyon, 1505 (item 391).

16mo. A-N⁸ a⁸; 104 leaves, ff. [1] 2-96 [8].

Bibliographies: Brunet IV, 691.

Copies: No other copy of this edition located.

394. Plumerey, Armand.

Vol. I.

LE PRINCIPAL | DE LA | CUISINE DE PARIS, | TRAITÉ | *DES ENTRÉES CHAUDES,* | DES ROTS EN GRAS ET EN MAIGRE, | DES ENTREMETS DE LÉGUMES, ENTREMETS SUCRÉS ET AUTRES; | PAR PLUMEREY, | Éleve de la maison du prince de Talleyrand, ancien chef des cuisines de madame | la princesse de Poniatowski, chef actuel des cuisines de Son Excellence le comte de Pahlen, | ambassadeur de Russie à Paris. | [short rule] | TOME PREMIER. | [short fancy rule] | PARIS. | AU DÉPOT, RUE THÉRÈSE, 11. | [in two columns: column one] DENTU, libraire, Palais-Royal, galerie d'Orléans. | TRESSE, libraire, 3, galerie de Chartres. | J. RENOUARD et Cie, libraires, 6, rue de Tournon. | [vertical rule] | [column two] MANSUT, libraire, 30, place St-André-des-Arts. | MAISON, libraire, 29, quai des Augustins. | AMYOT, libraire, rue de la Paix. [end columns] | ROUEN, café de France (M. Mériotte), place des Carmes; et à Londres, chez tous les Lib. | [short rule] | 1843

Vol. II.

LE PRINCIPAL | DE LA | CUISINE DE PARIS, | TRAITÉ | *DES ENTRÉES CHAUDES,* | DES ROTS EN GRAS ET EN MAIGRE, | DES ENTREMETS DE LÉGUMES, ENTREMETS SUCRÉS ET AUTRES; | OU | TOMES 4e ET 5e DE L'OUVRAGE DE CARÉME; | PAR PLUMEREY, | Éleve de la maison du prince de Talleyrand; ancien chef des cuisines de madame | la princesse de Poniatowski; chef actuel des cuisines de Son Excellence le comte de Pahlen, | ambassadeur de Russie à Paris. | [short rule] | TOME II ET DERNIER. | [short fancy rule] | PARIS. | AU DÉPOT, RUE THÉRÈSE, 11. | [in two columns: column one] DENTU, libraire, Palais-Royal, galerie d'Orléans. | J. RENOUARD et Cie, libraires, 6, rue de Tournon. | MANSUT, libraire, 30, place St-André-des-Arts. | [vertical rule] | [column two] GARNIER frères, Palais-Royal. | MAISON, libraire, 29, quai des Augustins. | AMYOT, libraire, rue de la Paix. [end columns] | À Londres, chez DULAU et Cie, lbr. – A Leipzig, chez J. RENOUARD et Cie, libr. | A Rome, chez MERLE, libraire. | [short rule] | 1844

First edition, Paris, 1843-1844. Continuation, forming volumes IV and V, of Carême's *L'art de la cuisine française* . . . (item 118).

214 x 132 mm. 2 vols. Vol. I. π^6 1-10^8 11^6 12-27^8; 220 leaves, pp. [i-v] vi-xi [xii] [1-3] 4-425 [426] [2]. Vol. II. [a]^2 b^8 c^4 1-25^8 26^4 27-34^8 35^2; 284 leaves pp. [4] [xiii] xiv-xxxv [xxxvi] [1] 2-539 [540].

Illustrations: Vol. I. Engraved frontispiece titled "Le cordon bleu d'une bonne petite maison," a lithographed half-title "Traité des Entrées chaudes," a copperplate engraving by Debucourt and an engraved portrait of Talleyrand. Vol. II. Engraved frontispiece portrait of Appert, a lithographed half-title "Traité des Entrées chaudes," and engraved portraits of Grimod de la Reynière and the Marquis de Cussy.

Bibliographies: Bitting, p. 374; Schraemli (1) 107; Simon BG 289; Vicaire 700; Wheaton and Kelly 4827.

Copies: *BMC*, *BNC*, and *NUC* (Boston Public Library and Library of Congress).

395. Poissardiana.

POISSARDIANA, | OU | CATÉCHISME DES HALLES; | OUVRAGE | Utile à la Jeunesse qui veut passer | joyeusement le CARNAVAL. | [short fancy rule] | A PARIS, | Rue du Carême Prenant, No. 34. | [short rule] | L'an II du retour de MARDI-GRAS.

First edition, Paris, ca. 1805.

119 x 75 mm. 1-12^6; 72 leaves, pp. [i-v] vi-xv [xvi] [17] 18-144. Bound with *Révolutioniana* (item 158) and *Gastronomiana* (item 206).

Illustration: Engraved handcolored frontispiece.

Bibliographies: Unrecorded in the bibliographies consulted.

Copies: No other copy located.

396. Poncelet, Polycarpe, ca. 1720-ca. 1780.

CHIMIE DU GOUT | ET | DE L'ODORAT, | *OU* | PRINCIPES | Pour composer facilement, & à peu de | frais, les Liqueurs à boire, & les Eaux | de senteurs. | *Avec Figures.* | [two short rules] | Ne quid Nimis. *Terence.* | [short rule] | [ornament] | A PARIS, | DE L'IMPRIMERIE DE P. G. LE MERCIER, | rue Saint Jacques, au Livre d'Or. | [two short rules] | M. D. CC. LV. | *AVEC APPROBATION, ET PRIVILEGE DU ROI.*

First edition, Paris, 1755.

8vo. A-Aa^8 Bb^4; 196 leaves, pp. [i-iii] iv-xxvi [27] 28-390 [2].

Illustrations: Engraved frontispiece of a chemist's shop and six engraved plates illustrating distilling aparatus.

Bibliographies: Blake, p. 358; Maggs 263; Oberlé (1) 1088; Oberlé (2) 402; Schraemli (1) 408; Simon BG 1212; Vicaire 171; Wheaton and Kelly 4831.

Copies: *BNC* and *NUC* (5 copies).

396a.   Porchon, A.

Part I:

LES REGLES │ DE LA SANTE', │ OU │ LE VERITABLE REGIME │ de vivre, que l'on doit │ observer dans la santé & │ dans la maladie. │ *Et une Table qui contient par* / *Alphabet les facultez &* / *vertus de tous les Alimens,* / *tirez des Plantes & des Ani-* / *maux dont on use ordinai-* / *rement.* │ Par A. P. Docteur en Medecine. │ [ornament] │ A PARIS, │ Chez MAURICE VILLERY, Quay │ des Augustins, proche l'Hostel │ de Luyne, à la décente du Pont │ S. Michel, à l'Image S. Jean │ Chrysostome. │ [rule] │ M. DC. LXXXVIII. │ *Avec Privilege du Roy.*

Part II:

LES REGLES │ DE LA SANTE', │ OU │ LE VERITABLE REGIME │ de vivre, que l'on doit │ observer dans la santé & │ dans la maladie. │ *Avec une Table qui contient* │ *par Alphabet les facultez &* │ *vertus de tous les Alimens,* / *corrigée & augmentée en* │ *cette seconde Edition d'un* / *grand nombre de Remarques* / *curieuses, de Medecine, de* / *Physique, de Moralle &* / *d'Histoire.* │ Par A. P. Docteur en Medecine. │ [ornament] │ A PARIS, │ Chez MAURICE VILLERY, Quay │ des Augustins, proche l'Hostel │ de Luyne, à la décente du Pont │ S. Michel, à l'Image S. Jean │ Chrysostome. │ [rule] │ M. DC. LXXXVIII. │ *Avec Privilege du Roy.*

Second edition, Paris, 1688. Originally published, Paris, 1684.

12mo. 2 parts in 1 volume. A-Q$^{8.4}$, ^{2}A-Y$^{8.4}$; 228 leaves, pp. [*18*] 1-111, 113-173, ^{2}[2] 1-48, 46-68, 68-260. Title-page of part II on ^{1}Q4^r.

Bibliographies: Bitting, p. 377; Vicaire 703. Bitting, Vicaire and Oberlé (1) 432 cite the first edition.

Copies: *BNC, NUC* (Library of Congress only).

397. R., J.-L.

LA LAITERIE. | ART | DE TRAITER LE LAITAGE, | DE FAIRE LE BEURRE, | ET DE FABRIQUER LES DIVERSES SORTES | DE FROMAGES; | PAR M. J.-L. R. | DEUXIÈME ÉDITION, | REVUE ET CORRIGÉE | PAR M. ✱✱✱. | [short fancy rule] | PARIS, | AUDOT, ÉDITEUR, | RUE DES MAÇONS-SORBONNE, No 11. | 1828.

Second edition, Paris, 1828. Originally published, Paris, 1823.

138 x 84 mm. 1-8$^{12.6}$ 9^6 10^2; 80 leaves, pp. [1-5] 6-159 [160].

Bibliographies: Simon BG 938; Vicaire 489.

Copies: No other copy of this edition located. *NUC* records the University of California, Berkeley, copy of the first edition.

398. Raisson, Horace-Napoléon, 1798-1854.

CODE | GOURMAND. | MANUEL COMPLET | DE | 𝕲astronomie. | CONTENANT | LES LOIS, RÈGLES, APPLICATIONS ET EXEMPLES | DE L'ART DE BIEN VIVRE; | PAR | L'AUTEUR DU CODE DES HONNÊTES GENS, ETC. | ✱ | *Les grandes pensées viennent de l'Estomac.* | ✱ | PARIS | AMBROIE DUPONT ET CIE, LIBRAIRES, | RUE VIVIENNE, N. 16. | ✱ | 1827

First edition, Paris, 1827.

139 x 84 mm. 1-22^6; 132 leaves, pp. [i-v] vi-xxxiv [35-37] 38-264.

Bibliographies: Maggs 415; Vicaire 729.

Copies: No other copy of the first edition located. *BNC* and *NUC* list the second and later editions; *BMC* lists the third edition.

399. Raymond, Emmeline, 1828-1902.

LA | BONNE MÉNAGÈRE | PAR | MME EMMELINE RAYMOND | [short fancy rule] | PARIS | LIBRAIRIE DE FIRMIN DIDOT FRÈRES, FILS ET CIE | IMPRIMEURS DE L'INSTITUT, RUE JACOB, 56 | 1867 | Tous droits réservés

First edition, Paris, 1867.

185 x 120 mm. π^2 1-30^6 31^8 32^2; 192 leaves, pp. [4] [1] 2-377 [378] [2]. Last three pages blank.

Illustrations: Thirteen wood engravings in the text showing techniques of carving.

Bibliographies: Vicaire 730 records the eighth edition, Paris, 1887, and refers to the first edition in a note.

Copies: *BNC*.

400. Reculet, C.

LE | CUISINIER | PRATICIEN | OU | LA CUISINE SIMPLE ET PRATIQUE | PAR | C. RECULET | CUISINIER DE MADAME LA COMTESSE D'AUTEROCHE ET DE MADAME LA MARQUISE DE COURTARVELLE | AUX CHATEAUX DE TOUCHAILLON ET DE LIERVILLE. | [short rule] | PARIS | [in two columns: column one] E. DENTU, LIBRAIRE | PALAIS-ROYAL, 13 | [verticle rule] | [column two] LACROIX ET BAUDRY, LIBRAIRES | QUAI MALAQUAIS, 15 [end columns] | ET CHEZ L'AUTEUR, BOULEVARD DU TEMPLE, 12 | [short rule] | 1859 | Droits de traduction réservés.

First edition, Paris, 1859.

215 x 131 mm. π^6 1-32^8 33^2; 264 leaves, pp. [i-v] vi-xii [1] 2-516.

Illustrations: Wood engravings in the text.

Bibliographies: Bitting, p. 391; Vicaire 733.

Copies: *BMC*, *BNC*, and *NUC* (Kansas State University and University of California, Berkeley).

401. Reflexions et observations sur la qualité des vins.

[head title] [ornament] | REFLEXIONS | ET | OBSERVATIONS | *Sur la qualité des Vins, & sur les analyses | que l'on en fait.*

First edition, Paris, de l'Imprimerie de Vincent, 1759.

4to. A-B⁴; 8 leaves, pp. [1] 2-14 [2]. Last leaf blank.

Bibliographies: Unrecorded in the bibliographies consulted.

Copies: No other copy located.

402. Regimen sanitatis salernitanum.

[head title] Incipit regimē sanitatis salernitanū excellentissimū pro [con]ser | uatiōe sanitatis toti[us] humani generis p[er] utliissimū. necnō a magi | stro Arnaldo de villa noua cathelano oim medico[rum] viuentiū gē | ma vtiliter ac scdm oim antiquo[rum] medico[rum] doctrinā veraciter ex | positū nouiter correctū ac emēdatū p[er] egregijssimos ac medicine | artis peritissimos doctores mōtispessulani regētes anno. M. | CCCC. octuagessmo. pdicto loco actu morā trabētes. | aNglo[rum] regi scripsit scola tota salerni.

New edition, Lyon? Johannes Siber? ca. 1495. Originally published, Cologne, 1480.

8vo. a-k⁸; 80 leaves, unpaginated. First leaf (blank?) wanting in this copy.

Bibliographies: Gambacorte and Giordano, p. 116, no. 10; Goff R-75; Pellechet 1282.

Copies: Goff (College of Physicians, Philadelphia, and Indiana University).

403. Regimen sanitatis salernitanum.

LE REGIME | DE SANTE' | DE L'ESCHOLE | DE SALERNE. | TRADVIT ET COM- | menté par M. MICHEL LE | LONG, Prouinois, Docteur | en Medecine. | *Auec l'Epistre de Diocle Carystien, touchant les | presages des maladeis à Antigon Roy d'Asie, | & le serment d'Hippocrate, mis de prose | en vers François par le mesme.* | [ornament] | A PARIS, | Chez NICOLAS & IEAN DE LA COSTE, au mont | S. Hilaire, à l'Escu de Bretagne, & en leur | boutique à la petite porte du Palais | deuant les Augustins. | [short rule] | M. DC. XXXIII. | *AVEC PRIVILEGE DV ROY.*

First edition, Paris, 1633, of Michel Le Long's translation into French. Originally published in Latin under the title *Regimen sanitatis salernitanum*, Cologne, 1480. Vicaire misdates this edition 1613 in a apparent typographical error for 1633 and also notes a second edition, 1637. Vicaire's error, along with his collation, is repeated by Gambacorta and Giordano. Copies in the Bibliothèque Nationale, Duke University, the National Library of Medicine and Yale are, like the Gernon copy, dated 1633.

8vo. a⁸ e⁸ A-Yy⁸; 376 leaves, pp. [*36*] 1-700 [*16*].

Bibliographies: Gambacorta and Giordano, p. 131, no. 36; Vicaire 511 (both misdating the first edition "1613").

Copies: *BNC* and *NUC* (Duke, National Library of Medicine, and Yale).

404. Regimen sanitatis salernitanum.

L'ART | *DE CONSERVER* | SA SANTÉ, | *COMPOSÉ* | PAR | L'ÉCOLE DE SALERNE, | *AVEC LA TRADUCTION* | EN VERS FRANÇOIS, | PAR MR. B. L. M. | [ornament] | A PARIS, | Chez PIERRE-ALEXANDRE LE PRIEUR, | Imprimeur-Libraire ordinaire du Roy, | rue S. Jacques, à la Croix d'Or. | [short rule] | M. DCC. XLIX. | *Avec Approbation & Privilege du Roy.*

New edition, Paris, 1749. Originally published in Latin under the title *Regimen sanitatis salernitanum*, Cologne, 1480, and in this translation by Antoine-Augustin Bruzen de la Martinière, The Hague, 1743. Gambacorta and Giordano state that this 1749 edition is a reprint from the 1660 edition which, on p. 89 of their bibliography, they attribute to Bruzen de la Martinière, clearly impossible as Bruzen de la Martinière was born in 1683. He died in The Hague in 1743.

12mo. a⁸ b⁴ c⁶ A-F⁸·⁴ G⁶ H²; 62 leaves, pp. [i-vi] vii-xxxvi [1] 2-77 [78] [*10*].

Bibliographies: Blake, p. 375; Gambacorta and Giordano, p. 93; Vicaire 45.

Copies: *BMC*, *BNC*, and *NUC* (6 copies).

405. Rendu, Victor, 1809-1877.

AMPÉLOGRAPHIE | FRANÇAISE | COMPRENANT | LA STATISTIQUE, | LA DESCRIPTION DES MEILLEURS CÉPAGES, | L'ANALYSE CHIMIQUE DU SOL, | ET LES PROCÉDÉS DE CULTURE ET DE VINIFICATION | DES

PRINCIPAUX VIGNOBLES DE LA FRANCE, | PAR | VICTOR RENDU | INSPECTEUR GÉNÉRAL DE L'AGRICULTURE. | Vitem nos caeleris stirpibus jure | praeponimus. | (COLUMELLA, lib. III, cap. 1.) | [short rule] | Deuxième Édition | [short fancy rule] | PARIS | LIBRAIRIE DE VICTOR MASSON | PLACE DE L'ÉCOLE-DE-MÉDECINE | M DCCC LVII | Droit de traduction réservé.

Second edition, Paris, 1857. This work originally was published in a much briefer version containing 160 pages, Paris, 1854. That version was reprinted in 1857, the same year this greatly expanded second edition was published.

227 x 142 mm. π^2 a^8 1-36^8; 298 leaves, pp. [*4*] [i] ii-xvi [1] 2-576.

Illustrations: Color lithographed map titled "Carte viticole de la France."

Bibliographies: Simon BV, p. 55.

Copies: *BMC*, *BNC*, and *NUC* (5 copies).

406. Richardin, Edmond, 1850-1917.

LA CUISINE FRANÇAISE | DU XIVe AU XXe SIÈCLE | [in red] L'Art du bien manger | SUIVI DE | L'ART DE CHOISIR LES VINS ET DE LES SERVIR A TABLE, | D'UN CHAPITRE SPÉCIAL, ORNÉ DE FIGURES EXPLICATIVES SUR | LE DÉCOUPAGE, | *et de Nombreux MENUS anciens et modernes*, | *puis des Aphorismes de BRILLAT-SAVARIN en 20 Compositions* | *hors-texte de A. ROBIDA.* | Preface d'André THEURIET | de l'Académie française | ÉDITION ACCOMPAGNÉE D'UNE SÉRIE DE REPRODUCTIONS D'ESTAMPES | D'APRÈS LES MAITRES DE LA PEINTURE; EN OUTRE, DE DESSINS | DE A. ROBIDA, GRAVÉS PAR A. LERONDEAU, | ET DE BOIS ORIGINAUX DU GRAVEUR PAUL E. COLIN | EXPLIQUÉS PAR | Gustave GEFFROY | de l'Académie Goncourt | [in red] Ouvrage adopté par le Ministère de l'Instruction publique et par la Ville de Paris. | *et contenant:* | DE CURIEUSES PRÉPARATIONS CULIANIRES DUES A DES ÉCRIVAINS ET DES AMATEURS, | LES CROQUIS GASTRONOMIQUES DE FULBERT-DUMONTEIL, | LES FORMULES PRATIQUES PERMETTANT DE PRÉPARER CHEZ SOI | LES PLATS RENOMMÉS DES GRANDS RESTAURANTS ET DES MAITRES-CUISINIERS, | DES RECETTES ORIGINALES DE VIEILLE CUISINE FRANÇAISE | FORMANT ENSEMBLE | [in red] plus de 2000 Recettes | Le tout recueilli et annoté | PAR | Edmond RICHARDIN | [short rule] | PARIS | [in red] ÉDITIONS D'ART ET DE LITTÉRATURE | [short rule] | EN VENTE A LA LIBRAIRIE NILSSON | *7, Rue de Lille*

Fourth edition, Paris, ca. 1913. Originally published, Paris, 1901.

185 x 134 mm. π^4 a^8 1-58^8; 476 leaves, pp. [8] [i-iii] iv-xvi [1] 2-926 [2]. First and last leaves blank. Publisher's green cloth stamped in gold and black.

Illustrations: Numerous reproductions of prints and photographs in the text.

Bibliographies: Bitting, p. 396; Maggs 629.

Copies: *BNC* and *NUC* (John Crerar Library, Library Company of Philadelphia, and Library of Congress).

407. Robert, le sieur.

L'ART | DE | BIEN TRAITER. | *DIVISE' EN TROIS PARTIES*. | OUVRAGE NOUVEAU, CURIEUX, | ET FORT GALANT, | UTILE A TOUTES PERSONNES, | ET CONDITIONS. | Exactement recherché, & mis en lumiere, | *Par L. S. R.* | [ornament] | A PARIS, | Chez JEAN DU PUIS, ruë S. Jacques | à la Couronne d'or. | [rule] | M. DC. LXXIV. | *Avec Privilege du Roy*.

First edition, Jean du Puis issue, Paris, 1674. Jean du Puis, to whom the royal privilege was granted, assigned part of this edition to Frédéric Léonard (see item 408).

12mo. a^2 A-R^{12} S^4; 210 leaves, pp. [4] [1] 2-413 [414] [2]. Last leaf blank.

Note: Barbier assigns this work to le sieur Robert and Vicaire 43 accepts the attribution. In a supplemental entry, 891, Vicaire reports that the Baron Pichon has since informed him that, the author is not le sieur Robert, but le sieur Rolland, one time officier de bouche to the Princesse de Carignan. *BNC* has followed Barbier's attribution; *NUC* has the work under Robert and under title.

Bibliographies: Bitting, p. 518; Maggs 173; Schraemli (1) 419; Schraemli (2) 31; Vicaire 891.

Copies: *BMC*, *BNC*, and *NUC* (Library of Congress only). Note: The *NUC* also records a copy in the John Crerar Library but they report this is an error and that they have only the Frédéric Léonard issue.

408. Robert, le sieur.

L'ART | DE | BIEN TRAITER. | *DIVISE' EN TROIS PARTIES*. | OUVRAGE NOUVEAU, CURIEUX, | ET FORT GALANT, | UTILE A TOUTES PERSONNES, | ET CONDITIONS. | Exactement recherché, & mis en lumiere, | *Par L. S. R.* |

[woodcut] | A PARIS, | Chez FREDERIC LEONARD, Imprimeur du | Roy, ruë S. Jacques, à l'Escu de Venise. | [rule] | M. DC. LXXIV. | *Avec Privilege du Roy.*

First edition, Frédéric Léonard issue, Paris, 1674. The royal privilege was granted to Jean du Puis who assigned part of the edition to Léonard. (See item 407).

12mo. a² A-R¹² S⁴; 210 leaves, pp. [*4*] [1] 2-413 [*414*] [*2*]. Last leaf, blank, wanting in this copy.

Bibliographies: Horn-Arndt 186; Vicaire 43.

Copies: *BNC* and *NUC* (John Crerar Library).

409. Robert, le sieur.

L'ART | DE | BIEN TRAITER. | *DIVISE' EN TROIS PARTIES.* | OUVRAGE NOUVEAU, CURIEUX, | ET FORT GALANT, | UTILE A TOUTES PERSONNES, | ET CONDITIONS. | Exactement recherché, & mis en lumiere, | *Par L. S. R.* | [publisher's monogram] | A LYON, | Chez CLAUDE BACHELU, Mar- | chand Libraire, ruë Merciere, vis-à-vis | Saint Antoine. | [rule] | M. DC. XCIII. | *Avec Permission.*

Second edition, Lyon, 1693. Originally published, Paris, 1674 (items 407 and 408).

12 mo. a² A-R¹² S⁴; 210 leaves, pp. [*4*] 1-413 [*414-416*].

For attribution of authorship see item 407.

Bibliographies: Schraemli (1) 420.

Copies: No other copy of this edition located.

410. Rolle, Pierre-Nicolas, 1770-1855.

RECHERCHES | SUR LE | CULTE DE BACCHUS, | SYMBOLE DE LA FORCE REPRODUCTIVE DE LA NATURE, | CONSIDÉRÉ | SOUS SES RAPPORT GÉNÉRAUX DANS LES MYSTÈRES | D'ÉLEUSIS, | ET SOUS SES RAPPORTS PARTICULIERS DANS LES DIONYSIAQUES | ET LES TRIÉTÉRIQUES. | PAR P. N. ROLLE, | Conservateur de la Bibliothèque de la ville de Paris, Membre de la |

Société royale Antiquaires de France, de la Société Philotechnique, | et associé libre de l'Athénée des Arts. | OUVRAGE QUI A REMPORTÉ LE PRIX PROPOSÉ EN 1819 | PAR L'INSTITUT (ACADÉMIE DES INSCRIPTIONS ET BELLES-LETTRES). | TOME PREMIER. [TOME SECOND.] [TOME TROISIÈME.] | PARIS, | J. S. MERLIN, LIBRAIRE, QUAI DES AUGUSTINS, No 7. | [short rule] | 1824.

First edition, Paris, 1824.

210 x 129 mm. 3 vols. Vol. I [a]^8 b-k^8 l^4 1-23^8 24^6; 274 leaves, pp. [6] [i] ii-clxi [clxii] [1] 2-379 [380]. Vol. II. π^2 1-29^8 30^6; 240 leaves, pp. [4] [1] 2-476. Vol. III. π^2 1-32^8 33^4; 262 leaves, pp. [4] [1] 2-517 [518] [2]. Last leaf in vol. III (blank?) wanting in this copy.

Bibliographies: Oberlé (2) 37; Simon BG 1302.

Copies: *BMC*, *BNC*, and *NUC* (8 copies).

411. Rose, Louis.

LA BONNE | FERMIÈRE, | OU | ÉLÉMENS ÉCONOMIQUES, | *Utiles aux jeunes Personnes destinées* | *à cet état*. | Travaillez, prenez de la peine; | C'est le fond qui manque le moins. *La Fontaine*. | *Par M. L. R. ancien Ech. de B ...* | Revue, corrigée & augmentée par l'Auteur. | [rule] | *Prix 24 sols broché*. | [rule] | [ornament] | A LILLE, | De l'Imprimerie de J. B. HENRY, sur la | grand'Place, près la rue de Tenremonde. | [two rules] | M. DCC. LXVII. | *Avec Approbation & Privilège du Roi.*

Second edition, Lille, 1767. Originally published, Paris, 1765.

12mo. π^4 A-L^{12}; 136 leaves, pp. [i-ii] iii-viii, 1-258 [6]. Last leaf blank.

Bibliographies: Unrecorded in the bibliographies consulted.

Copies: No other copy located.

412. Rumford, Sir Benjamin Thompson, 1753-1814.

ESSAIS | POLITIQUES, | ÉCONOMIQUES ET PHILOSPHIQUES; | PAR BENJAMIN Comte RUMFORD. | X.eme ESSAI, | ORNÉ DE SEPT PLANCHES | Sur la construction des cuisines publiques | et particulières, et la fabrication de leurs | ustensiles; avec diverses remarques et | observations indiquant la manière de |

perfectionner la cuisson de quelques | alimens. | TRADUIT DE L'ANGLAIS, | PAR TANNEGUY de COURTIVRON. | [short fancy rule] | PARIS, | CH. POUGENS, Imprimeur-Libraire, quai | Voltaire, n.° 10. | PICHON, Libraire, péristile du Théâtre Favart. | [short fancy rule] | AN X. (1802).

First edition in French, Paris, 1802, of Rumford's essay "On the construction of kitchen fire-places and kitchen utensils" originally published in volume II of his *Essays, Political, Economical, and Philosophical*, London, 1799-1802. Rumford's *Essais politiques, économiques et philosophiques* were published in French in six volumes, Geneva and Paris, 1799-1806, of which edition this is volume III.

218 x 138 mm. π^2 1-8^8; 66 leaves, pp. [*4*] [i] ii-xxxvi [37] 38-126 [*2*].

Illustrations: Seven engraved plates of kitchen fireplaces.

Bibliographies: Maggs 324; Schraemli (1) 429; Vicaire 760. Horn-Arndt 330 records vols. I and II only.

Copies: *BNC* (all 6 vols.) and *NUC* (6 sets of all 6 vols.).

413. Ruscelli, Girolamo, d. 1566.

LES | SECRETS | DV SEIGNEVR | ALEXIS | PIEMONTOIS. | *Reueu, & augmenté d'une infinité* | *de rares Secrets.* | [woodcut] | *A ROVEN,* | Chez IACQVES BESONGNE, dans la | Court du Palais. | [rule] | M. DC. LII.

New edition, Rouen, 1652. Originally published in Italian under the title *De Secreti del reverendo Donno Alessio Piemontese*, Venice, 1555, and in French, Antwerp, 1557, by Christopher Plantin.

8vo. A-Bbb^8 χ1; 385 leaves, pp. [1-2] 3-384, 349-675 [676-734].

Illustrations: Woodcuts in text illustrating distilling.

Bibliographies: This edition unrecorded in the bibliographies consulted. Wheaton and Kelly 5389 records a Rouen, R. Dare, 1652 edition.

Copies: No other copy of this edition located.

414. Saint-Surin, Marie-Caroline-Rosalie de Cendrecourt de.

L'HOTEL DE CLUNY │ AU MOYEN AGE, │ PAR Mme DE SAINT-SURIN, │
SUIVI │ DES CONTENANCES DE TABLE │ ET AUTRES POÉSIES INÉDITES │
DES XVe ET XVIe │ SIÈCLES. │ [ornament] │ PARIS. │ CHEZ J. TECHENER, │
PLACE DU LOUVRE. │ 1835

First edition, Paris, 1835.

199 x 110 mm. π^2 1-14$^{8.4}$ [15]^2 χ1; 89 leaves, pp. [*4*] [i] ii-vii [viii] [9] 10-174.

Bibliographies: Bitting, p. 415.

Copies: *BMC*, *BNC*, and *NUC* (5 copies).

415. Sallengre, Albert Henrik de, 1694-1723.

ÉLOGE │ DE │ L'IVRESSE. │ [rule] │ *Nullus eris, si sunt ignavae ad pocula vires;* │
Plurima ni sicces pocula, nullus eris. │ OBSOPAEUS, de arte bibendi. │ [rule] │
NOUVELLE ÉDITION, │ Revue, corrigée, et considérablement │ augmentée. │ [short
fancy rule] │ *A BACCHOPOLIS,* │ De l'Imprimerie du vieux SILÈNE, │ L'AN DE LA
VIGNE *5555.* │ *ET A PARIS,* │ Chez MICHEL, Libraire et Commissionnaire, │ rue de
l'Arbre Sec, No. 38. │ AN VI.

New edition, Paris, 1798. Originally published, The Hague, 1714.

12mo. A-K^{12} L^6; 126 leaves, pp. [1-5] 6-250 [2]. Last leaf (blank?) wanting in this
copy.

Illustrations: Engraved frontispiece by LeRoy after Binet showing mythological figures
drinking.

Bibliographies: Simon BG 1347.

Copies: *BMC*, *BNC*, and *NUC* (5 copies).

416. Scribe, Eugène, 1791-1861.

VATEL, │ OU │ LE PETIT-FILS D'UN GRAND HOMME, │ COMÉDIE-
VAUDEVILLE EN UN ACTE, │ PAR MM. SCRIBE ET MAZÈRES; │
REPRÉSENTÉE, POUR LA PREMIÈRE FOIS, A PARIS, SUR LE THÉÂTRE │ DE

MADAME, DUCHESSE DE BERRY, PAR LES COMÉDIENS ORDINAIRES | DE SON ALTESSE ROYALE, LE 18 JANVIER 1825. | [short fancy rule] | PRIX: I fr. 50 cent. | [short fancy rule] | [printer's monogram] | PARIS, | POLLET, LIBRAIRE, ÉDITEUR DE PIÈCES DE THÉATRE, RUE | DU TEMPLE, N. 36, VIS-A-VIS CELLE CHAPON. | [short rule] | 1825.

First edition, Paris, 1825.

222 x 135 mm. [1]⁸ 2⁸ 3²; 18 leaves, pp. [1-3] 4-35 [36].

Bibliographies: Vicaire 781.

Copies: *BNC* and *NUC* (Harvard, Indiana University, and Library of Congress).

416a.   Scriptores rei rusticae

Part I:

LIBRI DE RE RVSTICA, | M. CATONIS LIB. I. | M. TERENTII VARRO- | NIS LIB. III. | *Per Petrum Victoriū, ad ueterum exemplarium* | *fidem, suæ integritati restituti.* | [vignette] | PARISIIS. | *Ex officina Roberti Stephani typographi Regij.* | M.D.XLIII.

Colophon on P8ᵛ:

EX CVDEBAT ROB. STEPHANVS | TYPOGRAPHVS REGIVS, | PARISIIS. AN. M.D. | XLIII. XVI. CAL. | AVGVSTI.

8vo. A-P⁸; 120 leaves, ff. [1] 2-113 [114-120].

Part II:

L. IVNII MODERATI COLV- | MELLAE DE RE RVSTICA | LIBRI XII. | *Eiusdem de Arboribus liber separatus ab alijs.* | [vignette] | PARISIIS. |*Ex officina Roberti Stephani typographi Regij.* | M. D. XLIII.

Colophon on K3ᵛ:

EX CVDEBAT ROB. STEPHANVS | TYPOGRAPHVS REGIVS, | PARISIIS, AN. M. D. | XLIII. XI. CAL. | SEPTEMORIS.

8vo. a-z⁸ A-I⁸ K⁴; 260 leaves, pp. [1-2] 3-498 [*22*]. Last leaf, blank.

Illustrations: Line drawing of a pruning knife and diagrams in the text.

Part III:

PALLADII RVTILII TAVRI │ AEMILIANI, VIRIILLV- │ STRIS, DE RE RVSTI- │ CA LIBRI XIIII. │ [vignette] │ PARISIIS │ *Ex officina Roberti Stephani typographi* *Regij.* │ M. D. XLIII.

8vo. Aa⁸ B⁸ Cc-Mm⁸; 96 leaves, pp. [1-2] 3-186 [*6*].

Part IV:

ENARRATIONES VOCVM │ PRISCARVM IN LIBRIS │ DE RE RVSTICA, PERGE- │ ORGIVM ALEXANDRI- │ NVM. │ *Philippi Beroaldi in libros* XIII *Columellæ* │ *Annotationes.* │ *Aldus de Dierum generibus, simúlque de umbris,* │ *horis, quæ apud Palladium.* │ [vignette] │ PARISIIS. │ *Ex officina Roberti Stephani typographi Regij.* │ M. D. XLIII.

8vo. aa-kk⁸ ll⁴; 84 leaves, unpaginated.

Part V:

PETRIVICTORII EXPLICA- │ TIONES SVARVM IN CATO- │ NEM, VARRONEM, COLVMEL- │ LAM CASTIGATIONVM. │ PARISIIS. │ *Ex officina* *Roberti Stephani typographi Regij.* │ M. D. XLIII.

8vo. a-i⁸; 72 leaves, ff. [1] 2-70 [71-72].

New edition, Paris, 1543. Originally published, Venice, 1472.

Bibliographies: Renouard 1543.2.

Copies: *NUC* (8 copies).

417. Secrets concernant les arts et metiers.

SECRETS │ CONCERNANT │ LES ARTS │ ET METIERS. │ [ornament] │ A PARIS, │ Chez CLAUDE JOMBERT, Quay des │ Augustins, à la descente du Pont-Neuf, │ à l'Image Nôtre-Dame. │ [rule] │ M. DCCXVI. │ *AVEC PRIVILEGE DU ROY.*

First edition? Paris, 1716. The "privilege" is dated 5 December 1714, but no record of an edition earlier than this of 1716 has been found.

12mo. a^8 e^4 i^8 o^4 u^2 A-Ddd$^{8.4}$ Eee^6; 332 leaves, pp. [*52*] [1] 2-610 [*2*].

Bibliographies: Wheaton and Kelly 5509.

Copies: *BMC* and *NUC* (4 copies).

418. Sémélée et Bacchus.

SÉMÉLÉE | ET | BACCHUS, | OU | RECUEIL DE CHANSONS | DE TABLE, | EXTRAITES DES MEILLEURS AUTEURS. | [ornament] | PARIS, | CHEX LES MARCHANDS DE NOUVEAUTÉS.

First edition? Paris, ca. 1820.

140 x 89 mm. A-I^6; 54 leaves, pp. [1-3] 4-108.

Illustration: Etched frontispiece of Bacchus in a chariot.

Bibliographies: Maggs 831.

Copies: No other copy located.

418a. Suzanne, Alfred.

ALFRED SUZANNE | [short wavy rule] | [fancy] LA | [fancy] Cuisine et Pâtisserie | [fancy] Anglaise et Américaine | TRAITÉ DE L'ALIMENTATION EN ANGLETERRE ET EN AMÉRIQUE | [vignette] | DEUXIEME ÉDITION | [short rule] | Illustré de nombreux dessins par Gérard TANTET et FROMENT | [short rule] | PARIS | [short rule] | L'ART CULINAIRE, 4, PLACE SAINT-MICHEL | ET CHEZ L'AUTEUR, 48, RUE MONSIEUR-LE-PRINCE | 1904 | [short rule] | Tous droits réservés.

Second edition, Paris, 1904. Originally published, Paris, 1894.

239 x 155 mm. [1]^8 2-25^8; 200 leave, pp. [1-5] 6-394 [6]. Publisher's white paper covered boards printed on the front with a repeat of the title-page and on the back with the author's monogram; red cloth spine.

Illustrations: Wood and steel engravings after drawings by Gérard Tantet and Froment and halftone photographic illustrations, all in the text.

Bibliographies: Wheaton and Kelly 5866.

Copies: *NUC* (Radcliffe College and University of California).

419. Taillevent, Guillaume Tirel, called, ca. 1315-1395.

LE VIANDIER | DE | [in red] GUILLAUME TIREL | [in red] DIT | [in red] TAILLEVENT | *Enfant de cuisine de la reine Jehanne d'Evreux*, [in red] *queu du* | [in red] *Roi Philippe de Valois* [end red] *et du duc de Normandie, Dauphin de Viennois*, | *premier queu et* [in red] *Sergent d'armes de Charles V*, [end red] *Maistre* | *des* [in red] *garnisons de cuisine de Charles VI* | 1326-1395 | Publié sur le Manuscrit de la [in red] Bibliothèque Nationale. | avec les variantes des Mss. de la [in red] Bibliothèque Mazarine [end red] et des Archives | de la Manche, précédé d'une introduction et accmompagné de notes | PAR | LE BARON JÉRÔME PICHON | *Président de la Société des Bibliophiles François* | ET | GEORGES VICAIRE | On y a joint des [in red] pièces originales [end red] relatives à Taillevent, | les reproductions [in red] des ses sceaux et de son tombeau, [end red] la réimpression | de la [in red] plus ancienne édition connue [end red] de son livre, une édition nouvelle | du [in red] plus ancien Traité de cuisine [end red] écrit en françois | et une table des matières. | [in red: seal] | A PARIS | [in red] SE VEND CHEZ TECHENER | M. D. CCC. XCII

First edition thus, Paris, 1892. No. 5 of 50 copies on papier de Hollande of a total printing of 354 copies. This copy "imprimé pour Madame Georges Vicaire."

240 x 177 mm. π^6 *a-i*^{4} a-i^4 j-u^4 [x]^6; 132 leaves, pp. [12] [i-iii] iv-lxviii [1-3] 4-178 [6]. First three and last two leaves blank. Publisher's printed wrappers enclosed in publisher's printed silk covered boards.

Illustrations: Photogravure frontispiece of Taillevent's tomb, six photogravure plates (three folding) of his tomb and of his seal and, in the text, three facsimiles from early editions of *Le Viandier*.

Loose in this volume are two inserts of four pages each: (1) a supplement printing the text of a charter granting Taillevent land near Saint Germain en Laye; (2) "Deux nouvelles pièces relatives à Taillevent."

Accompanied by:

[wrapper title] SUPPLÉMENT AU VIANDIER DE TAILLEVENT | [rule] | LE MANUSCRIT | DE LA | BIBLIOTHEQUE VATICANE | PUBLIÉ | *Avec Avant-Propos, Notes et Tables* | PAR | LE BARON JÉRÔME PICHON | ET | GEORGES VICAIRE

Paris, H. Leclerc et P. Cornuau, 1892. One of 50 copies on papier de Hollande, not numbered, of a total printing of 354 copies.

4to. π^2 a-i^4 j-n^4 o^6; 62 leaves, pp. [181-183] 184-297 [298] [6], first two and last two leaves blank. Publisher's printed wrappers.

Illustrations: Facsimile of a page of the manuscript on p. 212 in the text.

Bibliographies: Oberlé (1) 51; Oberlé (2) 47.

Copies: Only the Oberlé copy located on Holland paper.

420. Taillevent, Guillaume Tirel, called, ca. 1315-1395.

Copy 2.

Title-page as in copy 1 (item 419).

First edition thus, Paris, 1892. No. 227 of 300 copies on vélin du Marais.

235 x 155 mm. π^6 a-i^4 j-u^4 v^4 x-ee^4 [ff]^6; 132 leaves, pp. [*12*] [i-iii] iv-lxviii [1-3] 4-178 [6]. First three and last two leaves blank. Note: In this copy conjugate leaves π1 and π6 were left unbound and laid in loosely. Publisher's printed wrappers.

Illustrations: As in copy 1.

Accompanied by the Supplement.

Title: As in item 419.

One of 300 copies on vélin du Marais, not numbered, of a total printing of 354 copies.

Collation: As in item 419.

Illustrations: As in item 419.

Bibliographies: Bitting, p. 370; Horn-Arndt 602; Maggs 30 (misdating the work 1891); Schraemli (1) 387; Wheaton and Kelly 6042.

Copies: *BMC*, *BNC*, and *NUC* (7 copies).

421. Tarenne de Laval, G. P., 1763-1847.

LE PATISSIER │ A TOUT FEU, │ OU │ NOUVEAUX PRINCIPES ÉCONOMIQUES DE PATISSERIE, │ A L'USAGE DES DAMES │ ET DES PERSONNES QUI S'OCCUPENT ELLES-MÈMES │ DE LEUR CUISINE. │ Ouvrage dans lequel on enseigne à fabriquer d'une manière facile, │ et à faire cuire, quand on le veut, sans aucune espèce de four, │ dans une cheminée de cuisine ou de chambre, toutes sortes de │ feuilletages, de pâtés froids ou chauds, de brioches, de biscuits, │ de gâteaux de Savoie, et d'accessoires ou ornements pour chacun │ d'eux. │ *On y a joint un Supplément sur l'emploi des pâtes manquées │ ou de rebut, et un Vobucalaire de cuisine pâtissière.* │ PAR G. P. L., ANCIEN PATISSIER RETIRÉ. │ DEUXIÈME ÉDITION, CONSIDÉRABLEMENT AUGMENTÉE; │ AVEC SIX PLANCHES. │ [short fancy rule] │ PARIS. │ AUDOT, LIBRAIRE-ÉDITEUR, │ RUE DU PAON, 8, ÉCOLE DE MÉDECINE. │ [short rule] │ 1838.

Second edition, Paris, 1838. Originally published, Paris, also 1838.

185 x 115 mm. 1-11^{12} 12^{10}(-12$_{10}$); 141 leaves, pp. [1-5] 6-282.

Illustrations: Six engraved plates by Durau of utensils and pastry designs.

Bibliographies: Bitting, p. 455 and p. 589; Maggs 455; Vicaire 664.

Copies: *BNC* and *NUC* (University of California, Berkeley, only).

422. Tendret, Lucien.

[in red] *LUCIEN TENDRET* │ AVOCAT A BELLEY │ [short fancy rule] │ [in red] LA TABLE │ AU PAYS DE │ BRILLAT-SAVARIN │ "L'homme a créé l'art culinaire, il ne │ mange pas comme une bête, il déjeune, │ il dine, il soupe." │ *La Bête.* │ CHERBULIEZ │ [ornament] │ BELLEY │ [in red] LOUIS BAILLY FILS, ÉDITEUR │ [short rule] │ 1892

First edition, Belley, 1892.

176 x 109 mm. π1 [1]⁸ 2-17⁸ 18⁶; 143 leaves, pp. [2] [1-5] 6-283 [284]. Ordinary paper copy, after 6 copies on Japon impériale and 70 copies on Hollande.

Bibliographies: Bitting, p. 458; Maggs 564; Oberlé (1) 256; Schraemli (1) 477; Wheaton and Kelly 5925.

Copies: *BMC*, *BNC*, and *NUC* (John Crerar Library and Library of Congress). Wheaton and Kelly (Boston Public Library only).

423. Tessereau, Auguste, b. 1813.

COURS ÉLÉMENTAIRE | D'HYGIÈNE | PAR | LE D A. TESSEREAU | Professeur d'Hygiène, | vice-président de l'Association polytechnique, | vice-président de la Commission d'Hygiène du 1er arrondissement, | chevalier de la Légion d'honneur, officier de l'Instruction publique. | OUVRAGE | COURONNÉ PAR L'ACADÉMIE IMPÉRIALE DE MÉDECINE | La santé est la félicité du corps. | THALÈS. | [short rule] | TROISIÈME ÉDITION | REVUE ET CORRIGÉE | [publisher's monogram] | PARIS | LIBRAIRIE CLASSIQUE DE PAUL DUPONT | Rue de Grenelle-Saint-Honoré, 45. | [short rule] | 1868

Third edition, Paris, 1868. Originally published under the title *Cours d'hygiène*, Paris, 1855.

174 x 107 mm. π⁴(-π1) 1-18¹².⁶ [19]⁶ (signature 19 signed "20"); 171 leaves, pp. [i-v] vi [1] 2-334 [2].

Bookplate: De la Bibliothèque du Comte de Chambord (Henri V de France, duc de Bordeaux) Né en 1820. Aquise par Maggs Bros. Ltd. de Londres.

Bibliographies: This edition unrecorded in the bibliographies consulted.

Copies: *BNC*.

423a. Thiébaut de Berneaud, Arsenne, 1777-1850.

MANUEL | THÉORIQUE ET PRATIQUE. | DU | VIGNERON FRANÇAIS, | OU | L'ART DE CULTIVER LA VIGNE, DE FAIRE. | LES VINS, LES EAUX-DE-VIE

ET VINAIGRES. | CONTENANT les différentes espèccs et variétés de la vigne, ses | maladies et les moyens de les prévenir: les meilleurs procé- | dés pour faire, perfectionner, régir et conserver les vins, les | eaux-de-vie et vinaigres, ainsi que la manière de préparer | avec ces substances toutes sortes de liqueurs, de gouverner | une cave, etc., etc.; enfin, de profiter avec avantage de tout | ce qui nous vient de la vigne; suivi d'un coup d'oeil sur les | maladies particulières au vigneron. | PAR M. THIÉBAUT DE BERNEAUD, | Secrétaire prepétuel de la Société Linnéenne de Paris, Membre de | plusieurs Sociétés Savantes et d'Agriculture de la France et de | l'Étranger. | TROISMÈME ÉDITION, | *Revue, corrigée, augmentée et ornée de figures.* | [short fancy rule] | PARIS, | RORET, LIBRAIRE, RUE HAUTEFEUILLE, | AU COIN DE CELLE DU BATTOIR. | 1827.

Third edition, Paris, 1827. Originally published, Paris, 1823.

147 x 89 mm. π1 χ1 1-29⁶ 30²; 178 leaves, pp. [4] [1] 2-351 [352]. Beige paper printed wrappers; 36 page publisher's catalog bound in at the end.

Illustrations: Engraved folding plate in three sections labeled *"Planche I."* *"Planche II."* and *"Planche III."* illustrating tools and equipment used by a vigneron.

Bibliographies: Oberlé (2) 200.

Copies: *BNC*; *NUC* (Franklin Institute, Philadelphia, and Harvard).

424. Le Thresor de sante.

LE | THRESOR | DE SANTE', | OV, | MESNAGE DE LA VIE | HVMAINE. | *Diuisé en dix Liures.* | Lesquels traictent amplement de toutes sortes de | Viandes & Breuuages, ensemble de leur | qualité & preparation. | *Oeuure nouuelle, autant curieuse & recerchee,* | *qu'vtile & necessaire.* | Faict par vn des plus celebres & fameux Medecins | de ce siecle. | [publisher's device with letter press to side, bottom to top: VNIVERSITAS RERVM, VT [top to bottom] PVLVIS, IN MANV IEHOVAE. | *A LYON,* | Chez Iean Ant. Hugnetan, ruë Merciere à la Sphere. | [short rule] | *M. DC. XVI.* | Auec Priuilege du Roy.

Second edition, Lyon, 1616. Originally published, Lyon, 1607.

Note: The colophon in this edition reads, "[within a border of type ornaments] *A LYON,* | De l'Imprimerie d'Estien- | ne Seruain. | [short rule] | M. DCVII." As the pagination in the 1607 and 1616 editions are the same, and as the colophon in each is dated 1607, it may be that the 1616 copies are a re-issue of the first edition, with a new title-page, rather than a second edition.

8vo. π1 A-Oo⁸; 297 leaves, pp. [2] 1-562 [30]. Last two leaves blank. Vicaire calls for ten unnumbered preliminary leaves, containing the dedicatory epistle, lacking in this copy and in the only other copy located (Folger Library).

Bibliographies: Vicaire 835. The first edition, Lyon, 1607, is recorded in Bitting, p. 607; Simon BG 1462; and Vicaire 834.

Copies: *NUC* (Folger Library only). The first edition is in *BMC* and *NUC* (Library of Congress only).

425. Traité de confiture.

TRAITE' | DE CONFITURE, | OU LE NOUVEAU | ET PARFAIT | CONFITURIER; | QUI ENSEIGNE LA MANIERE DE BIEN | faire toutes sortes de Confitures tant seches que | liquides, au sucre, à demy sucre, & sans sucre, | au miel, au moust, à l'eau, sel & vinaigre. | Des Compostes, des Pastes, des Sirops, & Gelées | de toutes sortes de fruits. | Des Dragées, Biscuits, Macaron, & Massepain. | Des Breuvages délicieux, des Eaux de liqueurs de | toute façon, & plusieurs autres délicatesses de | bouche. | *Avec l'Instruction & Devoirs des Chefs d'Office de* | *Fruiterie & de Sommelerie.* | [ornament] | A PARIS, | Chez THOMAS GUILLAIN, sur le Quay | des Augustins, à la descente du Pont-neuf, | à l'Image S. Loüis. | [rule] | M. DC. LXXXIX. | *AVEC PRIVILEGE DV ROY.*

First edition, Paris, 1689.

12mo. a⁸ A-Ee⁸·⁴ Ff⁴; 180 leaves, pp. [16] 1-168, 167-324 [18].

Bibliographies: Bitting, p. 608; Crahan 220; Drexel 503; Horn-Arndt 206; Vicaire 839.

Copies: *NUC* (John Crerar Library and Library of Congress).

426. Trifet, Hippolyte-Alexandre.

DU CAFÉ | DE | SON ACTION SUR L'HOMME | A L'ÉTAT DE SANTÉ ET A L'ÉTAT DE MALADIE, | PAR | LE DR TRIFET, | LAURÉAT DE LA FACULTÉ DE MÉDECINE DE PARIS, | ANCIEN INTERNE EN MÉDECINE ET EN CHIRURGIE DES HOPITAUX | ET HOSPICES CIVILS DE LA MÊME VILLE, | MEMBRE DE L'ÉCOLE PRATIQUE, ETC. | [ornament] | PRIX: 1 FRANC. |

[ornament] | PARIS. | MOQUET, LIBRAIRE-ÉDITEUR, | COUR DE ROHAN, 3, | PASSAGE DU COMMERCE; | ET CHEZ L'AUTEUR, RUE HAUTEVILLE, 18 BIS. | [short rule] | 1846.

First edition, second issue with a cancel title-page, Paris, 1846. Originally published under the title *Histoire et physiologie du café, de son action sur l'homme, à l'état de santé et à l'état de maladie*, Paris, 1846.

224 x 134 mm. [1]⁴ ($\pm 1_1$) 2-3⁸; 20 leaves, pp. [1-3] 4-40. Publisher's printed wrappers.

Bibliographies: This issue unrecorded in the bibliographies consulted. Oberlé (1) 750 records the first issue.

Copies: No other copy of the second issue located. Copies of the first issue are in *BMC*, *BNC*, and *NUC* (Boston Public Library and Harvard).

427. La Troupe des bons enfans.

LA TROUPE | DES | BONS ENFANS, | ASSEMBLÉS | A L'HOTEL DES RAGOUTS. | *Où les Curieux des bons repas auront une* | *satisfaction extraordinaire.* | [vignette] | A LELIS, | Chez GODERFE, rue de Nenemya.

First edition? Lille, ca. 1800. Note: The John Crerar catalogue record in the *NUC* dates this as from the third quarter of the seventeenth century, but the absence of the long "s" in the printer's font suggests it could not have been printed much before 1800.

151 x 90 mm. A⁶; 6 leaves, pp. [1-2] 3-11 [12].

Illustration: Woodcut vignette on title-page.

Bibliographies: Unrecorded in the bibliographies consulted.

Copies: *NUC* (John Crerar Library only). *BMC* records two reprints: Rouen [1840?] and London, 1931.

428. Venette, Nicolas, 1633-1698.

L'ART | DE TAILLER | LES ARBRES | FRUITIERS, | Avec un Dictionaire des mots dont se ser- | vent les Jardiniers, en parlant | des Arbres. | Et un Traité de l'usage des Fruits des Arbres, | pour se conserver en santé, ou pour | se guerir, lors que l'on est malade. | *Avec une liste des Fruits fondans pendant* | *toute l'Année.* | [publisher's monogram] | A PARIS, | Chez CHARLES DE SERCY, au sixiéme | Pilier de la Grand' Salle du Palais, vis-à- | vis la Montée de la Cour des Aydes, | à la Bonne-Foy couronnée. | [short rule] | M. DC. LXXXIII. | *Avec Privilege du Roy.*

First edition, Paris, 1683.

12mo. a^8 e^4 A-O$^{8.4}$; 96 leaves, pp. [*24*] 1-71 [72], ^{2}[*6*] 1-86 [87-90]. Bound with *Abregé pour les arbres nains et autres* by Jean Laurent (item 259).

Illustrations: Three folding woodcuts and four others in the text illustrating pruning.

Bibliographies: Unrecorded in the bibliographies consulted.

Copies: *BMC*, *BNC*, and *NUC* (Massachusetts Horticultural Society and National Agricultural Library).

429. Verdot, C.

HISTORIOGRAPHIE | DE LA TABLE, | OU | ABRÉGÉ HISTORIQUE, PHILOSOPHIQUE, | ANECDOTIQUE ET LITTÉRAIRE DES | SUBSTANCES ALIMENTAIRES ET DES | OBJETS QUI LEUR SONT RELATIFS, | DES PRINCIPALES FÊTES, MOEURS | USAGES ET COUTUMES DE TOUS | LES PEUPLES ANCIENS | ET MODERNES. | Dédié à l'Académie | DE L'INDUSTRIE AGRICOLE, MANUFACTURIÈRE | ET COMMERCIALE, | PAR C. VERDOT, | Membre de ladite Académie. | [ornament] | DEUXIÈME ÉDITION. | [ornament] | PARIS, | CHEZ L'AUTEUR, | RUE DE SEINE, FAUBOURG SAINT-GERMAIN, | N. 16, | SÉGUIEN, RUE DU FAUBOURG-SAINT-MARTIN, No 64, | ET CHEZ TOUS LES PRINCIPAUX LIBRAIRES. | 1833.

Second edition, Paris, 1833. Originally published, Paris, also 1833.

150 x 91 mm. π^6 2π^2 1-32^6; 200 leaves, pp. [i-v] vi-viii [ix-xvi] [1] 2-384. Publisher's printed wrappers.

Bibliographies: Bitting, p. 477; Drexel 548; Oberlé (1) 511; Vicaire 859; Wheaton and Kelly 6216.

Copies: *BNC* and *NUC* (5 copies).

430. Vergnaud, Armand-Denis, 1791-1885.

MANUELS-RORET. | [short rule] | NOUVEAU MANUEL COMPLET | DU | BRASSEUR | OU | L'ART DE FAIRE TOUTES SORTES DE BIÈRES | CONTENANT | Les Procédés de cet art tels qu'ils sont usités en Angleterre, en France, | en Belgique et en Allemagne, avec un exposé des altérations fraudu- | leuses de la bière, et des moyens de les découvrir; suivi d'un | exposé des perfectionnements les plus récents dans cet art, | et de l'analyse, la valeur réelle des houblons, et leur | conservation. | Par MM. RIFFAULT, VERGNAUD | ET | MALEPEYRE. | *Nouvelle Edition, revue, corrigée et augmentée.* | PARIS | A LA LIBRAIRIE ENCYCLOPÉDIQUE DE RORET, | RUE HAUTEFEUILLE, 12. | 1853

New edition, Paris, 1853. Originally published under the title *Manuel théorique et pratique du brasseur . . .* Paris, 1827. The other authors mentioned on the title-page are Jean-René-Denis Riffault des Hêtres, 1754?-1826, and François Malepeyre, 1794-1877.

145 x 89 mm. π^4 1-30^6 31^2 (-31$_2$); 185 leaves, pp. [i-v] vi-viii [1] 2-362. Folding letterpress table facing p. 106, not reckoned in the pagination.

Illustrations: Four lithographed folding plates and one wood engraving on p. 129 all showing brewing equipment.

Bibliographies: Unrecorded in the bibliographies consulted.

Copies: *BNC* and *NUC* (New York Public Library only).

431. Vergnette de Lamotte, Viscomte Alfred de.

LE VIN | PAR | A. DE VERGNETTE-LAMOTTE | Correspondant de l'Institut. | [short rule] | OUVRAGE ORNÉ DE 3 PLANCHES EN COULEUR ET DE 31 GRAVURES NOIRES | [short rule] | DEUXIÈME ÉDITION | [short rule] | PARIS | LIBRAIRIE AGRICOLE DE LA MAISON RUSTIQUE | 26, RUE JACOB, 26 | [short rule] | 1868 | Tous droits réservés.

Second edition, Paris, 1868. Originally published, Paris, 1867.

183 x 117 mm. 1-22$^{12.6}$ 23^4; 202 leaves, pp. [2] [i-v] vi-xiv [15] 16-402 [2]. First and last leaves, both blank, are pasted to the publisher's printed wrappers. 36 page publisher's catalogue, dated juillet 1869, bound in at the end.

Illustrations: Three sepia colored lithographed plates of microscope slides dated Mars 1858 and thirty-one wood engravings in the text.

Bibliographies: Simon BV, p. 22; Vicaire 859.

Copies: *BNC* and *NUC* (University of California, Berkeley, only).

432. Viala, Pierre, 1859-1936.

TRAITÉ GÉNÉRAL DE VITICULTURE | [short rule] | AMPÉLOGRAPHIE | PUBLIÉE SOUS LA DIRECTION DE | P. VIALA | Inspecteur général de la Viticulture, | Professeur de Viticulture à l'Institut national agronomique, | Membre de la Société nationale d'Agriculture, Docteur ès sciences naturelles. | [short rule] | SECRÉTAIRE GÉNÉRAL | V. VERMOREL | Sénateur, | Président du Comice agricole et viticole du Beaujolais, | Lauréat de la Prime d'honneur du Rhône, | Membre correspondant de la Société nationale d'Agriculture. | [short rule] | AVEC LA COLLABORATION DE | A. BACON, A. BARBIER, L. BELLE, A. BERGET, P. BESSON, A. BOUCHARD, A. BREIL, L. BRIN, R. BRUNET, | F. BUHL, M. CARLUCCI, D. L. DE CASTRO, G. CAZEAUX-CAZALET, L. CHAMBRON, R. CHANDON DE BRIAILLES, J.-B. CHAPELLE, | B. CHAUZIT, F. CONVERT, C. DA COSTA, G. COUANON, G. COUDERC, J. DUARTE D'OLIVEIRA, E. DURAND, G. FOËX, | V. GANZIN, P. GERVAIS, R. GOETHE, H. GORRIA, J. GREC, J. GUICHERD, J.-M. GUILLON, GY DE ISTWANFFI, R. JANINI, | V. KOSINSKI, H. DE LAPPARENT, R. MARÈS, MARQUÈS DE CARVALHO, P. MARSAIS, Abbé A. MATHIEU, C. MICHAUT, | A. MILLARDET, N. MINANGOIN, G. MOLON, P. MOUILLEFERT, T.-V. MUNSON, G. N. NICOLEANU, | J. NIEGO, G. NIKOLOFF, CH. OBERLIN, E. OTTAVI, P. PACOTTET, F. PAULSEN, F. PÉCHOUTRE, N. PETROVITCH, | P. PLAMENATZ, A. POTEBNIA, G. RABAULT, L. REICH, F. RICHTER, L.-H. ROBREDO, L. ROUGIER, Cte J. DE ROVASENDA, | J. ROY-CHEVRIER, G. DE LOS SALMONES, E. ET R. SALOMON, J. A. SANNINO, F. SEGAPELI, L. SÉMICHON, T. SIMPÉE, | G. SONCINI, A. TACUSSEL, B. TAÏROFF, CH. TALLAVIGNES, D. TAMARO, V. THIÉBAULT, T. TODOROVITCH, Dr L. TRABUT, | V. VANNUCCINI, A. VERNEUIL, Cte DE VILLENEUVE, XANTHOPOULOS, E. ZACHAREWICZ, V. C. M. DE ZUÑIGA. | [short rule] | TOME I | [short rule] | PARIS | MASSON ET Cie, ÉDITEURS | LIBRAIRES DE L'ACADÉMIE DE MÉDECINE | 120, BOULEVARD SAINT-GERMAIN (6e) | [short rule] | 1910

Title-page of second volume:

TRAITÉ GÉNÉRAL DE VITICULTURE | [short rule] | AMPÉLOGRAPHIE | PUBLIÉE SOUS LA DIRECTION DE | P. VIALA | Inspecteur général de la Viticulture, | Professeur de Viticulture à l'Institut national agronomique, | Membre de la Société nationale d'Agriculture, Docteur ès sciences naturelles. | [short rule] | SECRÉTAIRE GÉNÉRAL | V. VERMOREL | Président du Comice agricole et viticole du Beaujolais, | Lauréat de la Prime d'honneur du Rhône, | Membre correspondant de la Société nationale d'Agriculture. | [short rule] | AVEC LA COLLABORATION DE | A. BARBIER, A. BERGET, P. BESSON, D. BETHMONT, A. BOUCHARD, G. BOYER, L. BRIN, R. BRUNET, CARLUCCI, | G. CAZEAUX-CAZALET, R. CHANDON DE BRIAILLES, J.-B. CHAPELLE, B. CHAUZIT, F. CONVERT, C. DA COSTA, G. COUANON, | G. COUDERC, J. DUARTE D'OLIVEIRA, E. DURAND, A. C. FETWADJEFF, G. FOËX, V. GANZIN, GENNADIUS, P. GERVAIS, | R. GOETHE, H. GORRIA, J. GUICHERD, J.-M. GUILLON, R. JANINI, V. KOSINSKI, F. KÖVESSI, H. DE LAPPARENT, G. LAVERGNE, | J. LEVY-ZIVI, H. MARÈS, R. MARÈS, Abbé A. MATHIEU, Bon A. MENDOLA, C. MICHAUT, A. MILLARDET, | P. MOUILLEFERT, T.-V. MUNSON, NICOLEANU, J. NIEGO, NIKOLOFF, CH. OBERLIN, | E. OTTAVI, P. PACOTTET, A. POTEBNIA, G. RABAULT, L. REICH, F. RICHTER, L. ROUGIER, | Cte J. DE ROVASENDA, J. ROY-CHEVRIER, G. DE LOS SALMONES, E. ET R. SALOMON, F. G. SANNINO, B. SEGAPELI, | T. SIMPÉE, G. SONCINI, A. TACUSSEL, B. TAÏROFF, CH. TALLAVIGNES, D. TAMARO, Dr TRABUT, TROUARD-RIOLLE, | V. VANNUCCINI, A. VERNEUIL, Cte DE VILLENEUVE, E. ZACHAREWICZ, V. C. M. DE ZARRIGA. | [short rule] | PEINTURES DE A. KREŸDER ET J. TRONCY | [short rule] | TOME II | [short rule] | DIRECTION : 5, RUE GAY-LUSSAC, PARIS | ADMINISTRATION : VILLEFRANCHE-SUR-SAONE (RHÔNE) | [short rule] | 1901

Title-page of third volume:

TRAITÉ GÉNÉRAL DE VITICULTURE | [short rule] | AMPÉLOGRAPHIE | PUBLIÉE SOUS LA DIRECTION DE | P. VIALA | Inspecteur général de la Viticulture, | Professeur de Viticulture à l'Institut national agronomique, | Membre de la Société nationale d'Agriculture, Docteur ès sciences naturelles. | [short rule] | SECRÉTAIRE GÉNÉRAL | V. VERMOREL | Président du Comice agricole et viticole du Beaujolais, | Lauréat de la Prime d'honneur du Rhône, | Membre correspondant de la Société nationale d'Agriculture. | [short rule] | AVEC LA COLLABORATION DE | A. BACON, A. BARBIER, A. BERGET, P. BESSON, D. BETHMONT, A. BOUCHARD, G. BOYER, L. BRIN, F. BUHL, CARLUCCI, | G. CAZEAUX-CAZALET, L. CHAMBRON, R. CHANDON DE BRIAILLES, J.-B. CHAPELLE, B. CHAUZIT, F. CONVERT, C. DA COSTA | G. COUANON, G. COUDERC, J. DUARTE D'OLIVEIRA, E. DURAND, G. FOËX, V. GANZIN, GENNADIUS, | P. GERVAIS, R. GOETHE, H. GORRIA, J. GUICHERD, J.-M.

GUILLON, R. JANINI, V. KOSINSKI, F. KÖVESSI, H. DE LAPPARENT, | G. LAVERGNE, J. LEVY-ZIVI, R. MARÈS, Abbé A. MATHIEU, Bon A. MENDOLA, C. MICHAUT, A. MILLARDET, | P. MOUILLEFERT, T.-V. MUNSON, G. N. NICOLEANO, J. NIEGO, NIKOLOFF, CH. OBERLIN, | E. OTTAVI, P. PACOTTET, A. POTEBNIA, G. RABAULT, L. REICH, F. RICHTER, L. ROUGIER, | Cte J. DE ROVASENDA, J. ROY-CHEVRIER, G. DE LOS SALMONES, E. ET R. SALOMON, F. G. SANNINO, B. SEGAPELI, | T. SIMPÉE, G. SONCINI, A. TACUSSEL, B. TAÏROFF, CH. TALLAVIGNES, D. TAMARO, Dr L. TRABUT, G. TROUARD-RIOLLE, | V. VANNUCCINI, A. VERNEUIL, Cte DE VILLENEUVE, E. ZACHAREWICZ, V. C. M. DE ZUNIGA. | [short rule] | PEINTURES DE A. KREŸDER ET J. TRONCY | [short rule] | TOME III | [short rule] | PARIS | MASSON ET Cie, ÉDITEURS | LIBRAIRES DE L'ACADÉMIE DE MÉDECINE | 120, BOULEVARD SAINT-GERMAIN (6e) | [short rule] | 1902

Title-page of fourth volume:

TRAITÉ GÉNÉRAL DE VITICULTURE | [short rule] | AMPÉLOGRAPHIE | PUBLIÉE SOUS LA DIRECTION DE | P. VIALA | Inspecteur général de la Viticulture, | Professeur de Viticulture à l'Institut national agronomique, | Membre de la Société nationale d'Agriculture, Docteur ès sciences naturelles. | [short rule] | SECRÉTAIRE GÉNÉRAL | V. VERMOREL | Président du Comice agricole et viticole du Beaujolais, | Lauréat de la Prime d'honneur du Rhône, | Membre correspondant de la Société nationale d'Agriculture. | [short rule] | AVEC LA COLLABORATION DE | A. BACON, A. BARBIER, A. BERGET, P. BESSON, D. BETHMONT, A. BOUCHARD, G. BOYER, L. BRIN, F. BUHL, M. CARLUCCI, | G. CAZEAUX-CAZALET, L. CHAMBRON, R. CHANDON DE BRIAILLES, J.-B. CHAPELLE, B. CHAUZIT, F. CONVERT, C. DA COSTA, | G. COUANON, G. COUDERC, J. DUARTE D'OLIVEIRA, E. DURAND, G. FOËX, V. GANZIN, GENNADIUS, | P. GERVAIS, R. GOETHE, H. GORRIA, J. GUICHERD, J.-M. GUILLON, R. JANINI, V. KOSINSKI, F. KÖVESSI, H. DE LAPPARENT, | G. LAVERGNE, J. LEVY-ZIVI, R. MARÈS, Abbé A. MATHIEU, Bon A. MENDOLA, C. MICHAUT, A. MILLARDET, | P. MOUILLEFERT, T.-V. MUNSON, G. N. NICOLEANO, J. NIEGO, NIKOLOFF, CH. OBERLIN, | E. OTTAVI, P. PACOTTET, F. PAULSEN, A. POTEBNIA, G. RABAULT, L. REICH, F. RICHTER, L. ROUGIER, | Cte J. DE ROVASENDA, J. ROY-CHEVRIER, G. DE LOS SALMONES, E. ET R. SALOMON, J. A. SANNINO, F. SEGAPELI, | T. SIMPÉE, G. SONCINI, A. TACUSSEL, B. TAÏROFF, CH. TALLAVIGNES, D. TAMARO, Dr L. TRABUT, G. TROUARD-RIOLLE, | V. VANNUCCINI, A. VERNEUIL, Cte DE VILLENEUVE, E. ZACHAREWICZ, V. C. M. DE ZUÑIGA | [short rule] | PEINTURES DE A. KREŸDER ET J. TRONCY | [short rule] | TOME

IV | [short rule] | PARIS | MASSON ET Cie, ÉDITEURS | LIBRAIRES DE L'ACADÉMIE DE MÉDECINE | 120, BOULEVARD SAINT-GERMAIN (6e) | [short rule] | 1903

Title-page of fifth volume:

TRAITÉ GÉNÉRAL DE VITICULTURE | [short rule] | AMPÉLOGRAPHIE | PUBLIÉE SOUS LA DIRECTION DE | P. VIALA | Inspecteur général de la Viticulture, | Professeur de Viticulture à l'Institut national agronomique, | Membre de la Société nationale d'Agriculture, Docteur ès sciences naturelles. | [short rule] | SECRÉTAIRE GÉNÉRAL | V. VERMOREL | Président du Comice agricole et viticole du Beaujolais, | Lauréat de la Prime d'honneur du Rhône, | Membre correspondant de la Société nationale d'Agriculture. | [short rule] | AVEC LA COLLABORATION DE | A. BACON, A. BARBIER, A. BERGET, P. BESSON, D. BETHMONT, A. BOUCHARD, G. BOYER, L. BRIN, F. BUHL, M. CARLUCCI, | D. L. DE CASTRO, G. CAZEAUX-CAZALET, L. CHAMBRON, R. CHANDON DE BRIAILLES, J.-B. CHAPELLE, B. CHAUZIT, F. CONVERT, | C. DA COSTA, G. COUANON, G. COUDERC, J. DUARTE D'OLIVEIRA, E. DURAND, G. FOËX, V. GANZIN, GENNADIUS, | P. GERVAIS, R. GOETHE, H. GORRIA, J. GUICHERD, J.-M. GUILLON, R. JANINI, V. KOSINSKI, F. KÖVESSI, H. DE LAPPARENT, | C. LAVERGNE, J. LEVY-ZIVI, R. MARÈS, MARQUÈS DE CARVALHO, Abbé A. MATHIEU, Bon A. MENDOLA, C. MICHAUT, | A. MILLARDET, P. MOUILLEFERT, T.-V. MUNSON, G. N. NICOLEANO, J. NIEGO, NIKOLOFF, CH. OBERLIN, | E. OTTAVI, P. PACOTTET, F. PAULSEN, A. POTEBNIA, G. RABAULT, L. REICH, F. RICHTER, L. ROUGIER, | Cte J. DE ROVASENDA, J. ROY-CHEVRIER, G. DE LOS SALMONES, E. ET R. SALOMON, J. A. SANNINO, F. SEGAPELI, | T. SIMPÉE, G. SONCINI, A. TACUSSEL, B. TAÏROFF, CH. TALLAVIGNES, D. TAMARO, Dr L. TRABUT, G. TROUARD-RIOLLE, | V. VANNUCCINI, A. VERNEUIL, Cte DE VILLENEUVE, E. ZACHAREWICZ, V. C. M. DE ZUÑIGA. | [short rule] | PEINTURES DE A. KREŸDER ET J. TRONCY | [short rule] | TOME V | [short rule] | PARIS | MASSON ET Cie, ÉDITEURS | LIBRAIRES DE L'ACADÉMIE DE MÉDECINE | 120, BOULEVARD SAINT-GERMAIN (6e) | [short rule] | 1904

Title-page of sixth volume:

TRAITÉ GÉNÉRAL DE VITICULTURE | [short rule] | AMPÉLOGRAPHIE | PUBLIÉE SOUS LA DIRECTION DE | P. VIALA | Inspecteur général de la Viticulture, | Professeur de Viticulture à l'Institut national agronomique, | Membre de la Société nationale d'Agriculture, Docteur ès sciences naturelles. | [short rule] | SECRÉTAIRE GÉNÉRAL | V. VERMOREL | Président du Comice agricole et viticole du Beaujolais, | Lauréat de la Prime d'honneur du Rhône, | Membre correspondant de la Société nationale d'Agriculture. | [short rule] | AVEC LA

COLLABORATION DE │ A. BACON, A. BARBIER, L. BELLE, A. BERGET, P. BESSON, D. BETHMONT, A. BOUCHARD, G. BOYER, A. BREIL, L. BRIN, │ F. BUHL, M. CARLUCCI, D. L. DE CASTRO, G. CAZEAUX-CAZALET, L. CHAMBRON, R. CHANDON DE BRIAILLES, J.-B. CHAPELLE, │ B. CHAUZIT, F. CONVERT, C. DA COSTA, G. COUANON, G. COUDERC, J. DUARTE D'OLIVEIRA, E. DURAND, G. FOËX, │ V. GANZIN, GENNADIUS, P. GERVAIS, R. GOETHE, H. GORRIA, J. GREC, J. GUICHERD, J.-M. GUILLON, R. JANINI, │ V. KOSINSKI, F. KÖVESSI, H. DE LAPPARENT, G. LAVERGNE, J. LEVY-ZIVI, R. MARÈS, MARQUÈS DE CARVALHO, │ Abbé A. MATHIEU, Bon A. MENDOLA, C. MICHAUT, A. MILLARDET, N. MINANGOIN, P. MOUILLEFERT, │ T.-V. MUNSON, G. N. NICOLEANO, J. NIEGO, G. NIKOLOFF, CH. OBERLIN, E. OTTAVI, P. PACOTTET, │ F. PAULSEN, A. POTEBNIA, G. RABAULT, L. REICH, F. RICHTER, L.-H. ROBREDO, L. ROUGIER, │ Cte J. DE ROVASENDA, J. ROY-CHEVRIER, G. DE LOS SALMONES, E. ET R. SALOMON, J. A. SANNINO, F. SEGAPELI, │ T. SIMPÉE, G. SONCINI, A. TACUSSEL, B. TAÏROFF, CH. TALLAVIGNES, D. TAMARO, Dr L. TRABUT, G. TROUARD-RIOLLE, │ V. VANNUCCINI, A. VERNEUIL, Cte DE VILLENEUVE, E. ZACHAREWICZ, V. C. M. DE ZUÑIGA. │ [short rule] │ PEINTURES DE A. KREŸDER ET J. TRONCY │ [short rule] │ TOME VI │ [short rule] │ PARIS │ MASSON ET Cie, ÉDITEURS │ LIBRAIRES DE L'ACADÉMIE DE MÉDECINE │ 120, BOULEVARD SAINT-GERMAIN (6e) │ [short rule] │ 1905

Title-page of seventh volume:

TRAITÉ GÉNÉRAL DE VITICULTURE │ [short rule] │ AMPÉLOGRAPHIE │ PUBLIÉE SOUS LA DIRECTION DE │ P. VIALA │ Inspecteur général de la Viticulture, │ Professeur de Viticulture à l'Institut national agronomique, │ Membre de la Société nationale d'Agriculture, Docteur ès sciences naturelles. │ [short rule] │ SECRÉTAIRE GÉNÉRAL │ V. VERMOREL │ Sénateur │ Président du Comice agricole et viticole du Beaujolais, │ Lauréat de la Prime d'honneur du Rhône, │ Membre correspondant de la Société nationale d'Agriculture. │ [short rule] │ AVEC LA COLLABORATION DE │ A. BACON, A. BARBIER, L. BELLE, A. BERGET, P. BESSON, A. BOUCHARD, A. BREIL, L. BRIN, │ F. BUHL, M. CARLUCCI, D. L. DE CASTRO, G. CAZEAUX-CAZALET, L. CHAMBRON, R. CHANDON DE BRIAILLES, J.-B. CHAPELLE, │ B. CHAUZIT, F. CONVERT, C. DA COSTA, G. COUANON, G. COUDERC, J. DUARTE D'OLIVEIRA, E. DURAND, G. FOËX, │ V. GANZIN, P. GERVAIS, R. GOETHE, H. GORRIA, J. GREC, J. GUICHERD, J.-M. GUILLON, GY DE ISTWANFFI, R. JANINI, │ V. KOSINSKI, H. DE LAPPARENT, R. MARÈS, MARQUÈS DE CARVALHO, Abbé A. MATHIEU, C. MICHAUT, │ A. MILLARDET, N. MINANGOIN, G. MOLON, P. MOUILLEFERT, T.-V. MUNSON, │ G. N. NICOLEANU, J. NIEGO, G. NIKOLOFF, CH. OBERLIN, E. OTTAVI, P. PACOTTET, F. PAULSEN, F. PÉCHOUTRE, │ P. PLAMENATZ, A. POTEBNIA, G. RABAULT, L. REICH, F.

RICHTER, L.-H. ROBREDO, L. ROUGIER, Cte J. DE ROVASENDA, | J. ROY-CHEVRIER, G. DE LOS SALMONES, E. ET R. SALOMON, J. A. SANNINO, F. SEGAPELI, T. SIMPÉE, | G. SONCINI, A. TACUSSEL, B. TAÏROFF, CH. TALLAVIGNES, D. TAMARO, V. THIÉBAULT, T. TODOROVITCH, Dr L. TRABUT, | V. VANNUCCINI, A. VERNEUIL, Cte DE VILLENEUVE, XANTHOPOULOS, E. ZACHAREWICZ, V. C. M. DE ZUÑIGA. | [short rule] | TOME VII | [short rule] | PARIS | MASSON ET Cie, ÉDITEURS | LIBRAIRES DE L'ACADÉMIE DE MÉDECINE | 120, BOULEVARD SAINT-GERMAIN (6e) | [short rule] | 1909

First edition, Paris, 1901-1909.

344 x 247 mm. 7 vols. Vol. I. π^4 [1]^4 2-90^4 91^6; 370 leaves, pp. [i-v] vi-viii [1-3] 4-729 [730] [2]. Last leaf blank. Vol. II. π^2 1-50^4 51^2; 204 leaves, pp. [1-5] 6-408. Vol. III. π^2 1-48^4 49^2; 196 leaves, pp. [1-5] 6-392. Vol. IV. π^2 1-46^4 47^2; 188 leaves, pp. [1-5] 6-374 [2]. Last leaf blank. Vol. V. π^2 1-44^4 45^2; 180 leaves, pp. [1-5] 6-354 [2] [355] 356-358. Vol. VI. π^2 1-59^4; 238 leaves, pp. [1-5] 6-476. Vol. VII. π^4 1-50^4; 204 leaves, pp. [1-7] 8-408.

Illustrations. Vol. I. 70 black and white lithographed plates of varieties of grapes and numerous illustrations in the text. Vols. II-VI. 100 chromolithographed plates of varieties of grapes in each volume.

Bibliographies: Crahan 743; Nissen 2059; Oberlé (2) 276; Simon BV, p. 60.

Copies: *BMC* and *NUC* (8 copies).

433. Viard, Alexandre.

LE | CUISINIER IMPÉRIAL, | OU | L'ART DE FAIRE LA CUISINE | ET LA PATISSERIE | POUR TOUTES LES FORTUNES; | AVEC différentes Recettes d'Office et de Fruits | confits, et la manière de servir une Table | depuis vingt jusqu'à soixante Couverts. | PAR A. VIARD, Homme de bouche. | [short fancy rule] | A PARIS, | Chez BARBA, libraire, palais du Tribunal, galerie | derrière le Théâtre Français, no. 51, et galerie | des Libraires, vis-à-vis le passage Virginie, no. 14. | M. DCCCVI.

First edition, Paris, 1806.

195 x 120 mm. π^2 a^4 1-28^8 29^4 30^2; 236 leaves, pp. [i-v] vi-xii [1] 2-459 [460]. First leaf (blank or half-title) wanting in this copy.

Bibliographies: Crahan 471; Vicaire 860; Wheaton and Kelly 6232.

Copies: *BNC* and *NUC* (Radcliffe only).

433a. Viard, Alexandre.

LE │ CUISINIER ROYAL, │ OU │ L'ART DE FAIRE LA CUISINE │ ET LA
PÂTISSERIE, │ POUR TOUTES LES FORTUNES; │ Avec la manière de servir une
Table depuis vingt jusqu'à │ soixante Couverts. │ HUITIÈME ÉDITION, │ REVUE ET
CORRIGÉE; │ PAR A. VIARD, Homme de Bouche. │ AUGMENTÉE d'une Notice
sur les Vins, par M. M. S. U. │ [ornament] │ PARIS, │ CHEZ BARBA, LIBRAIRE,
PALAIS ROYAL, │ DERRIÈRE LE THÉATRE FRANÇAIS, No 51. │ 1814.

Eighth edition, Paris, 1814. Originally published under the title *Le Cuisinier impérial*,
Paris, 1806 (item 433). This is the first edition under this title.

199 x 123 mm. π^8 1-28^8; 232 leaves, pp. [i-vii] viii-xvi [1] 2-447 [448].

Bibliographies: Vicaire 860 in a note.

Copies: *BNC* and *NUC* (University of California, Berkeley, only).

434. Viard, Alexandre.

LE │ CUISINIER ROYAL, │ OU │ L'ART DE FAIRE LA CUISINE │ ET LA
PÂTISSERIE, │ POUR TOUTES LES FORTUNES; │ Avec la manière de servir une
Table depuis vingt jusqu'à │ soixante Couverts. │ NEUVIÈME ÉDITION, │ REVUE,
CORRIGÉE │ *Et augmentée de cent-cinquante Articlea,* │ PAR A. VIARD, Homme de
Bouche. │ SUIVIE D'UNE NOTICE SUR LES VINS, │ Par M. PIERHUGUE,
Sommelier du Roi. │ [short fancy rule] │ PARIS, │ CHEZ BARBA, LIBRAIRE,
PALAIS ROYAL, │ DERRIERE LE THÉATRE FRANÇAIS, No. 51. │ [short rule] │
De l'Imprimerie de HOCQUET, rue du Faubourg Montmartre, n. 4. │ 1817.

Ninth edition, Paris, 1817. Originally published under the title *Le Cuisinier impérial*,
Paris, 1806 (item 433), and under this title, Paris, 1814 (item 433a).

205 x 130 mm. π^4 [A]^4 B^4(-B$_4$) 1-28^8 29^4; 239 leaves, pp. [*8*] [i] ii-xiii [xiv] [1] 2-443,
474-485 [486] = 478.

Bibliographies: Maggs 354; Simon BG 1565; Vicaire 860 in a note; Wheaton and Kelly 6233.

Copies: *BNC* and *NUC* (Boston Public Library, Kansas State University, and Northwestern University).

435. Viard, Alexandre.

LE | CUISINIER ROYAL, | OU | L'ART DE FAIRE LA CUISINE, | LA PATISSERIE ET TOUT CE QUI CONCERNE L'OFFICE, | POUR TOUTES LES FORTUNES; | PAR MM. VIARD et FOURET, Hommes de Bouche. | ONZIÈME ÉDITION, | AUGMENTÉE DE 1100 ARTICLES, ET ORNÉE DE 9 PLANCHES POUR LE | SERVICE DES TABLES DEPUIS 12 JUSQU'A 60 COUVERTS. | SUIVIE D'UNE NOTICE SUR LES VINS, | Par M. PIERHUGUE, Sommelier du Roi. | [short fancy rule] | A PARIS, | CHEZ J.-N. BARBA, LIBRAIRE, | Éditeur des OEuvres de MM. PIGAULT-LEBRUN, PICARD | et ALEXANDRE DUVAL. | PALAIS-ROYAL, DERRIÈRE LE THÉATRE FRANÇAIS, No 51. | [short fancy rule] | 1822.

Eleventh edition, Paris, 1822. Originally published under the title *Le Cuisinier impérial*, Paris, 1806 (item 433), and under this title, Paris, 1814 (item 433a).

206 x 125 mm. π^4 1-34^8 35-37^4; 288 leaves, pp. [8] [1] 2-542 [i] ii-xxiii [xxiv] [2]. This copy wanting first leaf (half-title?) and last leaf (blank?).

Illustrations: Three lithographed folding plates, each with three table settings.

Bookplate: Westbury.

Bibliographies: Bitting, p. 478. Vicaire 860 in a note.

Copies: *BNC* and *NUC* (Cleveland Public Library only).

436. Viard, Alexandre.

LE | CUISINIER ROYAL, | OU | L'ART DE FAIRE LA CUISINE, | LA PATISSERIE ET TOUT CE QUI CONCERNE L'OFFICE, | POUR TOUTES LES FORTUNES; | PAR | MM. VIARD, FOURET ET DÉLAN, | HOMMES DE BOUCHE. | 14me ÉDITION, | AUGMENTÉE DE 300 ARTICLES NOUVEAUX |

PAR M. DÉLAN, │ SUIVIE D'UNE NOTICE COMPLÈTE DE TOUS LES VINS, │ PAR ORDRE DE SERVICE, │ DE M. G......, RESTAURATEUR. │ ORNÉE DE NEUF PLANCHES POUR LE SERVICE DES TABLES │ DEPUIS 12 JUSQU'A 60 COUVERTS. │ [short fancy rule] │ PARIS. │ J.-N. BARBA, PALAIS-ROYAL, │ GRANDE COUR, DERRIÈRE LE THÉATRE-FRANÇAIS, │ A CÔTÉ DE CHEVET; │ GUSTAVE BARBA, │ RUE MAZARINE, No 34. │ [short fancy rule] │ 1832.

Fourteenth edition, Paris, 1832. Originally published under the title *Le Cuisinier impérial*, Paris, 1806 (item 433), and under this title, Paris, 1814 (item 433a).

202 x 126 mm. π^4 1-38^8; 308 leaves, pp. [8] [1] 2-607 [608].

Illustrations: Three lithographed folding plates showing table settings.

Bibliographies: Vicaire 860 in a note stating, "en 1831, parait la 14e edition."

Copies: *BNC* and *NUC* (Library of Congress only).

437. Viard, Alexandre.

LE │ CUISINIER ROYAL │ PAR VIART, │ HOMME DE BOUCHE; │ DIX-HUITÈME ÉDITION, │ AUGMENTÉE DE DOUZE CENTS ARTICLES NOUVEAUX, │ PAR MM. FOURET ET DÉLAN, │ HOMMES DE BOUCHE. │ Contenant │ L'ART DE FAIRE LA CUISINE, LA PATISSERIE et tout ce qui concerne l'OFFICE, │ pour toutes les fortunes; │ Suivi d'une Notice complète de tous les Vins, par PIERRHUGUES, sommelier du roi; │ d'une Distribution des Vins par ordre de service, par M. GRIGNON. │ Orné de neuf planches pour le service des tables, depuis douze jusqu'à soixante couverts. │ D'une Table alphabétique de tous les mets, par ordre de service, etc., etc. │ [publisher's monogram] │ PARIS. │ GUSTAVE BARBA, │ ÉDITEUR DU CABINET LITTÉRAIRE, │ COLLECTION UNIVERSELLE DES MEILLEURS ROMANS MODERNES, │ RUE MAZARINE, 34, │ [short rule] │ 1842

Eighteenth edition, Paris, 1842. Originally published under the title *Le Cuisinier impérial*, Paris, 1806 (item 433), and under this title, Paris, 1814 (item 433a).

207 x 131 mm. π^4 1-38^8 39^4; 312 leaves, pp. [8] [1] 2-616.

Illustrations: Nine woodcuts in the text showing table settings.

Bibliographies: This edition unrecorded in the bibliographies consulted.

Copies: *NUC* (Kansas State University and University of California, Berkeley).

438. Vicaire, Georges, 1853-1921.

BIBLIOGRAPHIE | [in red] Gastronomique | PAR | [in red] GEORGES VICAIRE | AVEC UNE PRÉFACE | DE | [in red] PAUL GINISTY | *La cuisine. — La table. — L'office. — Les aliments. — Les vins. — Les cuisiniers | et les cuisinières. — Les gourmands et les gastronomes. — L'économie domestique. | Facéties. — Dissertations singulières. | Pièces de théâtre, etc., etc., depuis le XVe siècle jusque'à nos jours.* | [in red] AVEC DES FAC-SIMILES | [publisher's monogram] | PARIS | [in red] CHEZ P. ROUQUETTE ET FILS, ÉDITEURS | 69, PASSAGE CHOISEUL, 73 | [short rule] | 1890

Statement of limitation: JUSTIFICATION DU TIRAGE | [short rule] | TIRÉ A 50 EXEMPLAIRES SUR PAPIER DE HOLLANDE. | — 450 — SUR BEAU PAPIER VÉLIN. | [short rule].

First edition, Paris, 1890. Copy on beau papier vélin.

240 x 154 mm. $\pi^8 \chi 1$ 1-30^8 31^4; 253 leaves, pp. [i-vii] viii-xviii, numbered in columns, two to a page, [1-2] 3-972 [2].

Bibliographies: Bitting, p. 478; Oberlé (1) 1171; Schraemli (1) 492; Wheaton and Kelly 6240.

Copies: *BMC, BNC*, and *NUC* (8 copies).

439. Villars, Dominique, 1745-1814.

CATALOGUE | *DES* | SUBSTANCES VÉGÉTALES | *Qui peuvent servir à la Nourriture de | l'Homme, & qui se trouvent dans les | Départemens de l'Isere, la Drôme & | les Hautes-Alpes.* | PAR le Citoyen VILLAR, Officier de Santé de | l'Hôpital militaire de Grenoble, Professeur | de Botanique. | [Phrysian cap] | [rule] | *A GRENOBLE,* | De l'Imprimerie d'ALEXANDRE GIROUD, cader, | Place aux Herbes.

First edition, Grenoble, 1793.

8vo. A-C⁸; 24 leaves, pp. [1-3] 4-48. Bound with *Mémoire sur les aliments*, 1791 (item 332).

Bibliographies: Blake p. 474.

Copies: *BNC* and *NUC* (Harvard only).

440. Vontet, Jacques.

[manuscript title:] A Lecteur │ Lart de trancher la │ viande et toute sorte de │ fruicts a la modi Italienne │ A nouuelle a la francoise │ Par │ Jacques Vontet │ Escuyer tranchant

Engraved plates with manuscript text, Paris? ca. 1650.

Note: This series of plates illustrating carving has its origins in Mattia Giegher's *Il Trinciante*, Padua, 1621 (item 1146), and appears to have been published, probably in Paris, about 1650. The accompanying text, attributed to a carver named Jacques Vontet, was not printed but was written by hand and in some copies the plates are supplemented by additional hand drawn illustrations. Maggs, in their catalogue *Food and Drink Through the Ages* (London, 1937), assigns Lyon as the place of publication and circa 1647 as the date, this probably based on their identification of the printed coat of arms that appears at the beginning of most copies of the work as those of François Basset, sheriff of Lyon, 1646-1647. However, Pierre Berès has had the arms checked by the Bibliothèque Nationale and they report they are imaginary and belong to no real person. Berès, who at this writing owns two copies of these plates with the Vontet text, has dated them Paris? ca. 1650 and Paris? ca. 1660.

The plates were used again in the middle of the eighteenth century, this time with a hand written text by a carver named Pierre Petit (item 388).

4to. 53 leaves, unsigned. Folio 1, unidentified and probably made up coat of arms; f. 2, manuscript title; ff. 3-4, manuscript advice to the reader, written on rectos and versos; the remaining 49 leaves consist of 39 leaves with engraved plates (one leaf with two plates, printed on recto and verso, and ten with two plates printed on the recto of each leaf) and ten leaves blank on the recto and with manuscript carving instructions on the verso. Seventeen of the engraved plates also have manuscript carving instructions on the verso.

Bibliographies: Maggs 136; Oberlé (1) 552; Schraemli (1) 495; Schraemli (2) 79; Schraemli (3) 24; and Vicaire 870 describe similar works.

Copies: No two copies of this work are exactly alike. One similar to this is in the département des Etampes in the Bibliothèque Nationale and, at this writing, Pierre Berès has two copies in stock. See also Pierre Petit (item 388).

441. Vonlett, Jacques.

LA VRAYE METTODE | de bien trencher les viandes | tant à l'Italienne qu'à la main et | les différentes façons de peler et de | seruir touttes sortes de fruits et le | moyen den faire diverses figures | par JAQUE VONLETT | fribourgeois | Lyon 1647 | Recueilli, mis en ordre et préfacé par | CHARLES

DE SALVERTE | [fancy rule] | A DIJON | AUX ÉDITIONS DU RAISIN | 1926

First edition, Dijon, 1926. No. 99 of 100 copies on Auvergne of a total edition of 110 copies.

283 x 226 mm. π^4 1^4 $[1*]^4$ 2^4 $[2*]^4$ 3^4 χ^2; 26 leaves, pp. [8] [1] 2-37 [38] [6]. First two leaves and last leaf blank. Publisher's printed wrappers.

Illustrations: Numerous reproductions in the text from a set of 17th century engraved plates illustrating carving.

Bibliographies: Bitting, p. 480.

Copies: *BMC*, *BNC*, and *NUC* (John Crerar Library, Library of Congress, and New York Public Library).

442. Wirthe.

LE | CONFISEUR | NATIONAL ET UNIVERSEL, | CONTENANT | Les meilleurs procédés pour faire les confitures, compotes, dragées et | pâtes diverses; | PAR M. WIRTHE, | Ancien Confiseur; | SUIVI | DU DISTILLATEUR-LIQUORISTE | et du Limonadier, | TRAITÉ COMPLET ET PRATIQUE | DE LA DISTILLATION ET DES OPÉRATIONS DU LIMONADIER, | D'APRÈS LES DÉCOUVERTES MODERNES DE LA CHIMIE, | Pour frabriquer les liqueurs de table et autres, la préparation du café, | du thé, du chocolat, du punch, des sirops, glaces, sorbets, |

limonade, etc. | *PAR M. MATHIEU.* | [short rule] | AVEC PLANCHES GRAVÉES. | [short rule] | PARIS, | IMPRIMERIE DE P. BAUDOUIN, | rue et Hôtel Mignon, 2. | [short rule] | 1836.

First edition, Paris, 1836.

203 x 121 mm. π^2 1-19^8 20^6; 160 leaves, pp. [*4*] [1] 2-316.

Illustrations: Wood engraved frontispiece of two men in a laboratory and a lithographed folding plate illustrating the utensils of a confiseur and of a distiller.

Bibliographies: Bitting, p. 502; Maggs 452; Vicaire 877.

Copies: *BNC* and *NUC* (Library of Congress only).

443. Yahya' ibn Isa' ibn Jozlah, Abū Ali, al-Baghdādi, d. 1100.

[within an ornamental border] TACVI= | NI | AE GRITV= | DINVM | et Morborum ferme omnium Cor= | poris humani, cum curis co= | rundem. | BVHAHYLYHA BYN= | GEZLA Autore. | Christianissimo Regi CAROLO | eius nominis primo, nuncupati. | [below the border] [hand] Cum Priuilegio C AE S. Maiest. | ad Quinquennium. | ℂ ARGENT. apud Ioannem Schottum | librarium. M. D. XXXII.

First edition, Strassburg, 1532.

Folio. A^6 B-G^4 a^6 b-l^4; 76 leaves, pp. [i-ii] iii-lix [lx] [1] 2-89 [90] [2]. Last leaf blank. Bound with Ibn Bultan's *Tacvini sex rerum non naturalium* . . ., Strassburg, 1533 (item 244.)

Illustrations: Woodcut border, incorporating the German imperial arms, around the title-page by Hans Wechtelin and woodcut vignettes in the lower margins of many pages.

Bibliographies: Durling 4774.

Copies: *BNC*, *BMC*, and *NUC* (4 copies).

COLLECTION

DES

MÉMOIRES ET NOTICES

(AVEC DES PLANCHES),

Publiés depuis 1829 jusqu'en 1843,

RELATIVEMENT A L'EMPLOI ALIMENTAIRE

DE LA

GÉLATINE DES OS,

PAR M. D'ARCET,

Membre de l'Institut (Académie des Sciences), du Conseil de Salubrité, de la Société Centrale et Royale d'Agriculture, etc.

A PARIS,

Au Bureau de l'Administration de la Société Polytechnique,

RUE DE LA PAIX, Nº 20 ;

1843.

Item no.   38

L'ART
DU CUISINIER,

PAR A. BEAUVILLIERS,

Ancien Officier de Monsieur, comte de Provence, attaché aux Extraordinaires des Maisons royales, et actuellement Restaurateur, rue de Richelieu, n° 26, à la grande Taverne de Londres.

———

TOME PREMIER.

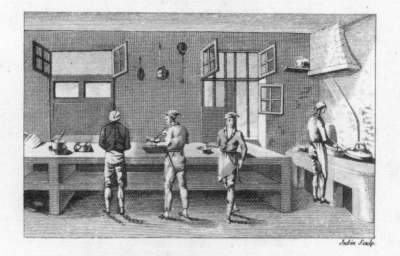

Jubin Sculp.

A PARIS,

CHEZ PILET, IMPRIMEUR-LIBRAIRE, RUE CHRISTINE, N° 5,

IL SE VEND AUSSI

CHEZ { COLNET, LIBRAIRE, QUAI DES PETITS-AUGUSTINS, ET LENOIR, LIBRAIRE, RUE DE RICHELIEU, N° 35.

1814.

ABREGÉ
DÈS TRAITEZ
DV CAFFE,
DV THE
ET DU
CHOCOLAT,

POUR LA PRESERVATION,
& pour la guerison des
maladies.

Ante languorem adhibe medicinam
Eccl. cap. 18. v. 20.

A LYON,
Chez ESPRIT VITALIS, ruë
Merciere.

M. DC. LXXXVII.
AVEC APPROBATION ET PERMISSION.

LE BON USAGE
DU THÉ'
DU CAFFE'
ET
DU CHOCOLAT
POUR LA PRESERVATION
& pour la guerison des Maladies.

Par Mr de Blegny, Conseiller, Medecin Artiste ordinaire du Roy & de Monsieur, & preposé par ordre de Sa Majesté, à la Recherche & Verification des nouvelles découvertes de Medecine.

A Lyon, & se vend
A PARIS,
Chez JACQUES COLLOMBAT, ruë
S. Jacques, au Pelican.

M. DC. LXXXVII.
AVEC PRIVILEGE DU ROY.

Chinois cueillant les feuilles, et
beuvant la liqueur de Thé.

Bouchet

A Lyon chez Thomas Amaulry, rue
Merciere au Mercure Galant

LES
DELICES DE
LA
Campagne

F. Chauueau fe.

PHYSIOLOGIE
DU GOUT,

OU

MÉDITATIONS DE GASTRONOMIE

TRANSCENDANTE;

OUVRAGE THÉORIQUE, HISTORIQUE ET A L'ORDRE DU JOUR,

Dédié aux Gastronomes parisiens,

PAR UN PROFESSEUR,

MEMBRE DE PLUSIEURS SOCIÉTÉS LITTÉRAIRES ET SAVANTES.

Dis-moi ce que tu manges, je te dirai qui tu es.
APHOR. DU PROF.

TOME PREMIER.

PARIS,

CHEZ A. SAUTELET ET Cie LIBRAIRES,

PLACE DE LA BOURSE, PRÈS LA RUE FEYDEAU.

———

1826.

Item no. 98

Das buch zu distillieren

die zusamen gethonen ding Composi∕
ta genant∕durch die eintzigē ding∕vnd das bůch Thesaurus pau
perū∕für die armen∕durch experiment von mir Jheronymo
Brunschwick vff geklubt vnd geoffenbart∕zů trost vñ
heil dē menschen vñ nutzlich ir leben vnd leib dar uß
zů erlengeren vnd in gesuntheit zů behalten.

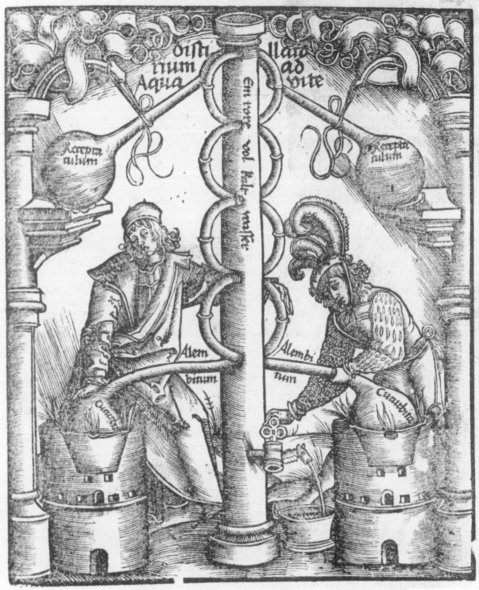

DU FESTIN

DU

ROI-BOIT.

A BESANÇON,

De l'Imprimerie de Jean-Felix
CHARMET.

M. DCC. LXII.

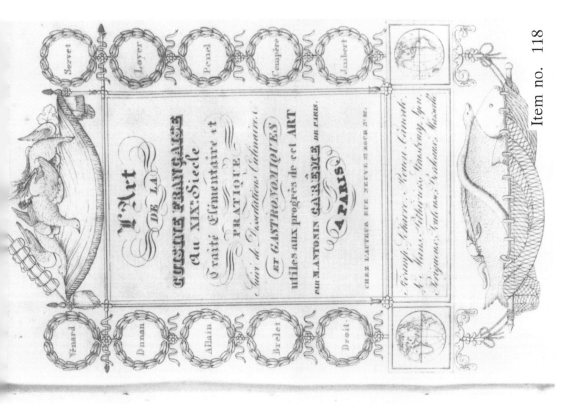

L'Art
DE LA
CUISINE FRANÇAISE
Au XIXe Siècle

Traité Élémentaire et
PRATIQUE

Suivi de Dissertations Culinaires et
et GASTRONOMIQUES
utiles aux progrès de cet ART

PAR M. ANTONIN CARÊME DE PARIS

A PARIS

CHEZ L'AUTEUR RUE NEUVE ST ROCH N° 82.

LE PATISSIER PITTORESQUE,

COMPOSÉ ET DESSINÉ

PAR M. A. CARÊME.

CONTENANT

Cent vingt-cinq Planches gravées au trait, dont cent dix représentent une variété de Modèles, de Pavillons, de Rotondes, de Temples, de Ruines, de Tours, de Belvéders, de Forts, de Cascades, de Fontaines, de Maisons de Plaisance, de Chaumières, de Moulins, et d'Hermitages ;

PRÉCÉDÉ

D'un traité des cinq Ordres d'Architecture, selon Vignole ; auquel on a joint des détails des Ordres Cariatide, Pœstum, Égyptien, Chinois et Gothiques ; tirés de l'Ouvrage de M. Durand, Parallèle des Monuments antiques et modernes.

A PARIS,

DE L'IMPRIMERIE DE FIRMIN DIDOT, LIBRAIRE,
IMPRIMEUR DU ROI, ET DE L'INSTITUT,
RUE JACOB, N° 24.

1815.

Normand fils sc.

Carême inven.

— Comment se fait-il que tes haricots aient été aujourd'hui si mal préparés, quand, ordinairement, tu me les sers de manière à me les faire goûter délicieusement ?

— C'est que, répondit le cuisinier en balbutiant, M. le marquis recevait M. le grand-vicaire.

— Et c'était une raison, maraud, pour te surpasser ! J'avais promis à l'abbé un régal, et tu nous as servi un plat que le plus mince bourgeois mangerait meilleur.

— C'est que, répondit le cuisinier de plus en plus troublé, M. le marquis a en effet mangé aujourd'hui des haricots.

— Et que me servais-tu donc auparavant ?

— Des rognons de coq, que je faisais passer à M. le marquis pour des haricots de Soissons.

— Imbécile ! Puisque tu avais pris sur toi la faute, n'en pouvais-tu prolonger la durée quelques jours encore ! »

LA CONTEMPLATION.

Item no. 134

NOUVEAU MANUEL

DU

CUISINIER.

CONTENANT

**LES RECETTES LES PLUS MODERNES
POUR FAIRE A PEU DE FRAIS UNE
CUISINE CONFORTABLE ;**

OUVRAGE

ENTIÈREMENT NEUF , RÉDIGÉ D'APRÈS LES
OBSERVATIONS DES PLUS CÉLÈBRES HOMMES DE
BOUCHE DU DIX-NEUVIÈME SIÈCLE ;

PAR M. CHEVRIER.

PARIS,

IMPRIMERIE DE Mme HUZARD (née VALLAT LA CHAPELLE);
Rue de l'Éperon, n° 7.

Les petites causes produisent souvent de grands effets.

RÉVOLUTIONIANA,

O U

ANECDOTES, ÉPIGRAMMES,

E T

saillies relatives à la révolution;

PAR PHILANA.

Sur les ailes du Temps la Tristesse s'envole.

LAFONTAINE.

A PARIS,

Chez MARADAN, Libraire, rue Pavée-
Saint-André-des-Arcs, n° 16.

A N X.

Item no. 158

Item no. 165

GRAND DICTIONNAIRE

DE

CUISINE

PAR

ALEXANDRE DUMAS

PARIS

ALPHONSE LEMERRE ÉDITEUR

PASSAGE CHOISEUL

DICTIONNAIRE DE CUISINE

PAR

Alexandre Dumas

REVU ET COMPLÉTÉ

PAR

J. VUILLEMOT, ÉLÈVE DE CARÊME

Ancien Cuisinier, Propriétaire de l'*Hôtel de la Cloche*, à Compiègne, etc.

———

PARIS

ALPHONSE LEMERRE, ÉDITEUR

27-31, PASSAGE CHOISSEUL, 27-31

Diffection de l'Efpaule de Mouton.

Cette diffection eft fi facile, fi ordinaire, & fi bien exprimée dans la figure que j'ay creu eftre inutile d'en faire vn long difcours.

Diffection de l'Efpaule de Mouton.

¶Marsili⁹ Ficin⁹ de triplici vita: Cū
textu Salerni ad vnguem castigato.

JEHAN PETIT

1489 (see last page)

LE

GASTRONOME

FRANÇAIS,

OU

L'ART DE BIEN VIVRE,

Par les anciens Auteurs du Journal des Gourmands,

MM. G. D. L. R***, D. D***, GASTERMANN,
G***, CLYTOPHON, CHARLES SARTROUVILLE, C. L. C***, C***,
MARIE DE SAINT-URSIN, B***, ETC.;

Ouvrage mis en ordre, accompagné de Notes, de
Dissertations et d'Observations

*Par M. C****.*

La découverte d'un mets nouveau fait plus pour le
bonheur de l'humanité que la découverte d'une étoile.
BRILLAT DE SAVARIN.
Veut mieux être ivrbes.
Gastronome.
Qui microscome.
GRITI.

PARIS.

CHARLES-BÉCHET, LIBRAIRE-COMMISSIONNAIRE,

QUAI DES AUGUSTINS, N° 57, PRÈS LE PONT-NEUF.

*

1828.

Promenade Nutritive.

cilius est esse pastozem locustaz aut pulicū in vanno ad solem exposito
rum q̃ custodire vxozem. Esto q̃ bis custodibus casta nó manserit: tu
tamen rationabiliter qd in te est fecisti:in culpa nó est: babebis quid re
spondeas cozam deo z bominibus. Et ammodo tunc tibi patientia ne
cessaria est:cogitās q̃ tu neq̃ prim⁹ neq̃ vltimus:qui impudicā z adul
teram babuit vxozem. memineris quia etiam maximi ex principibus
tales babuere vxozes. Quos si scire volueris: legito Franciscū Petrar
cham libzo. ij. cap. xxi. de remedio fortune aduerseaz te cum suis dictis
olar e. Rogemus dominū.

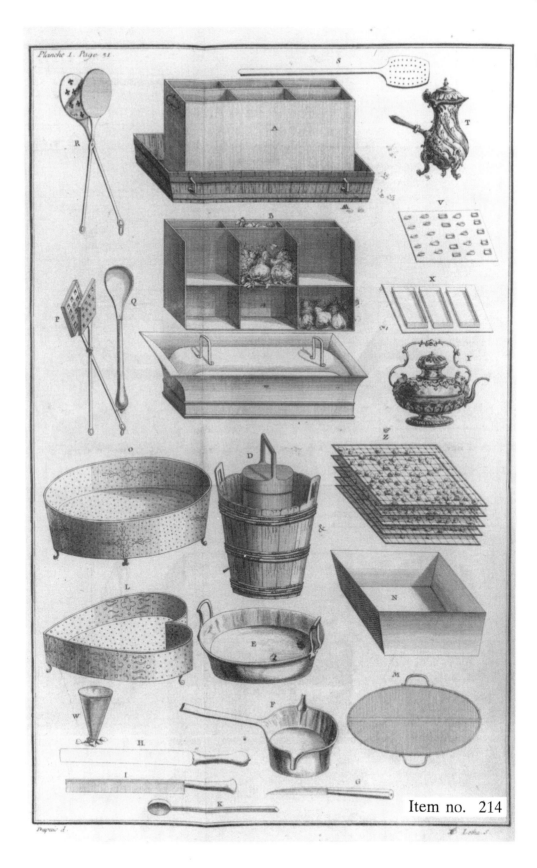

Item no. 214

Dupuis d.
Lotha s.

ALMANACH

DES GOURMANDS,

OU

CALENDRIER NUTRITIF,

SERVANT DE GUIDE DANS LES MOYENS DE FAIRE EXCELLENTE CHÈRE ;

Suivi de l'Itinéraire d'un Gourmand dans divers quartiers de Paris, et de quelques Variétés morales, apéritives et alimentaires, Anecdotes gourmandes, etc.

PAR UN VIEUX AMATEUR.

Tanquam leo rugiens, circuit quærens quem devoret.

S. Petr. epist. cap. vi, vers. 8.

A PARIS,

Chez Maradan , Libraire , rue Pavée—Saint-André-des-Arcs, n°. 16.

AN XI. — 1803.

Bibliothèque d'un Gourmand
du XIX Siècle.

LE GUIDE

DE SANTÉ,

OU

L'ART DE SE LA CONSERVER

Par les préceptes qui donnent la vie la plus longue
& exempte de maladies; avec différens préfervatifs,
& des moyens sûrs pour remédier promptement
aux divers accidens qui menacent la vie, & à une
foule d'incommodités dont on est journellement
attaqué:

SUIVI DES

DONS DE LA NATURE,

*Mis en ordre pour l'ufage de la Table fuivant
les Saifons de l'année;*

OU

Recueil contenant une idée des qualités & propriétés
des Alimens, tant animaux que végétaux, fer-
vant à la fubfiftance de l'homme.

Utile dulci. *Horat.*

A PARIS,

& fe trouve à LIÉGE,

Chez F. J. DESOER, Imprimeur-Libraire,
fur le Pont-d'Ifle.

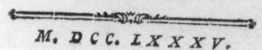

M. DCC. LXXXV.

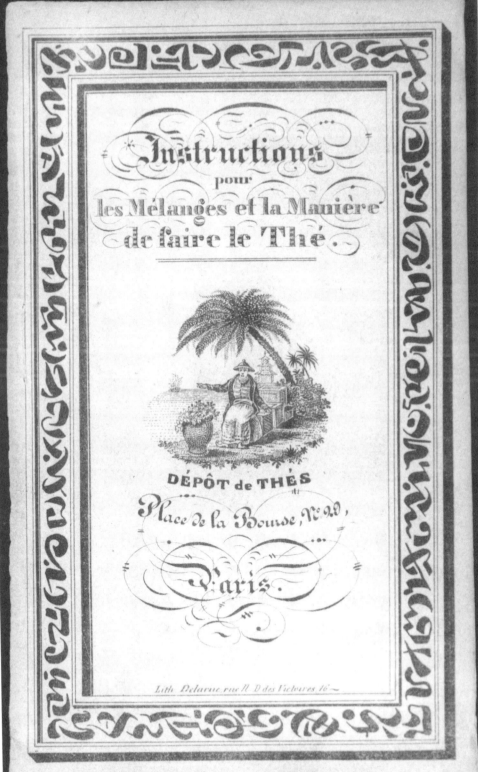

Instructions
pour
les Mélanges et la Manière
de faire le Thé.

DÉPÔT de THÉS
Place de la Bourse, No. 29,

Paris.

Lith. Delarue, rue N. D. des Victoires, 16.

MANUEL

DU

VINAIGRIER

ET

DU MOUTARDIER.

PAR M. JULIA-FONTENELLE.

PARIS,

RORET, LIBRAIRE, RUE HAUTEFEUILLE,

AU COIN DE CELLE DU BATTOIR.

LE
PASTISSIER
FRANCOIS;

Où est enseigné la maniere de faire
toute sorte de Pastisserie, tres-vtile
à toutes personnes.

ENSEMBLE

Le moyen d'aprester les œufs pour les
iours maigres , & autres, en plus
de soixante façons.

A PARIS,
Chez IEAN GAILLARD, ruë
Sainct Iacques, à la Diligence.

M. DC. LIII.
Auec Priuilege du Roy.

LE LIVRE
DE GLACE

OU

HISTOIRE CONCISE ET ABRÉGÉE

De tout ce qui regarde la Glace

Depuis son premier usage en Europe, comme article de luxe, jusqu'au temps présent.

AVEC DES INSTRUCTIONS

Sur la manière de produire de la Glace pure et solide, au moyen de l'Appareil frigorifique, suivies d'un recueil de recettes pour faire les glaces et les crêmes ou fromages glacés.

PARIS.

AU DÉPOT DES MACHINES FRIGORIFIQUES,

Chez LAHOCHE, *Palais-Royal, galerie Valois, N. 155.*

1845.

Item no. 287

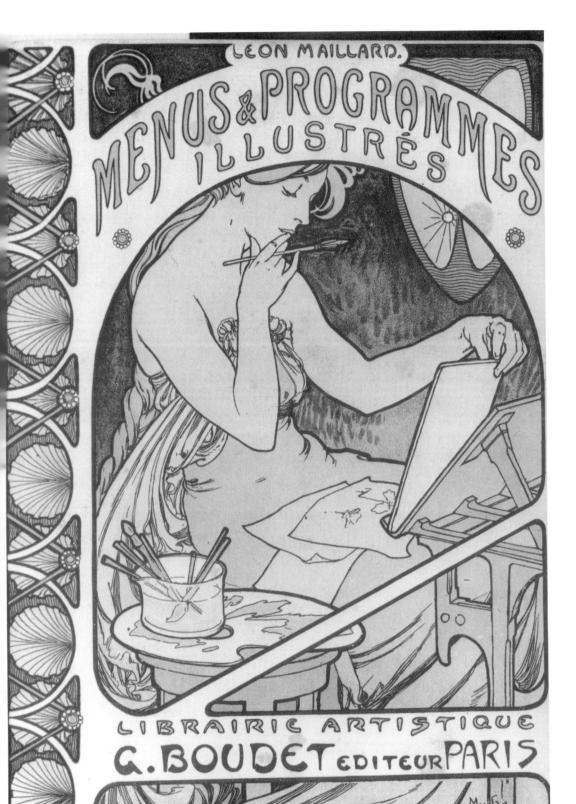

LEON MAILLARD.

MENUS & PROGRAMMES ILLUSTRÉS

LIBRAIRIE ARTISTIQUE
G. BOUDET EDITEUR PARIS

Mucha

Item no.   296

STATUTS,
PRIVILÉGES,
ORDONNANCES
ET
REGLEMENS
DE LA COMMUNAUTÉ
DES
MAISTRES BOULANGERS

de la ville, fauxbourgs & banlieue de Paris.

A PARIS,

De l'imprimerie de MOREAU, Libraire-Imprimeur
de la REINE & de Monseigneur le DAUPHIN.

M. DCC. LXVI.

LES DONS DE COMUS,

OU

LES DÉLICES DE LA TABLE.

OUVRAGE non-seulement utile aux Officiers de Bouche pour ce qui concerne leur art, mais principalement à l'usage des personnes qui sont curieuses de sçavoir donner à manger, & d'être servies délicatement, tant en gras qu'en maigre, suivant les saisons, & dans le goût le plus nouveau.

À PARIS,

Chez Prault, Fils, Quay de Conty, vis-à-vis la descente du Pont Neuf, à la Charité.

M. DCC. XXXIX.

Avec Approbation & Privilege du Roi.

Les attributs de la Bonne-Chere

MANUEL

DE

L'AMATEUR DE CAFE,

OU

L'ART DE PRENDRE TOUJOURS DE BON CAFÉ.

OUVRAGE

Contenant plusieurs procédés nouveaux, faciles et économiques, pour préparer le café et en rendre la boisson plus saine et plus agréable.

DÉDIÉ

AUX AMATEURS, AUX BONNES MÉNAGÈRES, etc., etc.

PAR M. H....,

Doyen des habitués du café de Foi.

PARIS.

AUDOT, LIBRAIRE-ÉDITEUR,
RUE DES MAÇONS-SORBONNE, Nº 11.

1828.

LE
CUISINIER
ROIAL
ET BOURGEOIS,

Qui apprend à ordonner toute
sorte de Repas, & la meilleure
maniere des Ragoûts les plus à
la mode & les plus exquis.

Ouvrage tres-utile dans les Familles, & sin-
gulierement necessaire à tous Maîtres
d'Hôtels, & Ecüiers de Cuisine.

C. Jeannel
1856.

A PARIS,
Chez CHARLES DE SERCY, au Palais,
au sixiéme Pilier de la Grand'Salle, vis-à-
vis la Montée de la Cour des Aides,
à la Bonne-Foi couronnée.

M. D C. X C I.
AVEC PRIVILEGE DU ROI.

MEMOIRE
POVR FAIRE
VN FESTIN.

ENSEMBLE LA VIE DE
puiſſante & tres-haute dame
Madame Gueline.

87

Reueue & augmentee de nouueau par
Monſieur Frippe ſaulce.

4

A ROVEN,

Chez IEAN PETIT, tenant ſaboutique
pres l'Orenger deuant S. Eloy.

M.DC.VII.

MÉMOIRE
SUR LES ALIMENTS.

LA matiere nutritive eſt diſſéminée ſur la ſurface de la terre avec une abondance & une profuſion vraiment admirable ; elle eſt répandue dans tous les végétaux, les plantes, leurs racines, leurs feuillages & leurs fruits ; il n'eſt pas juſqu'à leur tronc, à leur bois & à leur moëlle, qui ne puiſſent ſervir d'aliments.

Les animaux de toute eſpéce contiennent des chairs & des os, c'eſt-à-dire des ſubſtances propres à fournir des bouillons & des gelées nutritives : en un mot, par-tout où nous trouvons une ſubſtance propre à donner à l'eau cette apparence viſqueuſe de colle ou de gomme légere, là nous trouvons, ou nous pouvons trouver une matiere propre à réparer nos pertes, à entretenir nos forces, à ſervir enfin à notre nourriture. Il ne s'agit pour cela que d'extraire ou de ſéparer cette ſubſtance alimentaire, empriſonnée dans les corps végétaux & animaux, pour la rendre acceſſible à nos organes, & propres à la digeſtion.

Cette préparation, cette extraction de la gelée nutritive ſe fait au moyen de l'eau & du feu ; mais ces moyens ne ſuffiſent pas toujours. La bienfaiſante nature a donné aux ſubſtances alimentaires un goût, une ſaveur, une qualité particuliere à chacune : les unes trop fades, quoique très-nourriſſantes, ne ſe digéreroient pas ; elles peſeroient ſur nos organes, ne les agaceroient pas aſſez. Telles ſont les mauves, pluſieurs gommes & les farines non fermentées, ſur-tout celles des plantes légumineuſes. D'autres ont un goût âcre, piquant & aromatique, un goût acide, acerbe ou auſtere, qui, en frappant notre palais, le révoltent & le criſpent, & portent de même une impreſſion mordante & trop active ſur l'eſtomac, qui, au lieu d'exercer ſon action libre ſur ces aliments, ſe reſſerre & ſe raccornit. Ces mets en expriment alors les ſucs, comme une pincée de ſel l'exprimeroit d'un limaçon, au lieu de lui en fournir. Celles

LA NOUVELLE
CUISINIERE
BOURGEOISE,
SUIVIE DE L'OFFICE,

A L'USASE,

De tous ceux qui se mêlent des
dépenses de Maison.

A PARIS,

Chez G U I L L Y N, Quay des Augustins,
entre les ruës Pavée & Gît-le-Cœur,
au Lys d'or.

M. DCC. XLVI.

Avec Approbation & Privilege du Roy.

LES SOUPERS

DE

LA COUR,

OU

L'ART DE TRAVAILLER

TOUTES SORTES D'ALIMENS,

Pour fervir les meilleures Tables, fuivant
les quatre Saifons.

TOME I.

A PARIS,

Chez Guillyn, Libraire, Quai des Auguftins,
au Lys d'Or.

M. DCC. LV.

Avec Approbation & Privilége du Roi.

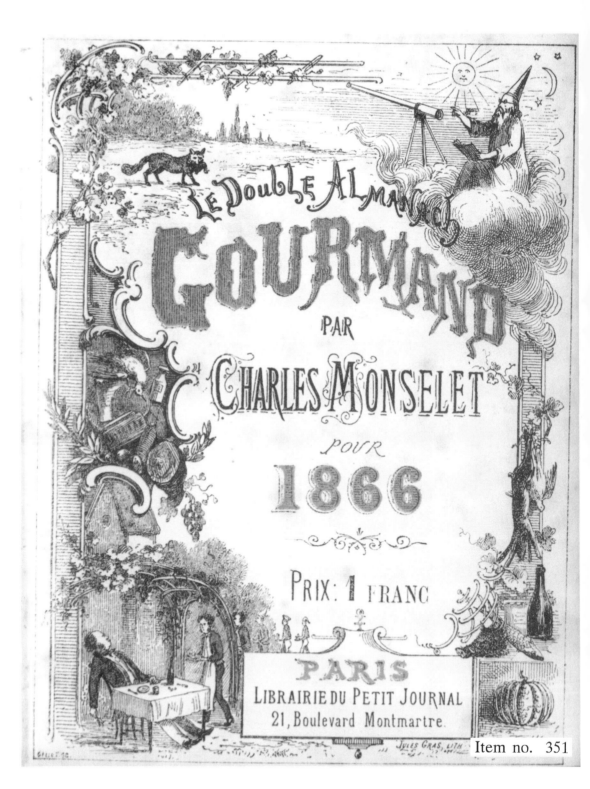

Le Double Almanach

GOURMAND

PAR

CHARLES MONSELET

POUR

1866

PRIX: 1 FRANC

PARIS
LIBRAIRIE DU PETIT JOURNAL
21, Boulevard Montmartre.

JULES GRAS, LITH.

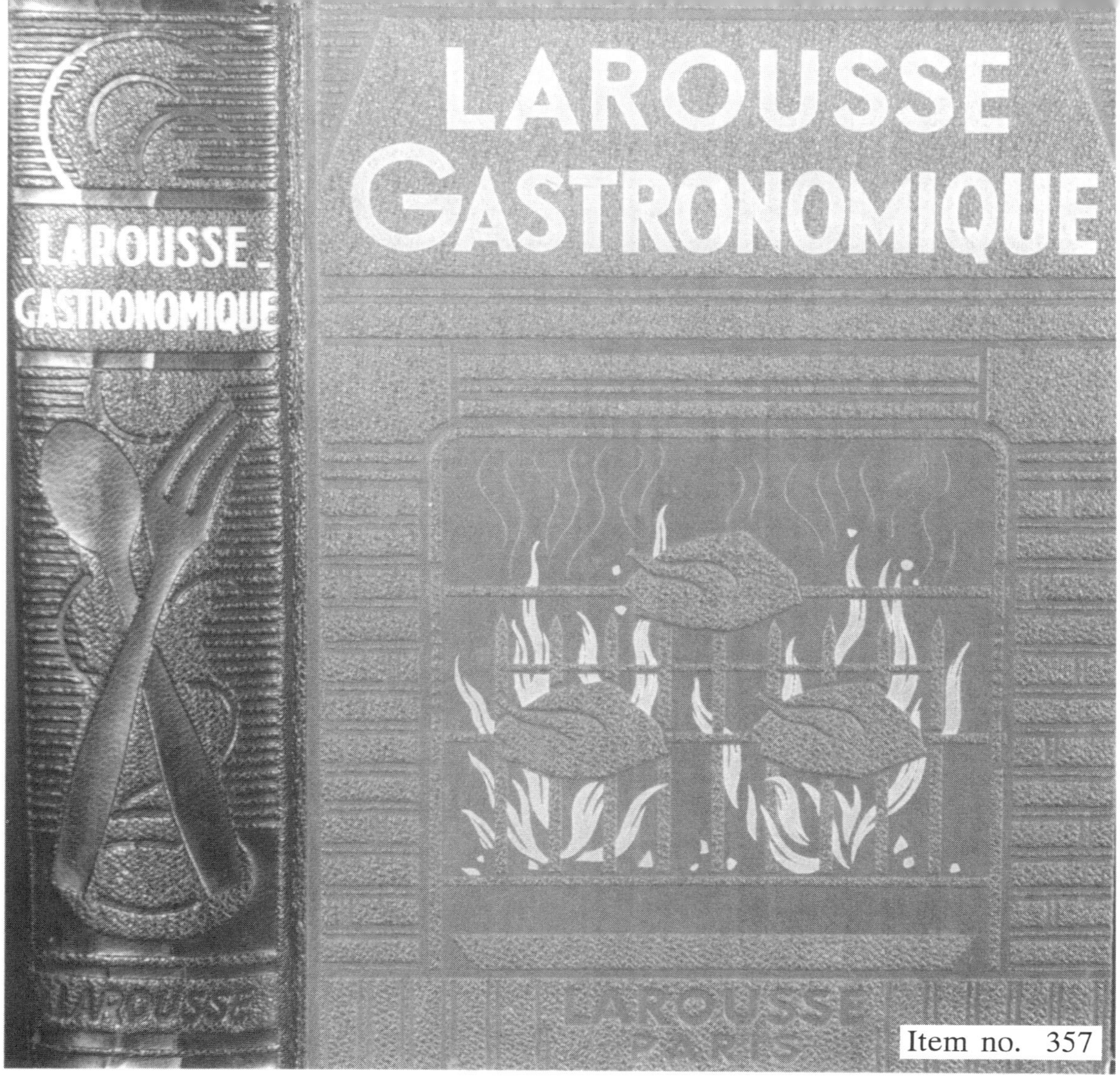

LAROUSSE GASTRONOMIQUE

LAROUSSE PARIS

LAROUSSE GASTRONOMIQUE

LAROUSSE

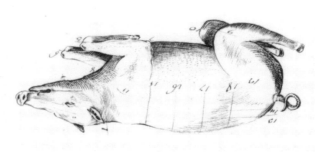

Le Cochon de lait.

Est bon en tout temps, et particulièrement au mois d'août, et de septembre, il est de difficile digestion, dont il se mange au sortir de la broche, autrement il incommode la faute. Luy [...] observer, il est farci d'accompagnée d'une farine du farcy, a partie du [...] Mais, sa tête [...] les jambes et les cuisses sont les parties que l'on fait ordinairement étant trop grasse, l'usage le [...] tranchées suivant l'ordre des chiffres de cette figure.

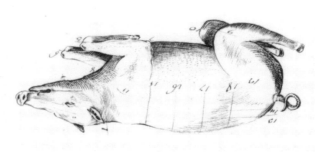

POISSARDIANA,

OU

CATÉCHISME DES HALLES;

OUVRAGE

Utile à la Jeunesse qui veut passer
joyeusement le CARNAVAL.

A PARIS,

Rue du Carême Prenant, N°. 34.

L'an II du retour de MARDI-GRAS.

Benoit Sculp.

*Parlez donc, monsieur : l'échanche l'est y pou
nous ficher la goaill qu'vous nous fisquez l'autre ...*

L'ART
DE
BIEN TRAITER.
DIVISÉ EN TROIS PARTIES.
OUVRAGE NOUVEAU, CURIEUX,
ET FORT GALANT,
UTILE A TOUTES PERSONNES,
ET CONDITIONS.

Exactement recherché, & mis en lumiere,

Par L. S. R,

A PARIS,
Chez JEAN DU PUIS, ruë S. Jacques
à la Couronne d'or.

M. DC. LXXV.

Avec Privilege du Roy.

165[?]

L'ART

DE

BIEN TRAITER.

DIVISE' EN TROIS PARTIES.

OU♥RAGE NOUVEAU , CURIEUX ;
ET FORT GALANT,

UTILE A TOUTES PERSONNES,
ET CONDITIONS.

Exactement recherché, & mis en lumiere,

Par L. S. R,

VIRTVTE INVIDIAM VINCE

PAX EVANGE
TIBI LISTA
MARC MEVS.

A PARIS,

Chez FREDERIC LEONARD , Imprimeur du
Roy, ruë S. Jacques, à l'Escu de Venise.

M. DC. LXXIV.

Avec Privilege du Roy.

LA TROUPE

DES
BONS ENFANS,

ASSEMBLÉS

'A L'HOTEL DES RAGOUTS.

*Où les Curieux des bons repas auront une
satisfaction extraordinaire.*

A LELIS,

Chez GODERFE, rue de Nenemya,

BIBLIOGRAPHIE
Gastronomique

PAR

GEORGES VICAIRE

AVEC UNE PRÉFACE

DE

PAUL GINISTY

La cuisine. — La table. — L'office. — Les aliments. — Les vins. — Les cuisiniers et les cuisinières. — Les gourmands et les gastronomes. — L'économie domestique. Facéties. — Dissertations singulières. Pièces de théâtre, etc., etc., depuis le XVe siècle jusqu'à nos jours.

AVEC DES FAC-SIMILÉS

PARIS

CHEZ P. ROUQUETTE ET FILS, ÉDITEURS

69, PASSAGE CHOISEUL, 73

—

1890

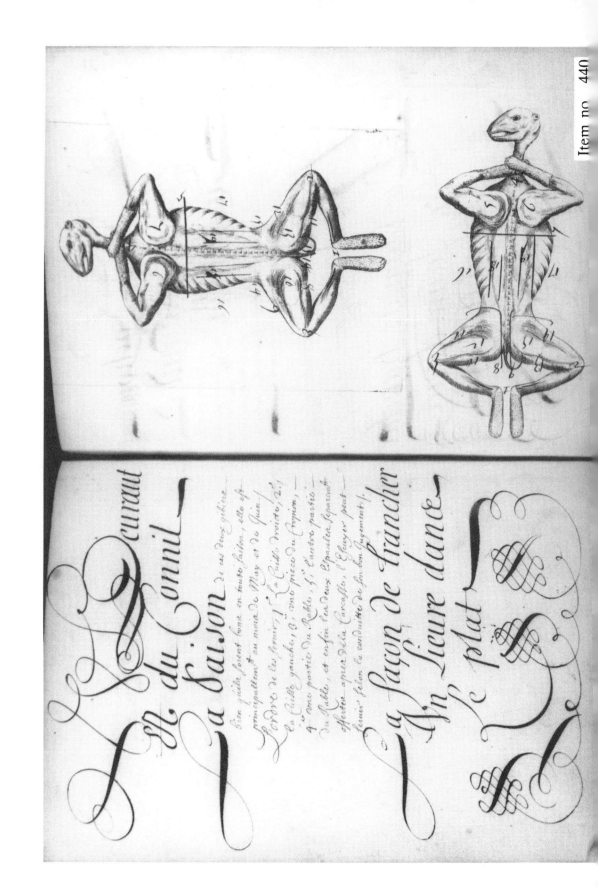

Levraut

St. du Connil

La Saison de ces deux gibiers
bien qu'elle soient sont en toute saison, elle est
principallement au mois de May et de Juin.

L'ordre de les servir; 1° La Cuisse droite, 2°.
La Cuisse gauche, 3°, une piece du Croupion
4° une partie du Rable, 5°. l'autre partie
du Rable, et enfin les deux Epaules séparant
effecter apres déla Carcasse, l'Esloyer peut
servir selon la conduitte de son Jugement;

La façon de Trancher
un Lievre dans
le plat.

GERMANY

444. Agrippa von Nettesheim, Heinrich Cornelius, 1486?-1535.

HENRICI | CORNELII AGRIPPAE AB NET- | tesheym, De incertitudine & Vanitate sciētia- | rum declamatio inuectiua, denuo | ab autore recognita & mar | ginalibus Annota- | tionibus aucta. | ❧ Capita tractandorum totius ope- | ris, sequétes indicant pagella. | [woodcut] | ❧ ANNO. M. D. XXXVII.

New edition, Köln, 1537. Originally published, Antwerp, 1530.

8vo. a⁴ A-Z⁸ &⁴; 192 leaves, unpaginated.

Note: This work is an attack on the state of science, the belief in witchcraft, and the accretions which had grown up around the simple doctrine of Christianity. In its encyclopaedic coverage there are brief sections on husbandry, including hunting and fishing, and on diet. Chapter LXXXIX, "De arte coquinaria" discusses those who have written on the subject of cookery and mentions some notable gluttons.

Bibliographies: This edition unrecorded in the bibliographies consulted. Durling lists other editions.

Copies: *BNC* and *NUC* (New York Public Library, Northwestern University, and University of Minnesota).

445. Agrippa von Nettesheim, Heinrich Cornelius, 1486?-1535.

HENRICI CORNELII | AGRIPPAE AB | NETTTESHEYM, DE | INCERTITVDINE ET | vanitate scientiarum declama | tio inuectiua, ex postre- | ma Authoris reco- | gnitione. | [woodcut] | *COLONIAE,* | *Apud Theodorum Baumium, sub si-* | *gno* *Arboris. Anno 1575.*

New edition, Köln, 1575. Originally published, Antwerp, 1530.

12mo. A-Cc¹²; 312 leaves, unpaginated. Last leaf (blank?) wanting.

Bibliographies: This edition unrecorded in the bibliographies consulted. Durling lists other editions.

Copies: *NUC* (5 copies).

446. Agrippa von Nettesheim, Heinrich Cornelius, 1486?-1535.

HENR. CORNELII │ AGRIPPAE │ AB NETTTESHEYM, │ DE INCERTITVDINE ET │ Vanitate omnium scientiarum │ & artium liber, lectu pla- │ ne iucundus & e- │ legans. │ *ACCEDVNT DVO EIVSDEM* │ *Auctoris libelli; quorum vnus est de Nobi-* │ *litate & praecellentia faeminei sexus, eius-* │ *demque supra virilem eminentia; Alter* │ *de matrimonio, seu coniugio,* │ *lectu etiam iucundis-* │ *simi.* │ [ornament] │ COLONIAE AGRIPPINAE, │ *Apud Antonium Hierat.* │ AN. M.D.XCVIII.

New edition, Köln, 1598. Originally published, Antwerp, 1530.

12mo. A-Cc^{12}; 312 leaves, unpaginated. Last leaf (blank?) wanting.

Bibliographies: This edition unrecorded in the bibliographies consulted. Durling lists other editions.

Copies: *NUC* (Hamilton College, Clinton, N.Y., only).

446a. Allgemeines Küchenlexikon für Frauenzimmer.

Allgemeines │ Küchenlexikon. │ für │ Frauenzimmer │ welche │ ihre Küche selbst besorgen │ order │ unter ihrer Aufsicht besorgen lassen │ [short rule] │ Erster Theil. [Zweiter Theil.] │ A-K. [L-Z.] │ [Tapered rule] │ Leipzig │ bei Voss und Compagnie 1794.

First edition, Leipzig, 1794.

8vo. 2 vols. Vol. I. ✳^{4} A-Uu^8 Xx-Yy^4; 356 leaves, pp. [i-iii] iv-vi [2], columns [1-2] 3-1408. Vol. II. A-Aaa^8; 376 leaves, pp. [4], columns [9-10] 11-1494, pp. [5]. Last two leaves, blank.

Illustrations: Woodcuts illustrating carving in the text in vol. II.

Bibliographies: Drexel 1074; Horn-Arndt 213.

Copies: *NUC* (New York Academy of Medicine only).

Amaranthes, 1677-1746. See Corvinus, Gottlieb Siegmund, 1677-1746.

447. Appert, Nicolas, 1750?-1841.

Die Kunst | alle thierische und begetabilische Nahrungsmittel | mehrere Jahre vollkommen geniessbar zu | erhalten | [short fancy rule] | herausgegeben aus Einladung S. E. des Ministers vom | Innern, nach vorheriger Prüfung und Genehmi= | gung des, bei dem Ministerium des Innern beste= | henden Raths der Künste und Manufacturen. | von | Appert, | Gutsbesitzer zu Massy, Department der Seine und Oise, | ehemaliger Conditor und Liquerfabrikant, Mundkoch | des herzogs Christian IV. | [fancy rule] | Aus dem Französischen übersetzt. | [rule] | Koblenz, 1810. | bei Pauli und Compagnie.

First edition in German, Koblenz, 1810. Originally published in French under the title *L'Art de conserver pendant plusieurs années toutes les substances animales et végétales*, Paris, 1810 (item 34).

8vo. π^4(-π4) 1-7^8 χ1; 60 leaves, pp. [6] [i] ii-xxiv [1] 2-89 [90].

Bibliographies: This edition unrecorded in the bibliographies consulted.

Copies: No other copy of this edition located.

448. Athenaeus.

ΑΘΗΝΑΙΟφ| ΔΕΙΠΝΟΣΟΦΙΣΤΩΝ | ΒΙΒΛΙΑ ΓΕΝΤΕΚΑΙΔΕΚΑ. | [ornament] | ATHENAEI | DEIPNOSOPHISTA- | RVM LIBRI XV. | [ornament] | ISAACVS CASAVBONVS recensuit, & ex antiquis | membranis suppleuit, auxítque. | *Adiecti sunt eiusdem CASAVBONI in eundem scriptorem* | *Animaduersionum libri XV.* | Addita est & IACOBI DALECHAMPII | CADOMENSIS, Latina interpreta- | tio, cum notis marginalibus. | Cum necessarijs indicibus. | [woodcut] | Apud Hieronymum Commelinum. | [short rule] | Anno M. D. XCVIII.

New edition, Heidelberg, 1598. Originally published, Venice, 1514 (item 1110). A second more reliable edition was published in Basle, 1535.

Folio: π^2 a-mmm^6 nnn^4 *-***^{6}; 372 leaves, pp. [4] 1-702 [38].

Bibliographies: Wheaton and Kelly 285.

Copies: *BMC*, *BNC*, and *NUC* (5 copies).

449. Bickelmann, George Conrad.

𝕷𝖊𝖍𝖗𝖇𝖚𝖈𝖍 | 𝖉𝖊𝖗 | 𝕶𝖔𝖈𝖍= 𝖚𝖓𝖉 𝕭𝖆𝖈𝖐𝖐𝖚𝖓𝖘𝖙, | 𝖔𝖉𝖊𝖗 | 𝖓𝖊𝖚𝖊𝖘𝖙𝖊𝖘 𝕯𝖗𝖊𝖘𝖉𝖓𝖊𝖗 𝕶𝖔𝖈𝖍𝖇𝖚𝖈𝖍, | 𝖊𝖓𝖙𝖍𝖆𝖑𝖙𝖊𝖓𝖉 | 𝖊𝖎𝖓𝖊 𝖕𝖗𝖆𝖐𝖙𝖎𝖘𝖈𝖍𝖊 𝕬𝖓𝖑𝖊𝖎𝖙𝖚𝖓𝖌 𝖟𝖚𝖗 𝕭𝖊𝖗𝖊𝖎𝖙𝖚𝖓𝖌 𝖛𝖔𝖓 𝖒𝖊𝖍𝖗 𝖆𝖑𝖘 1100 | 𝖆𝖚𝖘𝖊𝖗𝖑𝖊𝖘𝖊𝖓𝖊𝖓 𝖋𝖊𝖎𝖓𝖊𝖓 𝕾𝖕𝖊𝖎𝖘𝖊𝖓, 𝖆𝖑𝖑𝖊𝖓 𝕬𝖗𝖙𝖊𝖓 𝖅𝖚𝖈𝖐𝖊𝖗𝖇ä𝖈𝖐𝖊𝖗𝖊𝖎𝖊𝖓, | 𝖊𝖎𝖓𝖌𝖊𝖒𝖆𝖈𝖍𝖙𝖊𝖓 𝖚𝖓𝖉 𝖊𝖎𝖓𝖌𝖊𝖘𝖔𝖙𝖙𝖊𝖓𝖊𝖓 𝕴𝖗ü𝖈𝖍𝖙𝖊𝖓, 𝕾ü𝖑𝖟𝖊𝖓, 𝕲𝖊𝖑é'𝖘, | 𝕾ä𝖋𝖙𝖊𝖓, 𝕾𝖆𝖑𝖆𝖙𝖊𝖓, 𝕮𝖔𝖒𝖕𝖔𝖙𝖘, 𝕲𝖊𝖋𝖗𝖔𝖗𝖓𝖊𝖒 𝖚𝖓𝖉 𝖛𝖊𝖗= | 𝖘𝖈𝖍𝖎𝖊𝖉𝖊𝖓𝖊𝖓 𝕲𝖊𝖙𝖗ä𝖓𝖐𝖊𝖓, | 𝖓𝖊𝖇𝖘𝖙 | 𝖊𝖎𝖓𝖊𝖒, 𝖓𝖆𝖈𝖍 𝖉𝖊𝖓 𝕵𝖆𝖍𝖗𝖊𝖘𝖟𝖊𝖎𝖙𝖊𝖓 𝖊𝖎𝖓𝖌𝖊𝖗𝖎𝖈𝖍𝖙𝖊𝖙𝖊𝖓 | 𝕶ü𝖈𝖍𝖊𝖓𝖟𝖊𝖙𝖙𝖊𝖑=𝕭𝖚𝖈𝖍𝖊, | 𝖍𝖊𝖗𝖆𝖚𝖘𝖌𝖊𝖌𝖊𝖇𝖊𝖓 | 𝖛𝖔𝖓 | 𝕲𝖊𝖔𝖗𝖌 𝕮𝖔𝖓𝖗𝖆𝖉 𝕭𝖎𝖈𝖐𝖊𝖑𝖒𝖆𝖓𝖓, | 𝕷𝖊𝖍𝖗𝖊𝖗 𝖉𝖊𝖗 𝕶𝖔𝖈𝖍= 𝖚𝖓𝖉 𝕭𝖆𝖈𝖐𝖐𝖚𝖓𝖘𝖙 𝖟𝖚 𝕯𝖗𝖊𝖘𝖉𝖊𝖓. | 𝕯𝖚𝖗𝖈𝖍𝖌𝖊𝖘𝖊𝖍𝖊𝖓 𝖚𝖓𝖉 𝖊𝖒𝖕𝖋𝖔𝖍𝖑𝖊𝖓 | 𝖛𝖔𝖓 | 𝕵𝖔𝖍𝖆𝖓𝖓 𝕬𝖓𝖙𝖔𝖓 𝕲𝖗𝖎𝖒𝖒𝖊𝖗, 𝕮𝖆𝖗𝖑 𝕳𝖊𝖎𝖓𝖗𝖎𝖈𝖍 𝕳𝖎𝖙𝖟𝖘𝖈𝖍𝖔𝖑𝖉, | 𝕶ö𝖓𝖎𝖌𝖑. 𝕾ä𝖈𝖍𝖘. 𝕳𝖔𝖋𝖐ü𝖈𝖍𝖊𝖓𝖒𝖊𝖎𝖘𝖙𝖊𝖗, | 𝖚𝖓𝖉 | 𝕴𝖗𝖎𝖊𝖉𝖗𝖎𝖈𝖍 𝕴𝖌𝖓𝖆𝖙𝖟 𝕵𝖊𝖗𝖘𝖈𝖍𝖆𝖇𝖊𝖈𝖐, 𝕵𝖔𝖍𝖆𝖓𝖓 𝕲𝖔𝖙𝖙𝖑𝖔𝖇 𝖂𝖊𝖑𝖉, | 𝕶ö𝖓𝖎𝖌𝖑. 𝕾ä𝖈𝖍𝖘. 𝕳𝖔𝖋𝖒𝖚𝖓𝖉𝖐ö𝖈𝖍𝖊. | [fancy rule] | 𝕯𝖗𝖊𝖘𝖉𝖊𝖓, | 𝕻. 𝕲. 𝕳𝖎𝖑𝖘𝖈𝖍𝖊𝖗𝖘𝖈𝖍𝖊 𝕭𝖚𝖈𝖍𝖍𝖆𝖓𝖉𝖑𝖚𝖓𝖌. | [short rule] | 1827.

First edition, Dresden, 1827.

203 x 121 mm. π⁴ 1-26⁸ 27-28⁴; 220 leaves, pp. [i-iii] iv-viii [1] 2-432.

Bibliographies: Schraemli (3) 80.

Copies: *NUC* (Cornell only).

450. Buse, Gerhard Heinrich.

𝕶𝖚𝖓𝖘𝖙 | 𝖉𝖎𝖊 𝖂𝖊𝖎𝖓𝖊 | 𝖔𝖍𝖓𝖊 𝖆𝖑𝖑𝖊 | 𝖁𝖔𝖗𝖐𝖊𝖓𝖓𝖙𝖓𝖎𝖘𝖟 𝖚𝖓𝖉 𝖔𝖍𝖓𝖊 𝕹𝖆𝖈𝖍𝖙𝖍𝖊𝖎𝖑 | 𝖉𝖊𝖗 | 𝕲𝖊𝖘𝖚𝖓𝖉𝖍𝖊𝖎𝖙 𝖟𝖚 𝖛𝖊𝖗𝖇𝖊𝖘𝖘𝖊𝖗𝖓, | 𝖓𝖊𝖇𝖘𝖙 𝕬𝖓𝖟𝖊𝖎𝖌𝖊 𝖉𝖊𝖗 𝖇𝖊𝖘𝖙𝖊𝖓 𝕼𝖚𝖊𝖑𝖑𝖊𝖓, 𝖘𝖎𝖊 𝖜𝖔𝖍𝖑𝖋𝖊𝖎𝖑 𝖚𝖓𝖉 ä𝖈𝖍𝖙 | 𝖟𝖚 𝖊𝖗𝖍𝖆𝖑𝖙𝖊𝖓, 𝖘𝖈𝖍𝖆𝖉𝖍𝖆𝖋𝖙𝖊 𝖌𝖚𝖙 𝖟𝖚 𝖒𝖆𝖈𝖍𝖊𝖓 𝖚𝖓𝖉 | 𝖉𝖎𝖊𝖘𝖊𝖑𝖇𝖊𝖓 𝖛𝖔𝖗 𝕹𝖆𝖈𝖍𝖙𝖍𝖊𝖎𝖑 𝖟𝖚 𝖇𝖊𝖜𝖆𝖍𝖗𝖊𝖓, 𝖆𝖚𝖘 | 𝕰𝖗𝖋𝖆𝖍𝖗𝖚𝖓𝖌 𝖕𝖗𝖆𝖐𝖙𝖎𝖘𝖈𝖍𝖊𝖗 | 𝖂𝖊𝖎𝖓𝖍ä𝖓𝖉𝖑𝖊𝖗 𝖚𝖓𝖉 𝕮𝖍𝖊𝖒𝖎𝖐𝖊𝖗. | 𝕹𝖊𝖇𝖘𝖙 | 𝖊𝖎𝖓𝖊𝖒 𝕬𝖓𝖍𝖆𝖓𝖌, | 𝖆𝖑𝖑𝖊 𝕷𝖎𝖖𝖚𝖊𝖚𝖗𝖊 𝖘𝖊𝖑𝖇𝖘𝖙 𝖚𝖓𝖉 𝖆𝖚𝖋 𝖉𝖎𝖊 𝖒ö𝖌𝖑𝖎𝖈𝖍𝖘𝖙 𝖜𝖔𝖍𝖑𝖋𝖊𝖎𝖘𝖙𝖊 𝕬𝖗𝖙, | 𝖘𝖔 𝖜𝖎𝖊 𝖐ü𝖓𝖘𝖙𝖑𝖎𝖈𝖍𝖊 𝖂𝖊𝖎𝖓𝖊 𝖆𝖚𝖘 𝕭𝖊𝖊𝖗𝖊𝖓 𝖟𝖚 𝖛𝖊𝖗𝖋𝖊𝖗𝖙𝖎𝖌𝖊𝖓. | 𝕰𝖎𝖓 𝕳𝖆𝖓𝖉𝖇𝖚𝖈𝖍 | 𝖋ü𝖗 | 𝖂𝖊𝖎𝖓𝖍ä𝖓𝖉𝖑𝖊𝖗, 𝖂𝖊𝖎𝖓𝖙𝖗𝖎𝖓𝖐𝖊𝖗 𝖚𝖓𝖉 𝕷𝖎𝖖𝖚𝖊𝖚𝖗= | 𝖋𝖆𝖇𝖗𝖎𝖐𝖆𝖓𝖙𝖊𝖓, | 𝖍𝖊𝖗𝖆𝖚𝖘𝖌𝖊𝖌𝖊𝖇𝖊𝖓 | 𝖛𝖔𝖓 | 𝕲𝖊𝖗𝖍𝖆𝖗𝖉 𝕳𝖊𝖎𝖓𝖗𝖎𝖈𝖍 𝕭𝖚𝖘𝖊. | 𝕰𝖗𝖘𝖙𝖊𝖗 𝕭𝖆𝖓𝖉. | [fancy rule] | 𝕰𝖗𝖋𝖚𝖗𝖙 𝖚𝖓𝖉 𝕲𝖔𝖙𝖍𝖆, 1818. | 𝖎𝖓 𝖉𝖊𝖗 𝕳𝖊𝖓𝖓𝖎𝖓𝖌𝖘'𝖘𝖈𝖍𝖊𝖓 𝕭𝖚𝖈𝖍𝖍𝖆𝖓𝖉𝖑𝖚𝖓𝖌.

First edition, volume one only, Erfurt and Gotha, 1818. The second volume was published in 1820.

194 x 107 mm. π1 ✱⁸ ✱✱⁴ A-Dd⁸; 229 leaves, pp. [2] [i] ii-xxiv [1-3] 4-432.

Bibliographies: Horn-Arndt 402.

Copies: No other copy located.

450a. Cleef, Henny van.

𝕯𝖎𝖊 | [red, fancy] I [black] 𝖘𝖗𝖆𝖊𝖑𝖎𝖙𝖎𝖘𝖈𝖍𝖊 [red, fancy] K [black] 𝖚̈𝖈𝖍𝖊 | [short fancy rule] | 𝕶𝖔𝖈𝖍𝖇𝖚𝖈𝖍 | [medals] 𝖋𝖚̈𝖗 𝖉𝖆𝖘 [medals] | [red] 𝕴𝖘𝖗𝖆𝖊𝖑𝖎𝖙𝖎𝖘𝖈𝖍𝖊 𝕳𝖆𝖚𝖘𝖘 | 𝖛𝖔𝖓 | 𝕳𝖊𝖓𝖓𝖞 𝖛𝖆𝖓 𝕮𝖑𝖊𝖊𝖋. | [short double rule, top rule shorter than bottom] | [in red] 𝕱𝖚̈𝖓𝖋𝖙𝖊 𝕬𝖚𝖋𝖑𝖆𝖌𝖊. |[short rule, bottom rule shorter than top] | 𝕷𝖊𝖎𝖕𝖟𝖎𝖌. | 𝕸. 𝖂. 𝕶𝖆𝖚𝖋𝖒𝖆𝖓𝖓.

Fifth edition, Leipzig, [1910]. *NUC* records a third edition, Leipzig, 1896. No yearlier edition has been located.

224 x 146 mm. π^2 [1]^6 2-4^8 5^8 (5$_3$+χ^2) 6^8 7^8 (7$_5$ + 2χ1) 8-16^8 17^8 (17$_4$ + 3χ1) 18-21^8 22^4 [23]^8; 104 leaves, pp. [1-5] 6-70 [70a] 70b-70d 71⸳106 106a-106b 107-264 264a-264b 265-344 [i] ii-xvi. Publisher's brown cloth stamped in gold, black and two shades of green.

Bibliographies: Bitting, p. 91.

Copies: *NUC* (John Crerar Library only).

451. Coler, Johann, d. 1639.

OECONOMIA RURALIS ET DOMESTICA, | 𝕯𝖆𝖗𝖎𝖓̄ 𝖉𝖆𝖘 𝖌𝖆𝖓𝖙𝖟 | 𝖎𝖒𝖕𝖙 𝖆𝖑𝖑𝖊𝖗 𝖙𝖗𝖊𝖜𝖊𝖗 | 𝕳𝖆𝖚𝖘𝖟=𝖁𝖆̈𝖙𝖙𝖊𝖗/ 𝕳𝖆𝖚𝖘𝖟=𝕸𝖚̈𝖙𝖙𝖊𝖗/ | 𝖇𝖊𝖘𝖙𝖆̈𝖓𝖉𝖎𝖌𝖊𝖘 𝖛𝖓𝖉 𝖆𝖑𝖑𝖌𝖊𝖒𝖊𝖎𝖓𝖊𝖘 𝕳𝖆𝖚𝖘𝖘=𝕭𝖚𝖈𝖍/ 𝖛𝖔𝖒 𝕳𝖆𝖚𝖘𝖟= | 𝖍𝖆𝖑𝖙𝖊𝖓/ 𝖂𝖊𝖎𝖓= 𝕬𝖈𝖐𝖊𝖗= 𝕲𝖆̈𝖗𝖙𝖊𝖓= 𝕭𝖑𝖚𝖒𝖊𝖓 𝖛𝖓𝖉 𝕱𝖊𝖑𝖉=𝕭𝖆𝖜/ | 𝖇𝖊𝖌𝖗𝖎𝖋𝖋𝖊𝖓/ | 𝕬𝖚𝖈𝖍 𝖂𝖎𝖑𝖉= 𝖛𝖓𝖉 𝖁𝖔̈𝖌𝖊𝖑𝖋𝖆𝖓𝖌/ 𝖂𝖊𝖎𝖉= | 𝖂𝖊𝖗𝖈𝖐/ 𝕱𝖎𝖘𝖈𝖍𝖊𝖗𝖊𝖞𝖊𝖓/ 𝖁𝖎𝖊𝖍𝖟𝖚𝖈𝖍𝖙/ 𝕳𝖔𝖑𝖙𝖟𝖋𝖆̈𝖑𝖑𝖚𝖓𝖌𝖊𝖓/ 𝖛𝖓𝖉 𝖘𝖔𝖓𝖘𝖙𝖊𝖓 𝖛𝖔𝖓 | 𝖆𝖑𝖑𝖊𝖒 𝖜𝖆𝖘 𝖟𝖚 𝕭𝖊𝖘𝖙𝖊𝖑𝖑𝖚𝖓𝖌 𝖛𝖓𝖉 𝕽𝖊𝖌𝖎𝖊𝖗𝖚𝖓𝖌 𝖊𝖎𝖓𝖊𝖘 𝖜𝖔𝖍𝖑𝖇𝖊𝖘𝖙𝖊𝖑𝖙𝖊𝖓 𝕸𝖆𝖞𝖊𝖗𝖍𝖔𝖋𝖋𝖘/ | 𝕷𝖆̈𝖓𝖉𝖊𝖗𝖊𝖞/ 𝖌𝖊𝖒𝖊𝖎𝖓𝖊𝖓 𝕱𝖊𝖑𝖉= 𝖛𝖓𝖉 𝕳𝖆𝖚𝖘𝖟𝖜𝖊𝖘𝖊𝖓𝖘 𝖓𝖚̈𝖙𝖟𝖑𝖎𝖈𝖍 𝖛𝖓𝖉 𝖛𝖔𝖓𝖓𝖔̈𝖍𝖙𝖊𝖓 | 𝖘𝖊𝖞𝖓 𝖒𝖔̈𝖈𝖍𝖙𝖊. | 𝕾𝖆𝖒𝖕𝖙 𝖇𝖊𝖞𝖌𝖊𝖋𝖚̈𝖌𝖙𝖊𝖗 𝖊𝖎𝖓𝖊𝖗 𝖊𝖝𝖕𝖊𝖗𝖎𝖒𝖊𝖓𝖙𝖆𝖑𝖎𝖘𝖈𝖍𝖊𝖗 𝕳𝖆𝖚𝖘𝖟= 𝕬𝖕𝖔𝖙𝖊𝖈𝖐𝖊𝖓 𝖛𝖓𝖉 𝖐𝖚𝖗𝖙𝖟𝖊𝖗 | 𝖂𝖚𝖓𝖉𝖆𝖗𝖙𝖟𝖓𝖊𝖞= 𝕶𝖚𝖓𝖘𝖙/ 𝖜𝖎𝖊 𝖉𝖆𝖓𝖓 𝖆𝖚𝖈𝖍 𝖊𝖎𝖓𝖊𝖘 CALENDARII perpetui. | 𝕯𝖆𝖗𝖉𝖚𝖗𝖈𝖍 𝖛𝖓𝖉 𝖉𝖆𝖗𝖎𝖓𝖓𝖊𝖓/ 𝖜𝖎𝖊 𝖓𝖎𝖈𝖍𝖙 𝖆𝖑𝖑𝖊𝖎𝖓 𝕸𝖊𝖓𝖘𝖈𝖍𝖊𝖓/ 𝖁𝖎𝖊𝖍/ 𝕭𝖑𝖚= | 𝖒𝖊𝖓=𝕲𝖆𝖗𝖙𝖊𝖓 𝖛𝖓𝖉 𝕱𝖊𝖑𝖉𝖌𝖊𝖜𝖆̈𝖈𝖍𝖘𝖊𝖓/ 𝖒𝖎𝖙 𝖌𝖊𝖗𝖎𝖓𝖌𝖊𝖓 𝖀𝖓𝖐𝖔𝖘𝖙𝖊𝖓 𝖒𝖎𝖙 𝖉𝖊𝖗 𝕳𝖚̈𝖑𝖋𝖋 𝕲𝕺𝖙𝖙𝖊𝖘 𝖟𝖚 | 𝖍𝖊𝖑𝖋𝖋𝖊𝖓/ 𝖛𝖓𝖉 𝖛𝖔𝖒 𝖀𝖓𝖌𝖊𝖟𝖎𝖋𝖋𝖊𝖗 𝖟𝖓 𝖕𝖗𝖆𝖊𝖘𝖊𝖗𝖇𝖎𝖗𝖊𝖓/ 𝖛𝖓𝖉 𝖟𝖚 𝖘𝖆̈𝖚𝖇𝖊𝖗𝖓/ 𝖘𝖔𝖓𝖉𝖊𝖗𝖓 𝖆𝖚𝖈𝖍 𝖜𝖎𝖊𝖓𝖆𝖈𝖍 𝖉𝖊𝖓 influentiis | 𝖉𝖊𝖘𝖘

Gestirns Sonn vnd Monds/ zu rechter Zeit/ dem Liecht nach/ zu düngen/ säen/ pflanzen/ | erndten/ vnd zu bawen sey/ zu finden. | Von allerhand Kauff= vnd Handelsleut/ Auch Doctorn, Hauszbättern/ Apoteckern/ | Laboranten/ Balbierern/ Mahlern/ Goldschmied/ Müntzmeistern/ Ackerleut/ Gärtnern/ Vieh= | händlern/ Jägern/ Fischern/ Voglern/ vnd allen jeden/ so mit Handel vnd Wandel vmbgehen/ vnd | jhre Geschäfft/ Nahrung vnd Gewerb treiben. | Hiebevor von | M. JOANNE COLERO zwar beschrieben/ | Jetzo aber/ auff ein Newes in vielen Büchern mercklich corrigirt, | vermehret vnd verbessert/ in ZWEY THEIL abgetheilet vnd zum Er- | sten mahl mit schönen Kupfferstücken/ Sampt vollkommenem Register | in Truck verfertiget. | Cum Gratia & Privilegio Sac. Caesar. Majestatis. | [ornament] | Getruckt vnd Verlegt in der Churfürstlichen Stadt | Mäyntz/ | Durch Nicolaum Heyll/ Churfürstl. Mäyntzischen Hoff= | vnd Universität Buchtrucker. | [short rule] | ANNO M. DC. XLV.

Title-page of second part:

OECONOMIAE | RVRALIS ET DOMESTICAE, | Ander Theil/ | Das Erste Buch/ | Darinnen beschrieben vnd angezei= | get wird/ was zu Erhaltung/ auch Wiederbringung | Menschlichen Leibs Gesundheit nütz vnd dien= | lichen sey: | Als | 1. Von Lcamentis, wie die zu praepariren vnd zuzurichten seyen: auch wor= | zu ein jedes dienlich sey. | 3. Von mancherley Kranckheiten durch alle Gliedmassen desz Menschlichen | Leibs/ wannenhero dieselben kommen/ wie sie zu erkennen/ auch wie sie | füglichen durch innerliche vnd eusserliche Mittel können curirt werden/ | vnd zwar durch solche Artzney/ so ihm ein fleissiger Hauszwirth mehren= | theils selbsten machen vnd zurichten kan/ an vielen Orten mit fleisz cor= | rigiret/ vnd vielen bewehrten Stücklein verbessert. | 4. Ein sonderlicher Bericht von der abschewlichen Seuche der Pestilentz/ vnd | derselben Cura, die wol in acht zunehmen/ mit einem gantzen newen | Tractätlein von der Pest verbessert. | 5. Von schwangern Weibern/ wie mit denen vmbzugehen/ vor vnd nach der | Geburt/ vnd viel andere Stücke vor Mutter vnd Kinder nützlichen zu= | gebrauchen/ mit schönen newen Additionibus vnd Experimentis. | 6. Von Kindern/ wie dieselbe nützlich auff zuerziehen seynd. | Sampt einem besondern Register. | [ornament] | Mit Röm. Käys. Mayest. Gnad vnd Freyheit. | Mäyntz/ | In Verlegung Nicolai Heyllsz/ | [short rule] | ANNO M.DC.XXXXV.

First edition, Mainz, 1645.

Folio: π⁴ a-l⁶ m⁴ A-Ppp⁶, ²a-c⁴ d⁶, ³A-Gg⁶ Hh⁴; 642 leaves, pp. [*8*] 1-128 [*12*], ²1-732 [*36*], ³[*1*] 2-358 [*10*]. Last leaf blank.

Illustrations: Engraved title-page on π1ʳ and numerous woodcut and copperplate illustrations in the text.

Bibliographies: Graesse, II, 213, in a note.

Copies: *BMC* and *NUC* (4 copies).

452. Corvinus, Gottlieb Siegmund, 1677-1746.

Nutzbares, galantes und curiöses | [in red] Frauenzimmer= | LEXICON, | Worinnen nicht nur | [in red] Der Frauenzimmer geistlich= und | [in red] weltliche Orden, Aemter, Würden, Ehren= | Stellen/ Professionen, und Gewerbe, Privilegia, und | Rechtliche Wohlthaten, Hochzeiten und Trauer=Solennitäten, | Gerade und Erb=Stücken, Nahmen und Thaten der Göttinnen, | Heroinen, gelehrter Weibes=Bilder, Künstlerinnen, Prophetinnen, Affter= | Prophetinnen, Märtyrinnen, Poetinnen, Ketzerinnen, Qbackerinnen, Schwärmerinnen | und anderer Sectirischen und begeisterten Weibes=Personen, Zauberinnen und Hexen, auch | anderer beruffener, curiöser und merckens=würdiger Weibes=Bilder, Trachten und Moden, | Küchen= Tafel= Wochenstuben= Wäsch= Nehe= Hausz= Speisekammer= Keller= Kinder= Putz, Geräthe | und Vorrath, Juwelen und Schmuck, Galanterie, Seidne, Wollne und andere Zeuge, so zu ihrer | Kleidung und Putz dienlich, Rauch= und Peltzwerck, Haar=Putz und Auffsatz, Schmincken, kostbare | Olitäten und Seiffen, Bücher=Vorrath, Künste und Wissenschafften, Nahmen, Stamm= | Nahmen und besondere Benennungen, absonderliche Gewohnheiten und Gebräuche, Eigenschaften, | sonderbare Redens=Arten und Termini, Abergläubisches Wesen, Tändeleyen und Sprüchwörter, | Häuszliche Verrichtungen, Divertissements, Spiele und andere Ergötzlichkeiten, allgemeine Zufälle, | Beschwerungen und Gebrechen der Weiber, Jungfern und kleinen Kinder, Gesinde=Ordnung | und Arbeit, weibliche Straffen und absonderliche Züchtigungen, und alles dasjenige | was einem Frauenzimmer vorkommen kan, und ihm nöthig | zu wissen, | Sondern auch | Ein vollkommenes und auf die allerneueste Art verfertigtes | [in red] Koch= Torten= und Gebackens=Buch, | Samt denen darzu gehörigen Rissen, Taffel= | Auffsätzen und

Küchen=Zettuln, | Ordentlich nach dem Alphabeth kurtz und deutlich abgefaszt | und erkläret zu finden, | [in red] Dem weiblichen Geschlechte insgesamt zu | sonderbaren Nutzen, Nachricht und Ergötzlichkeit | auff Begehren ausgestellet | Von | [in red] Amaranthes. | [short rule] Leipzig, 1715. | bey Joh. Friedrich Gleditsch und Sohn.

First edition, Leipzig, 1715.

8vo.):(⁸ (folded. 1.8, 2-7) A-Yyy⁸ a-b⁸; 568 leaves, pp. [*16*], 1-2176 cols. [=1088 pp.] [*32*].

Illustrations: Engraved frontispiece on):(1ᵛ and sixteen pages with woodcuts showing table settings in the text.

Bibliographies: Unrecorded in the bibliographies consulted.

Copies: *BMC* and *NUC* (Cornell only).

453. Corvinus, Gottlieb Siegmund, 1677-1746.

Nutzbares, galantes und curiöses | [in red] Frauenzimmer= | LEXICON, | Worinnen der | [in red] Frauenzimmer geist= und weltliche | Orden, Aemter, | Würden, Ehren=Stellen, | Professionen, Rechte und Privilegia, Hochzeit= und | Trauer=Solennitäten, Gerade= und Erb=Stücken; die | Nahmen und Thaten der Göttinnen, Heroinnen, gelehrter | Frauenzimmer, Künstlerinnen, und | anderer merckwürdigen Personen | weiblichen Geschlechts; | [in red] Dererselben Trachten und Moden, und was | zum Putz und Kleidung des Frauenzimmers, und | Auszierung der Gemächer gehöret; ihre häusliche | Verrichtungen, Ergötzlichkeiten, Redens=Arten, und | was sonst einem Frauenzimmer zu wissen nöthig, | ordentlich nach dem Alphabet kurtz und deutlich erkläret zu finden, | wie auch | ein auf die allerneueste Art verfertigtes vollkommenes | [in red] Koch=Buch nebst Küchen=Zetteln | und Rissen von Tafel=Aufsätzen. | Vermehrte und verbesserte Auflage. | [rule] | Franckfurt und Leipzig, | [in red] bey. Joh. Friedrich Gleditschens seel. Sohn, | 1739.

Second edition, Frankfurt and Leipzig, 1739. Originally published, Leipzig, 1715 (item 452).

8vo. π^2)(^{4} A-Iii^8 Kkk^2 a-b^8; 464 leaves, pp. [*12*] 1-1768 cols. [=884 pp.] [*32*].

Illustrations: Engraved frontispiece by M. Bernioferothi filius after I. A. Richter showing ladies at various tasks on $\pi1^v$ and sixteen woodcuts, in the text, showing table settings.

Bibliographies: Holzmann und Bohatta VI 4850.

Copies: *NUC* (New York Public Library only).

454. Daisenberger, Maria Katharina.

𝔙𝔬𝔩𝔩𝔰𝔱ä𝔫𝔡𝔦𝔤𝔢𝔰 | 𝔅𝔞𝔶𝔢𝔯𝔦𝔰𝔠𝔥𝔢𝔰 𝔎𝔬𝔠𝔥𝔟𝔲𝔠𝔥 | 𝔣ü𝔯 𝔞𝔩𝔩𝔢 𝔖𝔱ä𝔫𝔡𝔢. | 𝔈𝔫𝔱𝔥ä𝔩𝔱: | 𝔏𝔢𝔦𝔠𝔥𝔱𝔣𝔞𝔰𝔰𝔩𝔦𝔠𝔥𝔢 𝔲𝔫𝔡 𝔟𝔢𝔴ä𝔥𝔯𝔱𝔢 𝔄𝔫𝔴𝔢𝔦𝔰𝔲𝔫𝔤𝔢𝔫 𝔞𝔲𝔣 𝔡𝔦𝔢 𝔳𝔬𝔯𝔱𝔥𝔢𝔦𝔩𝔥𝔞𝔣𝔱𝔢𝔰𝔱𝔢, 𝔰𝔠𝔥𝔪𝔞𝔠𝔨= | 𝔥𝔞𝔣𝔱𝔢𝔰𝔱𝔢 𝔲𝔫𝔡 𝔴𝔬𝔥𝔩𝔣𝔢𝔦𝔩𝔰𝔱𝔢 𝔄𝔯𝔱 𝔡𝔦𝔢 𝔉𝔩𝔢𝔦𝔰𝔠𝔥= 𝔲𝔫𝔡 𝔉𝔞𝔰𝔱𝔢𝔫𝔰𝔭𝔢𝔦𝔰𝔢𝔫, 𝔖𝔲𝔭𝔭𝔢𝔫, | 𝔖𝔬𝔰𝔷𝔢𝔫 𝔲𝔫𝔡 𝔊𝔢𝔪ü𝔰𝔢 𝔷𝔲 𝔨𝔬𝔠𝔥𝔢𝔫, 𝔅𝔞𝔠𝔨𝔴𝔢𝔯𝔨𝔢, 𝔆𝔬𝔪𝔭𝔬𝔱"𝔰, 𝔆𝔯𝔢𝔪𝔢"𝔰, 𝔊𝔢𝔩é𝔢"𝔰, | 𝔊𝔢𝔣𝔯𝔬𝔯"𝔫𝔢𝔰, 𝔐𝔞𝔯𝔪𝔢𝔩𝔞𝔡𝔢𝔫, 𝔖ä𝔣𝔱𝔢, 𝔴𝔞𝔯𝔪𝔢 𝔲𝔫𝔡 𝔨𝔞𝔩𝔱𝔢 𝔊𝔢𝔱𝔯ä𝔫𝔨𝔢, 𝔖𝔭𝔢𝔦𝔰𝔢𝔫 | 𝔣ü𝔯 𝔎𝔯𝔞𝔫𝔨𝔢 𝔲𝔫𝔡 𝔊𝔢𝔫𝔢𝔰𝔢𝔫𝔡𝔢 𝔷𝔲 𝔟𝔢𝔯𝔢𝔦𝔱𝔢𝔫, 𝔗𝔞𝔣𝔢𝔩𝔫 𝔫𝔞𝔠𝔥 𝔡𝔢𝔯 𝔫𝔢𝔲𝔢𝔰𝔱𝔢𝔫 𝔄𝔯𝔱 | 𝔷𝔲 𝔡𝔢𝔠𝔨𝔢𝔫, 𝔷𝔲 𝔱𝔯𝔞𝔫𝔰𝔠𝔥𝔦𝔯𝔢𝔫. 𝔉𝔢𝔯𝔫𝔢𝔯 𝔙𝔬𝔯𝔰𝔠𝔥𝔯𝔦𝔣𝔱𝔢𝔫 𝔷𝔲𝔪 𝔈𝔦𝔫𝔭ö𝔠𝔨𝔢𝔩𝔫 𝔲𝔫𝔡 | 𝔕ä𝔲𝔠𝔥𝔢𝔯𝔫 𝔡𝔢𝔰 𝔉𝔩𝔢𝔦𝔰𝔠𝔥𝔢𝔰, 𝔈𝔦𝔫𝔪𝔞𝔠𝔥𝔢𝔫 𝔳𝔢𝔯𝔰𝔠𝔥𝔦𝔢𝔡𝔢𝔫𝔢𝔯 𝔉𝔯ü𝔠𝔥𝔱𝔢, 𝔥𝔬𝔩𝔷𝔢𝔯𝔰𝔭𝔞𝔯𝔢𝔫, | 𝔏𝔦𝔠𝔥𝔱𝔢𝔯𝔷𝔦𝔢𝔥𝔢𝔫, 𝔖𝔢𝔦𝔣𝔢𝔫𝔰𝔦𝔢𝔡𝔢𝔫, 𝔉ä𝔯𝔟𝔢𝔫, 𝔅𝔩𝔢𝔦𝔠𝔥𝔢𝔫, 𝔅𝔯𝔬𝔡𝔟𝔞𝔠𝔨𝔢𝔫, 𝔚𝔞𝔰𝔠𝔥𝔢𝔫, | 𝔫𝔢𝔟𝔰𝔱 𝔫𝔬𝔠𝔥 𝔰𝔢𝔥𝔯 𝔳𝔦𝔢𝔩𝔢𝔫 𝔫ü𝔱𝔷𝔩𝔦𝔠𝔥𝔢𝔫 𝔥𝔞𝔲𝔰𝔥𝔞𝔩𝔱𝔲𝔫𝔤𝔰𝔳𝔬𝔯𝔱𝔥𝔢𝔦𝔩𝔢𝔫 𝔲𝔫𝔡 | 𝔐𝔦𝔱𝔱𝔢𝔩𝔫. | [short fancy rule] | 𝔖𝔢𝔠𝔥𝔷𝔢𝔥𝔫𝔱𝔢, | 𝔫𝔢𝔲𝔢𝔯𝔡𝔦𝔫𝔤𝔰 𝔳𝔦𝔢𝔩𝔣𝔞𝔠𝔥 𝔳𝔢𝔯𝔟𝔢𝔰𝔰𝔢𝔯𝔱𝔢 𝔲𝔫𝔡 𝔰𝔢𝔥𝔯 𝔳𝔢𝔯𝔪𝔢𝔥𝔯𝔱𝔢, | 𝔞𝔲𝔣 𝔳𝔦𝔢𝔯𝔷𝔦𝔤𝔧ä𝔥𝔯𝔦𝔤𝔢 𝔈𝔯𝔣𝔞𝔥𝔯𝔲𝔫𝔤 𝔤𝔢𝔤𝔯ü𝔫𝔡𝔢𝔱𝔢 𝔄𝔲𝔣𝔩𝔞𝔤𝔢. | 𝔙𝔬𝔫 | 𝔐𝔞𝔯𝔦𝔞 𝔎𝔞𝔱𝔥𝔞𝔯𝔦𝔫𝔞 𝔇𝔞𝔦𝔰𝔢𝔫𝔟𝔢𝔯𝔤𝔢𝔯, | 𝔤𝔢𝔟𝔬𝔯𝔫𝔢 𝔖𝔦𝔢𝔤𝔢𝔩 𝔦𝔫 𝔕𝔢𝔤𝔢𝔫𝔰𝔟𝔲𝔯𝔤. | [short rule] | 𝔝𝔴𝔢𝔦 𝔗𝔥𝔢𝔦𝔩𝔢. | 𝔐𝔦𝔱 𝔢𝔦𝔫𝔢𝔪 𝔦𝔫 𝔖𝔱𝔞𝔥𝔩 𝔤𝔢𝔰𝔱𝔬𝔠𝔥𝔢𝔫𝔢𝔫 𝔗𝔦𝔱𝔢𝔩𝔨𝔲𝔭𝔣𝔢𝔯. | [fancy rule] | 𝔑ü𝔯𝔫𝔟𝔢𝔯𝔤, 1843. | 𝔠. ℌ. 𝔝𝔢𝔥𝔰𝔠𝔥𝔢 𝔅𝔲𝔠𝔥𝔥𝔞𝔫𝔡𝔩𝔲𝔫𝔤. | 𝔉𝔯ü𝔥𝔢𝔯 𝔙𝔢𝔯𝔩𝔞𝔤 𝔳𝔬𝔫 𝔍. 𝔐. 𝔇𝔞𝔦𝔰𝔢𝔫𝔟𝔢𝔯𝔤𝔢𝔯 𝔦𝔫 𝔕𝔢𝔤𝔢𝔫𝔰𝔟𝔲𝔯𝔤.

Sixteenth edition, Nürnberg, 1843. Date of the original edition unknown.

182 x 111 mm. 1-30^8, ^{2}1-8^8 9^4; 308 leaves, pp. [1-5] 6-480, ^{2}[1-3] 4-136.

Illustration: Frontispiece, etched with engraving, of a kitchen scene.

Bibliographies: Horn-Arndt 414.

Copies: No other copy of this edition located. *NUC* records only an undated seventeenth edition.

455. De generibus ebriosorum et ebrietate vitanda.

De generibus Ebriosorum | et ebrietate vitanda. | Questio facetiarum et vrbanitatis plena: q[uod] pulcerrimis | optimorum scriptorum flosculis referta: in conclu= | sione Quodlibeti Erphurdiensis. Anno | Christi. M.D.XV. Circa autumna= | le equinoctium Scolastico | more explicata. | [woodcut]

Colophon: Impressum Nurnberge per Hieronymum Holczel | Anno dn̄i. Millesimo quingētesimo decimosexto

Second edition, Nürnberg, 1516. Originally published, Erfurt, 1515.

The authorship of this anonymous work has been variously attributed to Jakob Wimpheling, Jacob Hartlieb and others.

4to. A-B⁴ C⁶; 14 leaves, unpaginated.

Illustrations: Satirical woodcut of animals seated around a table on title-page.

Bibliographies: Holzmann und Bohatta I 10846.

Copies: *BMC*.

456. Dedekind, Friedrich, d. 1598.

GROBIANVS, ET | Grobiana. | DE | MORVM | SIMPLICITATE, LIBRI TRES, | Ingratiam omnium rusticitatis aman- | tium conscripti, Per | FRIDERICVM DEDEKINDVM. | *Iam denuò ab autore emendati, & plerisq;* | *in locis cùm praeceptis tum exem-* | *plis aucti.* | IRON EPISCOPTES STV- | *diosae Iuuentuti ciuilitatem optat.* | *Ethica concedant ueterum morosa sophorum,* | *Cedat Aristoteles, cumq;* | *Platone Cato.* | *Concedat Cicero Latius, concedat Erasmus,* | *Et quotquot morum de grauitate docent.* | *Hic liber exactam dat morum simplicitatem,* | *Eq; noua nuper prodijt ille schola.* | *Hunc, studiose puer, uigili perdisce labore,* | *Qui cupis ornatus moribusesse bonis.* | FRANC. *Apud Chr. Egenolphum.*

Colophon: FRANCOFORTI, *Apud Chr. Egenol-* | *phum, Anno* M.D.LIIII.

Fifth edition, Frankfurt, 1554. Originally published, Frankfurt, 1549.

8vo. A-M⁸; 96 leaves, ff. [1] 2-96.

Bibliographies: Brunet II, 560; Simon BG 452. Vicaire 255 records a Frankfurt, 1575, edition.

Copies: *NUC* (Columbia only).

457. Dedekind, Friedrich, d. 1598.

Der Grobianer | und | Die Grobianerin/ | Das ist/ | Drey Bücher | Von Einfalt der Sitten: | zu gefallen | Allen denen die grobheit lieb haben/ vor | vielen Jahren in Lateinischen ver= | sen beschrieben/ | Durch | FRIDERICUM DEDEKINDUM. | An jetzo aber der Teutschen Poeterey vernünff= | tigen Liebhabern/ in Alexandrinische Reime/ | nach anweisung H. Opitij gegebenen reguln | genaw vnd vleissig gebracht/ an vielen orten | vermehret/ vnd mit einem zu ende begge= | fügten ausführlichen Register | heraus gegeben/ | Durch | Wencel Scherffern Leobsch. Siles. | [rule] | Im Jahr M. DC.LIV.

Colophon: [four rows of type ornaments] In der Fürstlichen Residentz | Stadt Briegk | druckts | Balthasar Klose. | [rule] | M. DC. XL.

New edition, Brieg, 1654. Originally published in Latin under the title *Grobianus. De morum simplicitate, libri tres*, Frankfurt, 1549.

8vo. A-B⁸ ²A-T⁸; 168 leaves, pp. [*34*] 1-281 [282-300] [*2*]. Last leaf blank.

Bibliographies: This edition unrecorded in the bibliographies consulted.

Copies: *NUC* (Indiana University and University of California, Berkeley).

458. Dodoens, Rembert, 1517-1585.

HISTORIA | VITIS VI= | NIQVE: | *ET* | STIRPIVM NONNVLLA- | *rum aliarum.* | *ITEM* | *Medicinalium Obseruationum* | EXEMPLA. | *Auctore* | Remb. Dodonaeo Medico Caesareo. | [within ornamental wreath: BENEDICES | CORONAE ANNI | BENIGNITATIS | TVAE. PSAL. 64.] | [below the ornamental wreath] COLONIAE | *Apud Maternum Cholinum.* | cI . I . LXXX. | *Cum Gratia & Priuilegio Caes Maiest.*

First edition, Köln, 1580.

8vo.)(⁸ A-L⁸; 96 leaves, pp. [16] 1-169 [170-176]. Bound with Henri Rantzau"s *De Conservanda valitudine liber*, Leipzig, 1580 (item 500).

Bibliographies: Crahan 35; Simon BB II 197; Simon BG 514; Vicaire 284.

Copies: *BMC*, *BNC*, and *NUC* (5 copies).

459. Eobanus, Helius *Hessus*, 1488-1540.

DE CON- | SERVANDA BONA VALETVDINE | Opusculum Scholae Salernitanae, ad Re= | gem Angliae, uersibus conscriptum: Cum | *Arnoldi Nouicomensis, Medici & Philosophi cele-* / *berrimi, breuissimis ac utilissimis Enarrationibus. Et* / *haec omnia à barbarie, & infinitis, quibus scatebant,* / *mendis, tam accuratè repurgata, ut iam quasi* / *nouam faciem induerint, citraq; offen-* / *sionem legi possint.* / Opera & studio Ioannis Curionis, & / Iacobi Crellij. / *ACCESSERE* / De electione meliorum Simplicium, ac Spe- / cierum Medicinalium, Rhytmi M.O. / thonis Cremonensis. / ITEM, | S. Augustini Concio, de uitanda ebrietate, / *Carmine reddita.* / Cum Priuilegio Imper. / FRANC. Apud Chr. Egen.

Colophon: FRANC. *Apud Chr. Egenolphum.* | *Mense Martio.* | M. D. LI.

New edition, Frankfurt, 1551. Originally published under the title *Bonae valetudinis conservandae praecepta*, Erfurt, 1524.

8vo. A-O⁸ P⁴; 116 leaves, ff. [1] 2-114 [2].

Bibliographies: This edition unrecorded in the bibliographies consulted.

Copies: *BNC*, and *NUC* (Duke University only).

460. Eobanus, Helius *Hessus*, 1488-1540.

[in red] DE TVEN= | [in red] DA BONA VALETV= | DINE, LIBELLVS EOBANI | HESSI, COMMENTARIIS DOCTIS | simis [in red] à Ioanne Placotomo, [end red] Profes- | sore Medico quondam in Aca- | demia Regiomontana | illustratus. | ☞ [in red]) [in black] ✧ | [in red] *In quibus multa eruditè explicantur, studiosis* | [in red] *Philosophie plurimum profutura.* | Accesserunt & alia nonnulla lectu | non indigna,

quae uersa pa- | gina indicabit. | [ornament in red and black] | *Cum Gratia &* *Priuilegio Imperiali nouo.* | [in red] FRANC. Apud Haered. Chr. Egen. | *Anno* M. D. LXIIII.

Colophon: FRANCOFORTI EXCVDE= | bant Haeredes Christiani | *Egenolphi.* | M. D. LXIIII. | [woodcut] | [three type ornaments]

New edition, Frankfurt, 1564. Originally published under the title *Bonae valetudinis conservandae praecepta*, Erfurt, 1524.

8vo. A-Aa^8; 192 leaves, ff. [*4*] 1-183 [*5*]. Last two leaves blank.

Illustrations: Numerous woodcuts in the text.

Bibliographies: Schraemli (1) 231.

Copies: *BMC*, *BNC*, and *NUC* (National Library of Medicine, New York Academy of Medicine and University of Washington).

461. Eupel, Johann Christian.

Der | vollkommene Conditor, | oder | gründliche Anweisung | zur Zubereitung aller Arten Bonbons, Stangenzucker, | Conserven, Zuckerkuchen, Essenzpasten, Gefrornen, | Cremes, Gelees, Marmeladen, Compotts, u. s. w., so | wie auch zum Einmachen und Glasiren der Früchte, | nebst Abhandlungen vom Zucker, den Graden bei dem | Zuckerkochen und von den zur Conditorei nöthigen | Gefäszen und Geräthschaften, | im gleichen | erprobte Vorschriften und Rezepte | zu allen Gattungen der | Kunstbäckerei, | als zu Torten, Makronen, Marzipan, Biscuit, Auf= | läufen, Leb= oder Pfefferkuchen, Hohllippen, Hobel= | spähnen, Schmalz und anderm Backwerk, so wie auch den | schmackhaftesten Pasteten; | Ferner | zu den beliebetesten Arten | künstlicher Getränke und Chokoladen, | als zu den verschiedenen Obstweinen, Punschen, Eier= | punsch, Bischoff, Vin brulé, Rikus, Limonade, Mandel= | milch u. s. w. u. s. w. | von | Johann Christian Eupel, | Conditor in Gotha. | [short rule] | Dritte vermehrte und verbesserte Auflage. | [rule] | Ilmenau, 1823. | Gedruckt und verlegt bei Bernhard Friedrich Voigt.

Third edition, Ilmenau, 1823. Originally published, Sonderhausen, 1819.

171 x 100 mm. π^2 1-15^8 16^6 17^4; 132 leaves, pp. [*4*] [1-4] 5-252, 255-260 [*2*].

Note: This copy lacks signature 12 containing pp. 177-192.

Bibliographies: Schraemli (3) 315. Drexel 72 records the first edition.

Copies: No other copy of this edition located. *NUC* (Library of Congress only) records the first edition.

462. Förster, Johann Christian.

Vollständiger Unterricht | in der | Koch= und Haushaltungskunst | oder | gründliche Anweisung | für junge | Köche und Köchinnen | sich die | Zufriedenheit ihrer Herrschaft | zu erwerben. | [short rule] | Nebst einem Anhange | über die | Zubereitung der Speisen für Kranke | über das | Serviren einer Tafel | und über | die wohlfeilste Art | alle Gattungen | Federvieh zu mästen. | Von | Johann Christian Förster | Küchenmeister Ihrer Königl. Hoheit der letztverstorbenen Frau Herzoginn | von Braunschweig. | [short rule] | Mit einer Kupfertafel. | [rule] | Braunschweig, 1817 | in der Schulbuchhandlung.

New edition, Braunschweig, 1817. Originally published under the title *Braunschweigisches Kochbuch für angehende Köche*, 2 vols., Braunschweig, 1789-1790.

187 x 110 mm. π^6 1-47^8 48^2; 384 leaves, pp. [i-iii] iv-xii [1] 2-756.

Illustration: Etched folding plate of seven table settings.

Bibliographies: Unrecorded in the bibliographies consulted.

Copies: No other copy of this edition located. *NUC* locates the first edition (New York Academy of Medicine only).

462a. Gänsschopff, Tobias.

Kleine | Chronica/ | das ist | Einfältige Beschreibung der | Würtembergischen Frucht und Wein- | rechnung; Darinnen vornämlich zu finden/ wie | Jährlich Frucht und Wein gerathen/ die Käuff und | Schläg derselben/ insonderheit wie hoch die Wein-Rech- | nungen/ in den vornembsten Ampt-Stätten/ zu | Würtemberg/ da es Weinwachs | hat gewesen. | Neben ein und andern hin und wider/ | von Jahr zu Jaren/ vorgange- | nen Welthändeln: | wie auch | Einer Vermeldung aller im | Land Würtemberg habender Kostli- | cher Saurbronnen/ auch fürnemmer und | heilsamer Bäder und verselben | Gebrauch. | hievebor von Tobiâ Gänssschopffen/ Teutschen | Schulmeister zu Gröningen/ an Tag gegeben/ | anjetzo aber vermehrt/ und verbes- | sert durch. | N.S. | Stuttgart Gedruckt und verlegt | Bey Johann Weyrich Rösslin/ | [short rule] | ANNO M. DC. LX.

Second edition, Stuttgart, 1660. Originally published under the title *Chronicon, oder eigentliche Beschreibung vieler denkwürdigen Geschichten, die sich in dem… Fürstenthum Würtemberg, und dero Nachbarschafften… mitgeführt… von ungefahr Anno 1129 biss auff 1656 continuirt*, Stuttgart, 1656.

8vo. a² b⁶ A-Xx⁸ χ²; 362 leaves, pp. [*16*] 1-682 [*26*]. Last leaf, blank.

Illustrations: Engraved title-page with a portrait of Eberhardus III at the head and a view of Würtemberg at the foot.

Bibliographies: Unrecorded in the bibliographies consulted.

Copies: No other copy of this edition located. The British Library and Columbia hold the 1656 edition.

463. Gebauer, Georg Christian, 1690-1773.

GEORGII CHRISTIANI | GEBAUERI | DE | CALDAE | ET | CALDI | APVD VETERES | POTV | LIBER SINGVLARIS. | *LIPSIAE,* | APUD JACOBUM SCHUSTER | MDCCXXI.

First edition, Leipzig, 1721.

8vo. π²)(⁴ A-F⁸; 54 leaves, pp. [*12*] [1] 2-96.

Illustrations: Engraved frontispiece on π1ᵛ of a "Thermopolium Romanum," an engraved folding plate of three vessels and one engraving in the text on D1ᵛ.

Bibliographies: Horn-Arndt 258; Schraemli (1) 199; Vicaire 397.

Copies: *BMC* and *NUC* (Department of Interior Geological Survey Library, University of Pennsylvania and University of Texas).

464. Gespassiger Wort-Krieg.

Gespassiger | Wort-Krieg/ | Bestehend in einer lächerlichen Schertz=Frag/ ob denen | Brat: oder Leber=Würsten; oder Bluntzen? denen Sau=Köpf: oder | Schunken die Vorgangs=Ehre gebühre? | Von denen Eypeltauern in vergangenem Fasching mündlich durchge= | gribelt; dann einer Nährsamen Sau=Schneider=Zunfft schrifftlich | zugewidmet; | [woodcut] | Und nun bey eingeruckt=Oesterlicher Fleisch=Zeit/ allen Neu=Begierigen | zur Lust/ für ein | ROTHES=AYR | Druk= verfaster überreichet im Jahr 1708.

First edition? n.p., 1708.

4to. A⁴; 4 leaves, unpaginated.

Illustration: Woodcut of swineherd and swine on title-page.

Bibliographies: Unrecorded in the bibliographies consulted.

Copies: No other copy located.

465. Götz, Friedrich.

Die Kunst | Gefrornes | zu machen; | oder | gründliche Anweisung, künstliches Eis zu bereiten, | nebst einer Abhandlung über den Zucker, von den | Graden des Zuckerkochens, von der Mischung und | Auftragung der Farben auf das Gefrorne, von der | Entstehung, des künstlichen Eises und von dem, was | die berühmtesten Physiker seit dreihundert Jahren | darüber geschrieben haben, mit Bemerkungen, wie | jede Frucht, jede Flüssigkeit, so wie saure und süsze | Säfte, Liqueure u. s. w. zu diesem Behufe behan= | delt werden müssen, mit Aufschlüssen über Ab= | stammung und Beziehung aller Früchte, welche zum | künstlichen Eise gebraucht werden, nebst Vorschriften | und lithographischen Zeichnungen, dem Gefrornen | alle nur mögliche Formen zu geben und einem An= | hange über kühlende Getränke &c. | von | Friedrich Götz. | [publisher's monogram] | 𝔐it 4 lithographirten 𝔗afeln. | [two rules] | 𝔍lmenau, 1830. | 𝔇ruck, 𝔙erlag und 𝔏ithographie von 𝔅ernh. 𝔉r. 𝔙oigt.

First edition, Ilmenau, 1830.

8vo. π^4 $1\text{-}7^8$ 8^4; 64 leaves, pp. [i-iii] iv-viii [1] 2-119 [120].

Illustrations: Four engraved plates illustrating molds.

Note: From the library of Ian Fleming.

Bibliographies: Unrecorded in the bibliographies consulted.

Copies: No other copy located.

466. Graman, Georg, fl. 1618.

CEORGI GRAMANNI, | Ph. & Med. Doctoris, weiland 𝔠hur = | und 𝔉ürstl. 𝔖ächs. löbl. 𝔏andschafft 𝔥en = | neberg Medici ordinarii, zu | 𝔐einigen/ | 𝔑eu zugerichte/ sehr nützliche 𝔠hymische | 𝔯eise= und 𝔥ausz = | 𝔄potheca/ | 𝔖amt auszführlichem 𝔅ericht/ | was für 𝔘nterscheid zwischen der | 𝔊alenischen und 𝔓aracelsischen/ oder 𝔠hy= | mischen Medicin sey/ und wie mit denen/ | nach 𝔖pagirischer 𝔎unst bereiteten Subti- | litäten und Extracten, durch 𝔊ottes | 𝔖egen/ die 𝔊esundheit ein lange | 𝔷eit zu erhalten. | 𝔘nd dann auch allerhand gefährli= | che 𝔎ranckheiten/ mit kleiner Dosi, subtiler | 𝔐asse und wenigen 𝔗röpfflein gantz sicher/ | lieblich und anmutig von männiglichen | selbst curirt werden können/ l.a.laborirt/ | experimentirt/ und zum virdten | mahl verbessert. | [rule] | 𝔍ena/ bey 𝔍oh. 𝔍acob 𝔅auhofern/ 1670.

New edition, Jena, 1670. The date of the original edition is not known. *NUC* records an Erfurt, 1618, edition with a note that the imprint is supplied from J. Benzing's *Die Buchdrucker . . . im deutschen Sprachgebiet* (1963), p. 106.

12mo. A-L^{12}; 132 leaves; pp. [6] 1-229 [230-258]. Bound with Hannah Wolley's *Frauen Zimmers Zeit Vertreib*, Nürnberg, 1688 (item 525) and Johann Staricius's *Neu reformirt- und vermehrtet Helden-Schatz* [n.p.] 1676.

Bibliographies: This edition unrecorded in the bibliographies consulted.

Copies: No other copy of this edition located.

467. Hagger, Conrad.

[in red] Neues | Saltzburgisches | [in red] Koch=Buch/ | für | [in red] Hochfürstliche und andere vornehme Höfe/ Clöster/ | Herren=Häuser/ Hof= und Hausz=Meister/ | Köch und Einkäuffer; | Wie auch | [in red] Für einschichtige/ gesund und krancke Persohnen/ nicht allein | zu Hausz/ sondern auch im Feld. | [in red] Mit mehr dann 2500. Speisen/ und 318. in schönen Kupffer | gestochenen Formen/ aus eigener langwieriger praxi | also eingerichtet/ | [in red] Dasz man auch bey Hoch=Fürstl. und vornehmer Höfe Tafeln/ | bey grossen Gastereyen und gemeinen Mahlzeiten die Tische | auf das Zierlichste mit annehmlichsten Abwechslungen täglich | versehen und bestellen kan/ | Bestehend | [in red] Aus 4. Theilen/ in 8. Büchern eingetheilt/ bey deren | jeden ein doppelt Register mit angehänger. | Durch | [in red] Conrad Hagger/ Hoch= Fürstlich= Saltzburgischer | Stadt= und Landschafft= Koch. | [in red] Mit Röm. Rays. Maj. allergnädigstem Privilegio. | [rule] | [in red] AUGSPURG/ | Druckts und verlegts Johann Jacob Lotter/ | 1719.

Second edition, Augsburg, 1719. Originally published, Augsburg, 1718.

4to.)(⁴ (-)(4))( )(-)( )( )( )( )( )(⁴)( )( )( )( )( )(² A-Ee⁴ Ff², ²A-N⁴ O², ³A-D⁴ E², ⁴A-M⁴ N², ⁵)(⁴ a⁴ b⁴ (b2+ †²) c-d⁴ e⁴ (e2+H1) f-n⁴ c1 o-x⁴ ✱1 y-bb⁴ cc² dd-ee⁴ O⁴ ff-nn⁴ pp-qq⁴ rr², ⁶π1 A-Hh⁴ Ii⁴ (-Ii4), ⁷A-R⁴, ⁸A-FF⁴ Gg², ⁹A-Ff⁴ Gg²; 854 leaves, pp. [*42*] 1-206 [*22*], ²1-100 [*8*], ³1-32 [*4*], ⁴1-88 [*12*], ⁵[*8*] 1-12 [*4*] 13-36 [*2*] 37-104 [*2*] 105-168 [*2*] 169-220 [*8*] 221-284, 287-295, 300-301, 298-299, 296-297, 302-305, 285 [i.e.304], ⁶[*2*] 1-216 [*38*], ⁷1-116 [*20*], ⁸1-199 [200-236], ⁹1-203 [204-236].

Illustrations: Etched frontispiece of a kitchen scene and 303 etched plates showing dishes, designs for dishes and table settings.

Bibliographies: Crahan 325; Horn-Arndt 268; Vicaire 435. Schraemli (1) 225 and Schraemli (2) 67 record the first edition.

Copies: *NUC* (Library of Congress and New York Academy of Medicine).

468. Hamburgisches Kochbuch.

Hamburgisches | Kochbuch | oder | vollständige Anweisung | zum Kochen | insonderheit | für Hausfrauen in Hamburg | und Niedersachsen | verfaszt von | einigen Frauenzimmern in Hamburg. | [rule] | Mit Churfürstl. Sächsischer Freyheit. | [fancy rule] | Dritte, vermehrte und verbesserte Auflage. | [rule] | Hamburg, | bey Johann Henrich Herold. | 1798.

Third edition, Hamburg, 1798. Originally published, Hamburg, 1788.

8vo. ✱⁴ A-Pp⁸ Qq⁴; 312 leaves, pp. [8] [1] 2-615 [616].

Bibliographies: This edition unrecorded in the bibliographies consulted. Drexel 265 records the first edition.

Copies: No other copy of this edition located. *NUC* records the first edition (New York Academy of Medicine only).

469. Harsdörfer, Georg Philipp, 1607-1658.

[within a border of type ornaments] Vollständiges | TRINCIR- | Büchlein/ | handlend: | *I,* Von den Tafeldecken/ und was demselbigen anhängig. / *II,* Von Zerschneidung und Vorlegung der Speisen. | *III,* Von rechter Zeitigung aller Mundkoste/ oder von dem | Kuchenkalender durch das gantze Jahr. | Nach Italianischer und dieser Zeit üblichen Hofart mit fleisz be= | schrieben/ und mit vielen nohtwendigen Kupffern kunst= | richtig auszgebildet. | Und zu finden in Nürnberg/ bey Paulus Fürsten Kunsthändlern.

First edition, Nürnberg, ca. 1649.

Oblong 4to. A-T⁴; 76 leaves, pp. [14] [1-2] 3-135 [136-138].

Illustrations: Engraved title, two etched folding plates illustrating carving utensils and forty-one etched plates integral with the text and reckoned in the collation and pagination, illustrating napkin folding and carving. The carving illustrations derive from those in Mathias Giegher's *Il Trinciante*, Padoua, 1621 (item 1146).

This, the original edition, contains only three parts and was printed for Fürst by Christoff Lochner. The work, expanded to four parts and adding twenty-four Gast-

oder Tischfragen, was reprinted for Fürst by Heinrich Pillenhofer in 1652 with the title changed to *Vollständig vermehrtes Trincir-Buch* and the number of plates expanded to sixty-three, two of them folding. The engraved title-page was altered, the oval containing the original title changed to a rectangle with the new title, and the imprint and date added at the bottom of the page. The *NUC* records a further edition dated 1654 which was followed by a 1657 edition (item 470) and later editions of 1662, 1663 and 1665.

Bibliographies: Wheaton and Kelly 2697.

Copies: *NUC* and Wheaton and Kelly (Harvard only).

470. Harsdörfer, Georg Philipp, 1607-1658.

[within a border of type ornaments] Vollständiges und von neuem vermehrtes | Trincir-Buch. | Handlend: | I. Von den Tafeldecken/ und was demselbigen anhängig. | II. Von Zerschneidung und Vorlegung der Speisen. | III. Von rechter Zeitigung aller Mundkoste/ oder von dem | Kuchen-Calender/ durch das gantze Jahr. | IV. Von den Schaugerichten/ und etlichen Denckwürdigen | Banncketen. | V. XXV. Gast- oder Tischfragen/ Und ist ferners neurlich beyge= | bracht/ was in den ersten Theilen/ und sonderlich von dem Tafeldecken/ | auszsgelassen worden. | Nach Italianischer und dieser Zeit üblichen Hof-Art mit fleisz beschrieben/ | und mit Kupffern lehrartig auszgebildet. | [rule] | In Verlegung Paulus Fürsten/ Kunsthändlers. | Nürnberg/ Gedruckt bey Christoff Gerhard.

Fourth edition, Nürnberg, 1657. Originally published, Nürnberg [ca.1649] (item 469).

Oblong 4to. A-Ddd⁴; 200 leaves, pp. [8] [1-3] 4-379 [380-392].

Illustrations: Engraved title-page, two etched folding plates illustrating carving utensils, two engraved plates, one with two allegorical figures holding a wreath of laurel over the head of Count Wolffegg and the other of a primitive feast, and fifty-nine etched plates illustrating napkin folding and carving.

Bibliographies: Oberlé (1) 553; Schraemli (1) 228; Vicaire 844.

Copies: Only the Oberlé copy of this edition located.

Hessus, Helius Eobanus, 1488-1540. See Eobanus, Helius *Hessus*, 1488-1540 (item 459).

471. Huber, Johanna Maria.

Bayerisches | Kochbuch | für | Fleisch = und Fasttäge. | [short fancy rule] | Enthält: | leichtfaszliche und bewährte Anweisungen, um für alle | Stände auf die vortheilhafteste und schmackhafteste | Art zu kochen, zu backen, und einzumachen. | [short fancy rule] | Nebst einem Abschnitte | von | besondern Speisen für Kranke, | und | ökonomischen Hausmitteln. | [short fancy rule] | Herausgegeben | von | Johanna Maria Huberinn. | [rule] | Mit Bewill. der Kurfl. Bücherzensurspezialkommission. | [fancy rule] | Stadtamhof, | bei Joh, Mich. Daisenberger, bürgerl. Buchhändler. | 1800.
First edition, Stadtamhof, 1800.

8vo. π^2 A-Ii^8 Kk^6 Ll^4; 268 leaves, pp. [*4*] [1] 2-530 [*2*]. Last leaf blank.

Illustration: Etched frontispiece of a kitchen scene on $\pi1^v$.

Bibliographies: Horn-Arndt 475.

Copies: No other copy located.

472. Kartoffelbüchlein und Kartoffel-Kochbuch.

Kartoffelbüchlein | und | Kartoffel-Kochbuch | für Reich und Arm | oder | die Kartoffel in ihrer mehrhundertfältigen er = | probten Anwendung zu den mannichfaltigsten | Suppen, Gemüsen, Zuspeisen, Salaten, Mehl = | speisen, Backwerken und andern schmackhaften | Zubereitungen für die Tafel, | wie auch | nach ihrer vielfachen Nutzbarkeit für den Viehstand | und bei technischen Gewerben, namentlich zu Grütze, | Sago, Brot, Butter, Käse, Bier, Wein, Kaffee, Seife, | Lichtern und andern menschlichen Bedürfnissen. | Nach | vieljähriger eigner Erfahrung herausgegeben | von | einem Menschenfreunde. | [fancy rule] | Weimar, 1839. | Druck. und Verlag von Bernh. Friedr. Voigt.

First edition, Weimar, 1839.

12mo. π^{10} 1-5^{12} 6^6 7^2; 78 leaves, pp. [i-iii] iv-xx [1] 2-135 [136].

Bibliographies: Drexel 339.

Copies: No other copy located.

473. Klett, Andreas.

Neues | Trenchir-Büchlein. | Wie man nach rechter Art/ und ietzigem Gebrauch | nach/ allerhand Speisen ordentlich auff die Taffel setzen/ zier= | lich zerschneiden und vorlegen/ auch artlich wiederumb | abheben soll. | Alles mit schönen Kupfferstücken beygebracht und | mit Fleiss auffgesetzt | Durch | Andraeas Kletten/ Cyg. Misn. & Jur. Stud. | [rule] WEIMAR/ | Drukkts in Matthaei Birckners Verlag Thomas Eyliker/ | Anno 1659.

Second edition, Weimar, 1659. Originally published, Jena, 1657.

Oblong 12mo. A-K^6; 60 leaves, pp. [*12*] [1] 2-26 [*2*] 27-106.

Illustrations: Etched title-page showing an upper class family at table on A1^r and twenty-three inserted copperplate etchings illustrating carving. The copperplates derive from the plates in Mathias Giegher's *Il Trinciante*, Padoua, 1621 (item 1146).

Bibliographies: This edition unrecorded in the bibliographies consulted. Drexel 10 records the first edition.

Copies: No other copy located.

474. Klett, Andreas.

Neues | Trenchier= und Plicatur=Büchlein/ | Darinnen begriffen: | Wie/ nach jetziger Hof=Art/ allerhand Speisen und Früch= | te/ künstlicher Weise zerschnitten/ vorgeleget/ aufgetragen/ gesetzet/ | eingeschoben/ und wiederum abgehoben/ auch wie an Keyserl. Königl. Fürstl. und | Herrl. Tafeln/ das Tafel=Zeug nettiret/ frichiret/ zubereitet/ daraus al= | lerhand Plicaturn gearbeitet und gebildet wer= | den können. | Aufs fleissigste corrigiret/ mit gantz neuen Kupffer=Stücken ge= | zieret/ und ans Tage=Liecht gebracht/ |

Durch | ANDREAM Kletten/ Exercitiorum Magistrum. | [rule] | Nürnberg/ | In Verlegung Leonhard Loschge/ Buchändlern, 1677.

New edition, Nürnberg, 1677. Originally published, Jena, 1657.

Oblong 12mo. A-H⁸; 64 leaves, pp. [8] 1-120. Three letterpress folding charts showing table settings tipped in facing pp. 68, 70 and 92 and not reckoned in the collation or pagination.

Illustrations: Etched title-page by P. Froschel showing three people at table in a garden with a carver in attendance and twenty-eight inserted copperplate etchings illustrating carving and napkin folding. The copperplates derive from the plates in Mathias Giegher's *Il Trinciante*, Padoua, 1621 (item 1146).

Bibliographies: Drexel 11; Horn-Arndt 145; Vicaire 476.

Copies: *NUC* (John Crerar Library only).

475. Klett, Andreas.

[in red] ANDREAE Klettens/ N.P.C. | Wohl=informirter | [in red] Tafel-Decker und Trenchant/ | Welchem | Kurtz/ doch deutlich gewiesen wird/ wie er an Grosser Herren Tafeln/ | auch sonsten bey Gastereyen/ nach der allerneuesten Art/ nicht allein | [in red] Das Tafel-Zeug künstlich brechen/ | und in gar bielerley Figuren berwandeln, sondern auch | [in red] Allerhand Speisen/ Confect und Früchte | zierlich und nach der Ordnung auftragen/ zerschneiden/ borlegen und wieder abtragen soll. | [in red] Bey dieser neuen Auflage mit darzu dienlichen Kupffer-Stichen und berschiedenen | Historischen Gemüths= Belustigungen bersehen/ auch durch und durch nach des AUTORIS Tode/ | auf die heutige Art eingerichtet und berbessert | bon | [in red] Carl Christoph Neumann'/ N.P.C. | [rule] | Nünberg/ | [in red] Verlegts Buggel und Seitz Buchhändlere, 1724.

New edition, Nürnberg, 1724. Originally published, Jena, 1657.

Oblong 12mo.)(⁴ (-)(4) A-K⁸ Ll; 84 leaves, pp. [6] 1-162. This copy is imperfect, lacking the last (three?) leaves of signature L. There also should be two folding letterpress charts showing table settings facing pp. 100 and 132 present only in fragments in this copy.

Illustrations: Twenty-eight inserted copperplate etchings illustrating carving and napkin folding derived from the plates in Mathias Giegher's *Il Trinciante*, Padoua, 1621 (item 1146).

Bibliographies: Horn-Arndt 148; Simon BG 921.

Copies: No other copy located.

476. Knoer, R. Christine (Dortinger) d. 1809.

Sammlung | bieler | Vorschriften | bon allerley | Koch= und Backwerk | für | junges Frauenzimmer, | bon | einer Freundin der Kochkunst | in Göppingen. | [ornament] | Neue berbesserte Ausgabe. | [rule] | Stuttgart, | bey Erhard und Löflund | 1790.

New edition, Stuttgart, 1790. Date of the original edition unknown.

8vo.)(^{4} A-Bb^8; 196 leaves, pp. [8] [1] 2-374 [26]. Last leaf blank.

Bibliographies: Unrecorded in the bibliographies consulted.

Copies: No other copy of this edition located. *NUC* (Cornell and New York Academy of Medicine) locates a "neue Auflage," Stuttgart, 1787.

477. Kuss, Johanna.

Die | Holsteinische Küche | oder | Anleitung zur Führung des Hausstandes | in einer Anzahl | auf | Erfahrung begründeter, bewährter Anweisungen. | Herausgegeben | bon | Johanna Kusz. | [short rule] | [bar] Zweiundzwanzigste Auflage. [bar] | [short rule] | Leipzig, | Verlag der Dürr'schen Buchhandlung.

Twenty-second edition, Leipzig, ca. 1900. Date of the original edition unknown. Earliest edition recorded is the seventh, Altona, 1871 (Horn-Arndt 494).

188 x 128 mm. [1]^8 (-1$_1$) 2-25^8; 199 leaves, pp. [i-iii] iv-xxxiii [xxxiv] [1] 2-364. Publisher's red pictorial cloth lettered in gold and black.

Bibliographies: This edition unrecorded in the bibliographies consulted.

Copies: No other copy located.

478. Liber cure cocorum.

LIBER CURE COCORUM. | [short rule] | COPIED AND EDITED FROM THE
SLOANE MS. 1986 | BY | RICHARD MORRIS, | AUTHOR OF "THE
ETYMOLOGY OF LOCAL NAMES", | MEMBER OF THE PHILOLOGICAL
SOCIETY. | PUBLISHED FOR THE PHILOLOGICAL SOCIETY | BY | A. ASHER
& CO., BERLIN. | 1862.

First edition, Berlin, 1862.

8vo. π^4 a-c^8 d^4 χ1; 33 leaves, pp. [i-iii] iv [1] 2-61 [62].

Bibliographies: Vicaire 905; Wheaton and Kelly 3661.

Copies: *BMC* and *NUC* (13 copies).

479. Lissner, Erich.

WURSTOLOGIA | oder | 𝕰𝔰 𝔤𝔢𝔥𝔱 𝔲𝔪 𝔡𝔦𝔢 𝔚𝔲𝔯𝔰𝔱 | Eine Monographie über die Wurst
| von | ERICH LISSNER | vom Hause Kalle & Co. Aktiengesellschaft |
Wiesbaden-Biebrich | MCMXXXIX | *Cum Privilegio Farciminali & Consensu*
Porcorum

First edition, Wiesbaden, 1939.

4to. [1^6 2-5^8 6^6 7^4 8^6 9^8 10^{10} 11-12^8 13^4 14^6 15^4 16-17^8 18^6 19^2]; 126 leaves, pp. [1-2]
3-250 [2]. Last leaf blank. Publisher's marbled boards with printed label on front
cover and spine.

Illustrations: Black and white photolithographed illustrations reproduced from other
works in the text; three colored illustrations tipped onto text pages; a colored
reproduction of *Münchener Bilderbogen* no. 74 tipped in at end.

Bibliographies: Horn-Arndt 1066.

Copies: *NUC* (Harvard and University of California, Berkeley).

480. Lobera d'Avila, Luis.

Ein nutzlich Regiment der gesundt | heyt/ Genant das Vanquete/ oder Gastmal der Edlen diener | von der Complexion/ Eigenschafft/ Schad/ und nutz allerley | Speysz Trancks/ uñ von allem/ darmit sich der mensch in ge= | sundtheyt enthelt/ Mit sampt einem kurtzen Regiment/ | Wye man sich in der Pestilentz/ Pestilentzischen fieber | unnd Schweysz halten soll. | Gemacht durch den Hochgeachten Doctoré Ludouicum De Abila/ Keyserlicher Maye- | stat Leybartzt/ ehemals in Lateynischer und Hyspanisher sprach beschriben/ Un durch | den Hochgelerten Herren Michaelem Krautwadel/ der Freyen Künst unnd Artzney | Doctoré zu Landsperg verteütscht/ mit berenderüg alle dem/ so Teütscher Com= | plexió etwas hert/ bnleydlich/ oder swyder ist/ Auch mit hinzusetzung bilerley | leer/ sprüch/ und zeugknus Hochberümpter ärtzt/ dauon etwan im text | zu kurtze meldunng beschicht/ Als eyn yetlicher berstendiger | Leser an der seytten des texts wol abnemen mag. | [woodcut] | Mit Keyserlicher Mayestat Gnad und Priuilegio.

Colophon: Gedruckt in der Kayserlichen Statt Augspurg durch | Heynrich Steyner am 20. tag Februarij im | M. D. XXXI.

First edition in German, Augsburg, 1531, translated by Michael Krautwadel from Lobera d'Avila's *Vanquete de nobels cavalleros*, Augsburg, 1530.

4to. A-Z⁴ a² b⁴; 98 leaves, ff. [5] 1-90 [3].   Last leaf blank.

Illustrations: Six woodcuts in the text attributed to Hans Burgkmaie, Hans Weiditz, and Jörg Breu.

Bibliographies: Crahan 56; Durling 2835; Schraemli (1) 288; Vicaire 533.

Copies: *BMC*, *BNC*, and *NUC* (7 copies).

481. Löhr, Johann Andreas Christian, 1764-1823.

Der | vollständige Haushalt | mit seinen | Vortheilen, Hülfsmitteln und Kenntnissen | und | bielen entdeckten Geheimnissen | für | Hauswirthe und Hauswirthinnen | insonderheit für angehende. | bon | Carl Friedrich Schmidt. | [fancy rule] | Leipzig, bei Gerhard Fleischer | 1821.

First edition, Leipzig, 1821.

8vo. A-Mm⁸ Nn² (✱)⁸; 290 leaves, pp. [1-3] 4-564, [i] ii-xvi. Three folding letterpress tables tipped in facing p. 564 (though probably intended to face p. 560) not reckoned in collation or pagination.

Carl Friedrich Schmidt is a pseudonym used by Löhr in his work titled *Vollständiger und gründlicher Gartenunterricht* . . ., Leipzig, Gerhard Fleischer, 1816, according to *NUC* cataloging supplied by the National Agricultural Library.

Bibliographies: Unrecorded in the bibliographies consulted.

Copies: No other copy located.

482. Malortie, Ernst von, 1804-1887.

𝕯𝖆𝖘 𝕸𝖊𝖓𝖚. | 𝖁𝖔𝖓 | 𝕰𝖗𝖓𝖘𝖙 𝖛𝖔𝖓 𝕸𝖆𝖑𝖔𝖗𝖙𝖎𝖊, | 𝕺𝖇𝖊𝖗𝖍𝖔𝖋𝖒𝖆𝖗𝖘𝖈𝖍𝖆𝖑𝖑 𝖚𝖓𝖉 𝕲𝖊𝖍𝖊𝖎𝖒𝖗𝖆𝖙𝖍, Dr. phil. | Manger est un besoin, mais | savoir manger est un art! — | *Larochefoucauld.* | 𝕯𝖗𝖎𝖙𝖙𝖊, 𝖇𝖊𝖉𝖊𝖚𝖙𝖊𝖓𝖉 𝖊𝖗𝖜𝖊𝖎𝖙𝖊𝖗𝖙𝖊 𝕬𝖚𝖘𝖌𝖆𝖇𝖊. | [short rule] | 𝕰𝖗𝖘𝖙𝖊𝖗 𝕿𝖍𝖊𝖎𝖑. [𝖅𝖜𝖊𝖎𝖙𝖊𝖗 𝕿𝖍𝖊𝖎𝖑. | 𝕬𝖓𝖜𝖊𝖎𝖘𝖚𝖓𝖌 𝖟𝖚𝖗 𝕭𝖊𝖗𝖊𝖎𝖙𝖚𝖓𝖌 𝖉𝖊𝖗 𝕲𝖊𝖗𝖎𝖈𝖍𝖙𝖊. | 𝕸𝖎𝖙 29 𝕿𝖆𝖋𝖊𝖑𝖓 𝕬𝖇𝖇𝖎𝖑𝖉𝖚𝖓𝖌𝖊𝖓.] | 𝕬𝖓𝖑𝖊𝖎𝖙𝖚𝖓𝖌. 𝕸𝖚𝖘𝖙𝖊𝖗-𝕸𝖊𝖓𝖚𝖘. 𝕳𝖎𝖘𝖙𝖔𝖗𝖎𝖘𝖈𝖍𝖊 𝕸𝖊𝖓𝖚𝖘. | 𝕮𝖚𝖑𝖎𝖓𝖆𝖗𝖎𝖘𝖈𝖍𝖊 𝕷𝖎𝖙𝖙𝖊𝖗𝖆𝖙𝖚𝖗. | [short fancy rule] | 𝕳𝖆𝖓𝖓𝖔𝖛𝖊𝖗 1888. | 𝕶𝖑𝖎𝖓𝖉𝖜𝖔𝖗𝖙𝖍'𝖘 𝖁𝖊𝖗𝖑𝖆𝖌.

Third edition, Hanover, 1888. Originally published, Hannover, 1879, in one volume and enlarged to two volumes, Hanover, 1881.

2 vols. 225 x 142 mm. Vol. I. [1]⁸ 2-28⁸ 29² 30⁸; 234 leaves, pp. [1-5] 6-468. Vol. II. [1]⁸ 2-30⁸; 240 leaves, pp. [1-5] 6-480. Publisher's red cloth stamped in gold and black.

Illustrations: Vol. I. Lithographed plate with vignette of items for a feast on the recto and chromolithographed facsimile of a dinner menu on the verso as a frontispiece. Vol. II. Lithographed frontispiece of kitchen and twenty-eight wood engraved plates, largely pastry designs and the twenty-eighth a floor plan for a kitchen. Also some wood engravings in the text.

Bibliographies: Bitting, p. 305; Horn-Arndt 512.

Copies: *NUC* (Library of Congress and New York Public Library).

483. Marperger, Paul Jakob, 1656-1730.

[in red] PAUL JACOB MARPERGERS, | Königlich = Polnisch. und Chur = Sächsisch. Hoff = und Commercien-Rahts/ wie auch | Mitglieds der Königlich = Preuszischen Societät der Wissenschafften/ | Vollständiges | [in red] Küch = und Keller = | [in red] DICTIONARIUM, | In welchem allerhand | Speisen und Geträncke/ | [in red] Bekannte und unbekannte/ gesunde und ungesunde/ einheimische | und ausländische/ wohlfeile und kostbare/ nothwendige und entbehr = | liche/ und andere/ wie sie Nahmen haben mögen/ mehr beschrieben/ | [in red] Ihr rechter Einkauffs = und Erzielungs = Ort/ Zeit un Preisz/ wie auch ihre | Auslesung/ Zubereitung/ Conservation, nützliche und schädliche Würckung/ mässiger und | unmässiger Gebrauch/ nach gewissen Monaten/ Jahrs = Zeiten/ Witterungen und Ländern/ item nach der | Menschlichen Leibes = Constitution und Verrichtungen/ Alter/ Stand und Vermögen gewiesen; | Ferner | [in red] Allerhand nützliche Haushaltungs = Gesundheits = Lebens = und | Policey-Regeln/ mit Moralischen Anmerckungen/ gegeben/ | Unterschiedlicher Nationen ihre gewöhnliche Speis = Arten und Mahlzeiten | erzehlet/ | [in red] Grosser Herren Banquets, solenne Festins und Tractirungen/ | Adelicher und Bürgerlicher auch geringer Standes = Personen Convivia | wohl einzurichten/ die Tafeln zierlich anzuordnen/ zu garniren/ und zu bese = | tzen/ gelehret/ | Und in Summa alles dasjenige/ was zum splendiden so wohl/ als was zum moderaten | Leben an Speis und Getränck vorhanden seyn musz/ vorgestellet wird. | [in red] Allen Hoff- Küchen- und Keller-Meistern/ Schreibern/ Christl. Haus-Vä- | tern und Haus = Müttern/ zu sonderbaren Nutzen aufgesetzet. | [rule] | Hamburg/ in Verlegung BENJAMIN SCHILLERS seel. Wittwe/ ANNO 1716.

First edition, Hamburg, 1716.

4to. π^2)(^{2})( )(^{4} A-Hhhhhhh^4; 684 leaves, pp. [16] [1] 2-1352.

Illustration: Emblematic frontispiece etched with engraving on $\pi 1^v$.

Bibliographies: Bitting, p. 310; Drexel 24; Horn-Arndt 293; Schraemli (1) 320.

Copies: NUC (Library of Congress, New York Public Library, and New York Academy of Medicine.)

484. Mensa philosophica.

[title with ornamental bar on left and right] IA hoc Opusculo tra= | ctatur de his quibus | vtimuri mensa De naturis rerum videlicet cibi & po | tus De questionibus mensalibus varijs ac iucundis | quibus in mensa recreamur. Deq[ue] conditonibus eo[rum] | quibus in mensa conuersamur. Philosophice bilari= | terq[ue] proceditur. Quare hoc opus merito appelatur | Mensa Philosophica. | [woodcut] | [ornament]

Colophon: ¶ Presens liber (qué mensaz philosophicā vocant) | vnicuiq[ue] perutilis copēndiose p[er]tractans. in primis | quid in cōuiuijs pro cibis & potibus sumenduz est. | deinde qui sermones in illis [cu]m exigentia p[er]sonaruz | babendi sunt & q̄ questiones discuriende que insup[er] | facecie siue ioci interserendi feliciter explicit. ¶ Im- | pressus Colonie apud predicatores. Per me Lor | neliū de zyrvckzee alme vniuersitat[is] Colonieñ. sup | positū Anno salutis nostre. m.ccccc.viii. Mensis | vero Martij. die. xvij.

New edition, Köln, 1508. Originally published, Köln, ca. 1480.

4to. π^4 A^8 B^4 C^8 D^4 E^6 F^4 G^6 H^8; 52 leaves, unpaginated.

Illustrations: Armorial woodcut on $\pi1^v$ and repeated on $H8^v$.

Note: This work has been attributed variously to Theobald Anguilbert, an Irish physician, and to Michael Scott, a late 12th-early 13th century mathematician, physician, and scholar.

Bibliographies: Brunet III, 1636 in a note; Schraemli (1) 348; Schraemli (3) 9.

Copies: *NUC* (College of Physicians of Philadelphia and Yale).

485. Metzger, Johann.

Der | Rheinische Weinbau | in | theoretischer und praktischer Beziehung bearbeitet | von | Joh. Metzger, | Universitätsgärtner in Heidelberg; ordentlichem Mitgliede der Gesellschaft | für Naturwissenschaft und Heilkunde zu Heidelberg; ordentlichem und cor= | respondirendem Mitgliede der Königl. Hannöbersch. Landwirthschafsge= | sellschaft; Ehrenmitglied des Königl. Preuszisch. Gartenbereins; correspon= | direndem Mitgliede der Wetterauischen Gesellschaft für die gesammte Na= | turkunde und des Groszherzogl. Badischen landwirthschaftlichen | Vereins. | [short rule] | Mit 17 Steintafeln und einer groszen Untersuchungstabelle | verschiedener Weinberge im Rheinthale. | [fancy rule] | Heidelberg, 1827. | Bei August Oszwald.

First edition, Heidelberg, 1827.

8vo. π^8 1-16^8 17^2; 138 leaves, pp. [i-iii] iv-xvi [1] 2-260.

Illustrations: Seventeen lithographed plates on pull-out folds and one folding lithographed chart.

Bibliographies: Simon BV, p. 122.

Copies: *NUC* (Harvard, National Agricultural Library, and University of California, Berkeley).

485a. Morgenstern-Schulze, Johanna Katharina, d. 1796.

Left hand title-page:

Magdeburgisches | Kochbuch | für | angehende | Hausmütter Haushälterinnen | und | Köchinnen | [short rule] | Nebst einer | Unterweisung | in andern | zu einer guten Haushaltung | gehörigen | Wissenschaften | [short rule] | [...] (Preis 1 Thlr. 4 Gr.)

Right hand title-page:

Unterricht | für ein | junges Fruenzimmer | das | Küche | und | Haushaltung | selbst besorgen will | aus eigener Erfahrung ertheilt | von | einer Hausmutter | [short rule] | Erster Band | Mit zwei Kupfertafeln | [rule] | Neue rechtmassige verbesserte und | vermehrte Ausgabe | [rule] | Magdeburg 1802 | im Verlag des Buchhandlers Creutz,

New edition, Magdeburg, 1802. Volume I only of three published. Originally published, Magdeburg, 1782.

180 x 107 mm. π^2 χ^6 A-Ll^8; 280 leaves, pp. [2] [i-v] vi-xiv [1-3] 4-543 [544].

Illustrations: Two engraved folding copperplate illustrations, one of table settings and the other of carving.

Bibliographies: This edition unrecorded in the bibliographies consulted. Drexel, Holzmann/Bohatta, Horn-Arndt and Malortie cite other editions.

Copies: No other copy of this edition located.

486. Morgenstern-Schulze, Johanna Catharine, d. 1796.

Left hand title-page:

Magdeburgisches | Kochbuch | für | angehende | Hausmütter Haushälterinnen | und | Köchinnen | [short fancy rule] | Nebst einer | Unterweisung | in andern | zu einer guten Haushaltung | gehörigen | Wissenschaften | [short fancy rule] | Erster Band [Zweiter Band] [Dritter Band] | [volume one only: Mit zwei Kupfertafeln] [volume three only: Mit Einer Wäschtabelle] | [fancy rule] | Neue rechtmäszige verbesserte und | vermehrte Ausgabe | [fancy rule] | Magdeburg 1806 [1804] [1804] | im Verlag des Buchhändlers Creutz.

Right hand title-page:

Unterricht | für ein | junges Frauenzimmer | das | Küche | und | Haushaltung | selbst besorgen will | aus eigener Erfahrung ertheilt | von | einer Hausmutter | [short fancy rule] | Erster Band [Zweiter Band] [Dritter Band] | [volume one only: Mit zwei Kupfertafeln] [volume three only: Mit Einer Wäschtabelle] | [fancy rule] | Neue rechtmäszige verbesserte und | vermehrte Ausgabe | [fancy rule] | Magdeburg 1806 [1804] [1804] | im Verlag des Buchhändlers Creutz.

Fifth edition, Magdeburg, 1804-1806. Originally published, Magdeburg, 1782.

8vo. 3 vols. Vol. I. π^2 $^2\pi^6$ A-Ll^8; 280 leaves, pp. [2] [i-v] vi-xiv [1-3] 4-543 [544]. Vol. II. π^2)(^{4} A-Gg^8 Hh1; 247 leaves, pp. [2] [i-iii] iv-x [1-3] 4-482. Vol. III. π^2)(^{4} A-Cc^8 Dd^2 Ee^8; 224 leaves, pp. [4] [i] ii-viii [1-3] 4-435 [436].

Illustrations: Vol. I. Two etched folding plates showing table settings and carving instructions tipped on to the leading edges of pp. 245 and 251. Vol. III. Engraved chart of washing charges.

Bibliographies: This edition unrecorded in the bibliographies consulted. Drexel 50 records a Madgeburg, 1792, edition in two volumes.

Copies: No other copy of this edition located.

487. Neues lehrreiches und vollständiges Magazin.

Neues lehrreiches und vollständiges | Magazin, | vor junges Frauenzimmer | die ganze | Koch=Kunst, | und | Zuckerbeckerei, | samt allem, was damit verknüpft ist, | vollkommen zu erlernen. | [short rule] | Nach Art derer | Magazins | der | Madame le Prince de Beaumont, | in Fragen und Antworten eingekleidet, | und mit | alphabetischem Register zum bequemen Aufschlagen derer | darinnen enthaltenen mehr | als 4500 Speisen | [volume two only: sodann wieder mit einem besondern Register | der Fastern=Speisen] | auch einem | Trenchir-Buch mit Figuren | versehen. | Erster Theil. [Zweyter Theil.] | [volume one only: rule | Neue Auflage.] | [fancy rule] | Carlsruhe, 1771. [1770.] | gedruckt und verlegt bey Michael Macklot. [volume two: Maklot.]

Second edition of part one and first edition of part two, Carlsruhe, 1771, 1770. Originally published, Carlsruhe, 1769-1770; second edition, Carlsruhe, 1771-1773.

8vo. 2 vols. Vol. I.)(^{4} A-Zz^8 Aaa-Bbb^4; 380 leaves, pp. [8] [1] 2-750 [2]. Vol. II. Ccc-Fffff^8 a-e^8; 432 leaves, pp. [2] [751] 752-860, 863-1097, 1080-1404, 1415-1542, ^{2}1-76 [4] = 864 pp. Last two leaves blank.

Illustrations: Four folding woodcuts of table settings and woodcuts in the text illustrating carving.

Bibliographies: The first edition is unrecorded in the bibliographies consulted. Horn-Arndt 307 records second edition of both parts.

Copies: No other copy of the second edition located. *NUC* locates the first edition (New York Academy of Medicine and New York Public Library).

488. Neumann, Kaspur, 1683-1737.

LECTIONES PUBLICAE | Von Bier | SUBJECTIS DIAETETICIS, | Nehmlich von den in hiesigen Gegenden gewöhnlichsten und durch | Menschliche Hülffe zu Stande gebrachten | biererley Geträncken, | Vom | THÉE, CAFFÉE, | Bier, und

𝔚ein, | 𝔚ie solche | 𝔅ey dem in 𝔅erlin gestiffteten | 𝔎önigl. COLLEGIO
MEDICO-CHIRURGICO | abgehandelt worden | von | D. 𝔠aspar 𝔑eumann, |
𝔎önigl. 𝔓reuszischen 𝔥off = 𝔯ath und *Profess. publ. Chemiae pract.* | 𝔐it = 𝔊lied
des 𝔒ber-Collegii-Medici, der 𝔯öm. 𝔎ays. Academiae Nat. Curios, beyder 𝔎önigl.
So- | cietäten der 𝔚issenschafften zu 𝔅erlin und London, deszgleichen des
𝔓äbstlichen In- | stituti in Bologna, wie auch erster 𝔥off = 𝔄pothecker. | [rule] |
Sanior esse potes, si cum moderamine potes, | *Non quantum velis, sed quantum*
debeas, non quid cupias, sed quid conveniat. | [rule] | 𝔏𝔈𝔍𝔓𝔝𝔍𝔊, bey 𝔊ottlob
𝔅enjamin 𝔉romman, 𝔅uchhändl. des | 𝔚aisenhauses in 𝔷üllichau, 1735.

First edition, Leipzig, 1735.

4to. π⁴)(-)( )(⁴)( )( )(² A-Mmm⁴ Nnn²; 252 leaves, pp. [*28*] [1] 2-468.

Bibliographies: Unrecorded in the bibliographies consulted.

Copies: *BMC* and *NUC* (Harvard only).

489. New complementir und trenchier Büchlein.

[engraved title-page] *New Complementir vnd trenchier Büchlein: Darinnen aüch von*
Taffeldecken. | [banqueting scene] | *Rinteln: Gedruckt vnd verlegt bey Petro Lucio.*
Typogr. Acad. 1650.

New edition, Rinteln, 1650. The *Complementier Büchlein* originally was published,
Rinteln, 1648. The eighty page section on carving is reprinted from Harsdörfer's
Vollständiges Trincir-Büchlein (Nürnberg, ca.1649).

Oblong 12mo.)(⁸ A-E⁸, ²A⁴ B-D⁸; 76 leaves, pp. [*16*]; [*80*]; [9-11] 12-64. The first
sixteen pages, containing the engraved title, dedication and instructions for decorative
napkin folding, are followed by two parts, each with its own title-page:

Part one:

𝔑ew 𝔙ermehrtes | 𝔗rincier = 𝔅üchlein: | 𝔚ie man nach rechter 𝔍talienischer
auch jtziger | 𝔄rt und 𝔐anier allerhand 𝔖peisen zierlich zerschnei = | den/ und
höflich fürlegen soll. | 𝔄lles mit zugehörigen 𝔑ewen 𝔎upfferstücken gezieret. |
[ornament] | 𝔯inteln/ | 𝔇ruckts und verlegts 𝔓etrus 𝔏ucius/ der 𝔘niversität
bestalter 𝔅uchdrucker | [short rule] | daselbst/ 𝔍m 1650. 𝔍ahr

Part two:

Höfliches und Vermehrtes | Complementier Büchlein/ | Oder | Richtige Art und grundformliche Weise; | Wie man mit Hohen Fürstlichen: So wohl auch | Niedrigen und Gemeinen Stands Personen/ und sonsten bey Gesellschafften/ | Jungfrawen und Frawen/ zierlich und höflich conversiren/ reden | und umbgehen möge | [three ornaments] | Rintel/ Druckts und verlegts Petrus Lucius/ der Universität Buchdrucker/ | [short rule] | Im Jahr 1650.

Illustrations: Engraved title-page with illustration of people at table, a folding engraving of carving utensils, and forty engraved plates illustrating carving.

Bibliographies: Unrecorded in the bibliographies consulted.

Copies: No other copy located.

490. Nürnberger Kochbuch.

Der | aus dem Parnasso ehmals entlauffenen | vortrefflichen | Köchin/ | Welche | Bey denen Göttinnen Ceres, Diana und | Pomona viele Jahre gedienet/ | Hinterlassene | Und bishero/ bey unterschiedlichen der Löbl. Koch= | Kunst beflissenen Frauen zu Nürnberg/ zerstreuet und | in grosser Geheim gehalten gewesene | Germerck=Zettul; | Woraus zu erlernen/ | Wie man tausend neun hundert acht und zwanzig/ sowol | gemeine/ als rare Speisen; in Suppen/ Musen/ Pasteten/ Brühen/ | Essigen/ Saläten/ Salsen/ Sultzen/ Vor-richten/ Neben=Essen/ Ey= | ern/ gebraten=gebachen=gesotten= und gedämpfften Fischen/ Wildpret/ | Geflügel/ Fleisch/ auch eingemachten Sachen/ Dorten und | Zucker=werck bestehend; | Wohlgeschmack und Leckerhafft/ nach eines jeden Belieben/ zu zubereiten | und zu kochen; auch zu welcher Zeit man alle Zugehörungen einkauffen/ | und bemeldete Speisen auftragen solle. | Mit unermüdeten Fleisz zusammen gesammlet/ und denen wohl=geübten Künstler= | innen zu beliebiger Censur, denen unerfahrnen aber zur Lehr und Unterricht durch | alle Titul mercklich vermehret und nun durch öffentlichen Druck in dieser | zweyten Edition vom neuen mitgetheilet. | [rule] | Nürnberg/ | In Verlegung Wolffgang Moritz Endters. | Gedruckt bey Joh. Ernst Adelbulner. 1702.

Second edition, Nürnberg, 1702. Originally published, Nürnberg, 1691.

4to. [)(]⁴)( )(⁴(-)( )(4) A-Ssssss⁴ Tttttt-Bbbbbbb² Ccccccc³ Ddddddd-Lllllll⁴; 588 leaves, pp. [*14*] 1-1098 [*64*]. Leaves 6T1-7C1 are double leaves, tipped in by the edge and folded. Signature 7C is composed of one double leaf signed Ccccccc followed by two single leaves, the first signed Ccccccccii.

Illustrations: Engraved allergorical title-page and two engraved folding plates illustrating cuts of meat.

Bibliographies: Horn-Arndt 103; Malortie 213.

Copies: No other copy of this edition located.

491. Nürnberger Kochbuch.

Die │ so kluge als künstliche │ von │ ARACHNE und PENELOPE │ getreulich unterwiesene │ Hausz=Halterin/ │ Oder │ Dem Frauen=Zimmer wohlanständiger │ Kunst=Bericht │ und │ Gründlicher Hauszhaltungs=Unterricht. │ Als │ Desz Nürnbergischen Koch=Buchs Zweyter Theil/ │ bestehend │ In schicklicher Auferziehung der Töchter/ curieuser Anwei= │ sung zu sechs=und dreyssigerley dem Frauen=Zimmer wohl=anständigen │ Künsten und Galanterien/ vernünfftiger Einrichtung einer Neuen Hauszhaltung/ │ vortheilhaffter Anschaffung/ Einkauffung und Aufbehaltung allerley Victualien von Getreyd/ │ Zugemüsz/ Obst/ Fleisch/ Gewürtz/ Brod und Geträncken/ samt andern zu Feuer/ Holtz und Licht │ gehörigen/ wie auch allerley Gespinst/ Leinwat/ dero Bleich und Reinigung betreffenden Dingen; │ nebst einer Zugabe/ von denen bewährtesten Hausz=Mitteln wider die fürnehmste Frauen= und │ Kinder=Kranckheiten/ Verbesserung der Schönheit/ Anrichtung zierlicher Hausz Gärten und │ Altanen/ Zieh= und Verpflegung der singenden Vögel/ samt einem wohl= │ bewehrten Vieh=Artzney=Büchlein. │ Aus vielfältiger Erfahrung meistens zusammen getragen/ │ und zu allgemeinen Nutzen durch offentlichen Druck │ bekannt gemacht. [rule] │ Nürnberg/ │ In Verlegung Wolffgang Moritz Endters. │ Gedruckt bey Johann Ernst Adelbulner. │ AN. MDCCIII.

Third edition, Nürnberg, 1703. Originally published, Nürnberg, 1691.

4to. a⁴(-a1) b-c⁴ d² A-Kkkkkk⁴ Lllllll² (a3 signed "a2" and a4 signed "a3"); 515 leaves, pp. [*26*] 1-955 [*956-1004*].

Illustrations: Twenty-six etched and engraved plates, two of them folding, of plants and household implements.

Bibliographies: Horn-Arndt 340.

Copies: No other copy of this edition located.

492. Nürenberger Kochbuch.

Die | In ihrer Kunst vortrefflich geübte Köchin. | Oder | Auserlesenes und vollständig-vermehrtes | Allgemeines | Koch-Buch, | Darinnen | Eine deutliche Anweisung zu finden, wie man über | Drithalb Tausend, so wohl gemeine, als rare Speisen, wohlge= | schmack, und nach eines jeden Belieben, zubereiten und kochen, auch | zu welcher Zeit man alle Zugehörungen einkauffen, und jede Art der | Speisen auftragen solle. | Nebst einem *accuraten* Kupferstich/ | in welchen | Die Zertheilung und Aufhauung eines Ochsen und Kalbs | vorgestellet wird. | Alles mit unermüdeten Fleisz zusammen getragen, und nun bey dieser Vierdten Auflage, | nochmahl ansehnlich vermehrt und so viel möglich vollkommen gemacht. | [woodcut] | Nürnberg, | Verlegts Wolfg. Moritz Endters seel. Erben, Tochter Mayrin und Sohn. | Gedruckt bey Lorenz Bieling. 1734.

Fourth edition, Nürnberg, 1734. Originally published, Nürnberg, 1691.

4to. π^2)(^{2})( )(^{4} A-Qqqqqq^4 Rrrrr-Aaaaaaa^2 Bbbbbbb-Nnnnnnn^4; 596 leaves, pp. [*16*] 1-1084 [1085-1176]. Pages 1049-1080 are folding charts.

Illustration: Engraved frontispiece of kitchen scene by M. Rossier.

Bibliographies: Horn-Arndt 274; Malortie 262.

Copies: *NUC* (Cornell and New York Public Library).

493. Die Nürnbergische wohl unterwiesene Koechin.

[in red] Die Nürnbergische | wohl unterwiesene | [in red] Koechin | welche so wohl | an Fleisch= als Fast=Tägen, | zu geschickter Bereitung | [in red]

wohlschmeckender Speisen | deutliche Anweisung giebt. | Mit allergnädigsten Privilegien. | [ornament] | Nürnberg, | [in red] bey Joh. Adam Stein und Gabr. Nic. Raspe | 1752.

First edition, Nürnberg, 1752.

8vo. π1)(^{6})( )(^{4} A-Ooo^8; 491 leaves, pp. [*22*] [1] 2-906 [*54*].

Illustration: Engraved frontispiece of a woman handing fowls to a cook standing before an open fire with a spit in hand, not reckoned in the collation or pagination.

Bound with part two:

[in red] Die Nürnbergische | wohl unterwiesene | [in red] Köchin | zweyter Theil/ | Oder | [in red] der geschickte und wohlerfahrne | Pasteten= Torten= | und | [in red] Zucker=Becker | oder | Conditor. | Mit Römisch=Kayserl. wie auch Königl. Pohln. und | Churfürstl. Sächsz. Freyheit. | [in red: short triple rule] | Nürnberg, | bey Stein und Raspe. 1753.

First edition, Nürnberg, 1753.

8vo.)(^{4} A-Bbb^8 Ccc^4; 392 leaves, pp. [*8*] [1] 2-724 [*52*]. Last leaf blank.

Bibliographies: Drexel 261.

Copies: No other copy located.

494. Operation Vittles Cook Book.

OPERATION | *VITTLES* | COOK BOOK | compiled by | THE AMERICAN WOMEN | in | BLOCKADED BERLIN | January 1949

Second edition, Berlin, 1949. The verso of the tenth unnumbered page reads: "Published by | DEUTSCHER VERLAG | 2nd EDITION". No record of the first edition has been found.

8vo. [1-6^8 7^{10}]; 58 leaves, pp. [*14*] 1-96 [*6*]. First and last leaves pasted down. Publisher's printed boards.

Illustrations: Five half-tone photos of air lift scenes at front; line drawings and facsimile of title-page and one page of text of *Das Brandenburgische Koch-Buch*, (Berlin, 1732); five half-tone photos of children's drawings of air lift scenes at the end.

Bibliographies: Unrecorded in the bibliographies consulted.

Copies: *NUC* (Cornell only).

495. Opsopoeus, Vincentius.

DE ARTE | BIBENDI | LIBRI TRES, AV- | TORE VINCENTIO | OBSOPOEO. | *Denuo ab autore recognitum, & plus quam sexcentis* | *uersibus locupletatum.* | D. SEBASTIANI HAMAXVRGI APVD | *Fontes salutares frumentatoris, Hexastichon.* | Naso quidem pulchrè leges praescribit amandi, | Vt certa insanus curreret arte furor. | Pulchrius at multo tradit Vincentius artem | Potandi, quo sit certus ubiq[ue] modus. | Vt sit amare nephas, tamen est potare uoluptas, | Ex qua uirtutem regula iuncta facit. | Θεόγνιδος | οἶνος πινόμενος πουλὺς κακὸς, ἤν δέ τις αὐτον | πίνη ἐπισταμένως οὐκ κακὸς, ἀλλ᾽ ἀγαθός.

Colophon: Norimbergae apud Ioh. Petreium, | Anno M. D. XXXVII.

Second edition, Nürnberg, 1537. Originally published, Nürnberg, 1536.

4to. a⁶ b-n⁴; 54 leaves, unpaginated.

Bibliographies: Simon BG 1113; Vicaire 636.

Copies: *BNC* and *NUC* (University of Pennsylvania only).

496. Pechlin, Johann Nicolas, 1644-1706.

JOHANNIS NICOLAI | PECHLINI, | Med. D. P. | Serenissimi Cimbriae Principis Reg. | Archiatri, | THEOPHILUS BIBACULUS *Sive* | *De* | POTU THEAE | DIALOGUS. | [rule] *FRANCOFURTI,* | Impensis Johannis Sebastiani Riechelii, Bibliopolae | Kiloniensis, Anno M DC LXXXIV.

First edition, Frankfurt, 1684.

4to. ✱⁴ A-N⁴; 56 leaves, pp. [*8*] [1] 2-103 [*104*].

Bibliographies: Crahan 190; Horn-Arndt 181; Vicaire 668.

Copies: *BMC, BNC*, and *NUC* (4 copies).

497. Platina, Bartholomeo, 1421-1481.

BAP. PLA | TINAE CREMONENSIS, DE | HONESTA VOLVPTATE | ET VALETVDINE LI | BRI DECEM. | Cum indice gemino, rerum pariter | ac uerborum ita locuplete, ut mo | mento, quod uelis, inuenias. | [ornament] | *Coloniae ex officina Eucharij Ceruicorni,* | M. D. XXXVII.

New edition, Köln, 1537. Originally published, Rome, 1474 or 1475.

8vo. A⁸ a-q⁸ r⁴; 140 leaves, pp. [*16*] [1] 2-232 [*32*].

Bibliographies: Schraemli (1) 398; Simon BB II 524; Vicaire 691.

Copies: *BMC, BNC*, and *NUC* (Library of Congress and New York Academy of Medicine).

498. Procacci, Giacomo.

[in a compartment within an engraved border] TRINCIER | Oder | Vorleg=Buch/ | Darinnen berichtet wird/ | Wie man allerhand gebratene | und gesottene Speisen/ so auff Fürst= | liche und andere Taffeln getragen werden mögen/ | Nach Italianischer/ und vornemlich Romanischer | Arth/ anschneiden/ und auff der Gabel zierlich | zerlegen soll. | Vor dessen/ Von | GIACOMO. PROCACCHI. | In Italianischer Sprach beschrieben. | An jetzo aber | In das hochdeutsche trewlichen versetzet/ und | mit den signirten Kupfferstichen auffs best und | fleissigste gezieret/ etc. | [row of type ornaments] | Leipzig/ | In Verlegung Henning Groszen des Jüngern | Buchhändlers. | [short rule] | ANNO M DC XXI.

Colophon: [ornament] | Leipzig/ | In verlegung Henning Groszen/ | des Jüngern Buchhändlers. | [printer's device] | [ornament] | TYPIS GROSIANIS. | Gedruckt durch Georgium Liger/ | [rule] | Im Jahr: M. DC. XX.

First edition in German, Leipzig, 1621. According to Horn-Arndt, the original Italian edition was published in Rome, 1601, but no loction for this or any other Italian edition has been found. Neither B.In.G. nor Westbury record any edition of this work. Schraemli (1) 409 records a "Leipzig, 1620" edition but this appears to be an error caused by the 1620 date in the colophon of the 1621 edition.

Folio: "(?)"² A-I⁴ K²; 40 leaves, pp. [8] 1-69 [70] [2]. Last leaf blank.

Illustrations: Engraved border on title-page and seventeen etched plates, two of them folding, illustrating the art of carving. Woodcut printer's device on p. 70.

Bibliographies: Simon BG 1224; Vicaire 710. Schraemli (1) 409 mistakenly records a "Leipzig, 1620," edition; Drexel 9, Horn-Arndt 183 and Schraemli (1) 410 record a 1624 edition.

Copies: *NUC* (Cornell and New York Academy of Medicine).

499. Quaestiones naturales philosophorum.

Tractatus de variis anti | quo[rum] philosophorum questionibus naturalibus cum earū | dē solutionibus phice acuaturaliter pulcherrime declarate | [woodcut surrounded by names of twelve philosophers]

First edition, Köln, ca. 1500

4to. a-b⁶; 12 leaves, unpaginated.
Illustration: Woodcut depiciting famous philosophers on title-page.

Bibliographies: Crahan 76; Goff Q9.

Copies: *NUC* (Boston Public Library and University of California, Berkeley). Goff locates copies in the Boston Medical Library, the Huntington Library and the National Library of Medicine.

500. Rantzau, Henrik, 1526-1598.

HENRICI RANTZOVII | EQVITIS HOLSATI | DE CONSERVANDA | VALETVDINE LIBER, IN | priuatum liberorum suorum vsum | ab ipso conscriptus, ac | editus à | Dethleuo Syluio Holsato. | IN QVODE DIAETA, ITINE- | RE, ANNIS CLIMACTERICIS, | & antidotis praestantissimis, breuia & | vtilia praecepta continentur. | [woodcut] | LIPSIAE. | CVM PRIVILEGIO.

Colophon: LIPSIAE, | IMPRIMEBAT IOANNES | STEINMAN | Anno | [short rule] | M. D. LXXX.

Second edition? Leipzig, 1580. Originally published, Leipzig, 1576.

8vo. A-L⁸ M⁴; 92 leaves, [*12*] 1-169 [170] [2]. Last leaf blank. Bound with Rembert Dodoens' *Historia vitis vinique et stirpium nonnullarum aliarum*, Cologne, 1580 (item 458).

Bibliographies: This edition unrecorded in the bibliographies consulted.

Copies: *BMC.*

501.   Recepte für Lehrlinge der Kochkunkst, Hausfrauen und Köchinnen.

Recepte | für | Lehrlinge | der | Kochunkst, | Hausfrauen und Köchinnen. | [ornament] | [double rule] | Eisenach 1803. | Im Verlage der Wittekindtschen Hofbuchhandlung.

First edition? Eisenach, 1803.

8vo. ✳⁸ ✳✳⁸ A-T⁸; 168 leaves, pp. [*32*] [1] 2-304.

Bibliographies: Unrecorded in the bibliographies consulted.

Copies: No other copy located.

502.   Regimen sanitatis salernitanum.

DE CON- | SERVANDA BONA VALETVDINE | Opusculum Scholae Salernitanae, ad Re= | gem Angliae, uersibus conscriptum: Cum | *Arnoldi Nouicomensis, Medici &* | *Philosophi cele-* | *berrimi, breuissimis ac utilissimis Enarrationibus. Et* | *haec omnia à* | *barbarie, & infinitis, quibus scatebant,* | *mendis, tam accuratè repurgata, ut iam quasi* | *nouam faciem induerint, citraq; offen-* | *sionem legi possint.* | *Opera & studio* | *Ioannis Curionis, &* | *Iacobi Crellij.* | ACCESSERE | *De electione meliorum* | *Simplicium, ac Spe-* | *cierum Medicinalium, Rhytmi M.O=* | *thonis Cremonensis.* | ITEM, | *S. Augustini Concio, de uitanda ebrietate,* | *Carmine reddita.* | *Cum* | *Priuilegio Imper.* | FRANC. *Apud Chr. Egen.*

New edition, Frankfurt, 1551, of Johann Curion and Jacob Crell's revision of the *Regimen sanitatis salernitatum*, originally published, Frankfurt, 1545.

8vo. $*^8$ χ1 A-T^8; 161 leaves, ff. [9] 1-147 [148-252].

Illustrations: Numerous woodcuts in the text.

Bibliographies: Renzi, p. 78.

Copies: *BMC* and *NUC* (7 copies).

503. Riem, Johann, 1739-1807.

Joh. Riem's | Lehrbuch | die natürlichen und künstlichen | Getränke der | Menschen | näher kennen und zubereiten zu lernen. | [short fancy rule] Zweyte | Auflage | nach des Verfassers Tode unverändert | herausgegeben. | [rule] | mit | einem vollständigen Register. | [fancy rule] | Dresden, | in der Waltherschen | Hofbuchhandlung | 1809.

Second edition, Dresden, 1809. Originally published, Dresden, 1803.

8vo. π^2 A-Ii^8 Kk^6; 264 leaves, pp. [4] [1] 2-524.

Bibliographies: The edition unrecorded in the bibliographies consulted. Drexel 61 records the first edition.

Copies: No other copy located.

504. Rumpolt, Marx.

Ein new Kochbuch/ | Das ist/ | [in red] Ein Gründtli= | [in red] che | Beschreibung/ wie man recht vnd | wol/ nicht allein von vierfüssigen/ | heymischen vnd wilden Thie= | ren/ sondern auch von mancherley Vögel vnnd | Federwildpret/ darzu von allem | grünen vnd dürren Fischwerck/ allerley | Speisz/ als gesotten/ gebraten/ gebacken/ Presolen/ Carbonaden/ mancher= | ley | Pasteten vnd Füllwerck/ Gallrat/ etc. auff Teutsche/ Ungerische/ Hispanische/ | Italianische vnd Frantzö= | sische weisz/ kochen vnd zubereiten solle: Auch wie allerley Gemüsz/ Obs/ Salsen/ Senff/ | Confect vnd Latwergen/ zuzurichten seye. | [in red] Auch ist darinnen zu vernemmen/ wie man herrliche grosse Pancketen/ sampt | gemeinen Gastereyen/ ordentlich anrichten vnd bestellen soll. | [in red] Allen Menschen/ hohes vnd nidriges Standts/ Weibs vnd Manns Personen/ zu nutz jetzunde zum | ersten in Druck gegeben/ dergleichen vor nie ist auszgegangen/ | Durch | [in red] M. Marxen Rumpolt/ Churf. Meintzischen Mundtkoch. | Mit Röm. Keyserlicher Maiestat special Priuilegio. | 15 [woodcut] 87. | [in red] Sampt einem gründtlichen Bericht/ wie man alle Wein vor allen zufällen | bewaren/ die bresthafften widerbringen/ Kräuter vnd andere Wein/ Bier/ Essig/ vnd alle | andere Getränck/ machen vnd bereiten soll/ dasz sie natürlich/ vnd allen | Menschen vnschädtlich/ zu trincken seindt. | [in red] Gedruckt zu Franckfort am Mayn/ In verlegung | Sigmundt Feyerabendt/ Peter Fischer/ vnd | Heinrich Tack.

Second edition, Frankfurt, 1587. Originally published, Frankfurt, 1581. Graesse records editions of 1576, 1581, and 1583 but of these only that of 1581 is verifiable. Schraemli records the first edition, 1581, and notes he also owns the second edition, 1587, and the third, 1604.

Folio:)(^{6} a-k^4 χ1 A-Ddd^4 2χ1; 248 leaves, ff. [6] 1-41, i-cc [cci]. Note: This collation is tentative with reference to signature k and Ddd and the leaves χ1 and 2χ1. These two signatures are signed on four leaves rather than on three as are the others in the volume and it is likely, therefore, that the two disjunct leaves designated χ1 and 2χ1 are placed within the signatures k and Ddd. In this tightly bound copy it is not possible to tell which are the disjunct and which the conjugate leaves.

Illustrations: Numerous woodcuts by Jost Amman and Virgil Solis in the text.

Bibliographies: Crahan 78; Schraemli (1) 431; Schraemli (2) 59 in a note; Vicaire 761.

Copies: *NUC* (Cornell, John Crerar Library, and New York Academy of Medicine).

505. Ryff, Walther Hermann, d. 1548.

Confect Buch/ | Vnd Hausz Apoteck. | KVnstlich zuberaiten/ | Einmachen/ vnnd gebrauchen/ Wes inn | Ordenlichen Apotecken/ vnd Hauszhaltungen/ | zur Artznei/ Täglicher notturfft/ vnnd auch zum | Lust/ dienlich vnd nutz/

Trewliche Underrich= | tung/ So vil dem Gemainen man nötig/ | In acht Theyl kürtzlich abgetheylt. | Inhalt volkomnen Registers/ | am volgenden blat. | *Gualtherus Ryff, Argent. Medicus.* | *Cum Gratia & Priuilegio Imp.* | [woodcut] | Zu Franckfort/ Bei Christian Egenolff.

Third edition, Frankfurt, 1549. Originally published, Frankfurt, 1544.

8vo. *^{8} a-e^8 A-Z^8, ^{2}a-r^8; 368 leaves, ff. [*48*] 1-319 [*1*].

Illustrations: Numerous small woodcuts in the text.

Bibliographies: Benzing 137; Oberlé (1) 62; Simon BG 1335; Simon BBII 574.

Copies: *BMC* and *NUC* (National Library of Medicine only).

506. Ryff, Walther Hermann, d. 1548.

[in red] Confect Buch/ | [in red] vnd Hausz Apoteck. | K[in red]Unstlich zubereiten/ | [in red] Einmachen/ vnd gebrauchen/ Wes | in Ordenlichen Apotecken/ vnd Hauszhaltun | gen zur Artznei/ täglicher notturfft/ vnd auch | zum Lust/ dienlich vnd nutz/ Trewliche Un= | derrichtung/ So vil dem Gemaynen Man nö | tig/ in Acht Theyl kürtzlich abgetheylt. | Inhalt volkomnen Registers/ am | volgenden blat. | [in red] *Gualtherus Ryff, Argent. Medicus.* | *Cum gratia & priuilegio Imp.* | [in red and black: woodcut] | | Zu Franckfort/ Bei Christian Egenolff.

Fourth edition, Frankfurt, 1554. Originally published, Frankfurt, 1544.

8vo. *^{8} A-Z^8 a-v^8; 352 leaves, ff. [*8*] 1-343 [1]. Last leaf (blank?) wanting in this copy.

Illustrations: Numerous small woodcuts in the text.

Bibliographies: Benzing 138.

Copies: *NUC* (Kansas State University and Yale).

507. Ryff, Walther Hermann, d. 1548.

[in red] 𝕮𝖔𝖓𝖋𝖊𝖈𝖙 𝕭𝖚𝖈𝖍/ | [in red] 𝖛𝖓𝖉 𝕳𝖆𝖚𝖘𝖟 𝕬𝖕𝖔𝖙𝖊𝖈𝖐. | 𝕶[in red]𝖀𝖓𝖘𝖙𝖑𝖎𝖈𝖍 𝖟übereiten/ | [in red] 𝕰𝖎𝖓𝖒𝖆𝖈𝖍𝖊𝖓/ 𝖛𝖓𝖉 𝖌𝖊𝖇𝖗𝖆𝖚𝖈𝖍𝖊𝖓/ 𝖂𝖊𝖘 | in 𝕺𝖗𝖉𝖊𝖓𝖑𝖎𝖈𝖍𝖊𝖓 𝕬𝖕𝖔𝖙𝖊𝖈𝖐𝖊𝖓/ 𝖛𝖓𝖉 𝕳𝖆𝖚𝖘𝖟𝖍𝖆𝖑𝖙𝖚𝖓= | gen 𝖟𝖚𝖗 𝕬𝖗𝖙𝖟𝖓𝖊𝖎/ 𝖙ä𝖌𝖑𝖎𝖈𝖍𝖊𝖗 𝖓𝖔𝖙𝖙𝖚𝖗𝖋𝖋𝖙/ 𝖛𝖓𝖉 𝖆𝖚𝖈𝖍 | 𝖟𝖚𝖒 𝖑𝖚𝖘𝖙/ 𝖉𝖎𝖊𝖓𝖑𝖎𝖈𝖍 𝖛𝖓𝖓𝖉 𝖓ü𝖙𝖟/ 𝕿𝖗𝖊𝖜𝖑𝖎𝖈𝖍𝖊 𝖁𝖓= | 𝖉𝖊𝖗𝖗𝖎𝖈𝖍𝖙𝖚𝖓𝖌/ 𝕾𝖔 𝖛𝖎𝖑 𝖉𝖊𝖒 𝖌𝖊𝖒𝖊𝖎𝖓𝖊𝖓 𝕸𝖆𝖓 𝖓ö= | 𝖙𝖎𝖌/ in 𝕬𝖈𝖍𝖙 𝖙𝖍𝖊𝖞𝖑 𝖐ü𝖗𝖙𝖟𝖑𝖎𝖈𝖍 𝖆𝖇𝖌𝖊𝖙𝖍𝖊𝖞𝖑𝖙. | 𝕴𝖓𝖍𝖆𝖑𝖙 𝖛𝖔𝖑𝖐𝖔𝖒𝖒𝖊𝖓 𝕽𝖊𝖌𝖎𝖘𝖙𝖊𝖗𝖘/ | am 𝖛𝖔𝖑𝖌𝖊𝖓𝖉𝖊𝖓 𝖇𝖑𝖆𝖙. [in red] *Gualtherus Ryff, Argent. Medicus.* | *Cum gratia & priuilegio Imp.* | [in red and black: woodcut] | 𝖅𝖚 𝕴𝖋𝖗𝖆𝖓𝖈𝖐𝖋𝖚𝖗𝖙/ 𝕭𝖊𝖎 𝕮𝖍𝖗𝖎. 𝕰𝖌𝖊𝖓. 𝕰𝖗𝖇𝖊𝖓.

Fifth edition, Frankfurt, 1558. Originally published, Frankfurt, 1544.

8vo. ✳⁸ A-Z⁸ a-v⁸: 352 leaves, ff. [8] 1-343 [1]. Last leaf (blank?) wanting in this copy.

Illustrations: Numerous small woodcuts in the text.

Bibliographies: Benzing 139; Bitting, p. 412.

Copies: *NUC* (John Crerar Library and New York Academy of Medicine).

508. Ryff, Walther Hermann, d. 1548.

𝕷𝖚𝖘𝖙𝖌𝖆𝖗𝖙𝖊𝖓 𝖉𝖊𝖗 | 𝕲𝖊𝖘𝖚𝖓𝖉𝖙𝖍𝖊𝖎𝖙. | 𝖁𝖔𝖓 𝕳𝖆𝖚𝖘𝖟𝖌𝖊𝖒𝖆𝖈𝖍/ 𝖁𝖎𝖊𝖍𝖟𝖚𝖈𝖍𝖙/ 𝖛𝖓𝖉 𝕴𝖋𝖊𝖑𝖉𝖙= | 𝖇𝖆𝖜/ 𝖅𝖚𝖒 𝕲𝖊𝖇𝖗𝖆𝖚𝖈𝖍/ 𝕹𝖔𝖙𝖚𝖗𝖋𝖋𝖙 𝖛𝖓𝖉 𝖑𝖚𝖘𝖙 𝖉𝖊𝖗 𝖒𝖊𝖓𝖘𝖈𝖍𝖊𝖓 𝕹𝖆𝖈𝖍 𝖗𝖊𝖈𝖍= | 𝖙𝖊𝖗 𝖆𝖗𝖙/ 𝖇𝖊𝖖𝖚𝖊𝖒𝖑𝖎𝖈𝖍 𝖆𝖓𝖟𝖚𝖗𝖎𝖈𝖍𝖙𝖊𝖓/ 𝖊𝖗𝖟𝖎𝖊𝖍𝖊𝖓/ | 𝖛𝖓𝖉 𝖊𝖗𝖇𝖆𝖚𝖜𝖊𝖓. | [ornamental letter 𝕽] | 𝕽𝖊𝖚𝖙𝖙𝖊𝖗/ 𝕭ä𝖚𝖒/ 𝕲𝖊𝖘𝖙𝖊𝖚𝖉/ 𝖛𝖓𝖉 𝕴𝖋𝖗ü𝖈𝖍𝖙/ | 𝕯𝖊𝖘 𝖌𝖑𝖊𝖎𝖈𝖍𝖊𝖓 𝕲𝖊𝖙𝖍𝖎𝖊𝖗/ 𝖟𝖆𝖒 𝖛𝖓𝖉 𝖜𝖎𝖑𝖉/ 𝕴𝖓 𝖑𝖚𝖋𝖋𝖙/ | 𝖜𝖆𝖘𝖘𝖊𝖗/ 𝖛𝖓𝖉 𝕰𝖗𝖉𝖙𝖗𝖎𝖈𝖍 𝖑𝖊𝖇𝖊𝖓𝖉𝖊/ 𝕴𝖋𝖑𝖊𝖎𝖘𝖘𝖎𝖌 𝖇𝖊𝖘𝖈𝖍𝖗𝖎𝖇𝖊𝖓 𝖛𝖓𝖉 𝖋ü𝖗𝖌𝖊= | 𝖇𝖎𝖑𝖉𝖊𝖙. | 𝕸𝖎𝖙 𝖆𝖓𝖟𝖊𝖞𝖌𝖊 𝖛𝖎𝖑𝖋𝖆𝖑𝖙𝖎𝖌𝖘 𝕲𝖊𝖇𝖗𝖆𝖚𝖈𝖍𝖘 𝖉𝖊𝖗𝖘𝖊𝖑𝖇𝖊𝖓/ 𝖅𝖚𝖗 𝕾𝖕𝖊𝖎𝖘𝖊 𝖛𝖓𝖓𝖉 | 𝕬𝖗𝖙𝖟𝖓𝖊𝖎/ 𝕴𝖓 𝕶𝖚𝖈𝖍𝖊𝖓/ 𝕶𝖊𝖑𝖑𝖊𝖗/ 𝖛𝖓𝖉 𝕬𝖕𝖔𝖙𝖊𝖈𝖐𝖊𝖓. 𝖅𝖚𝖘𝖆𝖒𝖊𝖓 𝖇𝖗𝖆𝖈𝖍𝖙 𝖛𝖓𝖓𝖉 | 𝖇𝖊𝖘𝖈𝖍𝖗𝖎𝖇𝖊𝖓 𝖉𝖚𝖗𝖈𝖍 𝖂𝖆𝖑𝖙𝖍𝖊𝖗𝖚𝖒 𝕽𝖊𝖎𝖋𝖋. | [woodcut] | 𝕸𝖎𝖙 𝕶𝖊𝖞𝖘𝖊𝖗𝖑𝖎𝖈𝖍𝖊𝖓 𝕻𝖗𝖎𝖚𝖎𝖑𝖊𝖌𝖎𝖊𝖓/ 𝕲𝖊𝖙𝖗𝖚𝖈𝖐𝖙 𝖟𝖚 𝕴𝖋𝖗𝖆𝖓𝖈𝖐𝖋𝖚𝖗𝖙 𝖇𝖊𝖎 𝕮𝖍𝖗𝖎𝖘𝖙𝖎𝖆𝖓 𝕰𝖌𝖊𝖓𝖔𝖑𝖋𝖋𝖊𝖓.

First edition, Frankfurt, 1546.

Folio: ✳⁶ A-Z⁶ a-z⁶ Aa-Gg⁶ Hh⁸; 332 leaves, ff. [6] i-cccxxvi.

Bibliographies: Benzing 179.

Copies: *BMC* and *NUC* (New York Academy of Medicine, University of Delaware and University of Michigan).

509. Scheibler, Sophie Wilhelmine, b. 1793.

Allgemeines | deutsches Kochbuch | für | bürgerliche Haushaltungen | oder | gründliche Anweisung | wie man ohne Vorkenntnisse alle Arten Speisen und | Backwerk auf die wohlfeilste und schmackhafteste Art | zubereiten kann. | [short fancy rule] | Ein | unentbehrliches Handbuch | für | angehende Hausmütter, Haushälterinnen und | Köchinnen. | Herausgegeben | von | Sophie Wilhelmine Scheibler. | [publisher's monogram] | [rule] | Vierte stark vermehrte und verbesserte Auflage. | Mit einem Titelkupfer. | [double rule] | Berlin, 1821. | Druck und Verlag von Carl Friedrich Amelang. | (Brüderstrasze Nro. II.)

"Fourth edition," Berlin, 1821. There is also a "fourth edition" from the same publisher dated 1820. London bookseller Stephanie Hoppen's catalogue, *Four Centuries of Food and Drink*, vol. II, item 65, describes an edition dated 1819. No edition before 1819 has been located.

8vo. π^2 ✳^{8} ✳✳^{6} A-Bb^8 Cc^2; 218 leaves, pp. [4] [i] ii-xxviii [1-3] 4-402 [2].

Illustration: Engraved frontispiece of kitchen on $\pi 1^v$.

Bibliographies: This edition unrecorded in the bibliographies consulted. Drexel, I. 78, records the sixth edition, 1826.

Copies: No other copy of this edition located. *NUC* records a fourth edition from the same publisher dated 1820 at Cornell.

510. Scheibler, Sophie Wilhelmine, b. 1793.

Allgemeines | Deutsches Kochbuch | für alle Stände. | [short rule] | Ein unentbehrliches Handbuch | für | Hausfrauen, Haushälterinnen und Köchinnen. | Von | Sophie Wilhelmine Scheibler. | [short rule] | Neu bearbeitet von Luise

Quaas. | [short rule] | 𝕸𝖎𝖙 𝖛𝖎𝖊𝖗 𝕱𝖆𝖗𝖇𝖊𝖓𝖉𝖗𝖚𝖈𝖐𝖙𝖆𝖋𝖊𝖑𝖓 𝖉𝖊𝖗 𝖛𝖊𝖗𝖘𝖈𝖍𝖎𝖊𝖉𝖊𝖓𝖊𝖓 | 𝕱𝖑𝖊𝖎𝖘𝖈𝖍𝖆𝖗𝖙𝖊𝖓 𝖚𝖓𝖉 𝖛𝖎𝖊𝖑𝖊𝖓 | 𝕿𝖊𝖝𝖙=𝕬𝖇𝖇𝖎𝖑𝖉𝖚𝖓𝖌𝖊𝖓. | 𝕾𝖎𝖊𝖇𝖊𝖓𝖚𝖓𝖉𝖉𝖗𝖊𝖎𝖘𝖟𝖎𝖌𝖘𝖙𝖊 𝕬𝖚𝖋𝖑𝖆𝖌𝖊 | [ornament] | 𝕷𝖊𝖎𝖕𝖟𝖎𝖌, | 𝕮. 𝕱. 𝕬𝖒𝖊𝖑𝖆𝖓𝖌𝖘 𝖁𝖊𝖗𝖑𝖆𝖌. | 1901.

Thirty-seventh edition, Leipzig, 1901. The earliest edition located is, Berlin, 1819.

188 x 124 mm. I-II^8 1-36^8; 304 leaves, pp. [1a-4a] 5a-32a [1] 2-574 [2]. Publisher's green pictorical cloth lettered in black.

Illustrations: Four chromolithographed plates illustrating cuts of meat and wood engravings in the text.

Bibliographies: This edition unrecorded in the bibliographies consulted.

Copies: No other copy of this edition located.

511. Schellhammer, Maria Sophia.

𝕯𝖆𝖘 | 𝕭𝖗𝖆𝖓𝖉𝖊𝖓𝖇𝖚𝖗𝖌𝖎𝖘𝖈𝖍𝖊 | [in red] 𝕶𝖔𝖈𝖍=𝕭𝖚𝖈𝖍/ | 𝕺𝖉𝖊𝖗: | 𝕯𝖎𝖊 𝖜𝖔𝖍𝖑= | 𝖚𝖓𝖙𝖊𝖗𝖜𝖎𝖊𝖘𝖊𝖓𝖊 | 𝕶𝖔𝖈𝖍𝖎𝖓𝖓/ | 𝕯𝖆𝖘 𝖎𝖘𝖙: | [in red] 𝖀𝖓𝖙𝖊𝖗𝖗𝖎𝖈𝖍𝖙/ 𝖜𝖎𝖊 𝖒𝖆𝖓 𝖆𝖑𝖑𝖊𝖗𝖑𝖊𝖞 | 𝖜𝖔𝖍𝖑𝖘𝖈𝖍𝖒𝖊= | 𝖈𝖐𝖊𝖓𝖉𝖊 𝕾𝖕𝖊𝖎𝖘𝖊𝖓 𝖆𝖚𝖋𝖋𝖘 𝖋ü𝖌𝖑𝖎𝖈𝖍𝖘𝖙𝖊 𝖟𝖚𝖇𝖊𝖗𝖊𝖎𝖙𝖊𝖓/ 𝖘𝖈𝖍𝖒𝖆𝖈𝖐= | 𝖍𝖆𝖋𝖋𝖙𝖊 | 𝕾𝖚𝖕𝖕𝖊𝖓, 𝕻𝖔𝖙𝖆𝖌𝖊𝖓, 𝕻𝖆𝖘𝖙𝖊𝖙𝖊𝖓, 𝕿𝖆𝖗𝖙𝖊𝖓 𝖚𝖓𝖉 𝖆𝖑𝖑𝖊𝖗𝖍𝖆𝖓𝖉 | 𝕲𝖊𝖇𝖆𝖈𝖐𝖊𝖓𝖊𝖘 𝖒𝖆𝖈𝖍𝖊𝖓, 𝖓𝖆𝖈𝖍 | 𝖉𝖊𝖗 𝖏𝖊𝖙𝖟𝖙=ü𝖇𝖑𝖎𝖈𝖍𝖊𝖓 𝕬𝖗𝖙 𝖆𝖚𝖋𝖋𝖙𝖗𝖆𝖌𝖊𝖓 𝖚𝖓𝖉 | 𝖌𝖆𝖑𝖆𝖓𝖙 𝖆𝖓𝖇𝖗𝖎𝖓𝖌𝖊𝖓, 𝖆𝖚𝖈𝖍 𝕱𝖑𝖊𝖎𝖘𝖈𝖍, 𝕱𝖎𝖘𝖈𝖍𝖊, | 𝕲𝖆𝖗𝖙𝖊𝖓=𝕱𝖗ü𝖈𝖍𝖙𝖊 | 𝖚𝖓𝖉 𝖆𝖓𝖉𝖊𝖗𝖊 𝕾𝖆𝖈𝖍𝖊𝖓 &c. 𝖜𝖔𝖍𝖑 𝖊𝖎𝖓𝖒𝖆𝖈𝖍𝖊𝖓/ 𝖉ü𝖗𝖗𝖊𝖓 | 𝖔𝖉𝖊𝖗 | 𝖛𝖊𝖗𝖜𝖆𝖍𝖗𝖊𝖓 𝖘𝖔𝖑𝖑𝖊, | [in red] 𝕾𝖆𝖒𝖒𝖙 𝖛𝖎𝖊𝖑𝖊𝖓 𝖇𝖎𝖘𝖟𝖍𝖊𝖗 𝖜𝖊𝖓𝖎𝖌 𝖇𝖊𝖐𝖆𝖓𝖉𝖙𝖊𝖓 | 𝕶𝖚𝖓𝖘𝖙=𝕲𝖗𝖎𝖋𝖋𝖊𝖓/ 𝖘𝖔 𝖎𝖓 | 𝖉𝖊𝖗 𝕶𝖔𝖈𝖍=𝕶𝖚𝖓𝖘𝖙 𝖎𝖍𝖗𝖊𝖓 𝖘𝖔𝖓𝖉𝖊𝖗𝖇𝖆𝖍𝖗𝖊𝖓 𝕹𝖚= | 𝖙𝖟𝖊𝖓 𝖍𝖆𝖇𝖊𝖓, | 𝕸𝖎𝖙 𝖛𝖎𝖊𝖑𝖊𝖓 𝖉𝖆𝖟𝖚 𝖌𝖊𝖍ö𝖗𝖎𝖌𝖊𝖓 𝕶𝖚𝖕𝖋𝖋𝖊𝖗𝖓 𝖌𝖊𝖟𝖎𝖊𝖗𝖊𝖙. | [rule] | [in red] 𝕭𝖊𝖗𝖑𝖎𝖓, | 𝕭𝖊𝖞 | 𝕵𝖔𝖍𝖆𝖓𝖓 𝕬𝖓𝖉𝖗𝖊𝖆𝖘 𝕽ü𝖉𝖎𝖌𝖊𝖗, 1723.

Fifth edition, Berlin, 1723. Originally published under the title *Die wohl unterwiesene Köchinn*, Braunschweig, 1692.

4to π^2)(^{2} A-Ffff^4; 304 leaves, pp. [8] [1] 2-599 [600].

Illustrations: Engraved frontispiece of kitchen on π1^v and nineteen etched and engraved plates, eight of them folding, illustrating cooking utensils, pastry designs and table settings.

Bibliographies: Schraemli (1) 451; Schraemli (2) 64 in a note.

Copies: *NUC* (Cornell only).

512. Schidl, Johann Georg.

Der gesunde │ Zehr=Gaden, │ Dasz ist: │ Kurtze/ doch gründlich= und
ausführli= │ che Untersuchung deren Eigenschafften/ Kräff= │ ten/ Tugend/
und Würckungen/ des Nutzen und │ Schadens deren VICTUALIen, │
Speisen/ und Geträncken/ welche so= │ wohl bey Fürnemben= als gemeinen
Taflen pfle= │ gen aufgesetzt zu werden/ nebst Erklärung deren übri= │ gen
sogenannten nit natürlichen Sachen/ │ Nemlich: │ Des Luffts/ der Bewegung/
und Ruhe/ des │ Schlaffs/ und der Wachtbarkeit/ des Ausgeworffen= und │
Behaltenen/ und deren Gemüths=Leidenschafften. │ Einer │ Hochlöbl.
Landschafft in Bayrn Unter= │ Lands/ bey dero Solennen Herbst=Convent │
Unterthänigist dediciert. │ Von JOANNE GEORGIO SCHIDL, Phil. & Med.
Doctore │ Practico zu Landshut. │ [rule] │ Gedruckt bey Simon Golowitz/
Landschaffts=Buchdruckern allda.

First edition, Landshut, ca. 1700.

4to. A-L⁴ M²; 46 leaves, pp. [*8*] 1-83 [*84*].

Bibliographies: Drexel 874; Horn-Arndt 333.

Copies: No other copy located.

513. Schreger, Odilo.

[in red] Odilo Schregers, │ der vorsichtige │ und │ nach heutigem Geschmacke │
wohlerfahrne │ [in red] Speismeister. │ Sammt einer Anweisung │ zum Kochen,
Trenchiren │ und │ einigen sonderheitlichen Complimenten. │ [rule] │ Mit
beygefügten │ [in red] allgemeinen Tischregeln. │ [publisher's monogram] │ [fancy
rule] │ [in red] Augsburg, │ bey Matthäus Riegers sel. Söhnen. 1778.

First edition, Augsburg, 1778.

8vo. π² a⁶ b⁸ A-Ii⁸; 272 leaves, pp. [*32*] [1] 2-484 [*28*]. Last leaf blank.

Illustration: Engraved frontispiece of kitchen on π1ᵛ.

Bibliographies: Drexel 38; Horn-Arndt 337; Malortie 318.

Copies: No other copy located.

514. Schuppe, Johann.

Neu=verbesserter │ [in red] TRAITEUR A LA MODE, │ Welcher itzo zum drittenmahl der delicaten und neu begierigen Welt zu sonderbahren Nutzen darleget │ sein mit Fleisz zusammen getragenes/ und woleingerichtetes │ [in red] Koch Buch/ │ Worinnen mit sonderbahren Vergnügen zu finden/ │ [in red] Wie man/ so woll Hochfürstliche/ als anderer vornehmer Höfe Taffeln/ nach │ bester Manier des heutigen Etats, nicht weniger bey grossen Gastereyen/ oder Hoch= │ zeiten/ die Tische mit wollschmeckenden Speisen galant, bestellen/ und versehen könne │ Vornemlich/ │ [in red] Mit Potagen von allerhand Wildpret und zahmen Fleisch/ wild und zahmen Geflügelwerck/ │ Fisch/ und Gartengewächsen/ wie auch Tarten/ Pasteten/ und andern Gebackens; imgleichen Milch= │ Speisen/ Gallerten/ Fricasseen, Ragouts, Mandeln/ Eyern/ Morcheln und Champignons, │ Dann auch │ [in red] Mit allerhand schönen und wolgarnirten Braten/ │ Auch wie dieselben Speisen woll ordinirt/ angerichtet/ und vorgetragen werden sollen/ │ Anitzo mit dem Anhang auff 480. Species versehen/ mit hinzugefügten │ [in red] Ein und zwantzig Taffeln/ │ Samt deutlichen Bericht/ wie nach jeder Taffel Grösze/ und Form die angerichtete Speisen schicklich darauff in einander zu setzen/ wie │ auch/ auff vieler Begehren/ eine Verdeutschung der in diesem Buch vorkommenden Frantzösischen und andern frembden Wörtern/ │ benebst einem vollkommenen Register │ Auff Ersuchen/ denen Liebhabern zu Dienst mitgetheilet │ Von │ [in red] Hansz Schuppen/ Hochfürstl. Schleszw. Holstein. Mundkoch. │ [short rule] │ [in red] Lübeck und Leipzig/ bey Peter Böckmann, 1709. │ PLOEN/ Gedruckt durch Tobias Schmidt.

New edition, Lübeck and Leipzig, 1709. Originally published Lübeck and Leipzig, 1702.

4to. π1)(²)( )(² A-Hh⁴ Ii²; 131 leaves, pp. [*10*] 1-190 [*62*]. π1 is a folding title-page comprising half a quarto sheet tipped in by the edge.

Illustrations: Twenty-one woodcuts showing table settings on the rectos of the last 21 leaves.

Bibliographies: Drexel 19.

Copies: No other copy of this edition located. *BNC* records a 1727 edition.

515. Ain sehr Künstlichs unnd Fürtrefflichs Kochbüch.

[in red] Ain sehr Künstlichs vnnd Fürtrefflichs | [in red] Kochbuch/ von allerlay Speysen/ auch wie man | Latwergen vnnd Zucker einmachen soll/ vnd | sunst von anderen gutten haimlichen Kün- | sten/ Ainem yeden im Hausz sehr notwendig | vnnd nutzlich zu gebrauchen. | [in red] Durch ainen Fürnemen vnd berumbten Koch | [in red] seinem Ehegemahel zu der Letze geschenckt. | [woodcut of a kitchen scene] | [in red] Mit Rö: Kay: May: Freyhait/ in zway Jaren nit nach zu trucken. | 1559.

Colophon: Gedruckt zü Augspurg durch | Valentin Othmar.

First edition, Augsburg, 1559.

4to. π⁴ A-F⁴; 28 leaves, unpaginated.

Illustration: Woodcut of kitchen on title-page.

Bibliographies: Bitting, p. 570; Vicaire 479.

Copies: *NUC* (Library of Congress only).

516. Seidenburg, J. G.

Anweisung | zum | Seifensieden, Lichtziehen, Eszigbrauen, Einmachen | von Früchten, Einpöckeln, Räuchern des Flei= | sches, Brodbacken, Bierbrauen, Stärkemachen, | Holzersparen, Färben unnd Bleichen. | [short rule] | Für |

Frauenzimmer │ die ihrer │ Wirthschaft selbst vorstehen wollen. │ Von │ J. G. S. │ Nebst einem in Kupfer gestochenen Holzsparofen. │ [short double rule] │ Berlin, 1790.

First edition, Berlin, 1790.

8vo. π^2 A^6 B-H^8 I^4 (A1-A4 signed "A2"-"A5"); 68 leaves, pp. [2] [1-5] 6-131 [132] [2]. Last leaf blank.

Illustration: Engraved frontispiece, on $\pi1^v$ illustrating woodburning stove.

Bibliographies: Drexel 318; Malortie 247.

Copies: No other copy located.

517. Spitzweg, Karl, 1808-1885.

Die [in pink] Leibgerichte [end pink] des weiland │ Apothekers und Malerpoeten [in pink] Carl Spitzweg [end pink] │ von ihm eigenhändig aufgeschrieben │ und illustriert │ ENTDECKT UND HERAUSGEGEBEN VON │ SIEGFRIED WICHMANN │ VERLEGT BEI BRUCKMANN │ [in pink: short rule]

First edition, Munich, 1962.

8vo. 48 leaves, perfect bound and unpaginated. Printed paper covered boards.

Illustrations: Black and white and colored photolithographed reproductions in the text.

Bibliographies: Horn-Arndt 1213.

Copies: *BMC Supplement 1956-1965* and *NUC Supplement 1963-1967* (4 copies).

518. Staindl, Balthasar.

E[in red] In sehr Künstlichs │ [in red] vnnd nutzliches Kochbuch/ vor= │ mals nye in so leicht/ Mannen vnd Frawen perso= │ nen/ von ihnen selbst zu lernen/ inn Truck verfaszt │ vnd auszgangen ist/ Artlich in acht Bücher ge= │ theilt/

𝔰𝔞𝔪𝔭𝔱 𝔢𝔱𝔩𝔦𝔠𝔥𝔢𝔫 𝔣𝔞𝔰𝔱 𝔫𝔲𝔱𝔷𝔢𝔫 𝔟𝔢𝔴𝔢𝔯𝔱𝔢𝔫 │ ℌ𝔞𝔲𝔰𝔷𝔫𝔬𝔱𝔱𝔲𝔯𝔣𝔣𝔱𝔢𝔫 𝔬𝔡𝔢𝔯 𝔨𝔲𝔫𝔰𝔱𝔢𝔫. 𝔄𝔲𝔠𝔥 │ 𝔴𝔦𝔢 𝔪𝔞𝔫 𝔈𝔰𝔰𝔦𝔤 𝔪𝔞𝔠𝔥𝔢𝔱/ 𝔟𝔫𝔫𝔡 │ 𝔚𝔢𝔦𝔫 𝔤𝔲𝔱 𝔟𝔢𝔥𝔢𝔩𝔱. │ [in red] 𝔅𝔞𝔩𝔱𝔥𝔞𝔰𝔞𝔯 𝔖𝔱𝔞𝔦𝔫𝔡𝔩 𝔟𝔬𝔫 𝔇𝔦𝔩𝔩𝔦𝔫𝔤𝔢𝔫. │ [woodcut of a kitchen scene] │ [in red] Anno M. D. LXXXII.

New edition, Augsburg, 1582. The earliest edition located is Augsburg, 1544.

4to. A-O⁴; 56 leaves, ff. [*4*] 1-51 [52]. [folio 51 misnumbered "50"]

Illustration: Woodcut of kitchen scene on title-page.

Bibliographies: Vicarie 479.

Copies: No other copy of this edition located.

519. Entry deleted.

520. Syngrapheus, Polyonimus, *pseud.*

[within ornamental border] SCHOLA │ APICIA/ │ NA. │ E*x optimis quibusdam authoribus dili= / genter constructa. qua continentur offi= / cia Conuiuatoris. Cultus & Habitus bo / ni Couiuij, Qualitates & Regulae Opso / niorum, Rationes Secandi uel Scrutan / di in mensa, Sermones conuiuales, Quae / stiones conuiuales iucundissimae, / & alia item plura. / Polyonimo Syngrapheo authore. /* Δειπνειν με διδασκε. │ [below the ornamental border] FRANCOFORTI, A*pud C*hristianum E*genolphum.*

First edition, Frankfurt, 1534.

8vo. A-F⁸ G⁴; 52 leaves, ff. [1] 2-47 [*5*]. Last leaf blank.

Bibliographies: Oberlé (1) 64; Schraemli (3) 13; Vicaire 701.

Copies; *BMC, BNC,* and *NUC* (John Crerar Library, Library of Congress, and University of Michigan).

521. Trojano, Massimo, fl. 1565.

DISCORSI / DELLITRI= / OMFI, GIOSTRE, APPA / rati, é delle cose piu notabile fatte nelle / sontuose Nozze, dell' Illustrissimo & / Eccellentissimo Signor / Duca

Guglielmo. / PRIMO GENITO DEL GENEROSISSIMO | *Alberto* Quinto, C*onte*
Palatino D*el* Reno, *e* Duca della / *Bauiera alta e* Bassa, nell' Anno 1568, / à 22. di
Febraro. / *Compartiti in tre libri,* C*on vno* Dialogo, della an- / *tichita del felice ceppo*
di Bauiera. / ALLA | SERENISSIMA REGINA CHRISTIER- | NA
DANISMARCHI. | D*i* Massimo Troiano da Napoli. M*usico dell'* Illu- / *strissimo, &*
Eccellentissimo Signor / *Duca di* Bauiera. / [ornament] | In Monaco appresso Adamo
Montano. | M. D. LXVIII.

First edition, Munich, 1568.

4to. A-Bb^4; 100 leaves, pp. [*8*] [*1*] 2-40, 51-191 [192-202].

Illustration: Woodcut of arms of Bavaria and the Palatinate of the Rhein on p. 201.

Bookplate: Ex-libris Franc. Com. A. Thun-Hohenstein Tetschen.

Bibliographies: Unrecorded in the bibliographies consulted.

Copies: *BMC*, *BNC*, and *NUC* (Library of Congress only).

522. Thiemen, Johann Christoph.

[in black] H [in red] aus= [in black] J [in red] eld= [in black] A [in red] rtzney=
[in black] K [in red] och= [in black] K [in red] unst= | [in black] und | W [in red]
under= [in black] B [in red] uch. | [in black] Das ist: | A [in red] usführliche [in
black] B [in red] eschreib= und [in black] V [in red] orstellung/ | Wie ein kluger
Haus=Vatter und sorgfältige Haus=Mutter/ | wes Standes und Würden sie
auch immermehr seyn mögen/ mit vor= | trefflichem Nutzen und erprieszlichem
Nahrungs=Aufnehmen/ ihr Haus= | Wesen führen/ und/ durch GOttes reichen
Seegen/ auf ihre Nachkommen | höchst=glücklich fortpflantzen möge. | Alles/
um richtiger Ordnung willen/ | [in red] in Zwantzig Abtheilungen enthalten/ |
Darinn folgende Sachen abgehandelt werden: | [in two columns: column one] I.
Von der Haushaltung insge= | mein. | II. Vom Feld= und Ackerbau. | III. Vom
Gartenbau. | IV. Vom Weinbau. | V. Vom Haus= Feld= und Garten= |
Calender. | VI. Vom Bierbrauen. | VII. Vom Kochen. | IIX. Vom Trinchiren. |
IX. Vom Confitiren/ Candiren | und Zuckerbachen. | X. Von den Bienen. |
[vertical rule] | [column two] XI. Vom Wild= und Waidwerck. | XII. Von Pfleg=
und Wartung der | XIII. Von der Viehzucht. (Pferde. | XIV. Vom Vogelfang. |

XV. Von der Fischerey. | XVI. Von bewährten Artzneyen/ | so wohl für Manns= als | Weibs=Personen. | XVII. Vom Distilliren. | XIIX. Von heilsamen Kräutern. | XIX. Von Raritäten und Wun= | der=Künsten. | XX. Von zierlicher Briefstellung. [end columns] | Wohlmeinend zusamm getragen/ und mit schönen hierzu dienlichen Kupffern gezieret/ | von | [in red] Johann Christoph Thiemen. | [rule] | Nürnberg. | [in red] In Verlegung Joh. Hofmanns/ Buch= und Kunsthändlers. 1694.

New edition, Nürnberg, 1694. Originally published, Nürnberg, 1682.

4to. π1):o:(^{2}):o:( ):o:(^{2} A-Uuuuuuuuu^4 Xxxxxxxxx^2; 823 leaves, pp. [*10*] 1-1587 [1588-1636].

Illustrations: Engraved title-page and forty-one engraved plates, one folding.

Bibliographies: This edition unrecorded in the bibliographies consulted. Horn/Arndt 204 records the Nürnberg, 1682, edition.

Copies: *NUC* (New York Academy of Medicine only).

523. Trotti, Alberto.

[head title on 1$_3$^{r}] Alberti trotti ferrariensis ad reuerendissimum antistitem de | padua in tractatu de Jeiunio prohemium incipit.

Colophon: Summula breuis Alberti trotti ferrariēsis Ad reuerēdissimū | antistitēde padua de ieiunio explicit feliciter. Anno domini. M.CCCC.LXXVii. Laus deo clementissimo. | Impressum per Fridericum Creüssner ciuem Nürmm̄bergensem

First edition, Nürnberg, 1477.

Folio: [1-3]^8; 24 leaves, unpaginated. Last leaf, blank, missing in this copy.

Bibliographies: Goff T477.

Copies: *BMC*, *BNC*, and *NUC* (4 copies), Goff (the four copies in *NUC* plus Yale).

523a. Villiers, Mme. A. de.

[grey-green ornamental heading] | Mal was andres. | Eine | Sammlung erprobter fremdländischer | Kochrezepte für Feinschmecker | von | Mme A. de Villiers. | [publisher's device lettered SCHOEN UND WAHR 1806] | Leipzig, | C. S. Amelangs Verlag. | 1901. | [grey-green vertical and horizontal rules]

First edition, Leipzig, 1901. Text printed within upper and outer ornamental borders printed in green.

195 x 126 mm. π^4 χ1 1-11^8; 93 leaves, pp. [i-v] vi-viii [ix-x] [1-3] 4-166 [*10*]. Last ten pages blank except for upper green border and, on the first of these pages, the heading "Persönlisch gesammelte Rezepte." This copy lacks leaf π1. Publisher's burgundy cloth stamped in white.

Bibliographies: Bitting, p. 479.

Copies: *NUC* (Library of Congress and New York Public Library).

524. Vollkommne und neueste Tranchier=Kunst.

Vollkommne und neueste | Tranchier=Kunst | oder | doppelte Anweisung | alle Gattungen | sowohl gesottener als gebratener Speisen | Geflügel, Wildpret, Schlegel, Keulen &c. | auf die geschickteste Art nicht allein zu zerlegen | sondern | mit der besten Wohlanständigkeit | bey allen | vornehmen Tafeln oder Tischen | der Gesellschaft | vorzulegen. | [short fancy rule] | Alles auf das deutlichste nach doppelter Art | beschrieben | und | in Figuren | vorgestellt. | Neuste Auflage. | [fancy rule] | Carlsruhe, | in Macklots Hofbuchhandlung 1797.

New edition, Carlsruhe, 1797. Originally published, Carlsruhe, 1769.

8vo. A-D^8; 32 leaves, pp. [1-3] 4-62 [2]. Last leaf blank.

Illustrations: Woodcuts illustrating carving in the text. These illustrations are the same as those in *l'Ecole parfaite des Officiers de Bouche*, Paris, 1680.

Bibliographies: This edition unrecorded in the bibliographies consulted. Drexel 36 and Vicaire 841 record the first edition.

Copies: No other copy of this edition recorded. *NUC* locates a 1774 edition at Cornell.

525. Woolley, Hannah.

Frauen=Zimmers | Z [in red] eit= [in black] V [in red] ertreib/ | oder | Reiches Gemach von auszerlesenen Experi- | menten vnd Curiositäten bestehend | in einen neuen | [in red] Vollkommenen Koch=Buch/ | Zeigend die rechte Art und Weise/ wie man aller= | hand Fleisch/ Fische und Geflügel künst= | lich zubereiten könne/ | sampt einer | [in red] Präservier= und Candir=Kunst/ | Wie man beydes Früchte und Blumen in | Zucker einmachen/ und lange Zeit | erhalten könne | Dazu auch angehänget ist eine kleine | [in red] Frauen=Zimmers Apothecke, | Anfänglich in Englischer Sprache | beschrieben | von | [in red] ANNA WOLLEY, | Jetzo aber den Teutschen, Frauen=Zimmer | zu Nutzen in ihre Sprache versetzet/ und | dieser dritte Druck viel vermehret. | Mit Chur. Sächsischer Freyheit. | [rule] | [in red] HAMBURG/ | Verlegts Gottfried Schultzens Wittwe/ 1688.

Third edition of this translation, Hamburg, 1688. Originally published in English under the title *The Queen-like Closet*, London, 1670 (item 1062) and in this translation, Hamburg, 1674.

12mo. π^2 A^{10} $B\text{-}N^{12}$ O^6 (A1-A6 signed "A2"-"A7"); 174 leaves, pp. [1-4] 5-113 [114-122], ^{2}[1] 2-138 [*10*], ^{3}1-47 [48-52] [2]. Last leaf blank. Bound with Georg Graman's *Chymische Reise- und Hauss-Apotheca*, Jena, 1670 (item 466), and Johann Staricius *Neu reformirt- und vermehrtet Helden Schatz* [n.p.] 1676.

Illustration: Engraved frontispiece of an apothocary's shop.

Bibliographies: This edition unrecorded in the bibliographies consulted. Schraemli (1) 510 records the Hamburg, 1674, edition.

Copies: No other copy of this edition located. *BMC* and *NUC* (John Crerar Library) located the Hamburg, 1674, edition.

526. Ziehnert, Johann Gottlich, 1780-1856.

[engraved title-page; within a border of one thick and five thin rules] Gemälde | aus dem weiblichen Geschäftskreise. | [two short rules] | 𝔈𝔦𝔫𝔢 𝔅𝔦𝔩𝔡𝔢𝔯𝔰𝔠𝔥𝔲𝔩𝔢 𝔬𝔡𝔢𝔯 𝔢𝔦𝔫 𝔏𝔢𝔥𝔯𝔟𝔲𝔠𝔥 | *über die ersten, nöthigen Kenntnisse in der häuslichen* | *Wirthschaft* | *für junge Mädchen von 9-15 Jahren,* | *von J.G.Ziehnert, Pastor in Schlettau.* | [short fancy rule] | *Neue, sehr billige Ausgabe, mit 16 illuminirten u.* | *schwarzen Kupfertafeln,* | *welche 143 Abbildungen* | *von Wildpret, Vögeln, Fischen, Küchengewächsen,* | *Wirthschaftsgeräthschaften, etc. enthalten.* | [woodcut] | Pirna, | *Verlag von August Robert Friese.*

New edition. Pirna, 1832. No other edition known.

12mo. π^6 A-G^{12} H^6; 96 leaves, pp. [i-vii] viii-xii [1] 2-179 [180]. This copy lacks leaves π1-3.

Illustrations: Sixteen engraved plates, five of them hand colored.

Bibliographies: Gumuchian 5877 (this copy).

Copies: *NUC* (New York Public Library only).

526a. Zückert, Johann Friedrich, 1737-1778.

𝔍𝔬𝔥𝔞𝔫𝔫 𝔉𝔯𝔦𝔢𝔡𝔯𝔦𝔠𝔥 𝔷𝔲𝔠𝔨𝔢𝔯𝔱𝔰 | 𝔡𝔢𝔯 𝔄𝔯𝔷𝔫𝔢𝔶𝔤𝔢𝔩𝔞𝔥𝔯𝔱𝔥𝔢𝔦𝔱 𝔇𝔬𝔠𝔱𝔬𝔯𝔰, 𝔡𝔢𝔯 𝔯𝔬𝔪𝔦𝔰𝔠𝔥𝔨𝔞𝔶𝔰𝔢𝔯𝔩𝔦𝔠𝔥𝔢𝔫 | 𝔄𝔠𝔞𝔡𝔢𝔪𝔦𝔢 𝔡𝔢𝔯 𝔑𝔞𝔱𝔲𝔯𝔣𝔬𝔯𝔰𝔠𝔥𝔢𝔯, 𝔲𝔫𝔡 𝔡𝔢𝔯 𝔠𝔥𝔲𝔯𝔪𝔞𝔶𝔫𝔷𝔦𝔰𝔠𝔥𝔢𝔫 | 𝔄𝔠𝔞𝔡𝔢𝔪𝔦𝔢 𝔫𝔲𝔷𝔩𝔦𝔠𝔥𝔢𝔯 𝔚𝔦𝔰𝔰𝔢𝔫𝔰𝔠𝔥𝔞𝔣𝔱𝔢𝔫 𝔐𝔦𝔱𝔤𝔩𝔦𝔢𝔡𝔰 | 𝔐𝔢𝔡𝔦𝔠𝔦𝔫𝔦𝔰𝔠𝔥𝔢𝔰 | 𝔗𝔦𝔰𝔠𝔥𝔟𝔲𝔠𝔥, | 𝔬𝔡𝔢𝔯 | 𝔠𝔲𝔯 𝔲𝔫𝔡 𝔓𝔯𝔞𝔰𝔢𝔯𝔟𝔞𝔱𝔦𝔬𝔫 | 𝔡𝔢𝔯 𝔎𝔯𝔞𝔫𝔨𝔥𝔢𝔦𝔱𝔢𝔫 | 𝔡𝔲𝔯𝔠𝔥 𝔡𝔦𝔞𝔱𝔢𝔱𝔦𝔰𝔠𝔥𝔢 𝔐𝔦𝔱𝔱𝔢𝔩. | [vignette] | [fancy rule] | 𝔅𝔢𝔯𝔩𝔦𝔫, | 𝔟𝔢𝔦 𝔄𝔲𝔤𝔲𝔰𝔱 𝔐𝔶𝔩𝔦𝔲𝔰 1771.

First edition, Berlin, 1771.

8vo. a^8 b^4 A-Y^8 Z^4; 192 leaves, pp. [i-iii] iv-xxiv [1] 2-354 [6].

Bibliographies; This edition unrecorded in the bibliographies consulted. Vicaire 884 cites the second edition, Frankenthal, 1785.

Copies: *BMC.*

527. Zückert, Johann Friedrich, 1737-1778.

D. Johann Friedrich Zückert | der Römischkayserlichen Academie der Naturforscher, der Chur= | maynzischen Academie nützlicher Wissenschaften zu Erfurt, | und der Gesellschaft Naturforschender Freunde zu | Berlin Mitglied, | von den | Speisen | aus dem | Pflanzenreich. | [short double rule] | Oder | Zwote Fortsetzung | seiner Abhandlung | von den | Nahrungsmitteln. | [fancy rule] | Berlin, | bey August Mylius, 1778.

First edition, Berlin, 1778.

8vo. π^2 A-R^8 S^6 T^4; 148 leaves, pp. [4] [1] 2-292.

A sequel to his *Von den Speisen aus dem Thierreich, oder erste Fortsetzung seiner Abhandlung von den Nahrungsmitteln,* Berlin, 1777 (item 527a).

Bibliographies: Schraemli (3) 46 in a note. Vicaire 884 records the second edition, Berlin, 1785.

Copies: *NUC* (Joint University Libraries, Nashville, Tennessee, only).

527a. Zückert, Johann Friedrich, 1737-1778.

D. Johann Friedrich Zückert | des Teltowschen Creises aszistirender Physikus der Römischkayser- | lichen Academie der Naturforscher, der Churmaynzischen Aca- | demie nützlicher Wiffenschaften zu Erfurt, und der Gesellschaft | Naturforschender Freunde zu Berlin Mitglied, | von den | Speisen | aus dem | Thierreich, | [short thick-thin rule] | Oder, | Erste Fortsetzung | seiner Abhandlung | von den | Nahrungsmitteln. | [fancy rule] | Berlin, | bey August Mylius, 1777.

First edition, Berlin, 1777.

8vo. ✱^{4} A-K^8 L-M^4; 92 leaves, pp. [8] [1] 2-176.

Bibliographies: Unrecorded in the bibliographies consulted.

Copies: *NUC* (Joint University Libraries, Nashville, Tennessee, only).

De generibus Ebriosorum et ebrietate vitanda.

Questio facetiarum et vrbanitatis plena: & pulcerrimis
optimorum scriptorum flosculis referta: in conclu-
sione Quodlibeti Erphurdiensis. Anno
Christi. M.D.XV. Circa autumna-
le equinoctium Scolastico
more explicata.

Geispassiger
Wort-Krieg/
Bestehend in einer lächerlichen Schertz-Frag / ob denen
Brat: oder Leber-Würsten ; oder Bluntzen ? denen Sau-Köpf: oder
Schunken die Vorgangs-Ehre gebühre ?
Von denen Eypel-auern in vergangenem Fasching mündlich durchge-
gribelt; dann einer Nährsamen Sau-Schneider-Zunfft schrifftlich
zugewidmet;

Und nun bey eingeruckt-Oesterlicher Fleisch-Zeit/allen Neu-Begierigen
zur Lust/ für ein
ROTHES-AYR
Druk-verfaster überreichet im Jahr 1708.

Item no. 464

Item no. 470

Bayerisches Kochbuch

für Fleisch= und Fasttäge.

Enthält:

leichtfaßliche und bewährte Anweisungen, um für alle Stände auf die vortheilhafteste und schmackhafteste Art zu kochen, zu backen, und einzumachen.

Nebst einem Abschnitte

von

besondern Speisen für Kranke,

und

ökonomischen Hausmitteln.

Herausgegeben

von

Johanna Maria Huberinn.

Mit Bewill. der Kurfl. Bücherzensurspezialkommission.

Stadtamhof,

bei Joh. Mich. Daisenberger, bürgerl. Buchhändler.

1800.

Neü=vermehrtes
Trenchir=Büchlein.

Das, woran die Natur hat allen fleiß gewandt,
Zergliedert, Schöne, dir, deß Künstlers Liebe Hand.

Ein nutzlich Regiment der gesundt

heyt/ Genant das Vanquete/ oder Gastmal der Edlen diener
von der Complexion/ Eigenschafft/ Schad/ vnd nutz allerley
Speyß/ Trancks/ vñ von allem/ darmit sich der mensch in ge-
sundtheyt enthelt/ Mit sampt einem kurtzen Regiment/
Wye man sich in der Pestilentz/ Pestilentzischen fieber
vnnd Schweyß halten soll.

Gemacht durch den Hochgeach ten Doctorē Ludouicum De Auila/ Keyserlicher Mayestat Leybartzt/ ehemals in Lateynischer vnd Hyspanischer sprach beschriben/ Vñ durch
den Hochgelerten Herren Michaelem Krautwadel/ der Freyen Künst vnnd Artzney
Doctorē zü Landsperg vertentscht/ mit verenderũg allē dem/ so Teütscher Com-
plexiō etwas hert/ vnleydlich/ oder wyder ist/ Auch mit hinzü setzung vilerley
leer/ sprüch/ vnd zeugknus Hochberümpter ärtzt /dauon etwan im text
zü kurtze meldunng beschicht / Als eyn yetlicher verstendiger
Leser an der seytten des texts wol abnemen mag.

Mit Keyserlicher Mayestat Gnad vnd priuilegio.

PAUL JACOB MARPERGER,

Königlich-Polnisch- und Chur-Sächsisch- Hoff- und Commercien-Raths / wie auch Mitglieds der Königlich-Preußischen Societät der Wissenschafften/

Vollständiges

Küch- und Keller-

DICTIONARIUM

In welchem allerhand Speisen und Getränke/

Bekannte und unbekannte/ gesunde und ungesunde/ einheimische und ausländische/ wohlfeile und kostbare/ nothwendige und entbehrliche/ und andere/ wie sie für Nahmen haben mögen/ mehr beschrieben/

Ihrechter Einkauff- und Erzeugungs-Ort/ Zeit und Preiß/ wie auch ihre Auslesung/ Zubereitung/ Conservation, nützliche und schädliche Würckung/ mäßiger und unmäßiger Gebrauch/ nach gewissen Monaten/ Jahrs-Zeiten/ Witterungen und Ländern/ item nach der Menschen Leibes-Constitution und Verrichtungen/ Alter/ Stand und Kranckheit gewiesen;

Ferner

Allerhand nützliche Haußhaltungs- Gesundheits- Lebens- und Policey-Regeln/ mit Moralischen Anmerckungen/ gegeben/

Unterschiedlicher Nationen ihre gewöhnliche Speise-Arten und Mahlzeiten erzehlet/

Großer Herren Banquets, solenne Festins und Tractirungen/ wie auch der Bürgerlicher auch geringer Standes-Personen Convivia wohl einzurichten/ die Tafeln zierlich anzuordnen/ zu garniren/ und zu besten gen/ gelehret/

Und in Summa alles dasjenige/ was zum splendiden so wohl/ als was zum moderaten Leben an Speis und Getränck vorhanden seyn muß/vorgestellet wird/

Allen Hoff-Küchen- und Keller-Meistern/ Köchinnen/ Schreibern/ Christl. Haus-Vättern und Haus-Müttern/ zu sonderbaren Nutzen aufgesetzet.

Hamburg/ in Verlegung Benjamin Schillers sel. Wittwe/ ANNO 1716.

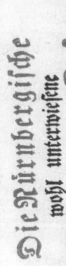

Die Nürnbergische
wohl unterwiesene
Köchin

welche so wohl

an Fleisch- als Fast-Tagen,

zu geschickter Bereitung

wohlschmeckender Speisen

deutliche Anweisung giebt.

Mit allergnädigsten Privilegien.

Nürnberg,

bey Joh. Adam Stein und Gabr. Nic. Raspe

1752.

TRINCIER
Oder
Vorleg-Buch/

Darinnen berichtet wird/
Wie man allerhand gebratene
vnd gesottene Speisen/ so auff Fürst-
liche vnd andere Taffeln getragen werden mögen/
Nach Italianischer/ vnd vornemlich Romanischer
Arth/anschneiden/vnd auff der Gabel zierlich
zerlegen soll.

Vor dessen/Von
GIACOMO. PROCACCHI.
In Italianischer Sprach beschrieben.

An jetzo aber
In das hochdeutsche trewlichen versetzet/vnd
mit den signirten Kupfferstichen auffs best vnd
fleissigste gezieret/etc.

Leipzig/
In Verlegung Henning Großen des Jüngern
Buchhändlers.

ANNO M DC XXI.

Ein new Kochbuch/
Das ist/
Ein Gründtli-
che Beschreibung / wie man recht vnd
wol/ nicht allein von vierfüssigen/ heymischen vnd wilden Thie-
ren/ sondern auch von mancherley Vögel vnnd Federwildpret / darzu von allem
grünen vnd dürren Fischwerck/ allerley Speiß/ als gesotten/ gebraten/ gebacken/ Presolen/ Carbonaden/ mancherley Pasteten vnd Füllwerck/ Gallrat/ etc. auff Teutsche/ Vngerische/ Hispanische/ Italianische vnd Frantzö-
sische weiß/ kochen vnd zubereiten soll: Auch wie allerley Gemüß/ Obs/ Saltzen/ Senff/
Confect vnd Latwergen/ zuzurichten seyt.

Auch ist darinnen zu vernemmen/ wie man herrliche grosse Pancketen/ sampt
gemeinen Gastereyen/ ordentlich anrichten vnd bestellen soll.

Allen Menschen/ hohes vnd nidriges Standts/ Weibs vnd Manns Personen/ zu nutz jetzunde zum
ersten in Druck gegeben/ dergleichen vor nie ist außgegangen.

Durch
M. Marxen Rumpolt/ Churf. Meintzischen Mundtkoch.

Mit Röm. Keyserlicher Maiestat special Priuilegio.

1 5 8 7.

Sampt einem gründtlichen Bericht/ wie man alle Wein vor allen zufällen
bewaren/ die breßhafften widerbringen/ Kräuter vnd andere Wein/ Bier/ Essig/ vnd alle
andere Getränck/ machen vnd bereiten soll/ daß sie natürlich/ vnd allen
Menschen vnschädlich/ zu trincken seindt.

Gedruckt zu Franckfort am Mayn/ In verlegung
Sigmundt Feyerabendt/ Peter Fischer/ vnd
Heinrich Tack.

Item no. 504

Ain sehr Künstlichs vnnd Fürtrefflichs

Kochbüch/ von allerlay Speysen/ auch wie man Latwergen vnnd Zucker einmachen soll/ vnd sunst von anderen gütten haimlichen Künsten/ Ainem yeden im Hauß sehr notwendig vnnd nutzlich zü gebrauchen.

Durch ainen Fürnemen vnd berümbten Koch seinem Ehegemahel zü der Letze geschenckt.

Mit Rö: Kay: May: Freyhait/ in zway Jaren nit nach zü trucken.

5 5 9.

Item no. 515

GREAT BRITAIN

528. Abbot, Robert.

THE | HOUSEKEEPER's | VALUABLE PRESENT: | OR, | *Lady's Closet Companion.* | BEING A | NEW AND COMPLETE | *ART OF PREPARING* | CONFECTS, | ACCORDING TO | *MODERN PRACTICE.* | *Comprized under the following Parts*; *viz.* | I. Different Methods and Degrees of boiling and | clarifying Sugar. | II. Methods of preserving various Fruits in Sy- | rups, &c. | III. Methods of making Marmalades, Jams, | Pastes, &c. | IV. Methods of making Syrups, Custards, Jellies, | Blanch-mange, Conserves, Syllabubs, &c. | V. Methods of preserving various Fruits in Brandy. | VI. Methods of making a Variety of Biscuits, rich | Cakes, &c. &c. | VII. Methods of mixing, freezing, and working Ice | Creams. | VIII. Methods of preparing Cordials and made | Wines. | With a Variety of other useful and elegant Articles. | [short fancy rule] | BY ROBERT ABBOT, | *Late Apprentice to Messrs.* NEGRI & GUNTER, | *Confectioners, in* Berkeley Square. | [short fancy rule] | PRINTED FOR THE AUTHOR; | And sold by C. COOKE, No. 17, Pater-noster Row; | and all other Booksellers in Town and Country. | [*Price* 2s. *sewed, or* 2s. 6d. *neatly bound.*]

First edition. Published, London, ca. 1790, according to Maclean, based on ownership inscription, "Anne Jones, Dec. 18, 1791," in the copy described in Pennell, p. 165.

12mo. A-H^6 I^2; 50 leaves, pp. [i-iii] iv-xii [13] 14-100.

Bibliographies: Maclean, p. 1; Oxford, p. 126; Pennell, p. 165; Simon BG 1.

Copies: *BMC* and *NUC* (New York Public Library only). Maclean records these copies and adds Wellcome Library and Brotherton Library in Britain and Kansas State University and Old Sturbridge Village, Mass., in North America.

529. Abercrombie, John, 1726-1806.

THE | British Fruit-Gardener; | AND | ART OF PRUNING: | COMPRISING, | The most approved Methods of PLANTING | and RAISING every useful FRUIT-TREE | and FRUIT-BEARING-SHRUB, whether for | Walls, Espaliers, Standards, Half-Standards, | or Dwarfs: | The true successful Practice of PRUNING, | TRAINING, GRAFTING, BUDDING, &c. | so as to render them abundantly fruitful: | AND | Full Directions concerning SOILS, SITUA- | TIONS, and EXPOSURES. | By JOHN ABERCROMBIE; | Of TOTTENHAM-COURT, Gardener: | AUTHOR OF | EVERY MAN HIS OWN GARDENER, | First published under the Name of Tho. MAWE. | LONDON: | Printed for LOCKYER DAVIS, in Holborn. | MDCCLXXIX.

First edition, London, 1779.

4to. [A]⁴ B-Xx⁴ Yy²; 178 leaves, pp. [2] [i] ii-iv [2] [1] 2-104, 104-119, 119-346.

Bibliographies: Henrey III, p. 1.

Copies: *BMC*, *BNC*, and *NUC* (8 copies).

530. The Accomplish'd Housewife.

THE | *Accomplish'd Housewife*; | OR, THE | GENTLEWOMAN'S COMPANION: | CONTAINING | [in two columns: column one] I. Reflections on the Education of | the Fair Sex; with Characters | for their Imitation. | II. The Penman's Advice to the | Ladies; or the Art of Writing | made easy, and entertaining. | III. Instruction for addressing | Persons of Distinction, in Writ- | ing or Discouse. | IV. An easy Introduction to the | Study of Practical Arithmetic. | V. Directions for copying Prints | or Drawings, and Painting either | in Oil or Water Colours, or with | *Crayons*. | VI. Directions for Marketing, with | respect to Butcher's Meat, Poul- | terer's Ware, and Fish. | VII. A Bill of Fare for every | Month in the Year. | VIII. Receipts in Cookery, Pa- | stry, &c. | [vertical double rule] | [column two] IX. Instructions for Carving and | placing Dishes on the Table. | X. All Sorts of Pickles, Made | Wines, &c. | XI. Remarks on the Nature and | Qualities of the most common | Aliments. | XII. Recipes in Physick and Sur- | gery. | XIII. Remarks on the Causes and | Symptons of most Diseases. | XIV. The Florist's Kalendar. | XV. Familiar Letters on several | Occasions in common Life; with | Instructions to young Orphan | Ladies how to judge of Propo- | sals of Marriage made to them | without the Consent of their | Friends or Guardians. | XVI. A Dictionary serving for the | Translation of ordinary *English* | Words into more scholastic ones. [end columns] | CONCLUDING | With some serious Instructions for the Conduct of the FAIR SEX, | with regard to their Duty towards GOD, and towards their | NEIGHBOURS. | [two rules] | *LONDON:* | Printed for J. NEWBURY, at the *Bible* and *Sun* near the | *Chapter-House* in St. *Paul's Church-yard*, and B. COLLINS, | Bookseller, in *Salisbury*. | [short rule] | MDCCXLVIII.

Second edition, London, 1748. Originally published, London, 1745.

12mo. π² A-Ff⁶ Gg² χGg⁶ Hh-Kk⁶ Ll² χ1 2χ1 Mm-Pp⁶; 230 leaves, pp. [*16*] 1-431 [432-444]. First leaf blank. χGg1 signed "Gg3".

Illustrations: Two engraved plates by L. Bickham showing specimens of round hand and Italian hand and six woodcuts in the text on Y5, Y6 and Z1 rectos and versos (pp. 249-254) showing table settings.

Bibliographies: Pennell, p. 156. Axford, p. 4, Bitting, p. 513, Maclean, p. 2, Oxford, p. 75 and Roscoe A1 all record the first edition, 1745, only.

Copies: No other copy of this edition located.

531. Accum, Friedrich Christian, 1769-1838.

𝕮𝖚𝖑𝖎𝖓𝖆𝖗𝖞 𝕮𝖍𝖊𝖒𝖎𝖘𝖙𝖗𝖞, | EXHIBITING | THE | *SCIENTIFIC PRINCIPLES* | OF | COOKERY, | WITH CONCISE INSTRUCTIONS FOR PREPARING GOOD AND WHOLESOME | PICKLES, VINEGAR, CONSERVES, FRUIT JELLIES, | MARMALADES, | AND VARIOUS OTHER ALIMENTARY SUBSTANCES EMPLOYED | IN | 𝕯𝖔𝖒𝖊𝖘𝖙𝖎𝖈 𝕰𝖈𝖔𝖓𝖔𝖒𝖞, | WITH OBSERVATIONS ON THE CHEMICAL CONSTITUTION AND NUTRITIVE | QUALITIES OF DIFFERENT KINDS OF FOOD. | [short rule] | *WITH COPPER PLATES.* | [hand-colored copperplate engraving] | BY FREDRICK ACCUM, | Operative Chemist, Lecturer on Practical Chemistry, on Mineralogy, and on Chemistry applied | to the Arts and Manufactures; Member of the Royal Irish Academy; Fellow of the Linnaean Society; | Member of the Royal Academy of Sciences, and of the Royal Society of Arts Berlin &c. &c. | 𝕷𝖔𝖓𝖉𝖔𝖓: | PUBLISHED BY R. ACKERMANN, 101, STRAND; | 1821.

First edition, London, 1821.

190 x 110 mm. a^{12} B-Q^{12} (a2 and a3 signed "a" and "a2"); 192 leaves, pp. [i] ii-xxii [xxiii-xxiv] [1] 2-336, ^{2}[i] ii-xxiii [xxiv], p. 336 misnumbered "356." Publisher's boards with printed paper label on spine.

Illustrations: Hand-colored copperplate engraved title-page and frontispiece showing types of stoves, not reckoned in collation or pagination.

Bibliographies: Axford, p. 106; Bitting, p. 2; Craig 2; Oxford, p. 150; Schraemli (1) 4; Vicaire 4; Wheaton and Kelly 18.

Copies: *BMC*, *BNC*, and *NUC* (10 copies).

532. Accum, Friedrich Christian, 1769-1838.

A TREATISE | ON | ADULTERATIONS OF FOOD, | AND | 𝕮𝖚𝖑𝖎𝖓𝖆𝖗𝖞 𝕻𝖔𝖎𝖘𝖔𝖓𝖘, | EXHIBITING | *THE FRAUDULENT SOPHISTICATIONS* | OF | BREAD, BEER, WINE, SPIRITUOUS LIQUORS, TEA, COFFEE, | Cream, Confectionery, Vinegar, Mustard, Pepper, Cheese, Olive Oil, Pickles, | AND OTHER ARTICLES EMPLOYED IN DOMESTIC ECONOMY. | AND | 𝕸𝖊𝖙𝖍𝖔𝖉𝖘 𝖔𝖋 𝖉𝖊𝖙𝖊𝖈𝖙𝖎𝖓𝖌 𝖙𝖍𝖊𝖒. |

[in red: vignette] | 𝕭𝖄 𝕱𝕽𝕰𝕯𝕽𝕴𝕮𝕶 𝕬𝕮𝕮𝖀𝕸, | 𝕺𝔭𝔢𝔯𝔞𝔱𝔦𝔳𝔢 𝕮𝔥𝔢𝔪𝔦𝔰𝔱, | 𝕷𝔢𝔠𝔱𝔲𝔯𝔢𝔯 𝔬𝔫 𝕻𝔯𝔞𝔠𝔱𝔦𝔠𝔞𝔩 𝕮𝔥𝔢𝔪𝔦𝔰𝔱𝔯𝔶, 𝕸𝔦𝔫𝔢𝔯𝔞𝔩𝔬𝔤𝔶, 𝔞𝔫𝔡 𝔬𝔫 𝕮𝔥𝔢𝔪𝔦𝔰𝔱𝔯𝔶 | 𝔞𝔭𝔭𝔩𝔦𝔢𝔡 𝔱𝔬 𝔱𝔥𝔢 𝒜𝔯𝔱𝔰 𝔞𝔫𝔡 𝕸𝔞𝔫𝔲𝔣𝔞𝔠𝔱𝔲𝔯𝔢𝔰; 𝕸𝔢𝔪𝔟𝔢𝔯 𝔬𝔣 𝔱𝔥𝔢 𝕽𝔬𝔶𝔞𝔩 𝕴𝔯𝔦𝔰𝔥 𝒜𝔠𝔞𝔡𝔢𝔪𝔶; | 𝕱𝔢𝔩𝔩𝔬𝔴 𝔬𝔣 𝔱𝔥𝔢 𝕷𝔦𝔫𝔫𝔞𝔢𝔞𝔫 𝖘𝔬𝔠𝔦𝔢𝔱𝔶; 𝕸𝔢𝔪𝔟𝔢𝔯 𝔬𝔣 𝔱𝔥𝔢 𝕽𝔬𝔶𝔞𝔩 𝒜𝔠𝔞𝔡𝔢𝔪𝔶 𝔬𝔣 | 𝖘𝔠𝔦𝔢𝔫𝔠𝔢𝔰, 𝔞𝔫𝔡 𝔬𝔣 𝔱𝔥𝔢 𝕽𝔬𝔶𝔞𝔩 𝖘𝔬𝔠𝔦𝔢𝔱𝔶 𝔬𝔣 𝒜𝔯𝔱𝔰 𝔬𝔣 𝕭𝔢𝔯𝔩𝔦𝔫, &𝔠. &𝔠. | [short double rule] | 𝕷𝔬𝔫𝔡𝔬𝔫: | Printed by J. Mallett, 59, Wardour Street, Soho. | SOLD BY LONGMAN, HURST, REES, ORME, AND BROWN, | PATERNOSTER ROW. | [short fancy rule] | 1820.

First edition, London, 1820.

191 x 115 mm. π1 A^8 B-Q^{12} R^6; 195 leaves, pp. [2] [i] ii-xvi [1] 2-372. Publisher's green and white printed boards.

Bibliographics: Axford, p. 397; Bitting, p. 2; Craig 1; Gabler, p. 3; Noling, p. 21; Schraemli (1) 3; Simon BG 17; Wheaton and Kelly 20.

Copies: *BMC* and *NUC* (12 copies).

533. Accum, Friedrich Christian, 1769-1838.

A | TREATISE | ON THE | 𝒜𝔯𝔱 𝔬𝔣 𝕭𝔯𝔢𝔴𝔦𝔫𝔤, | EXHIBITING | THE LONDON PRACTICE | OF | BREWING, | 𝕻𝔬𝔯𝔱𝔢𝔯, 𝕭𝔯𝔬𝔴𝔫 𝖘𝔱𝔬𝔲𝔱, 𝒜𝔩𝔢, 𝕿𝔞𝔟𝔩𝔢 𝕭𝔢𝔢𝔯, | AND | *VARIOUS OTHER KINDS OF MALT LIQUORS.* | [short rule] | *WITH COPPER PLATES.* | [hand-colored engraved vignette signed *W. Read. Sculpt.*] | BY FREDRICK ACCUM. | Operative Chemist, Lecturer on Practical Chemistry, on Mineralogy, and on Chemistry applied | to the Arts and Manufactures; Member of the Royal Irish Academy; Fellow of the Linnaean | Society; Member of the Royal Academy of Sciences, and of the Royal Society of Arts of | Berlin, &c. &c. | *LONDON.* | LONGMAN, HURST, REES, ORME, AND BROWN, PATERNOSTER-ROW. | *Green, Printer, Leicester Street, Leicester Square.* | 1820.

First edition, London, 1820.

176 x 103 mm. π^2 A^6 B-M^{12} N^2 χN^{12}; 152 leaves, pp. [2] [i-iii] iv-xiv [1] 2-268.

Note: Signature χN comprises a notice to the public of a new edition of Accum's *Treatise on Adulterations of Food.*

Illustrations: Hand-colored engraved illustrations of dome-brewing; coppers and portable brewing apparatus on the frontispiece and title-page, π1^v and π2^r.

Bibliographies: Noling, p. 21; Simon BG 19.

Copies: *BMC, BNC*, and *NUC* (4 copies).

534. Accum, Friedrich Christian, 1769-1838.

[engraved title-page] A | TREATISE | ON THE | 𝔄rt of 𝔅re𝔴ing, | EXHIBITING | THE LONDON PRACTICE | OF | BREWING, | ℜorter, 𝔅ro𝔴n 𝔖tout, 𝔄le, | 𝔗able 𝔅eer, | AND | VARIOUS OTHER KINDS OF MALT LIQUORS. | SECOND EDITION. | With Copper Plates. | [hand-colored engraved vignette signed *W. Read, Sculp.*] | 𝔅y 𝔍redrick 𝔄ccum, | *Operative Chemist, Lecturer on Practical Chemistry, on Mineralogy, & on Chemistry* | *applied to the Arts & Manufacturers; Member of the Royal Irish Academy; Fellow of* | *the Linnaean Society; Member of the Royal Academy of Sciences, & of the Royal Society* | *of Arts of Berlin, &c. &c.* | LONDON. | LONGMAN, HURST, REES, ORME, & BROWN, PATERNOSTER ROW. | MDCCCXXI.

Second edition, London, 1821. Originally published, London, 1820 (item 533).

190 x 109 mm. a^6 B-L^{12} M^6 N^{12}; 144 leaves, pp. [iii] iv- xiii [xiv] [1] 2-252, ^{2}[i] ii-xxiii [xxiv]. Note: Signature N comprises a notice to the public of a new edition of Accum's *Treatise on Adulteration of Food*.

Illustrations: Engraved, hand-colored, title-page, frontispiece, and one plate showing brewing equipment, not reckoned in the collation or pagination.

Bibliographies: This edition unrecorded in the bibliographies consulted. Simon BG 19 records the first edition.

Copies: *BMC* and *NUC* (7 copies).

535. Accum, Friedrich Christian, 1769-1838.

A TREATISE | ON THE ART OF | MAKING GOOD AND WHOLESOME | BREAD | OF | WHEAT, OATS, RYE, BARLEY, | AND | OTHER FARINACEOUS GRAIN, | EXHIBITING | THE ALIMENTARY PROPERTIES AND CHEMICAL CONSTITUTION | OF DIFFERENT KINDS OF BREAD CORN, AND OF THE | VARIOUS SUBSTITUTES USED FOR BREAD, IN | DIFFERENT

PARTS OF THE WORLD. | [hand-colored engraving] | BY FREDRICK ACCUM, | *OPERATIVE CHEMIST*, | Lecturer on Practical Chemistry, on Mineralogy, and on Chemistry applied to the Arts and | Manufactures; Member of the Royal Irish Academy; Fellow of the Linnaean Society; | Member of the Royal Academy of Sciences, and of the Royal Society | of Arts of Berlin, &c. &c. | [short rule] | 𝔏𝔬𝔫𝔡𝔬𝔫: | PRINTED FOR THOMAS BOYS, 7, LUDGATE HILL, | By C. Green, Leicester Street, Leicester Square. | 1821.

First edition, London, 1821.

187 x 110 mm. $\pi 1$ a^2 B-G^{12} H^8 N^{12}; 95 leaves, pp. [2] [i] ii-iii [iv] [1] 2-160, ^{2}[i] ii-xxiii [xxiv]. Publisher's boards, with printed paper label on spine. Note: Signature N comprises a notice to the public of a new edition of Accum's *Treatise on Adulterations of Food*.

Illustration: Hand-colored lithograph of an oven on $\pi 1^r$ (title-page).

Bibliographies: Axford, p. 398; Bitting, p. 2; Wheaton and Kelly 24.

Copies: *BMC* and *NUC* (6 copies).

536. Accum, Friedrich Christian, 1769-1838.

A | TREATISE | ON THE | 𝔄𝔯𝔱 𝔬𝔣 𝔐𝔞𝔨𝔦𝔫𝔤 𝔚𝔦𝔫𝔢 | FROM | NATIVE FRUITS; | EXHIBITING THE | CHEMICAL PRINCIPLES UPON WHICH THE ART OF WINE MAKING | DEPENDS; THE FRUITS BEST ADAPTED FOR | 𝔥𝔬𝔪𝔢 𝔪𝔞𝔡𝔢 𝔚𝔦𝔫𝔢𝔰, | AND | *THE METHOD OF PREPARING THEM*. | [hand-colored illustration of wine press] | BY FREDRICK ACCUM. | Operative Chemist, Lecturer on Practical Chemistry, on Mineralogy, and on Chemistry applied | to the Arts and Manufactures; Member of the Royal Irish Academy; Fellow of the Linnaean | Society; Member of the Royal Academy of Sciences, and of the Royal Society of Arts of | Berlin, &c. &c. | *LONDON*. | LONGMAN, HURST, REES, ORME, AND BROWN, PATERNOSTER-ROW | *Green, Printer, Leicester Street, Leicester Square*. | 1820.

First edition, London, 1820.

186 x 109 mm. $\pi 1$ a^2 b^2 B-D^{12} E^6 N^{12}; 59 leaves, pp. [2] [i-iii] iv-viii [9] 10-92, ^{2}[i] ii-xxiii [xxiv]. Note: Signature N comprises a notice to the public of a new edition of Accum's *Treatise on Adulterations of Food*.

Illustration: Hand colored engraving of a wine press on π1^r (title-page).

Bibliographies: Gabler, p. 4; Noling, p. 21; Simon BG 16.

Copies: *BMC* and *NUC* (8 copies).

537. Acton, Eliza, 1799-1859.

THE │ ENGLISH BREAD-BOOK │ FOR DOMESTIC USE, │ ADAPTED TO │
FAMILIES OF EVERY GRADE: │ CONTAINING THE │ PLAINEST AND MOST
MINUTE INSTRUCTIONS TO THE LEARNER; │ PRACTICAL RECEIPTS │ FOR
MANY VARIETIES OF BREAD; │ WITH │ NOTICES OF THE PRESENT SYSTEM
OF ADULTERATION, │ AND ITS CONSEQUENCES; │ AND OF THE │
IMPROVED BAKING PROCESSES AND INSTITUTIONS │ ESTABLISHED
ABROAD. │ BY │ ELIZA ACTON, │ AUTHOR OF "MODERN COOKERY." │
LONDON: │ LONGMAN, BROWN, GREEN, LONGMANS, & ROBERTS. │ 1857. │
The right of translation is reserved.

First edition, London, 1857.

173 x 113 mm. A^6 B-N^8 O^4 P^2; 108 leaves, pp. [i-v] vi-xii [1] 2-204. Publisher's
cloth. Publisher's 24 page catalogue bound in at end.

Bibliographies: Axford, p. 134; Bitting, p. 3; Simon BG 25; Wheaton and Kelly 25.

Copies: *BMC*, *BNC*, and *NUC* (5 copies).

538. Acton, Eliza, 1799-1859.

MODERN COOKERY, │ IN ALL ITS BRANCHES: │ REDUCED TO │ A SYSTEM
OF EASY PRACTICE, │ FOR THE USE OF PRIVATE FAMILIES. │ IN A SERIES
OF RECEIPTS, WHICH HAVE BEEN STRICTLY │ TESTED, AND ARE GIVEN
WITH THE MOST │ MINUTE EXACTNESS. │ BY ELIZA ACTON. │
ILLUSTRATED WITH NUMEROUS WOODCUTS. │ [short rule] │ FOURTH
EDITION. │ [short rule] │ LONDON: │ LONGMAN, BROWN, GREEN AND
LONGMANS, │ PATERNOSTER ROW. │ [short rule] │ 1845.

Fourth edition, London, 1845. Originally published, London, also 1845.

165 x 98 mm. π^8 [A]^8 B-QQ^8; 320 leaves, pp. [i-vii] viii-xi [xii] [2] [xiii] xiv-xxx [1] 2-607 [608]. Publisher's cloth.

Bibliographies: This edition unrecorded in the bibliographies consulted. Bitting, pp. 2-3, Craig 3, Oxford, p. 175, Schraemli (1) 5, and Simon BG 20-24 list other editions.

Copies: No other copy of this edition located.

539. Adair, Arthur Henry.

DINNERS | LONG AND SHORT | *by* | A. H. ADAIR | *WITH AN INTRODUCTION* | *by* | X. MARCEL BOULESTIN | *AND A PORTRAIT* | *by* | MARIE LAURENCIN | LONDON | *VICTOR GOLLANCZ LTD* | 14 Henrietta Street Covent Garden | 1928

First edition, London, 1928.

185 x 125 mm. [A]^8 B-Q^8; 128 leaves, pp. [1-8] 9-252 [*4*]. Last two leaves blank. Publisher's black cloth stamped in red.

Illustrations: Photogravure portrait of the author after a drawing by Marie Laurencin.

Bibliographies; Axford, p. 118; Bitting, p. 3.

Copies: *BMC* and *NUC* (4 copies).

540. Adams, Samuel and Sarah.

THE | COMPLETE SERVANT; | BEING A | PRACTICAL GUIDE | TO THE | PECULIAR DUTIES AND BUSINESS | OF ALL DESCRIPTIONS OF | Serbants, | FROM THE HOUSEKEEPER TO THE SERVANT OF ALL- | WORK, AND FROM THE LAND STEWARD | TO THE FOOT-BOY; | WITH | USEFUL RECEIPTS AND TABLES, | [short rule] | BY SAMUEL AND SARAH ADAMS, | *Fifty years Servants in different Families*. | [short rule] | LONDON: | PRINTED FOR KNIGHT AND LACEY, | PUBLISHERS OF BOOKS CONNECTED WITH THE USEFUL ARTS, | At the James Watt, in Paternoster=Row | [short rule] | MDCCCXXV. | *Price Seven Shillings and Sixpence*.

First edition, London, 1825.

190 x 110 mm. π1 [A]² B-S¹² T¹² (-T12=π1) *B-D*¹²; 254 leaves, pp. [i-iii] iv-vi [1] 2-430, ²[1] 2-72. Publisher's printed boards.

Bibliographies: Attar 351.1; Axford, p. 75; Bitting, p. 3; Oxford, p. 156.

Copies: *BMC* and *NUC* (Kansas State University and Library of Congress).

541. Adam's Luxury and Eve's Cookery.

ADAM's LUXURY, | AND | *EVE*'s COOKERY; | OR, THE | Kitchen-Garden display'd. | In Two Parts. | I. Shewing the best and most approved Methods | of raising and bringing to the greatest Perfection, | all the Products of the Kitchen-Garden; with a | Kalendar shewing the different Products of each | Month, and the Business proper to be done in it. | II. Containing a large Collection of RECEIPTS for | dressing all Sorts of Kitchen-Stuff, so as to afford | a great Variety of cheap, healthful, and palata- | ble Dishes. | To which is Added, | *The Physical Virtues of every Herb and Root.* | [rule] | Designed for the Use of all who would live Cheap, and pre- | serve their Health to old Age; particularly for Farmers and | Tradesmen in the Country, who have but small Pieces of | Garden Ground, and are willing to make the most of it. | [rule] | *LONDON:* | Printed for R. DODSLEY, in *Pall-Mall*; and Sold | by M. COOPER, at the *Globe* in *Pater-noster Row.* | [short rule] | MDCCXLIV.

First edition, London, 1744.

12mo. A⁶ B-K¹²; 114 leaves, pp. [i-v] vi-xii [1] 2-216.

Bibliographies: Axford, p. 4; Bitting, p. 514; Craig 4; Maclean, p. 3; Oxford, p. 74; Pennell, p. 151; Simon BG 64; Wheaton and Kelly 38.

Copies: *BMC* and *NUC* (6 copies). Maclean adds Brotherton Library, Glasgow University, Guildhall Library, New York Public Library and Radcliffe.

542. Agrippa von Nettesheim, Heinrich Cornelius, 1486?-1535.

[within a border of type ornaments] ¶ Henrie Cornelius | Agrippa, of the Vanitie and | *vncertaintie of Artes and* | Sciences: Englished by | Ia. San. Gent. | *Ecclesiastes.* I. | All is but most vaine Vanitie: and all | is most vaine, and but plaine | Vanitie. | *Seene and allowed according to the* | *order appoynted* | ¶ Imprinted at London, by | *Henrie Bynneman, dwelling* | in Knightryder streete, at the | signe of the Mer- | mayde. | *Anno.* 1575.

Second edition, London, 1575, of the English translation by James Sanford originally published, London, 1569.

4to. ¶⁴ A-Bbb⁴; 196 leaves, ff. [8] 1-187 [188].

Bookplate: The Right Honble. Algernon Capell, Earl of Essex, Viscount Maldon, & Baron Capell of Hadham. 1701.

Bibliographies: *STC* 205.

Copies: *BMC* and *NUC* (14 copies). *STC* (10+ copies).

543. The American Family Receipt Book.

THE | AMERICAN | FAMILY RECEIPT BOOK: | CONSISTING OF | SEVERAL THOUSAND | MOST VALUABLE | RECEIPTS, EXPERIMENTS, | &c. &c. | COLLECTED FROM | VARIOUS PARTS OF EUROPE, AMERICA, | AND | OTHER PORTIONS OF THE GLOBE. | LONDON: | RE-PRINTED FROM THE AMERICAN EDITION. | [short rule] | 1854.

Second edition, London, 1854. Originally published, London, 1850. This edition in the publisher's series "The Cottage Library." There was an American work with this title published in 1847 and reprinted several times through 1851 but it contains "nearly 500" recipes and is only 100 pages. The American edition from which this London edition claims to have been reprinted is unidentified.

125 x 77 mm. [A]⁸ B-2E⁸; 224 leaves, pp. [i-iii] iv [5] 6-447 [448]. Publisher's cloth.

Illustrations: Engraved frontispiece of a sick man and his nurse.

Bibliographies: This edition unrecorded in the bibliographies consulted. Axford, p. 10 and Bitting, p. 515, record the 1850 edition.

Copies: No other copy of this edition located. Of the 1850 edition only the Bitting copy in the Library of Congress is recorded.

544. Apicius.

[in red] APICII COELII | DE | [in red] OPSONIIS | ET | [in red] CONDIMENTIS, | Sive | [in red] Arte Coquinaria, | LIBRI DECEM. | [rule] | Cum Annotationibus [in red] MARTINI LISTER, | è Medicis domesticis serenissimae Ma- | jestatis Reginae

Annae. | ET | Notis selectioribus, variisque lectionibus integris, | [in red]
HUMELBERGII, CASPARI BARTHII, | & [in red] VARIORUM. | [rule] | [in red]
LONDINI: | Typis *Gulielmi Bowyer*. MDCCV.

First edition edited by Martin Lister, London, 1705.

8vo. A-P^8 Q-T^4; 136 leaves, pp. [2] i-xiv, 1-231 [232] [*24*]. Last leaf blank.

Bibliographies: Bitting, p. 13; Maclean, p. 4; Oxford, p. 49; Schraemli (1) 24; Simon
BG 125; Vicaire 32; Wheaton and Kelly 182.

Copies: *BMC*, *BNC*, and *NUC* (5 copies). Maclean locates three copies in Britain and
three in North America.

545. Appert, Nicolas, 1750-1841.

THE ART | OF | PRESERVING | ALL KINDS OF | *Animal and Vegetable*
Substances | FOR | SEVERAL YEARS. | [short fancy rule] | A WORK PUBLISHED
BY ORDER OF THE | *FRENCH MINISTER OF THE INTERIOR*, | On the Report of
the Board of Arts and Manufactures, | BY | M. APPERT. | [short fancy rule] |
TRANSLATED FROM THE FRENCH. | [short fancy rule] | LONDON: | PRINTED
FOR BLACK, PARRY, AND KINGSBURY, | BOOKSELLERS TO THE HON.
EAST-INDIA COM- | PANY, LEADENHALL STREET. | [short rule] | 1811.

First edition in English, London, 1811. Originally published in French, Paris, 1810
(item 34).

188 x 111 mm. A-H^{12}; 96 leaves, pp. [i-v] vi-xx [xxi-xxiv] [1] 2-164 [*4*].

Illustration: Engraved folding plate illustrating instruments for corking bottles.

Bibliographies: Axford, p. 20; Bitting, p. 14; Craig 5; Oxford, p. 141; Simon BG
135; Wheaton and Kelly 195.

Copies: *BMC* and *NUC* (11 copies).

546. Arbuthnot, John, 1667-1735.

AN | ESSAY | CONCERNING THE | NATURE | OF | *ALIMENTS*, | And the
CHOICE of THEM, | According to the different Constitutions of | HUMAN BODIES,
| In which the different Effects, Advantages, and | Disadvantages of Animal and

Vegetable | Diet, are explain'd. | [rule] | The SECOND EDITION. | To which are added, | PRACTICAL RULES of DIET | In the various Constitutions and Diseases of | HUMAN BODIES. | [rule] | By *JOHN ARBUTHNOT*, M. D. | Fellow of the *College of Physicians*, and of the | *Royal Society*. | [two rules] | *LONDON:* | Printed for J. TONSON in the *Strand*. | [short rule] | M DCC XXXII.

Second edition, London, 1732. Originally published, London, 1731.

8vo. A^8 a^4 B-Q^8 *R^4 R^8 (-R8) S-Ee^8; 231 leaves, pp. [*24*] 1-239 [*240*] [*8*] [*243*] 244-430 [*2*].

Bibliographies: Maclean, p. 5; Wheaton and Kelly 204.

Copies: *BNC* and *NUC* (8 copies). Maclean locates copies in the British Museum (though this edition is not recorded in *BMC*) and the Wellcome Library and, in the United States, at Harvard, the Library of Congress and Yale.

547. Arcana Fairfaxiana.

[in red] A [in black] rcana [in red] F [in black] airfaxiana | [in red] M [in black] anuscripta. | A manuscript volume of Apothecaries' Lore and | Housewifery nearly three centuries old, | used, and partly written by the | Fairfax Family. | [short rule] | Reproduced in fac=simile of the handwritings. | [in red: short rule] | An Introduction by | [in red] G [in black] eorge [in red] W [in black] eddell. | [in red: short rule] | Newcastle=on=Tyne: | Mawson, Swan, & Morgan. | [short rule] | mdcccxc.

First edition, Newcastle upon Tyne, 1890.

226 x 168mm. [1-7]^4 χ1 [8-33]^4; pp. [i-ix] x-xlviii [xlix-l] 1-206 [2]. Last leaf blank. Publisher's calf, stamped in gold.

Bibliographies: Bitting, p. 516; Driver 24.1; Schraemli (1) 500; Wheaton and Kelly 205.

Copies: *BMC* and *NUC* (8 copies).

548. Armstrong, John.

THE | YOUNG WOMAN'S GUIDE | TO | *Virtue, Economy, and Happiness;* | Being an improved and pleasant Directory | FOR | CULTIVATING THE HEART AND UNDERSTANDING; | WITH | *A COMPLETE AND ELEGANT SYSTEM OF* | DOMESTIC COOKERY, | Formed upon Principles of Economy; | ALSO, | [in two columns: column one] The Art of Carving and Decorating a | Table, explained by Engravings. | Confectionary in all its Branches. | Proper Directions for Marketting, and | Bills of Fare for every Day in the | Year. | [two rules] | [column two] Best Method of Brewing for large or | small Families. | Making and managing British Wines. | Valuable Medical Directions. | A great Variety of useful Family Re- | ceipts. [end columns] | TO WHICH ARE ADDED, | *Instructions to Female Servants in every Situation;* | APPROVED RULES FOR NURSING AND EDUCATING CHILDREN, | AND FOR | PROMOTING MATRIMONIAL HAPPINESS: | ILLUSTRATED | *By interesting Tales and Memoirs of celebrated Females;* | The whole combining all that is essential to the Attainment of | EVERY | DOMESTIC, ELEGANT, | AND | *INTELLECTUAL ACCOMPLISHMENT.* | [short rule] | *BY MR JOHN ARMSTRONG,* | And Assistants of unquestionable Experience in Medicine, Cookery, Brewing, and | all the Branches of Domestic Economy | [short rule] | FIFTH EDITION. | *Embellished and illustrated with twelve appropriate Engravings.* | [short fancy rule] | *Newcastle upon Tyne:* | PRINTED BY MACKENZIE AND DENT, ST. NICHOLAS' | CHURCH-YARD.

Fifth edition, Newcastle upon Tyne, ca. 1820.

206 x 125 mm. [A]^4 B^2 a-b^4 C-4Q^4 4R^2; 348 leaves, pp. [i-v] vi-xii, ^{2}[i] ii-xii [13] 14-684.

Bibliographies: This edition unrecorded in the bibliographies consulted. Attar, 4.1, 4.2, and 4.3, records an undated and unnumbered edition as well as the sixth and eighth editions from *BMC*.

Copies: No other copy of this edition located. A copy of the fourth edition, in the private collection of John C. Craig, is dated 1817 on the last page. *BMC* lists a sixth edition [1825?] and an eighth edition, 1828.

549. The Art and Mystery of Curing.

THE ART AND MYSTERY | OF | CURING, PRESERVING, AND POTTING | ALL KINDS OF | MEATS, GAME, AND FISH; | ALSO | THE ART OF | PICKLING AND THE PRESERVATION | OF | FRUITS AND VEGETABLES. |

ADAPTED AS WELL FOR THE WHOLESALE DEALER AS ALL
HOUSEKEEPERS. | | [short rule] | BY A WHOLESALE CURER OF
COMESTIBLES. | [short rule] | LONDON: | CHAPMAN AND HALL, 193,
PICCADILLY. | 1864.

First edition, London, 1864.

190 x 120 mm. A^4 b^2 B-M^8 N-O^2; 98 leaves, pp. [i-iii] iv-xii [1] 2-184. Publisher's
green cloth, stamped in gold.

The preface of this work is signed "J.R., Junior." *BMC* lists it under R., J., Junior and
the *NUC* under title with a cross reference under James Robinson, practical curer,
supposed author.

Bibliographies: Axford, p. 16; Bitting, p. 517.

Copies: *BMC* and *NUC* (Library of Congress only).

Atkyns, Arabella. See *The Family Magazine*.

550. Athenaeus.

THE | DEIPNOSOPHISTS | OR | BANQUET OF THE LEARNED | OF |
ATHENAEUS. | LITERALLY TRANSLATED | BY C. D. YONGE, B. A. | WITH
AN APPENDIX OF POETICAL FRAGMENTS, | RENDERED INTO ENGLISH
VERSE BY VARIOUS AUTHORS, | AND A GENERAL INDEX. | IN THREE
VOLUMES. | VOL. I. [VOL. II.] [VOL. III.] | LONDON: | HENRY G. BOHN,
YORK STREET, COVENT GARDEN. | MDCCCLIV.

First edition, London, 1854, of this translation into English, published in Bohn's
Classical Library, volumes 13-15.

176 x 108 mm. 3 vols. Vol. I. $[A]^4$ (-A1) B-EE^8; 219 leaves, pp. [i-iii] iv-vi [1]
2-432. Vol. II. π^2 FF-$3F^8$; 194 leaves, pp. [4] 433-815 [816]. Vol. III. $\pi1$ 3G-$4K^8$
$4L^2$; 219 leaves, pp. [2] [817] 818-1252.

Bibliographies: Bitting, p. 18; Simon BG 147; Wheaton and Kelly 297.

Copies: *BMC* and *NUC* (42 copies).

551. Austen, Ralph, d. 1676.

Observations upon some part of | Sr FRANCIS BACON'S | NATVRALL HISTORY |
as it concernes, | Fruit-trees, Fruits, and Flowers: | *especially the* | Fifth, Sixth, and
Seaventh CENTURIES, | Improving the Experiments mentioned, | to the best
Advantage. | [rule] | By RA*:* AUSTEN Practiser in the Art of Planting. | [rule] | Gen:
2. 8. | *And the Lord God planted a Garden Eastward in* Eden, *and there* | *he put the
man whom he had formed.* | *And out of the ground made the Lord God to grow every
tree that* | *is pleasant to the sight, and good for foode.* | Gen: I. 29. | *And God said:
behold I have given you every hearb bearing seede,* | *which is upon the face of all the
Earth: and every Tree, in which is the* | *fruit of a tree bearing seede, to you it shall be
for meate.* | [rule] | OXFORD, | Printed by *Hen: Hall*, for *Thomas Robinson*. 1658.

First edition, Oxford, 1658.

4to. A-G⁴; 28 leaves, pp. [*8*] 1-46 [*2*].

Bibliographies: Fussell (1) p. 49; Henrey I, p. 229; Wing A4234.

Copies: *BMC* (4 copies), *BNC* and *NUC* (10 copies). Wing (10 copies).

552. Austen, Ralph, d. 1676.

A Treatise of | FRUIT-TREES, | Shewing | The manner of *Grafting, Planting,
Pruning,* | and *Ordering* of them in all respects, according to | new and easy Rules of
Experience. | With Divers *Divine*, and *Humane Arguments*, of the | *Dignity* of
Fruit-trees, and *Art* of *Planting.* | Discovering some *Errors* in the *Theory*, and |
Practise of this *Art* to be avoyded. | With the *Alimentall*, and *Physicall* use of *Fruits.* |
Also concerning planting *Fruit-trees* in the *Fields*, and *Hedges,* | without hindrance of
any present profits. | Of *Cider*, and *Perry*; Liquors found by Experience, most |
conducing to HEALTH, and LONG-LIFE. | Of *VINEYARDS* in *ENGLAND.* | *Herein
likewise is laid downe some Encouragements, and directions for* | planting of WOOD;
for Building, Fuell, and other uses. | *By all which the value of Lands may be much
improved in a short time, with small cost, and little* | labour; *to the great advantage of
the Owners, and of the* COMMON-WEALTH. | To which may be annexed the second
part, viz. | *The spirituall use of an Orchard, or Garden: in divers* Similitudes *between*
Naturall | *and* Spirituall Fruit-trees, *according to* Scripture, *and* Experience. | [rule] |
The second Edition; with the addition of many new | Experiments, and Observations. |
[rule] | Deu.20.19. *Thou shalt not destroy the Trees being Trees for meat, for the tree
of the field is mans life.* | Ezek.24.27. *The tree of the field shall yeild her fruit.* | Amos

4.4. *They shall plant Gardens, and eate the fruits of them.* | *OXFORD*. | Printed by HENRY HALL Printer to the UNIVERSITY, | for THOMAS ROBINSON. M.DC.LVII.

Title-page of second part:

The Spirituall use of an | Orchard, or Garden of | FRUIT-TREES. | Set forth in divers *Similitudes* betweene | *Naturall* and *Spirituall* fruit-trees, in their | Natures, and ordering, according to | Scripture and Experience. | [rule] | The second Impression; with the Addition of many *Similitudes*. | By *RA: AUSTEN*, Author of the first part. | [rule] | Hos:12.10. *I have used* Similitudes *by the Ministrie of the Prophets.* | Jer:17.8. *He shall be as a Tree planted by the waters, and that spread-* | *eth out her Roots by the River, and shall not see when heat cometh, but* | *her leafe shall be greene, and shall not be carefull in the year of drought,* | *neither shall cease from yeilding fruit.* | Rom:11.23. *And they also, if they abide not still in unbeleife, shall be* | *grafted in, for God is able to graft them in againe.* | Joh:15.1,2. *I am the true Vine, and my Father is the husbandman.* | *Every branch that beareth fruit he purgeth it, that it may bring forth* | *more fruit.* Cant.2.3. *Like the Apple-tree among the Trees of the forrest, so is my* | *beloved among the sonnes. I sate downe under his shadow with great* | *delight, and his fruit was sweet to my tast.* | *OXFORD*, | Printed by HEN: HALL, Printer to the UNIVERSITY, | for THO: ROBINSON. M.DC.LVII.

Second edition, Oxford, 1657. Originally published Oxford, 1653. While Wing records the two parts separately, the title-page of *A Treatise of Fruit Trees* mentions *The Spiritual Use of an Orchard, or Garden of Fruit Trees* as part of the whole work and, therefore, the first part must have contained the second when published. It is possible the second part also was offered separately.

4to. a-c⁴ A-R⁴ S², ²†–††⁴ †††² A-Cc⁴; 196 leaves, pp. [*24*] 1-140, ²[*20*] 1-208.

Illustration: Engraved general title-page with an illustration of a formal garden.

Bibliographies: Fussell (1) pp. 48-49; Henrey I, p. 229; Wing A4239 and A4236.

Copies: *A Treastise*, BMC (3 copies), *BNC* and *NUC* (12 copies), Wing (11 copies); *The Spiritual Use*, BMC (2 copies), *BNC* and *NUC* (5 copies recorded separately), Wing (8 copies).

553. B., M.

THE | [in red] LADIES CABINET | *ENLARGED* and | *OPENED:* | *Containing* |
Many Rare [in red] Secrets [in black] and Rich [in red] Orna- | [in red] ments, [in
black] of several kindes, and | different uses. | Comprized | *Under three general*
Heads. | *Viz.* | of { [in red] 1. Preserving, Conserving, Candying, &c | [in red] 2.
Physick and Chirurgery. | [in red] 3. Cookery and Houswifery. | *Whereunto is added,*
| Sundry [in red] Experiments [in black] and choice Ex- | tractions of [in red] Waters,
Oyls, [in black] &c. | Collected and practised; | *By* | the late Right Honorable and |
Learned Chymist, | [in red] The Lord RUTHUEN. | [rule] | [in red] *The second Edit.*
with Additions; | AND | A particular Table to each Part. | [rule] | *LONDON,* Printed
by T.M. for [in red] *G. Bedell,* | and [in red] *T. Collins* [in black] at the [in red]
middle Temple- | [in red] Gate, [in black] Fleet-street. 1655.

Third edition, styled "second edition" on the title-page, London, 1655. Originally
published under the title *The Ladies' Cabinet Opened*, London, 1639, and greatly
enlarged for the London, 1654, and later editions.

12mo. A^4 B-L^{12} M^6 N^8; 138 leaves, pp. [8] 1-252 [*16*].

The preface is signed M.B. Wing and *BMC* enter this work under these initials and
NUC enters it under title. There is a cross reference in *BMC* from Thomas, baron
Ruthven to B., M.

Bibliographies: Oxford, p. 21; Pennell, p. 136; Wing B136.

Copies: *NUC* (4 copies). Wing (Bodleian Library and Folger Library).

554. Badham, Charles David.

PROSE HALIEUTICS | OR | ANCIENT AND MODERN | FISH TATTLE. | BY
THE | REV. C. DAVID BADHAM, M.D., | FELLOW OF THE ROYAL COLLEGE
OF PHYSICIANS, CURATE OF EAST BERGHOLT, | AUTHOR OF `INSECT
LIFE,' `THE ESCULENT FUNGUSES OF ENGLAND,' ETC. | [device] |
LONDON: | JOHN W. PARKER AND SON, WEST STRAND. | MDCCCLIV.

First edition, London, 1854.

200 x 124 mm. [A]^6 B-2A^{12}; 282 leaves, pp. [i-vii] viii-xii [1] 2-552. Publisher's
green cloth stamped in gold.

Bibliographies: Simon BG 160; Wheaton and Kelly 366.

Copies: *BMC* and *NUC* (10 copies).

555. Bailey, Nathan, d. 1742.

Dictionarium Domesticum, | Being a NEW and COMPLEAT | Houshold Dictionary. | For the Use both of | CITY and COUNTRY. | SHEWING, | I. The whole Arts of BREWING, BAKING, COOKERY, | and PICKLING. Also CONFECTIONARY in its | several Branches. | II. The Management of the KITCHIN, PANTRY, LAR- | DER, DAIRY, OLITORY, and POULTRY. With | the proper Seasons for Flesh, Fowl and Fish. | III. The HERDSMAN: Giving an Account of the Diseases of | Cattle, Poultry, &c. And the most approved Remedies | for their Cure. | IV. The *English* VINEYARD; being the best Method of | making *English* Wines and of Distilling most Kinds | of Simple and Compound Cordial Waters. | V. The APIARY: Or, The Manner of Breeding, Hiving | and managing of BEES. | VI. The *Family* PHYSICIAN and HERBALIST. Containing | the choicest Collection of Receipts for most Distempers, | incident to Human Bodies, hitherto made Publick; with | the Qualities and Uses of Physical Herbs and Plants of | *English* Growth. | [rule] | By *N. BAILEY*, | Author of the Universal Etymological *English* Dictionary. | [two rules] | *LONDON:* | Printed for C. HITCH at the *Red-Lion*, and C. DAVIS, both in *Pater-* | *Noster-Row*; and S. AUSTEN at the *Angel* and *Bible*, in St. *Paul's* | *Church-Yard*. | [short rule] | M,DCC,XXXVI.

First edition, London, 1736.

8vo. π^2 A-Pp^8; 306 leaves, unpaginated.

Illustration: Engraved frontispiece showing domestic scenes.

Bibliographies: Axford, p. 114; Bitting, p. 24; Maclean, p. 7; Noling, p. 47; Oxford, p. 69; Simon BG 161; Wheaton and Kelly 376.

Copies: *BMC* and *NUC* (6 copies). Maclean locates three additional copies in Britain and records three of the six *NUC* copies.

556. Barry, Sir Edward, 1696-1776.

OBSERVATIONS | HISTORICAL, CRITICAL, and MEDICAL, | ON THE | WINES OF THE ANCIENTS. | AND THE | ANALOGY between them and MODERN WINES. | WITH | General OBSERVATIONS on the PRINCIPLES and

QUALITIES | of WATER, and in particular on those of BATH. | Indagatio ipsa rerum tum maximarum tum etiam occultissimarum habet oblectationem. Si | vero aliquid occurret quod verisimile videatur, humanissima completur animus vo- | luptate. CIC. in Lucullo. | By Sir EDWARD BARRY, BART. | Fellow of the ROYAL COLLEGE of PHYSICIANS, and of the ROYAL SOCIETY. | [vignette signed *Isaac Taylor sculp.*] | LONDON, | Printed for T. CADELL, in the STRAND. 1775.

First edition, London, 1775.

4to. π^2 a^4 B-Ppp^4 χ^2; 248 leaves, pp, [i-iii] iv-xii, 1-479 [480] [*4*]. Last two leaves contain a list of new books sold by John Donaldson.

Illustrations: Engraved frontispiece and an engraved vignette on the title-page. The binder's instructions on page 480 call for a plate between pp. 160-161 not present in this copy.

Bibliographies: Gabler, p. 22; Maclean, p. 8; Noling, p. 53; Simon BG 168; Vicaire 66.

Copies: *BMC* (3 copies). *BNC* and *NUC* (14 copies). Maclean adds Brotherton Library, National Library of Scotland, and University of British Columbia.

556a. Bartlett, John Sherren, 1790-1863.

MAIZE, | OR | INDIANA CORN. | [short rule] | ITS ADVANTAGES AS A CHEAP AND NUTRITIOUS | ARTICLE OF FOOD. | With Directions for its Use. | [short fancy rule] | BY JOHN S. BARTLETT, M.D., | EDITOR OF THE "NEW YORK ALBION." | LONDON: | WILEY & PUTNAM, 6, WATERLOO PLACE. | [short rule] | MDCCCXLVI.

First British edition, London, 1846. Originally published as portion of the author's "A Letter to the Right Honourable Baron Ashburton...on the importance of the corn and flour trade with England...and the advantages of introducing maize into Great Britain," New York, 1842, and separately New York, 1845.

169 x 105 mm. B^{12}; 12 leaves, pp. [1-5] 6-24.

Bibliographies: Sabin 3755.

Copies: *NUC* (Library of Congress only).

557. Battam, Anne.

THE | LADY's Assistant | IN THE | Oeconomy of the Table: | A Collection of scarce and valuable | RECEIPTS, | Taken from the *Manuscripts* of divers PERSONS | *of the most refin'd Taste and greatest Judgment* | in the ARTS *of* COOKERY, PRESERVING, &c. | To which is added, | The AUTHOR'S own Method of PICKLING, | together with Directions for making several Sorts | of WINES, MEAD, SHERBET, PUNCH, &c. after | the most approved Manner. Also Directions for | MARKETING, Instructions for CARVING, BILLS | of FARE for every Month in the Year, &c. | Concluding with many excellent PRESCRIPTIONS, of | singular Efficacy in most DISTEMPERS incident | to the HUMAN BODY. | ORIGINALLY PUBLISHED, | *By the late Mrs.* ANNE BATTAM. | THE SECOND EDITION, | *With near* One Hundred and Fifty *additional* RECEIPTS, | *from several LADIES, never before published.* | *LONDON:* | for R. and J. DODSLEY, in *Pall-mall.* 1759. | [PRICE BOUND THREE SHILLINGS.]

Second edition, London, 1759. Originally published under the title *A Collection of Scarce and Valuable Receipts . . .*, London, 1750.

12mo. A⁶ B-N¹² O⁶; 156 leaves, pp. [*12*] 1-300.

Bibliographies: Maclean, p. 9; Oxford, p. 80, in a note; Simon BG 176.

Copies: *NUC* (Kansas State University and Vassar College). Maclean records these and adds the Brotherton Library copy.

558. Bautte, A.

MODERN | FRENCH AND ENGLISH | COOKERY | FOR | 𝔓𝔯𝔦𝔟𝔞𝔱𝔢 𝔉𝔞𝔪𝔦𝔩𝔦𝔢𝔰, 𝔥𝔬𝔱𝔢𝔩𝔰, 𝔯𝔢𝔰𝔱𝔞𝔲𝔯𝔞𝔫𝔱𝔰, 𝔞𝔫𝔡 𝔠𝔩𝔲𝔟𝔰, | CONTAINING OVER 3500 RECIPES. | BY | A. BAUTTE, | CHEF, HANS CRESCENT HOTEL, LONDON; | *Late Chef to H.I.H. The Archduchesse Stephanie;* | *The Austro-Hungarian Embassy, London; The Russian Embassy, Copenhagen;* | *The Khedivial Club, Cairo,* | &c. | LONDON: | MALCOMSON & CO., LIMITED, 74, GREAT QUEEN STREET, W.C. | 1901.

First edition, London, 1901.

245 x 160 mm. [A]⁸ B-QQ⁸ RR⁶; 318 leaves, pp. [i-iii] iv-xvi [1] 2-619 [620]. Publisher's wine coloured cloth over bevelled boards, stamped in gold.

Illustrations: Halftone photograph of the author as frontispiece and twenty-one lithographed plates showing utensils and prepared dishes.

Bibliographies: Driver 49.1; Wheaton and Kelly 452.

Copies: *BMC*; Wheaton and Kelly (Radcliffe only).

559. Beauvilliers, Antoine, 1754-1817.

THE | ART | OF | FRENCH COOKERY. | BY | A. B. BEAUVILLIERS, | RESTAURATEUR, PARIS. | [short rule] | *LONDON:* | PRINTED FOR | LONGMAN, HURST, REES, ORME, BROWN, AND GREEN, | PATERNOSTER-ROW. | 1824.

First edition in English, London, 1824. Originally published in French, Paris, 1814 (item 66).

174 x 100 mm. A^6 a^2 B-Q^{12} R^{10}; 198 leaves, pp. [i-iii] iv-xv [xvi] [1] 2-380. Publisher's boards with printed paper label on spine.

Bibliographies: Axford, p. 19; Bitting, p. 31; Oxford, p. 155; Schraemli (1) 47; Wheaton and Kelly 474.

Copies: *BMC* and *NUC* (Boston Public Library and Library of Congress).

560. Beauvilliers, Antoine, 1754-1817.

THE | ART | OF | FRENCH COOKERY. | BY | A. B. BEAUVILLIERS, | RESTAURATEUR, PARIS. | [short rule] | *THIRD EDITION.* | [short rule] | LONDON: | PRINTED FOR | LONGMAN, REES, ORME, BROWN, AND | GREEN, | PATERNOSTER-ROW. | 1827.

Third edition in English, London, 1827. Originally published in French, Paris, 1814 (item 66) and in English, London, 1824 (item 559). Note: While this is described on the title-page as the third edition, neither any bibliographical record nor any copy of a second edition has been found.

164 x 100 mm. A^6 a^2 B-R^{12}; 200 leaves, pp. [i-iii] iv-xv [xvi] [1] 2-380 [4]. Last two leaves blank.

Bibliographies: Oxford, p. 155, in a note; Simon BG 185; Wheaton and Kelly 476.

Copies: *BMC*. Wheaton and Kelly (American Antiquarian Society).

560a.   Beeton, Isabella Mary, 1836-1865.

THE BOOK │ OF │ HOUSEHOLD MANAGEMENT; │ Comprising Information for the │ [in three columns: column one] MISTRESS, │ HOUSEKEEPER, │ COOK, │ KITCHEN-MAID, │ BUTLER, │ FOOTMAN, │ [vertical rule] │ [column two] COACHMAN, │ VALET, │ UPPER AND UNDER │ HOUSE-MAIDS, │ LADY'S-MAID, │ MAID-OF-ALL-WORK, │ [vertical rule] │ [column three] LAUNDRY-MAID, │ NURSE AND NURSE- │ MAID, │ MONTHLY, WET, AND │ SICK NURSES, │ ETC. ETC. [end columns] │ ALSO, SANITARY, MEDICAL, & LEGAL MEMORANDA; │ WITH A HISTORY OF THE ORIGIN, PROPERTIES, AND USES OF ALL THINGS │ CONNECTED WITH HOME LIFE AND COMFORT. │ BY MRS. ISABELLA BEETON. │ Nothing lovelier can be found │ In Woman, than to study household good. – MILTON. │ LONDON: │ S. O. BEETON, 248, STRAND, W.C. │ 1861.

First edition, London, November 1859-October 1861. Issued in 24 monthly parts. The publisher's address on the front wrapper of Parts I-VIII is 18 Bouverie Street E.C., the printer is Cox and Wyman; the first line of the errata correctly refers to p. 57, not p. 657. Because of the growth in popularity of this work, the earlier issues had to be reprinted; the reprints of Parts I-VIII carry the publisher's later address, 248, Strand, W.C.

190 x 120 mm. Part I, B-D^8; 24 leaves, pp. [1] 2-48. Part II, E-G^8; 24 leaves, pp. 49-96. Part III, H-K^8; 24 leaves, pp. 97-144. Part IV, L-N^8; 24 leaves, pp. 145-192. Part V, O-Q^8; 24 leaves, pp. 193-240. Part VI, R-T^8; 24 leaves, pp. 241-288. Part VII, U-Y^8; 24 leaves, pp. 289-336. Part VIII, Z-2B^8; 24 leaves, pp. 337-384. Part IX, 2C-2E^8; 24 leaves, pp. 385-432. Part X, 2F-2H^8; 24 leaves, pp. 433-480. Part XI, 2I-2L^8; 24 leaves, pp. 481-528. Part XII, 2M-2O^8; 24 leaves, pp. 529-576. Part XIII, 2P-2R^8; 24 leaves, pp. 577-624. Part XIV, 2S-2U^8; 24 leaves, pp. 625-672. Part XV, 2X-2Z^8; 24 leaves, pp. 673-720. Part XVI, 3A-3C^8; 24 leaves, pp. 721-768. Part XVII, 3D-3F^8; 24 leaves, pp. 769-816. Part XVIII, 3G-3I^8; 24 leaves, pp. 817-864. Part XIX, 3K-3M^8; 24 leaves, pp. 865-912. Part XX, 3N-3P^8; 24 leaves, pp. 913-960. Part XXI, 3Q-3S^8; 24 leaves, pp. [961] 962-1008. Part XXII, 3T-3X^8; 24 leaves, p. 1009-1056. Part XXIII, 3Y-4A^8; 24 leaves, pp. 1057-1104. Part XXIV, 4B^8 b-c^8; 24 leaves, pp. 1105-1108, [i-iii] iv-viii, 1109-1112, ix-xxxix [x1].

Parts I and II in beige paper wrappers printed in black; Parts III-XXIV in terra cotta paper wrappers printed in black. All parts have a wood engraved title on the outer front wrapper and advertisements on the inner front and inner and outer back wrappers. There are also the following inserted ads: Part I, one leaf beforethe back wrapper; Part II, two leaves of yellow paper before the back wrapper; Part V, one leaf before back wrapper; Part XIV, small leaf of terra cotta paper before back wrapper; Part XVII, small leaf inside front wrapper; Part XIX, two leaves inside front wrapper; Part XXI, small leaf of stiff gray paper inside front wrapper; Part XXIII, two leaves inside front wrapper; part XXIV, small leaf of terra cotta paper inside front wrapper. The wrappers for Parts XI-XV, and XVII are numbered by hand; the others have printed Parts numbers.

Illustrations: Chromolithographed frontispiece and title-page in Part I and 12 chromolithographed plates showing prepared dishes in Parts II-XI, XIII, and XVI. Plates are from the first printing before the salmon colored background was added. Numerous wood engravings in the text.

Bibliographies: The parts issue is unrecorded in the bibliographies consulted.

Copies: *NUC* (Harvard's imperfect copy only).

561. Beeton, Isabella Mary, 1836-1865.

THE BOOK | OF | HOUSEHOLD MANAGEMENT; | 𝕮omprising 𝕴nformation for t𝔥e | [in three columns: column one] MISTRESS, | HOUSEKEEPER, | COOK, | KITCHEN-MAID, | BUTLER, | FOOTMAN, | [vertical rule] | [column two] COACHMAN, | VALET, | UPPER AND UNDER | HOUSE-MAIDS, | LADY'S-MAID, | MAID-OF-ALL-WORK, | [vertical rule] | [column three] LAUNDRY-MAID, | NURSE AND NURSE- | MAID, | MONTHLY, WET, AND | SICK NURSES, | ETC. ETC. [end columns] | ALSO, SANITARY, MEDICAL, & LEGAL MEMORANDA; | WITH A HISTORY OF THE ORIGIN, PROPERTIES, AND USES OF ALL THINGS | CONNECTED WITH HOME LIFE AND COMFORT. | BY MRS. ISABELLA BEETON. | Nothing lovelier can be found | In Woman, than to study household good. – MILTON. | LONDON: | S. O. BEETON, 248, STRAND, W.C. | 1861.

First edition in book form, London, 1861. First printing, with Cox and Wyman the printers and with the first line of the errata correctly referring to p. 57, not p. 657. This work originally was published in 24 monthly parts, 1859-1861.

175 x 110 mm. [a]⁴ b-c⁸ B-4A⁸ 4B⁴; 576 leaves, pp. [i-iii] iv-xxxix [xl] [1] 2-1112.

Illustrations: Chromolithographed frontispiece and title-page, 12 chromolithographed plates showing 48 prepared dishes; numerous wood engravings in the text. The plates are from the first printing, before the salmon colored background was added.

Bibliographies: Axford, p. 38; Bitting, p. 32; Craig 8; Simon BG 186.

Copies: *BMC* and *NUC* (4 copies).

562. Beeton, Isabella Mary, 1836-1865.

[within a single rule border] *THE "ALL ABOUT IT" BOOKS.* | [short fancy rule] | MRS. BEETON'S | DICTIONARY | OF | EVERY-DAY COOKERY. | [publisher's device] | LONDON: | S. O BEETON, 248, STRAND, W.C. | 1865.

First edition, London, 1865.

190 x 122 mm. π^2 1-23^8 24^4 (-24$_4$); 189 leaves, pp. [2] [vii] viii [1] 2-371 [372] [2].

Illustrations: Numerous wood engravings in the text.

Bibliographies: Unrecorded in the bibliographies consulted.

Copies: *BMC* and *NUC* (New York Public Library only).

563. Beeton, Isabella Mary, 1836-1865.

BEETON'S "ALL ABOUT IT " BOOKS. | [short rule] | ALL ABOUT COOKERY. | BY MRS. ISABELLA BEETON. | A Collection of Practical Recipes, | ARRANGED IN ALPHABETICAL ORDER. | NEW EDITION. | *ENLARGED, REVISED, AND THOROUGHLY* | *BROUGHT UP TO DATE.* | CONTAINING | MANY NEW RECIPES FOR EVERY BRANCH OF COOKERY. | NEW MENUS FOR ALL MEALS FOR ALL MONTHS IN THE YEAR. | VALUABLE COLOURED PLATES. | NEW FULL-PAGE AND OTHER ILLUSTRATIONS. | [short rule] | LONDON: | WARD, LOCK & CO., LIMITED, | WARWICK HOUSE, SALISBURY SQUARE, E.C., | NEW YORK AND MELBOURNE | 1903 | (*All Rights Reserved.*)

New edition, London, 1903. Originally published under the title *Mrs Beeton's Dictionary of Every-day Cookery*, London, 1865 (item 562).

199 x 130 mm. $\pi^4 \chi^2$ 1-29^8 30^4; 244 leaves, pp. [i-v] vi-viii [*4*] [1] 2-40 [2] 41-60 [2] 61-64 [2] 65-68 [2] 69-144 [2] 145-146 [2] 147-188 [2] [189] 190-200 [2] 201-252 [2] 253-320 [2] 321-326 [2] 327-332 [2] 333-396 [2] 397-424 [2] 425-444.

Illustrations: Chromolithographed frontispiece and three chromolithographed plates plus numerous wood engravings in the text, fourteen of them full page with versos blank as plates but on unnumbered text pages.

Bibliographies: This edition unrecorded in the bibliographies consulted.

Copies: No other copy of this edition located.

564. Bell, Joseph.

A | TREASTISE | ON | CONFECTIONARY, | *IN ALL ITS BRANCHES,* | WITH PRACTICAL NOTES, | *AND ILLUSTRATED WITH APPROPRIATE ENGRAVINGS.* | [short double rule] | IN FOUR PARTS. | [short double rule] | BY JOSEPH BELL, NEWCASTLE, | *Formerly Confectioner to their Royal Highnesses the Prince* | *of Wales and Duke of York.* | [short double rule] | WRITTEN FROM A KNOWLEDGE ACQUIRED BY A PRACTICE OF | THIRTY-FIVE YEARS AND UPWARDS. | [short double rule] | 𝔈𝔫𝔱𝔢𝔯𝔢𝔡 𝔞𝔱 𝔖𝔱𝔞𝔱𝔦𝔬𝔫𝔢𝔯'𝔰 ℌ𝔞𝔩𝔩. | [short fancy rule] | *NEWCASTLE:* | PRINTED FOR THE AUTHOR, BY G. ANGUS, IN THE SIDE. | [short rule] | 1817.

First edition, Newcastle upon Tyne, 1817.

225 x 144 mm. π^4 A-Ff^4 χ1; 121 leaves, pp. [i-iii] iv-viii [1] 2-223 [224-234].

Illustrations: Engraved frontispiece of a cake incorporating the lion, the unicorn, and the three plumes of the Prince of Wales, and four engraved plates, one folding and one printed in blue ink.

Bibliographies: Noling, p. 61; Simon BG 189.

Copies: *BMC*.

564a. Bennett, Arnold, 1867-1931.

Title at the head of text: N.K. 25. | [within a single rule frame] THOUGHTS ON NATIONAL KITCHENS. | By ARNOLD BENNETT. | [Reprinted form the *Daily News* by Kind permission of the | Editor and of the Author.]

First edition, London, 1918.

196 x 125 mm. π^2; 2 leaves unpaginated. At foot of last page: 2398. Wt. /850. 12 pfs. 10,000 (*4*). 5/18. S.O., F. Rd.

Bibliographies: Wheaton & Kelly 601.

Copies: *NUC* and Wheaton & Kelly (Harvard only).

565. Berchoux, Joseph de, 1762-1838.

GASTRONOMY, | OR | THE BON-VIVANT'S GUIDE. | *A POEM,* | IN FOUR CANTOS. | [short double rule] *FROM THE FRENCH OF J. BERCHOUX.* | [short double rule] | 𝔏𝔬𝔫𝔡𝔬𝔫: | PRINTED FOR J. BOOTH, DUKE STREET, PORTLAND PLACE, | BY T. HARPER, JUN. CRANE COURT, FLEET STREET. | [short rule] | 1810.

First edition in English, London, 1810, of Berchoux's "La Gastronomie, ou l'homme des champs à table" originally published in French, Paris, 1801.

270 x 210 mm. [A]^2 B-F^4 G^2; 24 leaves, pp. [*4*] [1] 2-42 [*2*]. Uncut in publisher's printed wrappers.

Bibliographies: Simon BG 197; Vicaire 85.

Copies: *BMC* and *NUC* (National Agricultural Library only).

566. Bishop, Frederick.

THE | ILLUSTRATED LONDON | COOKERY BOOK, | CONTAINING UPWARDS OF | FIFTEEN HUNDRED FIRST-RATE RECEIPTS | SELECTED WITH GREAT CARE, AND A PROPER ATTENTION TO ECONOMY; | AND EMBODYING ALL THE LATEST IMPROVEMENTS IN THE CULINARY ART: |

ACCOMPANIED BY IMPORTANT REMARKS AND COUNSEL ON THE | ARRANGMENT AND WELL-ORDERING OF THE KITCHEN, | COMBINED WITH | USEFUL HINTS ON DOMESTIC ECONOMY. | THE WHOLE BASED ON MANY YEARS' CONSTANT PRACTICE AND EXPERIENCE; | AND ADDRESSED TO | 𝔓𝔯𝔦𝔟𝔞𝔱𝔢 𝔣𝔞𝔪𝔦𝔩𝔦𝔢𝔰 𝔞𝔰 𝔴𝔢𝔩𝔩 𝔞𝔰 𝔱𝔥𝔢 𝔥𝔦𝔤𝔥𝔢𝔰𝔱 ℭ𝔦𝔯𝔠𝔩𝔢𝔰. | BY | FREDERICK BISHOP. | LATE CUISINIER TO ST. JAMES'S PALACE, EARL GREY, THE MARQUIS OF STAFFORD, | BARON ROTHSCHILD, EARL NORBURY, CAPTAIN DUNCOMBE, AND | MANY OF THE FIRST FAMILIES IN THE KINGDOM. | PROFUSELY ILLUSTRATED WITH ENGRAVINGS ON WOOD. | [short rule] | LONDON: 227, STRAND. | MDCCCLII.

First edition, London, 1852.

208 x 130 mm. a-b⁸ B-GG⁸; 248 leaves; pp. [i-iii] iv-xxi [xxxii] [1] 2-460 [461-464].

Illustrations: Wood engraved frontispiece and title-page, a folding wood engraving of "The Royal Kitchen, Windsor Castle," and numerous wood engravings in the text.

Bibliographies: Axford, p. 224; Bitting, p. 40; Craig 9.

Copies: *NUC* (Library of Congress, New York Public Library, and University of Massachusetts).

567. Bishop, Frederick.

THE | WIFE'S OWN BOOK | OF | COOKERY, | CONTAINING UPWARDS OF | FIFTEEN HUNDRED ORIGINAL RECEIPTS, | PREPARED WITH GREAT CARE, AND A PROPER ATTENTION TO ECONOMY, | AND EMBODYING ALL THE LATEST IMPROVEMENTS IN THE CULINARY ART; | ACCOMPANIED BY IMPORTANT REMARKS AND COUNSEL ON THE | ARRANGEMENT AND WELL-ORDERING OF THE KITCHEN, | COMBINED WITH | USEFUL HINTS ON DOMESTIC ECONOMY. | THE WHOLE BASED ON MANY YEARS' CONSTANT PRACTICE AND EXPERIENCE; | AND ADDRESSED TO | 𝔓𝔯𝔦𝔟𝔞𝔱𝔢 𝔉𝔞𝔪𝔦𝔩𝔦𝔢𝔰 𝔞𝔰 𝔴𝔢𝔩𝔩 𝔞𝔰 𝔱𝔥𝔢 𝔥𝔦𝔤𝔥𝔢𝔰𝔱 ℭ𝔦𝔯𝔠𝔩𝔢𝔰. | BY | FREDERICK BISHOP. | LATE CUISINIER TO ST. JAMES'S PALACE, EARL GREY, THE MARQUIS OF STAFFORD, | BARON ROTHSCHILD, EARL NORBURY, CAPTAIN DUNCOMBE, AND | MANY OF THE FIRST FAMILIES IN THE KINGDOM. | [short rule] | ILLUSTRATED WITH 250 DESCRIPTIVE ENGRAVINGS. | [short rule] | LONDON: | WARD AND LOCK, 158, FLEET STREET, | AND ALL BOOKSELLERS.

New edition, London, ca. 1856. The advertisements for new Ward and Lock books on leaf BB8 list *The Family Friend for 1855* and quote a review of that book in the *Edinburgh News* of January 26, 1856. In this copy, there is an ownership inscription on the front fly-leaf, "L. Belcher 1858." This edition, therefore, could not have been published before 1856 nor after 1858. Originally published under the title *The Illustrated London Cookery Book*, London, 1852 (item 566).

190 x 120 mm. π^8 A-BB^8; 208 leaves, pp. [i-iii] iv-xvi [1] 2-398 [2]. Publisher's rose cloth, stamped in gold.

Illustrations: Wood engraved frontispiece and title-page and 250 wood engravings in the text.

Bibliographies: Bitting, p. 40.

Copies: *BMC* and *NUC* (Library of Congress only).

568. Bonnefons, Nicolas de

The French | GARDINER: | INSTRUCTING | How to Cultivate all sorts of | FRUIT-TREES, | AND | HERBS for the GARDEN: | TOGETHER | With directions to *dry* and *conserve* them | in their *Natural*; | An accomplished Piece, | Written Originally in *French*, and now Trans- | planted into *English*, | [rule] | By *JOHN EVELYN* Esq; | Fellow of the Royal Society. | [rule] | Illustrated with Sculptures. | [rule] | Whereunto is annexed, The *English Vineyard* Vindicated | by *John Rose*, now Gardiner to his Majesty: with a | Tract of the making and ordering of Wines in *France*. | [rule] | *LONDON*, | Printed by *J. M.* for *John Crooke*, and are to be | sold at his Shop in *Duck-Lane,* 1669.

Second title-page:

THE *ENGLISH* | VINEYARD | VINDICATED | BY | *JOHN ROSE* | *Gard'ner* to His *MAJESTY*, | at His Royal *GARDEN* | in St. *James's*. | Formerly *Gard'ner* to her Grace | the *Dutchess* of *Somerset*. | *With an* Address, | *Where the best* Plants *are to be had at* | easie *Rates*. | [rule] | *LONDON,* | Printed by *J. M.* for *John Crook*, and are | to be sold at his Shop in *Duck-Lane*, 1669.

Second edition, London, 1669. Originally published in French under the title *Le Jardinier français*, Paris, 1651, and in English, London, 1658, of which edition Keynes records three issues.

8vo. A-T⁸, ²A-D⁸; 184 leaves, pp. [*10*] 1-294, ²[1-12] 13-48 [*16*]. A1 (blank) wanting in this copy.

Illustrations: Engraved frontispiece and four plates after those in the original French edition. The frontispiece and the first plate are signed A. Hertochs.

Bibliographies: Keynes 8; Wheaton and Kelly 735; Wing B3600.

Copies: *BMC* and *NUC* (5 copies). Wing (11 copies).

569.   Bonnefons, Nicolas de

THE FRENCH | GARDINER: | INSTRUCTING | How to Cultivate all sorts of | FRUIT-TREES, | AND | HERBS for the GARDEN. | TOGETHER | With Directions to Dry, and Conserve | them in their Natural. | An Accomplished Piece, | Written Originally in *French*, and now | Translanted into *English*. | By *JOHN EVELYN* Esquire, | Fellow of the Royal Society. | [rule] | *The third Edition illustrated with Sculptures.* | [rule] | Whereunto is annexed, The *English Vineyard* Vin- | dictated by *J. Rose*, now Gardiner to his Majesty: with | a Tract of the making and ordering of Wines in *France*. | [rule] | *London*, Printed by *T.R. & N.T.* for *B. Tooke*, and | are to be sold at the Ship in St. *Pauls* Church-yard. 1675.

Second title-page:

THE | English Vineyard | VINDICATED | By *JOHN ROSE*, | *Gardiner* to His | Majesty, | At His Royal | Garden in ST. JAMES'S. | Formerly *Gard'ner* to Her Grace | the Dutchess of *Somerset*. | With an Address, Where the best *Plants* | are to be had at easie *Rates*. | [rule] | *LONDON*, | Printed by *T.R. & N.T.* for *B. Tooke*, and are to | be sold at the Ship in St. *Pauls* Church-yard. 1675.

Fourth edition, styled third on the title-page, London, 1675. Originally published in French under the title *Le Jardinier français*, Paris, 1651, and in English, London, 1658.

8vo. A-T⁸, ²A-D⁸; 184 leaves, pp. [*10*] [*1*] 2-294, ²[1-13] 14-48 [*16*].

Illustrations: Engraved title-page on A1ʳ and three engraved plates in *The French Gardiner* and one engraved folding plate in *The English Vineyard Vindicated*.

Bibliographies: Henrey, p. 231; Keynes 10; Wheaton and Kelly 737; Wing B3602.

Copies: *BMC* and *NUC* (7 copies). Wing (10 copies).

570. A Book of Fruits and Flowers.

A | BOOK | OF | Fruits & Flovvers. | SHEWING | The Nature and Use of them, either | for Meat or Medicine. | AS ALSO: | To Preserve, Conserve, Candy, and in Wedges, | or Dry them. To make Powders, Civet bagges, | all sorts of Sugar-works, turn'd works in Sugar, | Hollow, or Frutages; and to Pickell them. | *And for Meat.* | To make Pyes, Biscat, Maid Dishes, Marchpanes, Leeches, | and Snow, Craknels, Caudels, Cakes, Broths, Fritter- | stuffe, Puddings, Tarts, Syrupes, and Sallets. | *For Medicines.* | To make all sorts of Poultisses, and Serecloaths for any member | swell'd or inflamed, Ointments, Waters for all Wounds, and Cancers, Salves | for Aches, to take the Ague out of any place Burning or Scalding; | For the stopping of suddain Bleeding, curing the Piles, | Ulcers, Ruptures, Coughs, Consumptions, and killing | of Warts, to dissolve the Stone, killing the | Ring-worme, Emroids, and Dropsie, | Paine in the Ears and Teeth, | Deafnesse. | [rule] | *Contra vim mortis, non est Medicamen in hortis.* | [rule] | *LONDON:* | Printed by *M. S.* for *Tho: Jenner* at the South entrance of the *Royall* | *Exchange*, London. 1653.

First edition, London, 1653.

4to. A-F⁴ G²; 26 leaves, pp. [2] 1-49 [50].

Illustrations: Eleven engraved illustrations of flowers and fruits in the text.

Bibliographies: Axford, p. 38; Bitting, p. 521; Oxford, p. 24; Wing B3708.

Copies: *BMC* and *NUC*. (Library Company of Philadelphia and New York Public Library). Wing (the same 3 copies).

571. Boorde, Andrew, 1490?-1549.

The Fyrst Boke of the | Introduction of Knowledge | made by | Andrew Borde | of Physycke Doctor. | [short fancy rule] | A Compendyous Regyment | or | A Dyetary of Helth | made in Mountpyllier, compyled by | Andrewe Boorde | of Physycke Doctour. | [short fancy rule] | Barnes | in the Defence of the Herde: | a Treatyse made, answerynge the Treatyse of | Doctor Borde upon Herdes. | [short fancy rule] | EDITED, WITH A LIFE OF ANDREW BOORDE,

AND LARGE EXTRACTS FROM HIS | *BREUYARY*, BY | F. J. FURNIVALL, M.A., TRIN. HALL, CAMB., | EDITOR OF *THE BABEES BOOK, &c.* | [short fancy rule] | LONDON: | PUBLISHED FOR THE EARLY ENGLISH TEXT SOCIETY, | BY N. TRÜBNER & CO., 60, PATERNOSTER ROW. | [short rule] | MDCCCLXX.

First edition thus, London, 1870. Early English Text Society, Extra Series, No. X. Originally published, London, 1548.

242 x 168 mm. [1]⁸ 2-24⁸; 192 leaves, pp. [1-8] 9-384.

Bibliographies: Bitting, p. 49; Wheaton and Kelly 765.

Copies: *BMC*, *BNC*, and *NUC* (28 copies).

572. Borella.

THE | COURT AND COUNTRY | CONFECTIONER: | OR, THE | HOUSE-KEEPER'S GUIDE; | To a more speedy, plain, and familiar method of understanding | the whole art of confectionary, pastry, distilling, and the | making of fine flavoured English wines from all kinds of | fruits, herbs, and flowers; comprehending near four hundred | and fifty easy and practical receipts, never before made known. | PARTICULARLY, | [in two columns: column one] PRESERVING. | CANDYING. | ICING | TRANSPARENT MARMALADE, | ORANGE, | PINE-APPLE, | PISTACHIO, and other Rich Creams. | CARAMEL. | PASTILS. | BOMBOONS. | [vertical rule] | [column two] PUFF, SPUN, and FRUIT-PASTES. | LIGHT-BISCUITS. | PUFFS. | RICH SEED-CAKES. | CUSTARDS. | SYLLABUBS. | FLUMMERIES. | TRIFLES. WHIPS. FRUITS, | and other JELLIES. | PICKLES, &c. &c. [end columns] | ALSO | New and easy directions for clarifying the different degrees of | sugar, together with several bills of fare of deserts for pri- | vate gentlemen's families. | To which is added, | A dissertation on the different species of fruits, and the art of | distilling simple waters, cordials, perfumed oils, and essences. | By an INGENIOUS FOREIGNER, now head confectioner | to the Spanish Ambassador in England. | LONDON. | Printed for G. RILEY, and A. COOKE, at their Circu- | lating Library, *Queen Street, Berkley Square*; J. BELL, | near *Exeter-Exchange*, in the *Strand*; J. WHEBLE, | at No. 20. *Pater-noster-row*; and C. ETHERING- | TON, at *York*. | M.DCC.LXX.

First edition, London, 1770.

8vo. [A]^4 a^8 b^4 B-X^8; 176 leaves, pp. [2] [i] ii [1] 2-3 [4], ^{2}[i] ii-xxiii [xxiv] [1] 2-271 [272], ^{3}[1] 2-46 [2].

Bibliographies: Axford, p. 103; Bitting, p. 49 and p. 538; Maclean, p. 10; Oxford, p. 102.

Copies: *NUC* (5 copies). Maclean adds the British Library and Brotherton Library.

573. Bradley, Edith.

[within green rule border] [in red] THE BOOK OF │ [in red] FRUIT BOTTLING │ [green rule] │ [in green] BY │ [in red] EDITH BRADLEY │ [in green] AND │ [in red] MAY CROOKE │ [green rule] │ [next nine lines in green] A PRACTICAL MANUAL ON THE PROCESS │ OF FRUIT BOTTLING. JAMS, JELLIES, AND │ MARMALADE MAKING: CHAPTERS ON FRUIT │ DRYING, HOME-MADE WINES AND CIDER │ MAKING, WITH PREFACE URGING UPON │ COUNTY COUNCILS THE IMPORTANCE OF │ FOSTERING THESE INDUSTRIES IN RURAL │ DISTRICTS. INTRODUCTION BY REV. W. │ WILKES, SECRETARY, ROYAL HORTICULTURAL SOCIETY │ [green rule] │ [in red] LONDON: JOHN LANE, THE BODLEY HEAD │ [in green] NEW YORK: JOHN LANE COMPANY. MCMVII

First edition, London, 1907.

190 x 127 mm. π^8 [A]^8 B-F^8 G^4; 60 leaves, pp. [i-vi] [vii-xvi] 1-99 [100] [*4*]. Publisher's light green cloth, stamped in dark green.

Illustrations: Halftone frontispiece and ten halftone plates plus ten wood engravings in the text.

Bibliographies: Bitting, p. 54, misdating the book 1906; Driver 115.1; Noling, p. 76. The Bitting copy, in the Library of Congress, is dated 1907.

Copies: *BMC* and *NUC* (7 copies).

574. Bradley, Martha.

THE │ BRITISH HOUSEWIFE: │ OR, THE │ COOK, HOUSEKEEPER's, │ AND │ GARDINER's COMPANION. │ CALCULATED FOR THE │ Service both of

LONDON and the COUNTRY; | And directing what is necessary to be done in the *Providing for, Con-* | *ducting*, and *Managing* a FAMILY throughout the Year. | CONTAINING | A general Account of fresh Provisions of all Kinds. Of the several *foreign* | *Articles* for the Table, pickled, or otherwise preserved; and the different Kinds of *Spices*, | *Salts, Sugars*, and other *Ingredients* used in *Pickling* and *Preserving* at Home: Shew- | ing *what* each is, *whence* it is brought, and what are its *Qualities* and *Uses*. | Together with the *Nature* of all Kinds of *Foods*, and the Method of *suiting* | *them to different* CONSTITUTIONS; | A BILL of FARE for each Month, the Art of *Marketing* and *chusing* fresh Provisions of all | Kinds; and the making as well as chusing of *Hams, Tongues*, and other *Store Dishes*. | Also DIRECTIONS for plain *Roasting* and *Boiling*; and for the Dressing of all Sorts of *Made* | *Dishes* in various Tastes; and the preparing the *Desert* in all its Articles. | Containing a greater Variety than was ever before publish'd, of the most | Elegant, yet least Expensive RECEIPTS in | [in four columns: column one] COOKERY, | PASTRY, | PUDDINGS, | PRESERVES, | PICKLES, | [column of seven type ornaments] | [column two] FRICASSEES, | RAGOUTS, | SOUPS, | SAUCES, | JELLIES, | [column of seven type ornaments] | [column three] TARTS, | CAKES, | CREAMS, | CUSTARDS, | CANDIES, | [column of seven type ornaments] | [column four] DRY'D FRUITS, | SWEETMEATS, | MADE WINES, | CORDIALS, And | DISTILLERY. [end columns] | *To which are annexed*, | The Art of CARVING; and the Terms used for cutting up various Things; | and the polite and easy Manner of *doing the Honours of the Table:* The whole Prac- | tice of *Pickling* and *Preserving:* And of preparing *made Wines, Beer*, and *Cyder*. | As also of *distilling* all the useful Kinds of *Cordial* and *Simple* Waters. | With the *Conduct of a Family* in Respect of *Health*; the *Disorders* to which they | are every *Month* liable, and the most approved *Remedies* for each. | And a Variety of other valuable Particulars, necessary to be known in *All Families*; and | nothing inserted but what has been *approved* by EXPERIENCE. | Also the Ordering of all Kinds of profitable *Beasts* and *Fowls*, with respect to their *Choice*, their | *Breeding* and *Feeding*; the *Diseases* to which they are severally liable each Month, and *Receipts* | for their *Cure*. Together with the Management of the *pleasant, profitable*, and *useful Garden*. | THE WHOLE | Embellished with a great Number of *curious* COPPER PLATES, shewing the | Manner of *Trussing* all Kinds of GAME, wild and tame FOWLS, *&c.* as also the Order of | setting out TABLES for *Dinners, Suppers*, and *Grand Entertainments*, in a Method never before | attempted; and by which even *those who cannot read* will be able to instruct themselves. | [rule] | *By Mrs.* MARTHA BRADLEY, *late of*, BATH: | Being the Result of upwards of *Thirty Years Experience*. | [rule] | [volume one only] The whole (which is deduc'd from Practice) compleating the careful Reader, | from the highest to the lowest Degree, in every Article of *Engish* Housewifery. | [volume two only] VOL. II. | [rule] [both volumes] | *LONDON:* | Printed for *S. Crowder* and *H. Woodgate*, at the *Golden Ball* in *Paternoster Row*.

First edition, London, 1756. Authorities have varied widely is assigning dates to this work: Kitchiner, 1755; Maclean, ca. 1760; Oxford, ca. 1770; Simon, ca. 1800.

Maclean located an advertisement in *Scots Magazine*, January, 1756, announcing "The British housewife, No. 1, To be continued weekly. 3d. Crowder." While no copy of the work has survived unbound in parts, the parts numbers I-XLI are designated in the signatures. If the weekly schedule was maintained, publication would have been completed late in 1756.

8vo. 2 vols. Vol. I. A-5B⁴; 376 leaves, pp. [1-2] 3-752. Vol. II. π1 A-Qqq⁴ Rrr⁴ (-Rrr4=π1); 252 leaves, pp. [2] 1-469 [470-502].

Illustrations: Vol. I. Engraved frontispiece of a kitchen. Vol. II. Seven engraved plates showing trussing and table settings.

Bibliographies: Axford, p. 45; Bitting, p. 54; Maclean, p. 11; Oxford, p. 104; Pennell, p. 167; Simon BG 236; Vicaire 111.

Copies: *BMC* and *NUC* (Harvard, Lehigh and Library of Congress). Maclean locates copies in the British Library, the Brotherton Library and the National Library of Scotland and, in the United States, at Colonial Williamsburg, the New York Public Library, and Radcliffe.

575. Bradshaw, Penelope.

THE | FAMILY JEWEL | AND | Compleat Housewife's Companion: | OR, THE | Whole ART of COOKERY made | Plain and Easy. | In a Method entirely new, and suited to every Capacity. | Calculated for the Preservation of Health, and upon the | Principles of Frugality, including Things useful, substantial, and | splendid. | Containing about Five Hundred RECEIPTS. | [in two columns: column one] In various Branches of Cookery, Pick- | ling, Preserving, Candying, &c. also, | in making Cakes, Jellies, Soops, Pastes. | Made Wines, &c. being the Result of | forty Years Experience, and an atten- | tive Observation upon all the Books | of Cookery yet published. | Various Ways of dressing *British* Pickled | Herrings; Directions for Marketting; | also, for brewing Beers and Ales; how | to manage a Beer Cellar, to keep Ale | very fine, to restore sour Beer to Per- | fection, and to preserve a Stock of | Yeast even in the scarcest Seasons. | [two vertical rules] | [column two] Mrs. *Stephens*'s Receipt for the Stone, | Dr. *Mead*'s, and others, for the Bite | of a mad Dog, Sir *Hans Sloane*'s for | sore Eyes, &c. curious Extracts from a | celebrated Treatise on the Teeth, their | Disorders and Cure. | Mons. *Milliens*'s Method of preserving | Metals, such as Guns, Grates, Candle- | sticks, &c. from Rust. Several excel- | lent Receipts for taking Ironmoulds, | Ink, &c. out of the finest Linen, to | clean Gold or Silver Lace. An effec- | tual Method for clearing a Room from | Bugs, and useful Directions for Ser- | vants to clean Plate, China, &c. [end columns] | With an INDEX directing to every RECEIPT. | By Mrs. PENELOPE BRADSHAW, Housekeeper | forty Years to a noble Family of great Taste, but | proper OEconomy. | The Whole Revised by a *London* Pastry-Cook of long | Practice, with Corrections; with the Addition of about Two Hun- | dred New RECEIPTS, and a BILL of FARE for every Month in | the Year, with the Manner of placing the Dishes. | LONDON: | printed for R. WHITWORTH, at the *Feathers*, in the | *Poultry*. M.DCC.LIV.

Revised and enlarged edition, London, 1754. Originally published under the title *Bradshaw's Valuable Family Jewel . . .*, London, 1748, a copy of which is in the private collection of John C. Craig. Other surviving copies include fifth and sixth editions, London, 1749, a tenth edition, 1748 (presumably misdated; Bitting records a tenth edition, 1751) and a twelfth edition, 1752. Evidently Mrs. Bradshaw died either in 1752 or 1753, after which the book was revised and enlarged "by a London Pastry-cook," conjectured by Virginia Maclean to be Edward Lambert, and published under the title *The Family Jewel*, as in this copy. The additions, which the prefatory letter states number "about two hundred new receipts," appear in a fifty page supplement that increases the book by more than half again its original length.

12mo. A-N⁶; 78 leaves, pp. [*12*] [1] 2-144.

Bibliographies: This edition unrecorded in the bibliographies consulted. Maclean, p. 14, records a variant of this edition with the same publisher and date but styled "sixth edition."

Copies: No other copy of this edition located. Of Maclean's variant "sixth edition." *NUC* locates copies at John Crerar Library and New York Academy of Medicine and Maclean adds the Brotherton Library.

575a. Brady, Margaret Y., b. 1900.

HEALTH FOR ALL | WARTIME | RECIPE BOOK | BY | MARGARET Y. BRADY, M.Sc. | *(Editor, Mother and Child Dept.* HEALTH FOR ALL) | LONDON: | HEALTH FOR ALL PUBLISHING COMPANY | HENRIETTA HOUSE, | 17-18 HENRIETTA STREET, LONDON, W.C.2

First edition, London, 1942.

183 x 120 mm. [A]⁸ B-H⁸; 64 leaves, pp. [*8*] 1-116 [*4*]. First two leaves and last two leaves, blanks, with the first leaf and the last leaf pasted down and the second leaf and the penultimate leaf serving as free endpapers. Publisher's blue cloth stamped in black. Publisher's white paper dust jacket printed in magenta and black.

Bibliographies: Unrecorded in the bibliographies consulted.

Copies: *NUC* (National Library of Medicine only).

576. Brande, W.

THE | *Town and Country Brewery Book;* | OR, | EVERY MAN HIS OWN BREWER, | AND | CELLARMAN, MALSTER AND HOP-MERCHANT: | CONDUCTED ON PRINCIPLES OF | HEALTH, PROFIT, & ECONOMY: | EXPLAINING | THE MOST APPROVED METHODS OF PRODUCING, AT THE LEAST EXPENCE, | THE RICHEST AND BEST-FLAVOURED | TOWN AND COUNTRY MALT DRINKS, | AND TO | PRESERVE AND FIT THEM FOR IMMEDIATE OR REMOTE USE, | AT ALL SEASONS OF THE YEAR; | FOR HOME CONSUMPTION OR EXPORTATION. | INCLUDING | The Management of the Beer-Cellar, Cooperage, Sweetening, and | Seasoning Old and New Casks; Regulation of the Temperature to be | observed during the Winter and Summer Months, &c. with a variety of | Original Instructions, Recipes, Estimates, and Calculations | IN THE VARIOUS PROCESSSES OF | BREWING DIFFERENT SOUND AND FAVOURITE BEERS, ALES, &c. | As adopted in the several counties of England, Scotland, and Wales. | [short rule] | BY W. BRANDE, MALSTER AND BREWER. | [short rule] | *"Let the man who drugs his beer, beware of the competition which will* | *soon rob him of all his customers."* | CHANCELLOR OF THE EXCHEQUER. | Vide Budget, 1829. | [short rule] | LONDON: | PUBLISHED BY DEAN AND MUNDAY, THREADNEEDLE-STREET. | [short rule] | *Price Four Shillings.*

First edition, London, ca. 1830.

172 x 104 mm. [A]⁶ aA⁶ B-Z⁶ Aa⁴; 148 leaves, pp. [1-4] 5-10 [iii] iv-xvi [13] 14-284.

Bibliographies: Noling, p. 77 dating the publication ca.1840.

Copies: *BMC* and *NUC* (Harvard and New York Public Library).

577. Briggs, Richard.

THE | English Art of Cookery, | ACCORDING TO THE | PRESENT PRACTICE; | BEING A | Complete Guide to all Housekeepers, | ON A | PLAN ENTIRELY NEW; | CONSISTING OF | THIRTY-EIGHT CHAPTERS. | CONTAINING, | [in two columns: column one] Proper Directions for Marketing, and | Trussing of Poultry. |

The making Soups and Broths. | Dressing all Sorts of Fish. | Sauces for every Occasion. | Boiling and Roasting. | Baking, Broiling, and Frying. | Stews and Hashes. | Made Dishes of every Sort. | Ragous and Fricasees. | Directions for dressing all Sorts of Roots | and Vegetables. | All Sorts of Aumlets and Eggs. | Puddings, Pies, Tarts, &c. | Pancakes and Fritters. | Cheesecakes and Custards. | [vertical double rule] | [column two] Blancmange, Jellies, and Syllabubs. | Directions for the Sick. | Directions for Seafaring Men. | Preserving, Syrups, and Conserves. | Drying and Candying. | All Sorts of Cakes. | Hogs Puddings, Sausages, &c. | Potting, and little cold Dishes. | The Art of Carving. | Collaring, Salting, and Sousing. | Pickling. | To keep Garden Vegetables, &c. | A Catalogue of Things in Season. | Made Wines and Cordial Waters. | Brewing. | English and French Bread, &c. [end columns] | WITH | BILLS OF FARE | FOR | EVERY MONTH IN THE YEAR, | Neatly and correctly engraved on TWELVE COPPER-PLATES. | [rule] | BY RICHARD BRIGGS, | MANY YEARS COOK AT THE GLOBE TAVERN, FLEET-STREET, | THE WHITE HART TAVERN, HOLBORN, | AND NOW AT THE TEMPLE COFFEE-HOUSE. | [rule] | LONDON: | PRINTED FOR G. G. J. AND J. ROBINSON, | PATER-NOSTER-ROW. | M.DCC.LXXXVIII.

First edition, London, 1788.

8vo. a^8 b^4 B-Tt^8; 340 leaves, pp. [i-iii] iv, ^{2}[i] ii-xx [1] 2-656.

Illustrations: Twelve engraved plates presenting bills of fare for each month of the year.

Bibliographies: Axford, p. 134; Maclean, p. 15; Wheaton and Kelly 844. Bitting, p. 60 and Vicaire 116 record the London, 1791, edition.

Copies: *NUC* (Library of Congress only). Maclean locates copies at the Bodleian Library, the Dorset County Library and the National Library of Wales and adds Radcliffe to the *NUC* holdings.

578. Entry deleted.

579. Briggs, Richard.

THE | English Art of Cookery, | ACCORDING TO THE | PRESENT PRACTICE; | BEING A | Complete Guide to all Housekeepers, | ON A | PLAN ENTIRELY NEW; | CONSISTING OF | THIRTY-EIGHT CHAPTERS. | CONTAINING, | [in two columns: column one] Proper Directions for Marketing, and | Trussing of Poultry, | The making of Soups and Broths, | Dressing all Sorts of Fish, | Sauces for every Occasion, | Boiling and Roasting, | Baking, Broiling, and Frying, | Stews and Hashes, | Made Dishes of every Sort, | Ragous and Fricasees, | Directions for dressing all Sorts of Roots | and Vegetables, | All Sorts of Aumlets and Eggs, | Puddings, Pies, Tarts, &c. | Pancakes and Fritters, | Cheesecakes and Custards, | [two vertical rules] | [column two] Blancmange, Jellies, and Syllabubs, | Directions for the Sick, | Directions for Seafaring Men, | Preserving, Syrups, and Conserves, | Drying and Candying, | All Sorts of Cakes, | Hogs Puddings, Sausages, &c. | Potting, and little cold Dishes, | The Art of Carving, | Collaring, Salting, and Sousing, | Pickling, | To keep Garden Vegetables, &c. | A Catalogue of Things in Season, | Made Wines and Cordial Waters, | Brewing, | English and French Bread, &c. [end columns] | WITH | BILLS OF FARE | FOR | EVERY MONTH IN THE YEAR, | Neatly and correctly engraved on TWELVE COPPER-PLATES. | [rule] | THE THIRD EDITION. | [rule] | BY RICHARD BRIGGS, | MANY YEARS COOK AT THE WHITE-HART TAVERN, HOLBORN, | TEMPLE COFFEE-HOUSE, AND OTHER TAVERNS IN LONDON. | [two rules] | LONDON: | PRINTED FOR G. G. AND J. ROBINSON, | PATER-NOSTER-ROW. | [short rule] | M,DCC,XCIV.

Third edition, London, 1794. Originally published, London, 1788 (item 577).

8vo. a⁸ b⁴ B-Nn⁸ Oo²; 294 leaves, pp. [i-iii] iv, ²[i] ii-xx [1] 2-564.

Illustrations: Twelve engraved plates presenting bills of fare for each month of the year.

Bibliographies: Axford, p. 134; Maclean, p. 16; Noling, p. 80; Oxford, p. 115; Pennell, p. 166; Wheaton and Kelly 843 (misdated 1744) and 845.

Copies: *BMC* and *NUC* (Iowa State University, Vassar and Yale). Maclean reports copies at the Wellcome Library, the Detroit Public Library and the Library of Congress.

580. Brillat-Savarin, Jean-Anthelme, 1755-1826.

THE | HANDBOOK OF DINING | OR | HOW TO DINE | THEORETICALLY, PHILOSOPHICALLY, AND HISTORICALLY CONSIDERED. | BASED CHIEFLY UPON | THE PHYSIOLOGIE DU GOÛT OF BRILLAT-SAVARIN. | BY LEONARD FRANCIS SIMPSON | M.R.S.L. | LONDON | LONGMAN, BROWN, GREEN, LONGMANS, & ROBERTS. | 1859.

First edition, London, 1859, of this translation and abridgement. Originally published in French, Paris, 1826 (item 98).

170 x 103 mm. A^8 a^2 B-Q^8 R^2; 132 leaves, pp. [i-vii] viii-xv [xvi] [ix] x-xi [xii] [1] 2-244. Publisher's black cloth with a pattern of white dots, stamped in gold.

Bibliographies: Axford, p. 195; Craig 14; Wheaton and Kelly 855.

Copies: *BMC* and *NUC* (7 copies).

581. Brillat-Savarin, Jean-Anthelme, 1755-1826.

BRILLAT-SAVARIN'S PHYSIOLOGIE DU GOÛT | [short rule] | A HANDBOOK | OF | [in red] GASTRONOMY | New and Complete Translation | [in red] *WITH FIFTY-TWO ORIGINAL ETCHINGS* | BY A. LALAUZE | LONDON | [in red] J. C. NIMMO AND BAIN | 14, KING WILLIAM STREET, STRAND, W.C. | 1884

First edition, London, 1884, of this translation. No. 168 of 300 copies issued in England. An additional 200 copies were issued in the United States by J. W. Bouton of New York.

217 x 145 mm. $[a]^4$ b^4 A-$3S^4$ $3T^2$; pp. [i-ix] x-xvi [1] 2-516. Publisher's half red morocco.

Illustrations: 52 original etchings by A. Lalauze printed on china paper and mounted as frontispiece and head and tail pieces for chapters.

Bibliographies: Driver 120.1.

Copies: *BMC* and *NUC* (9 copies).

582. The British Jewel.

THE | BRITISH JEWEL, | OR | COMPLETE HOUSEWIFE's | BEST COMPANION; | CONTAINING | [in two columns: column one] I. A number of the most | useful and uncommon Re- | ceipts in Cookery, with the | Manner of trussing Poultry, | Rabits, Hares, &c. illustrated | with curious Cuts, shewing | how each is to be trussed. | II. The best and most fa- | shionable receipts for all man- | ner of Pastry, Pickling, &c. | with some general rules to be | observed therein. | III. Directions for making | all sorts of English Wines, | Shrub, Vinegar, Varjuice, | Catchup, Sauces, Soups, Jel- | lies, &c. | IV. A Table to cast up ex- | pences by the day, week, | month or year. | V. Every Man his own | Physician; a valuable col- | [vertical rule] | [column two] lection of the most approved | Receipts for the cure of most | disorders incident to human | bodies, from the most emi- | nent English physicians. | VI. The manner of pre- | paring the Elixir of Life, | Turlington's Balsam, Fryar's | Balsam, the Court or Lady's | Black Sticking Plaster, Lip- | Salve, Lady York's Receipt | to preserve from the Small- | Pox or Plague, &c. the Roy- | al patent Snuff for the Head | and Eyes; Dr. Braken's | Powder for the Teeth, a Se- | cret for the cure of the Tooth | Ach, a speedy method to de- | stroy Warts or Corns, &c. | VII. Directions for de- | stroying Rats, Mice, Bugs, | Fleas, &c. | WITH | A choice Variety of useful FAMILY RECEIPTS. | Together with | A Method of restoring to Life People drowned, or in | any other Manner Suffocated, | To which is added | The COMPLETE FARRIER, being the Me- | thod of Buying, Selling, Managing, &c. and of the | Diseases and Cures incident to Horses. | [rule] | LONDON: | Printed and Sold by J. MILLER, at the Blue Anchor in | Mint Street, near St. George's Church, Southwark, 1769.

First edition, London, 1769.

4to. [A]⁴ B-N⁴; 52 leaves, pp. [1-5] 6-104.

Illustrations: Woodcuts in the text illustrating trussing.

Bibliographies: Axford, p. 45; Bitting, p. 524; Maclean, p. 16. Oxford and Simon BG list later editions.

Copies: *NUC* (Library of Congress only). Maclean locates only Library of Congress copy.

583. The British Jewel.

THE | BRITISH JEWEL; | OR | *Complete Housewife's best Companion.* | CONTAINING | [in two columns: column one] I. A Number of the most un- | common and useful Recipes in | Cookery, with the Manner of trus- | ing Poultry, Rabbits, Hares, &c. | illustrated with curious Cuts, shew- | ing how each is to be trussed. | II. The best and most fashion- | able Recipe for all Manner of | Pastry, Pickling, &c. with some | general Rules to be observed there- | in; with a Cut, and proper Direc- | tions how to lay a Table for four dif- | ferent Courses, in the present Taste, | by the Author, and others. | III. Directions for making all | Sorts of English Wines, Shrub, | Vinegar, Verjuice, Catchup, Sau- | ces, Soups, Jellies, &c. | IV. A Table to cast up Expen. | ces by the Day, Week, Month or | Year. | [vertical rule] |

[column two] | V. Every Man his own Physi- | cian; a valuable Collection of the | most approved Recipes for the | Cure of most Disorders incident to | Man or Woman, by the most emi- | nent Physicians in all Europe. | VI. The Manner of preparing | the Elixir of Life, Turlington's | Balsam, Friar's Balsam, the Court | or Ladies Black Sticking Plaister, | Lip-Salve, Lady York's Recipe to | preserve from the Small-Pox or | Plague, &c. the Royal Patent Snuff | for the Head and Eyes; Dr. Bra- | ken's Powder for the Teeth, a Se- | cret for the Cure of the Tooth-ach, | a speedy Method to destroy Warts | or Corns, &c. | VII. Directions for destroying | Rats, Mice, Bugs, Fleas, &c. | &c. &c. [end columns] | AND | A choice Variety of useful Family Recipes: | TOGETHER WITH | A Method of restoring to Life, People apparently | drowned, or in any other Manner suffocated. | ALSO | The COMPLETE FARRIER, | Being the Method of buying, selling, managing, &c. and | of the diseases incident to Horses, with their Cures. | TO WHICH IS ADDED, | THE ROYAL GARDENER, or Monthly | Calendar. | With the particular Months when River Fish Spawn, and | are most in Season; and the best Method of Brewing. | [rule] | *LONDON:* | Printed and Sold by T. SABINE, No. 81, *Shoe Lane,* | *Fleet Street.*

Seventh of seven editions listed in Maclean, London, ca. 1790. Originally published, London, 1769 (item 582).

4to. A-R⁴; 68 leaves, pp. [1] 2-136.

Illustrations: Engraved frontispiece captioned, "Engraved for the Prudent Housewife, & Published as the Act directs, July 21, 1788."

Bibliographies: Maclean, p. 16; Wheaton and Kelly 891.

Copies: *NUC* (Harvard and University of Pittsburgh). Maclean locates Kansas State University copy only.

584. Brooke, Humphrey, 1617-1693.

[within a double rule border] ϒΓΙΕΙΝΗ. | *OR A* | Conservatory | OF | HEALTH. | Comprized in a plain and practicall | Discourse upon the six particulars neces- | sary to Mans Life, *viz.* 1. Aire. 2. Meat | and Drink. 3. Motion and Rest. 4 Sleep | and Wakefulness. 5. The Excrements. | 6. The Passions of the Mind. With the | discussion of divers Questions pertinent | thereunto. Compiled and published for | the prevention of Sickness, and prolon- | gation of Life. | [rule] | *By* H. Brooke. *M. B.* | [rule] | *Mihi verò, & qui ambitionis, aut cujusvis* | *Cupiditatis gratiâ, impeditam negotiis vi-* | *tam delegerunt, quo minus corporicurando* | *vacare queant, ii quoq[ue], servire ultro do-* |

minis, & quidem pessimis videntur. Gal. | [rule] | *London*, Printed by *R.W.* for *G. Whittington*, | and are to be sold at the Blew-Anchor in | *Cornhill*, near the Exchange. 1650.

First edition, London, 1650.

12mo. A¹² a⁴ B-L¹² M⁸; 144 leaves, pp. [*32*] 1-256.

Bibliographies: Bitting, p. 61; Wing B4905.

Copies: *BMC* and *NUC* (5 copies). Wing (9 copies).

585. Brooks, Catharine.

THE | Complete *English* Cook; | OR | PRUDENT HOUSEWIFE. | Being an entire New COLLECTION of the | Most Genteel, yet least Expensive RECEIPTS in | every Branch of Cookery and good Housewifery. | VIZ. | [in three columns: column one] Roasting, | Boiling, | Stewing, | Ragoos, | Soups, | Sauces, | [two vertical rules] | [column two] Fricaseys, | Pies, Tarts, | Puddings, | Cheesecakes, | Custards, | Jellies, | [two vertical rules] | [column three] Potting | Candying, | Collaring | Pickling, | Preserving, | Made Wines, &c. [end columns] | Together with the ART of MARKETTING. | And Directions for placing Dishes on Table for | Entertainments: Adorned with proper Cuts. | And many other Things equally Necessary. | The Whole made Easy to the Meanest Capacity, | and far more Useful to Young Beginners than | any Book of the Kind ever yet published. | [rule] | *In cooking Fowl, or Flesh, or Fish,* | *Or any nice, or dainty Dish,* | *With Care peruse this useful Book,* | *'Twill make you a soon a perfect Cook.* | [rule] | *By* CATHARINE BROOKS *of* Red-Lyon-Street. | [rule] | To which is added, | The PHYSICAL DIRECTOR; being near Two | Hundred safe and certain Receipts for the Cure | of most Disorders incident to the Human Body. | Also the whole Art of Clear-Starching, Ironing, &c. | [rule] | The SECOND EDITION, with the Addition of a great | variety of Made Dishes, &c. | [rule] | LONDON: Printed for the AUTHORESS, and sold by | J. COOKE, at Shakespear's-head, in Pater- | noster-Row. | [Price One Shilling.]

Second edition, London, ca. 1765 No copy of the first edition is known but, as the preface is dated Jan. 20, 1762, it may be presumed to have been published in London, 1762. Maclean dates the second edition [ca. 1762], the British Library [1765] and Harvard [1767].

12mo. [A]² B-L⁶ M⁴; 66 leaves, pp. [1-4] 5-132. Signed on the verso of the title-page by C. Brooks and J. Cooke.

Illustration: Engraved frontispiece of a kitchen scene.

Bibliographies: Axford, p. 74; Bitting, p. 61; Maclean, p. 17; Oxford, p. 93; Wheaton and Kelly 894.

Copies: *BMC* and *NUC* (Harvard and Library of Congress). Maclean cites these copies and adds Brotherton and John Rylands copies.

586. Brownrigg, William.

THE | ART | OF MAKING | COMMON SALT, | As now Practised in | Most Parts of the World; | WITH SEVERAL | IMPROVEMENTS | PROPOSED in that ART, | For the USE of the | BRITISH DOMINIONS. | [rule] | BY | WILLIAM BROWNRIGG, *M.D.F.R.S.* | [two rules] | LONDON, | Printed, and sold by C. DAVIS, in *Holborn*; | A. MILLAR, in the *Strand*; and | R. DODSLEY, in *Pall-mall.* | [short rule] | MDCCXLVIII.

First edition, London, 1748.

8vo. a^8 b^4 B-S^8 T^4 U^8 χ1; 161 leaves, pp. [i-iv] v-xxiv, 1-295 [296] [2].

Illustrations: Six etched folding plates illustrating methods of making salt.

Bibliographies: Unrecorded in the bibliographies consulted; Driver 164.1; Wheaton and Kelly 947.

Copies: *BMC*, *BNC*, and *NUC* (13 copies).

587. Buckland, Anne Walbank.

OUR VIANDS | WHENCE THEY COME AND | HOW THEY ARE COOKED | WITH A BUNDLE OF OLD | RECIPES FROM COOKERY BOOKS | OF THE LAST CENTURY | BY ANNE WALBANK BUCKLAND | MEMBER OF THE ANTHROPOLOGICAL INSTITUTE, AUTHOR OF | `ANTHROPOLOGICAL STUDIES,' `THE WORLD BEYOND | THE ESTERELLES,' ETC. | `*Tell me what thou eatest and I will tell thee who thou art*.' | OLD PROVERB. | `*Viands of various kinds allure the taste* | *Of choicest sort and savour; rich repast*.' – POPE. | LONDON | WARD & DOWNEY | 12 YORK STREET COVENT GARDEN W.C. | 1893

First edition, London, 1893.

189 x 122 mm. [A]⁸ B-T⁸ U²; 154 leaves, pp. [i-v] vi [7] 8-308. Bound in publisher's green cloth, stamped in gold.

Bibliographies: Axford, p. 311; Bitting, p. 67; Driver 164.1; Wheaton and Kelly 947.

Copies: *BMC* and *NUC* (5 copies).

588. Caird, John.

THE | COMPLETE | CONFECTIONER | AND | FAMILY COOK; | INCLUDING | ALL THE LATE IMPROVEMENTS | IN | [in three columns: column one] CONFECTIONARY, | PRESERVING, | PICKLING, | [vertical rule] | [column two] JELLIES, | CREAMS, | PASTRY, | [vertical rule] | [column three] BAKING, | COOKERY, | &c. &c. [end columns] | WITH | MANY VALUABLE RECEIPTS, | AND AMPLE DIRECTIONS FOR | *MARKETING, TRUSSING, CARVING, &c.* | THE WHOLE BEING THE RESULT OF | MANY YEARS PRACTICE AND EXPERIENCE. | [short double rule] | BY J. CAIRD. | [short double rule] | ILLUSTRATED WITH COPPERPLATES AND WOODEN CUTS. | 𝔈𝔡𝔦𝔫𝔟𝔲𝔯𝔤𝔥: | PRINTED FOR W. CREECH, A. CONSTABLE & CO. J. ANDERSON, | JOHN THOMSON JUNR. & CO. OLIPHANT & BALFOUR, | AND ARCHIBALD ALLARDICE, LEITH; | LONGMAN, HURST, REES, & ORME, | AND CRADDOCK & JOY, | LONDON. | 1809.

First edition, London, 1809.

183 x 115 mm. π⁴ A-Pp⁶; 232 leaves, pp. [2] [i-iii] iv-vi [1] 2-454 [2]. First leaf (half-title or blank?) wanting in this copy; last leaf blank.

Illustrations: Engraved frontispiece; seven tipped in engravings, two folding, showing table settings; and woodcuts in the text.

Bibliographies: Axford, p. 73; Bitting, p. 72; Oxford, p. 137.

Copies: *BMC* and *NUC* (Library of Congress only).

589. Carême, Antonin, 1784-1833.

FRENCH COOKERY: | COMPRISING | *L'ART DE LA CUISINE FRANÇAISE;* | *LE PATISSIER ROYAL; LE CUISINIER PARISIEN.* | BY THE LATE | M. CARÊME, | SOME TIME CHEF OF THE KITCHEN OF HIS MAJESTY GEORGE IV., | TRANSLATED BY | WILLIAM HALL, | COOK TO T.P. WILLIAMS, ESQ., | M.P., AND CONDUCTOR OF THE PARLIAMENTARY DINNERS | OF THE RIGHT HONOURABLE LORD VISCOUNT CANTERBURY, G. C. B., | LATE SPEAKER OF THE HOUSE OF COMMONS. | [short rule] | WITH SEVENTY-THREE PLATES ILLUSTRATIVE OF THE ART. | [short rule] | LONDON: | JOHN MURRAY, ALBEMARLE STREET. | [short rule] | MDCCCXXXVI.

First edition, London, 1836, of this translation.

219 x 140 mm. [a]^2 b^8χb^8 c^4 B-2D^8 2E^4; 234 leaves, pp. [1-3] 4, v-xliii [xliv] [1] 2-422 [2]. Publisher's purple cloth with printed paper label on spine. Bound in at end are eight page and four page publisher's catalogs, each dated May 1836.

Illustrations: 73 lithographed folding plates illustrating elaborate dishes.

Bibliographies: Craig, 16; Oxford, p. 169; Simon BG 285; Wheaton and Kelly 1062.

Copies: *BMC.* Wheaton and Kelly (Radcliffe only).

590. Carter, Charles.

THE COMPLEAT | CITY and COUNTRY COOK: | OR, | Accomplish'd HOUSEWIFE. | Containing, | Several Hundred of the most approv'd RECEIPTS in | [in two columns: column one] COOKERY, | CONFECTIONARY, | CORDIALS, | COSMETICKS, | JELLIES, | [two vertical rules] | [column two] PASTRY, | PICKLES, | PRESERVING, | SYRUPS, | ENGLISH WINES, &c. [end columns] | Illustrated with Forty-nine large COPPER PLATES, | directing the regular placing the various Dishes on | the Table, from one to four or five Courses: Also, | Bills of Fare according to the several Seasons for | every Month of the Year. | LIKEWISE, | The *Horse-shoe Table* for the Ladies at the late In- | stalment at *Windsor*, the *Lord Mayor's Table*, and | other Hall Dinners in the City of *London*; with | a *Fish Table*, &c. | [rule] | By CHARLES CARTER, | Lately COOK to his Grace the Duke of *Argyle*, the Earl of | *Pontefract*, the Lord *Cornwallis*, &c. | [rule] | *To which is added by way of* Appendix, | Near *Two Hundred* of the most approv'd Receipts in Physick | and Surgery, for the Cure of the most common Diseases incident | to Families: | THE

COLLECTION OF A NOBLE LADY DECEASED. | *A* WORK *design'd for the Good, and absolutely Necessary* | *for all Families.* | [rule] | *LONDON:* | Printed for A. BETTESWORTH and C. HITCH; and C. DAVIS, in | *Pater-noster Row:* T. GREEN at *Charing-Cross*; and S. AUSTEN | in St. *Paul's* Church-yard. M.DCC.XXXII.

First edition, London, 1732.

8vo. A⁴ B-S⁸ T⁴; 144 leaves, pp. [i-ii] iii-viii, 1-280.

Illustrations: Engraved folding plate of an Installment Dinner and forty-eight plates, two folding, of bills of fare and table settings.

Bibliographies: Axford, p. 70; Bitting, p. 78; Maclean, p. 22; Noling, p. 98; Oxford, p. 62; Pennell, p. 148; Simon BG 297; Vicaire 150; Wheaton and Kelly 1086.

Copies: *BMC* and *NUC* (Harvard and Library of Congress). Maclean adds Bath College, Brotherton, Wellcome, New York Public Library, and University of Southern California.

591. Carter, Charles.

THE COMPLEAT | CITY and COUNTRY COOK: | OR, | Accomplish'd HOUSEWIFE. | CONTAINING, | Several Hundred of the most approv'd RECEIPTS in | [in two columns: column one] COOKERY, | CONFECTIONARY, | CORDIALS, | COSMETICKS, | JELLIES, | [two vertical rules] | [column two] PASTRY, | PICKLES, | PRESERVING, | SYRUPS, | ENGLISH WINES, &c. [end columns] | Illustrated with Forty-nine large COPPER PLATES, | directing the regular placing the various Dishes on the | Table, from one to four or five Courses: Also, Bills of | Fare according to the several Seasons for every Month | of the Year. | LIKEWISE, | The *Horse-shoe Table* for the Ladies at the late Instalment at | *Windsor*; the *Lord Mayor's Table*; and other Hall Dinners in | the City of *London*; with a Fish Table, &c. | [rule] | By CHARLES CARTER. | Lately COOK to his Grace the Duke of *Argyle*, the Earl of | *Pontefract*, the Lord *Cornwallis*, &c. | [rule] | *To which are added,* | Near *Two Hundred* of the most approved Receipts in Physick | and Surgery, for the Cure of the most common Diseases inci- | dent to Families; with several sovereign Receipts for the Cure | of the Bite of a Mad Dog. | [rule] | 𝕿𝖍𝖊 𝕾𝖊𝖈𝖔𝖓𝖉 𝕰𝖉𝖎𝖙𝖎𝖔𝖓, 𝖜𝖎𝖙𝖍 𝖑𝖆𝖗𝖌𝖊 𝕬𝖉𝖉𝖎𝖙𝖎𝖔𝖓𝖘. | [rule] | *LONDON:* Printed for A. BETTESWORTH and C. HITCH; | and C. DAVIS, in *Pater-noster-Row:* and S. AUSTEN in | St *Paul's* Church-yard. 1736.

Second edition, London, 1736. Originally published, London, 1732 (item 590).

8vo. A⁴ B-D⁸ ✱D⁸ E-X⁸ Y⁴; 176 leaves, pp. [i-iii] iv-viii [1] 2-329 [330-340] [*4*].

Illustrations: Forty-nine engraved plates, four of them folding, showing table settings.

Bibliographies: Bitting, p. 78; Maclean, p. 23; Simon BG 298.

Copies: *BMC* and *NUC* (Cornell, Library of Congress and National Agricultural Library). Maclean adds Bodleian Library and Wellcome Library.

592. Carter, Charles.

The COMPLETE | [in red] Practical COOK: | Or, A NEW | SYSTEM | Of the Whole ART and MYSTERY of | [in red] COOKERY. | Being a SELECT COLLECTION of | Above Five Hundred RECIPES for Dressing, after | the most Curious and Elegant Manner (as well FOREIGN as | ENGLISH) all Kinds of FLESH, FISH, FOWL, &c. | As also DIRECTIONS to make all Sorts of excellent *Pottages* and *Soups*, | fine *Pastry*, both sweet and savoury, delicate *Puddings*, exquisite *Sauces*, and rich | *Jellies*. With the best RULES for PRESERVING, POTTING, PICKLING, &c. | [rule] | [in red] FITTED FOR ALL OCCASIONS: | But more especially for the most *Grand* and *Sumptuous* ENTERTAINMENTS. | [rule] | [in red] Adorned with Sixty Curious COPPER PLATES; | Exhibiting the full SEASONS of the YEAR, and *Tables* proper for *Every* | *Month*; As also Variety of *large Ovals* and *Rounds*, and *Ambogues* | and *Square Tables* for CORORNATION-FEASTS, INSTALMENTS, &c. | [rule] | [in red] The WHOLE intirely NEW; | And none of the RECIPES ever published in any Treatise of this Kind. | [rule] | [in red] Approved by divers of the Prime NOBILITY; | And by several MASTERS of the ART and MYSTERY of COOKERY. | [rule] | [in red] *By* CHARLES CARTER, | Lately Cook to his Grace the Duke of *Argyll*, the Earl of *Pontefract*, | the Lord *Cornwallis*, &c. | [rule] | [in red] *LONDON:* | Printed for W. MEADOWS, in *Cornhill*; C. RIVINGTON, in St. *Paul's* | *Church-Yard*; and R. HETT, in the *Poultry*. M.DCC.XXX.

First edition, London, 1730.

4to. [A]⁴ a⁴ B-Ff⁴; 120 leaves, pp. [*16*] [1] 2-224.

Illustrations: Sixty engraved plates (five folding) showing table settings.

Bibliographies: Axford, p. 75; Bitting, p. 77; Craig 17; Maclean, p. 23; Oxford, p. 61; Wheaton and Kelly 1085.

Copies: *BMC* and *NUC* (5 copies). Maclean adds Brotherton Library, National Library of Scotland, Kansas State University and the Salem Institute.

593. Carter, E.

THE | FRUGAL COOK. | CONTAINING AN ASSORTMENT OF | ECONOMICAL AND USEFUL FAMILY RECEIPTS | IN | COOKERY, CONFECTIONARY, WINES, | PRESERVING, PICKLING, ETC. | WITH ALL NECESSARY INFORMATION CONNECTED WITH THE ABOVE ARTS. | EMBELLISHED WITH | UPWARDS OF FIFTY-ENGRAVINGS, | ILLUSTRATIVE OF | ORNAMENTING PASTRY, TRUSSING, SETTING TABLE, CARVING, ETC. | BY E. CARTER. | LONDON: | PUBLISHED BY J. T. WOOD, HOLYWELL STREET, STRAND. | 1851.

First edition? London, 1851.

143 x 116 mm. [A]^2 [B]^{12} C-I^8 K^2; 72 leaves, pp. [i-v] vi-viii [ix-xii] [1] 2-132.

Illustrations: Wood engravings in the text.

Bibliographies: Unrecorded in the bibliographies consulted.

Copies: Bodleian Library and Brotherton Library.

594. Carter, Susannah.

THE | FRUGAL HOUSEWIFE, | OR, | *Complete Woman Cook.* | WHEREIN | THE ART OF DRESSING ALL SORTS OF | VIANDS | WITH CLEANLINESS, DECENCY AND ELEGANCE, | IS EXPLAINED IN | *FIVE HUNDRED APPROVED RECEIPTS* | IN | Gravies, Sauces, Roasting, Boiling, Frying, Broiling, Stews, | Hashes, Soups, Fricassees, Ragouts, Pastries, Pies, | Tarts, Cakes, Puddings, Syllabubs, Creams, | Flummery, Jellies, Giams, and | Custards. | TOGETHER WITH THE BEST METHODS OF | Potting, Collaring, Preserving, Drying, Candying, Pickling, | AND | MAKING OF ENGLISH WINES; | TO WHICH ARE ADDED | TWELVE NEW PRINTS, | Exhibiting a proper Arrangment of Dinners, Two Courses | for every Month in the Year. | *WITH VARIOUS BILLS OF FARE.* | [two rules] | BY SUSANNAH CARTER, | OF CLERKENWELL. | [two rules] | *LONDON:* | PRINTED FOR E. NEWBERY, THE CORNER OF | ST. PAUL'S CHURCH-YARD. | 1795.

Third London edition, 1795. Originally published, London, ca. 1765.

12mo. A^6 $B-I^{12}$; 102 leaves, pp. [*12*] [1] 2-180 [181-192].

Illustrations: Two copper plates illustrating trussing and twelve woodcuts in text showing placement of dishes.

Bibliographies: Maclean, p. 24; Oxford, p. 122; Wheaton and Kelly 1090.

Copies: *BMC* and *NUC* (Center for Research Libraries and Vassar). Maclean adds Wellcome Library and Brotherton Library. Wheaton and Kelly (Radcliffe and Massachusetts Historical Society).

595. Carter, W.

THE | COOK AND CONFECTIONER'S | GUIDE; | OR | FEMALE'S INSTRUCTOR, | IN | COOKERY, CONFECTIONARY, | MAKING WINES, | PRESERVING, PICKLES, &c. | With every necessary information connected with the | above Arts. | [short rule] | BY W. CARTER. | [short rule] | LONDON: | BAILEY AND CO., BOOKSELLERS. | *Price Sixpence.*

First edition?, London, ca. 1840. Oxford assigns date [ca. 1800], Simon [c. 1830] and Kansas State University [1849?]. The physical appearance of the pamphlet suggests the 1840s.

170 x 108 mm. $[1]^{16}$ (fifth leaf signed "B"); 16 leaves, pp. [1-5] 6-32. Publisher's printed wrapper.

Bibliographies: Oxford, p. 126; Simon BG 299. Noling, p. 98, describes an edition, London, Bailey and Co., 1800 with 260 pages which, clearly, is either wrong in the number of pages or is another work.

Copies: *NUC* (Kansas State University only).

596. Cassell's Book of the Household.

Titles in volumes I and III:

CASSELL'S | BOOK OF THE HOUSEHOLD | A | 𝔚𝔬𝔯𝔨 𝔬𝔣 ℜ𝔢𝔣𝔢𝔯𝔢𝔫𝔠𝔢 | ON | DOMESTIC ECONOMY | VOLUME I. [VOLUME III.] | [short rule] | SPECIAL

EDITION | [short rule] | WITH COLOURED PLATES | KENNETH MACLENNAN | *75, PICCADILLY, MANCHESTER* | ALL RIGHTS RESERVED

Half-titles only in volumes II and IV:

CASSELL'S | BOOKS OF THE HOUSEHOLD | VOL. II. [VOL. IV.]

New edition, Manchester, 1890-1891, a re-issue of the London, Cassell, 1889-1891, edition with cancel title-pages. This is a "new edition" in the sense that the *Encyclopaedia Britannica* appears in new editions. The work began as *Cassell's Household Guide* (London, 1869-1871) (item 596a) but this "edition" published twenty years later is entirely re-written and resembles the original no more than do the various "editions" of the *Encyclopaedia Britannica*. A label in the front of each of the double volumes reads: THIS EDITION, | *being specially prepared for Subscription, is not* | *obtainable through the general Booksellers.* | CASSELL & COMPANY, LIMITED.

230 x 159 mm. 4 vols. Vol. I. π^2 ($\pm\pi$1) A-D^{16} 9-10^8 F-I^{16} J-K^{16} L^{14}; 192 leaves, pp. [i-iii] iv [1] 2-380. Vol. II π^2 M-U^{16} V-W^{16} X^{14}; 192 leaves, pp. [i-iii] iv [1] 2-380. Vol. III. π^2 ($\pm\pi$1) Y-2I^{16} 2J^{14}; 192 leaves, pp. [i-iii] iv [1] 2-380. Vol. IV. π^2 2K-2U^{16} 2V^{14}; 192 leaves, pp. [i-iii] iv [1] 2-380. Four volumes bound as two.

Illustrations: Vol. I. Three chromolithograph plates and one folding chart printed in blue and gold. Vol. II. Four chromolithograph plates. Vol. III. Four chromolithograph plates. Vol. IV. Three chromolithograph plates. All volumes contain numerous wood engravings in the text.

Bibliographies: This issue unrecorded in the bibliographies consulted. Attar 44.6 cites the London, Cassell, issue.

Copies: No other copy of this issue located. Attar locates copies of the Cassell issue in the Bodleian Library and the National Library of Scotland.

596a. Cassell's Household Guide.

CASSELL'S | HOUSEHOLD GUIDE: | BEING | A Complete Encyclopædia | OF | DOMESTIC AND DOCIAL ECONOMY, | AND FORMING | *A Guide to Every Department of Practical Life.* | VOLUME I. [II. III. IV.] | [publisher's monogram] | LONDON: | CASSELL, PETTER, AND GALPIN, | LUDGATE HILL, E. C.; | AND 596, BROADWAY, NEW YORK.

The title-pages of volumes II, III and IV replace the publisher's monogram with "[short rule] | 𝔚𝔦𝔱𝔥 𝔑𝔲𝔪𝔢𝔯𝔬𝔲𝔰 𝔍𝔩𝔩𝔲𝔰𝔱𝔯𝔞𝔱𝔦𝔬𝔫𝔰. | [short rule]".

First edition, London, 1869-1871. Originally issued in twenty-four monthly parts, 1869-1871. This set, in the publisher's cloth binding, is bound from the monthly parts. A portion of the parts issue wrapper appears in the margin of p. 128. See item 596 for a later "edition," completely re-written, of this work.

227 x 189 mm. 4 vols. Vol. I. π^2 1-23^8 24^6; 192 leaves, pp. [i-ii] iii-iv [1] 2-380. Vol. II. π1 25-48^8 χ^8 (-χ1=π1); 200 leaves, pp. [2] [1] 2-398. Vol. III. π1 49-71^8 χ^8(-χ1=π1); 192 leaves, pp. [2] [1] 2-381 [382]. Vol. IV. π1 72-95^8 96^8 (-96$_1$=π1); 200 leaves, pp. [2] [1] 2-397 [398]. Publisher's terra cotta cloth stamped in gold, black and blind. Note: Vol. I. in this set lacks pp. [381-382] 383-394 containing the "Analytical Index to the First volume of Cassell's Household Guide..."

Illustrations: Vol. I. Chromolithograph frontispiece and one chromolitograph plate, each showing eight prepared dishes. Vol. II. Chromolithograph frontispiece showing five desserts and one chromolithograph plate showing seven vegetable dishes. Vol. III. Chromolitograph frontispiece showing eight prepared dishes and a centre stand for fruit and flowers and custards in a tray, and an embossed block print of a design for a collar in point lace. Vol. IV. Chromolithograph frontispiece of a window decoration and a chromolitograph plate of a conservatory and aquarium. All volumes contain numerous wood engravings in the text.

Bibliographies: Attar 44.1.

Copies: *BMC, NUC* (5 copies); Attar locates copies in the Bodleian Library, the British Library, the National Library of Scotland and the Victoria and Albert Museum.

597. Charleton, Walter, 1619-1707.

[within a border of two rules] TWO | DISCOURSES. | I. Concerning | The Different WITS of MEN: | Written at the Request of a Gen- | tleman Eminent in Vertue, Learn- | ing, Fortune. | II. | The Mysterie of VINTNERS, | Or a Discourse concerning the | Various *Sicknesses* of *Wines*, and | their Respective Remedies at this | Day commonly Used. | [rule] | Delivered to the | ROYAL SOCIETY, | Assembled in | *Gresham=Colledge.* | [rule] | *LONDON,* | Printed by *R. W.* for *William Whitwood*, at | the Sign of the *Golden-Lion* in *Duck-* | *Lane*, near *Smithfield*, 1669.

First edition, London, 1669.

8vo. A-P⁸ Q⁴; 124 leaves, pp. [*16*] 1-230 [*2*]. A1 and Q4, blanks, wanting in this copy.

Bibliographies: Gabler, p. 57; Noling, p. 103; Simon BG 335; Wing C3694.

Copies: *BMC, BNC,* and *NUC* (11 copies). Wing (10 copies).

598. Charleton, Walter, 1619-1707.

[within a border of two rules] TWO | DISCOURSES. | The first, Concerning the different | WITS of MEN. | The second, A brief Discourse con- | cerning the various Sicknesses of | Wines, and their respective reme- | dies; at this day commonly used: | Delivered to the | 𝕽𝖔𝖞𝖆𝖑 𝕾𝖔𝖈𝖎𝖊𝖙𝖞. | [rule] | By *Walt. Charleton*, M. D. | [rule] | To which is added in this Third Edition, the | Art and Mystery of Vintners, and Wine-Coop- | ers: Containing approved Directions for Con- | serving and curing all manner and sorts of | Wines; whether, *Spanish, Greek, Italian, Por-* | *tugall,* or *French*: As it is now practised in | the City of *London.* | [rule] | *London,* Printed for *Will. Whitwood,* at the | *Angel* and *Bible* in *Little Britain,* 1692.

Fourth edition, styled the third, London, 1692. Originally published, London, 1669 (item 597).

12mo. [A]⁴ B-I¹² K²; 102 leaves, pp. [*8*] 1-183 [*184*] [*12*].

Bibliographies: Wing C3697.

Copies: *BMC* and *NUC* (Clark Library and Yale). Wing (5 copies).

599. Child, Samuel.

Every Man his own Brewer; | OR, A | COMPENDIUM | OF THE | ENGLISH BREWERY. | CONTAINING | The Best Instructions for the Choice of HOPS, | MALT, and WATER; and for the Right Ma- | nagement of the BREWING UTENSILS. | LIKEWISE, | The Most Approved Methods of Brewing LONDON | PORTER and ALE. Of Brewing AMBER, BURTON, | WESTERN and OAT ALES. Of Good TABLE | BEER, and MARLBOROUGH, DORCHESTER, NOT- | TINGHAM, and BRISTOL BEERS. | AND | Of manufacturing Pure Malt Wines. Of

Fermenta- | tion; Casual Distemperature in Brewing, with the | Cause and Remedy.
The Theory of British Fruits, | as applied to the Improvement of Malt Liquours | Of
AIR; its Properties and Effects on Malt Liquour. | Of the THERMOMETER, its Use
and Application | in Brewery. Of FIRE, and its Action on Malt | and Vinous Extracts.
| Together with | A Variety of MAXIMS and OBSERVATIONS deduced from |
Theory and Practice. And some Useful HINTS to the | Distillery, for Extracting a
Fine Spirit from Malt and other | Ingredients. | The Whole Illustrated by Several
EXPERIMENTS. | [rule] | By a GENTLEMAN, lately retired from the | Brewing
Business. | [two rules] | LONDON: | Printed for the AUTHOR: And Sold by J.
ALMON, | opposite Burlington House, in Piccadilly; and | Mess. ROBINSON and
ROBERTS, in Pater-noster Row. | [short rule] | MDCCLXVIII.

First edition, London, 1768. Uncancelled state of leaves A6 and B11.

12mo. A^6 B-L^{12} M^6; 132 leaves, pp. [4] i-vi, 29-30, ix-xxviii, 29-256 [4]. Note:
From this copy with leaves A6 in place and B11 uncancelled it can be seen that the
printer began setting type with the "Introduction" (p. ix) at signature B, but at some
point before printing the preliminaries in signature A it was decided to lengthen the
head title on page 29 (B11^r) from "The Philosophy of Brewing" to "The Philosophy of
Brewing; or, a Compendium of the English Brewery." The last leaf of signature A was
used to print the cancelan for pages 29-30 (B11), thereby causing a hiatus in the
pagination at the corrected copies between pages vi and ix.

Bibliographies: Maclean, p. 26.

Copies: No other copy with leaves A6 and B11 in their uncancelled state located.

600. Child, Samuel.

Every Man his own Brewer; | OR, A | COMPENDIUM | OF THE | ENGLISH
BREWERY. | CONTAINING | The Best Instructions for the Choice of HOPS, |
MALT, and WATER; and for the Right Ma- | nagement of the BREWING
UTENSILS. | LIKEWISE, | The Most Approved Methods of Brewing LONDON |
PORTER and ALE. Of Brewing AMBER, BURTON, | WESTERN and OAT ALES.
Of Good TABLE | BEER, and MARLBOROUGH, DORCHESTER, NOT- |
TINGHAM, and BRISTOL BEERS. | AND | Of manufacturing Pure Malt Wines. Of
Fermenta- | tion; Casual Distemperature in Brewing, with the | Cause and Remedy.
The Theory of British Fruits, | as applied to the Improvement of Malt Liquours | Of
AIR; it Properties and Effects on Malt Liquour. | Of the THERMOMETER, its Use
and Application | in Brewery. Of FIRE, and its Action on Malt | and Vinous Extracts.

| Together with | A Variety of MAXIMS and OBSERVATIONS deduced from | Theory and Practice. And some Useful HINTS to the | Distillery, for Extracting a Fine Spirit from Malt and other | Ingredients. | The Whole Illustrated by Several EXPERIMENTS. | [rule] | By a GENTLEMAN, lately retired from the | Brewing Business. | [two rules] | LONDON: | Printed for the AUTHOR: And Sold by J. ALMON, | opposite Burlington House, in Piccadilly; and | Mess. ROBINSON and ROBERTS, in Pater-noster Row. | [short rule] | MDCCLXVIII.

First edition, London, 1768. Cancelled states of leaves A6 and B11.

12mo. A^6 (-A6=B11) B^{12} (±B11) C-L^{12} M6; 131 leaves, pp. [*4*] i-vi, ix-xxviii, 29-256 [*4*]. See note on the collation under item 599.

Bibliographies: Maclean, p. 26.

Copies: *NUC* (Harvard and New York Public Library). Maclean adds Cambridge.

601. Child, Samuel.

EVERY | MAN HIS OWN BREWER: | A TREATISE | EXPLAINING THE ART AND MYSTERY OF BREWING | PORTER, | ALE, TWOPENNY, & TABLE-BEER, | Recommending and proving the Ease and Possibility | OF EVERY MAN'S BREWING HIS OWN BEER, | IN ANY QUANTITY, | *From One Peck to a Hundred Quarters of Malt.* | Intended to | REDUCE THE EXPENSE OF FAMILIES. | [two rules] | By SAMUEL CHILD, BREWER. | [two rules] | Some COOPERS attempt to extend their Art so far as to add | Strength to the BEER; but let it be remembered, that the | Principal Constituent Parts of BEER *should be* MALT and HOPS; | when Strength is given to the Liquor by any other Means, its | Nature is altered, and it is no more BEER that we drink. | COMBRUNE'S THEORY OF BREWING. | [short fancy rule] | LONDON: | PRINTED FOR R. LEA, GREEK-STREET, SOHO, | AND J. NUNN, GREAT QUEEN-STREET, | LINCOLN'S INN FIELDS. | 1808. | [PRICE SIXPENCE.]

New edition, London, 1808. Originally published, London, ca. 1790. This is an entirely different work from that with the same title published in 1768.

165 x 100 mm. [A]^2 (A1+B^{12}); 14 leaves, pp. [1-3] 4-28.

Bibliographies: This edition unrecorded in the bibliographies consulted. Noling, p. 105, records the third edition, undated, the fourth edition, 1794, the fifth edition, 1798, and the seventh edition, 1799.

Copies: No other copy of this edition located.

602. Chomel, Noel, 1632-1712.

[within a border of two rules] [in red] *DICTIONNAIRE* | *OECONOMIQUE:* | OR, |
[in red] The Family Dictionary. | CONTAINING | [in red] THE most experienced
Methods of improving ESTATES and of preserving HEALTH, | with many approved
Remedies for most *Distempers* of the Body of Man, Cattle and other Creatures, | and
the best *Means* for attaining long Life. | [in red] THE most advantageous Ways of
Breeding, Feeding and Ordering all Sorts of DO- | MESTICK ANIMALS, as *Horses,
Kine, Sheep, Swine, Poultry, Bees, Silkworms,* &c. | [in red] THE different Kinds of
NETS, SNARES and ENGINES for taking all Sorts of *Fish,* | *Birds,* and other Game.
| [in red] GREAT Vareity of Rules, Directions, and new Discoveries, relating to
GARDENING, | HUSBANDRY, SOILS and MANURES of all Sorts; the Planting and
Culture of *Vines,* | *Fruit Tress, Forest Trees, Underwoods, Shrubs, Flowers,* and their
several Uses; the Knowledge of | Foreign *Drugs, Dies,* Domestick and Exotick *Plants*
and *Herbs,* with their specifick Qualities and | medicinal Virtues. | [in red] THE best
and cheapest Ways of providing and improving all manner of MEATS and | DRINKS;
of preparing several Sorts of *Wines, Waters* and *Liquors* for every Season, both | by
Distillation and otherwise: Of preserving all kind of *Fruits* as well dry as liquid, and
making | divers *Sweetmeats* and *Works* of *Sugar,* and other profitable Curiosities, both
in the Confectionary | and Culinary Arts of *Housewifery.* | [in red] MEANS of making
the most Advantage of the Manufactures of SOAP, STARCH, | SPINNING,
COTTON, THREAD, &c. | [in red] THE Methods to take or destroy VERMIN and
other Animals, injurious to Garden- | ing, Husbandry, and all rural Oeconomy; with a
Description of Garden and other Country | *Tools* and *Utensils.* | [in red] AN Account
of the several WEIGHTS, MEASURES, &c. of METALS and MI- | NERALS, with
their *Preparations* and *Uses.* | [in red] ALL Sorts of RURAL SPORTS and
EXERCISES, conducing to the Benefit and | innocent Enjoyments of Life; as also
PAINTING in MINIATURE, and divers other *Arts* | and *Terms of Art* explained, for
the Entertainment and Amusement of Gentlemen, Ladies, &c. | [in red] THE whole
illustrated throughout with very great Variety of FIGURES, for the rea- | dier
understanding and practising of things to which they belong. | [rule] | *Done into*
English *from the Second Edition, lately printed at* Paris, *in two* | *Volumes, Folio,*
written by [in red] M. CHOMEL: | *With considerable* [in red] *ALTERATIONS* [in
black] *and* [in red] *IMPROVEMENTS.* | [rule] | Revised and Recommended by [in red]
Mr. R. BRADLEY, [in black] Professor of Botany in the | University of *Cambridge,*
and F. R. S. | [rule] | IN TWO VOLUMES. | [short rule] | [in red] VOL. I. [in
black] From [in red] A [in black] —— [in red] to [in black] —— [in red]H. [[in red]
VOL. II. [in black] From [in red] H [in black] —— [in red] to [in black] —— [in red]
Z.] | [two rules] | *LONDON:* | Printed for [in red] D. MIDWINTER, [in black] at the
Three Crowns in St. *Paul's Church-Yard.* | [short rule] | [in red] M. DCC. XXV.

First edition in English, London, 1725. Originally published in French, Lyon and Paris, 1709.

Folio. 2 vols. Vol. I. A-R⁴ Aa-Tt⁴ Uu² Xx1 Aaa-Aaaa⁴ Bbbb²; 245 leaves, unpaginated. Vol. II. π1 Aaaa-Ssss⁴ Tttt² 5A-5R⁴ 5S² Ttttt⁴ 5U⁴ 5W⁴ 5X-5Y⁴ 5Z² 6A-6L⁴ 6M⁶ 6N-6P⁴ 6Q² 7A-7N⁴; 282 leaves, unpaginated.

Illustrations: Numerous woodcuts in the text.

Bibliographies: Axford, p. 115; Bitting, p. 87; Fussell (1) p. 109; Maclean, p. 27; Oxford, p. 57; Wheaton and Kelly 1231.

Copies: *BMC* and *NUC* (14 copies). Maclean adds Cambridge and Edinburgh University.

603. Clarke, Edith Nicolls, 1844-1926.

THE NATIONAL | *TRAINING SCHOOL FOR COOKERY,* | BUCKINGHAM PALACE ROAD, S.W. | [two short rules] | HIGH-CLASS COOKERY | RECIPES, | AS TAUGHT IN THE SCHOOL. | BY | MRS. CHARLES CLARKE, | THE LADY SUPERINTENDENT. | *SIXTH EDITION.* | LONDON: | PRINTED AND PUBLISHED FOR | THE LADY SUPERINTENDENT OF THE NATIONAL TRAINING | SCHOOL FOR COOKERY, | BY WILLIAM CLOWES AND SONS, LIMITED, 13, CHARING CROSS, S.W. | [short rule] | 1893. | (*All rights reserved.*)

Sixth edition, London, 1893. Originally published, London, 1885.

180 x 120 mm. [A]² B-R⁸ S⁴ T²(-T2); 135 leaves, pp. [i-iii] iv [1] 2-265 [266].

Bibliographies: Driver 203.6; Wheaton and Kelly 1263.

Copies: *NUC* and Wheaton and Kelly (Boston Public Library only).

604. Cleland, Elizabeth, fl. 1755-1770.

A | NEW AND EASY | METHOD | OF | COOKERY. | TREATING, | [in two columns: column one] I. Of GRAVIES, SOUPS, | BROTHS, &c. | II. Of FISH, and their | SAUCES. | III. To Pot and Make HAMS, | &c. | [two vertical rules] | [column two] IV. Of PIES, PASTIES, | &c. | V. Of PICKLING and | PRESERVING. | VI.

Of Made WINES, DI- | STILLING and BREW- | ING, &c. [end columns] | By ELIZABETH CLELAND. | *Chiefly intended for the Benefit of the Young* LADIES | *who attend Her* SCHOOL. | [two rules] | *EDINBURGH:* | Printed for the Author by W. GORDON, C. WRIGHT, | S. WILLISON and J. BRUCE: | And sold at Her House in the *Luckenbooths.* | [short rule] | M. DCC. LV.

First edition, Edinburgh, 1755.

8vo. [a]⁴ b² A-Bb⁴ Cc²; 108 leaves, pp. [*12*] 1-204. Leaf a4 wanting in this copy.

Bibliographies: Maclean, p. 27. Noling, p. 108, Oxford, p. 88, Pennell, p. 157, and Vicaire 181 cite the second edition, Edinburgh, 1759. Axford, p. 290 , and Bitting, p. 91 cite the third edition, 1770.

Copies: *NUC* (New York Public Library only). Maclean adds a copy in the Abbotsford Library.

605. Clermont, B.

THE | PROFESSED COOK: | OR THE MODERN ART OF | *Cookery, Pastry,* and *Confectionary,* | Made PLAIN and EASY. | Consisting of the most approved Methods in the | FRENCH as well as ENGLISH COOKERY. | In which the French Names of all the different Dishes are given and | explained, whereby every Bill of Fare becomes intelligible and | familiar. | CONTAINING | [in two columns: column one] I. Of Soups, Gravy, Cullis and | Broths | II. Of Sauces | III. The different Ways of Dressing | Beef, Veal, Mutton, Pork, | Lamb, &c. | IV. Of First Course Dishes | V. Of Dressing Poultry | VI. Of Venison | VII. Of Game of all Sorts | VIII. Of Ragouts, Collops and | Fries | IX. Of Dressing all Kinds of Fish | X. Of Pastry of different Kinds | XI. Of Entremets, or Last Course | Dishes | [vertical rule] | [column two] XII. Of Omelets | XIII. Pastes of different Sorts | XIV. Dried Conserves | XV. Cakes, Wafers and Biscuits | XVI. Of Almonds and Pistachias | made in different Ways | XVII. Marmalades | XVIII. Jellies | XIX. Liquid and Dried Sweetmeats | XX. Syrups and Brandy Fruits | XXI. Ices, Ice Creams and Ice | Fruits | XXII. Ratafias, and other Cor- | dials, &c. &c. [end columns] | Translated from *Les Soupers de la Cour*; with the Addition | of the best Receipts which have ever appear'd in the | *French* Language. | And adapted to the *London Markets* by the EDITOR, who | has been many Years Clerk of the Kitchen in some of | the first Families in this Kingdom. | [rule] | THE SECOND EDITION. | [rule] | LONDON: | Printed for R. DAVIS, in *Piccadilly*; and T. CASLON, | opposite *Stationers-Hall*. MDCCLXIX.

Second edition, London, 1769. Originally published under the title *The Art of Modern Cookery Displayed*, London, 1767, in two volumes. This is, in part, a translation and adaptation of Menon's *Les Soupers de la Cour*, Paris, 1755 (item 344).

8vo. a^8 $^\pi$a^8 b^4 $^\pi$b^8 c^4 B-S^8 T^8 (-T8) U-Pp^8; 327 leaves, pp. [i-iii] iv-xvi [*48*] [1] 2-588 [*2*]. Last leaf (blank?) wanting in this copy.

Bibliographies: Bitting, p. 519; Maclean, p. 99; Oxford, p. 101; Simon BG 354; Wheaton and Kelly 4126.

Copies: *NUC* (Radcliffe). Maclean adds British Library, Wellcome Library, Library of Congress.

606. Clermont. B.

THE | PROFESSED COOK: | OR, THE MODERN ART OF | Cookery, Pastry, and Confectionary, | MADE PLAIN AND EASY. | Consisting of the most approved Methods in the | FRENCH as well as ENGLISH COOKERY. | IN WHICH | The French Names of all the different Dishes are given and explained, | whereby every Bill of Fare becomes intelligible and familiar. | CONTAINING | [in two columns: column one] I. Of Soups, Gravy, Cullis and Broths. | II. Of Sauces. | III. The different Ways of dressing Beef, | Veal, Mutton, Pork, Lamb, &c. | IV. Of First Course Dishes. | V. Of dressing Poultry. | VI. Of Venison. | VII. Of Game of all Sorts. | VIII. Of Ragouts, Collops and Fries. | IX. Of Dressing all Kinds of Fish. | X. Of Pastry of different Kinds. | XI. Of Entremets, or last Course Dishes. | [vertical rule] | [column two] XII. Of Omelets. | XIII. Pastes of different Sorts. | XIV. Dried Conserves. | XV. Cakes, Wafers and Biscuits. | XVI. Of Almonds and Pistachios made | in different Ways. | XVII. Marmalades. | XVIII. Jellies. | XIX. Liquid and Dried Sweetmeats. | XX. Syrups and Brandy Fruits. | XXI. Ices, Ice Creams, and Ice Fruits. | XXII. Ratafias, and other Cordials, &c. [end columns] | INCLUDING | A TRANSLATION of LES SOUPERS DE LA COUR; | WITH THE | Addition of the best Receipts which have ever appeared in the French or | English Languages, and adapted to the London Markets. | By B. CLERMONT, | Who has been many Years Clerk of the Kitchen in some of the first Families in this | Kingdom, and lately to the Right Hon. the Earl of ABINGDON. | The THIRD EDITION, revised and much enlarged. | LONDON: | Printed for W. DAVIS, in Piccadilly; T. CASLON, opposite Stationer's-Hall; G. | ROBINSON, in Paternoster-Row; F. NEWBERY, the Corner of St. Paul's Church- | Yard; and the AUTHOR, in Princes-Street, Cavendish-Square. | [short rule] | M.DCC.LXXVI.

Third edition, London, 1776. Originally published under the title *The Art of Modern Cookery Displayed*, London, 1767, in two volumes. This is, in part, a translation and adaptation of Menon's *Les Soupers de la Cour*, Paris, 1755 (item 344).

8vo. a^8 b-f^4 g^2 B-Qq^8 Rr^2; 336 leaves, pp. [i-iii] iv-x [xi-lx] [1] 2-610 [2].

Bibliographies: Maclean, p. 99; Roscoe A84; Simon BG 355; Wheaton and Kelly 4127.

Copies: *NUC* (6 copies). Maclean adds Brotherton Library.

607. A Closet for Ladies and Gentlewomen.

[within a border of type ornaments] A | CLOSET | for LADIES and | GENTLEVVOMEN. | OR, | The Art of Preserving, | Conserving, and | Candying. | *With the manner how to* | make diverse kindes of Sy- | rupes*:* and all kinde of | *banqueting stuffes.* | Also divers soveraigne Medi- | *cines and Salues for sundry* | *Diseases.* | [rule] | LONDON | Printed for *Arthur Iohnson*, | dwelling neare the great | *North dore of Paules.* | 1611.

Second edition, London, 1611. Originally published, London, 1608.

16mo. A-M^8; 96 leaves, pp. [2] 1-190.

Bibliographies: *STC* 5435. Craig 73, Oxford, p. 14, and Vicaire 183 record the 1608 edition (misdated 1618 in Vicaire).

Copies: *NUC* (Huntington Library only) and *STC* (7 copies).

608. A Closet for Ladies and Gentlewomen.

[within a border of type ornaments] A | CLOSET | for LADIES and | GENTLEVVOMEN. | OR, | The Art of preserving, | Conserving, and | Candying. | *With the manner how to* | make diverse kindes of Sy- | rupes*:* and all kinde of | *banqueting stuffes.* | Also divers soveraigne Medi- | *cines and Salues for sundry* | *Diseases.* | [rule] | LONDON | Printed for *Arthur Iohnson*, | dwelling neare the great | *North dore of Paules.* | 1614.

Third edition, London, 1614. Originally published, London, 1608.

16mo. A-M^8; 96 leaves, pp. [2] 1-190.

Bibliographies: *STC* 5436.

Copies: *STC* (Huntington Library and David Segal).

609. A Closet for Ladies and Gentlewomen.

[within a border of type ornaments] A | CLOSET | for Ladies and | *Gentlewomen.* | OR, | The Art of preseruing, | Conseruing, and | Candying. | *With the manner how to* | make diuerse kindes of | sirups, and all kinde of | *banqueting stuffs.* | Also diuerse soueraign Medi- | *cines and Salues for sun-* | *dry Diseases.* | [rule] | LONDON, | Printed for *Iohn Parker*, in | Pauls Church-yard at the | signe of the three Pi- | geons. 1624.

Fifth edition, London, 1624. Originally published, London, 1608.

12mo. A-H^{12}; 96 leaves, unpaginated. Bound with Sir Hugh Platt's *Delights for Ladies* . . . London, 1624 (item 930).

Bibliographies: *STC* 5436.5.

Copies: *STC* (British Library, imperfect, and Texas Woman's University).

610. A Closet for Ladies and Gentlewomen.

[within a border of type ornaments] A | CLOSET | for Ladies and | *Gentlewomen.* | OR, | The Art of preseruing, | Conseruing, and | Candying. | With the manner how | to make diuers kinds of | Sirups, and all kinde of | banqueting stuffes. | Also diuers soueraigne Medi- | cines and Salues for sundry | Diseases. | [rule] | LONDON, | Printed by *Iohn Hauiland.* | *1627.*

Sixth edition, London, 1627. Originally published, London, 1608.

12mo. A-H^{12}; 96 leaves, unpaginated.

Bibliographies: *STC* 5436.7.

Copies: *BMC* and *NUC* (Folger Library only). *STC* (4 copies).

611. Cobbett, Anne.

THE | ENGLISH HOUSEKEEPER: | OR, | MANUAL OF DOMESTIC MANAGEMENT: | CONTAINING | ADVICE ON THE CONDUCT OF HOUSEHOLD AFFAIRS, IN A SEPARATE | TREATISE ON EACH PARTICULAR DEPARTMENT, AND | 𝔓ractical 𝔍nstructions | CONCERNING | [in two columns: column one] THE STORE-ROOM, | THE PANTRY, | THE LARDER, | [vertical rule] | [column two] THE KITCHEN, | THE CELLAR, | THE DAIRY. [end columns] | TOGETHER WITH | *Remarks on the best Means of Rendering Assistance to Poor* | *Neighbours; and Hints for Laying Out Small Ornamental* | *Gardens;* *directions for Cultivating Herbs.* | THE WHOLE BEING INTENDED | FOR THE USE OF YOUNG LADIES WHO UNDERTAKE THE | SUPERINTENDENCE OF THEIR OWN HOUSEKEEPING. | [short rule] | BY ANNE COBBETT. | [short rule] | LONDON: | PUBLISHED BY ANNE COBBETT, 10, RED LION COURT, FLEET STREET; | W. TAIT, EDINBURGH; T. O'GORMAN, DUBLIN; | AND W. WILLIS, MANCHESTER

First edition, London, 1835.

12mo. [A]^{12} B-K^{12} [L]^{12} M-X^{12} [Y]^6 χ1; 259 leaves, pp. [i-iii] iv-xxiii [xxiv] [1] 2-480, ^{2}i-xii [2]. Recto of last leaf misnumbered 480.

Illustrations: Wood engraved frontispiece of game and wood engravings in the text illustrating carving.

Bibliographies: This edition unrecorded in the bibliographies consulted. Axford, p. 134, records the second edition, London, n.d.

Copies: *BMC* and *NUC* (New York Public Library only).

612. Cobbett, William, 1763-1835.

THE | AMERICAN GARDENER; | OR, | A TREATISE | On the Situation, Soil, Fencing and Laying-Out of | Gardens; on the Making and Managing of Hot- | Beds and Green-Houses; and on the Propagation | and Cultivation of the several sorts of Vegetables, | Herbs, Fruits and Flowers. | [two short rules] | BY WILLIAM COBBETT. | [two short rules] | "I went by the field of the Slothful and by the vineyard of the | "man void of understanding : and, lo! it was all grown over with | "thorns, and nettles covered the face thereof, and the stone-wall | "thereof was broken down. Then I saw and considered it well : | "I looked upon it, and received instruction." | Proverbs: Chap. XXIV. Ver. 30. | STEREOTYPE EDITION. | LONDON: | *PUBLISHED BY C. CLEMENT*, 1, *CLEMENT'S INN.* | [short rule] | 1821.

First edition, London, 1821. Cobbett revised this work and republished it as *The English Gardner*, London, 1829 (item 616).

190 x 108 mm. A-Y⁶; 132 leaves, unpaginated. Bound in publisher's boards with printed paper label on the spine.

Illustrations: Three woodcuts in the text.

Bibliographies: Pearl 114.

Copies: *BMC* and *NUC* (16 copies).

613. Cobbett, William, 1763-1825.

COTTAGE ECONOMY: | CONTAINING | Information relative to the brewing of BEER, making | of BREAD, keeping of COWS, PIGS, BEES, EWES, GOATS, | POULTRY and RABBITS, and relative to other matters | deemed useful in the conducting of the Affairs of a | Labourer's Family. | [short fancy rule] | BY WILLIAM COBBETT. | [short fancy rule] | *LONDON:* | Printed and Published by C. Clement, No. 183, Fleet Street | [short rule] | 1822.

First edition, London 1822, bound from the seven monthly parts published between 1 August 1821 and 1 March 1822 (with no number for February, 1822).
194 x 110 mm. π^2 A-E¹² G-H¹² I⁸ χ^2; 96 leaves, pp. [4] [1] 2-120 [145] 146-207 [208] [i] ii-iv. Published in seven monthly numbers, August 1821-January 1822 and March 1822 (there was no February 1822 number).

Illustrations: Engraved plate illustrating Needham & Co.'s Patent Brewing Machine facing B1ʳ.

Bibliographies: Attar 46.1; Pearl 115; Wheaton and Kelly 1276.

Copies: *BMC* and *NUC* (8 copies). Attar adds National Library of Scotland.

614. Cobbett, William, 1763-1825.

COTTAGE ECONOMY: | CONTAINING | Information relative to the brewing of BEER, making | of BREAD, keeping of COWS, PIGS, BEES, EWES, GOATS, | POULTRY and RABBITS, and relative to other matters | deemed useful in the conducting of the Affairs of a | Labourer's Family; to which are added, instructions | relative to the selecting, the cutting and the bleaching | of the Plants of ENGLISH GRASS and GRAIN, for the | purpose of making HATS and BONNETS. | [short fancy rule] | BY WILLIAM COBBETT. | [short fancy rule] | A NEW EDITION. | [short fancy rule] | *LONDON:* | Printed for J. M. Cobbett, Fleet Street | [short rule] | 1823.

Second edition, London 1823. Originally published, London, 1822 (item 613).

190 x 110 mm. [A]² B-I¹²; 98 leaves, unpaginated. A four page list of Cobbett's publications is bound in at the beginning. Bound in publisher's boards with a printed paper label on the spine.

Illustrations: Engraved frontispiece illustrating three types of English grass.

Bibliographies: Attar 46.2; Pearl 115 in a note; Wheaton and Kelly 1277.

Copies: *BMC* and *NUC* (7 copies). Attar adds Central District Library, Blackburn, Lancashire.

615. Cobbett, William, 1763-1825.

COTTAGE ECONOMY: | CONTAINING | Information relative to the brewing of BEER, making of BREAD, | keeping of COWS, PIGS, BEES, EWES, GOATS, | POULTRY, and | RABBITS, and relative to other matters deemed useful in the con- | ducting of the Affairs of a Labourer's Family; to which are | added, Instructions relative to the selecting, the cutting and the | bleaching of the Plants of ENGLISH GRASS and GRAIN, for the | purpose of making HATS and BONNETS; and also Instructions for | erecting and using Ice-houses, after the Virginian manner. | | [short rule] | BY WILLIAM COBBETT. | [short rule] | A NEW EDITION. | [two short rules] | LONDON: | PUBLISHED BY WILLIAM COBBETT, | 11, BOLT-COURT, FLEET-STREET. | [short rule] | 1831.

New edition, London, 1831. Originally published, London, 1822 (item 613).

185 x 108 mm. A-H^{12} I^4; 100 leaves, unpaginated. Publisher's boards, cloth spine, with printed paper label.

Illustration: Woodcut of an icehouse on H9^r.

Bibliographies: Pearl 115 in a note.

Copies: *BMC*.

616. Cobbett, William, 1763-1835.

THE │ ENGLISH GARDENER; │ OR, │ A TREATISE │ On the Situation, Soil, Enclosing and Laying-Out of Kitchen Gardens; │ on the Making and Managing of Hot-Beds and Green-Houses; and │ on the Propagation and Cultivation of all sorts of Kitchen-Garden │ Plants, and of Fruit-Trees whether of the Garden or the Orchard. │ And also │ On the Formation of Shrubberies and Flower-Gardens; and on the │ Propagation and Cultivation of the several sorts of Shrubs and │ Flowers; concluding with │ A Kalendar, │ Giving Instructions relative to the Sowings, Plantings, Prunings, and │ other labours, to be performed in the Gardens, in each Month of │ the Year. │ [two short rules] │ BY WILLIAM COBBETT. │ [two short rules] │ "I went by the field of the slothful, and by the vineyard of the man void │ "of understanding: and, lo! it was all grown over with thorns, and nettles │ "covered the face thereof, and the stone-wall thereof was broken down. │ "Then I saw and considered it well: I looked upon it, and received in- │ "struction." − Proverbs: Chap. XXIV. Ver. 30. │ PRINTED BY B. BENSLEY, ANDOVER, │ AND │ PUBLISHED BY THE AUTHOR, 183, FLEET STREET, LONDON; │ AND SOLD BY ALL BOOKSELLERS. │ [short rule] │ 1829.

First revised edition, London, 1829, under the new title. Originally published under the title *The American Gardener*, London, 1821 (item 612).

171 x 111 mm. [A]^2 B-U^{12} X^{10}; 240 leaves, unpaginated.

Illustrations: Woodcuts in the text.

Bibliographies: Pearl 150.

Copies: *BMC* and *NUC* (10 copies).

617. Cobbett, William, 1763-1835.

THE | ENGLISH GARDENER; | OR, | A TREATISE | On the Situation, Soil, Enclosing and Laying-Out, of Kitchen Gardens; on the | Making and Managing of Hot-beds and Green-Houses; and on the Propaga- | tion and Cultivation of all sorts of Kitchen-Garden Plants, and of Fruit-Trees | whether of the Garden or the Orchard. | AND ALSO, | On the Formation of Shrubberies and Flower-Gardens; and on the Propagation | and Cultivation of the several sorts of Shrubs and Flowers. | CONCLUDING WITH | A KALENDAR, | Giving Instructions relative to the Sowings, Plantings, Prunings, and other | labours, to be performed in the Gardens, in each Month of the Year. | [short rule] | BY WILLIAM COBBETT, M. P. | FOR OLDHAM. | [short rule] | "I went by the field of the slothful, and by the vineyard of the man void of understanding | "and, lo! it was all grown over with thorns, and nettles covered the face thereof, and the stone- | "wall thereof was broken down. Then I saw and considered it well: I looked upon it, and | "received instruction." – *Proverbs:* chap. xxiv. ver. 30. | [two short rules] | LONDON: | PUBLISHED AT 11, BOLT-COURT, FLEET-STREET; | AND MAY BE HAD OF ALL BOOKSELLERS. | [short rule] | 1833.

Second revised edition, London, 1833. Originally published under the title *The American Gardener*, London, 1821 (item 612) and in the revised edition under this title, London, 1829 (item 616).

202 x 126 mm. [A]² B-Y⁸ Z1; 171 leaves, pp. [4] [1] 2-338.

Illustrations: Engraved folding plate of a garden plan and numerous woodcuts in the text.

Bibliographies: Pearl 150 in a note.

Copies: *BMC* and *NUC* (8 copies).

618. Cobbett, William, 1763-1835.

A TREATISE | ON | COBBETT'S CORN, | Containing Instructions for Propagating and Cultivating the | Plant, and for Harvesting and Preserving the Crop; | AND ALSO | An Account of the several Uses to which the Produce is | applied, with Minute Directions relative to each Mode of | Application. | [short rule] | BY WILLIAM COBBETT. | [short rule] | "Men of the greatest learning, have spent their time in contriving instruments | "to measure the immense distance of the stars, and in finding out the dimensions | "and even the weight of the planets. They think it more eligible to study the │ "art of ploughing the sea with ships, than of tilling the land with ploughs. │ "They bestow the utmost of their skill, learnedly to pervert the natural use of │ "all the elements, for the destruction of their own species by the bloody art of │ "war; and some waste their whole lives in studying how to arm death with │ "new engines of horror, and inventing an infinite variety of slaughter, but think │ "it *beneath* men of learning (who only are capable of doing it), to employ their │ "learned labours in the invention of new, or even in improving the old, means │ "for the increasing of bread." – *Tull's Husbandry.* │ [two short rules] │ LONDON: │ PUBLISHED BY WILLIAM COBBETT, 183, FLEET-STREET. │ [short rule] │ 1828.

First edition, London, 1828.

186 x 112 mm. [A]^2 B-N^{12} O^2; 148 leaves, unpaginated.

Illustrations: Woodcuts of Cobbett's corn on B6^v, F12^r, and G8^r.

Bibliographies: Pearl 154; Wheaton and Kelly 1285.

Copies: *BMC* and *NUC* (17 copies).

619. Cochrane, James.

THE │ MODERN RECEIPT BOOK: │ BEING A COLLECTION OF NEARLY │ EIGHT HUNDRED VALUABLE RECEIPTS, │ *ARRANGED UNDER THEIR RESPECTIVE HEADS:* │ VIZ. │ DOMESTIC ECONOMY, BLEACHING AND SCOURING, DYEING, TANNING, │ CEMENTS, VARNISHES, LACKERS, │ RURAL ECONOMY, MANAGEMENT OF BEES, GARDENING, BREWING, │ DISTILLING, PERFUMERY, MAKING WINES, │ THE METALLIC ARTS, (INCLUDING GILDING, SILVERING, AND PLATING,) │ DRAWING AND PAINTING, &c. &c. │ [short rule] │ THE │ Whole carefully selected from the latest and best Authorities, │ AND ENRICHED BY │ MANY ORIGINAL AND VALUABLE COMMUNICATIONS, │ Confirmed by actual Experiment or Personal Observation. │ [short rule] │ BY JAMES COCHRANE. │ [short rule] │ LONDON: │ PRINTED FOR │ *A. K NEWMAN AND CO. LEADENHALL-STREET; AND DEAN AND* │ *MUNDAY, THREADNEEDLE-STREET.* │ [short rule] │ 1824.

Engraved title:

ARCANA OF THE ARTS, │ *OR* │ MODERN RECEIPT BOOK. │ A COLLECTION OF NEARLY │ *Eight Hundred Valuable Receipts* │ *WRITTEN, SELECTED &*

ARRANGED | 𝔅𝔶 𝔍𝔞𝔪𝔢𝔰 ℭ𝔬𝔠𝔥𝔯𝔞𝔫𝔢. | [vignette] | LONDON, | *PRINTED FOR A.K. NEWMAN & Cᵒ. LEADENHALL STREET* | AND | DEAN & MUNDAY, THREADNEEDLE STREET

First edition, London, 1824. Oxford, p. 149 dates this work 1821. However, as the preface is dated 1 March 1824 and the engraved frontispiece is dated June 1, 1824, Oxford must have misread the date.

168 x 115 mm. [A]² B-Aa⁶ Bb⁴; 144 leaves, pp. [*4*] [13] 14-295 [296]. Bound in publisher's printed boards.

Illustrations: Engraved frontispiece and title-page by H. Adlard after drawings by W. H. Brooke and H. Corbould, dated June 1, 1824.

Bibliographies: Oxford, p. 149, misdating the book 1821.

Copies: *BMC* and *NUC* (New York Public Library only).

620.   Cocke, Thomas.

[with a border of two rules] Kitchin-Physick. | OR, | Advice to the POOR, | By way of | DIALOGUE | Betwixt | [in two columns: column one] *Philanthropos*, | *Eugenius*, | *Lazarus* | [between the columns] }{ | [column two] Physician, | Apothecary, | Patient. [end of columns] | WITH | Rules and Directions, how to prevent sick- | ness, and cure Diseases by Diet, and such | things as are daily sold in the Market: | As also, for the better enabling of Nurses, | and such as attend sick people; there be- | ing nothing as yet extant (though much | desired) of this Nature. | [rule] | *Parve nec invideo*, &c. Ovid de Trist. | [rule] | *London*, Printed for *J. B.* who desires the | Reader to take notice, that he is the next | week to return this Book to the | Clark, or pay 12d.

Title-page of the second part:

[within a border of two rules] *Miscelanea Medica:* | OR, A | SUPPLEMENT | TO | Kitchin-Physick; | To which is added, | A short DISCOURSE | ON | STOVING | AND | BATHING: | WITH | Some transient and occasional | Notes on Dr. *George Thomp-* | *sons* Γαλήνο – Μεμψίς. | [rule] | — *Nec lex est justior ulla* | *Quam necis artificis arte perire sua.* | [rule] |*LONDON,* | Printed in the year 1675.

First edition of each part, London, 1675. Note: While Wing gives separate numbers of each part, *Kitchin-Physick* ends with the statement "Finis part the first" and the two are consistenly found together. The first (and only) edition of *Miscelanea Medica* was issued with the several later editions of *Kitchin-Physick*.

8vo. [A]⁴ B-F⁸ G⁴, ²A-D⁸; 80 leaves, pp. [8] 1-87 [88], ²[8] 1-52 [4]. First leaf (blank or half-title?) wanting in this copy.

Illustration: Folding woodcut, with letterpress text, showing and explaining a "Vaporarium." Supplied in facsimile in this copy.

Bibliographies: Wing C4791A and Wing C4793. Oxford, p. 38, cites a London, 1676, edition.

Copies: *NUC* (Folger Library, National Library of Medicine, and Yale). Wing records two copies of the first edition of *Kitchin-Physick* (Folger Library and National Library of Medicine) and eight copies of *Miscelanea Medica* issued with later editions of the first work.

621. Cogan, Thomas, 1545?-1607.

THE HAVEN │ OF HEALTH: │ Chiefely gathered for the comfort of Stu- │ dents, and consequently of all those that haue a │ care of their health, amplified vpon fiue words of │ *Hippocrates*, written *Epid. 6. Labour, Cibus,* │ *Potio, Somnus, Venus:* By *Thomas Coghan* │ master of Artes, & Bacheler │ of Phisicke. │ *Hereunto is added a Preseruation from the Pestilence,* │ *With a short Censure of the late sicknes at Oxford.* │ *Ecclesiasticus, Cap.*37. 30. │ By surfet haue manie perished: but he that dieteth │ himselfe prolongeth his life. │ [woodcut] │ AT LONDON │ Printed by Henrie Midleton, │ *for William Norton.* │ 1584.

First edition, London, 1584.

4to. ¶-¶¶⁴ A-P⁴; 160 leaves, pp. [16] 1-284 [20].

Illustration: Woodcut device of William Norton on the title-page and arms of Edward Seymor, Earl of Hertford on verso of title-page.

Bibliographies: Noling, p. 110; *STC* 5478.

Copies: *BMC* and *NUC* (5 copies). *STC* (10 copies).

622. Cogan, Thomas, 1545?-1607.

[ornament] | THE HAVEN OF | HEALTH, | Chiefly made for the comfort of
Students, | *and consequently for all those that haue a care of* | their health, amplified
vpon fiue words of | HIPPOCRATES, *written* Epid. 6. | Labour, Meat, Drinke, |
Sleepe, Venus: | *By* THOMAS COGAN, *Master of Artes, and* | *Bacheler of Physicke:*
and now of late | *corrected and augmented.* | Hereunto is added a Preseruation from
the Pestilence: | with a short censure of the late sicknesse | at *Oxford.* | *Ecclesiasticus,*
cap. 37.30. | By surfet haue many perished: but he that dieteth | himselfe prolongeth
his life. | [ornament] | LONDON, | Printed by MELCH. BRADVVOOD | for IOHN
NORTON. | 1605.

Fifth edition, London, 1605. Originally published, London, 1584 (item 621).

4to. ❧⁸ A-P⁸ Q² R-S⁸; 146 leaves, pp. [*16*] 1-272, 272-275 [i.e. 276] [*12*].

Bibliographies: Craig 19; *STC* 5482; Simon BG 360.

Copies: *BMC, BNC,* and *NUC* (Huntington and 3 copies at Folger). *STC* (10 copies).

623. Cole, Mary.

THE THIRD EDITION VERY MUCH IMPROVED. | [short fancy rule] | THE |
LADY's COMPLETE GUIDE; | OR, | COOKERY | IN ALL ITS BRANCHES. |
CONTAINING | The most approved Receipts, confirmed by Observation and Practice,
| in every reputable English Book of Cookery now extant; besides a | great Variety of
others which have never before been offered to the | Public. Also several translated
from the Productions of COOKS of | Eminence who have published in FRANCE,
particularly the DUKE | DE NIVERNOIS's, M. COMMO's HISTORIE DE
CUISINE, M. DI- | SANG's MAITRE D'HOTEL, M. VALOIS, and M.
DELATOUR, with | their respective Names to each Receipt; which, with the
ORIGINAL | ARTICLES, form the most complete System of Cookery ever yet |
exhibited, under the following Heads, viz. | [in three columns: column one]
ROASTING, | BOILING, | MADE-DISHES, | FRYING, | BROILING, | POTTING,
| FRICASSEES, | RAGOUTS, | [column two] SOUPS, | SAUCES, | GRAVIES, |
HASHES, | STEWS, | PUDDINGS, | CUSTARDS, | CAKES, | [column three]
TARTS, | PIES, | PASTIES, | CHEESECAKES. | JELLIES, | PICKLING, |
PRESERVING, | CONFECTIONARY, &c. [end columns] | To which is added, in
order to render it as complete and perfect as possible, | A LIST OF EVERY THING
IN SEASON, | SEVERAL BILLS OF FARE, AND AN ELEGANT COLLECTION
OF | LIGHT DISHES FOR SUPPER. | ALSO | THE COMPLETE BREWER; |

CONTAINING | Familiar Instructions for brewing all Sorts of Beer and Ale; including the proper | Management of the Vault or Cellar. | LIKEWISE | THE FAMILY PHYSICIAN; | Consisting of a considerable Collection of approved Prescriptions by MEAD, | SYDENHAM, TISSOT, FOTHERGIL, ELLIOT, BUCHAN, and Others. | [two rules] | BY MRS. MARY COLE, | COOK TO THE RIGHT HON. THE EARL OF DROGHEDA. | [two rules] | LONDON: | PRINTED FOR G. KEARSLEY, NO. 46, FLEET-STREET. | 1791.

Third edition, London, 1791. Originally published, London, 1788. See also item 734.

8vo. "[A]"-"[C]"^{8} "[D]"^{4} B-Ee^8 Ff-Hh^4 Ii^2; 258 leaves, pp. [i-iv] v-lvi [1] 2-460. This copy wanting B8 and C1 (pp. xxxi-xxxiv).

Bibliographies: Maclean, p. 29; Noling, p. 111. Axford, p. 244, Bitting, p. 94, and Simon BG 363 cite 1788 edition and Oxford, p. 117, cites the 1789 edition.

Copies: *NUC* (Kansas State University, New York Academy of Medicine, and New York Public Library). Maclean adds Brotherton Library and Wellcome Library.

624. A Collection of Ordinances.

A COLLECTION | OF | ORDINANCES AND REGULATIONS | FOR THE | GOVERNMENT OF THE ROYAL HOUSEHOLD, | MADE IN DIVERS REIGNS. | FROM KING EDWARD III. TO KING WILLIAM AND QUEEN MARY. | ALSO | RECEIPTS IN ANCIENT COOKERY. | [seal] | LONDON, | PRINTED FOR THE SOCIETY OF ANTIQUARIES BY JOHN NICHOLS: | SOLD BY MESSIEURS WHITE AND SON; ROBSON; LEIGH AND SOTHEBY; | BROWNE; AND EGERTON'S. | MDCCXC.

First edition, London, 1790.

4to. a^2 b-c^4 d^2 B^4 C^4 (C1 + *C^4 *D^6 *E^4 *F^2) D-Ooo^4 Ppp^2; pp. [i- ii] iii-xxii [1-2] 3-27 [28] [2] 27-39 [40] [2] 15-170, 169-476 (=532 pp.).

Bibliographies: Bitting, p. 532; Maclean, p. 30; Oberlé (1) 97; Oxford, p. 119; Pennell, p. 164; Wheaton and Kelly 3757.

Copies: *BMC* and *NUC* (20 copies). Maclean locates six copies, three in Britain and three in the United States.

625. Collingwood, Francis, and John Woollams.

THE | UNIVERSAL COOK, | AND | *City and Country Housekeeper.* | CONTAINING ALL THE | VARIOUS BRANCHES OF COOKERY: | THE DIFFERENT METHODS OF DRESSING | *Butchers Meat, Poultry, Game, and Fish;* | AND OF PREPARING | GRAVIES, CULLICES, SOUPS, AND BROTHS; | TO DRESS | ROOTS AND VEGETABLES, | AND TO PREPARE | *Little elegant Dishes for Suppers or light Repasts:* | TO MAKE ALL SORTS OF | PIES, PUDDINGS, PANCAKES, AND FRITTERS; | CAKES, PUFFS, AND BISCUITS; CHEESECAKES, TARTS, AND | CUSTARDS; CREAMS AND JAMS; BLANC MANGE, FLUMMERY, | ELEGANT ORNAMENTS, JELLIES, AND SYLLABUBS. | *The various Articles in* | CANDYING, DRYING, PRESERVING, AND PICKLING. | THE PREPARATION OF | HAMS, TONGUES, BACON &c. | DIRECTIONS FOR | TRUSSING POULTRY, CARVING, AND MARKETING. | THE MAKING AND MANAGEMENT OF | *Made Wines, Cordial Waters, and Malt Liquours.* | Together with | Directions for Baking Bread, the Management of Poultry and the Dairy, and the | Kitchen and Fruit Garden; with a Catalogue of the various Articles | in Season in the different Months of the Year. | *Besides a Variety of* | USEFUL AND INTERESTING TABLES. | The Whole Embellished with | The Heads of the Authors, Bills of Fare for every Month in the Year, and | proper Subjects for the Improvement of the Art of Carving, | elegantly engraved on fourteen Copper-Plates. | [rule] | BY FRANCIS COLLINGWOOD, AND JOHN WOOLLAMS, | Principal Cooks at the Crown and Anchor Tavern in the Strand, | *Late from the London Tavern.* | [two rules] | LONDON: | PRINTED BY R. NOBLE, FOR J. SCATCHERD AND J. WHITAKER, | NO. 12, AVE-MARIA-LANE. | [short rule] | 1792.

First edition, London, 1792.

8vo. A^8 b^4 c^2 B-Ff^8 Gg^2; 240 leaves, pp. [28] [1] 2-451 [452].

Illustrations: Engraved frontispiece portraits of the authors, twelve engraved plates showing bills of fare and one illustrating carving.

Bibliographies: Craig 20; Maclean, p. 30; Noling, p. 113; Oxford, p. 120; Pennell, p. 165; Simon BG 365; Wheaton and Kelly 1309.

Copies: *BMC* and *NUC* (Radcliffe and New York Academy of Medicine). Maclean adds the National Library of Scotland and Glasgow University Library in Scotland and Cornell, Kansas State University and Radcliffe in the United States.

626. Collingwood, Francis, and John Woollams.

THE | UNIVERSAL COOK, | AND | *City and Country Housekeeper.* | CONTAINING ALL THE | VARIOUS BRANCHES OF COOKERY: | THE DIFFERENT METHODS OF DRESSING | *Butchers Meat, Poultry, Game, and Fish;* | AND OF PREPARING | GRAVIES, CULLICES, SOUPS, AND BROTHS; | TO DRESS | ROOTS AND VEGETABLES, | AND TO PREPARE | *Little elegant Dishes for Suppers or light Repasts*: | TO MAKE ALL SORTS OF | PIES, PUDDINGS, PANCAKES, AND FRITTERS; | CAKES, PUFFS, AND BISCUITS; CHEESECAKES, TARTS, AND | CUSTARDS; CREAMS AND JAMS; BLANC MANGE, FLUMMERY, | ELEGANT ORNAMENTS, JELLIES, AND SYLLABUBS. | *The various Articles in* | CANDYING, DRYING, PRESERVING, AND PICKLING. | THE PREPARATION OF | HAMS, TONGUES, BACON, &c. | DIRECTIONS FOR | TRUSSING POULTRY, CARVING, AND MARKETING. | THE MAKING AND MANAGEMENT OF | *Made Wines, Cordial Waters, and Malt Liquours.* | Together with | Directions for Baking Bread, the Management of Poultry and the Dairy, and | Kitchen and Fruit Garden; with a Catalogue of the various Articles | in Season in the different Months of the Year. | *Besides a Variety of* | USEFUL AND INTERESTING TABLES. | The Whole Embellished with | The Heads of the Authors, Bills of Fare for every Month in the Year, and | proper Subjects for the Improvement of the Art of Carving, | elegantly engraved on fourteen Copper-Plates. | [rule] | BY FRANCIS COLLINGWOOD, AND JOHN WOOLLAMS, | Principal Cooks at the Crown and Anchor Tavern in the Strand, | *Late from the London Tavern.* | [short fancy rule] | THE SECOND EDITION. | [two rules] | LONDON: | PRINTED BY R. NOBLE, FOR J. SCATCHERD, | NO. 12, AVE-MARIA-LANE. | [short rule] | 1797.

Second edition, London, 1797. Originally published, London, 1792 (item 625).

8vo. A⁸ b⁶ B-Ff⁸ Gg²; 240 leaves, pp. [*28*] [1] 2-451 [452].

Illustrations: Engraved frontispiece of the two authors and twelve engraved plates of bills of fare.

Bibliographies: Maclean, p. 30; Oxford, p. 120, in a note; Schraemli (1) 118; Simon BG 365; Wheaton and Kelly 1310.

Copies: *NUC* (Boston Public Library and Yale).

627. Collins, John, 1625-1683.

[within a border of two rules] SALT │ AND │ FISHERY, │ *A Discourse thereof* │ Insisting on the following HEADS. │ 1. The several *ways* of making *Salt* in *England*, and Foreign │ Parts. │ 2. The *Character* and *Qualities* good and bad, of these several │ sorts of *Salt*, English refin'd asserted to be much better than │ any Foreign. │ 3. The *Catching* and *Curing*, or *Salting* of the most Eminent or │ Staple sorts of *Fish*, for long or short keeping. │ 4. The Salting of *Flesh*. │ 5. The Cookery of *Fish* and *Flesh*. │ 6. Extraordinary Experiments in preserving *Butter, Flesh, Fish,* │ *Fowl, Fruit,* and *Roots,* fresh and sweet for long keeping. │ 7. The Case and Sufferings of the *Saltworkers*. │ 8. Proposals for their *Relief*, and for the advancement of the │ *Fishery*, the *Woollen, Tin*, and divers other *Manufactures*. │ [rule] │ By *JOHN COLLINS*, Accomptant │ to the ROYAL FISHERY Company. │ *E Reg. Soc. Philomath.* │ [rule] │ *LONDON*, Printed by *A. Godbid*, and *F. Playford*, and are to be Sold by │ Mr. *Robert Horne* at the *Royal Exchange*, Mr. *John Kersey*, and Mr. *Hen-* │ *ry Faithorn*, at the *Rose* in St. *Pauls Church-yard*, Mr. *William Bury, Globe-* │ *maker*, at the *Globe* near *Charing-Cross*, 1682.

First edition, London, 1682. Third of three variant imprints recorded in Wing.

4to. A-V⁴; 80 leaves, pp. [*8*] 1-32, 49-164 [*4*].

Bibliographies: Wing C5380B.

Copies: *BMC* and *NUC* (9 copies). Wing adds Christ Church, Oxford, Magdalene College, Cambridge, and Wellcome Library.

The Compleat Cook see M., W (items 834-837).

628. The Complete Family-Piece.

THE │ Complete Family-Piece: │ AND, │ Country GENTLEMAN, and FARMER'S, │ BEST GUIDE. │ [rule] │ In Three PARTS. │ [rule] │ PART I. Containing, │ A very choice and valuable COLLECTION of above │ *One Thousand* well-experienced *Practical* Family-RECEIPTS in *Physick* │ and *Surgery*; *Cookery, Pastry* and *Confectionary*, with a complete Bill of │ *Fare* for every Month in the Year, and *Instructions* for placing the Dishes on │ a Table; for *Pickling* and *Preserving* all Sorts of *Fruits, Tongues, Hams,* &c. │ for *Distilling* and *Fermenting* of all *Compound, Simple Waters* and *Spirits*; │ for making *Mum, Cyder* and *Perry, Mead* and *Metheglin*; and for making │ and preserving all Sorts of excellent *English Wines*; with good and useful │ *Instructions* for *Brewing* fine, strong, good, wholesome and palatable *Drinks*, │ as

Beers, Ales, &c. in *small Quantities*, and at *easy Rates*, for the Use of all | *private Families*; with divers other useful and valuable *Receipts* interspersed | through the Whole, particularly *Dr. Mead's* for the Cure of the Bite of a | *Mad Dog*: Many of which were never before *Printed*, and the other expe- | rimentally taken from the latest and very best *Authorities*; and being all | regularly digested under their proper *Heads*, are divied into six different | *Chapters*. | PART II. Containing, | I. Full Instructions to be observed in HUNTING, COURSING, | SETTING and SHOOTING; with an *Account* of the several *Kinds* of | DOGS necessary for those *Diversions*, and RECEIPTS for the Cure of | all common Distempers to which they are liable; as also Receipts for the | *Cleaning* and *Preserving* of *Boots, Fire-Arms*, &c. | II. Cautions, Rules and Directions to be taken and observed | in FISHING; with the Manner of making and preserving of *Rods*, | *Lines, Floats, Artificial Flies*, &c. and for chusing and preserving several | *Sorts* of curious BAITS. | III. A full and complete *Kalender* of all WORK necessary | to be done in the FRUIT, FLOWER, and KITCHEN GARDENS, | GREEN-HOUSE &c. with the PRODUCE of each, in every *Month* | throughout the whole Year. | PART III. Containing, | Practical Rules, and Methods, for the *Improving* of | LAND, and *Managing* a FARM in all its *Branches*; with several curious | Receipts for *Brining, Liming* and preparing *Wheat, Barley, Oats*, &c. for | *Sowing*; excellent Receipts for destroying of *Moles, Rats* and *Mice*; a great | Number of choice RECEIPTS for the Cure of all common Distempers in- | cident to all Sorts of CATTLE; Directions of *Painting*; Instructions | for keeping *Bees, Tame Rabbits*, and *Pidgeons*; and a complete *Kalender* | of all *Business* necessary to be done in the FIELD, YARD, &c. by the | *Farmer*, in every *Month* throughout the Year. | With a complete Alphabetical INDEX to each PART. | [rule] | The SECOND EDITION Improved. | [rule] | *LONDON*: Printed for *A. Bettesworth and C. Hitch*; *C. Rivington*; | *S. Birt*; *T. Longman*; and *J. Clarke* in *Duck-Lane*. 1737. | (Price bound 3 *s.* 6 *d.*)

"Second edition," London, 1737. Originally published, London, 1736. Maclean records two editions, one published by J. Roberts and the other by T. Longman, J. Clarke and S. Birt, dated 1736, followed by this edition of 1737.

12mo. A^6 B-Z^{12} Aa-Ee^6; 300 leaves, pp. [i-ii] iii-xii [1] 2-526 [62].

Bibliographies: Bitting, p. 534; Maclean, p. 33; Vicaire 199; Wheaton and Kelly 1349. Axford, p. 74, Oxford, p. 66, and Simon BG 374 record the London, Longman, 1736 edition.

Copies: *BMC* (lacking title-page and incorrectly cataloged as 1736 edition) and *NUC* (Harvard, Kansas State University, and Yale). Maclean adds Brotherton and Wellcome Libraries.

629. Cook, Ann.

PROFESSED | COOKERY: | CONTAINING | [in two columns: column one]
BOILING, | ROASTING, | PASTRY, | PRESERVING, | [two vertical rules] |
[column two] POTTING, | PICKLING, | MADE-WINES, | GELLIES, and [end
columns] | Part of CONFECTIONARIES. | WITH | An ESSAY upon the LADY's
ART | of COOKERY. | [rule] | By *ANN COOK*, | Teacher of the true ART of
COOKERY. | [rule] | [ornament] | | [two rules] | *NEWCASTLE UPON TYNE:* |
Printed by J. WHITE, and sold by the AUTHOR, | at her House in the *Groat-market*.
M.DCC.LIV. | Price FIVE SHILLINGS.

First edition, Newcastle upon Tyne, 1754.

8vo. $\pi 1$ a^4 A-Y^4 Z^4 (-Z4=$\pi 1$); 96 leaves, pp. [i-ii] iii-x [1] 2- 173 [174-182].

Bibliographies: Maclean, p. 35, locating no copies of the first edition. Axford, p.
334. Bitting, p. 98, and Craig 25, record the second edition, London, 1755, and
Oxford, p. 91, Simon BG 383 and Vicaire 210 record the third edition, London
[ca.1760].

Copies: No other copy of the first edition located. *NUC* records the second edition
(Library of Congress only) and the third edition (Wellesley College only).

630. Cookery and Domestic Economy.

A WORK OF PLAIN PRACTICAL UTILITY. | [short rule] | COOKERY | AND
DOMESTIC ECONOMY, | FOR | YOUNG HOUSEWIVES. | 𝔍𝔫𝔠𝔩𝔲𝔡𝔦𝔫𝔤
𝔇𝔦𝔯𝔢𝔠𝔱𝔦𝔬𝔫𝔰 𝔣𝔬𝔯 𝔖𝔢𝔯𝔟𝔞𝔫𝔱𝔰. | BY THE MISTRESS OF A FAMILY. | [publisher's
monogram] | EDINBURGH: | PUBLISHED BY WILLIAM AND ROBERT
CHAMBERS. | 1845.

New edition, Edinburgh, 1845. Bitting, p. 537, records a "new and improved
edition," London [1862] which she describes as the second edition, stating that the first
was published in 1841. The preface in the Gernon copy is dated March 1838 which
may argue an earlier date for the first edition.

169 x 104 mm. [A]^8 B-H^8; 64 leaves, pp. [i-iii] iv [5] 6-128.

Bibliographies: Wheaton and Kelly 1381.

Copies: Wheaton and Kelly (Radcliffe only).

631. Cooper, Ambrose.

THE | COMPLETE | DISTILLER: | CONTAINING, | [in two columns: column one]
I. The Method of perform- | ing the various Processes of | Distillation, with Descrip- |
tions of the several Instru- | ments: The whole Doc- | trine of Fermentation: | The
manner of drawing | Spirits from Malt, Raisins, | Molosses, Sugar, &c. and | of
rectifying them: With | Instructions for imitating | to the greatest Perfection | [two
vertical rules] | [column two] both the Colour and Fla- | vour of *French* Brandies. | II.
The manner of distilling | all Kinds of Simple Wa- | ters from Plants, Flowers, | &c. |
III. The Method of making | all the compound Waters | and rich Cordials so largely |
imported from *France* and | *Italy*; as likewise all those | now made in *Great Britain*.
[end columns] | To which are added, | Accurate Descriptions of the several Drugs, |
Plants, Flowers, Fruits, &c. used by Distil- | lers, and Instructions for chusing the best
of | each Kind. | The Whole delivered in the plainest manner, for the | Use both of
Distillers and *Private Families*. | [rule] | By *A.* COOPER, DISTILLER. | [rule] |
LONDON: | Printed for P. VAILLANT in the *Strand*; and R. | GRIFFITHS in
Pater-Noster-Row. | [short rule] | M. DCC. LVII.

First edition, London, 1757. Maclean records two issues of the first edition, one with
a briefer title and this, listed second, with a more extended title. The second edition
appeared in 1760.

8vo. A-S^8 T^4; 148 leaves, pp. [*16*] [1] 2-266 [267-280].

Bibliographies: Gabler, p. 65; Maclean, p. 35; Maggs, 266; Simon BB II. 153; Simon
BG 388.

Copies: *BMC* and *NUC* (6 copies). Maclean adds Wellcome Library.

631a. Cooper, Ambrose.

THE | COMPLETE | DISTILLER: | CONTAINING, | [in two columns, column one]
I. The Method of performing | the various Processes of Distil- | lation, with
Descriptions of | the several Instruments: The | whole Doctrine of Fermenta- | tion:
The manner of draw- | ing Spirits from Malt, Rai- | sins, Molasses, Sugar, &c. and |
of rectifying them: With In- | structions for imitating, to the | greatest Perfection,
both the | [vertical double rule] | [column two] Colour and Flavour of *French* |

Brandies. | II. The manner of distilling | all Kinds of Simple Waters | from Plants, Flowers, &c. | III. The Method of making | all the compound Waters and | rich Cordials so largely im- | ported from *France* and *Italy*; | as likewise all those now made | in *Great Britain*. [end columns] | To which are added, | Accurate Descriptions of the several Drugs, Plants, | Flowers, Fruits, &c. used by Distillers, and Instruc- | tions for chusing the best of each Kind. | The whole delivered in the plainest manner, for the Use both of | *Distillers* and *Private Families* | [rule] | By AMBROSE COOPER, DISTILLER. | [rule] | The SECOND EDITION, | With many ADDITIONS. | [double rule] | *LONDON:* | Printed for P. VAILLANT, and R. GRIFFITHS, | in the *Strand*. 1760.

Second edition, London, 1760. Originally published, London, 1757 (item 631).

8vo. A-T^8 U^4; 156 leaves, pp. [*16*] [1] 2-280 [*16*]. P. 280 misnumbered "283". Last leaf, blank?, wanting in this copy.

Illustrations: Folding copperplate frontispiece illustrating distilling apparatus.

Bibliographies: Maclean, p. 36.

Copies: *NUC* (Library of Congress, Union Library Catalog of Pennsylvania, and University of Wisconsin). Maclean adds Wellcome Institute.

632. Copley, Esther Hewlett.

THE | COOK'S COMPLETE GUIDE, | ON THE PRINCIPLES | OF | 𝔉rugality, 𝔠omfort, and 𝔈legance | INCLUDING THE | ART OF CARVING, | AND | THE MOST APPROVED METHOD OF SETTING-OUT A TABLE | EXPLAINED BY NUMEROUS COPPER-PLATE ENGRAVINGS, | INSTRUCTIONS FOR | PRESERVING HEALTH, AND ATTAINING OLD AGE; | WITH DIRECTIONS FOR BREEDING AND FATTENING ALL SORTS OF POULTRY, AND FOR THE | MANAGEMENT OF BEES, RABBITS, PIGS, &c. &c. | RULES FOR CULTIVATING A GARDEN, | AND | NUMEROUS USEFUL MISCELLANEOUS RECEIPTS. | [short rule] | BY A LADY, | AUTHORESS OF "COTTAGE COMFORTS." | [short rule] | 𝔏ondon: | GEORGE VIRTUE, 26, IVY LANE, | PATERNOSTER-ROW.

Engraved title-page:

THE | NEW LONDON COOKERY. | *AND* | COMPLETE DOMESTIC GUIDE, | BY A LADY. | [vignette] | LONDON: | PUBLISHED BY G. VIRTUE, 26, IVY LANE.

First edition, printing with George Virtue imprint on the printed title-page, London, ca. 1827.

214 x 130 mm. [A]² π1 B-5N⁴ 5O⁴ (-5O₄=π1); 422 leaves, pp. [i- iii] iv [v-vi] [1] 2-838.

Illustrations: Engraved frontispiece, title-page, and ten plates illustrating trussing, carving and bills of fare. The first bill of fare plate has the imprint: *London, Published by G. Virtue, 26 Ivy Lane & Bath St. Bristol, 1827.* The part of the imprint after Ivy Lane is buffed out on the next five plates.

Bibliographies: Bitting, p. 99, describes three copies, one as this copy and the other two adding Bath Street, Bristol, to the publisher's imprint; Craig 26.

Copies: *NUC* (New York Public Library only).

633. Copley, Esther Hewlett.

THE | COOK'S COMPLETE GUIDE, | ON THE PRINCIPLES | OF | 𝔉rugality, Comfort, and 𝔈legance | INCLUDING THE | ART OF CARVING, | AND | THE MOST APPROVED METHOD OF SETTING-OUT A TABLE, | EXPLAINED BY NUMEROUS COPPER-PLATE ENGRAVINGS. | INSTRUCTIONS FOR | Preserving Health, and attaining Old Age, | WITH | DIRECTIONS FOR BREEDING AND FATTENING ALL SORTS OF POULTRY, AND FOR THE MANAGEMENT OF | BEES, RABBITS, PIGS, &c. &c. | RULES FOR CULTIVATING A GARDEN, | AND | NUMEROUS USEFUL MISCELLANEOUS RECEIPTS. | [short rule] | BY A LADY, | AUTHORESS OF "COTTAGE COMFORTS." | [short rule] | London: | PUBLISHED BY TALLIS AND CO. | AND SOLD BY G. VIRTUE, 26, IVY LANE.

Engraved title-page:

THE | NEW LONDON COOKERY. | *AND* | COMPLETE DOMESTIC GUIDE, | BY A LADY. | [vignette] | LONDON: | PUBLISHED BY G. VIRTUE, 26, IVY LANE. | AND BATH STREET BRISTOL.

First edition, later printing with Tallis and Co. and G. Virtue imprint on the printed title-page, London, ca. 1836. Originally published, London, ca. 1827 with G. Virtue imprint (item 632).

215 x 130 mm. [A]^2 B-5O^4; 422 leaves, pp. [i-iii] iv [1] 2-838 [2].

Illustrations: Engraved frontispiece, title-page, and ten plates illustrating trussing, carving and bills of fare. The plate facing p. 11 has the imprint: *London. Published by Geo. Virtue, 26 Ivy Lane 1836.* Of the six plates with bills of fare, three have the imprint: *London Published by G. Virtue, 26, Ivy Lane & Bath St. Bristol, 1827* and the other three have everything after Ivy Lane buffed out.

Bibliographies: This printing unrecorded in the bibliographies consulted. Bitting, p. 99, describes three copies, one as item 632, the other two adding Bath Street, Bristol, to the publisher's imprint.

Copies: No other copy with this imprint located. *NUC* (Library of Congress only) describes the Bitting copy with the G. Virtue imprint in which the plate facing p. 11 is dated 1836.

634. Copley, Esther Hewlett.

COTTAGE COOKERY. | [short rule] | BY ESTHER COPLEY, | AUTHOR OF "COTTAGE COMFORTS" ETC., ETC. | [short rule] | 𝕽𝖊𝖕𝖗𝖎𝖓𝖙𝖊𝖉 𝖋𝖗𝖔𝖒 𝖙𝖍𝖊 "𝕱𝖆𝖒𝖎𝖑𝖞 𝕰𝖈𝖔𝖓𝖔𝖒𝖎𝖘𝖙." | [short rule] | LONDON: | GROOMBRIDGE & SONS, PATERNOSTER ROW. | [short rule] | 1849.

First edition, London, 1849. Reprinted from *The Family Economist*, a London periodical.

146 x 90 mm. [A]^2 B-K^6 L^8(L4+1); 65 leaves, pp. [i-iii] iv [3] 4-127 [128].

Bibliographies: Simon BG 392.

Copies: No other copy of the first edition located. *NUC* records an undated edition (New York Public Library only).

635. Copley, Esther Hewlett.

THE | HOUSEKEEPER'S GUIDE; | OR | A PLAIN AND PRACTICAL SYSTEM | OF | 𝔇𝔬𝔪𝔢𝔰𝔱𝔦𝔠 𝔠𝔬𝔬𝔨𝔢𝔯𝔶. | [short rule] | BY THE AUTHOR OF "COTTAGE COMFORTS." | [two short rules] | LONDON: | JACKSON AND WALFORD, | ST. PAUL'S CHURCH YARD. | [short rule] | 1834.

Engraved title-page:

THE | *HOUSEKEEPER'S GUIDE,* | OR | A PLAIN & PRACTICAL SYSTEM | OF | 𝔇𝔬𝔪𝔢𝔰𝔱𝔦𝔠 𝔠𝔬𝔬𝔨𝔢𝔯𝔶, | *BY ESTHER COPLEY,* | *Author of "Cottage Comforts" &c.* | [vignette] | 𝔏𝔬𝔫𝔡𝔬𝔫. | *PRINTED FOR* | JACKSON & WALFORD, 18 ST. PAULS CHURCH YARD | 1834.

First edition, London, 1834.

160 x 102 mm. [a]² b⁴ B-CC⁸ DD⁴; 210 leaves, pp. [i-iii] iv-xi [xii] [1] 2-407 [408].

Illustrations: Engraved frontispiece, title-page, and five plates illustrating carving.

Bibliographies: Axford, p. 213; Bitting, p. 98; Oxford, p. 167; Simon BG 391.

Copies: *NUC* (Library of Congress only).

636. The Country Magazine.

THE | COUNTRY MAGAZINE: | OR, | GENTLEMAN and LADY'S | POCKET COMPANION; | CONTAINING | The COOK'S KALENDAR, being Rules and | Directions in every Part of COOKERY, taken from | the best Authors both *English* and *French*, with | some choice Receipts never before made publick; | ample and elegant BILLS of FARE for every Month | in the Year; the whole in such a Method as makes | it one of the completest Books of *Cookery* ever yet | published. | To which are added, | Receipts in PASTRY, PICKLING, PRESERVING, DI- | STILLING all Sorts of *Cordials* for the Closet; making all | Sorts of *English* Wines; brewing Beers, Ales, making *Mum,* | *Mead, Metheglin,* &c. | Curious and approved Receipts in *Physick,* useful and necessary | to be had in every Family, particularly for the *Gout,* the *Rheuma-* | *tism, Ague, Asthma, Consumption, Jaundice, Bite of Mad Dogs,* &c. | with Rules taken from Dr. *Cheyne* and others for the Preservation of | *Health* and *Long-Life.* | A GARDENER'S KALENDAR; for every Month in the Year, | shewing all that is to be done in the *Kitchen, Fruit* and *Pleasure* | *Garden,* the *Wilderness,*

Green-House and *Stove.* | Directions in HUSBANDRY and HORSEMANSHIP, with Re- | ceipts for the Cure of all Diseases incident to *Horses, Cows,* and all | other Cattle, *&c.* | ESSAYS on various Subjects, *Religious, Moral,* and | *Political.* | A Collection of SONGS, Epigrams, and other curious Pieces | of Poetry. | [two rules] | *LONDON:* | Printed and Sold by J. READ, in *White-Friar's, Fleetstreet.*

First edition, London, March 1736-February 1737. Twelve monthly issues (all published) with a general title-page and an index added.

8vo. π1 [A]² B-K⁴ [L]² M-S⁴ T² U-Bb⁴ Cc² Dd⁴ [Ee]² Ff-Ll⁴ Mm² Nn⁴ Oo² Pp-Vv⁴ Yy⁴ Zz² 3A-3F⁴ 3G² 3H⁴ 3I² 3K-3P⁴ 3Q² 3R⁴ 3S² 3T-4A⁴ 4B² 4C⁴ 4D² 4E-4K⁴ 4L² 4M⁴ 4N² 4O-4T⁴ 4V² 4X-5O⁴ 5P⁴ (-5P1) b⁴ c²; 398 leaves, pp. [2] [i-iii] iv, 5-540, 539-774 [*18*].

Illustrations: Woodcut representing the four seasons at the head of each monthly issue and a woodcut of a table setting on X2ʳ (p. 151).

Bibliographies: Maclean. p. 36.

Copies: *BMC* and *NUC* (New York Academcy of Medicine and New York Public Library).

637. The Court and Kitchin of Elizabeth, Commonly called Joan, Cromwel.

[within a border of two rules] THE | COURT & KITCHIN | OF | *ELIZABETH,* | Commonly called | *Joan Cromwel,* | THE | Wife of the late Usurper, | Truly | Described and Represented, | And now | Made Publick for general | Satisfaction. | [rule] | *London,* Printed by *Tho. Mil-* | *bourn,* for *Randal Taylor* in | St. *Martins Le Grand,* 1664.

First edition, London, 1664.

12mo. A⁸ B¹² C⁴ D⁸ E¹² F-G⁶ πG¹² H¹² I⁴; 84 leaves, pp. [*22*] 1-90, 97-151 [*152*] = 168 pp. This copy trimmed and inlaid throughout.

Illustration: Woodcut frontispiece portrait of Elizabeth Cromwell.

Bibliographies: Oxford, p. 33; Vicaire 216; Wing C7036; Wheaton and Kelly 1469.

Copies: *BMC* (2 copies) and *NUC* (Harvard only). Wing adds Trinity College, Cambridge, John Rylands Library, and John Crerar Library.

638. Crawford, Frances.

FRENCH COOKERY | ADAPTED FOR | ENGLISH FAMILIES | BY | MISS CRAWFORD. | LONDON: | RICHARD BENTLEY, NEW BURLINGTON STREET. | 1853.

First edition, London, 1853.

171 x 106 mm. [a]⁸ b⁶ B-O⁸ P²; 120 leaves, pp. [i-v] vi-xxviii [1] 2-209 [210] [2]. Last leaf blank. Bound in publisher's green cloth stamped in gold.

Bibliographies: Axford, p. 171; Bitting, p. 105.

Copies: *BMC* and *NUC* (Library of Congress only).

639. Dalgairns, Mrs.

THE | PRACTICE OF COOKERY, | ADAPTED TO | THE BUSINESS OF EVERY DAY LIFE. | BY | MRS DALGAIRNS. | SECOND EDITION. | EDINBURGH: | PRINTED FOR | CADELL & COMPANY, EDINBURGH; | SIMPKIN AND MARSHALL, LONDON; | AND ALL BOOKSELLERS. | [short rule] | 1829.

Second edition, Edinburgh, 1829. Originally published, Edinburgh, also 1829.

174 x 105 mm. [a]⁸ b⁸ c⁴ A-2K⁸ 2L²; 286 leaves, pp. [i-v] vi-xxix [xxx] [2] [1] 2-532. Publisher's boards with printed label.

Bibliographies: This edition unrecorded in the bibliographies consulted. Oxford, p. 163, records the first edition, also London, 1829. Bitting, p. 113, records the sixth edition, London, 1836.

Copies: *NUC* (Library Company of Philadelphia only).

640. Dalrymple, George.

THE | PRACTICE | OF | MODERN COOKERY; | ADAPTED TO | FAMILIES OF DISTINCTION, | As well as to those of | THE MIDDLING RANKS OF LIFE. | To which is added, | A GLOSSARY explaining the TERMS of ART. | *BY GEORGE*

DALRYMPLE, | Late Cook to SIR JOHN WHITEFOORD, Bart. | [short fancy rule] | EDINBURGH: | Printed for the AUTHOR. | Sold by C. ELLIOT, EDINBURGH; | and T. LONGMAN, LONDON. | [short rule] | MDCCLXXXI.

First edition, Edinburgh, 1781.

8vo. π^4 A-Ff^8 Gg^4 Hh^2; 242 leaves, pp. [2] [i-v] vi [1] 2-475 [476].

Bibliographies: Axford, p. 330; Bitting, p. 114; Maclean, p. 37; Oxford, p. 113; Vicaire 244.

Copies: *BMC* and *NUC* (Kansas State University and Library of Congress). Maclean adds Glasgow Public Libraries (Mitchell Library) and National Library of Scotland.

640a. Darling, George, 1782?-1862.

INSTRUCTIONS | FOR MAKING | UNFERMENTED BREAD. | WITH | OBSERVATIONS. | BY | A PHYSICIAN. | [short fancy rule] | LONDON: | TAYLOR AND WALTON, | UPPER GOWER STREET. | [short rule] | 1846.

First edition, London, 1846.

204 x 131 mm. [1]^8; 8 leaves, pp. [1-5] 6-15 [16].

Bibliographies: Unrecorded in the bibliographies consulted. RLIN records a tenth edition, London, 1847.

Copies: *BMC.*

640b. David, Elizabeth, b. 1913.

[pictorial title-page, reproducing hand-lettering, on a background of a Mediterranean coastal scene] *A Book of* / *Mediterranean* / FOOD | *by* / *Elizabeth David* / *Decorated by* / *John Minton* /*John Lehmann Ltd.* / *London*

First edition, London, 1950.

197 x 129 mm. [A]^8 B-M^8; 96 leaves, pp. [i-iv] v-xi [xii] [13-14] 15-191 [192].

Publisher's peach-colored cloth stamped in brown and gold. White paper dust jacket with a pictorial Mediterranean coastal scene printed in blue, red, yellow, green and black.

Illustrations: Drawings by John Minton reproduced in the text.

Bibliographies: Axford, p. 38.

Copies: *BMC* and *NUC* (8 copies).

640c. David, Elizabeth, b. 1913.

[pictorial title-page, reproducing hand-lettering, on a background of a grape arbor and a table of food] FRENCH COUNTRY | COOKING | *by* / *Elizabeth David* / *decorated by* / *John Minton* / *John Lehmann Ltd* / *London*

First edition, London, 1951.

197 x 129 mm. [A]^8 B-N^8 O^{12} P^8; 124 leaves, pp. [i-iv] v-x [xi-xii] [13-14] 15-247 [248]. Publisher's oatmeal-colored cloth stamped in brown and gold. White paper dust jacket with a pictorial scene of a French country kitchen printed in yellow, red, blue and black.

Illustrations: Drawings by John Minton reproduced in the text.

Bibliographies: Unrecorded in the bibliographies consulted.

Copies: *NUC* (New York Public Library and University of Virginia).

641. Davies, John.

THE | *INNKEEPER AND BUTLER'S* | GUIDE, | OR | *A DIRECTORY* | IN THE | *Making and Managing* | OF | BRITISH WINES; | TOGETHER WITH | DIRECTIONS | FOR THE | MANAGING, COLOURING, AND FLAVOURING, | OF | FOREIGN WINES AND SPIRITS, | AND FOR MAKING | *BRITISH COMPOUNDS,* | PEPPERMINT, ANISEED, SHRUB, &c. &c. | [short fancy rule] | By JOHN DAVIES. | [short fancy rule] | 𝔏𝔦𝔟𝔢𝔯𝔭𝔬𝔬𝔩, | PRINTED BY J. NUTTALL, DUKE STREET. | [two short rules] | 1805.

First edition, Liverpool, 1805.

8vo. [A]² B-P⁴ Q² χ1; 61 leaves, pp. [1-5] 6-120 [2].

Bibliographies: The first edition is unrecorded in the bibliographies consulted. Noling, p. 127, records the fifth edition, Leeds, 1807 and another edition dated 1809. Bitting, p. 117, and Schraemli (1) 137 record the eighth edition, 1808. Simon BG 435-437 records the 1811, 1822, and 1829 editions.

Copies: *BMC*.

642. Dawson, Thomas.

THE | GOOD HVS- | wifes Iewell. | *Wherein is to bee found most* | excellent and rare Deuises, for conceits | in Cookery, found out by the prac- | *tise of Thomas Dawson.* | Whereunto are adioyned sundry appro- | ued receits for many soueraign Oyles, | *and the way to distill many precious* | *Waters, with diuers approoued* | *Medicines for many* | *Diseases.* | *Also certaine approued pointes of husbandry, ve-* | *ry necessary for all Husbandmen to know.* | Newly set forth with additions. 1605. | Imprinted at London, by *I. W.* for Ed- | *ward White, dwelling at the little North* | *doore of Paules, at the Signe of* | *the Gun.*

Third edition, London, 1605. Originally published, London, 1585? This work was registered with the Stationers' Company in December 1584 and copies of *The Second Part of the Good Huswifes Jewell* exist dated 1585. However, the earliest copy of *The Good Huswifes Jewell* recorded in the *STC* is dated 1587.

8vo. A-F⁸ G⁶; 54 leaves, ff. [*1*] [1-2] 3-50 [*3*].

Bibliographies: *STC* 6392.5.

Copies: *STC* (Gernon copy only).

643. Dawson, Thomas.

THE | Second part of | *the good Hus-wiues* | IEWELL. | *Where is to be found most apt and readiest* | wayes to distill many wholesome | *and sweete waters.* | In which (likewise) is shewed the best | manner in preseruiug diuers sortes of | fruites, and making of Sirrops. | *With diuers conceites in Cookerie: with the* | *Booke of Caruing.* |

[ornament] | *LONDON* / *Printed by* E. Allde *for* Ed. White, *and* | are to be solde at his shope neere the | *little North doore of S. Paules Church* | *at the signe of the Gun.* | 1606.

Second title-page:

THE | Booke of Car- | *uing and sewing.* | *And all the feastes in the* | yeere, for the seruice of a Prince or | any other estate, as yee shall finde | each Office, the seruice accor- | ding in the booke fol- | lowing. | [ornament] | *LONDON* | Printed by Ed. Allde for Edward | *White, and are to be solde at the little* | *North doore of S. Paules,* *at the* | *Signe of the Gunne.*

Third edition, London, 1606. Originally published, London, 1585.

8vo. A-E^8, ^{2}A-B^8 C^4; 60 leaves, pp. [*8*] 1-72 [*40*].

Note: *The Booke of Carving and Sewing* has a separate title-page and separate signatures but is mentioned on the main title-page and is an integral part of this work.

Bibliographies: *STC* 6396.

Copies: *NUC* (Huntington Library only). *STC* adds Gernon copy.

644. A Decree Lately Made.

A | DECREE | Lately made in the High | Court of Starre-Chamber, after | consultation had among the | Iudges, and Certificate of their | opinions in diuers things, &c. | *And also a Confirmation of that Decree by* | His Sacred Maiestie; together with His | Maiesties Command that the same be | Printed, Published, and put in | due execution. | [rule] | [ornament] | | [rule] | ¶ Imprinted at London by ROBERT BARKER, | Printer to the Kings most Excellent | MAIESTIE: And by the | Assignes of IOHN BILL. | M.DC.XXXIII.

First edition, London, 1633. This decree concerns regulation of tavern keepers, bakers, city cooks, and victuallers.

4to. A-D^4; 32 leaves, unpaginated.

Bibliographies: *STC* 7755.

Copies: *BMC* and *NUC* (University of Michigan only). *STC* (10 copies).

645. Dedekind, Friedrich, d. 1598.

GROBIANUS; | OR, THE | Compleat Booby. | AN | IRONICAL POEM. | [rule] | In THREE BOOKS. | [rule] | Done into *English*, from the | Original *Latin* of *Friderick Dedekindus*, | [rule] | By *ROGER BULL*, Esq; | [rule] | *Acta cano, veniam da turpiter acta canenti,* | *Fas mihi sit crasso crassa referre modo.* | Grobian. Lib. 3. Cap. 3. | [rule] | [ornament] | [rule] | *LONDON:* | Printed for T. COOPER, at the *Globe* in Pater- | *Noster-Row*. MDCCXXXIX. | [Price Bound Four Shillings.]

First edition of this translation into English, London, 1739. Originally published in Latin under the title *Grobianus. De morum simplicitate, libri tres*, Frankfurt, 1549, and in English under the title *The School of Slovenrie*, London, 1605. Roger Bull, the reported translator of this edition, may be a pseudonym.

8vo. A-T^8; 152 leaves, pp. [i-v] vi-xiii [xiv-xvi] [1] 2-276 [*12*].

Bibliographies: Foxon B564.

Copies: *BMC* (2 copies), *BNC* and *NUC* (11 copies). Foxon (9 copies).

645a. Digby, Sir Kenelm, 1603-1665.

[within a border of type ornaments] | THE | CLOSET | Of the Eminently Learned | Sir *Kenelme Digbie Kt.* | OPENED: | Whereby is DISCOVERED | Several ways for making of | *Metheglin, Sider, Cherry-Wine, &c.* / *TOGETHER WITH* | Excellent Directions | FOR | COOKERY: | As also for | *Preserving, Conserving, Candying, &c.* | [rule] | Published by his Son's Consent. | [rule] | *London,* Printed by *E.C.* for *H. Brome,* at | the Star in *Little Britain*. 1669.

First edition, London, 1669.

8vo. [A]^2 B-X^8 Y^2; 164 leaves, pp. [*4*] 1-312 [*12*].

Illustrations: Engraved frontispiece portrait of the author.

Bibliographies: Bitting, p. 124; Oxford, p. 34; Simon BG 502; Wing D1427.

Copies: *BMC* and *NUC* (5 copies); Wing locates 9 copies.

646. Digby, Sir Kenelm, 1603-1665.

THE | CLOSET | Of the Eminently Learned | Sir *Kenelme Digby* Kt. | OPENED: | Whereby is Discovered | Several ways for making of | *Metheglin, Syder, Cherry-Wine,* &c. | TOGETHER WITH | Excellent Directions | FOR | COOKERY: | As also for | *Preserving, Conserving, Candying,* &c. | [rule] | Published by his Son's Consent. | [rule] | The Third Edition Corrected. | [rule] | LONDON: | Printed by *H. C.* for *H. Brome,* at the | West-end of St. *Pauls,* 1677.

Third edition, London, 1677. Originally published, London, 1669 (item 645a).

8vo. A-Q^8 R^4; 132 leaves, pp. [*4*] 1-251 [252-260].

Illustration: Engraved frontispiece portrait of Digby.

Bibliographies: Wing D1429. Axford, p. 66, in a note, Bitting, p. 124, Oxford, p. 34, and Simon BG 502 all record the first edition, London, 1669.

Copies: *BMC* and *NUC* (6 copies). Wing (10 copies).

647. Dods, Margaret (i.e. Christian Isabel Johnstone, 1781-1857).

THE | COOK AND HOUSEWIFE'S | MANUAL: | A PRACTICAL SYSTEM OF MODERN DOMESTIC COOKERY | AND FAMILY MANAGEMENT. | [short rule] | THE FOURTH EDITION, | REVISED AND ENLARGED: | CONTAINING A COMPENDIUM OF FRENCH COOKERY, AND OF FASHION- | ABLE CONFECTIONARY, PREPARATIONS FOR INVALIDS, A SELECTION | OF CHEAP DISHES, AND NUMEROUS USEFUL MISCELLANEOUS | RECEIPTS IN THE VARIOUS BRANCHES OF | DOMESTIC ECONOMY. | [short rule] | BY MISTRESS MARGARET DODS, | OF THE CLEIKUM INN, ST. RONAN'S | [short rule] | PUBLISHED BY OLIVER & BOYD, EDINBURGH; | AND SIMPKIN & MARSHALL, LONDON. | MDCCCXXIX.

Fourth edition, Edinburgh, 1829. Originally published, Edinbrugh, 1826.

12mo. π^2 a-c^2 A-X^{12} Y^6 Z^4 2A^4 2B^6; 280 leaves, pp. [*4*] [i] ii-xii [13] 14-132, 131-552, ^{2}[1] 2.

Illustrations: Wood engravings in the text illustrating carving.

Bibliographies: Noling, p. 135; Oxford, p. 158, in a note; Simon BG 515; Wheaton and Kelly 3213.

Copies: *NUC* (John Crerar Library, Kansas State University, and National Library of Medicine). Wheaton and Kelly (Harvard only).

648. Dolby, Richard.

THE | COOK'S DICTIONARY, | AND | HOUSE-KEEPER'S DIRECTORY: | A | NEW FAMILY MANUAL | OF | COOKERY AND CONFECTIONERY, | ON A PLAN OF READY REFERENCE | NEVER HITHERTO ATTEMPTED. | [short rule] | BY RICHARD DOLBY, | COOK AT THE THATCHED-HOUSE TAVERN, | ST. JAMES'S STREET. | [short rule] | LONDON: | HENRY COLBURN AND RICHARD BENTLEY, | NEW BURLINGTON STREET. | [short rule] | 1830.

First edition, London, 1830.

12mo. [A]² B-2X⁶; 260 leaves, pp. [i-iii] iv [1] 2-516. Publisher's cloth with gold stamped label on spine.

Bibliographies: Axford, p. 98; Bitting, p. 126; Oxford, p. 164; Simon BG 517; Wheaton and Kelly 1728.

Copies: *BMC* and *NUC* (4 copies).

649. Domestic Economy and Cookery.

DOMESTIC ECONOMY, | AND | COOKERY, | FOR RICH AND POOR; | CONTAINING | AN ACCOUNT OF THE BEST ENGLISH, SCOTCH, | FRENCH, ORIENTAL, AND OTHER FOREIGN | DISHES; | PREPARATIONS OF BROTHS AND MILKS FOR CONSUMPTION; | RECEIPTS FOR SEA-FARING MEN, TRAVELLERS, | AND CHILDREN'S FOOD. | TOGETHER WITH | ESTIMATES AND COMPARISONS | OF DINNERS AND DISHES. | [short rule] | THE WHOLE COMPOSED WITH THE UTMOST ATTENTION TO | HEALTH, ECONOMY, AND ELEGANCE. | BY A LADY. | [short rule] | LONDON: | PRINTED FOR | LONGMAN, REES, ORME, BROWN, AND GREEN, | PATERNOSTER-ROW. | 1827.

First edition, London, 1827.

180 x 109 mm. [A]^2 B-EE^{12} FF^{12} (-FF11,12) GG^{12} (GG1 signed ")FF11-GG"); 348 leaves, pp. [i-iii] iv [1] 2-691 [692].

Bibliographies: Axford, p. 121; Bitting, p. 544; Oxford, p. 162; Vicaire 284.

Copies: *NUC* (5 copies).

650. Donovan, Michael, d. 1876.

Volume one:

THE | CABINET OF USEFUL ARTS. | CONDUCTED BY THE | REV. DIONYSIUS LARDNER, LL.D. F.R.S. L.&E. | M.R.I.A. F.L.S. F.Z.S. Hon. F.C.P.S. M.Ast.S. &c. &c. | ASSISTED BY | EMINENT SCIENTIFIC MEN. | [short rule] | DOMESTIC ECONOMY. | VOL. I. | [in two columns: column one] BREWING. | DISTILLING. | [vertical rule] | [column two] WINE-MAKING. | BAKING &c. [end columns] | BY | MICHAEL DONOVAN, ESQ. M.R.I.A. | PROFESSOR OF CHEMISTRY | TO THE COMPANY OF APOTHECARIES IN IRELAND. | [short rule] | LONDON: | PRINTED FOR | LONGMAN, REES, ORME, BROWN, AND GREEN, | PATERNOSTER-ROW; | AND JOHN TAYLOR, | UPPER GOWER STREET. | 1830.

Engraved title-page:

DOMESTIC ECONOMY. | VOL. I. | CONTAINING | [in two columns: column one] BREWING. | DISTILLING. | [vertical rule] | [column two] WINE-MAKING. | BAKING &c. [end columns] | 𝔅𝔜 | MICHAEL DONOVAN, ESQ. M.R.I.A. | *PROFESSOR OF CHEMISTRY* | *to the company of Apothecaries in Ireland.* | [vignette signed, *H. Corbould del. E. Finden sculp.*] | 𝔏𝔬𝔫𝔡𝔬𝔫: | PRINTED FOR LONGMAN, REES, ORME, BROWN & GREEN, PATERNOSTER ROW; | AND JOHN TAYLOR, UPPER GOWER STREET. | 1830.

First edition, London, 1830. For volume II see item 651.

165 x 98 mm. A^6 B-AA^8 BB^4; 194 leaves, pp. [iii-v] vi-xiv [1] 2-376.

Illustrations: Engraved title-page with vignette of cherubs gathering food.

Bibliographies: Attar 66.1; Bitting, p. 127; Oxford, p. 164; Simon BG 521; Wheaton and Kelly 1748.

Copies: *BMC*, *BNC*, and *NUC* (18 copies). Attar adds Polytechnic Library, Oxford.

651. Donovan, Michael, d. 1876.

Volume one:

THE | CABINET CYCLOPAEDIA. | CONDUCTED BY THE | REV. DIONYSIUS LARDNER, LL.D. F.R.S. L.&E. | M.R.I.A. F.L.S. F.Z.S. Hon. F.C.P.S. M.Ast.S. &c. &c. | ASSISTED BY | EMINENT LITERARY AND SCIENTIFIC MEN. | [short rule] | Useful Arts. | [short rule] | DOMESTIC ECONOMY. | VOL. I. | [in two columns: column one] BREWING. | DISTILLING. | [vertical rule] | [column two] WINE-MAKING. | BAKING &c. [end columns] | BY | MICHAEL DONOVAN, ESQ. M.R.I.A. | PROFESSOR OF CHEMISTRY | TO THE COMPANY OF APOTHECARIES IN IRELAND. | [short rule] | A NEW EDITION. | LONDON: | PRINTED FOR | LONGMAN, ORME, BROWN, GREEN, & LONGMANS, | PATERNOSTER-ROW. | AND JOHN TAYLOR, | UPPER GOWER STREET. | 1837.

Engraved title-page:

New Edition. | DOMESTIC ECONOMY. | VOL. I. | CONTAINING | [in two columns: column one] BREWING. | DISTILLING. | [vertical rule] | [column two] WINE-MAKING. | BAKING &c. [end columns] | BY | MICHAEL DONOVAN, ESQ. M.R.I.A. | *PROFESSOR OF CHEMISTRY* | *to the company of Apothecaries in Ireland.* | [vignette signed, *H. Corbould del. E. Finden sculp.*] | London: | PRINTED FOR LONGMAN, REES, ORME, BROWN & GREEN, PATERNOSTER ROW; | AND JOHN TAYLOR, UPPER GOWER STREET. | 1830.

Volume two:

THE | CABINET CYCLOPAEDIA. | CONDUCTED BY THE | REV. DIONYSIUS LARDNER, LL.D. F.R.S. L.&E. | M.R.I.A. F.R.A.S. F.L.S. F.Z.S. Hon. F.C.P.S. &c. &c. | ASSISTED BY | EMINENT LITERARY AND SCIENTIFIC MEN. | [short rule] | Useful Arts. | [short rule] | DOMESTIC ECONOMY. | VOL. II. | ANIMAL AND VEGETABLE ALIMENTS USED BY THE | VARIOUS NATIONS OF THE WORLD; | AND THE PROCESSES TO WHICH THEY ARE SUBJECTED. | BY | MICHAEL DONOVAN, ESQ. | LATE PROFESSOR OF CHEMISTRY, MATERIA MEDICA, AND PHARMACY. | TO THE COMPANY

OF APOTHECARIES IN IRELAND. | [short rule] | LONDON: | PRINTED FOR | LONGMAN, ORME, BROWN, GREEN, & LONGMANS, | PATERNOSTER-ROW; | AND JOHN TAYLOR, | UPPER GOWER STREET. | 1837.

Engraved title-page:

DOMESTIC ECONOMY. | VOL. II. | HUMAN FOOD | *Animal and Vegetable* | 𝔅𝔜 | MICHAEL DONOVAN, ESQ. M.R.I.A. | *PROFESSOR OF CHEMISTRY* | *to the company of Apothecaries in Ireland.* | [vignette signed, *H. Corbould del. E. Finden sculp.* | 𝔏𝔬𝔫𝔡𝔬𝔫: | PRINTED FOR LONGMAN, ORME, BROWN, GREEN AND LONGMANS, PATERNOSTER ROW. | AND JOHN TAYLOR, UPPER GOWER STREET. | 1837.

New edition of volume I; first edition of volume II, both London, 1837. Volume I originally published, London, 1830 (item 650).

171 x 150 mm. 2 vols. Vol. I. π1 A⁶ B-AA⁸ BB⁴ χ1; 196 leaves, pp. [i-v] vi-xiv [1] 2-376 [2]. Vol. II. π1 A⁴ B-BB⁸ CC² χ1; 200 leaves, pp. [i-vii] viii-x [1] 2-388 [2]. Publisher's purple cloth with printed paper labels on the spines.

Illustrations: Engraved title-page in each volume with vignettes of cherubs gathering and preparing foods.

The complete *Cabinet Cyclopaedia* extended to 133 volumes published between 1830 and 1849.

Bibliographies: Attar, 66.2; Axford, p. 121 (undated edition); Bitting, p. 127 (first edition of volume I; "new edition" of Vol. II); Oxford, p. 164 (first editions of each volume); Simon BG 521 (first edition of Vol. I only); Wheaton and Kelly 1748 (first editions of each volume).

Copies: *BMC* (first editions), *BNC* (first editions), and *NUC* (18 copies of first editions).

652. Doran, John, 1807-1878.

TABLE TRAITS | WITH | SOMETHING ON THEM. | BY | DR. DORAN. | "Je suis aujourd'hui en train de conter; plaise à Dieu que cela ne | soit pas une calamité publique," – BRILLAT SAVARIN. | 𝔖𝔢𝔠𝔬𝔫𝔡 𝔈𝔡𝔦𝔱𝔦𝔬𝔫. | LONDON: | RICHARD

BENTLEY, NEW BURLINGTON STREET; | OLIVER & BOYD, EDINBURGH; HODGES & SMITH, DUBLIN; | AND TO BE HAD OF ALL BOOKSELLERS, AND AT THE RAILWAY STATIONS. | 1854.

Second edition, London, 1854. Originally published, London, also 1854.

180 x 112 mm. [A]² B-MM⁸ NN²; 276 leaves, pp. [4] [1] 2-547 [548].

Bibliographies: Axford, p. 386; Bitting, p. 128; Wheaton and Kelly 1751.

Copies: *NUC* (13 copies).

653. Drope, Francis, 1629?-1671.

[within a rule border] A | SHORT and SURE | GUID | in the Practice | Of Raising and Ordering | OF | Fruit-Trees. | Being the many years Recreation | and Experience of | *FRANCIS DROPE,* | Bachelour in Divinity, late fellow | of *Magdalen* Colledge in *Oxford.* | [rule] | *OXFORD,* | Printed for *Ric. Davis,* An. Dom. 1672.

First edition, Oxford, 1672.

8vo. A⁶(A5+1) B-H⁸ I⁴; 67 leaves, pp. [14] 1-120.

Bibliographies: Fussell (1), p. 59; Henrey I, p. 243; Wing D2188.

Copies: *BMC* and *NUC* (9 copies). Wing (10 copies).

654. Dufour, Philippe Sylvestre (1622-1687?).

[within a border of two rules] THE | Manner of Making | OF | COFFEE, TEA, | AND | CHOCOLATE. | As it is used | In most parts of *Eu-* | *rope, Asia, Africa,* | and *America.* | With their Vertues. | [rule] | Newly done out of French | and Spanish. | [rule] | *LONDON:* | Printed for *William Crook* at the *Green* | *Dragon* without *Temple Bar* near *De-* | *vereux* Court, 1685.

First edition in English, London, 1685, translated by John Chamberlayne. Originally published in French under the title *De l'usage de caphé, du thé, et du chocolate,* Lyon, 1671 (item 150). Wing enters this work under Dufour but for a discussion of the authorship see the note in item 150.

12mo. π² A-B¹² D-E¹² F¹⁰; 60 leaves, pp. [*12*] 1-20, 29-116. B3 and B5 are missigned "C3" and "C5."

Illustration: Woodcut on p. 9 showing coffee tree and an instrument for roasting coffee.

Bibliographies: Axford, p. 258; Bitting, p. 134; Noling, p. 140; Wheaton and Kelly 1822; Wing D2454.

Copies: *BMC*, *BNC*, and *NUC* (7 copies). Wing (11 copies).

655. Duncan, Daniel, 1649-1735.

[within a border of two rules] WHOLESOME │ ADVICE │ Against the ABUSE of │ Hot Liquors, │ PARTICULARLY OF [in two columns: column one] *Coffee,* │ *Chocolate,* │ *Tea,* │ [two fancy vertical rules] │ [column two] *Brandy,* │ AND │ *Strong-Waters.* [end columns] │ WITH DIRECTIONS │ To know what Constitutions they Suit, │ and when the Use of them may be │ Profitable or Hurtful. │ [rule] │ By Dr. *DUNCAN* of the Faculty of *Montpelier.* │ [rule] │ Done out of *French.* │ [rule] │ *LONDON,* │ Printed for *H. Rhodes* at the Star, the Corner of *Bride-* │ *Lane* in *Fleetstreet*, and *A. Bell* at the Cross-Keys │ and Bible in *Cornhil*, near the *Royal-Exchange*. 1706.

First edition in English, London, 1706. Originally published in French under the title *Avis salutaire à toute le monde, contre l'abus des choses chaudes, et particulièrement du café, du chocolate et du thé*, Rotterdam, 1705.

8vo. A⁴ B-S⁸ T⁴; 144 leaves, pp. [8] 1-280.

Bibliographies: Craig 30; Maclean, p. 39; Noling, p. 140; Simon BG 534; Wheaton and Kelly 1845.

Copies: *BMC* and *NUC* (10 copies). Maclean adds Brotherton Library and National Library of Scotland.

656. Dundonald, Archibald Cochrane, 9th earl of, 1749?-1831.

LETTERS, │ BY THE │ *EARL OF DUNDONALD,* │ ON │ MAKING BREAD FROM POTATOES, │ TO THE │ INHABITANTS OF GREAT BRITAIN; │ AND

PARTICULARLY TO THE | *INHABITANTS OF IRELAND,* | Who have been the first to Cultivate and Bring into | General Use, the Invaluable Plant or Root, | called the POTATOE. | [short fancy rule] | EDINBURGH: | PRINTED FOR WILLIAM CREECH, | [short rule] | M DCC XCI.

First edition, Edinburgh, 1791.

8vo. π^2 A-B^4 C^6; 16 leaves, pp. [*4*] [1] 2-24 [*4*]. Last leaf (blank?) wanting in this copy.

Inscribed "Mr Caventry from the Author"

Bibliographies: Unrecorded in the bibliographies consulted.

Copies: *NUC* (Yale only).

657. Dundonald, Archibald Cochrane, 9th earl of, 1749?-1831.

THE | PRESENT STATE | OF THE | Manufacture of Salt explained; | AND | A new Mode suggested of refining BRITISH SALT, | so as to render it equal, or superior to | the finest FOREIGN SALT. | To which is subjoined, | A PLAN for abolishing the present Duties and Restrictions on | the Manufacture of SALT, and for substituting other Duties, | less burthensome to the Subjects, more beneficial to the | Revenue, and better qualified to promote the Trade of | GREAT BRITAIN. | [short fancy rule] | By the Earl of DUNDONALD. | [two rules] | LONDON: | Printed by W. and A. STRAHAN: | For T. CADELL, in the Strand; J. STOCKDALE, in Piccadilly; | G. and T. WILKIE, No. 71, St. Paul's Church-Yard; | and W. RICHARDSON, Royal Exchange. | MDCCLXXXV. | [Price Two Shillings.]

First edition, London, 1785.

8vo. [A]^2 (A1+B-L^4 M^2); 44 leaves, pp. [2] [1] 2-84 [2].

Bibliographies: Maggs 297

Copies: *BMC*. *NUC* locates second edition only.

658. Dundonald, Archibald Cochrane, 9th earl of, 1749?-1831.

THOUGHTS | ON THE | Manufacture and Trade of Salt, | ON THE | HERRING FISHERIES, | AND ON | *The* COAL-TRADE *of Great Britain,* | SUBMITTED | To the Consideration of the Right Honourable WIL- | LIAM PITT, Chancellor of the Exchequer, &c. | and of every Lover of his Country. | BY | THE EARL OF DUNDONALD. | [short fancy rule] | EDINBURGH: | PRINTED FOR WILLIAM CREECH. | [short rule] | M,DCC,LXXXIV.

First edition, Edinburgh, 1784.

8vo. π^2 A-F^4 G^2; 28 leaves, pp. [*4*] [1] 2-52.

Bibliographies: Unrecorded in the bibliographies consulted.

Copies: *NUC* (8 copies).

659. Eales, Mary.

Mrs *Mary Eales*'s | RECEIPTS. | [rule] | CONFECTIONER to her late | MAJESTY Queen *ANNE.* | [rule] | [ornament] | [rule] | *LONDON:* | Printed by H. MEERE in *Black-* | *Fryers*, and to be had at Mr. *Cooper*'s at the | *Three Pidgeons* the lower End of *Bedford-* | *Street*, near the *New Exchange* in the *Strand.* | MDCCXVIII.

First edition, London, 1718.

8vo. A-N^4 O^2; 54 leaves, pp. [*8*] 1-100.

Bibliographies: Axford, p. 282; Bitting, p. 139; Maclean, p. 40; Noling, p. 143; Oxford, p. 55; Pennell, p. 146; Vicaire 305.

Copies: *BMC* and *NUC* (John Crerar Library and Library of Congress). Maclean adds Bodleian, Edinburgh University, Wellcome Library, Kansas State University, and Radcliffe.

660. Eales, Mary.

Mrs. *Mary Eales*'s | RECEIPTS. | [rule] | CONFECTIONER to her late | MAJESTY Queen *ANNE.* | [rule] | [ornament] | [rule] | *LONDON:* | Printed for J. BRINDLEY, Bookseller, at the *King's-* | *Arms* in *New Bond-Street*, and Bookbinder to Her | Majesty and His Royal Highness the Prince of *Wales*; | and R. MONTAGU at the *General Post-Office*, the | Corner of *Great Queen-Street*, near *Drury-Lane.* | MDCCXXXIII.

Second edition, London, 1733. Originally published, London, 1718 (item 659).

8vo. A-O⁴; 56 leaves, pp. [*8*] [*1*] 2-100 [*4*]. Last four pages contain publisher's advertisements.

Bibliographies: Maclean, p. 40; Oxford, p. 55; Simon BG 541.

Copies: *BMC* and *NUC* (New York Academy of Medicine, New York Public Library, and Wellesley College). Maclean adds Brotherton Library.

661. Eaton, Mary.

THE | COOK AND HOUSEKEEPER'S | COMPLETE AND UNIVERSAL | *DICTIONARY;* | INCLUDING | A SYSTEM OF MODERN COOKERY, | IN ALL ITS VARIOUS BRANCHES, | ADAPTED TO THE USE OF | *PRIVATE FAMILIES*: | ALSO A VARIETY OF | ORIGINAL AND VALUABLE INFORMATION, | RELATIVE TO | [in two columns: column one] BAKING, | BREWING, | CARVING, | CLEANING, | COLLARING, | CURING, | ECONOMY OF BEES, | —— OF A DAIRY, | [two vertical rules] | [column two] ECONOMY OF POULTRY, | FAMILY MEDICINE, | GARDENING, | HOME-MADE WINES, | PICKLING, | POTTING, | PRESERVING, | RULES OF HEALTH, [end columns] | AND EVERY OTHER SUBJECT CONNECTED WITH | DOMESTIC ECONOMY. | [short rule] | BY MRS. MARY EATON. | [short rule] | *EMBELLISHED WITH ENGRAVINGS.* | [two short rules] | BUNGAY: | PRINTED AND PUBLISHED BY J. AND R. CHILDS. | 1823.

Engraved title-page.

THE / *Cook and Housekeeper's* | Complete & Universal | 𝔇𝔦𝔠𝔱𝔦𝔬𝔫𝔞𝔯𝔶 | Including | *A system of Modern Cookery* / *in all its various Branches,* | adapted to the use of | PRIVATE FAMILIES, | *Also a variety of Original & Valuable Information* | [short fancy rule] *RELATIVE TO* [short fancy rule] | [in two columns: column one] *Baking*................ / *Brewing*.................. / *Carving*................ / *Cleaning*................ / *Collaring*............... / *Curing*................... / *Economy of Bees* / *– of a Dairy* | [vertical fancy rule] | [column two] *Economy of Poultry* / *Family Medicine* / *Gardening*................. / *Home-made Wines* / *Pickling*.................. / *Potting*..................... / *Preserving*.............. / *Rules of Health* | And every other Subject connected with | 𝔇𝔬𝔪𝔢𝔰𝔱𝔦𝔠 𝔈𝔠𝔬𝔫𝔬𝔪𝔶. | BY MRS. MARY EATON. | [shorty fancy rule] | BUNGAY | *Printed & Published by I. & R. Childs* | 1822.

First edition, Bungay, 1823. Note: The signatures indicate this work may have been published in parts. Signatures E-G are labelled no. 2, H-K are no. 3, and so on through 3Q, 3R and a which are no. 21 and b-d as no. 22. Part no. 1, signatures B-D, is not labelled. This could explain the discrepancy in the 1822 date on the engraved title-page and the 1823 date on the printed title.

211 x 130 mm. [a]⁴ b-d⁴ B-3R⁴; 264 leaves, pp. [i-v] vi-xxxii, 1-495 [496].

Illustrations: Engraved frontispiece portrait of the author, engraved title-page and four engraved plates of a patent brewing machine, two of carving and one of quartering veal, mutton, venison, beef, and pork.
Bibliographies: Axford, p. 79; Bitting, p. 139; Craig 31; Oxford, p. 152; Schraemli (1) 157; Simon BG 542.

Copies: *BMC* and *NUC* (Library of Congress and National Agricultural Library).

662. Edlin, Abraham.

A | TREATISE | ON | *THE ART* | OF BREAD-MAKING. | Wherein, | THE MEALING TRADE, | ASSIZE LAWS, | AND EVERY CIRCUMSTANCE CONNECTED WITH THE ART, | IS PARTICULARLY EXAMINED. | [two short rules] | BY A. EDLIN. | [two short rules] | *LONDON:* | Printed by J. Wright, St. John's Square, | FOR VERNOR AND HOOD, POULTRY. | [short rule] | 1805.

First edition, London, 1805.

188 x 108 mm. A-K¹²; 120 leaves, pp. [i-v] vi-xxiv [1] 2-216.

Large folding letterpress sheet at the end containing five tables of bread prices.

Bibliographies: Axford,p. 397; Bitting, p. 140; Simon BG 584; Wheaton and Kelly 1912.

Copies: *BMC* (2 copies) and *NUC* (5 copies).

663. Edmonds, George.

THE | Country Brewer's ASSISTANT, | AND | English Vintner's INSTRUCTOR, | In TWO PARTS. | PART the FIRST treating | [in three columns: column one] 1. The choice of | Water, | 2. Grinding the | Malt, | 3. Use and Na- | ture of the Hops, |

[vertical rule] | [column two] | 4. Instructions for | private Families, | 5. Brewing
good | Small-beer. | 6. General Instruc- | tions for brewing, | [vertical rule] | [column
three] 7. Mashing. | 8. Cooling and | Working, | 9. Casking the | Drink. [end
columns] | PART the SECOND | Containing general Instructions for making
ENGLISH WINES, | exemplified in a select Number of original choice Receipts | for
producing excellent WINES from the following BRITISH | Fruits, Herbs, and
Flowers: | [in four columns: column one] Grapes, | Raspberries, | Mulberries, |
Currants, | [vertical rule] | [column two] Cherries, | Gooseberries, | Quinces, |
Damsins, | [vertical rule] | [column three] Apricots, | Elder Berries, | Birch, | Sage, |
[vertical rule] | [column four] Cowslips, | Gilliflowers, | Strawberries, | Blackberries.
[end columns] | To which are added, Two excellent Receipts for making | ORANGE
and PALERMO Wines, | With Instructions for making (after the most improved
Method) | MEAD, CYDER, and METHEGLIN, | The celebrated IRISH and Green
USQUEBAUGHS, | The admired BRUNSWICK MUM (taken from the Record in |
the Town-house at *Brunswick*,) | And the genuine Receipt for making Dr. *Stevens's*
justly- | famous CORDIAL WATER. | With an APPENDIX, containing the Distiller's
Assistant. | [rule] | By GEORGE EDMONDS. | [rule] | LONDON: | printed for
ISAAC FELL, at No. 14, in *Pater-noster Row*, | MDCCLXIX.

Title-page of part two:

PART the SECOND: | OR, THE | English Vintner's INSTRUCTOR, | Containing |
GENERAL INSTRUCTIONS | For making | ENGLISH WINES: | Exemplified | In a
select Number of Original choice Receipts | for producing Wines from the following
Bri- | *tish* Fruits, Herbs, and Flowers; | [in four columns: column one] Grapes, |
Raspberries, | Mulberries, | Currants, | [vertical rule] | [column two] Cherries, |
Gooseberries, | Quinces, | Damsins, | [vertical rule] | [column three] Apricots, | Elder
Berries, | Birch, | Sage, | [vertical rule] | [column four] Cowslips, | Gilliflowers, |
Strawberries, | Blackberries. [end columns] | To which are added, | Two excellent
receipts for making ORANGE | and PALERMO Wines. | With Instructions for making
(after the most improved Method) | MEAD, CYDER, and METHEGLIN, | The
celebrated *Irish* and Green Usquebaughs, | The admired *Brunswick* Mum (taken from
the Re- | cord in the Town-house at *Brunswick*,) | And, The genuine Receipt for
making Dr. | *Stephens*'s justly-famous Cordial Water. | [rule] | By JEREMIAH
THOMPSON. | [rule] | LONDON: | Printed for ISAAC FELL, at No. 14, in
Pater-noster Row. | MDCCLXIX.

First edition, London, 1769.

12mo. [A]1 B-F^{12} G^6 H1; 68 leaves, pp. [2] [1] 2-134.

Note: Jeremiah Thompson, author of *The English Vintner's Instructor*, published as
the second part of *The Country Brewer's Assistant*, appears to have drawn on a work

titled *A New and Easy Way of Making Wines From Herbs, Fruits and Flowers*, by W. Edmonds of Hereford, published in 1767. Edmonds, for example, writes that from "... your ordinary white grapes you make a good white sort of wine, of the red grapes a Claret, and if want of colour, heighten it with a little Brazeil, boiled in about a quart of it, and strained very clear." Thompson similarly observes "... you make a very pretty flavored white-wine, from our native white grapes, and a good claret from the red ones; Brasil wood, boiled in a small quantity of the juice of the latter, and carefully strained into the cask, will greatly contribute to heighten its colour, if it needs it." Though similar, however, they are not the same work as is stated in Stephanie Hoppen's catalogue, *Four Centuries of Food and Drink*, Vol. III, item 32.

Bibliographies: Gabler, p. 83; Noling, p. 143 (misdating the work 1749).

Copies: No other copy located.

664. Ellis, William.

THE | COUNTRY HOUSEWIFE's | Family Companion: | OR | PROFITABLE DIRECTIONS for whatever relates | to the Management and good OEconomy | OF THE | *Domestick Concerns of a Country Life,* | According to the | PRESENT PRACTICE of the Country Gentleman's, the | Yeoman's, the Farmer's, &c. Wives, in the Counties | of *Hertford, Bucks,* and other Parts of *England:* | SHEWING | How great SAVINGS may be made in Housekeeping: | And wherein, among many other, | The following HEADS are particularly treated of and explained: | [in two columns: column one] I. The Preservation and Improve- | ment of Wheat, Barley, Rye, Oats, | and other Meals; with Directions | for making several Sorts of Bread, | Cakes, Puddings, Pies, &c. | II. Frugal Management of Meats, | Fruits, Roots, and all Sorts of | Herbs; best Methods of Cookery; | and a cheap Way to make Soups, | Sauces, Gruels, &c. | III. Directions for the Farm Yard; | with the best Method of increasing | and fatning all Sorts of Poultry, as | Turkies, Geese, Ducks, Fowls, &c. | [two vertical rules] | [column two] IV. The best Way to breed and | fatten Hogs; sundry curious and | cheap Methods of preparing Hogs | Meat; Directions for curing | Bacon, Brawn, pickled Pork, | Hams, &c. with the Management | of Sows and Pigs. | V. The best Method of making | Butter and Cheese, with several | curious Particulars containing the | whole Management of the Dairy. | VI. The several Ways of making | good Malt; with Directions for | brewing good Beer, Ale, &c. [end columns] | With Variety of CURIOUS MATTERS, | Wherein are contained frugal Methods for victualling Harvest-men, | Ways to destroy all Sorts of Vermine, the best Manner of suckling | and fattening Calves, Prescriptions for curing all Sorts of Distempers | in Cattle, with Variety of curious Receits for Pickling, Preserving, | Distilling, &c. | [rule] | *The Whole founded on near thirty Years Experience by* | W. ELLIS, *Farmer, at* Little

Gaddesden, *near* Hempsted, Hertfords. | [rule] | *LONDON:* | Printed for JAMES HODGES, at the *Looking-glass*, facing *St. Magnus* | Church, *London-Bridge*; and B. COLLINS, Bookseller, at *Salisbury*. 1750.

First edition, London, 1750.

8vo. π^2 A^4 B-Cc^8; 206 leaves, pp. [2] [i] ii-x [1] 2-379 [380-398] [2]. Last leaf (blank?) wanting in this copy.

Bibliographies: Axford, p. 102; Bitting, p. 143; Maclean, p. 43; Noling, p. 146; Oxford, p. 79; Simon BG 588.

Copies: *BMC* and *NUC* (5 copies). Maclean adds Brotherton Library, National Library of Wales, Wellcome Library, Kansas State University, New York Public Library, and Vassar College.

664a. Ellis, William.

THE | *London* and *Country* | BREWER: | Containing an ACCOUNT, | [in two columns, column one] I. Of the Nature of the Barley | Corn, and of the proper Soils | and Manures for the Improve- | ment thereof. | II. Of making Malts. | III. To know good from bad | Malts. | IV. Of the Use of the Pale, Am- | ber and Brown Malts. | V. Of the Nature of several Wa- | ters and their Use in Brewing. | VI. Of Grinding Malts. | VII. Of Brewing in General. | VIII. Of the *London* Method of | Brewing Stout Butt Beer, Pale | and Brown Ales. | IX. Of the Country or private | Way of Brewing. | X. Of the Nature and Use of the | Hop. | XI. Of Boiling Malt Liquors and | to Brew a Quantity of Drink | in a little Room, and with a | few Tubs. | XII. Of Foxing or Tainting of | [vertical rule] | [column two] Malt Liquors, their Preventi- | on and Cure. | XIII. Of Fermenting and Work- | ing of Beers and Ales, and the | unwholsome Practice of Beat- | ing in the Yeast Detected. | XIV. Of Several Artificial Lees | for feeding, fining, preserving | and relishing Malt Liquors. | XV. Of several pernicious In- | gredients put into Malt Li- | quors to encrease their Strength. | XVI. Of the Cellar or Reposito- | ry for keeping Beers and Ales. | XVII. Of Sweetning and Clean- | ing Casks. | XVIII. Of Bunging Casks and | Carrying them to some Dis- | tance. | XIX. Of the Age and Strength | of Malt Liquors. | XX. Of the Profit and Pleasure | of private Brewing, and the | Charge of buying Malt Li- | quors. [end columns] | To which is added, | A Philosophical Account of Brewing strong *October* Beer, by an Inge- | nious Hand. | [rule] | By a Person formerly concern'd in a common Brewhouse | at *London,* but for near twenty Years past has resided in | the Country. | [double rule] | *LONDON:* | Printed and Sold by *W. Meadows,* at the *Angel* in *Corn-* / *hil,* Mr. *Astley* at the *Rose* in St. *Paul's* Church-Yard, | *W. Bickerton* at *Lord Bacon's-Head* without *Temple-Bar,* | and *A. Parker in Pall-mall.*

First edition, London, 1734, of the first part of this work. Two additional parts were published between 1734 and 1738 and a supplement appeared in 1740.

8vo. A⁴ B-I⁸ K⁴ L²; 74 leaves, pp. [8] 1-138 [2].

Bibliographies: Kress 4285; Maclean, p. 43.

Copies: *BMC.*

664b. Ellis, William.

THE | London *and* Country | BREWER. | CONTAINING | The WHOLE ART of BREWING all SORTS | OF | MALT-LIQUORS, | As practised both in TOWN and COUNTRY; ac- | cording to OBSERVATIONS made by the AUTHOR in | FOUR YEARS TRAVELS through the several COUN- | TIES in *England.* | ALSO, | The METHOD of preserving LIQUORS in the CASK, | and DIRECTIONS to be observed in BOTTLING | them. | In THREE PARTS. | To which is added, | A | SUPPLEMENT, | By a Person formerly concerned in a PUBLIC BREW- | HOUSE in *London.* | [rule] | The FOURTH EDITION. | [two rules] | *LONDON:* | Printed for THOMAS ASTLEY, at the *Rose* in St. *Paul's* | Church-Yard. MDCCXLII. | [Price Four Shillings Stitched, Five Shillings Bound.]

Divisional title-pages:

Part I:

THE | London *and* Country | BREWER. | Containing an Account | [in two columns: column one] I. Of the NATURE of the BAR- | LEY-CORN, and of the proper | SOILS and MANURES for the | IMPROVEMENT thereof. | II. Of making GOOD MALTS. | III. To know GOOD from BAD | MALTS. | IV. Of the Use of the PALE, | AMBER, and BROWN MALTS. | V. Of the NATURE of several | WATERS, and their USE in | BREWING. | VI. Of GRINDING MALTS. | VII. Of BREWING in general. | VIII. Of the LONDON METHOD | of Brewing STOUT, BUTT- | BEER, PALE and BROWN | ALES. | IX. Of the COUNTRY or PRI- | VATE WAY of BREWING. | X. Of the NATURE and USE of | the HOP. | XI. Of BOILING MALT-LI- | QUORS, and to Brew a Quanti- | ty of Drink in a little Room, | and with a few Tubs. | XII. Of FOXING or TAINTING | of MALT-LIQUORS; their |

PREVENTION and CURE. | [two vertical rules] | [column two] XIII. Of FERMENTING and | WORKING of BEERS and | ALES, and the unwholesome | PRACTICE of BEATING in the | YEAST, detected. | XIV. Of several ARTIFICIAL | LEES for FEEDING, FINING, | PRESERVING, and RELISH- | ING MALT-LIQUORS. | XV. Of several PERNICIOUS IN- | GREDIENTS put into MALT- | LIQUORS to increase their | STRENGTH. | XVI. Of the CELLAR or | VALUT for keeping BEERS | and ALES. | XVII. Of SWEETENING and | CLEANING CASKS. | XVIII. Of BUNGING CASKS and | CARRYING them to some DIS- | TANCE. | XIX. Of the AGE and STRENGTH | of MALT-LIQUORS. | XX. Of the PROFIT and PLEA- | SURE of PRIVATE BREWING, | and the CHARGE of BUYING | MALT-LIQUORS. [end columns] | To which is added, | A PHILOSOPHICAL ACCOUNT of Brewing | strong OCTOBER BEER. | [rule] | By a Person formerly concerned in a Common Brewhouse at LON- | DON, but for Twenty Years past has resided in the Country. | [rule] | PART I. The FOURTH EDITION, Corrected. | [two rules] | *LONDON:* | Printed for T. ASTLEY, at the *Rose* in St. *Paul*'s Church-Yard. 1742. | [Price One Shilling.]

Part II:

THE | London *and* Country | BREWER. | Containing an ACCOUNT of | [in two columns: column one] I. Several ERRORS commit- | ted in making MALTS. | II. Of Brewing WHEAT- | MALT. | III. Of the Good and Bad | PROPERTIES of the HOP. | IV. Of the Nature, Preven- | tion, and Cure of Foxed | MALT-LIQUORS, and | UTENSILS. | V. Several WAYS of Reco- | vering stale or pricked | MALT-LIQUORS. | VI. Of FERMENTATION. | VII. Of Brewing DORCHES- | TER BEER, SHROPSHIRE | [two vertical rules] | [column two] DRINK, and a WEST- | INDIA LIQUOR. | VIII. Of Brewing MALT- | DRINKS without Boiling | Water, Wort, or Hops. | IX. Sir *Thomas Seabright*'s Me- | thod of Brewing a Pipe of | PALE OCTOBER. | X. The Fraudulent Practice | by short-measured CASKS | exposed. | XI. A LETTER from one | BREWER to another, con- | cerning CONCEALMENTS | of MALT-DRINKS. [end columns] | *To which is added,* | A DISSERTATION on the BREWERY, | Wherein is shewn, | The ill Consequence of CLAY-WELLS, and CLAY-BUNGS; how to | brew a clear, sound DRINK, with nasty, foul WATER; the | prejudicial Nature of FAECES; with several other serviceable | Matters. | [rule] | *By a Person formerly concerned in a public Brewhouse in* | London, *but for Twenty Years past has resided in the Country.* | [rule] | PART II. | The SECOND EDITION, Corrected. | [two rules] | *LONDON:* | Printed for THOMAS ASTLEY, at the *Rose* in St. *Paul*'s | Church-Yard. MDCCXLIII. | [Price One Shilling.]

Part III:

THE | London *and* Country | BREWER. | CONTAINING, | [in two columns: column one] I. Of the four QUARTERS of the | Year as they relate to Brewing | MALT-LIQUORS. | II. The State of BARLEY for the | Year 1737. | III. Of MALT-KILNS. | IV. Of FUELS for drying the | several Sorts of MALT. | V. Of the great public BREW- | HOUSE. | VI. Of the small private BREW- | HOUSE. | VII. An excellent Way of Brew- | ing a Butt of Pale strong BEER, | by an Inn-keeper. | VIII. Brewing a Hogshead and a | Half of PALE-ALE from fresh | MALT, by a private Person. | IX. The best Way to make EL- | DERBERRY-BEER (called EBU- | LUM) CHINA-ALE, and several | other Sorts. | [two vertical rules] | [column two] X. Of the DEVONSHIRE white | ALE. | XI. A SCHEME for Brewing strong | MALT-LIQUORS after a new | improved Method. | XII. Of WORTS, and their Im- | provements after a new Method. | XIII. The BARNSTABLE Way of | Brewing a Hogshead of fine | Pale ALE. | XIV. Of Working BEER and ALE | after a new Way, to their great | Advantage. | XV. Of Brewing BUTT-BEER | called PORTER. | XVI. An Account of the destruc- | tive WEEVILS, with several | Ways to destroy them. | XVII. Common PURL improv'd, | by a famous new cheap Receipt | now in Use, rendring it far more | wholesome and pleasant than by | the common Way. [end columns] | *To which is added,* | The CELLAR-MAN, | Or many Receipts to cure, preserve, and improve DRINKS in the | Cask; wherein the Case of CLOUDY-BEER is accounted for, and its | effectual Cure amply prescribed. A new advantageous Way to get | out the SAP of new CASKS, and to Season them at once; likewise | particular DIRECTIONS for BOTTLING MALT-DRINKS; with | many other useful Matters, never before Published; truly necessary | for those who are concerned in *Brewing* or *Selling* MALT-LIQUORS. | [rule] | *By a Person formerly concerned in a public Brewhouse at* | London, *but who for Twenty Years past has resided in the Country.* | [rule] | PART III. The SECOND EDITION, Corrected. | [two rules] | *LONDON:* | Printed for THOMAS ASTLEY, at the *Rose* in St. *Paul*'s | Church-Yard. MDCCXLIII. | [Price One Shilling.]

Supplement:

A | SUPPLEMENT | TO THE | LONDON *and* COUNTRY | BREWER. | CONTAINING, | [in two columns: column one] I. An Account of BARLEY and | MALT, and the Method of destroy- | ing that mischievous Insect the | WEVIL. | II. The Method of Brewing ALE and | BEER, as practised throughout *Eng-* | *land.* | III. A Receipt for making BALLS for | fining, relishing, colouring, and pre- | serving MALT LIQUORS. | IV. The Business of the CELLAR- | MAN, and the Method of preserving | Vessels sweet, and improving them | in the Cask. | V. Of colouring PALE-DRINK | BROWN, and BROWN PALE. | VI. Of WATER and its PROPER- | TIES in Brewing. | [two vertical rules] | [column two] VII. Of curing ROPY, FOXED, | MUSTY, PRICKED BEER. | VIII. Two Ways of Brewing OC- | TOBER

BEER. | IX. Of ELDER-TREES, and the | Method of procuring LARGE BER- |
RIES. | X. Of SCURY-GRASS ALE, and | SHIP-BEER. | XI. Of Brewing MALT
LIQUORS | by private Persons. | XII. Of the WIRE MALT-KILN. | XIII. Of
WATER. | XIV. Of MISCELLANEOUS MAT- | TERS relating to the BREWING, |
WORKING, and ADULTERA- | TING MALT LIQUORS. [end columns] | WITH |
Several curious OBSERVATIONS taken upon the Spot, by the AU- | THOR, in his
four Years Travels through the several Counties in | *England:* Likewise a curious
Letter from a Physician discover- | ing some ABUSES in the BREWERY, explaining
the Nature of | Yeasts, and the unwholsome Effects of it, when beat up with | MALT
LIQUORS. | [rule] | PART the Fourth and last. | [rule] | *By the* AUTHOR *of the
three former Parts.* | [rule] | The SECOND EDITION, with large ADDITIONS. |
[two rules] | *LONDON:* | Printed for THOMAS ASTLEY, at the *Rose* in St. *Paul*'s |
Church-Yard. MDCCXLIII. | [Price One Shilling.]

Fourth edition, London, 1742, of the first part and second editions, London 1743, of
parts two, three and four. Originally published, London, 1734-1738.

8vo. A⁴ B-Q⁸ R⁴ S-Y⁸ Z⁴, ²A⁸; 184 leaves, pp. [8] 1-332 [4] ²[1] 2-16. The last
signature consists of a 16 page publisher's catalogue.

Note: Maclean attributes this work to William Ellis, d. 1758, who was the author of
several books on farming. *BMC* indicates there were two authors named William Ellis,
the farmer who died in 1758 and another William Ellis who was a brewer. Both this
work and the preceding one are assigned by *ESTC* to William Ellis, brewer.

Bibliographies: Maclean, p. 46.

Copies: *NUC* (4 copies).

665. Elyot, Sir Thomas, 1490-1546.

[within a woodcut border] THE CASTEL | OF HELTHE, | Gathered, and made by
syr | Thomas Elyot knight, out | of the chief authors of Phi= | syke, whereby
every man | may knowe the state of his | owne body, the preservati= | on of
helthe, and how to | instruct well his phi= | sition in sickness, | that he be | not
| deceyved. | M.D.XXXIX.

Colophon: Londini in aedibus Thomae Berthe- | leti typis impress. | Cum priuilegio
ad imprimen- | dum solum. | ANNO M. D. XXXIX.

Second edition, London, 1539. Originally published, according to the *STC*, [London, 1537?].

4to. A-B^4 ^{2}A-X^4 Y^6; 98 leaves, ff. [8] 1-90.

Illustrations: Woodcut arms with motto "face aut tace" on A3^v and woodcut printer's device on B3^v.

Bibliographies: Oxford, p. 2; *STC* 7642.7; Wheaton and Kelly 1944.

Copies: *BMC* and *NUC* (6 copies). *STC* (5 copies).

666. Escoffier, Auguste, 1846-1935.

A GUIDE TO | MODERN COOKERY | BY | A. ESCOFFIER | OF THE CARLTON HOTEL | [publisher's device] | LONDON | WILLIAM HEINEMANN | 1907

First edition, London, 1907.

245 x 150 mm. [A]^8 B-3K^8; 448 leaves, pp. [i-v] vi-xvi [1] 2-880. Publisher's green cloth stamped in gold.

Illustration: Frontispiece portrait of the author.

Bibliographies: Craig 33; Driver 364.1. Axford, p. 192, and Bitting, p. 146, describe later editions.

Copies: *BMC* and *NUC* (District of Columbia Public Library, Drexel Institute, and University of Tennessee).

667. An Essay on the Nature and Properties of Porter.

AN ESSAY | ON THE NATURE AND PROPERTIES OF | PORTER: | WHEREIN IS SHEWN, | THE DELUSION OF THE POPULAR FALLACY, | THAT | MALT LIQUOR | IS A | NECESSARY ARTICLE OF CONSUMPTION | FOR THE | *WORKING CLASSES* | [short rule] | "The best drink is water." – DR. HUFELAND. | [short rule] | London: | Published by J. PASCO, Temperance Tract Depository, No. 90, | Bartholomew Close; LIVESEY, Preston; ROTHERY, Liverpool; | ELLERBY,

Manchester; W. PALLISTER, Leeds; THOMPSON, | Darlington; TAYLOR, Birmingham; REWCASTLE & SHEPHERD, | Newcastle-upon-Tyne; and all other Booksellers.

First edition, London, ca. 1830.

169 x 105 mm. [1-2]^{12}, signed [A]^2 B^4 C-E^6; 24 leaves, pp. [i-iii] iv [1] 2-44.

"Temperance Tract Depository, no. 90"

Bibliographies: Unrecorded in the bibliographies consulted.

Copies: *NUC* (New York Public Library only).

668. Estienne, Charles, 1504-1564.

Maison Rustique, | OR | THE COVNTRIE | FARME. | Compiled in the French tongue by | *Charles Steuens* and *Iohn* | *Liebault* Doctors of | Physicke. | And translated into English by RICHARD | SVRFLET Practitioner in | Physicke. | Also a short collection of the hunting of the Hart, | *wilde Bore, Hare, Foxe, Gray, Conie*; *of* | Birds and Faulconrie. | *The Contents whereof are to be seene in* | *the Page following.* | [woodcut] | Printed at London by Edm. Bollifant, | for *Bonham Norton.* | 1600

First edition in English, London, 1600. Originally published in French under the title *L'Agriculture et maison rustique*, Paris, 1564.

4to. A^8 b^8 B-Nnn^8; 480 leaves, pp. [*32*] 1-901 [*902-928*]. First leaf blank. This copy lacks leaves A8 and b1.

Illustrations: Woodcuts illustrating patterns for formal gardens on pp. 328-347, distilling apparatus, pp. 565-566, 569-572, and measuring land on pp. 654, 656, and 660.

Note: This work deals largely with agriculture and farming but also contains information on preserving fruit, baking, distilling, and making wine.

Bibliographies: Fussell (1) p. 13; *STC* 10547; Wheaton and Kelly 2005.

Copies: *BMC* and *NUC* (12 copies). *STC* (10 copies).

669. Evelyn, John.

[within a border of two rules] *ACETARIA.* | A | DISCOURSE | OF | SALLETS. | [rule] | By *J.E.* S.R.S. Author of | the *Kalendarium.* | [rule] | Οὐ παντὸς ἀνδρὸς ἔστιν ἀρτῦσαι καλῶς. | Crat. in Glauc. | [rule] | *LONDON,* | Printed for *B. Tooke* at the *Middle-* | *Temple* Gate in *Fleetstreet*, 1699.

First edition, London, 1699.

8vo. π^2 A^8 a^8 b^4 B-P^8 R^8; 142 leaves, pp. [*44*] 1-192 [48]. Folding letter press chart of species of "sallets" not reckoned in collation or pagination. First leaf, blank, wanting in this copy.

Bibliographies: Bitting, p. 149; Craig 34; Keynes 105; Oberlé (1) 691; Oxford, p. 46; Schraemli (1) 173; Whaton and Kelly 2020; Wing E3480.

Copies: *BMC* and *NUC* (25 copies). Wing (14 copies).

670. Eyton, Thomas Campbell, 1809-1880.

A HISTORY | OF | THE OYSTER | AND | THE OYSTER FISHERIES. | BY | T. C. EYTON, F.L.S., F.Z.S., | ETC. ETC. | [publisher's monogram] | LONDON: | JOHN VAN VOORST, PATERNOSTER ROW. | MDCCCLVIII.

First edition, London, 1858.

224 x 140 mm. a^4 B-C^8 D^4; 24 leaves, pp. [i-iii] iv [v-viii] [1] 2-40. Publisher's blue cloth, stamped in gold. Eight page publisher's catalogue dated July 1871 bound in at end.

Illustrations: Six lithographed plates, four of them tinted, by T.C. Eyton, of Oysters.

Bibliographies: Simon BG 646.

Copies: *BMC* and *NUC* (7 copies).

671. The Family Economist.

[within triple ruled border with proverbs within rules: Volume 5: TAKE HEED WILL SURELY SPEED. | THE TRUEST JESTS SOUND WORST IN GUILTY EARS. |

AS IS THE GARDEN, SUCH IS THE GARDENER. | LIFE IS HALF SPENT BEFORE WE NOW ITS USE AND VALUE. [Volume 6: AN OBEDIENT WIFE COMMANDS HER HUSBAND. | IT IS WIT TO PICK A LOCK AND STEAL A HORSE BUT WISDOM TO LET THEM ALONE. | IT COSTS MORE TO REVENGE INJURIES THAN TO BEAR THEM. | IF YOU WOULD ENJOY THE FRUIT PLUCK NOT THE FLOWER.] THE | FAMILY ECONOMIST; | A Penny Monthly Magazine, | FOR THE INDUSTRIOUS CLASSES. | [short rule] | VOLUME FIFTH. [VOLUME SIXTH.] | [short rule] | [vignette] | [in two columns: column one] The Cottage Homes of England! | By thousands on her plains, | They are smiling o'er the silvery brook, | And round the hamlet fanes: | From glowing orchards forth they peep, | Each from its nook of leaves; | And fearless there the lowly sleep, | As the bird beneath their eaves. | [vertical rule] | [column two] The free fair homes of England! | Long, long in hut and hall; | May hearts of native proof be reared | To guard each hallowed wall. | And green for ever be the groves, | And bright the flowery sod, | Where first the child's glad spirit loves | Its country and its God. | [short rule] | LONDON: | GROOMBRIDGE AND SONS, PATERNOSTER ROW. | 1852. [1853.] | RICHARD BARRETT, Printer,] [13, Mark Lane, London.

First edition, London, 1852-1853. Volumes V and VI of six published between 1848 and 1853.

184 x 118 mm. 2 vols. Vol. V. [A]^2 B-M^{10} N^8; 120 leaves, pp. [i-iii] iv [1] 2-236. Signature B (pp. 1-20) and L (pp. 181-200) wanting in this copy. Vol. VI. [A]^2 B-M^{10} N^8; 120 leaves, pp. [i-iii] iv [1] 2-236. Signature L missigned "M"; signature B (pp. 1-20) wanting in this copy.

Illustrations: Numerous wood engravings in the text.

Bibliographies: *ULS*, p. 1523.

Copies: *BMC*, *NUC* (4 copies), and *ULS* (New York Public Library, Vol. I only; Newberry Library, Vols. I-IV; Princeton, Vols, I-III; University of Minnesota, Vols. I-IV).

672. The Family Economist.

[within a single rule border] NEW ILLUSTRATED SERIES. | [short fancy rule] | THE | FAMILY ECONOMIST; | AND | ENTERTAINING COMPANION FOR TOWN & COUNTRY. | TO WHICH IS ADDED | The Boys' and Girls'

𝔗reasury | [vignette] | VOLUME FIRST. [SECOND.] | 𝔏ondon: |
GROOMBRIDGE AND SONS, PATERNOSTER ROW. | [short fancy rule] | 1854.

First edition, London, 1854. Vols I-II only of eleven published between 1854 and
1860.

184 x 118 mm. 2 vols. Vol. I. [A]² B-F¹⁶ [G]¹⁴; 96 leaves, pp. [i-iii] iv [1] 2-178 [2]
179-186. Vol. II. [A]² B¹⁶ [C-F]¹⁶ [G]¹⁴; 96 leaves, pp. [i-iii] iv [1] 2-188. Each
volume is made up of six separately published monthly parts.

Illustrations: Numerous wood engravings in the text.

Bibliographies: *ULS* p. 1523.

Copies: *BMC, NUC* (4 copies), and *ULS* (New York Public Library, Vols. I-IX;
Newberry Library, Vols, I-IV, VII-X).

673. The Family Magazine.

THE | Family MAGAZINE: | In TWO PARTS. | [rule] | PART I. | Containing
Useful *Directions* in All the BRANCHES of | HOUSE-KEEPING *and* COOKERY. |
Particularly Shewing | How to Buy-in the Best of all Sorts of PROVISIONS; | As
Poultry-Ware, Butchers-Meat, Fish, Fruit, &c. | With several Hundred RECEIPTS in |
[in two columns: column one] COOKERY, | PASTRY, | PICKLING, |
CONFECTIONARY, | [two vertical rules] | [column two] DISTILLING, |
BREWING, | COSMETICKS, *&c.* [end columns] | Together with the ART of |
MAKING *ENGLISH WINES,* &c. | [rule] | PART II. | Containing A Compendious |
BODY *of* PHYSICK; | Succinctly TREATING of | All the DISEASES and
ACCIDENTS | INCIDENT TO | MEN, WOMEN, and CHILDREN: | WITH |
Practical *Rules* and *Directions* for the Preserving and | Restoring of HEALTH, and
Prolonging of LIFE. | [rule] | In a METHOD intirely New and Intelligible; in which
every | Disease is *rationally* and *practically* considered, in its several STAGES | and
CHANGES; and approved RECIPE's inserted under every | Distemper, in
Alphabetical Order. | Being principally the *Common-place Book* of a late able
PHYSICIAN, | by which he successfully, for many Years, regulated his PRACTICE. |
[rule] | With a SUPPLEMENT, containing a great Variety of *Experienced Receipts,* |
from Two Excellent FAMILY COLLECTIONS. | [rule] | Now First communicated for
the PUBLICK BENEFIT. | [rule] | To which is Added, | *An* Explanation *of such*
TERMS OF ART *used in the* WORK, *as could not be so* | *easily reduced to the*

Understanding of common Readers. | [two rules] | *LONDON:* | Printed for J. OSBORN, at the *Golden-Ball* in *Paternoster-Row.* | [short rule] | MDCCXLI.

Title-page of Part I:

THE | Family Magazine. | [rule] | PART I. | [rule] | Containing Useful | DIRECTIONS | In All the BRANCHES of | *HOUSE-KEEPING* | AND | COOKERY. | Particularly Shewing | How to Buy-in the Best of all Sorts of | PROVISIONS; As *Poultry-Ware, Butchers-* | *Meat, Fish, Fruit,* &c. | With several Hundred RECEIPTS in | [in two columns: column one] COOKERY, | PASTRY, | PICKLING | CONFECTIONARY, | [two vertical rules] | [column two] DISTILLING, | BREWING, | COSMETICKS, &c. [end columns] | Together with the ART of | Making *ENGLISH WINES,* &c. | [rule] | [ornament] | [rule] | *LONDON:* | Printed in the YEAR MDCCXLI.

Title-page of Part II:

THE | Family Magazine. | PART II. | [rule] | Being a Compendious | BODY *of* PHYSICK; | Succinctly Treating of | All the DISEASES and ACCIDENTS | Incident to | MEN, WOMEN, *and* CHILDREN: | WITH | Practical RULES and | DIRECTIONS for the | Preserving and Restoring of HEALTH, and | Prolonging of LIFE. | [rule] | In a METHOD intirely New and Intelligible; in which | every Disease is *rationally* and *practically* considered in its several | STAGES and CHANGES; and approved RECIPE's inserted | under every Distemper, in *Alphabetical Order.* | [rule] | Being principally the Collection and Common-place Book of a | late able Physician, by which he successfully for many Years | regulated his Practice. | [rule] | With a SUPPLEMENT, containing a great Variety of *experienced Receipts,* | from two excellent Family Collections. | [rule] | To which is Added, | *An* Explanation *of such* TERMS OF ART *used in the Work, as could not be* / *so easily reduced to the Understanding of common Readers.* / [two rules] | *LONDON:* | Printed in the YEAR MDCCXLI.

First edition, London, 1741.

8vo. A-I⁸, ²A-U⁸ X²; 234 leaves, pp. [i-ii] iii-xiv [2] [1] 2-123 [124-126] [2], ²1-324.

Note: The preface of this work concludes: P.S. Being still teized for some Name, I will, tho' not my right one, subscribe That of Arabella Atkyns.

Bibliographies: Axford, p. 143; Bitting, p. 550; Craig 7; Maclean, p. 49; Oxford, p. 71; Pennell, p. 150; Simon BG 658; Wheaton and Kelly 2051.

Copies: *NUC* (5 copies). Maclean adds British Library, Guildhall Library and Leads Public Library.

674. The Family Receipt-Book.

THE | Family Receipt-Book; | OR, | UNIVERSAL REPOSITORY | OF | Useful Knowledge and Experience in all the various Branches of | DOMESTIC OECONOMY. | INCLUDING | *SCARCE, CURIOUS, AND VALUABLE, SELECT RECEIPTS, AND CHOICE SECRETS, IN* | [in four columns: column one] COOKERY, | MEDICINE, | CONFECTIONARY, | PASTRY, | BREWING, | [two vertical rules] | [column two] DISTILLING, | PICKLING, | PRESERVING, | PERFUMERY, | DYEING, | [two vertical rules] | [column three] GILDING, | PAINTING, | VARNISHING, | AGRICULTURE, | FARRIERY, | [two vertical rules] | [column four] GARDENING, | HUNTING, | FISHING, | FOWLING, | &c. &c. &c. [end columns] | WITH | SPECIFICATIONS OF APPROVED PATENT MEDICINES; | ALL THE MOST SERVICEABLE PREPARATIONS FOR | 𝔇omestic 𝔓urposes; | AND NUMEROUS SUCCESSFUL | *Improvements in the Ornamental as well as Useful Arts, Manufactures, &c.* | EXTRACTED FROM THE | RECORDS OF THE PATENT OFFICE; | AND | *TRANSLATED FROM FOREIGN BOOKS AND JOURNALS, IN ALL THE LANGUAGES OF EUROPE.* | THE WHOLE FORMING | A COMPLEAT LIBRARY of VALUABLE DOMESTIC KNOWLEDGE, and GENERAL OECONOMY; selected from the | EXPERIENCE of AGES, and combined with all the chief MODERN DISCOVERIES and IMPROVEMENTS | of our own and other COUNTRIES, in those Useful and Elegant ARTS which not | only contribute to the HAPPINESS, the CONVENIENCE, and the COMFORT, | of CIVILIZED and SOCIAL LIFE, but even to the | PRESERVATION and PROLONGATION | of LIFE itself. | [two short rules] | 𝔏ondon: | PRINTED FOR THE EDITORS, | *AND* | PUBLISHED BY ODDY AND CO. 27, OXFORD STREET; AND C. LA GRANGE, LONDON. | [*THIRD EDITION, PRICE 25s. BOARDS.*]

Third edition, London, ca. 1814, based on ownership inscription in this copy dated 22 February 1814. No earlier edition has been located. See item 766 for an abridged edition by D. Hughson.

264 x 205 mm. π1 [A]² B-7H² a-e²; 303 leaves, pp. [2] [i] ii [3] 4-584 [*20*].

Bibliographies: Oxford, p. 144, describing this edition and assigning the date ca. 1817. Bitting, p. 550, describes a copy with no mention of edition, assigning the date ca. 1810.

Copies: No other copy described as third edition located. *BMC* and *NUC* (Detroit Public Library and University of Wisconsin) describe copies with no mention of edition, assigning the date ca. 1820. The Bitting copy is not recorded in the *NUC*.

675. Farley, John.

THE | London Art of Cookery, | AND | HOUSEKEEPER's COMPLETE ASSISTANT. | On a NEW PLAN. | Made Plain and Easy to the Understanding of every HOUSEKEEPER, | COOK, and SERVANT in the Kingdom. | CONTAINING, | [in two columns: column one] Proper Directions for the Choice of all | Kinds of Provisions. | Roasting and Boiling all Sorts of | Butchers Meat, Poultry, Game, | and Fish. | Sauces for every Occasion. | Soups, Broths, Stews, and Hashes. | Made Dishes, Ragoos, and Fricassees. | All Sorts of Pies and Puddings. | Proper Instructions for dressing Fruits | and Vegetables. | [two vertical rules] | [column two] Pickling, Potting, and Preserving. | The Preparation of Hams, Tongues, | and Bacon. | The whole Art of Confectionary. | Tarts, Puffs, and Pasties. | Cakes, Custards, Jams, and Jellies. | Drying, Candying, and Preserving | Fruits, &c. | Made Wines, Cordial Waters, and | Malt Liquors. [end columns] | To which is added, | AN APPENDIX, | Containing | Considerations on Culinary Poisons; Directions for making | Broths, &c. for the Sick; a List of Things in Season in the | different Months of the Year; Marketing Tables, &c. &c. | Embellished with | A HEAD of the AUTHOR, and a BILL of FARE for every Month in | the Year, elegantly engraved on Thirteen Copper-plates. | [rule] | By JOHN FARLEY, | PRINCIPAL COOK AT THE LONDON TAVERN. | [two rules] | LONDON: | Printed for JOHN FIELDING, No. 23, Pater-noster Row; and J. SCAT- | CHERD and J. WHITAKER, No. 12, Ave Maria Lane, 1783. | [Price Six Shillings Bound.]

First edition, London, 1783.

Note: *Petits Propose Culinaires*, nos. 42 and 43, give a detailed account by Fiona Lucraft of Farley's plagiarism from Mrs. Raffald and Mrs. Glasse, which accounts for over 90% of the recipes in this book.

8vo. A⁸ a² B-Ff⁸ Gg⁶; 240 leaves, pp. [i-iii] iv-xx [1] 2-459 [460].

Illustrations: Engraved frontispiece portrait of the author dated Jan. 1, 1783, and twelve engraved plates of bills of fare for each month.

Bibliographies: Maclean, p. 50; Oxford, p. 114; Wheaton and Kelly 2066.

Copies; *BMC* and *NUC* (Harvard and New York Public Library). Maclean adds Boston Public Library, Library of Congress, and National Library of Scotland.

676. Farley, John.

THE | London Art of Cookery, | AND | HOUSEKEEPER's COMPLETE
ASSISTANT. | On a NEW PLAN. | Made Plain and Easy to the Understanding of
every HOUSEKEEPER, | COOK, and SERVANT in the Kingdom. | CONTAINING,
| [in two columns: column one] Proper Directions for the Choice of all | Kinds of
Provisions. | Roasting and Boiling all Sorts of | Butchers Meat, Poultry, Game, | and
Fish. | Sauces for every Occasion. | Soups, Broths, Stews, and Hashes. | Made
Dishes, Ragoos, and Fricassees. | All Sorts of Pies and Puddings. | Proper Instructions
for dressing Fruits | and Vegetables. | [two vertical rules] | [column two] Pickling,
Potting, and Preserving. | The Preparation of Hams, Tongues, | and Bacon. | The
whole Art of Confectionary. | Tarts, Puffs, and Pasties. | Cakes, Custards, Jams, and
Jellies. | Drying, Candying, and Preserving | Fruits, &c. | Made Wines, Cordial
Waters, and | Malt Liquors. [end columns] | To which is added, | AN APPENDIX, |
Containing | Considerations on Culinary Poisons; Directions for making | Broths, &c.
for the Sick; a List of Things in Season in the | different Months of the Year;
Marketing Tables, &c. &c. | Embellished with | A HEAD of the AUTHOR, and a
BILL of FARE for every Month in | the Year, elegantly engraved on Thirteen
Copper-plates. | [rule] | THE SECOND EDITION. | [rule] | By JOHN FARLEY, |
PRINCIPAL COOK AT THE LONDON TAVERN. | [two rules] | LONDON: |
Printed for J. SCATCHERD and J. WHITAKER, No. 12, Ave- | Maria-Lane, and
JOHN FIELDING, No. 23, Pater-noster-Row, 1784. | [Price Six Shillings Bound.]

Second edition, London, 1784. Originally published, London, 1783 (item 675).

8vo. A⁸ a² B-Ff⁸ Gg⁶; 240 leaves, pp. [i-iii] iv-xx [1] 2-459 [460].

Illustrations: Engraved frontispiece portrait of the author dated Jan. 1, 1783, and
twelve engraved plates of bills of fare for each month.

Bibliographies: Maclean, p. 50; Oxford, p. 114 in note.

Copies: Maclean locates Dorset County Library copy only.

677. Farley, John.

THE | London Art of Cookery, | AND | HOUSEKEEPER's COMPLETE
ASSISTANT. | On a NEW PLAN. | Made Plain and Easy to the Understanding of
every HOUSEKEEPER, COOK | and SERVANT in the Kingdom. | CONTAINING, |
[in two columns: column one] Proper Directions for the Choice of all | Kinds of
Provisions. | Instructions for trussing Poultry. | Roasting and Boiling all Sorts of But-

| chers Meat, Poultry, Game, and | Fish. | Baking, Broiling, and Frying. | Sauces for every Occasion. | Soups, Broths, Stews, and Hashes. | Ragoos and Fricassees. | Made Dishes, both plain and elegant. | All Sorts of Pies and Puddings. | Pancakes and Fritters. | Proper Instructions for dressing Fruits | and Vegetables. | Pickling, Potting, and Preserving. | [two vertical rules] | [column two] | The Preparation of Hams, Tongues, | and Bacon. | To keep Garden Stuffs and Fruits in | Perfection. | The whole Art of Confectionary. | The preparation of Sugars. | Tarts, Puffs, and Pasties. | Cakes, Custards, Jams, and Jellies. | Drying, Candying, and Preserving | Fruits, &c. | Elegant Ornaments for Entertain- | ments. | Instructions for Carving. | Necessary Articles for Sea-faring Per- | sons. | Made Wines, Cordial Waters, and | Malt Liquors. [end columns] | To which is added, | AN APPENDIX, | CONTAINING | Considerations on Culinary Poisons; Directions for making Broths, &c. | for the Sick; a List of Things in Season in the different | Months of the Year; Marketing Tables, &c. &c. | Embellished with | A HEAD of the AUTHOR, and a BILL of FARE for every Month | in the Year, elegantly engraved on Thirteen Copper-plates. | [rule] | By JOHN FARLEY, | PRINCIPAL COOK AT THE LONDON TAVERN. | [rule] | THE SEVENTH EDITION. | With the Addition of many new and elegant RECEIPTS in the various | Branches of COOKERY. | [two rules] | LONDON: | Printed for J. SCATCHERD and J. WHITAKER, No. 12, B. LAW, No. 13, | Ave-Maria-Lane; and G. and T. WILKIE, St. Paul's Church-Yard, 1792. | [Price Six Shillings Bound.]

Seventh edition, London, 1792. Originally published, London, 1783 (item 675).

8vo. A⁸ a⁸ B-Gg⁸ Hh⁴; 252 leaves, pp. [i-iii] iv-vi [vii-xxxii] [1] 2-467 [468-472].

Illustrations: Engraved frontispiece portrait of the author with the facade of the London Tavern and twelve engraved plates of bills of fare for each month. In this frontispiece Farley's name appears in the oval frame around the portrait.

Bibliographies: Maclean, p. 50; Oxford, p. 114 in note. Vicarie 355 describes the eighth edition, London, 1790 [sic.].

Copies: *NUC* (New York Public Library only). Maclean adds Brotherton Library, Cambridge University Library, Guildhall Library, and Kansas State University.

678. Farley, John.

THE | London Art of Cookery, | AND | HOUSEKEEPER's COMPLETE ASSISTANT. | On a NEW PLAN. | Made Plain and Easy to the Understanding of every HOUSEKEEPER, COOK, | and SERVANT, in the Kingdom. | CONTAINING, | [in two columns: column one] Proper Directions for the Choice of all | Kinds of

Provisions. | Instructions for trussing Poultry. | Roasting and Boiling all Sorts of But- | chers Meat, Poultry, Game, and | Fish. | Baking, Broiling, and Frying. | Sauces for every Occasion. | Soups, Broths, Stews, and Hashes. | Ragoos and Fricassees. | Made Dishes, both plain and elegant. | All Sorts of Pies and Puddings. | Pancakes and Fritters. | Proper Instructions for dressing Fruits | and Vegetables. | Pickling, Potting, and Preserving. | [two vertical rules] | [column two] The Preparation of Hams, Tongues, | and Bacon. | To keep Garden Stuffs and Fruits in | Perfection. | The whole Art of Confectionary. | The Preparation of Sugars. | Tarts, Puffs, and Pasties. | Cakes, Custards, Jams, and Jellies. | Drying, Candying, and Preserving | Fruits, &c. | Elegant Ornaments for Entertainments. | Instructions for Carving. | Necessary Articles for Sea-faring Per- | sons. | Made Wines, Cordial Waters, and | Malt Liquors. [end columns] | To which is added, | AN APPENDIX, | CONTAINING | Considerations on Culinary Poisons; Directions for making Broths, &c. | for the Sick; a List of Things in Season in the different | Months of the Year; Marketing Tables, &c. &c. | EMBELLISHED WITH | A HEAD of the AUTHOR, and a BILL of FARE for every Month | in the Year, elegantly engraven on Thirteen Copper-plates. | [rule] | By JOHN FARLEY, | PRINCIPAL COOK AT THE LONDON TAVERN. | [rule] | THE NINTH EDITION. | With the Addition of many new and elegant RECEIPTS in the various | Branches of COOKERY. | [two rules] | LONDON: | PRINTED BY JOHN BARKER, No. 6, OLD BAILEY, | FOR JAMES SCATCHERD, No. 12, Ave-Maria-Lane; T. WILKIE; | Messrs. RICHARDSONS; LONGMAN and REES; LACKINGTON | and Co. CADEL and DAVIES; DARTON and Co. | J. WALKER; J. WHITAKER. 1800. | [Price Six Shillings Bound.]

Ninth edition, London, 1800. Originally published, London, 1783 (item 675).

8vo. a⁸ b⁴ B-Ff⁸; 236 leaves, pp. [i-iii] iv-xxiv [1] 2-448.

Illustrations: Engraved frontispiece portrait of the author with the facade of the London Tavern and twelve engraved plates of bills of fare for each month. In this frontispiece Farley's name appears below the oval portrait.

Bibliographies: Maclean, p. 50; Oxford, p. 114 in note; Wheaton and Kelly 2069.

Copies: *NUC* (Radcliffe and Oregon State Univerity). Maclean adds Brotherton Library, Strathclyde Library, and Wellcome Library.

679. Farley, John.

THE | *London Art of Cookery,* | AND | HOUSEKEEPER's COMPLETE ASSISTANT. | *ON A NEW PLAN.* | MADE PLAIN AND EASY TO THE

UNDERSTANDING | OF EVERY | HOUSEKEEPER, COOK, AND SERVANT, | *IN THE KINGDOM.* | CONTAINING, | [in two columns: column one] Proper Directions for the Choice of all Kinds | of Provisions. | Instructions for Trussing Poultry. | Roasting and Boiling all Sorts of Butcher's | Meat, Poultry, Game, and Fish. | Baking, Broiling, and Frying. | Sauces for every Occasion. | Soups, Broths, Stews, and Hashes. | Ragoos and Fricassees. | Made Dishes, both plain and elegant. | All Sorts of Pies and Puddings. | Pancakes and Fritters. | Proper Instructions for dressing Fruits and | Vegetables. | [two vertical rules] | [column two] Pickling, Potting, and Preserving. | The Preparation of Hams, Tongues, and Bacon. | To keep Garden Stuffs and Fruits in Per- | fection. | The whole Art of Confectionary. | The Preparation of Sugars. | Tarts, Puffs, and Pasties. | Cakes, Custards, Jams, and Jellies. | Drying, Candying, and Preserving Fruits, &c. | Elegant Ornaments for Entertainments. | Instructions for Carving. | Necessary Articles for Sea-faring Persons. | Made Wines, Cordial Waters, and Malt Liquors. [end columns] | TO WHICH I ADDED, | AN APPENDIX, | CONTAINING | [in two columns: column one] Considerations on Culinary Poisons. | Directions for making Broths, &c. for the | Sick. | [two vertical rules] | [column two] A List of Things in Season in the different | Months of the Year. | Marketing Tables, &c. &c. [end columns] | EMBELLISHED WITH | A HEAD OF THE AUTHOR, | AND A BILL OF FARE FOR EVERY MONTH IN THE YEAR. | [short fancy rule] | *BY JOHN FARLEY,* | PRINCIPAL COOK AT THE LONDON TAVERN. | [short fancy rule] | THE TENTH EDITION. | *With the Addition of many new and elegant Recipts in the various Branches of Cookery.* | [two short rules] | *LONDON:* | PRINTED BY C. WHITTINGHAM, | *Dean Street Fetter Lane,* | FOR JAMES SCATCHERD, NO. 12, AVE-MARIA-LANE; | T. WILKIE; MESSRS. RICHARDSONS; LONGMAN AND REES; LACKINGTON AND CO.; | CADELL AND DAVIES; DARTON AND CO.; J. WALKER; AND J. NUNN. 1801. | [short fancy rule] | [*Price Six Shillings Bound.*]

Tenth edition, London, 1801. Originally published, London, 1783 (item 675).

213 x 126 mm. A^8 a^4 B-Aa^8; 196 leaves, pp. [i-iii] iv-xxiv [1] 2-366 [2].

Illustrations: Engraved frontispiece portrait of the author with the facade of the London Tavern and twelve plates of bills of fare for each month printed on the rectos and versos of six leaves. In this frontispiece Farley's name appears below the oval portrait.

Bibliographies: Maclean, p. 152; Oxford, p. 114 in note.

Copies: *BMC* and *NUC* (Library of Congress only).

680. The Farmer's Wife.

THE | FARMER's WIFE; | OR COMPLETE | COUNTRY HOUSEWIFE. | CONTAINING | [in two columns: column one] Full and ample DIREC- | TIONS for the Breed- | ing and Management of | TURKIES, FOWLS, | GEESE, DUCKS, | PIGEONS, &c. | INSTRUCTIONS for fatten- | ing HOGS, pickling of | PORK, and curing of | BACON. | How to make SAUSAGES, | HOGS- PUDDINGS, &c. | Full INSTRUCTIONS for | making WINES from va- | rious Kinds of English | Fruits, and from Smyrna | Raisins. | The METHOD of making | CYDER, PERRY, | MEAD, MUM, CHER- | RY-BRANDY, &c. | DIRECTIONS respecting | [two vertical rules] | [column two] the DAIRY, containing | the best Way of making | BUTTER, and likewise | *Gloucestershire, Cheshire,* | *Stilton, Sage,* and *Cream* | CHEESE, &c. | How to pickle common | English FRUITS and | VEGETABLES, with | other useful Receipts for | the FARMER's WIFE | and Country HOUSE- | KEEPER. | Full INSTRUCTIONS how | to brew BEER and ALE, | of all the various Kinds | made in this Kingdom. | Ample DIRECTIONS re- | specting the Management | of BEES, with an Ac- | count of the Use of HO- | NEY. [end columns] | To which is added | The Art of Breeding and Managing SONG BIRDS | in General: | Likewise a Variety of RECEIPTS in COOKERY, | And other Particulars well worthy the Attention of | Women of all Ranks residing in the COUNTRY. | [rule] | *Instructions, full and plain,* *we give,* | *To teach the* Farmer's Wife, | *With Satisfaction, how to live* | *The happy Country Life.* | [rule] | LONDON: | Printed for ALEX. HOGG, No. 16, in Pater-noster | Row. | [Price One Shilling and Six-pence.]

First edition? London, ca. 1780. Two editions of this book exist, both printed for Alex. Hogg and both undated. One, described by Maclean, has 125 pages and the other, described here and in Oxford, has 132 pages. The title-pages are from different settings of type, varying in line length, word division and punctuation plus the addition of "No. 16" to the publisher's address in the imprint in the 132 page edition. Priority between the editions has not been determined.

12mo. A-L⁶; 66 leaves, pp. [1-9] 10-132.

Illustrations: Engraved frontispiece of a farmyard.

Bibliographies: Maclean, p. 52 (125 page edition); Oxford, p. 111 (132 page edition).

Copies: *BMC* (no. of pages not stated) and *NUC* (125 page edition, New York Public Library only). Maclean adds the Brotherton Library copy of the 125 page edition.

681. The Female Instructor.

THE | FEMALE | INSTRUCTOR; | OR, | Young Woman's Companion: | BEING | *A GUIDE TO ALL THE ACCOMPLISHMENTS WHICH* | *ADORN THE FEMALE* *CHARACTER,* | EITHER AS | A USEFUL MEMBER OF SOCIETY – A PLEASING AND | INSTRUCTIVE COMPANION, | OR, A | RESPECTABLE MOTHER OF A FAMILY. | WITH MANY | 𝔓leasing 𝔈xamples of illustrious females. | [short fancy rule] | TO WHICH ARE ADDED, | USEFUL MEDICINAL RECEIPTS, | AND A CONCISE | *SYSTEM OF COOKERY,* | WITH OTHER VALUABLE INFORMATION IN THE DIFFERENT | BRANCHES OF DOMESTIC ECONOMY. | [short fancy rule] | "Favour is deceitful, and Beauty is vain; but a Woman that feareth the | Lord, she shall be *praised.*" SOLOMON. | [short fancy rule] | LIVERPOOL: | PRINTED BY NUTTALL, FISHER, AND DIXON, DUKE STREET. | [two short rules] | Stereotype Edition.

"Stereotype Edition," Liverpool, 1812.

210 x 133 mm. [A]⁴ B-4A⁴; 280 leaves, pp. [i-iii] iv [5] 6-560.

Illustrations: Engraved frontispiece titled "Female Accomplishments" dated Sept. 1, 1812 and three engraved plates, one titled "Death of Lady Jane Grey" dated April 1, 1812 and two showing table settings dated May 5, 1812 and May 6, 1812.

Bibliographies: Simon BG 666. Oxford, p. 143, cites editions of [1815] and [1816] and Bitting, p. 551, describes an 1837 edition.

Copies: *BMC* and *NUC* (New York Public Library, University of Illinois, and University of Pennsylvania).

682. The Female Instructor.

THE | FEMALE | INSTRUCTOR; | OR, | Young Woman's Companion: | BEING | *A GUIDE TO ALL THE ACCOMPLISHMENTS WHICH* | *ADORN THE FEMALE* *CHARACTER,* | EITHER AS | A USEFUL MEMBER OF SOCIETY – A PLEASING AND | INSTRUCTIVE COMPANION, | OR, A | RESPECTABLE MOTHER OF A FAMILY. | WITH MANY | 𝔓leasing 𝔈xamples of illustrious females. | [short fancy rule] | TO WHICH ARE ADDED, | USEFUL MEDICINAL RECEIPTS, | AND A CONCISE | *SYSTEM OF COOKERY,* | WITH OTHER VALUABLE INFORMATION IN THE DIFFERENT | BRANCHES OF DOMESTIC ECONOMY. | [short fancy rule] | "Favour is deceitful, and Beauty is vain; but a Woman that feareth the | Lord, she shall be *praised*." SOLOMON. | [short fancy rule] | LIVERPOOL: | PRINTED BY NUTTALL, FISHER, AND DIXON, DUKE STREET. | [two short rules] | Stereotype Edition.

"Stereotype Edition," Liverpool, 1815.

198 x 122 mm. [A]⁴ B-4A⁴; 280 leaves, pp. [i-iii] iv [5] 6-560.

Illustrations: Engraved title-page, seven engraved pictorial plates dated from October 1811 through October 1815 and two undated engraved plates showing table settings.

Bibliographies: Axford, p. 154; Oxford, p. 143. Simon BG 666 describes the [1812] edition and Bitting an 1837 edition.

Copies: No other copy of this edition located.

683. The Female Servant's Adviser.

THE | FEMALE | SERVANT'S ADVISER, | OR | 𝕿𝖍𝖊 𝕾𝖊𝖗𝖛𝖎𝖈𝖊 𝕴𝖓𝖘𝖙𝖗𝖚𝖈𝖙𝖔𝖗; | CONTAINING, | AMONG OTHER USEFUL AND NECESSARY INSTRUCTION, | 1. Maxims of Prudence to be recollected in Service. | 2. Directions for Arranging the Breakfast and Tea Tables. | 3. Instructions for Setting out a Family Dinner Table and Side- | board. | 4. Instructions for Setting out a Dinner Table for Company, as | also the Side-board and Side-table. | 5. Instructions for Serving up and Attending at Dinners. | 6. Instructions for Setting out a Supper Table. | 7. Directions for Dressing Meat, Fish, Poultry, Game, Vegetables, | &c.; and for making Hashes, Gravies, &c. | 8. Directions for the Preservation and Management of Meat, | Fish, Poultry, Game, Vegetables, &c. | 9. The best Methods of Cleaning Furniture, Looking Glasses, Gilt | Frames, Carpets, Floor Cloths, Steel and Brass Ornaments, | Knives and Forks, Decanters and Glasses, Plate of all kinds, | Cleaning and Trimming Lamps, &c. &c. | 10. Approved Methods of Washing Laces, Muslins, Linens, Flannels, | and of removing Iron Moulds, Ink Spots, Fruit and Wine | Stains, &c. &c. | 11. The Law of Master and Servant. | [short rule] | ILLUSTRATED WITH PLATES. | 𝕰𝖝𝖍𝖎𝖇𝖎𝖙𝖎𝖓𝖌 𝖙𝖍𝖊 𝕸𝖊𝖙𝖍𝖔𝖉𝖘 𝖔𝖋 𝕾𝖊𝖙𝖙𝖎𝖓𝖌 𝖔𝖚𝖙 𝕯𝖎𝖓𝖓𝖊𝖗 𝕿𝖆𝖇𝖑𝖊𝖘, &c. | [two short rules] | LONDON: | PRINTED FOR SHERWOOD, GILBERT, AND PIPER, | 23, PATERNOSTER ROW. | [short rule] | *Price Three Shillings.*

First edition? London, ca. 1837.

170 x 105 mm. [A]⁴ B-F¹²; 64 leaves, pp. [4] [i] ii [2] [1] 2-119 [120]. Publisher's boards with cloth spine and printed label on front cover. 24 page publisher's catalogue dated January 1837.

Illustrations: Two lithographed plates showing table settings on A1ᵛ and A4ʳ.

Bibliographies: Attar 375.1.

Copies: *BMC* dated [1830?] and *NUC* (Newberry Library only, dated [1829?]).

684. Fisher, Lydia.

[within a border of type ornaments] THE | PRUDENT HOUSEWIFE; | OR, COMPLETE | ENGLISH COOK, | For TOWN and COUNTRY. | Being the newest Collection of the most genteel, | and least expensive Recipes in every Branch of | COOKERY, viz. | GOING TO MARKET; | [in three columns: column one] | For | ROASTING, | BOILING, | [vertical rule] | [column two] FRYING, | HASHING, | STEWING | [vertical rule] | [column three] BROILING, | BAKING, and | FRICASSEEING. [end columns] | Also, for | [in three columns: column one] MAKING PUD- | DINGS, | CUSTARDS, | CAKES | [vertical rule] | [column two] CHEESE CAKES, | PIES, | TARTS, | RAGOUTS, | [vertical rule] | [column three] SOUPS, | JELLIES, | SYLLABUBS, | WINES, &c. [end columns] | To which are added, selected from the Papers of a Lady | of Distinction, lately deceased, New and infallible | Rules to be observed in | PICKLING, [vertical rule] PRESERVING, [vertical rule] BREWING, &c. | And, in order to render it still more valuable than any | other Publication that hath appeared, a Treasure of va- | luable Medicines, for the Cure of every Disorder, crowns | the whole of the Work; which contains every Instruc- | tion that relates to the pleasing of the Palate, and the | Preservation of that inestimable Blessing, HEALTH. | [rule] | Written by Mrs, FISHER, of RICHMOND. | [rule] | The TWELFTH EDITION, with Additions. | [rule] | LONDON: | Printed by T. SABINE, No. 81, Shoe-Lane, Fleet- | street, where Printing is expeditiously performed in | all its various Branches. | [short fancy rule] | PRICE ONE SHILLING.

Twelfth edition, London, ca. 1798. Originally published, London, ca. 1750.

4to. A-S⁴; 72 leaves, pp. [1-2] 3-144.

Illustrations: Woodcuts in the text illustrating carving and table settings.

Bibliographies: Maclean, p. 54; Wheaton and Kelly 2159. Bitting, p. 159, and Oxford, p. 82, describe the first edition. Bitting also records a fourth edition with a frontispiece dated July 21, 1788. Maclean dates the twelfth edition [c.1758] but this appears to be too early. William B. Todd in his *Directory of Printers and Others in Allied Trades, London and Vicinity 1800-1840*, gives Thomas Sabine's dates at 81 Shoe Lane as 1785-1804 which, combined with the dated frontispiece in Bitting's fourth edition, suggests a date closer to 1798 than 1758. The type face and design of the book also support the later date.

Copies: Maclean and Wheaton and Kelly locate only the Radcliffe College copy of the twelfth edition.

685. Forsyth, J. S.

A | DICTIONARY OF DIET; | BEING | A PRACTICAL TREATISE | ON | ALL PABULARY AND NUTRITIVE SUBSTANCES, | SOLID AND FLUID, | WITH THEIR COMPOUNDS, | USED AS FOOD; | INCLUDING THE OBSERVATIONS OF | EMINENT PHILOSOPHERS, PHYSICIANS, GASTRONOMERS, AND OTHER | INDUSTRIOUS INQUIRERS INTO THE TRUE SCIENCE OF EATING, | DRINKING, AND PRESERVING HEALTH, | THROUGH THE MEDIUM OF WELL REGULATED AND EASILY DIGESTIBLE | FOOD, FOUNDED ON THE KNOWN SPECIFIC PROPERTIES | OF ALL KINDS OF HUMAN ALIMENT; | WITH | THE MEANS OF PREVENTION, AND CURE, OF THE DISEASES RESULTING | FROM A DERANGED CONDITION OF THE ORGANS OF | DIGESTION, ETC. ETC. | BY J. S. FORSYTH, SURGEON, | AUTHOR OF THE "LONDON MEDICAL AND SURGICAL DICTIONARY;" "TREATISE ON DIET | AND REGIMEN;" "NEW DOMESTIC MEDICAL MANUAL," ETC. ETC. | [short rule] | "Health depends chiefly on the choice of food; and he who would treat | skillfully the subject of health, must consider the nautre of man, the nautre of | aliments, and the constitution of the person who takes them." – HIPPOCRATES. | "We should beware of such food as may tempt us to eat when we are not | hungry; and of such liquors as may entice us to drink when we are not thirsty." | SOCRATES. | [short rule] | *Second Edition.* | LONDON: HENRY CREMER, 19, CORNHILL. | 1834.

Second edition, London, 1834. Originally published, London, 1833. Another "second edition," in the private collection of John C. Craig, has the imprint, London, John Churchill, 1835.

205 x 124 mm. a² b⁶ c⁴ d² B-2L⁶ 2M⁴; 216 leaves, pp. [i-iii] iv-xxviii [1] 2-403 [404].

Illustration: Engraved frontispiece portrait of John Abernethy, F.R.S.

Bibliographies: Axford, p. 114; Bitting, p. 162; Simon BG 702; Vicaire 48.

Copies: *BMC* and *NUC* (Library of Congress only).

686. Forsyth, William, 1737-1804.

A | TREATISE | ON THE | CULTURE AND MANAGEMENT OF | FRUIT-TREES; | IN WHICH | A NEW METHOD OF PRUNING AND TRAINING IS FULLY DESCRIBED. | TO WHICH IS ADDED, A NEW AND IMPROVED EDITION OF | "OBSERVATIONS ON THE DISEASES, DEFECTS, AND INJURIES, | IN ALL KINDS OF FRUIT AND FOREST TREES:" | WITH AN | ACCOUNT OF A PARTICULAR METHOD OF CURE, | *Published by Order of Government.* | [two short rules] | BY WILLIAM FORSYTH, F. A. S. AND F. S. A. | GARDENER TO HIS MAJESTY AT KENSINGTON AND ST. JAMES'S, MEMBER | OF THE OECONOMICAL SOCIETY AT ST. PETERSBURG, &c. &c. | [two short rules] | LONDON: | *Printed by Nichols and Son, Red-Lion Passage, Fleet-Street,* | FOR T. N. LONGMAN AND O. REES, PATERNOSTER- ROW; T. CADELL, JUN. AND | W. DAVIES, STRAND; AND J. DEBRETT, PICCADILLY. | 1802.

First edition, London, 1802.

267 x 215 mm. A-AAA⁴ BBB²; 190 leaves, pp. [i-iii] iv-viii [1] 2-371 [372].

Illustrations: Thirteen engraved folding plates illustrating pruning.

Bibliographies: This edition unrecorded in the bibliographies consulted. Noling, p. 160, records the third edition, London, 1803.

Copies: *BMC*, *BNC*, and *NUC* (11 copies).

687. Francatelli, Charles Elmé.

THE MODERN COOK; | A PRACTICAL GUIDE TO THE CULINARY ART | IN ALL ITS BRANCHES, | COMPRISING, | IN ADDITION TO ENGLISH COOKERY, THE MOST APPROVED AND RECHERCHÉ | SYSTMES OF FRENCH, ITALIAN, AND GERMAN COOKERY; | ADAPTED AS WELL FOR THE LARGEST ESTABLISHMENTS AS | FOR THE USE OF PRIVATE FAMILIES. | BY CHARLES ELMÉ FRANCATELLI, | PUPIL TO THE

CELEBRATED CARÊME, | AND LATE MAÎTRE-D'HÔTEL AND CHIEF COOK
TO HER MAJESTY THE QUEEN. | WITH SIXTY ILLUSTRATIONS. | NINTH
EDITION. | *CAREFULLY REVISED, AND CONSIDERABLY ENLARGED.* |
LONDON: | RICHARD BENTLEY, NEW BURLINGTON STREET. | 1855.

Ninth edition, London, 1855. Originally published, London, 1846.

220 x 140 mm. [A]⁸ B-2K⁸ 2L⁴ 2M-2N⁸; 284 leaves, pp. [i-v] vi-xv [xvi] [1] 2-552.
Publisher's blue cloth, stamped in gold.

Illustrations: Numerous wood engravings in the text.

Bibliographies: Oxford, p. 177 in a note. Axford, p. 273, Craig 36, and Simon BG
703 record the first edition.

Copies: *BMC*.

688. Francatelli, Charles Elmé.

[in red] THE ROYAL | ENGLISH AND FOREIGN | [in red] CONFECTIONER: | A
PRACTICAL TREATISE ON THE | ART OF CONFECTIONARY IN ALL ITS
BRANCHES; | COMPRISING | ORNAMENTAL CONFECTIONARY
ARTISTICALLY DEVELOPED; | DIFFERENT METHODS OF PRESERVING
FRUITS, FRUIT PULPS, AND JUICES IN | BOTTLES, THE PREPARATION OF
JAMS AND JELLIES, FRUITS, AND | OTHER SYRUPS, SUMMER BEVERAGES,
AND A GREAT VARIETY OF | NATIONAL DRINKS; WITH DIRECTIONS FOR
MAKING DESSERT CAKES, | PLAIN AND FANCY BREAD, CANDIES,
BONBONS, COMFITS, SPIRITUOUS | ESSENCES, AND CORDIALS. | ALSO, |
THE ART OF ICE-MAKING, AND THE ARRANGEMENT AND | GENERAL
ECONOMY OF FASHIONABLE DESSERTS. | BY | [in red] CHARLES ELMÉ
FRANCATELLI. | PUPIL TO THE CELEBRATED CARÊME, AND LATE
MAÎTRE-D'HÔTEL TO HER MAJESTY THE QUEEN; | AUTHOR OF "THE
MODERN COOK," "THE COOK'S GUIDE," AND | "COOKERY FOR THE
WORKING CLASSES." | With numerous Illustrations in Chromo=
Lithography. | LONDON: | [in red] CHAPMAN AND HALL, 193, PICCADILLY.
| 1862. | [*The right of Translation is reserved.*]

First edition, London, 1862.

195 x 125 mm. π² a⁸ b⁴ B-EE⁸ FF⁴; 234 leaves, pp. [i-v] vi-xxvii [xxviii] [1] 2-422, ²[1] 2-18. Publisher's brown cloth, stamped in gold. The 18 page catalogue at the end is titlted "Francatelli's Royal Confectioner Advertiser."

Illustrations: Chromolithograph frontispiece of a wedding cake, five wood engraved plates, and eight chromolithograph plates.

Bibliographies: Axford, p. 353; Bitting, p. 164; Schraemli (1) 182.

Copies: *BMC* and *NUC* (Library of Congress only).

689. Frazer, Mrs.

THE | PRACTICE | OF | *COOKERY, PASTRY, PICKLING,* | *PRESERVING,* &c. | CONTAINING | FIGURES OF DINNERS, | FROM | FIVE TO NINETEEN DISHES, | AND | A FULL LIST OF SUPPER DISHES; | ALSO | A LIST OF THINGS IN SEASON, | *For every month in the Year,* | AND | DIRECTIONS FOR CHOOSING PROVISIONS: | WITH | TWO PLATES, showing the method of placing Dishes upon | a Table, and the manner of Trussing Poultry, *&c.* | BY MRS FRAZER, | SOLE TEACHER OF THESE ARTS IN EDINBURGH, | Several years COLLEAGUE, and afterwards SUCCESSOR | to Mrs. M'IVER deceased. | EDINBURGH: | PRINTED FOR PETER HILL, EDINBURGH, | AND | T. CADELL, LONDON. | M, DCC, XCI.

First edition, Edinburgh, 1791. Based on Susanna Maciver's *Cookery and Pastry* (Edinburgh, 1773).

12mo. π1 b⁶ A-X⁶ Y1 (b6 folded to precede b1); 134 leaves, pp. [i-iii] iv-xiii [xiv] [1] 2-254.

Illustrations: Two engraved plates illustrating trussing and table setting.

Bibliographies: Craig 38; Maclean, p. 55; Oxford, p. 120; Vicaire 375. Simon BG 711 and 712 for other editions.

Copies: *BMC* and *NUC* (New York Public Library only). Maclean adds Brotherton Library and National Library of Scotland.

689a. Frazer, Mrs.

THE | PRACTICE | OF | *COOKERY, PASTRY, CONFECTIONARY,* | *PICKLING,*
PRESERVING, &c. | CONTAINING | FIGURES OF DINNERS, | FROM | FIVE TO
NINETEEN DISHES, | A | FULL LIST OF SUPPER DISHES, | A | LIST OF
THINGS IN SEASON, | *For every Month in the Year,* | AND | DIRECTIONS FOR
CHOOSING PROVISIONS: | *WITH TWO COPPER PLATES,* | Showing the manner
of placing Dishes upon a Table, | and of Trussing Poultry, &c. | [double rule] | BY
MRS FRAZER, | TEACHER OF THESE ARTS IN EDINBURGH. | [double rule] |
THE SECOND EDITION, CORRECTED, | CONTAINING MANY ADDITIONAL
RECEIPTS, | NEVER BEFORE PUBLISHED. | [short thick-thin rule] |
EDINBURGH: | PRINTED FOR PETER HILL, AND VERNOR AND HOOD, |
LONDON. | [short rule] | 1795.

Second edition, Edinburgh, 1795. Based on Susanna Maciver's *Cookery and Pastry*
(Edinburgh, 1773). Originally published, Edinburgh, 1791 (item 689).

12mo. a^6 b^2 A-Y^6 Z^2; 142 leaves, pp. [i-iii] iv-xv [xvi] [1] 2-268.

Illustrations: Two copperplate engravings illustrating trussing and table setting.

Bibliographies: Maclean, p. 55; Oxford, p. 120.

Copies: *BMC, NUC* (American Antiquarian Society and Folger Library), Maclean
(Bodleian Library, National Library of Scotland, and New York Public Library).

690. Frazer, Mrs.

THE | PRACTICE | OF | [in two columns: column one] COOKERY, | PASTRY, |
CONFECTIONARY, | [two vertical rules] | [column two] PICKLING, | AND |
PRESERVING. [end columns] | WITH | Directions for choosing Provisions, Trussing
| Poultry, &c. | TO WHICH IS ADDED, | An APPENDIX, | containing, | Receipts
for making VINEGAR, KETCHUPS, | WINES, CORDIALS, &c. | LIKEWISE | The
ART of CARVING. | Also, | LISTS OF SUPPER AND DINNER DISHES, | AND |
Of Articles in seasons in the different Months of the Year; | *WITH PLATES,* | Shewing
the Manner of Trussing Poultry, and Placing | Dishes on a Table. | [two rules] | BY
MRS FRAZER, | *TEACHER OF THESE ARTS IN EDINBURGH,* | [two rules] | THE
THIRD EDITION. | IMPROVED AND ENLARGED. | [two short rules] |
EDINBURGH: | PRINTED FOR PETER HILL; | *By J. Ruthven & Sons.* | [short
rule] | 1800.

Third edition, Edinburgh, 1800. Originally published, Edinburgh, 1791 (item 689).

180 x 107 mm. π^2 a^6 A-Y^6 Z^4; 144 leaves, pp. [i-iii] iv-xvi [1] 2-270 [2], last leaf blank.

Illustrations: Two engraved plates showing table setting and trussing.

Bibliographies: Axford, p. 330; Bitting, p. 166; Maclean, p. 55; Oxford, p. 120 in a note.

Copies: *BMC* and *NUC* (National Library of Medicine only). Maclean adds National Library of Scotland.

691. Frazer, Mrs.

THE | PRACTICE | OF | COOKERY, PASTRY, | AND | CONFECTIONARY; | IN THREE PARTS: | CONTAINING, | [in two columns: column one] PART I. Receipts for mak- | ing up all kinds of plain and | dressed Dishes; Soups, Sauces, | Ragoos, Fricassees, &c. | PART II. Pies, Pastries, Pud- | dings, Dumplings, Custards, | Pancakes, Fritters, &c. | [two vertical rules] | [column two] PART III. Pickling and Preserv- | ing; Barley Sugars, Tablets, | Cakes, Biscuits, Cheese-Cakes, | Tarts, Jellies, Creams, Syl- | labubs, Blamange: Fowls, | Fishes, &c. in Jelly, with | other elegant Deserts. | [end columns] | AN | APPENDIX; | *Containing Receipts for making* | WINES, VINEGARS, KETCHUPS, SYRUPS, CORDIALS, POSSETS, &c. | DINNER AND SUPPER DISHES; ARTICLES IN SEASON; | DIRECTIONS FOR CARVING, &C. | ALSO, | *NEW PLATES,* | Shewing the manner of trussing Poultry, and placing | Dishes on a Table. | AND TO WHICH IS NOW ADDED, | *An* INDEX *to the whole, arranged Alphabetically.* | [two rules] | BY MRS FRAZER, | TEACHER OF THESE ARTS IN EDINBURGH. | [two rules] | *THE FOURTH EDITION:* | With large Additions and Improvements. | [two short rules] | *EDINBURGH:* | PRINTED FOR PETER HILL, | BY J. RUTHVEN AND SONS. | [short rule] | 1804.

Fourth edition, Edinburgh, 1804. Based on Susanna Mciver's *Cookery and Pastry* (Edinburgh, 1773). Originally published, Edinburgh, 1791 (item 689).

174 x 105 mm. π^2 A-Bb^6 cc^2; 154 leaves, pp. [4] [1] 2-304.

Illustrations: Two engraved plates showing table setting and trussing.

Bibliographies: Axford, p. 330 in a note.

Copies: *NUC* (New York Public Library only).

692. Furnivall, Frederick James, 1825-1910.

𝕰𝖆𝖗𝖑𝖞 𝕰𝖓𝖌𝖑𝖎𝖘𝖍 | 𝕸𝖊𝖆𝖑𝖘 𝖆𝖓𝖉 𝕸𝖆𝖓𝖓𝖊𝖗𝖘: | [short fancy rule] | 𝕵𝖔𝖍𝖓 𝕽𝖚𝖘𝖘𝖊𝖑𝖑'𝖘 𝕭𝖔𝖐𝖊 𝖔𝖋 𝕹𝖚𝖗𝖙𝖚𝖗𝖊, | 𝖂𝖞𝖓𝖐𝖞𝖓 𝖉𝖊 𝖂𝖔𝖗𝖉𝖊'𝖘 𝕭𝖔𝖐𝖊 𝖔𝖋 𝕶𝖊𝖗𝖚𝖞𝖓𝖌𝖊, | 𝕿𝖍𝖊 𝕭𝖔𝖐𝖊 𝖔𝖋 𝕮𝖚𝖗𝖙𝖆𝖘𝖞𝖊, | 𝕽. 𝖂𝖊𝖘𝖙𝖊'𝖘 𝕭𝖔𝖔𝖐𝖊 𝖔𝖋 𝕯𝖊𝖒𝖊𝖆𝖓𝖔𝖗, | 𝕾𝖊𝖆𝖌𝖊𝖗'𝖘 𝕾𝖈𝖍𝖔𝖔𝖑𝖊 𝖔𝖋 𝖁𝖊𝖗𝖙𝖚𝖊, | 𝕿𝖍𝖊 𝕭𝖆𝖇𝖊𝖊𝖘 𝕭𝖔𝖔𝖐, 𝕬𝖗𝖎𝖘𝖙𝖔𝖙𝖑𝖊'𝖘 𝕬 𝕭 𝕮, 𝖀𝖗𝖇𝖆𝖓𝖎𝖙𝖆𝖙𝖎𝖘, | 𝕾𝖙𝖆𝖓𝖘 𝕻𝖚𝖊𝖗 𝖆𝖉 𝕸𝖊𝖓𝖘𝖆𝖒, 𝕿𝖍𝖊 𝕷𝖞𝖙𝖞𝖑𝖑𝖊 𝕮𝖍𝖎𝖑𝖉𝖗𝖊𝖓𝖊𝖘 𝕷𝖞𝖙𝖎𝖑 𝕭𝖔𝖐𝖊, | 𝕵𝖔𝖗 𝖙𝖔 𝖘𝖊𝖗𝖇𝖊 𝖆 𝕷𝖔𝖗𝖉, 𝕺𝖑𝖉 𝕾𝖞𝖒𝖔𝖓, 𝕿𝖍𝖊 𝕭𝖎𝖗𝖈𝖍𝖊𝖉 𝕾𝖈𝖍𝖔𝖔𝖑-𝕭𝖔𝖞, | &c. &c. | [short fancy rule] | 𝖜𝖎𝖙𝖍 𝖘𝖔𝖒𝖊 | 𝖋𝖔𝖗𝖊𝖜𝖔𝖗𝖉𝖘 𝖔𝖓 𝕰𝖉𝖚𝖈𝖆𝖙𝖎𝖔𝖓 𝖎𝖓 𝕰𝖆𝖗𝖑𝖞 𝕰𝖓𝖌𝖑𝖆𝖓𝖉. | [short fancy rule] | EDITED BY | FREDERICK J. FURNIVALL, M.A., | TRIN. HALL, CAMBRIDGE. | LONDON: | N. TRÜBNER & CO., 60, PATERNOSTER ROW. | [short rule] | MDCCCLXVIII.

First edition, London, 1868.

268 x 200 mm. [A]⁴ B-N⁴ O⁴ (-O4) 1-49⁴; 251 leaves, pp. [8] [i] ii-c [ci-cvi] [1] 2-388. Publisher's quarter black morocco stamped in gold.

Illustrations: Sixteen plates showing scenes from medieval life bound in at the end.

Bibliographies: Axford, p. 124; Bitting, p. 172; Schraemli (1) 192.

Copies: *NUC* (4 copies).

693. Gayton, Edmund, 1608-1666.

[within a border of type ornaments and a rule] THE | Art of Longevity, | OR, | A Diaeteticall INSTITUTION. | [rule] | *Written by* Edmund Gayton, | *Bachelor in PHYSICK, of St.* John Bapt. | *Coll.* OXFORD. | [rule] | [ornament] | [rule] | *LONDON,* | Printed for the *Author.* 1659.

First edition, London, 1659.

4to. A⁴ a⁴ B-M⁴ N²; 54 leaves, pp. [*16*] 1-80, 83-94.

Bibliographies: Wing G406.

Copies: *BMC* (2 copies) and *NUC* (5 copies). Wing (11 copies).

694. The Gentleman's Companion.

THE | *Gentleman*'s Companion: | OR, | *Tradesman's Delight.* | CONTAINING, | The Mystery of DYING in all it Branches. The Manner | of preparing Colours. The Method of cleaning and ta- | king out Stains from Silks, Woollen or Linnen. To clean | Gold or Silver Lace, and Plate. To prepare a Cement for | China, or Glass. | The Art of Drawing, Limning, Painting, Etching Engrav- | ing, Carving, Gilding, Enamelling, and Refreshing | PICTURES. | Likewise the Quality of Natural and Artificial METALS. | How to harden or soften them. The Art of soldering, | burnishing and guilding Metals. To make all Sorts of | Ink. To prepare Gold and Silver for Writing. To make | Sealing Wax, or Wafers. To know the Purity of Gold | or Silver, and detect counterfeit Coins. | The Great Mr. *Boyle*'s Method of Writing in such a Manner | as cannot be discovered without the Help of Fire, Water, | &c. To take Blott out of Paper. The Art of dressing, | cleaning, and perfuming Gloves and Ribbons; and washing | all Sorts of Lace. | To which is added, | The Method of curing and preserving all Sorts of WINES | in the best Manner. Also, some excellent Receipts in | Cookery, Physick, and Surgery. Observations on Silk | Worms, with Directions how to manage and keep them | to Advantage. With many other useful Things never be- | fore Printed. | [rule] | *LONDON:* | Printed for *J. Stone*, at *Bedford-Row*, near *Gray's-Inn*; | and Sold by *G. Strahan*, at the *Royal Exchange*; | *W. Mears*, on *Ludgate-hill*; *J. Jackson*, in *Pall-* | *Mall*, and *C. Corbet*, at *Temple-Bar*, 1735. | (Price 2 s. 6 d.)

First edition, London, 1735.

12mo. A-M^{12}; 144 leaves, pp. [1-4] 5-257 [258-284] [*4*]. Page 257 misnumbered "259."

Bibliographies: Axford, p. 180; Bitting, p. 556; Maclean, p. 56; Oxford p. 65; Wheaton and Kelly 2355.

Copies: *NUC* (4 copies).

695. Glasse, Hannah, 1708-1770.

THE | ART | OF | COOKERY, | Made PLAIN and EASY; | Which far exceeds any THING of the Kind ever yet Published. | CONTAINING, | [in two columns: column one] I. Of Roasting, Boiling, &c. | II. Of Made-Dishes. | III. Read this Chapter, and you will find how | Expensive a *French* Cook's Sauce is. | IV. To make a Number of pretty little Dishes fit | for a Supper, or Side-Dish, and little Corner- | Dishes for a great Table; and the rest you have | in the Chapter for *Lent*. | V. To dress Fish. | VI. Of Soops and Broths. | VII. Of Puddings. | VIII. Of Pies. | IX. For a Fast-Dinner, a Number of good Dishes, | which you may make use for a Table at any | other Time. | X. Directions for the Sick. |

XI. For Captains of Ships. | XII. Of Hog's Puddings, Sausages, &c. | [two vertical rules] | [column two] XIII. To Pot and Make Hams, &c. | XIV. Of Pickling. | XV. Of making Cakes, &c. | XVI. Of Cheesecakes, Creams, Jellies, Whip | Syllabubs, &c. | XVII. Of Made Wines, Brewing, *French* Bread, | Muffins, &c. | XVIII. Jarring Cherries, and Preserves, &c. | XIX. To Make Anchovies, Vermicella, Ketchup, | Vinegar, and to keep Artichokes, French- | Beans, &c. | XX. Of Distilling. | XXI. How to Market, and the Seasons of the | Year for Butcher's Meat, Poultry, Fish, Herbs, | Roots, &c. and Fruit. | XXII. A certain Cure for the Bite of a Mad Dog. | By Dr. *Mead.* [end columns] | [rule] | BY A LADY. | [rule] | [ornament] | [two rules] | *LONDON:* | Printed for the AUTHOR; and sold at Mrs. *Ashburn*'s , a China-Shop, the | Corner of *Fleet-Ditch.* MDCCXLVII. | [*Price 3 s. stitch'd, and 5 s. bound.*]

First edition, London, 1747.

Folio: π^2 a-c^2 A-N^2 O1 P-Ss^2; 89 leaves, pp. [*16*] [i] ii [3] 4-65, 68-135, 138-166.

Bibliographies: Bitting, p. 186; Craig 39; Maclean, p. 59; Noling, p. 172; Oxford, p. 76; Pennell, p. 151: Simon BG 761; Wheaton and Kelly 2404.

Copies: *BMC* and *NUC* (9 copies). Maclean adds Brotherton Library and National Library of Scotland.

696. Glasse, Hannah, 1708-1770.

THE | Art of Cookery, | MADE | PLAIN and EASY; | Which far exceeds any Thing of the Kind every yet published. | CONTAINING, | [in two columns: column one] I. Of Roasting, Boiling, &c. | II. Of Made-Dishes. | III. Read this Chapter, and you | will find how Expensive a | *French* Cook's Sauce is. | IV. To make a Number of pretty | little Dishes fit for a Supper, or | Side-Dish, and little Corner- | Dishes for a great Table; and | the rest you have in the Chap- | ter for *Lent.* | V. To dress Fish. | VI. Of Soops and Broths. | VII. Of Puddings. | VIII. Of Pies. | IX. For a Fast-Dinner, a Number | of good Dishes, which you may | make use of for a Table at any | other Time. | X. Directions for the Sick. | XI. For Captains of Ships. | XII. Of Hog's Puddings, Sau- | sages, &c. | [two vertical rules] | [column two] XIII. To Pot and Make Hams, | &c. | XIV. Of Pickling. | XV. Of Making Cakes, &c. | XVI. Of Cheesecakes, Creams, | Jellies, Whip Syllabubs, &c. | XVII. Of Made Wines, Brewing, | *French* Bread, Muffins, &c. | XVIII. Jarring Cherries, and Pre- | serves, &c. | XIX. To Make Anchovies, Ver- | micella, Catchup, Vinegar, and | to keep Artichokes, French- | Beans, &c. | XX. Of Distilling. | XXI. How to Market, and the | Seasons of the Year for But- | cher's Meat, Poultry, Fish, | Herbs, Roots, &c. and Fruit. | XXII. A certain Cure for the Bite | of a Mad Dog. By Dr. *Mead.* | XXIII. A Receipt to keep clear | from Buggs. [end columns] | [rule] | *By a LADY.* |

[rule] | *The* SECOND EDITION. | [rule] | *LONDON:* | Printed for the AUTHOR, and sold at Mrs. *Wharton*'s Toy-Shop, | the *Bluecoat-Boy*, near the *Royal-Exchange*; at Mrs. *Ashburn*'s | China-Shop, the Corner of *Fleet-Ditch*; at Mrs. *Condall*'s Toy-Shop, | the *King's Head and Parrot*, in *Holborn*; at Mr. *Underwood*'s Toy- | Shop, near St. *James's-Gate*; and at most Market-Towns in *England.* | [short rule] | M.DCC.XLVII. | [*Price* 3 s. 6 d. *stitch'd, and* 5 s. *bound.*]

Second edition, London, 1747. Originally published, London, also 1747 (item 695).

8vo. [A]⁴ (A3 + a-c⁴ d²) B-Tt⁴; 182 leaves, pp. [2] [i] ii-iv [28] [1] 2-330.

Bibliographies: Axford, p. 17; Bitting, p. 187; Maclean, p. 59; Oxford, p. 77; Schraemli (1) 207; Simon BG 762.

Copies: *NUC* (Library of Congress only). Maclean adds Brotherton Library, Dorset County Library, and Kansas State University copies.

697. Glasse, Hannah, 1708-1770.

THE | Art of COOKERY, | MADE | PLAIN and EASY; | Which far exceeds any Thing of the Kind | ever yet published. | CONTAINING. | [in two columns: column one] | I. Of Roasting, Boiling, *&c.* | II. Of Made-Dishes. | III Read this Chapter, and you | will find how Expensive a | *French* Cook's Sauce is. | IV. To make a Number of pretty | little Dishes fit for a Supper, or | Side-Dish, and little Corner- | Dishes for a great Table; and | the rest you have in the Chapter | for *Lent.* | V. To dress Fish. | VI. Of Soops and Broths. | VII. Of Puddings. | VIII. Of Pies. | IX. For a Fast-Dinner, a Number | of good Dishes, which you may | make use of for a Table at any | other Time. | X. Directions for the Sick. | XI. For Captains of Ships. | XII. Of Hog's Puddings, Sau- | sages, *&c.* | [two vertical rules] | [column two] XIII. To Pot and Make Hams, | *&c.* | XIV. Of Pickling. | XV. Of Making Cakes, *&c.* | XVI. Of Cheesecakes, Creams, | Jellies, Whip Syllabubs, *&c.* | XVII. Of Made Wines, Brewing, | *French* Bread, Muffins, *&c.* | XVIII. Jarring Cherries, and Pre- | serves, *&c.* | XIX. To Make Anchovies, Ver- | micella, Catchup, Vinegar, | and to keep Artichokes, French- | Beans, *&c.* | XX. Of Distilling. | XXI. How to Market, and the | Seasons of the Year for Butcher's | Meat, Poultry, Fish, Herbs, | Roots, *&c.* and Fruit. | XXII. A certain Cure for the Bite | of a Mad Dog. By Dr. *Mead.* | XXIII. A Receipt to keep clear | from Buggs. [end columns] | [rule] | *By a* LADY. | [rule] | *The* THIRD EDITION. | [rule] | *LONDON:* | Printed for the AUTHOR, and Sold at Mrs. *Wharton*'s Toy-Shop, the | *Bluecoat-Boy*, near the *Royal-Exchange*; at Mrs. *Ashburn*'s China- | Shop, the Corner of *Fleet-Ditch*; at Mrs. *Condall*'s Toy-Shop, the | *King's-Head* and *Parrot*, in *Holborn*; at Mr. *Underwood*'s Toy-Shop | near St. *James's-Gate*; and at most Market-Towns in *England*. | MDCCXLVIII. | [*Price* 3 s. 6 d. *stitch'd, and* 5 s. *bound*.]

Third edition, London, 1748. Originally published, London, 1747 (item 695).

8vo. [A]⁴ (A3 + a-c⁴ d²) B-Tt⁴; 182 leaves, pp. [2] [i] ii-iv [28] [1] 2-330.

Bibliographies: Bitting, p. 187; Maclean, p. 59; Oxford, p. 77 in a note; Simon BG 763; Wheaton and Kelly 2405.

Copies: *NUC* (John Crerar Library and Stanford). Maclean adds Birmingham Public Library, Cambridge University, Brotherton Library, Kansas State University, and Radcliffe College.

698. Glasse, Hannah, 1708-1770.

THE | ART of COOKERY, | MADE | PLAIN and EASY; | Which far exceeds any Thing of the Kind ever | yet published. | CONTAINING, | [in two columns: column one] I. Of Roasting, Boiling, *&c.* | II. Of Made-Dishes. | III. Read this Chapter, and you | will find how Expensive a | *French* Cook's Sauce is. | IV. To make a Number of pretty | little Dishes fit for a Supper or | Side-Dish, and little Corner- | Dishes for a great Table; and | the rest you have in the Chap- | ter for *Lent*. | V. To dress Fish. | VI. Of Soops and Broths. | VII. Of Puddings. | VIII. Of Pies. | IX. For a *Lent* Dinner, a Number | of good Dishes, which you may | make use of for a Table at any | other Time. | X. Directions for the Sick. | XI. For Captains of Ships. | XII. Of Hogs Puddings, Sau- | sages, *&c.* | [two vertical rules] | [column two] XIII. To pot and make Hams, | *&c.* | XIV. Of Pickling. | XV. Of making Cakes, *&c.* | XVI. Of Cheesecakes, Creams, | Jellies, Whip Syllabubs, *&c.* | XVII. Of Made Wines, Brewing, | *French* Bread, Muffins, *&c.* | XVIII. Jarring Cherries, and | Preserves, *&c.* | XIX. To make Anchovies, Ver- | micella, Catchup, Vinegar, | and to keep Artichokes, | *French* Beans, *&c.* | XX. Of Distilling. | XXI. How to Market; the Sea- | sons of the Year for Butchers | Meat, Poultry, Fish, Herbs, | Roots, *&c.* and Fruit. | XXII. A certain Cure for the Bite | of a Mad Dog. By Dr. *Mead*. | XXIII. A Receipt to keep clear | from Buggs. [end columns] | To which are added, | By Way of APPENDIX, | I. To dress a Turtle, the *West-India* Way. II. To make Ice Cream. | III. A Turkey, *&c.* in Jelly. IV. To make Citron. V. To candy | Cherries or Green Gages. VI. To take Ironmolds out of Linnen. | [rule] | *By a* LADY. | [rule] | *The* FOURTH EDITION, *with* ADDITIONS. | [rule] | *LONDON:* | Printed for the AUTHOR, and sold at Mrs. *Ashburn*'s China-Shop, the | Corner of *Fleet-Ditch*; at the *Bluecoat-Boy*, near the *Royal-Exchange*; | at the *Leg and Dial*, in *Fleet-Street*; at the *Prince of Wales's Arms*, in | *Tavistock-Street, Covent-Garden*; by *W. Innys*, in

Pater-noster Row; | *J. Hodges*, on *London-Bridge*; *T. Trye*, near *Gray's-Inn-Gate, Hol-* | *born*; *J. Brotherton*, in *Cornhill*; and by the Booksellers in Town | and Country. | [short rule] | M.DCC.LI. | [*Price* 4 s. *stitch'd, and* 5 s. *bound.*] | *)* This BOOK is publish'd with His MAJESTY's Royal | Licence; and whoever prints it, or any Part of it, will be | prosecuted.

Fourth edition, London, 1751. Originally published, London, 1747 (item 695).

8vo. [A]² (A1 + a-c⁴) B-Tt⁴ Uu²; 180 leaves, pp. [2] [i] ii-iv [20] [1] 2-334.

Illustration: Engraved frontispiece advertising Hannah Glasse Habit Maker to Her Royal Highness the Princess of Wales.

Note: Signed "H. Glasse" on p. 1.

Bibliographies: Craig 40; Maclean, p. 59; Oxford, p. 77 in a note; Pennell, p. 154; Vicaire 414; Wheaton and Kelly 2406 and 2407.

Copies: *BMC* and *NUC* (Radcliffe only). Maclean adds Brotherton Library, Wellcome Library, and New York Public Library.

699. Glasse, Hannah, 1708-1770.

THE | ART of COOKERY, | MADE | PLAIN and EASY; | Which far exceeds any Thing of the Kind ever yet published. | CONTAINING, | [in two columns: column one] I. Of Roasting, Boiling, &c. | II. Of Made-Dishes. | III. Read this Chapter, and you | will find how Expensive a | *French* Cook's Sauce is. | IV. To make a Number of pretty | little Dishes fit for a Supper or | Side-Dish, and little Corner- | Dishes for a great Table; and | the rest you have in the Chap- | ter for *Lent*. | V. To dress Fish. | VI. Of Soops and Broths. | VII. Of Puddings. | VIII. Of Pies. | IX. For a *Lent* Dinner, a Number | of good Dishes, which you may | make use of for a Table at any | other Time. | X. Directions for the Sick. | XI. For Captains of Ships. | XII. Of Hogs Puddings, Sau- | sages, &c. | [two vertical rules] | [column two] XIII. To pot and make Hams, | &c. | XIV. Of Pickling. | XV. Of making Cakes, &c. | XVI. Of Cheesecakes, Creams, | Jellies, Whip Syllabubs, &c. | XVII. Of Made Wines, Brewing, | *French* Bread, Muffins, &c. | XVIII. Jarring Cherries, and | Preserves, &c. | XIX. To make Anchovies, Ver- | micella, Catchup, Vinegar, and | to keep Artichokes, *French* | Beans, &c. | XX. Of Distilling. | XXI. How to Market; the Sea- | sons of the Year for Butchers | Meat, Poultry, Fish, Herbs, | Roots, &c. and Fruit. | XXII. A certain Cure for the Bite | of a Mad Dog. By Dr. *Mead*. | XXIII. A Receipt to keep clear | from Buggs. [end columns] | To which are added, | By Way of

APPENDIX, | I. To dress a Turtle, the *West-India* Way. II. To make Ice Cream. | III. A Turkey, *&c.* in Jelly. IV. To make Citron. V. To candy | Cherries or Green Gages. VI. To take Ironmolds out of Linnen. | VII. To make *India* Pickle. VIII. To make *English* Catchup. | IX. To prevent the Infection among horned Cattle. | [rule] | *By a* LADY. | [rule] | *The* FIFTH EDITION, *with* ADDITIONS. | [rule] | *LONDON*: | Printed, and sold at Mrs. *Ashburn*'s China-Shop, the Corner of *Fleet-* | *Ditch*; at the *Bluecoat-Boy*, near the *Royal-Exchange*; at the *Prince of* | *Wales's Arms*, in *Tavistock-Street, Covent-Garden*; by *W. Innys*, in | *Pater-noster Row*; *J. Hodges*, on *London-Bridge*; *T. Trye*, near *Gray's-* | *Inn-Gate, Holborn*; *B. Dod*, in *Ave-Mary-Lane*; *J. Brotherton*, in | *Cornhill*; and by the Booksellers in Town and Country. | [short rule] | M.DCC.LV. | *** This BOOK is publish'd with His MAJESTY's Royal | Licence; and whoever prints it, or any Part of it, will be | prosecuted.

Fifth edition, London, 1755. Originally published, London, 1747 (item 695).

8vo. π^2 a-c^4 d^2 B-Tt^4 Uu^2; 182 leaves, pp. [*4*] [i] ii-vi [*20*] [*1*] 2-334.

Note: Signed "H. Glasse" on p. 1.

Bibliographies: Maclean, p. 59; Oxford, p. 77 in a note; Wheaton and Kelly 2408.

Copies: *BMC* and *NUC* (Historical Society of Pennsylvania, University of California, Berkeley, and Yale). Maclean adds Brotherton Library, Guildhall Library, and Kansas State University. Wheaton and Kelly (Radcliffe only).

700. Glasse, Hannah, 1708-1770.

THE | ART of COOKERY, | MADE | PLAIN and EASY; | Which far exceeds any Thing of the Kind yet published. | CONTAINING, | [in two columns: column one] I. How to Roast and Boil to perfection | every Thing necessary to be sent up to | Table. | II. Of Made-Dishes. | III. How expensive a French Cook's Sauce | is. | IV. To make a Number of pretty little | Dishes for a Supper or Side-dish, and | little Corner-dishes for a great Table. | V. To dress Fish. | VI. Of Soops and Broths. | VII. Of Puddings. | VIII. Of Pies. | IX. For a Lent Dinner; a Number of | good Dishes, which you may make use | of at any other Time. | X. Directions to prepare proper Food for | the Sick. | XI For Captains of Ships; how to make | all useful Things for a Voyage; and | setting out a Table on board a Ship. | [two vertical rules] | [column two] XII. Of Hogs Puddings, Sausages, &c. | XIII. To pot and make Hams, &c. | XIV. Of Pickling. | XV. Of making Cakes, &c. | XVI. Of Cheesecakes, Creams, Jellies, | Whip-Syllabubs, &c. | XVII. Of Made Wines, Brewing, French | Bread, Muffins, &c.

| XVIII. Jarring Cherries and Preserves, | &c. | XIX. To make Anchovies, Vermicella, | Catchup, Vinegar, and to keep Arti- | chokes, French Beans, &c. | XX. Of Distilling. | XXI. How to Market; the Seasons of | the Year for Butchers Meat, Poultry, | Fish, Herbs, Roots, and Fruit. | XXII. A certain cure for the Bite of a | Mad Dog. By Dr. Mead. | XXIII. A Receipt to keep clear from | Buggs. [end columns] | To which are added, | By Way of APPENDIX, | One hundred and fifty New and Useful RECEIPTS, | and a COPIOUS INDEX. | [rule] | By a LADY. | [rule] | The SEVENTH EDITION. | [rule] | LONDON, | Printed for A. MILLAR, J. and R. TONSON, W. STRAHAN, | P. DAVEY and B. LAW. 1760. | [Price bound Five Shillings.]

Seventh edition, London, 1760. Originally published, London, 1747 (item 695).

8vo. A⁸ a⁸ B-Cc⁸ Dd⁴; 220 leaves, pp. [2] [i] ii-vi [24] [1] 2-384 [24].

Note: Signed "H. Glasse" on p. 1.

Bibliographies: Maclean, p. 59; Oxford, p. 77 in a note.

Copies: *BMC* and *NUC* (Vassar and Virginia State Library). Maclean adds Brotherton Library and Kansas State University.

701. Glasse, Hannah, 1708-1770.

THE | ART of COOKERY, | MADE | PLAIN and EASY; | Which far exceeds any Thing of the Kind yet published. | CONTAINING, | [in two columns: column one] I. How to Roast and Boil to perfec- | tion every Thing necessary to be | sent up to Table. | II. Of Made-dishes. | III. How expensive a French Cook's | Sauce is. | IV. To make a Number of pretty little | Dishes for a Supper or Side-dish, and | little Corner-dishes for a great Table | V. To dress Fish. | VI. Of Soops and Broths. | VII. Of Puddings. | VIII. Of Pies. | IX. For a Lent Dinner; a Number | of good Dishes, which you may | make use of at any other Time. | X. Directions to prepare proper Food | for the Sick. | XI. For Captains of Ships; how to | make all useful Things for a Voy- | age; and setting out a Table on | board a Ship. | [two vertical rules] | [column two] XII. Of Hogs Puddings, Sausages, | &c. | XIII. To pot and make Hams, &c. | XIV. Of Pickling. | XV. Of making Cakes, &c. | XVI. Of Cheesecakes, Creams, Jel- | lies, Whip-Syllabubs, &c. | XVII. Of made Wines, Brewing, | French Bread, Muffins, &c. | XVIII. Jarring Cherries and Pre- | serves, &c. | XIX. To make Anchovies, Vermicel- | la, Catchup, Vinegar, and to keep | Artichokes, French Beans, &c. | XX. Of Distilling. | XXI. How to Market; the Seasons of | the Year for Butchers Meat, Poul- | try, Fish, Herbs, Roots, and Fruit. | XXII. A certain Cure for the Bite of | a

Mad-Dog. By Dr. Mead. | XXIII. A Receipt to keep clear from | Buggs. [end columns] | To which are added, | By Way of APPENDIX, | One hundred and fifty New and Useful RECEIPTS, | and a COPIOUS INDEX. | [rule] | By a LADY. | [rule] | The EIGHTH EDITION. | [rule] | LONDON: | Printed for A. MILLAR, J. and R. TONSON, W. STRAHAN, | T. CASLON, B. LAW, and A. HAMILTON. | M.DCC.LXIII. | [Price bound Five Shillings.]

Eighth edition, London, 1763. Originally published, London, 1747 (item 695).

8vo. A^8 a^8 B-Cc^8 Dd^4; 220 leaves, pp. [2] [i] ii-vi [*24*] [1] 2-384 [*24*].

Note: Signed "H. Glasse" on p. 1.

Bibliographies: Maclean, p. 59; Oxford, p. 77 in a note; Pennell, p. 154; Vicaire 414; Wheaton and Kelly 2409.

Copies: *NUC* (6 copies). Maclean adds British Library, Brotherton Library, and Wellcome Library.

702. Glasse, Hannah, 1708-1770.

THE | ART of COOKERY, | MADE | PLAIN and EASY; | Which far exceeds any Thing of the Kind yet published. | CONTAINING, | [in two columns: column one] I. How to Roast and Boil to Perfec- | tion every Thing necessary to be | sent up to Table. | II. Of Made-dishes. | III. How expensive a French Cook's | Sauce is. | IV. To make a Number of pretty little | Dishes for a Supper or Side-dish, and | little Corner-dishes for a great Table. | V. To dress Fish. | VI. Of Soops and Broths. | VII. Of Puddings. | VIII. Of Pies. | IX. For a Lent Dinner; a Number of | good Dishes, which you may make | use of at any other time. | X. Directions to prepare proper Food | for the Sick. | XI. For Captains of Ships; how to | make all useful Things for a Voy- | age; and setting out a Table on | board a Ship. | [two vertical rules] | [column two] XII. Of Hogs Puddings, Sausages, | &c. | XIII. To pot and make Hams, &c. | XIV. Of Pickling. | XV. Of making Cakes, &c. | XVI. Of Cheese-cakes, Creams, Jel- | lies, Whip-Syllabubs, &c. | XVII. Of made Wines, Brewing, | French Bread, Muffins, &c. | XVIII. Jarring Cherries and Preserves, | &c. | XIX. To make Anchovies, Vermicel- | la, Catchup, Vinegar, and to keep | Artichokes, French Beans, &c. | XX. Of Distilling. | XXI. How to Market; the Seasons of | the Year for Butchers Meat, Poultry, | Fish, Herbs, Roots, and Fruit. | XXII. A certain Cure for the Bite of a | Mad Dog. By Dr. Mead. | XXIII. A Receipt to keep clear from | Buggs. [end columns] | To which are added, | By Way of APPENDIX, | One hundred and fifty New and Useful RECEIPTS, | And a COPIOUS INDEX. | [rule] | By a LADY. |

[rule] | A NEW EDITION. | [rule] | LONDON: | Printed for A. MILLAR, R. TONSON, W. STRAHAN, | T. CASLON, T. DURHAM, and W. NICOLL. | M.DCC.LXVII. | [Price bound Five Shillings.]

New edition (no. 16 of 36 recorded in Maclean), London, 1767. Originally published, London, 1747 (item 695).

8vo. A^8 a^8 B-Cc^8 Dd^4; 220 leaves, pp. [2] [i] ii-vi [*24*] [1] 2-384 [*24*].

Note: Facsimile signature "H. Glasse" printed on p. 1.

Bibliographies: Maclean, p. 59; Oxford, p. 77 in a note; Vicaire 414; Wheaton and Kelly 2411.

Copies: *NUC* (Radcliffe only). Maclean adds British Library, Brotherton Library, Cleveland Public Library, Kansas State University, and New York Public Library.

703. Glasse, Hannah, 1708-1770.

THE | ART of COOKERY, | MADE | PLAIN and EASY; | Which far exceeds any Thing of the Kind yet published. | CONTAINING, | [in two columns: column one] I. How to Roast and Boil to Perfec- | tion every Thing necessary to be | sent up to Table. | II. Of Made-dishes. | III. How expensive a French Cook's | Sauce is. | IV. To make a Number of pretty little | Dishes for a Supper or Side-dish, and | little Corner-dishes for a great Table. | V. To dress Fish. | VI. Of Soops and Broths. | VII. Of Puddings. | VIII. Of Pies. | IX. For a Lent Dinner; a Number of | good Dishes, which you may make | use of at any other time. | X. Directions to prepare proper Food | for the Sick. | XI. For Captains of Ships; how to | make all useful Things for a Voy- | age; and setting out a Table on | board a Ship. | [two vertical rules] | [column two] XII. Of Hogs Puddings, Sausages, | &c. | XIII. To pot and make Hams, &c. | XIV. Of Pickling. | XV. Of making Cakes, &c. | XVI. Of Cheese-cakes, Creams, Jel- | lies, Whip-Syllabubs, &c. | XVII. Of made Wines, Brewing, | French Bread, Muffins, &c. | XVIII. Jarring Cherries and Preserves, | &c. | XIX. To make Anchovies, Vermicella, | Catchup, Vinegar, and to keep Arti- | chokes, French Beans, &c. | XX. Of Distilling. | XXI. How to market; the Seasons of | the Year for Butchers Meat, Poultry, | Fish, Herbs, Roots, and Fruit. | XXII. A certain Cure for the Bite of a | Mad Dog. By Dr. Mead. | XXIII. A Receipt to keep clear from | Buggs. [end columns] | To which are added, | One hundred and fifty New and useful RECEIPTS, | And a COPIOUS INDEX. | [rule] | By a LADY. | [rule] | A NEW EDITION. | WITH | The ORDER of a MODERN BILL of FARE, for each Month, in the | Manner the Dishes are to be placed upon the Table. | [rule] | LONDON, | Printed for *W.*

Strahan, J. and *F. Rivington, J. Hinton, Hawes* and Co. *W. John-* | *ston, T. Longman, W. Owen, S. Crowder, B. White, T. Caslon, J. Wilkie, G.* | *Robinson, T. Davies, J. Robson, T. Cadell, T. Becket* and Co. *W. Davis, J.* | *Knox, W. Nicoll, W. Cornish, T. Lowndes, R. Dymott, H. Gardner, B. Dom-* | *ville, J. Richardson, T. Durham, R. Baldwin,* and *J. Bell*. 1774. | [Price Five Shillings bound.]

New edition (no. 20 of 36 recorded in Maclean), London, 1774. Originally published, London, 1747 (item 695).

8vo. A⁸ a⁸ B-Cc⁸ Dd⁴; 220 leaves, pp. [2] [i] ii-vi [24] [1] 2-384 [24]. Folding letterpress chart of "The Order of a Modern Bill of Fare" facing p. 1 not reckoned in the collation or pagination.

Note: Facsimile signature "H. Glasse" printed on p. 1.

Bibliographies: Horn-Arndt 261; Maclean, p. 60; Oxford, p. 77 in a note; Schraemli (1) 209; Wheaton and Kelly 2413.

Copies: *BMC* and *NUC* (8 copies). Maclean adds Wellcome Library.

704. Glasse, Hannah, 1708-1770.

THE | ART OF COOKERY, | MADE | PLAIN and EASY; | Which far exceeds any Thing of the Kind yet published. | CONTAINING, | [in two columns: column one] I. How to Roast and Boil to Perfection | every Thing necessary to be sent up to | Table. | II. Of Made Dishes. | III. How expensive a French Cook's | Sauce is. | IV. To make a Number of pretty little | Dishes for a Supper or Side dish, and | little Corner-dishes for a great Table. | V. To dress Fish. | VI. Of Soups and Broths. | VII. Of Puddings. | VIII. Of Pies. | IX. For a Lent Dinner; a Number of | good Dishes, which may be made use | of at any other Time. | X. Directions to prepare proper Food for | the Sick. | XI. For Captains of Ships; how to make | all useful Dishes for a Voyage; and | setting out a Table on board. | [two vertical rules] | [column two] XII. Of Hogs Puddings, Sausages, &c. | XIII. To pot and make Hams, &c. | XIV. Of Pickling. | XV. Of making Cakes, &c. | XVI. Of Cheesecakes, Creams, Jellies, | Whipt-Syllabubs, &c. | XVII Of Made Wines, Brewing, French | Bread, Muffins, &c. | XVIII. Jarring Cherries and Preserves, | &c. | XIX. To make Anchovies, Vermicelli, | Catchup, Vinegar, and to keep Arti- | chokes, French Beans, &c. | XX. Of Distilling. | XXI. How to market; the Seasons of | the Year for Butchers Meat, Poultry, | Fish, Herbs, Roots, and Fruit. | XXII. A certain Cure for the Bite of a | Mad Dog. By Dr. Mead. | XXIII. A Receipt to keep clear from | Bugs. [end columns] | TO WHICH ARE ADDED, | One Hundred and Fifty new and useful RECEIPTS. |

And also Fifty RECEIPTS for different Articles of PERFUMERY. | WITH A
COPIOUS INDEX. | [rule] | By Mrs. GLASSE. | [rule] | A NEW EDITION, | With
all the MODERN IMPROVEMENTS: | And also the ORDER of a BILL of FARE for
each Month, in the Manner | the Dishes are to be placed upon the Table, in the present
Taste. | [two rules] | LONDON: | Printed for W. Strahan, J. Rivington and Sons, L.
Davis, W. Owen, T. Long- | man, B. Law, T. Payne, B. White, J. Robson, J.
Johnson, G.Robinson, T. Ca- | dell, T. and W. Lowndes, T. Wilkie, E. Newberry,
W. Nicoll, H. Gardiner, | W. and C. Domville, R. Baldwin, J. Bew, William
Goldsmith, J. Sewell, | T. Evans, J. Knox, W. Fox, and D. Ogilvy. |
MDCCLXXXIV.

New edition (no. 25 of 36 recorded in Maclean), London, 1784. Originally published,
London, 1747 (item 695).

8vo. A⁶ a⁸ B-Ee⁸ Ff²; 232 leaves, pp. [2] [i] ii-vi [20] [1] 2-409 [410] [26]. Folding
letterpress chart for bill of fare not included in collation or pagination.

Note: Facsimile signature "H. Glasse" printed on p. 1.

Bibliographies: Maclean, p. 60; Oxford, p. 77 in a note; Pennell, p. 155; Simon BG
768; Vicaire 414.

Copies: *BMC* and *NUC* (6 copies). Maclean adds Brotherton Library, Reading
University, Kansas State University, and New York Public Library.

705. Glasse, Hannah, 1708-1770.

THE | ART of COOKERY, | MADE | PLAIN and EASY; | Which far exceeds any
Thing of the Kind yet published, | CONTAINING | [in to columns: column one] I.
How to Roast and Boil to Perfec- | tion every Thing necessary to be | sent up to Table.
| II. Of Made Dishes. | III. How expensive a French Cook's | Sauce is. | IV. To make
a Number of pretty little | Dishes for a Supper or Side-dish, and | little Corner dishes
for a great Table. | V. To dress Fish. | VI. Of Soups and Broths. | VII. Of Puddings.
| VIII. Of Pies. | IX. For a Lent Dinner; a number of | good Dishes, which you may
make | Use of at any other Time. | X. Directions to prepare proper Food | for the
Sick. | XI. For Captains of Ships; how to | make all useful Things for a Voy- | age;
and setting out a Table on | board a Ship. | [two vertical rules] | [column two] XII. Of
Hogs Puddings, Sausages, | &c. | XIII. To pot and make Hams, &c. | XIV. Of
Pickling. | XV. Of making Cakes, &c. | XVI. Of Cheesecakes, Creams, Jel- | lies,
Whip-Syllabubs, &c. | XVII. Of made Wines, Brewing, | French Bread, Muffins, &c.
| XVIII. Jarring Cherries and Preserves, | &c. | XIX. To make Anchovies,

Vermicella, | Catchup, Vinegar, and to keep Ar- | tichokes, French Beans, &c. | XX. Of Distilling. | XXI. How to Market; the Seasons of | the Year for Butchers Meat, Poultry, | Fish, Herbs, Roots, and Fruit. | XXII. A certain cure for the Bite of a | Mad Dog. By Dr. Mead. | XXIII. A Receipt to keep clear from | Buggs. [end columns] | To which are added, | One hundred and fifty New and useful RECEIPTS. | And a COPIOUS INDEX. | [rule] | By a LADY. | [rule] | A NEW EDITION. | WITH | The ORDER of a MODERN BILL of FARE for each Month, and | the Manner the Dishes are to be placed upon the Table. | [rule] | LONDON: | Printed for a Company of Booksellers, and sold by L. WANGFORD, in | Fleet-Street, and all other Booksellers in Great Britain and Ireland. | [hand] Be careful to observe (Mrs. GLASS being dead) that the Genuine Edition | of her Art of Cookery is thus signed, by | W. Wangford.

New edition (no. 36 of 36 recorded in Maclean), London, ca. 1790. Originally published, London, 1747 (item 695). Note: Ownership signature in the Gernon copy, "Isabella Tindall, 1790," shows this edition is earlier than the date [c.1800] assigned by Maclean. Changing the date to [c.1790] would move this edition to 29 in Maclean's list.

8vo. A^8 b^4 B-X^8; 172 leaves, pp. [2] [i] ii-iv [*18*] [1] 2-298 [*22*].

Illustration: Engraved frontispiece of a housewife and her cook with the engraved caption: *The* Fair, *who's Wise and oft consults our* BOOK, | *And thence directions gives her Prudent Cook,* | *With* CHOCIEST VIANDS, *has her Table Crown'd,* | *And* Health, *with* Frugal Ellegance *is found.*

Bibliographies: Bitting, p. 187 misdating this edition [c. 1750]; Maclean, p. 60, dated [c. 1800]; Wheaton and Kelly 2417 dated [c. 1781].

Copies: *NUC* (Library of Congress only) dating the edition [177-?]. Maclean locates Kansas State University only. Wheaton and Kelly (imperfect copy at Harvard only).

706. Glasse, Hannah, 1708-1770.

THE | ART OF COOKERY, | MADE | PLAIN and EASY; | Which far excels any Thing of the Kind yet published. | CONTAINING, | [in two columns: column one] I. A List of the various Kinds of Meat, | Poultry, Fish, Vegetables, and Fruits, | in Season, in every Month of the | Year. | II. Directions for Marketing. | III. How to Roast and Boil to Perfec- | tion. | IV. Sauces for all plain Dishes. | V. Made Dishes. | VI. To dress Poultry, Game, &c. | VII. How expensive a French Cook's | Sauce is. | VIII. To make a Number of pretty | little Dishes for Suppers, or Side or | Corner

Dishes. | IX. To dress Turtle, Mock-turtle, &c. | X. To dress Fish. | XI. Sauces for Fish. | XII. Of Soups and Broths. | XIII. Of Puddings and Pies. | XIV. For a Lent Dinner; a Number | of good Dishes, which may be made | use of at any other Time. | [two vertical rules] | [column two] XV. Directions for the Sick. | XVI. For Captains of Ships; how to | make all useful Dishes for a Voyage; | and setting out a Table on board. | XVII. Of Hog's Puddings, Sausages, | &c. | XVIII. To pot, make Hams, &c. | XIX. Of Pickling. | XX. Of making Cakes, &c. | XXI. Of Cheesecakes, Creams, Jellies, | Whipt Syllabubs. | XXII. Of Made Wines, Brewing, | Baking, French Bread, Muffins, | Cheese, &c. | XXIII. Jarring Cherries, Preserves, &c. | XXIV. To make Anchovies, Vermi- | celli, Catchup, Vinegar, and to keep | Artichokes, French Beans, &c. | XXV. Of Distilling. | XXVI. Directions for Carving. | XXVII. Useful and valuable Family | Receipts. | XXVIII. Receipts for Perfumery, &c. [end columns] | IN WHICH ARE INCLUDED, | One Hundred and Fifty new and useful RECEIPTS, not inserted | in any former Edition. | WITH A COPIOUS INDEX. | [rule] | By Mrs. GLASSE. | [rule] | A NEW EDITION, | With all the MODERN IMPROVEMENTS: | And also the ORDER of a BILL of FARE for each Month; the Dishes | arranged on the Table in the most fashionable Style. | [two rules] | LONDON: | Printed for T. Longman, B. Law, J. Johnson, G. G. and J. Robinson, | H. Gardner, T. Payne, F. and C. Rivington, J. Sewell, W. Richardson, | W. Lane, W. Lowndes, G. and T. Wilkie, W. Nicoll, W. Fox, | Ogilvy and Speare, J. Debrett, J. Scatcherd, Vernor and Hood, | Clarke and Son, J. Nunn, J. Barker, B. Crosby, Cadell and Davies, | and E. Newbery. | 1796.

New edition (no. 32 of 36 recorded in Maclean), London, 1796. Originally published, London, 1747 (item 695).

8vo. π^2 A^8 (-A1) a^8 b^4 B-Dd^8 Ee^2; 231 leaves, pp. [2] [i-iii] iv-xl [1] 2-419 [420].

Note: Facsimile signature "H. Glasse" printed on p. 1.

Bibliographies: Maclean, p. 60; Oxford, p. 77 in a note; Schraemli (1) 210; Simon BG 771; Wheaton and Kelly 2418.

Copies: *BMC* and *NUC* (5 copies). Maclean adds Brotherton Library, National Library of Scotland, and Wellcome Library.

707. Glasse, Hannah, 1708-1770.

THE | *Compleat Confectioner:* | OR, THE | Whole Art of Confectionary | Made PLAIN and EASY. | SHEWING, | The various Methods of PRESERVING and CANDYING, | both dry and liquid, all Kinds of FRUIT, FLOWERS | and HERBS;

the different Ways of CLARIFYING SU- | GAR; and the Method of Keeping FRUIT, NUTS | and FLOWERS fresh and fine all the Year round. | ALSO | DIRECTIONS for making | [in two columns: column one] ROCK-WORKS and CANDIES, | BISCUITS, | RICH CAKES, | CREAMS, | CUSTARDS, | JELLIES, | WHIP SYLLABUBS, and CHEESE- | CAKES of all SORTS, | ENGLISH WINES of all Sorts, | [two vertical rules] | [column two] STRONG CORDIALS, | SIMPLE WATERS, | MEAD, OILS, &c. | SYRUPS of all Kinds, | MILK PUNCH that will keep | twenty Years. | KNICKNACKS and TRIFLES for | DESERTS, &c. [end columns] | LIKEWISE, | The Art of making ARTIFICIAL FRUIT, with the Stalks in it, | so as to resemble the natural Fruit. | To which are added, | Some BILLS of FARE for DESERTS for private FAMILIES. | [rule] | By H. GLASSE, Author of the ART of COOKERY. | [rule] | LONDON | Printed: And Sold at Mrs. ASHBURNER's China Shop, the Corner of *Fleet Ditch*; | at YEWD's Hat Warehouse, near *Somerset House*; at KIRK's Toyshop, in *St.* | *Paul*'s Church Yard; at DEARD's Toyshop, facing *Arlington-Street, Piccadilly*; | By I. POTTINGER, at the *Royal Bible*, in *Pater-noster Row*; and by | J. WILLIAMS, opposite *St. Dunstan*'s Church, *Fleet-street.*

First edition, first issue, with Mrs. Ashburner's China Shop imprint. London, ca. 1760.

8vo. [A]² B-Ss⁴; 162 leaves, pp. [i-iii] iv [1] 2-304, ²[i] ii-xv [xvi].

Note: Facsimile signature "H. Glasse" printed on p. iv and p. 1.

Bibliographies: Craig, 41; Maclean, p. 61; Noling, p. 172; Pennell, p. 155; Schraemli (1) 212; Simon BG 774.

Copies: *BMC* and *NUC* (5 copies). Maclean adds Bodleian Library.

708. Glasse, Hannah, 1708-1770.

THE | Complete Confectioner: | OR THE | WHOLE ART OF CONFECTIONARY | Made PLAIN and EASY. | SHEWING | The various Methods of PRESERVING and CANDYING, | both dry and liquid, | All Kinds of Fruit, Flowers, and Herbs; | The different WAYS of | CLARIFYING SUGAR; | And the Method of | Keeping FRUIT, NUTS, and FLOWERS, | FRESH AND FINE ALL THE YEAR ROUND. | Also DIRECTIONS for making | [in two columns: column one] Rock-works and Candies, | Biscuits, | Rich Cakes, | Creams and Ice Creams, | Custards, | Jellies, | Blomonge | Whip Syllabubs, and Cheese- | cakes of all Sorts, | Sweetmeats, | [two vertical rules] | [column two] English Wines of all Sorts, | Strong Cordials, | Simple Waters, | Mead, Oils, &c. | Syrups of all Kinds, | Milk Punch that will keep | twenty Years, |

Knicknacks and Trifles for De- | serts &c. &c. &c. [end columns] | LIKEWISE | The Art of making Artificial FRUIT, | With the Stalks in it, so as to resemble the natural Fruit. | To which are added, | Some Bills of Fare for Deserts for Private Families. | [rule] | By H. GLASSE, Author of the *Art of Cookery*. | [two rules] | LONDON: | Printed for J. COOKE, No. 17, Pater-noster Row.

First edition, second issue, with J. Cooke imprint. London, ca. 1765.

8vo. [A]² (±A1) B-Ss⁴; 162 leaves, pp. [i-iii] iv [1] 2-304, ²[i] ii-xv [xvi].

Note: Facsimile signature "H. Glasse" Printed on p. iv and p. 1.

Bibliographies: Maclean, p. 62; Oxford, p. 90.

Copies: *NUC* (Detroit Public Library and Wellesley College). Maclean adds Dorset County Library and East Essex County Library.

709. Glasse, Hannah, 1708-1770.

THE | Servant's Directory, | OR | HOUSEKEEPER's COMPANION: | Wherein the Duties of the | [in two columns: column one] CHAMBER-MAID, | NURSERY-MAID, | HOUSE-MAID, | [column two] LANDERY-MAID, | SCULLION, *or* | UNDER-COOK, [end columns] | Are fully and distinctly explained. | To which is annexed | A Diary, or House-keeper's Pocket-Book | For the whole YEAR. | WITH | Directions for keeping Accounts with Tradesmen, and | many other Particulars, fit to be known by the Mistress | of a Family. | [rule] | BY H. GLASS, | Author of *The Art of Cookery made plain and easy*. | [two rules] | LONDON: | Printed for the AUTHOR; and sold by W. JOHNSTON in *Ludgate Street*; | at Mrs. WHARTON's, the *Blue Coat-Boys* near the *Royal-Exchange*, at | Mrs. ASHBURNHAM's China-Shop the Corner of *Fleet-Ditch*, | Mr. VAUGHAN's, Upholder in *Prince's street, Leicester-Fields*, and by | all the Booksellers in Town and Country. M DCC LX. | N.B. *This Book is entered in the Hall-book of the Company of Stationers*.

First edition, London, 1760.

8vo. A⁴ a² B-Hh⁸ Ii-Mm⁴; 262 leaves, pp. [i-iii] iv-viii [*4*] [1-3] 4-80, ²[1] 2-432.

Bibliographies: Axford, p. 363; Bitting, p. 190; Craig 42; Maclean, p. 62; Pennell, p. 155; Wheaton and Kelly 2425.

Copies: *BMC* and *NUC* (4 copies). Maclean adds Brotherton Library, National Library of Scotland and Kansas State University.

710. The Good Housewife.

THE | GOOD HOUSEWIFE; | OR, | Cookery Reformed: | CONTAINING | A Select Number of the best RECEIPTS | IN | COOKERY, PASTRY, PRESERVING, | CANDYING, PICKLING, &c. | TOGETHER WITH | A distinct ACCOUNT of the Nature of ALIMENTS. | Collected from the most approved Authors, and from the | Papers of several GENTLEMEN and LADIES | eminent for their good Sense and Oeconomy. | [rule] | Published at the Request of a Physician of great Experience, | who, for the Benefit of the Purchaser, has carefully correct- | ed this Work; and shewn why several Things heretofore | used in COOKERY, and inserted in other Books, | have been prejudicial to Mankind. | [rule] | The SECOND EDITION. | [two rules] | *LONDON:* | Printed for P. DAVEY and B. LAW, at the *Bible* and *Ball*, | in *Avemary-Lane.* | [short rule] | MDCCLVI.

Second edition, London 1756. No record of the first edition found.

8vo. A-R^8, 136 leaves, pp. [*16*] [1] 2-254 [*2*]. Last leaf blank.

Bibliographies: Unrecorded in the bibliographies consulted.

Copies: *NUC* (New York Public Library only).

711. Good Things Made, Said & Done, for Every Home & Household.

[within a border of two rules and corner ornaments] GOOD THINGS | *MADE, SAID & DONE,* | FOR EVERY | HOME & HOUSEHOLD. | [two short rules] | *TWENTY-FOURTH EDITION.* | [two short rules] | [vignette labeled TRADE MARK YORKSHIRE RELISH] | LEEDS: | GOODALL, BACKHOUSE & Co., | WHITE-HORSE STREET. | [short rule] | 1887.

Twenty-fourth edition, Leeds, 1887. Originally published, Leeds, 1879.

138 x 91 mm. [A]^8 B-E^8 F^{12}; 52 leaves, pp. [1-2] 3-103 [104]. Publisher's blue cloth stamped in gold and black.

Illustrations: Numerous wood engravings in the text.

Bibliographies: Driver 436.13 but stating "title as twentieth edition."

Copies: Driver (British Library only).

712. Goold, Joseph.

AËRATED WATERS | AND | HOW TO MAKE THEM; | TOGETHER WITH | Receipts for Non-Alcoholic Cordials, | AND A SHORT ESSAY ON | THE ART OF FLAVOURING. | BY | JOSEPH GOOLD | *(Being a Revised and Enlarged Edition of previous Works by the same Author.)* | [ALL RIGHTS RESERVED.] | LONDON: | J. GILBERT SMITH, 141, QUEEN VICTORIA STREET, E.C. | [short rule] | 1880.

First edition, London, 1880.

219 x 135 mm. [A]^8 B-H^8 I^{10}; 74 leaves, pp. [*12*] [i] ii [*2*] [*1*] 2-118 [*14*]. First and last leaves pasted down as endpapers. Publisher's blue cloth stamped in gold and black.

Illustrations: Wood engravings in advertisements at front and back of the book.

Bibliographies: Axford, p. 5; Bitting, p. 193; Noling, p. 179.

Copies: *NUC* (Library of Congress only).

713. Gouffé, Jules, b. 1807.

THE | BOOK OF PRESERVES | (LE LIVRE DE CONSERVES) | CONTAINING INSTRUCTIONS FOR | PRESERVING MEAT, FISH, VEGETABLES, AND FRUIT | AND FOR THE PREPARATION OF | TERRINES, GALANTINES, LIQUEURS, SYRUPS, PETITS-FOURS, &c. | BY | JULES GOUFFÉ | CHEF OF THE PARIS JOCKEY CLUB; AUTHOR OF `THE ROYAL COOKERY BOOK' | TRANSLATED FROM THE FRENCH | BY | ALPHONSE GOUFFÉ | HEAD PASTRYCOOK TO HER MAJESTY THE QUEEN | Illustrated with 34 Woodcuts | LONDON | SAMPSON LOW, SON, AND MARSTON | CROWN BUILDINGS, 188 FLEET STREET | 1871 | *(All rights reserved)*

First edition in English, London, 1871. Originally published in French under the title *Le Livre des conserves*, Paris, 1869 (item 220).

224 x 146 mm. [A]⁴ B-UU⁴; 172 leaves, pp. [i-v] vi-viii [1] 2-333 [334-336].
Publisher's quarter green morocco stamped in gold with maroon cloth covered boards.

Illustrations: Engraved frontispiece portrait of the author and thirty-four wood engravings in the text.

Bibliographies: Axford, p. 39; Bitting, p. 195; Noling, p. 176; Wheaton and Kelly 2467.

Copies: *BMC* and *NUC* (10 copies).

714. Gouffé, Jules, b. 1807.

THE | [in red] ROYAL COOKERY BOOK | (LE LIVRE DE CUISINE) | BY | [in red] JULES GOUFFÉ | CHEF DE CUISINE OF THE PARIS JOCKEY CLUB | TRANSLATED FROM THE FRENCH AND ADAPTED FOR ENGLISH USE | BY | [in red] ALPHONSE GOUFFÉ | HEAD PASTRY-COOK TO HER MAJESTY THE QUEEN | COMPRISING | DOMESTIC AND HIGH-CLASS COOKERY | ILLUSTRATED WITH SIXTEEN LARGE PLATES | PRINTED IN COLOURS, AND ONE HUNDRED AND SIXTY-ONE WOODCUTS FROM | DRAWINGS FROM NATURE BY E. RONJAT | [[woodcut] | LONDON | [in red] SAMPSON LOW, SON, AND MARSTON | CROWN BUILDINGS, 188 FLEET STREET | 1868 | (*All rights reserved.*)

First edition in English, London, 1868. Originally published in French under the title *Le Livre de cuisine*, Paris, 1867 (item 218).

245 x 170 mm. π⁴ a⁴ b² B-4U⁴; 362 leaves, pp. [2] [i-v] vi- xviii [1-3] 4-702 [2].
Publisher's red cloth, stamped in black and gold.

Illustrations: Sixteen chromolithographed plates and 161 woodcuts in the text.

Bibliographies: Axford, p. 352; Craig 43; Schraemli (1) 214.

Copies: *BMC* and *NUC* (6 copies).

715. Graham, William.

THE | ART | OF | MAKING WINES, | OF | FRUITS, FLOWERS, and HERBS, | All the native Growth of ENGLAND: | Particularly of | [in three columns: column one] GRAPES, | GOOSE-BERRIES, | CURRANTS, | RASP-BERRIES, | MUL-BERRIES, | ELDER-BERRIES, | [column two] BLACK-BERRIES, | STRAW-BERRIES, | DEW-BERRIES, | APPLES, | PEARS, | CHERRIES, | [column three] PEACHES, | APRICOTS, | QUINCES, | PLUMBS, | DAMASCENS, | FIGS. [end columns] | AND | ROSES, COWSLIPS, SCURVY-GRASS, MINT, | MO- | RELLA, BAUM, &c. | WITH | A succinct Account of their *Medicinal Virtues*, and the | most approv'd Receipt for making RAISIN WINE. | To which are annex'd | Many Secrets relative to the MYSTERY of VINTNERS, never | yet made publick: Shewing not only how to prevent those | Accidents to which all WINES are liable, but absolutely to | retrieve those which are actually tainted; and give them the | most agreeable Flavour and Colour. | Written, after upwards of Thirty Years Experience, | By WILLIAM GRAHAM, Esq; | Late of *Ware*, in *Hertfordshire*. | And intended, according to the Words of the Poet, to | *Lift on high the human soul*; | *Leave no Poison in the Bowl*. ANON. | *LONDON:* | Printed for J. WILLIAMS, under St. *Dunstan's* Church in | *Fleet-Street*; and M. COOPER, at the *Globe* in *Pater-Noster-Row*.

First edition, London, ca. 1750.

8vo. [A]⁴(-A4) B-F⁴ G1(=A4); 24 leaves, pp. [i-v] vi [1] 2-42.

Bibliographies: Maclean, p. 63; Noling, p. 176.

Copies: *NUC* (Yale only).

716. Gunter, William.

GUNTER'S | CONFECTIONER'S ORACLE | CONTAINING | RECEIPTS FOR DESSERTS | ON THE | MOST ECONOMICAL PLAN FOR PRIVATE FAMILIES, AND | ALL FOUNDED ON THE ACTUAL EXPERIMENTS | OF THIRTY YEARS. | WITH AN APPENDIX, CONTAINING THE BEST RECEIPTS FOR | PASTRY-COOKS, AND AN ELUCIDATION OF THE | PRINCIPLES OF GOOD CHEER. | BEING | A COMPANIONS TO | DR. KITCHINER'S COOK'S ORACLE. | BY | W. GUNTER. | [short rule] | Palmam qui meruit ferat. | [short rule] | LONDON: | ALFRED MILLER, 137, OXFORD STREET. | [short rule] | 1830.

First edition, London, 1830.

167 x 105 mm. πB⁸ c⁸ B-M⁸ O-R⁸; 136 leaves, pp. [i-iii] iv-xxxii [1] 2-238 [2]. Last leaf (blank?) wanting in this copy.

Illustration: Lithographed frontispiece portrait.

Bibliographies: Simon BG 809. Noling, p. 183, incorrectly lists a London, Alfred Miller, 1817 edition with 122 pages citing a copy in the British Library. The *BMC*, however, records the first edition as this dated 1830.

Copies: *BMC* and *NUC* (Kansas State University and Yale).

717. H., M.

[within a single rule border] The Young | COOKS | MONITOR: | OR, | DIRECTIONS | FOR | Cookery and Distilling. | BEING | A choice Compendium of Excellent | Receipts. | Made Publick for the Use and Benefit | of my Schollars. | [rule] | By *M. H.* | [rule] | *LONDON,* | Printed by *William Downing* in Great | St. *Bartholomew-Close,* 1683.

First edition, London, 1683.

8vo. A-K⁸; 80 leaves, pp. [*4*] 1-149 [150] [*6*].

Bibliographies: Noling, p. 184; Oxford, p. 43; Wing H95; Vicaire 881.

Copies: *BMC*. Wing records only the British Library copy.

718. Hackwood, Frederick William b. 1851.

[in red] GOOD CHEER | THE ROMANCE OF FOOD AND | FEASTING | BY | [in red] FREDERICK W. HACKWOOD | AUTHOR OF "THE GOOD OLD TIMES," "INNS, ALES AND DRINKING CUSTOMS | OF OLD ENGLAND," ETC. | [in red] T. FISHER UNWIN | LONDON: ADELPHI TERRACE | LEIPSIC: INSELSTRASSE 20 | 1911

First edition, London, 1911.

215 x 140 mm. [1]^8 2-26^8 27^4; 212 leaves, pp. [1-7] 8-424.

Illustrations: Colored half-tone frontispiece reproducing William Hogarth's "The Election Entertainment" and twenty half-tone black and white plates reproducing other art works.

Bibliographies: Bitting, p. 207; Driver 457.1; Gabler, p. 114; Noling, p. 185.

Copies: *BMC* and *NUC* (7 copies).

719. Hall, T.

[within a border of two rules] THE | QUEEN's Royal | COOKERY: | OR, | Expert and ready Way for the Dressing | of all Sorts of Flesh, Fowl, Fish: Either | Bak'd, Boil'd, Roasted, Stew'd, Fry'd, | Broil'd, Hash'd, Frigasied, Carbonaded, | Forc'd, Collar'd, Sous'd, Dry'd, &c. After | the Best and Newest Way. With their | several Sauses and Salads. | And making all sorts of PICKLES. | ALSO | Making Variety of Pies, Pasties, Tarts, | Cheese-Cakes, Custards, Creams, &c. | WITH | The ART of Preserving and Candying | of Fruits and Flowers; and the making of | Conserves, Syrups, Jellies, and Cordial Waters. | Also making several Sorts of English Wines, | Cyder, Mead, Metheglin. | TOGETHER, | With several Cosmetick or Beautifying | Waters: And also several sorts of Essences and | Sweet Waters, by Persons of the highest Quality. | [rule] | *By* T. Hall, *Free Cook of* London. | [rule] | 𝕿𝔥𝔢 𝔖𝔢𝔠𝔬𝔫𝔡 𝔈𝔡𝔦𝔱𝔦𝔬𝔫 | [rule] | *London:* Printed for *C. Bates*, at the *Sun* and *Bible* | in *Gilt-spur-street*, in *Pye-corner*: And *A. Bettesworth*, | at the *Red Lion* on *London-Bridge*, 1713. | [between the rules of the border] | 𝔏𝔦𝔠𝔢𝔫𝔰𝔢𝔰 𝔞𝔠𝔠𝔬𝔯𝔡𝔦𝔫𝔤 𝔱𝔬 𝔒𝔯𝔡𝔢𝔯.

Second edition, London, 1713. Originally published, London, 1709.

12mo. A-G^{12} H^6; 90 leaves, pp. [1-6] 7-180.

Illustrations: Woodcut frontispiece with the head of Queen Anne above three compartments showing a kitchen, a pastry maker and a chemist, and a woodcut on p. 132 of pies.

Bibliographies: Craig, 44; Maclean, p. 65; Oxford, p. 51; Pennell, p. 145; Vicaire 436.

Copies: *BMC*. Maclean adds Brotherton Library, Wellcome Library, Harvard, and Vassar.

720. Hammond, Elizabeth.

MODERN | Domestic Cookery, | AND | 𝔘𝔰𝔢𝔣𝔲𝔩 𝔑𝔢𝔠𝔢𝔦𝔭𝔱 𝔅𝔬𝔬𝔨; | [short fancy rule] | CONTAINING MOST APPROVED | DIRECTIONS FOR PURCHASING, PRESERVING, | AND COOKING | *Meat, Fish, Poultry, Game, &c.* | IN ALL THEIR VARIETIES. | *TRUSSING AND CARVING;* | PREPARING | SOUPS, GRAVIES, SAUCES, MADE DISHES, | POTTING, PICKLING, &c. | with all the Branches of | PASTRY AND CONFECTIONARY. | A COMPLETE | FAMILY PHYSICIAN. | INSTRUCTIONS TO SERVANTS | For the best Methods of performing their various Duties. | ART OF MAKING | BRITISH WINES, BREWING, BAKING &c. | [short fancy rule] | BY ELIZABETH HAMMOND. | [short fancy rule] | *LONDON:* | PRINTED AND SOLD BY | DEAN AND MUNDAY, 35, THREADNEEDLE-STREET. | [short rule] | 1815.

Engraved title-page:

𝔐𝔬𝔡𝔢𝔯𝔫 | DOMESTIC COOKERY, | AND | 𝔘𝔰𝔢𝔣𝔲𝔩 𝔑𝔢𝔠𝔢𝔦𝔭𝔱 𝔅𝔬𝔬𝔨 | adapted for | *Families in the Middling, & Genteel Ranks of Life,* | *with a complete* | 𝔉𝔞𝔪𝔦𝔩𝔶 𝔓𝔥𝔶𝔰𝔦𝔠𝔦𝔞𝔫. | instructions for making | BRITISH WINES, BREWING, BAKING, &c. &c. | *By Elizabeth Hammond.* | [vignette] | LONDON. | PRINTED & SOLD BY DEAN & MUNDAY, | *35, Threadneedle Street,* | 1816.

First edition, London, 1816.

160 x 97 mm. B-Bb⁶; 144 leaves, pp. [i-iii] iv [5] 6-288. O3 and O4 (pp. 149-152) wanting in this copy.

Illustrations: Engraved frontispiece and title-page, the latter with the date 1816, and four engraved plates, three illustrating carving and one table settings.

Bibliographies: The first edition unrecorded in the bibliographies consulted. Oxford, pp. 143-144, cites an 1817 edition and mentions undated seventh and ninth editions. Axford, p. 274, and Bitting, p. 211, record an 1818 edition.

Copies: No other copy of this edition located.

721. Hammond, Elizabeth.

MODERN | DOMESTIC COOKERY, | AND | 𝔘𝔰𝔢𝔣𝔲𝔩 𝔕𝔢𝔠𝔢𝔦𝔭𝔱 𝔅𝔬𝔬𝔨. | [short rule] | CONTAINING | THE MOST APPROVED DIRECTIONS FOR PURCHASING, PRESERVING, | AND COOKING | MEAT, FISH, POULTRY, GAME, &c. | IN ALL THEIR VARIETIES; | TRUSSING AND CARVING; | PREPARING SOUPS, GRAVIES, SAUCES, MADE DISHES, | POTTING, PICKLING, &c. | with all the Branches of | *PASTRY & CONFECTIONARY;* | A COMPLETE | FAMILY PHYSICIAN; | INSTRUCTIONS TO SERVANTS, | FOR THE BEST METHODS OF PERFORMING THEIR VARIOUS DUTIES | THE ART OF | MAKING BRITISH WINES, | BREWING, BAKING &c. | [short rule] | BY ELIZABETH HAMMOND. | [short rule] | FOURTH EDITION, WITH ADDITIONS. | [short fancy rule] | 𝔏𝔒𝔑𝔇𝔒𝔑: | PRINTED FOR | DEAN & MUNDAY, THREADNEEDLE STREET; AND | A. K. NEWMAN & Co. LEADENHALL STREET. | [short rule]

Fourth edition, London, ca.1820. Originally published, London, 1816 (item 720).

170 x 104 mm. B-Aa⁶ [Bb]⁶; 144 leaves, pp. [i-iii] iv [5] 6-287 [288].

Note: This edition has no illustrations.

Bibliographies: This edition unrecorded in the bibliographies consulted.

Copies: *NUC* (New York Public Library only).

722. Hammond, Elizabeth.

MODERN | DOMESTIC COOKERY, | AND | 𝔘𝔰𝔢𝔣𝔲𝔩 𝔕𝔢𝔠𝔢𝔦𝔭𝔱 𝔅𝔬𝔬𝔨. | [short rule] | CONTAINING APPROVED DIRECTIONS FOR PURCHASING, PRESERVING, | AND COOKING, | MEAT, FISH, POULTRY, GAME, &c. | THE ART OF | TRUSSING AND CARVING: | *PREPARING SOUPS, GRAVIES, SAUCES, AND MADE DISHES,* | POTTING, PICKLING, &c. | THE BRANCHES OF | PASTRY AND CONFECTIONARY; | A | COMPLETE FAMILY PHYSICIAN; | *INSTRUCTIONS TO SERVANTS,* | FOR THE BEST METHOD OF PERFORMING THEIR VARIOUS DUTIES: | THE ART OF | MAKING BRITISH WINES, | BREWING, BAKING &c. | [short rule] | *BY ELIZABETH HAMMOND.* | [short rule] | SIXTH EDITION, IMPROVED. | [short fancy rule] | 𝔏𝔒𝔑𝔇𝔒𝔑: | PRINTED FOR A. K. NEWMAN & Co., LEADENHALL-STREET. | [short rule] | 1828.

Engraved title-page:

Modern | DOMESTIC COOKERY | AND | *USEFUL RECEIPT BOOK,* | *Adapted for Families* | in the Middling and Genteel Ranks of Life | BY | Elizabeth Hammond | [vignette] | LONDON, | *Printed for Dean & Munday, Threadneedle Street,* | AND | *A. K. Newman & Co. Leadenhall Street.* | Price Four Shillings in Boards.

Sixth edition, London, 1828. Originally published, London, 1816 (item 720).

174 x 104 mm. B-Aa⁶ [Bb]⁶; 144 leaves, pp. [i-iii] iv [5] 6-287 [288]. Publisher's printed boards.

Illustrations: Engraved frontispiece and title-page and four engraved plates showing carving and table settings.

Bibliographies: This edition unrecorded in the bibliographies consulted.

Copies: No other copy of this edition located.

723. Harrison, Sarah.

THE | *House-keeper's Pocket-Book;* | And Compleat | FAMILY COOK. | CONTAINING | Above Seven Hundred curious and | Uncommon RECEIPTS, in | [in two columns: column one] COOKERY, | PASTRY, | PRESERVING, | [two vertical rules] | PICKLING, | CANDYING, | COLLARING, &c. [end columns] | With plain and easy | INSTRUCTIONS for preparing and dressing | every Thing suitable for an Elegant Entertainment, | from Two Dishes to Five or Ten, &c. And Directions | for ranging them in their proper Order. | To which is prefix'd, | Such a copious and useful BILL of *Fare* of all manner of | Provisions in Season for every Month of the Year, that | no Person need be at a Loss to provide an agreeable | Variety of Dishes, at a moderate Expence. | With Directions for making all Sorts of WINES, MEAD, | CYDER, SHRUB, &c. and distilling STRONG- | WATERS, &c. after the most approv'd Method. | Concluding with many excellent PRESCRIPTIONS, of singular | Efficacy in most Distempers incident to the Human Body, | extracted from the Writings of the most eminent Physicians. | [rule] | By Mrs. SARAH HARRISON, of *Devonshire.* | [rule] | The SECOND EDITION, Corrected and Improv'd, with | the Addition of Four Hundred *Genuine* Receipts, sent to the | Author by several worthy Persons. | [rule] | *LONDON:* | Printed for R. WARE, at the *Bible* and *Sun* in *Amen-Corner,* | *Warwick Lane.* 1739. [Price 2 *s.* 6 *d.*]

"Second edition," London, 1739. Originally published, London, T. Worrall, 1733, and followed by a second edition, London, T. Worrall, 1738, before this edition, also styled the second.

12mo. A^4 B-M^{12} N^8; 144 leaves, pp. [i-iii] iv [v-viii] [1] 2-263 [264] [*16*].

Illustrations: Twenty woodcuts of table settings on K10^v- L8^r (pp. 212-231).

Bibliographies; Maclean, p. 66; Oxford, p. 64 in a note; Schraemli (1) 226; Wheaton and Kelly 2694. Bitting, p. 217, and Simon BG 816 for the 1755 edition and Vicaire 438 for the 1751 and 1755 editions. Axford, p. 214, records a "sixth edition" dated 1775 (an error for 1755).

Copies: *BMC* and *NUC* (Folger, Harvard, and New York Public Library).

724. Harrison, Sarah.

THE │ *House-keeper's Pocket-Book,* │ And Compleat │ FAMILY COOK: │ CONTAINING │ Above TWELVE HUNDRED Curious │ and Uncommon RECEIPTS in │ [in three columns: column one] COOKERY, │ PASTRY, │ [vertical rule] │ [column two] PRESERVING, │ PICKLING, │ [vertical rule] │ [column three] CANDYING, │ COLLARING, *&c.* [end columns] │ WITH │ Plain and easy Instructions for Preparing and Dressing every │ Thing suitable for an Elegant Entertainment, from Two │ Dishes to Five or Ten, *&c.* and Directions for ranging │ them in their proper Order. │ Also a copious and useful Bill of Fare, of all Manner of Provisions in │ Season, for every Month in the Year; so that no Person need be at a │ Loss to provide an agreeable Variety, at a moderate Expence. │ Together with Directions for making all Sorts of Wine, Mead, Cyder, │ Shrub, *&c.* and Distilling Strong-Waters, *&c.* after the most approved │ Methods: For Brewing Ale and Small-Beer in a cleanly, frugal Man- │ ner: And for Managing and Breeding Poultry to Advantage. │ Likewise several useful Family Receipts for taking out Stains, preserving │ Furniture, cleaning Plate, taking Iron-moulds out of Linen, *&c.* │ As also easy Tables, of Sums ready cast up, from one Farthing to one │ Pound, for the Use of those not conversant in Arithmetic: And │ Table shewing the Interst of Money from 3, 3 1/2, 4, and 5 *per Cent.* │ from one Day to a Year. │ The Whole is so contrived as to contain as much as any Book of double │ the Price; and the Excellency of the Receipts renders it the most │ useful Book of the Kind. │ [rule] │ By Mrs. *SARAH HARRISON*, of *Devonshire.* │ [rule] │ The SEVENTH EDITION, revised and corrected. │ To which are now added several modern Receipts, by very good Judges │ of the separate Articles, particularly to dress Turtle *&c.* │ Also, *Every one their own Physician:* A collection of the most approved | Receipts for the Cure of most Disorders incident to Human Bodies. | Carefully compiled by MARY MORRIS. | [two rules] | *LONDON:* | Printed for C. and R. WARE, at the *Bible and Sun* on *Ludgate-Hill.* | M.DCC.LX. [*Price 2s. 6d.*

Seventh edition, London, 1760. Originally published, London, 1733.

12mo. [A]^2 B-T^6 a-c^6 d^4 "[A]"-"[B]"^{6}; 144 leaves, pp. [*4*] [1-5] 6-215 [216], ^{2}[1] 2-36 [*32*].

Illustrations: Twenty woodcuts of table settings on K6^v- M4^r (pp. 108-127).

Bibliographies: Maclean, p. 66; Oxford, p. 64 in a note. Bitting, p. 217, and Simon BG 816 for the 1755 edition and Vicaire 438 for the 1751 and 1755 editions.

Copies: *BMC*. Maclean adds Brotherton Library and Glasgow University.

724a. Hart, Mrs. J.

HIGH-CLASS COOKERY | MADE EASY. | BY MRS. HART. | [ornament] | EDINBURGH: | LORIMER & CHALMERS, PRINTERS, | 31 ST. ANDREW SQUARE.

First edition, Edinburgh [ca. 1890].

184 x 115 mm. [A]^8 B-D^8; 32 leaves, pp. [1-6] 7-63 [64]. Publisher's greenish blue cloth stamped in gold and blind.

Bibliographies: Driver 480.1.

Copies: Not listed in *BMC*, *BNC*, or *NUC*. Driver locates two copies at the Polytechnic Library, Oxford.

725. Hart, James.

[within a border of two rules] KΛINIKH, | *OR* | THE DIET OF THE | DISEASED. | [rule] | *Divided into Three BOOKES.* | [rule] | Wherein is set downe at length the whole matter and | nature of Diet for those in health, but especially for the sicke; | the Aire, and other Elements; Meat and Drinke, with divers | other things; various controversies concerning | this Subject are discussed: | Besides many pleasant practicall and historicall relations, both of │ the Authours owne and other mens, &c. as by the Argument │ of each Booke, the Contents of the Chapters, and a large │ Table, may easily appeare. │ *Collected as well out of the Writings of ancient Philosophers,* │ *Greeke, Latine,* and *Arabian,* and other moderne Writers; │ as out of divers other Authours. │ [rule] │ Newly published by IAMES HART, Doctor in Physicke. │ [rule] │ [ornament] │ [rule] │ *LONDON,* │ Printed by IOHN BEALE, for ROBERT ALLOT, │ and are to be sold at his shop at the signe of the blacke Beare │ in Pauls Church-yard, 1633.

First edition, London, 1633.

Folio: ¶⁴ ✱⁴ a⁶ aa⁴ A-V⁴ Aa-Vu⁴ Aaa-Lll⁴ Mmm⁶ ✱✱⁴ Ooo⁴; 236 leaves, pp. [*16*] 1-28, ²1-411 [412] [*16*]. First leaf blank.

Bibliographies: Craig 45; Noling, p. 192; Oxford, p. 20; *STC* 12888.

Copies: *BMC* and *NUC* (15 copies). *STC* (10 copies).

726. Hartlib, Samuel, d. 1662.

A │ DESIGNE │ FOR │ *PLENTIE,* │ By an Vniversall Planting of │ FRVIT-TREES*:* │ Tendred by some Wel-wishers to │ the Publick. │ [rule] │ GEN. I.20. │ *And God said,* *Behold, I have given you every herb bearing seed* │ *which is upon the face of the earth,* *and every* Tree *in the which is* │ *the fruit of a* Tree *yielding seed, to you it shall be for* *meat.* │ [rule] │ [ornament] │ [rule] │ LONDON, │ Printed for *Richard Wodenothe* in Leaden-hall street, over │ against Leaden-hall.

First edition, London, 1652.

4to. A-D⁴; 16 leaves, pp. [*8*] 1-24.

Bibliographies: Fussell (1) p. 46; Henrey I, p. 248; Wing H984.

Copies: *BMC, BNC,* and *NUC* (8 copies). Wing (12 copies).

727. Hartman, George.

[within a border of two rules] THE TRUE │ PRESERVER and RESTORER │ OF │ HEALTH: │ BEING A │ CHOICE COLLECTION │ OF │ Select and Experienced REMEDIES for │ all Distempers incident to Men, Women and Children. │ Selected from, and Experienced by the most Famous | Physicians and Chyrurgeons of *Europe.* | TOGETHER WITH | Excellent DIRECTIONS for | COOKERY; | AS ALSO FOR | *PRESERVING,* and *CONSERVING,* | and making all Sorts of *METHEG-* | *LIN, SIDER, CHERRY-WINE,* &c. | WITH THE | Description of an Ingenious and Useful *ENGIN* | for Dressing of Meat, and for Distilling the Choicest | Cordial Waters, without Wood, Coals, Candle, or Oyl. | [rule] | *Published for the Publick Good, by* G. Hartman, *Chymist.* | [rule] | *London,* Printed by T. B, for the Author, and are to be sold | at his House in *Hewes-Court* in *Black-Friers,* 1682.

First edition, London, 1682.

8vo. A-Ee⁸, ²A-B⁸; 240 leaves, pp. [*16*] 1-351 [352], ²[1-2] 3-80, ³1-32.

Illustration: Woodcut of device for distilling on Aa4ʳ.

Bibliographies: Oxford, p. 41; Wing H1004. Bitting, p. 218, describes the 1684 edition.

Copies: *BMC* and *NUC* (National Library of Medicine only). Wing records these and six additional copies.

728. Haslehurst, Priscilla.

THE | FAMILY FRIEND, | OR | *Housekeeper's Instructor:* | CONTAINING | A VERY COMPLETE COLLECTION | OF | *ORIGINAL & APPROVED* | 𝕽eceipts | IN | *EVERY BRANCH* | OF | COOKERY, CONFECTIONARY, | &c. | [two short rules] | BY PRISCILLA HASLEHURST, | Who lived *Twelve Years* as Housekeeper | in the families of *Wm. Bethell, Esq.* of Rice Park, near Beverley; *Mrs. Joddrell,* of Manchester; | and others of the greatest respectability. | [two short rules] | 𝔖heffield: | Printed by J. Montgomery, Iris-Office, Hartshead; | 1802.

First edition, Sheffield, 1802.

190 x 115 mm. π² A-T⁴ V²; 80 leaves, pp. [*4*] [1] 2-156.

Bibliographies: Axford, p. 142; Bitting, p. 218; Oxford, p. 132.

Copies: *NUC* (Kansas State University and Library of Congress).

729. Haslehurst, Priscilla.

THE | FAMILY FRIEND, | AND | YOUNG WOMAN's COMPANION; | OR | *Housekeeper's Instructor:* | CONTAINING | A VERY COMPLETE COLLECTION | OF | *ORIGINAL AND APPROVED* | Receipts | IN | EVERY BRANCH OF | COOKERY, | CONFECTIONARY, &c. &c. | [short fancy rule] | BY PRISCILLA HASLEHURST, | Late of Sheffield. | [short fancy rule] | ALBION OFFICE: | Printed by C. & W. Thompson, Westbar and Cornmarket, Sheffield. | [short fancy rule] | 1814.

Second edition, Sheffield, 1814. Originally published, Sheffield, 1802 (item 728).

218 x 129 mm. [A]^4 B-2D^4; 108 leaves, pp. [i-iii] iv [5] 6-215 [216], p. iv misnumbered "v."

Illustrations: Engraved frontispiece and one other engraved plate, both illustrating carving.

Bibliographies: This edition unrecorded in the bibliographies consulted.

Copies: No other copy located.

730. Haslehurst, Priscilla.

THE | FAMILY FRIEND, | AND | YOUNG WOMAN's COMPANION; | OR | *Housekeeper's Instructor:* | CONTAINING A VERY | COMPLETE COLLECTION OF ORIGINAL AND APPROVED | Receipts, | IN EVERY BRANCH OF | COOKERY, CONFECTIONARY, &c. &c. | [short fancy rule] | THIRD EDITION. | [short fancy rule] | *BY PRISCILLA HASLEHURST,* | LATE OF SHEFFIELD. | [short fancy rule] | ALBION OFFICE: | PRINTED BY C. & W. THOMPSON, WESTBAR AND CORNMARKET, | SHEFFIELD. | [short fancy rule] | 1816.

Third edition, Sheffield, 1816. Originally published, Sheffield, 1802 (item 728).

204 x 122 mm. [A]^4 B-2D^4; 108 leaves, pp. [i-iii] iv [5] 6-215 [216].

Illustrations: Two engraved plates illustrating carving.

Bibliographies: This edition unrecorded in the bibliographies consulted.

Copies: No other copy located.

731. Hassall, Arthur Hill, 1817-1894.

FOOD | AND ITS | ADULTERATIONS; | COMPRISING THE REPORTS OF THE | ANALYTICAL SANITARY COMMISSION OF | "THE LANCET" | FOR THE YEARS 1851 TO 1854 INCLUSIVE, | REVISED AND EXTENDED: | BEING RECORDS OF THE RESULTS OF SOME THOUSANDS OF | ORIGINAL MICROSCOPICAL AND CHEMICAL ANALYSES OF THE SOLIDS AND | FLUIDS CONSUMED BY ALL CLASSES OF THE PUBLIC; | AND CONTAINING | THE NAMES AND ADDRESSES OF THE VARIOUS MERCHANTS, MANUFACTURERS, AND | TRADESMEN OF WHOM THE ANALYSED ARTICLES WERE PURCHASED. | [short rule] | BY ARTHUR HILL HASSALL, M.D., | CHIEF ANALYST OF THE COMMISSION: | DOCTOR OF MEDICINE IN THE UNIVERSITY OF LONDON; LICENTIATE OF THE ROYAL COLLEGE | OF PHYSICIANS OF LONDON; FELLOW OF THE ROYAL MEDICAL AND CHIRURGICAL SOCIETY; | FELLOW OF THE MEDICAL SOCIETY OF LONDON; FELLOW OF THE LINNAEAN SOCIETY; | MEMBER OF THE COUNCIL OF THE BOTANICAL SOCIETY OF LONDON; | CORRESPONDING FELLOW OF THE MEDICAL SOCIETY OF MUNICH AND OF THE NATURAL | HISTORY SOCIETIES OF MONTREAL AND DUBLIN; | LECTURER ON MEDICINE AT THE ROYAL FREE HOSPITAL MEDICAL COLLEGE; | PHYSICIAN TO THE ROYAL FREE HOSPITAL. | [short rule] | Illustrated by One hundred and fifty-nine Engravings, | SHOWING THE MINUTE STRUCTURES OF THE GREATER NUMBER OF THE | VEGETABLE SUSTANCES EMPLOYED AS ARTICLES OF FOOD, ALSO THOSE OF THE | MAJORITY OF THE SUBSTANCES USED FOR ADULTERATION. | LONDON: | LONGMAN, BROWN, GREEN, AND LONGMANS. | 1855.

First edition, London, 1855.

221 x 142 mm. A^8 a-b^8 c^2 B-TT^8 UU^8 (UU3 + πB^{12}) XX-ZZ^8; 398 leaves, pp. [4] [i-iii] iv-xlviii [1] 2-659 [660], ^{2}[1] 2 ([1-7] 8-24) [3] 4-59 [60]. UU3-ZZ8 contain advertisements and πB^{12} is a "Descriptive Catalogue of Highley's Educational Collections of Specimens, Apparatus, Models, etc. selected for facilitating the study of the Natural and Medical Sciences and Art" dated 1854 and called for in the instruction to the binder on $ZZ8^v$. Publisher's brown cloth stamped in gold, with a 24 page publisher's catalogue, dated September 1854, bound in at the end.

Illustrations: One hundred fifty-nine wood engravings in the text.

Inscribed: "To Viscount Palmerston From the Author."

Bibliographies: Unrecorded in the bibliographies consulted.

Copies: *BMC* and *NUC* (10 copies).

732. Hayward, Abraham.

THE | ART OF DINING; | OR, | GASTRONOMY AND GASTRONOMERS. | *SECOND EDITION.* | LONDON: | JOHN MURRAY, ALBEMARLE STREET. | 1853.

Second edition, London, 1853. Originally published, London, 1852.

161 x 97 mm. [A]^4(-A1) B-I^8 K^4 χ1(=A1); 72 leaves, pp. [i- iii] iv-vi [1] 2-137 [138].

Preface signed: "A. H. The Temple, January 1853."

Bibliographies: Simon BG 825; Wheaton and Kelly 2733.

Copies: *BMC* and *NUC* (9 copies).

732a. Haywood, Eliza Fowler, 1693?-1756.

A | PRESENT | FOR A | *Servant-Maid:* | OR, THE | Sure Means of gaining LOVE and ESTEEM. | Under the following Heads. | [in two columns: column one] Observance. | Avoiding Sloth. | Sluttishness. | Staying on Errands. | Telling Family Affairs. | Secrets among Fellow-Servants. | Entring into their Quarrels. | Tale-bearing. | Being an Eye-Servant. | Carelessness of Children. | Of Fire, Candle, Thieves. | New Acquaintance. | Fortune-Tellers. | Giving saucy Answers. | Liquorishness. | Apeing the Fashion. | Dishonesty. | The Market Penny. | Delaying to give Change. | [two vertical rules] | [column two] Giving away Victuals. | Bringing in Chair-women. | Wasting Victuals. | Quarrels with Fellow-Servants. | Behaviour to the Sick. | Hearing Things against a Master | or Mistress. | Being too free with Men Servants. | Conduct toward Apprentices. | Mispending Time. | Publick Shews. | Vails. | Giving Advice too freely. | Chastity. | Temptations from the Master. | If a single Man. | If a married Man. | If from the Master's Son. | If from Gentlemen Lodgers. [end columns] | To which are Added, | DIRECTIONS for going to *MARKET*; | ALSO, | For *Dressing* any *Common Dish*, whether FLESH, | FISH, or FOWL. | With some *Rules* for

WASHING, *&c.* | [rule] | *The Whole calculated for making both the* | Mistress *and the* Maid *happy.* | [rule] | *LONDON:* | Printed and Publish'd by T. GARDNER, at *Cowley's* | Head, without *Temple-Bar*; and sold by the Book- | sellers of Town and Country, 1743. | [Price One Shilling.]

First edition, London, 1743.

8vo. [A]² B-K⁴ L²; 40 leaves, pp. [*4*] 1-76.

Bibliographies: Maclean, p. 67; Oxford, p. 73; Pennell, p. 150.

Copies: *BMC* and *NUC* (Harvard and New York Public Library). Maclean adds National Library of Scotland.

733. Haywood, Mrs.

A | NEW PRESENT | FOR A | SERVANT-MAID: | CONTAINING | RULES for her MORAL CONDUCT both with respect to | Herself and her Superiors: | The Whole ART of COOKERY, PICKLING, PRESERVING, | *&c. &c.* and every other Direction necessary to be known | in order to render her a Complete, Useful, and Valuable | Servant. | In TEN BOOKS. | [in two columns: column one] I. Necessary *Cautions* and *Pre-* | *cepts* for gaining Goodwill and | Esteem. | II. *Directions* for *Marketing,* | or the Method of Chusing all | Kinds of Butchers Meat, Fish, | Fowl, &c. with Instructions for | Carving. | III. The *Whole Art of Cookery* | fully displayed, both with regard | to Dressing plain Victuals, and | also that of made Dishes, Soups, | Broths, &c. Together with the | best Methods of *Pickling* all Kinds | of Fruits, Buds, Flowers, &c. | IV. The *Art* of *Preserving* the | most useful Fruits, &c. | V. The Method of *Candying* | [vertical rule] | [column two] the *Fruits,* &c. generally kept in | a Family. | VI. The best Methods of *Mak-* | *ing all Kinds of English Wines,* | and giving them the true Flavour | of those imported from abroad. | VII. The *Whole Art of Distil-* | *lation*; with the Methods of mak- | ing the Cordial and Sweet-scented | Waters hitherto used in England, | and also those imported from other | Countries. | VIII. Useful *Family Receipts.* | IX. Some general *Rules* and | *Directions* for Maid-Servants. | X. *Instructions* for *Carving* ac- | cording to the Terms of Art. [end columns] | With *Marketing Tables*, and *Tables* for *Casting-up Expences,* &c. | The Whole interspersed with a great Number of ORIGINAL | RECEIPTS, never before published. | [rule] | By Mrs. HAYWOOD. | [two rules] | LONDON: | Printed for G. PEARCH, No. 12, Cheapside; and | H. GARDNER, opposite St. Clement's Church, in the Strand. | M.DCC.LXXI. | [Price Two Shillings bound.]

First edition, London, 1771.

12mo. A^6 χ1 B-M^{12} N^4; 143 leaves, pp. [i-iii] iv-xiii [xiv] [1] 2-272.

Illustration: Engraved frontispiece of a kitchen scene.

Note: This work appears in Maclean and in the *NUC* as by Eliza Fowler Haywood, 1693?-1756, but this attribution of authorship is doubtfull. Eliza Haywood did publish a book titled *A Present for a Servant-Maid*, London, 1743 (item 732a), but, as Maclean points out, this is a guide for a servant's behavior, not a cookery book as is the present work. *A New Present for a Servant-Maid* appeared fifteen years after Eliza Haywood died. The title-page ascribes it to Mrs. Haywood which may have been an attempt to associate the work with the well known author or may have referred to another Mrs. Haywood.

Bibliographies: Axford, p. 296; Bitting, p. 220; Maclean, p. 67; Noling, p. 196; Simon BG 828.

Copies: *NUC* (Huntington Library and Library of Congress). Maclean adds Brotherton Library, Kansas State University, and New York Public Library.

734. Hazlemore, Maximilian.

DOMESTIC ECONOMY; | OR, | A COMPLETE SYSTEM | OF | *ENGLISH HOUSEKEEPING:* | CONTAINING | The most approved Receipts, confirmed by Observation and Practice, in every | reputable English Book of Cookery now extant; besides a great Variety of | others which have never before been offered to the Public. Also a va- | luable Collection, translated from the Production of COOKS of Eminence | who have published in *France*, with their respective Names to each Receipt; | which, together with the ORIGINAL ARTICLES, form the most com- | plete System of HOUSEKEEPING ever yet exhibited, under the following | Heads, *viz.* | [in three columns: column one] ROASTING, | BOILING, | MADE-DISHES, | FRYING, | BROILING, | POTTING, | FRICASSEES, | RAGOUTS, | [two vertical rules] | [column two] SOUPS, | SAUCES, | GRAVIES, | HASHES, | STEWS, | PUDDINGS, | CUSTARDS, | CAKES, | [two vertical rules] | [column three] TARTS, | PIES, | PASTIES, | CHEESECAKES, | JELLIES, | PICKLING, | PRESERVING, and | CONFECTIONARY. [end columns] | To which is prefixed, in order to render it as complete and perfect as possible, | AN ELEGANT COLLECTION OF LIGHT DISHES FOR SUPPER, | ADAPTED FOR EVERY MONTH IN THE YEAR. | ALSO | THE COMPLETE BREWER; | CONTAINING | Familiar Instructions for brewing all Sorts of Beer and Ale; including the proper | Management of the Vault or Cellar. | LIKEWISE | *THE FAMILY PHYSICIAN*; | Being a Collection of the most valuable and approved Prescriptions by MEAD, |

SYDENHAM, TISSOT, FOTHERGILL, ELLIOT, BUCHAN, and Others. | [two rules] | BY MAXIMILIAN HAZLEMORE. | [two rules] | *LONDON:* | PRINTED FOR J. CRESWICK, AND CO. | [short rule] | 1794.

First edition thus, London, 1794. In fact, this is a word for word reprint of Mary Cole's *Lady's Complete Guide, or Cookery in all its Branches*, London, 1791 (item 623).

8vo. a-b^8 B-Bb^8 Cc^4; 212 leaves, pp. [1-3] 4 [v] vi-xxxii [1] 2-392.

Bibliographies: Maclean, p. 68; Noling, p. 196; Oxford, p. 123; Schraemli (1) 229; Wheaton and Kelly 2739.

Copies: *BMC* and *NUC* (Boston Public Library and New York Public Library). Maclean adds Brotherton Library. Wheaton and Kelly adds American Antiquarian Society.

735. Hazlitt, William Carew, 1834-1913.

[in red] O [in black] LD [in red] C [in black] OOKERY [in red] B [in black] OOKS | AND | ANCIENT CUISINE | BY | W. CAREW HAZLITT | *SECOND EDITION* | [ornament] | [in red] LONDON | ELLIOT STOCK, 62 PATERNOSTER ROW | 1893

Second edition, London, 1893. Originally published, London, 1886.

164 x 103 mm. [A]^2 B-S^8; 138 leaves, pp. [4] [1] 2-271 [272]. Publisher's printed boards and printed cloth spine.

Illustrations: Reproductions of woodcuts on P1^r and Q5^r (pp. 209 and 235).

Bibliographies: Driver 484.2.

Copies: *NUC* (5 copies).

735a. Heath, Ambrose.

[within a border of type ornaments] | COOKING IN WAR TIME | BY | AMBROSE HEATH | NICHOLSON AND WATSON

First edition, London, 1939.

184 x 121 mm. A-D^{16}; 64 leaves, pp. [1-8] 9-128. Publisher's white paper covered boards printed in red and blue; red paper spine printed in black.

Bibliographies: Unrecorded in the bibliographies consulted.

Copies: *BMC* and *NUC* (New York Public Library only).

735b. Heath, Ambrose.

[Pictorial title-page, reproducing hand-lettering, within an oval frame above a table set for dinner] GOOD FOOD | ON THE | AGA | *BY* / *Ambrose Heath* | WITH A NOTE ON | *Jam making, Fruit & Vegetable Bottling* / *and Bread making* / *by Miss M. FROOD, M.B.E.* / *decorated by* / *Edward Bawden* / *LONDON* / *FABER & FABER LIMITED* / *24 RUSSELL SQUARE*

First edition, London, 1933.

200 x 132 mm. [A]^8 B^4 C-P^8 Q^6; 122 leaves, pp. [1-4] 5-243 [244]. Publisher's beige cloth printed in brown, blue and black.

Illustrations: Line drawings by Edward Bawden in the text.

Bibliographies: Unrecorded in the bibliographies consulted.

Copies: *BMC* and *NUC* (Brooklyn Public Library and New York Public Library).

736. Heath, John Benjamin, baron.

Some Account of the Worshipful | [ornamental letter in red] C [in black] ompany of [ornamental letter in red] G [in black] rocers | *OF THE CITY OF LONDON* | BY BARON HEATH, | F.R.S., F.A.S. | Mercibus hic Italis mutat sub Sole recenti | Rugosúm Piper et pallentis Grana Cymini. | PERSIUS. Sat. v. | [short rule] | [in red] Third Edition. | [arms of the Worshipful Company of Grocers] | LONDON, 1869. | [Privately Printed.]

Third edition, London, 1869. Originally published, London, 1829.

275 x 184 mm. [a]⁴ b⁴ B-4G⁴ 4H²; 310 leaves, pp. [i-vii] viii-xvi [1] 2-601 [602] [2]. Last leaf blank. Full blue morocco with the arms of the Company stamped on the front.

Illustrations: Seven steel engraved plates, one chromolithographed folding plate and numerous vignettes and coats of arms in the text.

This copy contains an illuminated manuscript page presenting the book to Sir Henry Bartle Edward Frere, 22 April 1874.

Bibliographies: Unrecorded in the bibliographies consulted.

Copies: *BMC* and *NUC* (17 copies).

737. Heath, William, 1795-1840.

[engraved handcolored title-page] GOOD DINNERS. | *Dress'd by W Heath* | *and Served by* | *Thoˢ Mᶜ Lean* / *at his Hotel in the* / *Haymarket* / *Pub Janʸ 10 1824 by Thoˢ MᶜLean 26 Haymarket*

First edition, London, 1824.

245 x 338 mm. Nine leaves, unpaginated.

Illustrations: Nine lithographed hand colored plates. Bound in full green morocco with publisher's printed front wrapper bound in.

Bibliographies: Unrecorded in the bibliographies consulted.

Copies: *NUC* (Harvard only).

738. Henderson, William Augustus.

THE | HOUSEKEEPER's INSTRUCTOR; | OR, | *UNIVERSAL FAMILY COOK.* | BEING AN AMPLE AND CLEAR DISPLAY OF THE | ART OF COOKERY | *IN ALL ITS VARIOUS BRANCHES.* | CONTAINING | PROPER DIRECTIONS for DRESSING all Kinds of | BUTCHER'S MEAT, POULTRY, GAME, FISH, &c. | ALSO, THE | *Method of preparing Soups, Hashes, and Made Dishes;* | WITH | The Whole Art of Confectionary, Pickling, Preserving, &c. | LIKEWISE | *The making and keeping in Perfection British Wines*; | AND | PROPER RULES FOR BREWING MALT LIQUOR, | As well for Family Consumption as the Regale of private Visitants. | TO WHICH IS ADDED, | The Complete Art of Carving, | ILLUSTRATED WITH ENGRAVINGS, | *Explaining, by proper References, the Manner in which the Young Practitioner* | *may acquit himself at Table with Elegance and Ease.* | ALSO, | BILLS OF FARE FOR EVERY MONTH IN THE YEAR; | WITH COPPER-PLATES, DISPLAYING | *The Best Manner of decorating a Table;* | Whereby every Person will be enabled to add to the Art of Cookery the proper | Disposition of each Article in its respective Season. | TOGETHER WITH | *DIRECTIONS FOR MARKETING,* | AND THE | MANAGEMENT OF THE KITCHEN AND FRUIT-GARDEN. | The WHOLE formed on so NEW a PLAN, that the Inexperienced will be | instructed, and the professed Cook receive that Information which has | never been made known by any preceding Publication. | [short fancy rule] | By WILLIAM AUGUSTUS HENDERSON, | *Who has made the* Culinary Art *his Study for upwards of Forty Years.* | [short fancy rule] | *LONDON:* | PRINTED AND SOLD BY W. AND J. STRATFORD, | HOLBORN-HILL.

First edition, London, 1791. Note: Maclean records two editions of Henderson's *The Housekeeper's Instructor* without either date or edition statement. One is described as having 448 pages with the assigned date [c.1790] and the other, for which the number of pages is not given, with the assigned date [c.1793]. Resolution of the dating problem is helped by the ownership inscription in the Crahan copy: "M.A. Thornhill, 1791." The Crahan copy is from the edition with 456 + 24 pages. Further evidence is found in the publisher's advertisement on the verso of the last page of subscribers announcing Charles Alfred Ashburton's *A New, Genuine, and Complete History of England . . . to the Year 1793* which was published in parts from 1791 to 1794. The ownership inscription shows this edition of Henderson could not have been published *after* 1791 and the advertisement makes it unlikely it was published *before* 1791.

8vo. A-3O⁴; 240 leaves, pp. [1-2] 3-456 [*24*].

Illustrations: Engraved frontispiece of a kitchen scene, seven engraved plates illustrating carving, and four (two folding) showing table settings.

Bibliographies: Crahan 330; Craig, 46; Maclean, p. 68.

Copies: *NUC* (Harvard and University of Oregon) assigning the date [1800?]. Maclean adds National Library of Scotland and Wellcome Library.

739. Henderson, William Augustus.

THE | HOUSEKEEPER's INSTRUCTOR; | OR, | *UNIVERSAL FAMILY COOK.* |
BEING AN AMPLE AND CLEAR DISPLAY OF THE | ART OF COOKERY | *IN
ALL ITS VARIOUS BRANCHES.* | CONTAINING | PROPER DIRECTIONS for
DRESSING all Kinds of | BUTCHER'S MEAT, POULTRY, GAME, FISH, &c. |
ALSO, THE | *Method of preparing Soups, Hashes, and Made Dishes*; | WITH | The
Whole Art of Confectionary, Pickling, Preserving, &c. | LIKEWISE | *The making and
keeping in Perfection British Wines;* | AND | PROPER RULES FOR BREWING
MALT LIQUOR, | As well for Family Consumption as the Regale of private Visitants.
| TO WHICH IS ADDED, | The Complete Art of Carving, | ILLUSTRATED WITH
ENGRAVINGS, | *Explaining, by proper References, the Manner in which the Young
Practitioner* | *may acquit himself at Table with Elegance and Ease.* | ALSO, | BILLS
OF FARE FOR EVERY MONTH IN THE YEAR; | WITH COPPER-PLATES,
DISPLAYING | *The Best Manner of decorating a Table;* | Whereby every Person will
be enabled to add to the Art of Cookery the proper | Disposition of each Article in its
respective Season. | TOGETHER WITH | *DIRECTIONS FOR MARKETING,* | AND
THE | MANAGEMENT OF THE KITCHEN AND FRUIT-GARDEN. | The Whole
formed on so NEW a PLAN, that the Inexperienced will be | instructed, and the
professed Cook receive that Information which has | never been made known by any
preceding Publication. | [short fancy rule] | THE FIFTH EDITION. | [two short rules]
| By WILLIAM AUGUSTUS HENDERSON, | *Who has made the* Culinary Art *his
Study for upwards of Forty Years.* | [two short rules] | *LONDON:* PRINTED AND
SOLD BY W. AND J. STRATFORD, | No. 112 HOLBORN-HILL.

Fifth edition, London, ca.1793. Originally published, London [1791] (item 738).

8vo. [A]⁴ B-3L⁴ 3M⁶; 234 leaves, pp. [1-2] 3-448 [20].

Illustrations: Engraved frontispiece of a kitchen scene, seven engraved plates
illustrating carving, and four (two folding) showing table settings.

Bibliographies: Maclean, p. 69; Simon BG 832; Wheaton and Kelly 2774.

Copies: *NUC* (Harvard, Louisiana State University, and University of Texas).
Maclean adds Brotherton Library. Wheaton and Kelly adds Boston Public Library.

740. Henderson, William Augustus.

THE | HOUSEKEEPER's INSTRUCTOR; | OR, | *UNIVERSAL FAMILY COOK.* |
BEING AN AMPLE AND CLEAR DISPLAY OF THE | ART OF COOKERY | *IN
ALL ITS VARIOUS BRANCHES.* | CONTAINING | PROPER DIRECTIONS for

DRESSING all Kinds of | BUTCHER's MEAT, POULTRY, GAME, FISH, &c. |
ALSO, THE | *Method of preparing Soups, Hashes, and Made Dishes*, | WITH | The
Whole Art of Confectionary, Pickling, Preserving, &c. | LIKEWISE | *The Making
and Keeping in Perfection British Wines;* | AND | PROPER RULES FOR BREWING
MALT LIQUOR, | As well for Family Consumption as the Regale of private Visitants.
| TO WHICH IS ADDED, | The Complete Art of Carving, | ILLUSTRATED WITH
ENGRAVINGS, | *Explaining, by proper References, the Manner in which the Young
Practitioner* | *may acquit himself at Table with Elegance and Ease.* | ALSO, | BILLS
OF FARE FOR EVERY MONTH IN THE YEAR; | WITH COPPER-PLATES,
DISPLAYING | *The Best Manner of decorating a Table;* | Whereby every Person will
be enabled to add to the Art of Cookery the proper | Disposition of each Article in its
respective Season. | TOGETHER WITH | *DIRECTIONS FOR MARKETING,* | AND
THE | MANAGEMENT OF THE KITCHEN AND FRUIT-GARDEN. | The Whole
formed on so NEW a PLAN, that the Inexperienced will be | instructed, and the
professed Cook receive that Information which | has never been made known by any
preceding Publication. | [short fancy rule] | THE SIXTH EDITION. | [two short
rules] | By WILLIAM AUGUSTUS HENDERSON, | *Who has made the* Culinary Art
his Study for upwards of Forty Years. | [two short rules] | *LONDON:* PRINTED AND
SOLD BY W. AND J. STRATFORD, | No. 112, HOLBORN-HILL.

Sixth edition, London, ca.1795. Originally published, London [1791] (item 738).

8vo. [A]⁴ B-3L⁴; 228 leaves, pp. [1-2] 3-440 [*16*].

Illustrations: Engraved frontispiece of a kitchen scene, seven engraved plates
illustrating carving, and four (two folding) showing table settings. The two folding
plates are wanting in this copy.

Bibliographies: Maclean, p. 69.

Copies: *NUC* (Columbia and New York Public Library). Maclean adds Brotherton,
Kansas State University, and Radcliffe.

741. Henderson, William Augustus.

THE | HOUSEKEEPER's INSTRUCTOR; | OR, | *UNIVERSAL FAMILY COOK.* |
BEING AN AMPLE AND CLEAR DISPLAY OF THE | ART OF COOKERY | *IN
ALL ITS VARIOUS BRANCHES.* | CONTAINING | PROPER DIRECTIONS for
DRESSING all Kinds of | BUTCHER's MEAT, POULTRY, GAME, FISH, &c. |
ALSO, THE | *Method of preparing Soups, Hashes, and Made Dishes,* | WITH | The
Whole Art of Confectionary, Pickling, Preserving, &c. | LIKEWISE | *The Making*

and Keeping in Perfection British Wines; | AND | PROPER RULES FOR BREWING MALT LIQUOR, | As well for Family Consumption as the Regale of private Visitants. | TO WHICH IS ADDED, | The Complete Art of Carving, | ILLUSTRATED WITH ENGRAVINGS, | *Explaining, by proper References, the Manner in which the Young Practitioner* | *may acquit himself at Table with Elegance and Ease.* | ALSO, | BILLS OF FARE FOR EVERY MONTH IN THE YEAR; | WITH COPPER-PLATES, DISPLAYING | *The Best Manner of decorating a Table;* | Whereby every Person will be enabled to add to the Art of Cookery the proper | Disposition of each Article in its respective Season. | TOGETHER WITH | *DIRECTIONS FOR MARKETING,* | AND THE | MANAGEMENT OF THE KITCHEN AND FRUIT-GARDEN. | The Whole formed on so NEW a PLAN, that the Inexperienced will be | instructed, and the professed Cook receive that Information which | has never been made known by any preceding Publication. | [short fancy rule] | THE EIGHTH EDITION. | [two short rules] | By WILLIAM AUGUSTUS HENDERSON, | *Who has made the* Culinary Art *his Study for upwards of Forty Years.* | [two short rules] | *LONDON:* PRINTED AND SOLD BY W. AND J. STRATFORD, | No. 112, HOLBORN-HILL.

Eighth edition, London, ca. 1800. Originally published, London [1791] (item 738).

8vo. [A]^4 B-3K^4 3L^6; 230 leaves, pp. [1-2] 3-440 [*20*].

Illustrations: Engraved frontispiece of a kitchen scene, seven engraved plates illustrating carving, and four (two folding) showing table settings.

Bibliographies: Maclean, p. 69; Wheaton and Kelly 2775.

Copies: *NUC* and Wheaton and Kelly (Boston Public Library only).

742. Henderson, William Augustus.

THE | HOUSEKEEPER's INSTRUCTOR; | OR, UNIVERSAL | *FAMILY- COOK;* | BEING AN FULL AND CLEAR | *Display of the Art of Cookery in all it Branches;* | CONTAINING | [in two columns: column one] Proper Directions for Dressing all | Kinds of Butcher's Meat, Poultry, | Game, Fish, &c. | The Method of preparing all the Va- | rieties of Soups, Hashes, and made | Dishes. | [two vertical rules] | [column two] The whole Art of Confectionary, Pick- | ling, Preserving, &c. | The making and keeping in Perfection | British Wines; and | Proper Rules for Brewing Malt Liquor | for large or small Families. [end columns] | [two short rules] | TO WHICH IS ADDED, | The Complete Art of Carving, | ILLUSTRATED WITH ENGRAVINGS, | *Explaining, by proper References, the Manner in which Young Practitioners may* | *acquit themselves at Table with Elegance and Ease.* | ALSO, | [in two columns:

column one] Bills of Fare for every Month in the | Year. | The Manner of decorating a Table, | displayed by Copper-plates. | [two vertical rules] | [column two] Directions for Marketing. | Observations on Culinary Poisons, and | The Management of the Kitchen and | Fruit Garden. [end columns] | [two short rules] | BY W. A. HENDERSON, | *Many Years eminent in the Culinary Profession.* | [short fancy rule] | 𝕿𝖍𝖊 𝕾𝖊𝖛𝖊𝖓𝖙𝖊𝖊𝖓𝖙𝖍 𝕰𝖉𝖎𝖙𝖎𝖔𝖓. | [short fancy rule] | CORRECTED, REVISED, AND CONSIDERABLY IMPROVED, | *By every modern Addition and Variation in the Art,* | BY JACOB CHRISTOPHER SCHNEBBELIE, | LATE APPRENTICE TO MESSRS. TUPP AND PERRY, | *Oxford Street; afterwards* | PRINCIPAL COOK AT MELUN'S HOTEL, BATH; AND OF | MARTELLI'S, THE ALBANY, LONDON. | [two rules] | 𝕷𝖔𝖓𝖉𝖔𝖓. | PRINTED FOR THOMAS KELLY, 17, PATERNOSTER-ROW, | *By W. Clowes, Northumberland-Court, Strand.*

Seventeenth edition, London, 1811. Originally published, London [1791] (item 738).

210 x 132 mm. [A]⁴ B-3M⁴; 232 leaves, pp. [1-2] 3-464.

Illustrations: Engraved frontispiece portrait of J. C. Schnebbelie, seven engraved plates illustrating carving, and four showing table settings.

Bibliographies: Bitting, p. 224; Oxford, p. 134; Vicaire 441.

Copies: *BMC* assigning date [1823].

743. Hibberd, Shirley, 1825-1890.

PROFITABLE GARDENING; | A PRACTICAL GUIDE | TO | THE CULTURE OF VEGETABLES, FRUITS, | AND | OTHER USEFUL OUT-DOOR GARDEN PRODUCTS; | INTENDED FOR THE USE OF | AMATEURS, GENTLEMEN'S GARDENERS, ALLOTTEES, | AND GROWERS FOR MARKET. | BY SHIRLEY HIBBERD, F.R.H.S., | AUTHOR OF "RUSTIC ADORNMENTS," "GARDEN FAVOURITES," "BRAMBLES AND | BAY LEAVES," ETC., ETC. | NEW EDITION. | LONDON: | GROOMBRIDGE AND SONS, | PATERNOSTER ROW.

New edition, London, n.d. Originally published, London, 1863.

183 x 119 mm. [A]² B-T⁸ V⁴; 150 leaves, pp. [i-iii] iv [1] 2-296. Publisher's green cloth, stamped in gold. Four pages of publisher's advertisements bound in at the back.

Illustrations: Numerous wood engravings in the text.

Bibiliographies: Unrecorded in the bibliographies consulted.

Copies: *NUC* (5 copies).

744. Hill, Benson Earle, 1795-1845.

THE | EPICURE'S ALMANAC; | OR | 𝔇𝔦𝔞𝔯𝔶 𝔬𝔣 𝔊𝔬𝔬𝔡 𝔏𝔦𝔟𝔦𝔫𝔤; | CONTAINING | A CHOICE AND ORIGINAL RECEIPT OR A VALUABLE HINT FOR | EVERY DAY IN THE YEAR. | THE | RESULT OF ACTUAL EXPERIENCE, | APPLICABLE TO THE ENJOYMENT OF THE GOOD THINGS OF THIS LIFE, | CONSISTENTLY WITH THE VIEWS OF THOSE WHO STUDY | GENTEEL ECONOMY. | [short rule] | BY | BENSON E. HILL, | AUTHOR OF "RECOLLECTIONS OF AN ARTILLERY OFFICER," | "A PINCH OF SNUFF," &c. &c. | [short rule] | "Pan *shall* remain." – MIDAS. | LONDON: | HOW AND PARSONS, 132, FLEET STREET. | [short rule] | 1841.

First edition, London, 1841 Also published for 1842 (item 745) and 1843.

160 x 102 mm. [A]⁴ B-H¹² [I]²; 90 leaves, pp. [i-v] vi-viii [1] 2-172. Publisher's brown cloth, stamped in gold.

Bibliographies: Axford, p. 136; Bitting, p. 227; Oxford, p. 171; Simon BG 843.

Copies: *BMC* and *NUC* (Library of Congress only).

745. Hill, Benson Earle, 1795-1845.

THE | EPICURE'S ALMANAC | FOR | 1842; | CONTAINING A | CALENDAR OF THE MONTHS, ADORNED WITH CUTS; | TABLES OF THE VARIOUS DISHES IN SEASON: | WITH A | 𝔊𝔬𝔩𝔩𝔢𝔠𝔱𝔦𝔬𝔫 𝔬𝔣 𝔒𝔯𝔦𝔤𝔦𝔫𝔞𝔩 𝔞𝔫𝔡 𝔊𝔥𝔬𝔦𝔠𝔢 𝔉𝔢𝔠𝔦𝔭𝔢𝔰. | BY | BENSON E. HILL, ESQ. | [short rule] | "*Chief Justice.* There is not a hair on your face, but should have his | effect of gravity. | *Falstaff.* His effect of gravy, gravy, gravy!" – *Henry 4, Part 2, Act 1, Scene 2.* | [short rule] | LONDON: | HOW AND PARSONS, 132, FLEET STREET. | [short rule] | 1842.

First edition, London, 1842. Also published for 1841 (item 744) and 1843.

160 x 102 mm. B-Q⁶; 90 leaves, pp. [i-v] vi-viii [ix-x] [1] 2-169 [170]. Publisher's brown cloth, stamped in gold.

Illustrations: Wood engravings in the text.

Bibliographies: Axford, p. 136; Bitting, p. 227; Oxford, p. 171, Simon BG 844; Wheaton and Kelly 2836.

Copies: *BMC* and *NUC* (4 copies).

746. Hill, Georgiana.

ONIONS | 𝔇𝔯𝔢𝔰𝔰𝔢𝔡 𝔞𝔫𝔡 𝔖𝔢𝔯𝔟𝔢𝔡 | IN A HUNDRED DIFFERENT WAYS. | BY | GEORGIANA HILL, | AUTHOR OF "THE COOK'S OWN BOOK," "HOW TO COOK APPLES," | "HOW TO COOK RABBITS," ETC. | LONDON: | GEORGE ROUTLEDGE & SONS, | THE BROADWAY, LUDGATE; | NEW YORK: 416, BROOME STREET. | 1867.

First edition, London, 1867.

165 x 104 mm. [A]⁴ B-D⁸ E⁴; 32 leaves, pp. [i-iii] iv-vii [viii] [1] 2-55 [56]. Publisher's blue cloth printed in black.

Bibliographies: Axford, p. 308, Bitting, p. 228.

Copies: *BMC* and *NUC* (Library of Congress and U.S. Patent Office).

747. Hill, Thomas.

[a border of type ornaments above and on both sides] The Gardeners Labyrinth. | *Containing a discourse of the Gardeners life, in* | the yearly trauels to be bestowed on his plot of | earth, for the vse of a Garden: with instructions for | the choise of Seedes, apt times for sowing, set- | ting, planting, and watering, and the ves- | sels and instrumentes seruing to | that vse and purpose: | *Wherein are set forth diuers Herbers,* *Knots and Mazes,* | cunningly handled for the beautifying of Gardens. | Also the Phisicke benefit of ech Herb, Plant, and Floure, | with the vertues of the distilled Waters of euery of them, | *as by the sequele may further appeare.* | Gathered out of the best approoued Writers of Garde- | ning, Hushandrie, and Phisicke: by | *Dydymus Mountain.* | [woodcut] | LONDON. | Printed by Adam Islip, 1594.

Fourth edition, London, 1594. Originally published, London, 1577.

4to. A^4 A-Ii^4 Kk^2; 134 leaves, pp. [8] [1] 2-80, ^{2}[1-3] 4-180.

Illustrations: Four leaves, printed on one side only, with woodcuts of garden patterns after K4 not recknoned in signatures or pagination and numerous woodcuts in text.

Bibliographies: Fussell (1) p. 18; *STC* 13488.

Copies: *BMC* and *NUC* (4 copies). *STC* (9 copies).

748. Hill, Thomas.

The Gardeners Labyrinth, | OR, | A NEW ART | OF | GARDNING: | Wherein is laid down New and | Rare inventions and secrets of Gard- | ning not heretofore known. | For Sowing, Planting, and Setting all man- | ner of Roots, Herbs, and Flowers, both for the | use of the Kitchin Garden, and a Garden of plea- | sure, with the right ordering of all Delectable and | Rare Flowers, and fine Roots; As the like hath | not been heretofore published by any. | Likewise, here is set forth divers knots for the beau- | tifying of an GARDEN for Delight. | Lastly, here is set down the Physical benefit of each | Herbe, with the commodities of the Waters distilled | out of them, for the use and benefit of all. | [rule] | Collected from the best approved Authors, besides forty | years experience in the Art of Gardning: By *D. M.* | And now newly Corrected and inlarged. | [rule] | *London*, Printed by *Jane Bell*, and are to be sold at the | East-end of *Christ-Church*, 1652.

Second title-page:

THE SECOND PART | OF THE | Gardeners Labyrinth, | Vttering such skilfull Experience, and | worthy secrets, about the particular sowing and | removing of the most Kitchin Herbs, with the witty or- | dering of other dainty Herbs, delectable Flowers, pleasant | Fruits, and fine Roots, as the like hath not heretofore | been uttered of any. Besides, the Physick benefits of | each Herb annexed, with the commodity of waters distil- | led out of them, right profitable to be known. | [woodcut] | *LONDON,* | Printed by *Jane Bell*, and are to be sold at the East-end | of *Christ-Church*, 1651.

New edition, London, 1652. Originally published, London, 1576.

4to. [A]⁴ B-Ll⁴ Mm⁶; 142 leaves, pp. [*8*] 1-90, ²[1-3] 4-173 [*174*] [*12*]. First leaf (blank or half-title?) wanting in this copy.

Illustrations: Numerous woodcuts, mostly geometric garden designs, in text in Part One.

Bibliographies: Henrey I, p. 261; Wing H2016.

Copies: *BMC* and *NUC* (3 copies). Wing (10 copies).

749. Hill, Thomas.

THE | Profitable Arte of Gardening: to | which is added much necessarie matter, and | a number of secrets, with the Phisicke helps | belonging to each hearbe, and that easily | prepared. | To this is annexed two proper Treatises, the one en- | titutled, *The meruailous gouernment, propertie, and benefite of* | Bees, with the rare secretes of the honnie and waxe. And | the other, *The yerely coniectures meete for* | Husbandmen. | To these is likewise added a Treatise of the Arte of | Graffing and Planting of trees. | *Gathered by* Thomas Hyll, *Citizen of* | London. | [ornament] | LONDON, | *Imprinted by Edward Allde.* | 1593.

Second title-page:

[ornament] | A profitable instruction of the per- | *fect ordering of Bees, with the maruel-* | lous nature, property, and gouernement of them: and | the necessary vses, both of their Honnie and Waxe, | *seruing diuerslie, as well in inward, as outward causes:* | gathered out of the best writers. | To which is annexed a Treatise, intituled: cer- | taine Husbandly coniectures of dearth and plenty | *for euer, and other matters also meet for husband-* | men to know, &c. | By *Thomas Hill* Londoner. | [ornament] | ¶ *Imprinted at London by* | Edward Alde. | 1593.

Seventh edition, London, 1593. Originally published under the title *A Most Briefe and Pleasaunt Treatise, Teachynge Howe to Dress a Garden*, London, 1563.

4to. A-Y⁴ Aa-Mm⁴; 136 leaves, pp. [*8*] 1-164, ²[*8*] 1-92. Leaf I1 (pp. 57-58) lacking in this copy.

Illustrations: Woodcuts showing geometric garden designs on C1ᵛ, C2ʳ, C4ʳ, and X4ᵛ.

Bibliographies: Fussell (1) p. 18; *STC* 13496.

Copies: *BMC* and *NUC* (9 copies). *STC* (10 copies).

750. Hitt, Thomas, d. 1770?

A | TREATISE | OF | FRUIT-TREES. | BY | THOMAS HITT, | Formerly Gardener to the Right Honourable | Lord ROBERT MANNERS, at Bloxholme, in | Lincolnshire; and to Lord ROBERT BERTIE, | at Chislehurst, in Kent. | The THIRD EDITION. | [two rules] | LONDON: | Printed for ROBINSON and ROBERTS, at No 25. | in Pater-Noster-Row. | MDCCLXVIII.

Third London edition, 1768. Originally published, London, 1755; second edition, London 1757; third edition, Dublin, 1758.

8vo. A⁴ B-Cc⁸; 204 leaves, pp. [i-iii] iv-viii [1] 2-394 [6].

Illustrations: Seven engraved folding plates, largely illustrating espaliered fruit trees on garden walls.

Bibliographies: Henrey III, p. 60.

Copies: *BMC* and *NUC* (five copies).

751. Hoare, Clement, 1789-1849.

A PRACTICAL TREATISE | ON THE | CULTIVATION | OF | THE GRAPE VINE | ON OPEN WALLS. | BY CLEMENT HOARE. | LONDON: | LONGMAN, REES, ORME, BROWN, GREEN AND LONGMAN: | AND | MASON AND SON, CHICHESTER. | 1835.

First edition, London, 1835.

223 x 135 mm. [A]⁴ B-U⁴ X²; 82 leaves, pp. [1-9] 10-164; p. 4 is misnumbered vi.

Illustrations: Seven illustrations in the text of grape vines trained on walls.

Bibliographies: Gabler, p. 131 in a note.

Copies: *BMC* and *NUC* (Cornell only).

752. Holland, Mary.

THE COMPLETE | ECONOMICAL COOK, | AND | FRUGAL HOUSEWIFE; | AN ENTIRE NEW SYSTEM OF | DOMESTIC COOKERY; | CONTAINING APPROVED DIRECTIONS FOR | PURCHASING, PRESERVING, AND COOKING. | ALSO, | 𝔗𝔯𝔲𝔰𝔰𝔦𝔫𝔤 𝔞𝔫𝔡 𝔠𝔞𝔯𝔟𝔦𝔫𝔤; | PREPARING SOUPS, GRAVIES, SAUCES, MADE DISHES, | *POTTING, PICKLING, &c.* | WITH DIRECTIONS FOR | PASTRY AND CONFECTIONARY. | LIKEWISE THE | ART OF MAKING BRITISH WINES, | BREWING, BAKING, GARDENING, &c. | [short fancy rule] | BY MRS. MARY HOLLAND, | PROFESSED COOK. | [short rule] | "I had rather you would marry a Young Women without a Farthing, who is | "mistress of the art of Domestic Economy, than one who has Ten Thousand | "Pounds, and unacquainted with that necessary appendage to a good Wife." | DR. JOHNSON. | [short rule] | THE FOURTH EDITION, | Considerably amended and enlarged, the result of thirty years practice. | [two short rules] | 𝔏𝔬𝔫𝔡𝔬𝔫. | PRINTED FOR THOMAS TEGG, No. 111, CHEAPSIDE; W. SHARPE, KING | STREET; SIMPKIN AND MARSHALL; SHERWOOD, NEELY AND | JONES; ALSO R. GRIFFIN & CO. GLASGOW; AND | J. CUMMING, DUBLIN.

Engraved title-page:

THE | ECONOMICAL COOK | and | 𝔉𝔯𝔲𝔤𝔞𝔩 𝔥𝔬𝔲𝔰𝔢𝔴𝔦𝔣𝔢. | *a New System of* / *DOMESTIC COOKERY.* | 𝔅𝔶 | MRS. MARY HOLLAND. | [vignette signed Fussell delt., Davenport sculpt.] | *A NEW EDITION.* | [short rule] | *Steel Plate* / 𝔏𝔬𝔫𝔡𝔬𝔫. | PRINTED FOR THOMAS TEGG, CHEAPSIDE, | R. GRIFFIN & C°. GLASGOW, & J. CUMMING, DUBLIN.

Fourth edition, London, ca.1820.

168 x 98 mm. π^6 $2\pi^6$ $[A]^6$ B-BB^6; 162 leaves, pp. [1-3] 4 [iii] iv-xxxiii [xxxiv] [1] 2-288.

Illustrations: Steel engraved frontispiece of a kitchen scene, steel engraved title-page and four steel engraved plates illustrating carving, trussing, and table settings.

Bibliographies: Oxford, p. 166, records a "sixth edition" dated 1830 and states: "It is apparently a later edition of 'The Complete British Cook' of 1800." The latter is only one third the length of *The Complete Economical Cook*, so, even if one did grow out of the other, they are substantially different works.

Copies: No other copy of this edition located.

753.   Holland, Mary.

THE COMPLETE | ECONOMICAL COOK. | AND | FRUGAL HOUSEWIFE: | AN ENTIRE NEW SYSTEM OF | DOMESTIC COOKERY, | CONTAINING APPROVED DIRECTIONS FOR | PURCHASING, PRESERVING, AND COOKING. | ALSO, | 𝔗russing & 𝔠arving; | PREPARING SOUPS, GRAVIES, SAUCES, MADE DISHES, | *POTTING, PICKLING, &c.* | WITH DIRECTIONS FOR | PASTRY AND CONFECTIONARY. | LIKEWISE THE | ART OF MAKING BRITISH WINES, | BREWING, BAKING, GARDENING, &c. | [short fancy rule] | BY MRS. MARY HOLLAND, | PROFESSED COOK. | [short rule] | "I had rather you would marry a Young Woman without a Farthing, who is | "mistress of the art of Domestic Economy, than one who has Ten Thousand | "Pounds, and unacquainted with that necessary appendage to a good Wife." | DR. JOHNSON. | [short rule] | THE SIXTH EDITION. | Considerably amended and enlarged, the result of thirty years' practice. | [two short rules] | 𝔏ondon: | PRINTED FOR THOMAS TEGG, 73, CHEAPSIDE; SIMPKIN AND | MARSHALL; SHERWOOD, JONES AND CO. ALSO | R. GRIFFIN AND CO. GLASGOW; AND | J. CUMMING, DUBLIN. | [short rule] | 1827.

Engraved title-page:

THE | ECONOMICAL COOK | and | 𝔉rugal 𝔥ousewife. | *a New System of* / *DOMESTIC COOKERY.* | 𝔅y | MRS. MARY HOLLAND. | [vignette signed Fussell delt., Davenport sculpt.] | *A NEW EDITION.* | [short rule] | *Steel Plate* / 𝔏ondon. | PRINTED FOR THOMAS TEGG, CHEAPSIDE, | R. GRIFFIN & Cº. GLASGOW, & J. CUMMING, DUBLIN.

Sixth edition, London, 1827.

170 x 106 mm. π⁶ 2π⁶ [A]⁶ B-BB⁶; 162 leaves, pp. [1-3] 4 [i] ii-ix [x] [xix] xx-lx [1] 2-288. Publisher's printed boards repeating title-page information but substituting seventh edition for sixth and 1826 for 1827.

Illustrations: Steel engraved frontispiece of a kitchen scene, steel engraved title-page and four steel engraved plates illustrating carving, trussing, and table settings.

Bibliographies: Oxford, p. 166, records a "sixth edition" dated 1830. See note under item 752.

Copies: No other copy of this edition located.

754. The Home Book.

THE HOME BOOK; | OR, | YOUNG HOUSEKEEPER'S ASSISTANT: | FORMING | A COMPLETE SYSTEM OF DOMESTIC ECONOMY, | AND HOUSEHOLD ACCOUNTS. | WITH ESTIMATES OF EXPENDITURE, &c. &c. | IN EVERY DEPARTMENT OF HOUSEKEEPING, | FOUNDED ON FORTY-FIVE YEARS PERSONAL EXPERIENCE. | BY A LADY. | [short rule] | "Let these my counsels be a guide to you, | And my experience teach your lack of judgment; | So shall your Home become a Paradise, | Rich in Earth's purest bliss, Domestic Comfort!" | [short rule] | LONDON: | SMITH, ELDER, AND CO. 65, CORNHILL. | 1829.

First edition, London, 1829.

188 x 110 mm. π^2 A^2 B-H^{12} I^4; 92 leaves, pp. [i-iii] iv-vii [viii] [1] 2-175 [176]. Publisher's boards, uncut, with printed label on the spine.

Bibliographies: Attar 126.1; Oxford, p. 163.

Copies: *NUC* (New York Public Library only). Attar adds Bodleian Library, British Library, and Polytechnic Library, Oxford.

755. Hooper, Thomas.

THE | *NEW* | ROYAL | CONFECTIONER | IN WHICH IS GIVEN | THE IMPROVED ART | OF MAKING EVERY ARTICLE IN | MODERN CONFECTIONERY. | [short fancy rule] | By THOMAS HOOPER, Confectioner to Her Majesty. | [short fancy rule] | Second Edition. | [British royal arms] | London: |PRINTED AND PUBLISHED BY W. MASON, | 22, CLERKENWELL GREEN. | [short fancy rule] | EIGHT PENCE.

Second edition, London, ca.1840.

189 x 115 mm. [1]^6 [2]^{12}; 18 leaves, pp. [1-3] 4-36. Publisher's printed wrappers.

Bibliographies: Unrecorded in the bibliographies consulted.

Copies: No other copy located.

756. Houdlston, Thomas.

A | NEW METHOD | OF | COOKERY, | OR, | Expert and ready Way for the
Dressing of all Sorts | of Flesh, Fowl, Fish, either Baked, Boiled, Roast- | ed, Stewed,
Fried, Hashed, Frigasied, Carbonad- | ed, Forced, Collared, Soused, &c. after the best
| and newest Way, with their several Sauces and | Sallads, And making all Sorts of
PICKLES. | ALSO | Making Variety of Pies, Pasties, Tarts Cheese- | Cakes,
Custards, Creams, &c. | WITH | The ART of Preserving, Candying of Fruits and |
Flowers; and the making of Conserves, Syrups, | Jellies and Cordial Waters. Also
making several | Sorts of English Wines, Cyder, Mead, Metheglin. | TOGETHER |
With several Cosmetick or Beautifying Waters: | And also several Sorts of Essences
and Sweet Wa- | ters: By Persons of the highest Quality. | By THOMAS
HOUDLSTON, Cook in | DUMFRIES. | EDINBURGH: | Printed by DAVID
GRAY, for EBEN. WILSON | Bookseller in DUMFRIES. M. DCC. LX.

Second edition, Edinburgh, 1760.

8vo in half-sheets. π^2 A-R^4; 70 leaves, pp. [*4*] [1] 2-136.

Bibliographies: Maclean, p. 71, records two editions: (1) [Dumfries] printed for the
author, ca.1760, with 186 pages, locating only the National Library of Scotland copy;
(2) Edinburgh, Printed for E. Wilson at Dumfries, ca.1760, number of pages not given
and noting that there once was a copy in the British Library, now reported destroyed.
This latter copy, listed in *BMC*, is described as having 135 pages and, presumably, was
the same edition as the Gernon copy.

Copies: *BMC*, reported destroyed. No other copy of this edition located.

757. The Housekeeper's Assistant.

[engraved title-page] THE | *Housekeeper's Assistant,* | OR | 𝕸𝕺𝕯𝕰𝕽𝕹
𝕾𝖄𝕾𝕿𝕰𝕸 | OF | *Economical* | COOKERY, | *Particularly adapted to* | the |
MIDDLE CLASS of SOCIETY. | *By a Lady.* | Selected with care from the most
approved works. | [short fancy rule] | 𝕷𝖔𝖓𝖉𝖔𝖓 | *Published & Sold by all the
Booksellers.* | Price 3s. 6d.

First edition? London, ca. 1840.

139 x 88 mm. B-T$^{12.6}$ U^{12} V^6 X^6 (-X6); 185 leaves, pp. [iv] v-vi [vii] [8] 9-373.

Note: Even numbers are on the rectos and odd numbers on the versos of the leaves throughout this volume.

Illustrations: Engraved frontispiece of game in a larder and engraved title-page.

Bibliographies: Unrecorded in the bibliographies consulted.

Copies: No other copy located.

758. The Housekeeper's Pocket Book.

THE | *House-keeper's Pocket Book,* | AND COMPLETE | FAMILY COOK. | CONTAINING | Several HUNDRED Curious RECEIPTS in | [in two columns: column one] COOKERY, | PASTRY, | PRESERVING, | PICKLING, | [two vertical rules] | [column two] BREWING, | BAKING, | MADE WINES, | &c. [end columns] | With PLAIN and EASY | Instructions for preparing and dressing every thing | suitable for an elegant Entertainment, from Two | Dishes to Five or Ten, &c. | To which is Added. | Every Man his own Doctor, shewing the Nature | and Faculties of the different sorts of Foods, where- | by every Man and Woman may know what is Good | or Hurtful to them. | [rule] | *LONDON:* | Sold at H. FENWICK's Wholesale Book Warehouse | SNOW HILL.

Third edition, London, ca.1785. Originally published, London, 1776.

12mo. A-O⁶ (A2 and A3 missigned "A" and "A2"); 84 leaves, pp. [1-3] 4-168.

Illustration: Engraved frontispiece of a kitchen scene with the caption "Engraved for Mrs. Harrisons Cookery Book 1783." Mrs. Harrison's book titled *The House-keeper's Pocket Book, and Compleat Family Cook* was originally published, London, 1733, and is similar to this work only in title. The last edition of Mrs. Harrison's book recorded by Maclean is London, 1777, and none of the editions is recorded as having a frontispiece. It is likely this frontispiece was engraved for the second edition, London, 1783, of this work, the engraver mistakenly identifying this book with Mrs. Harrison's.

Bibliographies: Maclean, p. 72. Oxford, p. 115, records the London, 1783, edition.

Copies: Maclean records Yale copy only. There also are copies in the British Library, the Library of Congress and the New York Academy of Medicine.

759. The Housekeeper's Receipt Book.

THE | HOUSEKEEPER's | RECEIPT BOOK, | OR, THE | *Repository of Domestic Knowledge;* | CONTAINING A | COMPLETE SYSTEM OF HOUSEKEEPING, | FORMED ON PRINCIPLES OF | EXPERIENCE AND ECONOMY, | AND | *ADAPTED TO GENERAL USE.* | [two rules] | 𝔏𝔬𝔫𝔡𝔬𝔫: | PUBLISHED BY THE EDITOR; | SOLD BY S. A. ODDY, 2, IVY LANE, PATERNOSTER ROW; and | J. WALLIS, 77, BERWICK STREET, SOHO. | [short rule] | 1813.

First edition, London, 1813.

198 x 125 mm. [A]⁴ B-C⁴ D-I⁸ K-2R⁴ 3S⁴ *3S² 3T⁴; 192 leaves, pp. [*4*] [i] ii-iv [1] 2-360 [*12*] [369] 370-376.

Illustrations: Seven engraved plates, six of bills of fare (four of these six plates are missing in this copy) and one illustrating quartering of beef, veal, pork, and mutton. A frontispiece titled "A Domestic Scene" present in the 1818 edition (item 760) is not present in this copy.

Bibliographies: Simon BG 865.

Copies: No other copy of this edition located.

760. The Housekeeper's Receipt Book.

THE HOUSEKEEPER'S | RECEIPT BOOK; | OR, THE | *REPOSITORY OF DOMESTIC KNOWLEDGE*; | CONTAINING | A COMPLETE SYSTEM OF HOUSEKEEPING, | formed upon priciples of | EXPERIENCE AND ECONOMY, | AND | *ADAPTED TO GENERAL USE.* | INCLUDING | [in two columns: column one] DOMESTIC COOKERY, | COOKERY FOR THE SICK, | FAMILY MEDICINE, | *Treatment of Local Affections,* | *Cure of common Disorders,* | *Rules of Health.* | SYSTEMS OF BREWING, | [vertical fancy rule] | [column two] CONDUCT OF A DAIRY, | MANAGEMENT of POULTRY, | BEES, &c. &c. | KITCHEN GARDENING, | *Plants, Shrubs, Trees, &c.* | MISCELLANEOUS RECEIPTS, | &c. &c. | [ornament] | *TO WHICH IS ADDED, A* | COLLECTION OF MARKETING TABLES, | A | SYSTEM OF DOMESTIC BOOK-KEEPING, | *&c. c.* | EMBELLISHED WITH A FRONTISPIECE AND PLATES. | [short fancy rule] | LONDON: | PUBLISHED BY THE EDITOR; | And Sold by all PERIODICAL PUBLISHERS in Town and Country. | *Printed by J. Haddon, Tabernacle Walk.* | [short rule] | 1818

New edition, London, 1818. Originally published, London, 1813 (item 759).

209 x 123 mm. [A]² B-C⁴ D-I⁸ K-2Q⁴ 2R⁸ 3S² 3T⁴; 192 leaves, pp. [*4*] [1] 2-360 [*12*] [369] 370-376.

Illustrations: Engraved frontispiece titled "A Domestic Scene" and seven engraved plates, six of bills of fare and one illustrating quartering of beef, veal, pork, and mutton.

Bibliographies: This edition unrecorded in the bibliographies consulted. Simon BG 865 records an 1813 edition and Axford, p. 214, and Bitting, p. 564, an 1816 edition.

Copies: No other copy of this edition located. There is a copy of a London, 1815, edition in the private collection of John C. Craig.

761. The Housewife's Cookery Book.

THE | HOUSEWIFE'S | Cookery Book, | CONTAINING | DIRECTIONS FOR | Roasting, Boiling, Frying, Broiling, | Stewing, Hashing, Soups, Sauces, | Cakes, Vinegars, Puddings, Jellies, | Pies, Tarts, Catchups, Wines, | AND ALL THE | *Necessary Branches of Cookery.* | [vignette] | FALKIRK: | PRINTED FOR THE BOOKSELLERS.

First edition, published ca.1820.

170 x 104 mm. [1]¹²; 12 leaves, pp. [1-2] 3-24.

Illustration: Woodcut vignette of family scene on title-page.

Bibliographies: Unrecorded in the bibliographies consulted.

Copies: *BMC.*

762. Howard, Henry.

[within a border of two rules] *ENGLAND's* | NEWEST WAY in all | SORTS | OF | COOKERY, PASTRY, | AND | All PICKLES that are fit to be used. | ADORNED | With Copper Plates, setting forth the Manner | of placing Dishes upon Tables; and the Newest Fashions | of Mince-Pies. | [rule] | *By* HENRY HOWARD, | Free Cook of

London, and late Cook to his Grace the Duke of | *Ormond*, and since to the Earl of *Salisbury*, and Earl of *Winchelsea*. | [rule] | To which is added, | The Best Receipts for making Cakes, Mackroons, | Biskets, Ginger-Bread, French-Bread: As also for Preserving, | Conserving, Candying and Drying Fruits, Confectioning and | making of Creams, Syllabubs, and Marmalades of several | Sorts. | Likewise, Additions of Beautifying Waters, and other Cu- | riosities. | As also above Fifty new Receipts are added which renders the | whole Work compleat. | [rule] | The FIFTH EDITION. | [rule] | *LONDON:* | *Printed for* J. Knapton, R. Knaplock, J. *and* | B. Sprint, D. Midwinter, B. Lintot, | A. Bettesworth, W. *and* J. Innys, J. Osborn, | R. Robinson *and* A. Ward. 1726.

Fourth edition, second issue, styled "fifth edition," London, 1726. This is a reissue of the sheets of the fourth edition, London, C. Coningsby, 1717, with a cancel title-page. Originally published, London, 1703.

8vo. A^8 ($\pm$A1) a^4 B-P^8; 124 leaves, pp. [*24*] 1-224.

Illustrations: Three engraved folding plates, two of table settings and one of "several fashions of mince pies."

Bibliographies: Maclean, p. 73; Wheaton and Kelly 3016. Vicaire 447 records the 1703 edition; Oxford, p. 51, the 1708 edition; Axford, p. 134, and Bitting, p. 235, the 1717 edition.

Copies: *BMC* and *NUC* (Radcliffe only). Maclean adds Boston Public Library and Cornell.

763. Howard, Henry.

THE | British Cook's | COMPANION: | BEING A | COLLECTION of Four Hundred of | the newest and best RECEIPTS, in | [in two columns: column one] COOKERY. | PASTRY. | PICKLES. | CAKES. | MACKROONS. | BISKETS. | GINGER-BREAD. | FRENCH- BREAD. | PRESERVING. | CONSERVING. | CANDYING, and | DRYING FRUITS. | [vertical rule] | [column two] CONFECTIONING, and | MAKING of CREAMS. | SYLLABUBS, and | MARMALADES of seve- | ral Sorts. | JELLIES. | MADE WINES. | CORDIALS. | BEAUTIFYING WATERS. | OINTMENTS. | POWDERS, &c. [end columns] | With Copper Plates setting forth the manner | of placing Dishes upon Tables. | The proper Seasons for Fish, Fowls and Rabbets; with | Bills of Fare for every Month in the Year. Receipts | for Twenty-five different sorts of Puddings; and one, | excellent for curing the Spleen. | *Fitted for the Use of all publick and private* | *Families.* | [rule] | By

HENRY HOWARD, Free Cook of *London*. | [rule] | The FIFTH EDITION. | [rule] | *LONDON:* | Printed for R. KNAPLOCK, D. MIDWINTER, J. KNAPTON, | B. LINTOT, J. OSBORN, A. BETTESWORTH, B. SPRINT, | W. INNYS, R. ROBINSON, and A WARD. 1729.

Fourth edition, third issue, styled "fifth edition," London, 1729, of Howard's *England's Newest Way in all Sorts of Cookery* . . ., London, C. Coningsby, 1717, with a new title and new title-page. For another issue of the same sheets see item 762. Originally published, London, 1703.

8vo. A^8 ($\pm$A1) a^4 B-P^8; 124 leaves, pp. [*24*] 1-224.

Illustrations: Three engraved folding plates, two of table settings and one of "several fashions of mince pies."

Bibliographies: Maclean, p. 72.

Copies: *NUC* (New York Public Library only).

764. Hudson, Mrs.

THE | NEW PRACTICE | OF | COOKERY, PASTRY, BAKING, | AND | *PRESERVING:* | BEING | THE COUNTRY HOUSEWIFE'S | *BEST FRIEND.* | BY MRS HUDSON & MRS DONAT, | PRESENT AND LATE HOUSEKEEPERS AND COOKS | TO | *MRS BUCHAN HEPBURN* | OF SMEATON, | *And Published by Her Permission.* | 𝔈𝔡𝔦𝔫𝔟𝔲𝔯𝔤𝔥: | [two short rules] | PRINTED BY J. MOIR, ROYAL BANK CLOSE, | AND SOLD BY THE EDITORS. | 1804.

First edition, Edinburgh, 1804. Oxford, p. 134, comments, "Watt gives 1798 as the date, but there is no indication that the 1804 edition is not the first." No 1798 edition has been located and the work is not recorded in Maclean.

185 x 109 mm. π^2 a^4 A-U^6 χ1; 127 leaves, pp. [i-iii] iv-xii [3] 4-242 [2].

Bibliographies: Oxford, p. 134; Wheaton and Kelly 3065.

Copies: *NUC* (Radcliffe only).

765. Hughes, William, 1803-1861.

A | PRACTICAL TREATISE | ON THE | CHOICE AND COOKERY | OF | FISH. | BY PISCATOR. | SECOND EDITION. | LONDON: | LONGMAN, BROWN, GREEN, AND LONGMANS. | 1854.

Second edition, London, 1854. Originally published under the title *Fish, How to Choose and How to Dress*, London, 1843.

171 x 105 mm. [A]² B-T⁸ U²; 148 leaves, pp. [i-iii] iv [1] 2-291 [292]. Publisher's dark red cloth, stamped in gold, with 24 page publisher's catalogue bound in at end.

Bibliographies: Axford, p. 330; Bitting, p. 237 and p. 593; Wheaton and Kelly 3074. Oxford, p. 173, describes the original edition and cites this edition in a note.

Copies: *BMC* and *NUC* (4 copies).

766. Hughson, David.

THE NEW | *FAMILY* | RECEIPT-BOOK: | OR | *UNIVERSAL REPOSITORY OF DOMESTIC ECONOMY,* | INCLUDING A FUND OF | USEFUL KNOWLEDGE AND EXPERIENCE | *IN ALL THE VARIOUS BRANCHES OF* | COOKERY, MEDICINE, CONFECTIONERY, PASTRY, BREWING, DISTILLING, PICKLING, PRESERVING, PER- | FUMERY, DYEING, GILDING, PAINTING, VARNISHING, AGRICULTURE, FARRIERY, | GARDENING, HUNTING, FISHING, FOWLING, &c. &c. &c. | *From scarce, curious, and valuable select Receipts and choice Memorandums,* | WITH | SPECIFICATIONS OF APPROVED PATENT MEDICINES, | EXTRACTED FROM THE | *RECORDS OF THE PATENT OFFICE;* | ALL THE MOST SERVICEABLE PREPARATIONS FOR | 𝔇omestic 𝔓urposes, | AND NUMEROUS SUCCESSFUL IMPROVEMENTS IN THE | ORNAMENTAL AND USEFUL ARTS, MANUFACTURES, &c. | COLLECTED | FROM PRIVATE SOURCES OF INFORMATION, AS WELL AS FROM FOREIGN BOOKS AND JOURNALS IN | ALL THE LANGUAGES OF EUROPE: | THE WHOLE FORMING AN | *EXTENSIVE LIBRARY OF VALUABLE DOMESTIC KNOWLEDGE AND GENERAL ECONOMY;* | Selected from the Experience of Ages, and combined with all the chief Modern Discoveries and Improvements of our own and other Coun- | tries, in those useful and elegant Arts which not only contribute to the Happiness, the Convenience, and the | Comfort of Civilized and Social Life, but even to the Preservation and Prolongation of Life itself. | [two short rules] | *By D.*

HUGHSON, L.L.D. | [two short rules] | *LONDON:* | PRINTED FOR W. PRITCHARD, 36, WARWICK-LANE, NEWGATE STREET; | AND J. BYSH, 52, PATERNOSTER ROW. | [short rule] | 1817.

First edition thus, London, 1817. This work, as Oxford, p. 145, notes, is an abbreviated edition of *The Family Receipt-Book* (item 674). Hughson's name is not associated with the earlier work, which was published by a different publisher, and it appears he was the preparer of this version but not necessarily the earlier one. *BMC* records David Hughson, L.L.D., as the pseudonym of David Pugh, author of several early nineteenth century books about London. *NUC* states that David Hughson is the pseudonym of Edward Pugh, the same author *BMC* refers to as David Pugh, and includes *The New Family Receipt Book* among his works. Both *BMC* and *NUC* enter the earlier work, *The Family Receipt-Book*, under title.

258 x 211 mm. [A]^2 B-3X^2 3Z^2 $^\pi$4A^2 4A-5C^2 $^\pi$C^2; 192 leaves, pp. [1-5] 6-384.

Illustration: Engraved frontispiece titled "Truth pointing to the light of philosophy."

Bibliographies: Axford,, p. 294; Bitting, p. 237; Oxford, p. 145; Wheaton and Kelly 4895.

Copies: *NUC* (Harvard, Library of Congress, and William and Mary).

767. Huish, Robert.

[engraved title-page] THE ALPHABETICAL | Receipt Book, | AND | DOMESTIC ADVISER, | BEING | *The only arrangement of the kind ever printed;* | *and forming so complete a Book of reference in all matters* | OF | HOUSE KEEPING, | *That any article may in one instant be referred to* | *the same as in a common Dictionary.* | AMONG THE INNUMERABLE SUBJECTS TREATED UPON, | are | [in three columns: column one] *Advice upon* | *Abdominal Herniae;* | *or* | *Ruptures in the Navel, the* | *Thigh, and the Scrotum.* | *Adulterations* | *Agues* | *Antidotes for Poisons* | *Asthmas* | *Baking* | *Bathing* |*Bees, Treatise on* | [column two] *Bleaching* | *Botany (Domestic)* | *Brewing* | *Carving* | *Childbearing* | *Cooking* | *Cordial Making* | *Culinary Affairs* | *Distilling* | [column three] *Dress Making* | *Dyeing* | *Gardening* | *Marketing* | *Medicine* | *Perfumery* | *Pickling* | *Preserving* | *Teething* | *Wine Making* | *Windy Cholic, &c.* [end columns] | BY | ROBERT HUISH ESQR. | Aided by a professional Gentleman of the First ability. | *London, Published by John Williams,* | *44, Paternoster Row.* | And may be had of all Booksellers. | 1826.

First edition, London, 1826. The British Library has a copy of pages 1-80 in a printed wrapper with the title, "The Female's Friend; and the General Domestic Advertiser, Part I," indicating the book originally appeared in parts.

215 x 134 mm. B-5M⁴; 412 leaves, pp. 1-822 [2].

215 x 134 mm. B-5M^4; 412 leaves, pp. 1-822 [2].

Illustrations: Engraved title-page, lithographed frontispiece and thirty-five additional plates, the frontispiece and seventeen plates hand colored, and occasional wood engravings in the text.

This copy has the ownership signature of A.W. Oxford.

Bibliographies: Oxford, p. 159.

Copies: *BMC*, Part I only. *NUC* records only an 1837 edition, titled *The Female's Friend, and General Domestic Advertiser* (New York Public Library and Yale).

768. Humelbergius Secundus, Dick.

APICIAN MORSELS; | OR, | TALES OF THE | TABLE, KITCHEN, AND LARDER: | CONTAINING, | A NEW AND IMPROVED CODE OF *EAT*ICS; | SELECT EPICUREAN PRECEPTS; | NUTRITIVE MAXIMS, REFLECTIONS, ANECDOTES, &c. | ILLUSTRATING | THE VERITABLE SCIENCE OF THE MOUTH; | WHICH INCLUDES | THE ART OF NEVER BREAKFASTING AT HOME, AND | ALWAYS DINING ABROAD. | [short rule] | BY | DICK HUMELBERGIUS SECUNDUS. | [short rule] | "O vos qui stomacho laboratis, accurrite, et ego vos restaurabo!" | *Vide* p. 202. | "Always breakfast as if you did not intend to dine; and dine as if you | had not broken your fast." – *Code Gourmand.* | [short rule] | LONDON: | WHITTAKER, TREACHER AND CO. | AVE-MARIA LANE. | [short rule] | 1829.

First edition, London, 1829.

169 x 105 mm. π² [A]² B-Y⁸ Z⁶; 178 leaves, pp. [i-v] vi-viii [1] 2-348. Publisher's cloth with paper label on spine.

169 x 105 mm. π^2 [A]^2 B-Y^8 Z^6; 178 leaves, pp. [i-v] vi-viii [1] 2-348. Publisher's cloth with paper label on spine.

Illustration: Engraved frontispiece (unsigned) and one plate signed with the initials RC, both attributed to Robert Cruikshank in the American Art Association catalogue of the Townsend sale (4-6 February 1919).

Bibliographies: Axford, p. 14; Bitting, p. 237; Oxford, p. 164; Wheaton and Kelly 3080. Vicaire 448 cites an 1834 edition.

Copies: *NUC* (10 copies).

769. Hunter, Alexander, 1729-1809.

CULINA | FAMULATRIX MEDICINAE: | OR, | RECEIPTS IN COOKERY, | WORTHY THE NOTICE OF | Those MEDICAL PRACTITIONERS, who ride in their | CHARIOTS with a FOOTMAN behind, and who receive | TWO-GUINEA FEES from their RICH and LUXURIOUS | PATIENTS. | [short rule] | BY IGNOTUS. | [short rule] | ———Propera Stomachum laxare Saginis, | Et tua servatum consume in Saecula Rhombum. JUV. | [short rule] | *YORK:* | Printed by T. WILSON and R. SPENCE, High- | Ousegate: and sold by J. MAWMAN, Bookseller in the | Poultry, London. 1804.

First edition, York, 1804.

192 x 110 mm. A-T^6 U^4; 118 leaves, pp. [1-5] 6-235 [236].

Illustration: Etched frontispiece of a hog, titled "Transmigration."

Bibliographies: Axford, p. 105; Craig 47; Oxford, p. 133; Vicaire 240; Wheaton and Kelly 3090.

Copies: *BMC* and *NUC* (Radcliffe, New York Public Library, and Yale).

769a. Hunter, Alexander, 1729-1809.

CULINA | FAMULATRIX MEDICINÆ: | OR, | RECEIPTS IN MODERN COOKERY; | WITH A MEDICAL COMMENTARY, | WRITTEN BY | *IGNOTUS,* | AND REVISED BY | A. HUNTER, M.D. F.R.S. L. & E. | [two rules] | Qui Stomachum regem totius corporis esse contendunt, vera | niti ratione videntur. .... SERENDUS SAMMONICUS. | [two rules] | THE SECOND EDITION. | [short fancy rule] | *YORK:* | Printed by T. Wilson and R. Spence, High-Ousegate: | For J. MAWMAN, in the Poultry, London, and for | WILSON and SPENCE, York; | Sold also by J. WHITE, Fleet-street, and J. HARDING, St. James's | Street, London; A. CONSTABLE and Co. Edinburgh; | and by J. TODD, SOTHERAN and SON, and | J. WOLSTENHOLME, York. | 1805.

Second edition, York, 1805. Originally published, York, 1804 (item 769).

190 x 110 mm. A-Y^6 Z^2; 134 leaves, pp. [1-5] 6-268.

Illustration: Etched frontispiece of a hog, titled "Transmigration."

Bibliographies: Oxford, p. 133, in a note.

Copies: *BMC* and *NUC* (4 copies).

770. Hunter, Alexander, 1729-1809.

CULINA | FAMULATRIX MEDICINAE: | OR, | RECEIPTS IN MODERN
COOKERY; | WITH | A MEDICAL COMMENTARY, | WRITTEN BY |
IGNOTUS, | AND REVISED BY | A. HUNTER, M.D. F.R.S. L. & E. | [two rules]
| Qui Stomachum regem totius corporis esse contendunt, vera | niti ratione videntur.
.... SERENUS SAMMONICUS. | [two rules] | THE THIRD
EDITION. | [short fancy rule] | *YORK:* | Printed by T. Wilson and R. Spence, High-
Ousegate: | For J. MAWMAN, in the Poultry, London, and for | WILSON and
SPENCE, York; | Sold also by J. WHITE, Fleet-street, and J. HARDING, St. James's
| Street, London; A. CONSTABLE and Co. Edinburgh; | and by J. TODD,
SOTHERAN and SON, and | J. WOLSTENHOLME, York. | 1806.

Third edition, York, 1806. Originally published, York, 1804 (item 769).

168 x 99 mm. A-Z^6 Aa^4; 142 leaves, pp. [1-5] 6-284.
Illustration: Etched frontispiece of a hog, titled "Transmigration."

Bibliographies: Wheaton and Kelly 3091.

Copies: *NUC* (John Crerar Library only). Wheaton and Kelly (Radcliffe only).

771. Hunter, Alexander, 1729-1809.

CULINA | FAMULATRIX MEDICINAE: | OR, | Receipts in Modern Cookery; |
WITH | A MEDICAL COMMENTARY, | WRITTEN BY | *IGNOTUS,* | AND
REVISED BY | A. HUNTER, M.D. F.R.S. L. & E. | [short rule] | Magister artis,
Ingeniique largitor | Venter .... PERSIUS. | [short rule] |
THE FOURTH EDITION. | [short fancy rule] | *YORK:* | Printed by T. Wilson and R.

Spence, High-Ousegate: | For J. MAWMAN, in the Poultry, London, and for | WILSON and SPENCE, York; | Sold also by J. WHITE, and J. MURRAY, Fleet-street, | and J. HARDING, St. James's Street, London; A. CONSTABLE and Co. | Edinburgh; and by J. TODD, SOTHERAN and SON, | and J. WOLSTENHOLME, York. | 1806.

Fourth edition, York, 1806. Originally published, York, 1804 (item 769).

192 x 112 mm. Aa-Bb⁶ Cc⁴; 154 leaves, pp. [1-5] 6-308. Publisher's boards with printed label.

Illustration: Etched frontispiece of a hog, titled "Transmigration."

Bibliographies: Oxford, p. 133, in a note; Vicaire 240.

Copies: *BMC*.

772. Hunter, Alexander, 1729-1809.

CULINA | FAMULATRIX MEDICINAE: | OR, | Receipts in Modern Cookery; | WITH | A MEDICAL COMMENTARY, | WRITTEN BY | *IGNOTUS,* | AND REVISED BY | A. HUNTER, M.D. F.R.S. L. & E. | [short rule] | Magister artis, Ingeniique largitor | Venter. .... PERSIUS. | [short rule] | THE FIFTH EDITION, CONSIDERABLY ENLARGED. | [short fancy rule] | *YORK:* | Printed by T. Wilson and R. Spence, High-Ousegate: | For J. MAWMAN, in the Poultry, London, and for | WILSON and SPENCE, York; | Sold also by J. WHITE, and J. MURRAY, Fleet-street, | and J. HARDING, St. James's Street, London; A. CONSTABLE and Co. | Edinburgh: and by J. TODD, SOTHERAN and SON, | and J. WOLSTENHOLME, York. | 1807.

Fifth edition, first issue, York, 1807. Originally published, York, 1804 (item 769).

172 x 110 mm. A-Cc⁶ Dd⁴ (Dd3 + Ee⁶) (Dd4 signed "Ff"); 166 leaves, pp. [1-5] 6-310, ²[1] 2-22.

Illustration: Engraved frontispiece, titled "A Roman Stewpan from the Cabinet of Mons. Boisot."

Presentation copy, inscribed "To Sir Joshua Merrideth from his affect friend A. Hunter. July 22, 1808" and with Merrideth's bookplate.

Bibliographies: Horn-Arndt 477; Oxford, p. 133, in a note; Schraemli (1) 67; Wheaton and Kelly 3092.

Copies: *BMC* and *NUC* (7 copies).

773. Hunter, Alexander, 1729-1809.

CULINA FAMULATRIX MEDICINAE; | OR, | RECEIPTS | IN | MODERN COOKERY; | WITH A | 𝔐𝔢𝔡𝔦𝔠𝔞𝔩 ℭ𝔬𝔪𝔪𝔢𝔫𝔱𝔞𝔯𝔶, | BY | A. HUNTER, M.D. F.R.S. L. & E. | [short rule] | Magister artis, Ingeniique largitor | Venter. .... *Persius.* | [short rule] | A NEW EDITION. | [two short rules] | YORK: | *Printed by Wilson and Son, High-Ousegate;* | FOR JOHN MURRAY, NO. 32, FLEET-STREET, | LONDON; | Wilson & Son, York; and A. Constable & Co. Edinburgh. | 1810. | *Price Six Shillings in Boards* | [short rule] | [Entered at Stationers' Hall.]

Fifth edition, second issue, with a cancel title styled "A New Edition," York, 1810. Originally published, York, 1804 (item 769).

191 x 110 mm. A⁶ (-A1,2 + A1.2) B-Cc⁶ Dd⁴ (Dd3 + Ee⁶) (Dd4 signed "Ff"); 166 leaves, pp. [1-5] 6-310, ²[1] 2-22.

Illustration: Engraved frontispiece, titled "A Roman Stewpan from the Cabinet of Mons. Boisot."

Bibliographies: Oxford, p. 133, in a note; Wheaton and Kelly 3093.

Copies: *NUC* (4 copies).

774. Hunter, Alexander, 1729-1809.

RECEIPTS | IN | MODERN COOKERY; | WITH A | 𝔐𝔢𝔡𝔦𝔠𝔞𝔩 ℭ𝔬𝔪𝔪𝔢𝔫𝔱𝔞𝔯𝔶, | BY | A. HUNTER, M.D. F.R.S. L. & E. | [short rule] | Magister artis, Ingeniiique largitor | Venter...................... PERSIUS. | [short rule] | A NEW EDITION. | LONDON: | [two short rules] | JOHN MURRARY, ALBEMARLE-STREET: | SOLD ALSO BY | LONGMAN, BALDWIN, RICHARSON, LACKINGTON, WHITTAKER, | UNDERWOOD, LONDON; WILSON, YORK; MOZLEY, DERBY;

| MANNERS AND MILLER, AND OLIVER AND BOYD, | EDINBURGH; CUMMING, KEENE, AND | MILLLIKEN, DUBLIN: | And by every Bookseller and Newsman in Town and Country. | [short rule] | 1820.

New edition, London, 1820. Originally published under the title *Culina Famulatrix Medicinae*, York, 1804 (item 769).

178 x 115 mm. [A]⁸ B-M¹²; 140 leaves, pp. [i-v] vi-xiii [xiv-xvi] [1] 2-262 [2]. Last leaf blank.

Illustration: Engraved frontispiece of a cook and a beef roast.

Bibliographies: Axford, p. 342; Bitting, p. 248; Noling, p. 215.

Copies: *BMC* and *NUC* (Iowa State University, Library of Congress, and Yale).

774a. Jack, Florence B.

GOOD HOUSEKEEPING | INVALID | *Cookery Book* / *By* | Florence B. Jack | *Author of "Good Housekeeping Cookery Book"* / *and "Cookery for every Household"* / *Editor of "The Woman's Book"* / *GOOD HOUSEKEEPING MAGAZINE* / *153 Queen Victoria Street, London, E.C.4.*

First edition, London, 1926.

185 x 121 mm. [A]⁸ B-Q⁸; 128 leaves, pp. [1-6] 7-254 [2]. First leaf and last leaf, blank. Publisher's light blue cloth stamped in darker blue. White paper dust jacket printed in red, yellow, blue and green.

Bibliographies: Unrecorded in the bibliographies consulted.

Copies: *BMC*.

775. Jackson, Sarah.

THE | DIRECTOR: | OR, | YOUNG WOMAN's | BEST COMPANION. | CONTAINING| Above THREE HUNDRED easy Receipts in | Cookery, Pastry, Preserving, Candying, Pickling, | Collaring, Physick, and Surgery. | To which are added, | Plain and easy INSTRUCTIONS for chusing | Beef, Mutton, Veal, Fish, Fowl, and all other Eat- | ables: | ALSO, | DIRECTIONS | for Carving, and Made

Wines: | Likewise Bills of Fare for every Month in the YEAR. | With a complete
INDEX to the Whole. | A BOOK necessary for all Families. | By SARAH JACKSON.
| Collected for the Use of her own Family, and printed | at the Request of her Friends.
| Being one of the Plainest and Cheapest of the Kind. | The WHOLE makes a complete
Family COOK | and PHYSICIAN. | LONDON: | Printed for S. CROWDER and H.
WOODGATE, at the | *Golden Ball* in *Pater-noster Row*; J. FULLER in *Butcher-* |
hall-lane, Newgate-street; and J. NEALE, Bookseller, | at *Chatham*. M.DCC.LIV.
[Price I*s*. 6*d*.

First edition, London, 1754.

12mo. [A1] B-K⁶ L⁶ (-L6 = A1); 60 leaves, pp. [2] [1] 2-112 [6].

Bibliographies: Maclean, p. 74; Oxford, p. 86; Vicaire 459 recording the title as
Complete Family Cook; or, Young Woman's Best Companion.

Copies: *BMC* and *NUC* (New York Academy of Medicine only). Maclean adds
Brotherton Library and National Library of Scotland.

776. Jarrin, William Alexis.

THE | ITALIAN CONFECTIONER, | OR, | *Complete Economy of Desserts:* |
CONTAINING THE | 𝔈lements of t𝔥e 𝔄rt, | ACCORDING TO THE MOST
MODERN AND APPROVED PRACTICE. | FULL AND EXPLICIT DIRECTIONS,
| RESPECTING | DISTILLATION, | *DECORATION, AND MODELLING,* | IN ALL
THEIR BRANCHES: | INCLUDING | FIGURES, FRUITS, FLOWERS, AND
ANIMALS, | IN | 𝔊um 𝔓aste; | AND THE ART OF MOULDING, CASTING,
AND GILDING | COMPOSITION PASTES| OF NEW AND SUPERIOR QUALITY.
| THE WHOLE COMPRISING EVERY INFORMATION REQUISITE TO FORM |
THE COMPLETE CONFECTIONER, AND TO ENABLE HIM TO | ARRANGE
THE EMBELLISHMENTS OF THE TABLE | WITH TASTE AND ELEGANCE. |
[short rule] | BY G. A. JARRIN. | *ORNAMENTAL CONFECTIONER,* | AT |
MESSRS, GUNTERS, in BERKELEY SQUARE. | [short rule] | LONDON: |
PRINTED FOR JOHN HARDING, 36, ST. JAMES'S STREET. | [short rule] | 1820.

First edition, London, 1820.

234 x 147 mm. [a]⁴ b⁸ B-S⁸ T⁴; 152 leaves, pp. [i-v] vi-xxiv [1] 2-280. First leaf
blank. Publisher's boards with printed label on spine.

Illustrations: Engraved portrait of the author and two engraved folding plates of confectioner's equipment.

Bibliographies: Axford, p. 230; Craig 48; Wheaton and Kelly 3174. Oxford, p. 149, describes the 1827 edition and mentions the 1820 edition in a note.

Copies: *NUC* (John Crerar Library and Kansas State University). Wheaton and Kelly (Harvard only).

777. Jarrin, William Alexis.

THE | ITALIAN CONFECTIONER; | OR | COMPLETE ECONOMY | OF | DESSERTS, | ACCORDING TO THE MOST MODERN AND APPROVED PRACTICE. | [short rule] | BY G. A. JARRIN, | CONFECTIONER, NEW BOND STREET. | [short rule] | *NEW EDITION, REVISED AND ENLARGED.* | short rule] | LONDON: | JOHN EBERS AND CO., OLD BOND-STREET. | SOLD ALSO BY | HURST AND CO.; AND SIMPKIN AND MARSHALL, LONDON; WILSON AND | SONS, YORK; H. MOZLEY, DERBY; W. AND W. CLARKE, AND T. | GREGSON, MANCHESTER; G. AND J. ROBINSON, LIVER- | POOL; BELL AND BRADFUTE, EDINBURGH; | GRIFFIN, GLASGOW; J. CUMMING, | DUBLIN; AND BOLSTER, | CORK. | [short rule] | MDCCCXXIX.

Fourth edition, London, 1829. Originally published, London, 1820 (item 776), with the second edition in 1823 and the third in 1827.

200 x 127 mm. [a]^{12} b^6 B-L^{12}; pp. [i-v] vi-viii [2] [ix] x-xxx [1] 2-239 [240]. Publisher's boards with printed label on spine.

Illustrations: Lithographed frontispiece portrait of the author and two engraved folding plates of confectioner's equipment.

Bibliographies: Simon BG 883; Wheaton and Kelly 3177. Bitting, p. 244, and Oxford, p. 149, describe the 1827 edition.

Copies: *NUC* (Library of Congress only). Wheaton and Kelly (Radcliffe only).

778. Jeaffreson, John Cordy, 1831-1901.

A BOOK ABOUT THE TABLE. | BY | JOHN CORDY JEAFFRESON, | AUTHOR OF | "A BOOK ABOUT DOCTORS," "A BOOK ABOUT LAWYERS," | "A BOOK

ABOUT THE CLERGY." | &c. &c. | IN TWO VOLUMES. | VOL I. [VOL. II.] | LONDON: | HURST AND BLACKETT, PUBLISHERS, | 13, GREAT MARLBOROUGH STREET, | 1875. | *The Right of Translation is reserved.*

First edition, London, 1875.

222 x 137 mm. 2 vols. Vol. I. [A]^2 π1 B-X^8 Y^2; 165 leaves, pp. [6] [1] 2-324. Vol. II. [A]^2 π1 B-Z^8; 179 leaves, pp. [6] [1] 20-352. Publisher's purple cloth stamped in gold and black. Undated sixteen page publisher's catalogue bound in at end of volume one.

Bibliographies: Axford, p. 37; Bitting, p. 245; Driver 548.1; Wheaton and Kelly 3183.

Copies: *BMC* and *NUC* (13 copies).

779. Jeanes, William.

THE | MODERN CONFECTIONER: | A PRACTICAL GUIDE | TO THE | LATEST AND MOST IMPROVED METHODS FOR MAKING | THE VARIOUS KINDS OF CONFECTIONERY; | WITH | 𝕿𝖍𝖊 𝕸𝖆𝖓𝖓𝖊𝖗 𝖔𝖋 𝕻𝖗𝖊𝖕𝖆𝖗𝖎𝖓𝖌 𝖆𝖓𝖉 𝕷𝖆𝖞𝖎𝖓𝖌 𝖔𝖚𝖙 𝕯𝖊𝖘𝖘𝖊𝖗𝖙𝖘; | ADAPTED FOR PRIVATE FAMILIES, OR LARGE | ESTABLISHMENTS. | BY WILLIAM JEANES, | CHIEF CONFECTIONER AT MESSRS. GUNTER'S, CONFECTIONERS TO | HER MAJESTY, BERKELEY SQUARE. | WITH NUMEROUS ILLUSTRATIONS. | LONDON: | JOHN CAMDEN HOTTEN, PICCCADILLY. | 1861.

First edition, London, 1861.

197 x 120 mm. [A]^8 B-P^8; 120 leaves, pp. [i-iii] iv-xv [xvi] [1] 2-224. Publisher's green cloth stamped in gold. Six pages of advertisements bound in at the end and other advertisements pasted to front and back end papers.

Illustrations: Fourteen lithographed plates illustrating table settings and kitchen utensils.

Bibliographies: Axford, p. 273; Bitting, p. 245; Noling, p. 225.

Copies: *BMC* and *NUC* (Cleveland Public Library and Harvard).

780. Jenks, James.

THE | Complete Cook: | TEACHING THE | Art of COOKERY in ALL its Branches; | And to SPREAD a TABLE, | In a *Useful, Substantial* and *Splendid* MANNER, | At all SEASONS in the YEAR. | With Practical Instructions | TO CHOOSE, BUY, DRESS and CARVE all Sorts of | PROVISIONS. | *Far exceeding any Thing of the Kind yet Published.* | CONTAINING | The greatest Variety of Approved RECEIPTS in | [in two columns: column one] COOKERY, | PASTRY, | CONFECTIONARY, | [two vertical rules] | [column two] PRESERVING, | PICKLING, | COLLARING, &c. [end columns] | AND | DISHES for LENT and FAST-DAYS, | A Variety of MADE DISHES, | And to Dress both the REAL and MOCK TURTLE. | With an APPENDIX | Teaching the ART of Making | WINE, MEAD, CYDER, SHRUB, | STRONG, CORDIAL and MEDICAL WATERS; | Brewing MALT LIQUOR; | The Management and Breeding of POULTRY and BEES: | AND RECEIPTS | For Preserving and Restoring HEALTH and Relieving PAIN; and for | Taking out STAINS, Preserving FURNITURE, Cleaning PLATE, &c. | [rule] | For the USE of FAMILIES. | [rule] | By JAMES JENKS, Cook. | [rule] | LONDON: | Printed for E. and C. DILLY in the POULTRY. | M DCC LXVIII.

First edition, London, 1768.

12mo. a^{10} B-Q^{12} R^{2}; 192 leaves, pp. [i-iii] iv-xx [1] 2-364.

Bibliographies: Axford, p. 73; Bitting, p. 245; Maclean, p. 75; Noling, p. 226; Oxford, p. 97.

Copies: *BMC* and *NUC* (Columbia, Kansas State University, and Library of Congress). Maclean adds National Library of Scotland and New York Public Library.

781. Jennings, James.

TWO THOUSAND FIVE HUNDRED | Practical Recipes | IN | FAMILY COOKERY; | In which the whole Art of | PREPARING FOOD AND DRINK FOR THE HUMAN STOMACH | IS SIMPLIFIED AND EXPLAINED, | IN ACCORDANCE TO THE BEST KNOWLEDGE OF THE AGE, | *And most conductive to the Health and Happiness of our Species,* | WITH AN | INTRODUCTION | ON THE | DUTIES OF COOKS AND OTHER SERVANTS; | Observations on the Implements employed in Cooking; | INSTRUCTIONS FOR MARKETING, FOR TRUSSING, | AND FOR PERFORMING THE | HONOURS OF THE TABLE WITH GRACE AND PROPRIETY | IN THE WHOLE | Art of

𝔊𝔞𝔯𝔟𝔦𝔫𝔤. | [short rule] | BY JAMES JENNINGS, | *Author of the Family Cyclopaedia.* | [short rule] | LONDON: | SHERWOOD, GILBERT, AND PIPER, | PATERNOSTER-ROW. | [short rule] | 1837.

First edition, London, 1837.

192 x 110 mm. [a]² b-e¹² f² B-U¹² X¹⁰; 290 leaves, pp. [i-iii] iv, ²[i] ii-xcix [c] [1] 2-476. Dark blue cloth with printed label on spine.

Illustrations: Engraved frontispiece of kitchen scene titled "The Cook's Guide" dated Dec. 1836, and wood engravings illustrating quartering, trussing and carving in the text.

Bibliographies: Axford, p. 403; Bitting, p. 245.

Copies: *BMC* and *NUC* (Imperfect copy in Library of Congress only).

782. Johnson, Mary.

Madam JOHNSON's Present: | OR, EVERY | YOUNG WOMAN's | COMPANION, | IN | Useful and Universal KNOWLEDGE. | Digested under the following Heads: | [in two columns: column one] I. Spelling, Reading, Wri- | ting, and Arithmetick | taught without the Help | of a Master. | II. The Compleat Market- | Woman. | III. The Cook's Guide for | dressing all Sorts of Flesh, | Fowl and Fish. | IV. For Pickling, | Pastry, | and Confectionary. | V. An Estimate of the Ex- | pences of a Family in the | middling Station of Life. | [two vertical rules] | [column two] VI. The Art and Terms of | Carving Fish, Fowl, and | Flesh. | VII. A Bill of Fare for e- | very Month in the Year | for Dinner and Supper, | and also for extraordinary | Occasions. | VIII. The Young Woman's | Instructor for the right | Spelling of Words used in | Marketing, Cookery, Pick- | ling, Preserving, &c. [end columns] | To this Edition is added, | Several Useful TABLES, being the compleatest | Book of the Kind ever published. | [rule] | The Compiler, Madam JOHNSON, in order to make this | Book come as cheap as possible to the Purchasers, has, out | of her Benevolence, fixed the Price at 1*s*. 6*d*. Bound; | though it contains double the Quantity that is usually sold | for that Sum. | [rule] | The SECOND EDITION. | [two rules] | *LONDON:* | Printed for *J. FULLER,* in *Blowbladder-* | *Street, Cheapside.* 1759. | Price sewed 1 *s*. 3 *d*. Bound 1 *s*. 6 *d*.

"Second edition," London, 1759. Originally published, London, 1754, and reprinted in 1755 and twice in 1759, once with the imprint of J. Fuller and once with the imprint of H. Owen, both styled "second edition." Oxford, p. 83, records Mary Johnson's *The*

Young Woman's Companion; or, the Servant-Maid's Assistant. . . London, H. Jeffery, 1753, and states that a second edition was published in 1759 as *Madam Johnson's Present; or, Every Young Woman's Companion*, but Maclean treats these as separate works.

12mo. A² B-S⁶ T⁴; 108 leaves, pp. [i-ii] iii-iv [1] 2-192 [193-212].

Illustration: Engraved frontispiece portrait of the author.

Bibliographies: Maclean, p. 75; Vicaire 465. Axford, p. 156, and Bitting, p. 247, describe the "second edition" with the H. Owen imprint.

Copies: Maclean locates copies with the J. Fuller imprint in the Brotherton Library, the National Library of Scotland, and Kansas State University. *NUC* locates only one copy, with the H. Owen imprint, in the Library of Congress.

783. Justice, Sir James, 1698-1763.

THE │ BRITISH GARDENER'S │ DIRECTOR, │ Chiefly adapted to the │ Climate of the Northern Counties: │ DIRECTING │ The NECESSARY WORKS │ IN THE │ KITCHEN, FRUIT and PLEASURE GARDENS, │ AND IN THE │ NURSERY, GREEN-HOUSE, and STOVE. │ By JAMES JUSTICE, F. R. S. one of the principal │ Clerks of Session. │ *EDINBURGH:* │ Printed for A. KINCAID and J. BELL, and R. FLEMING, │ MDCCLXIV.

Second edition, Edinburgh, 1764. Originally published under the title *The Scots Gardiners* [sic] *Director*, Edinburgh, 1754. The first edition was reissued with a cancel title-page, calling it the second edition, Edinburgh, 1759.

8vo. π² A-Iii⁴ Kkk⁴(Kkk3+1); 227 leaves, pp. [4] [1] 2-443 [444] [6].

Illustration: Engraved folding plate titled "Plan of the Pine Apple Stove at Chighton Anno 1732," and an engraved plate of the "Plan of the Nursery Bed for the Crowns and Suckers of the Pine Apples."

Bibliographies: Henrey III.883.

Copies: *BMC, BNC,* and *NUC* (4 copies).

784. Kennedy, John, d. 1790.

A | TREATISE | UPON | *PLANTING*, | GARDENING, | AND THE | MANAGEMENT OF THE HOT-HOUSE. | CONTAINING | [in two columns: column one] I. The Method of planting Forest-Trees | in gravelly, poor, mountainous, and | heath Lands; and for raising the | Plants in the Seed-Bed, previous to | their being planted. | II. The Method of Pruning Forest-Trees, | and how to improve Plantations that | have been neglected. | III. On the Soils most proper for the | different Kinds of Forest-trees. | IV. The Management of Vines; their | Cultivation upon Fire-Walls and in the | Hot-House; with a new Method of | dressing, planting, and preparing the | Ground. | V. A new and easy Method to propagate | Pine Plants, so as to gain Half a Year | [two vertical rules] | [column two] in their Growth; with a sure Method | of destroying the Insect so destructive | to Pines. | VI. The best Method to raise Mushrooms | without Spawn, by which the Table | may be plentifully supplied every Day | in the Year. | VII. An improved Method of cultivating | Asparagus. | VIII. The best Method to cultivate Field | Cabbages, Carrots, and Turnips for | feeding of Cattle. | IX. A new Method of managing all | Kinds of Fruit-Trees, viz. of proper Soils | for planting, of pruning and dressing | them; with a Receipt to prevent | Blights, and cure them when blighted. [end columns] | [rule] | BY JOHN KENNEDY, | GARDENER TO SIR THOMAS GASCOIGNE, BART. | [rule] | THE SECOND EDITION, | CORRECTED AND GREATLY ENLARGED. | [rule] | IN TWO VOLUMES. | [rule] | VOL. I. [VOL. II] | [two rules] | LONDON: | PRINTED FOR S. HOOPER, N° 25, LUDGATE-HILL; | and G. ROBINSON, PATERNOSTER-ROW. | M DCC LXXVII.

Second edition, London, 1777. Originally published, York, 1776.

8vo. 2 vols. Vol. I. a⁶ A-R⁸ S⁴; 146 leaves, pp. [i-iii] iv-xi [xii] [1] 2-280. Vol. II. π² A-R⁸ S⁴; 142 leaves, pp. [4] [1] 2-279 [280].

Note: Blanche Henrey attributes this work to a John Kennedy who died in 1790 while the *NUC* attributes it to John Kennedy, 1759-1842. The author, in his preface, writes of giving directions "he has followed with the greatest success for many years." On the title-page Kennedy is decribed as gardener to Sir Thomas Gascoigne. As it seems improbable that Sir Thomas's gardener, with his many years of experience, was a lad of seventeen when he first published this two volume work of more than five hundred pages in 1776, I have accepted Henrey's John Kennedy as the correct author.

Bibliographies: Henrey III.894.

Copies: *BMC*, *BNC*, and *NUC* (Library of Congress, Massachusetts Horticultural Society, and New York Public Library).

785. Kent, Elizabeth Talbot Grey, countes of, 1581-1651.

[within a single rule border] A | *CHOICE MANVAL* | OF | Rare and Select |
SECRETS | IN | PHYSICK | AND | CHYRURGERY; | Collected and practised by
the Right | Honourable, the Countesse of | *Kent* late deceased. | As also most
Exquisite ways of Pre- | serving, Conserving, Candying, &c. | [rule] | Published by
W. J. GENT. | [rule] | *LONDON,* | Printed by *R. Norton,* 1653.

Second of three editions without edition statement recorded by Wing as published
London, 1653.

12mo. A⁴ B-E¹² F⁴; 56 leaves, pp. [*8*] 1-102 [*2*]. Last leaf (blank?) wanting in this
copy. Bound with *A True Gentlewomans Delight,* London, 1653 (item 788).

Bibliographies: Oxford, p. 22; Wing K310A.

Copies: *BMC.* Wing adds the Brotherton Library.

786. Kent, Elizabeth Talbot Grey, countess of, 1581-1651.

[within a border of two rules] A | *CHOICE MANVAL* | OF | Rare and Select |
SECRETS | IN | PHYSICK | AND | CHYRURGERY; | Collected and Practised by
the | Right Honorable, the Countesse of | KENT, late deceased. | As also most
Exquisite ways of Preserving, | Conserving, Candying, &c. | [rule] | Published by *W.*
I. GENT. | [rule] | *LONDON,* | Printed by *G. D.* and are to be sold by | *William*
Shears, at the Sign of the Bible in St. | *Pauls* Church-yard, 1653.

Third of three editions without edition statement recorded by Wing as published
London, 1653.

8vo. A-M⁸; 96 leaves, pp. [*16*] 1-176.

Bibliographies: Wing K310B.

Copies: *NUC* (Vassar and Yale). Wing adds the Wellcome Library.

787. Kent, Elizabeth Talbot Grey, countess of, 1581-1651.

[within a border of two rules] *A Choice Manual,* | Or Rare | SECRETS | IN |
PHYSICK | AND | CHIRURGERY: | Collected, & practised by the | Right

Honorable the Coun- | tess of *Kent*, late deceased. | Whereto are added several | Experiments of the Vertue | of *Gascons* powder, and La- | pis contra Yarvam by a | Professor of Physick. | As also most exquisite ways | of Preserving, Conserv- | ing, Candying, &c. | [rule] | *The Nineteenth Edition.* | [rule] | *London*, Printed for *H. Mort-* | *lock* at the Phoenix in St. | *Pauls* Churchyard. 1687.

Title-page of the second part:

[within a border of two rules] A | *True Gentlewomans* | DELIGHT. | Wherein is contain'd all | manner of COOKERY. | Together | with { *Preserving,* | *Conserving,* | *Drying,* and | *Candying.* | Very necessary for all Ladies | and Gentlewomen. | [rule] | Published by *W. G.* Gent. | [rule] | *LONDON,* | Printed for *Henry Mortlock,* | at the Phoenix in St. *Paul's* | Church-yard, 1682.

"Nineteenth edition," London, 1687. (Wing records only fifteen editions prior to this one.) As the "eighteenth edition" of *A Choice Manual* was published in 1682, it appears the printer followed copy from that title-page of the second part without changing the date.

24mo. A-R^{12} S^6; 210 leaves, pp. [*18*] 1-190 [*2*] 191-233 [*234*] [*6*], ^{2}[*20*] 1-140.

Bibliographies: Wing K317. Oxford, p. 23, in a note.

Copies: *BMC* and *NUC* (John Crerar Library only). Wing adds Glasgow University, National Library of Wales, and Royal College of Surgeons.

788. Kent, Elizabeth Talbot Grey, countess of, 1581-1651.

[within a single rule border] A | *True Gentlewomans* | DELIGHT. | Wherein is contained all | manner of COOKERY: | Together with { *Preserving,* | *Conserving,* | *Drying* | *and* | *Candying,* | Very necessary for all Ladies | and Gentlewomen. | [rule] | Published by *W. J.* GENT. | [rule] | *LONDON,* | Printed by *R. Norton,* 1653.

Second of two editions without edition statement recorded by Wing as published London, 1653.

12mo. A^4 B^8 C-D^{12} E^4; 40 leaves, pp. [*8*] 1-40, 65-96. Bound with the Countess of Kent's *A Choice Manual*. . . London, 1653 (item 785).

Bibliographies: Oxford, p. 22; Wing K317B.

Copies: Wing (Vassar College only).

789. Kettilby, Mary.

[within a border of two rules] A | COLLECTION | Of above Three Hundred | RECEIPTS | IN | Cookery, | Physick *and* Surgery; | For the Use of all | Good Wives, Tender Mothers, | and Careful Nurses. | [rule] | *By several Hands.* | [two rules] | *LONDON,* | Printed for RICHARD WILKIN, at the | *King's Head* in *St. Paul's Church-yard.* | MDCCXIV.

First edition, London, 1714.

8vo. A-P⁸ Q⁴; 124 leaves, pp. [*16*] 1-218 [219-232].

Bibliographies: Axford, p. 67; Craig 53; Maclean, p. 79; Oxford, p. 54: Schraemli (1) 242.

Copies: *BMC* and *NUC* (Duke and Huntington Library). Maclean adds Brotherton Library, National Library of Scotland, Cornell, and Detroit Public Library.

790. Kettilby, Mary.

[within a border of two rules] A | COLLECTION | Of above Three Hundred | RECEIPTS | IN | Cookery, | Physick *and* Surgery; | For the Use of all | Good Wives, Tender Mothers, and | Careful Nurses. | [rule] | *By several Hands.* | [rule] | 𝔗𝔥𝔢 𝔖𝔢𝔠𝔬𝔫𝔡 𝔈𝔡𝔦𝔱𝔦𝔬𝔫. | [rule] | To which is Added, | A Second PART, Containing a great Number of | Excellent Receipts, for Preserving and Con- | serving of Sweet-Meats, *&c.* | [rule] | *LONDON,* Printed for *Mary Kettilby,* and Sold by | *Richard Wilkin,* at the *King's Head* in *St. Paul's* | *Church-Yard.* MDCC XIX.

Title-page of the second part:

[within a border of two rules] A | COLLECTION | OF | RECEIPTS | IN | Cookery, | Physick *and* Surgery. | [rule] | PART II. | [rule] | CONTAINING LIKEWISE | A great Number of Excellent Receipts for Preser- | ving and Conserving of Sweet-Meats, *&c.* | [rule] | *By several Hands.* | [rule] | *LONDON,* | Printed for RICHARD WILKIN, at the | *King's Head* in *St. Paul's Church-Yard.* | M DCC XIX.

Second edition, London, 1719. Originally published, London, 1714 (item 789).

8vo. A-M⁸, ²A-F⁸; 144 leaves, pp. [*16*] 1-163 [164-176], ²[1-6] 7-86 [*10*]. First and last leaves (blanks?) wanting in this copy.

Bibliographies: Maclean, p. 79; Oxford, p. 54, in a note; Pennell, p. 146.

Copies: *BMC* and *NUC* (8 copies). Maclean adds Brotherton, National Museum of Wales and Wellcome and Kansas State University.

791. Kettilby, Mary.

[within a border of two rules] A │ COLLECTION │ Of above Three Hundred │ RECEIPTS │ IN │ Cookery, │ Physick *and* Surgery; │ For the USE of all │ Good WIVES, Tender MOTHERS, │ and Careful NURSES. │ [rule] │ *By several Hands.* │ [rule] │ The FOURTH EDITION. │ [rule] │ To which is ADDED, │ A SECOND PART, │ Containing a great Number of Excellent Receipts, for │ Preserving and Conserving of Sweet-Meats, *&c.* │ [rule] │ *LONDON:* Printed for MARY KETTILBY, │ and Sold by RICHARD WILKIN, at the *King's Head* │ in *St. Paul's Church-Yard.* M.DCC.XXVIII.

Title-page of the second part:

[within a border of two rules] A │ COLLECTION │ OF │ RECEIPTS │ IN │ Cookery, │ Physick *and* Surgery. │ [rule] │ PART II. │ [rule] │ CONTAINING LIKEWISE, │ A great Number of Excellent Receipts for Preserving │ and Conserving of Sweet-Meats, *&c.* │ *By several Hands.* │ [rule] │ The THIRD EDITION. │ [rule] │ *LONDON:* │ Printed for RICHARD WILKIN, at the │ *King's Head* in St. *Paul's Church-Yard.* │ [short rule] │ M.DCC.XXVIII.

Fourth edition of the first part, third edition of the second part, London, 1728. Originally published, London, 1714 (item 789).

8vo. A-R^8 S^2; 138 leaves, pp. [i-iii] iv-viii [9] 10-272 [*4*].

Bibliographies: Maclean, p. 82; Oxford, p. 54, in a note; Simon BG 904; Wheaton and Kelly 3273.

Copies: *BMC* and *NUC* (Radcliffe, New York Public Library, and University of Pennsylvania). Maclean adds Brotherton Library , Cambridge University, Wellcome Library, and Virginia State Library.

792. Kettilby, Mary.

[within a border of two rules] A | COLLECTION | Of above Three Hundred | RECEIPTS | IN | *Cookery, Physick* and *Surgery*; | For the USE of all | Good WIVES, Tender MOTHERS, | and Careful NURSES. | [rule] | *By Several Hands.* | [rule] | The FIFTH EDITION. | [rule] | To which is Added, | A SECOND PART, | CONTAINING | A great Number of Excellent Receipts, for *Preserving* | and *Conserving* of SWEET-MEATS, &c. | [two rules] | *LONDON:* | Printed for the Executrix of MARY KETTILBY; and sold | by W. PARKER, at the *King's Head* in *St. Paul's Church-yard.* | [short rule] | M DCC XXXIV.

Title-page of the second part:

[within a border of two rules] A | COLLECTION | OF | RECEIPTS | IN | Cookery, | Physick *and* Surgery. | [rule] | PART II. | [rule] | CONTAINING LIKEWISE | A great Number of Excellent Receipts, for *Preserving* | and *Conserving* of SWEET-MEATS, &c. | [rule] | *By Several Hands.* | [rule] | THE FOURTH EDITION. | [two rules] | *LONDON:* | Printed for W. PARKER, at the *King's-Head* | in St. *Paul's Church-Yard.* | MDCCXXXIV.

Fifth edition of the first part and fourth edition of the second part, London, 1734. Originally published, London, 1714 (item 789).

8vo. A-R^8 S^2; 138 leaves, pp. [i-iii] iv-viii [9] 10-272 [4].

Bibliographies: Bitting, p. 258; Maclean, p. 82; Oxford, p. 54, in a note.

Copies: *BMC* and *NUC* (John Crerar Library and Library of Congress). Maclean adds Brotherton Library, Wellcome Library, Cornell, and Huntington Library.

793. Kidder, Edward, 1666-1739.

[within a border of two rules] *E. Kidder's* | *RECEIPTS* | OF | PASTRY | *AND* | COOKERY, | For the Use of his Scholars. | *Who teaches at his School in* | Queen Street near S.t Thomas Apostles. | *On Mondays, Tuesdays & Wednesdays,* | In the Afternoon. | ALSO | *On Thursdays, Fridays & Satrudays,* | In the Afternoon, | *at his School next to* | Furnivals Inn in Holborn. | *Ladies may be taught at* | *their own Houses.*

First edition, London, ca. 1720

43 disjunct leaves of text, signed [-] A, A1, A2, B, B1, C, C1, C2, C3, D, D1, D2, D3, E, E1, E2, F, F1, F2, F3, F4, F5, F6, F7, F8, G, G1, G2, H, H1, I, I1, I2, K, K1, K2, L, L1, L2, L3 [-] [-]; ff. [*1*] 1-4 [*1*] 5 [*1*] 6-8 [*3*] 9 [*1*] A, 10 [2] 11 [*7*] 12 [*1*] 13-14 [*1*] 15 [2] 16 [17] 18 [*3*]. The text is engraved throughout and printed on the rectos of the leaves only. This copy lacks the page of Kidder's advertisement called for by Bitting.

Illustrations: Engraved frontispiece portrait of the author and eight engraved plates (three folding) of patterns and ornamental designs for pies and pastries.

Bibliographies: Axford, p. 124; Bitting, p. 259; Craig 51; Maclean, p. 82; Oxford, p. 71; Pennell, p. 151; Schraemli (1) 243; Simon BG 907; Vicaire 475; Wheaton and Kelly 3283.

Copies: *BMC* and *NUC* (Folger, Library of Congress, and University of Oregon). Maclean adds Wellcome Library. Wheaton and Kelly adds Boston Public Library.

793a. King, James Frederick Marsden.

YACHT COOKERY | and | Hints to Small Boat Sailors | BY | J. F. MARSDEN KING | GLASGOW | BROWN, SON & FERGUSON, LIMITED | 52 TO 58 DARNLEY STREET

First edition, Glasgow, 1935.

151 x 124 mm. [A]⁸ B-E⁸; 40 leaves, pp. [2] [1-4] 5-22 [2] 23-69 [70] [6]. Last 6 pages contain advertisements. Publisher's white paper covered boards printed in red and blue; blue cloth spine printed in black.

Illustrations: Sketch of a sailboat facing the title-page and of storage lockers facing p. 22, both in the text.

Bibliographies: This edition unrecorded in the bibliographies consulted. Axford, p. 430, records the third edition, Glasgow, 1966.

Copies: *BMC* and *NUC* (New York Public Library only).

794. King, William, 1663-1712.

[within a border of two rules] THE | Art of Cookery, | In Imitation of | *Horace*'s Art of Poetry. | WITH SOME | LETTERS | TO | Dr. *LISTER*, and Others: | Occasion'd principally by the Title of | a Book publish'd by the Doctor, being the | Works of *Apicius Coelius*, | *Concerning the Soups and Sauces of the* | *Antients*. | With an Extract of the greatest Curiosities contain'd | in that Book. | To which is added, | HORACE'S Art of Poetry, in *Latin*. | [rule] | *By the Author of the Journey to* LONDON. | [rule] | Humbly inscrib'd to the Honourable BEEF | STEAK CLUB. | [rule] | *LONDON:* | Printed for BERNARD LINTOTT at the *Cross-* | *Keys* between the two *Temple* Gates in *Fleet-* | *street*.

First authorized edition, London, 1708. There was also an unauthorzied folio edition printed in December 1707 but dated 1708 (Foxon K55).

8vo. [A]⁴ B-L⁸; 84 leaves, pp. [*8*] 1-160.

Bibliographies: Bitting, p. 260; Foxon K57; Maclean, p. 84; Oxford, p. 51; Pennell, p. 142; Schraemli (1) 244; Simon BG 908; Vicaire 475; Wheaton and Kelly 3294.

Copies: *BMC*, *BNC*, and *NUC* (30 copies). Maclean records six copies and Foxon ten copies.

795. King, William, 1663-1712.

[within a border of two rules] The ART of | COOKERY, | In Imitation of | *Horace*'s Art of Poetry. | WITH SOME | LETTERS | TO | Dr. *LISTER*, and Others: | Occasion'd principally by the Title of | a Book publish'd by the Doctor, being the | Works of *Apicius Coelius*, | *Concerning the Soups and Sauces of the* | *Ancients*. | With an Extract of the greatest Curiosities contain'd | in that Book. | To which is added | HORACE'S Art of Poetry, in *Latin*. | [rule] | *By the Author of the Journey to* LONDON. | [rule] | Humbly inscrib'd to the Honourable BEEF | STEAK CLUB. | [rule] | 𝔗𝔥𝔢 𝔖𝔢𝔠𝔬𝔫𝔡 𝔈𝔡𝔦𝔱𝔦𝔬𝔫. | [rule] | *LONDON:* | Printed for BERNARD LINTOTT, at the *Cross-Keys* between the | two *Temple* Gates in *Fleetstreet*.

Second edition, London, ca.1712. Originally published in an unauthorized folio edition printed December 1707 but dated 1708 and in an authorized edition, London, 1708 (item 794). Maclean dates this edition 1710, Foxon, in his *English Verse 1701-1750*, dates it 1712.

8vo. A-G⁸ [H]⁴; 60 leaves, pp. [4] 1-112 [4].

Illustrations: Engraved frontispiece by Van der Gucht after that by G. Goeree done for Lister's edition of Apicius, Amsterdam, 1709 (item 1076).

Bibliographies: Foxon K59; Maclean, p. 84; Simon BG 909; Wheaton and Kelly 3296.

Copies: *BMC* and *NUC* (7 copies). Maclean adds Brotherton Library and Colonial Williamsburgh and Foxon locates six copies.

796. Kirwan, Andrew Valentine, 1804-1870.

HOST AND GUEST. | A BOOK ABOUT DINNERS, WINES, | AND DESSERTS. | BY A. V. KIRWAN, | OF THE MIDDLE TEMPLE, ESQ. | [ornament] | [publisher's device] | LONDON: | BELL AND DALDY, 186, FLEET STREET. | 1864.

First edition, London, 1864.

180 x 117 mm. [a]⁸ b² B-CC⁸ DD⁴ EE1 (a1 folded to follow b2); 215 leaves, pp. [iii-v] vi-xxii [1] 2-410.

Bibliographies: Axford, p. 210; Bitting, p. 261; Gabler, p. 156; Noling, p. 240.

Copies: *BMC* and *NUC* (6 copies).

797. Kitchiner, William, 1775?-1827.

APICIUS REDIVIVUS; | OR, | THE COOK'S ORACLE: | Wherein especially | THE ART OF COMPOSING SOUPS, SAUCES, AND FLAVOURING ESSENCES | IS MADE SO CLEAR AND EASY, BY THE QUANTITY OF EACH | ARTICLE BEING ACCURATELY STATED BY WEIGHT AND | MEASURE, THAT EVERY ONE MAY SOON LEARN | TO DRESS A DINNER, AS WELL AS THE | MOST EXPERIENCED COOK; | 𝔅𝔢𝔦𝔫𝔤 𝔖𝔦𝔵 𝔥𝔲𝔫𝔡𝔯𝔢𝔡 𝔯𝔢𝔠𝔢𝔦𝔭𝔱𝔰, | THE | RESULT OF ACTUAL EXPERIMENTS | INSTITUTED IN | THE KITCHEN OF A PHYSICIAN, | FOR THE PURPOSE OF COMPOSING | A CULINARY CODE FOR THE RATIONAL EPICURE, | AND AUGMENTING | 𝔗𝔥𝔢 𝔄𝔩𝔦𝔪𝔢𝔫𝔱𝔞𝔯𝔶

𝔈𝔫𝔧𝔬𝔶𝔪𝔢𝔫𝔱𝔰 𝔬𝔣 𝔓𝔯𝔦𝔟𝔞𝔱𝔢 𝔍𝔞𝔪𝔦𝔩𝔦𝔢𝔰; | COMBINING ECONOMY WITH
ELEGANCE; | AND SAVING EXPENSE TO HOUSEKEEPERS, | AND TROUBLE
TO SERVANTS. | [rule] | "I have taken as much pains in describing, in the fullest
manner, how to make, in | the easiest, most agreeable, and most economical way,
those Dishes which daily con- | tribute to the comforts ot the middle rank of Society,
as I have in directing the | preparation of those *piquante* and elaborate relishes, the
most ingenious and accom- | plished "Officers of the Mouth" have invented for the
amusemenst of *Grands* | *Gourmands*. These are so composed, as to be as agreeable and
useful to the stomach, | as they are inviting to the appetite; nourishing without being
inflammatory, and | savoury without being surfeiting." – *Vide* PREFACE, *page* 3. |
[rule] | *LONDON:* | PRINTED FOR SAMUEL BAGSTER, | NO. 15,
PATERNOSTER-ROW, | By J. Moyes, Greville Street. | [short rule] | 1817.

First edition, London, 1817.

154 x 98 mm. a-b^{12} [c]^2 B-Q^{12} R^4; 210 leaves, unpaginated.

Illustrations: Four engraved plates, two with illustrations, two with text, describing
quartering the ox, the calf, the sheep and the pig.

Bibliographies: Noling, p. 240; Oxford, p. 145; Schraemli (1) 245; Wheaton and
Kelly 3335.

Copies: *BMC* and *NUC* (5 copies).

798. Kitchiner, William, 1775?-1827.

APICIUS REDIVIVUS. | [two short rules] | THE COOK'S ORACLE: |
CONTAINING | PRACTICAL RECEIPTS | FOR | [in two columns: column one]
ROASTING, | BOILING, | FRYING, | BROILING, | [fancy vertical rule] | [column
two] VEGETABLES, | FISH, | HASHES, | MADE DISHES, &c. &c. [end columns]
| *On the most Economical Plan for Private Families;* | ALSO, | THE ART OF
COMPOSING | THE MOST SIMPLE, AND MOST HIGHLY FINISHED |
BROTHS, GRAVIES, SOUPS, SAUCES, | AND FLAVOURING ESSENCES: | *The
Quantity of each Article* | BEING ACCURATELY STATED BY WEIGHT OR
MEASURE; | THE HUMBLEST NOVICE | MAY WORK WITH THE SAME
CERTAINTY AS THE | EXPERIENCED COOK. | *THE RESULT OF ACTUAL
EXPERIMENTS* | MADE IN | THE KITCHEN OF A PHYSICIAN, | FOR THE
PURPOSE OF COMPOSING | *A Culinary Code for the Rational Epicure,* | AND
AUGMENTING | THE ALIMENTARY ENJOYMENTS OF PRIVATE FAMILIES; |

COMBINING ECONOMY WITH ELEGANCE; | AND SAVING EXPENSE TO HOUSEKEEPERS, | AND TROUBLE TO SERVANTS. | [rule] | THE SECOND EDITION, | CAREFULLY REVISED. | [two short rules] | *LONDON:* | PRINTED FOR JOHN HATCHARD, PICCADILLY; | AND SOLD BY | MESSRS. SIMPKIN AND MARSHALL, STATIONERS' COURT; | UNDERWOODS, FLEET STREET; OGLE AND CO. HOLBORN; | OTRIDGE, 39, STRAND; AND STODART, 81, STRAND; | *And by all Booksellers and Newsmen in Town or Country.* | [short rule] | 1818.

Second edition, London, 1818 Originally published, London, 1817 (item 797).

161 x 101 mm. [A]² B-3C⁶ 3D⁸; 298 leaves, [4] [i-xxxvi] xxxvii-lvii [58] 59-592. Publisher's boards with cloth spine and printed label.

Illustrations: Engraved marketing table as frontispiece and eight pages of music, titled "Anacreontic Song" bound at the end.

Bibliographies: Axford, p. 99; Bitting, p. 262; Oxford, p. 146, in a note.

Copies: *BMC* and *NUC* (Library of Congress only).

799. Kitchiner, William, 1775?-1827.

THE | COOK'S ORACLE; | CONTAINING | RECEIPTS FOR PLAIN COOKERY | ON THE | MOST ECONOMICAL PLAN FOR PRIVATE FAMILIES: | ALSO | THE ART OF COMPOSING THE MOST SIMPLE AND | MOST HIGHLY FINISHED | Broths, Gravies, Soups, Sauces, Store Sauces, | AND FLAVOURING ESSENCES: | PASTRY, PRESERVES, PUDDINGS, PICKLES, &c. | CONTAINING ALSO | A COMPLETE SYSTEM OF COOKERY | FOR CATHOLIC FAMILIES. | *The Quantity of each Article is* | ACCURATELY STATED BY WEIGHT AND MEASURE; | *BEING THE RESULT OF* | Actual Experiments | INSTITUTED IN THE KITCHEN OF | WILLIAM KITCHINER, M.D. | AUTHOR OF | THE ART OF INVIGORATING LIFE BY FOOD; | THE HOUSEKEEPER'S LEDGER; | THE ECONOMY OF THE EYES, AND RULES FOR CHOOSING | AND USING SPECTACLES, OPERA GLASSES, AND | TELESCOPES; OBSERVATIONS ON SINGING, &c., AND | EDITOR OF THE NATIONAL, AND | SEA SONGS OF ENGLAND. | [short rule] | "Miscuit utile dulci." | [short rule] | A NEW EDITION. | [short rule] | LONDON: | PRINTED FOR CADELL AND CO.

EDINBURGH; SIMPKIN | AND MARSHALL, AND G. B. WHITTAKER, LONDON; | AND JOHN CUMMING, DUBLIN. | *To be had of all Booksellers.* | [short rule] | 1827.

Eighth edition, London, 1827. Originally published under the title *Apicius redivivus; or, the cook's oracle*, London, 1817 (item 797).

190 x 108 mm. A^{10} (A5+1) B^{12} C^{12} ($\pm$C7) D-X^{12} Y^6; 257 leaves, pp. [2] [i-v] vi-xix [xx] [1] 2-491 [492].

Bibliographies: Oxford, p. 146, in a note; Simon BG 914; Wheaton and Kelly 3341.

Copies: *BMC* and *NUC* (Harvard and University of California, Berkeley).

800. Kitchiner, William, 1775?-1827.

THE | COOK'S ORACLE; | CONTAINING | RECEIPTS FOR PLAIN COOKERY, | ON THE | MOST ECONOMICAL PLAN FOR PRIVATE FAMILIES: | ALSO | THE ART OF COMPOSING THE MOST SIMPLE AND | MOST HIGHLY FINISHED | Broths, Grabies, Soups, Sauces, Store Sauces, | AND FLAVOURING ESSENCES: | PASTRY, PRESERVES, PUDDINGS, PICKLES, &c. | CONTAINING ALSO | A COMPLETE SYSTEM OF COOKERY | FOR CATHOLIC FAMILIES. | *The Quantity of each Article is* | ACCURATELY STATED BY WEIGHT AND MEASURE; | *BEING THE RESULT OF* | Actual Experiments | INSTITUTED IN THE KITCHEN OF | WILLIAM KITCHINER, M.D. | AUTHOR OF | THE ART OF INVIGORATING LIFE BY FOOD; | THE HOUSEKEEPER'S LEDGER; | THE HORSE AND CARRIAGE-KEEPER'S ORACLE; | THE TRAVELLER'S ORACLE; | THE ECONOMY OF THE EYES, AND RULES FOR CHOOSING | AND USING SPECTACLES, OPERA GLASSES, AND | TELESCOPES; OBSERVATIONS ON SINGING, &c., AND | EDITOR OF THE NATIONAL, AND | SEA SONGS OF ENGLAND. | [short rule] | "Miscuit utile dulci." | [short rule] | *A NEW EDITION.* | [short rule] | LONDON: | PRINTED FOR CADELL AND CO. EDINBURGH; | SIMPKIN AND MARSHALL, AND G. B. WHITTAKER, LONDON; | AND JOHN CUMMING, DUBLIN. | *To be had of all Booksellers.* | [short rule] | 1829.

Ninth edition, London, 1829. Originally published, London, 1817 (item 797).

191 x 110 mm. A^{10} B-Y^{12} Z^6; 268 leaves, pp. [i-v] vi-xix [xx] [1] 2-512 [513-516]. Publisher's boards with printed label on spine.

Bibliographies: This edition unrecorded in the bibliographies consulted.

Copies: No other copy of this edition located.

801. Kitchiner, William, 1775?-1827.

THE ART | OF INVIGORATING AND PROLONGING | LIFE, | BY | FOOD, CLOTHES, AIR, EXERCISE, WINE, SLEEP, &c. | AND | PEPTIC PRECEPTS, | POINTING OUT | *AGREEABLE AND EFFECTUAL METHODS* | TO PREVENT AND RELIEVE | INDIGESTION, | AND TO | *REGULATE AND STRENGTHEN THE ACTION* | OF THE | STOMACH AND BOWELS. | [short rule] | Suaviter in modo, sed fortiter in re. | [short rule] | BY | THE AUTHOR OF "THE COOK'S ORACLE," | *&c. &c. &c.* | [short fancy rule] | *SECOND EDITION.* | [short rule] | LONDON: | PRINTED FOR HURST, ROBINSON, AND CO. | AND A. CONSTABLE AND CO., EDINBURGH. | [short rule] | 1821.

Second edition, London, 1821. No record of the first edition has been located.

179 x 103 mm. [A]² (A1 +ₓ1) B-M¹² N⁶; 141 leaves, pp. [6] [1] 2-276.

Bibliographies: This edition unrecorded in the bibliographies consulted.

Copies: *BMC* and *NUC* (Library Company of Philadelphia, National Library of Medicine, and University of British Columbia). The Wellcome Library has the second through the sixth editions, 1821-1828.

802. Kitchiner, William, 1775?-1827.

THE ART | OF INVIGORATING AND PROLONGING | LIFE, | BY FOOD, CLOTHES, AIR, EXERCISE, WINE, SLEEP, &c. | AND | PEPTIC PRECEPTS, | POINTING OUT | *AGREEABLE AND EFFECTUAL METHODS* | TO PREVENT AND RELIEVE | INDIGESTION, | AND TO | *REGULATE AND STRENGTHEN THE ACTION* | OF THE | STOMACH AND BOWELS. | Suaviter in modo, fortiter in re. | [short fancy rule] | TO WHICH IS ADDED, | THE PLEASURE OF MAKING A WILL. | Finis coronat opus. | [short rule] | BY WILLIAM KITCHINER, M.D. | AUTHOR OF THE COOK'S ORACLE; | THE ECONOMY OF THE EYES, AND RULES FOR CHOOSING | AND USING SPECTACLES, OPERA GLASSES, AND | TELESCOPES; OBSERVATIONS ON SINGING, &c., AND | EDITOR OF THE LOYAL, NATIONAL, AND SEA | SONGS OF ENGLAND. | [short rule] | *NEW EDITION.* | [short rule] | LONDON: | PRINTED FOR HURST, ROBINSON, AND CO. | AND A. CONSTABLE AND CO. EDINBURGH. | 1824.

Fifth edition, London, 1824. The earliest edition located is the second, London, 1821 (item 801).

159 x 100 mm. [A]⁴ B-Y⁸ Z⁴; 176 leaves, pp. [i-v] vi [vii-viii] [1] 2-341 [342] [2].

Bibliographies: *A Catalogue of Printed Books in the Wellcome Historical Meidcal Library*, III, 399.

Copies: *NUC* (College of Physicians of Philadelphia, Library Company of Philadelphia, and Library of Congress). Also in the Wellcome Library.

803. Kitchiner, William, 1775?-1827.

THE | HOUSEKEEPER'S ORACLE; | OR, | ART OF DOMESTIC MANAGEMENT: | CONTAINING | A COMPLETE SYSTEM OF CARVING | WITH ACCURACY AND ELEGANCE; | HINTS RELATIVE TO | DINNER PARTIES; | THE ART OF MANAGING SERVANTS; | AND THE | 𝔈𝔠𝔬𝔫𝔬𝔪𝔦𝔰𝔱 𝔞𝔫𝔡 𝔈𝔭𝔦𝔠𝔲𝔯𝔢'𝔰 𝔠𝔞𝔩𝔢𝔫𝔡𝔞𝔯, | SHEWING THE SEASONS WHEN ALL KINDS OF | MEAT, FISH, POULTRY, GAME, VEGETABLES, | AND FRUITS, | FIRST ARRIVE IN THE MARKET – EARLIEST TIME FORCED – WHEN | MOST PLENTIFUL – AND WHEN BEST AND CHEAPEST. | [short fancy rule] | BY THE LATE | WILLIAM KITCHINER, M.D. | [short rule] | *To which is added a Variety of useful and Original Receipts.* | [short rule] | "First for the Kitchen, as without that we shall look lean, and grow faint | quickly." – HANNAH WOOLEY'S *Cabinet*, 12mo. 1684, p. 255. | [short rule] | LONDON: | PRINTED FOR WHITTAKER, TREACHER, AND CO. | AVE MARIA LANE. | [short rule] | M.DCCC.XXIX.

First edition, London, 1829.

187 x 110 mm. [A]² B-P¹² Q⁴; 174 leaves, pp. [4] [1] 2-344. Publisher's blind stamped purple cloth with printed paper label on spine.

Illustration: Engraved frontispiece portrait of the author.

Bibliographies: Craig 52; Oxford, p. 162; Simon BG 920; Wheaton and Kelly 3349.

Copies: *BMC* and *NUC* (Duke, Kansas State University, and Yale). Wheaton and Kelly (Essex Institute only).

803a. La Chapelle, Vincent.

THE | MODERN COOK: | CONTAINING | INSTRUCTIONS | For Preparing and Ordering Publick Enter- | tainments for the Tables of Princes, Am- | bassadors, Noblemen, and Magistrates. | As also the least Expensive Methods of providing | for private Families, in a very elegant Manner. | New Receipts for Dressing of Meat, Fowl, and Fish, | and making Ragoûts, Fricassées, and Pastry of all Sorts, | in a Method never before publish'd. | Adorn'd with COPPER-PLATES, | Exhibiting the Order of Placing the different Dishes, &c. | on the Table, in the most polite Way. | [rule] | By Mr. *VINCENT LA CHAPELLE,* | Late Chief Cook to the Right Honourable the Earl | of CHESTERFIELD: | And now Chief Cook to his Highess the | Prince of ORANGE. | [rule] | In THREE VOLUMES. | [rule] | The THIRD EDITION. | [rule] | VOL. I. [VOL. I.I] [VOL. I.II] | [rule] | *LONDON:* | Printed for THOMAS OSBORNE, in *Gray's-Inn.* | [short rule] | MDCCXXXVI.

Note: The second and third numerals in "VOL. I.I" and "VOL. I.II" were stamped by hand after printing.

Third edition, London, 1736. Originally published, London, 1733.

8vo. 3 vols. Vol. I. π^2 A-C^4 D^2, ^{2}B-Y^8; 184 leaves, pp. [4] [i] ii-viii [20] [1] 2-240, 229-323, 328. Two letterpress folding charts with bills of fare not included in the collation or pagination. Vol. II. a-c^4 A-U^8; 172 leaves, pp. [i-iii] iv-xxii [2] [1] 2-316 [4]. Two letterpress folding charts with bills of fare not included in the collation or pagination. Vol. III. A^8 a^4 B-U^8 X^2 *A-*B^8 *C^4; 186 leaves, pp. [24] 1-307 [308], ^{2}1-38 [2]. Three letterpress folding charts with bills of fare not included in the collation or pagination.

Illustrations: Vol. I. Two engraved folding plates showing table settings and three engraved folding plates showing elaborate serving dishes. Vol. II. Two engraved folding plates showing table settings. Vol. III. Two engraved folding plates showing table settings and one showing ten serving platters.

Bibliographies: Maclean, p. 85; Oxford, p. 63, in a note; Simon BG 932.

Copies: *NUC* (John Crerar Library and Kansas State University). Maclean adds Wellcome Library.

The Ladies Cabinet Englarged and Opened. See B., M.

804. The Lady's Companion.

THE | Lady's Companion: | Or, an infallible | GUIDE to the *FAIR SEX.* | CONTAINING, | RULES, DIRECTIONS, and OBSERVATIONS, for their | Conduct and Behaviour through all Ages and Circumstances of | Life, as VIRGINS, WIVES, or WIDOWS. | WITH | DIRECTIONS, how to obtain all Useful and Fashionable Ac- | complishments suitable to the SEX. In which are comprised all Parts of GOOD | HOUSEWIFRY, particularly RULES and above one thousand different | RECEIPTS in every Kind of COOKERY. | [in two columns: column one] 1. Making all Sorts of Soops and Sauces. | 2. Dressing Flesh, Fish, and Fowl; this | last illustrated with Cuts, shewing how | every Fowl, Wild or Tame, is to be | trust for the Spit: Likewise all other | Kind of Game. | 3. Making above 50 different Sorts of | Puddings, which are double the Number | to be met with in any Book of this Kind. | [vertical rule] | [column two] 4. The whole Art of Pastry in making | Pies, Tarts, and Pasties. | 5. Receipts for all Manner of Pickling, | Collaring, &c. | 6. For Preserving, making Creams, Jel- | lies, and all Manner of Confectionary | 7. Rules and Directions for setting out | Dinners, Suppers, and Grand Enter- | tainments. [end columns] | To which is added, | BILLS of FARE for every Month in the Year, curiously | engraven on COPPER PLATES, with the Forms of Tables and Dishes, and | the Shapes of Pies, Tarts, and Pasties. | With Instructions for Marketing. | ALSO | RULES and RECEIPTS for making all the choicest Cordials for | the Closet: Brewing Beers, Ales, &c. Making all Sorts of *English* Wines, | Cyder, Mum, Mead, Metheglin, Vinegar, Verjuice, Catchup, &c. With some | fine Perfumes, Pomatums, Cosmeticks and other Beautifiers. | [rule] | The SECOND EDITION. | [rule] | LONDON: Printed for T. READ, in *Dogwell-Court, White-Fryers, Fleet-Street.* | [short rule] | MDCCXL.

Second edition, London, 1740. Originally published under the title *The Whole Duty of a Woman*, London, 1737. The first edition was published in parts and the part numbers still appear in the bottom margin on every third signature in the 1740 edition.

4to. A-Xxx⁴ Yyy² Zzz-4K⁴ 4L1 4M-4R⁴ 4S⁴ (-4S4=4L1); 342 leaves, pp. [1-3] 4-528, 527-538, 541-653, 664-694 (=684).

Illustrations: Ten woodcuts in the text illustrating trussing and thirty-nine etched plates, fifteen illustrating shapes of pies and other dishes and twenty- four of bills of fare.

Note: This is not the same work as that described under items 1052 and 1053.

Bibliographies: Maclean, p. 151; Oxford, p. 70, in a note.

Copies: *NUC* (Library Company of Philadelphia, New York Academy of Medicine, and William Andrews Clark Library).

805. The Lady's Companion.

THE | LADY'S COMPANION. | CONTAINING | Upwards of Three Thousand different RECEIPTS | in every Kind of | COOKERY: | AND | Those the best and most fashionable; | BEING | Four Times the Quantity of any Book of this Sort. | [in two columns: column one] I. Making near two Hundred diffe- | rent Sorts of Soops, Pottages, | Broths, Sauces, Cullises, &c. af- | ter the *French, Italian, Dutch,* | and *English* Way; also making | Cake-Soop for the Pocket. | II. Dressing Flesh, Fish, and Fowl; | this last illustrated with Cuts, | shewing how every Fowl is to be | truss'd. | III. Directions for making Ragoos | and Fricaseys. | IV. Directions for Dressing all | Manner of Kitchen Garden | Stuff, &c. | V. Making two Hundred different | Sorts of Puddings, Florendines, | Tanzeys, &c. which are four | Times the Number to be met | [two vertical rules] | [column two] with in any other Book of this | Kind. | VI. The whole Art of Pastry, in | making upwards of two Hundred | Pies, (with the Shapes of them | engraven on Copper-Plates) Tarts, | Pasties, Custards, Cheese-Cakes, | *Yorkshire* Muffins, &c. | VII. Receipts for all Manner of | Pickling, Potting, Collaring, &c. | VIII. For Preserving, making | Creams, Jellies, and all Manner | of Confectionary, with particular | Receipts for making Orgeat and | Blanc Manger. | IX. Rules and Directions for setting | out Dinners, Suppers, and grand | Entertainments. [end columns] | To which is added, | BILLS of FARE for every Month in the Year. | ALSO | DIRECTIONS for Brewing Beers, Ales, &c. making all Sorts | of *English* Wines, Cyder, Mum, Perry, Mead, Metheglin, | Vinegar, Verjuice, Catchup, &c. | WITH | The Receipts of Mrs. STEPHENS for the *Stone*; Dr. MEAD | for the *Bite of a Mad Dog*; The Recipe, sent from *Ireland,* | for the *Gout*; Sir HANS SLOANE's Receipt for *Sore Eyes*; | and the Receipt for making *Tar-Water.* | [rule] | The FIFTH EDITION, with large ADDITIONS. | [rule] | VOL. I. [VOL. II] | [rule] | *LONDON:* | Printed for T. READ, in *Dogwell-Court, White-Fryars, Fleet-Street*; | and R, BALDWIN, at the *Rose,* in *Pater-noster-row.* 1751.

Fifth edition, London, 1751. Originally published under the title *The Whole Duty of a Woman . . .*, London, 1737.

8vo. 2 vols. Vol. I. π1 B-Bb⁸ Cc²; 195 leaves, pp. [2] [1] 2-384 [4]. Vol. II. π1 B-Ee⁸; 217 leaves, pp. [2] [1] 2-422 [*10*].

Illustrations: Vol. I. Woodcuts in the text illustrating trussing. Vol. II. Four engraved folding plates, printed on rectos and versos, illustrating shapes of pies and other pastries.

Bibliographies: Maclean, p. 151; Oxford, p. 70, in a note.

Copies: *NUC* (Cornell only). Maclean adds Brotherton Library, Wellcome Library, Detroit Public Library, and Old Sturbridge Village (Mass.) Library.

806. The Lady's Companion.

THE | LADY'S COMPANION. | CONTAINING | Upwards of Three Thousand different RECEIPTS | in every Kind of | COOKERY: | AND | Those the best and most fashionable; | BEING | Four Times the Quantity of any Book of this Sort. | [in two columns: column one] I. Making near two Hundred diffe- | rent Sorts of Soops, Pottages, | Broths, Sauces, Cullises, &c. af- | ter the *French, Italian, Dutch,* | and *English* Way; also making | Cake Soop for the Pocket. | II. Dressing Flesh, Fish, and Fowl; | this last illustrated with Cuts, | shewing how every Fowl is to be | truss'd. | III. Directions for making Ragoos | and Fricaseys. | IV. Directions for Dressing all | Manner of Kitchen Garden | Stuff, &c. | V. Making two Hundred different | Sorts of Puddings, Florendines, | Tanzeys, &c. [Vol. II: Tanseys] which are four | Times the Number to be met | [two vertical rules] | [column two] with in any other Book of this | Kind. | VI. The whole Art of Pastry, in | making upwards of two Hundred | Pies, (with the Shapes of them | engraven on Copper-Plates) Tarts, | Pasties, Custards, Cheese-Cakes, | *Yorkshire* Muffins, &c. | VII. Receipts for all Manner of | Pickling, Potting, Collaring, &c. | VIII. For Preserving, making | Creams, Jellies, and all Manner | of Confectionary, with particular | Receipts for making Orgeat and | Blanc Manger. | IX. Rules and Directions for setting | out Dinners, Suppers, and grand | Entertainments. [end columns] | To which is added, | BILLS of FARE for every Month in the Year. | ALSO | DIRECTIONS for Brewing Beers, Ales, &c. making all | Sorts of *English* Wines, Cyder, Mum, Metheglin, Vinegar, | Verjuice, Catchup, &c. | WITH | The Receipts of Mrs. STEPHENS for the *Stone*; Dr. MEAD | for the *Bite of a Mad Dog*; the Recipe, sent from *Ireland,* | for the *Gout*; Sir HANS SLOANE's Receipt for *Sore Eyes*; | and the Receipt for making *Tar Water.* | [rule] | The SIXTH EDITION, with large Additions. | [rule] | VOL. I. [VOL. II] | [rule] | *LONDON:* | Printed for J. HODGES, on *London-Bridge*; and R. BALDWIN, | at the *Rose*, in *Pater-noster Row.* 1753.

Sixth edition, London, 1753. Originally published under the title *The Whole Duty of a Woman . . .*, London, 1737.

12mo. 2 vols. Vol. I. π1 B-S^{12} T^{12}(-T12=π1); 216 leaves, pp. [2] [1] 2-413 [414] [16]. Vol. II. π1 B-S^{12} T^8(-T8=π1); 212 leaves, pp. [2] [1] 2-389, 400-414 [18]. Note: Collation of volume two, not present in the Gernon collection, was supplied by John C. Craig from his copy.

Illustrations: Vol. I. Engraved frontispiece of a kitchen scene.

Bibliographies: Axford, p. 244; Bitting, p. 571; Maclean, p. 150; Wheaton and Kelly 3421.

Copies: *NUC* (5 copies). Maclean adds Brotherton Library.

807. The Lady's Guide.

THE LADY'S GUIDE | TO THE | ORDERING OF HER HOUSEHOLD, | AND
THE ECONOMY OF | THE DINNER TABLE. | BY A LADY. | LONDON: |
SMITH, ELDER AND CO., 65, CORNHILL. | [short rule] | M.DCCC.LXI. | [*The
Right of Translation is reserved.*]

First edition, London, 1861.

190 x 126 mm. π^8 1-31^8 32^2; 258 leaves, pp. [i-v] vi-xvi [1] 2-500. Publisher's purple
cloth, stamped in gold.

Illustrations: Illustrations of table settings in the text.

Bibliographies: Axford, p. 244; Bitting, p. 571; Vicaire 430.

Copies: *BMC* and *NUC* (Library of Congress only).

808. The Laird and Farmer.

THE | LAIRD and FARMER. | A | DIALOGUE | UPON | FARMING, TRADE,
COOK- | ERY, and their Method of LIVING in | SCOTLAND, balanc'd with that of
ENG- | LAND. | [rule] | In SIXTEEN CHAPTERS. | [rule] | By the AUTHOR of
the *Familiar Catechism.* | [rule] | [ornament] | *LONDON:* | Printed for the AUTHOR,
and sold by R. GRIFFITHS, | at the *Dunciad* in *St. Paul's Church-Yard*, and other
Book- | sellers in *London, Edinburgh, Glasgow, Aberdeen,* &c. | 1740. | [Price One
Shillng.]

First edition, London, 1740.

8vo. A-P^4 Q^2; 62 leaves, pp. [i-ii] iii-viii [3] 4-118.

Bookplate: Westbury.

Bibliographies: Maclean, p. 87.

Copies: *BMC* and *NUC* (Columbia and Harvard). Maclean adds John Rylands
Library.

809. Lamb, Patrick.

[within a border of two rules] *Royal Cookery*; *or, the Complete* | *Court-Cook.* | [rule] | CONTAINING THE | Choicest Receipts | In all the particular Branches of | COOKERY, | Now in Use in the QUEEN'S | PALACES | OF | [in two columns: column one] St. *James's,* | *Kensington,* | [two fancy vertical rules] | [column two] *Hampton-Court,* and | *Windsor.* [end columns] | With near Forty Figures (curiously engraven on *Copper*) | of the magnificent Entertainments at *Coronations, Instal-* | *ment, Balls, Weddings,* &c. at Court; Also Receipts for | making the *Soupes, Jellies, Bisques, Ragoo's, Pattys, Tan-* | *zies, Forc'd-Meats, Cakes, Puddings,* &c. | [rule] | *By* PATRICK LAMB, *Esq*; | Near 50 Years Master-Cook to their late Majesties | King *Charles* II. King *James* II. King *William* and Queen | *Mary,* and to Her Present Majesty Queen *ANNE.* | [rule] | To which are added, | Bills of Fare for every Season in the Year. | [rule] | *London,* Printed for *Maurice Atkins,* at the *Golden-Ball* in | S. *Paul's* Church-yard. 1710.

First edition, London, 1710. Maclean records two issues of the first edition published in 1710, one with the imprint, London, printed for Abel Roper and sold by John Morphew, and the other, London, printed for Maurice Atkins. She locates six copies of the former and one, in the New York Public Library, of the latter.

8vo. a^8 A-I^8; 80 leaves, pp. [*16*] [1] 2-127 [128] [*16*]. First leaf (blank or half-title?) wanting in this copy.

Illustrations: Thirty-four engraved plates (twenty-five folding) showing bills of fare.

Bibliographies: Bitting, p. 271 (Roper and Morphew issue); Maclean, p. 88 (both issues); Oxford, p. 52 (Roper and Morphew issue); Pennell, p. 144 (lacking title-page).

Copies: *BMC* (issue unspecified) and *NUC* (Folger, Harvard, and Library of Congress, Roper and Morphew issue). Maclean adds New York Public Library (both issues) and National Library of Scotland and Trinity College, Dublin (Roper and Morphew issue).

810. Lamb, Patrick.

[within a border of two rules] ROYAL-COOKERY: | OR, THE | *Compleat Court-Cook.* | CONTAINING THE | Choicest Receipts in all the several | Branches of Cookery, *viz.* for making of | Soops, Bisques, Olio's, Terrines, Surtouts, | Puptons, Ragoos, Forc'd-Meats, Sauces, | Pattys, Pies, Tarts, Tansies, Cakes, | Puddings, Jellies, &c. | As likewise | Forty Plates, curiously engraven on Copper, | of the Magnificent Entertainments at Coro- | nations, and Instalments; Balls, Weddings, |

&c. at Court; as likewise of City-Feasts. | *To which are added,* | Bills of Fare for every Month in the Year. | [rule] | *By* PATRICK LAMB, *Esq*; | Near Fifty Years Master-Cook to their late | Majesties King *Charles* II. King *James* II. King *William* and | Queen *Mary*, and Queen *Anne*. | [rule] | The 𝔖𝔢𝔠𝔬𝔫𝔡 𝔈𝔡𝔦𝔱𝔦𝔬𝔫, with the Addition of several new | Cuts, and above five Hundred new Receipts, all disposed | Alphabetically. | [two rules] | *LONDON*: | Printed for *J. Nutt*, and *A. Roper*; and to be sold by *E. Nutt* | at the *Middle-Temple-Gate* in *Fleetstreet*, 1716. Price *6s.*

Second edition, London, 1716. Originally published, London, 1710 (item 809).

8vo. A⁴ B-U⁸ X⁴; 160 leaves, pp. [*8*] 1-302 [*10*].

Illustrations: Forty engraved plates (thirty-five folding) showing bills of fare.

Bibliographies: Maclean, p. 88; Oxford, p. 53, in a note; Schraemli (1) 262; Vicaire 490.

Copies: *BMC* and *NUC* (Library Company of Philadelphia, New York State Library, and Wellesley). Maclean adds Brotherton Library, National Library of Scotland, and New York Public Library.

811. Langford, T.

[within a border of two rules] PLAIN and FULL | INSTRUCTIONS | To raise all sorts of | FRUIT-TREES | That prosper in | *ENGLAND*; | In that Method and Order, that every | thing must be done in, to give all the advan- | tage, may be, to every Tree as it is rising | from its Seed, till it come to its full growth. | TOGETHER | With all necessary directions about those seve- | ral ways of making *Plantations*, either of *Wall-Fruit*, or | *Dwarf-trees* in *Gardens*, or large *Standard-trees* in *Or-* | *chards* or *Fields*. | TOUCHING | Which last, because it's so vast an Improve- | ment of Land, all the profitable and practical ways are | here directed to with all exactness. | AND | In the last place the best directions are given for making | *liquors* of the several sorts of *Fruit*. | [rule] | By *T. LANGFORD*, Gent. | [rule] | *LONDON,* | Printed by *J.M.* for *Rich. Chiswel* at the *Rose* and | *Crown* in St *Paul's Church-Yard*, 1681.

First edition, London, 1681.

8vo. A⁸ a² B-K⁸ L⁶; 88 leaves, pp. [*20*] 1-148 [*8*].

Illustrations: Two engraved plates of trees. The first plate is conjugate with a leaf of explanation printed in letterpress which is not included in either the signature collation or the pagination statement.

Bibliographies: Fussell (1) pp. 62-63; Henrey I.215; Wing L388.

Copies: *BMC* (2 copies) and *NUC* (6 copies). Wing (12 copies).

812. Langham, William.

THE | GARDEN | OF | HEALTH: | CONTAINING THE | sundry rare and hidden vertues and | properties of all kindes of Simples | and Plants. | Together with the manner how they are to bee | vsed and applyed in medicine for the health of mans | body, against diuers diseases and infirmities most | common amongst men. | Gathered by the long experience and industry of WILLIAM | LANGHAM, Practitioner in Physicke. | [rule] | *The second Edition corrected and amended.* | [fancy rule] | *LONDON,* | Printed by THOMAS HARPER, with permission | of the Company of *Stationers.* | M. DC. XXXIII.

Second edition, London, 1633. Originally published, London, 1597.

4to. ¶⁴ A-Bbb⁸; 388 leaves, pp. [*8*] 1-702 [*66*].

Bibliographies: Craig 54; *STC* 15196.

Copies: *BMC* and *NUC* (19 copies). *STC* (10+ copies).

813. Lankester, Edwin (1814-1874).

ON FOOD. | BEING | LECTURES DELIVERED AT THE SOUTH KENSINGTON | MUSEUM. | BY | E. LANKESTER, M.D., F.R.S. | SUPERINTENDENT OF THE ANIMAL PRODUCT AND FOOD COLLECTIONS. | LONDON: | ROBERT HARDWICKE, 192, PICCADILLY. | 1864.

Second edition, first printing throughout, London, 1864. Originally published in two parts, London, 1861 and 1862.

186 x 123 mm. [A]⁴ B-2B⁸; 196 leaves, pp. [*5*] viii [*2*] [1-3] 4-174 [*2*] [*179*] 180-385 [*386*]. Publisher's rose cloth stamped in gold.

Illustrations: Numerous wood engravings in the text.

Bibliographies: See 813a.

Copies: See 813a.

813a. Lankester, Edwin (1814-1874).

ON FOOD. | BEING | LECTURES DELIVERED AT THE SOUTH KENSINGTON | MUSEUM. | BY | E. LANKESTER, M.D., F.R.S. | SUPERINTENDENT OF THE ANIMAL PRODUCT AND FOOD COLLECTIONS. | LONDON: | ROBERT HARDWICKE, 192, PICCADILLY. | 1864.

Second edition, London, 1864, with signatures D-M (pp. 61-174 [2]) reprinted with the following changes:

Original setting:	Reset:
p. 114 Fig. 4 Arachis hypogoea	no figure
p. 115 Olea europoea numbered Fig. 5	Olea europoea numbered Fig.4
p. 117 line 3 in col. 1: (ass's)	(apes)
p. 148 two short rules following text	no rules
facing p. 174 "SECOND COURSE"	blank

186 x 123 mm. [A]^4 B-C^8 "B2"^{14} "C2"^{16}(-"C2"1) "D2"-"F2"^{14} χ1 N-2B^8; 196 leaves, pp. [5] viii [2] [1-3] 4-174 [2] [179] 180-385 [386]. Publisher's rose cloth, spine stamped in gold.

Illustrations: Numerous wood engravings in the text.

Bibliographies: Wheaton and Kelly 3459 without distinguishing between the original printing and the partial reprinting.

Copies: *BMC* and *NUC* (6 copies). Partial reprinting not noted in *BMC* or *NUC*.

814. La Quintinie, Jean de, 1626-1688.

[within a border of two rules] THE | [in red] Compleat Gard'ner; | OR, | Directions for CULTIVATING | AND | Right ORDERING | OF | [in red] Fruit-GARDENS | AND | [in red] Kitchen-Gardens; | With Divers REFLECTIONS | On several Parts |

OF │ [in red] HUSBANDRY. │ [rule] │ In Six BOOKS. │ [rule] │ By the Famous Monsr. *De La Quintinye,* │ Chief director of all the [in red] *GARDENS* [in black] of the *French*-King. │ [rule] │ To which is added │ His Treatise of [in red] *ORANGE-TREES,* [in black] with │ the Raising of [in red] *MELONS,* [in black] omitted in the │ *French* [in red] Editions. │ [rule] │ Made English by [in red] *John Evelyn* [in black] Esquire, │ Illustrated with Copper Plates. │ [rule] │ [in red] *LONDON,* │ Printed for [in red] *Matthew Gillyflower,* [in black] at the *Spread Eagle* in │ *Westminster-Hall,* and [in red] *James Partridge,* [in black] at the *Post-* │ *house* at *Charing-Cross,* MDCXCIII.

First edition in English, London, 1693. Originally published in French under the title *Instructions pour les jardin fruitiers et potagers,* Paris, 1690.

Folio: π^2 a✱^{4} b^4 b✱✱1 c✱^{4} "[a]"^{4} "[b]"^{4}(-"[b]"4) B-O^4 P-Q^6 R-Aa^4 Bb^2, ^{2}B-P^4 Q^2 T-Dd^4 "[a]"^{2} ^{3}A-K^4; 256 leaves, pp. [*44*] 1-106, 106 [*107*] 108 [*1*] [109] [*1*] 110 [*1*] 111-115 [*1*] 116 [*1*] 117 [*1*] 116 [*1*] 119-184 [185-188], ^{2}1-116, 137-204 [*4*], ^{3}1-4, ^{4}1-80.

Illustrations: Engraved frontispiece portrait of the author, two double and nine single etched copperplate illustrations and additional etchings and woodcuts in the text.

Note: According to Keynes, John Evelyn oversaw this translation, probably with the assistance of George London. An abridged version was published in 1699 as translated by London and Henry Wise.

Bibliographies: Henrey I.218; Keynes 103; Wing L431.

Copies: *BMC* and *NUC* (31 copies). Wing (13 copies).

815. Laurence, John, 1668-1732.

[within a border of two rules] THE │ *Clergy-Man's Recreation:* │ Shewing the │ Pleasure *and* Profit │ Of the ART of │ GARDENING. │ [rule] │ *Quare agite ô proprios generatim discite Cultus,* │ *Agricolae, fructusque feros mollite colendo.* │ Virg. Georg. │ [rule] │ By *JOHN LAWRENCE,* A. M. │ Rector of *Yelvertoft* in *Northamptonshire,* and │ sometime Fellow of *Clare-Hall* in *Cambridge.* │ [rule] │ The FIFTH EDITION. │ [two rules] │ *LONDON:* │ Printed for BERNARD LINTOTT, between │ the *Temple Gates* in *Fleet-street,* 1717.

Fifth edition, London, 1717. Originally published, London, 1714.

8vo. A-F^8; 48 leaves, pp. [*12*] [1] 2-84.

Illustration: Engraved frontispiece on A1ᵛ and a small woodcut on C2ᵛ.

Bibliographies: Fussell (1) p. 100; Henrey III.937.

Copies: *BMC* (2 copies) and *NUC* (4 copies).

816. Laurence, John, 1668-1732.

[within a border of two rules] THE | FRUIT-GARDEN | KALENDAR: | OR, A |
SUMMARY | Of the ART of Managing the | *FRUIT-GARDEN.* | Teaching in order of
TIME what is to be | done therein every MONTH in the YEAR. | Containing several
new and plain Directions, | more particularly relating to the VINE. | [rule] | ——
Redit Horticolae *labor actus in Orbem*; | *Atque acer curas venientem extendit in
Annum,* | *Persequitur Vitem attondens, singit que putando.* | Virg. Georg. lib. 2. |
[rule] | To which is added, | An APPENDIX of the Usefulness of the | *Barometer*;
with some short Directions how | to make a right Judgment of the Weather. | [rule] |
By JOHN LAURENCE, M. A. | Rector of *Yelvertoft*, in *Northamptonshire.* | [rule] |
LONDON: | Printed for BERNARD LINTOT, at the *Cross-Keys,* | between the *Temple
Gates,* in *Fleetstreet.* 1718.

First edition, London, 1718.

8vo. A-K⁸ L⁴; 84 leaves, pp. [4] [i] ii-vi, ²i-v [vi] 1-149 [150-152].

Illustration: One engraved folding plate.

Bibliographies: Fussell (1) p. 100; Henrey III.939; Noling, p. 248.

Copies: *BMC* (5 copies) and *NUC* (19 copies).

817. Laurence, John, 1668-1732.

[within a border of two rules] THE | *Gentleman's Recreation:* | OR THE | SECOND
PART | OF THE | ART of GARDENING | IMPROVED. | Containing several NEW
EXPERIMENTS | and Curious OBSERVATIONS relating | to FRUIT-TREES: |
Particularly, a NEW METHOD of building | Walls with *Horizontal Shelters.* | [rule] |
Illustrated with Copper Plates. | [rule] | —*Si quid novisti rectius istis,* | *Candidus
imperti; si non, his utere mecum.* Hor. | [rule] | By *JOHN LAURENCE,* M. A. |
Rector of *Yelvertoft*, in *Northamptonshire.* | [rule] | To which is added by way of

APPENDIX, A new and | familiar way to find a most exact Meridian Line by the | Pole-Star; whereby Gentlemen may know the true Bear- | ings of their Houses and Garden Walls, and regulate their | Clocks and Watches, &c. By *Edward Laurence*, Brother | to the Author of this Book. | [rule] | *The* SECOND EDITION. | [rule] | *LONDON*: Printed for BERNARD LINTOTT | between the *Temple-Gates* in *Fleetstreet*. 1717.

Second edition, London, 1717. Originally published, London, 1716.

8vo. A⁸ a² B-H⁸ I²; 68 leaves, pp. [*20*] [1] 2-115 [116].

Illustrations: Engraved frontispiece on A1ᵛ and three engraved folding plates.

Bibliographies: Fussell (1) p. 101; Henrey III.943.

Copies: *BMC* (3 copies) and *NUC* (12 copies).

818. La Varenne, François.

[within a border of two rules] THE | French Cook, | Prescribing the way of making ready | of all sorts of Meats, Fish and flesh, with | the proper Sauce, either to procure Appe- | tite, or to advance the power of Digestion: | with the whole Skill of *Pastry-work*. | Together with about 200. excellent | Receits for the best sorts of | POTTAGES, | Both in *Lent*, and out of *Lent*. | *Also a Treatise of Conserves, both dry | and liquid, after the best fashion.* | The Third Edition. | With an Addition of some choice Receits | grown in Use amongst the Nobility and Gentry, | by a prime Artist of our own Nation. | [rule] | *Englished by* J. D. G. | [rule] | *LONDON,* | Printed for *Thomas Dring*, at the *Harrow* at Chan- | *cery Lane-end*, and *John Leigh*, at the *Blew* | *Bell* by *Flying-Horse* Court in | *Fleet-Street*. 1673.

Third edition in English, London, 1673. Originally published in French under the title *Le Cuisinier François*, Paris, 1651, and in English, London, 1653.

8vo. A⁸ a⁸ b⁴ B-T⁸ V⁴ (b4 folded to precede A1); 168 leaves, pp. [*40*] [1] 2-294 [2].

Bibliographies: Oxford, p. 24, in a note; Wing L625A.

Copies: Wing (Leeds University, National Library of Scotland, Wellcome Library, Huntington Library, and Wellesley College).

819. Lawrence, John, 1753-1839.

EVERY MAN HIS OWN BREWER. | [two short rules] | PRACTICAL
INSTRUCTIONS | IN | BREWING | ALE AND TABLE BEER, | FOR THE | USE
OF PRIVATE FAMILIES. | [two short rules] | BY BONINGTON MOUBRAY, ESQ.
| AUTHOR OF A TREATISE ON BREEDING, REARING, AND | FATTENING,
ALL KINDS OF DOMESTIC POULTRY. | [two short rules] | *LONDON:* |
PRINTED FOR SHERWOOD, JONES, AND CO. | PATERNOSTER ROW. | [short
rule] | 1824. | *Price One Shilling.*

First edition, London, 1824.

175 x 102 mm. A-B^{12} C^6; 30 leaves, pp. [1-5] 6-59 [60].

Note: Bonnington Moubray is a pseudonym of John Lawrence.

Bibliographies: Noling, p. 299.

Copies: *NUC* (Cornell University only).

820. Lawrence, John, 1753-1839.

A | Practical Treatise | ON | BREEDING, REARING, AND FATTENING, | ALL
KINDS OF | DOMESTIC POULTRY, | Pheasants, | PIGEONS, AND RABBITS |
INCLUDING | AN INTERESTING ACCOUNT OF THE | *EGYPTIAN METHOD* |
OF HATCHING EGGS BY ARTIFICIAL HEAT, | With the Author's Experiments
thereon. | [short fancy rule] | FOURTH EDITION; | WITH ADDITIONS, | *On the
Breeding, Feeding, and Management of Swine – on* | *Milch Cows for the Family Dairy
– and on Bees.* | From Memoranda made during Forty Years' Practice. | [two short
rules] | BY BONINGTON MOUBRAY, ESQ. | [two short rules] | London: |
PRINTED FOR SHERWOOD, NEELY, AND JONES, | PATERNOSTER ROW. |
[short rule] | 1822.

Fourth edition, London, 1822. Originally published, London, 1813.

175 x 102 mm. [A]^6 B-O^{12}; 162 leaves, pp. [i-v] vi-xii [1] 2-312.

Illustrations: Hand colored engraved frontispiece of a cock, a hen, a cow and a pig.

Note: Bonnington Moubray is a pseudonym of John Lawrence.

Bibliographies: Fussell (3) p. 29.

Copies: *BMC* and *NUC* (5 copies).

Lawson, William. *A New Orchard and Garden.* See items 851, 852, and 854, part six.

820a. Lebour-Fawssett, Emilie.

ECONOMICAL | FRENCH COOKERY FOR LADIES | *ADAPTED TO ENGLISH HOUSEHOLDS* | BY A "CORDON-BLEU" | [ornament] | LONDON | J. S. VIRTUE & CO., LIMITED, 26, IVY LANE | PATERNOSTER ROW | 1887

First edition, London, 1887. This collection of twelve essays went through six editions, the last published in 1902. They also were included in a larger work, *French Cooking for Ladies*, London, 1890, which contained thirty-six essays.

163 x 104 mm. A⁴ B-G⁸ H⁴; 56 leaves, pp. [2] [i-v] vi [1] 2-103 [104]. Publisher's light blue printed wrappers.

Bibliographies: Driver 606.1.

Copies: *BMC*.

821. Lémery, Louis, 1677-1743.

[within a border of two rules] A | TREATISE | OF | FOODS, | In GENERAL: | *First,* The *Difference* and *Choice* which | ought to be made of each Sort in parti- | cular. | *Secondly,* The *Good* and *Ill Effects* produced | by them. | *Thirdly,* The *Principles* wherewith they | abound. And, | *Fourthly,* The *Time, Age* and *Constitution* | they suit with. | To which are added, | *Remarks* upon each *Chapter*; wherein their | Nature and Uses are explained, according to | the Principles of *Chymistry* and *Mechanism.* | [rule] | Written in *French,* | By M. *LOUIS LEMERY,* Regent- | Doctor of the Faculty of *Physick* at *Paris,* | and of the Academy Royal of *Sciences.* | Now done into *English.* | [rule] | *LONDON,* Printed for *John Taylor,* at the | Ship in St. Paul's-Church-yard. M D CCIV.

First edition in English, London, 1704. Originally published in French under the title *Traité des aliments,* Paris, 1702 (item 276).

8vo. A⁸ a⁸ b⁴ B-X⁸ Y⁴; 184 leaves, pp. [*20*] i-xx, 1-320 [*8*].

Bibliographies: Axford, p. 397; Craig 56; Maclean, p. 89; Oberlé (1) 100; Oxford, p. 48; Vicaire 514; Wheaton and Kelly 3562.

Copies: *NUC* (9 copies). Maclean adds Brotherton Library, Edinburgh University, and Wellcome Library.

822. Lémery, Louis, 1677-1743.

A | [in red] TREATISE | OF ALL | [in red] SORTS of FOODS, | Both ANIMAL and VEGETABLE: | ALSO OF | [in red] DRINKABLES: | Giving an Account | How to chuse the best SORT of all KINDS; | [in red] Of the good and bad Effects they produce; the Prin- | [in red] ciples they abound with; the Time, Age and | [in red] Constitution they are adapted to. | Wherein their Nature and Use is explain'd according to | the Sentiments of the most eminent Physicians and | Naturalist Antient and Modern. | [in red] The Whole divided into one Hundred seventy-six Chapters. | With REMARKS upon each. | Written originally in FRENCH. | [in red] By the Leanred M. *L. LEMERY,* | Physician to the King, and Member of the Royal Academy. | [in red] Translated by D. HAY, M. D. | To which is added, | An Introduciton treating of FOODS in general: | A Table of the Chapters, and an Alphabetical Index. | [in red] A Work of universal Use to all who are inclin'd to know | [in red] the good or bad Qualities of what they eat or drink. | [rule] | [in red] *LONDON:* | Printed for T. OSBORNE, in *Gray's-Inn.* | [short rule] | MDCCXLV.

Fourth edition in English, London, 1745. Originally published in French under the title *Traité des aliments*, Paris, 1702 (item 276), and in English, London, 1704 (item 821).

12mo. A⁶ B-R¹² S⁶; 204 leaves, pp. [i-iv] v-xii, 1-372 [*24*].

Bibliographies: Axford, p. 397; Bitting, p. 281; Gabler, p. 165; Maclean, p. 89; Pennell, p. 145; Simon BG 948; Wheaton and Kelly 3561.

Copies: *NUC* (5 copies). Maclean adds British Library, Brotherton Library, and National Library of Scotland.

823. Lémery, Nicolas, 1645-1715.

[within a border of two rules] New Curiosities | IN | *Art* and *Nature:* | OR, A | COLLECTION | Of the most | Valuable *SECRETS* | IN ALL | *Arts* and *Sciences*; | As appears by the | CONTENTS. | [rule] | Composed and Experimented by the Sieur *Lemery*, | Apothecary to the *French* King. | [rule] | Translated into *English* from the Seventh Edition. Prin- | ted this last Year in *French*, in which is near one half | more than any former Edition. Illustrated with Cuts. | [rule] | To which is added a Supplement by the Translator. | [rule] | *London:* Printed for *John King*, at the *Bible and Crown* | in *Little Britain*; and Sold by *J. Morphew*, near | *Stationers-Hall*. 1711.

First edition of this translation into English, London, 1711. Originally published in French under the title *Recueil des Curiositez rare et nouvelles des plus admirables effets de la nature et de l'art*, Paris, 1674. The first edition in English appeared under the title *Modern Curiosities of Art and Nature*, London, 1685.

8vo. A-Aa⁸; 192 leaves, pp. [*16*] 1-354 [*14*].

Illustrations: Engraved frontispiece with five compartments showing "New Curiosities in Art, & Nature," and eight additional engraved plates.

Bibliographies: Maclean, p. 89 (describing a variant title); Noling, p. 252; Oxford, p. 53; Pennell, p. 144. Both Noling and Pennell incorrectly attribute this work to Louis, rather than Nicolas, Lémery.

Copies: *BMC* and *NUC* (9 copies).

824. Lessius, Leonardus, 1554-1623.

[within a border of type ornaments and rules] HYGIASTICON: | OR, | The right course of | preserving Life and | Health unto extream | old Age: | Together with soundnesse | and integritie of the | Senses, Judgement, | and Memorie. | [rule] | ¶ Written in Latine by | *Leonard Lessius*, | And now done into | English. | [rule] | *The second Edition.* | [rule] | [ornament] | [rule] | ¶ Printed by the Printers | to the Universitie of | *Cambridge*. 1634.

Second edition in English, Cambridge, 1634. Originally published in Latin, Antwerp, 1613, and first in English, Cambridge, also 1634.

24mo. ¶¹² χ² A-M¹² N⁴; 162 leaves, pp. [*44*] 1-210, ²1-70. First leaf blank.

Bibliographies: Craig 57; Oxford, p. 20; *STC* 15521; Wheaton and Kelly 3632.

Copies: *BMC* and *NUC* (8 copies). *STC* adds Oxford (English Faculty Library) and Cambridge.

825. Lessius, Leonardus, 1554-1623.

[within a border of type ornaments and rules] HYGIASTICON: | OR, | The right course of | preserving Life and | Health unto extream | old Age: | Together with soundnesse | and integritie of the | Senses, Judgement, | and Memorie. | [rule] | ¶ Written in Latine by | *Leonard Lessius,* | And now done into | English. | [rule] | *The third Edition.* | [rule] | [ornament] | [rule] | ¶ Printed by the Printers | to the Universitie of | *Cambridge.* 1636.

Third edition, Cambridge, 1636. Originally published in Latin, Antwerp, 1613, and in English, Cambridge, 1634.

24mo. ¶¹² χ² A-M¹² N⁴; 162 leaves, pp. [*44*] 1-210, ²1-70. First leaf blank.

Bibliographies: *STC* 15522; Wheaton and Kelly 3623.

Copies: *BMC* and *NUC* (4 copies). *STC* (10+ copies).

826. Lettsom, John Coakley, 1744-1815.

THE | NATURAL HISTORY | OF THE | TEA-TREE, | WITH OBSERVATIONS ON | THE MEDICAL QUALITIES OF TEA, | AND ON THE | EFFECTS OF TEA-DRINKING. | A NEW EDITION. | [two short rules] | BY JOHN COAKLEY LETTSOM, M.D. | [two short rules] | *LONDON:* | PRINTED BY J. NICHOLS; | FOR CHARLES DILLY. | [short rule] | 1799.

Third edition, London, 1799. Originally published, London, 1772.

4to. [a]⁴ b1 B-N⁴ O⁴(-O4=b1); 56 leaves, pp. [i-ii] iii-ix [x] 1-102.

Illustrations: Hand colored engraved frontispiece and four hand colored engraved plates of tea plants and one uncolored engraved plate of boxes for conveying plants by sea.

Bibliographies: Maclean, p. 90; Wheaton and Kelly 3643.

Copies: *BMC* and *NUC* (18 copies).

827. Lewer, Henry William, ed.

A BOOK OF | SIMPLES | [ornament] | *"Delirious persons here a cure may find,* | *To stem the phrensy and to calm the mind.'* | [ornament] | LONDON | SAMPSON LOW, MARSTON AND CO. LTD. | 100, SOUTHWARK STREET, S.E. | 1908

First edition, London, 1908.

226 x 146 mm. [A]^4 B-P^8 Q^2; 118 leaves, pp. [i-iv] v-viii, 1-225 [226]. Publisher's green Japanese vellum stamped in gold.

Introduction signed H.W. Lewer.

Bibliographies: Axford, p. 40; Driver 620.1.

Copies: *BMC*.

828. Lewis, W. G.

THE | GUIDE TO SERVICE. | [short rule] | THE COOK. | PLAIN AND PRACTICAL DIRECTIONS | FOR | COOKING AND HOUSEKEEPING; | WITH | UPWARDS OF 700 RECEIPTS. | [short rule] | LONDON: | CHARLES KNIGHT AND CO., LUDGATE STREET, | [short rule] | 1842.

First edition, London, 1842.

168 x 104 mm. [A]^2 B-T$^{12 \cdot 6}$ U^4; 168 leaves, pp. [i-iii] iv [1] 2-332. Publisher's brown cloth, spine stamped in gold.

Bibliographies: Axford, p. 193; Wheaton and Kelly 2573.

Copies: Wheaton and Kelly (Radcliffe only).

829. Llanover, Augusta Waddington Hall, lady, d. 1896.

GOOD COOKERY | ILLUSTRATED. | AND RECIPES COMMUNICATED BY THE WELSH HERMIT | OF THE CELL OF ST. GOVER, | *WITH VARIOUS REMARKS ON MANY THINGS* | *PAST AND PRESENT.* | BY | THE RIGHT HON.

LADY LLANOVER. | [publisher's monogram] | LONDON: | RICHARD
BENTLEY, NEW BURLINGTON STREET, | 𝔓𝔲𝔟𝔩𝔦𝔰𝔥𝔢𝔯 𝔦𝔫 𝔒𝔯𝔡𝔦𝔫𝔞𝔯𝔶 𝔱𝔬 ℌ𝔢𝔯
𝔐𝔞𝔧𝔢𝔰𝔱𝔶. | 1867.

First edition, London, 1867.

202 x 131 mm. [A]⁶ (±A2) B-HH⁸ II²; 248 leaves, pp. [i-v] vi-xii [1] 2-482 [2].
Publisher's brown cloth, stamped in gold.

Illustrations: Wood engraving titled "The First Meeting of the Hermit and the
Traveller" on A1ʳ (p. ii), and eleven plates illustrating utensils and scenes from the
narrative.

378 pages of narrative titled "The First Principles of Good Cookery" and "The
Traveller's Note Book" followed by a 102 page appendix containing recipes, many of
Welsh origin.

Bibliographies: Axford, p. 182; Bitting, p. 290.

Copies: *BMC* and *NUC* (Library of Congress only).

830. Locke, John, 1632-1704.

OBSERVATIONS UPON | THE GROWTH AND CULTURE | OF VINES AND
OLIVES: | THE PRODUCTION OF SILK: | THE PRESERVATION OF FRUITS. |
WRITTEN AT THE REQUEST OF | THE EARL OF SHAFTESBURY: | TO
WHOM IT IS INSCRIBED: | BY MR. JOHN LOCKE. | NOW FIRST PRINTED
FROM THE | ORIGINAL MANUSCRIPT IN | THE POSSESSION OF THE |
PRESENT EARL OF | SHAFTESBURY. | LONDON: | PRINTED FOR W.
SANDBY, IN FLEET STREET. | M DCC LXVI.

First edition, London, 1766.

8vo. A⁸ (-A1) B-E⁸ F⁴ χ1; 44 leaves, pp. [iii-v] vi-xv [xvi] [1] 2-73 [74].

Bibliographies: Bitting, p. 291; Gabler, p. 167; Henrey III.986; Maclean, p. 91;
Simon BG 962. Noling, p. 259, incorrectly dates this edition 1679.

Copies: *BMC* and *NUC* (10 copies).

831. Entry deleted.

832. London at Table.

LONDON AT TABLE; │ OR, │ HOW, WHEN, AND WHERE TO DINE AND │ ORDER A DINNER; │ AND WHERE TO AVOID DINING. │ WITH PRACTICAL HINTS TO COOKS. │ TO WHICH IS APPENDED │ THE BUTLER'S AND YACHT STEWARD'S MANUAL, AND │ TRUISMS FOR THE MILLION. │ LONDON: │ CHAPMAN AND HALL, 193, PICCADILLY. │ MDCCCLI.

First edition, London, 1851.

170 x 105 mm. [A]^2 B-D^8 E^6; 32 leaves, pp. [4] [1] 2-60. Publisher's green cloth, stamped in gold. 34 page publisher's catalogue, dated 1851, bound in at the end.

Illustrations: Engraved frontispiece by "Phiz" (H. K. Browne).

A revision of this work was published in 1858 under the title *London at Dinner*.

Bibliographies: Axford, p. 251; Bitting, p. 573; Simon BG 967; Wheaton and Kelly 3759.

Copies: *NUC* (4 copies).

833. Lovell, M. S.

THE │ EDIBLE MOLLUSKS │ OF │ GREAT BRITAIN AND IRELAND │ WITH │ RECIPES FOR COOKING THEM. │ BY │ M. S. LOVELL. │ "And the recipes and different modes of dressing │ I am prepared to teach the world for nothing, │ If men are only wise enough to learn." │ *Athenaeus, Deipnos*. Bk. iii. c. 69. │ [publisher's monogram] │ LONDON: │ REEVE & CO., 5, HENRIETTA STREET, COVENT GARDEN. │ 1867.

First edition, London, 1867.

189 x 125 mm. [A]^4 B-O^8; 108 leaves, pp. [8] [1] 2-207 [208]. Publisher's blue cloth, stamped in gold.

Illustrations: Twelve chromolithographed plates of snails and shell fish.

Bibliographies: Unrecorded in the bibliographies consulted.

Copies: *BMC* and *NUC* (13 copies).

834. M., W.

THE | COMPLEAT | COOK. | Expertly prescribing the | most ready wayes, | Whether, {*Italian*, | *Spanish*, | or *French*. | For dressing of *Flesh*, and *Fish*, | Ordering of *Sauces*, or making | OF | PASTRY. | [rule] | *LONDON*: | Printed for *Nath. Brook* at the | *Angel* in *Corn-hill*, 1655.

First edition, London, 1655. Oxford notes that this is the third part of *The Queen's Closet Opened* but that it "was sometimes published by itself." It is recorded separately in Wing and in this catalogue.

12mo. A-E^{12} F^4; 64 leaves, pp. [1-2] 3-123 [124-126] [2]. Last leaf (blank?) wanting in this copy.

Bibliographies: Axford, p. 71; Bitting, p. 533; Oxford, p. 26; Pennell, p. 134; Wing M88.

Copies: *BMC* and *NUC* (Huntington Library, Library of Congress, and University of Wisconsin). Wing adds Marischal College, Aberdeen.

835. M., W.

[within a single rule border] THE | COMPLEAT | COOK. | Expertly prescribing the | most ready wayes, | Whether, {*Italian*, | *Spanish*, | or *French*, | For dressing of *Flesh*, and *Fish*, | Ordering of *Sauces*, or making | OF | PASTRY. | [rule] | *LONDON*: | Printed by *E. B.* for *Nath. Brook*, at the | *Angel* in *Cornhill*, 1658.

Third edition, London, 1658. Originally published, London, 1655 (item 834).

12mo. A-F^{12}; 72 leaves, pp. [1-2] 3-123 [124-130] [*14*]. Bound with *The Queen's Closet Opened*, London, 1658 (item 838).

Bibliographies: Wheaton and Kelly 1333 and 1334; Wing M90.

Copies: *NUC* (Harvard only). Wing adds British Library and New York Public Library.

836. M., W.

[within a single rule border] The Compleat │ COOK: │ Expertly Prescribing │ The most ready Wayes, │ Whether, {*Italian*, │ *Spanish*, or │ *French*,} │ For dressing of *Flesh*, and │ *Fish*, Ordering of *Sauces*, │ or making of │ PASTRY. │ [rule] │ [ornament] │ [rule] │ *LONDON*, │ Printed by *J. Winter*, for *Nath. Brooke*, at │ the Angel in *Gresham*-College, 1668.

Seventh edition, London, 1668. Originally published, London, 1655 (item 834).

12mo. A-E^{12} F^6; 66 leaves, pp. [1-2] 3-123 [124-130] [2].

Bibliographies: Oxford, p. 26 in a note; Wing M93.

Copies: Wing (Folger Library only).

837. M., W.

The Compleat │ COOK: │ Prescribing │ The most Ready WAYS │ FOR │ Dressing *Flesh*, and *Fish*, │ Ordering │ *Sauces, Pickles, Jellies*, &c. │ And Making │ PASTRY │ After the *Newest Manner*. │ [two rules] │ *LONDON:* │ Printed for *J. Phillips, H. Rhodes*, and │ *J. Taylor*. 1710.

Tenth edition, London, 1710. Originally published, London, 1655 (item 834).

12mo. A-F^{12} G^4; 76 leaves, pp. [2] 1-138 [*12*]. Last leaf, G4, wanting in this copy. Bound with *The Queen's Closet Opened*, London, 1710 (item 840).

Bibliographies: Maclean, p. 31; Oxford, p. 26 in a note; Simon BG 373.

Copies: *BMC* and *NUC* (Clark Library, Duke, and University of California, Berkeley). Maclean adds Brotherton Library.

838. M., W.

[within a single rule border] THE │ QUEENS CLOSET │ OPENED: │ Incomparable Secrets in │ Physick, Chyrurgery, Preser- │ ving, Candying, and Cookery; │ As they were presented unto the | QUEEN | By the most Experienced Persons of our | times, many whereof were honoured with her | own Practise, when she pleased to descend to | these more private Recreations. | [rule] | The Fourth Edition corrected, with ma- | ny Additions: together with three ex- | act Tables, one of them never before | Printed. | [rule] | Transcribed from the true Copies of her | MAJESTIES own Receipt Books, | by *W. M.* one of her late Servants. | [rule] | *Vivit post funera Virtus* | [rule] | *London.* Printed for *Nathaniel Brooks* at | the Angel in *Cornhill,* 1658.

Title-page of second part:

[within a single rule border] A | QUEENS DELIGHT: | OR, | The ART | OF | *Preserving, Conserving,* | and *Candying*; | As also, | A right Knowledge of | making PERFUMES, and | Distilling the most | Excellent Waters. | [rule] | Never before Published. | [rule] | Printed by *R. Wood* for *Nath. Brooks,* at | the Angel in *Cornhill,* 1658.

Fourth edition, London, 1658. Originally published, London, 1655.

12mo. A⁶ C-P¹² Q⁶; 168 leaves, pp. [*12*] 1-300 [*24*]. Bound with *The Compleat Cook,* London, 1658 (item 835).

Illustration: Engraved portrait of Queen Henrietta Maria, widow of Charles I, on A1ᵛ.

Bibliographies: Wheaton and Kelly 3803; Wing M98.

Copies: *NUC* (Folger Library, Harvard, and National Library of Medicine). Wing (8 copies).

839. M., W.

[within a single rule border] THE | QUEENS | CLOSET | OPENED. | Incomparable Secrets in Phy- | sick, Chirurgery, Preser- | ving, and Candying, &c. | Which were presented unto the | QUEEN: | By the most Experienced Persons of the | Times, many whereof were had in esteem, | when She pleased to descend to private Recreations. | [rule] | Corrected and Reviewed, with many New and large | Additions: together with three exact Tables. | [rule] | *Vivit post Funera Virtus* | [rule] | *LONDON,* | Printed by *J.W.* for *Nath. Brooke,* at the | Angel in *Gresham*-College, near the *Ex-* | *change* in *Bishops-Gate-Street.* 1668.

Ninth edition, London, 1668. Originally published, London, 1655.

12mo. A^6 C-K^{12} L^4; 106 leaves, pp. [*12*] 1-191 [*192*] [*8*].

Illustration: Engraved portrait of Queen Henrietta Maria, widow of Charles I, on A1^v.

Bibliographies: Oxford, p. 26 in a note; Pennell, p. 136; Wing M100c. Bitting, p. 595, and Vicaire 184 record other editions.

Copies: Wing (British Library, Brotherton Library, and University of Delaware).

840. M., W.

[within a border of two rules] THE | Queen's Closet | OPENED. | BEING | Incomparable Secrets in PHYSICK, | SURGERY, PRESERVING, | CANDYING, and | COOKERY. | After the newest Mode now practi- | sed in *England*, | By the most experienc'd Persons of the Times. | [rule] / *The Eleventh Edition, Corrected, with many* New | *and* Large ADDITIONS *throughout the whole.* | [rule] | *Vivit post Funera Virtus.* | [rule] | *LONDON:* | Printed by *J. Phillips*, at the *King's-Arms* in | St. *Paul*'s Church-yard; *H. Rhodes* at the *Star*, | the corner of *Bride-lane* in *Fleet-street*; and | *J. Taylor*, at the *Ship* in *Pater-noster-Row*, | MDCCX.

Title-page of second part:

A | QUEEN's DELIGHT: | OR, A | SYSTEM | OF THE | *Confectionary* ART. | SHEWING | How to preserve all Sorts of FRUIT, | both Liquid and Dry, according to the | best Methods now in use; as also how | to make | [in two columns: column one] *Clear-Cakes,* | *Jellies,* | *Compotes,* | *Conserves,* | *Candy'd Confits,* | *Marmalets,* | *Quiddanies,* | *Pastes,* | *Pastils,* | *Sugar-works,* | [two fancy vertical rules] | [column two] *Biscotins,* | *Biskets,* | *March-panes,* | *Macaroons,* | *Wafers,* | *Liquors of several sorts,* | *Distilled Waters,* | *Essences,* | *Perfumes,* | *Syrups,* &c. [end columns] | [two rules] | *LONDON:* | Printed for *J. Phillips, H. Rhodes*, and | *J. Taylor*, 1710.

Eleventh edition, London, 1710. Originally published, London, 1655.

12mo. [A]^2 B-L^{12} M^4; 126 leaves, pp. [*4*] 1-240 [*8*]. Bound with *The Compleat Cook*, London, 1710 (item 837).

Bibliographies: Maclean, p. 119; Oxford, p. 26, in a note.

Copies: *BMC* and *NUC* (Huntington Library, Kansas State University, and the New York Academy of Medicine). Maclean adds Brotherton Library.

841. Macdonald, Duncan.

THE NEW | LONDON FAMILY COOK: | OR, | TOWN AND COUNTRY | *HOUSEKEEPERS' GUIDE;* | COMPREHENDING | DIRECTIONS FOR MARKETING, | With illustrative Plates, on a Principle entirely new; | *General Observations, and Bills of Fare for every Week in the Year*; | Practical Instructions for preparing | SOUPS, BROTHS, GRAVIES, SAUCES, AND MADE DISHES; | AND FOR DRESSING FISH, VENISON, HARES, BUTCHERS' MEAT, POULTRY, | GAME, &c. IN ALL THEIR VARIETIES. | With the respective branches of | PASTRY AND CONFECTIONARY, | THE ART OF POTTING, PICKLING, PRESERVING, &c. COOKERY FOR THE SICK, | AND FOR THE POOR. | Directions for Carving: | *And a Glossary of the most generally received French and English Terms in the Culinary Art.* | ALSO A SELECTION OF | *VALUABLE FAMILY RECIPES,* | IN DYEING, PERFUMERY, &c. | INSTRUCTIONS FOR BREWING, MAKING OF BRITISH WINES, DISTILLING, | MANAGING THE DAIRY, AND GARDENING. | AND | AN APPENDIX, | *Containing general Directions for Servants relative to the Cleaning of Household* | *Furniture, Floor-Cloths, Stoves, Marble Chimney-Pieces, &c.* | Forming in the whole a most complete | FAMILY INSTRUCTOR. | [short fancy rule] | *BY DUNCAN MACDONALD,* | HEAD COOK AT THE BEDFORD TAVERN AND HOTEL, CONVENT-GARDEN, | AND ASSISTANTS. | [two short rules] | Albion Press: | PRINTED FOR J. AND J. CUNDEE, IVY-LANE, | PATERNOSTER-ROW, LONDON.

Third edition, London, ca. 1811. Originally published, London, ca. 1800. The original edition was published by J. Robins. The second edition, published by John Cundee, has a preface dated 1808. In the third edition the preface is dated Dec. 1, 1811.

208 x 126 mm. [A]^4 B-4F^4 4G^2 4H-4K^4 4L^2; 316 leaves, pp. [i-iii] iv [5] 6-604, 609-634 [2].

Illustrations: Eight engraved plates, showing cuts of meat, table settings, carving and trussing. Six have the imprint of James Cundee and are dated from Jan. 1, 1808 through June 25, 1808; the other two have no imprint.

Bibliographies: This edition is unrecorded in the bibliographies consulted. Axford, Bitting, Maclean, and Oxford cite the J. Robins edition; Maclean also cites an edition published by John Cundee which she dates ca. 1800; Simon BG 978 describes an edition with the imprint "London, Albion Press, 1812" which, if correct, is the only edition with a dated title-page.

Copies: No other copy of this edition located. *NUC* locates J. Robins edition (Library of Congress only) and J. Cundee edition with the preface dated 1808 (Harvard, New York Public Library, and University of Missouri).

842. Maciver, Susanna.

COOKERY, | AND | PASTRY. | AS TAUGHT AND PRACTISED BY | MRS MACIVER, | TEACHER OF THOSE ARTS IN EDINBURGH. | [rule] | A NEW EDITION. | [rule] | TO WHICH ARE ADDED, FOR THE FIRST TIME, | FIGURES OF DINNER AND SUPPER | COURSES, FROM FIVE TO FIFTEEN DISHES. | ALSO, | A CORRECT LIST OF EVERY THING IN SEASON | FOR EVERY MONTH IN THE YEAR. | [short fancy rule] | EDINBURGH: | Printed for C. ELLIOT, EDINBURGH: | And G. G. J. and J. ROBINSON, LONDON. | [short rule] | MDCCLXXXVII.

Sixth edition, Edinburgh, 1787. Originally published, Edinburgh, 1773.

12mo. A^6 B-L^{12} M^6; 132 leaves, pp. [i-v] vi-xii [13] 14-264.

Bibliographies: Maclean, p. 92; Vicaire 546. Bitting, Oxford, and Simon BG cite other editions.

Copies: *NUC* (Vassar only). Maclean adds Bodleian, Cambridge, and National Library of Scotland.

843. Maciver, Susanna.

COOKERY | AND | PASTRY, | AS TAUGHT AND PRACTISED BY | MRS MACIVER, | TEACHER OF THOSE ARTS IN EDINBURGH. | [two short rules] | To which are Added, | FIGURES OF DINNER AND SUPPER COURSES, | FROM FIVE TO FIFTEEN DISHES; | also, | A CORRECT LIST OF EVERY THING IN SEASON | FOR EVERY MONTH IN THE YEAR. | [two rules] | A NEW EDITION, WITH ADDITIONS. | [two rules] | *EDINBURGH:* | Printed by D. Schaw and Co. Lawnmarket; | FOR J. FAIRBAIRN, N° 9. HUNTER'S SQUARE. | [short rule] | 1800.

Eighth edition, Edinburgh, 1800. Originally published, Edinburgh, 1773.

12mo. A^6 B-I^{12}; 102 leaves, pp. [i-vii] viii-xii [13] 14-204.

Bibliographies: Maclean, p. 92; Oxford, p. 106, in a note; Vicaire 546. Bitting and Simon BG cite other editions.

Copies: *NUC* (Florida State University only). Maclean adds British Library.

844. Macquin, Ange-Denis, 1756-1823.

𝕿𝖆𝖇𝖊𝖑𝖑𝖆 𝕮𝖎𝖇𝖆𝖗𝖎𝖆. | [short fancy rule] | THE BILL OF FARE: | A LATIN POEM, | *IMPLICITLY TRANSLATED AND FULLY EXPLAINED* | IN COPIOUS AND INTERESTING NOTES, | RELATING | TO THE PLEASRUES OF | GASTRONOMY, | AND THE MYSTERIOUS ART OF | COOKERY. | [short fancy rule] | Ipsa memor praecepta canam; celabitur auctor. – HOR. | [short fancy rule] | 𝕷𝖔𝖓𝖉𝖔𝖓: | PUBLISHED BY SHERWOOD, NEELY, AND JONES, PATER- | NOSTER ROW; J. ROBINS AND CO. IVY LANE, | PATERNOSTER ROW; AND SOLD BY | ALL BOOKSELLERS. | [short rule] | 1820.

First edition, London, 1820.

233 x 183 mm. [A]⁴ B-O⁴; 56 leaves, pp. [i-iii] iv-viii [1] 2-104.

Bibliographies: Axford, p. 385; Bitting, p. 300; Oxford, p. 148; Wheaton and Kelly 3884.

Copies: *BMC*, *BNC*, and *NUC* (5 copies).

845. Madden, Sir Frederick, 1801-1873, ed.

PRIVY PURSE EXPENSES | OF THE | [in red] 𝕻𝖗𝖎𝖓𝖈𝖊𝖘𝖘 𝕸𝖆𝖗𝖞, | DAUGHTER OF KING HENRY THE EIGHTH, | AFTERWARDS QUEEN MARY: | WITH | A MEMOIR OF THE PRINCESS, AND NOTES. | BY | FREDERICK MADDEN, ESQ. F.S.A., | ASSISTANT KEEPR OF THE MSS. IN THE | BRITISH MUSEUM. | [Tudor arms] | LONDON: | WILLIAM PICKERING. | MDCCCXXXI.

First edition, London, 1831.

215 x 132 mm. π² c-2d⁴ B-2N⁴ 2O⁴ (-2O4); 245 leaves, pp. [4] [ix] x-ccv [ccvi-ccviii] [1] 2-285 [286].

Bibliographies: Bitting, p. 303; Simon BG 987.

Copies: *BMC*, *BNC*, and *NUC* (15 copies).

846. The Magazine of Domestic Economy.

THE | MAGAZINE | OF | DOMESTIC ECONOMY. | VOLUME THE FIRST. [VOLUME THE SECOND.] [VOLUME THE THIRD.] [VOLUME THE FOURTH.] [VOLUME THE FIFTH.] [VOLUME THE SIXTH.] | [short rule] | WE ARE BORN AT HOME, WE LIVE AT HOME, AND WE MUST DIE AT HOME, SO THAT THE COMFORTS | AND ECONOMY OF HOME ARE OF MORE DEEP, HEART-FELT, AND PERSONAL INTEREST TO US, | THAN THE PUBLIC AFFAIRS OF ALL THE NATIONS IN THE WORLD. | [short rule] | LONDON: | PUBLISHED BY W. S. ORR & CO., PATERNOSTER ROW; | [Vols. 1-3] AND W. & R. CHAMBERS, EDINBURGH. [Vols. 4-5: AND FRASER & CRAWFORD, EDINBURGH. Vol. 6 has no Edinburgh publisher] | [short rule] | MDCCCXXXVI. [MDCCCXXXVI.] [MDCCCXXXVIII.] [MDCCCXXXIX.] [MDCCCXL.] [MDCCCXLI.]

First edition, volumes I-VI only, London, 1836-1841. Complete set consists of Vols. I-VII, July 1835-June 1842; new series, Vols I-II, July 1842-June 1844.

211 x 128 mm. Six volumes. Vol. I. [A]^2 B-BB^8 CC^2; 196 leaves, pp. [i-iii] iv, ^{2}[i] ii-iii [iv] 5-387 [388]. Vol. II. [A]^2 B-AA^8 BB^4 CC^2; 192 leaves, pp. [*4*] [1] 2-380. First leaf blank. Vol. III. [A]^2 B-AA^8 BB^6; 192 leaves, pp. [*4*] [1] 2-380. First leaf blank. Vol. IV. [A]^2 B-AA^8 BB^4 CC^2; 192 leaves, pp. [*4*] [1] 2-380. First leaf blank. Vol. V [A]^2 B-AA^8 BB^4 CC^2; 192 leaves, pp. [*4*] [1] 2-380. First leaf (blank) wanting in this copy. Vol. VI. [A]^2 B-AA^8 BB^4 CC^2; 192 leaves, pp. [*4*] [1] 2-380. First leaf blank.

Bibliographies: Axford, p. 256; Oxford, p. 169, records volume one only.

Copies: *BMC* and *ULS* (12 sets in varying degrees of completeness, at least four of which have these six volumes).

846a. Manual of Military Cooking.

[*Crown Copyright Reserved.* | 40 | [rule] | War Office. | [rule] | 1089 | MANUAL | OF | MILITARY COOKING. | PREPARED AT THE ARMY SCHOOL | OF COOKERY. | [short rule] | [British royal arms] | LONDON: | PRINTED UNDER

THE AUTHORITY OF HIS MAJESTY'S STATIONERY OFFICE | BY HARRISON AND SONS, 45-47, ST. MARTIN'S LANE, W.C., | PRINTER IN ORDINARY TO HIS MAJESTY. | [short rule] | To be purchased, either directly or through any Bookseller, from | WYMAN AND SONS, LTD., 29, BREAMS BUILDINGS. FETTER LANE E.C., and | 54, ST. MARY STREET, CARDIFF; or | H.M. STATIONERY OFFICE (SCOTTISH BRANCH), 23, FOURTH STREET, EDINBURGH; or | E. PONSONBY, LTD., 116, GRAFTON STREET, DUBLIN; | or from the Agencies in the British Colonies and Dependencies |the United States of America, the Continent of Europe and Abroad of | T. FISHER UNWIN, LONDON, W.C. | [short rule] | 1910. | *(Reprinted* 1915.) | *Price Sixpence.*

New edition, London, 1915. *BMC* records editions of 1895, 1899, 1904, 1910 and 1918. This appears to be a second printing of the 1910 edition.

Printer's information at the foot of p. 82: (B 11136) Wt. 42087-476 15,000 2/15 H&S P. 14/367

194 x 125 mm. A-E^8 F^2; 42 leaves, pp. [2] [1] 2-82. P. 76, unnumbered and blank, followed by a tipped-in folding chart numbered 76. Publisher's brown printed wrappers. 12 page publisher's catalog printed on pink paper pasted to the inner front wrapper and an 8 page publisher's catalog printed on pink paper pasted to the inner back wrapper.

Illustrations: Lithographed plate illustrating field cooking canisters tipped in facing p. 62. Line drawings in the text.

Bibliographies: Unrecorded in the bibliographies consulted.

Copies: No other copy of this printing located.

847. Markham, Gervase, 1568?-1637.

[A Way to Get Wealth. First edition. London, 1623. Part three]

COVNTREY | Contentments, | OR | The English Husvvife. | CONTAINING | The inward and outward Vertues which | ought to be in a compleate Woman. | *As her skill in Physicke, Surgerie, Extraction* | of Oyles, Banqueting-stuffe, Ordering of great Feasts, | Preseruing of all sorts of Wines, Conceited Secrets, | *Distillations, Perfumes, ordering of Wooll, Hempe, Flax,* | making Cloth, Dying, the knowledge of Dayries, | office of Malting, Oats, their excellent vses | in a Family, Brewing, Baking, and all | other things belonging to | an Houshold. | A Worke generally approued, and now much augmented, purged | and made most profitable and necessarie for all men, and

De- | dicated to the Honour of the Noble House of Exceter, | and the generall good of this Kingdome. | [rule] | By *G. M.* | [rule] | Printed at *London* by *I.B.*, for *R. Iackson*, and are to be sold at his shop | neere Fleet-streete Conduit. 1623.

Second edition, London, 1623, of *The English Housewife* published as the third part of Markham's *A Way to Get Wealth*. Originally published as book two of Markhams' *Countrey Contentments*, London, 1615.

4to. A-Hh⁴; 124 leaves, pp. [*8*] [*1*] 2-233 [*234*] [*2*]. Last leaf, blank, wanting in this copy.

Bibliographies: Poynter 34.1, part iii; *STC* 17343.

Copies: *BMC* and *NUC* (4 copies). *STC* (9 copies).

848. Markham, Gervase, 1568?-1637.

[A Way to Get Wealth. Sixth edition. London, 1637. Part three]

THE ENGLISH | HOVSE-WIFE, | Containing the inward and outward | Vertues which ought to be in a | compleate Woman. | As her skill in Physick, Surgery, Cookery, | Extraction of Oyles, Banquetting stuffe, Ordering of | great Feasts, Preserving of all sorts of Wines, Conceited Se- | crets, Distilations, Perfumes, ordering of Wooll, Hempe, Flax, | making Cloth, and Dying: the knowledge of Dayries, Office of | Malting, of Oates, their excellent uses in a Family, of | Brewing, Baking, and all other things belonging | to an Houshold. | A Worke generally approved, and now the fifth time much | augmented, purged and made most profitable and necessary for | all men, and the generall good of this Kingdome. | [rule] | By G. M. | [rule] | [publisher's device] | *LONDON,* | Printed by *Anne Griffin* for *Iohn Harrison*, at the Golden | Vnicorne in Pater-noster-row. 1637.

Fifth edition, London, 1637, of *The English Housewife* published as the third part of Markham's *A Way to Get Wealth*. Originally published as book two of Markhams' *Countrey Contentments*, London, 1615.

4to. A⁶ B-Q⁸ R⁶; 132 leaves, pp. [*12*] 1-252. First leaf, blank, wanting in this copy.

Bibliographies: Poynter 34.6, part iii; *STC* 17354.

Copies: *BMC* and *NUC* (4 copies). *STC* (7 copies).

849. Markham, Gervase, 1568?-1637.

[A Way to Get Wealth. Seventh edition. London, 1648. Part two]

Country Contentments: | OR, THE | HVSBANDMANS | RECREATIONS. |
CONTAYNING THE WHOLSOME | Experiences in which any man ought to Recre- |
ate himselfe, after the toyle of more serious businesse. | As namely, Hunting,
Hawking, Coursing with | Greyhounds, and the lawes of the Lease, Shooting in |
Longbow or Crosbow, Bowling, Tennis, Baloone. The | whole Art of Angling, and the
use of the Fighting Cock. | [rule] | *By* G. M. | [rule] | *The sixth Edition.* | Newly
Corrected, Enlarged, and adorned with many excellent | Additions, as may appeare by
this marke, ☞ | [publisher's monogram] | *LONDON,* | Printed by *William Wilson,* for
Iohn Harison, in | St. Pauls-Church-yard. 1649.

Sixth edition, London, 1649, of *Country Contentments* published as the second part of
Markham's *A Way to Get Wealth.* Originally published, London, 1615.

4to. A⁴ B-H⁸ I⁴; 64 leaves, pp. [8] 1-118 [2]. Last leaf, blank, wanting in this copy.

Bibliographies: Poynter 34.7, part ii; Wing M620.

Copies: *BMC, BNC,* and *NUC* (10 copies). Wing (13 copies).

850. Markham, Gervase, 1568?-1637.

[A Way to Get Wealth. Seventh edition. London, 1649. Part three]

THE | ENGLISH | HOUSE-WIFE, | CONTAINING | The inward and outward
Vertues which ought to be in a | compleat Woman. | As her skill in Physick, Surgery,
Cookery, Extraction of Oyles, | Banqueting stuffe, Ordering of great Feasts,
preserving of all sorts of | Wines, conceited Secrets, Distillations, Perfumes, ordering
of | Wooll, Hemp, Flax, making Cloth, and Dying, the know- | ledge of Dayries,
Office of Malting, of Oates, their | excelent uses in a Family, of Brewing, Ba- | king,
and all other things belonging | to an Houshold. | A Work generally approved, and
now the fifth time much aug- | mented purged, and made most profitable and necessary
for all men, | and the generall good of this KINGDOME. | [rule] | By *G. M.* | [rule] |
[ornament] | [rule] | *LONDON.* | Printed by B. ALSOP for JOHN HARISON, at are
to be sold at his | Shop in *Pauls* Church-yard, 1649.

Sixth edition, London, 1649, of *The English Housewife* published as the third part of Markham's *A Way to Get Wealth*. Originally published as book two of Markhams' *Countrey Contentments*, London, 1615.

4to. A^6 B-Q^8 R^6; 132 leaves, pp. [*12*] 1-252. First leaf blank.

Bibliographies: Bitting, p. 309; Poynter 34.7, part iii; Wing M629.

Copies: *BMC*, *BNC*, and *NUC* (10 copies). Wing (14 copies).

851. Markham, Gervase, 1568?-1637.

[A Way to Get Wealth. Seventh edition. London, 1648. Part six]

A new ORCHARD, and | GARDEN; | OR, | The best way for Planting, Grafting, and to | make any ground good, for a rich Orchard: Particularly | in the North, and generally for the whole Kingdom of *England*, | as in nature, reason, situation, and all probability, may and doth appear. | With the Country-houswifes Garden for Herbs of common use: | their Vertues, Seasons, Profits, Ornaments, variety of Knots, Models for | Trees, and Plots for the best ordering of Grounds and Walks. | AS ALSO, | The Husbandry of Bees, with their several Uses and Annoyances. | *All being the experience of Fourty and eight yeers labour, and now the second* | *time corrected and much enlarged, by* WILLIAM LAWSON. | Whereunto is newly added the Art of Propagating Plants; with | the true ordering of all manner of Fruits, in their gathering, | carrying home, and preservation. | [woodcut of three gardeners] | [bottom to top to left of woodcut] Skill and pains, bring fruitful gains. | [bottom to top to right of woodcut] *Nemo sibi natus.* | *London*, Printed for *W. Wilson*, for *John Harison*, and are to be sold | at his Shop in *Pauls* Church-yard. 1648.

Second title-page:

THE | COVNTRY HOVSE-WIVES | GARDEN, | Containing Rules for herbs, and Seeds, | of common use, with their times and seasons | when to set and sow them. | Together, | With the Husbandry of Bees, publi- | shed with secrets very necessary for every *House-* | *wife*: as also divers new Knots for Gardens. | The Contents see at large in the last Page. | Genes. 2.29. | *I have given unto you every Herb, and every tree,* | *that shall be to you for* | *meate.* | [publisher's device] | *LONDON* | Printed by *William Wilson*, for *John Harrison*, and are to be | sold at his Shop in Pauls-Church-yard. 1648.

Sixth edition, London, 1648, of William Lawson's *A New Orchard and Garden*, published as the sixth part of Markham's *A Way to Get Wealth*. Originally published, London, 1618.

4to. A⁴ B-I⁸ K⁴; 72 leaves, pp. [*8*] 1-134 [*2*]. Last leaf (blank?) wanting in this copy.

Illustrations: Woodcuts in the text.

Bibliographies: Poynter 34.7, part vi; Wing L730.

Copies: *BMC, BNC,* and *NUC* (9 copies). Wing (7 copies).

852. Markham, Gervasc, 1568?-1637.

[A Way to Get Wealth. Twelfth edition. London, 1668. Part six]

A NEW │ ORCHARD │ AND │ GARDEN: │ OR, │ The best way for Planting, Graffing, and to make any │ Ground good for a rich Orchard: Particularly in the North, and │ Generally for the whole Common-wealth, as in Nature, Reason, │ Situation, and all Probability, may and doth appear. │ With the Country Hous-wifes Garden for Herbs of Common use. │ Their Virtues, Seasons, Profits, Ornaments, variety of Knots, Models │ for Trees, and Plots, for the best ordering of Grounds and Walks. │ AS ALSO │ The Husbandry of Bees, with their several Uses and Annoyances: │ *All being the experience of Forty and eight years Labour, and now the fifth │ time Corrected, and much Enlarged. By* William Lawson. │ Whereunto is newly added the Art of Propagating Plants, with the true Or- │ dering of all manner of Fruits, in their Gathering, Carrying home, and Preservation. │ [woodcut of three gardeners] │ [bottom to top to left of woodcut] Skil and pains, bring fruitful gains. │ [bottom to top to right of woodcut] *Nemo sibi natus.* │ *London*, Printed for *George Sawbridge.* 1668.

Eleventh edition, London, 1668, of William Lawson's of *A New Orchard and Garden*, published as the sixth part of Markham's *A Way to Get Wealth*. Originally published, London, 1618.

4to. A-N⁴ O²; 54 leaves, pp. [*6*] 1-102.

Illustrations: Numerous woodcuts in the text.

Bibliographies: Poynter 34.12, part vi; Wing L735.

Copies: *BMC* and *NUC* (Harvard and Massachusetts Historical Society). Wing adds Bodleian Library, Wellcome Library, and Yale.

853. Markham, Gervase, 1568?-1637.

[A Way to Get Wealth. Thirteenth edition. London, 1676. Part three]

THE | ENGLISH | House-Wife, | CONTAING | The inward and outward Vertues
which | ought to be in a Compleat WOMAN. | As her Skill in *Physick, Chirurgery,*
Cookery, Extraction of Oyls, | *Banqueting stuff, Ordering of great Feasts, Preserving*
of all sort of | *Wides, conceited Secrets, Distillations, Perfimes,* Ordering of *Wool,* |
Hemp, Flax: Making *Cloth* and *Dying*; The knowledge of | *Dayries:* Office of *Malting*;
of *Oats*, their excellent uses in Fa- | milies: Of *Brewing, Baking,* and all other things
belonging to an | Houshold. | A *Work* generally approved, and now the | Eighth time
much Augmented, Purged and made most | profitable and necessary for all men, and
the general good | of this NATION. | [rule] | By *G. Markham.* | [rule] | *LONDON,* |
Printed by *George Sawbridge*, at the Sign of the *Bible* on | *Ludgate Hill.* 1675.

Twelfth edition, London, 1675, of *The English Housewife* published as the third part of
Markham's *A Way to Get Wealth.* Originally published as book two of Markhams'
Countrey Contentments, London, 1615.

4to. Aa⁴ Bbb-Bbbb⁴ Cccc²; 102 leaves, pp. [*8*] 1-80, 73-88, 97-104, 97-188.

Bibliographies: Poynter 34.13, part iii; Wing M681.

Copies: *BMC* and *NUC* (6 copies). Wing (12 copies).

854. Markham, Gervase, 1568?-1637.

[A Way to Get Wealth. Fourteenth edition. London, 1683. Parts one-six]

A | WAY | TO GET | WEALTH: | CONTAINING | Six Principal VOCATIONS, or
CALLINGS, In | which every good *Husband* or *House-wive* may lawfully | Imploy
themselves. | AS, | I. The Natures, Ordering, Curing, Breeding, Choice, Use and
Feeding | of all sorts of Cattel and Fowl, fit for the Service of Man: As also | the
Riding and Dieting of Horses, either for War or Pleasure. | II. The Knowledg, Use and
Laudable Practice of all the Recreations | meet for a *Gentleman.* | III. The Office of a
House-wife, in Physick, Chirurgery, Extraction of | Oyles, Banquets, Cookery,
Ordering of Feasts, Preserving of Wine, | conceited Secrets, Distillations, Perfumes,
Ordering of Wool, Hemp, | Flax, Dying, Use of Dayries, Maulting, Brewing, Baking:
and the | Profit of Oats. | IV. The Inrichment of the Weald in *Kent.* | V. The
Husbanding and Inriching of all sorts of barren Grounds, ma- | king them equal with
the most fruitful: With the Preservation of | Swine. And a Computation of Men and

Cattels Labours, &c. | VI. The making of Orchards, Planting and Graffing, the Office of Gar- | dening, and the Ornaments, with the best Husbanding of Bees. | [rule] | The first Five Books gathered by *G. M.* The last by Master | *W. L.* for the Benefit of *Great Britain.* | [rule] | *The Fourteenth time Corrected and Augmented by the Author.* | [rule] | *LONDON,* | Printed by *T. B.* for *Hannah Sawbridge*, at the Bible on *Ludgate-Hill*, 1683.

Sectional title-pages:

[Part one]

CHEAP and *GOOD* | HUSBANDRY, | FOR | The well-Ordering of all Beasts and Fowls, | and for the general Cure of their Diseases. | Containing the Natures, Breeding, Choice, Use, Feeding and | Curing of the Diseases of all manner of Cattel, as Horse, Oxe, Cow, | Sheep, Goats, Swine and tame Conies. | Shewing further the whole Art of Riding Great Horses, with | the breaking and ordering of them, and the Dyeting of the Running, | Hunting and Ambling Horse, and the manner how to use them in their | Travel. | Also, approved Rules for the Cramming, and fatting all sorts | of Poultry and Fowls, both tame and wild, &c. And divers good and | well approved Medicines, for the Cure of all the Diseases in Hawks, of | what kind soever. | Together with the Use and Profit of Bees, the manner of | Fish-Ponds, and the taking of all sorts of Fish. | Gathered together for the general Good and Profit of the | Common-wealth, by exact and assured Experience from English pra- | ctices, both certain, easie and cheap; differing from all former and | forraign Experiments, which either agreed not with our Clime, or were | too hard to come by, or over-costly, and too little purpose; all which | herein are avoided. Newly Corrected and Enlarged with many Ex- | cellent Additions. | [rule] | *The Fourteenth Impression.* | [rule] | *LONDON,* | Printed by *T.B.* for *Hannah Sawbridge*, at the Bible on | *Ludgate=Hill*, MDCLXXXIII.

[Part two]

Country Contentments; | OR THE | HUSBANMANS | Recreations. | CONTAINING | The Wholsome Experience, in which | any ought to Recreate himself, after the toyl | of more serious Business: | As namely, | Hunting, Hawking, Coursing with | Grey-Hounds, and the Laws of Leash, Shooting | in the Long-Bow or Cross-Bow, Bowling, | Tennis, Baloon; The whole Art of Angling, | And the use of the Fighting Cock. | [rule] | By *G. Markham.* | [rule] | *The Eleventh Edition.* | Newly Corrected, Enlarged, and adorned with ma- | ny Excellent Additions, as may appear by this Mark. ☞ | [rule] | *LONDON,* | Printed by *George Sawbridge*, at the Sign of the *Bible* | *Ludgate-Hill*-1683.

[Part three]

THE | ENGLISH | House-Wife, | CONTAINING | The inward and outward Vertues | which ought to be in a Compleat Woman. | As her Skill *in Physick, Chirurgery, Cookery, Extraction* of *Oyls,* | *Banqueting stuff, Ordering of great Feasts, Preserving of all sort* | of *Wines, conceited Secrets, Distillations, Perfums,* Ordering | of *Wool, Hemp, Flax:* Making *Cloath* and *Dying*; The | knowledge of *Dayries:* Office of *Malting*; of *Oats,* their | excellent uses in Families: Of *Brewing, Baking,* and all other | things belonging to an Houshold. | *A Work* generally approved, and now | the Ninth time much Augmented, Purged, and | made most profitable and necessary for all men, and | the general good of this NATION. | [rule] | By *G. Markham.* | [rule] | *LONDON,* | Printed by *Hannah Sawbridge,* at the Sign of the *Bible* | on *Ludgate-Hill.* 1683.

[Part four]

THE | INRICHMENT | OF THE | Weald of Kent. | OR, | A Direction to the Husbandman, | For the true Ordering, Manuring, and Inriching of | all the Grounds within the *Wealds* of *Kent,* and *Sus-* | *sex,* and may generally serve for all the Grounds in | of that Nature: As | 1 *Shewing the nature of* Wealdish *Ground, comparing it with the Soyl* | *of the Shires at large.* | 2 *Declaring what* Marle, *and the several sorts thereof, and where it* | *it is usually found.* | 3 *The profitable use of* Marle, *and other rich manuring, as well* | *in each sort of Arrable Land, as also for the encrease of Corn and* | *Pasture through the Kingdom.* | Painfully gathered for the good of this | Island, by a Man of great Eminence and Worth: | But Revised, Enlarged, and Corrected with the con- | sent, and by conference with the first Author. | [rule] | By *G. Markham.* | [rule] | *LONDON,* | Printed for *Hannah Sawbridge,* at the Sign of the *Bible* | on *Ludgate-Hill.* 1683.

[Part five]

Markham's Farewel to | HUSBANDRY: | OR, | The Enriching of all sorts of Barren and | Sterile Grounds in our Nation, to be as | Fruitful in all manner of Grain, Pulse, and | Grass, as the best Grounds whatsoever. | Together with the Annoyances and Preservation of all | Grain and Seed, from one year to many years. | As also a Husbandly computation of Men and Cattels | daily Labours, their Expences, Charges, and utmost profits. | Now newly the Eleventh time revis'd, corrected and a- | mended, together with many new Additions, and cheap Experiments. | For the bettering of Arable Pasture, and | Woody Grounds: Of making good all Grounds | again, spoiled with over-flowing of Salt water | by Sea-breaches; as also the enriching of the Hop- | Garden. And many other things never | published before. | [rule] | By *G. Markham.* | [rule] | *LONDON,* | Printed for *Hannah Sawbridge,* at the Sign of the *Bible* | on *Ludgate-Hill,* 1684.

[Part six]

A NEW | Orchard & Garden: | OR, | The best way for PLANTING, GRAFFING, and | to make any Ground good for a Rich *Orchard*: Particularly in | the North, and Generally for the whole Common-wealth, as in Nature, | Reason, Situation, and all Probability, may and doth appear. | With the Country House-wifes *Garden* for *Herbs* of Common use. | Their Virtues, Seasons, Ornaments, Variety of Knots, Models | for Trees, and Plots, for the best Ordering of Grounds and Walks. | AS ALSO | The Husbandry of *Bees*, with their several Uses and Annoyances: | *All being the Experience of Forty and Eight Years Labour, And now the* | *Sixth time Corrected, and much Enlarged, By* William Lawson. | Whereunto is newly added the Art of Propagating Plants, with the true | Ordering of all manner of Fruits, in their Gathering, Carrying home, and Preservation. | [woodcut of three gardeners] | [bottom to top to left of woodcut] Skill and Pains, bring fruitful gains. | [bottom to top to right of woodcut] *Nemo sibi natus.* | *London,* Printed for *Hannah Sawbridge,* at the Sign of the *Bible* | on *Ludgate-Hill.* 1683.

Fourteenth edition, London, 1683. Originally published, London, 1623.

4to. [A]⁴ B-X⁴ Aa-Mm⁴ Nn² Aaa-Bbbb⁴ Cccc² Dddd-Ffff⁴, ²A-R⁴, ³A-N⁴ O² (Aaa missigned "Aa"); 370 leaves, pp. [*12*] 1-146 [*10*], ²[*4*] 1-92 [*4*], ³[*8*] 1-80, 73-88, 97-104, 97-188, ⁴[*4*] [1] 2-19 [*20*], ⁵[*6*] 1-126 [*4*], ⁶[*6*] 1-102.

Illustrations: Woodcuts in the text in parts five and six.

Bibliographies: Poynter 34.14; Wing M682. Note: Wing also records Lawson's *A New Orchard and Garden* separately under Wing L737.

Copies: *NUC* (5 copies of Markham's *A Way to Get Wealth,* London, 1683, and 8 copies of Lawson's *A New Orchard and Garden,* London, 1683). Wing (9 copies M682 and 11 under L737).

855. Marnette.

THE | Perfect Cook: | BEING | The most exact Directions for the | making all kind of Pastes, with the | perfect way teaching how to Raise, Season and | make all sorts of Pies, Pasties, Tarts, and Flo- | rentines, &c. now practised by the most Famous | and Expert Cooks, both *French* and *English.* | AS ALSO | The Perfect *English* Cook, | Or

right method of the whole Art | of Cookery, with the true ordering | of *French,
Spanish,* and *Italian* Kickshaws, with | A-la-mode Varieties for Persons of Honour. |
To which is added, | The way of dressing all manner of Flesh, | Fowl, and Fish, and
making admirable Sauces, | after the most refined way of *French* and *English*. | The
like never extant. | [rule] | By Mounsier *Marnette*. | [rule] | *LONDON,* | Printed for
Obadiah Blagrave at the *Black Bear* and | *Star* in St. *Pauls Church-Yard*, over against
the | Little North-Door, 1686.

Second edition, London, 1686. Originally published, London, 1656. Pp. 1-154 are a
translation of *Le Patissier françois*, Paris, 1653 (item 266) attributed to La Varenne,
and pp. 155-213 are a new section titled "The Perfect English Cook."

12mo. π^2 A^6 B-K^{12}; 116 leaves, pp. [*16*] 1-213 [214-216].

Illustration: Engraved frontispiece titled "The French Pastery-Cooke" on $\pi1^v$. This is
the same frontispiece as was used in *Le Patissier François*, Amsterdam, 1655, which,
according to Oxford, was by R. Vaughn. This engraving is
unsigned but cross-hatching in the lower right corner could cover a removed signature.

Bibliographies: Oxford, p. 28, in a note; Vicaire 566; Wing M706A.

Copies: *NUC* (New York Public Library only). Wing also records only the New York
Public Library copy.

856. Marshall, Agnes Bertha, d. 1905.

FORTIETH THOUSAND | [short rule] | MRS A. B. MARSHALL'S | COOKERY
BOOK | REVISED AND ENLARGED EDITION | *WITH 125 ILLUSTRATIONS* |
𝔏onđon | MARSHALL'S SCHOOL OF COOKERY, 30 & 32 MORTIMER STREET
| SIMPKIN, MARSHALL, HAMILTON, KENT & CO. LIMITED | 4
STATIONERS'-HALL COURT | *Infringements of copyright will be prosecuted*

Fortieth thousand, London, ca. 1900. Originally published, London, 1888. The
original edition numbers 468 pages.

183 x 120 mm. [A]^4 B-QQ^8 RR^4; 312 leaves, pp. [*8*] [1] 2-576, ^{2}1-40. Leaves
PP1-RR4 contain advertisements; rear free end paper numbered as page 41 and, like
the other end papers, contains advertisements. Green cloth stamped in gold.

Illustrations: Engraved frontispiece portrait of the author printed on coated paper, and 125 wood engravings in the text plus additional wood engravings in the advertisements.

Bibliographies: This edition unrecorded in the bibliographies consulted.

Copies: No other copy described as fortieth thousand located, however the *NUC* does locate two copies (Kansas State University and National Agricultural Library) with 576 pages.

856a. Marshall, Agnes Bertha, d. 1905.

MRS A. B. MARSHALL'S | [red] LARGER COOKERY BOOK | OF | EXTRA RECIPES | [short rule] | [red] DEDICATED | BY PERMISSION | TO | [red] H.R.H. PRINCESS CHRISTIAN | [short rule] | *WITH TWO HUNDRED AND EIGHTY-FOUR ILLUSTRATIONS* | 𝕷𝖔𝖓𝖉𝖔𝖓 | MARSHALL'S SCHOOL OF COOKERY | 30 & 32 MORTIMER STREET, W. | AND SIMPKIN, MARSHALL, HAMILTON, KENT & CO. LTD. | STATIONERS'-HALL COURT, E.C.

First edition, London, 1891.

258 x 167 mm. [A]² B-UU⁸ XX⁶; 344 leaves, pp. [4] [1-5] 6-656, ²[1-2] 3-28. Publisher's dark green cloth stamped in blind and gold.

Note: Errata slip tipped in before p. 5, reading: *CORRECTION:* | Page 272, Line 8, for "pint" read "pinch."

Illustrations: Frontispiece portrait of the author printed on heavier stock and tipped in; 284 wood engravings in the text. The last 28 pages contain illustrated advertisements.

Bibliographies: Axford, p. 279; Bitting, p. 310.

Copies: *BMC* and *NUC* (Library of Congress only).

857. Marshall, Agnes Bertha, d. 1905.

ELEVENTH THOUSAND | MRS A. B. MARSHALL'S | [in red] LARGER COOKERY BOOK | OF | EXTRA RECIPES | [short rule] | [in red] DEDICATED | BY PERMISSION | TO | [in red] H.R.H. PRINCES CHRISTIAN | [short rule] | *WITH TWO HUNDRED AND EIGHTY-FOUR ILLUSTRATIONS* | 𝕷𝖔𝖓𝖉𝖔𝖓 |

MARSHALL'S SCHOOL OF COOKERY | 32 & 30 MORTIMER STREET, W. | AND SIMPKIN, MARSHALL, HAMILTON, KENT, & CO. LTD. | STATIONERS'-HALL COURT, E.C.

Eleventh thousand, London, 1902. Originally published, London, 1891 (item 856a).

258 x 165 mm. [A]^2 B-XX^8 YY^4; 350 leaves, pp. [*4*] [1-5] 6-622 [2] 623-656, ^{2}1-38. Publisher's dark green cloth, stamped in gold.

Illustrations: Frontispiece portrait of the author and 284 wood engravings in the text. The last 38 pages contain illustrated advertisements.

Bibliographies: Driver 688.8; Wheaton and Kelly 3976.

Copies: *NUC* (National Agricultural Library only). Driver (Texas Woman's University only). Wheaton and Kelly (Radcliffe only).

858. Marshall, Elizabeth.

THE | Young Ladies' Guide | IN THE | ART of COOKERY: | Being a COLLECTION of useful | RECEIPTS, | Published for the Convenience of the | LADIES committed to her Care. | [rule] | By ELIZ. MARSHALL. | [two rules] | *NEWCASTLE;* | Printed by T. SAINT, for the AUTHOR. | [short rule] | MDCCLXXVII.

First edition, Newcastle-upon-Tyne, 1777.

8vo. π^2 A-Cc^4; 106 leaves, pp. [i-iii] iv [1] 2-199 [200] [8]. Last leaf, blank.

Bibliographies: Axford, p. 432; Bitting, p. 311; Maclean, p. 94; Oxford, p. 108; Vicaire 568.

Copies: *NUC* (Library of Congress only). Maclean adds British Library and Newcastle-upon-Tyne Public Library.

859. Marshall's Improved Family Ledger.

MARSHALL'S | Improved Family Ledger, | AND | House=keeper's | ACCOUNT BOOK, | [two short rules] | FOR 1831. | [two short rules] | ADAPTED FOR | KEEPING A DAILY STATEMENT OF FAMILY EXPENCES. | [short fancy rule] |

WITH ENGRAVED ILLUSTRATIONS | *Of the Art of Carving, and a Dinner of Two Courses for every Month,* | VALUABLE RECIPES, A COLLECTION OF TABLES, &c. | [two short rules] | LONDON: | PRINTED BY W. J. RUFFY, 29, BUDGE ROW; | PUBLISHED BY W. MARSHALL, 1, MIDDLE ROW, HOLBORN BARS; | SOLD ALSO BY | THORP & BURCH, JEWRY STREET, ALDGATE; AND C. PENNY, BOW LANE. | [short fancy rule] | PRICE TWO SHILLINGS.

First edition, London, 1830.

198 x 158 mm. [A]⁴ B-M⁴; 48 leaves, pp. [1] 2-96. Publisher's printed wrappers.

Illustrations: Wood engravings in the text illustrating table settings and carving.

Bibliographies: Unrecorded in the bibliographies consulted.

Copies: *BMC.*

860. Martin, Sarah.

THE | NEW EXPERIENCED | ENGLISH-HOUSEKEEPER, | *FOR THE USE AND EASE* | OF | LADIES, HOUSEKEEPERS, COOKS, &c. | WRITTEN PURELY FROM HER OWN PRACTICE | *By Mrs. Sarah Martin,* | MANY YEARS HOUSEKEEPER | *TO THE LATE FREEMAN BOWER ESQ.* | OF BAWTRY. | BEING | AN ENTIRE NEW COLLECTION OF ORIGINAL | RECEIPTS WHICH HAVE NEVER APPEARED IN | PRINT, IN EVERY BRANCH OF | COOKERY, CONFECTIONARY, *&c.* | [two short rules] | DONCASTER: | *PRINTED FOR THE AUTHORESS* | BY D. BOYS. | AND SOLD BY MESS. F. & C. RIVINGTON, ST. PAUL's CHURCH-YARD, | LONDON. | MDCCXCV. | *(Entered at Stationers' Hall.)*

First edition, Doncaster, 1795.

8vo. [A]⁴ B⁴ C⁴ (-C4), ²B-Bb⁴; 107 leaves, pp. [22] [1] 2-173 [174] [*18*].

Bibliographies: Axford, p. 293; Bitting, p. 312; Maclean, p. 95; Oxford, p. 123; Pennell, p. 166.

Copies: *BMC* and *NUC* (Cornell, Harvard, and Library of Congress). Maclean adds Brotherton Library, Glasgow University, and New York Public Library.

861. Mason, Charlotte.

THE | LADY's ASSISTANT | FOR | REGULATING and SUPPLYING her TABLE; | CONTAINING | ONE HUNDRED AND FIFTY SELECT BILLS OF FARE, | Properly disposed for | FAMILY DINNERS | Of Five Dishes, to Two Courses of Eleven and Fifteen; | With upwards of | FIFTY BILLS OF FARE | FOR | SUPPERS, | From Five Dishes to Nineteen; | AND | SEVERAL DESERTS: | Including a considrable Number of | CHOICE RECEIPTS | OF VARIOUS KINDS, | WITH Directions for preparing them in the most | approved Manner: | Now First Published from the MANUSCRIPT COLLECTION of | A PROFESSED HOUSEKEEPER; | Who had upwards of Thirty Years Experience in Families of the First Fashion. | [two rules] | LONDON: | Printed for J. WALTER, at Homer's Head, Charing-Cross. | M.DCC.LXXIII.

First edition, London, 1773.

8vo. [A]² B-Dd⁸ Ee²; 212 leaves, pp. [i-iii] iv [1] 2-408 [*12*].

Bibliographies: Maclean, p. 95; Vicaire 572. Bitting records the Dublin, 1778, edition.

Copies: Maclean records National Library of Wales and Kansas State University copies only.

862. Mason, Charlotte.

THE | LADY's ASSISTANT | FOR | Regulating and Supplying her TABLE, | BEING A | COMPLETE SYSTEM OF COOKERY, | CONTAINING | One Hundred and Fifty select BILLS of FARE, properly | disposed for FAMILY DINNERS of Five Dishes, | to Two Courses of Eleven and Fifteen; | With upwards of | Fifty BILLS of FARE for SUPPERS, from Five Dishes to Nineteen; | AND | SEVERAL DESERTS: | Including likewise, | The fullest and choicest RECEIPTS of various Kinds, | WITH | Full Directions for preparing them in the most approved Manner, | from which a continual Change may be made, as wanted, in the | several BILLS of FARE: | [rule] | Published from the MANUSCRIPT COLLECTION of | Mrs. CHARLOTTE MASON, | A PROFESSED HOUSEKEEPER, who had upwards of Thirty Years | Experience in Families of the first Fashion. | [rule] | The SECOND EDITION corrected, and considerably enlarged. | [rule] | "The most refin'd understanding and the most exalted sentiments do not place a | "woman above the little duties of life." | Mrs. GRIFFITH. | [two rules] | LONDON: | Printed for J. WALTER, at Homer's-Head, Charing-Cross. | M.DCC.LXXV.

Second edition, London, 1775. Originally published, London, 1773 (item 861).

8vo. [A]^2 B-Ff^8 Gg^8 (-Gg8) Hh-Ii^8; 251 leaves, pp. [i-v] vi [vii-viii] [1] 2-471 [472-492] [2]. Last leaf (blank?) wanting in this copy.

Bibliographies: Maclean, p. 95; Oxford, p. 107; Pennell, p. 161; Vicaire 573; Wheaton and Kelly 4000. Bitting records the Dublin, 1778, edition.

Copies: Maclean locates Brotherton Library, Kansas State University, and New York Public Library. Wheaton and Kelly (Radcliffe only).

863. Mason, Charlotte.

THE | LADIES' ASSISTANT | FOR | Regulating and Supplying the TABLE, | BEING A | COMPLETE SYSTEM OF COOKERY, &c. | CONTAINING | The most SELECT BILLS of FARE, properly disposed, | For FAMILY DINNERS of Five Dishes | To Two Courses of Eleven and Fifteen; | WITH | BILLS of FARE for SUPPERS, from Five Dishes to Nineteen; | AND | SEVERAL DESERTS: | INCLUDING | The fullest and choicest RECEIPTS of various Kinds, | AND | Full Directions for preparing them in the most approved Manner, | by which a continual Change may be made, as wanted, from the | several BILLS of FARE. | LIKEWISE | Directions for Brewing, Making English Wines, Raspberry, Orange, | and Lemon-Brandies, &c. | ALSO | REMARKS on KITCHEN-POISONS, and necessary Cautions thereon. | [rule] | Originally published from the MANUSCRIPT COLLECTION of | Mrs. CHARLOTTE MASON, | A PROFESSED HOUSEKEEPER, | Who had upwards of Thirty Years Experience in Families of the first Fashion. | [rule] | A NEW EDITION, | ENLARGED, CORRECTED, AND IMPROVED, TO THE PRESENT TIME. | [rule] | "The most refin'd understanding and the most exalted sentiments do not place a | "woman above the little duties of life." Mrs. GRIFFITH. | [two rules] | LONDON: | Printed for J. WALTER, at Homer's-Head, Charing-Cross. | [short rule] | M.DCC.LXXXVI.

Fifth edition, London, 1786. Originally published, London, 1773 (item 861).

8vo. a^8 b^2 B-Ii^8 Kk^4; 262 leaves, pp. [20] [1] 2-484 [20].

Bibliographies: Maclean, p. 95; Oxford, p. 108, in a note; Wheaton and Kelly 4002. Bitting records the Dublin, 1778, edition.

Copies: *BMC, BNC,* and *NUC* (Harvard only). Maclean adds Brotherton Library, Wellcome Library, New York Academy of Medicine, and New York Public Library.

864. Mason, Charlotte.

THE | LADY's ASSISTANT | FOR | REGULATING AND SUPPLYING THE
TABLE; | BEING A | *COMPLETE SYSTEM OF COOKERY.* | CONTAINING THE
MOST | SELECT BILLS OF FARE, | PROPERLY DISPOSED, | FOR FAMILY
DINNERS OF FIVE DISHES TO TWO COURSES OF ELEVEN AND FIFTEEN; |
WITH BILLS OF FARE FOR SUPPERS, | FROM FIVE TO NINETEEN DISHES; |
AND | SEVERAL DESSERTS: | INCLUDING THE | FULLEST AND CHOICEST
RECEIPTS OF VARIOUS KINDS, | And full Directions for preparing them in the
most approved Manner, by which a continual Change | may be made, as wanted, from
the several Bills of Fare. | LIKEWISE, | DIRECTIONS FOR BREWING, | MAKING
ENGLISH WINES, RASPBERRY, ORANGE, AND LEMON-BRANDIES, &c. |
ALSO, REMARKS ON KITCHEN POISONS, | AND NECESSARY CAUTIONS
THEREON. | *WITH AN APPENDIX,* | CONTAINING GENERAL PARTICULARS
ON THE | BREEDING, REARING, AND MANAGEMENT OF POULTRY, | On the
Business of the DAIRY; and on the Management of the KITCHEN and FRUIT
GARDEN. | [two short rules] | Originally published from the Manuscript Collection of
| *Mrs. CHARLOTTE MASON,* | A PROFESSED HOUSEKEEPER, | Who had
upwards of Thirty Years Experience in Families of the First Fashion. | [short fancy
rule] | 𝕿𝔥𝔢 𝕰𝔦𝔤𝔥𝔱𝔥 𝕰𝔡𝔦𝔱𝔦𝔬𝔫, | ENLARGED, CORRECTED, AND IMPROVED, TO
THE PRESENT TIME. | [short fancy rule] | "The most refined understanding and the
most exalted sentiments do not place a woman above the | "little duties of life" *Mrs.
Griffith.* | [two short rules] | *LONDON:* | PRINTED BY C. WHITTINGHAM, | *Dean
Street, Fetter Lane,* | FOR J. WALTER; VERNOR AND HOOD; J. SCATCHERD;
E. NEWBERY; J. SEWELL; | T. HURST; R. LEA; LACKINGTON, ALLEN, AND
CO. W. J. AND J. RICHARDSON; | J. MATHEWS; P. M`QUEEN; CROSBY AND
LETTERMAN; T. KAY; AND J. TINDAL. | [short fancy rule] | 1801.

Ninth edition, styled "Eighth edition" on the title-page, London, 1801. Originally
published, London, 1773 (item 861).

210 x 130 mm. [A]^8 a^2 B-Gg^8 Hh^2; 244 leaves, pp. [1-3] 4 [5-20], ^{2}[1] 2-422, ^{3}[1-2]
3-25 [26] [*20*].

Bibliographies: Axford, p. 244; Roscoe A331; Simon BG 1015. Bitting records the
Dublin, 1778, edition and Maclean eight eighteenth century editions.

Copies: *BMC.*

865. Massialot, François, ca. 1660-1733.

[within a border of two rules] THE | *Court and Country Cook:* | GIVING | New and Plain DIRECTIONS | How to Order all manner of | ENTERTAINMENTS, | And the best sort of the | Most exquisite *a-la-mode* RAGOO'S. | Together with | NEW INSTRUCTIONS | FOR | *CONFECTIONERS:* | SHEWING | How to Preserve all sorts of FRUTIS, as well | dry as liquid: Also, | How to make divers SUGAR-WORKS, and other | fine Pieces of Curiosity; | How to set out a DESERT, or Banquet of | SWEET-MEATS to the best advantage; And, | How to Prepare several sorts of LIQUORS, that | are proper for every Season of the Year. | A WORK more especially necessary for Stewards, | Clerks of the Kitchen, Confectioners, Butlers, and | other Officers, and also of great use in private Families. | [rule] | *Faithfully translated out of French into English by* J.K. | [rule] | *London:* Printed by *W. Onley,* for *A.* and *J. Churchill,* at | the Black Swan in *Pater-noster-row,* and *M. Gillyflower* | in *Westminster-hall,* 1702.

First edition in English, London, 1702. The first part is translated from Massialot's *Le Cuisinier roial et bourgeois,* Paris, 1691 (item 316) and the second and third parts from his *Nouvelle Instruction pour les confitures, les liqueurs, et les fruits,* Paris, 1692 (item 320).

8vo. a-d⁴ B-S⁸ T⁸(T2+aa-bb⁴) V-Dd⁸ Ee⁴ Ff²; 238 leaves, pp. [*32*] 1-276, ²[*16*] 1-130, ³1-20 [2].

Illustrations: Nine engraved plates and two woodcuts in the text, all illustrating table settings.

Bibliographies: Axford, p. 103; Bitting, p. 538; Maclean, p. 97; Oxford, p. 47; Wheaton and Kelly 4072.

Copies: *NUC* (5 copies). Maclean adds the Brotherton Library, Kansas State University, and New York Public Library.

866. Masters, Thomas.

THE | ICE BOOK: | BEING | A COMPENDIOUS & CONCISE HISTORY | OF | EVERYTHING CONNECTED WITH ICE | FROM ITS FIRST INTRODUCTION INTO EUROPE AS AN ARTICLE | OF LUXURY TO THE PRESENT TIME; | WITH AN ACCOUNT OF THE | 𝔄𝔯𝔱𝔦𝔣𝔦𝔠𝔦𝔞𝔩 𝔐𝔞𝔫𝔫𝔢𝔯 𝔬𝔣 𝔓𝔯𝔬𝔡𝔲𝔠𝔦𝔫𝔤 𝔓𝔲𝔯𝔢 & 𝔖𝔬𝔩𝔦𝔡 𝔍𝔠𝔢, | AND | A VALUABLE COLLECTION OF THE MOST APPROVED

RECIPES FOR | MAKING SUPERIOR WATER ICES AND ICE CREAMS | AT A
FEW MINUTES' NOTICE. | BY THOMAS MASTERS. | "Tut! tut! thou art all *ice*, |
Thy kindness *freezes*. | RICHARD III. *– Act IV. Scene 2*. | LONDON: | SIMPKIN,
MARSHALL, & CO., STATIONERS' HALL COURT, | LUDGATE STREET. |
1844.

First edition, London, 1844.

222 x 141 mm. [a]⁴ b² B-N⁸ O⁶; 108 leaves, pp. [i-v] vi-xii [1] 2-198 [6]. Bound in
publisher's lavender cloth stamped in gold.

Illustrations: Six lithographed plates illustrating T. Masters' Patent Freezing
Apparatus, plus two plates illustrating a rotary knife-cleaner followed by three folding
plates of advertisements.

Bibliographies: Bitting, p. 315; Noling, p. 282; Oxford, p. 174; Wheaton and Kelly
4078.

Copies: *BMC* and *NUC* (8 copies).

867. May, Robert.

[within a single rule border] | THE | Accomplisht Cook, | OR THE | ART and
MYSTERY | OF | COOKERY. | Wherein the whole ART is revealed in a | more
easie and perfect Method, than hath | been publisht in any Language. | Expert and
ready Wayes for the Dressing of all Sorts of | FLESH, FOWL, and FISH, with variety
of SAUCES | proper for each of them; and how to raise all manner | of *Pastes*; the
best Directions for all sorts of *Kickshaws*; | also the *Tearms* of CARVING and
SEWING. | An exact Account of all *Dishes* for all *Seasons* of the | Year, with other *A
la mode Curiosities*. | The Third Edition, with large Additions throughout | the whole
Work; besides two hundred Figures of se- | veral Forms for all manner of bake't
Meats, (either | Flesh or Fish) as Pyes, Tarts, Custards, Cheesecakes, | and
Florentines, placed in Tables, and directed to the | Pages they appertain to. | [rule] |
Approved by the fifty five Years Experience and Industry | of *ROBERT MAY*, in his
Attendance on seve- | ral Persons of great Honour. | [rule] | *LONDON,* | Printed for
N. Brooke, and are to be sold by *Tho. Archer* | at his shop under the *Dyal* of St.
Dunstans Church | in *Fleet Street* 1671.

Third edition, London, 1671, the second of two issues, with variant imprints, recorded
in Wing. Originally published, London, 1660.

8vo. A-Ii⁸; 256 leaves, pp. [*32*] 1-461 [*462-472*] [*8*].

Illustrations: Woodcut portrait of the author on Alᵛ and numerous small woodcuts in the text. This copy wanting the four folding plates.

Bibliographies: Oxford, p. 30 in a note; Wing M1393aA. Vicaire 578 records the 1660 edition and Simon BG 1029 the 1678 edition.

Copies: *BMC*. Wing records only the British Library copy of this issue.

868. May, Robert.

[within a single rule border] | THE | Accomplisht Cook, | OR THE | ART & MYSTERY | OF | COOKERY. | Wherein the whole ART is revealed in a | more easie and perfect Method, than hath | been publisht in any language. | Expert and ready Ways for the Dressing of all Sorts | of FLESH, FOWL, and FISH, with variety of | SAUCES proper for each of them; and how to | raise all manner of *Pastes*; the best Directions for | all sorts of *Kickshaws*, also the *Terms* of CAR- | VING and SEWING. | An exact account of all *Dishes* for all *Seasons* of the | Year, with other *A-la-mode Curiosities* | The Fifth Edition, with large Additions throughout | the whole work: besides two hundred Figures of | several Forms for all manner of bak'd Meats, | (either Flesh, or Fish) as, Pyes Tarts, Custards; | Cheesecakes, and Florentines, placed in Tables, | and directed to the Pages they appertain to. | [rule] | Approved by the fifty five Years Experience and In- | dustry of *ROBERT MAY*, in his Atten- | dance on several Persons of great Honour. | [rule] | *London*, Printed for *Obadiah Blagrave* at the *Bear* and | *Star* in St. *Pauls Church-Yard*, 1685.

Fifth edition, London, 1685. Originally published, London, 1660.

8vo. A-Ii⁸; 256 leaves, pp. [*32*] 1-461 [*461-480*]. First leaf wanting in this copy.

Illustrations: Engraved frontispiece portrait of the author and numerous small woodcuts in the text. Four folding plates called for by Bitting wanting in this copy.

Bibliographies: Bitting, p. 318; Oxford, p. 30, in a note; Wheaton and Kelly 4093; Wing M1394. Vicaire 578 records the 1660 edition and Simon BG 1029 the 1678 edition.

Copies: *BMC* and *NUC* (5 copies). Wing (10 copies).

869. Meager, Leonard, 1624?-1704.

[within a border of two rules] THE │ English Gardener: │ OR, A │ Sure guide to young *PLANTERS* │ AND │ GARDENERS │ In three Parts. │ THE FIRST │ Shewing the way and order of Plant- │ ing and raising all sorts of Stocks, Fruit-trees, │ and Shrubs, with the divers ways and manners │ of Ingrafting and Inoculating them in their several Sea- │ sons, Ordering and preservation. │ THE SECOND, │ How to order the Kitchin-Garden, for all sorts of Herbs, │ Roots, and Sallads. │ THE THIRD, │ The ordering of the Garden of pleasure, with varietie of Knots, │ and Wilderness-work after the best fashion, all cut in Copper │ Plates ; also the choicest and most approved ways for the raising all sorts of │ Flowers and their seasons, with directions concerning Arbors, and hedges in Gar- │ dens; likewise several other very useful things fit to be known of all that delight │ in Orchards and Gardens. │ [rule] │ Fitted for the use of all such as delight in Gardning, whereby the meanest capa- │ city need not doubt of success (observing the rules herein directed) in their un- │ dertakings. │ [rule] │ By *Leonard Meager* above thirty years a Practitioner in the Art of │ *GARDENING.* │ [rule] │ *London*, Printed for *T. Peirrepoint*, and sold by the Booksellers of *London*, 1682.

Second edition, London, 1682. Originally published, London, 1670.

4to. A-T^4; 76 leaves, pp. [*8*] 1-144.

Illustrations: Twenty-four engraved plates, the first illustrating pruning and the others geometrical designs for gardens.

Bibliographies: Wing M1569.

Copies: *NUC* (4 copies). Wing (Library Company of Philadelphia, Massachusetts Horticultural Society, and National Agricultural Library).

870. Melroe, Eliza.

AN │ *ECONOMICAL,* │ AND │ NEW │ Method of Cookery; │ DESCRIBING UPWARDS OF │ *EIGHTY* │ Cheap, Wholesome, and Nourishing Dishes, │ CONSISTING OF │ ROAST, BOILED, AND BAKED MEATS; │ STEWS, FRIES, │ *And above Forty Soups*; │ A VARIETY OF │ *PUDDINGS, PIES, &c.* │ WITH NEW AND USEFUL │ OBSERVATIONS │ ON │ *Rice, Barley, Pease, Oatmeal, and Milk,* │ AND THE NUMEROUS DISHES THEY AFFORD, │ *Adapted to* │ THE NECESSITY OF THE TIMES, │ Equally in all Ranks of Society, │ [fancy rule] │ *By ELIZA MELROE,* │ [fancy rule] │ "OEconomy is the source of Plenty." │ "Bury not your Talent." │ [fancy rule] │ London: Printed and published for the Author, by C.

CHAPPLE, No. 66, | PALL-MALL; sold also by T. N. LONGMAN, | Paternoster-Row; | and all other Booksellers in Town and Country. | Price 2s. 6d. or six for 10.6d. if purchased by Clubs of the labouring | Poor, or intended for their Use. | [fancy rule] | 1798. | ENTERED AT STATIONER's-HALL.

First edition, London, 1798.

8vo. [A]² B-F⁸ G⁶; 48 leaves, pp. [1-2] 3-94 [2]. Last leaf (blank?) wanting in this copy.

Bibliographies: Axford, p. 128; Bitting, p. 319; Maclean, p. 99; Oxford, p. 125; Simon BG 1033; Vicaire 581; Wheaton and Kelly 4111.

Copies: *BMC* and *NUC* (6 copies). Maclean adds Brotherton Library, Dorset County Library, and Detroit Public Library.

871. Menon.

THE ART OF | MODERN COOKERY | DISPLAYED. | Consisting of the most approved METHODS of | *Cookery, Pastry,* and *Confectionary* | Of the PRESENT TIME. | TRANSLATED FROM | *Les Soupers de la Cour*, ou, *La Cuisine Reformée*; the | last and most complete Practice of Cookery published | in French. | To which are added, | Explanatory Notes and References, together with the Produce | of the London Markets; | By the TRANSLATOR, | A Foreigner, who has been several Years a Clerk of the Kit- | chen in Noble Families in this Kingdom. | In this Work the French Names are preserved, and explained, for | the mutual Ease and Instruction of Natives and Foreigners. | [rule] | VOL. I. | [rule] | LONDON: | Printed for the TRANSLATOR. | Sold by R. DAVIS, in Piccadilly. | MDCCLXVII.

Volume two has a half-title only:

[row of type ornaments] | THE | ART | OF | MODERN COOKERY | DISPLAYED. | VOL. II. | [row of type ornaments]

First edition, London, 1767, of this translation by Bernard Clermont of Menon's *Les Soupers de la Cour*. The French edition originally published, Paris, 1755 (item 344). For the second English edition, London, 1769, the title was changed to *The Professed Cook*.

8vo. 2 volumes bound as one with continuous signatures and pagination. a⁸ π a⁸ b⁴ π b⁸ c⁴ B-Pp⁸; 328 leaves, pp. [i-iii] iv-xvi [*48*] [1] 2-286 [*4*] 289-588 [2]. Last leaf blank.

Bibliographies: Axford, p. 20; Bitting, p. 519; Maclean, p. 99; Vicaire 49. Oxford, p. 101, records the 1769 edition; Wheaton and Kelly 4125.

Copies: *NUC* (Radcliffe, Library of Congress, and New York Academy of Medicine). Maclean adds Bodleian Library.

872. Menon.

THE │ French Family Cook: │ BEING │ A complete System of French Cookery. │ Adapted to the Tables not only of the Opulent, but of │ Persons of moderate Fortune and Condition. │ CONTAINING │ Directions for choosing, dressing, and serving up all Sorts of │ Butcher Meat, Poultry, &c. │ The different Modes of making all kinds of Soups, Ragouts, │ Fricandeaus, Creams, Ratafias, Compôts, Preserves, &c. &c. − │ as well as a great Variety of cheap and elegant Side Dishes, │ calculated to grace a Table at a small Expence. │ Instructions for making out Bills of Fare for the four Seasons of │ the Year, and to furnish a Table with few or any number of │ Dishes at the most moderate possible Expence. │ Necessary for Housekeepers, Butlers, Cooks, and all who are concerned │ in the Superintendence of a Family. │ [short fancy rule] │ TRANSLATED FROM THE FRENCH. │ [short fancy rule] │ LONDON: │ Printed for J. BELL, No. 148, Oxford Street, nearly │ opposite New Bond Street. │ M.DCC.XCIII.

First edition, London, 1793, in English of Menon's *La Cuisinière bourgeoise*, originally published in French, Paris, 1746 (item 336).

8vo. A⁴ a⁸ b⁴ B-Y⁸ Z⁴; 188 leaves, pp. [8] [iii] iv-xviii, xvii-xxiv [1] 2-342 [2].

Bibliographies: Axford, p. 172; Bitting, p. 554; Maclean, p. 101; Oxford, p. 121; Pennell, p. 166; Simon BG 714.

Copies: Maclean locates Bodleian Library, Brotherton Library, Cambridge, Cornell, Library of Congress, and New York Public Library.

873. Middleton, John.

[within a border of two rules] Five Hundred │ NEW RECEIPTS │ IN │ [in two columns: column one] COOKERY, │ CONFECTIONARY, │ PASTRY, │ }{ │ [column two] PRESERVING, │ CONSERVING, │ PICKLING; [end columns] │ AND THE │ Several Branches of these ARTS │ necessary to be known by all good │

HOUSEWIVES. | [rule] | By *JOHN MIDDLETON,* | Cook to his Grace the late Duke of *Bolton.* | [rule] | Revised and Recommended by | Mr. *HENRY HOWARD.* | [rule] | [publisher's device] | *LONDON:* | Printed for THO. ASTLEY, at the *Rose* | against the North Door of St. *Paul's.* | [short rule] | M DCC XXXIV.

First edition, London, 1734.

8vo. A^4 B-R^8; 132 leaves, pp. [2] i-iv, 1-249 [250-258].

Bibliographies: Axford, p. 159; Bitting, p. 324; Craig 61; Maclean, p. 101; Oxford, p. 64; Schraemli (1) 353; 64; Vicaire 598.

Copies: *BMC* and *NUC* (4 copies). Maclean adds Brotherton Library and Kansas State University.

874. Miles, Eustace Hamilton, b. 1868.

Muscle, Brain, and Diet | A | PLEA FOR SIMPLER FOODS | BY | EUSTACE H. MILES, M.A. (CAMB.) | *Winner of the Tennis Gold Prize 1897, 1898, 1899, Amateur* *Champion* | *1899; Winner of the Open Competition in the Amateur Racket Cham-* | *pionship 1899; Classical Honours Coach at Cambridge University;* | *Author of* *"Lessons in Lawn Tennis", "How to Learn* | *Philology", "How to Prepare Essays", etc.* | [publisher's monogram] | LONDON | SWAN SONNENSCHEIN & CO., LIM. | NEW YORK: THE MACMILLAN COMPANY | 1900

First edition, London, 1900.

188 x 120 mm. π^8 A-X^8 Y^2 Z^4; 182 leaves, pp. [i-iv] v-xv [xvi] [1] 2-345 [346] [2]. Last leaf blank.

Note: From the library of Ian Fleming.

Bibliographies: Wheaton and Kelly 4176.

Copies: *BMC.* Wheaton and Kelly (Harvard only).

875. Miller, Philip, 1691-1771.

THE | GARDENERS KALENDAR; | Directing what WORKS are necessary to be performed | EVERY MONTH | IN THE | *Kitchen, Fruit,* and *Pleasure-Gardens,* | As also in the | Conservatory *and* Nursery: | SHEWING | I. The particular SEASONS for PROPAGATING | all Sorts of ESCULENT PLANTS and FRUITS, with the | Time when each Sort is proper for the Table. | II. The proper SEASONS for Transplanting all Sorts of | TREES, SHRUBS, and PLANTS, with the Time of their | Flowering. | [rule] | BY PHILIP MILLER, F. R. S. | Member of the Botanick Academy at FLORENCE, and | Gardener to the Worshipful Company of APOTHECARIES, | at their Botanick Garden in *Chelsea.* | [rule] | The FOURTEENTH EDITION, | With a LIST of the MEDICINAL PLANTS, which | may be gathered for Use each MONTH. | To which is prefixed, | A short INTRODUCTION to the SCIENCE of | BOTANY, illustrated with Copper Plates. | [two rules] | *LONDON:* | Printed for the AUTHOR; | And sold by JOHN RIVINGTON in *St. Paul's Churh-Yard,* | H. WOODFALL, A. MILLAR, J. WHISTON and B. WHITE, | G. HAWKINS, J. HINTON, R. BALDWIN, L. HAWES and | W. CLARKE and R. COLLINS, W. JOHNSTON, T. LONG- | MAN, T. CASLON, B. LAW, C. RIVINGTON, Z. STUART, | J. DODSLEY, and M. RICHARDSON. 1765.

Fourteenth edition, London, 1765. Originally published, London, 1732.

8vo. A⁸ a-c⁸ d1 B-Bb⁸ Cc⁸(-Cc8=d1); 232 leaves, pp. [i-v] vi-xv [xvi] [1] 2-50, ²[1] 2-376 [22].

Illustrations: Engraved allegorical frontispiece and five engraved folding plates illustrating parts of plants.

Bibliographies: Henrey III.1141.

Copies: *BMC* and *NUC* (7 copies).

876. Modern Confectionary.

MODERN | CONFECTIONARY; | CONTAINING | RECEIPTS | FOR | DRYING AND CANDYING, COMFITS, CAKES, PRESERVES, | LIQUEURS, ICES, JELLIES, CREAMS, SPONGES, | PASTES, POTTED MEATS, PICKLES, | WINES, ETC. ETC. ETC. | [short rule] | BY THE | AUTHOR OF THE MODERN COOKERY. | [short rule] | DERBY: | PRINTED BY AND FOR H. MOZLEY, BROOK-STREET; | and sold | BY COWIE, LOW AND CO. POULTRY, LONDON. | 1826.

First edition, Derby, 1826.

152 x 91 mm. [A]² B-S⁶ T⁴; 108 leaves, pp. [1-5] 6-213 [214] [2]. Last leaf (blank?) wanting in this copy. Modern boards with original printed front paper cover preserved.

Bibliographies: Axford, p. 273, and Bitting, p. 2, attributing this work to Eliza Acton, probably on the strength of the statement on the title-page that this work is "by the author of the Modern Cookery." However, as Eliza Acton's *Modern Cookery in all its Branches* was not published until 1845 (item 533) it is more likely that the reference here is to *The Modern Cookery*, Derby, 1818, also published by Henry Mozley (item 877).

Copies: *NUC* (Library of Congress only).

877. The Modern Cookery.

THE | MODERN COOKERY, | WRITTEN UPON | THE MOST APPROVED | AND | ECONOMICAL PRINCIPLES, | AND IN WHICH | EVERY RECEIPT HAS STOOD THE TEST | OF EXPERIENCE. | [short fancy rule] | BY A LADY. | [short fancy rule] | [vignette] | DERBY: | PRINTED BY AND FOR HENRY MOZLEY. | 1818.

First edition, Derby, 1818.

153 x 95 mm. [A]² B-P⁶; 86 leaves, pp. [4] [13] 14-171 [172-180]. Publisher's printed paper covered boards.

Illustrations: Wood engraved frontispiece and vignette on title-page, and six illustrations in the text showing table settings.

Bibliographies: This edition unrecorded in the bibliographies consulted. Oxford, p. 149, records the second edition, 1820; Axford, p. 274, and Bitting, p. 579, the eighth edition, 1843; and Simon BG 1060 the tenth edition, 1856.

Copies: No other copy of this edition located.

878. The Modern Method of Regulating and Forming a Table.

THE | MODERN METHOD | OF | REGULATING and FORMING | A | TABLE, | EXPLAINED and DISPLAYED. | CONTAINING | A great Variety of DINNERS laid out in the most elegant Taste, | from two Courses of Five and Five, to Twenty-one and | Twenty-one Dishes; finely represented, | ON | ONE HUNDRED and

FIFTY-TWO COPPER PLATES. | TOGETHER WITH | Twelve elegant DINNERS for different Seasons of the Year. | AND | A correct LIST of such Particulars as are in Season during every Month. | THE WHOLE | Calculated for the Use and Ease of LADIES, CLERKS of the KITCHEN, | HOUSE-KEEPRS, &c. | [rule] | By several eminent COOKS, and others well acquainted with these Arts. | [rule] | Printed for J. HUGHES, opposite the Duke of Grafton's, in Old Bond-Street; and | S. CROWDER, N°. 12, Pater-noster-Row.

First edition, London, ca. 1760.

Folio: π² a⁴(-a4) [A]² B-4P² 4Q1(=a4) [R]² (R1+1); 177 leaves, pp. [i-iii] iv, ²i-vi, ff. [*1*] 1-39, 41-170 [*1*] 171. Ff. 170 and 171 and the plate between them are folding leaves, two with letterpress and one with engraved plates on recto and verso, showing table settings too large for the normal folio leaves of the volume.

Illustrations: Engraved plates of table settings on the versos of 168 leaves and the recto and verso of the folding leaf between folios 170 and 171.

Bibliographies: Bitting, p. 579; Maclean, p. 102; Oxford, p. 80; Wheaton and Kelly 4209.

Copies: *BMC* and *NUC* (Harvard and Library of Congress). Maclean adds Brotherton Library.

879. Moffett, Thomas, 1553-1604.

Healths Improvement: | *OR,* | RULES | Comprizing and Discovering | the *Nature, Method,* and *Manner* of | *Preparing* all sorts of | FOOD | Used in this NATION. | [rule] | Written by that ever Famous | *THOMAS MUFFETT,* | Doctor in PHYSICK: | [rule] | Corrected and Enlarged | BY | *CHRISTOPHER BENNET,* | Doctor in Physick, and Fellow of the | Colledg of Physitians in *London.* | [rule] | LONDON, | Printed by *Tho: Newcomb* for *Samuel Thomson,* at the | sign of the white Horse in *Pauls* Churchyard, 1655.

First edition, London, 1655.

4to. [A]⁴ B-Pp⁴; 152 leaves, pp. [1-7] 8, ²1-296.

Bibliographies: Axford, p. 198; Craig 63; Oxford, p. 27; Pennell, p. 133; Schraemli (1) 361; Simon BG 1063; Viacire 613; Wheaton and Kelly 4268; Wing M2382.

Copies: *BMC, BNC,* and *NUC* (15 copies). Wing (12 copies).

Note: The author's name is variously spelled Moffet, Moffett, Mouffet, Mouffett, Muffet, and Muffett. Moffett is preferred by *NUC*, Mouffet by *BMC*, and Muffett by *BNC*.

880. Moffett, Thomas, 1553-1604.

HEALTH's Improvement: | OR, | RULES | Comprizing and Discovering the | NATURE, METHOD and MANNER | Of PREPARING all sorts of | FOODS | Used in this NATION. | [rule] | Written by that ever Famous | *THOMAS MOFFET*, | Doctor in Physick. | [rule] | Corrected and Enlarged by CHRISTOPHER | BENNET, Doctor in Physick, and Fellow of | the College of Physicians in *London*. | [rule] | To which is now prefix'd, | A short View of the AUTHOR's LIFE and | WRITINGS, by Mr. OLDYS. | AND | An INTRODUCTION, by R. JAMES, M.D. | [two rules] | *LONDON:* | Printed for T. OSBORNE in *Gray's-Inn* | [short rule] | MDCCXLVI.

New edition, London, 1746. Originally published, London, 1655 (item 879).

12mo. a^{12} b^4 A-Q^{12} R^8; 216 leaves, pp. [i-vii] viii-xxxii [1] 2-398 [2]. Last leaf blank.

Bibliographies: Bitting, p. 327; Maclean, p. 104; Oxford, p. 28, in a note; Pennell, p. 134; Simon BG 1064; Wheaton and Kelly 4269.

Copies: *BMC* and *NUC* (4 copies). Maclean adds Brotherton Library and Edinburgh Royal College of Physicians.

881. Mollard, John.

THE | ART OF COOKERY | *MADE EASY AND REFINED*; | COMPRISING | AMPLE DIRECTIONS FOR PREPARING EVERY ARTICLE | REQUISITE FOR FURNISHING THE TABLES | OF THE | NOBLEMAN, GENTLEMAN, AND TRADESMAN. | BY | JOHN MOLLARD, COOK; | Lately one of the Proprietors of Freemasons' Tavern, Great | Queen Street, Lincoln's Inn Fields; now removed to | Dover Street, Picadilly, formerly THOMAS'S. | *SECOND EDITION.* | [two short rules] | *LONDON:* | PRINTED FOR THE AUTHOR, | AND SOLD BY J. NUNN, GREAT QUEEN STREET, LINCOLN'S | INN FIELDS, AND ALL BOOKSELLERS IN TOWN | AND COUNTRY. | [short rule] | 1802. | *T. Bensley, Bolt Court, Fleet Street*.

Second edition, London, 1802. Originally published, London, 1801.

211 x 128 mm. [a]^4 b^8 B-Y^8; 180 leaves, pp. [i-v] vi-xxiv [1] 2-314 [*22*].

Illustrations: Twelve engraved plates with bills of fare.

Bibliographies: Axford, p. 17; Bitting, p. 328; Oxford, p. 131, in a note; Wheaton and Kelly 4214.

Copies: *NUC* (Boston Public Library and Library of Congress).

882. Mollard, John.

THE | ART OF COOKERY | MADE EASY AND REFINED; | COMPRISING | AMPLE DIRECTIONS FOR PREPARING EVERY ARTICLE REQUISITE FOR | FURNISHING THE TABLES | OF THE | NOBLEMAN, GENTLEMAN, AND TRADESMAN. | [short fancy rule] | BY | MR. JOHN MOLLARD, | OF THE LONDON TAVERN. | [short fancy rule] | *FOURTH EDITION.* | [short fancy rule] | LONDON: | PRINTED FOR J. NUNN, GREAT QUEEN STREET, LINCOLN'S | INN FIELDS; LONGMAN, HURST, REES, AND ORME, PATER- | NOSTER ROW; RICHARDSONS, ROYAL EXCHANGE; AND J. | RIDGWAY, 170, PICCADILLY. | [short rule] | 1808. | Price 7*s*. 6*d*. in boards.

Fourth edition, London, 1808. Originally published, London, 1801.

224 x 134 mm. [a]^8 b^4 B-O^8 P^2; 118 leaves, pp. [i-v] vi-viii [*16*] [1] 2-211 [212].

Illustrations: Engraved dedication leaf and twelve engraved leaves with bill of fare for each month.

Bibliographies: Bitting, p. 328; Oxford, p. 131, in a note.

Copies: *NUC* (Library of Congress only).

883. Monteiro, Maria Josefa de.

THE | CONTINENTAL FISH COOK: | OR, | A FEW HINTS ON MAIGRE DINNERS. | BY | M. J. N. DE FREDERIC. | LONDON: | R. WASHBOURNE, 18 PATERNOSTER ROW. | 1874. | *Price One Shilling.*

First edition, London, 1874.

137 x 90 mm. 1-5^6 6^2; 32 leaves, pp. [i-iii] iv [5] 6-64.

Bibliographies: This edition unrecorded in the bibliographies consulted. Axford, p. 78, Bitting, p. 119, and Wheaton and Kelly 4234, cite the second edition, also London, 1874.

Copies: *BMC*.

884. Moore, Isabella.

The Useful and Entertaining | FAMILY MISCELLANY: | CONTAINING THE | Complete ENGLISH Housekeeper's Companion. | IN WHICH ARE | Near Five Hundred RECEIPTS | IN | [in two columns: column one] COOKERY, | PASTRY, | PRESERVING, | [vertical row of three type ornaments] | [column two] Making, WINES, | CANDYING, and | PICKLING. [end columns] | With plain and very easy INSTRUCTIONS for chusing | All Sorts of EATABLES. | ALSO, | Directions for Carving, with several CUTS explaining in the easiest | Manner, the best Way of trussing HARES, and FOWLS; with Forms | of placing Dishes on a Table, either in the middling or genteelest | Manner. | By Mrs. ISABELLA MOORE, | Who was Twenty Years a worthy and frugal Housekeeper in a private | Gentleman's Family, at DUFFIELD near DERBY. | TO WHICH ARE ADDED, | The GENUINE RECEIPTS | FOR | Preparing and Compounding the Principal Medicines | made Use of by the late Mr. WARD. | With OBSERVATIONS thereon by J. PAGE, Esq; | ALSO, | The SYREN; Or, CHEARFUL SONGSTER: | CONSISTING | Of a Collection of near SEVENTY approv'd SONGS, suited for | those who delight in Harmony, Decency, and good Sense. | [two rules] | *LONDON:* | Printed by and for ISAAC HOLROYD, in the Year 1764. | (Price One Shilling.)

First edition, London, 1764.

8vo. π^2 A-B^8 C^4 D-G^8 H^4; 58 leaves, pp. [i] ii-iv, 1-112.

Bibliographies: This edition unrecorded in the bibliographies consulted. Maclean records only the London, 1772, edition.

Copies: No other copy located.

885. Moore, Sir Jonas, 1617-1679.

[within a border of two rules] Englands Interest: | OR THE | 𝕲entlemen and 𝕱armers 𝕱riend, | SHEWING, | 1. How Land may be Improv'd from 20 *s.* to

8 *l*. and │ so to 100 *l. per* Acre, *per Annum*, with great Ease, │ and for an inconsiderable Charge. 2. How to make │ Cyder, Perry, Cherry, Currant, Gooseberry and │ Mulberry Wines, as Strong and Wholesome as │ *French* or *Spanish* Wines: And the Cyder and Wines │ so made to be Sold for 3 *d. per* Quart, tho' as good │ as Wine now Sold for 18 *d*. 3. The Best and │ Quickest way of Raising a Nursery. 4. Directions │ for Brewing the Finest Malt-Liquors, much Better │ and Cheaper than hitherto known: Shewing what │ Care is to be taken in the Choice of Water, Malt, │ and Hops; and how they are to be Mixed, Boyled │ and Fermented, for making the best *March* or │ *October* Beer, strong Ale, &*c*. 5. Instructions for │ Breeding Horses much Cheaper, and to a far grea- │ ter Advantage than ever yet know. 6. Of the │ Husbandry of Bees, and the great benefit thereby. │ 7. Instructions for the Profitable Ordering of Fish │ Ponds, and for Breeding of Fish. │ [rule] │ *The Third Edition, with Large Additions.* │ [rule] │ *By* Sir *J. More*. │ [rule] │ *LONDON*, │ Printed an Sold by *J. How*, at the *Seven-Stars* │ *Talbot-Court*, in *Grace-church-street*, 1705.

Third edition, London, 1705. Originally published, London, 1697.

12mo. A-G^{12}; 84 leaves, pp. [2] 1-166.

Bibliographies: Fussell (1) p. 70.

Copies: *BMC* and *NUC* (5 copies).

886. Moore, Sir Jonas, 1617-1679.

[within a border of two rules] *England*'s Interest: │ OR, THE │ 𝕲entlemen an𝖉 𝕵armer'𝖘 𝕵rien𝖉. │ SHEWING, │ I How Land may be improved from 20 s │ to 8 *l*. and so to 100 *l. per* Acre, *per Annum*, │ with great Ease, and for an inconsiderable │ Charge. 2. The best and quickest Way of rai │ sing a Nursery. 3. How to make Cyder, Per- │ ry, Cherry, Curran, Goose-berry, Mul-berry, │ and Birch Wines, as strong and wholesome as │ *French* and *Spanish* Wines; and the Cyder and │ Wines so made, to be sold at 3 *d. per* Quart, │ tho' as good as Wine now sold for 18 *d*. 4. Di- │ rections for Brewing the finest Malt Liquors, │ Better and Cheaper than hitherto known; shew- │ ing what Care is to be taken in the Choice of │ Water, Malt and Hops; and how they are to │ be mixed, boiled, and fermented, for making │ the best *March* or *October* Beer, strong Ale, &*c*. │ 5. Instructions for Breeding Horses much Chea │ per, and to a far greater Advantage than ever │ yet know. 6. Of the Husbandry of Bees, and │ the great Benefit thereby. 7. Instructions for │ the profitable ordering of Fish-Ponds, and for │ the Increase of Fish. 8. A Guide for young │ Anglers, teaching them the best Method of │ catching Trout, Carp, Barbels, Jacks, Pikes, │ Perch, Roach, Dace, &*c*. As also how to Dress │ them after the newest Fashion. Lastly, Physick │ for

Families, containing many useful Medicines | for several Distempers, particuarly the Plague. | [rule] | By Sir *J. MOORE.* | [rule] | *LONDON*, Printed for *A. Bettesworth*, at the | *Red Lion* in *Pater-noster-Row*. 1721.

Fifth edition, London, 1721. Originally published, London, 1697.

12mo. A-H^{12}; 96 leaves, pp. [1-3] 4-69, 71, 70, 70-188 [2].

Bibliographies: Fussell (1) p. 70-71; Simon BG 1069.

Copies: *BMC* and *NUC* (6 copies).

887. Moseley, Benjamin, 1742-1819.

A | TREATISE | CONCERNING THE | PROPERTIES AND EFFECTS | OF | COFFEE. | THE SECOND EDITION, | WITH LARGE ADDITIONS, AND A PREFACE. | BY BENJAMIN MOSELEY, M. D. | AUTHOR OF | "OBSERVATIONS ON THE DYSENTERY OF THE WEST-INDIES." | [short fancy rule] | LONDON: | PRINTED FOR THE AUTHOR: | AND SOLD BY JOHN STOCKDALE, | OPPOSITE | BURLINGTON-HOUSE, PICCADILLY. | M DCC LXXXV.

Second edition, London, 1785. Originally published under the title *Observations on the Properties and Effects of Coffee*, London, also 1785.

8vo. π1 a-d^4 B-I^4 K^4(-K4=π1); 52 leaves, pp. [2] [i] ii- xxxi [xxxii] [1] 2-69 [70].

Presentation copy, inscribed "John Wilkes Esq with the Authors Comp:"

Bibliographies: Maclean, p. 104; Wheaton and Kelly 4260.

Copies: *BMC* and *NUC* (4 copies).

887a. Moseley, Benjamin, 1742-1819.

A | TREATISE | CONCERNING THE | PROPERTIES AND EFFECTS | OF | COFFEE. | [short rule] | THE FIFTH EDITION, | WITH CONSIDERABLE ADDITIONS. | [short rule] | By BENJAMIN MOSELEY M.D. | Physician to Chelsea Hospital, Member of the College | of Physicians of London, of the University of

Leyden, | of the American Philosophical Society, &c. &c.; | Author of a Treatise on Tropical Diseases, Military | Operations, and the Climate of the West-Indies. | [short rule] | LONDON: | PRINTED FOR J. SEWELL, NO. 32, CORNHILL. | M.D.CC.XCII.

Fifth edition, London, 1792. Originally published under the title *Observations on the Properties and Effects of Coffee*, London, 1785.

8vo. π^2 a-f^8 g^4 h^2; 56 leaves, pp. [*4*] [i] ii-xxvii [xxviii] [1] 2-80.

Bibliographies: Maclean, p. 104.

Copies: *BMC, BNC, NUC* (14 copies), Maclean (5 copies).

887b. Mother's Own Book.

THE | MOTHER'S OWN BOOK, | CONTAINING | IMPORTANT AND USEFUL | [fancy] PREPARATIONS, &c. | With which every Housekeeper ought to | be acquainted. | [rule] | In presenting this little Work to the public, the publisher begs to state | that he can vouch for the goodness of the preparations, having witnessed | the trial of many of them with complete success; and he confidently | affirms without fear of contradition, that there never was any thing of | the kind offered for sale before, at the same price, that contained so much | real useful information, as many of the Recipes have often been sold at | from Twenty to Thirty Shillings each. | Ipswich: | PRINTED FOR AND PUBLISHED BY J. B. ROGERS. | *Price Sixpence.* | [short rule] | 1834.

First edition, Ipswich, 1834.

168 x 105 mm. [1]^{16}; 16 leaves, pp. [1-3] 4-32. Leaf 5$_r$ signed B. Publisher's light blue wrappers printed with a repeat of the title-page on the outer front wrapper.

Note: Most of this booklet treats cures for illnesses. There are a few paragraphs on preserving fruits and increasing the flavor of tea.

Bibliographies: Unrecorded in the bibliographies consulted, or in RLIN.

Copies: No other copy located.

Moubray, Bonington, see Lawrence, John, 1753-1839 (item 817).

888. Moxon, Elizabeth.

English Housewifry. | EXEMPLIFIED | In above four Hundred and Fifty | RECEITS, | Giving DIRECTIONS in most Parts of | COOKERY; and how to prepare | various Sorts of | [in two columns: column one] SOOPS, | MADE-DISHES, | PASTS, | PICKLES, | }{ | [column two] CAKES, | CREAMS, | JELLIES, | MADE-WINES, &c. [end columns] | With Cuts for the orderly placing the Dishes and | Courses; also Bills of Fare, for every Month in the | Year; and an alphabetical Index to the Whole. | A Book necessary for Mistresses of Families, higher and | lower Women Servants, and confined to Things | USEFUL, SUBSTANTIAL and SPLENDID, and cal- | culated for the Preservation of HEALTH, and upon | the Measures of FRUGALITY, being the Result of | thirty Years *Practice* and *Experience*. | [rule] | *By* ELISABETH MOXON. | [rule] | The SECOND EDITION, Corrected. | [rule] | *LEEDS:* | Printed by *James Lister*, and sold by *John Swale*, at | *Leeds*; *S. Birt*, in *Ave-Mary-Lane, London*; and | by the Booksellers in Town and Country.

Second edition, Leeds, ca. 1743. Originally published, Leeds, ca. 1741.

12mo. [A]² B-Q⁶; 92 leaves, pp. [4] 1-149 [150] [30].

Illustrations: Six woodcuts in the text and a seventh on a folding leaf showing table settings.

Bibliographies: Maclean, p. 105; Wheaton and Kelly 4271 (misdating the work 1685). Vicaire 612 records the fourth edition.

Copies: Maclean records Leeds Public Library and Kansas State University. Wheaton and Kelly adds Essex Institute.

889. Moxon, Elizabeth.

English Housewifry. | EXEMPLIFIED | In above Four Hundred and Fifty | RECEIPTS, | Giving DIRECTIONS in most Parts of | COOKERY; and how to | prepare | various Sorts of | [in two columns: column one] SOOPS, | MADE-DISHES, | PASTS, | PICKLES, | }{ | [column two] CAKES, | CREAMS, | JELLIES, | MADE-WINES, &c. [end columns] | With CUTS for the orderly placing the | DISHES and COURSES; also Bills of Fare | for every Month in the Year; and an Al- | phabetical INDEX to the Whole. | A BOOK necessary for Mistresses of Families, higher and | lower Women Servants, and confined to Things | USEFUL, SUBSTANTIAL and SPLENDID, and cal- | culated for the Preservation of HEALTH, and upon the | Measures of FRUGALITY, being the Result of thirty | Years *Practice* and *Experience.* | *By* ELIZABETH MOXON. | The FIFTH EDITION. | *LEEDES:* Printed, | And Sold by S. BIRT, in *Ave-Mary-Lane, London*; E. SWALE | and J. LISTER, in *Leedes*; Mr. MOXON, in *Pontefract*; and | J. LORD, in *Wakefield, Barnsley,* and *Pontefract.*

Fifth edition, Leeds, ca. 1752. Originally published, Leeds, ca. 1741.

12mo. A-S⁶ U⁶; 114 leaves, pp. [i-ii] iii [iv] 5-203 [204] [24]. Last leaf blank.

Illustrations: Six woodcuts in the text and a seventh on a folding leaf showing table settings.

Bibliographies: Maclean, p. 105.

Copies: *NUC* (New York Public Library only). Maclean adds Leeds Public Library, Manchester Public Library, and Library of Congress.

890. Moxon, Elizabeth.

English Housewifry | EXEMPLIFIED | In above Four Hundred and Fifty | RECEIPTS, | Giving Directions in most Parts of | COOKERY; | And how to prepare various SORTS of | [in two columns: column one] SOOPS, | MADE-DISHES, | PASTES, | PICKLES, | [two vertical rules] | [column two] CAKES, | CREAMS, | JELLIES, | MADE-WINES, &c. [end columns] | With CUTS for the orderly placing the DISHES and | COURSES; also Bills of Fare for every Month in the | Year; and an alphabetical INDEX to the whole. | A Book necessary for Mistresses of Families, higher and | lower Women Servants, and confined to Things | USEFUL, SUBSTANTIAL and SPLENDID, and calcula- | ted for the Preservation of HEALTH, and upon the | Measures of Frugality, being the Result of thirty | Years Practice and Experience. | *By* ELIZABETH MOXON. | WITH AN | APPENDIX, | Never before printed, CONTAINING | Upwards of Sixty Receipts, of the most valuable Kind, | communicated to the Publisher by several Gentle- | women in the Neighbourhood, distinguished by | their extraordinary Skill in HOUSEWIFRY. | The EIGHTH EDITION, Corrected. | *LEEDES:* Printed, | For GEORGE COPPERTHWAITE, Bookseller, and sold | at his Shop in *Leedes*; by T. WILSON, and | C. ETHERINGTON, in *York*; sold also by Mr. B. | DOD, Bookseller, in *Ave-Mary-Lane, London.* 1758.

Eighth edition, Leeds, 1758. Originally published, Leeds, ca. 1741.

12mo. π² A-X⁶ ᵖX⁶ Y⁴; 138 leaves, pp. [2] [1-4] 5-224 [22] 227-252 [2].

Illustrations: Six woodcuts in the text and a seventh on a folding leaf showing table settings. This copy lacks the second folding plate, A Dinner in Summer.

Bibliographies: Maclean, p. 105; Oxford, p. 78, in a note; Wheaton and Kelly 4272.

Copies: *BMC* (2 copies) and *NUC* (4 copies). Maclean adds Brotherton Library and Leeds Public Library. There are two editions styled "eighth edition" and the above record of copies includes both.

891. Moxon, Elizabeth.

English Housewifery, | EXEMPLIFIED IN ABOVE | Four Hundred and Fifty RECEIPTS, | Giving DIRECTIONS in most Parts of | COOKERY; | And how to prepare various SORTS of | [in two columns: column one] SOUPS, | MADE-DISHES, | PASTES, | PICKLES, | [vertical row of type ornaments] | [column two] CAKES, | CREAMS, | JELLIES, | MADE WINES, &c. [end columns] | With CUTS for the orderly placing the DISHES and | COURSES; also BILLS of FARE for every Month in | the Year; and an Alphabetical INDEX to the Whole. | A Book necessary for Mistresses of Families, higher and | lower Women Servants, and confined to Things *Use-* | *ful, Substantial,* and *Splendid,* and calculated for the | Preservation of Health, and upon the Measures of | Frugality, being the Result of Thirty Years Practice | and Experience. | [rule] | By ELIZABETH MOXON. | [rule] | WITH AN | APPENDIX, | Containing upwards of SEVENTY RECEIPS, of the | most valuable Kind, (many never before Printed) com- | municated to the Publisher by several Gentlewomen in | the Neighbourhood, distinguished by their extraordi- | nary Skill in Housewifery. | To this *Edition* is now added, an INTRODUCTION, | giving an Account of the Times when River Fish are | in Season; and a TABLE, shewing at one View the | proper Seasons for Sea Fish. | [rule] | THE THIRTEENTH EDITION, CORRECTED. | [rule] | LONDON: | PRINTED FOR W. OSBORNE, T. GRIFFIN, AND | H. MOZLEY, GAINSBRO'. | [short rule] | M.DCC.LXXXIX.

Fifteenth edition, London, 1789, styled thirteenth edition on the title-page. Originally published, Leeds, ca. 1741.

12mo. π^4 A-U^6 $_\chi$L^6($_\chi$L6+1) Y^4 (signature $_\chi$L composed of two double leaves wrapped around $_\chi$L1.2 plus one disjunct leaf); 135 leaves, pp. [i-ii] iii-viii, 5-203 [204], ^{2}[1] 2-33 [34-40] [double leaf] [*4*] [double leaf] [*10*].

Illustrations: Eight woodcuts in the text, two on the folding double leaves, showing table settings.

Bibliographies: Maclean, p. 105; Oxford, p. 78, in a note; Pennell, p. 160.

Copies: *NUC* (New York Academy of Medicine, Northwestern, and Yale).

892. Moxon, Elizabeth.

ENGLISH HOUSEWIFERY, | EXEMPLIFIED IN | *Above Four Hundred and Fifty Receipts,* | GIVING DIRECTIONS IN MOST PARTS OF | COOKERY; | AND HOW TO PREPAPRE VARIOUS SORTS OF | [in three columns: column one] SOUPS, | MADE DISHES, | PASTES, | [column two] | PICKLES, | CAKES, | CREAMS, | [column three] JELLIES, | MADE WINES, | &c. &c. &c. [end columns] | *WITH ELEGANT CUTS,* | For the orderly placing the dishes and courses; also bills of | fare for every month in the year; and an alphabetical index | to the whole. A book necessary for mistresses of families, | higher and lower women servants, and confined to things | useful, substantial, and splendid, and calculated for the pre- | servation of health, and upon the measures of frugality, | being the result of thirty years practice and experience. | [short fancy rule] | BY ELIZABETH MOXON. | [short fancy rule] | WITH AN APPENDIX, | Containing upwards of Eighty Receipts, of the most | valuable kind. | TO THIS EDITION IS NOW ADDED, | *AN INTRODUCTION,* | Giving an account of the times when River Fish are in season; | and a table, showing at one view the proper seasons | for Sea Fish. | [rule] | A NEW EDITION IMPROVED. | [rule] | LONDON: | PRINTED FOR J. BRAMBLES, A. MEGGITT, AND J. WATERS, | BY H. MOZLEY, GAINSBOROUGH. | 1808.

New edition, London, 1808. Originally published, Leeds, ca. 1741.

142 x 87 mm. A-X^6 Y^4; 130 leaves, pp. [i-iv] v-vii [viii] [9] 10-231 [232-260].

Illustrations: Six woodcuts in the text showing table settings.

Bibliographies: This edition unrecorded in the bibliographies consulted.

Copies: No other copy of this edition located.

Muffett, Thomas, see Moffett, Thomas.

892a. Murray, Ross.

THE | MODERN HOUSEHOLDER: | A MANUAL OF | DOMESTIC ECONOMY | IN ALL ITS BRANCHES. | COMPILED AND EDITED BY | ROSS MURRAY, | AND THE MEDICAL PORTION BY | A MEMBER OF THE ROYAL COLLEGE

OF SURGEONS. | *NEW EDITION.* | 𝔚𝔦𝔱𝔥 𝔒𝔯𝔦𝔤𝔦𝔫𝔞𝔩 𝔍𝔩𝔩𝔲𝔰𝔱𝔯𝔞𝔱𝔦𝔬𝔫𝔰 𝔓𝔯𝔦𝔫𝔱𝔢𝔡 𝔦𝔫 𝔠𝔬𝔩𝔬𝔲𝔯𝔰 𝔟𝔶 𝔎𝔯𝔬𝔫𝔥𝔢𝔦𝔪. | AND NUMEROUS WOODCUTS. | [publisher's device] | LONDON: | FREDERICK WARNE AND CO. | BEDFORD STREET, COVENT GARDEN. | NEW YORK: SCRIBNER, WELFORD, AND ARMSTRONG.

"New edition," London, 1872 or 1873; the preface is dated December 1872. This work was issued as a companion to *Warne's Model Cookery Book* (London, 1868). Although styled "new edition" on the title-page, no other edition is known. There was an abridged version published under the title *Warne's Model Housekeeper* (London, 1879).

190 x 128 mm. [A]^6 B-2Z^8 3A^8; 368 leaves, pp. [i-v] vi-xii [1] 2-722 [2]. Last leaf, blank?, wanting in this copy.

Illustrations: Chromolithographied frontispiece and 15 additional chromolithographed plates; numerous wood engravings in the text.

Bibliographies: Wheaton & Kelly 4299.

Copies: *BMC* and *NUC* (Cleveland Public Library, Harvard and U. S. Patent Office Library). Wheaton & Kelly adds New England Deposit Library.

893. Murray's Modern Cookery Book.

Murray's Modern Cookery Book. | [short fancy rule] | MODERN | DOMESTIC COOKERY: | BASED ON THE WELL-KNOWN WORK OF MRS. RUNDELL, | BUT INCLUDING ALL THE RECENT IMPROVEMENTS IN | THE CULINARY ART. | FOUNDED ON PRINCIPLES OF ECONOMY AND PRACTICAL KNOWLEDGE, | AND | 𝔄𝔡𝔞𝔭𝔱𝔢𝔡 𝔣𝔬𝔯 𝔓𝔯𝔦𝔳𝔞𝔱𝔢 𝔉𝔞𝔪𝔦𝔩𝔦𝔢𝔰. | BY A LADY. | WITH ILLUSTRATIVE WOODCUTS. | LONDON: | JOHN MURRAY, ALBEMARLE STREET. | 1851.

First edition, London, 1851.

172 x 111 mm. a^8 b^6 B-2U^8 2X^2; 352 leaves, pp. [i-ii] iii-xxviii [1] 2-675 [676]. Publisher's rose cloth stamped in gold. Thirty-two page publisher's catalogue dated Freburary 1851 bound in.

Illustrations: Wood engraved frontispiece of the larder and wood engraved plate of the kitchen plus numerous wood engravings in the text.

Bibliographies: The first printing unrecorded in the bibliographies consulted. Oberlé (1) 170 records an 1857 printing.

Copies: No other copy located.

894. Murrell, John.

[within a border of two rules] MVRRELS | TWO BOOKES | OF | COOKERIE | AND | CARVING. | [rule] | The fifth time printed, with | new Additions. | [rule] | LONDON, | Printed by *M. F.* for *Iohn Marriot,* | and are to be sold at his shop in St | Dunstans Churchyard in Fleetstreet. | 1641.

Fifth edition, London, 1641. Originally published under the title *A New Booke of Cookery*, London, 1615. *A New Booke of Carving and Sewing*, included in this work, reprints *The Boke of Kervynge*, London, 1508.

8vo. A-N⁸; 104 leaves, pp. [6] 1-188 [14]. Last leaf blank.

Bibliographies: Bitting, p. 336; Oxford, p. 19, in a note; Wing M3125.

Copies: *BMC, BNC,* and *NUC* (John Crerar Library only). Wing adds the Bodleian Library.

895. Natura exenterata.

[within a border of two rules] *NATURA EXENTERATA:* | OR | NATURE UNBOWELLED | By the most | *Esquisite Anatomizers of Her.* | *Wherein are contained,* | Her choicest SECRETS digested into | RECEIPTS, fitted for the Cure of all sorts | of Infirmities, whether Internal or External, | Acute or Chronical, that are In- | cident to the Body of Man. | Collected and preserved by several Persons of Quali- | ty and great Experience in the Art of Medicine, | whose names are prefixed to the Book. | Containing in the whole, One thousand seven | hundred and twenty. | Very necessary for such as regard their Owne | Health, or that of their friends. | [rule] | *Valetudinem tuam cura diligenter.* | [rule] | *VVhereunto are annexed,* | Many Rare, hitherto un-imparted Inventions, for | Gentlemen, Ladies and others, in the Recre- | ations of their different Imployments. | With an exact Alphabetical Table referring to the several | Diseases, and their proper Cures. | [rule] | *London,* Printed for, and are to be sold by *H. Twiford* at his shop in | Vine Court Middle Temple, *G. Bedell* at the Middel Temple | Gate Fleetstreet, and *N. Ekins* at the Gun neer the | West-end of S. *Pauls* Church, 1655.

First edition, London, 1655.

8vo. [A]⁴ B-Ii⁸; 252 leaves, pp. [8] 1-469 [470] [16]. Last leaf blank. P.469 misnumbered "369." First leaf wanting in this copy.

Illustration: Engraved frontispiece portrait of Lady Alathea Talbot, Countess of Arundell and Surrey.

Bibliographies: Wing N241.

Copies: *BMC* and *NUC* (8 copies). Wing (12 copies).

895a. The Natural History of Coffee, Thee, Chocolate, Tobacco.

[Within a border of two rules] THE | Natural History | OF | [in two columns, column one] COFFEE, | THEE, | [two facing pointed brackets] | [column two] CHOCOLATE, | TOBACCO. [end columns] | In four several Sections; | WITH A | TRACT | OF | ELDER and JUNIPER-BERRIES, | Shewing how Useful they may be in Our | *COFFEE-HOUSES:* | And also the way of making | MUM, | With some Remarks upon that LIQUOR. | [rule] | Collected from the Writings of the best Physicians, | and Modern Travellers. | [rule] | *LONDON:* | Printed for *Christopher Wilkinson,* at the *Black Boy* over | against St. *Dunstan's* Church in *Fleetstreet.* 1682.

First edition, London, 1682.

Note: Wing enters this work under John Chamberlayne, 1666-1723. The Arents catalog disputes this attribution as Chamberlayne was only sixteen when this work was published. The *BMC* enters it under History with a note, by J. Chamberlayne?, and the *NUC* enters it under title with a cross reference from Chamberlayne. Chamberlayne translated Dufour's *Traitez nouveaux & curieux du café, du thé et du chocolate* in 1685 (item 654).

4to. A-E⁴; 20 leaves, pp. [1-2] 3-36 [4].

Bibliographies: Arents 372; Wing C1859.

Copies: *BMC* (4 copies); *NUC* (17 copies); Wing (10 copies).

896. Nettleton, Joseph Alfred.

THE MANUFACTURE | OF | WHISKY AND PLAIN SPIRIT. | BY | J. A. NETTLETON, | *Author of* | "CONDENSING AND COOLING IN DISTILLATION," . . . 1897. | "THE FLAVOUR OF WHISKY," . . . . 1894. | "THE MANUFACTURE OF SPIRIT IN THE UNITED KINGDOM," 1893. | "THE MANUFACTURE OF VINEGAR," . . . . . 1892. | "THE PRESERVATION OF HOPS," . . . . . . 1891. | "EVERY BREWER HIS OWN ANALYST," . . . . . 1884. | "STUDY OF ORIGINAL GRAVITY," . . . . . . 1881. | "WHISKY" ("CHAMBERS' ENCYCLOPAEDIA"), ... 1891. | [two short rules] | Aberdeen: | G. CORNWALL & SONS. | [short rule] | 1913.

First edition, Aberdeen, 1913.

240 x 155 mm. [1]⁸ 2⁸ χ1 A-I⁸ J-U⁸ V⁸ W-2I⁸ 2J-2L⁸; 361 leaves, pp. [i-ix] x-xxxiv [1] 2-606 [2]. Last leaf blank. Advertisements bound in at the front: [1]⁶ χ1 2χ1; 8 leaves, pp. [1] 2-15 [16]. Brown cloth stamped in gold and blind.

Illustrations: Two folding maps facing p. 178, two folding wood engravings of distilling appartus facing pages 206 and 248, and numerous wood engravings in the text.

Bibliographies: Noling, p. 307.

Copies: *BMC* and *NUC* (Detroit Public Library only).

897. The New Domestic Cookery.

[within an ornamental rule border] THE NEW | DOMESTIC COOKERY, | OR THE | HOUSEWIFE'S SURE GUIDE. | CONTAINING | *Complete Instructions for Cooking every description of Viands* | WITH | CHEAPNESS AND ELEGANCE. | BY A LADY. | [short rule] | *REFERENCES TO THE FRONTISPIECE.* | [in four columns: column one] BEEF. | *Hind Quarter.* | 1 Sirloin. | 2 Rump. | 3 Edge Bone | 4 Buttock. | 5 Mouse ditto. | 6 Veiny Piece. | 7 Thick Flank. | 8 Thin ditto. | 9 Leg. | *Fore Quarter.* | 10 Fore Rib, 5 ribs | [vertical rule] | [column two] 11 Mid. Rib, 4 ribs | 12 Chuck, 3 do. | 13 Clod. | 14 Brisket. | 15 Shoulder, or Leg | Mutton Piece. | 16 Neck, or Stick- | ing Piece. | 17 Shin. | 18 Cheek. | VEAL. | 1 Loin, best end. | 2 Loin, Chump do. | [vertical rule] | [column three] 3 Fillet. | 4 Knuckle, hind. | 5 Ditto, fore. | 6 Neck, best end. | 7 Ditto, scrag end. | 8 Blade Bone. | 9 Breast, best end. | 10 Ditto, Brisket. | MUTTON. | 1 Leg. | 2 Loin, best end. | 3 Do. Chump do. | [vertical rule] | [column four] 4 Neck, best end. | 5 Neck, Scrag end. | 6 Shoulder. |

7 Breast. | Saddle, 2 Loins | PORK. | 1 The Sparerib. | 2 Hand. | 3 Belly, or Spring. | 4 Fore Loin. | 5 Hind ditto. | 6 Leg. [end columns] | [short rule] | DERBY: | THOMAS RICHARDSON; | SIMPKIN, MARSHALL, AND CO., LONDON.

First edition, Derby, ca. 1838. See also item 898.

192 x 115 mm. A^{12}; 12 leaves, pp. [1-3] 4-24. Recent blue buckram, publisher's cream printed wrappers preserved.

Illustrations: Wood engraving of farmyard on front wrapper and a lithographed, hand-colored, folding frontispiece of a kitchen scene flanked by illustrations for quartering beef, veal, mutton, and pork.

Bibliographies: Unrecorded in the bibliographies consulted.

Copies: No other copy with this imprint located.

898. The New Domestic Cookery.

THE NEW | DOMESTIC COOKERY, | OR THE | HOUSEWIFE'S SURE GUIDE. | CONTAINING | *Complete Instructions for Cooking every description of Viands* | WITH | CHEAPNESS AND ELEGANCE. | BY A LADY. | [short rule] | *REFERENCES TO THE FRONTISPIECE.* | [in four columns: column one] BEEF. | *Hind Quarter.* | 1 Sirloin. | 2 Rump. | 3 Edge Bone | 4 Buttock. | 5 Mouse ditto. | 6 Veiny Piece. | 7 Thick Flank. | 8 Thin ditto. | 9 Leg. | *Fore Quarter.* | 10 Fore Rib, 5 ribs | [vertical rule] | [column two] 11 Mid. Rib, 4 ribs | 12 Chuck, 3 do. | 13 Clod. | 14 Brisket. | 15 Shoulder, or Leg | Mutton Piece. | 16 Neck, or Stick- | ing Piece. | 17 Shin. | 18 Cheek. | VEAL. | 1 Loin, best end. | 2 Loin, Chump do. | [vertical rule] | [column three] 3 Fillet. | 4 Knuckle, hind. | 5 Ditto, fore. | 6 Neck, best end. | 7 Ditto, scrag end. | 8 Blade Bone. | 9 Breast, best end. 10 Ditto, Brisket. | MUTTON. | 1 Leg. | 2 Loin, best end. | 3 Do. Chump do. | [vertical rule] | [column four] 4 Neck, best end. | 5 Neck, Scrag end. | 6 Shoulder. | 7 Breast. | Saddle, 2 Loins | PORK. | 1 The Sparerib. | 2 Hand. | 3 Belly, or Spring. | 4 Fore Loin. | 5 Hind ditto. | 6 Leg. [end columns] | [short rule] | DERBY: | THOMAS RICHARDSON.

First edition, Derby, ca. 1839, later printing. This printing, with Thomas Richardson but not Simpkin, Marshall in the imprint, appears to post-date that with the combined imprint (item 897). There is more wear to the stereotype plates and the list of pamphlets on the back wrapper adds "Church-yard Gleanings," a title not present on the wrapper on the other copy.

190 x 115 mm. A^{12}; 12 leaves, pp. [1-3] 4-24. Recent green cloth, publisher's green printed wrappers preserved.

Illustrations: Wood engraving of farmyard on front wrapper and a lithographed, hand-colored, folding frontispiece of a kitchen scene flanked by illustrations for quartering beef, veal, mutton, and pork.

Bibliographies: Unrecorded in the bibliographies consulted.

Copies: *NUC* (New York Public Library and Yale).

899. The New Female Instructor.

THE NEW | FEMALE INSTRUCTOR: | OR, | Young Woman's | *GUIDE TO DOMESTIC HAPPINESS* | BEING | AN EPITOME OF ALL THE ACQUIREMENTS NECESSARY TO FORM | THE FEMALE CHARACTER, IN EVERY CLASS OF LIFE: | WITH | EXAMPLES OF ILLUSTRIOUS WOMEN | TO WHICH ARE ADDED, | ADVICE TO SERVANTS; | A COMPLETE | Art of Cookery, | AND | PLAIN DIRECTIONS FOR CARVING: | ALSO, | A GREAT VARIETY OF MEDICINAL AND OTHER USEFUL RECEIPTS | IN DOMESTIC ECONOMY; | *AND NUMEROUS OTHER INTERESTING ARTICLES,* | FORMING | A Complete Storehouse of Valuable Knowledge. | [two short rules] | London. | PRINTED FOR THOMAS KELLY, 17, PATERNOSTER-ROW,

Engraved title:

THE | FEMALE INSTRUCTOR; | *OR* | Young Woman's | COMPANION, | AND | Guide to Domestic Happiness; | *BEING* | AN EPITOME OF ALL THE ACQUIREMENTS | necessary to form the Female Character in every Class of Life, | *with* | EXAMPLES OF ILLUSTRIOUS WOMEN. | [woodcut of garden scene] | LONDON, | *Published by* THOS. KELLY, *17, Paternoster Row, March 20,* | 1824.

New edition, London, 1824. Originally published, London, R. Edwards [1814]. Bitting describes the original edition, noting that her copy has an ownership signature, "Susannah Brown Her Book-1816." The new edition described here has an author's Advertisement on pp. iii-iv dated Aug. 12th, 1818, and an engraved title-page dated 1824. This work is not the same as *The Female Instructor*, Liverpool, 1812 (items 681 and 682).

211 x 130 mm. [A]^4 B-3X^4; 268 leaves, pp. [i-iii] iv-vi [vii-viii] [1] 2-528.

Illustratons: Engraved frontispiece dated March 20, 1824, an engraved title-page dated 1824, two engraved pictorial plates dated April 28, 1818, and May 9, 1818, and four undated engraved plates illustrating handwriting, butcher cuts of beef, veal, mutton, and pork, and carving.

Bibliographies: This edition unrecorded in the bibliographies consulted. Attar records two editions, undated and 1834, with a variant title and with 672 pages.

Copies: *NUC* (Simmons College, Boston, only).

900. A New System of Practical Domestic Economy.

A | NEW SYSTEM | OF | PRACTICAL | DOMESTIC ECONOMY; | FOUNDED ON | MODERN DISCOVERIES, | AND THE | PRIVATE COMMUNICATIONS OF PERSONS OF EXPERIENCE | [short rule] | NEW EDITION, | REVISED AND ENLARGED; | WITH | ESTIMATES OF HOUSEHOLD EXPENSES, | ADAPTED TO | FAMILIES OF EVERY DESCRIPTION. | [short rule] | In every point of view, an Economist is a good character. – *Hunter's Culina.* | [short rule] | LONDON: | COLBURN AND BENTLEY, NEW BURLINGTON STREET. | 1831.

New edition, London, 1831. Originally published under the title *Practical Economy*, London, 1821.

183 x 113 mm. [A]^6 B-R^{12} S1 T-X^{12} X✱^{2} (X✱1+1) Y^{12} (-Y11,12); 246 leaves, pp. [i-v] vi-xii [1] 2-463 [464] [*20*]. First leaf wanting in this copy.

Bibliographies: Oxford, p. 167. Attar 251.1-251.7 records seven editions between 1821 and 1830. Axford, p. 297, and Bitting, p. 583, record the third edition, 1823.

Copies: No other copy of this edition located. *BMC* records the third edition, 1823 and a new edition, 1824. *NUC* locates editions of 1823, 1824, 1825, 1827, and 1828.

901. Nicol, Walter, d. 1811.

THE | FORCING, FRUIT, AND KITCHEN | GARDENER: | COMPREHENDING THE FORCING OF | [in three columns: column one] ASPARAGUS, | CUCUMBERS, | CHERRIES, | FIGS, | [column two] GRAPES, | MELONS, | MUSHROOMS, | NECTARINES, | [column three] PEACHES, | PINE APPLES, | AND | STRAWBERRIES. [end columns] | TOGETHER WITH THE | Management of the GREEN-HOUSE – Culture of | WALL and ORCHARD FRUITS – KITCHEN VE- | GETABLES, SALLADS and HERBS. | THIRD EDITION, WITH LARGE

ADDITIONS. | Illustrated with SIX NEW COPPERPLATES; | CONTAINING TEN DIFFERENT DESIGNS OF HOT-HOUSES, HOT-WALLS, &c. | ON THE NEWEST AND MOST IMPROVED CONSTRUCTIONS. | [two short rules] | BY WALTER NICOL, | Author of "THE PRACTICAL PLANTER," and of an "ESSAY ON GARDEN- | ING," drawn up by Desire, and for Consideration of the Board of | Agriculture; and Corresponding Member of the Natural | History Society of Edinburgh. | [short fancy rule] | EDINBRUGH: | PRINTED FOR WILLIAM CREECH; | AND SOLD IN LONDON BY T. CADELL JUN. & W. DAVIES | J. SCATCHERD, AND T. HURST. | [short fancy rule] | 1802.

Third edition, Edinburgh, 1802. Originally published under the title *The Scotch forcing gardener . . .* Edinburgh, 1797.

8vo. π^8 A-Cc^8 Dd^4 Ee^2; 222 leaves, pp. [i-ix] x-xvi [1] 2-427 [428]. P. 428 numberd "[2]".

Illustrations: Six engraved plates illustrating the construction of hot-houses.

Bibliographies: Henrey III.1182.

Copies: *BMC* and *NUC* (National Agricultural Library, University of California, Berkeley, and University of Delaware).

902. A Noble Boke off Cookry.

A | NOBLE BOKE | OFF COOKRY | FFOR A PRYNCE HOUSSOLDE | OR ENY OTHER ESTATELY HOUSSOLDE | [ornament] | REPRINTED VERBATIM FROM A RARE MS. | IN THE HOLKHAM COLLECTION | EDITED | BY MRS. ALEXANDER NAPIER. | [ornament] | LONDON: | ELLIOT STOCK, 62, PATERNOSTER ROW, E.C. | 1882.

First edition, London, 1882.

218 x 173 mm. [A]^8 B-I^8 K^4 χ1; 77 leaves, pp. [2] [i-v] vi-xiii [xiv] [1-3] 4-136 [2]. Publisher's Japanese vellum over boards, stamped in red and gold.

Illustrations: Wood engraved vignettes at beginning and end of volume and head and tailpieces in text.

Bibliographies: Axford, p. 299; Bitting, p. 339; Driver 751.1; Wheaton and Kelly 4463.

Copies: *BMC* and *NUC* (13 copies).

903. Nott, John.

THE | *Cook's* and *Confectioner's* | DICTIONARY: | Or, the Accomplish'd |
Housewife's Companion. | CONTAINING, | I. The choicest Receipts in all the
several Branches of | COOKERY; or the best and newst Ways of dressing all sorts of
Flesh, | Fish, Fowl, &c. for a Common or Noble Table; with their proper | Garnitures
and Sauces. | II. The best way of making Bisks, Farces, forc'd Meats, | Marinades,
Olio's, Puptons, Ragoos, Sauces, Soops, Potages, &c. ac- | cording to the *English,
French*, and *Italian* Courts. | III. All manner of Pastry-works, as Biskets, Cakes, |
Cheese-cakes, Custards, Pastes, Patties, Puddings, Pyes, Tarts, &c. | IV. The various
Branches of Confectionary; as Candying, | Conserving, Preserving, and Drying all
sorts of Flowers, Fruits, Roots, | &c. Also Jellies, Composts, Marmalades, and
Sugar-works. | V. The way of making all *English* potable Liquors; | Ale, Beer, Cider,
Mead, Metheglin, Mum, Perry, and all sorts of *Eng-* | *lish* Wines; Also Cordials, and
Beautifying Waters. | VI. Directions for ordering an Entertainment, or Bills of | Fare
for all Seasons of the Year; and setting out a Desert of Sweet- | meats to the best
Advantage; With an Explanation of the Terms us'd | in Carving. According to the
Practice of the most celebrated Cooks, | Confectioners, &c. in the Courts of *England,
France*, &c. and many | private and accomplish'd Housewives. | [rule] | Revised and
Recommended | By JOHN NOTT, *Cook to his Grace the Duke* | *of* BOLTON. | [rule]
| *LONDON:* | Printed for C. RIVINGTON, at the *Bible and Crown*, | in St. *Paul*'s
Church-yard. MDCCXXIII.

First edition, London, 1723.

8vo. A⁴ B-Rr⁸; 316 leaves, unpaginated.

8vo. A^4 B-Rr^8; 316 leaves, unpaginated.

Illustrations: Engraved frontispiece by J. Pine and woodcut of table setting on Qq7^r.

Bibliographies: Craig 65; Maclean, p. 107; Oxford, p. 56; Vicaire 631.

Copies: *BMC* and *NUC* (5 copies). Maclean adds Brotherton Library.

904. Nott, John.

THE | *Cooks* and *Confectioners* | [in red] DICTIONARY: | Or, the Accomplish'd |
[in red] Housewives Companion. | CONTAINING | [in two columns: column one] I.
The choicest Receipts in all the se- | veral Branches of COOKERY; or | the best and
newest Ways of dres- | sing all sorts of Flesh, Fish, Fowl, | &c. for a Common or
Noble Ta- | ble; with their proper Garnitures | and Sauces. | II. The best Way of
making Bisks, | Farces, forc'd Meats, Marinades, | Olio's, Puptons, Ragoos, Sauces, |
Soops, Pottages, &c. according to | the *English, French*, and *Italian* | Courts. All

Sorts of Pickles | III. All manner of PASTRY-WORKS, | as Biskets, Cakes, Cheese-cakes, | Custards, Pastes, Patties, Puddings, | Pyes, Tarts, &c. | IV. The various Branches of CON- | FECTIONARY; as Candying, Con- | serving, Preserving, and Drying all | [vertical rule] | [column two] sorts of Flowers, Fruits, Roots, | &c. Also Jellies, Composts, Mar- | malades, and Sugar-works. | V. The Way of making all *English* | potable Liquors; Ale, Beer, Cyder, | Mead, Metheglin, Mum, Perry, | and all sorts of *English* Wines: Al- | so Cordials, and Beautifying Waters. | VI. Directions for ordering an En- | tertainment, or Bills of Fare for | all Seasons of the Year; and set- | ting out a Desert of Sweet-meats | to the best Advantage: With an | Explanation of the Terms us'd in | Carving. According to the Practice | of the most celebrated Cooks, Con- | fectioners &c. in the Courts of | *England, France,* &c. and many | private and accomplish'd House- | wives. | [rule] | The [in red] SECOND EDITION [in black] with Additions. | [rule] | Revised and Recommended By [in red] JOHN NOTT, [in black] late Cook to | the Dukes of SOMERSET, ORMOND and BOLTON; Lord | LANSDOWN and ASHBURNHAM. | [rule] | [in red] *LONDON:* | Printed by *H.P.* for [in red] C. RIVINGTON, [in black] at the *Bible* and | *Crown*, in St. *Paul's* Church-yard. 1724. | [Price six Shillings.]

Second edition, London, 1724. Originally published, London, 1723 (item 903).

8vo. A⁴ B-Rr⁸; 316 leaves, unpaginated.

Illustrations: Engraved frontispiece by J. Pine and woodcut of table setting on Qq⁷ʳ.

Bibliographies: Axford, p. 98; Bitting, p. 346; Maclean, p. 107; Noling, p. 313: Oxford, p. 57, in a note; Simon BG 1102.

Copies: *NUC* (Lehigh University, Library of Congress, and Western Reserve University). Maclean adds British Library and Brotherton Library.

905. Nourse, Timothy, d. 1699.

[within a border of two rules] *Campania Foelix.* | [rule] | OR, A | DISCOURSE | OF THE | Benefits *and* Improvements | OF | 𝔥𝔲𝔰𝔟𝔞𝔫𝔡𝔯𝔶: | CONTAINING | DIRECTIONS for all manner | of *Tillage, Pasturage,* and *Plantation*; As | also for the making of *Cyder* and *Perry.* | With some CONSIDERATIONS upon | I. *Justices of the Peace, and Inferior Officers.* | II. *On Inns and Alehouses.* | III. *On Servants and Labourers.* | IV. *On the Poor.* | To which are Added, | Two ESSAYS: | I. *Of a Country-House.* | II. *Of the Fuel of* London. | [rule] | By *Tim. NOURSE,* Gent. | [rule] | *LONDON:* Printed for *Tho. Bennet,* at the | *Half-Moon* in St. *Paul's* Church-yard. 1700.

First edition, London, 1700.

8vo. A⁴ B-Z⁸ Aa⁴; 184 leaves, pp. [8] [1] 2-354 [6].

Illustrations: Engraved frontispiece on A1ᵛ.

Bibliographies: Fussell (1) p. 85; Wing N1416.

Copies: *BMC*, *BNC*, and *NUC* (13 copies). Wing (14 copies).

906. Nutt, Frederic.

THE | COMPLETE CONFECTIONER; | OR, | THE WHOLE ART OF | CONFECTIONARY: | FORMING | A Ready Assistant to all Genteel FAMILIES; | GIVING THEM A | PERFECT KNOWLEDGE OF CONFECTIONARY: | WITH | INSTRUCTIONS, | NEATLY ENGRAVED ON TEN COPPER-PLATES, | How to decorate a TABLE with TASTE and | ELEGANCE, | Without the Expence or Assistance of a CONFECTIONER. | BY A PERSON, | Late an APPRENTICE to the well-known Messrs. NEGRI | and WITTEN, of BERKLEY-SQUARE. | [two rules] | LONDON: | PRINTED FOR THE AUTHOR; | AND SOLD BY J. MATHEWS, NO. 18, STRAND, | M DCC LXXXIX. | [Price 10*s*. 6*d*. neatly bound.] | *Entered at Stationers Hall.*

First edition, London, 1789.

8vo. [a]⁴ b⁸ A-N⁸ O²; 118 leaves, pp. [i-iv] v-xxiv [1] 2-212.

Illustrations: Ten engraved plates, three folding, nine showing table settings, and the tenth a pastry decorating tool.

Bibliographies: Axford, p. 73; Maclean, p. 108; Oxford, p. 117; Simon BG 1107.

Copies: *BMC*. Maclean adds Aberdeen University, National Library of Scotland, and New York Public Library.

907. Nutt, Frederic.

THE | COMPLETE CONFECTIONER; | OR, | THE WHOLE ART OF | CONFECTIONARY: | FORMING | A Ready Assistant to all Genteel FAMILIES; | GIVING THEM A | PERFECT KNOWLEDGE OF CONFECTIONARY; | WITH |

INSTRUCTIONS, | NEATLY ENGRAVED ON TEN COPPER-PLATES, | HOW TO DECORATE | A TABLE with TASTE and ELEGANCE, | WITHOUT | The Expence or Assistance of a CONFECTIONER. | BY A PERSON, | Late an APPRENTICE to the well-known Messrs. NEGRI | and WITTEN, of BERKLEY-SQUARE. | [short rule] | SECOND EDITION. | [short rule] | 𝕷𝖔𝖓𝖉𝖔𝖓: | PRINTED FOR THE AUTHOR; | AND SOLD BY J. MATHEWS, No. 18, STRAND. | M,DCC,XC. | Price Seven Shillings neatly bound. | ENTERED AT STATIONERS HALL.

Second edition, London, 1790. Originally published, London, 1789 (item 906).

8vo. [a]⁴ b⁸ A-N⁸ O²; 118 leaves, pp. [i-iv] v-xxiv [1] 2-212.

Illustrations: Ten engraved plates, three folding, nine showing table settings, and the tenth a pastry decorating tool.

Bibliographies: Bitting, p. 347; Maclean, p. 108; Oxford, p. 117, in a note; Simon BG 1108.

Copies: *NUC* (4 copies). Maclean adds British Library, International Wine and Food Society in London, and Brotherton Library.

908. Nutt, Frederic.

THE | COMPLETE | CONFECTIONER, | OR | THE WHOLE ART OF | 𝕮𝕺𝕹𝕱𝕰𝕮𝕿𝕴𝕺𝕹𝕬𝕽𝖄 | MADE EASY: | *With Instructions to decorate a Table with Taste and* | *Elegance.* | THE RESULT OF MANY YEARS EXPERIENCE WITH THE | CELEBRATED NEGRI AND WITTEN. | [short fancy rule] | BY FREDERIC NUTT, ESQ. | [short fancy rule] | THIRD EDITION, WITH CONSIDERABLE ADDITIONS. | [two short rules] | *LONDON:* | PRINTED FOR | MATHEWS AND LEIGH, 18, STRAND. | 1806.

Third edition, London, 1806. Originally published, London, 1789 (item 906).

187 x 107 mm. A-K¹² L⁶; 126 leaves, pp. [i-v] vi-xxiii [xxiv] [1] 2-224 [225-228]. Quarter calf with publisher's printed boards.

Illustrations: Engraved frontispiece titled "Pomona" and ten engraved plates, three folding, nine showing table settings, and the tenth a pastry decorating tool.

Bibliographies: Oxford, p. 117, in a note; Vicaire 634.

Copies: No other copy of this edition located.

909. Nutt, Frederic.

THE | COMPLETE | CONFECTIONER, | OR | THE WHOLE ART OF | *CONFECTIONARY, MADE EASY;* | WITH | 𝕽𝖊𝖈𝖊𝖎𝖕𝖙𝖘 | FOR | LIQUEURES, HOME-MADE WINES, *&c.* | THE RESULT OF MANY YEARS EXPERIENCE WITH | THE CELEBRATED NEGRI AND WITTEN. | [short fancy rule] | BY FREDERIC NUTT, ESQ. | [short fancy rule] | SIXTH EDITION. | [two rules] | *LONDON:* | PRINTED BY J. SMEETON, | FOR MATHEWS AND LEIGH, 18, STRAND. | [short fancy rule] | 1809.
Sixth edition, London, 1809. Originally published, London, 1789 (item 906).

168 x 98 mm. A-M^{12} N^2; 146 leaves, pp. [i-v] vi-xxiv [1] 2-261 [262] [6].

Illustrations: Engraved frontispiece titled "Pomona" (a re-engraving after that in the third edition) and ten engraved plates, three folding, nine showing table settings, and the tenth a pastry decorating tool. Folding parts of plates 8 and 9 wanting in this copy.

Bibliographies: Noling, p. 314; Oxford, p. 117, in a note; Wheaton and Kelly 4499.

Copies: *NUC* (Harvard and Kansas State University).

910. Nutt, Frederic.

THE | *IMPERIAL* | AND | ROYAL COOK: | CONSISTING OF | *THE MOST SUMPTUOUS MADE DISHES,* | RAGOUTS, FRICASSEES, SOUPS, | GRAVIES, *&c.* | *Foreign and English:* | INCLUDING THE LATEST IMPROVEMENTS | IN | *FASHIONABLE LIFE.* | [short fancy rule] | BY | FREDERIC NUTT, ESQ. | *AUTHOR OF THE COMPLETE CONFECTIONER, &c.* | [two short rules] | *LONDON:* | PRINTED FOR MATHEWS AND LEIGH, STRAND, | BY JAMES MOYES, SHOE LANE. | [short rule] | 1809.

First edition, London, 1809.

172 x 97 mm. A-O^{12} P^6; 174 leaves, pp. [i-v] vi-xxiv [1] 2-311 [312-324]. First leaf wanting in this copy.

Illustration: Engraved frontispiece portrait of the author by Woodman after a drawing by Satchwell.

Bibliographies: Axford, p. 224; Craig 66; Oxford, p. 136; Simon BG 1110; Vicaire 634.

Copies: *BMC* and *NUC* (Iowa State University, New York Public Library, and University of Wisconsin).

911. The Oyster.

THE OYSTER; | WHERE, HOW, AND WHEN | TO | FIND, BREED, COOK | AND | EAT IT. | [woodcut of oysters] | LONDON: | TRÜBNER & CO., 60, PATERNOSTER ROW. | MDCCCLXI.

First edition, London, 1861.

182 x 102 mm. [A]⁴ B-G⁸; 52 leaves, pp. [i-v] vi-viii [9] 10-96, ²[1-2] 3-7 [8]. Half calf and marbled boards with publisher's colored pictorial wrappers bound in.

Illustrations: Wood engraved frontispiece and wood engravings on title-page and first page of text, all by George Cruikshank. Two of the wood engravings are repeated in colors on the front and back wrappers. There also is an anatomical wood engraving of an oyster on p. 30.

Note: Halkett and Laing attribute this work to Herbert Byng Hall (1805?-1883) and state that it has been incorrectly attributed to Eustace Clare Grenville Murray (1824-1881). *BMC* enters it under Hall and the *NUC* under Murray.

Bibliographies: Axford, p. 312 (misdated 1959); Bitting, p. 588; Cohn, 623.

Copies: *BMC* and *NUC* (9 copies).

912. Papin, Denys, 1647-1714.

[within a border of two rules] A | New Digester | OR | ENGINE | FOR SOFTNING | BONES, | CONTAINING THE | DESCRIPTION | Of its *Make* and *Use* in these Particulars: | *VIZ.* | Cookery, Voyages at Sea, Confectionary, Ma- | king of Drinks, Chymistry, and Dying. | WITH AN | Account of the Price a good big Engine will cost, | and of the Profit it will afford. | [rule] | By *DENYS PAPIN* M. D. Fellow of the | ROYAL SOCIETY. | [two rules] | *LONDON,* | Printed by *J. M.* for *Henry Bonwicke* at the *Red Lyon* | in S. *Paul's* Church-yard. 1681.

First edition, London, 1681.

4to. [A]⁴ B-H⁴; 32 leaves, pp. [*8*] 1-54 [*2*]. Last leaf blank.

Illustration: Engraved folding plate showing apparatus.

Bound with *A Continuation of the New Digester of Bones* . . ., London, 1687 (item 913).

Bibliographies: Craig 67; Noling, p. 320; Oxford, p. 40; Vicaire 653; Wheaton and Kelly 4598; Wing P309.

Copies: *BMC, BNC,* and *NUC* (14 copies). Wing (8 copies).

913. Papin, Denys, 1647-1714.

A | CONTINUATION | OF the NEW | DIGESTER | OF | BONES: | It's IMPROVEMENTS and new USES it hath | been applyed to, both for *SEA* and *LAND.* | Together with some Improvements and new Uses | of the *AIR-PUMP*, tryed both in *England* and | in *Italy.* | [rule] | By *DENYS PAPIN* M. D. Fellow of the | *ROYAL SOCIETY.* | [rule] | LONDON, | Printed by *Joseph Streater*, near *Pauls-Wharf* in *Thames-street,* | and are to be Sold by the *Book-Sellers* in *Loudon.* 1687.

First edition, London, 1687.

4to. A-Q⁴ R²; 66 leaves, pp. [*8*] 1-123 [*124*]. A3 missigned "A2."

Illustrations: Two engraved folding plates showing apparatus.

Bound with *A New Digester* . . ., London, 1681 (item 912).

Bibliographies: Oxford, p. 41; Wheaton and Kelly 4599; Wing P308.

Copies: *BMC* and *NUC* (13 copies). Wing (8 copies).

914. Parkes, Frances Byerley.

DOMESTIC DUTIES; | OR, | INSTRUCTIONS TO YOUNG MARRIED LADIES, | ON THE | MANAGEMENT OF THEIR HOUSEHOLDS | AND THE | REGULATION OF THEIR CONDUCT IN THE VARIOUS | RELATIONS AND DUTIES OF | MARRIED LIFE. | [short rule] | BY MRS. WILLIAM PARKES. | [short rule] | Every wise woman buildeth her house; but the foolish plucketh it down with | her hands. | Who can find a virtuous woman? for her price is far above rubies. | Her children arise up and call her blessed; her husband, also, and he praiseth | her. | PROVERBS. | [short rule] | *SECOND EDITION.* | LONDON: | PRINTED FOR | LONGMAN, HURST, REES, ORME, BROWN, AND GREEN, | PATERNOSTER-ROW. | 1825.

Second edition, London, 1825. Originally published, London, also 1825.

191 x 109 mm. A^6 B-X^{12} Y^4; 250 leaves, pp. [i-v] vi-ix [x-xii] [1] 2-487 [488]. A folding letterpress chart is tipped in facing p. 226 and is not reckoned in the collation or pagination.

Illustrations: Numerous wood engravings in the text.

Bibliographies: Attar 221.1. Oxford, p. 157, cites the first and third editions.

Copies: *BMC* and *NUC* (Library of Congress and University of Florida). Attar adds Brotherton Library.

915. Parkes, Frances Byerley.

DOMESTIC DUTIES; | OR, | INSTRUCTIONS TO YOUNG MARRIED LADIES, | ON THE | MANAGEMENT OF THEIR HOUSEHOLDS | AND THE | REGULATION OF THEIR CONDUCT IN THE VARIOUS | RELATIONS AND DUTIES OF | MARRIED LIFE. | [short rule] | BY MRS. WILLIAM PARKES. | [short rule] | Every wise woman buildeth her house; but the foolish plucketh it down with | her hands. | Who can find a virtuous woman? for her price is far above rubies. | Her children arise up and call her blessed; her husband also, and he praiseth | her. | PROVERBS. | [short rule] | *THIRD EDITION.* | LONDON: | PRINTED FOR | LONGMAN, REES, ORME, BROWN, AND GREEN, | PATERNOSTER-ROW. | 1828.

Third edition, London, 1828. Originally published, London, 1825.

180 x 106 mm. A⁶ B-Y¹² Z² χ1; 261 leaves, pp. [2] [v] vi-xiii [xiv] [1] 2-510. A2 and A3 missigned "A3" and "A4." A folding letterpress chart is tipped in facing p. 244 and is not reckoned in the collation or pagination.

Illustrations: Numerous wood engravings in the text.

Bibliographies: Attar 221.2; Oxford, p. 157, in a note dating this edition 1829; Wheaton and Kelly 4610.

Copies: *NUC* (Oregon State University only). Attar adds Brotherton Library. Wheaton and Kelly (American Antiquarian Society, Boston Public Library, and Harvard).

916. Party-Giving on Every Scale.

PARTY-GIVING │ ON │ EVERY SCALE. │ OR │ *THE COST OF ENTERTAINMENTS* │ WITH THE │ *FASHIONABLE MODES OF ARRANGEMENT.* │ BY THE AUTHOR OF │ "MANNERS AND TONE OF GOOD SOCIETY," │ "THE MANAGEMENT OF SERVANTS." │ ETC. │ [publisher's monogram] │ LONDON: │ FREDERICK WARNE AND CO., │ BEDFORD STREET, STRAND.

First edition, London, 1880.

180 x 115 mm. [A]⁸ B-P⁸; 120 leaves, pp. [i-vii] viii-xv [xvi] [1] 2-224.

Bibliographies: Unrecorded in the bibliographies consulted. Wheaton and Kelly records the second edition, London, 188-.

Copies: *BMC* and *NUC* (4 copies).

917. The Pastry-Cook's Vade-Mecum.

[within a border of two rules] THE │ 𝔓astry = 𝔒ook's │ *Vade-Mecum:* │ OR, A │ POCKET-COMPANION │ FOR │ Cooks, House-Keeprs, Coun- │ try Gentlewomen, *&c.* │ CONTAINING, │ Choice and Excellent Directions, and │ Receipts for making all Sorts of Pa- │ stry-Work; Dressing the most Dainty │ Dishes; Candying, Preserving and │ Drying all manner of Fruit. As also, │ the Art of *Distilling* and *Surgery.* │ *LONDON:* │ Printed for *Abel Roper,* at the *Black-Boy* │ in *Fleet-street,* 1705.

First edition, London, 1705.

12mo. A^4 B-E^{12} F^2, 54 leaves, pp. [*8*] 1-100.

Bibliographies: Axford, p. 316; Bitting, p. 589; Maclean, p. 111; Oxford, p. 49.

Copies: *BMC* and *NUC* (Library of Congress only).

918. Paulli, Simon, 1603-1680.

A | TREATISE | ON | [in two columns: column one] TOBACCO, | TEA, | [two vertical rules] | [column two] COFFEE, *and* | CHOCOLATE. [end columns] | IN WHICH | I. The Advantages and Disadvantages at- | tending the Use of these Commodities, are not | only impartially considered, upon the Princi- | ciples of *Medicine* and *Chymistry*, but also as- | certained by *Observation* and *Experience*. | II. Full and distinct Directions laid down for | knowing in what Cases, and for what particu- | lar Constitutions, these Substances are either | beneficial, or hurtful. | III. The *Chinese* or *Asiatic Tea*, shewn to be the | same with the *European Chamelaeagnus*, or | *Myrtus Brabantica*. | [rule] | *The Whole Illustrated with* COPPER PLATES, *exhibiting* | *the* Tea *Utensils of the* Chinese *and* Persians. | [rule] | Written originally by SIMON PAULI; | AND | Now Translated by Dr. *JAMES*. | [rule] | *Ante omnia scire convenit Naturam Corporis; quia alii graciles,* / *alii obesi sunt, alii calidi, alii frigidiores, alii humidi,* / *alii sicciores, alios adstricta, alios resoluta, alvus exer-* / *cet.* Celsus, *Lib. 1. Cap.* 3. | [rule] | *LONDON:* | Printed for T. OSBORNE, in *Gray's Inn*; | J. HILDYARD, at *York*; M. BRYSON, at *New-* | *castle*; and J. LEAKE, at *Bath.* | [short rule] | M,DCC,XLVI.

First edition in English, London, 1746. Originally published in Latin under the title *Commentarius de abusu tabaci Americanorum veteri, et herbae theé Asiaticorum in Europa novo*, Strassburg, 1665.

8vo. $[A]^2$ B-L^8 M^6; 88 leaves, pp. [*4*] [1] 2-171 [*172*].

Illustrations: Two engraved folding plates signed B. Cole of coffee and tea making apparatus.

Bibliographies: Maclean, p. 111; Noling, p. 323; Vicaire 667; Wheaton and Kelly 4688.

Copies: *BNC* and *NUC* (15 copies). Maclean adds Brotherton Library, Glasgow University, and Wellcome Library.

919. Peckham, Ann.

THE | Complete English COOK; | OR, | PRUDENT HOUSEWIFE. | BEING | An
entire new Collection of the most general, yet least | expensive RECEIPTS in every
Branch of | COOKERY and GOOD HOUSEWIFERY. | With DIRECTIONS for | [in
three columns: column one] Roasting, | Boiling, | Stewing, | Ragoos, | Soups, |
Sauces, | [fancy vertical rule] | [column two] Fricaseys | Pies, Tarts, | Puddings, |
Cheese-Cakes, | Custards, | Jellies, | [fancy vertical rule] | [column three] Potting, |
Candying, | Collaring, | Pickling, | Preserving, | Made-Wines, &c. [end columns] |
Together with Directions for placing Dishes on Tables of Entertainment: | And many
other Things equally necessary. The Whole made easy to | the meanest Capacity, and
far more useful to young Beginners than any | Book of the Kind extant. | *In cooking
Fowl, or Flesh, or Fish,* | *Or any nice, or dainty Dish,* | *With Care peruse this useful
Book,* | *'Twill make you soon a perfect Cook.* | [rule] | By ANN PECKHAM, of
LEEDS, | Who is well known to have been for Forty Years past one of the most |
noted COOKS in the Country of *York.* | [rule] | [fancy rule] | LEEDS: | Printed by
GRIFFITH WRIGHT, M,DCC,LXVII. | And Sold by | The Author, and J. OGLE, in
Leeds; and Messrs. | ROBINSON and ROBERTS, in Pater-noster-Row, London.

First edition, Leeds, 1767.

12mo. π^2 A-H^{12} I-M^6; 122 leaves, pp. [i-iii] iv, 5-201 [202-244].

Note: Maclean points out that the title-page of this work is almost identical with that of
a book by Catherine Brooks published ca. 1762. While the title-pages are the same,
she notes, the books are entirely different.

Bibliographies: Maclean, p. 112; Oxford, p. 95.

Copies: *BMC.* Maclean adds Cambridge, Edinburgh University, and New York
Public Library.

920. Pegge, Samuel, 1704-1796, editor.

THE | FORME OF CURY, | A ROLL | OF | ANCIENT ENGLISH COOKERY, |
Compiled, about A. D. 1390, by the | Master-Cooks of King RICHARD II, |
Presented afterwards to Queen ELIZABETH, | by EDWARD Lord STAFFORD, |
And now in the Possession of GUSTAVUS BRANDER, Esq. | Illustrated with
NOTES, | And a copious INDEX, or GLOSSARY. | A MANUSCRIPT of the
EDITOR, of the | same Age and Subject, with other congruous | Matters, are

subjoined. | "——— ingeniosa gula est." MARTIAL. | LONDON, | PRINTED BY J. NICHOLS, | PRINTER TO THE SOCIETY OF ANTIQUARIES. | M DCC LXXX.

First edition, second issue, London, 1785, erronerously dated 1780. Originally published, London, 1780.

4to. a²(±a1.2) b-e⁴ f² A-U⁴ Y² Z⁴ Aa-Bb⁴; pp. [i-ii] iii-iv, ²i-xxxvi, 1-188.

Illustrations: Engraved frontispiece portrait of the editor, by J. Basire, dated 1785, and an engraved facsimile of one recipe from the original manuscript, also by Basire.

This copy inscribed: Francis Grose Esqr. Capt:, Adjutant, and master of the Surry Millitia, with Mr: Brander's Complim:ts.

Note: In the first issue of *The Form of Cury* the editor, Samuel Pegge, was not named. On the title-page he was referred to as "AN ANTIQUARY" and the dedication to Gustavus Brander, who then owned the manuscript from which the work was edited, was signed, on p. iv, "THE EDITOR." Five years later the unsold sheets of the first edition were re-issued with a newly printed first signature containing a re-set title-page in which reference to the editor as "AN ANTIQUARY" is dropped and the re-set dedication is signed "S. PEGGE" rather than "THE EDITOR." The date on the new title-page, however, remained 1780. A portrait of Pegge dated 1785 was supplied for the re-issue. There was no portrait in the first issue.

The fact that four copies of the second issue (the Gernon copy and copies at Cornell University, the Detroit Public Library, and Kansas State University) are inscribed to their recipients by Gustavus Brander suggests he may have initiated this re-issue of the work. No inscribed copy of the first issue has been located. Two aberrant copies (at the Boston Public Library and a second Kansas State University copy) contain the first signature in both its cancelled and uncancelled states; neither is inscribed.

The title-page of the first issue reads as follows:

THE | FORME OF CURY, | A ROLL | OF | ANCIENT ENGLISH COOKERY, | Compiled, about A.D. 1390, by the | Master-Cooks of King RICHARD II, | Presented afterwards to Queen ELIZABETH, | By EDWARD Lord STAFFORD, | And now in the Possession of GUSTAVUS BRANDER, Esq. | Illustrated with NOTES, | And a copious INDEX, or GLOSSARY. | A MANUSCRIPT of the EDITOR, of the same Age and Subject, is subjoined. | BY AN ANTIQUARY. | "——— ingeniosa gula est." MARTIAL. | LONDON, | PRINTED BY J. NICHOLS. | M DCC LXXX.

Bibliographies: First issue: Maclean, p. 113; Oxford, p. 108; Simon BG 1143. Second issue: Axford, p. 169; Bitting, p. 361; Craig 69; Maclean, p. 112; Pennell, p. 162; Wheaton and Kelly 2212. Issue not noted: Vicaire 669.

Copies: First issue: *BMC* and Massachusetts Historical Society. Second issue: *BMC*, Bodleian Library, Cornell (2 copies), Detroit Public Library, Harvard, Kansas State University, Library of Congress, New York Public Library, University of Chicago, University of Minnesota, and University of North Carolina, Greensboro. Aberrant copies of the second issue with both cancelled and uncancelled printings of signature a are located in the Boston Public Library and Kansas State University.

921. Pennell, Elizabeth Robins, 1855-1936.

[woodcut title-page lettered] THE FEASTS | OF AUTOLYCUS | THE DIARY OF A GREEDY WOMAN | [woodcut of a man with a skillet at a stove] | EDITED | BY ELIZABETH ROBINS PENNELL | LONDON: JOHN LANE: | NEW YORK | THE MERRIAM CO | MDCCCXCVI

First edition, London, 1896.

176 x 117 mm. π1 [1]^8 2-10^8 [11-12]^8 13-16^8 17^4; 133 leaves, pp. [2] [1-5] 6-264. Publisher's light green cloth stamped in dark green, red, and gold.

Bibliographies: Axford, p. 153; Bitting, p. 363; Driver 821.1; Wheaton and Kelly 4718.

Copies: *BMC* and *NUC* (13 copies).

922. Percy, Henry Algernon, 5th Earl of Northumberland, 1478-1527.

THE | REGULATIONS AND ESTABLISHMENT | OF THE | HOUSHOLD | OF | HENRY ALGERNON PERCY, | THE FIFTH EARL OF | NORTHUMBERLAND, | AT HIS CASTLES OF | WRESILL AND LEKINFIELD | IN YORKSHIRE. | BEGUN ANNO DOMINI | M.D.XII. | [crown] | LONDON PRINTED | M.DCC.LXX.

First edition, London, 1770.

8vo. [A]^4 B-C^4 D^4 (-D4) b^4 ^{2}B-Nnn^4 Ooo^2; 253 leaves, pp. [i-v] vi-xxvi [xxvii-xxviii], ^{2}[i-ii] iii-x [1] 2-464 [465-468].

Bibliographies: Craig 70; Maclean, p. 114; Wheaton and Kelly 4730.

Copies: *BMC* and *NUC* (9 copies). Maclean adds National Library of Scotland.

923. Philips, John, 1676-1709.

[within a border of two rules] CYDER. | A | POEM. | In TWO BOOKS. | [rule] | —*Honos erit huic quoq; Pomo?* Virg. | [rule] | *LONDON:* | Printed for *Jacob Tonson*, within *Grays-Inn* | Gate next *Grays-Inn* Lane. 1708.

First edition, London, 1708, with catch word "When" on p. 68 complete and p. 74 so numbered.

8vo. [A]^2 B-F^8 G^4 H^2; 48 leaves, pp. [6] [1] 2-89 [90].

Illustration: Engraved frontispiece depicting gardeners at work by vander Gucht on A2^v.

Bibliographies: Bitting, p. 369; Foxon P237; Simon BG 1161.

Copies: *BMC*, and *NUC* (31 copies).

924. Philips, John, 1676-1709.

CYDER. | A | POEM. | [rule] | In TWO BOOKS. | [rule] | — *Honos erit huic quoq; Pomo?* Virg. | [rule] | WITH THE | SPLENDID SHILLING; | PARADISE LOST, | And Two SONGS, *&c.* | [rule] | *LONDON:* | Printed and Sold by *H. Hills*, in *Black-Fryars*, near | the Water-side. 1709.

Second edition, London, 1709. Originally published, London, 1708 (item 923).

8vo. A-C^8; 24 leaves, pp. [1] 2-48.

Bibliographies: Foxon P239; Noling, p. 328.

Copies: *BMC*, and *NUC* (10 copies).

925. Philips, John, 1676-1709.

CIDER, | A POEM | IN TWO BOOKS, | BY | *JOHN PHILIPS.* | [short fancy rule] | WITH NOTES PROVINCIAL, HISTORICAL, | AND CLASSICAL, | *BY CHARLES*

DUNSTER. | [short fancy rule] | LONDON: | *PRINTED BY GEORGE STAFFORD,* | FOR T. CADELL, IN THE STRAND. | MDCCXCI.

New edition, London, 1791. Originally published, London, 1708 (item 923).

8vo. [a]² b⁴ B-Aa⁴; 98 leaves, pp. [1-5] 6-8 [9-12], ²[1] 2-183 [184].

Bibliographies: Bitting, p. 369; Oberlé (1) 1083; Simon BG 1164.

Copies: *BMC, BNC,* and *NUC* (10 copies).

926. Phillips, Sarah.

THE | LADIES HANDMAID: | OR, A | COMPLEAT SYSTEM | OF | COOKERY; | ON THE | PRINCIPALS of ELEGANCE and FRUGALITY. | WHEREIN | The useful ART of COOKERY is rendered plain, easy | and familiar: | CONTAINING | The best approved, yet least expensive RECEIPTS in every | BRANCH of HOUSEWIFRY, *viz.* | [in three columns: column one] ROASTING, | BOILING, | MADE-DISHES, | SOUPS, | SAUCES, | [vertical rule] | [column two] JELLIES, | RAGOUTS, | FRICASSEES, | TARTS, | CAKES, | [vertical rule] | [column three] CREAMS, | CUSTARDS, | PASTRY, | PICKLING, | JARRING, *&c.* [end columns] | And every other Branch of COOKERY and good HOUSEWIFRY, too | tedious to be enumerated in a Title Page. | TOGETHER | With INSTRUCTIONS for CARVING and BILLS of FARE for every | Month in the Year. | Embellished with vareity of curious COPPER-PLATES, representing the | genteelest Method of Disposing or Placing the Dishes, Trussing Fowls, *&c.* | ALSO | The Best approved Method of CLEAR-STARCHING. | [rule] | *By Mrs.* SARAH PHILLIPS, *of* Duke-Street. | [two rules] | LONDON: | Printed for J. COOTE, at the *King's-Arms,* opposite *Devereux-Court,* | in the *Strand,* M,DCC,LVIII.

First edition, London, 1758.

8vo. A² a⁴(-a4) b-c⁴ B-Nnn⁴ Oool (=a4); 246 leaves, pp. [1-3] 4 [*18*] [5] 6-296, 295-472.

Illustrations: Engraved frontispiece of the author, dated 1758, and four engraved plates showing table settings and trussing fowls.

Bibliographies: Axford, p. 243; Bitting, p. 369; Craig 71; Maclean, p. 115; Simon BG 1167.

Copies: *NUC* (Library of Congress, New York Academy of Medicine, and New York Public Library). Maclean adds Brotherton Library and International Wine and Food Society.

927. Philp, Robert Kemp, 1819-1882.

THE | FAMILY SAVE-ALL | A SYSTEM OF | 𝔖econdary 𝔠ookery | SUPPLYING | EXCELLENT DISHES FOR BREAKFAST, LUNCHEON, | DINNER, AND SUPPER, FROM COLD AND | OTHER FRAGMENTS | WITH | INVALUABLE HINTS | FOR ECONOMY IN THE USE OF EVERY ARTICLE OF | HOUSEHOLD CONSUMPTION. | BY THE | EDITOR OF "ENQUIRE WITHIN," ETC. | [SALE OF THE AUTHOR'S WORKS: | IN GREAT BRITAIN, HALF-A-MILLION VOLUMES; AN EQUAL NUMBER IN AMERICA.] | [short rule] | LONDON | PUBLISHED FOR THE PROPRIETOR BY | W. KENT & CO., 23, PATERNOSTER ROW | AND SOLD BY ALL BOOKSELLERS. | 1861.

First edition, London, 1861.

186 x 122 mm. [a]^4 b^6 c^4 B-K^{16} L^2; 160 leaves, pp. [i-iii] iv-xxviii [1] 2-292. Publisher's brown cloth stamped in gold.

Bibliographies: Wheaton and Kelly 4772.

Copies: *NUC* (New York Public Library only). Wheaton and Kelly (Radcliffe only).

928. Philp, Robert Kemp, 1819-1882.

THE | FAMILY SAVE-ALL | A SYSTEM OF | 𝔖econdary 𝔠ookery | SUPPLYING | EXCELLENT DISHES FOR BREAKFAST, LUNCHEON, | DINNER, AND SUPPER, FROM COLD AND | OTHER FRAGMENTS | WITH | INVALUABLE HINTS | FOR ECONOMY IN THE USE OF EVERY ARTICLE OF | HOUSEHOLD CONSUMPTION. | BY THE | EDITOR OF "ENQUIRE WITHIN," ETC. | SALE OF THE AUTHOR'S WORKS | IN GREAT BRITAIN, HALF-A-MILLION VOLUMES; AN EQUAL NUMBER IN AMERICA. | SECOND EDITION. | LONDON | PUBLISHED FOR THE PROPRIETOR BY | W. KENT & Co., 23, PATERNOSTER ROW | AND SOLD BY ALL BOOKSELLERS. | 1861.

Second edition, London, 1861. Originally published, London, also 1861 (item 927).

186 x 122 mm. [a]⁴ b⁶ c⁴ B-K¹⁶ L²; 160 leaves, pp. [i-iii] iv-xxviii [1] 2-292. Publisher's blue-green cloth stamped in gold.

Bibliographies: Attar 237.1 and Simon BG 660.

Copies: *BMC*. Attar adds Bodleian Library.

929. Philp, Robert Kemp, 1819-1882.

THE | PRACTICAL HOUSEWIFE, | FORMING A COMPLETE | 𝔈𝔫𝔠𝔶𝔠𝔩𝔬𝔭𝔞𝔢𝔡𝔦𝔞 of 𝔇𝔬𝔪𝔢𝔰𝔱𝔦𝔠 𝔈𝔠𝔬𝔫𝔬𝔪𝔶, | COMPRISING | [in two columns: column one] THOUGHTS ON HOUSEKEEPING, | FAMILY MEDICAL GUIDE, | APERIENT MEDICINES, | FOOD FOR INVALIDS, | COOKERY FOR CHILDREN, | RUDIMENTS OF COOKERY, | DOMESTIC MANIPULATION, | LAYING-OUT TABLES, | [vertical rule] | [column two] TRUSSING AND CARVING, | FOOD FOR THE MONTHS, | SUMMER AND WINTER DRINKS, | USEFUL HINTS TO HOUSEKEEPERS, | HINTS ON FAMILIAR THINGS, | DOMESTIC AND USEFUL RECEIPTS, | A COPIOUS INDEX, MAKING THE RE- | FERENCE TO EACH ITEM MOST EASY. [end columns] | BY THE | EDITORS OF THE "FAMILY FRIEND." | [short fancy rule] | LONDON: | WARD AND LOCK, 158, FLEET STREET; | AND ALL BOOKSELLERS.

Engraved title-page:

[within a single rule border] THE | PRACTICAL HOUSEWIFE | BY THE | EDITORS | OF THE | FAMILY FRIEND | [vignette of kitchen scene] | LONDON | WARD & LOCK 158 FLEET STREET.

First edition, London, 1855.

186 x 122 mm. π⁸ A-I⁸ J-M⁸; 112 leaves, pp. [2] [i-iii] iv-xxix [xxx] [1] 2-192. Publisher's gray cloth stamped in gold.

Illustrations: Wood engraved frontispiece and title and numerous wood engravings in the text.

Bibliographies: Attar 243.1; Axford, p. 329; Bitting, p. 593.

Copies: *BMC* and *NUC* (Library of Congress only). Attar adds Bodleian Library and Polytechic Library, Oxford.

930. Plat, Sir Hugh, 1552-1611.

DELIGHTS | FOR | LADIES, | *TO* | ADORNE THEIR | *Persons, Tables, Closets,* | and Distillatories; | WITH | *Beauties, Banquets, Perfumes,* | *and Waters.* | [rule] | Reade, practise, and censure. | [rule] | LONDON, | Printed by *Humfrey Lownes.* | 1624.

Tenth edition, London, 1624. Originally published, London, 1600.

12mo. A-H^{12}; 96 leaves, unpaginated. This copy lacks leaves H3-H10.

Bound with *A Closet for Ladies and Gentlewomen*, London, 1624 (item 609).

Bibliographies: Bitting, p. 373; *STC* 19983.5.

Copies: *STC* (British Library and Horblit copies).

931. Plat, Sir Hugh, 1552-1611.

[within an ornamental border] DELIGHTES | FOR | LADIES | *by* | *Sir Hugh Plat* | With Introductions by | G. E. FUSSELL | and | KATHLEEN ROSEMARY FUSSELL | *LONDON* | CROSBY LOCKWOOD & SON LTD | 39 THURLOE STREET, S.W. 7 | 1948

First printing of this edition, London, 1948, reset from the edition of 1609.

216 x 138 mm. [a]^8 b-e^8 f^6 B-G^8 H^6; 100 leaves, pp. [i-v] vi-xci [xcii] [1-3] 4-106 [2]. Publisher's red cloth, stamped in silver, in a dust jacket.

Bibliographies: Wheaton and Kelly 4812.

Copies: *BMC* and *NUC* (14 copies).

932. Plat, Sir Hugh, 1552-1611.

[within a border of two rules] THE | GARDEN | OF | EDEN. | OR, | *An accurate* | *Description of* | *all* Flowers *and* Fruits *now* | *growing in* England, *with par-* | *ticular* | *Rules how to advance* | *their* Nature *and* Growth, *as* | *well in* Seeds *and* Herbs, *as* | *the secret ordering of* Trees | *and* Plants. | [rule] | By that learned and great |

Observer, | Sir HUGH PLAT, *Knight.* | And now published by the *Author's* | own Manuscript. | [rule] | LONDON, | Printed for *William Leake*, at the | Crown in Fleetstreet betwixt the | Two Temple Gates. | 1653.

Second edition, London, 1653. Originally published London, also 1653.

8vo. $^\pi$A^8 A-K^8; 88 leaves, pp. [1-2] 3-175 [176].

Bibliographies: Henrey I.293; Wing P2385.

Copies: *BMC, BNC,* and *NUC* (7 copies). Wing (6 copies).

933. Plat, Sir Hugh, 1552-1611.

[within a border of two rules] THE | GARDEN | OF | EDEN: | OR, | An accurate Description of all | *Flowers* and *Fruits* now growing | in *England*, with particular Rules | how to advance their Nature and | Growth, as well in *Seeds* and | *Herbs*, as the secret Ordering of | *Trees* and *Plants.* | [rule] | In Two Parts. | [rule] | By that Learned and great Obser- | ver, Sir *HUGH PLAT* Kt. | [rule] | *The Sixth Edition.* | [rule] | *LONDON,* | Printed for *William* and *John Leake,* | at the Crown in *Fleetstreet* betwixt | the two Temple Gates 1675.

Title-page of the second part:

[within a border of two rules] THE | SECOND PART | OF THE | Garden of Eden: | OR, | An accurate Description | of all *Flowers* and *Fruits* now | growing in *ENGLAND.* | WITH | Particular Rules how to advance | their Nature and Growth, as | well in *Seeds* and *Herbs*, as | the secret Ordering of | *Trees* and *Plants.* | [rule] | By that Learned and great Obser- | ver, Sir *HUGH PLAT* Kt. | [rule] | *LONDON,* | Printed for *William* and *John Leake,* | at the Crown in *Fleetstreet*, betwixt | the two Temple Gates 1675.

Seventh edition, London, 1675, styled "sixth edition" on the title-page. Originally published, London, 1653.

8vo. A-L^8, ^{2}A-L^8; 176 leaves, pp. [*28*] 1-148, ^{2}[*16*] 1-159 [160].

Bibliographies: Wing P2388.

Copies: *BMC* and *NUC* (6 copies). Wing (5 copies).

934. Plat, Sir Hugh, 1552-1611.

[The Jewell House of Art and Nature. London, 1594. Part three].

[within ornamental woodcut] Diuers Chimicall | *Conclusions concerning* | the Art of Distillation. | With many rare practises | *and vses thereof, according* | to the Authors own | experience. | Faithfully and familiarly set | *downe by H. Plat of Lin-* | colnes Inne Gent. | LONDON | *Printed by Peter Short.* | 1594.

First edition, London, 1594.

4to. A-I⁴ K²; 38 leaves, pp. [1-2] 3-76.

Illustrations: Numerous woodcuts in the text.

Bibliographies: Craig 72; Noling, p. 330; *STC* 19991; Wheaton and Kelly 4815.

Copies: *BMC, BNC*, and *NUC* (3 copies of this part recorded separately and 7 copies of the complete work). *STC* (10 copies).

935. Plat, Sir Hugh, 1552-1611.

[within a border of type ornaments] THE | JEVVEL HOUSE | OF | Art and Nature: | CONTAINING | Divers Rare and Profitable Inven- | tions, together with sundry new Experiments in | the Art of Husbandry. | *WITH* | Divers Chimical Conclusions concerning the Art | of Distillation, and the rare practices and uses thereof. | Faithfully and familiarly set down, according to | the Authours own experience. | [rule] | *By Sir Hugh Plat of Lincolns Inne, Knight.* | [rule] | Wherunto is added, A rare and excellent Discourse | of Minerals, Stones, Gums, and Rosins; with the vertues | and use thereof. *By D. B. Gent.* | [rule] | LONDON: Printed by *Bernard Alsop*, and are to be | sold at his house in Grubstreet, near the Upper Pump. 1653.

Second edition, London, 1653. Originally published, London, 1594 (item 934, for part three).

4to. A-Gg⁴; 120 leaves, pp. [*8*] 1-232.

Illustrations: Woodcut of an "Ear of Summer Barley" on the verso of the title-page and numerous woodcuts in the text.

Bibliographies: Bitting, p. 373; Simon BG 1186; Wheaton and Kelly 4814; Wing P2390.

Copies: *BMC* and *NUC* (26 copies). Wing (9 copies).

935a. Plumtre, Annabella.

DOMESTIC MANAGEMENT; | OR, THE HEALTHFUL | COOKERY-BOOK. | TO WHICH IS PREFIXED | *A TREATISE ON DIET,* | AS THE SUREST MEANS TO PRESERVE | HEALTH, LONG LIFE, &c. | WITH MANY | VALUABLE OBSERVATIONS | ON THE NUTRITIOUS AND BENEFICIAL AS WELL AS THE | INJURIOUS EFFECTS OF VARIOUS KINDS OF FOOD; | ALSO | REMARKS | ON THE | *WHOLESOME AND PERNICIOUS MODES OF COOKERY,* | Intended as an Antidote to modern Errors therein. | *To which is added,* | THE METHOD OF TREATING SUCH TRIFLING MEDICIAL CASES | AS PROPERLY COME WITHIN THE SPHERE OF | *DOMESTIC MANAGEMENT.* | [short tappered rule] | BY A LADY. | [short wavy rule] | SECOND EDITION, CORRECTED AND ENLARGED. | [short thin-thick rule] | *LONDON;* | PRINTED FOR B. AND R. CROSBY AND CO. STATIONER'S-COURT, | PATERNOSTER-ROW; | And Sold by every Bookseller in the United Kingdom. | 1813. | [short rule] | *Price 6s. extra boards.*

Second edition, second printing or issue, London, 1813. Originally published, London, 1810, and in the second edition, London, 1812. The Lilly Library copy is too tightly bound to determine whether it is a re-issue of the 1812 sheets with a cancel title-page or a new printing from the second edition setting of type.

Note: Watt attributes this work to Annabella Plumtre. Oxford mis-cites Watts and gives the author's first name as Arabella, a mistake that Bitting repeats. *NUC* has a cross reference from Bell Plumtre to Annabella Plumtre.

160 x 90 mm. A^{12} χB^6 $B-S^{12}$; 222 leaves, pp. [i-iii] iv-xxxvi [1] 2-375 [376] [*32*]. Last leaf wanting in this copy.

Illustrations: Engraved frontispiece illustrating a well-stocked larder.

Bibliographies: The 1813 issue or printing is unrecorded in the bibliographies consulted. Vicaire 700 records the second edition, London, 1812 and Axford, p. 121; Bitting, p. 374; Oxford p. 139, and Vicaire 700 all record the first edition, London, 1810.

Copies: No other copy of the 1813 issue or printing located. *NUC* locates only the Bitting copy of the first edition, London, 1810.

936. Poole, Watkin.

THE | FEMALE'S BEST FRIEND; | OR, THE | YOUNG WOMAN'S GUIDE | TO | VIRTUE, ECONOMY, AND HAPPINESS: | CONTAINING | *A COMPLETE MODERN* | 𝔖𝔶𝔰𝔱𝔢𝔪 𝔬𝔣 𝔠𝔬𝔬𝔨𝔢𝔯𝔶, | FORMED UPON PRINCIPES OF ECONOMY FOR PRIVATE FAMILIES: | ALSO | [in two columns: column one] Instructions for Marketing. | The best modes of Trussing, Carving, and De- | corating a Table, illustrated by Engravings. | The art of composing the most simple and | highly finished Broths, Gravies, Soups, | and Sauces. | The mysteries of Potting, Pickling, and Pre- | serving. | [two vertical rules] | [column two] The art of making all sorts of Confectionary | and Pastry. | Improved methods of making and manag- | ing, British Wines, also of Brewing and | Baking. | Valuable Medicinal Directions, and a great | variety of useful Family and Medical Re- | ceipts. [end columns] | TO WHICH ARE ADDED, | INSTRUCTIONS TO FEMALE SERVANTS OF EVERY DESCRIPTION; | *Advice to the Young Mother;* | RULES FOR THE TREATMENT OF INFANTS; DIRECTIONS FOR NURSING, AND | FOR THE MANAGEMENT AND EDUCATION | OF CHILDREN; | USEFUL HINTS FOR THE SICK CHAMBER; | AND FOR | PROMOTING MATRIMONIAL HAPPINESS: | ILLUSTRATED BY | *MORAL AND RELIGIOUS ESSAYS,* | TALES, | AND MEMOIRS OF ILLUSTRIOUS FEMALES, | EMINENT FOR THEIR PIETY, VIRTUE, AND ACCOMPLISHMENTS. | The whole being an improved and pleasant Directory for cultivating the Heart and Under- | standing, and a sure Guide to every acquirement for forming | *A PLEASING COMPANION,* | A RESPECTABLE MOTHER, AND A USEFUL MEMBER OF SOCIETY. | [short fancy rule] | A NEW EDITION, | EDITED AND COMPILED | BY WATKIN POOLE, ESQ. | FROM WRITERS OF UNQUESTIONABLE EXPERIENCE IN MEDICINE, COOKERY, BREW- | ING, AND EVERY OTHER BRANCH OF DOMESTIC ECONOMY. | [short fancy rule] | *Illustrated with beautiful appropriate Engravings.* | [two short rules] | 𝔐𝔞𝔫𝔠𝔥𝔢𝔰𝔱𝔢𝔯: | PRINTED AND PUBLISHED BY J. GLEAVE AND SON, 191, DEANSGATE. | 1826.

Engraved title-page:

[within an architectural border] PRACTICAL BOOK OF UTILITY &c. | *THE Females* | BEST FRIEND | or | 𝔜𝔬𝔲𝔫𝔤 𝔚𝔬𝔪𝔞𝔫𝔰 | GUIDE. | MANCHESTER. | *Published by J. Gleave & Son 191 Deansgate.* | *Engd. on Steel by J. Pigot & Son.*

"New edition," Manchester, 1826. This is the only edition mentioned by Attar and Oxford and no other record of any other edition has been found.

208 x 130 mm. π^4 A-4R^4; 348 leaves, pp. [i-iii] iv-viii [9] 10-694 [2].

Illustrations: Steel engraved frontispiece and title-page and twelve engraved plates illustrating handwriting, joints of meat, table settings, carving, and trussing.

Bibliographies: Attar 249.1; Oxford, p. 160.

Copies: Attar locates a copy at the Polytechnic Library, Oxford.

937. Price, Elizabeth.

THE | NEW BOOK OF COOKERY; | OR, | Every Woman a perfect Cook: | CONTAINING | The greatest Variety of approved Receipts in all | the Branches of COOKERY and CONFEC- | TIONARY, viz. | [in three columns: column one] | Boiling, | Roasting, | Broiling, | Frying, | Stewing, | Hashing, | Baking, | Fricassees, | Ragouts, | [vertical rule] | [column two] Made-Dishes, | Soups and Sauces, | Puddings, | Pies and Tarts, | Cakes, | Custards, | Cheesecakes, | Creams, | Syllabubs, | [vertical rule] | [column three] Jellies, | Pickling, | Preserving, | Candying, | Drying, | Potting, | Collaring, | English Wines, | &c. &c. &c. [end columns] | TO WHICH ARE ADDED, | The best instructions for Marketing, and sundry | Modern Bills of Fare; also Directions for Clear Starch- | ing, and the Ladies' Toilet, or, Art of preserving and | improving Beauty: Likewise a Collection of Physical | Receipts for Families, &c. | The Whole calculated to assist the *prudent Housewife* and her *Ser-* | *vants*, in furnishing the *cheapest* and *most elegant* Set of Dishes in the | various Departments of COOKERY, and to instruct Ladies in many | other Particulars of great Importance too numerous to mention in | this Title Page. | [rule] | By Mrs. ELIZ. PRICE, of BERKELEY-SQUARE, | Assisted by others who have made the Art of Cookery their | constant Study. | [rule] | A NEW EDITION for the PRESENT YEAR, with great | ADDITIONS. | [rule] | Here you may quickly learn with Care, | To act the Housewife's Part, | And dress a modern Bill of Fare | With Elegance and Art. | [two rules] | LONDON: | Printed for the AUTHORESS, and sold by ALEX. HOGG, | No 16, PATER-NOSTER-ROW. | [*Price only One Shilling.*]

Second edition, London, ca.1765. Originally published, London, ca.1760.

12mo. [A]^2 B-I^6 K^4; 54 leaves, pp. [i-iii] iv [13] 14-114 [2].

Illustrations: Engraved frontispiece of a kitchen scene.

Bibliographies: Maclean, p. 118.

Copies: Maclean (Brotherton Library copy only).

938. Price, Elizabeth.

THE | NEW, UNIVERSAL, AND | COMPLETE CONFECTIONER; | OR THE | WHOLE ART OF CONFECTIONARY | MADE PERFECTLY PLAIN AND EASY. | Containing *full Accounts* of all the various Methods of | PRESERVING and CANDYING, both dry and liquid, | *FRUIT, FLOWERS, GARDEN STUFF, HERBS, &c.* | ALSO THE SEVERAL WAYS OF | CLARIFYING SUGAR; | AND THE BEST METHODS OF | KEEPING FRUIT, NUTS, AND FLOWERS, | Fresh and Fine all the Year round: | TOGETHER WITH DIRECTIONS FOR MAKING | [in three columns: column one] Blomonge, | Biscuits, | Cakes, | Rock-Works, | Candies, | Tarts, | Possets, | Custards, | [vertical rule] | [column two] Jellies, | Creams, | Ices, | Whip Syllabubs, | Cheesecakes, | Sweetmeats, | Puffs & Pastes, | Oils, &c. | [vertical rule] | [column three] Syrups of all Kinds, | Jams, | Conserves, | Cordials, | Compotes, | Knicknacks, | Trifles, Comfits, | Drops, &c. &c. &c. [end columns] | Including various Modern and Original Receipts for | making LEMONADE, ORGEAT, ORANGEADE, | WATERS, and other REFRESHMENTS. | [short fancy rule] | *By Mrs. ELIZABETH PRICE,* | OF BERKELEY-SQUARE, | Author of The NEW BOOK OF COOKERY. | [short fancy rule] | Embellished with an Elegant Frontispiece. | [two rules] | 𝕃𝔬𝔫𝔡𝔬𝔫: | Printed for ALEX. HOGG, No. 16, *Paternoster-Row*, | by S. COUCHMAN, *Throgmorton-Street.* | [Price only 1s. 6d.]

First edition, London, ca.1790. Maclean gives the date of publication as ca.1760 but Alexander Hogg's dates at no. 16 Paternoster Row and S. Couchman's in Throgmorton Street only overlap from 1790 to 1804.

12mo. [A]^2 B-H^6 I^4; 48 leaves, pp. [1-5] 6-94 [95-96].

Illustrations: Engraved frontispiece of a lady and her maid.

Bibliographies: Axford, p. 297; Bitting, p. 382; Maclean, p. 118; Noling, p. 335; Oxford, p. 110.

Copies: *NUC* (Library of Congress only). Maclean adds Brotherton Library and National Library of Scotland.

939. Price, Elizabeth.

The NEW, UNIVERSAL, and | Complete Confectioner; | BEING THE | WHOLE ART of CONFECTIONARY | Made Perfectly PLAIN and EASY. | Containing a Full ACCOUNT of all the various Methods of | PRESERVING and CANDYING, both dry and liquid, | All Kinds of Fruit, Flowers and Herbs; | Also the various WAYS of | CLARIFYING SUGAR; | And the various METHODS of | Keeping FRUIT, NUTS, and FLOWERS, | FRESH AND FINE ALL THE YEAR ROUND. | Together with DIRECTIONS for making | [in three columns: column one] Blomonge, | Biscuits, | Rich-cakes, | Rock-works, and Can- | dies, | Custards, | Jellies, | Creams and Ice creams, | [two vertical rules] | [column two] Whip Syllabubs, and | Cheese-cakes of all | sorts. | Sweetmeats, | English Wines of all | Sorts, | Strong Cordials, | Simple waters, | [two vertical rules] | [column three] Mead, Oils, &c. | Syrups of all kinds, | Milk Punch that will | keep twenty years. | Knicknacks, and Tri- | fles, for Deserts, &c. | &c. &c. [end columns] | INCLUDING LIKEWISE | The Modern Art of making Artificial FRUIT, | With the STALKS in it, so as to resemble the natural FRUIT. | To which, among many other useful Articles, are added, | Several Bills of Fare for Deserts for Private Families, &c. &c. | [rule] | The whole Revised, Corrected, and Improved, | By Mrs. ELIZABETH PRICE, of Berkley Square; | Author of that excellent little cheap book entitled (to distinguish it | from all Old and Spurious Publications of the Kind) | The NEW BOOK of COOKERY, Price only 1s. | [rule] | Embellished with an Elegant Frontispiece. | [two rules] | LONDON: | Printed for A. HOGG, at the King's Arms, No. 16, Paternoster Row. | [Price only 2s.] | Altho' it Contains more in Quantity, and is better in Quality, than other | Books of the Kind, which are sold at 5s.

Third of four editions recorded by Maclean. London, ca.1800. Originally published, London, ca.1790 (item 938).

12mo. [A]⁴ B-O⁶ P²; 84 leaves, pp. [i-iv] v-viii [13] 14-171 [172]. pp. 169-171 misnumbered 369-371.

Illustrations: Engraved frontispiece of a lady and her maid.

Bibliographies: Maclean, p. 118.

Copies: *NUC* (Library of Congress and New York Public Library). Maclean adds Brotherton Library.

940. A Proper Newe Booke of Cokerye.

A PROPER NEWE | BOOKE OF COKERYE | EDITED BY | CATHERINE FRANCES FRERE | With Notes, Introduction and Glossary; | together with Some Account of Domestic | Life, Cookery and Feasts in Tudor Days, | and of the first owners of the Book, | Matthew Parker, Archbishop of Canterbury, | and Margaret Parker his Wife. | [ornament] | *Original title-page faces p. clxiv.* | CAMBRIDGE: | W. HEFFER & SONS LTD. | 1913.

First printing of this edition, Cambridge, 1913. Originally published, London, 1558.

212 x 138 mm. π^2 [A]^8 B-K^8 L^2 1 BB-HH^8 JJ^6; 147 leaves, pp. [4] [i-v] vi-clxiv [2] 1-124.

Illustration: Etched frontispiece portrait of Matthew Parker, signed Emery Walker.

Bibliographies: Axford, p. 335; Bitting, p. 168; Wheaton and Kelly 4891.

Copies: *BMC* (1914 printing) and *NUC* (9 copies).

941. Prynne, William, 1600-1669.

HEALTHES: | SICKNESSE. | OR, | A COMPENDIOVS AND | briefe Discourse; prouing, *the Drinking, and* | *Pledging of Healthes, to be Sinfull, and vtterly Vnlawfull* | *unto Christians*; by Arguments, Scriptures, Fathers, Moderne | Diuines, Christian Authors, Historians, Councels; Imperiall | Lawes and Constitutions; and by the voyce, and verdict of prophane, | and Heathen Writers: Wherein all those ordinary Obiections, | Excuses, or Pretences, which are made to Iustifie, Extenuate, or | excuse the Drinking, or Pledging of Healthes, are | likewise cleared and answered. | [rule] | By WILLIAM PRYNNE Gent. *Hospitii Lincolniensis.* | [rule] | Isay 5.11.22. Haback. 2. 15, 16. | *Woe vnto them that rise vp early in the morning, that they may follow strong* | *drinke: that continue vntill night till wine enflame them. Woe vnto them* | *that are mighty to drink wine, and men of strength to mingle strong drinke.* | *Woe vnto him that giueth his neighbour drinke: that puttest thy bottle to* | *him, and makest him drunken also, that thou maist looke on their naked-* | *nesse: the cup of the Lords right hand shall be turned towards thee, and* | *shamefull spuing shall be on thy glory.* | Ambrose. Epist. lib. 3. Epist. Vercellensi Ecclesiae. | *Non propter voluptatem bibendum est, sed propter infirmitatem: pro remedio igitur* | *parcius, non pro delicsis redundantius.* | Owen Epigram. Pars 1. lib. 2. Epigr. 42. | *Quo tibi potarum plus est in ventre* Salutum, | *Hoc minus epotis, hisce* Salutis *habes.* | Vna salus *sanis, nullam potare* Salutem | *Non est in pota vera* Salute *Salus.* | Printed in London. 1628.

Second edition, London, 1628. Originally published, London, also 1628. The first edition is a 4to in fours; the second a 4to in eights.

4to. A-H⁸; 64 leaves, pp. [*32*] 1-52, 55-62, 61-95 [96].

Bibliographies: Simon BG 1235; *STC* 20463.

Copies: *BMC* and *NUC* (19 copies without distinguishing between the first and second editions). *STC* records ten plus copies, adding Bodleian Library, Durham Cathedral Library, Peterborough Cathedral Library, and University of Glasgow for Britain.

942. Pyne, William Henry, 1769-1843.

WINE AND WALNUTS; | OR, | After Dinner Chit-Chat. | BY | EPHRAIM HARDCASTLE, | CITIZEN AND DRY-SALTER. | [short rule] | *SECOND EDITION.* | [short rule] | IN TWO VOLUMES. | VOL. I. [VOL. II.] | [short rule] | LONDON: | PRINTED FOR | LONGMAN, HURST, REES, ORME, BROWN, AND GREEN, | PATERNOSTER-ROW. | 1824.

Second edition, London, 1824. Originally published, London, 1823.

173 x 102 mm. 2 vols. Vol. I. [A]⁴ B-O¹² P⁶; 166 leaves, pp. [i-v] vi-viii [1] 2-324. Vol. II. [A]⁴ B-P¹² Q²; 174 leaves, pp. [i-v] vi-viii [1] 2-340.

Bibliographies: Gabler, p. 214.

Copies: *NUC* (8 copies). *BMC* has the 1823 edition.

The Queens Closet Opened. See M., W. (items 838-840)

943. Rabisha, William.

[within a border of two rules] The whole Body of | COOKERY | DISSECTED, | Taught, and fully manifested, | Methodically, Artifically, and ac- | cording to the best Tradition of the | *English, French, Italian, Dutch,* &c. | OR, | A Sympathy of all Varieties in Natural | Compounds in that Mystery. | Wherein is contained certain Bills of | Fare for the Seasons of the Year, for Feasts and | Common Diets. | Whereunto is annexed a Second Part of | Rare Receipts of Cookery: With certain use- | ful Traditions. | With a Book of Preserving, Conserving | and Candying, after the most Exquisite and | Newest manner: Delectable for Ladies and | Gentlewomen. | [rule] | *LONDON,* | Printed for *George Calvert* at the *Half-moon,* and | *Ralph Simpson* at the *Harp,* in St. *Paul's* | Church-yard, 1682.

Fourth edition, London, 1682. Originally published, London, 1661.

8vo. A⁸ a⁸ b⁴ B-T⁸ U⁴; 168 leaves, pp. [*40*] 1-288 [289-290] [*6*].

Bibliographies: Watt, 787i. Craig 76, Oxford, p. 30, Simon BG 1248 and Vicaire 727 record the 1661 edition. Wing records editions of 1661, 1673, and 1675 and a variant title, *The Whole Art of Cookery,* London, Eliza Calvert [1682].

Copies: *NUC* (Kansas State University only).

944. Raffald, Elizabeth Whitaker, 1733-1781.

The EXPERIENCED | English House-keeper, | For the Use and Ease of | Ladies, House-keepers, Cooks, &c. | Wrote purely from PRACTICE, | And dedicated to the | Hon. Lady ELIZABETH WARBURTON, | Whom the Author lately served as House-keeper. | Consisting of near 800 Original Receipts, most of which never | appeared in Print. | PART FIRST, Lemon Pickle, Browning for all Sorts of Made | Dishes, Soups, Fish, plain Meat, Game, Made Dishes both hot | and cold, Pyes, Puddings, &c, | PART SECOND, All Kind of Confectionary, particularly the | Gold and Silver Web for covering of Sweetmeats, and a Desert | of Spun Sugar, with Directions to set out a Table in the most | elegant Manner and in the modern Taste, Floating Islands, Fish | Ponds, Transparent Puddings, Trifles, Whips, &c. | PART THIRD, Pickling, Potting, and Collaring, Wines, Vi- | negars, Catchups, Distilling, with two most valuable Receipts, | one for refining Malt Liquors, the other for curing Acid Wines, | and a correct List of every Thing in Season in every Month of | the Year. | [rule] | By ELIZABETH RAFFALD. | [two rules] | MANCHESTER: | Printed by *J. Harrop,* for the Author, and sold by Messrs, *Fletcher* | and *Anderson,* in St. *Paul's* Church-yard, *London;* and by | *Eliz. Raffald,* Confectioner, near the *Exchange, Manchester,* 1769. | The Book to be signed by the Author's own Hand-writing, and | entered at Stationers Hall.

First edition, Manchester, 1769.

8vo. ᵖA⁴ A-Aaa⁴; 192 leaves, pp. [*4*] [i] ii-iii [iv] [1] 2-362, ²[1] ii-xi [xii] [2]. Last leaf (blank?) wanting in this copy.

Illustrations: Two engraved folding plates showing table settings.

Note: Signed Eliz. Raffald on p. 1.

Bibliographies: Craig 77; Maclean, p. 121; Oxford, p. 99; Pennell, p. 161; Simon BG 1249; Wheaton and Kelly 4950.

Copies: *BMC* and *NUC* (Kansas State University and Northwestern). Maclean adds Cambridge, National Library of Scotland, Wellcome Library, Cornell, and New York Public Library. Wheaton and Kelly (Radcliffe only).

945. Raffald, Elizabeth Whitaker, 1733-1781.

The EXPERIENCED | English Housekeeper, | For the USE and EASE of | Ladies, Housekeepers, Cooks, &c. | Wrote purely from PRACTICE, | And dedicated to the | Hon. Lady ELIZABETH WARBURTON, | Whom the Author lately served as House-keeper: | Consisting of near Nine Hundred Original Receipts, most of | which never appeared in Print. | [in two columns: column one] PART I. Lemon Pickle, Browning | for all Sorts of Made Dishes, Soups, | Fish, Plain Meat, Game, Made | Dishes both hot and cold, Pyes, | Puddings, &c. | PART II. All Kind of Confec- | tionary, particularly the Gold and | Silver Web for covering of Sweet- | meats, and a Desert of Spun Sugar, | with Directions to set out a Table | in the most elegant Manner and | [two vertical rules] | [column two] in the modern Taste, Floating | Islands, Fish-Ponds, Transparent | Puddings, Trifles, Whips, &c. | PART III. Pickling, Potting, and | Collaring, Wines, Vinegars, Catch- | ups, Distilling, with two most va- | luable Receipts, one for refining | Malt Liquors, the other for curing | Acid Wines, and a correct List of | every Thing in Season for every | Month in the Year. [end columns] | [rule] | THE THIRD EDITION. | WITH | Three COPPER PLATES of a curious new-invented FIRE STOVE, | wherein any common Fuel may be burnt instead of Charcoal, and | Two PLANS of a GRAND TABLE of Two Covers. | [rule] | By ELIZABETH RAFFALD. | [two rules] | LONDON: | Printed for the AUTHOR, and sold by R. BALDWIN, No. 47, in | Pater-noster-Row. 1773. | N.B. No Book is genuine but what is signed by the Author.

Third edition, London, 1773. Originally published, Manchester, 1769 (item 944).

8vo. A^4 B-Bb^8 $^\pi$Bb^8; 196 leaves, pp. [*4*] [i] ii-iii [iv] [1] 2-366 [*18*].

Illustrations: Three engraved folding plates, one of a stove and two of table settings.

Note: Signed Eliz. Raffald on p. 1.

Bibliographies: Maclean, p. 121; Oxford, p. 99, in a note; Vicaire 727; Wheaton and Kelly 4951.

Copies: *NUC* (New York Public Library, Simmons College, and University of Wisconsin). Maclean adds British Library, Brotherton Library, and Dorset County Library. Wheaton and Kelly (American Antiquarian Society only).

946. Raffald, Elizabeth Whitaker, 1733-1781.

The EXPERIENCED | English Housekeeper, | For the USE and EASE of | Ladies, Housekeepers, Cooks, &c. | Wrote purely from PRACTICE, | And dedicated to the | Hon. Lady ELIZABETH WARBURTON, | Whom the Author lately served as Housekeeper: | Consisting of near Nine Hundred Original Receipts, most of | which never appeared in Print. | [in two columns: column one] PART I. Lemon Pickle, Browning | for all Sorts of Made Dishes, Soups, | Fish, Plain Meat, Game, Made | Dishes both hot and cold, Pyes, | Puddings, &c. | PART II. All Kinds of Confec- | tionary, particularly the Gold and | Silver Web for covering of Sweet- | meats, and a Desert of Spun Sugar, | with Directions to set out a Table | in the most elegant Manner and | [two vertical rules] | [column two] in the modern Taste, Floating | Islands, Fish-Ponds, Transparent | Puddings, Trifles, Whips, &c. | PART III. Pickling, Potting, and | Collaring, Wines, Vinegars, Catch- | ups, Distilling, with two most va- | luable Receipts, one for refining | Malt Liquors, the other for curing | Acid Wines, and a correct List of | every Thing in Season for every | Month in the Year. [end columns] | [rule] | THE FIFTH EDITION. | WITH | Three COPPER PLATES of a curious new-invented FIRE STOVE, | wherein any common Fuel may be burnt instead of Charcoal, and | Two PLANS of a GRAND TABLE of Two Covers. | [rule] | By ELIZABETH RAFFALD. | [two rules] | LONDON: | Printed for the AUTHOR, and sold by R. BALDWIN, No. 47, in | Pater-noster-Row. 1776. | N.B. No Book is genuine but what is signed by the Author.

Fifth edition, London, 1776. Originally published, Manchester, 1769 (item 944).

8vo. A^4 B-Cc^8; 204 leaves, pp. [*4*] [i] ii-iii [iv] [1] 2-382 [*18*].

Illustrations: Three engraved folding plates, one of a stove and two of table settings.

Note: Signed Eliz Raffald on p. 1.

Bibliographies: Maclean, p. 121; Oxford, p. 99, in a note.

Copies: *BMC* and *NUC* (Harvard and New York Public Library). Maclean adds Brotherton and Wellcome Libraries.

947. Raffald, Elizabeth Whitaker, 1733-1781.

THE EXPERIENCED │ English Housekeeper, │ For the USE and EASE of │ Ladies, Housekeepers, Cooks, &c. │ Written purely from PRACTICE, │ AND DEDICATED TO THE │ Hon. Lady ELIZABETH WARBURTON, │ Whom the Author lately served as Housekeeper: │ Consisting of near Nine hundred Original Receipts, most of │ which never appeared in Print. │ [in two columns: column one] PART I. Lemon Pickle, Browning │ for all Sorts of Made Dishes, Soups, │ Fish, Plain Meat, Game, Made │ Dishes both hot and cold, Pyes, │ Puddings, &c. │ PART II. All Kinds of Confec- │ tionary, particularly the Gold and │ Silver Web for covering of Sweet- │ meats, and a Dessert of Spun Sugar, │ with Directions to set out a Table │ in the most elegant Manner, and │ [two vertical rules] │ [column two] in the modern Taste; Floating │ Islands, Fish-Ponds, Transparent │ Puddings, Trifles, Whips, &c. │ PART III. Pickling, Potting, and │ Collaring, Wines, Vinegars, Catch- │ ups, Distilling, with two most va- │ luable Receipts, one for refining │ Malt Liquors, the other for curing │ Acid Wines, and a correct List of │ every Thing in Season for every │ Month in the Year. │ [rule] │ THE EIGHTH EDITION. │ WITH AN ENGRAVED HEAD OF THE AUTHOR; │ Also Two PLANS of a GRAND TABLE of Two Covers; and │ A curious new invented FIRE STOVE, wherein any common Fuel may be │ burnt instead of Charcoal, │ [rule] │ By ELIZABETH RAFFALD. │ [two rules] │ LONDON: │ PRINTED FOR R. BALDWIN NO. 47, IN PATER- NOSTER-ROW. │ MDCCLXXXII.

Eighth edition, London, 1782. Originally published, Manchester, 1769 (item 944).

8vo. A⁴ B-Cc⁸; 204 leaves, pp. [*4*] [i] ii-iii [iv] [1] 2-384 [*16*].

Illustrations: Engraved frontispiece portrait of the author dated 1782, and three engraved folding plates, one of a stove and two of table settings.

Note: Printed facsimile of the author's signature on p. 1.

Bibliographies: Maclean, p. 123; Oxford, p. 99, in a note.

Copies: *BMC* and *NUC* (University of British Columbia and Yale). Maclean adds Brotherton Library and Cambridge.

948. Raffald, Elizabeth Whitaker, 1733-1781.

THE EXPERIENCED | English Housekeeper, | FOR THE USE AND EASE OF | Ladies, Housekeepers, Cooks, &c. | Written purely from PRACTICE, | DEDICATED TO THE | Hon. Lady ELIZABETH WARBURTON, | Whom the Author lately served as Housekeeper: | Consisting of several Hundred Original Receipts, most of which | never appeared in Print. | [in two columns: column one] PART I. Lemon Pickle, | Browning | for all Sorts of Made Dishes, Soups, | Fish, Plain Meat, Game, Made | Dishes both hot and cold, Pies, | Puddings, &c. | PART II. All Kinds of Confec- | tionary, particularly the Gold and | Silver Web for covering of Sweet- | meats, and a Desert of Spun Sugar, | with Directions to set out a Table | in the most elegant Manner and | [two vertical rules] | [column two] in the modern Taste, Floating | Islands, Fish-Ponds, Transparent | Puddings, Trifles, Whips, &c. | PART III. Pickling, Potting, and | Collaring, Wines, Vinegars, Catch- | ups, Distilling, with two most va- | luable Receipts, one for refining | Malt Liquors, the other for curing | Acid Wines, and a correct List of | every Thing in Season for every | Month in the Year. [end columns] | [rule] | By ELIZABETH RAFFALD. | A NEW EDITION, | In which are inserted some celebrated Receipts by other Modern Authors. | [rule] | [two rules] | LONDON: | PRINTED FOR A. MILLAR, W. LAW, AND R. CATER. | [short rule] | MDCCLXXXVII.

Fifteenth edition, London, 1787. Originally published, Manchester, 1769 (item 944).

8vo. A-Eee⁴; 204 leaves, pp. [4] [i] ii-iii [iv] [1] 2-384 [16]. Last leaf (blank?) wanting in this copy.

Illustrations: Engraved frontispiece portrait of the author and three engraved folding plates, one of a stove and two of table settings. The portrait is a simplified version, without lettering, of the 1782 portrait published in the eighth edition (item 947).

Bibliographies: Maclean, p. 123; Simon BG 1251.

Copies: Maclean locates Brotherton Library only.

949. Raffald, Elizabeth Whitaker, 1733-1781.

THE EXPERIENCED | English Housekeeper, | FOR THE USE AND EASE OF | Ladies, Housekeepers, Cooks, &c. | Written purely from PRACTICE; | DEDICATED TO THE | *Hon. Lady ELIZABETH WARBURTON,* | Whom the Author lately served as Housekeeper. | *Consisting of several Hundred* ORIGINAL RECEIPTS, *most of which* | *never appeared in Print.* | [in two columns: column one] PART I. Lemon Pickle,

Browning | for all Sorts of made Dishes, Soups, | Fish, plain Meat, Game, made | Dishes both hot and cold, Pies, | Puddings, &c. | PART II. All Kinds of Confection- | ary, particularly the Gold and Silver | Web for covering of Sweetmeats, | and a Dessert of Spun Sugar; with | Directions to set out a Table in the | most elegant Manner and in the | [vertical rule] | [column two] Modern Taste, Floating Islands, | Fish Ponds, Transparent Puddings, | Trifles, Whips, &c. | PART III. Pickling, Potting, and | Collaring, Wines, Vinegars, Catch- | ups, Distilling; with two most | valuable Receipts, one for refining | Malt Liquors, the other for curing | Acid Wines, and a correct List of | every Thing in Season for every | Month in the Year. [end columns] | [rule] | By ELIZABETH RAFFALD. | [rule] | A NEW EDITION. | In which are inserted some celebrated Receipts by other modern | Authors. | [short fancy rule] | *LONDON:* | PRINTED FOR A. MILLAR, W. LAW, AND R. CATER. | *Anno* 1799.

Twenty-eighth edition recorded by Maclean, London, 1799. Originally published, Manchester, 1769 (item 944).

8vo. A⁴ B-Cc⁸; 204 leaves, pp. [i-iii] iv-vii [viii] [1] 2-397 [398] [2]. Last leaf blank.

Illustrations: Engraved frontispiece portrait of the author and three engraved folding plates, one of a stove and two of table settings. The portrait is an even cruder version of that that appears in the fifteenth edition (item 948).

Bibliographies: Maclean, p. 123; Oxford, p. 99, in a note.

Copies: Maclean records British Library only.

950. Raffald, Elizabeth Whitaker, 1733-1781.

THE EXPERIENCED | ENGLISH HOUSEKEEPER, | FOR THE USE AND EASE OF | *Ladies,* | HOUSEKEEPERS, COOKS, &c. | Written purely from Practice; | DEDICATED TO | The Hon. Lady ELIZABETH WARBURTON, | Whom the Author lately served as Housekeeper. | [short fancy rule] | CONSISTING OF | SEVERAL HUNDRED ORIGINAL RECEIPTS, | Most of which never appeared in Print. | [short fancy rule] | [in two columns: column one] PART I. Lemon Pickle, Brown- | ing for all sorts of made Dishes, | Soups, Fish, plain Meat, Game, | made Dishes both hot and cold, | Pies, Puddings, &c. | PART II. All Kinds of Confec- | tionary, particularly the Gold | and Silver Web for covering of | Sweetmeats, and a Dessert of Spun | Sugar; with Directions to set out | a Table in the most elegant Man- | ner and in the modern Taste; | [two vertical rules] | [column two] Floating Islands, Fish Ponds, | Transparent Puddings, Trifles, | Whips, &c. | PART III. Pickling,

Potting, and | Collaring; Wines, Vinegars, | Catchups, Distilling; with two | most valuable Receipts, one for | refining Malt Liquors, the other | for curing Acid Wines; and a | correct List of every Thing in | Season for every Month in the | Year. [end columns] | [two short rules] | By ELIZABETH RAFFALD. | [two short rules] | *A New Edition,* | In which are inserted some celebrated Receipts by other Modern Authors. | TOGETHER WITH | THE COMPLETE ART OF CARVING, | and | MARKETING. | [within ornament] 𝔐𝔞𝔫𝔠𝔥𝔢𝔰𝔱𝔢𝔯: | G. BANCKS, Printer, 10, Exchange-street.

Twenty-ninth edition recorded by Maclean, Manchester, ca.1799. Originally published, Manchester, 1769 (item 944).

12mo. π^4 A^6 C-Oo^6 Pp^2; 222 leaves, pp. [i-iii] iv-vii [viii] [1] 2-434 [2]. Last leaf blank.

Illustrations: Engraved frontispiece portrait of the author and four engraved folding plates, one of a stove, two of table settings, and one of carving. This is yet another portrait depicting Mrs. Raffald as a younger, more attractive woman that the earlier versions.

Bibliographies: Maclean, p. 123, locating no copies and noting the *The Manchester Press before 1801* (Manchester, 1931) by the Manchester Libraries Committee claims this edition is spurious.

Copies: No other copy of this edition located.

951. Raffald, Elizabeth Whitaker, 1733-1781.

THE EXPERIENCED | ENGLISH HOUSEKEEPER, | For the USE and EASE of | LADIES, HOUSEKEEPERS, COOKS, &c. | Written purely from PRACTICE; | DEDICATED TO THE | *Hon. Lady ELIZABETH WARBURTON,* | Whom the Author lately served as Housekeeper: | *Consisting of several Hundred* ORIGINAL RECEIPTS, *most of* | *which never appeared in Print.* | [short rule] | PART I. Lemon-Pickle, Browning for all sorts of made | Dishes; Soups, Fish, plain Meat, Game, made Dishes, both | hot and cold, Pies, Puddings, &c. | PART II. All Kinds of Confectionary, particularly the | Gold and Silver Web for covering of sweetmeats, and a De- | sert of Spun Sugar; with Directions to set out a Table in | the most elegant Manner, and in the modern Taste, Float- | ing Islands, Fish Ponds, Transparent Puddings, Trifles, | Whips, &c. | PART III. Pickling, Potting, and Collaring; Wines, Vi- | negars, Catchups, Distilling; with two most valuable Re- | ceipts, one for refining Malt

Liquors, the other for curing | Acid Wines; and a correct List of every Thing in Season | for every Month in the Year. | [short rule] | BY ELIZABETH RAFFALD. | [short rule] | A NEW EDITION. | In which are inserted some celebrated Receipts by other | modern Authors. | [short fancy rule] | LONDON: | PUBLISHED FOR THE BOOKSELLERS; AND PRINTED AND SOLD | BY H. AND G. MOZLEY, MARKET-PLACE, GAINSBROUGH. | 1800.

Thirtieth edition recorded by Maclean, London, 1800. Originally published, Manchester, 1769 (item 944).

12mo. A^4 B-Q^{12} R^2; 186 leaves, pp. [i-iii] iv-vii [viii] [1] 2-364. This copy lacks leaves B5-B8 (pp. 9-16).

Illustrations: Engraved frontispiece portrait of the author and three engraved folding plates, one of a stove and two of table settings. This is yet another portrait, a young Mrs. Raffald but with a rounder face than in the portrait in the twenty-eighth edition (item 950).

Bibliographies: Maclean, p. 123.

Copies: Maclean records Brotherton Library only.

952. Raffald, Elizabeth Whitaker, 1733-1781.

THE EXPERIENCED | English Housekeeper, | FOR THE USE AND EASE OF | Ladies, Housekeepers, Cooks, &c. | Written purely from PRACTICE; | DEDICATED TO THE | *Hon. Lady ELIZABETH WARBURTON,* | Whom the Author lately served as Housekeeper. | *Consisting of several Hundred* ORIGINAL RECEIPTS, *most of which* | *never appeared in Print.* | [in two columns: column one] PART I. Lemon Pickle, Browning | for all Sorts of made Dishes, | Soups, Fish, plain Meat, Game, | made dishes, both hot and cold, | Pies, Puddings, &c. | PART II. All Kinds of Confection- | ary, particularly the Gold and | Silver Web for covering of Sweet- | meats, and a Dessert of Spun Su- | gar; with Directions to set out a | Table in the most elegant Man- | ner and in the Modern Taste, | [vertical rule] | [column two] Floating Islands, Fish Ponds, | Transparent Puddings, Trifles, | Whips, &c. | PART III. Pickling, Potting, and | Collaring, Wines, Vinegars, | Catchups, Distilling; with two | most valuable Receipts, one for | refining Malt Liquors, the other | for curing Acid Wines; and a | correct List of every Thing in | Season for every Month in the | Year. [end columns] | [short rule] | By ELIZABETH RAFFALD. | [short rule] | A NEW EDITION. | In which are inserted some celebrated Receipts by other | modern

Authors. | [short rule] | 𝕷𝖔𝖓𝖉𝖔𝖓: | Published and sold by all the BOOKSELLERS, and by T. WILSON | and R. SPENCE, Printers, High-Ousegate, York. | *Anno* 1801.

New edition, London, 1801. Originally published, Manchester, 1769 (item 944).

206 x 124 mm. A^4 B-Cc^8; 204 leaves, pp. [i-iii] iv-vii [viii] [1] 2-397 [398] [2]. Last leaf (blank?) wanting in this copy.

Illustrations: Engraved frontispiece portrait of the author and three folding plates, one of a stove, and two of table settings. This portrait is the same as that in the twenty-eighth edition (item 949).

Bibliographies: This edition unrecorded in the bibliographies consulted.

Copies: *BMC*.

953. Raffald, Elizabeth Whitaker, 1733-1781.

THE EXPERIENCED | English Housekeeper, | FOR THE USE AND EASE OF | Ladies, Housekeepers, Cooks, &c. | Written purely from PRACTICE; | DEDICATED TO THE | *Hon. Lady ELIZABETH WARBURTON,* | Whom the Author lately served as Housekeeper. | *Consisting of several Hundred* ORIGINAL RECEIPTS, *most of which* | *never appeared in print.* | [in two columns: column one] PART I. Lemon Pickle, Browning | for all Sorts of Made-Dishes, | Soups, Fish, plain Meat, Game, | Made-Dishes, both hot and cold, | Pies, Puddings, &c. | PART II. All Kinds of Confection- | ary, particularly the Gold and | Silver Web for covering of Sweet- | meats and a Dessert of Spun Su- | gar; with Directions to set out a | Table in the most elegant Man- | ner and in the Modern Taste, | [vertical rule] | [column two] Floating Islands, Fish Ponds, | Transparent Puddings, Trifles, | Whips, &c. | PART III. Pickling, Potting, and | Collaring; Wines, Vinegars, | Catchups, Distilling; with two | most valuable Receipts, one for | refining Malt Liquors, the other | for curing Acid Wines; and a | correct List of every Thing in | Season for every Month in the | Year. [end columns] | [short rule] | By ELIZABETH RAFFALD. | [short rule] | A NEW EDITION. | In which are inserted some celebrated Receipts by other | modern Authors. | [short rule] | 𝕷𝖔𝖓𝖉𝖔𝖓: | Published and sold by all the BOOKSELLERS, and by T. WILSON | and R. SPENCE, Printers, High Ousegate, York. | *Anno* 1803.

New edition, London, 1803. Originally published, Manchester, 1769 (item 944).

211 x 128 mm. A⁴ B-Cc⁸; 204 leaves, pp. [i-iii] iv-vii [viii] [1] 2-397 [398] [2]. Last leaf blank.

Illustrations: Engraved frontispiece portrait of the author signed "Hampton, Prince & Cattles, York," and three folding plates, one of a stove and two of table settings.

Bibliographies: This edition unrecorded in the bibliographies consulted.

Copies: *NUC* (John Crerar Library only).

954. Raper, Elizabeth, d. 1778.

[two rules] | THE | RECEIPT | BOOK | OF | *ELIZABETH RAPER* | [rule] | *And a portion of her Cipher Journal.* | *Edited by her great-grandson the* | *late* BARTLE GRANT | *with a portrait and decorations by* | DUNCAN GRANT | [rule] | Written 1756-1770 and never before printed. | [publisher's device] | *soho:* THE NONESUCH PRESS, 1924 | [two rules]

First edition, London, 1924, no. 589 of 850 copies printed.

233 x 148 mm. [1]⁴ [2-4]¹⁶; 52 leaves, pp. [8] 1-94 [95-96]. Publisher's blue buckram, stamped in gold, in dust jacket.

Illustrations: Pen drawings by Duncan Grant reproduced on half and sectional titles.

Note: *BMC* enters the author as Raper, Elizabeth; *NUC* as Grant, Elizabeth (Raper).

Bibliographies: Axford, p. 341; Noling, p. 339.

Copies: *BMC* and *NUC* (10 copies).

955. Read, George.

THE | GUIDE TO TRADE. | [short rule] | THE CONFECTIONER: | CONTAINING | THE METHOD OF MAKING| ALL SORTS OF PRESERVES, SUGAR-BOILING, | COMFIT MAKING, LOZENGES, ORNAMENTAL CAKES, ICES, | LIQUEURS, WATERS, | AND GUM-PASTE ORNAMENTS. | [short rule] | BY GEORGE READ. | [short rule] | LONDON: | CHARLES KNIGHT AND CO., LUDGATE STREET. | [short rule] | 1842.

First edition, London, 1842. The "Guide to Trade" series numbered ten volumes, published between 1838 and 1842.

164 x 101 mm. [A]^6 B-I$^{12.6}$ K^2; 80 leaves, pp. [i-v] vi-xii [1] 2-148. Modern calf stamped in gold; original printed wrappers preserved.

Bibliographies: Noling, p. 341; Simon BG 1262. Bitting cites the fifth edition and Oxford a work with the title *The Pastry Cook's and Confectioner's Assistant* which he dates c. 1842.

Copies: *BMC. NUC* records fifth, eighth, and fourteenth editions, each in a single copy.

956. Read, George.

THE | CONFECTIONER | BY | GEORGE READ |LONDON | HOULSTON AND SONS | PATERNOSTER ROW

New edition, London, ca. 1845. Reprint of the original 1842 edition (item 955), adding a new preface on pp. xiii-xvii and an Appendix of new recipes on pp. 149-160.

163 x 104 mm. [A]^8 B-L^8; 88 leaves, pp. [2] [v] vi-xvii [xviii] [1] 2-160. Publisher's brown cloth stamped in gold.

Bibliographies: This edition unrecorded in the bibliographies consulted.

Copies: No other copy of this edition located.

956a. Recipes for the Million.

RECIPES | FOR THE MILLION | A Handy Book for the Household | [publisher's monogram] | London | T. FISHER UNWIN | PATERNOSTER SQUARE | MDCCCXCI

First edition, London, 1891.

182 x 124 mm. [1]^2 2-27^4 28^2; 108 leaves, pp. [4] [1] 2-212. Publisher's red cloth stamped in blue and black; 24 page publisher's catalog bound in at the end.

Bibliographies: Driver 869.1.

Copies: *BMC* and *NUC* (Library of Congress only). Driver adds Bodleian Library and an unidentified private collection.

957. Redding, Cyrus, 1785-1870.

EVERY MAN | HIS OWN BUTLER. | [short rule] | BY THE AUTHOR OF THE | "HISTORY AND DESCRIPTION OF MODERN WINES." | [short rule] | [vignette] | Hermitage "for the stomach's sake." | [short rule] | LONDON: WHITTAKER AND CO., AVE-MARIA LANE. | [short rule] | MDCCCXXXIX.

First edition, London, 1839.

168 x 104 mm. b² [c]⁶ B-R⁶ [S]⁴; 108 leaves, pp. [i-iii] iv-xv [xvi] [1] 2-200. Publisher's purple cloth stamped in gold.

Illustration: Vignette of two monks drinking wine on title-page.

Bibliographies: Gabler, p. 221; Noling, p. 341.

Copies: *BMC* and *NUC* (Library Company of Philadelphia and Library of Congress).

958. Redding, Cyrus, 1785-1870.

A | HISTORY AND DESCRIPTION | OF | MODERN WINES. | [short rule] | BY | CYRUS REDDING. | [vignette] | LONDON: | WHITTAKER, TREACHER, & ARNOT, | AVE MARIA LANE. | [short rule] | 1833.

First edition, London, 1833.

225 x 135 mm. A⁸(A1+χ1) a⁸ b² B-Cc⁸ Dd⁴; 223 leaves, pp. [i-ii] [2] [iii-v] vi-xxxv [xxxvi] [1] 2-407 [408]. Publisher's green cloth, spine stamped in gold.

Note: The title leaf, χ1, is printed on heavier than text paper and is tipped in.

Illustrations: Engraved vignettes at the head of each chapter.

Bibliographies: Gabler, p. 221; Noling, p. 342; Simon BG 1265.

Copies: *BMC* and *NUC* (9 copies).

959. Regimen sanitatis Salernitanum.

[within a woodcut border] REGIMEN SA- | NITATIS SA- | LERNI. | [leaf] 𝔗𝔥𝔦𝔰 𝔟𝔬𝔨𝔢 𝔱𝔢𝔞𝔠𝔥𝔦𝔫𝔤𝔢 | 𝔞𝔩𝔩 𝔭𝔢𝔬𝔭𝔩𝔢 𝔱𝔬 𝔤𝔬𝔲𝔢𝔯𝔫𝔢 𝔱𝔥𝔢𝔪 | 𝔦𝔫 𝔥𝔢𝔩𝔱𝔥𝔢, 𝔦𝔰 𝔱𝔯𝔞𝔫𝔰𝔩𝔞𝔱𝔢𝔡 𝔬𝔲𝔱 | 𝔬𝔣 𝔱𝔥𝔢 𝔏𝔞𝔱𝔶𝔫𝔢 𝔱𝔬𝔫𝔤𝔢 𝔦𝔫 𝔱𝔬 | 𝔢𝔫𝔤𝔩𝔶𝔰𝔥𝔢 𝔟𝔶 𝔗𝔥𝔬𝔪𝔞𝔰 | 𝔓𝔞𝔶𝔫𝔢𝔩. | 𝔴𝔥𝔦𝔠𝔥𝔢 𝔟𝔬𝔨𝔢 𝔦𝔰 𝔞𝔪𝔢𝔫𝔡𝔢𝔡, | 𝔞𝔲𝔤𝔪𝔢𝔫𝔱𝔢𝔡, 𝔞𝔫𝔡 | 𝔡𝔦𝔩𝔦𝔤𝔢𝔫𝔱𝔩𝔶 𝔦𝔪= | 𝔭𝔯𝔦𝔫𝔱𝔢𝔡.

Colophon: LONDINI IN AEDIBVS THO. | BERTHELETI REGII IMPRES- | SORIS EXCVSVM. | AN. M. D. XXXV. | CVM PRIVILEGIO.

Third English edition, London, 1535. Originally published in Latin, Cologne, 1480. The English editions of 1528, 1530, 1535, and 1541 contain the original Latin text of the *Regimen sanitatis salernitanum* with a translation into English by Thomas Paynell of the extensive commentary by Arnaldus Villanova.

4to. A^6 B-Y^4 a-i^4; 126 leaves, ff. [6] 1-119 [1]. Last leaf (blank?) wanting in this copy.

Bibliographies: Durling 3836; *STC* 21598.

Copies: *BMC* and *NUC* (Indiana University, National Library of Medicine, and Yale). *STC* (6 copies).

960. Regimen sanitatis Salernitanum.

[within a woodcut border] [leaf] REGIMEN | SANITATIS SA- | LERNI. | [leaf] 𝔗𝔥𝔦𝔰 𝔟𝔬𝔨𝔢 𝔱𝔢𝔞𝔠𝔥𝔦𝔫𝔤𝔢 | 𝔞𝔩𝔩 𝔭𝔢𝔬𝔭𝔩𝔢 𝔱𝔬 𝔤𝔬𝔲𝔢𝔯𝔫𝔢 𝔱𝔥𝔢𝔪 | 𝔦𝔫 𝔥𝔢𝔩𝔱𝔥𝔢, 𝔦𝔰 𝔱𝔯𝔞𝔫𝔰𝔩𝔞𝔱𝔢𝔡 𝔬𝔲𝔱 | 𝔬𝔣 𝔱𝔥𝔢 𝔏𝔞𝔱𝔶𝔫𝔢 𝔱𝔬𝔫𝔤𝔢 𝔦𝔫 𝔱𝔬 | 𝔢𝔫𝔤𝔩𝔶𝔰𝔥𝔢 𝔟𝔶 𝔗𝔥𝔬𝔪𝔞𝔰 | 𝔓𝔞𝔶𝔫𝔢𝔩. | 𝔴𝔥𝔦𝔠𝔥𝔢 𝔟𝔬𝔨𝔢 𝔦𝔰 𝔞𝔪𝔪𝔢𝔫𝔡𝔢𝔡, | 𝔞𝔲𝔤𝔪𝔢𝔫𝔱𝔢𝔡, 𝔞𝔫𝔡 | 𝔡𝔦𝔩𝔦𝔤𝔢𝔫𝔱𝔩𝔶 𝔦𝔪= | 𝔭𝔯𝔦𝔫𝔱𝔢𝔡.

Colophon: [leaf] LONDINI IN AEDIBVS | THO. BERTHELETI TYPIS | IMPRES. | CVM PRIVILEGIO ADIM- | PRIMEDVM SOLVM. | ANNO. M. D. XLI. | [leaf]

Fourth English edition, London, 1541. See edition note under item 959.

4to. A^4 χ^2 B-Y^4 a-i^4; 126 leaves, ff. [6] [1] 2-119 [1]. Last leaf (blank?) wanting in this copy.

Bibliographies: Craig 68; Gambacorta/Giordano, p. 77; *STC* 21599.

Copies: *BMC* and *NUC* (9 copies). *STC* (10 copies).

961. Reynolds, Robert.

THE NEW | PROFESSED COOK, | ADAPTED TO THE FAMILIES OF EITHER | *NOBLEMEN, GENTLEMEN, OR CITIZENS;* | CONTAINING UPWARDS OF | SEVEN HUNDRED | FRENCH AND ENGLISH | PRACTICAL RECEIPTS IN COOKERY, | AND | ONE HUNDRED | IN | CONFECTIONARY; | TO WHICH IS ADDED, | [in two columns: column one] BOTTLING OF FRUITS AND | JUICES; | HOME-MADE WINES; | [vertical rule] | [column two] DISTILLING; | PICKLING AND PRE- | SERVING; [end columns] | *And many other Articles of Information necessary to be known* | by every MISTRESS *of a Family, and* SERVANT. | [short rule] | SECOND EDITION, | WITH CONSIDERABLE ADDITIONS. | [short rule] | BY ROBERT REYNOLDS, | COOK TO HIS GRACE THE DUKE OF PORTLAND, | AND PUPIL OF THE LATE MR. P. SIMON, COOK TO HIS MAJESTY, | AND TO THE KING OF FRANCE. | [short rule] | PRINTED FOR J. BOOTH, DUKE STREET, | PORTLAND PLACE. | [short rule] | 1829.

Second edition, London, 1829. Originally published under the title *The New French and English Professed Cook*, London, 1815.

169 x 105 mm. A⁶ A✻⁶ B-S⁸($4+1) T-2A⁶; 201 leaves, pp. [i- iii] iv-xxiii [xxiv] [1] 2-374 [4]. Last four pages, publisher's advertisements. Signatures B-S are 18mo. in half-sheets with the odd leaf tipped in following the fourth leaf of each signature.

Bibliographies: This edition unrecorded in the bibliographies consulted. Axford, p. 333 and Bitting, p. 395, record the third edition, 1849.

Copies: *NUC* (Kansas State University and New York Public Library).

962. Ricket, E.

[within a red ornamental border of two rules] THE | [in red] 𝕲entleman's 𝕿able 𝕲uide. | BEING PRACTICAL RECIPES FOR | WINE CUPS, AMERICAN DRINKS, | PUNCHES, CORDIALS, | SUMMER & WINTER BEVERAGES. | RECHERCHÉ BILLS OF FARE | WITH | SERVICE OF WINES, | &c., &c. | [short rule] | BY | [in red] E. RICKET AND C. THOMAS. | [short rule] | ENTERED AT

STATIONERS' HALL. | [short rule] | [*The Authors reserve the right of translation.*] | [short rule] | 𝕷𝖔𝖓𝖉𝖔𝖓: | AGENT – H. BORN, 115, LONDON WALL, E.C | [short rule] | 1871.

First edition, London, 1871.

157 x 110 mm. [A]⁴ χ⁴ B⁴ 2χ⁴ C⁴ 3χ⁴ D⁴ 4χ⁴ E⁴; 36 leaves, pp. [i-iii] iv-x [11] 12-53 [54-72]. Publisher's green cloth, stamped in gold. Twelve pages of advertisements bound in at the end.

Illustrations: Wood engraved illustrations in the text.

Bibliographies: Gabler, p. 225; Noling, p. 346.

Copies: No other copy located.

963. Roberts, George Edwin, 1831-1865.

CUPS AND THEIR CUSTOMS. | [short rule] | "Touch brim! touch foot! the wine is red, | And leaps to the lips of the free; | Our wassail true is quickly said, – | Comrade! I drink to thee! | "Touch foot! touch brim! who cares? who cares? | Brothers in sorrow or glee, | Glory or danger each gallantly shares, – | Comrade! I drink to thee! | "Touch brim! touch foot! once again, old friend, | Though the present our last draught be; | We were boys – we are men – we'll be true to the end – | Brother! I drink to thee!" | [short rule] | LONDON: | JOHN VAN VOORST, PATERNOSTER ROW. | MDCCCLXIII.

Engraved title-page:

CUPS AND THEIR CUSTOMS. | [hand colored vignette] | SPRIG OF BORAGE IN GLASS CUP, | OF THE THIRD OR FOURTH CENTURY. | London: Published by John Van Voorst, Paternoster Row.

First edition, London, 1863.

187 x 124 mm. [A]⁴ B-C¹² D²; 30 leaves, pp. [2] [i-iii] iv-vi [1] 2-52. Publisher's glazed blue-black boards, printed in gold.

Illustrations: Hand colored wood engraved title-page.

Bibliographies: Gabler, p. 226.

Copies: *BMC* and *NUC* (10 copies).

964. Roberts, William Henry.

THE | BRITISH WINE-MAKER, | AND | DOMESTIC BREWER; | A COMPLETE, PRACTICAL, AND EASY TREATISE ON THE ART AND | MANAGEMENT OF BRITISH WINES, AND LIQUEURS, | AND DOMESTIC BREWING. | BY W. H. ROBERTS. | SECOND EDITION. | OLIVER & BOYD, EDINBURGH; | AND | SIMPKIN, MARSHALL, & CO., LONDON. | MDCCCXXXV.

Second edition, Edinburgh, 1835. Originally published Edinburgh, also 1835.

166 x 94 mm. π^6 A-T^8 χ^6; 164 leaves, pp. [i-iii] iv-xii [1] 2-302 [2] [*12*]. χ1-6 contain critical notices of the book. Note: In this copy T8, on which is printed the half-title to Part I, has been left in signature T where it was printed. In an ideal copy it would have been removed and tipped in following π6 and the collation would read: π^6 χ1 A-S^8 T^8(-T8=χ1) 2χ^6; 164 leaves, pp. [i-iii] iv-xii [2] [1] 2-302 [*12*].

Bibliographies: Simon BG 1296.

Copies: *NUC* (Library of Congress, New York Botanical Garden, and New York Public Library).

965. Robertson, Hannah.

THE | YOUNG LADIES | SCHOOL OF ARTS. | CONTAINING, | A great Variety of practical Receipts, | IN | [in three columns: column one] GUM-FLOWERS | FILLIGREE | JAPANNING | SHELL-WORK | GILDING | PAINTING | [vertical rule] | [column two] COSMETICS | JELLIES | PRESERVES | CAKES | CORDIALS | CREAMS | [vertical rule] | [column three] JAMMS | PICKLES | CANDYING | MADE WINES | CLEAR STARCH | ING, &c. [end columns] | Also, a great many CURIOUS RECEIPTS, both useful | and entertaining, never before published. | [rule] | By Mrs HANNAH ROBERTSON. | [rule] | The Second Edition, with large Additions. | [rule] | *EDINBURGH:* | Printed by WAL. RUDDIMAN junior, | For Mrs ROBERTSON: Sold by her, and by all the | Booksellers in *Scotland* and *England*. | [short rule] | M,DCC,LXVII.

Title-page of Part II.

THE | YOUNG LADIES | SCHOOL OF ARTS. | CONTAINING, | A great Variety of practical Receipts, | IN | COOKERY, PASTRY, PUDDINGS, | MARKETING,

&c. &c. | [rule] | PART II. | [rule] | By Mrs HANNAH ROBERTSON. | [rule] | The Second Edition, with large Additions. | [rule] | *EDINBURGH:* | Printed by WAL. RUDDIMAN junior, | For Mrs ROBERTSON: Sold by her, and by all the | Booksellers in *Scotland* and *England.* | [short rule] | M,DCC,LXVII.

Engraved title-page:

[within an ornamental border] THE | *YOUNG LADIES* / *School of Arts* / *Calculated for the Improvement* / *of Female Education* / *Embelished with several* / *Prints of the most Beau=* / *tifull Flowers as large* / *as Nature* | By | *Mrs. Hannah Robertson* / *The Second Edition* / *with large Additions*

Second edition, Edinburgh, 1767. Originally published, Edinburgh, 1766.

12mo. 2 vols. Vol. I. a^6 b^4 A-O^6 P^2; 96 leaves, pp. [i-v] vi-xviii [2] 1-171 [172]. Vol. II. a-b^6 A-K^6; 72 leaves, pp. [i-iii] iv-xxi [xxii] [2] 1-120.

Illustrations: Vol. I. Engraved title-page and five engraved folding plates of flowers.

Bibliographies: Axford, p. 432; Bitting, p. 400; Maclean, p. 124; Oxford, p. 96.

Copies: *NUC* (Library of Congress and Michigan State University). Maclean adds National Library of Scotland.

966. Robertson, Hannah.

THE | YOUNG LADIES | SCHOOL of ARTS. | CONTAINING | A great Variety of Practical Receipts, | IN | [in three columns: column one] GUM-FLOWERS | FILLIGREE | JAPANNING | SHELL-WORK | GILDING | PAINTING | [vertical rule] | [column two] COSMETICS | JELLIES | PRESERVES | CAKES | CORDIALS | CREAMS | [vertical rule] | [column three] JAMMS | PICKLES | CANDYING | MADE WINES | CLEAR STARCH- | ING, &c. [end columns] | Together with | Directions for breeding CANARY BIRDS, and breed- | ing, nursing, and ordering of the SILK- WORM. | Also, a great many CURIOUS RECEIPTS, both use- | ful and entertaining, never before published. | [rule] | By Mrs. HANNAH ROBERTSON. | [rule] | The Fourth Edition, with large Additions. | [rule] | YORK: | Printed at the New PRINTING-OFFICE, in | COPPERGATE, for Mrs. ROBERTSON, | and sold by all the Booksellers in | England and Scotland. | [short fancy rule] | M,DCC,LXXVII.

Fourth edition, York, 1777. Originally published, Edinburgh, 1766.

12mo. πA^6 a^6 A-P^6 Q1; 103 leaves, pp. [2] [i] ii-xx [xxi-xxii] [1] 2-182.

Bibliographies: Axford, p. 432; Maclean, p. 124; Noling, p. 349; Oxford, p. 97, in a note.

Copies: *NUC* (Michigan State University only). Maclean adds Brotherton Library.

967. Robinson, James.

THE | WHOLE ART | OF | CURING, PICKLING, AND SMOKING | MEAT AND FISH, | BOTH IN | 𝔗𝔥𝔢 𝔅𝔯𝔦𝔱𝔦𝔰𝔥 𝔞𝔫𝔡 𝔉𝔬𝔯𝔢𝔦𝔤𝔫 𝔐𝔬𝔡𝔢𝔰; | WITH | MANY USEFUL MISCELLANEOUS RECEIPTS, | AND FULL DIRECTIONS FOR THE CONSTRUCTION OF | AN ECONOMICAL DRYING-CHIMNEY AND APPARATUS, | ON AN ENTIRELY ORIGINAL PLAN. | BY | JAMES ROBINSON, | EIGHTEEN YEARS A PRACTICAL CURER. | LONDON: | PRINTED FOR | LONGMAN, BROWN, GREEN, AND LONGMANS, | PATERNOSTER-ROW. | 1847.

First edition, London, 1847.

171 x 103 mm. A^6 B-K^8 L^4 M^2; 84 leaves, pp. [i-iii] iv-xii [1] 2-153 [154] [2]. Last leaf blank. Publisher's brown cloth, stamped in gold. 32 page publisher's catalogue, dated January 1847, bound in at the end.

Bibliographies: Axford, p. 421; Bitting, p. 401; Oxford, p. 177; Simon BG 1298; Wheaton and Kelly 5191.

Copies: *BMC* and *NUC* (Library of Congress and New York Public Library). Wheaton and Kelly (Radcliffe).

968. Robinson, James.

THE | WHOLE ART | OF MAKING | BRITISH WINES, | CORDIALS, AND LIQUEURS, | IN THE GREATEST PERFRECTION; | AS ALSO, | 𝔖𝔱𝔯𝔬𝔫𝔤 𝔞𝔫𝔡 𝔚𝔬𝔯𝔡𝔦𝔞𝔩 𝔚𝔞𝔱𝔢𝔯𝔰: | TO WHICH IS ADDED | A COLLECTION OF VALUABLE RECIPES FOR | BREWING FINE AND STRONG WELSH ALES, | AND MISCELLANEOUS ARTICLES CONNECTED | WITH THE PRACTICE. | BY | JAMES ROBINSON, | AUTHOR OF | "THE ART OF CURING, PICKLING, AND PRESERVING," | ETC. | LONDON: | PRINTED FOR | LONGMAN, BROWN, GREEN, & LONGMANS, | PATERNOSTER-ROW. | 1848.

First edition, London, 1848.

162 x 101 mm. A⁸ a² B-S⁸ T²; 148 leaves, pp. [i-v] vi-xx [1] 2-275 [276].   Publisher's rose colored cloth, stamped in gold.

Bibliographies: Gabler, p. 227; Noling, p. 349.

Copies: *BMC* and *NUC* (Cornell, Kansas State University, and University of California, Berkeley).

969. Rogers, John, 1752-1842.

THE | VEGETABLE CULTIVATOR: | CONTAINING | A PLAIN AND ACCURATE DESCRIPTION | OF | ALL THE DIFFERENT SPECIES AND VARIETIES OF | CULINARY VEGETABLES; | WITH | THE MOST APPROVED METHOD OF CULTIVATING THEM | BY NATURAL AND ARTIFICIAL MEANS, | AND THE BEST MODE OF COOKING THEM; | 𝔄lphabetically 𝔄rranged. | TOGETHER WITH | A DESCRIPTION OF THE PHYSICAL HERBS IN GENERAL USE, &c. | ALSO, | SOME RECOLLECTIONS OF | THE LIFE OF PHILIP MILLER, F.R.S. | Gardener to the Worshipful Company of Apothecaries at | Chelsea. | [short rule] | BY JOHN ROGERS, | AUTHOR OF "THE FRUIT CULTIVATOR." | [short rule] | LONDON: | LONGMAN, ORME, BROWN, GREEN, & LONGMANS, | PATERNOSTER-ROW. | 1839.

First edition, London, 1839.

171 x 103 mm. A-Y⁸ Z⁴; 180 leaves, pp. [i-iii] iv-xv [xvi] [1] 2-343 [344]. Publisher's green cloth stamped in gold. Sixteen page publisher's catalogue dated July 1839 bound in at end.

Bibliographies: Wheaton and Kelly 5204.

Copies: *BMC* and *NUC* (Massachusetts Horticultural Society, Peabody Institute, and Pennsylvania Horticultural Society). Wheaton and Kelly (Essex Institute).

970. Rose, Giles.

[within a single rule border] A perfect School of | INSTRUCTIONS | For the | *Officers of the Mouth:* | SHEWING | The Whole ART | OF | [in two columns:

column one] A Master of the │ Houshold, │ A Master Carver, │ A Master Butler, │ }{ │ [column two] A Master Confe- │ ctioner, │ A Master Cook, │ A Master Pastryman [end columns] │ Being a Work of singular Use for Ladies and │ Gentlewomen, and all Persons whatsoe- │ ver that are desirous to be acquainted with │ the most Excellent ARTS of Carving, │ Cookery, Pastry, Preserving, and Laying a │ Cloth for Grand Entertainments. The like │ never before extant in any Language. │ Adorned with Pictures curiously Ingraven, │ displaying the whole Arts. │ [rule] │ By *Giles Rose* one of the Master Cooks in │ His Majesties Kitchen. │ [rule] │ *LONDON*, │ Printed for *R. Bentley* and *M. Magnes*, in │ *Russel-street* in *Covent-Garden*, 1682.

First edition, London, 1682.

12mo. A-Aa^{12} Bb^6; 294 leaves, pp. [*24*] 1-563 [564].

Illustrations: Woodcuts in the text illustrating table settings and carving.

Bibliographies: Axford, p. 319; Bitting, p. 407; Craig, 78; Oxford, p. 42; Pennell, p. 141; Wing R1933.

Copies: *BMC.* Wing adds Bodleian Library and Cambridge.

971. Rundell, Maria Eliza Ketelby, 1745-1828.

A │ NEW SYSTEM │ OF │ DOMESTIC COOKERY; │ FORMED UPON │ PRINCIPLES OF ECONOMY, │ And adapted to the Use of │ *PRIVATE FAMILIES.* │ [short fancy rule] │ BY A LADY. │ [short fancy rule] │ A NEW EDITION, CORRECTED. │ [two short rules] │ *LONDON:* │ PRINTED FOR JOHN MURRAY, FLEET-STREET; J. HARDING, │ ST. JAMES'S-STREET; AND A. CONSTABLE AND CO. │ EDINBURGH; │ *At the Union Printing-Office, St. John's Square, by W. Wilson.* │ [short rule] │ 1807. │ [short rule] │ *Price Seven Shillings and Sixpence.*

Third edition, London, 1807. There was a "second edition, considerably enlarged and improved," also published by Murray, London, 1807. See the note at the end of this entry for an account of the publication of this work.

158 x 94 mm. a-b^{12} c^2(c1 +c✳) B-P^{12} Q^8; 203 leaves, pp. [22] [i] ii-xxviii, 28✳, 29✳, xxix-xxx [1] 2-351 [352].

Illustrations: Etched frontispiece titled "Art of Cookery" with the imprint "Published as the act directs, Novr. 1st, 1805, by J. Murray" and nine plates illustrating cuts of meat, carving, and trussing.

Bibliographies: Axford, p. 297; Oxford, p. 135.

Copies: *NUC* (4 copies).

Notes: No edition of this work dated earlier than 1807 has been located. The *NUC* records a "second edition, considerably enlarged and improved," also published by Murray, London, 1807, and Oxford records the "new edition" described here but nothing earlier. The imprint on the frontispiece, "Published as the act directs, Novr. 1st 1805, by J. Murray," suggests the first edition may have appeared late in 1805 or early in 1806, but no copy of this edition has been located.

The *DNB* gives the following account of the publication of this book:

"While living at Swansea in 1806 Mrs. Rundell collected various recipes for cookery and suggestions for household management for the use of her married daughters." She sent the manuscript to the publisher, John Murray (1778-1843), of whose family she was an old friend. He suggested the title "Domestic Cookery," and had the work carefully revised by competent editors, among whom was Dr. Charles Taylor, of the Society of Arts, and added engravings. It was published as "A New System of Domestic Cookery" in 1808, and had an immense success. From five to ten thousand copies were long [*sic*] printed yearly. It became one of Murray's most valuable properties, and in 1812, when he bought the lease of the house in Albemarle Street, part of the surety consisted of the copyright of the "Domestic Cookery." As the earliest manual of household management with any pretensions to completeness, it called forth many imitations.

"In 1808 Murray presented Mrs. Rundell with £150. She replied, `I never had the smallest idea of any return for what I considered a free gift to one whom I had long regarded as my friend.' In acknowledging a copy of the second edition, Mrs. Rundell begged Murray not to think of remunerating her further, and in the preface to the edition of 1810 she expressly stated that she would receive no emolument. But in 1814 Mrs. Rundell accused Murray of neglecting the book and of hindering its sale. After obtaining an injunction in the vice-chancellor's court to restrain Murray from republishing the book, she in 1821 placed an improved version of it in the hands of Messrs. Longman for publication. Murray retaliated by obtaining an injunction from the lord chancellor to prevent Mrs. Rundell from publishing the book with any of his additions and embellishments. On 3 Nov. the lord chancellor dissolved the injunction against Murray, but gave right to neither party, declaring that a court of law and not a court of equity must decide between them (*Gent. Mag.* 1821, ii. 465). After long delay, Mrs. Rundell accepted Murray's offer of £1,000 in full discharge of all claims, together with a similar sum to defray her costs and expenses (cf. MOORE, *Memoirs*, v. 118, 199). The book was translated into German in 1841; the sixty-fifth English edition appeared in the same year."

972. Rundell, Maria Eliza Ketelby, 1745-1828.

A | NEW SYSTEM | OF | DOMESTIC COOKERY; | FORMED UPON |
PRINCIPLES OF ECONOMY. | And adapted to the Use of | *PRIVATE FAMILIES.* |
[short fancy rule] | BY A LADY. | [short fancy rule] | A NEW EDITION,
CORRECTED. | [two short rules] | *LONDON:* | PRINTED FOR JOHN MURRAY,
FLEET-STREET; J. HARDING, | ST. JAMES'S-STREET; AND A. CONSTABLE
AND CO. | EDINBURGH; | *At the Union Printing-Office, St. John's Square, by W.
Wilson.* | [short rule] | 1808. | [short rule] | *Price Seven Shillings and Sixpence.*

Fourth edition, London, 1808. Originally published, London ca.1806 or 1807. See
note at end of item 971.

154 x 97 mm. a^{10} B-P^{12} Q^8; 186 leaves, pp. [*20*] [1] 2-351 [352]. a2-a5 missigned
"a3"-"a6".

Illustrations: Engraved frontispiece, after the etched frontispiece in the 1807 edition,

Bibliographies: This edition unrecorded in the bibliographies consulted.

Copies: *BMC* and *NUC* (College of William and Mary only).

973. Rundell, Maria Eliza Ketelby, 1745-1828.

A | NEW SYSTEM | OF | DOMESTIC COOKERY; | FORMED UPON |
PRINCIPLES OF ECONOMY: | AND ADAPTED TO THE | USE OF PRIVATE
FAMILIES. | BY A LADY. | A NEW EDITION, CORRECTED. | [short rule] |
LONDON: | JOHN MURRAY, ALBEMARLE-STREET: | SOLD ALSO BY |
LONGMAN, BALDWIN, RICHARDSON, WHITTAKER, UNDERWOOD,
SIMPKIN | AND MARSHALL, LONDON; WILSON, YORK; MOZLEY, DERBY; |
MANNERS AND MILLER, AND OLIVER AND BOYD, | EDINBURGH;
CUMMING, MILLIKEN, AND KEENE, | DUBLIN. | And by every Bookseller and
Newsman in Town and Country. | [short rule] | 1824. | [short rule] | *Price Seven
Shillings and Sixpence in Boards.*

New edition, London, 1824. Originally published, London ca.1806 or 1807. See note
at end of item 971.

152 x 98 mm. a-c^8 d^2(d1 + 1) B-C^8 D^8(D2 + 1) E-FF^8 G1; 253 leaves pp. [i-v] vi-liv [1]
2-36, 36✱, 37✱, 37-449 [450].

Illustrations: Engraved frontispiece titled "Domestic Cookery" dated August 1823, and nine engraved plates illustrating cuts of meat, carving, and trussing.

Bibliographies: Wheaton and Kelly 5358.

Copies: *BMC* and *NUC* and Wheaton and Kelly (Radcliffe only).

974. Rundell, Maria Eliza Ketelby, 1745-1828.

A | NEW SYSTEM | OF | DOMESTIC COOKERY; | FORMED UPON | PRINCIPLES OF ECONOMY, | AND ADAPTED TO THE | USE OF PRIVATE FAMILIES. | BY A LADY. | WITH THE ADDITION OF MANY NEW RECEIPTS. | [short rule] | LONDON: | PRINTED FOR THOMAS ALLMAN, 42, HOLBORN HILL, | AND SOLD BY ALL BOOKSELLERS. | [short rule] | 1839.

New edition, London, 1839 Originally published, London, ca.1806 or 1807. See note at end of item 971.

168 x 107 mm. [A]² [B]⁸ C-O⁸ [P]⁸ Q-2C⁸ [2D]²; 204 leaves, pp. [22] [i] ii-xxx [1] 2-28, 28✳, 29✳, 29-168, 168✳, 169, 169✳, 170-351 [352]. Publisher's black cloth, stamped in gold.

Illustrations: Engraved frontispiece titled "New System of Domestic Cookery" and nine engraved plates illustrating cuts of meat, carving, and trussing.

Bibliographies: Wheaton and Kelly 5359.

Copies: Wheaton and Kelly (Radcliffe only).

975. Rundell, Maria Eliza Ketelby, 1745-1828.

A | NEW SYSTEM | OF | DOMESTIC COOKERY; | FORMED UPON | PRINCIPLES OF ECONOMY, | AND ADAPTED TO THE | USE OF PRIVATE FAMILIES | BY A LADY. | WITH THE ADDITION OF MANY NEW RECEIPTS. | [short rule] | LONDON: | PRINTED FOR THOMAS ALLMAN, 42, HOLBORN HILL, | AND SOLD BY ALL BOOKSELLERS. | [short rule] | 1840.

New edition, London, 1840. Originally published, London, ca.1806 or 1807. See note at end of item 971.

168 x 107 mm. [A]² [B]⁸ C-O⁸ [P]⁸ Q-2C⁸ [2D]²; 204 leaves, pp. [22] [i] ii-xxx [1] 2-28, 28✱ [*1*] 29✱, 30-168, 168✱, 169, 169✱ [170] 171-351 [352]. Publisher's brown cloth, stamped in gold.

Illustrations: Engraved frontispiece titled "New System of Domestic Cookery" and nine engraved plates illustrating cuts of meat, carving, and trussing.

Bibliographies: Bitting, p. 411.

Copies: Not in *NUC* but presumably in the Bitting Collection in the Library of Congress.

976. Rundell, Maria Eliza Ketelby, 1745-1828.

A | NEW SYSTEM | OF | DOMESTIC COOKERY: | FOUNDED UPON | PRINCIPLES OF ECONOMY; | AND ADAPTED TO THE | USE OF PRIVATE FAMILIES. | BY A LADY. | SIXTY-SIXTH EDITION. | AUGMENTED AND IMPROVED BY THE ADDITION OF MORE THAN | *NINE HUNDRED* NEW RECEIPTS, | SUITED TO THE PRESENT STATE OF THE ART OF COOKERY. | [short fancy rule] | LONDON: | JOHN MURRAY, ALBEMARLE STREET. | [short rule] | 1842.

Sixty-sixth edition, London, 1842. Originally published, London, ca. 1806 or 1807. See note at end of item 971.

166 x 100 mm. a-c⁸ d² ₓ1 B-2N⁸ 2O⁶, leaf ₓ1 signed "d3"; 313 leaves, pp. [i-ii] iii-liv [1] 2-571 [572]. Dark green cloth stamped in gold and blind.

Illustrations: Engraved frontispiece by Alfred Adlard after a drawing by H. Corbould, titled "Domestic Cookery" and nine engraved plates illustrating cuts of meat, carving, and trussing.

Bibliographies: Wheaton and Kelly 5360.

Copies: *NUC* (Radcliffe College only).

977. Rundell, Maria Eliza Ketelby, 1745-1828.

A | NEW SYSTEM | OF | DOMESTIC COOKERY; | FORMED UPON | PRINCIPLES OF ECONOMY, | AND ADAPTED TO THE | USE OF PRIVATE

FAMILIES. | 𝔚𝔦𝔱𝔥 𝔗𝔢𝔫 𝔍𝔩𝔩𝔲𝔰𝔱𝔯𝔞𝔱𝔦𝔬𝔫𝔰. | [short rule] | BY A LADY. | [short rule] | LONDON. | PRINTED FOR THE BOOKSELLERS. | [short rule] | 1846.

New edition, London, 1846. Originally published, London, ca.1806 or 1807. See note at end of item 971.

158 x 101 mm. π^2 a-c^6 B-2G^6 [2H]^6 2I^2; 202 leaves, pp. [*4*] [i] ii-xii, ^{2}[i] ii-xxiv [1] 2-28, 28✳, 29✳, 29-361 [362].

Illustrations: Engraved frontispiece of a kitchen scene and nine lithographed plates illustrating cuts of meat, carving, and trussing.

Bibliographies: This edition unrecorded in the bibliographies consulted.

Copies: No other copy of this edition located.

978. Ruscelli, Girolamo, c. 1566.

The Secrets of the reuerend | Maister *Alexis* of Piemont, con- | *taining excellent remedies against diuerse* | diseases, wounds, and other accidents, with | *the maner to make Distillations, Par-* | fumes, Confitures, Dyings, Colours, Fu- | sions, and Meltings. A worke well ap- | proued, verie necessarie for | euerie man. | *Newly corrected and amended, and also* | somewhat inlarged in certaine places, | which wanted in the first | edition. | *Translated out of French into English by* | William Ward. | [vignette] | Imprinted at London by Peter Short, for | *Thomas Wight*. 1595.

First collected edition, London, 1595, of all four parts in English. Originally published in Italian under the title *De' Secreti del Reverendo Donno Alessio Piemontese*, Venice, 1555 or 1556, and in English in four separate parts, London 1558, 1560, 1562, and 1569.

4to. A-Zz^8; 368 leaves, ff, [*6*] 1-348 [*14*].

Bibliographies: *STC* 312.

Copies: *NUC* (4 copies). *STC* (10 copies).

979. Ruscelli, Girolamo, c. 1566.

[within a single rule border] THE | SECRETS | OF | ALEXIS: | *CONTAINING MANY* | EXCELLENT REMEDIES | *AGAINST DIVERS DISEASES,* | *wounds, and other Accidents.* | With the maner to make | [in two columns: column one] { | *Distillations,* | *Parfumes,* | *Confitures,* | *Dyings,* | }{ | [column two] *Colours,* | *Fusions,* | and | *Meltings.* | } [end columns] | A worke well approued, very necessarie | for euery man. | *Newly corrected and amended, and also* | somewhat more enlarged in certaine places, | *which wanted in the former* | Editions. | [two rules] | LONDON, | Printed by WILLIAM STANSBY for *Richard Meighen* | and *Thomas Iones*, and are to be sold at their shop with- | out Temple-barre vnder *S. Clements* | Church. 1615.

Second collected edition, London, 1615, here divided into five parts, in English.

4to. A-Zz⁸; 368 leaves, ff. [*6*] [*1*] 2-348 [*14*].

Bibliographies: *STC* 312.5.

Copies: *BMC* and *NUC* (7 copies). *STC* (10 copies).

Ruthven, Thomas, baron, see B., M. (item 553)

980. S., D.

[within a border of two rules] *Vinetum Angliae:* | OR, | A new and easy Way to make | Wine of *English* Grapes and other Fruit, e- | qual to that of *France, Spain, &c.* with their | Physical Virtues. | Also to make Artificial Wines, and to Order | and Recover them when damaged. | To make all sorts of Cyder, Mead, Metheglin, | Rum, Rack, and many other useful Liquors. | To Gather, Order and Keep Fruit in all Seasons. | The true Art of Distilling Brandy, Strong-waters | and Cordial-waters. | To make all sorts of Pickles, and sundry sorts | of Vinegars. | The whole Art and Mystery of a Confectioner. | The compleat Caterer, or how to know whether | Flesh, Fish or Fowl be Old or Young, New | or Stale. | Rules for frugal, cheap and well Living. | To destroy all sorts of Vermin; with divers o- | ther notable things, never before made pub- | lick. | [rule] | By *D. S.* | [rule] | Sold by *G. Conyers*, at the Gold Ring in *Little Britain.* | (*Price One Shilling.*)

First edition, London, ca.1690.

8vo. A-M⁸; 96 leaves, pp. [*18*] 1-174.

Bibliographies: Axford, p. 411; Bitting, p. 615; Simon BG 1579; Wing S16.

Copies: *BMC* and *NUC* (Library of Congress, Kansas State University, and University of California, Berkeley). Wing adds Cambridge.

980a. Sala, George Augustus, 1828-1895.

THE │ THOROUGH │ GOOD COOK │ A SERIES OF │ CHATS ON THE CULINARY ART │ AND │ NINE HUNDRED RECIPES │ BY │ GEORGE AUGUSTUS SALA │ CASSELL AND COMPANY, LIMITED │ *LONDON, PARIS & MELBOURNE* │ 1895 │ ALL RIGHTS RESERVED

First edition, London, 1895.

203 x 163 mm. A^{10} B-I^8 J-U^8 V^8 W-EE^8 FF^6; 256 leaves, pp. [i-v] vi-xvii [xviii-xx] [1] 2-492. Publisher's blue cloth stamped in gold.

Bibliographies: Axford, p. 391; Bitting, p. 415; Driver 926.1.

Copies: *BMC*, Driver (14 copies), *NUC* (5 copies).

980b. Sallengre, Albert Henrik de, 1694-1723.

Ebrietatis Encomium: │ OR, THE │ PRAISE │ OF │ DRUNKENNESS. │ WHEREIN │ Is authentically, and most evidently │ proved, The *Necessity* of frequently *getting* │ *Drunk*; and, That the *Practice* of *getting* │ *Drunk* is most *Antient, Primitive,* and *Ca-* │ *tholic.* │ CONFIRMED │ By the Example of *Heathens, Turks, Infidels,* │ *Primitive Christians, Saints, Popes, Bishops,* │ *Doctors, Philosophers, Poets, Free Masons,* │ and other Men of *Learning* in all Ages. │ [rule] │ BY │ BONIFACE OINOPHILUS, │ *de Monte* Fiascone, *A. B. C.* │ *Vinum latificans Cor hominis.* / *Narratur & Prisci* Cantonis, │ *Sape Mero caluisse virtus.* HORAT. │ *LONDON:* / *Printed for* E. CURLL, *over against* Catherine │ Street, *in the* Strand. 1723. Price *2 s. 6 d.*

First edition in English, London, 1723, translated by Robert Samber. Originally published in French, The Hague, 1714.

12mo. A^6 B-I^{12} K^6; 108 leaves, pp. [*12*] [1] 2-204. First leaf, blank.

Illustrations: Engraved frontispiece of a man drinking from a bottle, captioned: Vivimus dum Bibimus.

Bibliographies: Gabler G31100 misdating the book 1722 and misdiscribing it as having 151 pp.

Copies: *BMC* and *NUC* (8 copies).

981. Salmon, William, 1644-1713.

[within a border of two rules] THE │ Family-Dictionary; │ OR, │ *Houshold Companion:* │ Wherein are *Alphabetically* laid down Exact *Rules* │ and Choice *Physical RECEIPTS* │ FOR │ The Preservation of Health, Prevention of Sickness, and │ Curing the several Diseases, Distempers, and Grievances, │ incident to Men, Women, and Children. │ *Also,* Directions for Making Oils, Ointments, Salves, Cordial- │ Waters, Powders, Pills, Bolus's, Lozenges, Chymical Pre- │ parations, Physical-Wines, Ales, and other Liquors, *&c.* and │ Descriptions of the Virtues of Herbs, Fruits, Flowers, │ Seeds, Roots, Barks, Minerals, and Parts of Living Crea- │ tures, used in Medicinal Potions, *&c.* │ Likewise, 𝔇irections for 𝔊ookery, in Dressing Flesh, Fish, │ Fowl, Seasoning, Garnishing, Sauces, and Serving-up in │ the Best and most acceptable Manner. The *Whole ART* of │ Pastry, Conserving, Preserving, Candying, Confectioning, *&c.* │ *Also,* The Way of Making all sorts of Perfumes, Beautifying- │ Waters, Pomatums, Washes, Sweet-Balls, Sweet-Bags, and │ Essences: Taking Spots, and Stains out of Garments, Lin- │ nen, *&c.* and Preserving them from Moths, *&c.* Wash- │ ing Point, Sarsnets, and Restoring Faded Linnen; and Scowr- │ ing, or Brightning Tarnished Gold, or Silver Lace, Plate, *&c.* │ *Together,* VVith the Art of Making all sorts of English │ VVines, as Currants, Cherries, Gooseberries, and Cyder, │ Mead, Metheglin, *&c.* And the *ART* of Fining, and │ Recovering Foul or Faded Wines. The *MYSTERY* of │ Pickling, and keeping all Sorts of Pickles throughout the Year. │ *To which is Added, as an* APPENDIX, │ The Explanation of Physical Terms, Bills of Fare in all Sea- │ sons of the Year. With the *ART* of CARVING. │ And many other Useful Matters. │ [rule] │ By *J. H.* │ [rule] │ *London*, Printed for ℌ. ℜhodes, at the *Star*, the Corner of │ *Bride-lane*, in *Fleetstreet*, 1695.

First edition, London, 1695.

8vo. A⁴ B-T⁸ U⁸(U7+1) X-Aa⁸; 189 leaves, unpaginated.

Bibliographies: Axford, p. 142; Bitting, p. 416; Oxford, p. 45; Wheaton and Kelly 5431; Wing H66 and S428.

Copies: *NUC* (8 copies). Wing H66 adds Birmingham Central Reference Library, the British Library (but not in *BMC*) and St. John's College, Cambridge.

982. Salmon, William, 1644-1713.

[within a border of two rules] THE | Family Dictionary: | OR, | *Houshold Companion.* | CONTAINING, | I. COOKERY in Dressing Flesh, Fowl, Fish, Herbs, | Roots, making Sawces, &c. | II. PASTRY, making Pyes, Pasties, Puddings, | Pancakes, Cheesecakes, Custards, Tansies, &c. | III. CONFECTS, Candies, Conserves, Preserves, | Creams, Gellies, Pickles, &c. | IV. POTABLE Liquors, as Ale, Beer, Mum, Mead, | Cider, Perry, Rape, *English* Wines, Chocolet, Coffee, Tea, &c. | V. PERFUMING Sweet Balls, Pouders, Pomanders, | Essences, Sweet Waters, Beautifying Washes, &c. | VI. HUSBANDRY, as it relates to the Improvement | of Our Barren and Waste Lands, Manufactures &c. | VII. PREPARATIONS Galenick and Chymick' | relating to Physick and Chirurgery, as Cordial Waters, | Spirits, Tinctures, Elixirs, Syrups, Pouders, Electuaries, | Pills, Oils, Balsams, Cerecloths, and Emplasters, fitted | for Curing most Diseases Incident to Men, Women, and | Children. | [rule] | *The* FOURTH EDITION, *with above Eleven* | *Hundred Additions, intersperst through the Whole WORK.* | [rule] | By *WILLIAM SALMON*. M. D. | [rule] | *LONDON:* Printed for H. Rhodes, at the Star, the | Corner of *Bride-Lane*, in *Fleet-Street.* 1710.

Fourth edition, London, 1710. Originally published, London, 1695 (item 981).

8vo. A-Nn^8; 288 leaves, pp. [*16*] 1-560.

Bibliographies: Axford, p. 142; Bitting, p. 416, in a note; Maclean, p. 128; Oxford, p. 46, in a note; Simon BG 1350; Wheaton and Kelly 5433.

Copies: *BMC, BNC*, and *NUC* (Harvard, National Library of Medicine, and New York Academy of Medicine). Maclean adds Brotherton Library and Manchester Public Library. Wheaton and Kelly adds American Antiquarian Society.

983. Scot, Reginald, 1538?-1599.

A Perfite platforme | of a Hoppe Garden, | and necessarie Instructions for the | making and mayntenaunce thereof, | with notes and rules for reformation | of all abuses, commonly practised | therein, bery necessarie and | expedient for all men | to habe, which in any | wise habe to doe | with Hops. | *Nowe newly corrected and augmented* | By *Reynolde Scot.* | *Prouerbs*. II. | Who so laboureth after goodnesse, findeth his desire. | *Sapien.*7. | Wisedome is nymbler than all nymble things. | She goeth thorough and attayneth to all things. | [ornament] | [leaf] Imprinted at London by Henrie | *Denham, dwelling in Pater noster* | Rovve, at the Signe of | the Starre. | 1576. | *Cum priuilegio ad imprimendum solum.*

Second edition, London, 1576. Originally published, London, 1574.

4to. A-K⁴; 40 leaves, pp. [*14*] 1-63 [64] [*2*]. Last leaf (blank?) wanting in this copy.

Illustrations: Woodcuts in the text.

Bibliographies: Fussell (1), pp. 11-12; Henrey I.337; *STC* 21866.

Copies: *BMC* and *NUC* (7 copies). *STC* (9 copies).

984. Scott, William.

THE | HOUSE BOOK; | OR, | FAMILY CHRONICLE OF USEFUL KNOWLEDGE, | AND | COTTAGE PHYSICIAN: | COMBINING | [in two columns: column one] MEDICINE, | COOKERY, | DIET, | GENERAL ECONOMY, | HEALTH, | [vertical rule] [column two] SEA-BATHING, | GARDENING, | MANUFACTURES, | ARTS, &c. &c. [end columns] | WITH THE VARIOUS BRANCHES OF | 𝕯𝖔𝖒𝖊𝖘𝖙𝖎𝖈 𝕮𝖔𝖓𝖈𝖊𝖗𝖓𝖘; | INCLUDING UPWARDS OF | A THOUSAND SELECT RECIPES | AND PRESCRIPTIONS, | FROM THE BEST AUTHORITIES; AND A VAREITY OF OTHER | IMPORTANT INFORMATION, FOR THE USE OF FAMILIES, | INVALIDS, AND CONVALESCENTS. | [short rule] | EDITED | BY WILLIAM SCOTT, M. D. | [two short rules] | *LONDON:* | PRINTED FOR SHERWOOD, GILBERT, AND PIPER, | PATERNOSTER-ROW. | [short rule] | 1826.

First edition, London, 1826.

227 x 140 mm. a-b⁴ B-4H⁴; 312 leaves, pp. [i-iii] iv-xvi [1] 2-232, 239-614. Publisher's boards, with printed paper label on the spine.

Illustrations: Engraved frontispiece by Storer after Cruikshank and hand colored engraved plate of Common Purple Vervain facing p. 391.

Bibliographies: Attar 270.1.

Copies: *BNC* and *NUC* (John Crerar Library, Library of Congress, and Yale). Attar adds Wellcome Institute.

985. Shackleford, Ann.

THE | Modern Art of Cookery | IMPROVED; | OR, | Elegant, Cheap, and Easy Methods, of preparing | most of the DISHES now in Vogue; | In the Composition whereof | Both HEALTH and PLEASURE have been consulted, | BY, | Mrs. ANN SHACKLEFORD, of *Winchester*. | TO WHICH IS ADDED, | An APPENDIX; | Containing a Dissertation on the different Kinds of | Food, their Nature, Quality, and various Uses. | By a PHYCISIAN. | AND | A MARKETING MANUAL, | And other useful PARTICULARS. | By the EDITOR. | [rule] | She turns, on hospitable thoughts intent, | What choice to chuse for delicacy best; | What order, so contriv'd as not to mix | Tastes, not well join'd, inelegant, but bring | Taste after Taste, upheld with kindliest change. | MILTON. | [rule] | LONDON: | Printed for J. NEWBERY, at the Bible and Sun, in | St. Paul's Church-Yard; and F. NEWBERY, in | Pater-noster-Row. 1767.

First edition, London, 1767.

12mo. A-N^{12} O^6; 162 leaves, pp. [i-ii] iii-xxiv, 1-284 [*16*]. Last leaf (blank?) wanting in this copy.

Bibliographies: Axford, p. 273; Bitting, p. 430; Maclean, p. 131; Oxford, p. 95; Pennell, p. 160; Vicaire 791.

Copies: *NUC* (Library of Congress only). Maclean adds Brotherton Library and New York Public Library.

986. Sheen, James Richmond.

[within a red single rule border with ornamental corners] WINES | AND | [in red] OTHER FERMENTED LIQUORS; | FROM THE | 𝔈arliest 𝒜ges to the present 𝔗ime. | DEDICATED TO | [in red] ALL CONSUMERS IN THE UNITED KINGDOM. | BY | JAMES RICHMOND SHEEN. | [short rule] | "If it be true that a wise man, like a good refiner, can gather gold | out of the drossiest volume, and that a fool will be a fool with the best | book, — yea, or without a book; there is no reason that we should deprive | a wise man of any advantage to his wisdom, while we seek to

restrain | from a fool that which, being restrained, will be no hindrance to his | folly."
– MILTON'S `AREOPAGITICA,' sec. 28. (1644.) | [short rule] | [in red]
LONDON: | ROBERT HARDWICKE, 192, PICCADILLY. W. | AND ALL
BOOKSELLERS.

First edition, London, 1864.

170 x 105 mm. [a]² b⁴ B-T⁸ U²; 152 leaves, pp. [i-iii] iv-xii [1] 2-292.

Illustrations: Wood engravings in the text.

Bibliographies: Bitting, p. 431; Noling, p. 371, dating the book 1865.

Copies: *BMC* and *NUC* (5 copies).

987. Sigmond, George Gabriel, b. 1794.

TEA; | ITS EFFECTS, MEDICINAL | AND MORAL. | BY | G. G. SIGMOND,
M.D. F.S.A. F.L.S. | PROFESSOR OF MATERIA MEDICA TO THE ROYAL |
MEDICO-BOTANICAL SOCIETY. | [short rule] | LONDON: | PRINTED FOR |
LONGMAN, ORME, BROWN, GREEN, & LONGMANS, | PATERNOSTER-ROW.
| 1839.

First edition, London, 1839.

171 x 108 mm. [A]⁴ B-K⁸; 76 leaves, pp. [i-v] vi-viii [1] 2-144. Publisher's green
cloth stamped in gold. Sixteen page publisher's catalogue dated November 1839 bound
in at the end.

Bibliographies: Crahan 726; Noling, p. 374; Wheaton and Kelly 5593.

Copies: *BMC, BNC,* and *NUC* (12 copies).

988. Simon, André Louis, 1877-1970.

THE ART | OF GOOD LIVING | *A Contribution to the better Understanding* | *of*
Food and Drink | *together with a* | *Gastronomic Vocabulary* | *and a* | *Wine Dictionary*
| *by* | ANDRÉ L. SIMON | *with a frontispiece after Daumier* | *and a foreword by* |
Maurice Healy | *London* | CONSTABLE & CO LTD | *1929*

First edition, London, 1929, limited issue. No. 271 of 300 copies, signed by the author.

230 x 149 mm. π^8 [A]^8 B-M^8 N^6(N2 signed "O"); 110 leaves, pp. [i-viii] ix-xvi [1-2] 3-200 [201-202] [2]. Quarter Japan vellum, stamped in gold, and marbled boards.

Illustrations: Colored frontispiece and eleven black and white plates after works by well known artists.

Bibliographies: Axford, p. 19; Bitting, p. 436; Oberlé (1) 296; Noling, p. 375.

Copies: *BMC* (trade issue) and *NUC* (trade issue only, 9 copies).

989. Simon, André Louis, 1877-1970.

A CONCISE | ENCYCLOPAEDIA | OF *Gastronomy* | BY ANDRE L. SIMON | [two short rules] | *With decorations by John Leigh-Pemberton* | [two short rules] | COMPLETE AND UNABRIDGED | COLLECTOR'S BOOK CLUB | LONDON W.I. ENGLAND

Limitation statement:

This de luxe edition, limited to 100 copies, | is published by special arrangement with | Messrs Wm Collins Son & Co. Ltd, and the | Collectors Book Club, and forms part of | the first edition in one volume. This edition | contains the full text of the separate parts | published between 1939 and 1946, | thoroughly revised. | Five copies numbered I to V have been | struck off as presentation copies. | No.............. [23. written in ink] | [authors signature] | *Designed and produced* | *by Rainbird McLean Ltd* | *De Luxe Binding by* | *the Collectors Book Club* | *43 Crawford Place, London W I, England* | *Printed in Great Britain by Samuel Sidders & Son Ltd* | 1952

New edition, London, 1952. Originally published in nine parts, London, 1939-1946, and in book form, London, Collins, 1952. This copy is from the limited issue of 100 copies made up of sheets of the Collins edition with a cancel title leaf.

215 x 137 mm. [A]^{16}($\pm$A2) B-V^{16} W-Bb^{16} Cc^4; 420 leaves, pp. [i-vi] vii-xii [1-2] 3-827 [828].

Bibliographies: Unrecorded in the bibliographies consulted. Noling, p. 376, records a copy of part VIII dated 1948.

Copies: No other copy of this limited issue located.

990. Simpson, John.

A | COMPLETE | SYSTEM OF COOKERY, | ON A PLAN ENTIRELY NEW, | CONSISTING OF | EVERY THING THAT IS REQUISITE | FOR | COOKS TO KNOW | IN THE | KITCHEN BUSINESS; | CONTAINING | BILLS OF FARE | FOR | *EVERY DAY IN THE YEAR,* | AND | DIRECTIONS TO DRESS EACH DISH; | BEING | ONE YEAR's WORK, | AT THE MARQUIS OF BUCKINGHAM'S, | *From the* 1*st of January, to the* 31*st of December,* 1805. | [two short rules] | BY | JOHN SIMPSON, | PRESENT COOK TO THE MOST NOBLE | THE MARQUIS OF BUCKINGHAM. | [two short rules] | LONDON: | PRINTED FOR W. STEWART, OPPOSITE | ALBANY, PICCADILLY. | 1806.

First edition, London, 1806.

226 x 138 mm. [A]⁶ B-3B⁸ 3C²; 384 leaves, pp. [i-vii] viii-xi [xii] [1] 2-754 [2]. Last leaf blank. Publisher's boards with printed label on the spine.

Bibliographies: Axford, p. 76; Bitting, p. 436; Oxford, p. 134; Simon BG 1386; Vicaire 792; Wheaton and Kelly 5633.

Copies: *BMC* and *NUC* (5 copies).

991. Simpson, John.

A COMPLETE | SYSTEM OF COOKERY, | ON A PLAN ENTIRELY NEW; | CONSISTING OF EVERY THING REQUISITE FOR COOKS TO | KNOW IN THEIR DEPARTMENTS; | LIKEWISE | CONFECTIONARY AND PICKLING, | PROPER FOR HOUSE-KEEPERS TO HAVE A KNOWLEDGE OF; | Containing | Bills of Fare for every Day of the Year, | And Directions how to Dress each Dish: | BEING ONE YEAR'S WORK, | AT THE LATE MOST NOBLE | THE MARQUIS OF BUCKINGHAM'S, | *From the* 1*st of January to the* 31*st of December,* 1805; | INCLUDING THE | DINNERS AND ENTERTAINMENTS | GIVEN TO HIS ROYAL HIGHNESS | *THE PRINCE OF WALES.* | DURING A WEEK AT STOW; | AND TO | LOUIS XVIII. AND THE FRENCH PRINCES, | AT GOSFIELD. | [two rules] | BY JOHN SIMPSON, | *Then Cook to the late Marquis of Buckingham.* | [two rules] | BEING THE FOURTH EDITION, | Corrected and Enlarged with the Addition of Pickling, &c. | [short rule] | *LONDON:* | PRINTED FOR W. STEWART, 194, OPPOSITE ALBANY, PICCADILLY; | R. LEA, GREEK STREET, SOHO; P. MARTIN & Co. OXFORD-STREET; J. HATCHARD, | PICCADILLY; W. ANDERSON, PICCADILLY; T. HUGHES, LUDGATE-STREET; | & B. CROSBY & Co. STATIONER'S-COURT, LUDGATE-STREET.

Fourth edition, London, ca.1813. Originally published, London, 1806 (item 990).

210 x 128 mm. π1 [A]⁸ πB² B-Xx⁸ Yy⁴; 359 leaves, pp. [2] [i-v] vi-xx [1] 2-696.

Bibliographies: Oxford, p. 135, in a note, mentions undated editions of 1807 and 1816. The British Library dates the fourth edition [1813?].

Copies: *BMC*.

992. Simpson, John.

A | COMPLETE SYSTEM | OF | COOKERY, | *ON A PLAN ENTIRELY NEW;* | CONSISTING OF | AN EXTENSIVE AND ORIGINAL COLLECTION OF | RECEIPTS, | IN | 𝕮𝖔𝖔𝖐𝖊𝖗𝖞, 𝕮𝖔𝖓𝖋𝖊𝖈𝖙𝖎𝖔𝖓𝖆𝖗𝖞, 𝖊𝖙𝖈. | WITH | BILLS OF FARE | *FOR EVERY DAY IN THE YEAR*; | THE WHOLE AS ACTUALLY DRESSED AND SERVED UP, DURING FIVE | YEARS' RESIDENCE, AT THE MARQUIS OF BUCKINGHAM'S; | Including | SEVERAL ENTERTAINMENTS GIVEN TO | *HIS ROYAL HIGHNESS THE PRINCE OF WALES,* | AND OTHER ROYAL PERSONAGES. | To which are now added, | TABLES OF ARTICLES IN SEASON, | AND | 𝕿𝖍𝖊 𝕸𝖔𝖉𝖊 𝖔𝖋 𝕯𝖗𝖊𝖘𝖘𝖎𝖓𝖌 𝕿𝖚𝖗𝖙𝖑𝖊, | (NEVER BEFORE GIVEN IN ANY WORK OF THE KIND) | *BILLS OF FARE FOR DESERTS,* | AND A SERIES OF RECEIPTS AND BILLS OF FARE OF ECONOMICAL DISHES, | TO SUIT THE MOST PRIVATE FAMILIES. | [two short rules] | BY JOHN SIMPSON, | COOK TO THE LATE AND PRESENT MARQUIS OF BUCKINGHAM. | [two short rules] | 𝕷𝖔𝖓𝖉𝖔𝖓: | PRINTED FOR W. STEWART, 194, PICCADILLY; BALDWIN, CRADOCK, | AND JOY, PATERNOSTER-ROW; GALE AND FENNER, PATERNOSTER- | ROW; T. HUGHES, LUDGATE-HILL; J. HATCHARD, PICCADILLY; | A. ANDERSON, PICCADILLY; RODWELL AND MARTIN, NEW BOND- | STREET; J. BOOKER, NEW BOND-STREET; AND THE AUTHOR, 3, | PORTMAN-STREET, PORTMAN-SQUARE. | [short rule] | 1816.

New edition, London, 1816. Originally published, London, 1806 (item 990).

177 x 103 mm. [A]⁴ B-AA¹² BB⁸; 288 leaves, pp. [2] [i] ii-iii [iv-vi] [1] 2-568.

Bibliographies: Simon BG 1387; Wheaton and Kelly 5634.

Copies: *NUC* (Radcliffe and University of Oregon).

993. Skuse, E.

[Copyright. Fourth Edition.] [Price 7s. 6d.; Postage 4d.] | THE | CONFECTIONERS' HAND-BOOK | AND | PRACTICAL GUIDE | TO THE | ART OF SUGAR BOILING | *In all its branches.* | The Manufacture of Creams, Fondants, Liqueurs, Pastilles, Jujubes (Gelatine | and Gum), Comfits, Lozenges (Plain and Medicated), Chocolate, Chocolate | Creams, Drops, Bars, &c.; American Caramels, Ice Creams and Moulded | Ices of every description; | *JAMS, JELLIES AND MARMALADES* |(BY FIRE AND STEAM). | *Preserved and Crystalized Fruits, Candied Peel,* | ENGLISH AND SCOTCH PASTRY, | *Cordials and Syrups for American Hot & Iced Beverages.* | AERATED WATERS | Of every description, by Hand and Machine, for Bottle, Syphon, or Fountain, | Ginger Beer, Horehound, and other Fermented Beers. | [wood engraving] | The Recipes are accompanied with full and clear instructions in every | branch. Every information about Colours and Flavours; the best to use | and how to make them. Useful notes on Machinery for every purpose, and | About One Hundred Illustrations. | [two short rules] | PUBLISHED BY E. SKUSE, 30, PRAED, STREET, LONDON, W.; | SIMPKIN, MARSHALL & Co., STATIONERS' HALL COURT; | HAMILTON, ADAMS & Co., PATERNOSTER ROW.

Fourth edition, London, ca.1882. Originally published, London, 1878.

214 x 134 mm. [A]^4 B-2C^4 [2D]^4 χ1; 109 leaves, pp. [i-iv] v-viii [1] 2-184 [26]. Last 26 pages contain ads for confectionary goods. Bound in publisher's blue cloth stamped in gold and black.

Illustrations: Numerous wood engravings in the text.

Bibliographies: This edition unrecorded in the bibliographies consulted. Axford, p. 77, and Bitting, p. 437, record the third edition, London [1880?]. Noling, p. 381, and *BMC* date the third edition 1881.

Copies: No other copy of this edition located.

994. Skuse, E.

[10th Edition.] | *Copy-Right.*] [*Price 7/6, Postage 4d.* | SKUSE'S | COMPLETE CONFECTIONER | A | PRACTICAL GUIDE | TO THE | ART OF SUGAR BOILING IN ALL ITS BRANCHES | THE MANUFACTURE OF FONDANTS, CREAMS, | CHOCOLATES, PASTILLES, JUJUBES (GELATINE AND | GUM), COMFITS, LOZENGES (PLAIN AND | MEDICATED), CARAMELS, NOYEAUS, NOUGATS, | JAP NUGGETS, PRALINES &c., | ICE CREAMS AND ICES OF

EVERY DESCRIPTION, | JAMS, JELLIES AND MARMALADES (BY FIRE AND STEAM) | CONCENTRATED TABLE AND OTHER JELLIES, | PRESERVED AND CRYSTALLIZED FRUITS, CANDIED PEEL, &c. | ENGLISH AND SCOTCH PASTRY. | [short rule] | All Information Respecting Colours and Flavours; | the best to use and how to make them. | [short rule] | *USEFUL NOTES ON MACHINERY FOR EVERY PURPOSE.* | [short rule] | PUBLISHED BY | W. J. BUSH & CO., LTD., ASH GROVE, HACKNEY, LONDON.

Tenth edition, London, ca. 1900. Originally published, London, 1878.

214 x 140 mm. π^6 1-14^8; 118 leaves, pp. [*12*] [1] 2-222 [2]. First and last leaves pasted down as endpapers.

Illustrations: Numerous wood engravings in the text.

Bibliographies: This edition unrecorded in the bibliographies consulted. Bitting, p. 437, records an eleventh edition, London, 1911.

Copies: No other copy of this edition located.

995. Smith, Mrs.

THE | FEMALE ECONOMIST; | OR, | A PLAIN SYSTEM OF COOKERY: | FOR THE USE OF | FAMILIES. | CONTAINING | EIGHT HUNDRED AND FIFTY VALUABLE | *RECEIPTS.* | [two short rules] | BY MRS SMITH. | [two short rules] | "In every station, an ECONOMIST | is a respectable character." | *Hunter's Culinae.* | [short fancy rule] | 𝕋𝕙𝕚𝕣𝕕 𝔼𝕕𝕚𝕥𝕚𝕠𝕟. | [short fancy rule] | LONDON: | PRINTED FOR MATHEWS AND LEIGH, STRAND. | 1810. | FOUR SHILLINGS BOARDS.

Third edition, London, 1810. Originally published, London, also 1810.

194 x 115 mm. π^{12} A-O^{12}; 180 leaves, pp. [i-v] vi-xxiv [1] 2-330, ^{2}[i] ii-vi. Publisher's blue printed boards.

Illustrations: Engraved frontispiece.

Bibliographies: Axford, p. 154, records the second edition, London, 1810. Simon BG 1391, without mention of which edition.

Copies: *NUC* (Library of Congress only). A copy of the first edition is in the private collection of John C. Craig.

996. Smith, Eliza.

[within a border of two rules] The Compleat │ HOUSEWIFE; │ OR, │ *Accomplished Gentlewoman's* │ COMPANION: │ Being a COLLECTION of upwards of Five │ Hundred of the most approved RECEIPTS in │ [in two columns: column one] COOKERY, │ PASTRY, │ CONFECTIONARY, │ PRESERVING, │ PICKLES, │ [two vertical rules] │ [column two] CAKES, │ CREAMS, │ JELLIES, │ MADE WINES, │ CORDIALS. [end columns] │ With COPPER PLATES curiously engraven for the │ regular Disposition or Placing the various DISHES │ and COURSES. │ AND ALSO │ BILLS of FARE for every Month in the Year. │ To which is added, │ A Collection of near Two Hundred Family RECEIPTS of │ MEDICINES; *viz. Drinks, Syrups, Salves, Ointments,* and │ various other Things of soveraign and appoved Efficacy in │ most Distempers, Pains, Aches, Wounds, Sores, &c. never │ before made publick; fit either for private Families, or such │ publick-spirited Gentlewomen as would be beneficent to │ their poor Neighbours. │ [rule] │ By *E* ──── *S* ────. │ [rule] │ *LONDON:* │ Printed for J. PEMBERTON, at the *Golden Buck*, over- │ against St. *Dunstan's Church* in *Fleet-street.* │ [short rule] │ M. DCC. XXVII.

First edition, London, 1727.

8vo. A-X⁸ Y⁴ a⁸; 180 leaves. pp. [*16*] 1-326 [*18*]. Sixteen page publisher's catalogue bound in at the end.

Illustrations: Six engraved folding plates showing table settings.

Bibliographies: Axford, p. 71; Craig 82; Maclean, p. 133; Oxford, p. 60; Pennell, p. 146.

Copies: *NUC* (John Crerar Library only). Maclean adds Brotherton Library, Wellcome Library, and New York Public Library.

997. Smith, Eliza.

[within a border of two rules] The COMPLEAT │ HOUSEWIFE: │ OR, │ *Accomplish'd Gentlewoman's* │ COMPANION: │ Being a COLLECTION of upwards of Six │ Hundred of the most approved RECEIPTS in │ [in two columns: column one]

COOKERY, | PASTRY, | CONFECTIONARY, | PRESERVING, | PICKLES, | [two vertical rules] | [column two] CAKES, | CREAMS, | JELLIES, | MADE WINES, | CORDIALS. [end columns] | With COPPER PLATES curiously engraven for | the regular Disposition or Placing the various | DISHES and COURSES. | AND ALSO | BILLS of FARE for every Month in the Year. | To which is added, | A Collection of above Three Hundred Family RECEIPTS | of MEDICINES; *viz. Drinks, Syrups, Salves, Ointments,* | and various other Things of sovereign and approved Efficacy | in most Distempers, Pains, Aches, Wounds, Sores, *&c.* | never before made publick; fit either for private Families, or | such publick-spirited Gentlewomen as would be beneficent to | their poor Neighbours. | [rule] | By *E. SMITH.* | [rule] | *The* EIGHTH EDITION, *with very large Additions; not in any* | *of the former Impressions.* | [rule] | *LONDON:* | Printed for J. and J. PEMBERTON, at the *Golden Buck,* | against St. *Dunstan's Church* in *Fleetstreet.* 1737. | [within the border rules] Price Five Shillings.

Ninth edition recorded by Maclean, styled "Eighth edition" on the title-page, London, 1737. Originally published, London, 1727 (item 996).

8vo. A^8 (A1+1) B-Aa^8 Bb^2; 195 leaves. pp. [*18*] [1] 2-354 [i] ii-xv [xvi-xviii].

Illustrations: Engraved frontispiece of kitchen scene and six engraved folding plates showing table settings.

Bibliographies: Maclean, p. 134; Oxford, p. 60, in a note.

Copies: *NUC* (University of Iowa only). Maclean adds Dorset County Library and National Museum of Wales.

998. Smith, George.

A | Compleat Body | OF | DISTILLING, | Explaining the | MYSTERIES | OF THAT | SCIENCE, | IN | A most easy and familiar Manner; | Containing an | Exact and accurate Method of making all the | COMPOUND CORDIAL-WATERS now in Use, | WITH | A particular Account of their several Virtues: | As also a | DIRECTORY | Consisting of | All the INSTRUCTIONS necessary for learning the | *DISTILLERS ART*; with a Computation | of the original Cost of the several Ingredients, | and the Profits arising in Sale. | Adapted no less to the Use of private Families, than of Apo- | thecaries and Distillers. | [rule] | In two Parts. | [rule] | By G. SMITH, of *Kendall* in *Westmorland.* | [rule] | *LONDON:* | Printed for BERNARD LINTOT between the *Temple-Gates* | MDCCXXV.

First edition, London, 1725.

8vo. A-K^8; 80 leaves, pp. [*8*] 1-149 [150] [*2*]. Eight page publisher's catalogue bound in at the end.

Bibliographies: Gabler, p. 263; Maclean, p. 135.

Copies: *BMC* and *NUC* (Clark Library and University of California, Davis). Maclean adds National Library of Scotland and Wellcome Library.

999. Smith, George.

THE | NATURE | OF | FERMENTATION | EXPLAIN'D; | WITH THE | METHOD | Of Opening the BODY of any | GRAIN or VEGETABLE SUBJECT, | So as to obtain from it a | SPIRITUOUS LIQUOR: | EXEMPLIFIED | By the PROCESS of preparing RUM, as | 'tis manag'd in the *West-Indies.* | With many other useful REFLECTIONS and | OBSERVATIONS. | To which is added, | A COLLECTION of several *Compound Cor-* | *dial Waters*, with the ART of preparing some | *Artificial Wines*, not hitherto publish'd. | By Way of APPENDIX to the *Compleat Body of* | *Distilling.* | [rule] | By GEORGE SMITH of *Kendal* in *Westmoreland.* | [rule] | *LONDON:* | Printed for BERNARD LINTOT between the | *Temple-Gates.* MDCCXXIX. Price One Shilling.

First edition, London, 1729.

8vo. A^4 B-D^8 E^4; 32 leaves, pp. [*8*] 1-56.
Bibliographies: Gabler, p. 264; Maclean, p. 136; Noling, p. 383.

Copies: *BMC* and *NUC* (5 copies). Maclean adds National Library of Scotland.

1000. Smith, Mary.

THE | Complete House-keeper, | AND | PROFESSED COOK. | CALCULATED | For the greater Ease and Assistance of Ladies, | House-keepers, Cooks &c. &c. | Containing upwards of | SEVEN HUNDRED practical and approved RECEIPTS, | under the following Heads: | [in two columns: column one] I. Rules for Marketing. | II. Boiling, Roasting, and Broil- | ing Flesh, Fish, and Fowls; | and for making Soups and Sau- | ces of all Kinds. | III. Making made Dishes of all | Sorts, Puddings, Pies, Cakes, | Fritters &c. | IV. Pickling, Preserving, and | making Wines in the best Man- | ner and Taste. | [two vertical rules] | [column two] V. Potting and Collaring; As- | pikes in Jellies; Savoury | Cakes, Blamonge, Ice Creams | and other Creams, Whips, |

Jellies, *&c.* | VI. Bills of Fare for every Month | in the Year; with a cor- | rect List of every Thing in | Season for every Month; | illustrated with two elegant | Copper-plates of a First and | Second Course for a genteel | Table. [end columns] | [rule] | By MARY SMITH, | Late House-keeper to Sir Walter Blackett, Bart. and formerly | in the Service of the Right Hon. Lord Anson, Sir Tho. Sebright, | Bart. and other Families of Distinction, as House-keeper and | Cook. | [two rules] | *NEWCASTLE:* | Printed by T. SLACK, for the Author. 1772.

First edition, Newcastle upon Tyne, 1772.

8vo. [A]^4 B-Ccc^4; 196 leaves, pp. [i-ii] iii-v [vi] [7-9] 10-392.

Illustrations: Two engraved folding plates illustrating table settings. The second plate is wanting in this copy.

Bibliographies: Maclean, p. 136; Wheaton and Kelly 5696. Axford, p. 74; Bitting, p. 439, and Oxford, p. 106, cite the 1786 edition.

Copies: *BMC* and *NUC* (Radcliffe and New York Public Library). Maclean adds Brotherton Library, Newcastle upon Tyne Public Library, and Library of Congress.

1001. Smith, Robert.

[within a border of two rules] COURT COOKERY: | OR, THE | Compleat *English* COOK. | Containing the Choicest and Newest | RECEIPTS | For making SOOPS, POTTAGES, FRICAS- | SEYS, HARSHES, FARCES, RAGOOS, | CULLISES, SAUCES, FORC'D-MEATS | and SOUSES; with various Ways of Dres- | sing most Sorts of Flesh, Fish and Fowl, | Wild and Tame; with the best Methods of | POTTING and COLLARING. | AS LIKEWISE | Of Pastes, Pies, Pastys, Pattys, Puddings, | Tansies, Biskets, Creams, Cheesecakes, Floren- | dines, Cakes, Jellies, Sillabubs and Custards. | ALSO | Of Pickling, Candying and Preserving: With a Bill of Fare | for every Month in the Year, and the latest Improvements in | COOKERY, *&c.* | [rule] | By R. SMITH, Cook (under Mr. *Lamb*) to King *William*; as | also to the Dukes of *Buckingham, Ormond, D'Aumont* (the | *French* Ambassador) and others of the Nobility and Gentry. | [two rules] | *LONDON:* | Printed for T. WOTTON, at the *Three Daggers* in *Fleet-Street.* | MDCCXXIII.

First edition, London, 1723.

8vo. A^4 B-H^8 I^4, ^{2}A-F^8; 116 leaves, [8] [1] 2-112 [8], ^{2}1-82 [14].

Bibliographies: Craig 83; Maclean, p. 137; Oxford, p. 55.

Copies: *BMC* and *NUC* (John Crerar Library, New York Public Library, and University of Wisconsin). Maclean adds Brotherton Library.

1002. Smith, Robert.

[within a border of two rules] COURT COOKERY: | OR, THE | *Compleat* English *COOK*. | Containing the Choicest and Newest | RECEIPTS | FOR MAKING | [in two columns: column one] SOOPS, | POTTAGES, | FRICASSEYS, | HARSHES, | FARCES, | }{ | [column two] RAGOO'S, | CULLISES, | SAUCES, | FORC'D-MEATS, | And SOUSES: [end columns] | With various Ways of Dressing most Sorts of Flesh, | Fish, and Fowl, Wild, and Tame; with the best | Methods of *Potting*, *Collaring* and *Pickling*. | AS LIKEWISE | *Of Pastes, Pies, Pasties, Patties, Puddings,* *Tan-* | *sies, Biskets, Creams, Cheesecakes, Florendines, Cakes,* | *Jellies, Sillabubs and Custards.* | ALSO | Of Candying and Preserving: With a Bill of Fare for every | Month in the Year, and the latest Improvements in | COOKERY, PASTRY &c. | [rule] | By R. SMITH, Cook (under Mr. *Lamb*) to King *William*; as | also to the Dukes of *Buckingham, Ormond, D'Aumont* (the | *French* Ambassador) and others of the Nobility and Gentry. | [rule] | 𝕿𝖍𝖊 𝕾𝖊𝖈𝖔𝖓𝖉 𝕰𝖉𝖎𝖙𝖎𝖔𝖓, 𝖜𝖎𝖙𝖍 𝖑𝖆𝖗𝖌𝖊 𝕬𝖉𝖉𝖎𝖙𝖎𝖔𝖓𝖘. | [two rules] | *LONDON:* | Printed for T. WOTTON, at the *Three-Daggers* in *Fleet-Street*. | [short rule] | M.DCC.XXV.

Second edition, London, 1725. Originally published, London, 1723 (item 1001).

8vo. π1 A⁴ B-P⁸ Q⁴; 121 leaves, pp. [*10*] [1] 2-218 [*14*]. First leaf contains a lists of books sold by Tho. Wotton.

Bibliographies: Axford, p. 103; Bitting, p. 440; Maclean, p. 137.

Copies: *NUC* (4 copies). Maclean adds Brotherton Library and Wellcome Library.

1003. Soyer, Alexis, 1809-1858.

THE | 𝕲𝖆𝖘𝖙𝖗𝖔𝖓𝖔𝖒𝖎𝖈 𝕽𝖊𝖌𝖊𝖓𝖊𝖗𝖆𝖙𝖔𝖗: | A | SIMPLIFIED AND ENTIRELY NEW | SYSTEM OF COOKERY, | WITH NEARLY | TWO THOUSAND PRACTICAL RECEIPTS | SUITED TO THE INCOME OF ALL CLASSES. | ILLUSTRATED WITH | NUMEROUS ENGRAVINGS | AND CORRECT AND MINUTE PLANS

HOW KITCHENS OF EVERY SIZE, FROM THE | KITCHEN OF A ROYAL PALACE TO THAT OF THE HUMBLE COTTAGE, | ARE TO BE CONSTRUCTED AND FURNISHED. | BY | MONSIEUR A. SOYER, | OF THE REFORM CLUB. | LONDON: | SIMPKIN, MARSHALL, & CO., STATIONERS' HALL COURT: | AND SOLD BY | JOHN OLLIVIER, PALL-MALL. | 1846.

First edition, London, 1846.

220 x 141 mm. [a]⁴ b⁸ 1-45⁸ 46⁴ 47⁸; 384 leaves, pp. [i-v] vi-xxiv [1] 2-720, ²[1] 2-18, ³[1] 2-6. Publisher's rose cloth, stamped in gold.

Illustrations: Frontispiece portrait of the author drawn by Emma Soyer and engraved in steel by H. B. Hall and fifteen wood engraved plates, two folding, including six plates illustrating elaborate dishes, and others showing the kitchen of the Reform Club, a table of a wealthy family, Soyer's table at home, a drawing of two young Bavarians by Emma Soyer and a self-portrait of Emma Soyer engraved in steel by H. B. Hall.

Bibliographies: Bitting, p. 443; Craig 84; Oxford, p. 176; Schraemli (1) 462; Simon BG 1401; Vicaire 798.

Copies: *BMC* and *NUC* (5 copies).

1004. Soyer, Alexis, 1808-1858.

THE | 𝔐𝔬𝔡𝔢𝔯𝔫 𝔥𝔬𝔲𝔰𝔢𝔴𝔦𝔣𝔢 | OR | MÉNAGÈRE. | COMPRISING | NEARLY ONE THOUSAND RECEIPTS | FOR THE ECONOMIC AND JUDICIOUS | PREPARATION OF EVERY MEAL OF THE DAY, | AND THOSE FOR | THE NURSERY AND SICK ROOM; | WITH MINUTE DIRECTIONS FOR FAMILY MANAGEMENT | IN ALL ITS BRANCHES. | 𝔍𝔩𝔩𝔲𝔰𝔱𝔯𝔞𝔱𝔢𝔡 𝔴𝔦𝔱𝔥 𝔈𝔫𝔤𝔯𝔞𝔟𝔦𝔫𝔤𝔰, | INCLUDING THE | MODERN HOUSEWIFE'S UNIQUE KITCHEN, AND MAGIC STOVE. | BY | ALEXIS SOYER, | AUTHOR OF "THE GASTRONOMIC REGENERATOR," | (REFORM CLUB.) | *SECOND EDITION.* | LONDON: | SIMPKIN, MARSHALL, & CO., STATIONERS' HALL COURT; | OLLIVIER, PALL MALL. | 1849.

Second edition, London, 1849. Originally published, London, also 1849.

187 x 122 mm. [A]⁸ B-FF⁸; 232 leaves, pp. [i-v] vi-xvi [1] 2-441 [442-448]. Publisher's green cloth, stamped in gold.

Illustrations: Frontispiece portrait of the author engraved in steel by H. B. Hall after a drawing by Emma Soyer, wood engraved dedication leaf "To the fair daughters of Albion," three wood engravings at the end advertising Soyer's products, and two wood engravings in the text on pp. 229 and 389.

Bibliographies: Bitting, p. 443; Oberlé (1) 209; Oxford, p. 180; Simon BG 1402 (8th thousand); Vicaire 798.

Copies: *NUC* (Kansas State University and National Library of Medicine). *BMC* has 11th thousand, also 1849.

1005. Soyer, Alexis, 1809-1858.

[within a gold border of two rules with ornamental corners] THE │ [in gold] PANTROPHEON │ OR, │ HISTORY OF FOOD, │ [in gold] And its Preparation, │ FROM THE EARLIEST AGES OF THE WORLD │ [in gold] BY A. SOYER, │ AUTHOR OF │ "The Gastronomic Regenerator" and the "Modern Housewife, or Ménagère," &c. │ [short fancy rule] │ [in gold] EMBELLISHED WITH FORTY-TWO STEEL PLATES, │ [in gold] ILLUSTRATING THE GREATEST GASTRONOMIC MARVELS OF ANTIQUITY. │ [short fancy rule] │ LONDON: │ SIMPKIN, MARSHALL, & CO., STATIONERS' HALL COURT. │ MDCCCLIII. │ [short fancy rule] │ *The Author reserves his right of Translating this Work.*

First edition, London, 1853.

234 x 155 mm. π^8 [A]^4 B-I^8 J-U^8 V^8 W^8 X-Y^8 Z^8 (Z5+1) AA-DD^8 EE^2; 247 leaves, pp. [i-v] vi-xvi [1-3] 4-400 [2] [401] 402-474 [475-476]. Publisher's blue cloth, stamped in gold.

Illustrations: Frontispiece portrait of the author engraved in steel by Alfred Adams after a drawing by Emma Soyer, and forty-two steel engraved plates, two folding.

Bibliographies: Bitting, p. 443; Simon BG 1405; Vicaire 798; Wheaton and Kelly 5748.

Copies: *BMC* and *NUC* (7 copies).

1006. Soyer, Alexis, 1809-1858.

A | SHILLING COOKERY | FOR | THE PEOPLE: | EMBRACING | AN
ENTIRELY NEW SYSTEM OF PLAIN COOKERY | AND DOMESTIC
ECONOMY. | BY | ALEXIS SOYER, | AUTHOR OF "THE MODERN
HOUSEWIFE," | ETC. ETC. | 𝔈𝔦𝔤𝔥𝔱𝔦𝔢𝔱𝔥 𝔗𝔥𝔬𝔲𝔰𝔞𝔫𝔡. | LONDON: | GEO.
ROUTLEDGE & CO., FARRINGDON STREET. | NEW YORK: 18, BEEKMAN
STREET. | 1855. | *The Author of this work reserves the right of translating it.*]

Eightieth thousand, London, 1855. Originally published, London, 1854.

163 x 103 mm. [A]^8 B-N^8; 104 leaves, pp. [i-vii] viii-x [1] 2-194, ^{2}1-4. Last four
pages contain publisher's advertisements. Publisher's green boards printed in red and
blue. Sixteen pages of advertisements bound in at the end. Publisher's advertisements
on front and back end papers.

Illustrations: Wood engraved portrait of the author on A1^v and wood engravings of
Soyer's products in the appendix.

Bibliographies: Vicaire 799; Wheaton and Kelly 5752.

Copies: *BMC* and *BNC*. *NUC* records an 1854 10th thousand and various 1855
printings from the 30th thousand through 136th thousand, but not the 80th thousand.
Wheaton and Kelly locates a copy dated 1855 at Radcliffe but does not indicate which
printing.

1007. Soyer, Alexis, 1809-1858.

A | SHILLING COOKERY | FOR | THE PEOPLE | EMBRACING | AN
ENTIRELY NEW SYSTEM OF PLAIN COOKERY | AND DOMESTIC ECONOMY
| BY ALEXIS SOYER | AUTHOR OF "THE CULINARY CAMPAIGN" | ETC.
ETC. | 𝔗𝔴𝔬 𝔥𝔲𝔫𝔡𝔯𝔢𝔡 𝔞𝔫𝔡 𝔈𝔦𝔤𝔥𝔱𝔶-𝔢𝔦𝔤𝔥𝔱𝔥 𝔗𝔥𝔬𝔲𝔰𝔞𝔫𝔡. | LONDON | GEORGE
ROUTLEDGE AND SONS | THE BROADWAY, LUDGATE | NEW YORK: 416
BROOME STREET

Two hundred eighty-eighth thousand, London, ca.1862. Originally published, London,
1854.

163 x 100 mm. [A]^8 B-N^8; 104 leaves, pp. [*10*] [1] 2-198. Publisher's yellow boards
printed in red and green. Publisher's advertisements on front and back end papers.

Illustrations: Wood engraved portrait of the author by L. H. Michael on A1^v and wood engravings of Soyer's products in the appendix.

Bibliographies: Simon BG 1407.

Copies: No other copy of this printing located.

1008. Soyer, Alexis, 1809-1858.

SOYER'S │ CULINARY CAMPAIGN. │ BEING HISTORICAL REMINISCENCES │ OF THE LATE WAR. │ WITH │ THE PLAIN ART OF COOKERY │ FOR │ MILITARY AND CIVIL INSTITUTIONS, THE ARMY, NAVY, │ PUBLIC, ETC. ETC. │ BY ALEXIS SOYER, │ AUTHOR OF "THE MODERN HOUSEWIFE," "SHILLING COOKERY FOR THE PEOPLE," │ ETC. │ [short rule] │ LONDON: │ G. ROUTLEDGE & CO., FARRINGDON STREET. │ NEW YORK: 18, BEEKMAN STREET. │ 1857. │ [*The right of translation is reserved.*]

Wood engraved title-page:

[Wood engraving of the author with soldiers preparing food in camp, lettered] A CULINARY │ CAMPAIGN │ BY │ A. SOYER. │ ILLUSTRATED BY H. G. HINE │ P. 1.

First edition, London, 1857.

180 x 114 mm. [A]^4 B-PP^8 QQ^4; 304 leaves, pp. [i-vii] viii [1] 2-597 [598] [2]. Publisher's red cloth, stamped in gold.

Illustrations: Steel engraved frontispiece portrait of the author "from a photograph by Bingham (Paris)," a wood engraved title-page, seven wood engraved plates by H. G. Hine, and some wood engravings in the text.

Presentation copy, inscribed "with the author's compliments to Mr. T H Phillips A. Soyer"

Bibliographies: Bitting, p. 444; Craig 86; Schraemli (1) 465; Simon BG 1408; Wheton and Kelly 5756.

Copies: *BMC* and *NUC* (17 copies).

1008a. Soyer, Nicolas.

SOYER'S | PAPER-BAG COOKERY | BY | NICOLAS SOYER | LATE CHIEF, BROOK'S CLUB | LONDON: ANDREW MELROSE | 3 YORK STREET, COVENT GARDEN | 1911

First edition, first printing, London, 1911. There were three printings in 1911: June 6, June 30, and July 27.

160 x 100 mm. [A]⁸ B-H⁸; 64 leaves, pp. [6] [1-5] 6-112 [*10*]. First two leaves and last two leaves, blanks, with the first leaf and last leaf pasted down and the second leaf and the penultimate leaf serving as free endpapers. Publisher's red cloth stamped in blind and gold, in light blue dust jacket printed in dark blue.

Illustrations: Frontispiece halftone photographic portrait of the author printed on coated paper and tipped in.

Bibliographies: Bitting, p. 444; Driver 1007.1.

Copies: *BMC* and *NUC* (John Crerar Library, Library of Congress, and New York Public Library). Driver locates all of these copies and seven more in Britain.

1009. Stavely, S. W.

[within a border of type ornaments] THE | *NEW WHOLE ART* | OF | CONFECTIONARY, | SUGAR BOILING, | 𝔍𝔠𝔢𝔦𝔫𝔤, 𝔈𝔞𝔫𝔡𝔶𝔦𝔫𝔤, 𝔚𝔦𝔫𝔢𝔰, 𝔍𝔢𝔩𝔩𝔶 𝔐𝔞𝔨𝔦𝔫𝔤, &𝔠. | WHICH WILL BE FOUND | Very beneficial to Ladies, Confectioners, House- | keepers, &c. particularly to such as have not | a perfect knowledge of that art. | [short rule] | ELEVENTH EDITION. | [short rule] | *To which are now added several new and useful Receipts,* | NEVER BEFORE PUBLISHED. | [short rule] | BY S. W. STAVELY, NOTTINGHAM. | [short rule] | PRICE ONE SHILLING. | [short rule] | In this Edition several Pages of New Receipts are added, | never before introduced in the Work. | [short rule] | DERBY: PRINTED BY G. WILKINS & SON. | [short rule] | 1830

Eleventh edition, Derby, 1830.

177 x 107 mm. A-E⁶ (A3 missigned "A2"); 30 leaves, pp. [i-iii] iv-vi [7] 8-60. Publisher's printed wrappers.

Bibliographies: This edition unrecorded in the bibliographies consulted. Noling, p. 390, records a Derby, 1827, edition.

Copies: No other copy of this edition located. *BMC* and *NUC* record other editions.

1009a. Stewart, J. A.

THE | *Young Woman's Companion;* | OR, | FEMALE INSTRUCTOR: | BEING A SURE AND COMPLETE GUIDE TO EVERY ACQUIREMENT | ESSENTIAL IN FORMING | A PLEASING COMPANION, A RESPECTABLE MOTHER, | OR, | *A useful Member of Society.* | INTERSPERSED WITH | MORAL AND RELIGIOUS ESSAYS, | *Interesting Tales* | AND | MEMOIRS OF ILLUSTRIOUS WOMEN. | To which are subjoined, | SEVERAL VERY VALUABLE MEDICINAL RECEIPTS, AND OTHER USEFUL DIREC- | TIONS, REQUISITE FOR EVERY FEMALE TO WHOM DOMESTIC | ECONOMY IS A DESIRABLE OBJECT. | [short fancy rule] | A NEW EDITION, IMPROVED. | [short fancy rule] | A virtuous woman is above rubies – She openeth her mouth with wisdom, and | in her tongue is the law of kindness." KING LEMUEL | [two short rules] | LONDON: | PUBLISHED BY G. VIRTUE, | 26, IVY LANE; BATH STREET, BRISTOL; AND ST. VINCENT | STREET, LIVERPOOL. | 1828.

New edition, London, 1828. Originally published Oxford, Bartlett, and Newman [1814].

214 x 133 mm. [A]⁴ B⁴, B✲⁴-3A⁴, 3A✲⁴ 3B⁴ 3C⁴, 3C✲⁴; 384 leaves, pp. [8] [17] 18-776.

Note: This volume is gathered in fours with signatures signed B, B✲, C, C✲, D, D✲ etc.

Illustrations: Engraved frontispiece and title-page and seven engraved plates. The directions to the binder, on p. 776, call for eight plates. The titles for the plates given there do not correspond to the plates in this copy of the book although these plates do have the imprint of the publisher, G. Virtue.

Bibliographies: This edition unrecorded in the bibliographies consulted. Attar 289.1 and 289.2 record Oxford [1814] and third edition, Oxford, 1815.

Copies: No other copy of this edition located. The first and third editions recorded by Attar are in the Bodleian Library.

1010. Stopes, Henry, 1852-1902.

MALT AND MALTING. | An 𝔥istorical, 𝔖cientific, anꝺ 𝔓ractical 𝔗reatise, | SHOWING, AS CLEARLY AS EXISTING KNOWLEDGE PERMITS, | WHAT MALT IS, AND HOW TO MAKE IT. | *With full descriptions of all buildings and appliances, together with detailed* | *definitions of every matter connected therewith.* | [short rule] | ILLUSTRATED BY 150 WOODUCTS. | [short fancy rule] | BY | H. STOPES, | M. SOC. ENG. AND SOC. ARTS, F.G.S., F. SOC. CHEMICAL INDUSTRY, | F. R. HIST. SOC., ETC., ETC. | [two short rules] | LONDON: | F. W. LYON, | BREWERS' JOURNAL OFFICE, EASTCHEAP BUILDINGS, E.C. | [short rule] | 1885. | [*The Rights of Translation and Reproduction are Reserved.*] | *Déposé.*] [*Deponirt.*

Fore-title:

MALT AND MALTING. | [short fancy rule] | BY | H. STOPES. | [engraving] | PNEUMATIC MALTHOUSE, YEOVIL. | LONDON: | F. W. LYON, | BREWERS' JOURNAL OFFICE, EASTCHEAP BUILDINGS, E. C. | [short rule] | 1885.

First edition, London, 1885.

240 x 155 mm. [A]^8 B-UU^8; 344 leaves; pp. [i-vii] viii-xiv [1] 2-80, 83-226, 233-250, 253-286, 289-628, 631-662, ^{2}[*1*] i-xxiv [*1*]. Seven inserted plates, all but that for pp. 287-288 folding, are included in the pagination and account for pp. 81-82, 227-232, 251-252, 287-288, and 629-630.

Illustrations: Seven wood engraved plates, six folding, and 150 wood engravings in the text.

Bibliographies: Noling, p. 394.

Copies: *BMC*, *BNC*, and *NUC* (4 copies).

1011. Stubbe, Henry, 1632-1676.

THE | Indian Nectar, | OR A | DISCOURSE | CONCERNING | CHOCOLATA: | WHEREIN | The *Nature* of the *Cacao-nut*, and the other Ingredi- | ents of that Composition, is examined, and stated | according to the Judgment and Experience of the | *Indians*, and *Spanish* Writers, who lived in the *Indies*, | and others; with sundry additional Observations | made in *England*: The ways of *compounding* and | preparing *Chocolata* are enquired into; its Effects, as | to its *alimental* and *Venereal* quality, as well as *Medi-* | *cinal* (especially in *Hypochondriacal Melancholy*) are | fully debated. Together with a *Spagyrical Analysis* | of the *Cacao-nut*, performed by the excellent Chy- | mist, *Monsieur le Febure*, Chymist to His Majesty. | [rule] | *By* Henry Stubbe *formerly of* Ch. Ch. *in* Oxon. *Physician* | *for His Majesty, and the Right Honourable* Thomas *Lord* | Windsor *in the Island of* Jamaica *in the* West-Indies. | [rule] | *Thomas Gage,* Survey of the *West-Indies.* chap. 15. | *Here* [in a certain part of *Guaxaca*] *grow many Trees of* Cacao, *and* | Anchiote, *whereof is made the* Chocolatte, *and is a Commodity of* | *much trading in those parts, though our* English *and* Hollanders | *make little use of it, when they take a prize at Sea, as not knowing* | *the* secret virtue *and* quality *of it for the good of the Stomach.* | —— Videant, intrabescántque relictâ. | [rule] | *London*, Printed by *J.C.* for *Andrew Crook* at the Sign of the Green | Dragon in St. *Paul*'s Church-yard. 1662.

First edition, London, 1662.

8vo. A-M^8 N^4; 100 leaves, pp. [*16*] 1-184.

Bibliographies: Noling, p. 396; Wing S6049.

Copies *BMC* and *NUC* (7 copies). Wing adds Bodleian Library, Cambridge, College of Physicians in London, and Signet Library in Edinburgh.

1012. Sturgeon, Launcelot, *pseud.*

ESSAYS, | MORAL, PHILOSOPHICAL, | AND | STOMACHICAL, | On 𝕿𝖍𝖊 𝖎𝖒𝖕𝖔𝖗𝖙𝖆𝖓𝖙 𝕾𝖈𝖎𝖊𝖓𝖈𝖊 of | GOOD-LIVING. | [short rule] | Dedicated to the Right Worshipful | THE COURT OF ALDERMEN. | [short rule] | BY LAUNCELOT STURGEON, ESQ. | Fellow of the Beef-Steak Club, and an Honorary Member of several | Foreign Pic Nics, &c. &c. &c. | [short rule] | *"Eat! drink! and be merry! – for to-morrow you die."* | [short fancy rule] | *LONDON:* | PRINTED FOR G. AND W. B. WHITTAKER, | 13, AVE-MARIA LANE. | [short fancy rule] | 1822.

First edition, London, 1822.

176 x 100 mm. a^8 B-K^{12} L^6; 122 leaves, pp. [i-v] vi-xvi [1] 2-226 [2]. Last leaf (blank?) wanting in this copy.

Illustrations: Wood engraved frontispiece by William Hughes titled "Meditations of an Epicure."

Bibliographies: Axford, p. 137; Bitting, p. 452; Oxford, p. 151; Simon BG 1422.

Copies: *BMC* and *NUC* (Cornell, John Crerar Library, and New York Public Library).

1013. Switzer, Stephen, 1682?-1745.

A COMPENDIOUS │ METHOD │ For the RAISING of the │ *Italian* BROCOLI,
Spanish CARDOON, │ CELERIAC, FINOCHI, and │ Other Foreign
KITCHEH-VEGETABLES. │ As also an │ ACCOUNT │ OF THE │ LA LUCERNE,
St. FOYNE, CLOVER, │ And other *Grass-Seeds*. │ With the Method of *Burning of
Clay*, for the Im- │ provement of Land, made very perfect and │ compleat from the last
Summer's Experience. │ [rule] │ 𝕿𝖍𝖊 𝕱𝖔𝖚𝖗𝖙𝖍 𝕰𝖉𝖎𝖙𝖎𝖔𝖓. │ [rule] │ To which is added, │
A Farther Account of the *Burning of Clay*, lately │ Communicated to the Author by a
Person of Worth and Ho- │ nour of *North-Britain*, who has greatly experienced the
same. │ By which it appears, that *Burnt Clay* is not only the cheapest │ but the best
Discovery for the Improvement of Land (especially │ that which is cold and poor) ever
yet produced. │ [rule] │ By *STEPHEN SWITZER*, Author of the *Practical* │ *Fruit* and
Kitchen-Gardener. │ [rule] │ *Quare agite, ô, proprios generatim discite cultus,* │
Agricolae, ―― VIRG. │ [two rules] │ *LONDON:* │ Printed for THOMAS
ASTLEY, at the *Rose* in │ *St. Paul's-Churchyard*. 1729 [Price 1 *s*. 6 *d*.]

Fourth edition, London, 1729. Originally published, London, 1728.

8vo. π² a⁴ B-F⁴ χ² G-H⁴ I²; 38 leaves, pp. [i-v] vi-xii [1] 2-64. Leaf π1 (half-title or
blank?) wanting in this copy.

Illustrations: Two engraved plates, one on 2ʳ and the other an inserted folding plate,
illustrating a "kiln for burning of clay" and a third engraved folding plate illustrating
"the ornamental part of gardening."

Bibliographies: Fussell (1), p. 121; Henrey III. 1404; Wheaton and Kelly 5882.

Copies: *BMC* and *NUC* (8 copies).

1014. Switzer, Stephen, 1682?-1745.

[within a border of two rules] THE │ *Nobleman, Gentleman,* │ and *Gardener's* │
RECREATION: │ OR, AN │ INTRODUCTION │ TO │ GARDENING, PLANTING, │
AGRICULTURE, and the │ other *Business* and *Pleasures* of a │ *Country Life.* │ [rule] │

By STEPHEN SWITZER. | [rule] | ——*Inceptumq; unà decurre laborem:* | *O decus!*
O fama! merito pars maxima nostrae, | *Maecenas pelagoq; volans da vela petenti.* |
Virg. Geo. 2. | [two rules] | *LONDON:* Printed for B. BARKER, and | C. KING,
both is *Westminster-Hall.* 1715.

First edition, London, 1715.

8vo. π^4 a^8 $b^8(\pm b8)$ B-S^8 T^6; 162 leaves, pp. [*8*] i-xxxiv, 1-266 [*16*]. Note: The
collation given here is for an ideal copy. In fact, in the Lilly Library copy leaf b8
survives in both the cancelled and uncancelled states (π^4 a-b^8 χ1 B-S^8 T^6). In the
uncancelled state of b8^v (p. xxxii) the author makes a number of disparaging remarks
about those who have riches. He appears to have had second thoughts about these –
after all, it was those with riches most likely to buy his book – and replaces them with
more general observations, including his hope that the book will be well received, in
the cancel leaf.

Illustrations: Engraved frontispiece of a formal garden.

Bibliographies: Fussell (1), p. 118; Henrey III. 1410.

Copies: *BMC* and *NUC* (8 copies).

1015. Switzer, Stephen, 1682?-1745.

[within a border of two rules] THE | PRACTICAL | FRUIT-GARDENER. | Being the
best and newest Method of rais- | ing, Planting, and Pruning all Sorts of | Fruit-Trees,
agreeably to the Experience | and Practice of the most eiminent GAR- | DENERS and
NURSERY-MEN. | [rule] | By STEPHEN SWITZER. | [rule] | Revised and
recommended by the Revd. | Mr. LAURENCE and Mr. BRADLEY. | [rule] |
Adorn'd with proper Plans. | [rule] | *Honos erit huic quoque Pomo.* Virg. Georg. II. |
[rule] | *LONDON,* | Printed for *Tho. Woodward* at the Half- | Moon over against St.
Dunstan's Church | in *Fleet-street.* MDCCXXIV.

First edition, London, 1724.

8vo. π^2 a^8 b^4 B-Y^8 [Z]^2; 184 leaves, pp. [*28*] 1-323 [*324-340*]. P. 323 misnumbered
"333."

Illustrations: Three engraved folding plates with plans for gardens.

Bibliographies: Fussell (1) p. 120; Henrey III. 1413.

Copies: *BMC* and *NUC* (8 copies).

1016. Switzer, Stephen, 1682?-1745.

The Practical Kitchen Gardiner: | Or, A New and Entire | System of Directions | For the Employment in the | MELONRY, | KITCHEN-GARDEN, | AND | POTAGERY, | In the several Seasons of the Year. | Being chiefly | The OBSERVATIONS of a Person train'd | up in the Neat-Houses or Kitchen-Gardens | about *London.* | Illustrated with PLANS and DESCRIPTIONS | proper for the Situation and Disposition of | those GARDENS. | To which is added, by way of SUPPLEMENT, | The Method of Raising CUCUMBERS and MELONS, | MUSHROOMS, BORECOLE, BROCCOLI, POTATOES, | and other curious and useful Plants, as practised in | *France, Italy, Holland* and *Ireland.* | And also, An Account of the LABOURS and PROFITS of a | Kitchen-Garden, and what every Gentlemen may rea- | sonably expect therefrom in every Month of the Year. | In a METHOD never yet attempted. | [rule] | The Whole Methodiz'd and Improv'd, | By *STEPHEN SWITZER,* | Author of the *Practical Fruit Gardiner.* | [rule] | ———*Et quas Humus educat Herbis* | *Fortunata fuit*——— Ovid Metam. XV. | [rule] | *LONDON:* Printed for THO. WOODWARD, at the *Half-Moon* | over-against St. *Dunstan's* Church in *Fleetstreet.* 1727.

First edition, London, 1727.

8vo. A^8 a-b^8 B-Ee^8; 240 leaves, pp. [*16*] i-xx [*12*] 1-424 [*8*].

Illustrations: Three engraved folding plates of plans for gardens.

Bibliographies: Fussell (1) p. 120; Henrey III. 1417; Maclean, p. 139; Simon BG 1432; Wheaton and Kelly 5884.

Copies: *BMC* and *NUC* (9 copies). Maclean adds Brotherton Library.

1017. Taverner, John, d. 1606.

CERTAINE EXPERIMENTS | CONCERNING FISH | AND FRUITE: | Practised by Iohn Taverner | Gentleman, and by him pub- | lished for the benefit of others | *Anchora, Spei.* | LONDON, | PRINTED FOR WILLIAM PONSONBY. | 1600. | *With an Introduction by Eric Parker*

Imprint from the half-title:

MANCHESTER | SHERRATT & HUGHES | 1928 | Published for the Salmon and Trout Association | Fishmongers Hall, London.

First printing of this edition, Manchester, 1928. Originally published, London, 1600.

245 x 182 mm. [1-2]^8; 16 leaves, pp. [*4*] [i] ii-iv [1] 2-24. Publisher's gray paper boards with printed label on front.

Illustrations: Halftone of photograph of the title-page of the original edition.

Bibliographies: Unrecorded in the bibliographies consulted.

Copies: *BMC* and *NUC* (11 copies).

1018. Taylor, Martha.

THE | HOUSEWIFE'S GUIDE, | OR A | COMPLETE SYSTEM | OF | MODERN COOKERY, | CONTAINING | *DIRECTIONS how to ROAST and BOIL*, | Every thing necessary for the Table; | HOW TO MAKE | GRAVIES, SAUCES, FRICASSEES, | *And Various Dishes for Lent.* | TO WHICH IS PREFIXED, | *DIRECTIONS FOR CARVING*, | With beautiful Wood Engravings. | [short rule] | Particularly adapted to the Middle Class of Society. | [short rule] | BY MARTHA TAYLOR, | LATE COOK TO THE EARL OF SHAFTSBURY. | [short rule] | PRICE ONE SHILLING. | [short rule] | Printed and Sold by G. WILKINS and SON, Derby.

First edition? Derby, ca.1824.

180 x 103 mm. A^6 B-C^{12}; 30 leaves, pp. [1-3] 4-59 [60].

Illustrations: Wood engraved figures illustrating carving on the verso of the title-page.

Bibliographies: Unrecorded in the bibliographies consulted.

Copies: No other copy located.

1019. Thacker, John.

THE | ART | OF | COOKERY. | CONTAINING | Above SIX HUNDRED AND FIFTY of the | most approv'd RECEIPTS heretofore published, under the | following Heads, viz. | [in three columns: column one] ROASTING, | BOILING, | FRYING, | BROILING, | BAKING, | FRICASEES, | PUDDINGS, | CUSTARDS, | [two vertical rules] | [column two] CAKES, | CHEESE-CAKES, | TARTS, | PYES, | SOOPS, | MADE-WINES, | JELLIES, | CANDYING, | [two vertical rules] | [column three] PICKLING, | PRESERVING, | PASTRY, | COLLERING, | CONFECTIONARY, | CREAMS, | RAGOOS, | BRASING, &c. &c. [end columns] | ALSO, A | BILL OF FARE | For every MONTH in the YEAR. | WITH AN | ALPHABETICAL INDEX to the Whole: | BEING | A BOOK highly necessary for all FAMILIES, | having the GROUNDS of COOKERY fully display'd therein. | [rule] | By JOHN THACKER, | COOK to the Honourable and Reverend the DEAN and | CHAPTER in DURHAM. | [two rules] | NEWCASTLE UPON TYNE: | Printed by I. THOMPSON and COMPANY. | [short rule] | MDCCLVIII.

First edition, Newcastle upon Tyne, 1758.

8vo. π^4 $*^4$ A-2R^4 2S^2 a-d^4 (2A-2S signed "A2"-"S2"); 186 leaves, pp. [*16*] [1] 2-144, 143-322 [*32*].

Illustrations: Woodcuts, principally of pie shapes, in the text.

Bibliographies: Maclean, p. 140; Oxford, p. 88. Axford, p. 17, and Bitting, p. 458, cite the 1762 edition.

Copies: *BMC* and *NUC* (National Library of Medicine only). Maclean adds Brotherton Library, Newcastle upon Tyne Public Library, Cornell, and Library of Congress.

1020. Timbs, John, 1801-1875.

HINTS | FOR THE TABLE: | OR, THE | 𝔈conomy of 𝔊ood 𝔏iving. | [short rule] | To form a science and a nomenclature | From out the commonest demands of nature. – BYRON. | [short rule] | [woodcut of fork, plate, and knife] | LONDON: | SIMPKIN, MARSHALL, AND CO. | STATIONERS' HALL COURT. | [short rule] | 1838.

First edition, London, 1838.

142 x 92 mm. A-P⁶; 90 leaves, pp. [i-v] vi-xii [1] 2-167 [168]. Publisher's blue cloth, stamped in gold.

Authorship of this work is attributed to John Timbs in Allibone, Halkett and Laing, and *NUC*. It does not appear in the partial list of Timbs's works in the *DNB*.

Bibliographies: Oxford, p. 171, without attribution of authorship. Simon BG 1464 cites an 1859 edition under Timbs.

Copies: *NUC* (Kansas State University and University of Illinois). *BMC* records the 1859 edition under title.

1021. Toogood, Harriet.

THE │ TREASURY OF FRENCH COOKERY. │ A COLLECTION OF THE BEST │ FRENCH RECIPES, │ ARRANGED AND ADAPTED FOR ENGLISH HOUSEHOLDS. │ BY │ MRS. TOOGOOD. │ [publisher's monogram] │ LONDON: │ RICHARD BENTLEY, 8, NEW BURLINGTON STREET, │ 𝔓𝔲𝔟𝔩𝔦𝔰𝔥𝔢𝔯 𝔦𝔫 𝔒𝔯𝔡𝔦𝔫𝔞𝔯𝔶 𝔱𝔬 𝔥𝔢𝔯 𝔐𝔞𝔧𝔢𝔰𝔱𝔶. │ 1866.

First edition, London, 1866.

188 x 124 mm. [a]⁸ b² B-T⁸ U⁶; 160 leaves, pp. [i-v] vi-xix [xx] [1] 2-298 [299-300]. Publisher's terra cotta cloth, stamped in gold.

Bibliographies: Unrecorded in the bibliographies consulted.

Copies: *BMC*.

1021a. Traill, Catherine Parr (Strickland) 1802-1899.

THE LIBRARY OF ENTERTAINING KNOWLEDGE. │ [short rule] │ THE │ BACKWOODS OF CANADA: │ BEING │ LETTERS FROM THE WIFE OF AN │ EMIGRANT OFFICER, │ ILLUSTRATIVE OF THE DOMESTIC ECONOMY OF BRITISH AMERICA. │ [short rule] │ LONDON: │ CHARLES KNIGHT, 22, LUDGATE STREET. │ [short rule] │ MDCCCXXXVI.

First edition. London, 1836. Published as vol. 32 of "the Library of Entertaining Knowledge."

155 x 99 mm. [A]⁴ B-T¹²·⁶ U-X⁶ Y²; 180 leaves, pp. [i-vii] viii [1] 2-351 [352]. Publisher's black quarter calf with marbled board; spine stamped in gold.

Illustrations: Numerous woodcuts in the text.

Bibliographies: Sabin 96411.

Copies: *BMC* and *NUC* (24 copies).

1022. The Tricks of the Trade.

THE | TRICKS OF TRADE | IN THE | A̶d̶u̶l̶t̶e̶r̶a̶t̶i̶o̶n̶s̶ ̶o̶f̶ ̶F̶o̶o̶d̶ ̶a̶n̶d̶ ̶P̶h̶y̶s̶i̶c̶; | WITH | DIRECTIONS FOR THEIR DETECTION AND COUNTERACTION. | [short rule] | LONDON: | DAVID BOGUE, FLEET STREET. | [short rule] | MDCCCLVI.

First edition, London, 1856.

170 x 106 mm. [A]⁸ B-N⁸; 104 leaves, pp. [i-vii] viii-xvi [1] 2-191 [192]. Publisher's green cloth, stamped in gold. A 32 page publisher's catalogue dated February, 1856, and a 16 page publisher's catalogue of "Present Books for Youth" dated 1856 bound in at the end.

Bibliographies: Bitting, p. 610; Craig 90; Wheaton and Kelly 6083.

Copies: *BMC* and *NUC* (9 copies).

1023. La Troupe des bons enfans.

LA TROUPE | DES | BONS ENFANS | ASSEMBLÉS | À | L'HOTEL DES RAGOUTS | [two rules] | REPRINTED FROM | *The Very Rare Original Edition* | with | A PREFATORY NOTE | by | EDWIN MARION COX | [two rules] | *LONDON* | PRINTED AT THE *Chiswick Press* | [short rule] | MDCCCCXXXI

First printing of this edition, London, 1931, limited to 150 copies, reprinted from the original, Lelis (i.e. Lille) ca. 1800 (item 427). Cox claims the original edition, from which he reprinted the above, was published in the third quarter of the seventeenth century, but the absense of the long "s" in the printer's font suggests ca. 1800.

190 x 135 mm. [1]¹²; 12 leaves, pp. [2] [1-4] 5-18 [4]. First and last leaves, blank. Publisher's quarter buckram with boards and printed paper label on front cover.

Inscribed on the first page, "With best wishes to a recovered schoolmate. 1932 E. M. C."

Bibliographies: Unrecorded in the bibliograhies consulted.

Copies: *BMC* and *NUC* (John Crerar Library and University of Minnesota).

1024. The True Way of Preserving and Candying.

[within a border of two rules] THE │ TRUE WAY │ OF │ 𝔓𝔯𝔢𝔰𝔢𝔯𝔟𝔦𝔫𝔤 and ℭ𝔞𝔫𝔡𝔶𝔦𝔫𝔤, │ AND │ Making Several Sorts │ OF │ 𝔖𝔴𝔢𝔢𝔱=𝔐𝔢𝔞𝔱𝔰, │ According to the │ Best and Truest Manner. │ [rule] │ Made Publick for the Benefit │ of all *English* Ladies and │ Gentlewomen; especially │ for my Scholars. │ [two rules] │ *LONDON,* │ Printed for the 𝔄𝔲𝔱𝔥𝔬𝔯, in the │ Year, MDCXCV.

Second edition, London, 1695. Originally published, London, 1681.

8vo. A-K⁸; 80 leaves, pp. [1-6] 7-154 [6].

Bibliographies: Axford, p. 400; Oxford, p. 40, in a note. Bitting, p. 611; Oxford, p. 40; Vicaire 874; and Wing T3126A all record the 1681 edition.

Copies: *NUC* (Clark Library and Library of Congress).

1025. Trusler, John, 1735-1820.

THE │ Honours of the Table, │ OR, │ RULES FOR BEHAVIOUR DURING MEALS; │ WITH THE WHOLE │ ART OF CARVING, │ ILLUSTRATED BY A VAREITY OF CUTS. │ TOGETHER WITH │ Directions for going to Market, and the Method of │ distinguishing good Provisions from bad; │ TO WHICH IS ADDED │ A Number of Hints or concise Lessons for the Improvement of │ Youth, on all occasions in Life. │ [rule] │ By the AUTHOR of PRINCIPLES of POLITENESS, &c. │ [rule] │ "To do the honours of a table gracefully, is one of the out-lines of a well-bred │ "man; and to carve well, little as it my seem, is useful twice every day, │ "and the doing of which ill is not only troublesome to ourselves, but renders us │ "disagreeable and ridiculous to

others." | LORD CHESTERFIELD'S LETTERS. | [rule] | FOR THE USE OF
YOUNG PEOPLE. | [rule] | LONDON. | Printed for the AUTHOR, at the
𝕷𝖎𝖙𝖊𝖗𝖆𝖗𝖞 = 𝕻𝖗𝖊𝖘𝖘, No. 14, Red- | Lion-Street, Clerkenwell; and may be had of *H. D.*
Symmonds, | Paternoster-Row, and all Book-sellers in Town and Country. |
M,DCC,LXXXVIII.

First edition, London, 1788.

12mo. A-E^{12}; 60 leaves, pp. [1-3] 4-120. "A List of books published by the Rev. Dr.
Trusler, at the Literary-Press, No. 62, Wardour-Street, Soho. 1790" of ten pages
bound in at the end.

Illustrations: Woodcuts illustrating carving in the text.

Bibliographies: Craig 91; Maclean, p. 142; Oxford, p. 116; Pennell, p. 162;
Schraemli (1) 484; Simon BG 1475. Bitting, p. 466, cites the 1791 edition.

Copies: *BMC* and *NUC* (John Crerar Library, Kansas State University, and University
of California of Los Angeles). Maclean adds Brotherton Library, Wellcome Library,
Detroit Public Library, and Library of Congress.

1026. Trusler, John, 1735-1820.

THE | Honours of the Table, | OR, | RULES FOR BEHAVIOUR DURING MEALS;
| WITH THE WHOLE | ART OF CARVING, | ILLUSTRATED BY A VAREITY
OF CUTS. | TOGETHER WITH | Directions for going to Market, and the Method of
| distinguishing good Provisions from bad; | TO WHICH IS ADDED | A Number of
Hints or concise Lessons for the Improvement of | Youth, on all Occasions in Life. |
[rule] | BY the AUTHOR of PRINCIPLES of POLITENESS, &c. | [rule] | "To do the
honours of a table gracefully, is one of the out-lines of a well bred | "man; and to
carve well, little as it my seem, is useful twice every day, and the | "doing of which ill
is not only troublesome to ourselves, but renders us disagreeable | "and ridiculous to
others." | LORD CHESTERFIELD'S LETTERS. | [rule] | FOR THE USE OF
YOUNG PEOPLE. | [rule] | THE SECOND EDITION. | [rule] | LONDON. |
Printed for the Author, at the LITERARY-PRESS, No. 62, | Wardour-street, Soho;
and all Book-sellers in Town and | Country. | M,DCC,XCI.

Second edition, London, 1791. Originally published, London, 1788 (item 1025).

12mo. A-E^{12}; 60 leaves, pp. [1-3] 4-120.

Illustrations: Woodcuts illustrating carving in the text.

Bibliographies: Bitting, p. 466; Maclean, p. 142; Oxford, p. 117, in a note; Pennell, p. 163; Schraemli (1) 485; Simon BG 1476; Wheaton and Kelly 6092.

Copies: *BMC*, *BNC*, and *NUC* (4 copies). Maclean adds Brotherton Library, Guildhall Library in London, and National Library of Wales.

1027. Trusler, John, 1735-1820.

THE │ ART OF CARVING │ EXCERPTED │ FROM A WORK ENTITLED │ *The Honours of the Table* (1788) │ BY │ THE REVD DR JOHN TRUSLER │ Author of │ *The Principles of Politeness* │ &c. │ [two rules] │ "To do the honours of a table gracefully, is one of the │ out-lines of a well-bred man; and to carve well, little as │ it may seem, is useful twice every day, and the doing of │ which ill is not only troublesome to ourselves, but renders │ us disagreeable and rediculous to others." │ LORD CHESTERFIELD'S LETTERS │ [two rules] │ With a Biographical Note by S.M. │ and an Appreciation by S.C.R. │ CAMBRIDGE │ AT THE UNIVERSITY PRESS │ 1932

First edition thus, second printing, Cambridge, 1932. This edition originally printed for the Friends of the University Press, Cambridge, Christmas, 1931.

Note: S.M. is Stanley Morison and S.C.R. is S.C. Roberts.

171 x 103 mm π^6 1-4^8 5^6; 44 leaves, pp. [i-iv] v-xii, 1-75 [76]. Publisher's yellow cloth stamped in red, in dust jacket.

Bibliographies: Axford, p. 17; Bitting, p. 466.

Copies: *BMC* and *NUC* (4 copies).

1028. Tryon, Thomas, 1634-1703.

THE │ Good House-wife │ MADE A │ Doctor, │ Or, Health's Choice and sure Friend │ Being a Plain Way of *Nature's* own │ prescribing, to │ Prevent and Cure │ most *Diseases* incident to *Men, Wo-* │ men and *Children*, by *Diet* and │ *Kitchin-Physick* only. │ With some Remarks on the Practice of │ *Physick* and *Chymistry* │ [rule] │ By

Thomas Tryon, Student in Physick; And Author | of *The Way to Health, Long Life and Hap-* | *piness. Country-mans Companion. The New* | *Art of Brewing*, &c | [rule] | The Second Edition. To which is added some | Observations on the Tedious Methods of Un- | skilful Chyrurgions; with Cheap and Easie | Remedies. By the same Author. | [rule] | *London*, Printed for *H. N.* and *T. S.* And are | to be Sold at the *Kings-Arms* in the *Poultry*, | and at the *Crooked-Billet* in *Holywell-Lane*, | *Shoreditch*, 1692.

Second edition, London, 1692. Originally published, London, ca.1690.

12mo. A⁶ B-N¹²; 150 leaves, pp. [*12*] 1-285 [286] [2]. Last leaf blank.

Bibliographies: Oxford, p. 43, in a note; Wing T3181. Craig 92 and Simon BG 1482 record the first edition.

Copies: *BMC* and *NUC* (7 copies). Wing (5 copies).

1029. Tryon, Thomas, 1634-1703.

[within a single rule border] THE | 𝔚𝔞𝔶 𝔱𝔬 𝔥𝔢𝔞𝔩𝔱𝔥, | Long *LIFE* and | HAPPINESS, | Or, A Discourse of | Temperance | AND | The particular *Nature of all things* | requisit for the Life of Man, As | All sorts of *Meats, Drinks, Air, Exercise, &c.* with | special Directions how to use each of them to the best Advantage of the | BODY and MIND. | Shewing from the true ground of Nature whence most | Diseases proceed, and how to prevent them. | To which is added, A Treatise of most sorts of | 𝔈𝔫𝔤𝔩𝔦𝔰𝔥 𝔥𝔢𝔯𝔟𝔰, | With several other remarkable and most useful Obser- | vations, very necessary for all Families. The whole Treatise | displaying the most hidden secrets of *Philosophy*, and made easie and familiar | to the meanest Capacities, by various Examples and Demonstrances. | 𝔗𝔥𝔢 𝔩𝔦𝔨𝔢 𝔫𝔢𝔳𝔢𝔯 𝔟𝔢𝔣𝔬𝔯𝔢 𝔓𝔲𝔟𝔩𝔦𝔰𝔥𝔢𝔡. | [rule] | *Communicated to the World for a general Good*, | By 𝔓𝔥𝔦𝔩𝔬𝔱𝔥𝔢𝔬𝔰 𝔓𝔥𝔶𝔰𝔦𝔬𝔩𝔬𝔤𝔲𝔰. | [rule] | *London*, Printed and Sold by *Andrew Sowle*, at the Crooked-Billet in *Holloway-* | *Lane* near *Shoreditch*, 1683.

First edition, London, 1683.

8vo. [1-36]⁸ [37]⁴ [38-43]⁸ [44]⁴ signed [a]⁴ b⁴ B-Uuu⁴ [Xxx]⁴ Yyy-Qqqq⁴; 344 leaves, pp. [*16*] 1-669 [670-672]. First leaf (blank or half-title?) wanting in this copy.

Bibliographies: Bitting, p. 466; Craig 93; Oxford, p. 43; Wing T3200.

Copies: *NUC* (11 copies). Wing (9 copies).

1030. Tryon, Thomas, 1634-1703.

[within a border of two rules] The WAY To │ HEALTH, │ LONG │ Life and
Happiness: │ Or, A Discourse of │ TEMPERANCE, │ And the Particular │ Nature of
all Things requisite for the Life of │ Man; As, All sorts of *Meats, Drinks, Air,
Exercise*, &c. │ with special Directions how to use each of them to the │ best
Advantage of the BODY and MIND. │ Shewing from the true ground of Nature,
whence most │ Diseases proceed, and how to prevent them. │ To which is Added, │ A
Treatise of most sorts of ENGLISH HERBS, │ With several other remarkable and most
useful Observa- │ tions, very necessary for all Families. The whole Trea- │ tise
displaying the most hidden secrets of *Philosophy*, and │ made easie and familiar to the
meanest Capacities, by │ various Examples and Demonstrances. │ [rule] │ 𝕿𝔥𝔢 𝔩𝔦𝔨𝔢
𝔫𝔢𝔳𝔢𝔯 𝔟𝔢𝔣𝔬𝔯𝔢 𝕻𝔲𝔟𝔩𝔦𝔰𝔥𝔢𝔡. │ [rule] │ Communicated to the World for a general Good, │
By *THOMAS TRYON*, Student │ in PHYSICK. │ [rule] │ *The Second Edition, with
Amendments.* │ [rule] │ *LONDON:* │ Printed by *H. C.* for 𝕽. 𝕭𝔞𝔩𝔡𝔴𝔦𝔫, near the *Ox-* │
ford-Arms in *Warwick-Lane*, 1691.

Second edition, London, 1691. Originally published, London, 1683 (item 1029).

8vo. A-Kk^8 Ll^4; 268 leaves, pp. [*16*] 1-500 [*2*], ^{2}1-18.

Bibliographies: Oxford, p. 43, in a note; Simon BG 1480; Wing T3201.

Copies: *BMC* and *NUC* (12 copies). Wing (8 copies).

1031. Tryon, Thomas, 1634-1703.

[within a border of two rules] The WAY To │ HEALTH, │ LONG │ Life and
Happiness: │ Or, A Discourse of │ TEMPERANCE, │ And the Particular │ Nature of
all Things requisite for the LIFE of │ MAN; As, All sorts of *Meats, Drinks, Air,
Exercise*, &c. │ with special Directions how to use each of them to the │ best
Advantage of the BODY and MIND. │ Shewing from the true ground of Nature,
whence most │ Diseases proceed, and how to prevent them. │ To which is Added, │ A
Treatise of most sorts of ENGLISH HERBS, │ With several other remarkable and most
useful Obser- │ vations, very necessary for all Families. The whole │ Treastise
displaying the most hidden Secrets of *Philoso-* │ *phy*, and made easie and familiar to
the meanest Capa- │ cities, by various Examples and Demonstrances. │ [rule] │ 𝕿𝔥𝔢
𝔩𝔦𝔨𝔢 𝔫𝔢𝔳𝔢𝔯 𝔟𝔢𝔣𝔬𝔯𝔢 𝕻𝔲𝔟𝔩𝔦𝔰𝔥𝔢𝔡. │ [rule] │ Communicated to the World for a General
Good, │ By *THOMAS TRYON*, Student │ in PHYSICK. │ [rule] │ *The Third Edition.* │

To which is added a Discourse of the *Philosophers Stone*, or | *Universal Medicine*, Discovering the Cheats and Abuses | of those *Chymical* Pretenders. | [rule] | *LONDON,* | Printed and are to be Sold by most Booksellers. 1697.

Third edition, first issue, with the title dated 1697. The second issue (item 1032) has a cancel title dated 1698. Originally published, London, 1683 (item 1029).

8vo. A-U⁸ X⁴ ᵗX⁸ Y-Gg⁸ Hh-Ii⁴; 252 leaves, pp. [*16*] 1-312, 305-456, ²1-24.

Bibliographies: Oxford, p. 43, in a note; Simon BG 1481; Wing T3202.

Copies: *BMC* and *NUC* (9 copies). Wing (Glasgow University and Clark Library).

1032. Tryon, Thomas, 1634-1703.

[within a border of two rules] The WAY To | HEALTH, | LONG | Life and Happiness: | Or, A Discourse of | TEMPERANCE, | And the Particular | Nature of all Things requisite for the LIFE of | MAN; as All sorts of *Meats, Drinks, Air, Exercise*, &c. | with special Directions how to use each of them to the | best Advantage of the BODY and MIND. | Shewing from the true ground of Nature, whence most | Diseases proceed, and how to prevent them. | To which is Added, | A Treatise of most sorts of ENGLISH HERBS, | With several other remarkable and most useful Obser- | vations, very necessary for all Families. The whole | Treastise displaying the most hidden Secrets of *Philoso-* | *phy*, and made easie and familiar to the meanest Capa- | cities, by various Examples and Demonstrances. | [rule] | 𝔗𝔥𝔢 𝔗𝔥𝔦𝔯𝔡 𝔈𝔡𝔦𝔱𝔦𝔬𝔫. | To which is added a Discourse of the *Philosophers Stone*, or | *Universal Medicine*, Discovering the Cheats and Abuses | of those *Chymical* Pretenders. | [rule] | 𝔗𝔥𝔢 𝔩𝔦𝔨𝔢 𝔫𝔢𝔟𝔢𝔯 𝔟𝔢𝔣𝔬𝔯𝔢 𝔓𝔲𝔟𝔩𝔦𝔰𝔥𝔢𝔡. | [rule] | Communicated to the World for a General Good, By | *THOMAS TRYON*, Student | in PHYSICK. | [rule] | *LONDON* | Printed for *Edmund Richardson*, at the *Naked boy* in *Newgate* | Street over against *St. Martins Le grand* 1698.

Third edition, second issue, with a cancel title dated 1698. Originally published London, 1683 (item 1029).

8vo. A⁸(±A1) B-U⁸ X⁴ ᵗX⁸ Y-Gg⁸ Hh-Ii⁴; 252 leaves, pp. [*16*] 1-312, 305-456, ²1-24.

Bibliographies: Wing T3203.

Copies: *NUC* (Vassar College only). Wing (British Library only).

1033. Tryon, Thomas, 1634-1703.

[within a border of two rules] 𝔚𝔦𝔰𝔡𝔬𝔪'𝔰 𝔇𝔦𝔠𝔱𝔞𝔱𝔢𝔰: | *OR,* | APHORISMS & RULES, | *Physical, Moral,* and *Divine;* | For Preserving the *Health* of the *Body,* | and the *Peace* of the *Mind,* fit to be | regarded and practised by all that | would enjoy the Blessings of the pre- | sent and future World. | *To which is added,* | A BILL of FARE | OF | Seventy five Noble Dishes of Ex- | cellent Food, far exceeding those made | of Fish or Flesh, which Banquet I pre- | sent to the Sons of Wisdom, or such | as shall decline that depraved Custom | of Eating Flesh and Blood. | [rule] | *By* THO. TRYON, *Student in Physick, and Au-* | thor *of* Pythagoras's Mystick Philosophy Re- | vived, *wherein the Mysteries of Dreams, Vi-* | sions, Angels, and Spirits, are unfolded, and | their secret Communications to Mankind. | [rule] | *LONDON,* | Printed for *Tho. Salusbury,* at the Sign of the | *Temple* near *Temple-Bar* in *Fleetstreet.* 1691

First edition, London, 1691.

12mo. A² (A1+1) B-E¹² G¹² I¹² L⁶ (E8 and E9 signed "F2" and "F3," G6 and G7 signed "H" and "H2," I8 signed "K2"); 81 leaves, pp. [6] 1-153 [154-156].

Bibliographies: Oxford, p. 43; Wing T3205.

Copies: *BMC* and *NUC* (5 copies). Wing (5 copies).

1033a. Turnbull, William Barclay David Donald, 1811-1863, ed.

COMPOTA DOMESTICA. | FAMILIARUM DE BUKINGHAM ET D'ANGOULEME, | MCCCCXLIII, LII, LXIII. | QUIBUS ANNEXÆ | EXPENSÆ CUJUSDAM COMITIS IN ITINERE, | MCCLXXIII. | EDINBURGI. | MDCCCXXXVI.

First edition, Edinburgh, 1836. Presented to the members of the Abbotsford Club by William B. D. D. Turnbull who owned the original manuscript household books. The list of members of the Abbotsford Club printed in the preliminaries records twenty-five names, indicating that at least twenty-five copies were printed.

249 x 200 mm. π² χ⁴ [A]⁴ B-N⁴; 58 leaves, pp. [6] [i] ii-v [vi] [1-3] 4-104. Printed on vellum. Publisher's green silk covered boards rebacked in green morocco stamped in gold.

Bibliographies: Unrecorded in the bibliographies consulted.

Copies: *BMC* and *NUC* (8 copies).

1034. Tusser, Thomas, 1524?-1580.

[within an ornamental border] 1597 | 𝔉𝔦𝔳𝔢 𝔥𝔲𝔫𝔡𝔯𝔢𝔱𝔥 𝔭𝔬𝔦𝔫𝔱𝔢𝔰 𝔬𝔣 | 𝔤𝔬𝔬𝔡 𝔥𝔲𝔰𝔟𝔞𝔫𝔡𝔯𝔦𝔢, as well for the | Champion or Open countrie, as | also for the Woodland or Seuerall, | mixed in euerie month with Huswiferie, | ouer and besides the booke | of Huswiferie. | Corrected, better ordered, and newlie aug | mented to a fourth part more, with diuers other | lessons, as a diet for the farmer, of the properties | of winds, planets, hops, hearbs, bees, and approo= | ued remedies for sheepe and cattell, with ma= | nie other matters both profitable and | not unpleasant for the | Reader. | Also a table of Husbandrie at the begin= | ning of this booke: and another of Huswiferie | at the end, for the better and easier | finding of anie matter con= | teined in the same. | Newlie set foorth by Thomas | *Tusser Gentleman.* | *Imprinted at London by Peter Short* | dwelling on Bredstreet hill at the | signe of the Starre.

Colophon: *LONDON,* | Printed by Peter Short, dwelling on Bred- | *streethil, at the signe of the Starre.* | 1597.

Sixteenth edition, London, 1597. Originally published under the title *A Hundred Good Points of Good Husbandry,*, London, 1557, and expanded to *Five Hundred Points of Good Husbandry United to as Many of Good Wifeire*, London, 1573.

4to. A-K^8 L^2; 82 leaves, pp. [1-4] 5-162 [163-164]. Last two leaves in this copy supplied in facsimile.

Bibliographies: Fussell (1) pp. 8-9; *STC* 24385.

Copies: *STC* (Bodleian Library, John Rylands Library, University of St. Andrews, and Rutgers University).

1035. Tusser, Thomas, 1524?-1580.

[within a single rule border] Five Hundred Points | OF | Good Husbandry. | As well for the Champion or open | Countrey, as also for the Woodland or | Several, mixed in every Moneth, with Hous- | wifery, over and besides the Book | of Houswifery. |

[rule] | Corrected, better ordered, and newly augment- | ed to a fourth part more, with divers other lessons, as | a diet for the Farmer, of the properties of Winds, | Plants, Hops, Hearbs, Bees, and approved | Remedies for Sheep and Cattel; with | many other matters both profita- | ble, and not unpleasant to | the Reader. | [rule] | Also two Tables, one of Husbandry, and the other of | Houswifery, at the end of the Book, for the better | and easier finding out of any matter | contained in the same. | [rule] | Newly set forth by THOMAS TUSSER, Gent. | *LONDON,* | Printed by *T. R.* and *M. D.* for the Company | of Stationers. 1672.

Twenty-sixth edition, London, 1672. Originally published under the title *A Hundred Good Points of Good Husbandry*, London, 1557, and expanded to *Five Hundred Points of Good Husbandry United to as Many of Good Wifeire*, London, 1573.

4to. A-T⁴; 76 leaves, pp. [1] 2-144, 143-146 [4].

Bibliographies: Wing T3369.

Copies: *BMC, BNC,* and *NUC* (17 copies). Wing (11 copies).

1036. Twyne, Thomas, 1543-1613.

[within a border of type ornaments] The Schoolemaster, or Teacher | *of Table Philosophie.* | A most pleasant and merie com- | panion, wel worthy to be welcomed (for | a dayly Gheast) not onely to all mens boorde, to | guyde them with moderate & holsome dyet: | but also into euery mans companie at all | tymes, to recreate their mindes, with | honest mirth and delectable deuises: | to sundrie pleasent purposes of | pleasure and pastyme. | *Gathered out of diuers, the best ap-* | *proued Auctours: and deuided into* | foure pithy and pleasant Treatises, as | it may appeare by the contentes. | [rule] | [ornament] Imprinted at London, by | Richarde Jones: dwelling ouer= | agaynst S. Sepulchers Church | without Newgate. | 1576.

First edition, London, 1576.

4to. A-V⁴; 80 leaves, unpaginated.

This is the Christie-Miller copy, sold at the Britwell Court sale, March, 1926.

Bibliographies: Oxford, p. 7, in a note; *STC* 24411.

Copies: *NUC* (Folger Shakespeare Library, Huntington Library and John Crerer Library). *STC* adds Bodleian Library.

1037. Ude, Louis Eustache.

THE | 𝔉rench Cook; | OR, | *THE ART OF COOKERY* | DEVELOPED IN | ALL ITS VARIOUS BRANCHES. | [short rule] | BY LOUIS EUSTACHE UDE, | FORMERLY COOK TO LOUIS XVI. KING OF FRANCE, AND AT PRESENT | COOK TO THE RIGHT HON. EARL OF SEFTON. | [short rule] | LONDON: | PRINTED BY COX AND BAYLIS, | Great Queen Street, Lincoln's-Inn-Fields, | For the Author, and sold by J. EBERS, 27, Old Bond | Street; and may be had of all the Booksellers in the | United Kingdom. | [short rule] | 1813.

First edition, London, 1813.

213 x 131 mm. π1 a-c^8 d^2 B-2H^8; 267 leaves, pp. [2] [i] ii-lii [1] 2-480.

Illustrations: Engraved frontispiece portrait of the author and eight engraved plates with bills of fare.

Bibliographies: Axford, p. 171; Bitting, p. 471; Oxford, p. 142.

Copies: *BMC* and *NUC* (Library of Congress only).

1038. Ude, Louis Eustache.

THE | 𝔉rench Cook; | OR, | *THE ART OF COOKERY* | DEVELOPED IN | ALL ITS VARIOUS BRANCHES. | [short rule] | BY LOUIS EUSTACHE UDE, | FORMERLY COOK TO LOUIS XVI. KING OF FRANCE, AND AT PRESENT | STEWARD TO THE UNITED SERVICE CLUB. | [short rule] | FOURTH EDITION. | [short fancy rule] | LONDON: | PRINTED BY COX AND BAYLIS, | Great Queen Street, Lincoln's-Inn-Fields, | For the Author, and sold by J. EBERS, 27, Old Bond | Street; and may be had of all the Booksellers in the | United Kingdom. | [short rule] | 1816.

Fourth edition, London, 1816. Originally published, London, 1813 (item 1037).

213 x 127 mm. π1 a-c^8 d^2 B-2H^8; 267 leaves, pp. [2] [i] ii-lii [1] 2-480.

Illustrations: Engraved frontispiece portrait of the author and eight engraved plates with bills of fare.

Bibliographies: This edition unrecorded in the bibliographies consulted.

Copies: No other copy of this edition located.

1039. Ude, Louis Eustache.

THE │ FRENCH COOK. │ A │ SYSTEM │ OF │ *FASHIONABLE AND ECONOMICAL COOKERY,* │ FOR THE │ USE OF ENGLISH FAMILIES. │ "True *taste* is an excellent economist. – ROGERS. │ BY │ LOUIS EUSTACHE UDE, │ CI-DEVANT COOK TO LOUIS XVI. AND THE EARL OF SEFTON, AND LATE │ STEWARD TO HIS LATE ROYAL HIGHNESS THE DUKE OF YORK. │ NINTH EDITION, ENLARGED. │ LONDON: │ W. H. AINSWORTH, 23, OLD BOND-STREET; │ SOLD ALSO BY │ HURST AND CO., ST. PAUL'S CHURCHYARD; SHERWOOD AND CO., PA- │ TERNOSTER-ROW; SIMPKIN AND MARSHALL, STATIONERS'-HALL- │ COURT; J. ANDREWS, NEW BOND-STREET; AND W. SAMS, ST. JAMES'S- │ STREET: WILSON AND SONS, YORK; H. MOZLEY, DERBY; W. AND │ W. CLARKE, MANCHESTER; G. AND J. ROBINSON, LIVERPOOL: │ OLIVER AND BOYD, EDINBURGH; AND WESTLEY AND TYRRELL, │ DUBLIN. │ [short rule] │ 1827.

Ninth edition, London, 1827. Originally published, London, 1813 (item 1037).

194 x 118 mm. a^{12} b^6 c1 B-X^{12} Y^6 Z^2; 267 leaves, pp. [1-3] 4 [v] vi-xxxviii [1] 2-496.

Illustrations: Lithographed frontispiece portrait of the author and eight engraved plates showing bills of fare.

Bibliographies: Simon BG 1516.

Copies: No other copy of this edition located.

1039a. Vegetable Cookery.

VEGETABLE COOKERY; │ WITH AN │ INTRODUCTION, │ RECOMMENDING │ ABSTINENCE FROM ANIMAL FOOD │ AND │ *INTOXICATING LIQUORS.* │ BY A LADY. │ [vignette] │ *THE FOURTH EDITION.* │ LONDON: │ PUBLISHED BY

EFFINGHAM WILSON, | ROYAL EXCHANGE; | MESSRS, CLARKE, AND MESSRS, THOMSON, MANCHESTER; | F. W. WAKEMAN, DUBLIN; AND MESSRS., WAUGH | AND INNES, EDINBURGH. | [short rule] | MDCCCXXXIII.

Fourth edition, London, 1833. There was a second edition, London and Manchester, 1829. No earlier edition is recorded.

165 x 99 mm. [A]² B-2Q⁶; 236 leaves, pp. [*4*] [*1*] 2-451 [*452*] [*4*]. Last two leaves contain publisher's advertisements. Bound in dark brown boards with darker brown cloth spine with white paper label on the spine lettered: [two rules] | VEGETABLE | COOKERY | BY | A LADY | [short rule] | 6s. | [two rules]

Bibliographies: Bitting p. 613; Oxford p. 167.

Copies: *BMC* and *NUC* (Kansas State University and Library of Congress).

1040. Venner, Tobias, 1577-1660.

[within a border of two rules] VIA RECTA | *AD* | VITAM LONGAM, | *OR* | A PLAINE PHILOSOPHI- | CALL DISCOVRSE OF THE | Nature, faculties, and effects, of all such things | as by way of nourishments, and Dieteticall obserua- | tions, make for the preseruation of Health, with | their iust applications vnto euery age, con- | stitution of body, and time of | *YEARE.* | [rule] | WHEREIN ALSO BY WAY OF IN- | troduction, the Nature and Choise of Habita- | ble Places, with the true vse of our famous *Bathes* | of BATHE, is perspicuously demonstrated. | [rule] | The second Edition, corrected and enlarged: | *BY* | TO: VENNER, *Doctor of Physicke in* BATHE. | [rule] | [ornament] | [rule] | *LONDON:* | Printed by *T. S.* for *Richard Moore,* and are to be sold at | his shop in St. *Dunstans* Church-yard in Fleet-street. | 1622.

Second edition, London, 1622. Originally published, London, 1620.

4to. A² B-Cc⁴ Dd²; 104 leaves, pp. [*4*] 1-194 [*10*]. Last leaf blank.

Bibliographies: Oxford, p. 18, in a note; *STC* 24644; Simon BG 1531; Wheaton and Kelly 6208.

Copies: *BMC* and *NUC* (9 copies). *STC* (8 copies).

1041. Venner, Tobias, 1577-1660.

VIA RECTA │ AD │ Vitam Longam. │ OR, │ A plain Philosophicall Demonstration of │ the Nature, Faculties, and Effects, of all such things │ as by way of nourishments make for the preservation of │ health, with divers necessary dieticall observations; │ as also of the true use and effects of Sleep, Exer- │ cise, Excretions, and Perturbations, with │ just applications to every age, constituti- │ on of body, and time of yeere. │ [rule] │ *By* TO. VENNER, *Doctor of Physick in* Bathe. │ [rule] │ Whereunto is annexed by the same Author, a ne- │ cessary and compendious Treatise of the famous Baths of │ *Bathe*, with a Censure of the medicinable faculties │ of the water of Saint *Vincent's* Rocks │ neere the City of *Bristoll.* │ As also an accurate Treastise concerning TOBACCO. │ [rule] │ LONDON, │ Printed by *R. Bishop*, for *Henry Hood*, and are to be sold at his shop │ in Saint *Dunstans* Churchyard in Fleetstreet. 1638.

First sectional title-page:

THE │ BATHS │ OF │ BATHE: │ OR, │ A NECESSARY COMPENDIOVS │ Treatise concerning the Nature, Vse, and Effi- │ cacie of those famous Hot Waters. │ Published for the benefit of all such as yeerely │ for their health, resort to those Baths. │ With an Advertisement of the great utility that │ commeth to mans body, by the taking of Physick, in │ the Spring, inferred upon a Question moved, │ concerning the frequencie of sicknesse, and │ death of people more in that season, │ than in any other. │ Whereunto is also annexed a Censure, concerning the Water │ of Saint *Vincents* Rocks neere *Bristoll*, which is in great │ request and use against the Stone. │ [rule] │ *By* TO. VENNER *Doctor of Physick in Bathe.* │ [rule] │ LONDON, │ Printed by *R. Bishop* for *Henry Hood*, and are to be sold at │ his shop in Saint *Dunstans* Churchyard in │ Fleetstreet. 1637.

Second sectional title-page:

A │ Briefe and Accurate │ TREATISE │ *CONCERNING* │ The taking of the Fume of │ TOBACCO, │ Which very many, in these dayes, │ doe too too licenciously use. │ In which, the immoderate, irregular, and un- │ seasonable use thereof is reprehended, and │ the true nature and best manner of using it, │ perspicuously demonstrated. │ [rule] │ *By* TO. VENNER *Doctor of Physick in Bathe.* │ [rule] │ LONDON, │ Printed by *R. Bishop* for *Henry Hood*, and are to be │ sold at his shop in Saint *Dunstans* Churchyard │ in Fleetstreet. 1637.

Sixth edition, London, 1638. Originally published, London, 1620.

4to. A^2 a^4 B-Zz^4 $^\pi$Aa^2; 190 leaves, pp. [*16*] 1-364. First leaf blank.

Bibliographies: Bitting, p. 476; Oxford, p. 18, in a note; *STC* 24647; Wheaton and Kelly 6210.

Copies: *BMC* and *NUC* (6 copies). *STC* (10+ copies).

1042. Venner, Tobias, 1577-1660.

VIA RECTA | AD | Vitam Longam. | OR, | A Treatise wherein the right way and best | manner of living for attaining to a long and | healthfull life, is clearly demonstrated and punctually | applied to every age and constitution of body. | *Much more enlarged than the former Impressions.* | [rule] | By THO. VENNER Doctor of Physick in Bathe. | [rule] | Whereunto is annexed by the same Authour, | A very necessary, and compendious Treatise of the fa- | mous Baths of BATHE. | *WITH* | A Censure of the Medicinall faculties of the Water of | *St. Vincents-Rocks* neer the City of *Bristoll.* | As also | An accurate Treastise concerning TOBACCO. | *All which are likewise amplified since the former*

Impressions. | [rule] | LONDON, | Printed by *James Flesher*, for *Henry Hood*, and are to be sold at his Shop | in Saint *Dunstans* Church-yard in Fleetstreet. | 1650.

First sectional title-page:

THE | BATHS | OF | BATHE: | OR, | A necessary compendious *Treatise,* | concerning the Nature, Use, and Efficacy | of those famous Hot-Waters. | *Published for the benefit of all such as yearely, for* / *their health, resort to those Baths.* | With an Advertisement of the great utility that cometh to mans | body, by the taking of Physick in the Spring, inferred upon | a Question moved, concerning the frequency of sicknesse, and | death of people more in that season, than in any other. | *Whereunto is also annexed a* Censure, *concerning the Water* / *of Saint* Vincents *rocks near* Bristoll, *which is in great* / *request and use against the Stone.* | [rule] | By TO. VENNER Doctor of Physick in *Bathe.* | [rule] | *LONDON.* | Printed by *Iames Flesher* for *Henry Hood*, and are to be sold | at his shop in Saint *Dunstans* Church-yard | in Fleetstreet, 1650.

Second sectional title-page:

A | Brief and Accurate | TREATISE | *CONCERNING* | The taking of the Fume of | TOBACCO, | Which very many, in these dayes, | doe too too licenciously use. | In which the immoderate, irregular, and un- | seasonable use thereof is reprehended, and the | true nature and best manner of using it, | perspicuously demonstrated. | [rule] |

By TO. VENNER Doctor of Physick in *Bathe*. | [rule] | *LONDON*, | Printed by *Iames Flesher* for *Henry Hood*, and are to be sold | at his shop in Saint *Dunstans* Church-yard | in Fleetstreet, 1650.

Seventh edition, London, 1650. Originally published, London, 1620.

4to. A^2 a^4 B-Ccc^4 Ddd^2; 200 leaves, pp. [*12*] 1-55, 58-226, 237-331, 342-382, 391-417 [418].

Bibliographies: Oxford, p. 18, in a note; Wheaton and Kelly 6211; Wing V195.

Copies: *BMC* and *NUC* (13 copies). Wing (9 copies).

1043. Verral, William.

A | COMPLETE SYSTEM | OF | COOKERY. | In which is set forth, | A Variety of genuine RECEIPTS, | collected from several Years Experience | under the celebrated Mr. de ST. CLOUET, | sometime since COOK to his Grace the | Duke of *Newcastle*. | [rule] | By WILLIAM VERRAL, | Master of the *White-Hart* Inn in *Lewes, Sussex*. | [rule] | Together with an INTRODUCTORY PREFACE, | Shewing how every Dish is brought to Table, | and in what Manner the meanest Capacity shall | never err in doing what his Bill of Fare con- | tains. | To which is added, | A true Character of Mons. de ST. CLOUET. | [two rules] | LONDON, | Printed for the AUTHOR, and sold by him; | As also by EDWARD VERRAL Bookseller, in *Lewes:* | And by JOHN RIVINGTON in *St. Paul's Church-yard, London*. | [short rule] | M DCC LIX.

First edition, London, 1759.

8vo. [A]^8(-A8) B-S^8 T1 (=A8); 144 leaves, pp. [*14*] i-xxxiii [xxxiv] 1-240.

Bibliographies: Axford, p. 76; Bitting, p. 477; Maclean, p. 147; Oxford, p. 89; Pennell, p. 158; Schraemli (1) 490; Simon BG 1553; Vicaire 859; Wheaton and Kelly 6224.

Copies: *BMC* and *NUC* (6 copies). Maclean adds Brotherton Library and Wellcome Library.

1044. Vizetelly, Henry, 1820-1894.

A HISTORY | OF | [in red] CHAMPAGNE | WITH NOTES ON | THE OTHER SPARKLING WINES OF FRANCE. | [in red] BY HENRY VIZETELLY, |

CHEVALIER OF THE ORDER OF FRANZ-JOSEF, AUTHOR OF `THE WINES OF THE WORLD CHARACTERISED AND CLASSED,' | `FACTS ABOUT PORT AND MADEIRA,' `FACTS ABOUT CHAMPAGNE AND OTHER SPARKLING WINES,' | `FACTS ABOUT SHERRY,' ETC. | [vignette] | [in red] ILLUSTRATED WITH 350 ENGRAVINGS. | LONDON: | [in red] HENRY SOTHERAN & CO., | 136, STRAND; 36, PICCADILLY; 77 & 78, QUEEN STREET, CITY. | *MANCHESTER:* 49, CROSS STREET. | MDCCCLXXXII. | [*All rights reserved.*]

First edition, London, 1882.

272 x 211 mm. [a]⁴ b² B-P⁴ Q² R-MM⁴; 140 leaves, pp. [i-v] vi-xii [1] 2-263 [264] [*4*]. Publisher's green cloth stamped in gold; 8 pages of advertisements for champagne and books published by Vizetelly bound in at the end.

Illustrations: Lithographed frontispiece titled "A Supper under the Regency," five engraved plates, a colored lithographed map of the Champagne Vineyards and 350 engravings in the text.

Bibliographies: Gabler, p. 294; Noling, p. 426.

Copies: *BNC* and *NUC* (5 copies).

1044a. Walker, Thomas, 1784-1836.

THE ORIGINAL. | BY | THOMAS WALKER, M. A. | TRINITY COLLEGE, CAMBRIDGE; | BARRISTER AT LAW, AND ONE OF THE POLICE MAGISTRATES OF THE | METROPOLIS. | VOL. 1. | LONDON: | HENRY RENSHAW, 356, STRAND. | 1835.

First edition, London, 1835. Bound from the original 39 numbers of the periodical which appeared weekly from 20 May - 2 December 1835. The last number contains the statement, "The numbers, which were out of print, now being reprinted, complete sets of the `Original!' may now be had of the publisher." In this copy the stab holes and traces of the parts issue wrappers appear in numbers 6-39 indicating they are the original numbers; numbers 1-5 may be reprints.

209 x 133 mm. Vol. I [A]² B⁶ C-CC⁸ DD⁶, Vol. II B-C⁸ D²; 224 leaves, pp. Vol. I [i-iii] iv [1] 2-408, Vol. II [1] 2-36. The two volumes are bound as one and no title-page was printed for the aborted second volume.

Bibliographies: *ULS* p. 3206.

Copies: *BMC*; *ULS* (12 copies).

1045. Walsh, John Henry, 1810-1888.

THE | ENGLISH COOKERY BOOK: | UNITING | A GOOD STYLE WITH
ECONOMY, | AND | ADAPTED TO ALL PERSONS IN EVERY CLIME; |
CONTAINING | MANY UNPUBLISHED RECEIPTS IN DAILY USE | BY
PRIVATE FAMILIES. | COLLECTED BY A COMMITTEE OF LADIES. | AND
EDITED BY | J. H. WALSH, F.R.C.S., | AUTHOR OF "A MANUAL OF
DOMESTIC ECONOMY." | 𝔚𝔦𝔱𝔥 𝔈𝔫𝔤𝔯𝔞𝔟𝔦𝔫𝔤𝔰. | LONDON: | G. ROUTLEDGE
AND CO., FARRINDGON STREET; | AND 18, BEEKMAN STREET, NEW
YORK. | 1858.

First edition, London, 1858.

184 x 104 mm. [A]⁴ B-2A⁸ 2B⁴; 192 leaves, pp. [i-iii] iv-viii [1] 2-375 [376].
Publisher's quarter red morocco and green cloth, stamped in gold.

Illustrations: Eight wood engraved plates showing kitchen implements, trussing, and
carving.

Bibliographies: This edition unrecorded in the bibliographies consulted. Simon BG
1595 records the 1859 edition.

Copies: *BMC*.

1046. Warder, Joseph.

[within a border of two rules] THE TRUE | *AMAZONS:* | OR, | The MONARCY of |
BEES: | Being a new Discovery and Improvement | of those Wonderful *Creatures.* |
Wherein is Experimentally Demonstrated, | *I. That they are all governed by a QUEEN.*
| *II. The amazing Beauty and Dignity of her Person.* | *III. Her extraordinary Authority*
and Power. | *IV. Their exceeding Loyalty and unparallelled Love to* | *their QUEEN.* |
V. Their Sex, Male and Female. | *VI. The Manner of their Breeding.* | *VII. Their*
Wars. | *VIII. Their Enemies, with Directions plain and easy* | *how to manage them,*
both in Straw-hives and | *Transparent Boxes*; *so that with laying out but* / *Four of Five*
Pounds, in Three or Four Years, if the / *Summers are kind, you may get Thirty or Forty*
/Pounds per Annum. | Also how to make the *English* WINE or MEAD, | equal, if not
superior to the best of other *Wines.* | [rule] | By *JOSEPH WARDER* of *Croydon,*

PHYSICIAN. | [rule] | 𝕿𝖍𝖊 𝕾𝖊𝖈𝖔𝖓𝖉 𝕰𝖉𝖎𝖙𝖎𝖔𝖓 𝖜𝖎𝖙𝖍 𝕬𝖉𝖉𝖎𝖙𝖎𝖔𝖓𝖘. | [rule] | *Sic vos non vobis mellificatis Apes*. Virg. | [rule] | *LONDON*, Printed for *John Pemberton*, at the | *Buck* and *Sun* over-against St. *Dunstan*'s Church | in *Fleet-street*, and *William Taylor* at the *Ship* | in *Pater-noster-row*. 1713.

Second edition, London, 1713. Originally published, London, 1712.

8vo. A^8 (-A8) B-L^8; 87 leaves, pp. [i-ii] iii-xii [2] 1-160.

Illustrations: Engraved frontispiece portrait of the author.

Note: Chapter XXI. "How to make English Canary, no way inferior to the best of Spanish wines," on pp. 155-56, is the only part of this work not treating bees.

Bibliographies: Fussell (1) p. 117.

Copies: *BMC* and *NUC* (4 copies).

1047. Warm Beer.

[within a border of two rules] *Warm Beer:* | OR, A | TREATISE, | WHEREIN | Is declared by many Reasons, that | BEER so qualified, is far more Whole- | some than that which is drank COLD; | with a Confutation of such Objections | as are made against it. | INTERSPERST | With divers Observations, touching the drink- | ing of COLD WATER. | AND | Publish'd for the Preservation of HEALTH. | [row of type ornaments] | *LONDON:* | Printed for J. WILFORD, at the Three *Flower* | *De Luces* in *Little-Britain*. 1724.

Second edition, London, 1724. Originally published, Cambridge, 1641.

8vo. $^\pi$A^4 A-F^4; 28 leaves, pp. [8] [1] 2-48. 8 page publisher's catalogue bound in at the end.

Bibliographies: This edition unrecorded in the bibliographies consulted.

Copies: *BMC* and *NUC* (Yale only).

1048. Warner, Richard, 1763-1857.

[engraved title-page] 𝕬𝖓𝖙𝖎𝖖𝖚𝖎𝖙𝖆𝖙𝖊𝖘 𝕮𝖚𝖑𝖎𝖓𝖆𝖗𝖎𝖆𝖊 | or | CURIOUS TRACTS | *relating to the Culinary affairs* | of the | OLD ENGLISH, | *With a preliminary discourse, Notes, and Illustrations,* | By | *The Reverend Richard Warner,* | OF SWAY, | near Lymington, Hants. | Πολλ; τοι Πνεονασ λιμρυ κοροσ ;λεσεν ανδρασ. | *Non in Caro nidore voluptas* | *Summa, sed in teipso est; tu pulmentaria quaere* | *Sudando.* | [short rule] | LONDON, | *Printed for R. Blamire, Strand.* | 1791.

First edition, London, 1791. Printing on laid paper watermarked "WL." Large paper copy with the distance from the gutter of the fold to the left hand margin of the type page on B3^r measuring 65 mm.

4to. B-Cc^4; 100 leaves, pp. [i] ii-lx [1] 2-137 [138] [2]. Last blank leaf wanting in this copy.

Illustrations: Engraved title-page (there is no letterpress title) and two aquatint plates, one of two pages, tinted terra cotta, and an engraved tail piece on p. lvii. The double plate, "A Peacock Feast," which Maclean reports had to be withdrawn after publication because of copyright infringement, is present in this copy.

Bibliographies: Bitting, p. 485; Craig 97; Maclean, p. 149; Oxford, p. 120; Pennell, p. 164; Schraemli (1) 496; Simon BG 1607; Vicaire 873; Wheaton and Kelly 2213. Of the above bibliographies only Craig notes the large paper copies.

Copies: *BMC* (2 large paper and 1 smaller paper). *BNC* and *NUC* (20 copies). Neither *BNC* nor *NUC* indicate large or smaller paper copies. Maclean adds Bodleian Library and National Library of Scotland.

1049. Warner, Richard, 1763-1857.

[engraved title-page] 𝕬𝖓𝖙𝖎𝖖𝖚𝖎𝖙𝖆𝖙𝖊𝖘 𝕮𝖚𝖑𝖎𝖓𝖆𝖗𝖎𝖆𝖊 | or | CURIOUS TRACTS | *relating to the Culinary affairs* | of the | OLD ENGLISH, | *With a preliminary discourse, Notes, and Illustrations,* | By | *The Reverend Richard Warner,* | OF SWAY, | near Lymington, Hants. | Πολλ; τοι Πνεονασ λιμρυ κοροσ ;λεσεν ανδρασ. | *Non in Caro nidore voluptas* | *Summa, sed in teipso est; tu pulmentaria quaere* | *Sudando.* | [short rule] | LONDON, | *Printed for R. Blamire, Strand.* | 1791.

First edition, London, 1791. Printing on smaller wove paper, the distance from the gutter of the fold to the left margin of the type page on B3^r measuring 42 mm.

4to. B-Cc⁴; 100 leaves, pp. [i] ii-lx [1] 2-137 [138] [2].

Illustrations: Engraved title-page (there is no letterpress title) and two aquatint plates, one of two pages, tinted terra cotta, and an engraved tail piece on p. lvii. The double plate, "A Peacock Feast," which Maclean reports had to be withdrawn after publication because of copyright infringement, is present in this copy.

Bibliographies: Bitting, p. 485; Maclean, p. 149; Oxford, p. 120; Pennell, p. 164; Schraemli (1) 496; Simon BG 1607; Vicaire 873. None of the above bibliographies notes that there were two printings, one on large and one on smaller paper.

Copies: *BMC* (2 large paper and 1 smaller paper). *BNC* and *NUC* (20 copies). Neither *BNC* nor *NUC* indicate large or smaller paper copies. Maclean adds Bodleian Library and National Library of Scotland.

1050. Watson, John Edward.

THE | HOUSEWIFE'S DIRECTORY: | BEING | 𝕿𝖍𝖊 𝖒𝖔𝖘𝖙 𝕮𝖔𝖒𝖕𝖑𝖊𝖙𝖊 𝕾𝖞𝖘𝖙𝖊𝖒 | OF | DOMESTIC ECONOMY | EVER SUBMITTED TO PUBLIC NOTICE. | CONTAINING, | [in two columns: column one] 1. Instructions respecting Diet. | 2. Dishes for each Month. | 3. Choice of Butcher's Meat, Fish, Game, | and Poultry. | 4. To Dress Vegetables. | 5. Roasting and Boiling. | 6. To Dress Fish. | 7. Directions for Trussing. | 8. To Dress Poultry. | 9. The Art of Carving. | 10. Hashing and Mincing. | 11. Made Dishes. | 12. Soups, Gravies, &c. | 13. Puddings and Pies. | [two vertical rules] | [column two] 14. Mode of placing Dishes on the Table. | 15. Pastry and Confectionary. | 16. Dishes for Lent and Fridays. | 17. Bread, Biscuits, &c. | 18. Pickling and Preserving. | 19. Hams, Sausages, &c. | 20. Malt Liquors, Wines, and Cordials. | 21. Useful Family Medicines. | 22. Food, &c. for Invalids. | 23. Cosmetics and Perfumes. | 24. Management of a Kitchen Garden. | 25. Management of a Dairy, Cattle, and | Poultry. | 26. Miscellaneous Receipts. [end columns] | WITH COPIOUS | *MARKETING AND OTHER TABLES.* | [short fancy rule] | BY | JOHN EDWARD WATSON. | [short rule] | "In the choice of a wife, young men generally look upon beauty as the principal requisite; the | more prudent ones look out for a fortune; but, were I a young man in middling life, I would say, | `Give me, in preference, *a clean, obliging, and prudent housewife; for,* when beauty is faded, and | fortune diminished, I shall still preserve that which will render my lot superior to that of those whose | wives dissipate their income in folly or carelessness.'" − *Lord Chesterfield.* | [short rule] | 𝕷𝖔𝖓𝖉𝖔𝖓: | PRINTED FOR WILLIAM COLE, | No. 10, NEWGATE STREET.

First edition, London, 1825.

175 x 105 mm. [A]⁴ B-K¹²; 112 leaves, pp. [2] [i-iii] iv-vi [1] 2-212 [*4*]. This copy lacks leaves A1 and K9-12. In the Bitting copy in the Library of Congress, p. 212 is the last numbered page; the pages on K11 are unnumbered and K12 is missing but presumed to have been unnumbered.

Illustrations: The Bitting copy in the Library of Congress contains an engraved frontispiece of a kitchen scene not present in this copy.

Note: Two printings at least of the preliminaries of this work are known. The Bitting copy has a printer's imprint of G. H. Davidson, Ireland Yard, Doctors' Commons on the verso of the title-page while the Gernon copy has a table of contents listing twenty-seven section there.

Bibliographies: Bitting, p. 486.

Copies: *NUC* (Library of Congress and Michigan State University).

1051. White, John.

A | TREATISE | ON THE | ART OF BAKING, | WITH A | PRELIMINARY INTRODUCTION, | SHEWING | THE VARIOUS PRODUCTIONS OF THE DIFFERENT QUARTERS OF THE | GLOBE – OBSERVATIONS ON THE PRESENT STATE OF AGRICUL- | TURE – THE FARMER AND MIDDLEMAN. – STRICTURES | ON THE CORN BILL, &c. | WITH | A NUMBER OF VALUABLE RECEIPTS, | 𝔒riginal and 𝔖elected, | FOR THE | BAKER AND DOMESTIC CIRCLE. | [two short rules] | BY JOHN WHITE, BAKER, DUNBAR. | [short rule] | The bitterness is past, and what remains | Of life, life to come, I hope is joyfulness, | Not that false joy the unthinking only feel | When fortune smiles upon them, – but the joy | Arising from a consciousness of right | That I have done my duty to my King – | My Country – and to – Heaven. – *Temora, or the Last Field of Fingal.* | [short rule] | EDINBURGH: | PRINTED BY ANDERSON & BRYCE. | [short rule] | 1828.

First edition, Edinburgh, 1828.

224 x 135 mm. π¹⁰ χ² A-Z⁸ 2χ²; 198 leaves, pp. [i-iii] iv-xxiv [9] 10-376 [*4*]. Publisher's boards with printed label on the spine.

Bibliographies: Wheaton and Kelly 6471.

Copies: *BMC* and *NUC* (5 copies).

1052. The Whole Duty of a Woman.

[within a border of two rules] THE │ Whole Duty │ OF A │ WOMAN: │ Or a Guide to the 𝔉emale 𝒮ex. │ From the Age of Sixteen, │ to Sixty, &c. │ Being Directions, How Women of all Qua- │ lities and Conditions, ought to Behave │ themselves in the Various Circumstances │ of this Life, for their Obtaining not only │ Present, but Future Happiness. │ I. Directions how to Obtain the Divine │ and Moral Virtues, of Piety, Meekness, │ Modesty, Chastity, Humility, Compassion, │ Temperance and Affability, with their │ Advantages, and how to avoyd the Op- │ posite Vices. │ II. The Duty of Virgins. Directing them │ what they ought to do, and what to a- │ voyd, for gaining all the Accomplish- │ ments required in that State. With │ the Whole Art of Love, &c. 3. The │ Whole Duty of a Wife. 4. The Whole │ Duty of a Widow, &c. Also Choice │ Receipts in Physick, and Chirurgery. │ With the Whole Art of Cookery, Pre- │ serving, Candying, Beautifying, &c. │ [rule] │ *Written by a Lady.* │ [rule] │ *London,* Printed for *J. Gwillim,* against the │ *Great James Tavern* in *Bishopsgate-* │ *street,* 1695.

First edition, London, 1695.

12mo. [A]⁴ B-H¹² I⁸; 96 leaves, pp. [8] 1-184. First leaf wanting in this copy.

Bibliographies: Simon BG 1617. Maclean, p. 150, records the third-sixth and eighth editions and Oxford, p. 46, lists the third-fifth and eighth editions. Not recorded in Wing.

Copies: *BMC* (lacking title-page).

1053. The Whole Duty of a Woman.

[within a border of two rules] THE │ Whole Duty │ OF A │ WOMAN: │ OR, │ A *Guide* to the *Female Sex,* │ From the Age of *Sixteen* to *Sixty,* &c. │ Being Directions, How Women of all Qualities │ and Conditions ought to Behave themselves in │ the various Circumstances of this Life, for │ their obtaining not only Present, but Future │ Happiness. │ I. Directions how to obtain the Divine and Moral │ Vertues, of *Piety, Meekness, Modesty, Chastity,* │ *Humility, Compassion, Temperance,* and *Affabi-* │ *lity,* with their Advantages; and how to avoid | the opposite Vices. | II. The Duty of *Virgins*, directing them what they | ought to do, and what to avoid, for gaining | all the Accomplishments required in that State. | With the whole Art of *Love*. | III. The whole Duty of a Wife. | IV. The whole Duty of a Widow, *&c.* | Also choice Receipts in Physick and Chyrurgery. | With the whole Art of Cookery, Preserving, | Candying, Beautifying, *&c.* | [rule] | *Written by a Lady.* | [rule] | The Seventh EDITION. | [rule] | *LONDON:* Printed for, and Sold by *Edward* | *Midwinter*, at the *Looking-Glass* on *London-* | *Bridge*.

Seventh edition, London, ca.1720. Originally published, London, 1695 (item 1052).

12mo. [A]⁴ B-G¹² H⁸; 84 leaves, pp. [8] 1-154 [6].

12mo. [A]^4 B-G^{12} H^8; 84 leaves, pp. [8] 1-154 [6].

Illustrations: Woodcut on A1ᵛ of a woman at praycr and a woman in the kitchen.

Bibliographies: Craig 98. Craig assigns the date [1720]. The sixth edition is dated 1718 and the eighth 1735. The seventh is undated. Maclean, p. 150, records the third-sixth and eighth editions and Oxford, p. 46, lists the third-fifth and eighth editions.

Copies: Private collection of John C. Craig.

1054. Entry cancelled.

The Whole Duty of a Woman: see also The Lady's Companion (item 804-806).

1055. Wilkinson, Mrs.

THE | COMPLEAT | SERVANT MAID; | CONTAINING | All that is NECESSARY to be KNOWN | to be QUALIFIED for the | FOLLOWING PLACES, | *VIZ.* | [in two columns: column one] Ladies Maid, | Housekeeper, | Chamber Maid, | Nursery Maid, | Cook Maid, | [vertical row of type ornaments] | [column two] House Maid, | Laundry Maid, | Dairy Maid, | and | Scullery Maid. [end columns] | ALSO, | The best DIRECTIONS to qualify a Young Woman | for any COMMON SERVICE, and the most appro- | ved DIRECTIONS for Clear-Starching. | Together with INSTRUCTIONS how to manage | POULTRY, *&c.* | By Mrs. *WILKINSON*, | Who has gone through most of the above Services, in | which she has acquired a competent

Fortune. | [two rules] | *LONDON:* | Printed for J. COOKE and J. COOTE at the *King's Arms*, | opposite *Devereux Court* in the *Strand*. | MDCCLVII. | [Price One Shilling.]

First edition, London, 1757.

8vo. [A1] B-H⁴ I⁴(-I4=A1); 32 leaves, pp. [2] [1] 2-62.

Bibliographies: Maclean, p. 151. Maclean, noting the similarity of title, speculates this may be the same as Anne Barker's *The Complete Servant Maid: or, Young Woman's Best Companion* [ca.1762]. However, a comparison of the British Library's copy of Barker's work and this copy of Wilkinson's shows they are not related.

Copies: No other copy located. Maclean cites only this copy as described in the Sotheby Catalogue for 4 March 1968.

1056. Williams, Charles, 1796-1866.

SILVER-SHELL; | OR, | THE ADVENTURES OF AN OYSTER. | BY | CHARLES WILLIAMS. | "Dost know how an Oyster makes his shell?" | SHAKESPEARE. | [short rule] | LONDON: | WARD AND LOCK, 158, FLEET STREET. | [short rule] | 1856.

First edition, London, 1856.

170 x 105 mm. [A]⁴ B-I⁸ J-L⁸ M⁴; 96 leaves, pp. [i-vii] viii [1] 2-184. Publisher's green cloth, stamped in gold.

Illustrations: Frontispiece titled "Oyster dredging" and wood engraved illustrations in the text.

Bibliographies: Simon BG 1620.

Copies: *BMC* and *NUC* (Harvard only).

1057. Willis, Michael.

[within a border of two rules with ornaments at each corner] COOKERY MADE EASY: | BEING | *A COMPLETE SYSTEM* | OF | DOMESTIC MANAGEMENT, | UNITING | 𝔈𝔩𝔢𝔤𝔞𝔫𝔠𝔢 𝔴𝔦𝔱𝔥 𝔈𝔠𝔬𝔫𝔬𝔪𝔶. | [short rule] | TO WHICH ARE ADDED, |

INSTRUCTIONS FOR TRUSSING & CARVING, | *WITH SEVERAL DESCRIPTIVE PLATES;* | METHOD OF CURING & DRYING HAMS AND TONGUES; | HOW TO MAKE | MUSHROOM AND WALNUT KETCHUPS, | *QUIN'S SAUCE, VINEGARS, &c. &c.* | With other necessary Information, | THE WHOLE | BEING THE RESULT OF ACTUAL EXPERIENCE. | [short rule] | BY MICHAEL WILLIS, | *MANY YEARS COOK AT THE THATCHED-HOUSE TAVERN.* | [short rule] | *LONDON:* | ORLANDO HODGSON, CLOTH FAIR.

Third edition? London, ca.1830. Originally published, London, 1824.

164 x 101 mm. a^8 [B]^6 C-T^6; 116 leaves, pp. [i-iii] iv-xvi [1] 2-216. This copy lacks leaf a7.

Illustrations: Wood engraved frontispiece and five wood engraved plates illustating trussing and carving.

Bibliographies: Axford, p. 88; Bitting, p. 500; Oxford, p. 155, in a note; Vicaire 877. Simon BG 1623 records an 1829 edition.

Copies: *NUC* (Library of Congress and New York Public Library).

1058. Woolley, Hannah

[within a single rule border] The Accomplish'd | LADY'S DELIGHT | 𝕴𝖓 𝕻𝖗𝖊𝖘𝖊𝖗𝖛𝖎𝖓𝖌, 𝕻𝖍𝖞𝖘𝖎𝖈𝖐, 𝕭𝖊𝖆𝖚𝖙𝖎𝖋𝖞𝖎𝖓𝖌, | 𝖆𝖓𝖉 𝕮𝖔𝖔𝖐𝖊𝖗𝖞. | *CONTAINING,* | I. The ART of PRESERVING, | and CANDYING Fruits and Flow- | ers, and the making of all sorts of Con- | serves, Syrups, and Jellies. | II. The PHYSICAL CABINET, | Or, Excellent Receipts in Physick and | Chirurgery; Together with some Rare | Beautifying waters, to adorn and add | Loveliness to the Face and Body: And | also some New and Excellent Secrets | and Experiments in the ART of *AN-* | *GLING.* | III. The COMPLEAT COOKS GUIDE | Or, directions for dressing all sorts of Flesh, | Fowl, and Fish, both in the *English* and *French* | Mode, with all Sauces and Sallets; and the mak- | ing Pyes, Pasties, Tarts, and Custards, with the | Forms and Shapes of many of them. | [rule] | 𝕿𝖍𝖊 𝕾𝖊𝖈𝖔𝖓𝖉 𝕰𝖉𝖎𝖙𝖎𝖔𝖓 𝕰𝖓𝖑𝖆𝖗𝖌𝖊𝖉. | [rule] | *LONDON.* | Printed for *Nath. Crouch,* at the *George* at the | lower end of *Cornhil* over against | the *Stocks-Market*, 1677.

First sectional title-page:

[within a single rule border] THE | PHISICAL | Cabinet: | CONTAINING | Excellent Receipts | IN | Physick and Chyrurgery, | For Curing most Diseases Incident to | the

Bodies of Men and Women. | TOGETHER | VVith some Rare Beautifying | Waters, Oyls, Oyntments and Pow- | ders, to Adorn and add Loveliness | to the FACE and BODY. | AS ALSO | Some New and Excellent Secrets | and Experiements in the Art of | *ANGLING.* | *London* Printed in the Year 1677.

Second sectional title-page:

[within a single rule border] New and Excellent | EXPERIMENTS | AND | SECRETS | In the ART of Angling: | BEING | Directions for the whole | ART. | [two rules] | *LONDON,* | Printed in the Year 1677.

Third sectional title-page:

[within a single rule border] THE | Compleat Cook's | GUIDE. | OR | Directions for the Dressing of | all sorts of Flesh, Fowl, and Fish, | both in the *English* and *French* Mode; | with the preparing of all manner of | Sawces and Sallets proper thereunto. | TOGETHER | With the making of all Sorts of | Pyes, Pasties, Tarts, and Custards; | with the Forms and Shapes of many | of them. | WITH | Bills of Fare , both for Ordinary, and | Extraordinary. | [rule] | *London,* Printed in the Year 1667.

Second edition, London, 1677. Originally published, London, 1675.

12mo. A-Q^{12}; 192 leaves, pp. [*4*] 1-380.

Illustrations: Engraved frontispiece portrait of the author and engraved title-page (both supplied in photocopies in this copy), engraved frontispiece of anglers facing the title-page of the third part (p. 191), and three engraved plates, one of fish and two of pie shapes.

Note: Wing and *BMC* attribute this work to Hannah Woolley (under the variant spelling Wolley). Maclean and *NUC* enter it under title with no author attribution.

Bibliographies: Craig 100; Oxford, p. 37; Wing W3269.

Copies: *BMC* and *NUC* (John Crerar Library and Yale). Wing (Yale only).

1059. Woolley, Hannah

[within a border of two rules] The Accomplish'd | 𝕷𝖆𝖉𝖞's 𝕯𝖊𝖑𝖎𝖌𝖍𝖙, | IN | 𝕻𝖗𝖊𝖘𝖊𝖗𝖛𝖎𝖓𝖌, 𝕻𝖍𝖞𝖘𝖎𝖈𝖐, 𝕭𝖊𝖆𝖚𝖙𝖎𝖋𝖞𝖎𝖓𝖌 | 𝕮𝖔𝖔𝖐𝖊𝖗𝖞, 𝖆𝖓𝖉 𝕲𝖆𝖗𝖉𝖊𝖓𝖎𝖓𝖌. | CONTAINING, | I. The Art of *Preserving*, and *Candying.* | Fruits and Flowers, and making all sorts of |

Conserves, Syrups, Jellies, and Pickles. | II. The *Physical Cabinet:* Or, excellent | Receipts in *Physick* and *Chirurgery*. Also | some New Receipts relating to the Fair Sex, | whereby they may be richly furnish'd with all | manner of *Beautifying Waters*, to add Love- | liness to the Face and Body. | III. The *Compleat Cook's Guide:* Or, Di- | rections for Dressing all sorts of Flesh, Fowl, | and Fish, after the Newest Fashion now in | Use at the *British* Court; with the making | Sauces, of Pyes, Pasties, Tarts, Custards, *&c.* | IV. The *Female Angler*, instructing Ladies | and others, in the varous Methods of taking | all manner of Fish, in the Fish-Pond or River. | V. The *Lady's Diversion in her Garden:* | Or, the compleat Flowerist, with the Nature | and Use of all sorts of Plants and Flowers. | [rule] | 𝕿𝖍𝖊 𝕿𝖊𝖓𝖙𝖍 𝕰𝖉𝖎𝖙𝖎𝖔𝖓 𝕴𝖓𝖑𝖆𝖗𝖌𝖊𝖉. | [rule] | *LONDON*, Printed, for *Daniel Pratt*, at | the *Bible* and *Crown* against *Hungerford-* | *Market* in the *Strand*. 1719.

Engraved title-page:

[within a pictorial frame illustrating household tasks] THE | Accomplisht Ladys | 𝕭𝖊𝖑𝖎𝖌𝖍𝖙. | *In* Preserving Physick, Beau: | tifying *and* Cookery

Tenth edition, London, 1719. Originally published, London, 1675.

12mo. A-G^{12} H^6; 90 leaves, pp. [6] 1-134, 145-177 [178-184].

Illustrations: Engraved title showing women at domestic tasks. Woodcuts of pie shapes on pp. 122-123.

Bibliographies: Maclean, p. 3; Oxford, p. 38, in a note; Wheaton and Kelly 6612.

Copies: *NUC* (Harvard, John Crerar Library, and Kansas State University). Maclean adds Brotherton Library.

1060. Woolley, Hannah

THE | Compleat Servant-Maid: | OR, THE | COOK'*s* GUIDE. | CONTAINING | Directions for Dressing all Sorts of | *Flesh, Fowl,* and *Fish*, after the Newest Fa- | shion, from the *Highest Taste* to the most *Fru-* | *gal Method* of Private Families: With Di- | rections for making *Sauces, Pyes, Pasties,* | *Tarts, Custard,* &c. | ALSO | The Art of *Preserving, Candying Fruits* | and *Flowers*, and making all Sorts of *Conserves,* | *Syrups, Jellies,* and *Pickles*. Receipts in *Phy-* | *sick* and *Chirurgery*, and to make several *Simple* | *Waters* of excellent Use in Private Families. | To which is Added, |

Recreation for the *LADIES*, by | instructing them in the best Methods of *Catch-* | *ing* of *Fish*, either in Ponds or Rivers; and | Profitable Amusements in Managing of Gardens | for Pleasure, as well as for the Use of the | Kitchen. | [Price One Shilling.]

Eleventh (or later) edition, London, ca.1725. Originally published under the title *The Accomplish'd Lady's Delight* London, 1675.

12mo. A-G^{12} H^6; 90 leaves, pp. [6] [1] 2-163 [164-172] [2]. P. 163 misnumberd "162." Last leaf (blank?) wanting in this copy.

Bibliographies: Wheaton and Kelly 1336.

Copies: *NUC* (Harvard only).

1061. Woolley, Hannah

[within a border of two rules] $\mathfrak{The}$ $\mathfrak{compleat}$ | SERVANT-MAID: | OR, THE | Young Maidens Tutor. | Directing them how they may fit, | and qualifie themselves for any of | these Employments, | viz. | [in two columns: column one] *Waiting-Woman,* | *House-Keeper,* | *Chamber-Maid,* | *Cook-Maid,* | *Under-Cook-Maid,* | }{ | [column two] *Nursery-Maid,* | *Dairy-Maid,* | *Laundry-Maid,* | *House-Maid,* | *Scullery Maid.* [end columns] | [rule] | Whereunto is added a Supplement con- | taining the choicest Receipts [end columns] and rarest | Secrets in Physick and Chirurgery. | [rule] | Composed for the great benefit and ad- | vantage of all young Maidens. | [rule] | *The Fifth Edition Corrected and Amended.* | [rule] | *LONDON,* | Printed for *Tho.* *Passenger*, at the Three | *Bibles* and *Star* on *London-Bridge.* 1691.

Fifth edition, London, 1691. Originally published, London, 1677.

12mo. A-G^{12} H^6; 90 leaves, pp. [1-8] 9-178 [179-180].

Illustrations: Engraved frontispiece titled "The Compleat Sarvant Maid" on A1^v and two etched plates showing examples of calligraphy.

Note: This is an entirely different work than *The Compleat Servant Maid; or, The Cook's Guide* (item 1060) which is a retitled edition of *The Accomplish'd Lady's Delight*. Both contain recipes but this work also includes much general household information.

Bibliographies: Oxford, p. 40, in a note; Wheaton and Kelly 1335; Wing W3275. Wing records only the first edition, 1677, and the fifth edition, 1691.

Copies: Wing (Glasgow University only). Wheaton and Kelly (imperfect copy at Harvard only).

1062. Woolley, Hannah.

[within a border of two rules] THE | QUEEN-LIKE CLOSET; | OR, | RICH CABINET: | Stored with all manner of | RARE RECEIPTS | FOR | Preserving, Candying & Cookery. | Very Pleasant and Beneficial to all | Ingenious Persons of the | FEMALE SEX. | [rule] | By HANNAH WOLLEY. | [rule] | *LONDON,* | Printed for *R. Lowndes* at the | *White Lion* in *Duck-Lane,* | near *West-Smithfield,* | 1670.

First edition, London, 1670.

12mo. A^6 B-S^{12} T^6; 216 leaves, pp. [*12*] 1-383 [384] [*36*]. First leaf (blank?) and last leaf (blank?) wanting in this copy.

Illustrations: Engraved frontispiece of five kitchen scenes.

Bibliographies: Axford, p. 338; Oxford, p. 35; Vicaire 878; Wing W3282.

Copies: *BMC* and *NUC* (John Crerar Library and Kansas State University). Wing adds Glasgow University.

1063. Woolley, Hannah.

[within a border of two rules] 𝔗𝔥𝔢 𝔔𝔲𝔢𝔢𝔫=𝔩𝔦𝔨𝔢 ℭ𝔩𝔬𝔰𝔢𝔱, | OR | RICH CABINET: | Stored with all manner of | RARE RECEIPTS | FOR | *Preserving, Candying and Cookery.* | Very Pleasant and Beneficial to all | Ingenious Persons of the FEMALE SEX. | [rule] | To which is added, | A SUPPLEMENT, | *PRESENTED* | To all Ingenious LADIES, | and GENTLEWOMEN. | [rule] | By *Hannah Wolley.* | [rule] | The Third EDITION. | [rule] | *LONDON,* | Printed for *Richard Lowndes* at the *White* | *Lion* in *Duck-Lane,* near *West-* | *Smithfield,* 1675.

Title-page for the supplement:

[within a border of type ornaments] A | SUPPLEMENT | TO THE | *QUEEN-LIKE* | CLOSET; | OR | A LITTLE | OF | EVERY THING. | PRESENTED | To all

Ingenious Ladies, | and Gentlewomen. | [rule] | By *HANNA WOOLLEY*. | [rule] | *LONDON,* | Printed by *T.R.* for *Richard Lownds,* | and are to be Sold at the Sign of the | *White Lion* in *Duck-Lane*, 1674.

Third edition, London, 1675. Originally published, London, 1670 (item 1062).

12mo. A^6 B-P^{12} Q^{10}, ^{2}A^8 B-I^{12} K^4; 292 leaves, pp. [*12*] 1-344 [*12*], ^{2}[*16*] 1-200. This copy wants leaves A1, A2, ^{2}E1, ^{2}I1-4, 9-12 and ^{2}K1-4.

Illustrations: Engraved frontispiece of five kitchen scenes.

Bibliographies: Oxford, p. 35, in a note; Wing W3284.

Copies: *BMC* and *NUC* (Florida State University and William Andrews Clark Library). Wing adds Glasgow University.

1064. Woolley, Hannah.

[within a border of two rules] 𝔗𝔥𝔢 𝔔𝔲𝔢𝔢𝔫 = 𝔩𝔦𝔨𝔢 𝔠𝔩𝔬𝔰𝔢𝔱, | OR | RICH CABINET: | Stored with all manner of | RARE RECEIPTS | FOR | *Preserving, Candying, and Cookery.* | Very Pleasant and Beneficial to all | Ingenious Persons of the *Female Sex.* | [rule] | *To which is added,* | A SUPPLEMENT, | *PRESENTED* | To all Ingenious LADIES, | and GENTLEWOMEN. | [rule] | By *Hannah Wolley.* | [rule] | The Fourth EDITION. | [rule] | *LONDON,* | Printed for *R. Chiswel* at the *Rose* and | *Crown* in St. *Paul's Church-yard*, and | *T. Sawbridge* at the *Three Flowers-de-* | *luce* in *Little Britain*, 1681.

Title-page for the supplement:

[within a border of type ornaments] A | SUPPLEMENT | TO THE | *QUEEN-LIKE* | CLOSET, | OR | A LITTLE | OF | EVERYTHING. | PRESENTED | To all Ingenious Ladies, | and Gentlewomen. | [rule] | By *HANNAH WOOLLEY.* | [rule] | *LONDON,* | Printed for *R. Chiswel* at the *Rose* and | *Crown* in S. *Paul's Church-yard*, and | *T. Sawbridge* at the *Three Flowers-de-* | *Luce* in *Little-Britain*, 1680.

Fourth edition, London, 1681. Originally published, London, 1670 (item 1062).

12mo. A^6 B-Q^{12} R^6, ^{2}A^8 B-I^{12} K^4; 300 leaves, pp. [*12*] 1-337, 336, 337, 348, 341, 340, 341, 343[=344] [*28*], ^{2}[*16*] 1-200. A1 blank.

Bibliographies: Oxford, p. 35, in a note; Schraemli (1) 509; Wing W3285.

Copies: *BMC* and *NUC* (John Crerar Library and New York State Library). Wing adds Glasgow University.

1065. Worlidge, John.

[within a border of two rules] Systema Agriculturae; | The MYTSTERY of | HUSBANDRY | DISCOVERED: | Treating of the several New and most Advantagious Ways | OF | *Tilling, Planting, Sowing, Manuring, Ordering, Improving* | Of all sorts of | [in three columns: column one] GARDENS, | ORCHARDS, | }{ | [column two] MEADOWS, | PASTURES, | }{ | [column three] CORN-LANDS, | WOODS & COPPICES. [end columns] | As also of | FRUITS, CORN, GRAIN, PULSE, NEW-HAYS, CATTLE, | FOWL, BEASTS, BEES, SILK-WORMS, *&c.* | With an Account of the several *INSTRUMENTS* and | *ENGINES* used in the PROFESSION. | To which is added | *KALENDARIUM RUSTICUM:* | OR, | The HUSBANDMANS Monthly Directions. | ALSO | The PROGNOSTICKS of *Dearth,* *Scarcity, Plenty, Sickness, Heat,* | *Cold, Frost, Snow, Winds, Rain, Hail, Thunder,* *&c.* | AND | *DICTIONARIUM RUSTICUM:* | OR, | The Interpretation of RUSTICK TERMS. | The whole WORK being of great Use and Advantage to | all that delight in that most NOBLE PRACTICE. | [rule] | *The Second Edition, carefully Corrected and Amended*; *with many large* | *and useful Additions throughout the whole Work: By the* Author. | [rule] | Published for the Common Good: By *J. W.* Gent | [rule] | Virgil. *O fortunatos nimium, sua si bona norint,* | *Agricolas.* ——— | [rule] | *LONDON:* Printed by *J. C.* for *T. Dring*; and are to be sold by *Charles Smith* | and *Tho. Burrell,* at the *Angel* neer the Inner-Temple-gate, and the *Golden Bull* | under St. *Dunstans* Church in *Fleet-street*. 1675.

Title-page of the second part:

Kalendarium Rusticum: | OR, | MONETHLY DIRECTIONS | FOR THE | HUSBANDMAN. | [rule] | Being CHAP. XIII. | [rule] | SHEWING | The most Seasonable Times for the performing of his | Rural Affairs | Throughout the YEAR. | [rule] | *Operum memor esto tempestivorum* | *Omnium*———Hesiod. | [rule] | [ornament] | *LONDON:* | Printed by *J. C.* for *Tho. Dring*, in the Year 1675.

Title-page of the third part:

Dictionarium Rusticum; | OR, THE | INTERPRETATIONS | AND | SIGNIFICATIONS | OF SEVERAL | RUSTICK TERMS | Used in several places of |

ENGLAND: | And also the Names of several | INSTRUMENTS and MATERIALS | Used in this | MYSTERY of *AGRICULTURE;* | And other Intricate Expressions dispersed in our | Rural Authors. | [ornament] | *London:* Printed in the Year 1675.

Second edition, London, 1675. Originally published, London, 1669.

Folio: A² C-D⁴ E² e⁴ F-Zz⁴; 180 leaves, pp. [*32*] 1-324 [*4*].

Illustrations: Woodcuts in the text.

Bibliographies: Fussell (1) pp. 69-70; Wing W3599.

Copies: *BMC* and *NUC* (13 copies). Wing (10 copies).

1066. Worlidge, John.

[within a border of two rules] Systema Agriculturae; | The MYSTERY of | HUSBANDRY | DISCOVERED. | Treating of the several New and most Advantagious Ways | OF | *Tilling, Planting, Sowing, Manuring, Ordering, Improving* | Of all sorts of | [in three columns: column one] GARDENS, | ORCHARDS, | }{ | [column two] MEADOWS, | PASTURES, | }{ | [column three] CORN-LANDS, | WOODS & COPPICES. [end columns] | As also of | FRUITS, CORN, GRAIN, PULSE, NEW-HAYS, CATTLE, | FOWL, BEASTS, BEES, SILK-WORMS, FISH, &c. | With an Account of the several *INSTRUMENTS* and | *ENGINES* used in the PROFESSION. | To which is added | *KALENDARIUM RUSTICUM:* | OR, | The HUSBANDMANS Monthly Directions. | ALSO | The PROGNOSTICKS of *Dearth, Scarcity, Plenty, Sickness, Heat* | *Cold, Frost, Snow, Winds, Rain, Hail, Thunder,* &c. | AND | *DICTIONARIUM RUSTICUM:* | OR, | The Interpretation of RUSTICK TERMS. | The whole WORK being of great Use and Advantage to | all that delight in that most NOBLE PRACTISE. | [rule] | *The* Fourth Edition *carefully Corrected and Amended, with one whole Section* | *added, and many large and useful Additions throughout the whole Work.* | [rule] | By *J. W.* Gent. | [rule] | Virgil. *O fortunatos nimium, sua si bona norint,* | *Agricolas.*——— | [rule] | *LONDON,* Printed for *Tho. Dring*, at the *Harrow* at the corner | of *Chancery-lane* in *Fleetstreet,* 1687.

Title-page of the second part:

Kalendarium Rusticum: | OR, | MONTHLY DIRECTIONS | FOR THE | HUSBANDMAN. | [rule] | Being CHAP. XIII. | [rule] | SHEWING | The most SEASONABLE TIMES for the performing | OF HIS | RURAL AFFAIRS | Throughout the Year. | [rule] | *Operum memor esto tempestivorum* |

Omnium——Hesiod. | [rule] | [four rows of six, four, two and one fleur de lis] | [rule] | *LONDON*, | Printed for *Thomas Dring*, at the *Harrow* over against | the *Inner Temple-Gate* in *Fleetstreet*. 1687.

Title-page of the third part:

Dictionarium Rusticum; | OR, THE | INTERPRETATIONS | AND | SIGNIFICATIONS | OF SEVERAL | RUSTICK TERMS | Used in several Places of | ENGLAND: | And also the Names of several | INSTRUMENTS and MATERIALS | Used in this | MYSTERY of *AGRICULTURE*; | And other Intricate Expressions dispersed in our | Rural Authors. | [rule] | *LONDON*, | Printed for *Thomas Dring*, over against the Inner Temple-Gate in | *Fleet-Street*, 1687.

Fourth edition, London, 1687. Originally published, London, 1669.

Folio: $\pi^2 \chi^2 A^2 a\text{-}b^2 *^4 B\text{-}Ss^4 Tt^2$; 176 leaves, pp. [*28*] 1-72, 83-262 [*2*] [*263*] 264-326 [*6*].

Illustrations: Engraved frontispiece printed on $\pi 2^r$, one engraved plate before leaf D1 and woodcuts in the text.

Bibliographies: Fussell (1) pp. 69-70; Simon BG1633; Wing W3601.

Copies: *BMC* and *NUC* (7 copies). Wing (8 copies).

1067. Worlidge, John.

[within a border of two rules] *Systema Horti-culturae:* | OR, | The Art of Gardening. | In Three BOOKS. | The I. Treateth of the Excellency, Scituation, | Soil, Form, Walks, Arbours, Springs, Fountains, Wa- | ter-works, Grotto's, Statues, and other Ornaments of | Gardens, with many Rules, and Directions, concern- | ing the same. | The II. Treateth of all sorts of Trees planted for | Ornament of Shade, Winter-Greens, Flower-Trees, | and Flowers, that are propagated or preserv'd in the | Gardens of the best Florists, and the best Ways and | Methods of Raising, Planting, and Improving them. | The III. Treateth of the Kitchin Garden, and | of the variety of Plants propagated for Food, or for any | Culinary Uses: With many general and particular | Rules, and Instructions, for the making Hot Beds, al- | tering and enriching any sort of Garden ground, Wa- | tering, Cleansing, and Adapting all sorts of Earth to | the various Plants that are usually planted therein. To | the great Improvement of every sort of Land, as well | for Use and Profit, as for Ornament and Delight. | Illustrated with Sculptures, representing the Form of | Gardens, according to the newest Models.

| [rule] | By *J. Woolridge*, Gent. | [rule] | 𝕮𝖍𝖊 𝕮𝖍𝖎𝖗𝖉 𝕰𝖉𝖎𝖙𝖎𝖔𝖓, 𝖜𝖎𝖙𝖍 𝖑𝖆𝖗𝖌𝖊 𝕬𝖉𝖉𝖎𝖙𝖎𝖔𝖓𝖘. | [rule] | *London:* Printed for *Tho. Dring*, at the *Harrow* over against | the *Inner-Temple*-Gate in *Fleetstreet*. 1688.

Title-page of the second part:

THE | GARDENERS | Monthly Directions. | SHEWING | *What is Necessary to be done* | *throughout the Year*, | IN | Sowing, Planting, and Propagating, the | most valuable of the Shrubs, Flow- | ers, Esculents, and other Hortensian | Plants before Treated of. | AND | What Ornamental Trees | and Flowers, are in their Prime | in each MONTH. | [two rules] | *LONDON:* | Printed for *Tho. Dring*, at the *Harrow*, over against | the *Inner Temple-gate* in *Fleetstreet*. 1688.

Third edition, London, 1688. Originally published, London, 1677.

8vo. A-T^8 V^4; 156 leaves, pp. [*2*] i-x [*4*] 1-278 [*18*].

Illustrations: Engraved title-page and two engraved plates by F. H. Van Houe.

Bibliographies: Fussell (1) p. 71; Henrey I.374; Wing W3606.

Copies: *BMC* and *NUC* (7 copies). Wing (5 copies).

1068. Worlidge, John.

[within a border of two rules] *Systema Horti-culturae:* | OR, | The Art of Gardening. | In Three BOOKS. | The I. Treateth of the Excellency, Scituation, | Soil, Form, Walks, Arbours, Springs, Fountains, Wa- | ter-works, Grotto's, Statues, and other Ornaments of | Gardens, with many Rules, and Directions, concern- | ing the same. | The II. Treateth of all sorts of Trees planted for | Ornament of Shade, Winter-Greens, Flower-Trees, | and Flowers, that are propagated or preserv'd in the | Gardens of the best Florists, and the best Ways and | Methods of Raising, Planting, and Improving them. | The III. Treateth of the Kitchin-Garden, and of | the Variety of Plants propagated for Food, or for any | Culinary Uses: With many general and particular | Rules, and Instructions, for the making Hot Beds, al- | tering and enriching any sort of Garden-ground, Wa- | tering, Cleansing, and Adapting all sorts of Earth to | the various Plants that are usually planted therein. To | the great Improvement of every sort of Land, as well | for Use and Profit, as for Ornament and Delight. | Illustrated with Sculptures, representing the Form of | Gardens, according to the Newest Models. | [rule] | 𝕮𝖍𝖊 𝕱𝖔𝖚𝖗𝖙𝖍 𝕰𝖉𝖎𝖙𝖎𝖔𝖓. 𝕿𝖔 𝖜𝖍𝖎𝖈𝖍 𝖎𝖘 𝖆𝖉𝖉𝖊𝖉 𝖙𝖍𝖊 𝕲𝖆𝖗𝖉𝖊𝖓𝖊𝖗'𝖘 | 𝕸𝖔𝖓𝖙𝖍𝖑𝖞

𝕯𝖎𝖗𝖊𝖈𝖙𝖎𝖔𝖓𝖘. | [rule] | By *J. Woolridge*, Gent. | [rule] | *LONDON*, | Printed for *Will. Freeman*, at the *Bible* over against | the *Middle-Temple-Gate* in *Fleetstreet*, 1700.

Title-page of the second part:

THE | GARDENER'S | Monthly Directions, | Shewing what is | NECESSARY to be DONE | Throughout the | YEAR, | IN | Sowing, Planting, and Propagating | the most Valuable of the Shrubs, Flow- | ers, Esculents, and other Hortensian | Plants before treated of: | And what | Ornamental Trees and Flowers | Are in their | PRIME in each MONTH. | [rule] | *LONDON*, Printed for *William Freeman*, at | the *Bible* over against the *Middle Temple-gate* | in *Fleet-street*. 1700.

Fourth edition, London, 1700. Originally published, London, 1677.

8vo. A-T⁸ V⁴; 156 leaves, pp. [*4*] i-viii [*4*] 1-278 [*18*].

Illustrations: Engraved title-page on A1ʳ and three engraved plates by F. H. Van Houe.

Bibliographies: Wing W3606A.

Copies: *NUC* (8 copies).

1069. Worlidge, John.

[within a border of two rules] *Vinetum Britannicum*: | OR, A | TREATISE | OF | CIDER, | And such other Wines and Drinks that | are extracted from all manner of Fruits | Growing in this Kingdom. | Together with the Method of | Propagating all sorts of Vinous | FRUIT-TREES. | And a Description of the new-invented | INGENIO or MILL, | For the more expeditious and | better making of CIDER. | And also the right Method of making | Metheglin and Birch-Wine. | [rule] | With Copper-Plates. | [rule] | By *J. W.* Gent. | [rule] | *LONDON*: Printed by *J. C.* for *Tho. Dring*, over against the | Inner-temple-gate; and *Tho. Burrel*, at the Golden-ball under | St. *Dunstan's* Church in *Fleet-street*. 1676.

First edition, London, 1676.

8vo. [A]² B⁸ b² C-O⁸; 108 leaves, pp. [*24*] 1-186 [*6*].

Illustrations: Engraved frontispiece on A1ᵛ showing cider presses and two plates facing pp. 82 and 100.

Bibliographies: Bitting, p. 504; Fussell (1) p. 70; Gabler, p. 315; Simon BG 1632; Wing W3608.

Copies: *BMC* and *NUC* (9 copies). Wing adds Bodleian Library and Cambridge.

1070. Worlidge, John.

[within a border of two rules] *Vinetum Britannicum:* | OR A | TREATISE | OF | CIDER, | And other Wines and Drinks extracted | from Fruits Growing in this Kingdom. | With the Method of Propagating all | sorts of Vinous FRUIT-TREES. | And a DESCRIPTION of the New-Invented | INGENIO or MILL, | For the more expeditious making of *CIDER*. | And also the right way of making | METHEGLIN and BIRCH-WINE. | [rule] | The Second Impression, much Enlarged. | [rule] | To which is added, A Discourse teach- | ing the best way of Improving BEES. | [rule] | With Copper Plates. | [rule] | By *J. Worlidge*. Gent. | [rule] | *LONDON,* | Printed for *Thomas Dring*, over against the Inner-Tem- | ple-gate; and *Thomas Burrel*, at the Golden-ball under | St. *Dunstan*'s Church in *Fleet-street*. 1678.

Title-page of the second part:

APIARIUM; | OR A | DISCOURSE | OF THE | Government and Ordering | OF | BEES, | With their Nature and Properties, | Tending to the best Way of IMPROVING | them, and to the Discovery of the Falla- | cies that are imposed by some, for pri- | vate Lucre, on the Credulous Lovers | and Admirers of these Insects. | [rule] | The Second Edition. | [rule] | Written by *J. W. Gent*. | [rule] | *LONDON,* | Printed for and Sold by *Thomas Dring* Bookseller, | at the Sign of the *Harrow* at *Chancery*-lane-end | in *Fleet-street*. MDCLXXVIII.

Second edition of *Vinetum Britannicum* and first edition of *Apiarium*, London, 1678. *Vinetum Britannicum* originally published, London, 1676 (item 1069).

8vo. [A]⁴ B-R⁸,²A-D⁸; 164 leaves, pp. [*24*] 1-240, ²[*10*] 1-42 [*12*].

Illustrations: Engraved plate facing p. 106 and engraved illustrations in the text on Al^v, I2^r, K2^v and ²A1^v.

Bibliographies: Fussell (1) p. 70; Gabler, p. 315; Schraemli (1) 511; Wing W3609.

Copies: *BMC* and *NUC* (9 copies). Wing adds Royal Agricultural Society.

1071. Worrall, Joseph.

THE | DOMESTIC | RECEIPT BOOK, | IN TWO PARTS, | CONTAINING 866 AUTHENTICATED | RECIPES, | CHIEFLY ON | DOMESTIC ECONOMY; | PARTICULARLY ADAPTED TO FAMILY ESTABLISHMENTS, AND | CALCULATED TO PROMOTE A CONSIDERABLE SAVING | IN HOUSEHOLD EXPENDITURE. | [short rule] | BY JOSEPH WORRALL. | [short rule] | SECOND EDITION. | [short rule] | "Gather up the fragments that remain that nothing be lost." *− Jesus Christ.* | "The world has not yet learned the riches of frugality." *− Tully.* | "If you would be wealthy, think of saving as well as of getting." *− Dr. Franklin.* | "A penny saved, is two-pence clear." *− Ibid.* | [short rule] | Rochdale: | PRINTED BY J. HARTLEY, YORKSHIRE-STREET. | 1832.

Second edition, Rochdale, 1832. First published, London, also 1832.

175 x 108 mm. [A]⁴ B-N⁶; 76 leaves, pp. [1-9] 10-149 [150] [2]. First leaf and last leaf blank. Publisher's printed blue wrappers.

Bibliographies: Attar 243.2.

Copies: *BMC* and *NUC* (New York Public Library and New York State Library).

1072. Young, Hannah M., 1858-1949.

[Engraved title-page] [in blue] Liebig | [in blue] *Company's* | PRACTICAL | COOKERY | [in white on black] BOOK | [in blue] A collection of new and | [in blue] useful recipes in every | [in blue] branch of cookery | *Compiled by* | *MRS H.M. YOUNG.* | LONDON | *Liebig's Extract of Meat Company, Limited* | 9 FENCHURCH AVENUE, E. C. | 1893 | (All rights reserved). | [short rule] | PRINTED IN GERMANY.

First edition, London, 1893.

172 x 109 mm. [1]¹⁸ [2-3]²⁰; 58 leaves, pp. [2] i-viii [2] 1-104. Publisher's pictorial chromolithographed boards.

Illustrations: Numerous wood engravings in the text.

Bibliographies: Driver 1194.1.

Copies: Driver (Castle Museum, York; Polytechnic Library, Oxford; Swiss Cottage Library, London).

1073. Entry deleted.

1074. The Young Woman's Companion.

THE | 𝔜𝔬𝔲𝔫𝔤 𝔚𝔬𝔪𝔞𝔫'𝔰 ℭ𝔬𝔪𝔭𝔞𝔫𝔦𝔬𝔫: | OR, | FRUGAL HOUSEWIFE. | Containing the most approved Methods of | *PICKLING, PRESERVING, POTTING, COLLARING,* | *CONFECTIONARY,* | Managing and Colouring Foreign Wines and Spirits, making English Wines, | Compounds, &c. &c. | ALSO | THE ART OF COOKERY, | Containing Directions for dressing all kinds Butchers' Meat, Poultry, Game, | Fish, &c. &c. &c. | WITH | THE COMPLETE ART OF CARVING, | Illustrated and made plain by Engravings. | LIKEWISE | INSTRUCTIONS FOR MARKETING. | WITH THE THEORY OF | 𝔅𝔯𝔢𝔴𝔦𝔫𝔤 𝔐𝔞𝔩𝔱 𝔏𝔦𝔮𝔲𝔬𝔯. | TO WHICH ARE ADDED, | *DIRECTIONS FOR LETTER WRITING,* | DRAWING, PAINTING, &c. | AND | SEVERAL VALUABLE MISCELLANEOUS PIECES. | [two short rules] | *Manchester:* | PRINTED BY RUSSELL AND ALLEN, DEANSGATE. | 1811.

First edition, Manchester, 1811.

208 x 126 mm. π^2 a-b^4 A-3X^4 3Y^2 3Z-4A^4; 288 leaves, pp. [*4*] [i] ii-xvi [1] 2-540 [*16*].

Illustrations: Six engraved plates illustrating table settings and carving.

Bibliographies: Oxford, p. 140. Simon BG 1638 lists an 1816 edition.

Copies: No other copy located.

Culinary Chemistry,

EXHIBITING

THE

SCIENTIFIC PRINCIPLES

OF

COOKERY,

WITH CONCISE INSTRUCTIONS FOR PREPARING GOOD AND WHOLESOME
PICKLES, VINEGAR, CONSERVES, FRUIT JELLIES,
MARMALADES,

AND VARIOUS OTHER ALIMENTARY SUBSTANCES EMPLOYED

IN

Domestic Economy,

WITH OBSERVATIONS ON THE CHEMICAL CONSTITUTION AND NUTRITIVE
QUALITIES OF DIFFERENT KINDS OF FOOD.

WITH COPPER PLATES.

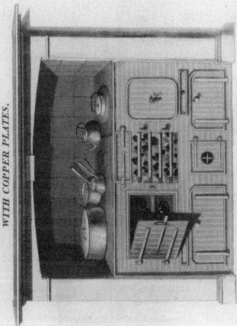

BY FREDRICK ACCUM,

Operative Chemist, Lecturer on Practical Chemistry, on Mineralogy, and on Chemistry applied
to the Arts and Manufactures; Member of the Royal Irish Academy; Fellow of the Linnean Society;
Member of the Royal Academy of Sciences, and of the Royal Society of Arts Berlin, &c. &c.

London:

PUBLISHED BY R. ACKERMANN, 101, STRAND;

1821.

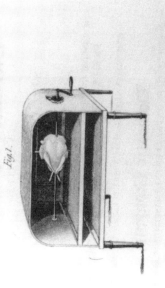

To face Title.

Fig 1.

A TREATISE

ON

ADULTERATIONS OF FOOD,

AND

Culinary Poisons,

EXHIBITING

THE FRAUDULENT SOPHISTICATIONS

OF

BREAD, BEER, WINE, SPIRITUOUS LIQUORS, TEA, COFFEE,

Cream, Confectionery, Vinegar, Mustard, Pepper, Cheese, Olive Oil, Pickles,

AND OTHER ARTICLES EMPLOYED IN DOMESTIC ECONOMY.

AND

Methods of detecting them.

BY FREDRICK ACCUM,

Operative Chemist, Lecturer on Practical Chemistry, Mineralogy, and on Chemistry
applied to the Arts and Manufactures; Member of the Royal Irish Academy;
Fellow of the Linnæan Society; Member of the Royal Academy of
Sciences, and of the Royal Society of Arts of Berlin, &c. &c.

London:

Printed by J. Mallett, 59, Wardour Street, Soho.

SOLD BY LONGMAN, HURST, REES, ORME, AND BROWN,

PATERNOSTER ROW.

1820.

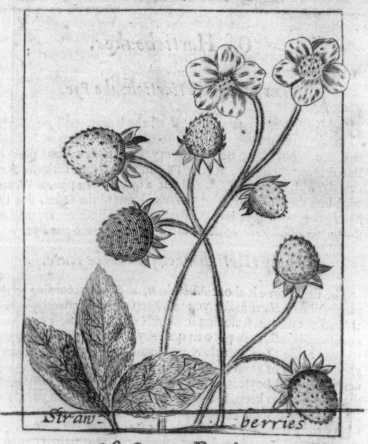

Straw- -berries

Of Straw-Berries.

A Tart of Straw-Berries.

PIck and wash your *Straw-Berries* clean, and put them in the past one by another, as thick as you can, then take *Sugar*, *Cinamon*, and a little *Ginger* finely beaten, and well mingled together, cast them upon the *Straw Berries*, and cover them with the lid finely cut into Lozenges, and so let them bake a quarter of an houre, then take it out, strewing it with a little *Cinamon*, and *Sugar*, and so serve it.

C

of

THE
Englifh Art of Cookery,

ACCORDING TO THE
PRESENT PRACTICE;

BEING A

Complete Guide to all Houfekeepers,

ON A

PLAN ENTIRELY NEW;

CONSISTING OF

THIRTY-EIGHT CHAPTERS.

CONTAINING,

Proper Directions for Marketing, and Truffing of Poultry.
The making Soups and Broths.
Dreffing all Sorts of Fifh.
Sauces for every Occafion.
Boiling and Roafting.
Baking, Broiling, and Frying.
Stews and Hafhes.
Made Difhes of every Sort.
Ragous and Fricafees.
Directions for dreffing ll Sorts of Roots and Vegetables.
All Sorts of Aumlets and Eggs.
Puddings, Pies, Tarts, &c.
Pancakes and Fritters.
Cheefecakes and Cuftards.

Blancmange, Jellies, and Syllabubs.
Directions for the Sick.
Directions for Seafaring Men.
Preferving, Syrups, and Conferves.
Drying and Candying.
All Sorts of Cakes.
Hogs Puddings, Saufages, &c.
Potting, and little cold Difhes.
The Art of Carving.
Collaring, Salting, and Soufing.
Pickling.
To keep Garden Vegetables, &c.
A Catalogue of Things in Seafon.
Made Wines and Cordial Waters.
Brewing.
Englifh and French Bread, &c.

WITH

BILLS OF FARE

FOR

EVERY MONTH IN THE YEAR,

Neatly and correctly engraved on TWELVE COPPER-PLATES.

By RICHARD BRIGGS,

MANY YEARS COOK AT THE GLOBE TAVERN, FLEET-STREET,
THE WHITE HART TAVERN, HOLBORN,
AND NOW AT THE TEMPLE COFFEE-HOUSE.

LONDON:
PRINTED FOR G. G. J. AND J. ROBINSON,
PATER-NOSTER-ROW.
M.DCC.LXXXVIII.

Item no. 578

FRONTISPIECE.

weth well to the ways of her Houshold, and eat the bread of Idleness. Prov. 31 N. 27.

THE
Complete *English* Cook;
OR
PRUDENT HOUSEWIFE.

Being an entire New COLLECTION of the Most Genteel, yet least Expensive RECEIPTS in every Branch of Cookery and good Housewifery.

VIZ.

Roasting,	Fricaseys,	Poting,
Boiling,	Pies, Tarts,	Candying,
Stewing,	Puddings,	Collaring
Ragoos,	Cheesecakes,	Pickling,
Soups,	Custards,	Preserving,
Sauces,	Jellies,	Made Wines, &c.

Together with the ART of MARKETTING. And Directions for placing Dishes on Table for Entertainments: Adorned with proper Cuts.

And many other Things equally Necessary. The Whole made Easy to the Meanest Capacity, and far more Useful to Young Beginners than any Book of the Kind ever yet published.

*In cooking Fowl, or Flesh, or Fish,
Or any nice, or dainty Dish,
With Care peruse this useful Book,
'Twill make you soon a perfect Cook.*

By CATHARINE BROOKS of Red Lyon-Street.

To which is added,

The PHYSICAL DIRECTOR; being near Two Hundred safe and certain Receipts for the Cure of most Disorders incident to the Human Body. Also the whole Art of Clear-Starching, Ironing, &c.

The SECOND EDITION, with the Addition of a great variety of Made Dishes, &c.

LONDON: Printed for the AUTHORESS, and sold by J. COOKE, at Shakespear's - head, in Paternoster-Row.

[Price One Shilling.]

Item no. 585

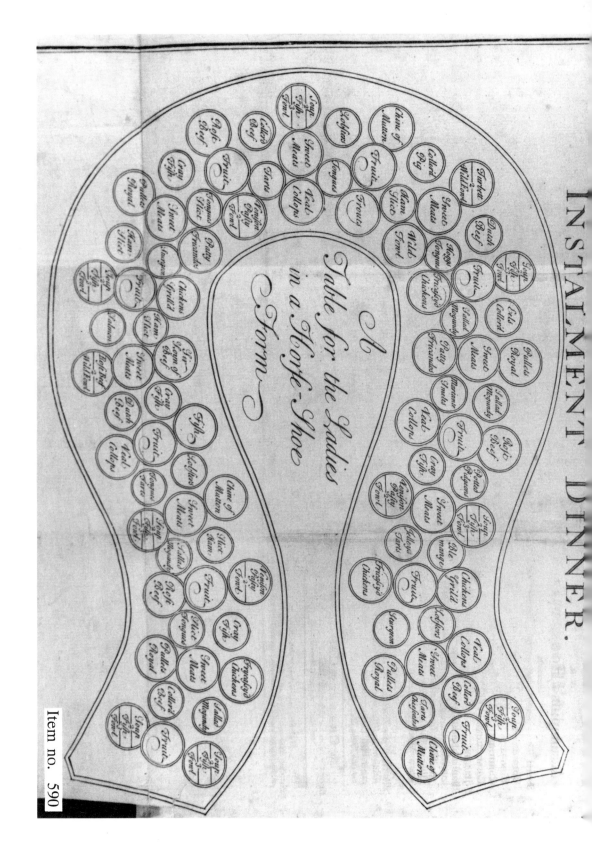

INSTALMENT DINNER.

A Table for the Ladies in a Horse-Shoe Form.

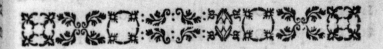

THE
PHILOSOPHY
OF
BREWING.

BY Philofophy here, is not intended that mode of fpeaking in words, and terms, unintelligible to nine tenths of thofe, who may defire a thorough acquaintance with the fubject, but merely that plain fenfe and reafon of things, whence fprings an accurate knowledge of the virtues and qualities of the feveral fpecies of Grain, Vegetables and Seeds that may be ufed in the Brewery, and how the fame may be in various cafes applied, for Health, Pleafure, and Profit.

Wheat is the prime feed, for the manufactures of Bread, Beer, and Spirits; and

The Philosophy of Brewing;

OR, A

COMPENDIUM

OF THE

ENGLISH BREWERY.

BY Philosophy here, is not intended that mode of speaking in words, and terms, unintelligible to nine tenths of those, who may desire a thorough acquaintance with the subject, but merely that plain sense and reason of things, whence springs an accurate knowledge of the virtues and qualities of the several species of Grain, Vegetables and Seeds that may be used in the Brewery, and how the same may be in various cases applied for Health, Pleasure, and Profit.

Wheat is the prime seed, for the manufactures of Bread, Beer, and Spirits;
and

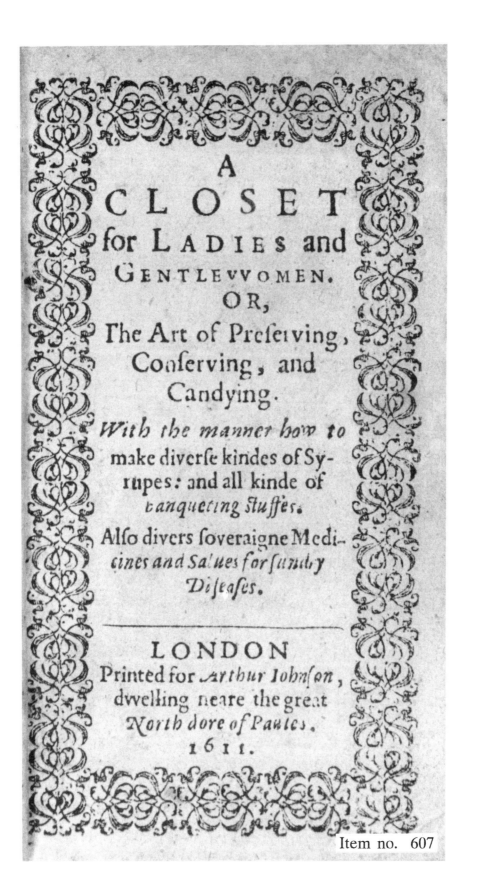

A
CLOSET
for LADIES and
GENTLEVVOMEN.
OR,
The Art of Preserving,
Conserving, and
Candying.

With the manner how to
make diverse kindes of Sy-
rupes: and all kinde of
banqueting stuffes.

Also divers soveraigne Medi-
cines and Salues for sundry
Diseases.

LONDON
Printed for *Arthur Iohnson*,
dvvelling neare the great
North dore of Paules.
1611.

Mᴿ F. COLLINGWOOD.

Mᴿ J. WOOLLAMS.

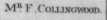

Published as the Act. Directs, by Scatchard, & Whitaker, Avemaria Lane, Apl 24, 1792.

THE
UNIVERSAL COOK,

AND

City and Country Housekeeper.

CONTAINING ALL THE

VARIOUS BRANCHES OF COOKERY:

THE DIFFERENT METHODS OF DRESSING

Butchers Meat, Poultry, Game, and Fish;

AND OF PREPARING

GRAVIES, CULLICES, SOUPS, AND BROTHS;

TO DRESS

ROOTS AND VEGETABLES,

AND TO PREPARE

Little elegant Dishes for Suppers or light Repasts:

TO MAKE ALL SORTS OF

PIES, PUDDINGS, PANCAKES, AND FRITTERS;

CAKES, PUFFS, AND BISCUITS; CHEESECAKES, TARTS, AND
CUSTARDS; CREAMS AND JAMS; BLANC MANGE, FLUMMERY,
ELEGANT ORNAMENTS, JELLIES, AND SYLLABUBS.

The various Articles in

CANDYING, DRYING, PRESERVING, AND PICKLING.

THE PREPARATION OF

HAMS, TONGUES, BACON, &c.

DIRECTIONS FOR

TRUSSING POULTRY, CARVING, AND MARKETING.

THE MAKING AND MANAGEMENT OF

Made Wines, Cordial Waters, and Malt Liquors.

Together with

Directions for Baking Bread, the Management of Poultry and the Dairy; and the
Kitchen and Fruit Garden; with a Catalogue of the various Articles
in Season in the different Months of the Year.

Besides a Variety of

USEFUL AND INTERESTING TABLES.

The Whole Embellished with

The Heads of the Authors, Bills of Fare for every Month in the Year, and
proper Subjects for the Improvement of the Art of Carving,
elegantly engraved on fourteen Copper-Plates.

By FRANCIS COLLINGWOOD, AND JOHN WOOLLAMS,

Principal Cooks at the Crown and Anchor Tavern in the Strand,
Late from the London Tavern.

LONDON:

PRINTED BY R. NOBLE, FOR J. SCATCHERD AND J. WHITAKER,
No. 12, AVE-MARIA-LANE.

1792.

Item no. 625

PROFESSED
COOKERY:

CONTAINING

BOILING,	POTTING,
ROASTING,	PICKLING,
PASTRY,	MADE-WINES,
PRESERVING,	GELLIES, and

Part of CONFECTIONARIES.

WITH

An ESSAY upon the LADY's ART of COOKERY.

By *ANN COOK,*
Teacher of the true ART of COOKERY.

NEWCASTLE UPON TYNE:

Printed by J. WHITE, and fold by the AUTHOR, at her Houfe in the *Groat-market.* M.DCC.LIV.

Price FIVE SHILLINGS.

THE NEW LONDON COOKERY,

AND

COMPLETE DOMESTIC GUIDE,

BY A LADY.

LONDON.

COOKERY.

LONDON.
PUBLISHED BY JANE AND WEBLEY, 11, IVY LANE, PATERNOSTER ROW.

THE
COURT & KITCHIN
Things of Reign of
ELIZABETH,

Commonly called
Joan Cromwel,

THE
Wife of the late Usurper,

Truly,
Described and Represented,

And now
Made Publick for general
Satisfaction.

London, Printed by Tho. Milbourn, for Randal Taylor in St. Martins Le Grand, 1664.

From feigned glory, & Usurped Throne
And all the Greatnesse to me falsly showne
And from the Arts of Government set free
See how Protectresse & a Drudge agree

THE CLOSET

Of the Eminently Learned

Sir *Kenelme Digby* Kt.

OPENED:

Whereby is Discovered

Several ways for making of

Metheglin, Syder, Cherry-Wine, &c.

TOGETHER WITH

Excellent Directions

FOR

COOKERY:

As also for

Preserving, Conserving, Candying, &c.

Published by his Son's Consent.

The Third Edition Corrected.

LONDON:

Printed by *H. C.* for *H. Brome,* at the
West-end of St. *Pauls,* 1677.

The truly Learned and Hono:ble
Sr. *Kenelme Digby* Kt. Chancellor
to the *Q: Mother*
Aged 6s.

Printed for *Henry Brome* 1674

Plaūts
Sun: Powder
his Cookery
Ree:ūm Phyſick &c
Sir Digby of Bodies

THE
Manner of Making
OF
COFFEE, TEA,
AND
CHOCOLATE.

As it is used

In most parts of *Europe, Asia, Africa,* and *America.*

With their Vertues.

Newly done out of French, and Spanish.

LONDON:

Printed for *William Crook* at the *Green Dragon* without *Temple Bar* near *Devereux* Court, 1685.

Harriet

Mrs *Mary Eales's*

RECEIPTS.

CONFECTIONER to her late MAJESTY Queen *ANNE*.

LONDON:

Printed by H. MEERE in *Black-Fryers*, and to be had at Mr. *Cooper's* at the *Three Pidgeons* the lower End of *Bedford-Street*, near the *New Exchange* in the *Strand*. MDCCXVIII.

ſone coꝛrupted being eaten. Of the iuyce of them may be made a ſyꝛope, very holſome agaynſt the diſtemperance of coler, wherof pꝛocedeth a ſtyn=kynge bꝛeathe, they be colde in the fyꝛſte degree, and moyſte in the ſeconde.

❡ Of Appulles.

AL appulles eaten ſone after that they be ga thered, are cold, hard to digeſt, and do make yll and coꝛrupted bloudde, but beinge well kepte vntyll the nexte wynter, oꝛ the yere folowyng, ea=ten after meales, they are right holſome, and doo confirme the ſtomake, and make good digeſtion, ſpecially if they be roſted oꝛ baken, moſt pꝛoperly in a cholerike ſtomake. They are beſte pꝛeſerued in hony, ſo ẙ one touch not an other. The roughe taſted appuls are holſome, where the ſtomake is weake by diſtemperance of heate oꝛ moche moy-ſture. The bytter appuls, where that griefe is in=creaced. The ſoure appuls, where the matter is congeled oꝛ made thycke with heate. In diſtem-perature of heate and dꝛythe by dꝛynkyng moch wine, they haue ben found cõmodious: being ea-ten at nyght, going to bedde, without dꝛynkynge to them: they be cold and moiſt in the firſt degree.

❡ Of Quynces.

QUynces be colde ⁊ dꝛye, eaten afoꝛe meale, they bynde and reſtrayne the ſtomake, that it may not digeſt well the mete, except that they be roſted oꝛ ſodden, the coꝛe taken out, and

myꝛt

THE
London Art of Cookery,

AND

HOUSEKEEPER's COMPLETE ASSISTANT.

On a NEW PLAN.

Made Plain and Easy to the Underſtanding of every HOUSEKEEPER, COOK, and SERVANT in the Kingdom.

CONTAINING,

Proper Directions for the Choice of all Kinds of Proviſions.

Roaſting and Boiling all Sorts of Butchers Meat, Poultry, Game, and Fiſh.

Sauces for every Occaſion.

Soups, Broths, Stews, and Haſhes.

Made Diſhes, Ragoos, and Fricaſſees.

All Sorts of Pies and Puddings.

Proper Inſtructions for dreſſing Fruits and Vegetables.

Pickling, Potting, and Preſerving.

The Preparation of Hams, Tongues, and Bacon.

The whole Art of Confectionary.

Tarts, Puffs, and Paſties.

Cakes, Cuſtards, Jams, and Jellies.

Drying, Candying, and Preſerving Fruits, &c.

Made Wines, Cordial Waters, and Malt Liquors.

To which is added,

AN APPENDIX,

Containing

Conſiderations on Culinary Poiſons; Directions for making Broths, &c. for the Sick; a Liſt of Things in Seaſon in the different Months of the Year; Marketing Tables, &c. &c.

Embelliſhed with

A HEAD of the AUTHOR, and a BILL of FARE for every Month in the Year, elegantly engraved on Thirteen Copper-plates.

By JOHN FARLEY,

PRINCIPAL COOK AT THE LONDON TAVERN.

LONDON:

Printed for JOHN FIELDING, No. 23, Pater-noſter Row; and J. SCAT-CHERD and J. WHITAKER, No. 12, Ave Maria Lane, 1783.

[Price Six Shillings Bound.]

Mr. JOHN FARLEY,

Principal Cook at the London Tavern.

Publiſhed Jan.1. 1783. by I. Fielding, N.º 23, Pater-noſter Row, I. Scatherd & I. Whitaker, N.º 12, Ave Maria Lane.

THE ROYAL

ENGLISH AND FOREIGN

CONFECTIONER:

A PRACTICAL TREATISE ON THE

ART OF CONFECTIONARY IN ALL ITS BRANCHES;

COMPRISING

ORNAMENTAL CONFECTIONARY ARTISTICALLY DEVELOPED;

DIFFERENT METHODS OF PRESERVING FRUITS, FRUIT PULPS, AND JUICES IN BOTTLES, THE PREPARATION OF JAMS AND JELLIES, FRUIT, AND OTHER SYRUPS, SUMMER BEVERAGES, AND A GREAT VARIETY OF NATIONAL DRINKS; WITH DIRECTIONS FOR MAKING DESSERT CAKES, PLAIN AND FANCY BREAD, CANDIES, BONBONS, COMFITS, SPIRITUOUS ESSENCES, AND CORDIALS.

ALSO,

THE ART OF ICE-MAKING, AND THE ARRANGEMENT AND GENERAL ECONOMY OF FASHIONABLE DESSERTS.

BY

CHARLES ELMÉ FRANCATELLI.

PUPIL TO THE CELEBRATED CARÊME, AND LATE MAITRE-D'HOTEL TO HER MAJESTY THE QUEEN;
AUTHOR OF "THE MODERN COOK," "THE COOK'S GUIDE," AND
"COOKERY FOR THE WORKING CLASSES."

With numerous Illustrations in Chromo-Lithography.

LONDON:

CHAPMAN AND HALL, 193, PICCADILLY.

1862.

[The right of Translation is reserved.]

FRONTISPIECE

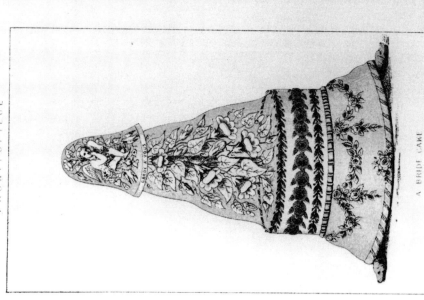

A BRIDE CAKE

THE
ART
OF
COOKERY,

Made PLAIN and EASY;

Which far exceeds any THING of the Kind ever yet Published.

CONTAINING,

BY A LADY.

LONDON:

Printed for the AUTHOR; and sold at Mrs. *Ashburn*'s, a China-Shop, the Corner of *Fleet-Ditch*. MDCCXLVII.

[*Price* 3 s. 6. *stitch'd, and* 5 s. *bound.*]

Item no. 695

THE
Compleat Confectioner:

OR, THE
Whole Art of Confectionary
Made PLAIN and EASY.

SHEWING,

The various Methods of PRESERVING and CANDYING, both dry and liquid, all Kinds of FRUIT, FLOWERS and HERBS; the different Ways of CLARIFYING SUGAR; and the Method of Keeping FRUIT, NUTS and FLOWERS fresh and fine all the Year round.

ALSO

DIRECTIONS for making

ROCK-WORKS and CANDIES,
BISCUITS,
RICH CAKES,
CREAMS,
CUSTARDS,
JELLIES,
WHIP SYLLABUBS, and CHEESE-CAKES of all SORTS,
ENGLISH WINES of all Sorts,

STRONG CORDIALS,
SIMPLE WATERS,
MEAD, OILS, &c.
SYRUPS of all Kinds,
MILK PUNCH that will keep twenty Years,
KNICKNACKS and TRIFLES for DESERTS, &c.

LIKEWISE,

The Art of making ARTIFICIAL FRUIT, with the Stalks in it, so as to resemble the natural Fruit.

To which are added,

Some BILLS of FARE for DESERTS for private FAMILIES.

By H. GLASSE, Author of the ART of COOKERY.

LONDON
Printed: And Sold at Mrs. ASHBURNER's China Shop, the Corner of *Fleet Ditch*; at YEWD's Hat Warehouse, near *Somerset House*; at KIRK's Toyshop, in *St. Paul's* Church Yard; at DEARD's Toyshop, facing *Arlington-Street, Piccadilly*; By I. POTTINGER, at the *Royal Bible*, in *Pater-noster Row*; and by J. WILLIAMS, opposite *St. Dunstan's* Church, *Fleet-street*.

Albinia Mathias. 1769

THE
Servant's Directory,

OR

HOUSEKEEPER's COMPANION:

Wherein the Duties of the

CHAMBER-MAID,		LANDERY-MAID,
NURSERY-MAID,		SCULLION, *or*
HOUSE-MAID,		UNDER-COOK,

Are fully and diſtinctly explained.

To which is annexed

A Diary, or Houſe-keeper's Pocket-Book

For the whole Y E A R.

W I T H

Directions for keeping Accounts with Tradeſmen, and
many other Particulars, fit to be known by the Miſtreſs
of a Family.

By H. G L A S S,

Author of *The Art of Cookery made plain and eaſy.*

L O N D O N:

Printed for the AUTHOR; and ſold by W. JOHNSTON in *Ludgate ſtreet*;
at Mrs. WHARTON's, the *Blue Coat-Boys* near the *Royal-Exchange*, at
Mrs. ASHBURNHAM's China-Shop the Corner of *Fleet-Ditch*,
Mr. VAUGHAN's, Upholder in *Prince's ſtreet, Leiceſter-Fields*, and by
all the Bookſellers in Town and Country. M DCC LX.

N. B. *This Book is entered in the Hall-book of the Company of Stationers.*

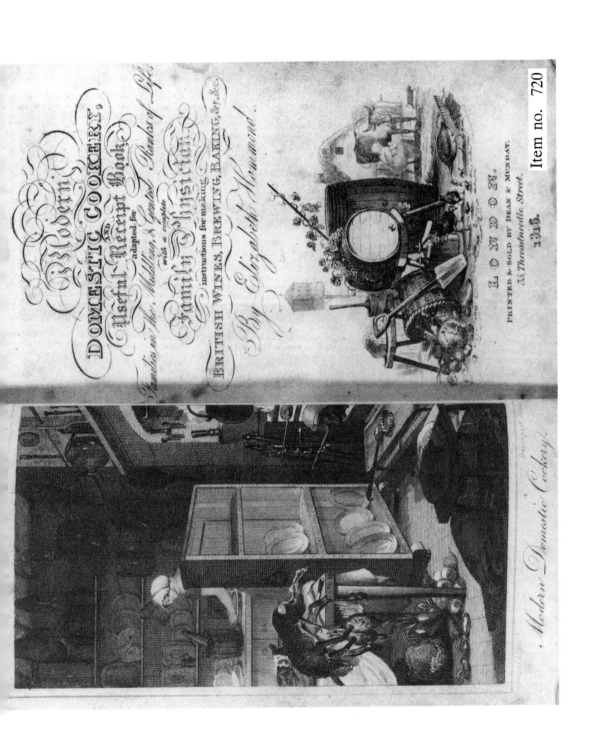

Modern
DOMESTIC COOKERY,
AND
Useful Receipt Book,
adapted for
Families in the Middling & Genteel Ranks of Life.

with a complete
Family Physician
instructions for making
BRITISH WINES, BREWING, BAKING, &c.&c.

By Elizabeth Hammond.

LONDON.
PRINTED & SOLD BY DEAN & MUNDAY,
35, Threadneedle Street.
1845.

Modern Domestic Cookery.

THE
FAMILY FRIEND,

OR

Housekeeper's Instructor:

CONTAINING

A VERY COMPLETE COLLECTION

OF

ORIGINAL & APPROVED

Receipts

IN

EVERY BRANCH

OF

COOKERY, CONFECTIONARY,

&c.

BY PRISCILLA HASLEHURST,

Who lived *Twelve Years* as Housekeeper
in the families of *Wm. Bethell, Esq.* of Rice Park, near Beverley ; *Mrs. Joddrell,* of Manchester ;
and others of the greatest respectability.

Sheffield:
Printed by J. Montgomery, Iris-Office, Hartshead,
1802.

Engrav'd for Haywoods New Present for a Servant Maid

NEW PRESENT
FOR A
SERVANT-MAID:

CONTAINING

RULES for her MORAL CONDUCT both with respect to Herself and her Superiors:

The Whole ART of COOKERY, PICKLING, PRESERVING, &c. &c. and every other Direction necessary to be known in order to render her a Complete, Useful, and Valuable Servant.

In TEN BOOKS.

I. Necessary *Cautions* and *Precepts* for gaining Goodwill and Esteem.

II. *Directions* for *Marketing*; er the Method of Chusing all Kinds of Butchers Meat, Fish, Fowl, &c. with Instructions for Carving.

III. The *Whole Art of Cookery* fully displayed, both with regard to Dressing plain Victuals, and also that of made Dishes, Soups, Broths, &c. Together with the best Methods of *Pickling* all Kinds of Fruits, Buds, Flowers, &c.

IV. The *Art of Preserving* the most useful Fruits, &c.

V. The Method of *Candying* the *Fruits*, &c. generally kept in a Family.

VI. The best Methods of *Making* all Kinds of *English Wines*, and giving them the true Flavour of those imported from abroad.

VII. The *Whole Art of Distillation*; with the Methods of making the Cordial and Sweet-scented Waters hitherto used in England, and also those imported from other Countries.

VIII. Useful *Family Receipts*.

IX. Some general *Rules* and *Directions* for Mail-Servants.

X. *Instructions* for Carving according to the Terms of Art.

With *Marketing Tables*, and Tables for *Casting-up Expences*, &c.

The Whole interspersed with a great Number of ORIGINAL RECEIPTS, never before published.

By Mrs. HAYWOOD.

LONDON:
Printed for G. PEARCH, No. 12, Cheapside; and H. GARDNER, opposite St. Clement's Church, in the Strand.
M.DCC.LXXI.
[Price Two Shillings.]

Item no. 733

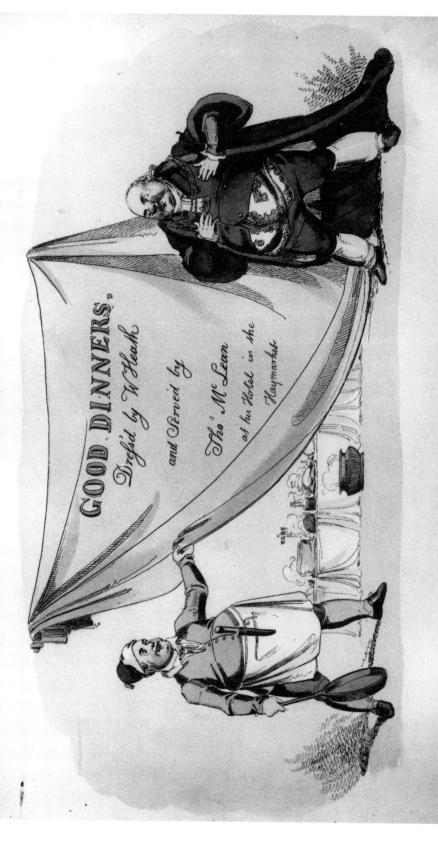

GOOD DINNERS.

Drefs'd by W Heath

and Served by

Tho's Mc Lean

at his Hotel in the

Haymarket

Pub for 1824 by Tho? Mc Lean 26 Haymarket

THE

HOUSEKEEPER's INSTRUCTOR;

OR,

UNIVERSAL FAMILY COOK.

BEING AN AMPLE AND CLEAR DISPLAY OF THE

ART OF COOKERY

IN ALL ITS VARIOUS BRANCHES.

CONTAINING

PROPER DIRECTIONS for DRESSING all Kinds of
BUTCHER's MEAT, POULTRY, GAME, FISH, &c.

ALSO, THE

Method of preparing Soups, Hashes, and Made Dishes;

WITH

The Whole Art of Confectionary, Pickling, Preserving, &c.

LIKEWISE

The making and keeping in Perfection British Wines;

AND

PROPER RULES FOR BREWING MALT LIQUOR,
As well for Family Consumption as the Requst of private Victuals.

TO WHICH IS ADDED,

The Complete Art of Carving,

ILLUSTRATED WITH ENGRAVINGS,
Explaining, by proper References, the Manner which the Young Practitioner
may acquit himself at Table with Elegance and Ease.

ALSO,

BILLS OF FARE FOR EVERY MONTH IN THE YEAR;

WITH COPPER-PLATES, DISPLAYING

The Best Manner of decorating a Table;

Whereby every Person will be enabled to add to the Art of Cookery the proper
Disposition of each Article in its respective Station.

TOGETHER WITH

DIRECTIONS FOR MARKETING,

AND THE

MANAGEMENT OF THE KITCHEN AND FRUIT-GARDEN.

The WHOLE formed on so NEW a PLAN, that the Inexperienced will be
instructed, and the practised Cook receive that Information which has
never been made known by any preceding Publication.

By WILLIAM AUGUSTUS HENDERSON,
Who has made the Culinary Art his Study for upwards of Forty Years.

LONDON:

PRINTED AND SOLD BY W. AND J. STRATFORD,
HOLBORN-HILL.

FRONTISPIECE.
Engraved for Henderson's Housekeepers Instructor.

Explanation

How to Cook Onions,

In a Hundred Different Ways.

GEORGIANA HILL.

ROUTLEDGE'S HOUSEHOLD MANUALS.

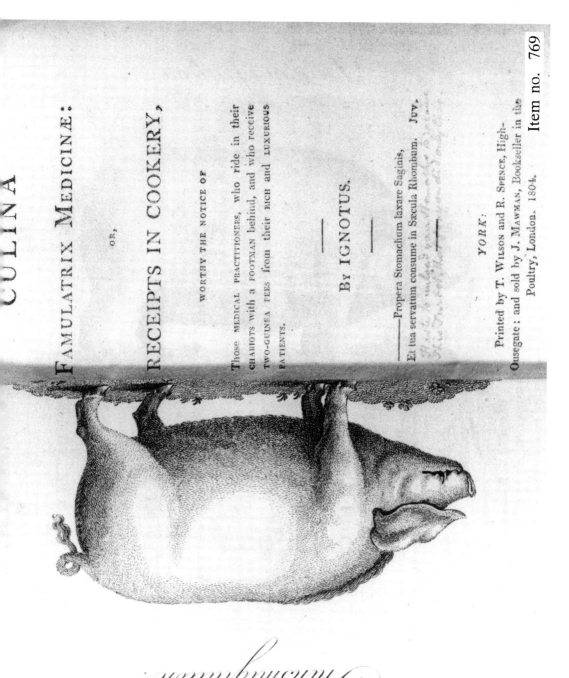

CULINA

FAMULATRIX MEDICINÆ:

OR,

RECEIPTS IN COOKERY,

WORTHY THE NOTICE OF

THOSE MEDICAL PRACTITIONERS, who ride in their CHARIOTS with a FOOTMAN behind, and who receive TWO-GUINEA FEES from their RICH and LUXURIOUS PATIENTS.

BY IGNOTUS.

———

Propera Stomachum laxare Saginis,
Et tua servatum consume in Sæcula Rhombum.   JUV.

———

YORK:

Printed by T. WILSON and R. SPENCE, High-Ousegate: and sold by J. MAWMAN, Bookseller in the Poultry, London. 1804.

Transmogrations

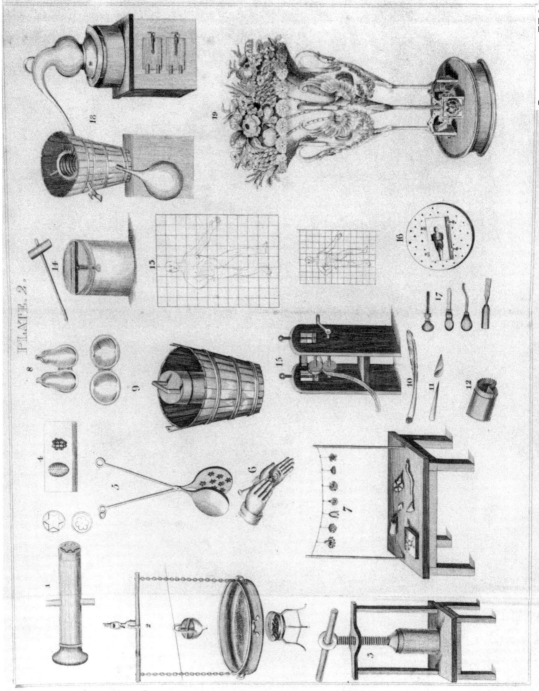

Item no. 781

TWO THOUSAND FIVE HUNDRED

Practical Recipes

IN

FAMILY COOKERY;

In which the whole Art of

PREPARING FOOD AND DRINK FOR THE HUMAN STOMACH

IS SIMPLIFIED AND EXPLAINED,

IN ACCORDANCE TO THE BEST KNOWLEGE OF THE AGE,

And most conducive to the Health and Happiness of our Species;

WITH AN

INTRODUCTION

ON THE

DUTIES OF COOKS AND OTHER SERVANTS:

Observations on the Implements employed in Cooking;

INSTRUCTIONS FOR MARKETING, FOR TRUSSING,

AND FOR PERFORMING THE

HONOURS OF THE TABLE WITH GRACE AND PROPRIETY

IN THE WHOLE

Art of Carving.

BY JAMES JENNINGS,

Author of the Family Cyclopædia.

THE COOKERY STUDY

London Published by Sherwood Gilbert & Piper Jan. 1836.

LONDON:

SHERWOOD, GILBERT, AND PIPER,

PATERNOSTER-ROW.

1837.

A
COLLECTION
Of above Three Hundred
RECEIPTS
IN
Cookery,
Physick *and* Surgery;

For the Use of all
Good Wives, Tender Mothers,
and Careful Nurses.

By several Hands.

LONDON,
Printed for RICHARD WILKIN, at the
King's Head in *St. Paul's Church-yard.*
MDCCXIV.

Royal Cookery; or, *the Complete Court-Cook.*

CONTAINING THE

Choiceſt Receipts

In all the particular Branches of

COOKERY,

Now in Uſe in the QUEEN's

PALACES

OF

St. *James's,* ⎱ *Hampton-Court,* and
Kenſington, ⎰ *Windſor.*

With near Forty Figures (curiouſly engraven on *Copper*)
of the magnificent Entertainments at *Coronations, Inſtal-
ment, Balls, Weddings,* &c. at Court; Alſo Receipts for
making the *Soupes, Jellies, Biſques, Ragoo's, Pattys, Tan-
zies, Forc'd-Meats, Cakes, Puddings,* &c.

By PATRICK LAMB, *Eſq;*

Near 50 Years Maſter-Cook to their late Majeſties
King *Charles* II. King *James* II. King *William* and Queen
Mary, and to Her Preſent Majeſty Queen *ANNE.*

To which are added,

Bills of Fare for every Seaſon in the Year.

London, Printed for *Maurice Atkins,* at the *Golden-Ball* in
S. *Paul's* Church-yard. 1710.

LONDON AT TABLE;

OR,

HOW, WHEN, AND WHERE TO DINE AND

ORDER A DINNER;

AND WHERE TO AVOID DINING.

WITH PRACTICAL HINTS TO COOKS.

TO WHICH IS APPENDED

THE BUTLER'S AND YACHT STEWARD'S MANUAL, AND

TRUISMS FOR THE MILLION.

LONDON:

CHAPMAN AND HALL, 193, PICCADILLY.

MDCCCLI.

THE QUEENS CLOSET

OPENED:

Incomparable Secrets in
Phyfick, Chyrurgery, Preferving, Candying, and Cookery;

As they were prefented unto the
QUEEN

By the moſt Experienced Perſons of our
times, many whereof were honoured with her
own Practiſe, when ſhe pleaſed to deſcend to
theſe more private Recreations.

The Fourth Edition corrected, with many Additions: together with three exact Tables, one of them never before
Printed.

Tranſcribed from the true Copies of her
MAJESTIES own Receipt Books,
by W. M. one of her late Servants.

Vivit poſt funera Virtus

London. Printed for *Nathaniel Brooks* at
the Angel in *Cornhill,* 1658.

Sold by Nat: Brook

COVNTREY
Contentments,
OR
The English Husvvife.

CONTAINING
The inward and outward Vertues which
ought to be in a compleate Woman.

As her skill in Physicke, Surgerie, Extraction
of Oyles, Banqueting-stuffe, Ordering of great Feasts,
Preseruing of all sorts of Wines, Conceited Secrets,
Distillations, Perfumes, ordering of Wooll, Hempe, Flax,
making Cloth, Dying, the knowledge of Dayries,
office of Malting, Oats, their excellent vses
in a Family, Brewing, Baking, and all
other things belonging to
an Houshold.

A Worke generally approued, and now much augmented, purged
and made most profitable and necessarie for all men, and Dedicated to the Honour of the Noble House of Exceter,
and the generall good of this Kingdome.

By G. M.

Printed at *London* by *I.B,* for *R. Iackson,* and are to be sold at his shop
neere Fleet-streete Conduit. 1623.

Perfect Cook:

BEING

The moſt exact Directions for the making all kind of Paſtes, with the perfect way teaching how to Raiſe, Seaſon, and make all ſorts of Pies, Paſties, Tarts, and Florentines, &c. now practiſed by the moſt Famous and Expert Cooks, both French and Engliſh.

AS ALSO

The Perfect Engliſh Cook,

Or right method of the whole Art of Cookery, with the true ordering of French, Spaniſh, and Italian Kickſhaws, with A-la-mode Varieties for Perſons of Honour.

To which is added,

The way of dreſſing all manner of Fleſh, Fowl, and Fiſh, and making admirable Sauces, after the moſt refined way of French and Engliſh. The like never extant.

By Monſieur Marnette.

LONDON,

Printed for Obadiah Blagrave at the Black Bear and Star in St. Pauls Church-Yard, ove Little North-Door, 1686.

The FRENCH Paſtery-Cooke

THE

NEW EXPERIENCED

ENGLISH-HOUSEKEEPER,

FOR THE USE AND EASE

OF

LADIES, HOUSEKEEPERS, COOKS, &c.

WRITTEN PURELY FROM HER OWN PRACTICE

By Mrs. Sarah Martin,

MANY YEARS HOUSEKEEPER

TO THE LATE FREEMAN BOWER ESQ.

OF BAWTRY.

BEING

AN ENTIRE NEW COLLECTION OF ORIGINAL

RECEIPTS WHICH HAVE NEVER APPEARED IN

PRINT, IN EVERY BRANCH OF

COOKERY, CONFECTIONARY, &c.

DONCASTER:

PRINTED FOR THE AUTHORESS

BY D. BOYS.

AND SOLD BY MESS. F. & C. RIVINGTON, ST. PAUL'S CHURCH-YARD,
LONDON.
M DCC XCV.
(Entered at Stationers' Hall.)

THE
Court and Country Cook:

GIVING
New and Plain DIRECTIONS
How to Order all manner of

ENTERTAINMENTS,

And the beſt ſort of the

Moſt exquiſite *a-la-mode* RAGOO's.

Together with

NEW INSTRUCTIONS
FOR
CONFECTIONERS:

SHEWING

How to Preſerve all ſorts of FRUITS, as well
dry as liquid: Alſo,

How to make divers SUGAR-WORKS, and other
fine Pieces of Curioſity;

How to ſet out a DESERT, or Banquet of
SWEET-MEATS to the beſt advantage; And,

How to Prepare ſeveral ſorts of LIQUORS, that
are proper for every Seaſon of the Year.

A WORK more eſpecially neceſſary for Stewards,
Clerks of the Kitchen, Confectioners, Butlers, and
other Officers, and alſo of great uſe in private Families.

Faithfully tranſlated out of French into Engliſh bv J. K.

London: Printed by *W. Onley*, for *A.* and *J. Churchill*, at
the Black Swan in *Pater-noſter-row*, and *M. Gillyflower*
in *Weſtminſter-hall*, 1702.

Item no. 865

MASTERS'
Patent Freezing Cooling Preserving
& CHURNING APPARATUS

OR MACHINE FOR THE RAPID AND ECONOMICAL PRODUCTION OF

CREAM AND WATER ICES,

ALSO CYLINDERS OF PURE ICE FROM SPRING WATER, FOR THE COOLING OF WINE, LEMONADE, BUTTER, LIQUEURS &c.&

AND FOR KEEPING A CONSTANT SUPPLY OF ICED WATER IN THE HOTTEST SEASONS

OR CLIMATES.

Nº1.

The Patent Freezing & Cooling Machine as ready for
Action. The lower part represented as open contains
a Wine Cooler into which the Freezing mixture passes
after it has frozen the Dessert Ices.

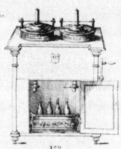

Nº2.

A Patent double Freezing Machine, by which two
Distinct Dessert Ices may be frozen at once by one
person.

Nº3.

The Patent Ice Safe when closed.

Nº4.

The Patent Ice Safe with doors open.

The Patent Ice Safe contains an Ice Well in the centre with a Water Well to which water may be constantly kept Ice cold. The closets
at each end & the Drawers at the bottom are for preserving Game, Fish, &c from the effects of heat & for cooling wine &c. An Air
Pump is fixed to the side for exhausting hot air when required.

Nº5.

A Patent Refrigerator by which a dozen of Wine, Water &c may
be cooled down to the freezing point in a few minutes, at a tri-
fling expense without the assistance of Ice, Snow or Acids.

Nº6.

The Patent Wine Cooler containing a Cylin-
der of Ice produced by the Machine from pure
water while freezing the Dessert Ices.

SOLD BY THE PATENTEE AT THE MANUFACTORY, 56, UPPER CHARLOTTE STREET, FITZROY SQUARE,
AT Nº 180, NEW BOND STREET, AND Nº 7, MANSION HOUSE STREET, OPPOSITE THE M

Item no. 866

Cay mayfey Mary Bailey

THE
Accomplisht Cook,
OR THE
ART and MYSTERY
OF
COOKERY.

Wherein the whole A R T is revealed in a
more easie and perfect Method, than hath
been publisht in any Language.

Expert and ready Wayes for the Dressing of all Sorts of
FLESH, FOWL, and FISH, with variety of SAUCES
proper for each of them; and how to raise all manner
of *Pastes*; the best Directions for all sorts of *Kickshaws*;
also the *Tearms* of CARVING and SEWING.

An exact Account of all *Dishes* for all *Seasons* of the
Year, with other *A la mode Curiosities*.

The Third Edition. with large Additions throughout
the whole Work; besides two hundred Figures of several Forms for all manner of bake't Meats, (either
Flesh or Fish) as Pyes, Tarts, Custards, Cheesecakes,
and Florentines, placed in Tables, and directed to the
Pages they appertain to.

Approved by the fifty five Years Experience and Industry
of ROBERT MAY, in his Attendance on seve-
ral Persons of great Honour.

LONDON,

Printed for N. Brooke, and are to be sold by Tho. Archer
at his shop under the Dyal of St. Dunstans Church
in Fleet Street 1671.

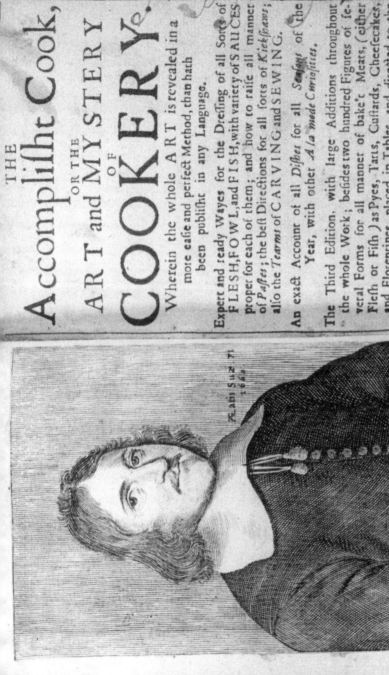

ÆTATIS SUÆ 71
1660

What: wouldst thou view but in one face
all hospitalitie the race
of those that for the Gusto stand,
whose tables a whole Ark comand
of Natures plentie wouldst thou see
this sight, peruse Maijs booke, tis hee.

Five Hundred

NEW RECEIPTS

IN

COOKERY,　　　　PRESERVING,
CONFECTIONARY,　CONSERVING,
PASTRY,　　　　　PICKLING;

AND THE

Several Branches of these ARTS
neceſſary to be known by all good
HOUSEWIVES.

By *JOHN MIDDLETON*,
Cook to his Grace the late Duke of *Bolton*.

Reviſed and Recommended by
Mr. *HENRY HOWARD*.

THOMAS ASTLEY.

LONDON:
Printed for THO. ASTLEY, at the *Roſe*
againſt the North Door of St. *Paul's*.

M DCC XXXIV.

THE

MODERN COOKERY,

WRITTEN UPON

THE MOST APPROVED

AND

ECONOMICAL PRINCIPLES,

AND IN WHICH

EVERY RECEIPT HAS STOOD THE TEST OF EXPERIENCE.

~~~~~~~~~~~~

BY A LADY.

~~~~~~~~~~~~

DERBY:

PRINTED BY AND FOR HENRY MOZLEY.

1818.

The Useful and Entertaining

FAMILY MISCELLANY:

CONTAINING THE

Complete ENGLISH Housekeeper's Companion.

IN WHICH ARE

Near Five Hundred RECEIPTS

IN

COOKERY,   ❀   Making WINES,
PASTRY,   ❀   CANDYING, and
PRESERVING,   ❀   PICKLING.

With plain and very easy INSTRUCTIONS for chusing

All Sorts of EATABLES.

ALSO,

Directions for Carving, with several CUTS explaining in the easiest Manner, the best Way of trussing HARES, and FOWLS; with Forms of placing Dishes on a Table, either in the middling or genteelest Manner.

By Mrs. ISABELLA MOORE,

Who was Twenty Years a worthy and frugal Housekeeper in a private Gentleman's Family, at DUFFIELD near DERBY.

TO WHICH ARE ADDED,

The GENUINE RECEIPTS

FOR

Preparing and Compounding the Principal Medicines made Use of by the late Mr. WARD.

With OBSERVATIONS thereon by J. PAGE, Esq;

ALSO,

The SYREN; Or, CHEARFUL SONGSTER:

CONSISTING

Of a Collection of near SEVENTY approv'd SONGS, suited for those who delight in Harmony, Decency, and good Sense.

LONDON:
Printed by and for ISAAC HOLROYD, in the Year 1764.
(Price One Shilling.)

Item no. 884

MVRRELS
TWO BOOKES
OF
COOKERIE
· AND
CARVING·

The fifth time printed, with
new Additions.

LONDON,
Printed by *M. F.* for *Iohn Marriot*,
and are to be fold at his fhop in St
Dunftans Churchyard in Fleetftreet.
1 6 4 1.

THE

Cook's and *Confectioner's*

DICTIONARY:

Or, the Accomplish'd

Houfewife's Companion.

CONTAINING,

I. The choiceſt Receipts in all the ſeveral Branches of Cookery; or the beſt and neweſt Ways of dreſſing all ſorts of Fleſh, Fiſh, Fowl, &c. for a Common or Noble Table; with their proper Garnitures and Sauces.

II. The beſt way of making Bisks, Farces, forc'd Meats, Marinades, Olio's, Pupltons, Ragoos, Sauces, Soops, Potages, &c. according to the *Engliſh, French,* and *Italian* Courts.

III. All manner of Paſtry-works, as Biskets, Cakes, Cheeſe-cakes, Cuſtards, Paſtes, Pattes, Puddings, Pyes, Tarts, &c.

IV. The various Branches of Confectionary; as Candying, Conſerving, Preſerving, and Drying all ſorts of Fowers, Fruits, Roots, &c. Alſo Jellies, Compoſts, Marmalades, and Sugar-works.

V. The way of making all *Engliſh* potable Liquors; Ale, Beer, Cider, Mead, Metheglin, Mum, Perry, and all ſorts of *Engliſh* Wines, Alſo Cordials, and Beautifying Waters.

VI. Directions for ordering an Entertainment, or Bills of Fare for all Seaſons of the Year; and ſetting out a Deſert of Sweet-meats to the beſt Advantage: With an Explanation of the Terms us'd in Carving. According to the Practice of the moſt celebrated Cooks, Confectioners, &c. in the Courts of *England, France,* &c. and many private and accompliſh'd Houſewives.

Reviſed and Recommended

By John Nott, *Cook to his Grace the Duke of* BOLTON.

L O N D O N :

Printed for C. Rivington, at the *Bible and Crown,* in St. *Paul's* Church-yard. MDCCXXIII.

THE OYSTER,

WHERE,
HOW AND WHEN
TO
FIND, BREED, COOK
AND
EAT IT.

LONDON:
TRÜBNER & C°., 60 PATERNOSTER ROW.

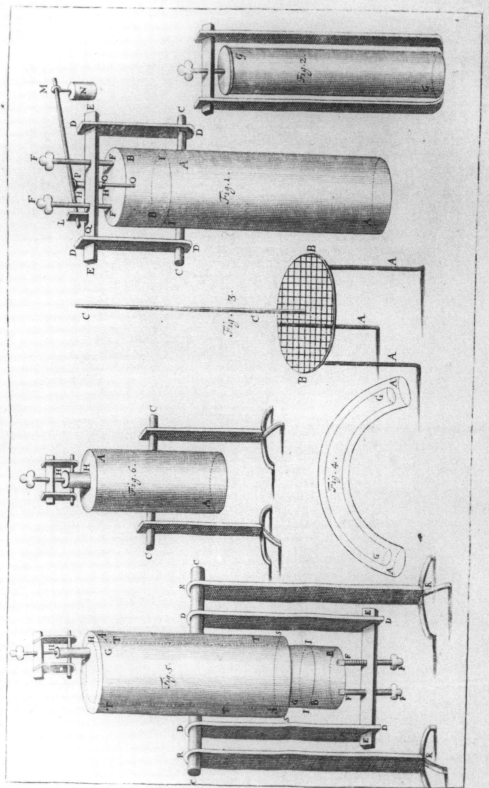

THE

FORME OF CURY,

A R O L L

OF

ANCIENT ENGLISH COOKERY,

Compiled, about A. D. 1390, by the
Master-Cooks of King RICHARD II,

Presented afterwards to Queen ELIZABETH,
by EDWARD Lord STAFFORD,

And now in the Possession of GUSTAVUS BRANDER, Esq.

Illustrated with N O T E S,

And a copious INDEX, or GLOSSARY.

A MANUSCRIPT of the EDITOR, of the
same Age and Subject, with other congruous
Matters, are subjoined.

" ————— ingeniosa gula est." MARTIAL.

with M.r Brandes
Compl.ts

PRINTED BY J. NICHOLS,
PRINTER TO THE SOCIETY OF ANTIQUARIES.

M DCC LXXX.

Samuel Pegge A.M. S.A.S.

A.D. MDCCLXXXVI. Æt. 81.

Impensis et in Ædes Gustavi Brander · tam ·

SIBI ET AMICIS.

THE
LADIES HANDMAID:

OR, A

COMPLEAT SYSTEM

OF

COOKERY;

ON THE

PRINCIPALS of ELEGANCE and FRUGALITY.

WHEREIN

The ufeful ART of COOKERY is rendered plain, eafy and familiar:

CONTAINING

The beft approved, yet leaft expenfive RECEIPTS in every BRANCH of HOUSEWIFRY, *viz.*

ROASTING,	JELLIES,	CREAMS,
BOILING,	RAGOUTS,	CUSTARDS,
MADE-DISHES,	FRICASSEES,	PASTRY,
SOUPS,	TARTS,	PICKLING,
SAUCES,	CAKES,	JARRING, &c.

And every other Branch of COOKERY and good HOUSEWIFRY, too tedious to be enumerated in a Title Page.

TOGETHER

With INSTRUCTIONS for CARVING and BILLS of FARE for every Month in the Year.

Embellifhed with variety of curious COPPER-PLATES, reprefenting the genteeleft Method of Difpofing or Placing the Difhes, Truffing Fowls, &c.

ALSO

The Beft approved Method of CLEAR-STARCHING.

By Mrs. SARAH PHILLIPS, *of* Duke-Street.

LONDON:

Printed for J. COOTE, at the *King's-Arms,* oppofite *Devereux-Court,* in the *Strand.* M,DCC,LVIII.

Mrs SARAH PHILLIPS 1758

Engraved for the Ladies Hand-Maid. Printed only for Xivote.

THE PRACTICAL HOUSEWIFE

BY THE EDITORS

OF THE

FAMILY FRIEND

LONDON:
WARD & LOCK 158 FLEET STREET.

THE

NEW, UNIVERSAL, AND

COMPLETE CONFECTIONER;

OR THE

WHOLE ART OF CONFECTIONARY

MADE PERFECTLY PLAIN AND EASY.

Containing *full Accounts* of all the various Methods of PRESERVING and CANDYING, both dry and liquid, *FRUIT, FLOWERS, GARDEN STUFF, HERBS, &c.*

ALSO THE SEVERAL WAYS OF

CLARIFYING SUGAR;

AND THE BEST METHODS OF

KEEPING FRUIT, NUTS, AND FLOWERS,

Fresh and Fine all the Year round:

TOGETHER WITH DIRECTIONS FOR MAKING

Blomonge,	Jellies,	Syrups of all Kinds,
Biscuits,	Creams,	Jams,
Cakes,	Ices,	Conserves,
Rock-Works,	Whip Syllabubs,	Cordials,
Candies,	Cheesecakes,	Compotes,
Tarts,	Sweetmeats,	Knicknacks,
Posset,	Puffs & Pastes,	Trifles, Comfits,
Custards, &c.	Oils, &c.	Drops, &c. &c. &c.

Including various Modern and Original Receipts for making LEMONADE, ORGEAT, ORANGEADE, WATERS, and other REFRESHMENTS.

By Mrs. ELIZABETH PRICE,
OF BERKELEY-SQUARE,
Author of THE NEW BOOK OF COOKERY.

Embellished with an Elegant Frontispiece.

London:

Printed for ALEX. HOGG, No. 16, *Paternoster-Row,*
by S. COUCHMAN, *Throgmorton-Street.*
[Price only 1s. 6d.]

FRONTISPIECE.

London, Published by Alex. Hogg, No. Paternoster Row.

The whole Body of

COOKERY
DISSECTED,

Taught, and fully manifested,
Methodically, Artificially, and according to the beſt Tradition of the
Engliſh, French, Italian, Dutch, &c.

OR,

A Sympathy of all Varieties in Natural
Compounds in that Myſtery.

Wherein is contained certain Bills of
Fare for the Seaſons of the Year, for Feaſts and
Common Diets.

Whereunto is annexed a Second Part of
Rare Receipts of Cookery : With certain uſeful Traditions.

With a Book of Preſerving, Conſerving
and Candying, after the moſt Exquiſite and
Neweſt manner : Delectable for Ladies and
Gentlewomen.

LONDON,

Printed for *George Calvert* at the *Half-moon,* and
Ralph Simpſon at the *Harp,* in St. *Paul's*
Church-yard, 1 6 8 2.

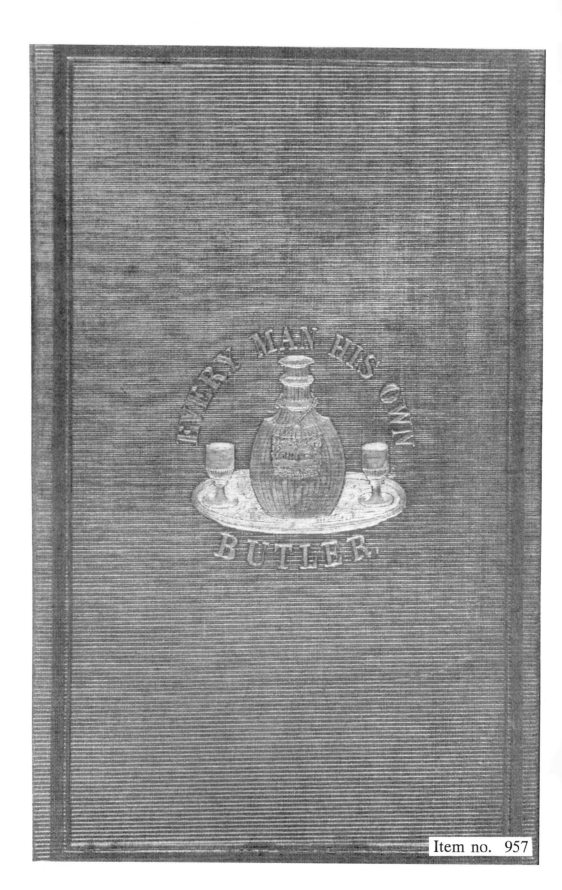

EVERY MAN HIS OWN BUTLER

The Dissection of a Turkey-Cock.

The dissection of a Turkey-Cock.

A Turkey-Cock may be cut up in two fashions, that is to say, either upon your Fork held up, or else lying in the Dish, as 'tis easie seen by the figure; you may also cut him into many pieces; for the doing of which, observe this order; the white of the Breast is always held for the most delicate piece, therefore you may present a piece of that with a piece of the rump for the first Plate; 2. a small Fork, with some more of the brawn of the breast; 3. the other side of the rump, with a little of the brawn of the brest; 4. the two little forkes, with some more of the brawn of the breast; 5. a wing; 6. another wing; but as this Fowl is big enough ordinarily of himself, so you may divide the wings or thighs into several pieces at your own discretion; and as it is easie for you to know what pieces are most delicate and best pleasing, so you may cut the brawn of the breast into as many pieces as you shall think fit, which are many more than I have here specified.   The

A

NEW SYSTEM

OF

DOMESTIC COOKERY;

FORMED UPON

PRINCIPLES OF ECONOMY,

And adapted to the Use of

PRIVATE FAMILIES.

BY A LADY.

A NEW EDITION, CORRECTED.

LONDON:

PRINTED FOR JOHN MURRAY, FLEET-STREET; J. HARDING,
ST. JAMES'S-STREET; AND A. CONSTABLE AND CO.
EDINBURGH;

At the Union Printing-Office, St. John's Square, by W. Wilson.

1807.

Price Seven Shillings and Sixpence.

ART
OF
COOKERY.

The Secrets of the reuerend

Maister *Alexis* of Piemont, con-
taining excellent remedies against diuerse
diseases, wounds, and other accidents, with
the maner to make Distillations, Par-
fumes, Confitures, Dyings, Colours, Fu-
sions, and Meltings. A worke well approued, verie necessarie for
euerie man.

Newly corrected and amended, and also
somewhat inlarged in certaine places,
which wanted in the first
edition.

Translated out of French into English by
William Ward.

Imprinted at London by Peter Short, for
Thomas Wight. 1595.

FRONTISPIECE.

HOUSE BOOK;

OR,

FAMILY CHRONICLE OF USEFUL KNOWLEDGE,

AND

COTTAGE PHYSICIAN:

COMBINING

MEDICINE,	SEA-BATHING,
COOKERY,	GARDENING,
DIET,	MANUFACTURES,
GENERAL ECONOMY,	ARTS, &c. &c.
HEALTH,	

WITH THE VARIOUS BRANCHES OF

Domestic Concerns;

INCLUDING UPWARDS OF

A THOUSAND SELECT RECIPES

AND PRESCRIPTIONS,

FROM THE BEST AUTHORITIES; AND A VARIETY OF OTHER
IMPORTANT INFORMATION, FOR THE USE OF FAMILIES,
INVALIDS, AND CONVALESCENTS.

EDITED

By WILLIAM SCOTT, M.D.

LONDON:

PRINTED FOR SHERWOOD, GILBERT, AND PIPER,

PATERNOSTER-ROW.

1826.

Mary Marsh

THE
Modern Art of Cookery
IMPROVED;
OR,

Elegant, Cheap, and Easy Methods, of preparing
most of the DISHES now in Vogue;

In the Composition whereof

Both HEALTH and PLEASURE have been consulted,

BY,

Mrs. ANN SHACKLEFORD, of *Winchester*.

TO WHICH IS ADDED,

An APPENDIX;

Containing a Differtation on the different Kinds of
Food, their Nature, Quality, and various Ufes.

By a PHYCISIAN.

AND

A MARKETING MANUAL,

And other ufeful PARTICULARS.

By the EDITOR.

She turns, on hofpitable thoughts intent,
What choice to chufe for delicacy beft;
What order, fo contriv'd as not to mix
Taftes, not well join'd, inelegant, but bring
Tafte after Tafte, upheld with kindlieft change.

MILTON.

LONDON:

Printed for J. NEWBERY, at the Bible and Sun, in
St. Paul's Church-Yard; and F. NEWBERY, in
Pater-nofter-Row. 1767.

THE
FEMALE ECONOMIST;

OR, A

PLAIN SYSTEM

OF

COOKERY:

For the Use of Families.

BY MRS. SMITH.

THIRD EDITION.

LONDON:

PRINTED FOR MATHEWS AND LEIGH, STRAND,

By Harrison and Leigh, 373, Strand.

[FOUR SHILLINGS BOARDS.]

THE KITCHEN DEPARTMENT OF THE REFORM CLUB.

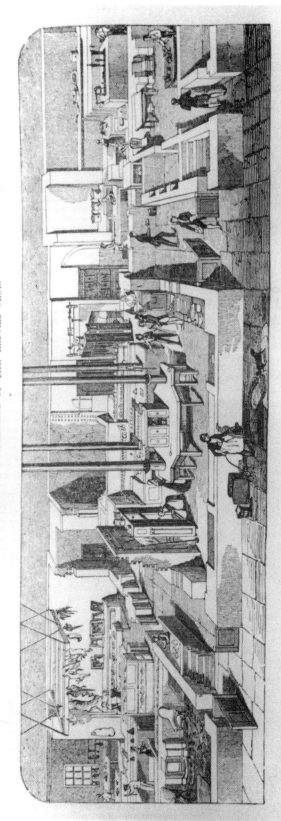

"This is a curious print, and unique of its kind: it presents on a large scale a coup-d'œil of the matchless culinary arrangements of the Reform Club, the various offices for which extend over the whole basement of the building. To show them at one glance, the partition-walls are cut away, and a bird's-eye view is given of the several kitchens, larders, sculleries, and batterie de cuisine; the different functionaries are all at their posts, and the accomplished chef, Monsieur Soyer, is in the act of pointing out to a favoured visitor the various contrivances suggested by his ingenuity and experience. With a plan of the building, there are references to a minute explanatory account of the uses of the multifarious apparatus here exhibited, for the admiration of the scientific gastronome and the envy of rival artistes."—Spectator.

Item no. 1003

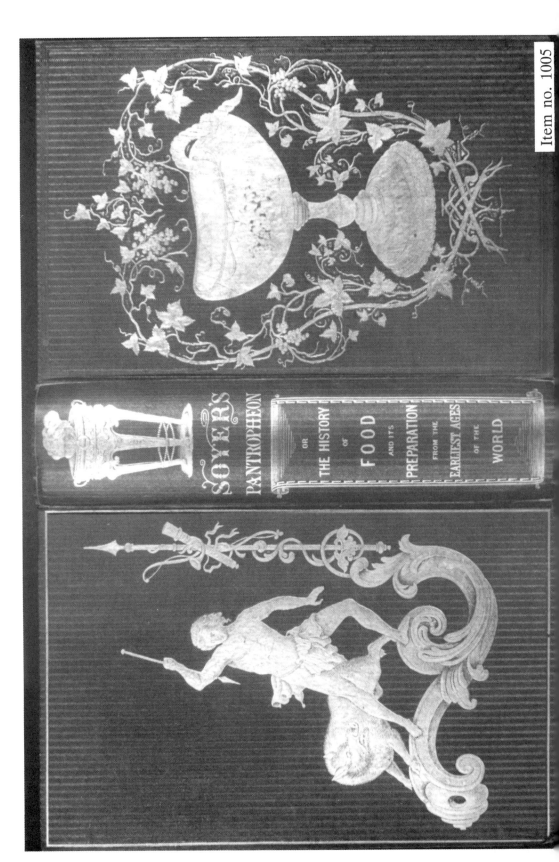

SOYER'S PANTROPHEON

OR THE HISTORY OF FOOD AND ITS PREPARATION FROM THE EARLIEST AGES OF THE WORLD

ONE SHILLING

SOYER'S COOKERY BOOK

LONDON: GEORGE ROUTLEDGE & SONS.

Item no. 1007

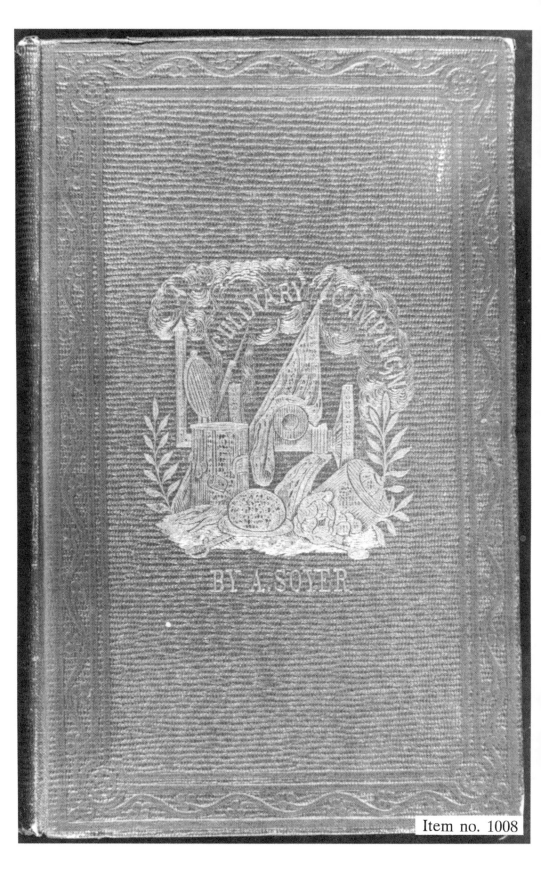

CULINARY CAMPAIGN

BY A. SOYER.

ESSAYS,

MORAL, PHILOSOPHICAL,

AND

STOMACHICAL,

On The important Science of

GOOD-LIVING.

Dedicated to the Right Worshipful

THE COURT OF ALDERMEN.

By LAUNCELOT STURGEON, Esq.

Fellow of the Beef-Steak Club, and an Honorary Member of several Foreign Pie Nics, &c. &c. &c.

" Eat! drink! and be merry!—for to-morrow you die."

LONDON:

PRINTED FOR G. AND W. B. WHITTAKER,
13, AVE-MARIA LANE.

1822.

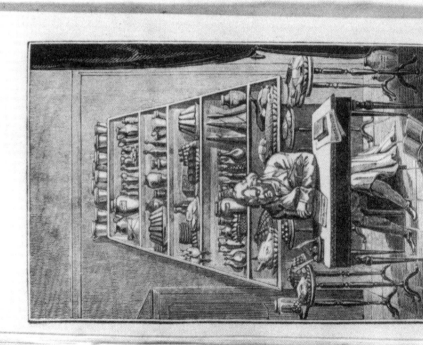

MEDITATIONS OF AN EPICURE.

W. HUGHES

Item no. 1012

THE
ART
OF
COOKERY.

CONTAINING

Above SIX HUNDRED AND FIFTY of the
most approv'd RECEIPTS heretofore published, under the
following Heads, viz.

ROASTING,	CAKES,	PICKLING,
BOILING,	CHEESE-CAKES,	PRESERVING,
FRYING,	TARTS,	PASTRY,
BROILING,	PYES,	COLLERING,
BAKING,	SOOPS,	CONFCTIONARY,
FRICASEES,	MADE-WINES,	CREAMS,
PUDDINGS,	JELLIES,	RAGOOS,
CUSTARDS,	CANDYING,	BRASING, &c. &c.

ALSO, A
BILL OF FARE
For every MONTH in the YEAR.

WITH AN
ALPHABETICAL INDEX to the Whole:

BEING
A BOOK highly necessary for all FAMILIES,
having the GROUNDS of COOKERY fully display'd therein.

By JOHN THACKER,
COOK to the Honourable and Reverend the DEAN and
CHAPTER in DURHAM.

NEWCASTLE UPON TYNE:
Printed by I. THOMPSON and COMPANY.
MDCCLVIII.

Wisdom's Dictates:
OR,
APHORISMS & RULES,

Physical, Moral, and *Divine*;

For Preserving the *Health* of the *Body*, and the *Peace* of the *Mind*, fit to be regarded and practised by all that would enjoy the Blessings of the present and future World.

To which is added,

A BILL of FARE
OF

Seventy five Noble Dishes of Excellent Food, far exceeding those made of Fish or Flesh, which Banquet I present to the Sons of Wisdom, or such as shall decline that depraved Custom of Eating Flesh and Blood.

By THO. TRYON, *Student in Physick,* and *Author of* Pythagoras's Mystick Philosophy Revived, *wherein the Mysteries of Dreams, Visions, Angels, and Spirits, are unfolded, and their secret Communications to Mankind.*

LONDON,

Printed for *Tho. Salusbury,* at the Sign of the *Temple* near *Temple-Bar* in *Fleetstreet.* 1691.

The Schoolemaster, or Teacher
of Table Philosophie.

A moſt pleaſant and merie companion, wel woꝛthy to be welcomed (foꝛ
a dayly Gheaſt) not onely to all mens booꝛde, to
guyde them with moderate ⁊ holſome dyet:
but alſo into euery mans companie at all
tymes, to recreate their mindes, with
honeſt mirth and delectable deuiſes:
to ſundꝛie pleaſant purpoſes of
pleaſure and paſtyme.

Gathered out of diuers, the beſt ap-
pꝛoued Auctours: and deuided into
foure pithy and pleaſant Treatiſes, as
it may appeare by the contentes.

Imprinted at London, by
Richarde Jones: dwelling ouer-
agaynſt S. Sepulchers Church
without Newgate.
1576.

Item no. 1036

Louis Eustache Ude

THE

French Cook:

OR,

THE ART OF COOKERY

DEVELOPED IN

ALL ITS VARIOUS BRANCHES.

BY LOUIS EUSTACHE UDE,

FORMERLY COOK TO LOUIS XVI. KING OF FRANCE, AND AT PRESENT
COOK TO THE RIGHT HON. EARL OF SEFTON.

PRINTED BY COX AND BAYLIS,
Great Queen Street, Lincoln's-Inn-Fields,

For the Author, and sold by J. EBERS, 27, Old Bond
Street; and may be had of all the Booksellers in the
United Kingdom.

1813.

THE

ENGLISH COOKERY BOOK:

UNITING

A GOOD STYLE WITH ECONOMY,

AND

ADAPTED TO ALL PERSONS IN EVERY CLIME;

CONTAINING

MANY UNPUBLISHED RECEIPTS IN DAILY USE

BY PRIVATE FAMILIES.

COLLECTED BY A COMMITTEE OF LADIES.

AND EDITED BY

J. H. WALSH, F.R.C.S.,

AUTHOR OF "A MANUAL OF DOMESTIC ECONOMY."

With Engravings.

LONDON:

G. ROUTLEDGE AND CO., FARRINGDON STREET;

AND 18, BEEKMAN STREET, NEW YORK.

1858

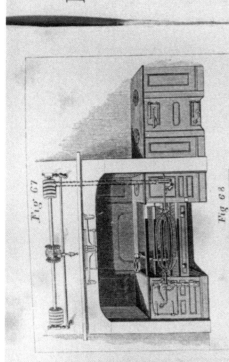

Fig 67

Fig 68

Fig 69

Fig 70

KITCHEN RANGES.

Antiquitates Culinariæ,

or

CURIOUS TRACTS

relating to the Culinary affairs

of the

OLD ENGLISH.

With a preliminary discourse, Notes, and Illustrations,

By

The Reverend Richard Warner,

OF SWAY,

near Lymington, Hants.

Πολλῷ τοι πλέονας λιμοῦ κόροσ ὤλεσεν ανδρασ.

*Non in Caro nidore voluptas
Summa, sed in teipso est; tu pulmentaria quære
Sudando.*

LONDON,

Printed for R. Blamire, Strand.

1791.

THE
COMPLEAT
SERVANT MAID;

CONTAINING

All that is NECESSARY to be KNOWN
to be QUALIFIED for the

FOLLOWING PLACES,

VIZ.

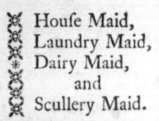

Ladies Maid,	House Maid,
Housekeeper,	Laundry Maid,
Chamber Maid,	Dairy Maid,
Nursery Maid,	and
Cook Maid,	Scullery Maid.

ALSO,

The best DIRECTIONS to qualify a Young Woman
for any COMMON SERVICE, and the most approved DIRECTIONS for Clear-Starching.

Together with INSTRUCTIONS how to manage
POULTRY, &c.

By Mrs. *WILKINSON,*

Who has góne through most of the above Services, in
which she has acquired a competent Fortune.

LONDON:

Printed for J. COOKE and J. COOTE at the *King's Arms,*
opposite *Devereux Court* in the *Strand.*

MDCCLVII.
[Price One Shilling.]

The Accomplish'd
LADY'S DELIGHT
In Preserving, Physick, Beautifying,
and Cookery.

CONTAINING,

I. The ART of PRESERVING,
and CANDYING Fruits and Flow-
ers, and the making of all sorts of Conserves, Syrups, and Jellies.

II. The PHYSICAL CABINET.
Or, Excellent Receipts in Physick and
Chirurgery; Together with some Rare
Beautifying waters, to adorn and add
Loveliness to the Face and Body: And
also some New and Excellent Secrets
and Experiments in the ART of AN-
GLING.

III. The COMPLEAT COOKS GUIDE
Or, directions for dressing all sorts of Flesh,
Fowl, and Fish, both in the *English* and *French*
Mode, with all Sauces and Sallets; and the mak-
ing Pyes, Pasties, Tarts, and Custards, with the
Forms and Shapes of many of them.

The Second Edition Enlarged.

LONDON,
Printed for *Nath. Crouch*, at the *George* at the
lower end of *Cornhil* over against
the *Stocks-Market*, 1677.

a

Item no. 1058

THE

QUEEN-LIKE CLOSET;

OR,

RICH CABINET:

Stored with all manner of

RARE RECEIPTS

FOR

Preferving, Candlying & Cookery.

Very Pleafant and Beneficial to all Ingenious Perfons of the FEMALE SEX.

By Hannah Wolley.

LONDON,

Printed for *R. Lowndes* at the *White Lion* in *Duck-Lane,* near *Weft-Smithfield,* 1670.

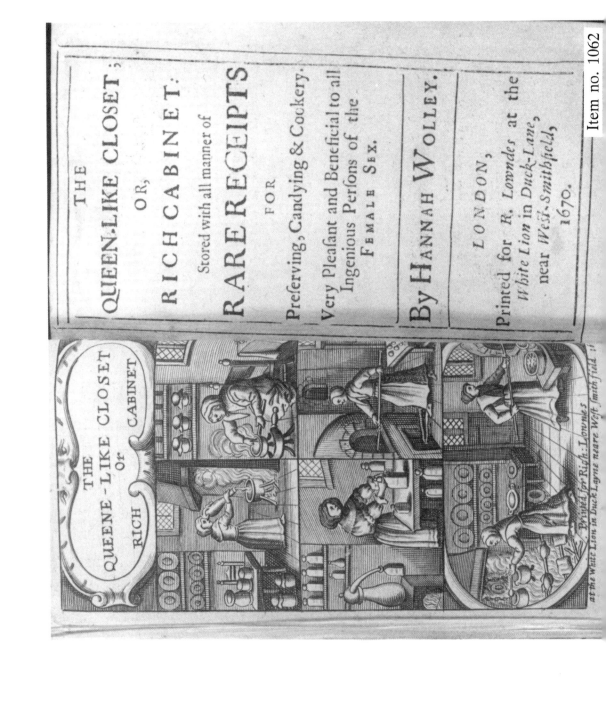

THE QUEENE-LIKE CLOSET OR RICH CABINET

Printed for Righ: Lownes at the White Lion in Duck Lyne neare Weft ſmith Field

HOLLAND

1075. Alkemade, Cornelis van, 1654-1737.

Title-page of volumes one and two:

NEDERLANDS | DISPLEGTIGHEDEN, | VERTOONENDE | DE PLEGTIGE GEBRUIKEN AAN DEN DIS, | IN | HET HOUDEN VAN MAALTYDEN, | EN | HET DRINKEN DER GEZONDHEDEN, | ONDER | DE OUDE BATAVIEREN, | EN VORSTEN, GRAAVEN, EDELEN, | EN ANDERE INGEZETENEN | DER NEDERLANDEN, | WELEER GEBRUIKELYK, | NEVENS | den oorsprongk dezer Gewoontens, en der zelver | overeenkomst met die van andere Volken. | DOOR | K. VAN ALKEMADE, | EN | Mr. P. VAN DER SCHELLING. | *EERSTE DEEL.* [*TWEEDE DEEL*, | *Met Plaaten.*] | *Met Platen.* | [row of five type ornaments] | *TE ROTTERDAM*, | By PHILIPPUS LOSEL, 1732.

Title-page of volume three:

NEDERLANDS | DISPLEGTIGHEDEN, | VERTOONENDE HET | GEBRUIK, EN MISBRUIK AAN DEN DIS, | IN HET | HOUDEN VAN MAALTYDEN, | EN HET | DRINKEN DER GEZONDHEDEN, ENZ. | ONDER DE OUDE BATAVIEREN, | VORSTEN, GRAA- | VEN, EDELEN, EN ANDERE NEDERLANDEREN; | NEVENS DE OORZAAKEN DEZER MISBRUIKEN; | DE WETTEN, EN MIDDELEN DAAR TEGEN; | EN DERZELVER OVEREENKOMST MET | DIE DER ANDERE VOLKEN; | *VOLGENS DE GESCHIEDENISSEN; EN GODGELEERDHEID*, | *EN ZEDEKUNDE; EN REGTSGELEERDHEID*, | *EN STAATKUNDE.* | DOOR | K. VAN ALKEMADE, | EN | Mr. P. VAN DER SCHELLING. | *DERDE DEEL.* | Met Plaaten. | [row of three type ornaments] | *TE ROTTERDAM*, | By PHILIPPUS LOSEL, 1735.

First edition, Rotterdam, 1732-1735.

8vo. 3 vols. Vol. I. $*^8$ $(*)^2$ $**-******^8$ $******^2$ (A)-(C)^8 A-Mm^8 Nn1; 349 leaves, pp. [*136*] 1-562. Vol. II. π^2 A-Kk^8 Ll^4(-Ll4) Mm-Qq^8 Rr^2; 311 leaves, pp. [*4*] 1-557 [*558-618*]. Vol. III. $*-***^8$ $****^6$ χ1 (A)^8 (B)^4 (C)^2 A-Ss^8 Tt^6; 379 leaves, pp. [*90*] 1-612 [*56*]. Last leaf blank.

Illustrations: Vol. I. Engraved title-page on $*1^r$ and etched plate of "Goude Bruilofts Penning" facing p. 209. Vol. II. Engraved title-page on $\pi1^r$ and eleven etched and engraved plates (three folding) numbered 1-13 but with 4-6 on one plate, all of drinking vessels. Vol. III. Three etched and engraved plates (two folding) of drinking vessels.

Bibliographies: Crahan 233; Oberlé (2) 485.

Copies: *BMC* and *NUC* (4 copies).

1076. Apicius.

[in red] APICII COELII | DE | [in red] OPSONIIS | ET | [in red] CONDIMENTIS, | Sive | [in red] ARTE COQUINARIA, | LIBRI DECEM. | Cum Annotationibus | [in red] MARTINI LISTER, | è Medicis domesticis Serenissimae Maje- | statis Reginae Annae, | ET | Notis selectioribus, variisque lectionibus integris, | [in red] HUMELBERGII, BARTHII, REINESII, | [in red] A. VAN DER LINDEN, & ALIORIUM, | ut & *Variarum Lectionum* Libello. | [in red] EDITIO SECUNDA, | *Longe auctior atque emendatior.* | [ornament] | [in red] AMSTELODAMI, | Apud JANSSONIO-WAESBERGIOS. | [short rule] | [in red] MDCCIX.

Second edition, Amsterdam, 1709, of the text as edited and annotated by Martin Lister. The Lister edition was originally published, London, 1705 (item 544).

8vo. π^2 ✳^{6} ✳✳^{8} ✳✳✳^{4} A-V^8; 180 leaves, pp. [40] 1-277 [278-320]. ✳1-✳4 mis-signed ✳2-✳5.

Illustration: Engraved frontispiece of ancient kitchen scene on $\pi1^v$.

Bibliographies: Bitting, p. 13; Horn-Arndt 9; Oberlé (2) 2; Pennell, p. 112; Schraemli (1) 25; Simon BG 126; Vicaire 32; Wheaton and Kelly 183.

Copies: *BMC, BNC,* and *NUC* (19 copies).

1077. Baudet, Florence Élise Joséphine Marguerite.

DE | MAALTIJD EN DE KEUKEN | IN DE | MIDDELEEUWEN | DOOR | DR. FLORENCE E. J. M. BAUDET. | [short rule] | GEÏLLUSTREERD MET AUTHENTIEKE AFBEELDINGEN. | [publisher's monogram] | A. W. SIJTHOFF. − LEIDEN.

New edition, Leiden, 1917. Originally published, Leiden, 1904.

222 x 147 mm. π^6 1-10^8 11^4(-11$_1$); 89 leaves, pp. [2] [i-vii] viii-ix [x] [1] 2-164 [2].

Illustrations: Half-tone frontispiece and three half-tone plates and numerous illustrations in the text.

Bibliographies: Unrecorded in the bibliographies consulted.

Copies: *BMC*.

1078. Bonnefons, Nicholas de.

LES │ DELICES │ DE LA │ CAMPAGNE, │ Suitte du │ JARDINIER │ FRANÇOIS, │
Où est enseigné à preparer pour l'usa- │ ge de la vie tout ce qui croist sur │ la Terre, &
dans les Eaux. │ *Dedié aux Dames Mesnageres.* │ SECONDE EDITION, │ augmentée
par l'Autheur. │ [ornament] │ A AMSTERDAM, │ Chez IEAN BLAEV. │ M. DC.
LXI.

Third Amsterdam edition, 1661, following those of 1655 and 1656. Originally
published, Paris, 1654 (item 86).

12mo. $*^{10}$ A-O^{12} P^6 Q^2; 186 leaves, pp. [*20*] 1-350 [2]. Last leaf (blank) wanting in
this copy.

Illustrations: Engraved title-page and three engraved plates after those by F. Chauveau
in the Paris editions on $*1^r$, $*10^v$, D9^v and I2^v.

Bibliographies: Vicaire 262.

Copies: No other copy of this edition located.

1078a. Bonnefons, Nicholas de.

LE │ IARDINIER │ FRANÇOIS. │ QVI ENSEIGNE A │ Cultiuer les Arbres, & Her- │
bes Potageres; Auec la manie- │ re de conseruer les Fruicts, & │ faire toutes sortes de
Confitu- │ res, Conserues, & Massepans. │ *DEDIE' AVX DAMES.* │ [ornament] │ A
AMSTELDAM. │ CHEZ RAPHAEL SMITH. │ [short rule] │ M. DC. LV.

New edition, Amsterdam, 1655. Originally published, Paris, 1651,

12 mo. a^{12} A-P^{12} [Q]^{12}; 204 leaves, pp. [*24*] 1-379 [380] [*4*]. Last two leaves blank. Q
1, 3, and 5 signed "G", "G3", and "GV"; Q 2 and 4 signed "R2" and "R4".

Bibliographies: Wheaton and Kelly 741.

Copies: *NUC* (Harvard, Library of Congress and National Agricultural Library).

Bourbon, Louis-Auguste de, Prince de Dombes, 1700-1755. See *Le Cuisinier Gascon* (item 1081).

1079. Chacón, Pedro, 1527-1581.

PETRUS CIACCONIUS | TOLETANVS | DE TRICLINIO | *Sive* | *De modo convivandi apud priscos Romanos,* | *& de conviviorum apparatu.* | Accedit | FULVI URSINI APPENDIX, | & | HIER. MERCURIALIS. | De accubitus in cena antiquorum | origine dissertatio | *In his Scriptores veteres quamplurimi explicantur,* | *& emendantur, nec non res ipsa adjectis* | *ancis figuris illustrantur.* | [vignette] OPTIMI CONSVLTORES MORTVI | AMSTELODAMI, | Apud ANDREAM FRISIUM. 1664.

New edition, Amsterdam, 1664. Originally published, Rome, 1588.

12mo. *✳*⁶ A-T¹² V⁶; 240 leaves, pp. [*12*] [1] 2-445 [446- 468].

Illustrations: Engraved title and fifteen engraved illustrations in the text and six engraved plates, five folding.

Bibliographies: Simon BG 344; Vicaire 174; Wheaton and Kelly 1123.

Copies: *BMC, BNC,* and *NUC* (9 copies).

1080. De cierlycke voorsnydinge aller tafel-gerechten.

DE CIERLYCKE | VOORSNYDINGE | Aller | TAFEL-GERECHTEN; | *Onderwijsende* | *Hoe allerhande Spijzen, zo wel op de Vork, als zonder de* | *zelve,* *aardiglik konnen voorgesneden, en in be-* | *quame ordre omgedient worden.* | [ornament] | T'AMSTERDAM, | [short rule] | By HIERONYMUS SWEERTS, voor-aan in de Kalver-straat, in de Dankbaarheyt. 1670.

Second edition, Amsterdam, 1670. Originally published, Amersterdam, 1664.

Oblong 4to. A-F⁸; 48 leaves, pp. [1-2] 3-96.

Illustrations: Engraved title-page of a gentleman at table with a carver presenting a fowl for carving and thirty-one engraved plates illustrating carving and one folding plate showing carving instruments.

Bibliographies: Wheaton and Kelly 1252. Bitting, p. 530; Horn-Arndt 114; Schraemli (1) 114; Schraemli (2) 82; and Vicaire 870 cite the Amsterdam, 1664, edition.

Copies: *NUC* and Wheaton and Kelly (Boston Public Library only). *BMC* records Amsterdam, 1664, edition.

1081. Le Cuisinier Gascon.

LE | *CUISINIER* | *GASCON.* | [ornament] | *A AMSTERDAM.* | [two rules] | M. DCC. XL.

First edition, Amsterdam, 1740.

12mo. a⁴ A-Q$^{8.4}$ S⁸; 108 leaves, pp. [*8*] [1] 2-208.

Bibliographies: Bitting, p. 540; Simon BG 421, in a note; Vicaire 233. Horn-Arndt 290 describes a facsimile edition, Paris, 1970, and claims the author of this work is Louis-Auguste de Bourbon, Prince de Dombes, to whom the dedicatory epistle is addressed.

Copies: *NUC* (John Crerar Library and Library of Congress).

1082. Le Cuisinier Gascon.

LE | *CUISINIER* | GASCON. | *NOUVELLE EDITION,* | A laquelle on a joint la Lettre | du Patissier Anglois. | [ornament] | *A AMSTERDAM.* | [two rules] | M. DCC. XLVII.

Third edition, Amsterdam, 1747. Originally published Amsterdam, 1740 (item 1081) followed by a second edition, Amsterdam, 1741.

12mo. π² a⁴(-a1) A-V$^{8.4}$ X²; 127 leaves, pp. [*10*] [1] 2- 244. First leaf blank.

The "Lettre d'un patissier anglois au nouveau cuisinier françois" (pp. 195-231) is by Desalleurs, l'aîné.

Bibliographies: Bitting, p. 540, in a note; Oberlé (1) 112; Schraemli (1) 132; Simon BG 421; Vicaire 234.

Copies: *NUC* (John Crerar Library and New York Academy of Medicine).

1083. Dufour, Philippe Sylvestre, 1622-1687.

[in red] TRAITEZ | Nouveaux & curieux | [in red] DU CAFE', | [in red] DU THE' | ET DU | [in red] CHOCOLATE, | Ouvrage également necessaire aux | Medecins, & à tous ceux qui | aiment leur santé. | Par PHILIPPE SYLVESTRE DuFour | *A quoy on a adjouté dans cette Edition, la meil-* | *leure de toutes les methodes, qui manquoit* | *à ce Livre, pour composer* | [in red] L'EXCELLENT CHOCOLATE, | Par Mr. St. DISDIER. | Troisiéme Edition. | [ornament] | [in red] A LA HAYE, | Chez ADRIAN MOETJENS, Mar- | chand Libraire prez la Cour, à la | Libraire Françoise. | [rule] | [in red] M. DC. XCIII.

Second edition printed in Holland, The Hague, 1693. Originally published, Lyon, 1685 (item 169) and reprinted The Hague, 1685, and Lyon, 1688 (item 170).

12mo. A-R^{12}; 204 leaves, pp. [1-14] 15-404 [405-408].

Illustrations: Engraved frontispiece and three engraved plates.

Bibliographies: Bitting, p. 134, in a note; Horn-Arndt 120; Vicaire 293.

Copies: *BMC*, *BNC*, and *NUC* (5 copies).

1084. De Geoeffende en Ervaren Keuken-Meester Of de Verstandige Kok.

De Geoeffende en Ervaren | KEUKEN-MEESTER, | *Of de Verstandige* KOK. | Onderwijsende, hoe dat in ENGELAND, | VRANKRIJK, ITALIEN, DUYTSLAND, &c. al- | derhande soorten van *Spijsen*, soo voor de | Tafelen der GROOTEN, als lagere en min- | dere STANTS-PERSOONEN, bereyd, gehan- | deld en toegemaakt werden. | [rule] | *Insgelijks ook een byzonder* | KOOK-BOEK, | Tot dienst der ROOMS gesinde in de VISCH | en VASTE DAGEN; en hoe men alder- | hande soort van VISCH kan berey- | den en voordienen. | [rule] | *Als mede* | Het Bereyden van verscheyde sagte *Spijsen*, tot | dienst der SIEKEN en KRANKEN: Mits- | gaders het mengen van veelder- | hande SAUZEN, &c. | [rule] | *Alles door Ervarendheyd goed bevonden, entenge-* | *meenen nutte uytgegeven, door zeekere Hof-* | *bediende van een* *Hoog Aanzienelijke* | PERSONAGIE. | *EERSTE DEEL.* | [rule] | [ornament] | TOT LEYDEN, | Gedrukt voor den Autheur, by de Weduwe van | BASTIAAN SCHOUTEN, wonende in de | Nieuwe-steeg, 1701.

Title-page of the second part:

HET NEDERLANDS | KOOK-BOEK, | ONDERWIJSENDE | Het Bereyden en Voordienen van | Alderhande Spijzen; | EN IN HET BYZONDER | *Hoedanig de* ROOMS - *gezinde, op de* VIS - *en* | VASTEN-DAGEN, *de hen geoorlofde* | SPIJSEN, *laaten toe-maken* | *en voordienen.* | [rule] | ALS MEDE | Het bereyden van verscheyde zagte *Spijzen,* | tot dienst der ZIEKEN en KRANKEN. | [rule] | *Alles door* *Ervarentheyt goed bevonden,* | *en ten gemeenen nutte uytgegeeven,* | DOOR | N. N. | *TWEEDE DEEL.* | [ornament] | TOT LEYDEN, | Gedrukt voor den Autheur, by de Weduwe van | BASTIAAN SCHOUTEN, woonende in de | Nieuwe-steeg, Anno 1701.

First edition, Leiden, 1701.

8vo. ✱⁴ A-V⁸, ²π1 A⁶ B-R⁸; 299 leaves, pp. [8] 1-320, ²[2] 5-272. ²A1-3 mis-signed A3-5.

Illustrations: Engraved frontispiece on ✱1ᵛ.

Bibliographies: Bitting, p. 556.

Copies: *NUC* (Library of Congress, New York Academy of Medicine, and Yale).

1085. Glauber, Johann Rudolf, 1604?-1668.

FURNI NOVI | PHILOSOPHICI, | *Sive* | DESCRIPTIO ARTIS | DESTILLATORIAE | NOVAE; | *Nec non* | Spirituum, Oleorum, Florum, aliorumque | Medicamentorum illius beneficio, facilimâ quâ- | dam & peculiari viâ è vegetabilibus, animalibus & minerali- | bus; conficiendorum & quidem magno cum lucro; agens quo- | que de illorum usu tàm chymico quàm medico, edita | & publicata in gratiam veritatis Studio- | sorum *Per* | JOANNEM RUDOLPHUM | GLAUBERUM. | [ornament] | *AMSTERODAMI,* | Prostant apud JOANNEM JANSSONIUM, | [short rule] | cIↃ Iↄc LI.

Title-page of the second part:

FURNORUM | PHILOSOPHICORUM, | *PARS ALTERA.* | *In quâ* | Describitur secundae fornacis proprietas; | cujus beneficio destillari possunt omnia volatilia, | subtilia & combustibilia; vegetablilia, animalia & mineralia; | viâ quâdam incognitâ hactenus & compendiosa; quâ nihil perdi- | tur omnino, sed spritus etiam subtilissimi capiuntur, | | quod aliàs per retortas, aliaque vasa | fieri nequit | *Per* | JOANNEM RUDOLPHUM | GLAUBERUM. | [ornament] | *AMSTERODAMI,* | Prostant apud JOANNEM JANSSONIUM, | [short rule] | cIɔ Iɔc LI.

Title-page of the third part:

FURNORUM | PHILOSOPHICORUM, | *PARS TERTIA.* | *In quâ* | Describitur tertiae fornacis natura, cujus | beneficio & quidem absque vesicis & ahenis, aliis- | que cupreis, ferreis, stanneis & plumbeis instrumentis, | spiritus varii vegetabiles ardentes, extracta, olea, | salia, &c. | Adminiculo autem exigui alicujus instrumenti | cuprei, vasorumque ligneorum, ad usus tam chymicos | quàm medicos praeparari possunt. | *Per* | JOANNEM RUDOLPHUM | GLAUBERUM. | [ornament] | *AMSTERODAMI,* | Prostant apud JOANNEM JANSSONIUM, | [short rule] | cIɔ Iɔc LI.

Title-page of the fourth part:

FORNACUM | PHILOSOPHICARUM, | *PARS QVARTA.* | *Continens* | Descriptionem Fornacis Quartae, cujus be- | neficio Mineralia & Metalla probantur & exa- | minantur viâ quâdam compendiosiore, quàm ha- | ctenus modo illo vulgari; item Metallorum separa- | tionem vi fusionis; aliaque necessaria vi fusio- | nis perpetranda. | *Vtilissima Chymicis, Mineralium probatoribus* | *& sossoribus.* | *Per* | JOANNEM RUDOLPHUM | GLAUBERUM. | [ornament] | *AMSTERODAMI,* | Prostant apud JOANNEM JANSSONIUM, | [short rule] | cIɔ Iɔc LI.

Title-page of the fifth part:

FORNACUM | PHILOSOPHICARUM, | *PARS QVINTA.* | Ubi agitur de natura Quintae Fornacis mi- | rabili; ut & de instrumentorum & materia- | lium ad praedictos. 4. Furnos pertinen- | tium, praeparatione facili. | *Vtilissima Medicinae Hermeticae sectatoribus.* | | *Per* | JOANNEM RUDOLPHUM | GLAUBERUM. | [ornament] | *AMSTERODAMI,* | Prostant apud JOANNEM JANSSONIUM, | [short rule] | cIɔ Iɔc LI.

Title-page of the appendix:

ANNOTATIONES | *IN* | APPENDICEM | Quintae Partis Fornacum Philosophica- | rum, ubi de variis agitur Secretis utilissimis, opti- | mis & incognitis, incredulorum &

natura- | lium Secretorum ignarorum gra- | ciâ publicatae. | *Per* | JOANNEM RUDOLPHUM | GLAUBERUM. | [ornament] | *AMSTERODAMI*, | Prostant apud JOANNEM JANSSONIUM, | [short rule] | cIɔ Iɔc LI.

Title-page of the final part:

DE AURI TINCTURA | Sive | AURO POTABILI | VERO. | Quid sit & quommodo differat ab auro | potab ili falso & Sophistico | *Quomodo Spagyrice praeparandum & quomodo* | *in Medicinâ usurpandum.* | *Per* | JOANNEM RUDOLPHUM | GLAUBERUM. | [ornament] | *AMSTERODAMI*, | Prostant apud JOANNEM JANSSONIUM, | [short rule] | cIɔ Iɔc LI.

First edition in Latin, Amsterdam, 1651. Originally published in German under the title *Furni novi Philosophici: oder Beschreibung einer New erfundenen Distillir-Kunst*, Amsterdam, 1646-1649.

8vo. A-D^8 E^4 Aa-Ii^8 Kk^4 Aaa-Ccc^8 Ddd^4 Aaaa-Eeee^8 Ffff^4 Aaaaa-Ccccc^8 Ddddd^4 a-d^8 e^4 aa^8 bb^4. Last leaf blank.

Illustrations: Three folding woodcuts following parts I, II, and III and woodcuts in the text in part V.

Bibliographies: Simon BG 777.

Copies: *BNC* and *NUC* (13 copies).

1086. La Chapelle, Vincent.

LE | [in red] CUISINIER | MODERNE, | *Qui apprend à donner toutes sortes* | [in red] DE REPAS, | En Gras & en Maigre, d'une manière plus délicate | que ce qui en a été écrit jusqu'à présent; | [in red] DIVISÉ EN CINQ VOLUMES, | Avec de nouveaux Modéles de Vaisselle, & des Des- | seins de Table dans le grand goût d'aujourd'hui, | gravez en Taille-douce; | [in red] *DEDIÉ* | *A Son Altesse Serenissime* | MONSEIGNEUR LE PRINCE | [in red] D'ORANGE ET DE NASSAU, &c. | PAR LE SIEUR | [in red] VINCENT LA CHAPELLE, | Son Chef de Cuisine. | [in red] *SECONDE EDITION* | *Revûe, corrigée & augmentée.* | [in red] TOME PREMIER. [SECOND.] [TROISIEME.] [QUATRIEME.] [CINQUIÈME.] | [ornament] | [in red] *A LA HAYE*, | Aux Dépens de L'AUTEUR. | [short rule] | [in red] M. DCC. XLII.

Second edition in French, The Hague, 1742. Originally published in English under the title *The Modern Cook*, London, 1733, in three volumes. The first edition in French was published in four volumes in The Hague with copies dated both 1735 and 1736.

8vo. 5 vols. Vol. I. a⁴(a1 + *²) A-R⁸ S⁴(-S4); 145 leaves, pp. [*12*] [1] 2-261 [262] [*16*]. Three folded half- sheets numbered I-IV, VIII-IX, with letterpress explanations of the folding plates are bound with the plates at the end of the volume. Vol. II. *² A-R⁸; 138 leaves, pp. [*4*] [1] 2-258 [*14*]. Vol. III. *² A-T⁸; 154 leaves, pp. [*4*] [1] 2-288 [*16*]. Single folded half-sheet, numbered V-VI, with letterpress explanations of the folding plates is bound with the plates at the end of the volume. Vol. IV. *² A-V⁸ X⁸(-X8); 169 leaves, pp. [*4*] [1] 2-313 [314] [*20*]. Single folded half-sheet, numbered VII, with letterpress explanations of the folding plates is bound with the plates at the end of the volume. Vol. V. π1 *⁴ (±)1) A-Y⁸ Z⁴ (cancellan *1 mis-signed "a2"); 185 leaves, pp. [*10*] [1] 2-346 [*14*].

Illustrations: Vol. I. Five engraved folding plates of table settings. Vol. II. Three engraved folding plates, two of table settings and one of an elaborate dish. Vol. III. Three engraved folding plates, two of table settings and one of a "Terrine or Olio." Vol. IV. Two folding plates, one of a table setting and one of a "Surtout, to be left upon the Table till the Dessert is serv'd."

Bibliographies: Vicaire 868; Wheaton and Kelly 3395. Bitting, p. 268, cites the La Haye, 1735, edition and Simon BG 933 a copy with the same imprint but dated 1736. Vicaire states the first edition appears with both dates.

Copies: *BMC* and *NUC* (Kansas State University and New York Public Library). Wheaton and Kelly (Radcliffe only).

1087. La Roque, Jean de, 1661-1745.

[in red] VOYAGE | DE | [in red] L'ARABIE HEUREUSE, | Par l'Ocean Oriental, & le Détroit de la Mer | Rouge. Fait par les François pour la premiere | fois, dans les années 1708, 1709 & 1710. | [in red] AVEC | La Relation particuliere d'un Voyage du Port de | MOKA à la Cour du Roi d'YEMEN, dans la seconde | Expedition des années 1711, 1712 & 1713. | Un Memoire concernant l'Arbre & le Fruit du CAFÉ, | dressé sur les Observations de ceux qui ont fait ce dernier | Voyage. Et un Traité historique de l'origine & du pro- | grès du Café, tant dans l'Asie que dans l'Europe; de son | introduction en France, & de l'établissement de son usage | à Paris. | [vignette] | [in red] A AMSTERDAM, | Chez STEENHOUWER ET UYTWERF, | Libraires sur le Rockin, vis à vis la Porte de la Bourse. | [short rule] | [in red] MDCCXVI.

New edition, Amsterdam, 1716. Originally published, Paris, 1715, and reprinted, Paris, 1716, and Amsterdam, 1716.

12mo. ✳⁸ A-O¹² P⁴ Q⁶ (-Q6); 185 leaves, pp. [*16*] 1-343 [344-354].

Illustrations: Engraved frontispiece on ✳1ᵛ, engraved folding map, and three engraved folding plates of coffee plants.

Bibliographies: Bitting, p. 274; Wheaton and Kelly 3484.

Copies: *BMC* and *NUC* (13 copies).

1088. La Varenne, Françoise Pierre de.

LE VRAY | CUISINIER | FRANCOIS, | ENSEIGNANT | Le Maniere de bien apprester & assaisonner tou- | tes sortes de Viandes, grasses & maigres, Lé- | gumes & Pastisseries en perfection, &c. | *Augementée d'un nouveau Confiturier, qui apprend à* | *bien faire* | *toutes sortes de Confitures, tant seches que liquides, de Com-* | *postes, de* | *Fruits, de Dragées, Breuvages dé-* | *licieux, & autres délicatesses de bouche.* | LE | MAISTRE d'HOSTEL | Et le Grand | ECUYER-TRANCHANT, | Ensemble d'une Table Alphabétique des Matieres qui | sont traitées dans tout le Livre. | *Par le Sieur* *DE LA VARENNE, Ecuyer de* | *Cuisine de Monsieur le Marquis d'Uxelles.* | NOUVELLE EDITION. | [ornament] | A AMSTERDAM, | Chez PIERRE MORTIER, Libraire, sur | le Vygendam, à la ville de Paris.

New edition, Amsterdam, ca. 1700. Originally published under the title *Le Cuisiniers françois*, Paris, 1651, and under this title, Paris, 1682, with later editions in 1698, 1712, 1721 and the above undated edition.

12mo. ✳¹² A-Q¹²; 204 leaves, pp. [*24*] 1-380 [*4*].

Illustrations: Engraved frontispiece of a man at table on ✩1ʳ, twelve woodcuts in the text illustrating carving, one folding etched plate illustrating table settings, and six etched plates, five of them folding, illustrating carving.

Bibliographies: Maggs 187; Pennell, p. 121; Schraemli (1) 275; Vicaire 500. Bitting, p. 276, cites the Paris, 1682, edition.

Copies: *BMC* and *NUC* (John Crerar Library only).

1089. Lémery, Nicolas, 1645-1715.

NOUVEAU | RECUEIL | DE | CURIOSITEZ, | Les plus Rares & admirables de tous | les Effects, que l'Art & la Nature | sont capables de produire. | AUGMENTÉ | De plus de moitié, | *De merveilleux & beaux Secrets* | *Gallands & autres*, | Tres-utiles & nécessaires à tous ceux, qui | sont curieux de conserver leur santé. | *Expérimentez & approuvez par Gens de* | *qualité, & Composez par le Sr. d'Emery*. | Derniére Edition augmentée, Re- | veüe, Corrigée & enrichie | de Tailles-douces. | [ornament] | *Suivant la Copie de PARIS* | *A LEYDE*, | Chez PIERRE VANDER Aa, | *Marchand Libraire*, 1688.

New edition, Leiden, 1688. Originally published under the title *Recueil des curiositez rare et nouvelles des plus admirables effets de la nature*, Paris, 1674. First published under this title, Leiden, 1685.

12mo. $*^4$ A-X^{12} Y^8; 264 leaves, pp. [*8*] 1-488 [*32*].

Illustrations: Engraved title-page and eight engraved plates.

Bibliographies: Horn-Arndt 160. Bitting, p. 144, Oberlé (1) 90, and Vicaire 327, cite the Leiden, 1685, edition.

Copies: *NUC* (Harvard, Harvard Arnold Arboretun, and National Library of Medicine).

1090. Liger, Louis, sieur d'Auxerre, 1658-1717.

[in red] OECONOMIE | GENERALE | DE | [in red] LA CAMPAGNE, | *OU* | NOUVELLE | [in red] MAISON RUSTIQUE. | *Par le Sieur LOUIS LIGER*, *d'Auxerre*, | [in red] TOME PREMIER. [SECOND.] | *Seconde Edition revêë & corrigee*. | [ornament] | A AMSTERDAM, | Chez [in red] HENRI DESBORDES, [in black] Marchand Libraire, | dans le Kalver-straat. | [short rule] | [in red] M. DCCI.

Second edition, Amsterdam, 1701. Originally published, Paris, 1700. The second Paris edition was published in 1708. Starting with the third edition, Paris, 1721, the work was retitled *La Nouvelle maison rustique*.

2 vols. 4to. Vol. I. $*$-$**^4$ A-Xx^4; 184 leaves, pp. [*16*] 1-342 [*10*]. Vol. II. $*^4$ A-Ss^4 Tt^2; 170 leaves, pp. [*8*] 1-320 [*12*].

Illustrations: Numerous woodcuts in the text.

Bibliographies: Oberlé (2) 83; Vicaire 520; Wheaton and Kelly 3689.

Copies: *BMC*, *BNC*, and *NUC* (6 copies).

1091. Martin, Louis.

L'ESCHOLE | DE | SALERNE | En vers Burlesques. | & | DUO POEMATA | MACARONICA; | DE BELLO | HUGUENOTICO: | Et de Gestis Magnanimi & Pruden- | tissimi Baldi. | [ornament] | *Suiuant la Copie imprimée* | A PARIS. | [short rule] | M. DC. LI.

New edition published by Bonaventure and Abraham Elzevier, Leiden, 1651. Originally published, Paris, 1647.

12mo. A-F^{12}; 72 leaves, pp. [1-24] 25-139 [140] [4]. First leaf and last leaf (blanks?) wanting in this copy.

Note: The first poem in this volume is by Louis Martin, the second by Remy Belleau, and the third by Girolamo Folengo.

Bibliographies: Vicarie 335.

Copies: *BMC*, *BNC*, and *NUC* (University of Michigan only).

1092. Massialot, François, ca. 1660-1733.

[in red] LE NOUVEAU | CUISINIER | [in red] ROYAL | ET | [in red] BOURGEOIS, | Qui apprend à ordonner toutes sortes de | Repas en gras & en maigre, & la meil- | leure maniere des Ragoûts les plus deli- | cats & les plus à la mode; & toutes sor- | tes de Pâtisseries: avec de nouveaux | desseins de Tables. | *Ouvrage très-utile dans les Familles, aux* | *Maîtres d'Hôtels & Officiers de Cuisine.* | [in red] TOME PREMIER. [TOME SECOND.] | NOUVELLE EDITION [in red] , [in black] , | Revûë & corrigée. | [ornament] | A AMSTERDAM [in red] , [in black] , | [in red] *AUX DEPENS DE LA COMPAGNIE.* | M. DCC. XXXIV.

New edition, Amsterdam, 1734. Originally published under the title *Le Cuisinier roial et bourgeois*, Paris, 1691 (item 316) and enlarged to two volumes, under the new title, Paris, 1712, and to three volumes, Paris, 1733-1734 (item 319).

12mo. 3 vols. (wanting vol. III). Vol. I. $*^4$ A-T^{12} V^6; 238 leaves, pp. [8] [1] 2-444 [24]. Last leaf blank. Vol. II. π1 A-S^{12}; 217 leaves, pp. [2] 1-384, 387-408 [26].

Illustrations: Vol. I. Nine etched plates, four of them folding, illustrating a surtout and table settings. Vol. II. Fourteen etched folding plates illustrating table settings and four woodcuts in the text.

Bibliographies: Vicaire 575.

Copies: *BNC*.

1093. Quélus, D. de.

[in red] HISTOIRE | NATURELLE | DU | [in red] CACAO, | ET DU | [in red] SUCRE; | *DIVISE'E EN DEUX TRAITEZ,* | Qui contiennent plusieurs faits nouveaux, | & beaucoup d'observations également | curieuses & utiles. | [in red] SECONDE EDITION | *Revuë & corrigée par l'Auteur.* | [ornament] | [in red] A AMSTERDAM, | Chez HENRI STRIK, Libraire à | côté de la Maison de Ville. | [short rule] | [in red] MDCCXX.

Second edition, Amsterdam 1720. Originally published, Paris, 1719.

8vo. $*^6$ A-O^8 P^2; 120 leaves, pp. [12] [1] 2-228.

Illustrations: Six engraved plates, four of them folding, illustrating the cacao plant, the sugar cane, and equipment used to produce sugar.

Bibliographies: Vicaire 445 under title but referring to the author as M. de Caïlus; Wheaton and Kelly 4941.

Copies: *BMC*, *BNC*, and *NUC* (6 copies).

1094. Sallengre, Albert Henrik de, 1694-1723.

L'ÉLOGE | DE | L'YVRESSE. | NOUVELLE EDITION. | *Revûë, Corrigée &* | *Augmentée.* | [vignette] | A LA HAYE, | Chez ADRIAN MOETJENS, | Marchand Libraire près de la Cour, | à la Librairie Françoise. | [short rule] | M. DCC. XV.

Second edition, The Hague, 1715. Originally published, The Hague, 1714.

12mo. A-S$^{8.4}$ T^6 (A3 and A4 mis-signed "A2" and "A3"); 114 leaves, pp. [*8*] 1-216 [*4*].

Illustration: Engraved frontispiece of Bacchus on A1^v.

Bibliographies: Bitting, p. 415; Simon BG 1346.

Copies: *BMC, BNC,* and *NUC* (5 copies).

1095. Sallengre, Albert Henrik de, 1694-1723.

[in red] HISTOIRE | DE | PIERRE DE | [in red] MONTMAUR, | Professeur Royal en Langue Grecque | dans l'Université de Paris. | PAR | [in red] M. DE SALLENGRE. | *Dùm nihil habemus majus, calamo ludimus.* | [in red] TOME PREMIER. [SECOND.] | [vignette] | [in red] A LA HAYE, | Chez CHR. VAN LOM, P. GOSSE | & R. ALBERTS. | [rule] | [in red] M DCC XV.

First edition, The Hague, 1715. A collection of satires on the gourmand Montmaur by various authors, edited by Sallengre.

8vo. 2 vols. Vol. I. π1 χ^2 ✳^{6} ✳✳^{8}-✳✳✳✳✳✳✳✳✳^{8} ✳✳✳✳✳✳✳✳✳✳^{4} A-T^8 V^4; 225 leaves, pp. [*6*] iii-cxxxii [*2*] 1-312; ✳1-✳4 signed "✳2"-"✳5". Vol. II. π1 A-T^8 V^6; 159 leaves, pp. [*2*] 1-316.

Illustrations: Vol. I. Engraved frontispiece and eight engraved plates; Vol. II. Engraved frontispiece.

Bibliographies: Brunet V, 78; Graesse VI, p. 234; Oberlé (1) 374.

Copies: *BMC, BNC,* and *NUC* (8 copies).

1095a. Schoock, Martin, 1614-1669.

[red] MARTINI SCHOOKII | LIBER | *DE* | [red] CERVISIA. | QUO | Omnia ad illam pertinentia | plenissime dicutiuntur. | [woodcut lettered in an arch over the top] ARS . NATVRAMIVVAT | *GRONINGÆ,* | Typis [red] FRANCISCA BRONCHORSTTI; [black] Civitatis | Groning. Ord. Typog. [red] ANNO 1661.

First edition, second issue, Groningen, 1661, The first issue title reads: *Martini Schoockii Liber de cervisia. Quo non modo omnia ad cerealem potum pertinentia comprehenduntur, sed varia quoque problemata, philosophiphica & philologica discutiuntur: Simul incidenter quaedam authorum antiquorum loca illustrantur.* The printer discovered the misspelling of "philosophica" and printed a considerably abridged cancel title-page for the unsold copies.

12mo. $*^8$ ($\pm*2$) A-S^{12} T^4; 156 leaves, pp. [*16*] 1-429 [430-438] [*2*]. First leaf and last leaf, blank.

Bibliographies: The second issue is unrecorded in the bibliographies consulted. Henssler 988; Horn-Arndt 198; and Vicaire 775 record the first issue.

Copies: No other copy of the second issue located. *BMC, BNC* and *NUC* (Northwestern and Princeton) locate the first issue.

1096. Swalve, Bernhard, ca. 1625-1680.

Querelae & Opprobria | VENTRICULI; | *SIVE* | ΠΡΟΣΟΠΟΠΟΙΙΑ | *Ejusdem* | Naturalia sua sibi vendicantis, | & Abusus | *Tam Diaeteticos, quam Pharmaceu-* | *ticos* *perstringentis.* | Operâ ac Studio | BERNHARDI SWALVE Med. | [ornament] | *AMSTELODAMI,* | [short rule] | Ex Officina *Joannis Janssonii à Waesberge,* | & *Elizei Weyerstraten.* ANNO 1664.

First edition, Amsterdam, 1664.

12mo. $*^8$ A-N^{12} O^6 P^4; 172 leaves, pp. [*16*] 1-321 [322-332].

Illustration: Engraved title-page on $*1^r$.

Bibliographies: Vicaire 811.

Copies: *BNC* and *NUC* (5 copies).

1096a. De Verstandige Kock

This work, described separately in Bitting, is a section of the third part of a Dutch housekeeping compendium covering gardening, husbandry, bee-keeping, and cookery. The cookery part is anonymous and may have been issued by itself as it has survived that way in several gastronomic collections. The full description of all three parts follows:

Part One, by Jan van der Groen:

𝕯en 𝕹ederlandtsen | HOVENIER, | Zijnde het I. Deel van *het Vermakelijck Landt-leven*. | 𝕭eschrijvende alderhande | Prinçelijcke en Heerlijcke Lust-hoven en Hofsteden, | en hoemen de selve, met veelderley uytnemende Boomen, | Bloemen en Kruyden, kan beplanten, bezaeyen, en verçieren. | Door *J. van der GROEN*, Hovenier van Sijn | Doorluchtige Hoogheydt, den HEERE | PRINCE van ORANGIEN, &c. | 𝕭errijckt met berscheyde Kopere Figuuren, uytbeeldende | Prinçelijcke Lust-hoven en Hofsteden, na de Nederlandtse en France | ordre; als oock eenige Fonteynen, maniere ban 𝕰nten/ | 𝕺culeren/ in-leggen en af-zuggen. | Met noch ontrent 200 Modellen van *Bloem-percken, Parterres,* / *Dool-hoven, Prieelen, Lat-wercken,* en *Zonne-wijsers.* / *Desen laetsten Druck is doorgaens verbetert.* | [ornament] | t'AMSTERDAM, | [short rule] | Voor MARCUS DOORNICK, Boeck-verkooper op den | Vygen-dam, in 't Cantoor Inct-vat. 1670. | 𝕸et 𝕻ribilegie boor 15 𝕵aren.

Part One section title on I4ʳ:

𝕿wee hondert | MODELLEN, | Voor de Lief-hebbers van | HOVEN en THUYNEN. | 𝕾eer dienstigh om alderley | BLOEM-PERKEN, PARTERRES of LOOF-WERCKEN | te leggen : noch eenige Modellen om *Prieelen, Lat-werc-* / *ken en Dool-hoven* na de konst op te stellen, als | oock verscheyden *Soone-wijsers.* | 𝕯ienende tot onderrechtinge boor alle 𝕷ief-hebbers en 𝕳oveniers/ | om 𝕳ofsteden en 𝕷usthoven konstelijck te berieren. | [woodcut] | t'AMSTERDAM, | [short rule] | Voor MARCUS DOORNICK, Boeckverkooper op den Vygen- | dam, in 't Kantoor Incktvat. 1670. | 𝕸et 𝕻ribilegie boor 15 𝕵aren.

Second edition, Amsterdam, 1670. Originally published, Amsterdam, 1669.

4to. A-Q⁴; 64 leaves, pp. [*30*] 1-96 [*2*].

Illustrations: Engraved title-page, fifteen engravings, and numerous woodcuts. All the illustrations are on text pages and included in the collation. Eleanour Rohde, in *The Story of the Garden* says the engravings are "the best illustrations of the famous gardens of Ryswyck, Honsholredyk, and the Huis 'ten Bosch (near the Hague) as they were before they were altered in imitation of Le Nôtre's designs."

Bibliographies: Hunt 317.

Copies: *BNC* and *NUC* (National Agricultural Library and Peabody Institute). Also Hunt.

Part two, by Petrus Nylandt.

𝔇𝔢 𝔑𝔦𝔢𝔲𝔴𝔢 𝔙𝔢𝔯𝔰𝔱𝔞𝔫𝔡𝔦𝔤𝔢𝔫 | HOVENIER, | Over de twaelf Maenden van't Jaer. | *Zijnde het* II DEEL *van het* | VERMAKELYCK LANDT-LEVEN. | 𝔅𝔢𝔰𝔠𝔥𝔯𝔦𝔧𝔟𝔢𝔫𝔡𝔢 / hoe men op de beste en bequaemste manier sal 𝔥𝔬𝔟𝔢𝔫/ 𝔗𝔥𝔲𝔶𝔫𝔢𝔫/ | 𝔏𝔲𝔰𝔱-𝔥𝔬𝔟𝔢𝔫 𝔢𝔫 𝔅𝔬𝔬𝔪𝔤𝔞𝔢𝔯𝔡𝔢𝔫 𝔳𝔢𝔯𝔬𝔯𝔡𝔦𝔫𝔢𝔢𝔯𝔢𝔫/ 𝔟𝔢𝔯𝔢𝔶𝔡𝔢𝔫/ 𝔟𝔢𝔭𝔩𝔞𝔫𝔱𝔢𝔫/ 𝔢𝔫 𝔟𝔢𝔷𝔞𝔢𝔶𝔢𝔫. | Met een Onderwijsinge van der selver aert, kracht, en gebruyck, tot onder- | houding van's Menschen gesontheyt. | 𝔖𝔢𝔢𝔯 𝔡𝔦𝔢𝔫𝔰𝔱𝔦𝔤𝔥 𝔟𝔬𝔬𝔯 𝔞𝔩𝔩𝔢 𝔡𝔢𝔫 𝔤𝔢𝔢𝔫𝔢𝔫/ 𝔡𝔦𝔢 𝔤𝔢𝔢𝔯𝔫𝔢 𝔰𝔠𝔥𝔬𝔬𝔫𝔢 𝔇𝔯𝔲𝔠𝔥𝔱𝔢𝔫 | 𝔢𝔫 𝔤𝔯𝔬𝔬𝔱 𝔭𝔯𝔬𝔣𝔦𝔧𝔱 𝔰𝔬𝔲𝔡𝔢 𝔱𝔯𝔢𝔠𝔨𝔢𝔫. | *Beschreven door* P. NYLAND, *der Medcijnen Doctor.* | [engraving of garden] | t'Amsterdam, Voor *Marcus Doornick*, Boeckverkooper op de Middeldam, 1672. | 𝔐𝔢𝔱 𝔓𝔯𝔦𝔟𝔦𝔩𝔢𝔤𝔦𝔢 𝔟𝔬𝔬𝔯 15 𝔍𝔞𝔯𝔢𝔫.

Third edition, Amsterdam, 1672. Originally published, Amsterdam, 1669, followed by a revised second edition, Amsterdam, 1670.

4to. A-L^4; 44 leaves, pp. [*8*] 1-76 [*4*].

Illustrations: Engraving on title-page and woodcuts in the text.

Bibliographies: This edition unrecorded in the bibliographies consulted. Hunt 317 records the second edition, 1670.

Copies: *BNC* and *NUC* (National Agricultural Library, Peabody Institute, and Temple University).

Part Three, by Petrus Nylandt.

𝔇𝔢𝔫 𝔈𝔯𝔟𝔞𝔯𝔢𝔫 | HUYS-HOUDER, | 𝔒𝔣 | MEDICYN-WINCKEL: | *Zijnde het* III. DEEL *van het* | VERMAKELYCK LANDT-LEVEN. | 𝔒𝔫𝔡𝔢𝔯𝔴𝔦𝔧𝔰𝔢𝔫𝔡𝔢/ 𝔥𝔬𝔢𝔪𝔢𝔫 binnen en buyten de 𝔖𝔱𝔢𝔡𝔢𝔫/ 𝔥𝔢𝔶𝔩𝔰𝔞𝔪𝔢 𝔐𝔢𝔡𝔦𝔠𝔦𝔧𝔫𝔢𝔫 | 𝔟𝔬𝔬𝔯 𝔡𝔢 𝔤𝔢𝔟𝔯𝔢𝔨𝔢𝔫 𝔟𝔞𝔫 𝔐𝔢𝔫𝔰𝔠𝔥𝔢𝔫 𝔢𝔫 𝔅𝔢𝔢𝔰𝔱𝔢𝔫/ 𝔰𝔞𝔩 𝔱𝔬𝔢𝔪𝔞𝔨𝔢𝔫 𝔢𝔫 𝔟𝔢𝔯𝔢𝔶𝔡𝔢𝔫. | *MET* | Een Onderrichtinge, hoe men uyt verscheyden Bloemen en Kruyden, nutte en | wel-ruyckende Wateren, sal konnen uyttrecken, en distilleren. | 𝔄𝔩𝔰 𝔪𝔢𝔡𝔢 | Den Naerstigen BYEN-HOUDER, | *Door* P. NYLAND, *der Medicijnen Doctor.* | 𝔑𝔬𝔠𝔥 𝔦𝔰 𝔥𝔦𝔢𝔯 𝔞𝔠𝔥𝔱𝔢𝔯 𝔟𝔶 𝔤𝔢𝔟𝔬𝔢𝔤𝔥𝔱 Den VERSTANDIGEN KOCK. | [engraving of vetrinarian] | t'Amsterdam, 𝔟𝔬𝔬𝔯 Marcus Doornick, 𝔅𝔬𝔢𝔠𝔨𝔟𝔢𝔯𝔨𝔬𝔬𝔭𝔢𝔯 𝔬𝔭 𝔡𝔢𝔫 𝔇𝔶𝔤𝔤𝔢𝔫𝔡𝔞𝔪/ | in't 𝔠𝔬𝔪𝔭𝔱𝔬𝔦𝔯 𝔍𝔫𝔠𝔨𝔱-𝔟𝔞𝔱. Met Privilegie.

Part Three section title on E4^r:

Den Naerstigen | BYEN-HOUDER, | Onderrechtende | Hoe men met nut en profijt de Byen re- | geeren en onderhouden sal. | *Als mede* / Hoedanigh men Honigh en Wasch, op een korte en bequame | manier sal vergaderen/ bereyden en suyveren. | [engraving of bee keeper] | t'Amsterdam, voor Marcus Doornick, Boeckverkooper op den Middeldam/ | in't Kantoor Jnckt-vat. Met Privilegie.

Part Three section title on H1^r:

DE | VERSTANDIGE KOCK, | *Of* Sorghvuldige Huys-houdster: | BESCHRYVENDE, | Hoe men op de beste en bequaemste manier alderhande Spijsen | sal koken/ stoven/ braden/ backen en bereyden; met de Saussen daer toe | dienende: Seer dienstigh en profijtelijck in alle Huys-houdingen. | Oock om veelderleye slagh van TAERTEN en PASTEYEN toe te stellen. | Vermeerdert met de | HOLLANDTSE SLACHT-TYDT. | Hier is noch achter by gevoeght/ de | VERSTANDIGE CONFITUURMAKER, | Onderwijsende/ hoe men van veelderhande Vruchten/ Wortelen/ Bloemen en Bladen/ &c. | goede en nutte Confituren sal konnen toemaken en bewaren. | [engraving of kitchen] | t'Amsterdam, voor Marcus Doornick, Boeckverkooper op den Dyggendam/ | in't Kantoor Jnct-vat. Met Privilegie. | H

Second edition, Amsterdam, undated but between 1670 and 1672. Originally published, Amsterdam, 1669.

4to. A-L⁴; 44 leaves, pp. [1-3] 4-88.

Illustrations: Engraved title-page, two engraved section titles, all included in the collation, and three woodcuts in the first section. The first and second engraved title-pages are signed G. V. Eeckhout.

Bibliographies: Hunt 317.

Copies: *BNC* and *NUC* (5 copies).

1097. De volmaakte geldersche keuken-meyd.

DE | VOLMAAKTE | *GELDERSCHE* | KEUKEN-MEYD, | *Onderwyzende* | Hoe men allerhande Spyzen op een smakelyke | en min kostbare wyze kan toerigten;

nament- | lyk; het koken, stoven, bakken en braden | van alle soorten van Vleesch en
Visch, | mitsgaders het stoven, inmaken en dro- | gen van allerley Groentens en an- |
dere Vrugten, als meede het In- | zouten en Roken van Vleesch, | het maken van
Worsten, en | eyndelyk eenige beproefde | HUYS-MIDDELEN, | Zeer dienstig in
veelderhande Qualen | en Toevallen; | *Waar by nog komt,* | Een Verzameling van
hondert agtien Uitgelezene | RECEPTEN, | *Ter extraordinaire toebereydinge van
delicate* | Spyzen, Confituren en Tincturen. | *Derden Druk* | Veel vermeerdert. | [rule]
| *Te NYMEGEN.* | By ISAAC VAN CAMPEN, | Boekdrukker en Boekverkoper, naast
| het Stadhuys, 1768.

Sixth edition, Nijmegen, 1768.

8vo. ✳⁶ A-Hh⁸, ²A-F⁸; 302 leaves, pp. [*12*] [1] 2-459 [460-496], ²1-91 [92-96].

Illustration: Etched title on ✳1ʳ.

Bibliographies: This edition unrecorded in the bibliographies consulted. Oberlé (1)
107 records a fourth edition, Amsterdam, 1752-1755, in 3 vols. under the title *De
volmaakte hollandsche Keuken-Meid.* Drexel 246 and Malortie, p. 863, record the fifth
edition, Amsterdam, 1761-1763, in 3 parts.

Copies: No other copy of this edition located.

Volmaakte grond-beginzelen der keuken-kunde (Amsterdam, 1769).
See item 1100.

Aanhangzel, van de volmaakte Hollandsche keuken-meid (Amsterdam, 1769). See
item 1099.

1098. De volmaakte Hollandsche keuken-meid.

DE VOLMAAKTE | HOLLANDSCHE | KEUKEN-MEID. | ONDERWYZENDE |
Hoe men allerhande *Spyzen, Confituren* en *Nage-* | *rechten,* zonder ongemeene kosten,
zelfs voor | de Roomsgezinden op Visdagen en in de Vas- | ten, gezond en smakelyk
kan toebereiden: | Hoe men alles tegen de winter inlegt. | Wat men in de
SLACHT-TYD doen moet: | En hoe men *Mol* en versch *Bier* des | zomers goed kan
houden. | BENEVENS | *Eenige vaste tekens waar aan men zien kan of het* | Vleesch,
ten tyde der Vee-Pest, *gezondi is of niet.* | EN | Hoe men een ordentelyke TAFEL zal
schikken wan- | neer men zyne vrienden onthaald, met eenige *Figu-* | *ren,* van

opgedischte Tafels, opgeheldert. | Als mede eenige | HUISMIDDELEN | *Voor de* Verkoudheid; *om allerhande* Koortzen *onfeil-* | *baar te geneezen; om bet* Gezicht *te versterken &c.* | *Nevens de toebereiding van eenige zagte Spyzen en* | *Dranken tot verkwikking van zieke Menschen.* | Beschreeven door | *EENE VOORNAAME MEVROUWE* | Onlangs in 's Gravenhage Overleeden. | ZEVENDE DRUK. | Verbeterd, en van zeer veele Drukfeilen gezuiverd. | *Gedrukt volgens haar eigen Handschrift.* | [rule] | *Te AMSTERDAM,* | By STEVEN VAN ESVELDT, | in de Kalverstraat, het derde Huys van de Room- | sche Kerk de Papegaay. 1772. | *Met Privilegie.*

Seventh edition, Amsterdam, 1772. The earliest recorded edition is the fourth, Amsterdam, 1752-1755.

8vo. *⁸(٭1 + π²) ٭٭⁶ A-I⁸ K²; 90 leaves, pp. [*32*] 1-148. Letterpress folding chart facing p. 147. Bound with *Aanhangzel van de volmaakte Hollandsche keuken-meid* (Amsterdam, 1769) and *Volmaakte grond-beginzelen der keuken-kunde* (Amsterdam, 1769).

Illustrations: Etched and engraved title `DE VOLMAAKTE HOLLANDSE | KEUKEN MEID.' similar, but not identical, to that in item 1100.

Bibliographies: This edition unrecorded in the bibliographies consulted. Oberlé (1) 107 records the fourth edition, Amsterdam, 1752-1755. Drexel 246 and Malortie, p. 363, record the Amsterdam, 1761-1763, edition.

Copies: *NUC* (American Philosophical Society only).

1099. Aanhangzel, van de volmaakte Hollandsche keuken-meid.

AANHANGZEL, | VAN DE | VOLMAAKTE | HOLLANDSCHE | KEUKEN-MEID. | ONDERWYZENDE | Veelerhande zaaken, omtrent het toebereiden der *Spy-* | *zen, Confituuren*, en *Nagerechten*, zelfs voor de | Roomsgezinden op Vischdagen en in de Vasten. | Het inleggen van alles tegens de Winter, en | wat verder de SLACHT-TYD aangaat; | behorende tot het voorige Stukje. | ALS MEEDE | Nog eenige zeer heilzaame | HUISMIDDELEN. | *Tegens veelerhande quaalen en Toevallen.* | *Neevens eenigen zeer dienstige Geheimen.* | Hier is in 't byzonder by gevoegt | DE KUNST. | Om allerhande Tafel gerechten | VOOR TE SNYDEN; | De Delikaatste stukken te kennen om aan de Gasten | VOOR TE DIENEN. | *Nevens de* Wyze *om allerhande Tafel-goed Konstig* | *en Cierlyk te Vouwen.* | Vergadert uit verscheidene Handschriften van eenige Hol- | landsche

Mevrouwen en Juffrouwen. | *Opgeheldert en Verciert met Koopere Plaaten.* | [rule] | Te *AMSTERDAM*, | By STEVEN VAN ESVELDT; | In de Kalverstraat, 1769. | *Met Previlegie.*

New edition, Amsterdam, 1769. The earliest recorded edition is Amsterdam, 1763.

8vo. ✳⁸ ✳✳⁴ ✳✳✳² A-H⁸ I⁶; 84 leaves, pp. [*28*] 1-140. Bound with *De volmaakte Hollandsche keuken-meid* (Amsterdam, 1772) and *Volmaakte grond-beginzelen der keuken-kunde* (Amsterdam, 1769).

Illustrations: Etched and engraved title "DE VOLMAAKTE HOLLANDSE | KEUKEN MEID." similar, but not identical, to that in item 1098, and two etched folding plates illustrating carving and napkin folding.

Bibliographies: This edition unrecorded in the bibliographies consulted. Drexel 246 and Malortie, p. 363, record the Amsterdam, 1763, edition.

Copies: No other copy of this edition located.

1100. Volmaakte grond-beginzelen der keuken-kunde.

VOLMAAKTE | GROND-BEGINZELEN | DER | KEUKEN-KUNDE. | Behelzende eene korte dog volledige verhande- | ling, van alles wat een Kok of Keuken-Meid, | weeten moet; en het geen zy in het *Kooken*, | *Braden, Stooven, Bakken, Droogen, Zouten,* | *Inleggen, Confyten,* &c. en het *aanrichten* | van een *Tafel* waar te neemen *heeft.* | *Zynde eene beknopte voorstelling en considerable ver-* | *meerdering van* | DE VOLMAAKTE | HOLLANDSCHE | KEUKEN-MEID. | Onderwyzende breedvoerig, het toebereiden | van allerhande *Spyzen, Confituuren, Nagerech-* | *ten* en *Huismiddelen.* Het bezorgen van den | *Slachttyd, Winter-provisien* en *Dranken.* | Het *Dekken* en *Schikken* van een orden- | telyke *Tafel,* &c | *Ten dienste van alle Koks en Keuken-Meisjes, om dezelve* | *in deeze Kunst te volmaken; zonder eenige andere* | *Boeken of onderrechtingen daar toe nodig* | *te hebben; opgegeeven* | DOOR | D'Autheur van de Hollandsche Keuken-Meid. | [ornament] | Te *AMSTERDAM*, | By STEVEN VAN ESVELDT, | Boekverkoper in de Kalverstraat, het 3de huis | van de Roomsche Kerk de Papegaay. 1769. | *Met Previlegie.*

New edition, Amsterdam, 1769. The earliest recorded edition is Amsterdam, 1758.

8vo. ✳⁸ A-I⁸; 80 leaves, pp. [*16*] 1-143 [144]. Bound with *De volmaakte Hollandsche keuken-meid* (Amsterdam, 1772) and *Aanhangzel van de volmaakte Hollandsche keuken-meid* (Amsterdam, 1769).

Illustration: Etched title `VOLMAAKTE KEUKEN GEREEDSCHAPPEN.'

Bibliographies: Horn-Arndt 346. Drexel 246 and Malorite, p. 363, record the Amsterdam, 1763, edition.

Copies: *NUC* (American Philosophical Society only).

De Cierlijcke
VOORSNYDINGE
Aller
TAFEL GERECHTEN

t'Amsterdam, by Hieronymus Sweerts, Boek- en Printverkooper in de Kalverstraat.

De Geoeffende en Ervaren
KEUKEN-MEESTER,
Of de Verstandige KOK.

Onderwijsende, hoe dat in ENGELAND,
VRANKRIJK, ITALIEN, DUYTSLAND, &c. alderhande soorten van *Spijsen*, soo voor de
Tafelen der GROOTEN, als lagere en min-
dere STANTS-PERSOONEN, bereyd, gehan-
deld en toegemaakt werden.

Insgelijks ook een byzonder
KOOK-BOEK,
Tot dienst der ROOMS gesinde in de VISCH
en VASTE DAGEN; en hoe men alderhande soort van VISCH kan bereyden en voordienen.

Als mede
Het Bereyden van verscheyde sagte *Spijsen*, tot
dienst der SIEKEN en KRANKEN: Mits-
gaders het mengen van veelder-
hande SAUZEN, &c.

Alles door Ervarendheyd goed bevonden, en ten ge-
meenen nutte uytgegeven, door zeekere Hof-
bediende van een Hoog Aanzienelijke
PERSONAGIE.
EERSTE DEEL.

TOT LEYDEN,
Gedrukt voor den Autheur, by de Weduwe van
BASTIAAN SCHOUTEN, wonende in de
Nieuwe-steeg, 1701.

Item no. 1084

Ventriculi QVERELÆ et Opprobria *Adornante Bernhardo Swalve Med. Doct.*

AMSTELODAMI, *Apud Ioannem a Waesberge et Elizeum Weyerstraten.* 1664.

Item no. 1096

DE
VOLMAAKTE
GELDERSCHE
KEUKEN MEYD

DE VOLMAAKTE HOLLANDSE
KEUKEN MEID.

T.J. walter sculp

INDIA

1101. Riddell, R.

INDIAN | DOMESTIC ECONOMY | AND | RECEIPT BOOK; | COMPRISING
NUMEROUS DIRECTIONS | FOR | PLAIN WHOLESOME COOKERY, | BOTH
ORIENTAL AND ENGLISH; | WITH MUCH MISCELLANEOUS MATTER |
ANSWERING FOR ALL GENERAL PURPOSES OF REFERENCE | CONNECTED
WITH | HOUSEHOLD AFFAIRS, | LIKELY TO BE IMMEDIATELY REQUIRED
BY | FAMILIES, MESSES, AND PRIVATE INDIVIDUALS, | RESIDING AT THE
PRESIDENCIES OR OUT-STATIONS. | [short rule] | BY THE AUTHOR OF |
"MANUAL OF GARDENING FOR WESTERN INDIA." | [short rule] | Third
Edition, Revised. | BOMBAY: | PRINTED AND SOLD AT THE BOMBAY
GAZETTE PRESS, | AND TO BE HAD OF ALL BOOKSELLERS. | [short rule] |
1852.

Third edition, Bombay, 1852. Originally published, Bombay, 1849.

216 x 135 mm. π^4 [1-5]^8 6-7^8 [8]^8 9-10^8 [11-27]^8 [28-29]^4 [30]^6 [31]^2 [32-36]^4 [37-42]^8
[43-46]^4; 320 leaves, pp. [i-v] vi-viii [1] 2-630 [2].

Bibliographies: This edition unrecorded in the bibliographies consulted. Axford, p.
226, cites the first edition.

Copies: No other copy of this edition located.

1102. Riddell, R.

INDIAN | DOMESTIC ECONOMY | AND | RECEIPT BOOK; | COMPRISING |
NUMEROUS DIRECTIONS FOR PLAIN WHOLESOME COOKERY, | BOTH
ORIENTAL AND ENGLISH; WITH MUCH MISCELLANEOUS MATTER |
ANSWERING FOR ALL GENERAL PURPOSES OF REFERENCE | CONNECTED
| WITH HOUSEHOLD AFFAIRS, LIKELY TO BE IMMEDIATELY | REQUIRED
BY FAMILIES, MESSES, AND PRIVATE INDIVIDUALS, | RESIDING AT THE
PRESIDENCIES OR OUT-STATIONS. | [short fancy rule] | BY THE AUTHOR OF
| "MANUAL OF GARDENING FOR WESTERN INDIA." | [short fancy rule] |
FOURTH EDITION – REVISED. | MADRAS: | PRINTED BY D. P. L. C.
CONNOR, AT THE CHRISTIAN KNOWLEDGE | SOCIETY'S PRESS, CHURCH
STREET, VEPERY. | 1853.

Fourth edition, Madras, 1853. Originally published, Bombay, 1849.

213 x 135 mm. π^4 A-V^4 W-Z^4, "A1"-"V1"^{4} "W1-Z1"^{4}, "A2"-"V2"^{4} "W2-Z2"^{4}, "A3"-"I3"^{4}; 328 leaves, pp. [i-vii] viii [1] 2-645 [646] [2]. First leaf and last leaf (blanks?) wanting in this copy.

Bibliographies: This edition unrecorded in the bibliographies consulted. Axford, p. 226, cites the first edition.

Copies: *NUC* (New York Public Library only).

INGREDIENTS FOR CURRY POWDER.

Four Receipts.

	No. 1.	No. 2.	No. 3.	No. 4.	
Coriander seeds.	lbs. 20	lbs. 12	lbs. 3	lbs. 1	{ To be well roasted.
Turmeric.	,, 4	2	1	1 2oz.	..Pounded.
Cummin seeds.	,, 1	,,	½	,,	{ Dried and ground.
Fenugreek.	,, 1	1	,,	0 4oz.	
Mustard seed.	,, 1	,,	⅕	,,	{ Dried and cleaned of husks.
Ginger, dried.	,, 2	2	,,	1	
Black pepper.	,, 2	1	1	1 ,,	
Dried Chillies.	,, 1	2	1	0 12oz.	
Poppy seed.	,, 2	2	,,	,,	
Garlic.	,, 2	1	,,	,,	
Cardamons.	,,	,,	,,	0 8oz.	
Cinnamon.	,,	,,	,,	0 8oz.	

IRELAND

1103. Briggs, Richard.

THE | English Art of Cookery, | ACCORDING TO THE | PRESENT PRACTICE; | BEING | A Complete GUIDE to all HOUSEKEEPERS, | on a PLAN entirely new; consisting of | Thirty-eight Chapters. | CONTAINING | [in two columns: column one] Proper Directions for Market- | ing, and Trussing of Poultry. | The making Soups and Broths. | Dressing all sorts of Fish. | Sauces for every Occasion. | Boiling and Roasting. | Baking, Broiling, and Frying. | Stews and Hashes. | Made Dishes of every sort. | Ragous and Fricasees. | Directions for dressing all sorts | of Roots and Vegetables. | All Sorts of Aumlets and Eggs. | Puddings, Pies, Tarts, &c. | Pancakes and Fritters. | Cheese-cakes and Custards. | Blanc'mange, Jellies, and Syl- | labubs. | [fancy verticle rule] | [column two] Directions for the Sick. | Directions for Seafaring Men. | Preserving, Syrups, and Con- | serves. | Drying and Candying. | All sorts of Cakes. | Hogs Puddings, Sausages, &c. | Potting, and little cold Dishes. | The Art of Carving. | Collaring, Salting, and Sousing. | Pickling. | To keep Garden Vegetables, &c. | A Catalogue of Things in Sea- | son. | Made Wines and Cordial Wa- | ters. | Brewing. | English and French Bread, &c. [end columns] | With BILLS of FARE for every MONTH in the YEAR, | NEATLY AND CORRECTLY PRINTED. | [rule] | BY RICHARD BRIGGS, | Many Years COOK at the GLOBE-TAVERN, | FLEET-STREET, the | WHITE-HART TAVERN, HOLBORN, and now at the | TEMPLE | COFFEE HOUSE, LONDON. | [two rules] | DUBLIN: | Printed for P. BYRNE No. 108, GRAFTON-STREET. | [short fancy rule] | 1791.

First Dublin edition, 1791. Originally published, London, 1788 (item 577).

12mo. A^{12} [a]^4 b-c^4 B-Z^{12} 2A^4 (2A signed "A2"); 292 leaves, pp. [i-v] vi-xxiv, 1-24, ^{2}[1] 2-533 [534] [2]. Last leaf blank.

Bibliographies: Maclean, p.15.

Copies: *NUC* (Buffalo and Erie County Public Library and Harvard).

1104. Cheap Receipts and Hints on Cookery.

[Within an ornamental border] 𝕮𝖍𝖊𝖆𝖕 𝕽𝖊𝖈𝖊𝖎𝖕𝖙𝖘 𝖆𝖓𝖉 𝕳𝖎𝖓𝖙𝖘 | ON | COOKERY; | COLLECTED FOR DISTRIBUTION | AMONGST THE | IRISH PEASANTRY | IN 1847. | [short fancy rule] | ARMAGH: | PRINTED BY J. M`WATTERS, ENGLISH-ST. | [short rule] | MDCCCXLVII.

First edition, Armagh, 1847.

170 x 104 mm. π^2 A-G^6 H^2 (π2 signed "A1"); 46 leaves, pp. [i-iii] iv-vi [7-9] 10-91 [92]. Publisher's purple cloth stamped in gold.

Bibliographies: Axford, p. 59; Bitting, p. 528.

Copies: *NUC* (Library of Congress only).

1105. Glasse, Hannah, 1707-1770.

THE | Compleat Confectioner: | OR, THE | *Whole Art of Confectionary* | Made PLAIN and EASY: | SHEWING, | The various Methods of PRESERVING and CANDYING, | both dry and liquid, all Kinds of FRUIT, FLOWERS and | HERBS; the different Ways of CLARIFYING SUGAR; | and the Method of Keeping FRUIT, NUTS and FLOW- | ERS fresh and fine all the Year round. | ALSO | DIRECTIONS for making | [in two columns: column one] ROCK-WORKS and CANDIES, | BISCUITS, | RICH CAKES, | CREAMS, | CUSTARDS, | JELLIES, | WHIP SYLLABUBS, and | CHEESE-CAKES of all Sorts. | ENGLISH WINES of all Sorts. | [two vertical rules] | [column two] STRONG CORDIALS, | SIMPLE WATERS, | MEAD, OILS &c. | SYRUPS of all Kinds, | MILK PUNCH, that will keep | twenty Yeras. | KNICKNACKS and TRIFLES | for DESERTS, &c. | LIKEWISE | The Art of making ARTIFICIAL FRUIT, with the Stalks | in it, so as to resemble the natural fruit. | To which are added, | Some BILLS of FARE for DESERTS for private FAMILIES. | [rule] | By H. GLASSE, Author of the ART of COOKERY. | [rule] | ALSO, The NEW ART OF BREWING. By Mr. ELLIS. | [two rules] | DUBLIN: | Printed by JOHN EXSHAW, at the Bible in Dame-street, | [short rule] | MDCCXLII.

Title-page of The New Art of Brewing on p. 193:

THE | New ART of Brewing | AND | Improving MALT LIQUORS | To the greatest Advantage. | CONTAINING | [in two columns: column one] The New Improvement of | the Barley Corn, for ma- | king the best, and palest | Malt. | The best Methods of brew- | ing all Sorts of fine Ale, | Strong Beer, and Table | Beer, in several Parts of | England and Wales. | An Account of Hops, and of | a new discovered Herb | growing wild, which for | its agreeable bitter, and | [two vertical rules] | [column two] wholesome qualities, is of- | ten preferred to the Hop. | Curious Methods of drying | Malt and Hops in the | greatest Perfection. | How to prevent the Damage | done by the Wevil Inscct, | to Malt, Wheat, &c. | To fine, relish, strengthen | and preserve Ale or strong | Beer, Wine or Cyder, and | to recover them if turned, | &c. &c. &c. [end columns] | With many other curious and very useful Matters rela- | ting to the BREWERY, never before published. | And absolutely necessary for all who would

brew their │ own MALT DRINK in the highest Perfection. │ [rule] │ *By* WILLIAM
ELLIS, │ Late of London, Brewer. │ [rule] │ *DUBLIN:* │ Printed by JOHN EXSHAW,
at the BIBLE in Dame- │ street, opposite Castle-lane. │ [short rule] │ MDCCLXI.

New edition Dublin, 1762, of *The Compleat Confectioner.* Originally published,
London, ca. 1760 (item 707). Note: The date on *The Compleat Confectioner* title-
page is printed MDCCXLII for MDCCLXII. No other edition of William Ellis's *The
New Art of Brewing* has been located. It is a much shorter and completely different
work than his *London and Country Brewer*, London, 1734-1738.

12mo. [A]² B-K¹² L⁶ M⁸; 124 leaves, pp. [i-iii] iv [1] 2- 228 [*16*].

Bibliographies: Maclean, p. 61.

Copies: *BMC* and *NUC* (Brooklyn Public Library and New York Public Library).
Maclean adds International Wine and Food Society and National Library of Ireland.

1106. Kennedy, John, d. 1790.

A │ TREATISE │ UPON │ *PLANTING*, │ GARDENING, │ AND THE │
MANAGEMENT OF THE HOT-HOUSE. │ CONTAINING │ [in two columns:
column one] I. The Method of planting Forest- │ Trees in gravelly, poor, moun- │
tainous, and heath Lands; and for │ raising the Plants in the Seed-Beds, │ previous to
their being planted. │ II. The Method of Pruning Forest- │ Trees, and how to improve
Plan- │ tations that have been neglected. │ III. On the Soils most proper for │ the
different kinds of Forest-trees. │ IV. The Management of Vines; │ their Cultivation
upon Fire-Walls, │ and in the Hot-House; with a new │ Method of dressing, planting,
and │ preparing the Ground. │ V. A new and easy Method to pro- │ pagate Pine Plants,
so as to gain │ Half a Year in their Growth; │ [two vertical rules] │ [column two] with a
sure Method of destroy- │ ing the Insect so destructive to │ Pines. │ VI. The best
Method to raise Mush- │ rooms without Spawn, by which │ the Table may be
plentifully sup- │ plied every Day in the Year. │ VII. An improved Method of culti- │
vating Asparagus. │ VIII. The best Method to culti- │ vate Field Cabbages, Carrots,
and │ Turnips for feeding of Cattle. │ IX. A new Method of managing all │ Kinds of
Fruit-Trees, viz. of pro- │ per soils for planting, of pruning │ and dressing them; with a
Receipt │ to prevent Blights, and to cure │ them when blighted. [end columns] │ [rule] │
BY JOHN KENNEDY, │ GARDENER TO SIR THOMAS GASCOIGNE, BART. │
[two rules] │ DUBLIN: │ Printed for W. WILSON, No. 6, Dame-street. │ [rule] │
M,DCC,LXXXIV.

Third edition, Dublin, 1784. Originally published, York, 1776.

8vo. A-Gg^8; 240 leaves, pp. [i-v] vi-xiii [xiv-xvi] [1] 2-462 [2].

Bibiliographies: Henrey III.895.

Copies: *BNC* and *NUC* (5 copies).

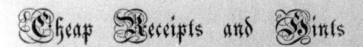

Cheap Receipts and Hints

ON

COOKERY;

COLLECTED FOR DISTRIBUTION

AMONGST THE

IRISH PEASANTRY

IN 1847.

ARMAGH:

PRINTED BY J. M'WATTERS, ENGLISH-ST.

MDCCCXLVII.

ITALY

1107. Adami, Antonio.

IL | [in red] NOVITIATO | DEL MAESTRO | DI CASA; | [in red] Nel qual si dà
notitia particolare di tutte le cose | [in red] necessarie per essercitare conuenientemen- |
[in red] te quest' Offitio nella Corte di Roma. | *Con vna instruttione generale, per*
conoscer le quali- | *tà della roba, fuggir le fraudi, e far le proui-* | *sioni con vantaggio*
co' loro prezzi. | [in red] Vi si mostrano in oltre le regole da misurare fabriche, e
diuerse | [in red] prattiche d'Agricoltura, e particolarmente per fare | [in red] diuerse
sorti di Vini, e conseruarli. | *OPERA* | [in red] DI DON ANTONIA ADAMI | [in red]
DALLA ROCCACONTRADA; | *Vtile sì à Prencipi, come ad ogni altra qualità di*
persone priuate | *per il buon gouerno delle lor Case.* | [ornament in red and black] |
[in red] In Roma, [in black] Appresso Pietr' Antonio Facciotti. [in red] 1636. | [rule] |
Con licenza de' Superiori, & Priuilegio.

First edition, Rome, 1636.

8vo. A-Q^8; 128 leaves, pp. [1-2] 3-252 [*4*].

Bibliographies: B. In. G. 10; Simon BG 1299; Vicaire 746; Westbury, p. 2.

Copies: B. In. G., *BNC* and *NUC* (Harvard only).

1108. Agnoletti, Vicenzo.

LE ARTI | DEL CREDENZIERE, CONFETTIERE | E LIQUORISTA | RIDOTTE
ALL' ULTIMA PERFEZIONE | DA | VINCENZO AGNOLETTI | CREDENZIERE
E LIQUORISTA | *All' attuale servizio di S. M. I. Maria Luisa* | *Duchessa di Parma,*
Piacenze e Guastalla. | PER USO DE' PROFESSORI E DILETTANTI. | [publisher's
monogram] | ROMA 1822. | [short rule] PRESSO PIO CIPICCHIA. | *Con*
Permesso.

First edition, Rome, 1822.

171 x 114 mm. [1]^8 ($\pm 1_1$) [2]^8 3-17^8 18-20^4 21^4 (-21$_1$); 151 leaves, pp. [1-2] 3-301
[302].

Bibliographies: Bitting, p. 4; Westbury, p. 2. B. In. G. records the Florence, 1826,
edition.

Copies: *BMC* and *NUC* (Kansas State University only).

Alessio Piemontese, see Ruscelli, Girolamo, d. 1566.

1109.　Apicius.

Apicii Celii de re Coquinaria libri decem. | Coquinariae capita Graeca ab Apitio prosita haec sunt. | Epimeles: Artoprus: Cepurica: Pandecter: Osprion | Trophetes: Polyteles: Tetrapas: Thalassa: Halicus. | Hanc Plato adulatricem medicinae appellat.

Colophon: ⅭⅠ Impressum uenetiis p Iohannem de Cereto de Tridino | alias Tacuinum. M.CCCCC.III. die tertio mensis Augusti

New edition, Venice, 1503. Originally published, Venice, ca.1482-1486.

4to. a-h^4; 32 leaves, unpaginated.

Bibliographies: Schraemli (1) 20; Schraemli (2) 7; Vicaire 30; Wheaton and Kelly 185.

Copies: *BMC*, *BNC*, and *NUC* (4 copies).

1110.　Athenaeus.

ATHENAEVS | ᾿ΑΘΗΝΑΙΟΥ Δειπνοσοφιστοῦ τὴν πολυμαθεστάτην πραγματείαν νῦν ἔξεστί σοι φιλόλογε μικροῦ | πριαμένῳ πολλῶν τε καὶ μεγάλων καὶ ἀξιομνημονεύτων καὶ Θαυμαστῶν καὶ ποικίλων καὶ δαι- | δάλων καὶ γλαφυρῶν καὶ ὧν ἴσως πρότερον οὐκ ᾔδεις, ἐς γνῶσιν ἐλθεῖν · καὶ ὅλως τῶν τῆς | ἑλληνικῆς παιδείας ἀποθέτων καὶ δυσευρέτων κειμηλίων ἐγκρατεῖ γενέσθαι. τῶν | δὲ βιβλίων πεντεκαίδεκα τὸν ἀριθμὸν ὄντων, τὰ μὲν τρισκαίδεκα, ὁλοσχερῆ, | τὸ δέ τοι πρῶτον καὶ δεύτερον ἐπιτετμηνένα σοι παρέχομεν. ἀκεφάλῳ | σώματι κεφαλὴν ἀναγκασθεντες ἐπιθεῖναι κολοβήν. ἀνδρῶν οὖν | ἐστιν συγνωμόνων τὸ ταυτὶ τὰ συγγράμα τ᾿ ἀναλεγομέ- | νους, μάλιστα μὲν τοῖς περὶ τὸν ᾿Αλδον τὸν πολύαθλόν | τε καὶ πολυγράμματον εὐχαριστειν. Οὐχ ἥ- | κιστα δὲ καὶ Μουσούρῳ τῷ διδασκάλῳ. | τῷ εἰ καὶ μὴ παντάπασιν ἰασα- | μένῳ τἀντίγραφον τῶνδε | τῶν τύπων ἀνηκέ- | στοις ἕλκεσι | πολλα- | χῆ |

διεφθο- | ρός, | ἀλλ᾽ οὖν | πολλὰς μὲν μυ- | ριάδας διορθώσαντι | σφαλμάτων πολλοὺς δὲ στί- | χους τῶν παρεισαγομένων κατα- | λογάδην πρότερον ἀναγινωσκομένους | καὶ χύδην, εἰς τὴν προσήκουσαν τῆς ἐμμέτρου τάξεως εὐκρίνειαν ἀποκαταστήσαντι, χάριν εἰδέναι. | [printer's device]

Colophon: VENETIIS APVD ALDVM, ET | ANDREAM SOCERVM | MENSE AVGVSTO. | M.D.XIIII.

First edition, Venice, 1514.

Folio: A-B^{10} a-s^8 t^4; 168 leaves, pp. [α1-α2] α3-α38 [2] 1-294 [2]. Leaf B10, blank, wanting in this copy.

Bibliographies: B. In. G. 112; Schraemli (1) 35; Schraemli (2) 9; Vicaire 50.

Copies: B. In. G., *BMC*, *BNC*, and *NUC* (8 copies).

1111. Athenaeus.

ATHENAEI | DIPNOSOPHISTARVM | siue Coenae sapientum | Libri XV. | NATALE DE COMITIBVS VENETO NVNC | primum è Graeca in Latinam linguam uertente. | COMPLVRIBVS EX MANVSCRIPTIS ANTIQVIS- | simis exemplaribus additis: quae in Graecè hactenus impressis | uoluminibus non reperiebantur. | Ad potentissimum Ferdinandum, Pannoniae, | Boemiae, ac Romanorum Regem. | Cum priuilegio summi Pontificis Pauli IIII. & Illustriss. | Senatus Veneti in annos XX. | [woodcut, lettered on three sides, vertically bottom to top] QVI BIBERIT EX HAC | [horizontally across the top] AQVA NON SI- | [vertically top to bottom] TIET IN AETERNVM. | Venetiis apud Andream Arriuabenum | ad signum Putei. MDLVI.

First edition in Latin, Venice, 1556. Originally published in Greek, Venice, 1514 (item 1110).

Folio: ✱^{6} A-AA^6 Aa^6; 156 leaves, pp. [*12*] 1-288 [*12*].

Bibliographies: B. In. G. 113; Oberlé (2) 3; Wheaton and Kelly 304.

Copies: B. In. G., *BMC* (2 copies), *BNC*, and *NUC* (10 copies).

1112. Avvertimenti sopra la fabrica della carne porcina.

AVVERTIMENTI | SOPRA LA FABRICA | Della Carne Porcina. | [ornament] | In Bologna, Per Nicolò Tebaldini. | M.DC.XXVII. | *Con Licennza de' Superiori.*

First edition? Bologna, 1627.

4to. A-C⁴; 12 leaves, pp. [1-2] 3-21 [22] [2]. Last leaf blank.

Bibliographies: Unrecorded in the bibliographies consulted.

Copies: No other copy located.

1113. Bacci, Andrea, 1524-1600.

[engraved title-page, with architectual designs and figures, lettered] DE NATVRALI | VINORVM HISTORIA | DE VINIS ITALIAE | *Et de Conuiuijs Antiquorum* | LIBRI SEPTEM | ANDREAE BACCII | *Elpidiani Medici, atq[ue] Philosophi,* | *Ciuis Romani* | ACCESSIT DE FACTITIIS, AC CERVISIIS, | *de q[ue] Rheni, Galliae, Hispaniae, et de totius* | *Europae Vinis et de omni Vinorum usu* | COMPENDIARIA TRACTATIO | AD AMPLISSIMVM | S.R.E. CARD. | ASCANIVM COLVMNAM | [on an oval frame surrounding portrait of the author] ANDREAE BACCII ELPIDIEN AETAT. SVAE ANNO LXXII | [below portrait] *Romae anno 1596* | SVMMO CONATV *ex officina Nicholai Mutis* AS SIDVITATE ET FERVORE.

First edition, Rome, 1596.

Folio: A⁴ †⁴ ††⁶ B-Aaa⁴ Bbb²; 200 leaves, pp. [28] 1-370 [2].

Bibliographies: B. In. G. 129; Bitting, p. 23; Schraemli (1) 42; Simon BG 155; Vicaire 60.

Copies: B. In. G., *BMC* (4 copies), *BNC*, and *NUC* (8 copies).

1114. Baldini, Baccio, d. 1585.

BACCII | BALDINII | IN LIBRVM | HYPPOCRATIS. | *DE AQVIS, AERE, ET LOCIS* | Commentaria. | *Eiusdem Tractatus de Cucumeribus.* | CVM LICENTIA SVPERIORVM. | [vignette] | FLORENTIAE, | *Ex Officina Bartholomaei Sermartillij.* | CI I LXXXVI.

Title-page of the treatise on cucumbers:

BACCII | BALDINII | Tractatus | DE CVCVMERIBVS. | [ornament] | *CVM LICENTIA SVPERIORVM.* | [vignette] | FLORENTIAE, | *Apud Bartholomaeum Sermartellium.* | MDLXXXVI.

First edition, Florence, 1586.

4to. a⁶ A-P⁸ Q⁶, ²A⁸; 140 leaves, pp. [*12*] 1-252, ²[1-2] 3-16.

Bibliographies: B. In. G. 138.

Copies: B. In. G., *BMC, BNC,* and *NUC* (4 copies).

1115. Barotti, Lorenzo, 1724-1801.

IL CAFFÈ. | [short rule] | *CANTI DUE.*

Colophon: PARMA | [fancy rule] | DALLA STAMPERIA REALE | CI . I CC. LXXXI. | *CON APPROVAZIONE.*

First edition, Parma, 1781.

4to. π⁴ a-e⁴; 24 leaves, pp. [*8*] 1-38 [2]. Last leaf blank.

Bookplates: Westbury; Marcus Crahan.

Bibliographies: B. In. G. 154; Crahan 244; Westbury p. 20.

Copies: B. In. G., *BMC* (2 copies) and *NUC* (Brown University and University of California, Berkeley).

1116. Benedictus de Nursia, (ca.) 1398-1469.

[Head title] ℂ Incipit libellus de conseruatione sanitatis. secun- | dum ordinez Alphabeti distinctus. Per erimiũ docto | rem magistrũ Benedictum compositus.

Fifth edition, Rome, Stephan Plannck, ca. 1487/88. Originally published, Rome, 1475.

4to. [a-b^8 c^4 d^8 e^4 f-g^8 h^6]; 54 leaves, unpaginated.

Bibliographies: *GKW* 3822; Goff B314.

Copies: *BMC*, *BNC*, and *GKW* (10 copies); Goff (College of Physicians, Philadelphia, and Walters Art Gallery).

1117. Benzi, Ugo, 1376-1439.

REGOLE │ [in red] DELLA SANITA │ ET NATVRA DE' CIBI, │ [in red] DI VGO BENZO │ [in red] SENESE. │ *ARRICCHITE DI VAGHE ANNOTATIONI,* │ *& di copiosi Discorsi, Naturali, & Morali* │ [in red] DAL SIG. LODOVICO BERTALDI │ *Medico delle Serenissime* │ [in red] ALTEZZE DI SAVOIA. │ *Et nuouamente in questa seconda impressione aggiontoui* │ *alle medeme materie i Trattati di* │ [in red] BALDASAR PISANELLI, [in black] esue Historie naturali; │ & Annotationi del Medico [in red] GALINA. │ [vignette] │ [in red] IN TORINO, MDCXX. │ [rule] │ Per gli Heredi di Gio. Domenico Tarino.

Second edition, Turin, 1620. Originally published, Turin, 1618.

8vo. †-††^{8} A-Ddd^8; 416 leaves, pp. [*32*] 1-704, 805-898 [899-900] (=800).

Bibliographies: B. In. G. 184; Horn-Arndt 107; Vicarie 82; Westbury, p. 23.

Copies: B. In. G., *BMC*, *BNC*, and *NUC* (Library of Congress and National Library of Medicine).

1118. Cavalcante, Ippolito,, duca di Buonvicino, d. 1859.

LA CUCINA │ TEORICO-PRATICA │ OVVERO │ IL PRANZO PERIODICO │ *DI OTTO PIATTI AL GIORNO* │ CUMULATIVAMENTE COL SUO CORRISPONDENTE RIPOSTO, E DETTAGLIO │ APPROSSIMATIVO DELLA SPESA GIORNALIERA, PRATICA DI SCALCARE │ E SERVIRE IN TAVOLA │ finalmente │ QUATTRO SETTIMANE │ SECONDO LE STAGIONI │ DELLA CUCINA CASARECCIA │ *IN DIALETTO NAPOLITANO* │ *del Cav. e Ippolito Cavalcante* │ 𝕯𝖚𝖈𝖆 𝖉𝖎 𝕭𝖚𝖔𝖓𝖛𝖎𝖈𝖎𝖓𝖔 │ QUARTA EDIZIONE │ NAPOLI │ STAMPERIA E CARTIERE DEL FIBRENO │ Strada Trinità Maggiore N° 26 │ [ornament] │ 1844

Fourth edition, Naples, 1844. Originally published, Naples, 1837.

201 x 121 mm. [1]⁸ 2-44⁸; 352 leaves, pp. [1-9] 10-702 [2]. Last leaf blank. Printed on alternating signatures of blue, white, and pink paper.

Binding: Full polished black calf, richly stamped in gold, the front and back center panels enclosing the crowned chiffres "MA" of Maria Amalia of Lüchtenberg (French: Marie-Amélie de Bourbon, 1782-1866) on the front and "LF" of Luigi Filippo (Louis-Philippe, 1773-1850) on the back. Marie-Amélie was the daughter of Ferdinand IV, King of Naples. She married Louis-Philippe in 1809 and reigned as queen of France from 1830 until Louis-Philippe was deposed in 1848.

Illustrations: Four folding lithographed plates showing a buffet and table settings.

Bibliographies: Bitting, p. 80; Vicaire 223; Westbury, p. 44.

Copies: *BMC* and *NUC* (Library of Congress only).

1119. Celebrino, Eustachio.

[within an ornamental border] Opera noua che in- | segna apparechiar | vna mensa a vno cōuito: & etiā a ta | gliar in tauola de ogni sorte | carne & dar li Cibi | secondo Lor- | dine che | vsa- | no gli scalchi p[er] far honore a Forestieri. | ℂ Intitulata. | Refetorio. | ℂ Appresso agiontoui alcuni secreti aper- | tinenti al cucinare/ & etiam a conseruare | carne e frutti longo tempo.

First edition, Cesena, Girolamo Soncino, ca. 1526.

4to. A-B⁴; 8 leaves, unpaginated.

Bibliographies: Sander 1898.

Copies: *BMC* (copy noted as missing).

1120. Cervio, Vincenzo.

IL TRINCIANTE | DI M. VINCENZO | C.ERVIO, | AMPLIATO, ET RIDOTTO A | PERFETTIONE DAL CAVALLIER REALE | FVSORITTO DA NARNI, | Trinciante dell'Illust.mo & Reuer.mo | Signor Cardinal Farnese. | CO' PRIVILEGII. | [vignette, lettered on three sides, vertically bottom to top] QVAL PIV FERMO |

[horizontally across the top] E IL MIO FOGLIO | [vertically top to bottom] EL MIO PRESAGIO.] | IN VENETIA, | Appresso gli Heredi di Francesco Tramezini. | M D LXXXI.

First edition, Venice, 1581.

4to. ✳⁴ A-L⁴; 48 leaves, ff. [*4*] 1-44.

Illustrations: Tipped in folding woodcut of carving knives and forks and two woodcuts on B2 recto and verso of serrated knife, fork and tongs and of two birds with carving indications.

Bibliographies: B. In. G. 454; Schraemli (1) 109; Schraemli (2) 74; Vicaire 159; Westbury, p. 45; Wheaton and Kelly 1117.

Copies: B. In. G., *BMC*, *BNC*, and *NUC* (Harvard, John Crerar Library, and New York Academy of Medicine).

1121. Cervio, Vicenzo.

IL TRINCIANTE | DI M. VINCENZO | CERVIO, | *AMPLIATO ET A PERFETTIONE* | *ridotto dal Caualier Reale Fusoritto* | *da Narni*, | Già Trinciante dell' Illustrissimo, & Reuerendissimo Signor | Cardinal Farnese, & al presente dell' Illustriss. | Signor Cardinal Mont'alto. | *Con diuerse aggiunte fatte dal Caualier Reale, & dall' istesso in questa vltima* | *Impressione, aggiuntoui nel fine vn breue Dialogo detto il MASTRO DI* | *CASA, per gouerno d'vna Casa di qual si voglia Principe con li* A, M. D. XCIII. | *Nella Stampa del Gabbia.*

Title-page of second part:

AGGIVNTA | FATTA AL TRINCIANTE | DEL CERVIO | DAL CAVALIER REALE | FVSORITTO DA NARNI, | TRINCIANTE DELL' ILLVSTRISS. | ET REVER. SIG. CARDINALE | MONT'ALTO. | Seconda Editione emendata, & Ampliate. | [woodcut] | *Con Priuilegio, e Licenza de' Superiori.* | [rule] | IN ROMA. | Ad Istanza di Giulio Burchioni. | [rule] | *Nella Stampa del Gabbia.* | *M. D. XCIII.*

Title-page of third part:

IL MASTRO DI CASA | RAGIONAMENTO | DEL CAVALIER REALE, | FVSORITTO DA NARNI: | TRINCIANTE. | DELL' ILLVSTRISS. ET REVEREND.MO | SIGNOR CARDINAL MONT'ALTO: | CON IL SIGNOR

CESARE PANDINI | Mastro di casa dell' Illustrissimo, & Reuerendissimo | Signor Cardinal Farnese. | [woodcut] | *Con Priuilegio, e Licenza de' Superiori.* | [rule] | IN ROMA. | Ad Istanza di Giulio Burchioni. | [rule] | *Nella Stampa del Gabbia.* | *M. D. XCIII.*

Second edition, Rome, 1593. Originally published, Venice, 1581 (item 1120).

4to. †⁴ A-H⁸ I⁶ K⁴ L⁸; 86 leaves, pp. [*8*] 1-162 [2].

Bound with Cesare Evitascandalo's *Dialogo del trenciante*, Rome, 1609 (item 1137) and *Libro dello scalco*, Rome, 1609 (item 1138).

Illustrations: Four full page woodcuts in the text showing carving instruments, a turkey and peacock ready for carving, a fish pond with two fishermen, and a laid table.

Bibliographies: B. In. G. 456; Horn-Arndt 30; Pennell, p. 117; Schraemli (1) 110; Schraemli (2) 75; Westbury, p. 46; Wheaton and Kelly 1118.

Copies: B. In. G., *BMC*, *BNC*, and *NUC* (8 copies).

1122. Cocchi, Antonio Celestino, 1695-1758.

[in red] DEL VITTO PITAGORICO | *PER USO DELLA MEDICINA* | [in red] DISCORSO | D'ANTONIO COCCHI | [in red] MUGELLANO. | [vignette] | [in red] IN FIRENZE. MDCCXXXXIII. | [rule] | Nella Stamperia di [in red] FRANCESCO MOÜCKE | *Con licenza de' Superiori.*

First edition, Florence, 1743.

4to. A-D⁸ E¹⁰; 42 leaves, pp. [1-4] 5-84.

Bibliographies: B. In. G. 492; Vicarie 185; Westbury, p. 48.

Copies: B. In. G., *BMC* (2 copies), *BNC*, and *NUC* (Countway Library, New York Academy of Medicine, and University of Wisconsin).

1123. Colle, Giovanni Francesco.

[within ornamental border] REFVGIO DE POVFRO GENTIL- | HVOMO COMPOSTO PER. IO. | FRANCISCO COLLE A LO | ILLVSTRIS. ET EXCELLEN | TIS.S.D. ALPHONSO DV | CA DI FERRARA. | [Estes arms]

Colophon: Stampato in Ferrara per Magistro Laurentio di Russi │ da Valētia. Adi IX. de Zugno. M.D.XX.

First edition, Ferrara, 1520.

4to. ¶⁴ A-K⁴; 44 leaves, ff. [*4*] [I] II-XLIIII. Leaves A2 and A3 wanting in this copy.

Illustrations: Woodcut border to title and A1 recto, woodcut arms of Este family on title and woodcut initial letters in the text. Brunet calls for a plate illustrating a knife and fork not present in this copy.

Bibliographies: B. In. G. 497; Brunet, II, 132. The second edition is retitled *Refugio ouer ammonitorio de gentilhuomo* (Ferrara, 1532) (item 1124).

Copies: B. In. G. The retitled second edition is in *BMC*, *BNC*, and *NUC* (John Crerar Library only).

1124. Colle, Giovanni Francesco.

[within a woodcut factotum] REFV │ GIO OVER │ ammonitorio de gen │ tilhuomo composto │ per Io. Francesco Col │ le a lo illustris. & eccel │ lentis. S.D. Alphon- │ so Duca di Ferrara. │ M D XXXII

Second edition, Ferrara, 1532. Originally published, Ferrara, 1520 (item 1123).

8vo. ✠⁴ A-H⁴; 36 leaves, ff. [*8*] 1-27 [1]. Last leaf (blank?) wanting in this copy.

Illustrations: Title-page within a woodcut factotum and woodcut of carving implements on A2ᵛ and A3ʳ.

Bibliographies: Simon BG 364; Vicaire 187; Westbury, p. 50.

Copies: *BMC*, *BNC*, and *NUC* (John Crerar Library only).

1124a. Collezione quanto si e' scritto...delle Patate

COLLEZIONE │ QUANTO SI E' SCRITTO DI PIU' IMPOR- │ TANTE, E DI PIU' ADATTO │ *INTORNO* │ ALLA COLTIVAZIONE ED USO │ *DELLE* │ PATATE │ Preceduta dal Sovrano generale Stabilimento per le │ Sovvenzioni Economiche de'

Poveri, e dalle | Istruzioni correlative per eseguirlo. | [vignette captioned *Gramola par le Patate*] | NAPOLI MDCCCIII. | NELLA STAMPERIA SIMONIANA | *Con licenza de' Superiori.*

First edition, Naples, 1803.

211 x 139 mm. π^4 A-R^8; 140 leaves, pp. [*8*] 1-267 [268-272].

Illustrations: Engraved folding plate of a furnace.

Bibliographies: B. In. G. 499.

Copies: B. In. G.

1125.   Compagnia della Lesina.

[within a frame of type ornaments and single rules] LA LESINA | [below the frame] DIALOGO, | CAPITOLI, | & Ragionamenti. | DELLA CELEBERRIMA | Compagnia de' LE SINANTI. | *Con alcune piaceuoli Dicerie in lode di detta* | *Compagnia, & altre Compositioni* | *nel medesimo genere.* | [within a frame of two rules] L'ASSOTIGLIARLA PIV' | [woodcut of an awl] | MEGLIO ANCO FORA. | [below the frame] *Stampata per Ordine de gli otto Operaij* | *di detta Compagnia.* *1601.*

Title-page of second part:

[within a border of type ornaments] LA | VERA REGOLA | PER MANTENERSI | MAGRO, | Con pochissima Spesa. | *Scritta da M. Spilorcion de' Stitichi, Corret-* | *tor della nobilissima Compagnia* | *delle* LESINE. | A Messer Agocchion Spontato | suo Compare. | Opera vtilissima per tutti coloro, che | patiscono strettezza di borsa. | *Di Guilio Cesare dalla Croce.* | [woodcut of an awl] | IN FERRARA. | [rule] | Per Vittorio Baldini, MDCI. | *Con licenza de' Superiuri.*

New edition, Ferrara, 1601.   Originally published [Florence? 1550?] according to *BMC*; Westbury suggests perhaps twenty years later.

8vo.   A-D^8 ^{2}D^4; 36 leaves, pp. [1-2] 3-64 [*8*].   P. 3 misnumbered "4".

Bibliographies: This edition unrecorded in the bibliographies consulted.   Vicaire 195 and Westbury pp. 96-101 record other editions.

Copies: No other copy of this edition located.

1126. Il confetturiere piemontese.

IL | CONFETTURIERE | PIEMONTESE | CHE INSEGNA | LA MANIERA DI CONFETTARE FRUTII | IN DIVERSE MANIERE | *Far Biscottini, Marzapani, Canestrelli,* | *Acquavita, Sorbetti, e molte altre cose* | *appartenenti a tal Arte.* | [vignette] | IN TORINO 1790. | [two rules] | PRESSO BELTRAMO ANTONIO RE.

First edition, Turin, 1790.

12mo. A-T^{12} V^8; 236 leaves, pp. [1-2] 3-471 [472]. Modern boards, original printed wrappers preserved.

Bibliographies: Schraemli (1) 124; Westbury p. 53.

Copies: No other copy of this edition located. *NUC* records four copies of a Milan, 1792, edition.

1127. Corrado, Vincenzo.

[within a border of type ornaments] IL CREDENZIERE | DI BUON GUSTO | OPERA MECCANICA | *DELL' ORITANO* | VINCENZO CORRADO | [woodcut] | [two rules] | NAPOLI MDCCLXXVIII. | NELLA STAMPERIA RAIMONDIANA.

First edition, Naples, 1778.

4to. a^4 b^6 A-G^4 H^4 (-H4); 41 leaves, pp. [20] 1-62.

Illustrations: Frontispiece engraved portrait of the author and an engraved folding plate of a dessert table.

Bibliographies: B. In. G. 546; Bitting, p. 101; Westbury, p. 57.

Copies: B. In. G.

1128. Corrado, Vincenzo.

[within a border of type ornaments] IL CUOCO | *GALANTE.* | [woodcut] | IN NAPOLI MDCCLXXIII. | NELLA STAMPERIA RAIMONDIANA.

First edition, Naples, 1773.

4to. a⁴ A-Ee⁴ Ff⁶; 122 leaves, pp. [*8*] 1-234 [*2*]. Last leaf blank.

Illustrations: Two engraved folding plates of table settings.

Bibliographies: B. In. G. 549; Westbury, p. 56.

Copies: B. In. G., *BMC* and *NUC* (John Crerar Library only).

1129. Corrado, Vincenzo.

IL CUOCO GALANTE | DI | F. VINCENZO CORRADO | *QUINTA EDIZIONE* | ACCRESCIUTA DEL TRATTATO | DELLE PATATE | *ED IN TUTTO MIGLIORATA* | PER VIEPPIU' SODDISFARE GLI UOMINI DI BUON SENSO, | E DI BUON GUSTO | [short fancy rule] | *Stulta est gloria, nisi utile est quod facimus* | Phaedri lib. III. fab. 17.. | [three short double rules, tiered] | *NAPOLI MDCCCI.* | [short rule] | *Dalla Stamperia Orsiniana* | PRESSO I FRATELLI TERRES | *Con Approvazione.*

Fifth edition, Naples, 1801. Originally published Naples, 1773 (item 1128).

240 x 190 mm. a⁴ A-Ff⁴; 120 leaves, pp. [i-ii] iii-viii, 1-232.

Illustrations: Frontispiece portrait of author etched with engraving and two engraved folding plates showing table setting.

Bibliographies: Vicaire 895; Westbury, p. 56.

Copies: No other copy of this edition located.

1130. Corrado, Vincenzo.

[within a border of type ornaments] DEL | CIBO PITAGORICO | OVVERO ERBACEO | PER USO DE' NOBILI, E DE' LETTERATI | OPERA MECCANICA | *DELL' ORITANO* | VINCENZO CORRADO | [woodcut] | [two rules] | IN NAPOLI MDCCLXXXI. | Nella Stamperia dei FRATELLI RAIMONDI | *Con licenza de' Superiori.*

First edition, Naples, 1781.

4to. a⁴ A-F⁴; 28 leaves, pp. [*8*] 1-47 [48].

Illustrations: Engraved frontispiece portrait of the author.

Bibliographies: B. In. G. 565; Bitting, p. 101; Schraemli (1) 125; Westbury, p. 58.

Copies: B. In. G. and *NUC* Supplement (Library of Congress only).

1131. Crisci, Giovanni Battista.

[engraved title-page; within a frame of architectural forms and figures] LVCERNA |
DE | Corteggiani | *Oue, in Dialogo si tratta diffusa=* | *mente delle Corti; cosi de uenti*
quatt- | *ro officii nobili, come de la uarieta* | *de cibi per tutto l'anno; e ciascu=* | *na*
Domenica Et altri Ban | *chetti Diuisa in sei Capitoli.* | *OPRA* | *DI GIO: BATTISTA*
CRISCI | *Napolitano* | *ALL' ALTEZZA SERMA. DEL GRAN* / *DVCA DI TOSCANA*
FERDINADO II. | [within an oval compartment] NON MIHI SEDTIBI | [at either side
of the compartment at base of architectural form, left] *Superiorum* [right] *permissu* |
Neap. apud Io. Dominicū Roncagliolū Anno 1634

First edition, Naples, 1634.

4to. a⁴ A-Yy⁴ Zz⁴(-Zz4); 187 leaves, pp. [*8*] 1-348 [*18*].

Illustration: Engraved title-page on a1ʳ.

Bibliographies: B. In. G. 595; Schraemli (1) 130; Simon BG 418; Vicaire 221;
Westbury, p. 62.

Copies: B. In. G. and *NUC* (Library of Congress only).

1131a. Dalla Bona, Giovanni, 1712-1786.

DELL' USO E DELL' ABUSO | DEL CAFFÈ | *DISSERTAZIONE* | STORICO-
FISICO-MEDICA | *DEL DOTTOR* | GIOVANNI | DALLA BONA. | SECONDA
EDIZIONE | *Con aggiunte, massime intorno la Cioccolata;* | *ed il Rosolì.* |
[ornament] | IN VERONA | C I ꓷ I ꓷ C C L X. | [short rule] | Per Pierantonio .Berno
Stampatore e Librajo sulla Via de'Leoni. | *CON LICENZA DE' SUPERIORI.*

Second edition, Verona, 1760. Originally published under the title *L'uso e l'abuso del*
caffe, Verona, 1751.

4to A-L⁴ M⁶; 50 leaves, pp. [1-4] 5-99 [100].

Bibliographies: Bitting, p. 114; Westbury, p. 73.

Copies: *BMC*, and *NUC* (5 copies).

1132. Davini, Giovanni Baptista, d. 1733.

DE POTU | VINI CALIDI | DISSERTATIO | *AUCTORE* | JOHANNE BAPTISTA | DAVINI | SERENISSIMI | RAYNALDI I. | Mutinae, Regii, Mirandulae, &c. Ducis | *MEDICO.* | [publisher's monogram] | MUTINAE, MDCCXX. | [rule] | Typis Antonii Capponi Impressoris Episcop. | *Superiorum Permissu.*

First edition, Modena, 1720.

4to. π² A-H⁴ I⁶; 40 leaves, pp. [*4*] 1-75 [76].

Bibliographies: B. In. G. 662; Simon BG 438. Bitting, Horn-Arndt, and Vicaire record only the second edition.

Copies: B. In. G. and *NUC* (Folger Library, National Library of Medicine, and UCLA).

1133. Durante, Castore, 1529-1590.

IL TESORO | DELLA SANITA. | *NEL QVALE SI DA IL MODO* | *da conseruar la* *Sanità, & prolungar la vita,* | *& si tratta della Natura de' Cibi, & de i* | *Rimedij de i* *Nocumenti loro.* | OPERA NVOVA DI CASTOR | Durante da Gualdo, Medico, & Cit- | tadino Romano. | [woodcut] | IN ROMA, | Ad instantia di Iacomo Tornieri, & Iacomo Biricchia. | Appresso Francesco Zannetti. 1586. | [rule] | *Con Priuilegio, &* *Licentia de' Superiori.*

First edition, Rome, 1586. Originally published in Latin, Pesaro, 1565, under the title *De benitate et vitio alimentorum.* This work was reprinted the same year by Andrea Muschio in Venice, an edition which is recorded as the first in Simon BG 537. Westbury states he discussed this with Simon and they agreed the Rome, Tornieri and Biricchia, edition is the first. Tornieri and Biricchia published Durante's *Herbario nuovo* earlier the same year.

4to. π⁴ A-Pp⁴; 156 leaves, pp. [*8*] 1-296 [*8*].

Illustrations: Woodcut vignette on title-page and on π2^r and a woodcut portrait of the author at age 56 on π4^v.

Bibliographies: B. In. G. 741; Pennell, p. 116; Westbury, p. 82; Wheaton and Kelly 1859. Bitting, Horn-Arndt, Simon BG, and Vicaire record later editions.

Copies: B. In. G., *BMC* and *NUC* (5 copies).

1134. Durante, Castore, 1529-1590.

IL TESORO │ DELLA SANITA, │ *Di Castor Durante da Gualdo, Medico,* │ & *Cittadino Romano.* │ Nel quale s'insegna il modo di conseruar │ la Sanità, & prolungar la vita, │ *Et si tratta* │ DELLA NATVRA DE' CIBI, │ & de' Rimedij de' nocumenti loro. │ CON LA TAVOLA DELLE COSE NOTABILI. │ [vignette] │ IN VENETIA, M D LXXXVIII. │ Appresso Andrea Muschio.

New edition, Venice, 1588. Originally published in Latin, Pesaro, 1565, under the title *De bonitate et vitio alimentorum*, and in Italian, Rome, 1586 (item 1133).

8vo. †^{8} A-V^8 X^4; 172 leaves, pp. [*16*] [1] 2-328.

Bibliographies: B. In. G. 744; Schraemli (1) 154; Simon BB II 201; Vicaire 303; Westbury, p. 83.

Copies: B. In. G., *BNC* and *NUC* (Baker University, Kansas, and National Library of Medicine).

1135. Evitascandalo, Cesare.

BREVE │ AGGIONTA │ AL DIALOGO │ DEL │ MAESTRO DI CASA │ DI │ CESARE EVITASCANDALO │ D'ALTRI NECESSARII RECORDI │ PER QVELL' OFFITIO. │ [woodcut] │ IN ROMA, Appresso Stefano Paolini. MDCX. │ [rule] │ *Con licenza de' Speriori.*

Third edition, Rome, 1610. Originally published, Rome, 1606.

4to. A-B^4 C^6; 14 leaves, pp. [1-2] 3-26 [2]. Last leaf blank.

Bound with Cesare Evitascandalo's *Dialogo del maestro di casa*, Rome, 1606.

Bibliographies: Horn-Arndt 129. Westbury, pp. 90-92, cites editions of 1606, 1609, and 1620 but not this of 1610.

Copies: *NUC* (4 copies).

1136. Evitascandalo, Cesare.

DIALOGO | DEL MAESTRO | DI CASA. | DI CESARE EVITASCANDALO | ROMANO. | Nel quale si conriene di quanto il Maestro di casa deue esser' | instrutto. Et quanto deue saper ciascun' altro che vo- | glia esercitar' officio in Corte. | *Di nuouo la terza volta restampato, & corretto, con aggiontione de altri officii, & | molti documenti, & recordi necessarii, come appare nel fine del libro.* | Vtile à tutti li Padroni, Cortegiani, Officiali, & seruitori della Corte: | & à qual si voglia Capo, & Padre di Famiglia. | [rule] | *CON PRIVILÉGIO.* | [woodcut] | IN ROMA, Appresso Carlo Vullietti. MDCVI. | [rule] | *Con licenza de' Superiori.*

Fourth edition, Rome, 1606. Originally published, Rome, 1596.

4to. ✱⁴ ✱✱⁴ A-T⁴ V²; 86 leaves, pp. [*16*] 1-154 [*2*].

Bound with the author's *Breve aggionta al dialogo del maestro de casa di Cesare Evitascandalo* (Rome, 1610).

Illustration: Woodcut portrait of the author on ✱✱4ᵛ.

Bibliographies: Horn-Arndt 129; Westbury, p. 90. See B. In. G. 787 for a record of other editions.

Copies: *BMC* and *NUC* (4 copies).

1137. Evitascandalo, Cesare.

DIALOGO | DEL TRENCIANTE, | DI CESARE | EVITASCANDALO | ROMANO. | Nel quale si legge quanto si deue operare, & osseruare | nel seruitio del Trenciante. | [woodcut in red and black] | IN ROMA, | Appresso Carlo Vullietti. 1609. | [rule] | *Con Licenza de' Superiori.*

First edition, Rome, 1609.

4to. π⁴ A-L⁴ M⁶; 54 leaves, pp. [*8*] 1-100.

Bound with Vincenzo Cervio's *Il trinciante*, Rome, 1593 (item 1121) and Evitascandalo's *Libro dello scalco*, Rome, 1609 (item 1138).

Bibliographies: B. In. G. 789; Westbury, p. 92.

Copies: B. In. G., *BMC* and *NUC* (Cornell and John Crerar Library).

1138. Evitascandalo, Cesare.

LIBRO │ DELLO SCALCO │ DI CESARE │ EVITASCANDALO. │ *Quale insegna quest' honorato seruitio* │ [woodcut, lettered on four sides, vertically bottom to top] QVINTVS │ [horizontally across the top] FAVSTA DIV │ [vertically top to bottom] PAVLVS TRADVCAT │ [horizontally upside down across the bottom] TEMPORA. │ IN ROMA. │ Appresso Carlo Vullietti. MDCIX. │ [rule] │ *Con licenza de Superiori.*

First edition, Rome, 1609.

4to. ✻⁴ A-S⁴; 76 leaves, pp. [*8*] 1-144.

Bound with Evitascandalo's *Dialogo del trenciante*, Rome, 1609 (item 1137) and Vincenzo Cervio's *Il trinciante*, Rome, 1593 (item 1121).

Illustration: Woodcut portrait of the author on ✻4ᵛ.

Bibliographies: B. In. G. 790; Westbury, p. 92.

Copies: B. In. G., *BMC* and *NUC* (4 copies).

1139. Felici, Giovanni Battista.

PARERE │ *INTORNO ALL' USO* │ DELLA │ CIOCCOLATA │ Scritto in una LETTERA │ DAL CONTE DOTTOR │ GIO: BATISTA │ FELICI │ *ALL'* │ *ILLUSTRISS. SIGNORA* │ LISABETTA │ GIROLAMI │ D' AMBRA. │ [ornament] │ IN FIRENZE. │ [rule] │ APPRESSO Giuseppe Manni MDCCXXVIII. │ *Con Licenza de' Superiori.*

First edition, Florence, 1728.

4to. §⁶ A-L⁴; 50 leaves, pp. [i-iv] v-xi [xii] 1-88.

Bibliographies: B. In. G. 812; Bitting, p. 155; Westbury, p. 102; Wheaton and Kelly 2110.

Copies: B. In. G., *BMC* and *NUC* (6 copies).

1140. Ferrari, Giovanni Battista, 1584-1655.

HESPERIDES | SIVE | DE MALORVM AVREORVM | CVLTVRA ET VSV | Libri Quatuor | IO: BAPTISTAE FERRARII SENENSIS | E SOCIETATE IESV. | [woodcut] | ROMAE, | Sumptibus Hermanni Scheus. | MDCXLVI. | [rule] | *SVPERIORVM PERMISSV.*

First edition, Rome, 1646.

Folio: ✠⁶ A-Qqq⁴; 254 leaves, pp. [*12*] 1-480 [*16*].

Illustrations: 102 full page engraved illustrations in the text, some depicting allegorical scenes and the others the known varieties of lemons.

Bibliographies: B. In. G. 815; Hunt 243; Vicaire 357.

Copies: B. In. G., *BNC* and *NUC* (12 copies).

1141. Frizzi, Antonio, 1736-1800.

LA | SALAMEIDE | POEMETTO GIOCOSO | CON | LE NOTE | [vignette] | VENEZIA MDCCLXXII | Appresso Guglielmo Zerletti | *Con Licenza de' Superiori e Privilegio.*

First edition, Venice, 1772.

8vo. ✱⁴ A-H⁸ I⁴; 76 leaves, pp. [*8*] [I] II-CXXXV [CXXXVI].

Illustrations: Engraved frontispiece and title-page, not reckoned in the signatures or pagination and engraved vignette at head of A1ʳ.

Bibliographies: B. In. G. 852; Westbury, p. 197; Wheaton and Kelly 2288.

Copies: B. In. G. and *NUC* (Harvard, New York Public Library, and University of California, Berkeley).

1142. Frugoli, Antonio.

PRATICA | E SCALCARIA | D'ANTONIO FRVGOLI LVCCHESE. | *Intitolata* | PIANTA DI DELICATI FRVTTI | Da seruirsi à qualsiuoglia Mensa di Prencipi e gran Signori, & à | Persone ordinarie ancora: con molti auuertimenti circa | all' honorato Officio di Scalco. | *Con le liste di tutti mesi dell' Anno, compartite nelle quattro Stagioni.* | Con vn Trattato dell' Inuentori delle viuande, e beuande, cosi antiche, come | moderne, nuouamente ritrouato, e tradotto di lingua Armenia in Italiana. | DIVISA IN SETTE LIBRI. | *Con la Tauola copiosa di tutto quello che al principio di ciaschedun libro* | *si contiene, à beneficio Uniuersale.* | CON PRIVILEGIO. | [vignette] | IN ROMA, Appresso Francesco Caualli. 1631. | *Con licenza de' Superiori.*

First edition, Rome, 1631.

4to. a-e⁴ A-Mmm⁴; 252 leaves, pp. [*40*] 1-464.

Illustrations: Engraved portrait of the author on a3ᵛ.

Bibliographies: B. In. G. 854; Westbury, p. 106. Vicaire 375 for the 1632 edition.

Copies: B. In. G., *BMC, BNC*, and *NUC* (New York Academy of Medicine only).

1143. Fuscone, Pietro Paolo, fl. 1605.

TRATTATO | DEL BERE CALDO, | E FREDDO | DI PIETRO PAOLO FVSCONE | ROMANO FILOSOFO, | E MEDICO. | Doue si disputa, se conuiene generalmente à tutti cosi sani, come amala- | ti, & in particolare a' Podagrosi il beuere del continouo l'acqua | col vino, tanto calda quanto si può sofferire, ouero | molto fredda con neue, ò pure come | ci vien data dalla natura. | *Aggiungendouisi in fine vn Capitolo, doue s'insegna il vero modo di conoscere* | *le acque buone, e di correggere le triste.* | [vignette] | In GENOVA, Appresso Giuseppe Pauoni. MDCV. | *Con licenza de' Superiori.*

First edition, Genoa, 1605.

4to. †⁴ A-DDD⁴; 204 leaves, pp. [*8*] 1-102 101-388 [*10*]. Last leaf blank.

Bibliographies: B. In. G. 857; Vicaire 378.

Copies: B. In. G., *BMC*, *BNC*, and *NUC* (National Library of Medicine only).

1144. Galen.

DI GALENO | DELLI MEZZI, CHE SI POSSONO | *tenere per conseruarci la sanita.* | RECATO IN QVESTA LINGVA | *nostra da M. Giouanni Tarcagnota.* | [ornament] | [vignette, lettered on three sides, vertically bottom to top] *QVAL PIV FERMO* | [horizontally across the top] *È IL MIO FIGOLO* | [vertically top to bottom] *È IL MIO PRESAGGIO.* | *Co'l priuilegio del sommo Pontefice Paulo* III. & | *dell' Illustrissimo Senato Veneto per anni* X.

Colophon: *In Venetia per Michele Tramezzino.* | M D XLIX.

First edition in Italian, Venice, 1549. Originally published in Latin under the title *De sanitate tuenda*, Paris, 1517.

8vo. ✱⁸ a-t⁸ π t⁸ u⁸; 176 leaves, ff. [8] 1-160, 153, 162, 155, 160, 157 [3]. Last three leaves blank.

Bibliographies: B. In. G. 872.

Copies: B. In. G. and *NUC* (5 copies).

1145. Giegher, Mattia, d. ca. 1630.

LO SCALCO | DI M. MATTIA GIEGHER | Bauaro di Mosburc; | Trinciante dell' Inclita Nazion' Alemanna in Padoua; | DEDICATO | *ALL' ILLVSTRISSIMO SIG. ENRICO RANZOVIO,* | *di Sconeuiede, ec.* | Dignissimo Consiglier dell' Inclita Nazion' Alemanna nell' Vniuersità de' Sign. Legisti in Padoua; | ed à tutta l'Inclita Nazion de' Nobilissimi Signori Alemanni della detta Vniuersita. | [woodcut] | *IN PADOVA, Per Guasparri Criuellari. M. DC. XXIII.* | Con licenza de' Superiori.

First edition, Padua, 1623.

4to. A-F⁴ †²; 26 leaves, pp. [1-2] 3-47 [48-52].

Illustrations: Three etched and engraved plates depicting table settings.

Bibliographies: B. In. G. 936; Westbury, p. 115.

Copies: B. In. G., *BMC* and *NUC* (Princeton Theological Seminary only).

1146. Giegher, Mattia, d. ca. 1630.

IL TRINCIANTE | Di Messer Mattia Gieger Bauaro di Mosburc, | Con le figure delle cose da trinciare, e de' Coltelli, e forcine, intagliate in ramo; | aggiuntiui alcuni breui, ed vtili ricordi sopra ciascuna figura. | *All' Illustrissimo Signor* | FEDERIGO DI POLENZ | NOBILE DI PRVSSIA, | Degnissimo Consiglier dell' Illustriss. Nazion Alamanna nell' Vni- | uersità de' Signori Legisti in Padoua. | *Ed à tutta l'Illustriss. Nazion de' nobilissimi Sig. Alamani della detta Vniuersità.* | [ornament] | *In Padoua per il Martini Stampator Camerale. Con lic. de' Superiori.* | M DC XXI.

First edition, Padua, 1621.

4to. A-B⁴ C² †²; 12 leaves, unpaginated.

Illustrations: Etched and engraved folding plate of carver's knives and forks; 28 etched and engraved plates depicting carving.

Note: This copy contains contemporary annotations in the text and on the plates.

Bibliographies: B. In. G. 938; Westbury, p. 114.

Copies: B. In. G., *BMC* and *NUC* (Princeton Theological Seminary only).

1147. Giegher, Mattia, d. ca. 1630.

LI TRE TRATTATI | DI MESSER MATTIA GIEGHER | BAVARO DI MOSBVRC, | *TRINCIANTE DELL' ILL.*MA. *NATIONE* | *ALEMANNA IN PADOVA.* | Nel primo si mostra con facilità grande il modo di piegare ogni sorte di panni li- | ni, cioè, saluiette, e touaglie, e d'apparecchiare vna tauola, con certe altre | galanterie degna d'effer sapute; le quali cose tutte son rappresentate in | figure di rame: e questa è inuenzion del tutto nuoua dell' autore, ne | mai più per addietro veduta. | Nel secondo, intitolato lo Scalco, s'insegna, oltr'al conoscere le stagioni di tutte le | cose, che si mangiano, la maniera di metterc in tauola le viuande; il che. con | tre differenti figure di tauole intagliate in rame, chiaramente si mostra | Nel terzo, detto il Trinciante, s'insegna il modo di trinciare ogni sorte di viuan- | de, con le sue figure medesimamente in rame; opera rinuouata, e di molte | cofe accresciuta. | [ornament] | [rule] | In PADOVA Per Paolo Frambotto M. DC. XXXIX. Con licenza de' Superiori

First collection edition, Padua, 1639.

Oblong 4to. A⁴ ﬡ⁴, ²A-G⁴(-G4), ³A² B-D⁴ E², ⁴A²; 53 leaves, pp. [*16*], ²[1] 2-54, ³[*32*], ⁴[*4*].

Illustrations: Engraved portrait of the author on ³E2ʳ and 48 plates as follows: two engraved folding plates showing carving utensils; six etched plates illustrating napkin folding; twelve etched plates illustrating carving pork; twenty-four etched plates illustrating carving fowl, fish, and fruits and four illustrating table settings.

Bibliographies: B. In. G. 937; Bitting, p. 182; Drexel 238; Schraemli (1) 203; Schraemli (2) 77; Vicaire 402; Westbury, p. 115.

Copies: B. In. G., *BMC*, *BNC*, and *NUC* (Cornell, Library of Congress, and New York Public Library).

1148. Giovane.

☙ OPERA-DI | gnissima: & vtile per chi si diletta di [Cuci] | nare: con molti bellissimi secreti de | compōere: & cōseruare viuan- | de: & molti altri secreti di | piu cose: Composto | p[er] il valēte Ma= | estro Gio | uane | De la Cucina dela Santtita dil | nostro Summo Pontefice. | [woodcut of kitchen scene]

Colophon: Stampata nela magnifica Citta di | Milano per Pietro Paulo | verini Fiorentino in la cō | drada delle bandiere | al ballone | [woodcut of tree with motto `FELICE PIANTA']

Note: Title-page restored. The original title-page has the spelling "DI | gnissima" which the restorer has modernized to "DE | gnissima" replacing the missing "I" with an "E". We have transcribed the original spelling. The restorer also failed to add "Cuci" missing in this copy's title-page and supplied in the transcription in brackets.

First edition, Milan, ca. 1530.

12mo. [a]⁴ b-g⁴; 28 leaves, unpaginated.

Bibliographies: Vicarie 406; Westbury, p. 117.

Copies: *BMC* and *BNC*.

1149. Grapaldi, Francesco Mario, 1464-1515.

FRANCISCI MARII GRAPALDI | DE PARTIBVS AEDIVM LI | BELLVS CVM ADDITA | MENTIS EMENDA | TISSIMVS.

Second edition, enlarged, Parma, Angelus Ugeletus, 1501. Originally published, Parma, ca. 1494.

4to. A-B⁶ a-p⁸ q-r⁶; 144 leaves, ff. [*12*] 1-132.

Bibliographies: Simon BB II. 315; Simon BG 787.

Copies: *BNC* and *NUC* (4 copies).

1150. Guidi, Azzo.

LA | SPEZIERIA | DOMESTICA. | [fancy rule] | *Sive Medicum adhibueris, sive non,* | *convalesces.* | Cicer. de Orat. | [ornament] | IN VENEZIA, | M. DCC. LXXXII. | [rule] | NELLA STAMPERIA GRAZIOSI | *Con Pubblica Approvazione, & Priv.*

First edition, Venice, 1782.

8vo. *⁸(-*1) A-I⁸ K⁸(-K8); 86 leaves, pp. [*14*] 1-157 [158].

Bibliographies: B.In.G. 128; Westbury, p. 119.

Copies: B.In.G. and *NUC* (New York Academy of Medicine only).

1151. Lancellotti, Vittorio.

LO SCALCO | PRATTICO | DI VITTORIO LANCELLOTTI | DA CAMERINO | All' Illustrissimo, e Reuerendiss. Prencipe | IL CARD. IPPOLITO | ALDOBRANDINO | CAMERLENGO DI SANTA CHIESA. | [woodcut] | IN ROMA, | Appresso Francesco Corbelletti. MDCXXVII. | [rule] | *Con Licenza de'* *Superiori.*

First edition, Rome, 1627.

4to. †⁴ A-Nn⁴ Oo⁶; 154 leaves, pp. [*8*] 1-300.

Bibliographies: Oberlé (1) 530; Simon BG 941; Vicaire 490; Westbury, p. 127; Wheaton and Kelly 3441.

Copies: *BMC*, *BNC*, and *NUC* (Harvard, John Crerar Library, and New York Academy of Medicine).

1152. Landi, Ortensio, ca. 1512-ca. 1553.

COMMENTARIO | DELLE PIV NOTABILI, | & mostruose cose d'Italia, & altri | luoghi: di lingua Aramea in | Italiana tradotto. | ✩ | CON VN BREVE CATALO- | *go de gli inuentori delle cose che si mangia=* | *no & beueno, nouamente ritrouato.* | [ornament] | [woodcut] | IN VINETIA *per Bartholomeo Cesano.* | [short rule] | M D LIII.

Third edition, Venice, 1553. Originally published, Venice, 1548.

8vo. A-I⁸; 72 leaves, ff. [1] 2-71 [72]. Last leaf (blank?) wanting in this copy.

Bibliographies: B. In. G. 1080; Brunet III, 812. Bitting, Horn-Arndt, Simon BG, and Westbury cite other editions.

Copies: B. In. G., *BMC* and *NUC* (Duke University and Newberry Library).

1153. Latini, Antonio.

LO SCALCO | ALLA MODERNA, | OVERO | *L' ARTE DI BEN DISPORRE I CONVITI,* | Con le regole più scelte di Scalcheria, insegnate, e poste in prat- | tica, à beneficio de' Professori, ed altri Studiosi, | DAL CAVALIER | ANTONIO LATINI | DA COLLE AMATO DI FABRIANO, | NELLA MARCA D'ANCONA, | *Essercitato nel Servigio di Varii Porporati,* | *e Prencipi Grandi.* | Dove s'insegna il modo facile, e nobile di Trinciare, fare Arrosti, Bol- | liti, Stufati, varie Minestre signorili, diverse Zuppe alla Reale, | Morselletti delicati, Brodi sostantiosi, Fritti appettitosi, Pa- | sticci d'ogni sorte, con la loro dosa proportionata, per | quante persone si vorrà, Piatti composti differenti, | Crostate, ò Pizze Reali, con la loro dosa, Sal- | se, e Sapori in variati modi. | *Con un facile modo di far Profumi, in diverse maniere, Aceti* | *odorosi, e salutiferi, di conservare ogni sorte di frutti per* | *tutto l'Anno, di fare vaghi, e nobili Trionfi, di bene* | *imbandire le Tavole, di conoscere i gradi qua-* | *litativi d'ogni sorte d'Animale comestibile;* | Et unitamente si tratta delli primi Inventori, che hanno posto in uso il | cibo di molti Animali, cosi Volatili, come Quadrupedi, | e formar di quelli varie Vivande. | *Et una nota de' Paesi di questo Regno, dove nascono Frutti, Vini, ed* | *altre cose simili, per uso de' Conviti.* | [ornament] | IN NAPOLI 1694. | [short rule] | *Con Licenza de' Superiori, e Privilegio.*

Colophon: IN NAPOLI. Nella nuova Stampa delli Socii | Dom. Ant. Parrino, e Michele Luigi Mutii 1692 | [rule] | *Con Licenza de' Superiori, e Privilegio.*

Second edition, Naples, 1694. Originally published, Naples, 1693.

4to. a² ᵀa⁴ A-Hhhh⁴; 314 leaves, pp. [*12*] 1-606 [*10*]. Last leave contains errata.

Illustrations: Etched frontispiece, engraved portrait of the author, two folding engraved plates illustrating carving implements and techniques of carving fruits, and a folding etched plate of a banquet table.

Note: A second part of this work, titled *Nella quale specialmente si tratta delle vivande di magro*, also was published, Naples, 1694.

Bibliographies: B. In. G. 1104; Schraemli (1) 265 (both parts); Vicaire 492 (not mentioning the second part); Westbury, p. 129 (both parts).

Copies: B. In. G., *BMC* and *NUC* (5 copies).

1154. Liberati, Francesco, fl. 1639-1669.

IL PERFETTO | MASTRO DI CASA | DI FRANCESCO LIBERATI | ROMANO. | *DISTINTO IN TRE LIBRI.* | *Opera vtilissima, e necessaria al buon* | *gouerno di* | *qualsiuoglia Corte,* | *e Casa priuata.* | ALL' ILLVSTRISS. SIGNORE | IL SIG. GALGANO | MARCHESE BICHI. | [ornament] | IN ROMA, Per Angelo Bernabò dal Verme. 1658. | [rule] | *Con licenza de' Superiori, et Priuilegio.*

First edition, Rome, 1658.

8vo. a⁸ A-R⁸; 144 leaves, pp. [*16*] 1-269 [*270-278*]. Letterpress folding table giving costs of supporting a family in Rome in 1658 bound in after H3.

Bibliographies: Vicarie 905; Westbury, p. 134.

Copies: *BMC* and *BNC*.

1155. Il libro della cucina.

IL | LIBRO DELLA CUCINA | DEL SEC. XIV | TESTO DI LINGUA | NON MAI
FIN QUI | STAMPATO | [short fancy rule] | BOLOGNA | Presso Gaetano
Romagnoli | 1863

First edition, Bologna, 1863. No. 146 of 202 copies. Vicaire gives the date 1862 in
error.

176 x 116 mm. [1]⁸ 2-3⁸ 4⁴; ²[1]⁸ 2-8⁸; 92 leaves, pp. [i-iii] iv-liii [liv] [2] [1] 2-127
[128].

Note: This work is printed from a manuscript different from, but closely related to,
that from which item 1156 derives.

Bibliographies: Vicaire 429.

Copies: *NUC* (6 copies).

1156. Libro di cucina.

LIBRO DI CUCINA | DEL SECOLO XIV | A CURA | DI | LUDOVICO FRATI |
[publisher's monogram] | LIVORNO | RAFFAELLO GIUSTI, EDITORE | 1899

Second edition, Livorno, 1899. Limited to 400 copies. Originally published, Livorno,
1890.

194 x 130 mm. [*]⁴ **⁴ 1-12⁴; 56 leaves, pp. [i-viii] viii-xv [xvi] [1] 2-92 [4]. First
two and last four pages, blank.

Bibliographies: B. In. G. 1158; Bitting, p. 166; Wheaton and Kelly 2259.

Copies: B. In. G., *BNC* and *NUC* (9 copies).

1157. Manelfi, Giovanni.

MENSA | ROMANA | *Siue* | VRBANA VICTVS RATIO. | *IOAN. MANELPHI*
ERETANI SA- | *bini, Archiatri Romani, atque in Almae Vrbis* | *Archigymnasio Primarij*
Medicinae | *Practicae Professoris.* | Ad Gloriosiss. & Sanctiss. Principem |

INNOCENTIVM X. | PONT. OPT. MAX. | [Papal arms] | ROMAE, Typis & Expensis Philippi de Rubeis, | Anno lubilaei M. DC. L. | [short rule] | *Superiorum Permissu.*

First edition, Rome, 1650.

4to. ✠⁶ A-Hh⁴ Ii⁶; 136 leaves, pp. [*12*] 1-239 [240] [*20*].

Bibliographies: B. In. G. 1219; Bitting, p. 306; Oberlé (1) 79; Vicaire 556; Wheaton and Kelly 3921.

Copies: B. In. G., *BMC, BNC,* and *NUC* (5 copies).

1158. Manetti, Saverio, 1723-1785.

DELLE SPECIE DIVERSE | DI FRUMENTO E DI PANE | SICCOME | DELLA PANIZZAZIONE | MEMORIA | DEL DOTTOR SAVERIO MANETTI | *Pubblicata sotto gli auspici dell' Illustriss. Sig.* | ANDREA GINORI | PATRIZIO FIORENTINO | Provveditore del Tribunale e Magistrato della Sanità, | e dell' Arte del Cambio, di quella Città, | *E ATTUALMENTE PRESIDENTE* | DELL' IMPERIAL SOCIETA' FISICO – BOTANICA | FIORENTINA. | [ornament] | IN VENEZIA | MDCCLXVI. | [short rule] | PRESSO ANTONIO ZATTA | *CON LICENZA DE' SUPERIORI, E PRIVILEGIO*

Second edition, Venice, 1766. Originally published, Florence, 1765.

4to. π⁴ A-Ff⁴ Gg⁴(-Gg4); 123 leaves, pp. [1-4] 5-7 [8], ²1-237 [238].

Bibliographies: B. In. G. 1222; Westbury, p. 140.

Copies: B. In. G., *BMC* and *NUC* (Library of Congress and National Agricultural Library).

1159. Manfredi, Girolamo, d. 1492.

LIBRO | INTITOLATO | IL PERCHE. | TRADOTTO DI LATINO | IN VOLGARE. | Dell' Eccell. Medico, & Astrologo, M. Gieronimo | de' Manfredi. | *Et dall' istesso in molti luochi dilucidato, & illustrato.* | Con mostrar le cagioni d'infinite cose, appartenenti | alla sanità. | *Con la dichiaratione delle virtù d' alcune herbe.* | Di nuouo ristampata, & repurgata da quelle cose, che | hauessero potuto offendere il simplice animo | del Lettore. | [publisher's device] | IN VENETIA, M. DC. XXIX. | [rule] | Appresso Ghirardo Imberti.

New edition, Venice, 1629. Originally published in Latin under the title *Liber de homine*, Bologna, 1474.

8vo. a-b⁸ A-V⁸; 176 leaves, pp. [*32*] 1-314 [*6*]. Last three leaves blank.

Bibliographies: Westbury, p. 143.

Copies: *BMC*.

1160. Massonio, Salvatore, 1554 or 5-1624.

ARCHIDIPNO, | OVERO | DELL' INSALATA, | E DELL' VSO DI ESSA, | *Trattato nuouo, curioso, e non mai più dato in luce*, | DA SALVATORE MASSONIO | Scritto, e diuiso in Sessanta otto Capi; | Dedicato a' molto Illustri Signori fratelli, | LVDOVICO, ANTONIO, E FABRITIO | COL' ANTONII. | [armorial woodcut] | IN VENETIA, MDCXXVII. | [rule] | APPRESSO MARC' ANTONIO BROGIOLLO. | *Con Licenza de' Superiori, e Priuilegio*.

First edition, Venice, 1627.

4to. a-b⁴ A-Hhh⁴ Iii⁴(-Iii4); 227 leaves, pp. [*16*] 1-249, 240-426 [*2*] = 454.

Bibliographies: B. In. g. 1266; Bitting, p. 315; Schraemli (1) 329; Simon BG 1023; Vicaire 577; Westbury, p. 146.

Copies: B. In. G., *BMC* (2 copies), *BNC* and *NUC* (6 copies).

1161. Mattei, Venantio.

TEATRO | NOBILLISSIMO | DI SCALCHERIA | DI | *VENANTIO MATTEI* | DA CAMERINO | Per apparecchio di Banchetti à gran | Prencipi, secondo il variar delle | stagioni. | Col modo di far diuerse viuande per il passato non | vsate à benefitio de Professori | *Con aggiunta di fare diuerse sorte di minestre* | DEDICATO | All' Eminentissimo, e Reuerendissimo | *SIG. CARDINALE* | GIACOMO | ROSPIGLIOSI. | [rule] | IN ROMA, Per Giacomo Dragondelli 1669. | *CON LICENZA DE' SVPERIORI*.

First edition, Rome, 1669.

4to. †⁶ A-2I⁴ 2K⁶; 140 leaves, pp. [1-3] 4-5 [6-12]; ²1-266 [2]. Last leaf blank.

Bibliographies: B. In. G. 1269; Bitting, p. 316; Schraemli (1) 334; Simon BG 1467; Vicaire 858; Westbury, p. 147.

Copies: B. In. G., *BMC, BNC*, and *NUC* (John Crerar Library and Library of Congress).

1162. Messisbugo, Christofore di.

[ornament] BANCHETTI [ornament] | COMPOSITIONI DI | VIVANDE, ET AP= | PARECCHIO GE= | NERALE, DI | CHRISTOFORO | DI MESSI | SBVGO, | [four type ornaments] | [leaf] ALLO ILLVSTRISSIMO [leaf] | ET REVERENDISSIMO | SIGNOR IL SIGNOR | DON HIPPOLITO | DA ESTE, | CARDINALE DI | FERRARA. | *Con gratia* [ornament] *Et Priuilegio.* | IN FERRARA PER GIOVANNI | *De Buglhat Et Antonio Hucher Compagni.* | *Nell' Anno.* M. D. XLIX.

First edition, Ferrara, 1549.

4to. ✳⁴ ᵖ✳⁴ A-Z⁴ &⁴ a-c² χ1; 111 leaves, ff. [8] 1-22 [2], ²1-71 [8].

Illustrations: Woodcut portrait of the author on ✳1ᵛ, woodcut of a banquet on ᵖ✳3ᵛ, woodcut of a kitchen scene on F3ʳ, and a woodcut of the printer's emblem on &2ᵛ and χ1ᵛ.

Bibliographies: B. In. G. 1286; Oberlé (1) 61; Schraemli (1) 349; Schraemli (2) 23; Simon BG 1048; Vicaire 596; Westbury, p. 150; Wheaton and Kelly 4150.

Copies: B. In. G., *BMC* and *NUC* (6 copies).

1163. Messisbugo, Cristoforo di.

LIBRO NOVO | NEL QVAL S'INSEGNA A' FAR | *d'ogni sorte di uiuanda secondo la diuersità de* | *i tempi, cosi di Carne come di Pesce.* | *Et il modo d' ordinar banchetti, apparecchiar Tauole,* | *fornir palazzi, & ornar camere* | *per ogni gran Prencipe.* | OPERA ASSAI BELLA, E MOLTO | *Bisogneuole à Maestri di Casa, à Scalchi, à* | *Credenzieri, & à Cuochi.* | *Composta per M. Christofaro di Messisbugo, & hora* | *di nouo corretta, & ristampata.* | *Aggiontoui di nuouo, il modo di saper*

tagliare / *ogni sorte di* Carne, & Vccellami. / *Con la sua* Tauola ordinata, oue
ageuol- / *mente si trouerà ogni cosa.* | [woodcut] | IN VENETIA MDLVII.

Third edition, Venice, 1557. Originally published, Venice, 1552.

8vo. A-P⁸ Q⁴; 124 leaves, ff. [1] 2-112, 105-112 [*4*]. Last leaf blank.

Bibliographies: B. In. G. 1287; Simon BG 1049; Westbury, p. 150.

Copies: B. In. G., *BMC* and *NUC* (Folger Library and New York Public Library).

1164. Pagliarini, Lorenzo Maria.

IL FVOCO | RISTRETTO, ET VNITO | DISCORSO PRATICO. | In cui si dimostra
con facilità nuoui modi di fa- | re il fuoco, e portare il suo calore con poli- | zia,
commodità, & vtilità singolare per | qualsiuoglia sorte di persona, | *Con nuoua*
aggiunta, & accresciuto con | *due Tauole distinte.* | Dato in luce à benefizio publico |
DA LORENZO MARIA | PAGLIARINI | D' AREZZO DI TOSCANA. | *DEDICATO*
| All' Illustriss. e Reuerendiss. Signore | MONSIG. CIAMPINI. | [ornament] | In
Roma, Per Dom. Ant. Ercole. 1695. | *Con licenza de' Superiori.* [rule] | Si Vendono
alla piazza della Minerua alla medesi- | ma Insegna dal sudetto Pagliarini Libraro.

Second edition, Rome, 1695. Originally published, Rome, 1694.

8vo. A⁸ B⁸(-B8), ²A⁴ [B]⁴; 23 leaves, pp. [1-2] 3-29 [30], ²[8] 1-6 [2].

Illustrations: Engraved title-page by N. Billy after Ferd. Fab. and five engraved plates
illustrating an apparatus for cooking.

Bibliographies: B. In. G. 1417 in a note.

Copies: B. In. G. and *BMC*.

1165. La pasticciera di compagna e di citta.

LA PASTICCIERA | DI COMPAGNA E DI CITTA | CON L'ARTE | DI FARE
PANI PEPATI, CIALDE, ED OBBLII | OPERA CHE FA SEGUITO | ALLA
CUCINIERA DI COMPAGNA | [short rule] | TRADUZIONE DAL FRANCESE |
[short rule] | TORINO 1845 | DALLA LIB. DELLA MINERVA SUBALPINA | DI
P. P. GIUS. VACCARINO | *contrada Doragrossa num. 2.*

First edition in Italian, Turin, 1845. Originally published in French under the title *La Patissière de la campagne et de la ville . . .*, Paris, 1818.

185 x 113 mm. [1]⁶ 2-8⁶ 9⁸; 56 leaves, pp. [1-5] 6-112.

Bibliographies: This edition unrecorded in the bibliographies consulted. Westbury, p. 169, cites a Turin, 1848, edition.

Copies: No other copy located.

1166. Persio, Antonio, fl. 1575-1613.

DEL | BEVER CALDO | COSTVMATO | da gli antichi Romani | TRATTATO D'ANTONIO | PERSIO. | *Nel quale si pruoua con l'historia, & essempio de gli* | *antichi, & con la ragione, che il bere fatto caldo al* | *fuoco, è di maggior giouamento,* *& forse anche gusto,* | *che non è il freddo hoggidi vsato.* | ALLA SANTITÀ DI N. S. | Clemente Ottauo | CON PRIVILEGIO. | [woodcut] | IN VENETIA, Presso Gio. Battista Ciotti, | alsegno della Minerua. 1593.

First edition, Venice, 1593.

8vo. a⁸ A-M⁸; 104 leaves, ff. [8] 1-86 [10].

Illustrations: Woodcut on E7ᵛ of an implement for heating water.

Bibliographies: B. In. G. 1464; Bitting, p. 366; Horn-Arndt 69; Oberlé (1) 916; Simon BB II. 497; Vicaire 676; Westbury, p. 171.

Copies: B. In. G., *BMC*, *BNC*, and *NUC* (5 copies).

1167. Petronio, Alessandro Trajano, d. 1585.

DEL VIVER | DELLI ROMANI, | ET DI CONSERVAR | LA SANITÀ | Di M. ALESSANDRO PETRONIO da Ciuita Castellana | LIBRI CINQVE | Doue si tratta del Sito di Roma, dell' Aria, de' Venti, delle Stagioni, | dell' Acque, de' Vini, delle Carni, de' Pesci, de' Frutti, delle Herbe, | & di tutte l'altre cose pertinenti al gouerno de gli Huomini, | & dclle Donne d'ogni età, & conditione. | *Opera vtile, & necessaria* *non solo a Roma, mà ancora ad ogn' altro Paese.* | CON DVI LIBRI APPRESSO DELL' ISTESSO AVTORE, | del mantenere il Ventre molle senza Medicine | *Tradotti* *dalla lingua Latina nella Volgare, dall' Eccellente Medico* | M. BASILIO PARAVINCINO, DA COMO. | Con molte postille in margine, & vna Tauola

copiosissima delle cose notabili. | [rule] | CON PRIVILEGIO DI N. S. CLEMENTE
VIII. | [engraved coat of arms] | IN ROMA, Appresso Domenico Basa. M. D. XCII.
| [rule] | CON LICENTIA DE' SVPERIORI.

First edition in Italian, Rome, 1592. Originally published in Latin under the title *De
victu Romanorum*, Rome, 1581.

4to. ✱✱⁶ A-Lll⁴; 234 leaves, pp. [*12*] 1-416 [*40*].

Bibliographies: B. In. G. 1471; Horn-Arndt 70; Oberlé (1) 69; Schraemli (2) 87;
Simon BB II. 499; Simon BG 1159; Vicarie 680; Westbury, p. 171; Wheaton and
Kelly 4756.

Copies: B. In. G., *BMC, BNC*, and *NUC* (5 copies).

1168. Pisanelli, Baldassare.

TRATTATO | DELLA NATVRA | DE CIBI ET DEL BERE, | DEL SIG.
BALDASSARE | Pisanelli, Medico Bolognese. | Nel quale non solo tutte le virtù, & i
vitij di quelli | minutamente si palesano; ma anco i rimedij per | correggere i loro
difetti copiosamente s'insegnano: | tanto nell' apparecchiarli per l'vso, quanto nell' or-
| dinare il modo di riceuerli. | *Distinto in vn vago, e bellissimo partimento, tutto
ripieno* | *della dottrina de' piu celebrati Medici, & Filosofi:* | *con molte belle Historie
Naturali.* | [woodcut] | M D LXXXIIII. | [rule] | IN VENETIA, Appresso Gio.
Battista Porta.

Second edition, Venice, 1584. Originally published, Rome, 1583.

4to. a⁴ A-T⁴; 80 leaves, pp. [*8*] 1-144, 155-162 (for 152).

Bibliographies: B. In. G. 1498; Horn-Arndt 72; Simon BB II.507; Simon BG 1171;
Vicaire 682; Westbury, p. 173.

Copies: B. In. G., *BMC* and *NUC* (5 copies).

1169. Platina, Bartolomeo, 1421-1481.

[head title on a1ʳ] PLATYNAE DE HONESTA VOLVPTATE: | ET VALITVDINE
AD AMPLISSIMVM AC | DOCTISSIMVM. D. B. ROVERELLAM. S. CLE |
MENTIS PRAESBITERVM CARDINALEM | LIBER PRIMVS.

Colophon on π4^v: VIRI DOCTISSIMI Pla | tynae opusculum de obso/ | niis ac honesta uoluptate: | impressum Venetiis Du/ | ce iclyto Petro Mocenico. | Idibus Iuniis. Mcccclxxv.

First dated edition, Venice, Laurentius de Aquila and Sibyllinus Umber, 1475, believed to be preceded by an undated edition printed in Rome by Ulrich Han, 1474 or 1475.

Folio: [π^4 a^{10} b-l^8]; 94 leaves, unpaginated. This copy lacks the last two leaves, the first of which is supplied in facsimile (the second is blank).

Bibliographies: Goff P762; Horn-Arndt 76; Simon BB I. 78; Simon BG 1187; Vicaire 688.

Copies: *BMC, BNC,* and *NUC* (4 copies). Goff (8 copies).

1170. Platina, Bartolomeo, 1421-1481.

Platynae de honesta uoluptate: & ualitudine: uel | de obsoniis: & Arte Coquinaria libri decem.

Colophon: Venetiis Bernardinus Venetus Impressit | Anno Domini. M.II.D.

New edition, Venice, 1498. Originally published, Rome, 1474 or 1475.

4to. a-y^4; 88 leaves, unpaginated.

Bibliographies: Goff P 764; Oberlé (1) 52; Simon BB. I. 81; Simon BG 1189; Vicaire 689.

Copies: *BMC* and *NUC* (8 copies). Goff (8 copies).

1171. Platina, Bartolomeo, 1421-1481.

Platine viri celeberrimi. De honesta | voluptate ac valitudine libri de | cem q[ue] emendatissime im= | pressi: cum noua ta= | bula & indice.

Colophon: Venetiis Per Ioānē Tacuinū de Trino. M.D.XVII. Die. II. Ianuarii.

New edition, Venice, 1517. Originally published, Rome, 1474 or 1475.

4to. A⁴ B-K⁸; 76 leaves, ff. [*4*] I-LXXII.

Bibliographies: B. In. G. 1517; Bitting, p. 373; Horn-Arndt 79, Simon BB II. 521; Simon BG 1196.

Copies: B. In. G. and *NUC* (4 copies).

1172. Possetto, Giovanni.

Dott. GIOVANNI POSSETTO │ PERITO CHIMICO IGIENISTA │ DEL MUNICIPIO DI TORINO │ [short rule] │ LA │ CHIMICA DEL VINO │ ANALISI, ALTERAZIONI, MANIPOLAZIONI, ADULTERAZIONI. │ CON APPENDICE │ SULLA FABBRICAZIONE E SUL'ANALISI DELL'ACETO │ CON FIGURE INTERCALATE NEL TESTO │ E TAVOLE │ [publisher's monogram] │ TORINO │ CARLO CLAUSEN │ [short rule] │ 1897

First edition, Turin, 1897.

239 x 160 mm. π4 χ4 1-31⁸; 256 leaves, pp. [i-v] vi-xvi [1] 2-496. Two folding charts not reckoned in the signatures or the pagination. Publisher's printed wrappers.

Illustrations: Numerous wood engravings in the text.

Bibliographies: Unrecorded in the bibliographies consulted.

Copies: *BNC.*

1173. Rabasco, Ottaviano.

IL │ CONVITO │ OVERO │ DISCORSI DI QVELLE MATERIE │ Che al Conuito s'Appartengono. │ *DEL SIG. OTTAVIANO RABASCO.* │ Nelle Accademie de gl'Incitati in Roma │ e de Gelati in Bologna detto l'Assicurato. │ Doue s'hanno sttettamente, con ordine diligente la Diffinitione l'Origine, │ la Materia, il Luogo, il Tempo, l'Apparato, i Ministri, le Feste, │ i Giuochi, i Ragionamenti, le Circostanze, gl' Effetti, le Deità, & │ imaginati Numi tutelari de' Conuiti tanto pubblici quan- │ to priuati, e di qualunque genere d' essi │ distintamente. │ *Con l'uso di varie nattioni di Greci, Romani, Egittij, Persiani, Ebrei,* │ *e d' altri, tanto de gl' antichi quanto de nostri tempi.* │ E con vn Discorso, a qual parte della Filosofia si subordini il Conuito. │ *AL MAGNANIMO DON CARLO MEDICI* │ *De' Serenissimi Principi di Toscana.* │ Aggiuntoui vn Indice Copiosissimo │ [woodcut] │ IN FIORENZA M.DC.XV. │ [rule] │ Per Gio: Donato, e Bernardino Giunti, & Compagni │ *Con Licenza de' Superiori, & Priuilegio.*

First edition, Florence, 1615.

4to. ✱⁴ †² A-Nn⁴ Oo²; 152 leaves, pp. [*12*] 1-253 [254-292].

Bibliographies: B. In. G. 1585; Simon BG 1244/1245; Vicaire 725; Westbury, p. 183.

Copies: B. In. G., *BMC*, *BNC*, and *NUC* (4 copies).

1174. Romoli, Domenico.

LA SINGOLARE | DOTTRINA DI M. DOMENICO | *Romoli sopranominato
Panunto,* | Dell' ufficio dello Scalco, de i condimenti di tutte le vi- | uande, le stagioni
che si conuengono a tutti gli ani- | mali, vecelli, & pesci, Banchetti di ogni tempo, & |
mangiare da apparecchiarsi di dì, in dì, per tutto | l'anno a Prencipi. | *Con la
dichiaratione della qualità della carni di* | *tutti gli animali, & pesci, & di tutte le* |
viuande circa la sanità. | Nel fine vn breue trattato del reggimento della sanità. |
Opera sommamente vtile a tutti. | [ornament] | [woodcut with motto on three sides
lettered, bottom to top] QVAL PIV FERMO | [across top] E IL. MIO FOGLIO | [top
to bottom] E IL MIO PRES AGIO | *Col Priuilegio del Sommo Pontefice, & dell'
Illustr.* | *Senato Veneto per anni XX.*

First edition, Venice, 1560.

8vo. a-b⁸ A-Aaa⁸; 392 leaves, ff. [*16*] 1-376.

Bibliographies: B. In. G. 1696; Bitting, p. 403; Pennell, p. 116; Schraemli (1) 421
(with date 1570); Simon BB II. 565; Simon BG 1307; Vicaire, 747; Westbury, p. 190.

Copies: B. In. G., *BMC*, *BNC*, and *NUC* (5 copies).

1175. Rosselli, Giovanne de.

[in red] Opera noua chiamata Epulario, | [in red] Quale tracta il modo de cucinare ogni
carne/ vcelli/ | [in red] pesci, de ogni sorte. Et fare sapori/ torte/ pastel/ | [in red] li/
al modo de tutte le prouince: & molte | [in red] altre gētilezze. Cōposta p[er] Maestro
| [in red] Giouāne de rosselli. Frācese. | [woodcut of a kitchen scene]

Colophon: ℭ Impresso in Venetia per industria e spesa de | Nicolo Zopino Et
Vincenzo compagni in | la chasa de Maistro Jacomo Penci | da Lecho Impressore
acuratissi/ | mo. Nel. M.D.xvii.adi.iii. | del Mese de Aprile. | [woodcut]

Third edition, Venice, 1517. Originally published Venice, 1516.

8vo. A-L⁴; 44 leaves, ff. [i] ii-xli [xlii-xliv].

Illustrations: Woodcut of kitchen scene on title-page.

Bibliographies: Vicaire 751.

Copies: *NUC* (John Crerar Library only).

1176. Rosselli, Giovanne de.

Epulario quale tratta del mo | [in red] do de cucinare ogni carne, Uccelli, | [in red] Pesci, de ogni sorte, & fare Sa | [in red] pori, Torte, & pastelli al mo- | [in red] do de tutte le Prouincie. | [woodcut of a kitchen scene]

Colophon: ℭ In Venetia appresso gli heredi di Gioanne | Padoano, Nel anno del Signore. 1555.

Sixteenth edition, Venice, 1555. Originally published, Venice, 1516.

8vo. A-F⁸; 48 leaves, ff. [1-2] 3-47 [48]. Last leaf (blank?) wanting in this copy.

Illustrations: Woodcut of kitchen scene on title-page.

Bibliographies: Westbury, p. 192. See B. In. G. 1710 for a list of other editions.

Copies: No other copy of this edition located.

1177. Rosselli, Giovanne de.

EPVLARIO | IL QVALE | TRATTA | DEL MODO DI CVCINARE | Ogni Carne, Vccelli, & Pesci | d'ogni sorte. | *ET DI PIV INSEGNA FAR SAPORI*, | *Torte, Pastelli,* *al modo di tutte le Prouin-* | *cie de Mondo.* | Con la gionta di molte altre cose bellissime. | [woodcut of a beehive] | In Venetia, & poi in Treuigi, | [rule] | Appresso Aurelio Righettini. M. DC. XXX.

Twenty-fourth edition, Venice, 1630. Originally published, Venice, 1516.

16mo. A-C¹⁶; 48 leaves, ff. [1] 2-43 [44-48]. Last leaf blank.

Bibliographies: This edition unrecorded in the bibliographies consulted and not in the list of editions in B. In. G.

Copies: No other copy of this edition located.

1178. Rossetti, Battista.

DELLO SCALCO | DEL SIG. GIO. BATTISTA | ROSSETTI, | *Scalco della Serenissima Madama Lucretia da Este* | *Duchessa d'Urbino,* | Nel quale si contengono le qualità di vno Scalco perfetto, | & tutti i carichi suoi, con diuersi vfficiali | à lui sottoposti: | *Et gli ordini di vna casa da Prencipe, e i modi di seruirlo,* | *cosi in banchetti, come in tauole ordinarie.* | Con gran numero di banchetti alla Italiana, & alla Alemana, di varie, e bellissime | inuentioni, e desinari, e cene familiari per tutti i mesi dell' anno. | con apparecchi diuersi di tauole non vsati, | *Et con molte varietà di viuande, che si possono cauare* | *di ciascuna cosa atta à mangiarsi.* | Et con tutto ciò che à buono cias cun mese: & con le prouisioni da farsi | da esso Scalco in tempo di guerra. | [woodcut] | IN FERRARA, | Appresso Domenico Mammarello, | MDLXXXIIII.

First edition, Ferrara, 1584.

4to. a-b⁴ A-Kk⁴ Ll⁶ Mm-Yyy⁴ Zzz²; 284 leaves, pp. [*16*] [1] 2-268 [*4*] 269-547 [548].

Note on front free end paper: Pierre Gauthier — vente Pichon. 21 Fev 98.

Bibliographies: B. In. G. 1713; Vicaire 752; Westbury, p. 193.

Copies: B. In. G.

1179. Ruscelli, Girolamo. d. 1566.

Title-page of Part One:

LA PRIMA PARTE | DE' SECRETI DEL | REVERENDO DONNO | ALESSIO PIEMONTESE, | NVOVAMENTE DALL' AVTTOR | MEDESIMO RIVEDVTI ET | RICORRETTI. | [vignette] | *Con Priuilegio dell'* Illustriss. *&* Eccellentiss. *Signor Duca d'Vrbino,* | *che niuno possa quest' opera stampare, ne altroue stampata uen-* | *dere per tutto il* Dominio *di sua* Eccellenza. | IN PESARO *Per Bartolomeo Cesano.* 1559.

Title-page of Part Two:

LA SECONDA PARTE | DE' SECRETI DEL | REVERENDO DONNO | ALESSIO PIEMONTESE, | & d'altri eccellentissimi huomini. | NVOVAMENTE MANDATI IN | LVCE A COMMVNE VTILITA | D'OGNIVNO. | [vignette lettered vertically, bottom to top] SICVI HIC SERPENTEM, | [top to bottom] SIC NOCENTES EXCVTIAM | *Con Priuilegio dell' Illustriss. & Eccellentiss. Signor Duca d'Vrbino,* / *che niuno possa quest' opera stampare, ne altroue stampata* / *uendere per tutto il Dominio di sua Eccellenza.* | IN PESARO *Per Bartolomeo Cesano.* 1559.

New edition, Pesaro, 1559. Originally published, Venice, 1555.

8vo. a⁸ A-N⁸ aa⁸ bb⁴ a-o⁸ p⁴; 240 leaves, first part ff. [*8*] 1-103 [*1*]; second part pp. 1-231 [24], [*232*]. P. 231 misnumbered "131".

Bibliographies: B. In. G. 1729 in the list of editions.

Copies: B. In. G. and *BNC*.

1180. Savonarola, Giovanni Michele, 1384?-1462?

Libreto delo Excellētissimo Physico | maistro Michele Sauonarola: de tu= | te le cose che se māzano comunamēte | e piu che comune: e di quelle se beue= | no per Italia: e de sei cose non natura | le: & le regule per conseruare la sanita | deli corpi humani, con dubij notabi | lissimi Nouamente Stampato.

Colophon: In Venetia per Simone de Lue- | re. adi. xxi. Agosto. M.D.VIII.

First edition, Venice, 1508.

4to. a-m⁴ n⁶; 54 leaves, ff. [1] 2-53 [*54*].

Bibliographies: B. In. G. 1772; Drexel 778; Bitting, p. 626; Simon BB II. 580; Westbury, p. 200.

Copies: B. In. G., *BMC* and *NUC* (4 copies).

1181. Savonarola, Giovanni Michele, 1384?-1462?

TRATTATO │ VTILISSIMO DI MOL │ TE REGOLE, PER CONSER= │ *uare la Sanità, dichiarando qual cose sia=* │ *no utili da mangiare, & quali triste:* │ *& medesimamente di quelle* │ *che si beuono per Italia.* │ *Aggiontoui alcuni dubij molto notabili.* │ *Composto per* M. M*ichele Sauonarola* / *Fisico Eccellentissimo.* │ * │ [vignette] │ VENETIIS.

Colophon: *In V*inegia per gli heredi di Gioanne Paduano. │ M D L IIII.

New edition, Venice, 1554. Originally published under the title *Libreto . . . de tute le cose che se manzano comunamente*, Venice, 1508 (item 1180).

8vo. A-K^8 L^4; 84 leaves, ff. [1] 2-84.

Bibliographies: B. In. G. 1774; Horn-Arndt 92; Maggs 36; Schraemli (1) 444; Simon BB II. 582; Vicaire 771; Westbury, p. 200.

Copies: B. In. G., *BNC* and *NUC* (Folger Library, National Library of Medicine, and New York Academy of Medicine).

1182. Scappi, Bartolomeo.

OPERA DI M. │ BARTOLOMEO │ SCAPPI, CVOCO SECRETO │ DI PAPA PIO V. │ *DIVISA IN SEI LIBRI,* │ *Nel primo si cotiene il ragionameto che fa l'autore con Gio. suo discepolo.* │ *Nel secondo si tratta di diuerse uiuande di carne sì* │ *di quadrupedi, come di uolatili.* │ *Nel terzo si parla della statura, e stagione de pesci.* │ *Nel quarto si mostrano le liste del presentar le uiuande in tauola* │ *cosi di grasso come di magro.* │ *Nel quinto si contiene l'ordine di far diuerse sorti di paste, & altri lauori.* │ *Nel sesto, & ultimo libro si ragiona de conualescenti, & molte* │ *altre sorti di uiuande per gli infermi.* │ *Con il discorso funerale che fu fatto nelle esequie de Papa Paulo III.* │ *Con le figure che fanno bisogno nella cucina, & alli Reuerendissimi nel Conclaue.* │ [vignette lettered on three sides │ [bottom to top] *QVAL PIV FERMO* │ [top] *E IL MIO FOGLIO* │ [top to bottom] *E IL MIO PRESAGGIO.*] │ *Col priuilegio del sommo Pontefice Papa Pio V. & dell' Illustrissimo* │ *Senato Veneto per anni XX.*

Colophon: *IN VENETIA,* │ *Appresso Michele Tramezzino. M D LXX.*

First edition, Venice, 1570.

4to. a⁶ A-V⁴ X-Vvv⁸, ²A⁴; 458 leaves, ff. [6] 1-56, 59-66, 65-304, 303-391 [6] 392-436 [437-440] [4].

Illustrations: Twenty-eight etched and engraved plates, one folding showing a banquet scene, and the others comprising a portrait of the author, six scenes of food preparation and twenty of kitchen implements and apparatus.

Bibliographies: B. In. G. 1779; Maggs 81; Pennell, p. 114; Schraemli (1) 446; Vicaire 771; Westbury, p. 202; Wheaton and Kelly 5455. Bitting and Simon BG cite undated editions, both with fewer pages than the original edition.

Copies: B. In. G., *BMC* and *NUC* (Kansas State University only).

1183. Scappi, Bartolomeo.

OPERA DI M. | BARTOLOMEO | SCAPPI, | CVOCO SECRETO | DI PAPA PIO QVINTO, | Diuisa in sei Libri. | Nel primo si contiene il ragionamento che fa l'Autore con Gio. suo discepolo. | Nel secondo si tratta di diuerse uiuande di carne, si di quadrupedi, come di uolatili. | Nel terzo si parla della statura, e stagione de' pesci. | Nel quarto si mostrano le liste del presentar le uiuande in tauola, cosi di grasso come di | magro. | Nel quinto si contiene l'ordine di far diuerse sorti di paste, & altri lauori. | Nel sesto, & ultimo libro si ragiona de' conualescenti, & molte altre sorti di uiuande | per gli infermi. | *Con il discorso funerale, che fu fatto nelle essequie* | *di PAPA* *PAVLO III.* | Con le Figure che fanno bisogno nella Cucina, & alli Re- | uerendissimi nel Conclaue. | [woodcut] | IN VENETIA, M D XCVIII. | [rule] | Appresso Alessandro Vecchi.

Fifth edition, Venice, 1598. Originally published, Venice, 1570 (item 1182). 4to. ✱⁴(-✱4) A-Rr⁸ Ss⁴; 327 leaves, ff. [3] 1-311 [312-324].

Illustrations: Twenty-seven woodcuts, one folding, all after the engravings in the 1570 edition. The folding plate shows a banquet scene and single page illustrations comprise a portrait of the author, six scenes of food preparation and nineteen pages of kitchen utensils and apparatus. The folding plates and portrait are tipped in and not reckoned in the collation; twenty-five woodcuts at the end are on leaves Qq8ʳ-Ss4ʳ.

Bibliographies: B. In. G. 1781; Pennell, p. 115; Schraemli (1) 447; Vicaire 773; Westbury, p. 202; Wheaton and Kelly 5457.

Copies: B. In. G., *BMC* and *NUC* (Harvard only).

1184. Scappi, Bartolomeo.

[etched title-page lettered] M. BORTOLOMEO SCAPPI DELL | ARTE DEL CVCINARE CON | IL MASTRO DI CASA E TRINCIANTE. | VENE | TIA | 1643 | COMBI | [signed] Astinenza.

Ninth edition, Venice, 1643. Originally published under the title *Opera*, Venice, 1570 (item 1182).

4to. [A]⁴ B-Iiii⁴ KKKK⁶; 318 leaves, pp. [1-3] 4-636.

Illustrations: Etched title-page showing Bacchus and other figures and twenty-seven etched and engraved plates, one folding showing a banquet scene, and the others comprising six scenes of food preparation and twenty of kitchen implements and apparatus.

Note: This edition, as others from 1605 forward, include *Il trinciante* by Vincenzo Cervio (pp. 551-662) and *Il mastro di casa* by Cesar Pandini (pp. 623-636).

Bibliographies: B. In. G. 1784; Maggs 38; Vicaire 775; Westbury, p. 203.

Copies: B. In. G., *BMC*, *BNC*, and *NUC* (New York Public Library, University of California, Berkeley, and University of Illinois).

1184a. Scriptores rei rusticae.

LIBRI DE RE RVSTICA | A NICOLAO *Angelio uiro consumatissimo nuper* / *maxima diligentia recogniti et typis excusi, cum in* / *dice & expositione omnium dictionumn. Ca/* / *tonis. Varronis. Collumellæ. Palla* / *dij quæ aliqua enucleatione* / *indigebant,* | M. *Catonis.* LIB. I. | M. *Terentij Varronis.* LIB. III. | L. *Iunij Moderati Columellæ.* LIB. XII. | *Eiusdem de arboribus Liber Separatus ab alÿs.* / *Palladij* LIB. XIIII. | *De duobus dierum generibus, simulq; de umbris* / & *oris, quæ apud Palladium.*

Colophon on Q11ʳ:

Impressum Florentiæ opera & impressa Philippi | *Iuntæ. Anno a natiuitate. D. X. V. Su/* | *pramille mense Iulio. Leone* | *Decimo Pontificæ.* | ΛΛ BB *abcdefghiklmnop qrstuxy [con]* & *[rum]* | ABCDEFGHIKLMNOPQ. | *Quaterniones omnes præter Q* & *B B qui sunt sesternoines.*

New edition, Florence, 1515. Originally published, Venice, 1472.

8vo. AA⁸ BB¹² a-z⁸ &⁸ ç⁸ ℞⁸ A-P⁸ Q¹²; 360 leaves, ff. [*20*] 1-339 [*340*]. The *NUC* records the following collation for this work: AA⁸ BB⁸ (BB4+BBy⁴) a-z⁸ &8 ç⁸ ℞⁸ A-P⁸ Q¹⁰ (Q5+Qy¹·²). As the colophon states that all gatherings are in 8s except BB and Q which are in 12s we can read the "y" in signatures BB and Q as "v" and "yi" as "vi" thus signing the first six leaves of these gatherings.

Bibliographies: B. In. G. 1800; Simon BB 594; Simon BG 311.

Copies: *NUC* (8 copies).

1185. Stefani, Bartolomeo.

L'ARTE | DI BEN CVCINARE, ET INSTRVIRE | i men periti in questa lodeuole professione. | *Doue anco s'insegna à far Pasticci, Sapori, Salse, Gelatine, Torte, & altro* | DI BARTOLOMEO STEFANI | Cuoco Bolognese. | *All' Ill.mo & Ecc.mo Sig. Marchese* | OTTAVIO GONZAGA | Prencipe del Sacro Romano Imperio, de' Marchesi | di Mantoua, e Signor di Vescouato, &c. | [etched portrait of author] | [rule] | IN MANTOVA, Appresso gli Osanna, Stampatori Ducali, 1662. | *Con licenza de' Superiori.*

First edition, Mantua, 1662.

4to. [A]⁴ B-T⁴; 76 leaves, pp. [1-2] 3-144 [*8*].

Illustration: Etched portrait of the author on the title-page.

Bibliographies: B. In. G. 1863; Vicaire 803; Westbury, p. 208.

Copies: B. In. G. and *BMC*.

1186. Stefani, Bartolomeo.

L'ARTE | DI BEN | CVCINARE, | ET INSTRVIRE | I men periti in questa lodeuole | professione. | *DOVE ANCO S' INSEGNA* | *A far Pasticci, Sapori, Salse,* | *Gelatine, Torte,* | *& altro.* | DI | BARTOLOMEO STEFANI | Cuoco di S.A.S. di Mantoua. | *Con nuoua aggionta in questa vltima* | *Impressione.* | [three type ornaments] | IN BOLOGNA, | [rule] | Per il Longhi. *Con licenza de' Superiori.*

New edition, Bologna, ca.1690. Originally published, Mantua, 1662 (item 1185).

12mo. A-K¹²; 120 leaves, pp. [1-2] 3-240.

Bibliographies: Westbury, p. 209. B. In. G. 1863 in the list of other editions.

Copies: *NUC* (Folger Library only).

1187. Tanara, Vincenzo, d. 1657.

L'ECONOMIA | DEL CITTADINO | IN VILLA | *DI VINCENZO TANARA.* | Libri VII. | Intitolati. Il Pane, e'l Vino. Le Viti, e l' Api. Il Cortile. | L'Horto. Il Giardino. La Terra. | La Luna, e'l Sole. | *Oue con erudita varietà si rappresenta, per mezo* | *dell' Agricoltura, vna Vita ciuile,* | *e con isparmio.* | [engraved land- and seascape signed *Il Coriolano*] | IN BOLOGNA, MDCXLIV. | [rule] | *CON LICENZA DE'* *SVPERIORI.*

First edition, Bologna, 1644.

4to. ¤⁴ A-Dddd⁴ Eeee⁶; 302 leaves, pp. [8] 1-594 [2].

Illustrations: Engraved illustration signed "Il Coriolano" on title-page; woodcut of printer's device on p. 595. Woodcuts chiefly illustrating grafting in the margins of the text.

Bookplate: Westbury.

Bibliographies: B. In. G. 1885; Oberlé (1) 78; Westbury, p. 211; Wheaton and Kelly 5891.

Copies: B. In. G. and *NUC* (5 copies).

1188. Togni, Michel.

RACCOLTA | Delle singolari qualità | DEL CAFFE' | DA MICHIEL TOGNI | DEDICATA | *Al Molto Illustre Sig. il Sig.* | FRANCESCO | PELEGRINO. | [vignette] | IN VENETIA, M. DC. LXXV. | [rule] | Per Gio: Francesco Valuasense. | *Con Licenza de' Superiori.*

First edition, Venice, 1675.

12mo. A-B¹²; 24 leaves, pp. [1-4] 5-48. First two pages blank.

Illustration: Engraved illustration of a coffee plant on p. 37.

Bibliographies: Vicaire 836; Westbury, p. 216; Wheaton and Kelly 6049.

Copies: *BNC* and *NUC* (Harvard and National Library of Medicine).

1189. Torrella, Gaspar, 1452-1520.

℄ Pro regimine seu preseruatiōe sanitatis │ ℄ De Esculentis & poculen/ │ tis dialogus.

Colophon: ℄ Finit │ dyalogus p[ro] │ gimine sanitatis val │ de vtilis: edit[us] a magistro │ Gaspare torrella natione valen │ tino Ēpo sancte Juste: ac. S. d.n. Ju │ lij. ij. medico ac prelato domestico: cum quo │ modum cognoscendi complexiones │ tā esculento[rum] q[uam] proculento[rum] do │ cet. Anno a n[a]ti[vi]tate dñi. │ M.d.vi. impressus │ per mag[ist]r[e]m Jo. │ Besickē.

First edition, Rome, 1506.

4to. a-k⁸ l⁶; 86 leaves, unpaginated. Last leaf (blank?) wanting in this copy.

Bibliographies: Unrecorded in the bibliographies consulted.

Copies: *BMC* and *NUC* (Folger Library and National Library of Medicine).

1190. Vasselli, Giovanni Francesco.

L' APICIO │ OVERO │ Il Maestro de' Conuiti │ DI │ *GIO. FRANCESCO VASSELLI.* │ DEDICATO │ All' Illustrissimo │ SENATO DI BOLOGNA. │ [armorial woodcut] │ IN BOLOGNA, MDCXLVII. │ [rule] │ Per gli HH. del Dozza. Con licenza de' Superiori.

First edition, Bologna, 1647.

Signature R², pp. [129-132] lacking in this copy. 4to. [a]⁴ b⁴ A-Q⁴; 72 leaves, pp. [*16*] 1-117 [118-128].

Bibliographies: B. In. G. 1977; Vicaire 857; Westbury, p. 222.

Copies: B. In. G., *BMC* and *BNC* (2 copies).

1191. Vettori, Pietro, 1499-1585.

[ornament] | TRATTATO | DI PIERO VETTORI | DELLE LODI, ET DELLA | COLTIVATIONE | De gl'Vliui. | *Di nuouo Ristampato.* | [ornament] | [woodcut] | IN FIRENZE | Nella Stamperia de'Giunti. | M D LXXIIII.

Second edition, Florence, 1574. Originally published, Florence, 1569.

4to. A-M⁴ N²; 50 leaves, pp. [*8*] 1-90 [*2*].

Bibliographies: B. In. G. 2032; Brunet V, 1180; Graesse VII, 302; Oberlé (1) 687.

Copies: B. In. G., *BMC*, *BNC*, and *NUC* (9 copies).

ΑΘΗΝΑΙΟΥ δειπνοσοφιστοῦ τὴν πολυμαθεστάτην πραγματείαν τῶν ἕξεις τίσοι φιλολόγ μικρῷ περιχμθίῳ πολλῶν τε καὶ μεγάλων καὶ ἀξιομνημονεύτων καὶ θαυμαστῶν καὶ ποικίλων καὶ σαφϐέλων καὶ γλαφυρῶν καὶ ὧν ἴσως πρότερον οὐκ ἤδεις, ἐς γνῶσιν ἐλθεῖν. καὶ ἕλως τῶν τῆς ἑλληνικῆς παιδείας ἀκρότητων ἢ δυσευρέτων κειμηλίων ἐγκρατεῖ γενέσθαι. τῶν δὲ βιβλίων πεντεκαίδεκα τὸν ἀριθμὸν ὄντων, τὰ μὲν τεσσαρακαίδεκα, ὅλος ὁρῇς. τὸ δέ τοι πρῶτον ἢ ἐδύ τὸ ἐν ἐπὶ πέντε μικρὰ σοι παρέξομεν. ἀκεφάλῳ σώματι κεφαλὴν ἀεκγκαθὼς τις ἐπιθεῖναι κολοβῷ ἀδ ρᾷ οὕτω ἔστιν εὐγνωμόνων τὸ ταυτὶ τὰ συγγράμματ᾽ ἀφαλεγομἑ νους, μάλιστα μὴ τοῖς περὶ ἢ ἄλλον τὸν πολύαθλόν τε καὶ πολυγράμματον εὐχαριστεῖν. ΟΥΧ ἥ κιστα δὲ καὶ μουσπύρῳ τῷ διδασκάλῳ. τῷ ἐι καὶ μὴ παντί τὰ πᾶσιν ἴσαμ μθίῳ τὰν τ᾽ γραφον τόνδε τῶν τύπων ἀφηκέ- σοις ἕλκεσι πολλα- χῇ διεφ, θο- ρός, ἀλλ᾽ ἐιω πολλὰς μὲν μυ- ριάδας διορθώσαντι σφαλμάτων πολλοὺς δὲ στί- χους τῶν παρεισαγομθίων κατὰ λογάδην πρότερον ἀεκγινωσκομθίους καὶ χύδην, εἰς τὴν προσήκουσαν τῆς ἑμμἱ δου τάξεως ἀνκείνδαι ἀποκαταστήσαντι, χάριν εἰδέναι.

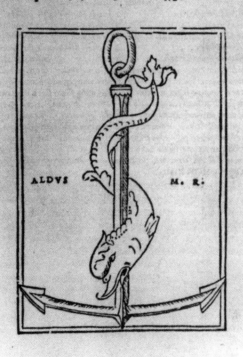

ALDVS   M. R.

Item no. 1110

VI

AVVERTIMENTI

SOPRA LA FABRICA

Della Carne Porcina.

In Bologna, Per Nicolò Tebaldini.

M.DC.XXVII.

Con Licennza de' Superiori.

DE NATVRALI
VINORVM HISTORIA
DE VINIS ITALIAE
Et de Conuiuijs Antiquorum
LIBRI SEPTEM
ANDREAE BACCII
Elpidiani Medici, atq; Philoſophi,
Ciuis Romani

ACCESSIT DE FACTITIIS, AC CERVISIIS,
de q; Rheni, Galliæ, Hiſpaniæ, & de totius
Europæ Vinis & de omni Vinorum uſu
COMPENDIARIA TRACTATIO
AD AMPLISSIMVM
S·R·E·CARD·
A SCANIVM COLVMNAM

Cum Gratia

et Priuilegio

ANDREAE BACCII ELPIDIEN · Æ TATV · SVÆ ANNO · LXXII

Superiorum

Romani

anno 1596

Permiſſum

SVMMO CONATV Ex officina Nicholai Mutij ASSIDVITA

Item no. 1113

BACCII
BALDINII
IN LIBRVM
HYPPOCRATIS.

DE AQVIS, AERE, ET LOCIS
Commentaria.

Eiusdem Tractatus de Cucumeribus.

CVM LICENTIA SVPERIORVM.

FLORENTIAE,
Ex Officina Bartholomaei Sermartellij.
CIƆ IƆ LXXXVI.

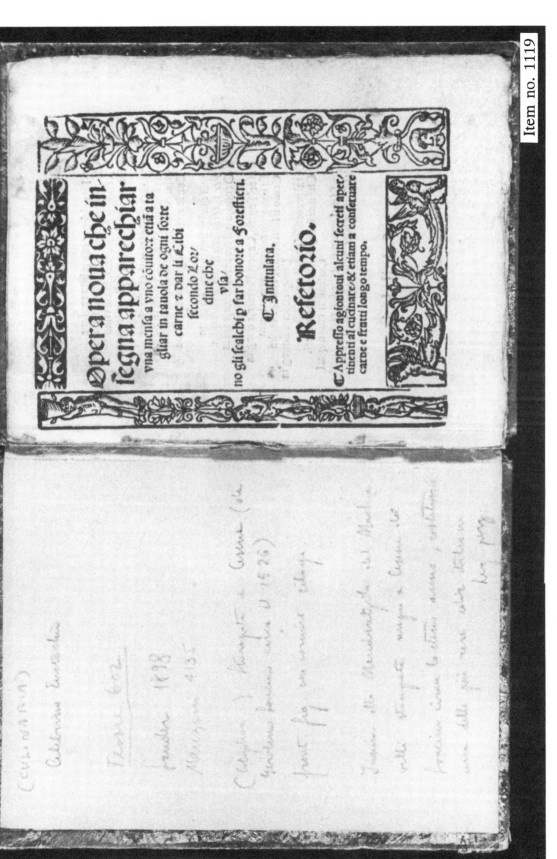

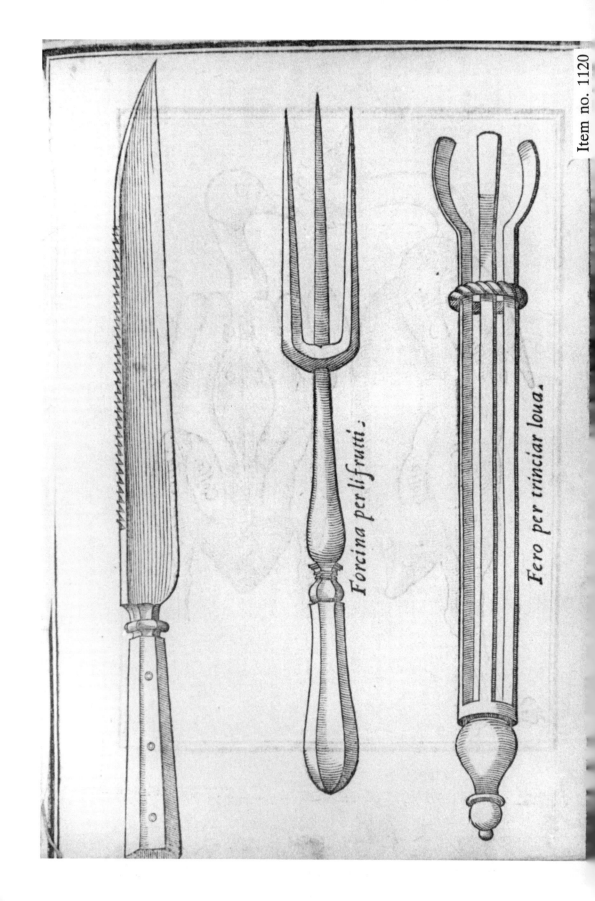

Forcina per li frutti.

Fero per trinciar loua.

IL CREDENZIERE

DI BUON GUSTO

OPERA MECCANICA

DELL'ORITANO

VINCENZO CORRADO

NAPOLI MDCCLXXVIII.

Nella Stamperia Raimondiana.

VINCENZO CORRADO D'ETA SUA D'ANNI XL.

IL CORRADO ORITAN VINCENZO E QUESTO,
MECCANICO INMORTAL DI PREGJ ONUSTO,
GALANTE IL CUOCO, E IL CREDENZIER DI GUSTO.
OPRE SON SUE: TI BASTA INTENDI IL RESTO.

LIMON

S. REMI

Item no. 1140

IL TRINCIANTE

Di Mefser Mattia Gieger Bauaro di Mosburc,

Con le figure delle cofe da trinciare, e de' Coltelli, e forcine, intagliate in rame; aggiuntiui alcuni breui, ed vtili ricordi fopra ciafcuna figura.

All'Illuftrifsimo Signor

FEDERIGO DI POLENZ NOBILE DI PRVSSIA.

Degniffimo Configlier dell'Illuftrifs. Nazion Alamanna nell'Vniuerfità de' Signori Legifti in Padoua.

Ed à tutta l'Illuft.ifs. Nazion de' nobiliffimi Sig. Alamäni della detta Vniuerfità.

In Padoua per il Martini Stampator Camerale. Con lic. de' Superiori.
M DC XXI.

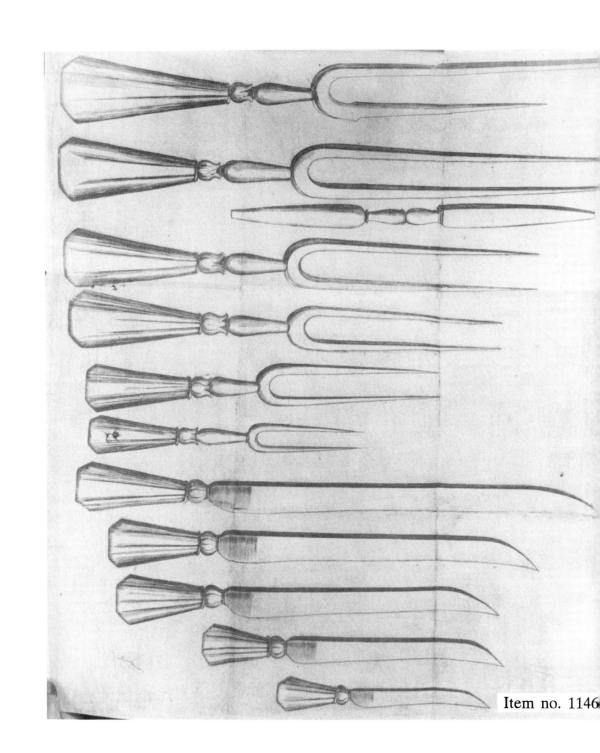

Item no. 1146

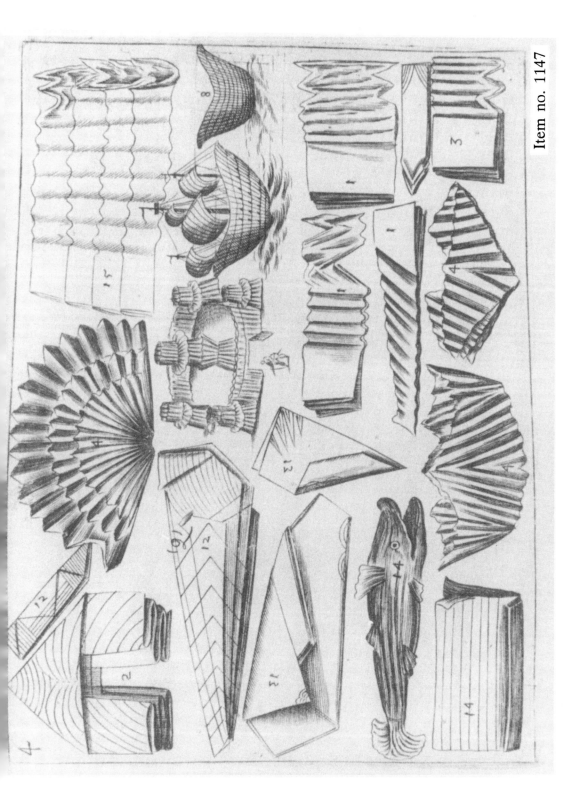

OPERA · DE

gniſſima: τ vtile per chi ſi diletta di
nare: con molti belliſſimi ſecreti de
compõere: τ cõſeruare vinan-
de: τ molti altri ſecreti di
piu coſe: Compoſto
p il valẽte Ma-
eſtro Gio
uane
De la Cucina dela Sanctita dil
noſtro Summo Pontefice.

Item no. 1162

Cucina principale

reduto da pani

lucerna

Camerino per garzoni

ordegno

Conserua

murcllo e pignatte

banco

Colonna col mortaro

Tauola per imbandire.

Item no. 1182

Item no. 1183

JAPAN

1192. Ehon konrei michishirube. Kyōto, Hishiya Jihei, 1813.

First edition?

217 x 159 mm. 2 vols. Vol. I. 8 double leaves. Vol. II. 8 double leaves and a single leaf pasted down at the end of the volume. Gathered in accordian folds in the oriental manner.

Illustrations: Woodcut illustrations of wedding ceremonies by Hotta Renzan printed in red, pink, blue, yellow, and green on all pages except the first in volume one and the last two in volume two.

Bibliographies: Unrecorded in the bibliographies consulted.

Copies: No other copy located.

1193. Irie, Jōan.

Hyakkō hijutsu. Edo [Tokyo] Takeda Tōsuke, 1724.

First edition?

227 x 161 mm. 3 vols. 25 double leaves. Vol. II. 23 double leaves. Vol. III. 33 double leaves. All three volumes gathered in accordian folds in the oriental manner.

Illustrations: Woodcut illustrations of handcrafts in all three volumes. One illustration in volume two shows the preparation and cooking of fish.

Bibliographies: Unrecorded in the bibliographies consulted.

Copies: No other copy located.

1194. Koshi, Kichirobei.

Shōjin kondate shū. Edo [Tokyo] Maekawa Rokuzaemon; Osaka, Kōchiya Mohei; Kyoto, Noleagawa Tōshirō, 1824.

First edition, Tokyo, 1824, of volume two of a two volume work. Volume one was published, Tokyo, 1819.

130 x 180 mm. Vol. II only of two volumes. 65 double leaves and a single leaf pasted down at the beginning of the volume. Gathered in accordian folds in the oriental manner.

Illustrations: Woodcuts of eating and cooking utensils on the pasted down leaf and of flowers in the text at the end of the volume.

Bibliographies:; Unrecorded in the bibliographies consulted.

Copies: No other copy located.

1195. Seitaien.

Gyokai nōdoku hinbutsu zukō. Edo [Tokyo] Suharaya Mohei, 1849.

New edition, Tokyo, 1849. Originally published, Tokyo, 1837. This edition is the first to contain colored illustrations.

180 x 120 mm. 76 double leaves and two single leaves pasted down at the front and back of the volume. Gathered in accordian folds in the oriental manner.

Illustrations: The first three double leaves printed in black, tinted in red and blue, with three pages of illustrations by Takashima Shunshō, one of a fishing scene and two of fish. Numerous woodcut illustrations of fish in the text.

Bibliographies: Unrecorded in the bibliographies consulted.

Copies: No other copy located.

1196. Yamakawa, Nenmu.

Kondate sen. Osaka, no publisher, 1760.

First edition?

213 x 147 mm. 27 double leaves and one single leaf. The first and last double leaves are pasted down. Gathered in accordian folds in the oriental manner.

Illustrations: Woodcut of a cook shop scene on the second double leaf.

Bibliographies: Unrecorded in the bibliographies consulted.

Copies: No other copy located.

▲ 一　諸〻白〻

▲ 一　糕〻初〻椒〻

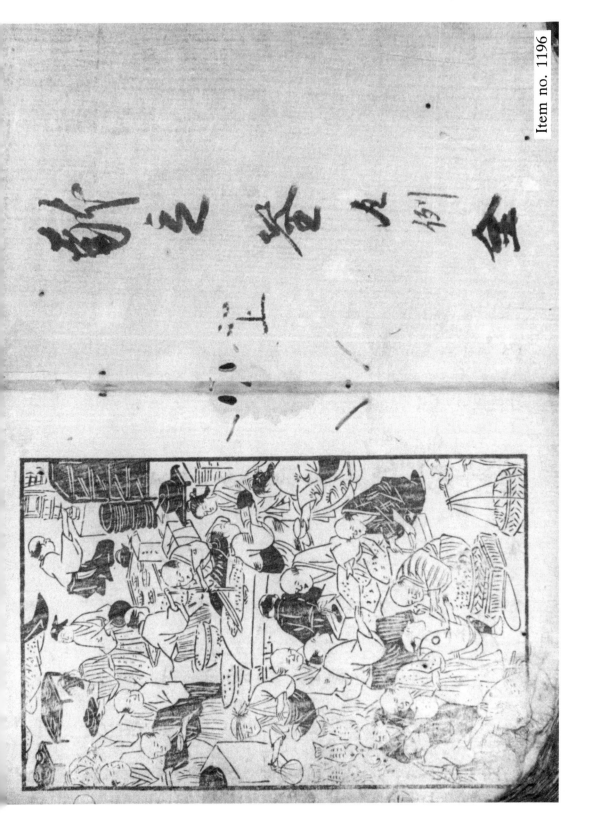

MEXICO

1197. Blanquel, Simón.

[within an ornamental border] NOVISIMO ARTE | DE | COCINA, | Ó |
ESCELENTE COLECCION | DE LAS MEJORES RECETAS | para que al menor
costo posible, y con la ma- | yor comodidad, pueda guisarse á la española, | francesa,
italiana é inglesa; sin omitirse cosa | alguna de lo hasta aquí publicado, para sazo- | nar
al estilo de nuestro país. | LLEVA AÑADIDO | lo mas selecto que se encuentra acerca
de la | repostería; el arte de trinchar &c., con dos | graciosísimas estampas que aclaren
mejor es- | te último tratadito. | *DEDICADO* | A LAS SEÑORITAS MEXICANAS. |
[short fancy rule] | MEXICO. | Impreso en la oficina del C. Alejandro Valdés. | [short
rule] | 1831.

First edition, Mexico City, 1831.

146 x 101 mm. [1]⁴ 2-34⁴ 35⁴ (-35₄); 139 leaves, pp. [1-2] 3-245 [246-250] [i]
ii-xxviii.

Illustrations: Two engraved illustrations on pp. 247 and 249 of carving.

Bibliographies: Unrecorded in the bibliographies consulted.

Copies: *NUC* (John Crerar Library and National Library of Medicine).

1198. Blanquel, Simón.

NOVISIMO ARTE | DE | [ornament] COCINA, [ornament] | Ó | ESCELENTE
COLECCION | de las | MEJORES RECETAS, | *Para que al menor costo posible y*
con la mayor co- | *modidad, pueda guisarse á la española, francesa,* | *italiana é*
inglesa; sin omitirse nada de lo hasta | *aqui publicado, para sazonar al estilo*
mexicano. | [short rule] | LLEVA AÑADIDO | Lo mas selecto que se encuentra
acerca de reposte- | ría, el arte de trinchar &c., con dos estampas | que aclaran mas
este último tratadito. | [short fancy rule] | MÉXICO. – 1845. | [short rule] | Imprenta
á cargo de Manuel N. de la Vega, | *calle de Tiburcio núm.* 21.

New edition, Mexico City, 1845. Originally published, Mexico City, 1831 (item
1197).

155 x 96 mm. [1]⁸ 2-19⁸ 20⁴; 156 leaves, pp. [1-2] 3-312.

Illustrations: Two lithographed plates illustrating carving.

Bibliographies: Unrecorded in the bibliographies consulted.

Copies: No other copy of this edition located.

1199. Brillat-Savarin, Jean Anthelme, 1755-1826.

FISIOLOGIA DEL GUSTO. | POR | BRILLAT SAVARIN, | y traducida del francés | POR EUFEMIO ROMERO. | ILUSTRADA | POR BERTALL. | PRECEDIDA | DE UNA NOTICIA BIOGRAFICA | POR ALF. KARR. | Grabados en madera intercalados en el texto por Midderigh. | [woodcut] | MÉJICO. | [short rule] | IMPRENTA DE JUAN R. NAVARRO, editor. | calle de Chiquis núm. 6. | [short rule] | 1852.

First Mexican edition, Mexico City, 1852. Originally published in French under the title *Physiologie du goût*, Paris, 1826 (item 98).

222 x 148 mm. [1]⁴ 2-52⁴; 208 leaves, pp. [i-iii] iv-viii [9] 10-414 [2].

Illustrations: Numerous woodcuts in the text after those in the first edition.

Bibliographies: Unrecorded in the bibliographies consulted.

Copies: No other copy located.

1200. El Cocinero Mexicano.

EL COCINERO MEXICANO, | Ó | COLECCION | DE LAS | *MEJORES RECETAS* | PARA GUISAR | AL ESTILO AMERICANO, | Y DE LAS MAS SELECTAS SEGUN EL METODO DE LAS | COCINAS ESPAÑOLA, ITALIANA, FRANCESA E INGLESA. | *Con los procedimientos mas sencillos para la fa-* | *bricacion de masas,* *dulces, licores, helados y to-* | *do lo necesario para el decente servicio de una* | *buena* *mesa.* | TOMO I. [TOMO II.] [TOMO III.] | MEXICO: 1831. | [short rule] | IMPRENTA DE GALVAN, A CARGO DE MARIANO AREVALO, CALLE DE | CADENA NUM. 2.

First edition, Mexico City, 1831.

152 x 100 mm. 3 vols. Vol. I. π² χ⁶ 1-21⁸ [22]²; 178 leaves, pp. [4] [i] ii-xi [xii] [1] 2-314 [26]. Vol. II. [1]⁸ 2-21⁸ 22⁴; 172 leaves, pp. [1-2] 3-323 [324-344]. Vol. III. 1-28⁸ 29²; 226 leaves, pp. [1-2] 3-428 [24].

Bibliographies: Unrecorded in the bibliographies consulted.

Copies: *NUC* (New York Public Library only).

1201. Manual del cocinero y cocinera.

MANUAL | DEL | COCINERO Y COCINERA, | tomado | DEL PERIODICO
LITERARIO | LA RISA. | [short rule] | SE DEDICA | *Al bello secso de Puebla.* |
[ornament] | PUEBLA: | [short rule] | IMPRENTA DE JOSÉ MARÍA MACÍAS, |
calle de Micieses número 2. | [short rule] | 1849.

First edition? Puebla, 1849.

146 x 95 mm. [1]^8 2-26^8; 208 leaves, pp. [1-3] 4-397 [398-416].

Illustrations: Eight lithographed plates, two hand colored.

Bibliographies: Unrecorded in the bibliographies consulted.

Copies: No other copy located.

NOVISIMO ARTE

DE

COCINA,

ó

ESCELENTE COLECCION

DE LAS MEJORES RECETAS

para que al menor costo posible, y con la mayor comodidad, pueda guisarse á la española, francesa, italiana é inglesa; sin omitirse cosa alguna de lo hasta aquí publicado, para sazonar al estilo de nuestro país.

LLEVA AÑADIDO

lo mas selecto que se encuentra acerca de la repostería; el arte de trinchar &c., con dos graciosísimas estampas que aclaren mejor este último tratadito.

DEDICADO

A LAS SEÑORITAS MEXICANAS.

MEXICO.

Impreso en la oficina del C. Alejandro Valdés.

1831.

MANUAL

DEL

COCINERO Y COCINERA,

tomado

DEL PERIODICO LITERARIO

LA RISA.

SE DEDICA

Al bello secso de Puebla.

PUEBLA:

IMPRENTA DE JOSÉ MARÍA MACÍAS,
calle de Micieses número 2.

1849.

POLAND

1202. Maciej z Miechowa, 1457-1523.

EDITIO VE- | NERABILIS D. MATHIE | DE MIECHOW ARTIVM ET ME- | *dicinae doctoris eximij. Canonici Cracouien. &c.* / *pro conseruanda hominum sanitate fami-* / *liarissimo collecta stilbo.* | *Iosephi Czimmermani Cracouiensis. Anno' suae etatis* / *decimoquinto. Immatura aeditio, in immortalem* / *candorem, illius magni Medici doctoris* / *Mathiae de Miechow.* / *Vos ego qui sapitis, Medicis qui fiditis omnes* / *Quos fluere in morbos, effluereq; leue est.* / *Hunc moneo doctum & frugalem sumite librune.* / *Carius hic nihil sit, nihil suerit melius.* / *Scilicet ille bonus de Miechow, ille Machaon* / *Noster, habet solus consilia Hippocratis.*

Colophon: *Impressum Cracouiae per Mathiam Scharffenberg.* / *Anno.* M. D. XXXV.

First edition, Cracow, 1535.

12mo. A-K$^{8 . 4}$ L^8; 68 leaves, unpaginated.

Bibliographies: Oberlé (1) 323.

Copies: *BMC* and *NUC* (Yale only).

EDITIO VE-
NERABILIS D. MATHIE
DE MIECHOW ARTIVM ET ME-
dicinæ doctoris eximij. Canonici Cracouien. &c.
pro conseruanda hominum sanitate fami-
liarißimo collecta stilbo.

Iosephi Czimmermani Cracouiensis. Anno' suæ ætatis
decimoquinto. Immatura æditio, in immortalem
candorem, illius magni Medici doctoris
Mathiæ de Miechow.

Vos ego qui sapitis, Medicis qui fiditis omnes
Quos fluere in morbos, effluereq; leue est.
Hunc moneo doctum & frugalem sumite librum.
Carius hic nihil sit, nihil fuerit melius.
Scilicet ille bonus de Miechow, ille Machaon
Noster, habet solus consilia Hippocratis.

PORTUGAL

1203. Annona, ou mixto-curioso.

Title-page of Volume One:

ANNONA, | OU | MIXTO-CURIOSO. | *Folheto Semanal*, | QUE ENSINA | O
METHODO DE COSINHA E COPA, | COM UM ARTIGO | DE |
𝕽𝕰𝕮𝕽𝕰𝕬𝕮𝕬𝕺. | TOMO. I. | [short fancy rule] | N.° 1. | [short fancy rule] |
Assigna-se na Loja de José Joaquim Nepomuceno, Rua | *Augusta N. ° 137, onde*
tambem se recebe a correspondencia | *das Provincias, franca de porte. Vende-se nas*
mais do cos- | *tume. Os preços de cada assinatura são os sequintes. Por* | 12 *N.os*
440 *réis, ou tambem a pagar no acto da entrega de* | *cada N. ° obrigando-se a acceitar*
os 12 40 *réis, avulso* 40 *réis.* | [ornament] | LISBOA. 1836. | [fancy rule] | NA
TYPOGRAFIA DA VIUVA SILVA E FILHOS. | Calçada de Santa Anna N.° 74.

Title-page of Volume Two:

ANNONA, | OU | MIXTO-CURIOSO. | *Folheto Semanal* | QUE ENSINA | O
METHODO DE COSINHA E COPA, | COM UM ARTIGO | DE |
𝕽𝕰𝕮𝕽𝕰𝕬𝕮𝕬𝕺. | TOMO II. | [short fancy rule] | N.° 13. | [short fancy rule] |
Assigna-se na Loja de José Joaquim Nepomuceno, Rua / *Augusta N. ° 137, onde*
tambem se recebe a correspondencia / *das Provincias, Franca de porte. Vende-se nas*
mais do cos- | *tume. Os preços de cada assinatura são os seguintes. Por* / 12 *N.*^{os}
440 *réis, ou tambem a pagar no acto da entrega de* / *cada N. ° obrigand-se a acceitar*
os 12, 40 *réis, avulso* 40 *réis.* | [ornament] | LISBOA. 1836. | [fancy rule] | NA
TYPOGRAFIA DA VIUVA SILVA E FILHOS. | Calçada de Santa Anna N.° 74.

Title-page of Volume Three:

ANNONA, | OU | MIXTO-CURIOSO. | *Folheto Semanal* | QUE ENSINA | O
METHODO DE COSINHA E COPA, | COM UM ARTIGO | DE |
𝕽𝕰𝕮𝕽𝕰𝕬𝕮𝕬𝕺. | TOMO III. | [short fancy rule] | N.° 25. | [short fancy rule] |
Assiana-se nas lojas de João Henriques, Rua Augusta N.° | 1; José Joaquim
Nepomuceno, dita rua N.° 137, onde se rece- | be a correspondencia das Provincias,
Franca de porte. Assi- | gna-se tambem e se vende nas mais do costume. Os preços de
| cada assinatura são os seguintes. Por cada 12. n.ºs 440 reis, | e tambem pagando no
acto da entrega de cada N.° obrigando-se | a acceitar 12, 40 réis, avulso 40 réis. |
[ornament] | 𝕷𝖎𝖘𝖇𝖔𝖆. | IMPRENSA DE C. A. S. CARVALHO | no um da calçada do
Garcia n.° 42. | [short rule] | 1837.

First edition, Lisbon, 1836-1837. Published in thirty-six numbers, paginated to form
three volumes. Volume I contains numbers 1-12; Volume II, numbers 13-24, and

Volume III, numbers 25-36. Each number has its own title-page. Only the title-page for the first number of each volume is transcribed.

145 x 98 mm. 3 vols. Vol. I. [1-12]^{12} [13]^2; 146 leaves, pp. [1-2] 3-288 [*4*]. All signatures in volume one signed). Vol. II. a-h^{12} i-k^8 l-n^{12}; 148 leaves, pp. [1-2] 3-291 [292-296]. Vol. III. A-M^{12} N^2; 146 leaves, pp. [1-2] 3-290 [2].

Bibliographies: *Livros Portugueses de cozinha* 339.

Copies: Biblioteca Nacional, Lisbon.

1204. Lebrun.

ARTE | DO | SALCHICHEIRO, | OU | METHODO | DE | PREPARAR E CONSERVAR AS DIFFERENTES | PEÇAS DE PORCO, SEGUNDO OS MAIS | MODERNOS PROCESSOS, | PRECEDIDA | DE UM TRATADO | SOBRE O MODO DE CRIAR, CEVAR E CURAR | O GADO SUINO, | Traduzida do francez. | [short fancy rule] | LISBOA. | NA TYPOGRAPHIA DE G. M. MARTINS, | Rua dos Capellistas n.° 62. | [short rule] | 1856.

First edition in Portuguese? Lisbon, 1856. Originally published in French under the title *Nouveau manuel complet du charcutier*, Paris, 1840 (item 272).

154 x 101 mm. π^4 1-19^8 20^4; 160 leaves, pp. [i-v] vi-vii [viii] [1] 2-309 [310] [2].

Bibliographies: This translation unrecorded in the bibliographies consulted.

Copies: No other copy located.

1204a. Novo Manual do Cozinheiro.

[hollow letter] NOVO MANUAL | DO COZINHEIRO, | OU | ARTE DA COZINHA | POSTA AO ALCANCE DE TODOS. | [ornament] | LISBOA. | VENDE-SE EM CASA DOS PRINCIPALS LIVREIROS | [short rule] | 1841.

First edition, Lisbon, 1841.

138 x 84 mm. π^2 1-18$^{12.6}$ 19^{12} 20^4; 180 leaves, pp. [1-5] 6-360.

Illustrations: Engraved frontispiece of a man sitting at table and an engraved folding plate illustrating carving.

Bibliographies: Unrecorded in the bibliographies consulted or in RLIN.

Copies: No other copy located.

1205. Rigaud, Lucas.

COZINHEIRO MODERNO | OU NOVA | ARTE DE COZINHA | ONDE SE ENSINA PELO METHODO | mais facil, e mais breve o modo de se prepara | rem varios manjares, tanto de carne, como de | peixe; Mariscos, legumes, ovos, lacticinios: | Varias qualidades de massas para pães, empa- | das, tortas, timbales, pasteis, bôlos, e outros | pratos de entremeio: Varias receitas de caldos | para differentes sopas: Caldos para doentes, e | hum caldo portativo para viagens longas. | *Com huma observaçaõ sobre algumas frutas; o tempo* | *de se colherem, tanto para se comerem na so-* | *bre mesa, como para doces, e se con-* | *servarem para o Inverno.* | OBRA MUITO UTIL, E NECESSARIA | a todas as pessoas de qualquer qualidade que se- | jaõ, e principalmente aos Professoras desta Ar- | te; aos Conserveiros, e a todos os que se achaõ | encarregados do governo das casas. | *DADO A' LUZ* | POR LUCAS RIGAUD | *Hum dos Chefes da Cozinha de Suas Magestades* | *Fidelissimas, &c.* | [ornament] | LISBOA | Na Offic. Patriarc. de FRANCISCO LUIZ AMENO. | [short rule] | M. DCC. LXXX. | *Com licença da Real Meza Consoria.*

First edition, Lisbon, 1780.

8vo. A-Hh^8 Ii^6; 254 leaves, pp. [1-6] 7-508. An eight page publisher's catalogue, dated 1781, is bound in at the end.

Bibliographies: *Livros Portugueses de cozinha* 277. Vicaire records the second edition, Lisbon, 1785.

Copies: *NUC* (Kansas State University only) and Biblioteca Nacional, Lisbon.

1206. Rodrigues, Domingos, 1637-1719.

ARTE | DE | COZINHA | DIVIDIDA EM TRES PARTES, | A primeira trata do modo de consinhar varios pratos de todo | o genero de carnes, e conserva, tortas, e empadas. A segun- | da de peixes, marisco, frutas, hervas, óvos, laticinios, doces, | e conserva, tocantes ao mesmo genero. A terceira da fòrma | de banquete para qualquet tempo do anno, e do modo com | que se hosped, aõ os Embaixadores, e como se guarnece hua | ma mesa redonda à Franceza. | *E nesta ultima impressaõ acccrescentada* | OFFERECIDA | AO S.R ANTONIO MONTEIRO | DE CAMPOS. |*AUTOR* | DOMINGOS RODRIGUES. | Mestre da cozinhª de Sua Magestade. | [ornament] | LISBOA: | Na Offic. de MANOEL ANTONIO, e a sua custa impresso | M.DCC.LVIII. | [rule] | *Com as licenças necessarias.*

New edition, Lisbon, 1758. Originally published, Lisbon, 1683.

8vo. π^2 A-S^8 T^6; 152 leaves, pp. [*4*] [1] 2-300.

Illustrations: Three folding woodcuts, printed on recto and verso, showing table settings.
Bibliographies: *Livros Portugueses de cozinha* 282.

Copies: *BMC* and Biblioteca Nacional, Lisbon.

ANNONA,

OU

MIXTO-CURIOSO.

Folheto Semanal,

QUE ENSINA

O METHODO DE COSINHA E COPA,

COM UM ARTIGO

DE

RECREAÇAÕ.

TOMO I.

N.º 12.

Assigna-se na Loja de José Joaquim Nepomuceno, Rua Augusta N.º 137, onde tambem se recebe a correspondencia das Provincias, franca de porte. Vende-se nas mais do costume. Os preços de cada assignatura são os seguintes. Por 12 N.ºˢ 440 réis, ou tambem a pagar no acto da entrega de cada N.º obrigando-se a acceitar os 12, 40 réis, avulso 40 réis.

LISBOA. 1836.

NA TYPOGRAFIA DA VIUVA SILVA E FILHOS.
Calçada de Santa Anna N.º 74.

RUSSIA

1207. Lobanov-Rostovsky, Aleksandr Yakovlevich, prince, 1788-1866.

Volume I:

TABLETTES GASTRONOMIQUES | DE | SAINT-PÉTERSBOURG, | RÉDIGÉES PAR UN AMATEUR, | ET | PRÉCÉDÉES D'UNE LISTE DES OUVRAGES A CONSULTER. | [vignette] | ST. PÉERSBOURG. | IMPRIMERIE D'ÉDOUARD PRATZ. | 1856.

Volume II, part one:

TABLETTES GASTRONOMIQUES | DE | SAINT-PÉTERSBOURG, | RÉDIGÉES PAR UN AMATEUR, | [short rule] | SECONDE PARTIE, | RECUEIL DE MENUS. | [vignette] | ST. PÉTERSBOURG. | IMPRIMERIE D'ÉDOUARD PRATZ. | 1858.

Volume II, part two:

TABLE DES MATIÈRES | DE LA SECONDE PARTIE | DES TABLETTES GASTRONOMIQUES.

First edition, St. Petersburg, 1856-1858, limited to 100 copies.

244 x 169 mm. 2 vols. in three parts. Vol. I. $\pi^4 \chi^2$ 1-6^8 7^4; 58 leaves, pp. [i-v] vi-ix [x-xii] [1] 2-102 [2]. Vol. II, part one. $\pi^2 \chi^4$ ($-\chi$4) 1-19^8 20^2; 159 leaves, pp. [i-v] vi-viii [ix-x] [1] 2-308. Vol. II, part two. π1 χ^6; 7 leaves, pp. [1-3] 4-14.

Bibliographies: Bitting, p.605; Schraemli (1) 260; Vicaire 815.

Copies: *BMC* and *NUC* (Library of Congress only).

TABLETTES GASTRONOMIQUES

DE

SAINT-PÉTERSBOURG,

RÉDIGÉES PAR UN AMATEUR,

ET

PRÉCÉDÉES D'UNE LISTE DES OUVRAGES A CONSULTER.

ST.-PÉTERSBOURG.
IMPRIMERIE D'ÉDOUARD PRATZ.
1856.

SPAIN

1208. Altimiras, Juan.

NUEVO ARTE | DE | COCINA, | SACADO | DE LA ESCUELA | DE LA |
EXPERIENCIA | ECONOMICA, | SU AUTHOR | *JUAN ALTAMIRAS.* | [fancy rule]
| *Con las Licencias necessarias.* | Barcelona: En la Imprenta de Maria Angela | Martí
Viuda, Plaza de San Jayme. | Año 1767.

Sixth edition, Barcelona, 1767. Originally published, Madrid, 1745.

8vo. π^8 A-L^8; 96 leaves, pp. [*16*] 1-176.

Bibliographies: Drexel 639; Malortie I.357; Palau I.252; Schraemli (1) 11.

Copies: *NUC* (Georgetown University only).

1209. Altimiras, Juan.

NUEVO ARTE | DE COCINA, | SACADO DE LA ESCUELA | DE LA
EXPERIENCIA ECONOMICA, | *Su Autor* Juan Altimiras, | *DEDICADO* | A SAN
DIEGO DE ALCALÁ. | [ornament] | MADRID: MDCCLXXXVIII. | [two rules] |
En la Imprenta de D. JOSEPH DO- | BLADO, calle de Barrio-Nuevo, | donde se
hallará.

New edition, Madrid, 1788. Originally published, Madrid, 1745.

8vo. A-L^8 M^2; 90 leaves, pp. [i-ii] iii-xv, xx-xxx [xxxi-xxxii] 1-152.

Illustration: Woodcut of kitchen utensils on B6^r.

Bibliographies: This edition unrecorded in the bibliographies consulted.

Copies: No other copy of this edition located.

1210. Carbonell y Bravo, Francisco, 1758-1837.

ARTE DE HACER | Y | *CONSERVAR EL VINO,* | CON UNA NOTICIA | ACERCA
LA FABRICACION DEL VINAGRE, | POR EL | *Dr. D. FRANCISCO CARBONELL*

Y BRAVO, | *CATEDRATICO DE QUIMICA, &c.* | [short fancy rule] | BARCELONA: EN LA OFICINA DE D. ANTONIO BRUSI | IMPRESOR DE CÁMARA DE S. M. AÑO DE 1820.

First edition, Barcelona, 1820.

200 x 138 mm. π^2 A-Nn^4 χ^2; 148 leaves pp. [*4*] 1-292.

Illustrations: Three engraved folding plates illustrating wine making apparatus.

Bibliographies: Palau III.153.

Copies: No other copy located.

Bound with:

ADICION | AL APÉNDICE | DEL ARTE DE HACÉR Y CONSERVAR EL VINO | POR EL | *Dr. D. FRNCISO CARBONELL Y BRAVO* | *Farmacéutico honorario de Cámara de S. M.* | *Catedrático de Quimica &c.* | [short fancy rule] | *BARCELONA:* | [short fancy rule] | EN LA IMPRENTA DE LA VIUDA É HIJOS DE BRUSE | AÑO 1824.

First edition, Barcelona, 1824.

4to. [1]^4 2^4; 8 leaves, pp. [1-2] 3-16.

Bibliographies: Palau III.153.

Copies: No other copy located.

1211. Duval, Henri-Louis-Nicolas, 1783-1854.

General title-page:

MANUAL | COMPLETO | Y GUIA GENERAL | DE | PASTELEROS, CONFITEROS, DESTILADORES, LICORISTAS | Y PERFUMADORES. | Dividido en cuatro tratados. | [short fancy rule] | CONTIENE | LOS MEJORES PROCEDIMIENTOS PARA PREPARAR EL CAFE, CHO- | COLATE, EL PONCHE, LOS HELADOS, BEBIDAS REFRESCANTES, | LICORES, FRUTAS EN AGUARDIENTE, CONFITURAS, PASTAS, | ESPIRITUS, ESENCIAS, VINOS

ARTIFICIALES, PASTELERIA LIGERA, | CERVEZAS, CIDRAS, AGUAS, POMADAS, Y POLVOS: VINAGRES | SALUDABLES PARA EL TOCADOR, LA DESTILACION DE TODAS ES- | PECIAS DE AGUARDIENTES, ETC. ETC. EL MODO DE HACER TODA | CLASE DE PASTELES, EMPANADAS, TORTAS, ETC. | POR MR. CARDELI, Y MADAMA GACON-DUFOUR. | Traducido de la cuarta edicion francesa. | *Barcelona.* | LIBERÍA DE SAURI Y COMP. CALLE DE ESCUDELLERS. | [short fancy rule] | 1832.

Title-page of the first part:

ARTE | ꝺe | DESTILADORES, LICORISTAS | Y | REPOSTEROS. | CONTIENE LOS MEJORES METODOS PARA PREPARAR | EL CAFE, CHOCOLATE, PONCHS, HELADOS, BEBI- | DAS REFRESCANTES, LICORES, FRUTAS EN AGUAR- | DIENTE, ESENCIAS, VINOS ARTIFICIALES, etc. | *Traducido de la cuarta edicion francesa.* | [vignette] | 𝔅arcelona. | [short fancy rule] | LIBERÍA DE SAURI Y COMPAÑIA, CALLE DE ESCUDELLERS | 1832

Title-page of the second part:

MANUAL | ꝺe | CONFITEROS, | Y | FABRICANTES DE DULCES, | CONTIENE LOS DESCUBRIMIENTOS MAS RECIENTES Y | UN SIN NUMERO DE SECRETOS NUEVOS. | TRADUCIDO DEL FRANCES. | [vignette] | 𝔅arcelona. | [short fancy rule] | LIBERÍA DE SAURI Y COMPAÑIA, CALLE DE ESCUDELLERS, | 1832.

Title-page of the third part:

MANUAL | ꝺe | PASTELEROS, | Ó | ARTE PARA PREPARAR | TODA CLASE DE PASTELES, PASTAS, PASTELILLOS, TORTAS, | EMPANADAS ETC., FRIO Ó CALIENTE. | POR MADAMA GACON-DUFOUR. | *Traducido del frances.* | [vignette] | 𝔅arcelona. | [short fancy rule] | LIBERÍA DE SAURI Y COMPAÑIA, CALLE DE ESCUDELLERS. | 1832.

The fourth part, a "Vocabulario general," has no title-page.

First edition in Spanish, Barcelona, 1832. Originally published in French under the titles *Manuel du cuisinier et de la cuisinière*, Paris, 1822, and *Manuel du limonadier, du confiseur et du distillateur*, Paris, 1822. (See items 175-177 for other French editions and item 1221 for a Spanish adaptation.)

167 x 106 mm. π² [1]⁸ 2-5⁸ 6⁶ [7]⁸ 8-12⁸ 13⁴ [14]⁸ 15-19⁸ [20]² 21⁸; 158 leaves, pp. [4] [1-6] 7-84 [8], ²[1-3] 4-98 [6], ³[1-3] 4-96 [4], ⁴[1] 2-16. In this copy signature 20 is misbound between π1 and π2 and signature 13 is misbound with 13₂.₃ before 13₁.₄.

Bibliographies: Palau III.156.

Copies: No other complete copy located. *NUC* records what appears to be a fragment of sixteen pages located at Kansas State University.

1212. Juan de Aviñon.

within a woodcut frame] [armorial woodcut with initials P V] │ ℭ [in red] Seuillana medici │ na. Que trata el modo cō seruati │ [in red] uo y curatiuo delos q̄ abitā en la │ muy insigne ciudad de Seuilla: │ [in red] la q̄l sirue y a puechapa q̄lquier │ otro lugar destos reynos. Obra │ [in red] ātigua digna & ser leyda. Va di= │ rigida al illustrissimo cabildo & │ [in red] la misma ciudad [in black] año. M.D.xlv [in black and red].

First edition, Seville, 1545.

4to. A⁴ B-S⁸; 140 leaves, ff. [4] 1-135 [1]. Last leaf blank.

Bibliographies: Palua I.588.

Copies: *BMC* and *NUC* (Hispanic Society of America and National Library of Medicine).

1213. Manual de la criada económica.

𝕸anual │ DE LA CRIADA │ ECONÓMICA, │ Y DE LAS MADRES DE FAMILIAS QUE DESEAN ENSEÑAR │ Á SUS HIJAS LO NECESARIO PARA EL GOBIERNO │ DE SU CASA. │ [vignette] │ MADRID: │ Se halla en la librería de Perez, │ *calle de Carretas.* │ [short rule] │ 1830.

First edition, Madrid, 1830.

141 x 93 mm. π² 1-12⁸ 13⁴; 102 leaves, pp. [4] [1] 2-199 [200].

Bibliographies: Palau VIII.143.

Copies: *NUC* (University of Illinois only).

1214. Martinez Montiño, Francisco.

ARTE DE COZINA, | PASTELERIA, VIZCO- | cheria, y Conserueria. | *Compuesta* | *por Francisco Martinez* | *Motiño, cozinero mayor del Rey* | *nuestro señor.* | [woodcut] | CON PRIVILEGIO. | *En Madrid por Luis Sanchez.* | Año M. DC. XI.

First edition, Madrid, 1611.

8vo. ¶⁸ A-Ss⁸; 336 leaves, ff. [*8*] 1-317 [*11*].

Illustrations: Woodcut with motto "VIGILI LABORE" on title-page and two woodcuts on R6ᵛ.

Bibliographies: Palau VIII.293.

Copies. No other copy located.

1215. Martinez Montiño, Francisco.

ARTE | DE | COCINA, | PASTELERIA, | VIZCOCHERIA, | Y CONSERVERIA: | COMPUESTA | *POR FRANCISCO MARTINEZ* | *Montiño, Cocinero Mayor del Rey* | *nuestro Señor.* | NUEVAMENTE CORREGIDA, | Y ENMENDADA. | [rule] | *CON* | *LICENCIA.* | *Barcelona*: En la Imprenta de Maria Angela | Martì viuda, en la plaza de S. Jayme. | Año 1763.

Twelfth edition, Barcelona, 1763. Originally published, Madrid, 1611 (item 1214).

8vo. π⁸ A-Kk⁸; 272 leaves, pp. [*16*] 1-510 [*18*]. Last leaf (blank?) wanting in this copy.

Bibliographies: Bitting, p. 329; Palau VIII.293.

Copies: *NUC* (Library of Congress and University of Wisconsin).

1216. Martinez Montiño, Francisco.

ARTE | DE COCINA, | PASTELERIA, | VIZCOCHERIA, | Y CONSERVERIA. | *COMPUESTO POR FRANCISCO* | *Martinez Montiño, Cocinero Mayor* | *del Rey.* | DECIMATERCIA IMPRESION. | [ornament] | CON LICENCIA. | [rule] | En Madrid, en la Imprenta de PANTALEON | AZNAR. Año 1778. | *A costa de la Real* *Compañia de Impresores,* | *y Libreros del Reyno.*

Thirteenth edition, Madrid, 1778. Originally published, Madrid, 1611 (item 1214).

8vo. ¶⁴ A-Gg⁸; 244 leaves, pp. [*8*] 1-480.

Bibliographies: Palau VIII.293.

Copies: *NUC* (4 copies).

1217. Martinez Montiño, Francisco.

ARTE DE COCINA, | PASTELERÍA, | VIZCOCHERÍA | Y CONSERVERI·A; | COMPUESTO | *POR FRANCISCO MARTINEZ MONTIÑO,* | *cocinero mayor del Rei.* | DÉCIMAQUNITA IMPRESION. | MADRID: 1800. | *EN LA IMPRENTA DE* *BARCO.* | *Con licencia.*

Eighteenth of the twenty-five editions recorded by Palau, styled fifteenth on the title-page, Madrid, 1800. Originally published, Madrid, 1611 (item 1214).

8vo. π⁴ A-Gg⁸; 244 leaves, pp. [*8*] 1-462 [*18*].

Illustration: Woodcut of cooking implements on π4ʳ.

Bibliographies: Palau VIII.293.

Copies: No other copy of this edition located.

1218. Mata, Juan de la.

[within a border of type ornaments] ✠ | ARTE | DE REPOSTERIA, | EN QUE SE CONTIENE TODO | genero de hacer Dulces secos, y en lìquido, | Vizcochos, Turrones, y Natas: | BEBIDAS HELADAS DE TODOS | generos, Rosolis, Mistelas,

&c. | CON UNA BREVE INSTRUCCION | para conocer las Frutas, y servirlas crudas. | Y DIEZ MESAS, CON | su explicacion. | SU AUTHOR | *JUAN DE LA MATA, REPOSTERO EN ESTA* | *Corte, natural del Lugar de Matalavilla, Concejo del* | *Sil de Arriba, Montañas, y Reyno de Leon,* | *y Obispado de Oviedo.* | QUIEN LE DEDICA AL EXC^mo. SEÑOR | Don Rodulfo Acquaviva y Aragon, Duque | de Atri, &c. | [rule] | CON LICENCIA: En Madrid, por Antonio Marin, | año M.DCCXLVII. | [rule] | *Se hallarà en casa de Simon Moreno, Mercader de Libros* | *frente las Gradas de San Phelipe el Real.*

First edition, Madrid, 1747.

8vo. ¶⁸ ¶¶⁴ A-M⁸ N²; 110 leaves, pp. [*24*] 1-196.

Illustrations: Engraved arms of Don Rodulfo Acquaviva y Aragon, duke of Atri, and ten etched folding plates showing table settings.

Bibliographies: Palau VIII.349; Schraemli (1) 330.

Copies: *NUC* (New York Public Library only).

1219. Mata, Juan de la.

✠ | ARTE | DE REPOSTERIA, | EN QUE SE CONTIENE TODO | genero de hacer Dulces secos, y en liquido, | Vizcochos, Turrones, y Natas: | BEBIDAS HELADAS DE TODOS GENEROS, | Rosolis, Mistelas, &c. | CON UNA BREVE INSTRUCCION | para conocer las Frutas, y servirlas crudas. | Y DIEZ MESAS, CON SU EXPLICACION. | SU AUTOR | *JUAN DE LA MATA, REPOSTERO EN ESTA CORTE,* | *natural del Lugar de Matalavilla, Concejo del Sil* | *de Arriba,* *Montañas, y Reyno de Leon,* | *y Obispado de Oviedo.* | Año [ornament] de 1755. | [line of type ornaments] | CON LICENCIA. En Madrid: En la Imprenta, y Li- | brerìa de Joseph Garcia Lanza, Plazuela del Angel, | donde se hallará.

Second edition, Madrid, 1755. Originally published, Madrid, 1747 (item 1218).

8vo. ¶⁴ A-Ff⁴ N²; 120 leaves, pp. [*8*] 1-232.

Bibliographies: Palau VIII.349.

Copies: *BMC* and *NUC* (5 copies).

1220. Mata, Juan de la.

ARTE | DE REPOSTERIA, | EN QUE SE CONTIENE | *todo gènero de hacer Dulces* *secos, y en lìquido,* | *Vizcochos, Turrones, Natas: Bebidas* | *heladas de todos generos,* *Rosolis,* | *Mistelas, &c.* | CON UNA BREVE INSTRUCCION | para conocer las Frutas, y servirlas crudas. | Y DIEZ MESAS CON SU EXPLICACION. | SU AUTOR | *JUAN DE LA MATA, REPOSTERO* | *en esta Corte, natural del Lugar de* *Matalavilla,* | *Concejo del Sil de Arriba, Montañas, y Reyno* | *de Leon, y Obispado de* *Oviedo.* | [ornament] | CON LICENCIA: | En Madrid: En la IMPRENTA de JOSEF HERRERA. | MDCCLXXXVI.

New edition, Madrid, 1786. Originally published, Madrid, 1747 (item 1218).

4to. π^2 A-Cc^4; 106 leaves, pp. [4] 1-208.

Bibliographies: Palau 157658; Schraemli (1) 332; Wheaton and Kelly 4079.

Copies: *NUC* (Boston Public Library, Indiana University, and New York Academy of Medicine).

1221. Rementeria y Fica, Mariano.

MANUAL | DEL COCINERO, COCINERA, REPOSTERO, PASTELERO, | CONFITERO Y BOTILLERO, | con el método para trinchar y servir toda clase de | viandas, y la cortesanía y urbanidad que se debe | usar en la mesa. | POR | DON MARIANO DE REMENTERÍA Y FICA. | *ULTIMA EDICION:* | aumentada con muchos articulos nuevos, el modo de con- | servar toda clase de sustancias alimenticias, los pesca- | dos frescos, y una noticia curiosa sobre toda clase de | vinos nacionales y estrangeros, sus propiedades y modo | de servirlos en las mesas. | [short fancy rule] | MADRID: 1845. | IMPRENTA DE DON NORBERTO LLORENCI, | *calle del Sacramento, número* 3. | [rule] | *Se hallará en la libreria de* Cuesta, *calle Mayor, núm.* 2, | *y en la de* Sanchez, *calle de la Concepcion.*
Fifth edition, Madrid, 1845. Originally published, Madrid, 1828.

148 x 101 mm. π^2 1-22^8 23^6 24^8 25^4; 196 leaves, pp. [4] [1] 2-388. Sixteen page publisher's catalogue bound in at the end.

Illustration: One engraved folding plate illustrating carving.

Bibliographies: Palau XVI.202.

Copies: No other copy of this edition located.

Note: *BMC* and *NUC* record this as a translation of Henri Louis Nicolas Duval's *Manuel du cuisinier et de la cuisinière* and title-pages of some editions state "traducido por D. Mariano de Rementeria y Fica." *BNC* and Palau enter the work under Renenteria y Fica and the introduction in the copy in hand describes it as inspired by, rather than translated from, the French original, which a comparison with the French edition bears out.

1222. Villena, Enrique de Aragon, Marqués de, 1384-1434.

[within a border of type ornaments] ARTE CISORIA, | Ó TRATADO | DEL ARTE DEL CORTAR | DEL CUCHILLO, | QUE ESCRIVIÓ | DON HENRIQUE DE ARAGON, | MARQUES DE VILLENA: | *LA DA A LUZ*, | CON LICENCIA DEL REY NUESTRO SEÑOR, | LA BIBLIOTHECA REAL | DE SAN LORENZO | DEL ESCORIAL. | [two short rules] | En Madrid en la Oficina de Antonio Marin. | Año de 1766.

First edition, Madrid, 1766, of this work on carving written in 1423.

4to. ¶-¶¶¶⁴ A-Bb⁴; 112 leaves, pp. [*24*] 1-197 [198] [2]. Last leaf (blank?) wanting in this copy.

Illustrations: Woodcuts of carving implements in the text.

Bibliographies: Palau XXVII.273; Simon BG 1578; Vicaire 864; Wheaton and Kelly 6251.

Copies: *BMC* and *NUC* (10 copies).

¶ Seuillana medici
na.Que trata el modo cõferuati
uo y curatiuo delos q̃ abitã en la
muy infigne ciudad de Seuilla:
la q̃l firue y a,puecha pa q̃lquier
otro lugar deftos reynos. Obra
ãtigua digna õ fer leyda.Ca dis
rigida al illuftriffimo cabildo õ
la mifma ciudad año,.M.D.xlv.

ARTE DE COZINA,

PASTELERIA, VIZCO-
cheria, y Conserueria.

Compuesta por Francisco Martinez
Motiño, cozinero mayor del Rey
nuestro señor.

VIGILI   LABORE

CON PRIVILEGIO.

En Madrid por Luis Sanchez,
Año M. D C. XI.

ARTE
DE REPOSTERIA,

EN QUE SE CONTIENE TODO
genero de hacer Dulces fecos, y en liquido,
Vizcochos, Turrones, y Natas:

BEBIDAS HELADAS DE TODOS
generos, Rofolis, Miftelas, &c.

CON UNA BREVE INSTRUCCION
para conocer las Frutas, y fervirlas crudas.

Y DIEZ MESAS, CON
fu explicacion.

SU AUTHOR

*JUAN DE LA MATA, REPOSTERO EN ESTA
Corte, natural del Lugar de Matalavilla, Concejo del
Sil de Arriba, Montañas, y Reyno de Leon,
y Obifpado de Oviedo.*

QUIEN LE DEDICA AL EXC.mo SEÑOR
Don Rodulfo Acquaviva y Aragon, Duque
de Atri, &c.

CON LICENCIA: En Madrid, por Antonio Marin,
año M.DCC XLVII.

*Se hallarà en cafa de Simon Moreno, Mercader de Libros
frente las Gradas de San Phelipe el Real.*

SWEDEN

1222a. Nylander, Margaretha.

𝕳𝖆𝖓𝖉𝖇𝖔𝖐 | mid den nu brukliga | 𝕱inare 𝕸atlagningen; | innehållande tillka |
𝕭eskrifning | på | 𝕮onfecturer, 𝕾ylter och 𝕲lacer; | samt ett | 𝕭ihang, | att
göra 𝕾oja, 𝕱ransk, 𝕾enap, 𝕬ttikor, | 𝕭är-𝖜iner, 𝕭är-safter, att inlägga
𝕬njobis, | m. m.; jemte några 𝖀nderrättelser om 𝕾lagt, | 𝕭rygd och
𝕭rödbakning. | [short tapered rule] | 𝕬𝕱 | MARGARETHA NYLANDER. | [short
rule] | 𝕾junde tillökta och förbättrade 𝖀pplagan. | [tapered rule] | 𝕾tockholm, |
𝕹ordströmska 𝕭oktryckeriet, 1838.

First edition, Stockholm, 1838.

184 x 107mm. π^4 A-U^8 W^8 X-Z^8; 196 leaves, pp. [8] [1] 2-384.

Bibliographies: Unrecorded in the bibliographies consulted.

Copies: No other copy located.

SWITZERLAND

1223. Apicius.

CAELII APITII | SVMMI ADVLATRICIS MEDI- | cinae artificis DE RE
CVLINARIA Libri X. re- | cens è tenebris eruti, & à mendis uindicati, | typisq[ue]
summa diligentia | excusi. | PRAETEREA, | P▸ PLATINAE CREMO | NENSIS
VIRI VNDECVNQVE DO | ctissimi, De tuenda ualetudine, Natura rerum, & Popinae
| scientia Libri X. ad imitationem C. API- | TII ad unguem facti. | AD HAEC, |
PAVLI AEGINETAE DE | FACVLTATIBVS ALIMENTORVM TRA | CTATVS,
ALBANO TORINO | INTERPRETE. | *Cum* INDICE *copiosissimo.* | BASILEAE▸ |
[short rule] | M. D. XLI.

First printing of this edition, Basel, 1541. Originally published, Venice, ca.
1483-1486.

4to. α⁴ β⁴ a-z⁴ A-Z⁴; 192 leaves, pp. [*16*] 1-366 [2]. Last leaf blank.

Bibliographies: B. In. G. 77; Bitting, p. 11; Horn-Arndt, 7; Schraemli (1) 21;
Schraemli (2) 8: Simon BB II.51; Simon BG 122; Vicaire 30.

Copies: B. In. G., *BMC, BNC,* and *NUC* (5 copies).

1224. Apicius.

IN HOC OPERE CONTENTA. | APICII CAELII | DE OPSONIIS ET
CONDIMENTIS, | SIVE ARTE COQVINA = | RIA, LIBRI X. | ITEM, | Gabrielis
Humelbergij Medici, Physici | Isnensis in Apicij Caelij libros X. | Annotationes. |
TIGVRI IN OFFICINA | Froschouiana. Anno, | M. D. XLII.

First printing of the Gabriel Humelberg edition, Zürich, 1542. Originally published
Venice, ca. 1483-1486.

4to. A-Hh⁴; 124 leaves, ff. [1] 2-123 [124]. Last leaf blank.

Bibliographies: B. In. G. 79; Horn-Arndt 8; Schraemli (1) 23; Simon BB II.53; Simon
BG 124; Vicaire 31; Wheaton and Kelly 181.

Copies: B. In. G., *BMC, BNC* and *NUC* (4 copies).

1225. Chavannes, Cornélie.

COURS | D'ÉCONOMIE DOMESTIQUE, | PAR | *Cornélie Chavannes,* | DIRECTRICE DE L'ÉCOLE NORMALE DES INSTITUTRICES | DU CANTON DE VAUD. | Toute femme sage bâtit sa maison, | mais la folle la ruine de ses mains. | PROV. XIV. V. I. | [short fancy rule] | LAUSANNE. | IMPRIMERIE DES FRÈRES BLANCHARD. | [short rule] | 1840.

First edition, Lausanne, 1840.

203 x 131 mm. [1]^8 2-19^8 20^2; 154 leaves, pp. [i-iii] iv-vi [1] 2-296 [6].

Bibliographies: Unrecorded in the bibliographies consulted.

Copies: No other copy located.

1226. La Cuisinière de Genève.

LA | CUISINIÈRE | DE GENÈVE. | Enseignant la manière de préparer toutes sortes | de viandes, de volailles, de gibiers, de pois- | sons du Lac Léman, de légumes, de fruits, &c. | La façon de faire toutes sortes de gelées, de | pâtes, de gâteaux, de tourtes, de pâtés, &c. | Et de composer divers sirops, glaces, crêmes, | essences, &c. à la genevoise. | *PARTICULIÈREMENT* | *A l'usage des jeunes Cuisinières qui veulent se* | *pousser pour des repas un peu recherchés,* | *comme pour des tables bourgeoises.* | Nouvelle Edition, revue, corrigée et | augmentée. | [vignette] | *A GENÈVE,* | Chez BONNANT, Imprimeur-Libraire, | au bas de la vallée du Collège. | [short fancy rule] | 1803.

Second edition, Geneva, 1803. Originally published Geneva, 1798.

142 x 89 mm. A-I^{12}; 108 leaves, pp. [1-3] 4-215 [216].

Bibliographies: This edition unrecorded in the bibliographies consulted.

Copies: No other copy of this edition located.

1227. Curchod, Henri, b. 1820.

ESSAI | THÉORIQUE ET PRATIQUE | SUR | LA CURE DE RAISINS | ÉTUDIÉE
PLUS SPÉCIALEMENT | à | VEVEY | SUIVI DE | QUELQUES REMARQUES
SUR LES CONDITIONS HYGIÉNIQUES | DE CETTE VILLE ET DE PLUSIEURS
TABLEAUX MÉTÉOROLOGIQUES | PAR | H. CURCHOD | DOCTEUR EN
MÉDECINE DE L'UNIVERSITÉ DE BERLIN, | MEMBRE ORDINAIRE DU
CONSEIL DE SANTÉ DU CANTON DE VAUD, | MEMBRE DES SOCIÉTÉS
VAUDOISE ET HELVÉTIQUE DES SCIENCES NATURELLES, | DE LA
SOCIÉTÉ DE MEDECINE DE LAUSANNE ET MEMBRE CORRESPONDANT |
DE LA SOCIÉTÉ MÉDICALE DE GENÈVE. | [short rule] | [in two columns,
column one] VEVEY | LIBRAIRIE SCHWEIGHAUSER | [vertical rule] | [column
two] BERLIN | AUGUSTE HIRSCHWALD [end columns] | 1860

First edition, Vevey and Berlin, 1860.

218 x 149 mm. π^8 1-8^8 8)^2 (8)1 + 9^4) χ1 [10]^4; 83 leaves, pp. [i-v] vi-xiii [xiv] [1]
2-134 [*16*]. Leaves 9$_{3\text{-}4}$, χ1 and 10$_{1\text{-}4}$ contain letterpress tables, leaf χ1 is a 3/8 sheet
folding table. Bound in publisher's printed boards.

Inscribed by the author to Prof. W. Lachmann.

Bibliographies: Unrecorded in the bibliographies consulted.

Copies: *BMC*, *BNC*, and *NUC* (Yale and National Library of Medicine).

1227a. Kümicher, Caroline.

Die | Kartoffelküche. | [short wavy rule] | Enthaltend: | verschiedene der
schmackhaftesten Kartoffelsuppen, Pasteten, | Knödel, Krapfen,
Kartoffelnudeln, Kartoffelbrei, Omeletten, | Aufläufe, Pudding, Strudel,
verschiedene Gemüse von kar- | toffeln, Würste, Hefenbackerei,
Kartoffelcoteletten, verschiedene | Schmalzbackereien von Kartoffeln, Torten,
kleine Backereien, | Kuchen, Salate, verschiedene wholfeile Gerichte, |
Kartoffelsaucen & c. | Von | Caroline Kümicher, | Verfasserin des Constanzer
Kochbuchs, der bürgerlichen Küche und des | eleganten und bürgerlichen
Theetischs. | Vierte Auflage. | [short fancy rule] | Bern, 1859. | Verlag von J.
Heuberger's Buchhandlung.

Fourth edition, Bern, 1859. Originlly published, Constanz and St. Gallen, 1848.

184 x 114 mm. π^4 1-6^8; 52 leaves, pp. [i-iii] iv-viii [viii] [1] 2-96. Publisher's yellow paper wrappers printed on the outer front wrapper with a repeat of the title-page within an ornamental border; outer back wrapper contains publisher's advertisement.

Bibliographies: This edition unrecorded in the bibliographies consulted. Drexel 102 cites a fifth edition, Bern, 1859.

Copies: No other copy of this edition located. *BMC* records a tenth edition, Bern, 1890.

1228. Rytz-Dick, Lina.

LA | BONNE CUISINIÈRE | BOURGEOISE, | OU | INSTRUCTION | A PRÉPARER DE LA MEILLEURE MANIÈRE LES METS USITÉS | SOIT DANS LA VIE ORDINAIRE, SOIT POUR DES | OCCASIONS DE FÊTES, | ACCOMPAGNÉE | D'UN TABLEAU REPRÉSENTANT LA MANIÈRE D'ARRANGER | AGRÉABLEMENT LES PLATS SUR LA TABLE. | PAR | *L. Rytz née Dick.* | [short fancy rule] | *Traduit d'après la seconde édition allemande* | par | *G. de B.* | BERNE. | Chez *C. Rätzer*, imprimeur, rue des juifs, No. 112. | [short rule] | 1837.

First edition in French, Bern, 1837. Originally published in German under the title *Neues Berner Kochbuch*, Bern, 1835.

193 x 120 mm. π^2 χ^4 1-20^8 21^4 [22]^2; 172 leaves, pp. [i-v] vi-xii [1] 2-332.

Bibliographies: This edition unrecorded in the bibliographies consulted.

Copies: No other copy of this edition located.

1229. Simeo Sethus, fl. 1071-80.

SIMEONIS | SETHI MAGISTRI | ANTIOCHIAE SYNTAGMA | PER ELEMENTORVM ORDINEM, DE ALI- | mentorum facultate ad Michaelem Du- | cam Imperatorem à Lilio Grego- | rio Giraldo Ferrariense o- | lim latinitate do- | natum: | NVNC VERO PER DOMINICVM | *Monthesaurum* V*eronensem correctum* | *& penè reformatum.* | BASILEAE | Apud Petrum Pernam, | M. D. LXI.

Second edition, Basel, 1561. Originally published, Basel, 1538.

8vo. a-k^8; 80 leaves, pp. [1-2] 3-144 [*16*].

Bibliographies: B. In. G. 1834; Durling 4211; Schraemli (1) 457; Schraemli (2) 85; Simon BB II.621; Vicaire 790.

Copies: B. In. G., *BMC*, *BNC*, and *NUC* (National Library of Medicine, Ohio State University and Yale).

1230. Stuck, Johann Wilhelm, 1542-1607.

ANTIQVITATVM | CONVIVIALIVM | LIBRI III. | IN QVIBVS HEBRAEO- | RVM. GRAECORVM, ROMANORVM ALIA= | RVMQVE NATIONVM ANTIQVA CONVIVIORVM GENERA, | mores, consuetudines, ritus ceremoniae q[ue] conviviales atque etiam alia ex= | plicantur; & cumijs, quae hodie cúm apud Christianos, tum apud alias gen | tes, a Christiano nomine alienas, in usu sunt, conferuntur: multa Gramma= | tica, Physica, Medica, Ethica, Oeconomica, Politica, Philosophica deniq[ue] atq[ue] Hi= | storica cognitu jucunda simul & utilia tractantur: plurima sacrorum pro= | phanorumq[ue] Auctorum veterum loca obscura illustrantur, cor= | rupta emendantur: deniq[ue] desperatus deploratusq[ue] no= | strorum temporum luxus atq[ue] luxuria gra= | vi censura damnatur. | AVCTORE IO. GVILIELMO | STVCKIO, TIGVRINO. | EDITIO SECVNDA, | *Auctoris ipsius curâ auctior, melior & longè emendatior:* | *Cum totius operis Indice novo eoq[ue]* *copiosissimo.* | [woodcut] | TIGVRI | APVD IOHANNEM VVOLPHIVM, TYPIS | FROSCH. ANNO M. D. XCVII.

Second edition, Zürich, 1597. Originally published, Zürich, 1582.

Folio. α-β^6 φ^8 a-z^6 A-Zz^6 AA^6; 440 leaves, ff. [*20*] 1-419 [420].

Bibliographies: Schraemli (1) 471; Simon BB II.629; Vicaire 805; Wheaton and Kelly 5845.

Copies: *BMC*, *BNC*, and *NUC* (9 copies).

1231. Wecker, Anna.

Neu/ köstlich und nutzliches | [in red] Koch=Buch/ | In welchem kurtzlich begriffen/ | [in red] Wie allerhand künstliche Spei= | sen/ so wol von zahmen als wilden Thieren: | Vögel bñ Federwildprät/ grün= bñ gedörrtem Fischwerck: | Wie auch allerley Gebachens/ als Barten/ Marci= | panen=Pasteten bñ dergleichen: | [in red] Beneben von biel= bñ mancherley Obs/ | von Gemüsz/ für Gesunde bnd Krancke/ in allerley | Beschwärungen bñ Gebrästen: Auch für schwangere | Weiber/ Kindbetterinnen/ Alt=betagte schwache Personen/ | kunst= bñ nutzlich in der Eyl/ bnd mit geringem Kosten zuberei= | ten bñ zu zurichten. | Weyland fleissig beschrieben | Durch | [in red] Frau Anna Weckerin. | Diese letste Edition mit bielen Speisen von Garten= | und Feldgewächs/ von Eyern: Item Milch bñ Butter/ | sehr bieler Gattungen/ allerley Geflügel bñ bierfüssigen Thieren/ | wie auch bielerley Art von Fischen auff neueste Französische Manier | köstlich bñ wol zu zurichten sehr biel bermehrt/ bñ durch einen | sonderbaren berleckerten Liebhaber an Tag | gegeben. | [in red: ornament] | Gedruckt zu Basel, | [two fancy rules] | [in red] In Verlag Emanuel Königs bñ Söhnen/ | Im Jahr Christi 1679.

Second title-page:

Parisische | Küchemeister/ | Das ist: | Jetziger Zeit berleckerte | Französische Art | bñ Manier, Allerhand Spei= | sen bey köstlichen Pancketen bñ | Hauszhaltungen zu kochen bñ | zuzurichten. | [ornament] | Gedruckt im Jahr [rule] | 1679.

New edition, Basel, 1679. Originally published under the title *Ein köstlich new Kochbuch von allerhand Speisen . . .*, Amberg, 1598. Graesse cites an Amberg, 1597, edition, but no copy of this has been traced.

8vo.):(^{8} A-Rr^8; 328 leaves, pp. [*16*] 1-459 [460], ^{2}[1-2] 3-161 [162-178] [2]. Last leaf blank.

Bibliographies: Schraemli (1) 499; Schraemli (2) 71. Horn-Arndt 96 and Schraemli (2) 70 describe the Amberg, 1598, edition, the former noting that it is the first German cookbook by a woman.

Copies: *NUC* (Lilly Library only).

1231a. Wecker, Johann Jacob, 1528-1586.

ANTIDOTARIUM | GENERALE | ET | SPECIALE: | *EX / OPT. AUTHORUM /*
tàm veterum, quàm recentiorum | SCRIPTIS | fideliter & methodicè | à | JOAN.
JACOBO WECKERO | BASIL. | congestum & dispositum: | *NUNC VERÒ SUPRA*
PRIORES / editiones omnes multis novis & optimis FORMULIS, | *maximè verò*
EXTRACTIS / auctum. | Adjectis INDICIBUS locupletissimis. | [crown] | BASILEAE,
| Typis JOAN. JACOBI GENATHI, | Sumptibus haeredum LUDOVICI KÖNIG. |
Anno cIɔ Iɔ c XLII.

Title-page of the *Antidotarium speciale*:

ANTIDOTARIUM | SP[ECIALE, | à | JOAN. JACOBO WECKERO |
BASILIENSE, | *EX / OPT. AUTHORUM / tàm veterum, quàm recentiorum /*
SCRIPTIS / Fideliter congestum, & tandem methodicè, | supra priores Editiones,
uberrimè au- | ctum, conjunctim editum, | & exornatum. | *Adjectis ELENCHIS*
locupletissimis. | [crown] | BASILEAE, | Typis JOAN. JACOBI GENATHI, |
Sumptibus haeredum LUDOVICI KÖNIG. | Anno cIɔ Iɔ c XLII.

New edition, Basil, 1642. The *Antidotarium generale* originally was published, Basil,
1576, and the *Antidotarium speciale*, Basil, 1577. The latter work includes information
on wines and on distilling eau-de-vie.

4to. α^8 a-z^8 A-Q^8 R^6):(^{4}):( ):(^{2} aa-gg^8 hh^2; 390 leaves, pp. [*16*] [*605*] numbered in
columbs 1-1210 [*31*] [*12*] [*111*] numbered in columns 1-222 [*5*] = 780.

Illustrations: Numerous woodcuts in the text in the *Antidotarium speciale* illustrating
distilling apparatus.

Bibliographies: This edition unrecorded in the bibliographies consulted. Simon BB II
705 records the first edition of the *Antidotorium speciale*.

Copies: *NUC* (National Library of Medicine and University of British Columbia,
Vancouver).

1232. Wecker, Johann Jacob, 1528-1586.

DE | SECRETIS | LIBRI XVII. | EX VARIIS AUTHORIBUS | Collecti,
methodicéque digesti, | & auci | PER | *JOAN. JACOBUM WERKERUM,* |
Basiliensem, Medicum Colma- | *viensem.* | Accessit INDEX Iocupletissimus. |

[printer's device] | *BASILEAE,* | [rule] | Sumptibus JOHANNIS REGIS. | *Excudebat* JOH. RODOLPHUS GENATH. | M. DC. LXII.

New edition, Basel, 1662. First published, Basel, 1559, as a translation of the six books of Girolamo Ruscelli's *De' secreti del reverendo donna Alessio Piedmontese.* In later editions Wecker added new material, expanding the work to seventeen books by 1582.

8vo.)(⁸ A-Vu⁸ Xx⁴; 356 leaves, pp. [*16*] 1-667 [668-694] [*2*]. Last leaf blank.

Illustrations: Woodcuts in the text.

Bibliographies: This edition unrecorded in the bibliographies consulted.

Copies: *NUC* (7 copies).

1233. Wecker, Johann Jacob, 1528-1586.

JOH. JAC. WECKERI, | Basiliensis, Medici Colm. | DE | SECRETIS | LIBRI XVII. | *Ex variis Auctoribus collecti,* | *methodicè digesti,* | Atque | Tertia hâc Editione | *Non solùm ab innumeris mendis,* | *Obscuritateq[ue] purgati, sed &* | THEODORI ZVINGERI, | Philos. & Medic. Basiliens. | *ADDITIONIBUS* | *E Pharmacia &* *Chymiâ* | *Utilissimis aucti.* | | Accessit INDEX Iocupletissimus. | [ornament] | *BASILEAE.* | [fancy rule] | Impensis JOHAN. LUDOVICI KÖNIG. | *Typis* JOH. CONRADI à MECHEL. | Ann. 1701.

New edition, Basel, 1701. See item 1232.

8vo.)o(⁸ χ² A-Ddd⁸; 406 leaves, pp. [*12*] 1-764 [*38*]. Last three leaves blank.

Illustrations: Woodcuts in the text.

Bibliographies: Horn-Arndt 98.

Copies: *BMC* and *NUC* (8 copies).

1234. Willich, Jodocus, 1501-1552.

ARS MAGIRICA | HOC EST, | COQVINARIA, | DE CIBARIIS, FERCVLIS
OPSO- | nijs, alimentis & potibus diuersis parandis, eo- | rumq; facultatibus. Liber
Medicis, philolo- | gis, & sanitatis tuendae studiosis om- | nibus apprimè vtilis. |
IODOCO VVILLICHIO RESELLI A- | *no Medico & Theologo, Academiae Francfordia-*
| *nae cis Viadrum professore doctissima,* | *nunc primùm editus.* | Huic accedit, |
IACOBI BIFRONTIS RHAETI | DE OPERIBVS LACTA- | RIIS EPISTOLA. | *Cum*
indice rerum & verborum. | *TIGVRI APVD IACO-* | *bum Gesnerum.*

First edition, Zürich, 1563.

8vo. ✱⁸ a-o⁸ P⁸ †⁸; 136 leaves, pp. [*16*] 1-227 [228-256].

Bibliographies: B. In. G. 2059; Bitting, p. 499; Schraemli (1) 501; Schraemli (2) 69;
Simon BB II.708; Simon BG 1622; Vicaire 875.

Copies: B. In. G., *BMC, BNC,* and *NUC* (5 copies).

1234a. Zimmermann, P.

𝕯𝖎𝖊 𝕵𝖚𝖓𝖌𝖊 | 𝕳𝖆𝖚𝖘𝖍ä𝖑𝖙𝖊𝖗𝖎𝖓𝖓, | 𝖊𝖎𝖓 𝕭𝖚𝖈𝖍 | 𝖋ü𝖗 | 𝕸ü𝖙𝖙𝖊𝖗 𝖚𝖓𝖉 𝕿ö𝖈𝖍𝖙𝖊𝖗, | 𝖛𝖔𝖓 | 𝕻.
𝖅𝖎𝖒𝖒𝖊𝖗𝖒𝖆𝖓𝖓. | [short fancy rule] | 𝕰𝖗𝖘𝖙𝖊𝖘 [𝖅𝖜𝖊𝖞𝖙𝖊𝖘] [𝕯𝖗𝖎𝖙𝖙𝖊𝖘] 𝕭ä𝖓𝖉𝖈𝖍𝖊𝖓. |
[ornament] | 𝕯𝖗𝖎𝖙𝖙𝖊 𝕬𝖚𝖋𝖑𝖆𝖌𝖊. | [fancy rule] | 𝕷𝖚𝖟𝖊𝖗𝖓, | 𝖌𝖊𝖉𝖗𝖚𝖈𝖐𝖙 𝖚𝖓𝖉 𝖛𝖊𝖗𝖑𝖊𝖌𝖙 | 𝖇𝖊𝖞
𝕵𝖔𝖘𝖊𝖕𝖍 𝕬𝖑𝖔𝖞𝖘 𝕾𝖆𝖑𝖟𝖒𝖆𝖓𝖓, | 1789.

Third edition, Luzern, 1789. The second edition was published, in 2 vols., Luzern,
1785. No record of the first edition has been found.

8vo. 3 vols. Vol. I. ✱⁴ A-Z⁸; 188 leaves, pp. [*8*] [1] 2-367 [368]. Vol. II. ✱² A-U⁸
X⁶; 168 leaves, pp. [*4*] [1-3] 4-332. Vol. III. ✱² A-O⁸ Aa-Hh⁸ πI⁶; 184 leaves, pp. [i-
iii] iv [1] 2-224, ²[1-5] 6-140.

Illustration: Vol. II. One engraved plate facing p. 94.

Bibliographies: Unrecorded in the bibliographies consulted.

Copies: No other copy located. Case Western Reserve has the second edition, Luzern,
1785.

CAELII APITII DE CVLI

NARIAE REI DISCIPLINA LI
BER PRIMVS, QVI EPI
meles inscribitur.

LA
CUISINIÈRE
DE GENÈVE.

Enseignant la manière de préparer toutes sortes de viandes, de volailles, de gibiers, de poissons du Lac Léman, de légumes, de fruits, &c.

La façon de faire toutes sortes de gelées, de pâtes, de gâteaux, de tourtes, de pâtés, &c.

Et de composer divers sirops, glaces, crêmes, essences, &c. à la genevoise.

PARTICULIÈREMENT

A l'usage des jeunes Cuisinières qui veulent se pousser pour des repas un peu recherchés, comme pour des tables bourgeoises.

Nouvelle Edition, revue, corrigée et augmentée.

A GENÈVE,

Chez BONNANT, Imprimeur-Libraire, au bas de la vallée du Collège.

1803.

ARS MAGIRICA
HOC EST,
COQVINARIA,

DE CIBARIIS, FERCVLIS OPSO-
nijs, alimentis & potibus diuersis parandis, eo-
rumq́; facultatibus. Liber Medicis, philolo-
gis, & sanitatis tuendæ studiosis om-
nibus apprimè vtilis.

*IODOCO VVILLICHIO RESELLIA-
no Medico & Theologo, Academiæ Francfordia-
næ cis Viadrum professore doctissimo,
nunc primùm editus.*

Huic accedit,
IACOBI BIFRONTIS RHAETI
DE OPERIBVS LACTA-
RIIS EPISTOLA.

Cum indice rerum & verborum.

TIGVRI APVD IACQ-
bum Gesnerum.

Caroli Osleuij

MANUSCRIPTS

FRANCE

1235. Manuscript title at head of text: Memoire de ce que jay fourni | pour Monsieur Ferrier

252 x 167 mm. 2 leaves. One sheet, folded; undated but circa 1580.

Note: This is a priced list, probably presented as a bill, for food (partridge, hares, ox-tongues, quails, fieldfares, vermicelli, tunny-fish, soles, mullets, etc.) served at the wedding feast of M. Ferrier.

1236. Marin, François.

Manuscript title: [within a single ruled frame] Les Dons de Comus. | ou | Les Délices de la Table. [pen trial] | Ouvrage non seulement utile aux Officiers de Bouche | pour ce qui concerne leur art, mais principalement | à l'usage des personnes qui sont curieuses de | scavoir donner à manger, et d'être servies | délicatement, tant en gras qu'en maigre, | suivant les saisons, & dans le goût | le plus nouveau. [pen trial] | A Paris | Chez Prault, Fils, Quay de Conty, vis-à-vis | la descente du Pont Neuf, à la Charité. | 1739. | Avec approbation & Privilege du Roy [pen trial]

196 x 153 mm. 127 leaves, pp. [4] [1-2] 3-27 [28], ^{2}1-220 [2].

Note: Complete transcription in an unknown copperplate hand of Marin's *Les Dons de Comus* (item 301).

1237. Manuscript title: Etat | et Menu général de la | Dépense ordinaire de la | Chambre aux deniers | du Roy | Année 1764 | [scroll]

238 x 180 mm. 186 leaves, 182 with text and 4 blank, unpaginated.

Note: This manuscript, in the hand of a professional scribe, records the household expenses of Louis XV during the year 1764. It includes a list of the persons who were entitled to sit at various tables at court, menus at the different tables with expenses, and accounts for bread and wine distributed on feast days.

1238. Manuscript title: Etat | et Menu Général | de la Depense ordinaire | de la Chambre aux deniers | du Roy. | Année 1773. | [scroll]

237 x 180 mm. 171 leaves, 169 with text and 2 blank, unpaginated.

Note: This manuscript, in the hand of a professional scribe, records the household expenses of Louis XV during 1773, the last full year of his reign. It includes a list of the persons who were entitled to sit at various tables at court, menus at the different tables, and various other household expenses.

1239. Engraved invoice, filled in by pen and ink, listing items of food supplied to the comtesse de Vologer, dated 28 February 1831, and receipted by Corcellet. Vignette on upper half depicts a man seated at a table greedily carving a fish and surrounded by more food and bottles. Below the vignette: AV GOVRMAND, | *Corcellet, Md de Comestible Palais Royal No. 104.*

296 x 194 mm. Single sheet printed on one side.

1240. Apicius

Manuscript title: Les dix Livres | d'Apicius Coelius | de la Chose Culinaire | *traduits en français pour la première fois* | *par Bertrand Guégan* | *avec des notes, des commentaires et des* | *interprétions d'Edouard Nignon.* | [two short rules] | *Se vendent à Paris* | [two short rules] | 1918.

201 x 156 mm. 194 leaves, ff. [2] 1-192.

Note: Written in an unidentified hand (Guégan's?) in red and black ink on the rectos only. The notes, commentaries and interpretations by Edouard Nignon mentioned on the manuscript title appear neither in this manuscript nor in the published edition of Guégan's translation, Paris, 1933 (item 33). This manuscript varies substantially from the published version.

GREAT BRITAIN

1241. Manuscript volume of recipes and medical remedies from the library of Henry Frederick, Prince of Wales (1594-1612).
314 x 204 mm. 245 leaves, 224 with text and 21 blank, unpaginated; undated but circa 1610.

Binding: Contemporary calf, front and back covers ruled and stamped in gold with corner decorations and the arms of Henry Frederick, Prince of Wales, eldest son of James I.

Note: The manuscript, in an unknown hand, is divided under the following heads: Preserves; Conserves; Marmaledds; Dryed fruites; Quiddemocks; Candyes; Gellyes; Serrops; Bakemeates; Cookery; Chirurgery. It concludes with a four page list of "Severall sort of sweet meates fitting for a Bankquett."

1242. Manuscript volume of recipes with ownership signature on the recto of the first leaf: "[Joan?] Macies Book 1691 | Melbury Osmond". First word damaged and obscure.

231 x 170 mm. 143 leaves, pp. [2], ff. 1-10, pp. 11-21, 21, 24-70, 80, 90, 100, 102-127 [*176*].

Contents: f. [1] ownership signature; verso, blank; ff. [2-60] recipes in several hands, principally seventeenth century but some later; ff. [61-135r] blank; f. [135v] poem beginning "O thou who Absent all my thoughts employ"; ff. [136-139] blank; ff. [140-141r] recipes; ff. [141v- 143] table of contents.

1243. Manuscript, headed: A Christning Dinner for the heir of Mr. Westby of Ranfield in janry | 1696 and sarved by his Ladys mother then wife to a third Husband assisted | only by a Cooke maid & her own sarvant and servad up with soe littel | noize at the sight of soe vast a banquett as follows

277 x 192 mm. Single sheet, written on one side, mounted on a later sheet of laid paper.

Note: Ranfield is located in West Riding, Yorkshire. Dishes served include: "boyled Salmon," "whole roasted Lamb," "boyled gamon of bacon," "Calved head hasht," and "two roasted udders."

1244. Manuscript volume of recipes with ownership signature on the front fly leaf: "Elizabeth Maynard | her Book of receits | :1696:"

198 x 152 mm. 139 leaves, pp. 1-100, 102-208, 210-221, 223-281.

Contents: pp. 1-2, index; pp. 3-52, confectionary recipes; pp. 53-66, blank; pp. 67-70, index; pp. 71-89, blank; pp. 90-152, cookery recipes; pp. 153-155, blank; pp. 156-177, beverage recipes; pp. 178-181, index; pp. 182-258, blank; pp. 259-281, medical recipes.

1245. Dashwood, Dorothea Read, d. 1753.

Manuscript title: Reciepts | *Confectionary &c* | *Collected by* | *Dorothea Dashwood* | *Anno Dom* | 1718

200 x 155 mm. 142 leaves, pp. [i-xii] 1-84 [85-98] [*174*].

Contents: p. [i], blank; p. [ii], title; pp. [iii-vi], table of contents; pp. [vii-xii], blank; pp. 1-84, recipes; pp. [85, 87, 89, 91, 93, 95, 97], recipes; pp. [86, 88, 90, 92, 94, 96, 98] and remaining 174 pages, blank.

Note: On p. 81 of this manuscript is a copy of a poem headed "To Make a Soope by Mr. Pope to Dr. Swift." D.F. Foxon, in his *English Verse 1701-1750* (Vol. I, item P952) enters the poem under Pope and cites a broadside printing in the Bodleian Library which he tentatively dates 1726. He comments, "For a discussion of the authorship see *Twickenham Pope* VI. 253-5 and references. Originally written in a composite letter to Swift from Pope, Gay and others." It also was published in *Atterburyana*, London: 1717, as "Mr. Pope's Receipt to make Soup. For the Use of Dean Swift."

Dorothea Dashwood, daughter and co-heir of Sir James Read, of Brocket Hall, Hertfordshire, married Sir Robert Dashwood, Bart., of Northbooke in Oxfordshire.

1246. Kidder, Edward, 1666-1739.

Manuscript volume of recipes loosely transcribed from *E. Kidder's Receipts of Pastry and Cookery for the Use of his Scholars*, London, ca. 1720 (item 793).

183 x 115 mm. 37 leaves, pp. [4] 1-45 [2] 46-54, 46-50 [8]. First and third leaves blank, verso of second leaf contains printed advertisement for Kidder's school, transcribed below. Undated, but soon after 1722, the date of the watermark, number 1805 in Edward Heawood's *Watermarks*, Monumenta Chartae Papyraceae, vol. I, Hilversum Paper Publications Society, 1950.

Kidder's advertisement: [within an oval frame surrounded by scrolls and topped with a crowned head of a lion] *TO ALL YOUNG LADIES* | *At Edw. Kidders Pastry-School* | *in little Lincolns Inn-fields, are taught all* | *Sorts of Pastry & Cookery, Dutch-hollow* | *works,* | *& Butter works, on Thursday, Frydays,-Saturday,* | *in the afternoon: and on* | *the same days, in the* | *morning at this School, in Norris- street in St.* | *James's* | *Market, & at his School, in St. Martins le* | *Grand, on Monday, Tuesday, and* | *Wednesday, in the* | *afternoon.*

Note: The transcriptions of the recipes in this volume follow the information in Kidder's printed book but not the exact wording or spelling. The recipes are grouped under the same general headings in both though the order within the group varies. Here are the variant forms of one of the recipes.

In the printed book:

Forc'd Meat Balls.
Sweet Balls.

Take part of a Leg of Lamb or Veal & Scrape it | fine & shred the same quantity of Beef Suet; put | thereto a good quantity of Currants, Season it with | Sweet Spice, a little Lemon Peel, 3 or 4 Yolks of eggs, | & a few Sweet- herbs; mix it well together & make it | into little balls

In the manuscript:

Force meat Balls
Sweet Balls.

Take part of a Leg of Lamb or Veale and mince it | small with the same quantity of Beef suit putt thereto | a good quantity of currants, season with cloves mace | nuttmegg cinnamon and sugar a little Lemon peile 3 | or 4 yolks of Eggs and a few sweetherbs mix it well together | then make it into little Balls.

NUC records a similar manuscript in the John Crerar Library. It is possible these were copied by and for the use of Kidder's students. In the Gernon manuscript, five of the final eight unnumbered pages contain recipes not from Kidder and in a second hand. The inside front cover has the ownership signature of Mrs. Anne Mills in a hand not similar to either that of the copyist or the writer of the supplementary recipes.

1247. Manuscript title, first part: Receipts, | For All Sorts | Of Preserves, | Biskets, & Creams,

Manuscript title, second part: Receipts | For All Manner | Of Cookery | [ornamental scroll]

416 x 263 mm. 188 leaves, pp. [i-viii] 1-217 [218-242], ^{2}1-120 [6]. First and last leaves pasted down. Undated but, based on the watermark, number 1845 in Edward

Heawood's *Watermarks*, Monumenta Chartae Papyracae, vol. I, Hilversum, Paper Publications Society, 1950, from the early eighteenth century.

Contents: pp. [i-iv], blank; p. [v], title; pp. [vi-viii], blank; pp. 1-218, recipes; pp. [219-226], blank; pp. [227-235], index; pp. [236-240], blank; p. [241], title; p. [242], blank; pp. ²1-120, recipes; last six pages, blank.

1248. Gerry, Samuel. Songbook and recipe book, dos à dos style. Ownership name on first leaf: SAMUEL GERRY. | February 27th 1767 | [five rules].

191 x 148 mm. 24 leaves, unpaginated, last leaf pasted down.

Note: This volume began as a songbook and contains fifteen pages of neatly copied lyrics and music to "Barby," "Parindon," "Burnham," "Evening Hymn-new," "Evening Hymn-old," "The King's Anthem--Psalm LXXII," and "An Anthem for Christmas Day." These, presumably, were copied into the book by Samuel Gerry in 1767. Later owners turned the book upside down and, beginning at the back, copied recipes into it. The recipes, in several later unknown hands, are written in ink and in pencil. A number of later recipes, clipped from newspapers, are pasted in.

1249. Manuscript volume of recipes with ownership initials on the inside front cover: "D=S=C- | Haigh Sepr. 1779".

198 x 160 mm. 130 leaves, unpaginated. First and last leaves pasted down as endpapers.

Contents: f. 1, pasted down; ff. 2-58r., recipes numbered 1-229, at end of which is written "The above receipts from Lady Bradshaighs Book," referring to Elizabeth (Pennington) Bradshaigh (d. 1695), the wife of Sir Roger Bradshaigh of Haigh; f. 58v, blank; ff. 59-67r, index; f. 67v, blank; ff. 68-78, recipes; ff. 79-80, index; ff. 81-101r, recipes numbered 1-64; ff. 101v-128r, additional unnumbered recipes in various hands; ff. 128v-130, blank.

1250. Manuscript volume of recipes with ownership signature on inside front cover: "Anna Seward 1786".

73 leaves, pp. 12-13, 8-11, 6-7, 14-15 [*4*] 18-23, 26-27, 24-25, 48-49, 40-43, 57-61 [*62*] [*110*]. Some pages missing and several misbound when the volume was repaired. Recipes, possibly in Anna Seward's hand, begin on the inside front cover and continue on the next thirty-three pages. The thirty-fifth page contains an index and the last three pages in the volume contain medical recipes. The other pages are blank. The paper has a watermark corresponding with number 205 in Edward Heawood's *Watermarks*, Monumenta Chartae Papyraceae, vol. I, Wilversum, Paper Publications Society, 1950, where it is dated 1776.

Anna Seward (1747-1809) was a poet and author and a friend of Dr. Samuel Johnson, James Boswell and Hester Piozzi.

1251. Manuscript title: Reciepts [sic] approv'd

90-151 mm. 188 leaves, 117 with manuscript recipes for wines, medicines and cookery in several hands, dos à dos style, and 71 blank, unpaginated. English, undated, but eighteenth century.

Bookplate: From the books of Crosby Gaige.

1252. Manuscript volume of recipes with ownership signature on inside front cover "Lockhart Neilson".

183 x 111 mm. 72 leaves, pp. 1-61 [*62*] [*10*].

Undated but, based on the consistent use of the long s in the handwriting, probably late eighteenth to early nineteenth century.

1253. Manuscript volume of recipes in several English hands, undated but late eighteenth through mid-nineteenth century.

200 x 158 mm. 156 leaves, pp. [*30*] 1-281 [282]. First page, recipe "To make Daffy's"; second page, blank; third- eighteenth pages, contents; nineteenth-thirtieth pages, blank; pp. 1-281, recipes on 210 pages and 71 pages blank.

Note: Bookplate of Thomas Prinsep, Esq.

1254. Manuscript volume of recipes in several English hands, undated but late eighteenth through mid-nineteenth century. A few individual recipes are dated, the earliest 15 March 1811 and the latest 13 February 1828.

158 x 202 mm. 144 leaves, pp. [i-viii] 1-227 [228-280].

Contents: pp. [i-vii], table of contents; p. [viii], blank; pp. 1-226, recipes; pp. 227, [228-239], blank; pp. [240-253], alphabetical index; pp. [254-256], blank ruled; pp. [257-276] written dos a dos: pp. [276-274] "Forms of Conclusions and Attestations of Wills and Codicils"; p. [273], blank; pp. [272-264], "The Last Will and Test. of J.J. of &c."; pp. [261-257], "The Will of R.O. of &c."

1255. Manuscript volume dos à dos style, of recipes with ownership signature on inside front cover: *"Miss Tyndale | Her Book | 1806"*.

229 x 185 mm. 106 leaves, pp. 1-26, 29-56, 61-82, 162- 163, 166-277, 180, 190, 193-204 [241] 242-260 [*90*]. Several pages removed. Paper bears watermark date 1802.

Bookplate: *Sold by* | GIBBONS, | Bookseller | *& Binder,* | -No. *5.-* | Argyle Street, | BATH.

1256. Manuscript volume of recipes.

221 x 181 mm. 43 leaves, unpaginated, of lined paper with watermark date 1837. Recipes on pp. [1-24], [45-48], [52-55], [74-80] [82-86]. List of furnishings in pencil on p. [57] and another list of furnishings in a different hand in black ink on p. [61] under heading: "J.G. Perigoe, 32 Alexandra Rd., Aug 13th 1930 to Mr. Tanton Sale Room". Several pages removed.

1257. Soyer, Alexis Benôit, 1809-1858.

Visiting book, 1841-1857.

340 x 272 mm. 32 leaves, unpaginated, with authographs and pasted in correspondence. An undated etching of Soyer and "Soyer's Symposium Season

Ticket," 1851, pasted on front free endpaper; pamphlet titled *Innovation culinaire: La Crême de la Grande Bretagne; Macédoine Terrestrocélestial* pasted on back free endpaper.

Correspondents include: brewer Michael Thomas Bass; Benjamin Disraeli; general Sir John Fox Burgoyne; George William Frederick Howard, 7th earl of Carlisle; philanthropist William Cotton; George Cruikshank whose letter to Soyer dated 26 October 1846 incorporates a drawing of the artist chained to his desk on which lies a note reading "works preparing for Xmas"; Richard Doyle; general Sir George de Lacy Evans; poet Sir John Hanmer; Augustus Frederick Fitzgerald, 3rd duke of Leinster; Charlotte Augusta (Stanhope) Fitzgerald, duchess of Leinster; Nathanial Clements, 2nd earl of Leitrim; William Lowther, 2nd earl of Lonsdale; general Sir James Macdonell; Sir John Benjamin Macneill; Hector John Graham Toler, 3rd earl of Norbury; Irish politicain Daniel O'Connell; Count Alfred Guillaume Gabriel d'Orsay; architect Sir Joseph Paxton; journalist Samuel Phillips; Prince Albert's private secretary Sir Charles Beaumont Phipps; John Russell, 1st earl Russell; dramatist Charles Selby; Margaret (Shaw-Stewart) Seymour, duchess of Somerset; author Albert Richard Smith; Edward Stanley, bishop of Norwich; medical reformer Thomas Wakley; Richard Grosvenor, 2nd marquis of Westminster; and actor Edward Richard Wright.

1258. Manuscript volume of recipes.

185 x 115 mm. 16 leaves, unpaginated, of lined paper with watermark date 1849. Recipes on pp. [1-21]; other pages blank.

1259. Underwood, C.

Manuscript receipt book of C. Underwood, butcher, Hornsey Road (London), issued to Mr. Young, of 1 Claremont Villas, Tollington Park, covering the period from 21 December 1859 to 24 October 1863, with Inland Revenue receipt stampes affixed.

152 x 93 mm. 35 leaves, unpaginated, last three blank. Entries note kinds and amounts of meat purchased and prices.

1260. Grant, Sir James Hope, 1808-1875.

Album of menus, invitations and music programs, 1866-1874.

240 x 176 mm. 40 leaves, unpaginated.

Contains twenty-nine printed and nine holograph items, mostly pasted on rectos with holograph notes, including lists of attendees, on facing pages. Many of the invitations and programs are for state occasions hosted by members of the Royal family. General Sir Hope Grant, who assembled this album, served with the 9th lancers in both China and India before becoming quartermaster-general at the Horse Guards in 1865.

ITALY

1261. Manuscript title: [ornament] │ REGO= │ LE │ [ornament]

At head of text on p. 4: Interrogazioni da farsi alli Putti che vorrano essere ascritti Confrattelli Nell' Arte nostra de formaggieri

194 x 144 mm. 30 leaves, unpaginated, sewn in a single gathering with contemporary stiff wrappers. ca. 1761.

Note: On page 5, at the end of the introduction, is written "Li Presenti Esami fà Stampati sotto la Massaria del Signor Francesco Albarello nel' Anno MDCCLXI" which may indicate this was copied from a printed document. No trace, however, of a printed progenitor has been found. The work is a book of instruction in the form of question and answer for aspirants to admission to the guild of cheesemakers, saussage-makers and fish-curers. The text is decorated with broad red and green rules.

AUTHOR INDEX

All items indexed by item number not by page number.

TITLE INDEX

All items indexed by item number not by page number.

966

The Queen-like Closet. 1062-1064.
The Queens Closet Opened. 838-840.
The Queen's Royal Cookery. 719.
Querelae et opprobria ventriculi. 1096.

Raccolta delle singolari qualità del caffé. 1188.
Recipes for the Million. 956a.
The Receipt Book of Elizabeth Raper. 954.
Receipts in Modern Cookery, With a Medical Commmentary. 769-774.
Recepte für Lehrlinge der Kochkunst, Hausfrauen und Köchinnen. 501.
Recherches sur le culte de Bacchus. 410.
Recherches sur les substances nutritives que renferment les os. 39.
Recherches sur les végétaux nourrissans. 376.
Recipes for the Million. 956a.
Recueil de diverses notes relatives à la gélatine extraite des os provenant de la viande de boucherie. 40.
Recueil pratique d'économie rurale et domestique. 197.
Reflexions et observations sur la qualité des vins. 401.
Refugio de povfro gentilhuomo. 1123.
Refugio over ammonitorio de gentilhuomo. 1124.
Le Regime du Caresme. 30.
Regimen sanitatis salernitanum. 402-404, 502, 959, 960.
Regles pratiques sur la diète. 37.
Les Regles de la santé. 396a.
Regole della sanita et natura de' cibi. 1117.
The Regulations and Establishment of the Houshold of Henry Algernon Percy, the Fifth Earl of Northumberland. 922.
Révolutioniana. 158.
Der Rheinische Weinbau. 485.
Rosa gallica. 130.
Royal Cookery. 809, 810.
The Royal Cookery Book. 714.
Les Royal-diners. 238.
The Royal English and Foreign Confectioner. 688.
Le Royal syrop de pommes. 164.

La Salameide. 1141.
Salt and Fishery. 627.
Sammlung vieler Vorschriften von allerley Koch- und Backwerk für junges Frauenzimmer. 476.
Lo Scalco. 1145.
Lo Scalco alla moderna. 1153.
Lo Scalco prattico. 1151.

Tablettes gastronomiques de Saint-Pétersbourg. 1207.

Tacvini ae gritudinum et morborum ferme omnium corporis humani. 443.

Tacvini sanitatis. 243, 244.

Tea; Its Effects, Medical and Moral. 987.

Teatro nobillissimo di scalcheria. 1161.

Il Tesoro della sanita. 1133, 1134.

Teütsche Speiszkammer. 85.

Le Thé et le chocolat dans l'alimentation publique. 386.

Theophilus Bibaculus, sive de potu theae dialogus. 496.

The Thorough Good Cook. 980a.

Le Thresor de santé. 424.

Thoughts on the Manufacture and Trade of Salt, on the Herring Fisheries, and on the Coal-trade of Great Britian. 658.

Thoughts on National Kitchens. 564a.

Toutes les oeuvrres charitables (Guybert). 236.

The Town and Country Brewery Book. 576.

Tractatus de cucumeribus. 1114.

Tractatus novi de potu caphé, de chinensium thé, et de chocolata. 168.

Traité de l'alimentation en Angleterre et en Amérique. 418a.

Traité complet de l'art de la distillation. 15.

Traité de confiture. 425.

Traité de l'alimentation en Angelterre et en Amérique. 418a.

Traité de l'office (Berthe). 78.

Traité de l'office (Etienne). 187.

Traité des alimens (Gautier). 207.

Traité des alimens de Caresme. 31.

Traité des aliments (Lémery). 276-278.

Traité des champignons comestibles, suspect et vénéneux. 365.

Traité des festins. 361.

Traité des liqueurs et de la distillation des alcools. 173.

Traité du lait. 314.

Traité général de viticulture. 432.

Traité historique et pratique de la cuisine. 346.

Traité medico-gastronomique sur les indigestions. 313.

Traité pratique des champignons comestibles. 260.

Traité raisonné de la distillation. 239a, 239b, 240.

Traité sur l'art de fabriquer les sirops et les conserves de raisins. 377.

Traité sur les propriétés et les effets du café. 358.

Traité théorique et pratique sur la culture de la vigne. 132.

Traitez nouveaux et curieux du café, du thé et du chocolate. 169, 170.

Traitez singuliers et nouveaux contre le paganisme du roy-boit. 156.

Trattato del bere caldo e freddo. 1143.

Trattato della natura de cibi et del bere. 1168.

SUBJECT INDEX

All items indexed by item number not by page number.

CHRONOLOGICAL INDEX

All items indexed by item number not by page number.

Chronological Index[*]

1475: It. 1169.
1477: G. 523.
ca.1487-1488: It. 1116.
ca.1495: F. 402
ca.1495-1500: F. 191.
1498: It. 1170.
ca.1500: G. 499.
1501: It. 1149.
1503: It. 1109.
1505: F. 391.
1506: It. 1189.
1508: F. 223; G. 494; It. 1180.
1510: F. 211.
1511: F. 212.
1514: F. 209; It. 1110.
1515: I. 1184a.
1516: G. 455.
1517: It. 1171, 1175.
1518: F. 130.
1519: F. 103.
1520: It. 1123.
ca.1526: It. 1119.
1530: F. 198.
ca.1530: It. 1148.
1531: F. 243, 253; G. 480.
1532: F. 104, 384, 443; It. 1124.
1533: F. 183a, 244.
1534: F. 210; G. 520.
1535: G.B. 959; Pol. 1202.
1537: F. 105; G. 444, 495, 497.
1539: F. 392; G.B. 665.
1541: F. 32; G.B. 960; Swi. 1223.
1543: F. 416a.
1545: Sp. 1212; Swi. 1224.
1546: G. 508.

---

[*]Abbreviations: A., Austria; B., Belgium; C., Canada; Cz., Czechoslovakia; F., France; G., Germany; G.B., Great Britain; H., Holland; In., India; Ir., Ireland; It., Italy; J., Japan; M., Mexico; Ph., Philippines; Pol., Poland; Por., Portugal; R., Russia; Sp., Spain; Swe., Sweden; Swi., Switzerland.

1549: G. 505; It. 1144, 1162.
1550: F. 85.
1551: G. 459, 502.
1553: It. 1152.
1554: G. 456, 506; It. 1181.
1555: It. 1176.
1556: It. 1111.
1557: It. 1163.
1558: G. 507.
1559: G. 515; It. 1179.
1560: F. 106; It. 1174.
1561: Swi. 1229.
1563: Swi. 1234.
1564: G. 460.
1568: G. 521.
1570: It. 1182.
1574: It. 1191.
1575: F. 350; G. 445; G.B. 542.
1576: G.B. 983, 1036.
1580: G. 458, 500.
1581: It. 1120.
1582: F. 27; G. 518.
1584: G.B. 621; It. 1168, 1178.
1586: It. 1114, 1133.
1587: G. 504.
1588: It. 1134.
1592: It. 1167.
1593: G.B. 749; It. 1121, 1166.
1594: G.B. 747, 934.
1595: G.B. 978.
1596: It. 1113.
1597: G.B. 1034; Swi. 1230.
1598: G. 446, 448; It. 1183.
1600: G.B. 668.
1601: It. 1125.
1602: F. 393.
1605: G.B. 622, 642; It. 1143.
1606: G.B. 643; It. 1136.
1607: F. 331.
1608: F. 258.
1609: It. 1137, 1138.
1610: It. 1135.
1611: G.B. 607; Sp. 1214.

1612: F. 359.
1614: G.B. 608.
1615: F. 59, 164; G.B. 979; It. 1173.
1616: F. 424.
1618: F. 144, 188.
1620: It. 1117.
1621: G. 498; It. 1146.
1622: G.B. 1040.
1623: G.B. 847; It. 1145.
1624: G.B. 609. 930.
1626: B. 13.
1627: B. 18; F. 93; G.B. 610; It. 1112, 1151, 1160.
1628: G.B. 941.
1629: It. 1160.
1630: It. 1177.
1631: It. 1142.
1633: F. 403; G.B. 644, 725.
1634: G.B. 824; It. 1131.
1636: G.B. 825; It. 1107.
1637: G.B. 848.
1638: G.B. 1041.
1639: It. 1147.
1641: G.B. 894.
1642: Swi. 1231a.
1643: It. 1184.
1644: It. 1187.
1645: G. 451.
1646: B. 19; It. 1140.
1647: It. 1190.
ca.1647: F. 388, 440.
1648: G.B. 851.
1649: G.B. 849, 850.
ca.1649: G. 469.
1650: F. 315; G. 489; G.B. 584, 1042; It. 1157.
1651: H. 1085, 1091.
1652: F. 261, 413; G.B. 726, 748.
1653: F. 262, 266; G.B. 570, 785, 786, 788, 932, 935.
1654: F. 86; G. 457.
1655: F. 43; G.B. 553, 834, 879, 895; H. 1078a.
1656: F. 87, 89.
1657: F. 267, G. 470; G.B. 552.
1658: G.B. 551, 835, 838; It. 1154.
1659: F. 90, 297; G. 473; G.B. 693.

1660: F. 184, 290; G. 462a.

1661: H. 1078, 1095a.

1662: F. 88, 179, 273; G.B. 1011; It. 1185; Swi. 1232.

1664: F. 155; G.B. 637; H. 1079, 1096.

1665: F. 44, 63, 91; H. 1078a.

1667: F. 265.

1668: F. 396a; G.B. 836, 839, 852.

1669: F. 236; G.B. 568, 645a, 597; It. 1161.

1670: F. 156; G. 466; G.B. 1062; H. 1080, 1096a.

1671: F. 150; G.B. 867.

1672: B. 22; F. 178; G.B. 653, 1035.

1673: G.B. 818.

1674: F. 407, 408.

1675: F. 61, 259; G.B. 569, 620, 853, 933, 1063, 1065; It. 1188.

1676: F. 62; G. 519; G.B. 1069.

1677: G. 474; G.B. 646, 1058.

1678: G.B. 1070.

1679: Swi. 1231.

1681: G.B. 811, 912, 1064.

1682: B. 23; F. 361, 369; G.B. 627, 727, 869, 895a, 943, 970.

1683: F. 194, 428; G.B. 717, 812, 854, 1029.

1684: G. 496.

1685: F. 168, 169, 263; G.B. 654, 868.

1686: G.B. 855.

1687: F. 82, 83; G.B. 787, 913, 1066.

1688: F. 170, 192, 396a; G. 525; G.B. 1067; H. 1089.

1689: F. 193, 425.

ca.1690: G.B. 980; It. 1186.

1691: F. 316; G.B. 1030, 1033, 1061.

1692: F. 49, 320, G.B. 598, 1028; It. 1153.

1693: F. 317, 409; G.B. 814; H. 1083.

1694: G. 522.

1695: G.B. 981, 1024, 1052; It. 1164.

1697: G.B. 1031.

1698: F. 321; G.B. 1032.

1699: F. 264; G.B. 669.

1700: F. 50, 286a; G.B. 905, 1068.

ca.1700: G. 512; H. 1088.

1701: H. 1084, 1090; Swi. 1233.

1702: F. 276; G. 490; G.B. 865.

1704: G.B. 821.

1705: B. 14; F. 277, 318, 325; G. 491; G.B. 544, 886, 917.

1706: F. 314; G.B. 655.

1708: F. 180; G. 464; G.B. 794, 923.
1709: G. 514; G.B. 924; H. 1076.
1710: F. 30; G.B. 809, 837, 840, 982.
1711: G.B. 823.
1712: B. 16.
ca.1712: G.B. 795.
1713: F. 31; G.B. 719, 1046.
1714: F. 284; G.B. 789.
1715: F. 283; G. 452; G.B. 1014; H. 1094, 1095.
1716: F. 181, 417; G. 483; G.B. 810; H. 1087.
1717: G.B. 815, 817.
1718: G.B. 659, 816.
1719: G. 467; G.B. 790, 1059.
1720: H. 1093; It. 1132.
ca.1720: G.B. 793, 1053.
1721: G. 463; G.B. 886.
1723: G. 511; G.B. 903, 980a, 1001.
1724: G. 475; G.B. 904, 1015, 1047; J. 1193.
1725: B. 17; G.B. 602, 998, 1002.
ca.1725: G.B. 1060.
1726: F. 322; G.B. 762.
1727: G.B. 996, 1016.
1728: G.B. 791; It. 1139.
1729: G.B. 763, 999, 1013.
1730: G.B. 592.
1732: F. 323; G.B. 546, 590; H. 1075.
1733: F. 319; G.B. 660.
1734: F. 319; G. 492; G.B. 664a, 792, 873; H. 1092.
1735: G. 488; G.B. 694; H. 1075.
1736: F. 286; G.B. 555, 591, 636, 803a.
1737: G.B. 628, 636, 997.
1738: F. 269.
1739: F. 285, 301, 340; G. 453; G.B. 645, 723.
1740: G.B. 808, 804; H. 1081.
1741: G.B. 673.
1742: F. 302, 340, 341; G.B. 664a; H. 1086.
1743: G.B. 732a; It. 1122.
ca.1743: G.B. 888.
1744: G.B. 541.
1745: G.B. 822.
1746: F. 336; G.B. 880, 918.
1747: G.B. 695, 696; H. 1082; Sp. 1218.
1748: G.B. 530, 586, 697.

1749: F. 243, 404.

1750: F. 96, 342; G.B. 664.

ca.1750: G.B. 715.

1751: F. 214, 257a, 341a; G.B. 698, 805.

1752: F. 143a, 337; G. 493.

ca.1752: G.B. 889.

1753: F. 239a; G. 493; G.B. 806.

1754: G.B. 575, 629, 775.

1755: F. 37, 92, 278, 344, 396; G.B. 604, 699; Sp. 1219.

1756: F. 258a, 338; G.B. 574, 710.

1757: F. 289; G.B. 631, 1055.

1758: F. 142, 303, 335, 346; G.B. 890, 926, 1019; Por. 1206.

1759: F. 239b, 401; G.B. 557, 782, 1043.

1760: G.B. 631a, 700, 709, 724, 756; I. 1131a; J. 1196.

ca.1760: A. 2; G.B. 707, 878.

1761: Ir. 1105.

1762: F. 109, 160.

1763: F. 28a; G.B. 701; Sp. 1215.

1764: F. 160; G.B. 783, 884.

1765: F. 128a, 131; G.B. 657.

ca.1765: G.B. 585, 708, 875, 937.

1766: F. 298, 347; G.B. 830; It. 1158; Sp. 1222.

1767: F. 162, 411; G.B. 702, 871, 919, 965, 985; Sp. 1208.

1768: F. 28c, 182, 215; G.B. 599, 600, 750, 780; H. 1097.

1769: F. 29, 153; G.B. 582, 605, 663, 944; H. 1099, 1100.

1770: F. 69; G. 487; G.B. 572, 922.

1771: F. 108; G. 487, 526a; G.B. 733.

1772: F. 163; G.B. 1000; H. 1098; It. 1141.

1773: G.B. 861, 945; It. 1128.

1774: G.B. 703.

1775: F. 68a, 68b, 304; G.B. 556, 862.

1776: F. 324; G.B. 606, 946.

1777: A. 6; F. 240, 339; G. 527a; G.B. 784, 858, 966.

1778: F. 345, 374; G. 513, 527; It. 1127; Sp. 1216.

1779: F. 167a, 372; G.B. 529

1780: F. 326, 328; G.B. 920; Por. 1205.

ca.1780: F. 329; G.B. 680.

1781: F. 327, 376; G.B. 640; It. 1115, 1130.

1782: F. 274, 281; G.B. 947; It. 1150.

1783: F. 107, 254; G.B. 675.

1784: F. 28b; G.B. 658, 676, 704; Ir. 1106.

1785: A. 8; B. 15a; Cz. 26a; F. 186, 235; G.B. 657, 887, 920.

ca.1785: G.B. 758.

1786: F. 79, 358; G.B. 863; Sp. 1220.

1787: G.B. 842, 948.

1788: G.B. 577, 1025; Sp. 1209.

1789: F. 246; G.B. 891, 906.

1790: G. 476, 516; G.B. 624, 907; It. 1126.

ca.1790: G.B. 528, 583, 705, 938.

1791: A. 1; F. 332; G.B. 623, 656, 689, 738, 925, 1026, 1048, 1049; Ir. 1103.

1792: A. 1a; F. 247; G.B. 625, 677, 887a.

1793: F. 249, 439; G.B. 739, 872.

1794: F. 348; G. 446a; G.B. 579, 734.

1795: G.B. 594, 689a, 860.

ca.1795: G.B. 740.

1796: G.B. 706.

1797: G. 524; G.B. 626.

1798: F. 415; G. 468.

ca.1798: G.B. 684, 870.

1799: A. 3; F. 375; G.B. 826, 949.

ca.1799: G.B. 950.

1800: B. 20; G. 471; G.B. 678, 690, 843, 951; Sp. 1217.

ca.1800: F. 183, 427; G.B. 741, 939.

1801: F. 131a, 132, 371; G.B. 679, 864, 952; It. 1129.

1802: F. 158, 412; G. 485a; G.B. 686, 728, 881, 901.

1803: F. 71, 129, 159, 161, 224, 291; G. 501; G.B. 953; I. 1124a; Swi. 1226.

1804: F. 72, 197, 225; G. 486; G.B. 691, 764, 769.

1805: F. 73, 226, 280, 395; G.B. 641, 662, 769a.

1806: F. 114, 221, 227, 292, 433; G. 486; G.B. 770, 771, 908, 990.

1807: F. 115, 228; G.B. 772, 971.

1808: F. 116, 229, 233; G.B. 601, 882, 892, 972.

1809: F. 112, 206; G. 503; G.B. 588, 909, 910.

1810: A. 4; F. 34, 117, 230, 337; G. 447; G.B. 565, 773, 995.

ca.1810: F. 48, 143.

1811: A. 5; F. 147, 231; G.B. 545, 742,1074.

ca.1811: G.B. 841.

1812: F. 320; G.B. 681.

1813: F. 35, 373; G.B. 759, 935a, 1037; J. 1192.

ca.1813: G.B. 991.

1814: F. 66, 433a; G.B. 729.

ca.1814: G.B. 674.

1815: A. 7; F. 124, 126, 146, 275; G.B. 682, 720.

1816: F. 66, 66a, 149, 195; G.B. 730, 992, 1038.

1817: F. 66, 434; G. 462; G.B. 564, 766, 797.

1818: F. 45, 52, 113, 133, 334; G. 450; G.B. 760, 798, 877.

1819: F. 74, 152.

1820: B. 24; F. 237, 305; G.B. 532, 533, 536, 774, 776, 844; Sp. 1210.

ca.1820: F. 418; G.B. 548, 721, 752, 761.

1821: F. 36, 41, 151, 293; G. 481, 509; G.B. 531, 534, 535, 612, 801.

1822: F. 122, 252, 330, 435; G.B. 613, 820, 1012; It. 1108.

1823: F. 46, 53; G. 461; G.B. 614, 661.

1824: F. 67, 410; G.B. 559, 619, 737, 802, 819, 899, 942, 973; J. 1194; Sp. 1210.

ca.1824: G.B. 1018.

1825: B. 15; F. 42, 174, 196, 202, 248, 300, 366, 416; G.B. 540, 914, 1050.

1826: F. 98, 175, 213, 367; G.B. 767, 876, 936, 984.

1827: F. 199, 201, 251, 282, 310, 368, 423a; G. 449, 485; G.B. 560, 649, 753, 799, 1039.

ca.1827: G.B. 632.

1828: B. 12; F. 120, 125, 127, 139, 200, 204, 207, 250a, 306, 307, 309, 312, 313, 397, 398; G.B. 618, 722, 915, 1051, 1009a.

1829: B. 10, F. 39, 47, 308, 311; G.B. 616, 639, 647, 754, 768, 800, 803, 961.

ca.1829: F. 40.

1830: F. 141; G. 465; G.B. 648, 650, 716, 859, 1009, Sp. 1213.

ca.1830: G.B. 576, 595, 667, 1057.

1831: F. 357a; G.B. 615, 845, 900; M. 1197, 1200.

1832: F. 241, 436; G. 526; G.B. 1071; Sp. 1211.

1833: F. 28, 118, 429; G.B. 617, 958, 1039a.

1834: F. 164a; G.B. 635, 685, 887a.

1835: F. 118, 414; G.B. 611, 751, 964, 1044a.

1836: F. 54, 64, 70, 110, 137, 138, 360, 442; G.B. 589, 846, 1021a, 1033a; Por. 1203.

ca.1836: G.B. 633.

1837: F. 65; G.B. 651, 781; Swi. 1228.

ca.1837: G.B. 683.

1838: F. 177, 421; G.B. 848, 1020; Swe. 1222a.

ca.1838: G.B. 897.

1839: F. 57, 145, 167, 205; G. 472; G.B. 777, 848, 957, 969, 974, 987.

ca.1839: G.B. 898.

1840: F. 272; G.B. 848, 975; Swi. 1225.

ca.1840: F. 148; G.B. 755, 757.

1841: F. 84, 128; G.B. 744, 848; Por. 1204a.

1842: F. 121, 123, 437; G.B. 745, 828, 955, 976.

1843: F. 38, 242, 394; G. 454.

1844: B. 11; F. 134, 157, 394; G.B. 866; It. 1118.

1845: F. 76, 187, 190, 287; G.B. 538, 630; It. 1165; M. 1198; Sp. 1221.

ca.1845: G.B. 956.

1846: F. 97, 187, 294, 333, 426; G.B. 556a, 640a, 977, 1003.

1847: G.B. 967; Ir. 1104.

1848: F. 119, 176; G.B. 968.

1849: B. 9; G.B. 634, 1004; J. 1195; M. 1201.

1850: F. 140.

1851: F. 349; G.B. 593, 832, 893.

1852: F. 260; G.B. 566, 671; In. 1101; M. 1199.

1853: F. 239, 430, G.B. 638, 671, 732, 1005; In. 1102.

1854: B. 21; F. 51, 136; G.B. 543, 550, 554, 652, 672, 765.

1855: F. 136, 288; G.B. 687, 721, 929, 1006.

1856: F. 58; G.B. 1022, 1056; Por. 1204; R. 1207.

ca.1856: G.B. 567.

1857: F. 405; G.B. 537, 1008.

1858: F. 173, 360a; G.B. 670, 1045.

1859: F. 400; G.B. 560a, 580; Swi. 1227a.

1860: F. 31a, 383, 387; G.B. 560a; Swi. 1227.

ca.1860: F. 56, 216.

1861: C. 26; F. 386; G.B. 560a, 561, 779, 807, 911, 927, 928.

1862: F. 299, 365a; G. 478; G.B. 688.

ca.1862: G.B. 1007.

1863: G.B. 963; It. 1155.

1864: F. 99, 245; G.B. 549, 796, 813, 813a, 986.

1865: C. 25; F. 351, 385; G.B. 562.

ca.1865: F. 81, 295.

1866: F. 222, 352, 379; G.B. 1021.

1867: F. 218, 353, 399; G.B. 746, 829, 833.

1868: F. 354, 362, 381, 423, 431; G.B. 692, 714.

ca.1868: F. 95.

1869: F. 220, 355; G.B. 596a, 736.

1870: F. 111; G.B. 571, 596a.

1871: G.B. 596a, 713, 962.

1872: F. 165; G.B. 892a.

1873: F. 171, 219, 380; G.B. 892a.

1874: F. 94, 100, 165; G.B. 883.

1875: G.B. 778.

1876: F. 55, 75, 78, 378.

1877: F. 68, 356.

1878: F. 77, 212a, 238, 271.

1879: F. 60, 101, 382.

1880: F. 208; G.B. 712, 916.

ca.1880: F. 102.

1882: F. 172; G.B. 902, 1044.

ca.1882: G.B. 993.

1884: F. 279; G.B. 581.

1885: G.B. 1010.

1887: F. 202a; G.B. 711, 820a.

1888: G. 482.
1889: F. 203.
1890: F. 438; G.B. 547.
ca.1890: G.B. 596, 724a.
1891: G.B. 856a, 956a.
1892: F. 419, 422.
1893: F. 217, 255; G.B. 587, 603, 735, 1072.
1894: F. 135, 189.
1895: G.B. 980a.
1896: G.B. 921.
1897: It. 1172.
1898: F. 296.
ca.1898: F. 80.
1899: It. 1156.
1900: G.B. 874.
ca.1900: G. 477; G.B. 856, 994.
1901: F. 432; G. 510, 523a; G.B. 558.
1902: F. 256, 432; G.B. 857.
1903: F. 185a, 257, 432; G.B. 563.
1904: F. 418a, 432.
1905: F. 432.
1907: F. 57a, 390; G.B. 573, 666.
1908: G.B. 827.
1909: F. 432.
ca.1909: F. 166.
1910: F. 185, 270, 432; G. 450a.
1911: F. 389; G.B. 718, 1008a.
1912: F. 185b.
1913: G.B. 896, 940.
ca.1913: F. 406.
1915: G.B. 846a.
1917: C. 24a; H. 1077.
1918: G.B. 564a.
1920: F. 234.
1921: F. 234.
1924: G.B. 954.
1926: F. 441; G.B. 774a.
1928: G.B. 539, 1017.
1929: G.B. 988.
1930: F. 250, 364.
1931: F. 268; G.B. 1023.
1932: G.B. 1027.

1933: F. 33, 363; G.B. 735b.
1935: G.B. 793a.
1936: F. 154.
1938: F. 357, 365.
1939: G. 479; G.B. 735a.
1942: G.B. 575a.
1946: F. 232.
1948: G.B. 931.
1949: G. 494.
1950; G.B. 640b.
1951: G.B. 640c.
1952: G.B. 989.
1962: G. 517.